dedicated to all lovers of the great outdoors

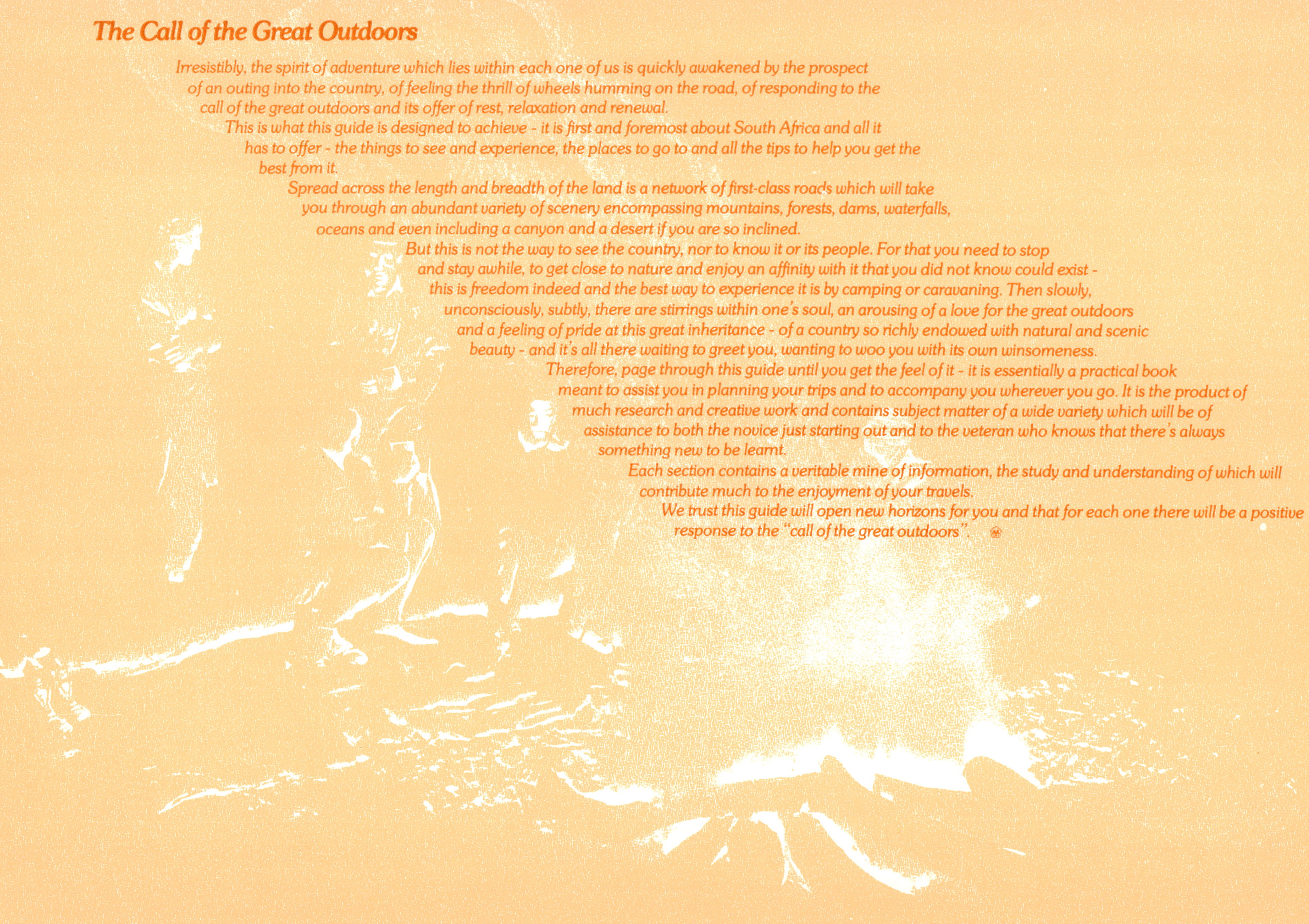

The Call of the Great Outdoors

Irresistibly, the spirit of adventure which lies within each one of us is quickly awakened by the prospect of an outing into the country, of feeling the thrill of wheels humming on the road, of responding to the call of the great outdoors and its offer of rest, relaxation and renewal.

This is what this guide is designed to achieve - it is first and foremost about South Africa and all it has to offer - the things to see and experience, the places to go to and all the tips to help you get the best from it.

Spread across the length and breadth of the land is a network of first-class roads which will take you through an abundant variety of scenery encompassing mountains, forests, dams, waterfalls, oceans and even including a canyon and a desert if you are so inclined.

But this is not the way to see the country, nor to know it or its people. For that you need to stop and stay awhile, to get close to nature and enjoy an affinity with it that you did not know could exist - this is freedom indeed and the best way to experience it is by camping or caravaning. Then slowly, unconsciously, subtly, there are stirrings within one's soul, an arousing of a love for the great outdoors and a feeling of pride at this great inheritance - of a country so richly endowed with natural and scenic beauty - and it's all there waiting to greet you, wanting to woo you with its own winsomeness.

Therefore, page through this guide until you get the feel of it - it is essentially a practical book meant to assist you in planning your trips and to accompany you wherever you go. It is the product of much research and creative work and contains subject matter of a wide variety which will be of assistance to both the novice just starting out and to the veteran who knows that there's always something new to be learnt.

Each section contains a veritable mine of information, the study and understanding of which will contribute much to the enjoyment of your travels.

We trust this guide will open new horizons for you and that for each one there will be a positive response to the "call of the great outdoors".

ACKNOWLEDGEMENTS

The Automobile Association of South Africa expresses its grateful acknowledgements for the invaluable and authoritative contributions, information and advice which it has received from government, provincial and municipal departments, private organisations and bodies, and numerous individuals in the provision of much of the material which made possible the preparation of this guide.

In particular, the following bear special mention:

Mr Peter Johnson for the superb cover illustration "Dawn Sky"

The Geological Society of South Africa; Dr P.D. Toens; Dr F.J. Coertzee and Mr F. Walraven of the Department of Geological Survey for assistance with the Geological Map of South Africa, and to Dr C. Jennings for the provision of the list of geological sites of tourist interest

Mr E.G. Buckley of Map Studios for permission to reproduce the artist's impression of Southern Africa

Mr James Clarke of The Star's CARE campaign and the S.A. Council for Conservation and Anti-Pollution for some of the material included in the article on "Environmental Care for the Caravaner and Camper"

Dr D.J.B. Killick of The Botanical Research Institute, Pretoria for the feature on "Roadside Identification of Trees", and to Mrs R. Holcroft for the tree illustrations

Mr W.A. Wright, Fire Prevention Officer of the Johannesburg Fire Department for the material used in the article on "Fire Prevention for the Caravaner and Camper"

The South African Red Cross Society for assistance with "First Aid for the Caravaner and Camper"

The South African Institute for Medical Research for information on snake bites and for base information from which the Bilharzia and Malaria maps were prepared

Mr S.G. Weyer of Cadac SA for assistance with the feature on "Gas Appliances"

Mr Luke Schoeman of Caravan Mecca, Pretoria for information on "Family Camping"

The Automobile Association of Rhodesia and Mrs M.J. Buckley of the Caravan Club of Southern Africa for assistance with the feature "Your Caravaning Holiday" and also the list of recommended Caravan Parks

Mr Trevor Short of Simpsons, Pretoria, for information on "Backpacking"

The Departments of Forestry, Nature Conservation and both the National and Natal Parks Board for information and assistance in the preparation of the maps and text in the National Hiking Way and Wilderness Trail sections

Mr Barney Paris of Juta and Co. for permission to base the feature "The Constellations as seen from South Africa on any night in the year" on Arthur W. Long's book of similar title; to Dr Patrick Moore, Mr Pete Collins and Mr Tom Geary for vetting and correcting the text where necessary; to the Johannesburg Planetarium for the supply of and permission to reproduce transparencies in this section; to Hamish Campbell for his transparency on page 42; to Mr T.W. Russo of the Astronomical Society of South Africa and finally to Mr Jack Bennett of Pretoria who inspired this article

The National Road Safety Association for material used in the preparation of the section on "Road Signs"

The Government Printer, Pretoria, for copyright authority to base AA maps on official publications

To the many organisations and individuals, particularly provincial roads engineers and inspectors for the provision of road information, and to those who have assisted with the wealth of detail included on the maps

To the Surveyors-General, the respective municipalities, engineers, traffic departments and other officials for the information used in the preparation of the town plans and for copyright authority to reproduce the coats-of-arms of each city/town included

To Professor J.J. Oberholster for the information on National Monuments

To the South African Tourist Corporation (SATOUR) for the provision of and permission to use photographs included in the guide

Dr N. Strydom, Mr Peter Charman and Mr Trevor Babich for checking and advising on the sections dealing with fishing, which were compiled with the assistance of a host of people throughout the country

The Pretoria News for copyright authority to reproduce some illustrations of fish included in the above sections

Mr Val Duke of the Boy Scouts Association for material from which the section on "Useful Knots and Hitches" was prepared

The many officials who co-operated in supplying information from which the individual sections on "Dams and Lakes", "Waterfalls", "Mountain Passes" and "Golf Courses" were prepared

The Stellenbosch Wine Farmers Association for assistance with the Four Passes Drive map

The hundreds of caravan park and camping site managers, proprietors and other officials who co-operated in the supply of the information from which the various sections included in the gazetteer were compiled, including Mr Alan Roberts of the South African Youth Hostels Association

Mr Eddie Andriés and the SA Caravan and Camping Council for their interest, encouragement and advice with the preparation of this guide

Special thanks are due to the individual members of the AA staff, who in their respective capacities have played their invaluable parts in the gathering, collating, preparation, translation, editing and presentation of all the information contained in this guide

Last but not least, the AA accords its grateful appreciation to the artists, cartographers and printers whose co-operation, assistance and advice greatly facilitated the production of this book

CONTENTS AND INDEX TO AA OUTDOOR HOLIDAY GUIDE

Printed by Keartland Press, P.O. Box 9221, Johannesburg 2000

HIERDIE BOEK IS OOK IN AFRIKAANS VERKRYGBAAR

Although all possible care has been taken in compiling the information included in this book, the Association cannot accept responsibility for any errors or omissions.

Users discovering any errors, or wishing to compliment the AA or to suggest any improvements are invited to write to:

The Director-General, The Automobile Association of South Africa, P.O. Box 596, Johannesburg 2000

SPECIAL PRICE TO ALL MEMBERS
R11,50 PER COPY PLUS 46c SALES TAX = R11,96

Environmental Care

for the Camper and Caravaner

The poisoning of our planet by industrial waste and chemical products is of serious concern to all, for the future of nature conservation depends upon each individual's awareness of the environment and of his place in it. Although preventive plans are conceived by governments, individuals all have a role to play in the protection of our surroundings.

Man engages in many amusements to broaden his culture or occupy his time, including activities such as camping and caravaning. Because so much time is spent in houses, offices or workshops, his reaction is to take advantage of every free minute to return to nature. The protection of our natural resources - green girdles of forests and natural landscapes, vast areas of water, and fauna and flora - is therefore of concern to everyone.

All caravaners and campers can assist by observing the anti-pollution code of the SA Council for Conservation and Anti-Pollution (SACCAP).

Air

- ☐ Burn rubbish only when and where permitted
- ☐ Avoid burning anything that will create poisonous fumes or a lot of smoke
- ☐ Report instances of industrial air, water or land pollution to the local authorities, newspapers and SACCAP

Soil

- ☐ Take great care when using pesticides and weed killers
- ☐ Only bury or dump rubbish which is bio-degradable*
- ☐ Place all other rubbish in disposal bins or take to municipal dumping grounds

* "Bio-degradable" *means substances which rot quickly and easily*

Water (sea, rivers, lakes and dams)

- ☐ Never throw rubbish, oil or poisonous chemical substances into open water or down drains
- ☐ Keep gutters and storm water drains free of litter
- ☐ Always use bio-degradable* detergents
- ☐ Report instances of agricultural or industrial pollution to the local authorities, your local newspaper and SACCAP
- ☐ Help to prevent any soil erosion whenever and wherever you can

Homes, Cities, Places of Recreation

- ☐ Always dispose of rubbish as requested by the authorities
- ☐ Make yourself responsible for picking up all litter
- ☐ Encourage your families and friends to buy those commercial products which are packed in returnable or bio-degradable* containers
- ☐ Never write, carve or paint on plants, trees or on anyone else's property

Noise

- ☐ Always keep the volume of radios and tape-recorders at levels which do not disturb anyone else
- ☐ Ensure that any vehicle you own is operated as silently as possible

The following DOs and DON'Ts will also serve as a guide in achieving the above objectives:

DOs

- ☐ Do encourage others to promote the interests of conservation and anti-pollution
- ☐ Do guard against all risks of fire
- ☐ Do close all gates properly
- ☐ Do keep dogs under proper control

"Man has enough objective reasons to safeguard nature. But in the last analysis it will only be saved by our hearts. It will only be saved if man loves it simply because it is beautiful and we need beauty, in whatever form our background and training enable us to appreciate it."

(J Durst - Before Nature Dies)

- ☐ Do keep to the paths or roads across farm land
- ☐ Do avoid damaging fences, hedges and walls
- ☐ Do leave no litter
- ☐ Do safeguard water supplies
- ☐ Do protect wildlife, plants and trees
- ☐ Do travel carefully on country roads
- ☐ Do respect the life of the countryside

DON'Ts

- ☐ Don't antagonise animals in game parks by throwing empty containers at them
- ☐ Don't show your lack of regard for others by emptying ashtrays, paper bags etc from the window of your car
- ☐ Don't litter roadside picnic places by leaving empty tins or papers lying around
- ☐ Don't deface caves and rock paintings
- ☐ Don't pick or remove flowers, plants or shrubs from the veld: besides spoiling the countryside, you can be prosecuted
- ☐ Don't disfigure trees or rocks by carving or painting your initials on them
- ☐ Don't be careless with matches or cigarettes - veld fires destroy
- ☐ Don't abandon old prams, chairs, cars etc anywhere except in a junk yard or dumping ground

Let every man, woman and child decide to act as an honorary caretaker, never wilfully destroying or damaging any part of our great heritage so that it may be preserved intact for future generations.

(Environmental problems may be reported to the National Anti-Pollution Secretariat, P.O. Box 2744, Durban, 4000. Tel. 41-7062/3 or the Witwatersrand Office, P.O. Box 28911, Sandringham, 2131, Tel. Johannesburg 45-6886)

Code of Behaviour

To obtain the maximum enjoyment and benefit from caravaning and camping remember the important "DOs" and "DON'Ts" both on and off the road.

Off the Road

DOs

- ☐ Do reserve stands in advance during peak holiday periods - the AA will do this for you on request
- ☐ Do obey the rules of the caravan park/camping site and of the local authorities
- ☐ Do camp on authorised stands and pay the requisite dues
- ☐ Do be courteous and considerate to others
- ☐ Do respect the property and peace of others
- ☐ Do observe sanitary regulations
- ☐ Do keep the stand neat and tidy
- ☐ Do leave the stand as clean as you would wish to find it - dispose of rubbish or waste where facilities are available for doing so or if there are no such facilities, remove the rubbish from the stand and bury it in a proper manner
- ☐ Do be careful when making an open fire - particularly in the veld and forests. Clear away undergrowth before making a fire
- ☐ Do respect the rules relating to dress at caravan parks and camping sites

DON'Ts

- ☐ Don't camp on sites without the prior permission of the land owner - or municipal or district authority in the case of communal land
- ☐ Don't offend others by word or bearing
- ☐ Don't make undue noise particularly between 22 h 00 and 06 h 00
- ☐ Don't foul the ground with waste water
- ☐ Don't leave litter or rubbish on the stand
- ☐ Don't make an open fire unless permission has been given
- ☐ Don't damage in any way the trees, shrubs, hedges or other plants on the site
- ☐ Don't damage fences

On the Road

DOs

- ☐ Do keep your car and caravan in a roadworthy condition - car and caravan tyre pressures are important
- ☐ Do check all controls - stop lights, indicators, mirrors, coupling etc before driving off
- ☐ Do make sure that you have a clear view to the rear along both sides of the caravan
- ☐ Do ensure that the gas tap, all windows and air vents of the caravan are closed and the door locked before driving off
- ☐ Do obey the traffic regulations
- ☐ Do keep well to the left and allow faster traffic to pass

DON'Ts

- ☐ Don't tow a caravan larger or heavier than your car can safely manage under all conditions
- ☐ Don't follow too closely behind other traffic
- ☐ Don't park where your car or caravan will inconvenience others
- ☐ Don't stop on narrow roads, bends or other places where you could endanger yourself or other road users. If you have to stop always pull well off the road, and signal your intention to do so well in advance
- ☐ Don't drive when you are tired - rather change drivers if you can or find the nearest resting place and take a break
- ☐ Don't drive in close convoy with other caravans

Note: Members who wish to apply for the AA camping carnet (see gazetteer for full details) are required to undertake to observe the rules of good camping - many of which are incorporated in the "DOs" and "DON'Ts" in the "Off the Road" section above.

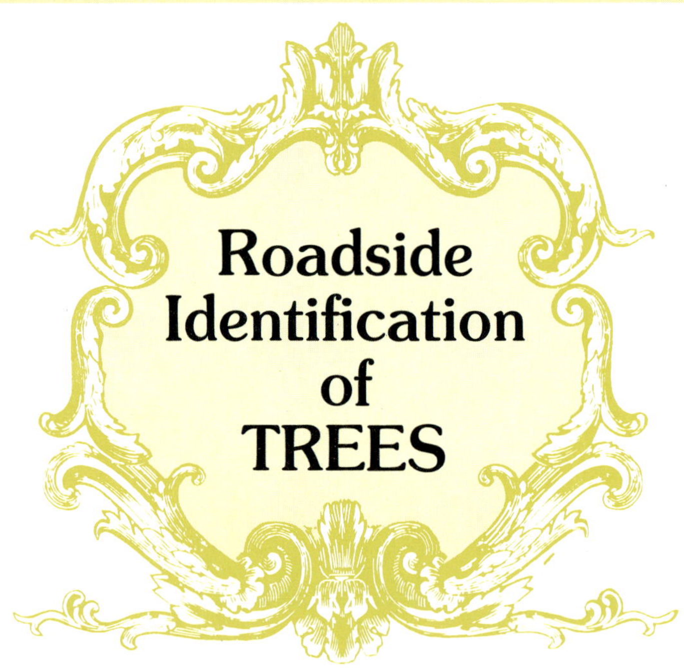

Roadside Identification of TREES

The trees illustrated here are among the most likely of the nearly 1 000 tree species in Southern Africa to be encountered by motorists at roadsides and in caravan and camping sites. Some of the trees selected have rather similar habit and leaf shapes, so it has been necessary in some cases to illustrate fruits as well. The number appearing next to the name of each tree is the number allocated to it in the National List of Trees (1972). The numbering of trees along roadsides and in parks and reserves is to enable the public to identify them simply by referring to the National List. Apart from the scientific names, common names in both English and Afrikaans, where available, are given. Brief descriptions of the trees together with spot maps showing their distribution are also provided. A short list of books and articles on trees is appended for those members who may wish to know more about the subject. It is hoped that this guide will stimulate the interest of members in one of our most priceless assets, our indigenous trees.

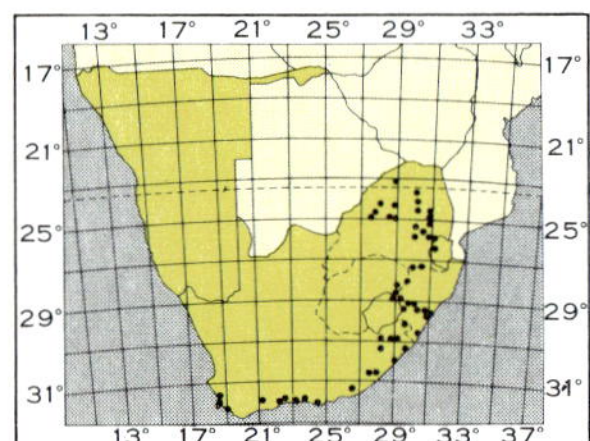

MAP INDICATING GENERAL DISTRIBUTION OF TREES IN SOUTH AFRICA AND SOUTH WEST AFRICA (NAMIBIA)

SUGGESTED READING

CARR, J.D., 1976. The South African Acacias. Johannesburg: Conservation Press.

COATES PALGRAVE, K., 1977. Trees of Southern Africa. Cape Town: C. Struik.

CODD, L.E.W., 1951. Trees and shrubs of the Kruger National Park. Memoirs of the Botanical Survey of South Africa, No. 26.

DE WINTER, B., DE WINTER, M. & KILLICK, D. J. B., 1966. Sixty-six Transvaal trees. Johannesburg: Voortrekkerpers.

DE WINTER, B. & VAHRMEIJER, J., 1972. The national list of trees. Pretoria: Van Schaik.

DYER, R.A., 1965. The cycads of Southern Africa. Bothalia 8: 405-515.

ELIOVSON, S., 1965. South African wild flowers for the garden. Cape Town: Timmins.

GALPIN, E. E., 1925. The native timber trees of the Springbok Flats. Memoirs of the Botanical Survey of South Africa, No. 7.

HENKEL, J. S., 1934. The woody plants of Natal and Zululand. Durban: Natal University Development Fund Committee.

HENNESSEY, E. F., 1973. South African Erythrinas. Durban: Natal Branch of the Wildlife Protection and Conservation Society of South Africa.

IMMELMAN, W. F. E., WICHT, C. L. & ACKERMAN, D. P. (ed.), 1973. Our green heritage. Cape Town: Tafelberg-Uitgewers.

KROMHOUT, C. P., 1967. Twenty kinds of Transvaal timbers. Fauna & Flora 18: 1-29.

KRUGER, T. J., 1973. Bome, struike en rankplante. Bethal: Kruger.

LEISTNER, 1970. Trees and Shrubs of the Willem Pretorius Game Reserve. Bloemfontein: O.F.S. Prov. Admin.

LETTY, C., 1962. Wild flowers of the Transvaal. Pretoria: Trustees of the Wild Flowers of the Transvaal Bookfund.

MOLL, E. J., 1967. Forest trees of Natal - a field guide to 200 species. Durban: Wildlife Protection and Conservation Society of South Africa.

PALMER, E., 1977. A field guide to the trees of Southern Africa. London: Collins.

PALMER, E. & PITMAN, N., 1972-1973. Trees of Southern Africa. Cape Town: A. A. Balkema. 3 vols.

POYNTON, R. J., 1963. A guide to the characteristics and uses of trees and shrubs. Forestry Dept. Bulletin No. 39. Pretoria: Department of Forestry.

ROSS, J. H., 1972. The *Acacia* species of Natal. Durban: Natal Branch of the Wildlife Protection and Conservation Society of South Africa.

SIM, T. R., 1907. The forests and forest flora of the Colony of the Cape of Good Hope. Aberdeen: Taylor & Henderson.

SMITH, C. A., 1966. Common names of South African plants. Memoirs of the Botanical Survey of South Africa, No. 35

STOKES, H., 1967. What tree is that? Cape Town: Purnell.

TREE SOCIETY OF SOUTHERN AFRICA, 1964. Trees and shrubs of the Witwatersrand. Johannesburg: Witwatersrand University Press.

URTON, N. R., 1962. Guide to the indigenous trees of the Eastern Cape. Port Elizabeth: Port Elizabeth Technical College.

VAN DER SPUY, U., 1971. South African shrubs and trees for the garden. Johannesburg: Hugh Keartland Publishers.

VAN WYK, P., 1973-1974. Trees of the Kruger National Park. Johannesburg: Perskor. 2 vols.

WATT, J. M. & BREYER-BRANDWIJK, M. G., 1962. The medicinal and poisonous plants of Southern and Eastern Africa. Edinburgh: Livingstone.

18 *Podocarpus latifolius* (True Yellowwood, Opregte Geelhout)
Evergreen tree up to 33 m high. *Leaves* narrow, linear-elliptic, 3,5 - 6 cm long, 0,6 - 0,8 cm wide. *Male cones* catkin-like, 1 - 2 cm long. *Female cones* with fleshy receptacles, 8 - 14 mm long; cones produced between October and January.

39 *Celtis africana* (White Stinkwood, Witstinkhout)
Deciduous tree, usually about 13 m high, with pale grey bark. *Leaves* egg-shaped, 4 - 10 cm long with 3 prominent basal veins. *Flowers* small, yellow-green, appearing mostly in September. *Fruits* spherical, 6 mm in diameter, yellow.

122 ***Boscia albitrunca*** **(Shepherd's Tree, Witgatboom)**
Evergreen tree, usually about 5 m high, with white trunk. *Leaves* narrowly oblong, tapered at base, 5 cm long, 1,3 cm wide. *Flowers* small, star-shaped in clusters, appearing from August to October. *Fruit* round, 5 - 10 mm in diameter, light brown.

187 ***Acacia sieberana*** **var.** ***woodii*** **(Paperback-thorn, Papierbasdoring)** Deciduous tree, 4 - 8 m high, with umbrella-shaped crown, peeling bark and paired, white, straight thorns. *Leaves* feathery, 5 - 15 cm long. *Flowers* in creamy white, spherical heads about 13 mm in diameter, appearing from October to January. *Pods* thick and woody, 10 - 25 cm long, 2,5 cm wide.

148 ***Albizia adianthifolia*** **(Flat-crown, Platkroon)**
Deciduous, markedly flat-topped tree, about 10 m high with white twigs. *Leaves* feathery, up to 23 cm long and 15 cm wide. *Flowers* creamy green, in heads, appearing in September and October. *Pods* parallel-sided, 18 cm long, 2,5 cm wide.

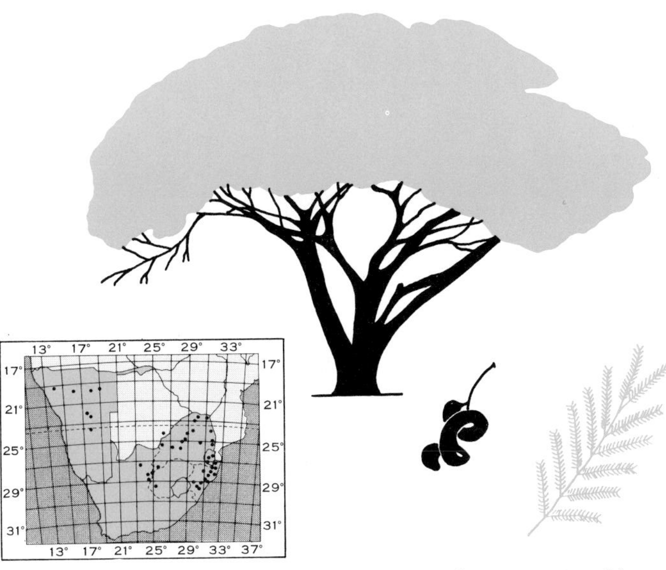

188 ***Acacia tortilis*** **subsp** ***heteracantha*** **(Haak-en-Steek)**
Deciduous, round or flat-topped tree, 5 - 8 m high, with paired hooked and straight thorns. *Leaves* feathery, 5 cm long. *Flowers* in cream, spherical heads, about 5 mm in diameter, appearing from November to February. *Pods* curled or corkscrew-shaped, up to 5 cm long.

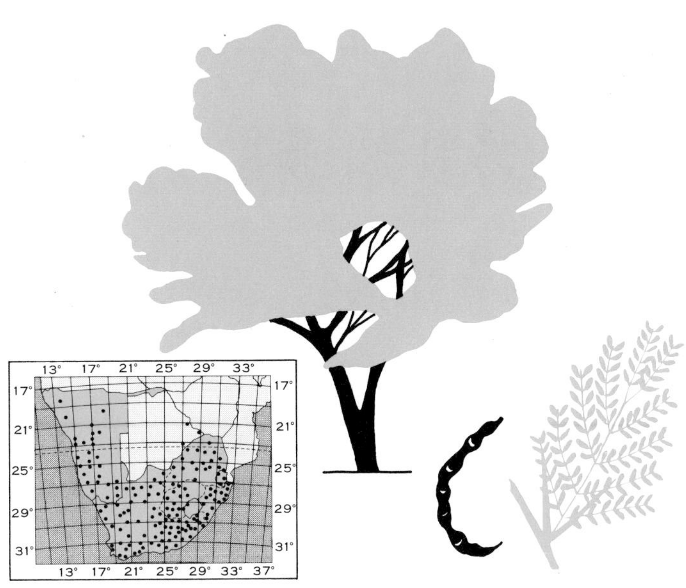

172 ***Acacia karroo*** **(Sweet-thorn, Soetdoring)**
Deciduous, round or flat-topped tree, 5 - 10 m tall, with paired straight white thorns. *Leaves* feathery, up to 12 cm long, 5 cm wide. *Flowers* in yellow spherical heads, 1 cm in diameter, appearing from November to April. *Pods* sickle-shaped, narrow, 5 - 8 cm long, in clusters.

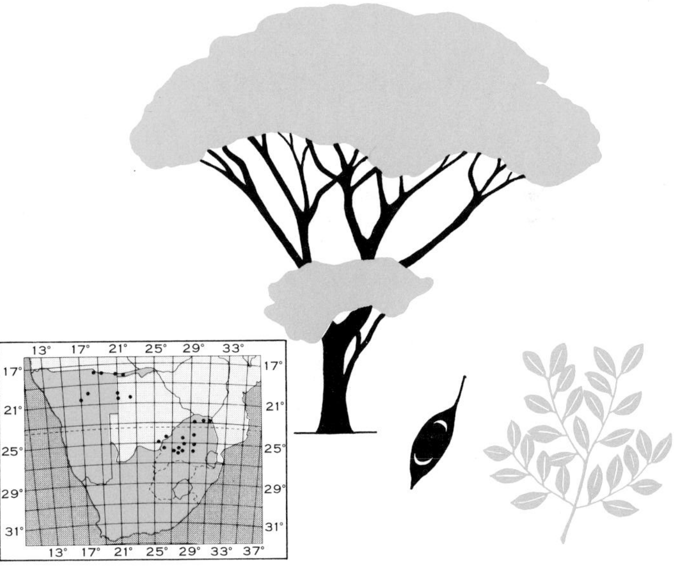

197 ***Burkea africana*** **(Wild Seringa, Wildesering)**
Deciduous, round or flat-topped tree, 8 - 10 m high. *Leaves* twice-branched, 30 - 37 cm long. *Flowers* small, cream, in drooping tassels 15 - 20 cm long, appearing in October and November. *Pods* oval, with pointed ends, up to 8 cm long, flat.

202 ***Schotia brachypetala*** **(Weeping Boerboon, Huilboerboon)**
Evergreen, round-topped tree, 6 - 10 m high. *Leaves* once-branched, 7 - 15 cm long, with oblong asymmetrical-based leaflets. *Flowers* cup-like, deep red, in clusters, appearing in September and October. *Pods* oblong, up to 12 cm long and 5 cm wide, flat.

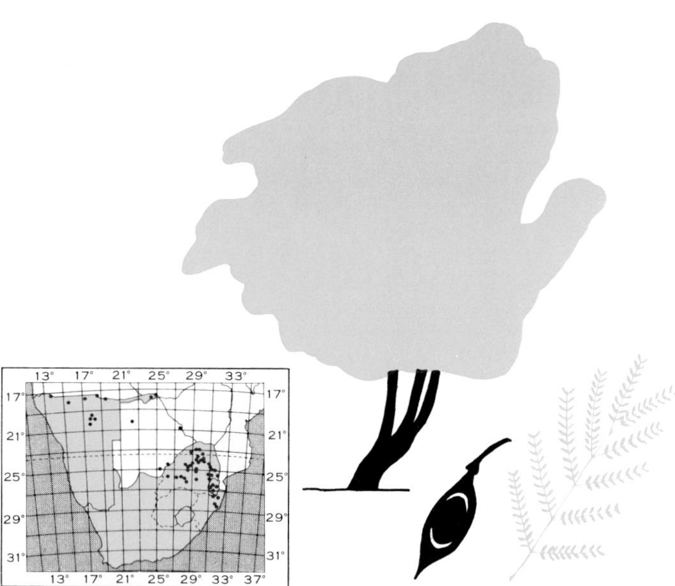

215 ***Peltophorum africanum*** **(African Wattle, Huilboom)**
Deciduous tree, 6 - 13 m high with spreading crown. *Leaves* feathery, about 10 cm long. *Flowers* in erect sprays at ends of branchlets, up to 2 cm in diameter, yellow, appearing from October to February. *Pods* flat, 5 cm long, 1,3 - 1,9 cm wide, tapered at both ends.

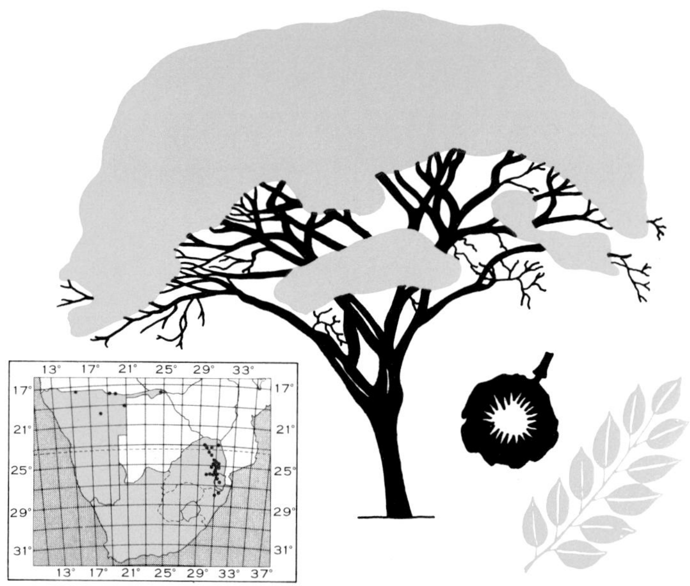

236 ***Pterocarpus angolensis*** **(Kiaat)**
Deciduous, spreading tree, 10 - 15 m high. *Leaves* drooping, once-branched, up to 38 cm long. *Flowers* pea-like, 1,3 cm long, cream-yellow, in sprays at ends of branches, appearing in September and October. *Pods* circular, 8 cm in diameter, with bristly central portion.

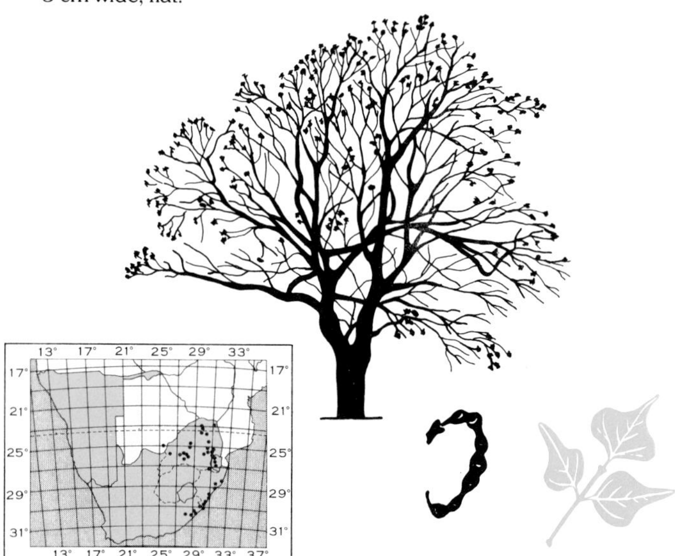

245 ***Erythrina lysistemon*** **(Transvaal Kaffirboom, Transvaalse Kafferboom)** Deciduous tree, 3 - 8 m high, with narrow crown and scattered thorns. *Leaves* long-stalked with 3 heart-shaped leaflets up to 10 cm long. *Flowers* scarlet, in triangular bunches, appearing from July to September. *Pods* 8 - 15 cm long, constricted between seeds.

301 ***Trichilia emetica*** **(Natal Mahogany, Rooi Essenhout)**
Evergreen, spreading tree, 10 - 13 m high. *Leaves* once-branched, up to 30 cm long, with 3 - 5 pairs of leaflets and 1 terminal leaflet, deep green. *Flowers* bell-shaped, creamy white, in bunches at ends of branches, appearing in September and October. *Fruit* stalked, almost spherical, 2,5 cm in diameter.

351 ***Euphorbia ingens*** **(Candelabra Tree, Naboom)**
Candelabra-shaped, succulent tree, 10 - 15 m high, with angled branches and milky juice. *Leaves* small, produced only on young plants. *Flowers* male and female borne in clusters at ends of branches, reddish, fleshy, appearing from April to June. *Fruit* roundish, 8 - 10 cm in diameter.

360 ***Sclerocarya caffra*** **(Marula, Maroela)**
Deciduous tree, usually 8 - 13 m high, with spreading or rounded crown. *Leaves* once-branched, 15 - 30 cm long, blue-green. *Flowers* minute, male and female on separate trees, appearing mainly from September to November. *Fruit* plum-like, 3 - 4 cm in diameter, yellow.

536 ***Combretum erythrophyllum*** **(River Bush Willow, Vaderlandswilg)** Deciduous tree, up to 13 m high. *Leaves* lance-shaped to oblong, narrowed at both ends, up to 10 cm long and 5 cm wide. *Flowers* small, yellow or green, clustered in spherical heads, appearing in September to November. *Fruit* 4-winged, about 1,3 cm long.

386 ***Rhus lancea*** **(Karee)**
Evergreen tree or shrub, about 8 m high, with rounded crown. *Leaves* digitate, consisting of 3 lance-shaped leaflets. *Flowers* very small, yellow-green, in sprays in axils of leaves and at ends of branches, appearing from late summer to winter. *Fruit* roundish, slightly flattened, about 6 mm in diameter.

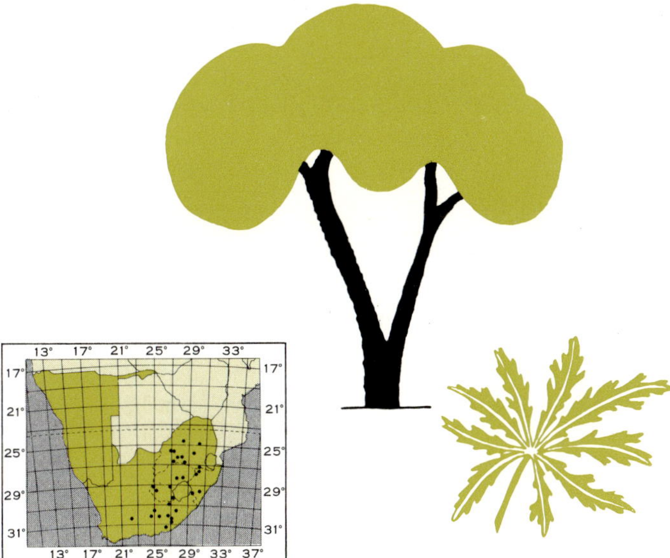

563 ***Cussonia paniculata*** **(Highveld Cabbage Tree, Hoëveld-Kiepersol)**
Evergreen tree, 3 - 5 m high with corky bark and mop-like crown of leaves. *Leaves* large, digitate, consisting of 15 - 17 leaflets, grey or blue-green. *Flowers* small, greenish in short stalked spikes arranged in sprays.

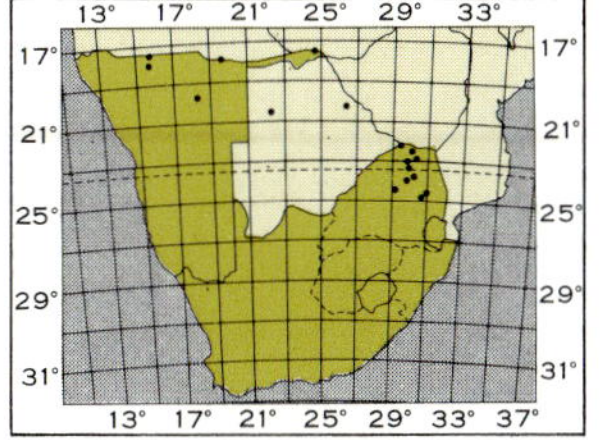

467 ***Adansonia digitata*** **(Baobab, Kremetartboom)**
Deciduous tree, up to 15 m high with spreading crown and huge trunk. *Leaves* digitate, consisting of 5 - 7 leaflets on long stalk. *Flowers* large, pendulous, white, 13 - 15 cm in diameter, appearing from October to December. *Fruit* egg-shaped, 10 - 25 cm long.

617 ***Olea africana*** **(Wild Olive, Olienhout)**
Evergreen, spreading tree or shrub, 2 - 10 m high. *Leaves* lance-shaped or oblong, tapering at both ends, up to 8 cm long and 1,3 cm wide. *Flowers* small, white or cream, in sprays in leaf axils, appearing from October to March. *Fruit* roundish, up to 1 cm in diameter, black.

The Law and The Caravaner

The caravaner, as well as obeying the laws relating to motorists, should exercise special care when towing a caravan. In addition, he must comply with the regulations relating to the caravan itself. The following information will assist.

Registration and Licensing

Caravans must be registered. They must be licensed annually and the clearance certificate must be affixed in a waterproof mounting in a conspicuous position on the left side of the caravan so that it is clearly legible from that side.

The licence issued is to own a caravan, whether used on a public road or not. Exemption from a licence will be granted only under certain circumstances. When buying a second-hand caravan, a roadworthy test and certificate are required for transfer of the caravan into your name.

The cost of the licence is based on the tare (T) of the caravan, and varies in the different provinces, adjacent countries and in South West Africa/Namibia. A valid licence covers the caravan for holiday visits to all provinces, S W A/Namibia and adjacent countries, including Rhodesia.

If the owner moves his place of residence to another town or territory, he must immediately notify the local licensing authority of both his old and new address, failure to do so is an offence.

Insurance

Caravans must be covered by Third Party (MVA) Insurance. The premium is nominal and the insurance is renewable on the 1st May each year. The token of insurance must be displayed on the front of the caravan so it is clearly visible from the lefthand side. Comprehensive insurance is not compulsory. The premium is generally related to the value of the caravan and not to its size or mass.

The Caravan Itself

There are certain important requirements applicable to caravans which must be adhered to. Reputable caravan manufacturers ensure that their caravans, as sold to the public, comply with these requirements but the following details are given so that if a used caravan is purchased or alterations are made to an existing caravan, the provisions of the basic legal requirements may be verified.

Information to be Displayed

The following information must be displayed on the caravan in letters and figures not less than 40 mm in height:

Tare (in kilograms) - designated "T"

The permissible maximum laden vehicle mass (in kilograms) - designated "V"

The manufacturer of the caravan will supply particulars of tare and permissible maximum vehicle mass if these are not already displayed on the caravan.

Direction Indicators

If the towing vehicle's indicators are obscured by the caravan or if the overall length of the combination of vehicles exceeds 7,6 m the rear end of the caravan must be fitted with indicators, one on each side, at a height of not less than 450 mm and not more than 2,1 m from ground level. This, in effect, requires all caravans to be fitted with flasher direction indicators at the rear. They are connected to the car's direction indicator control system.

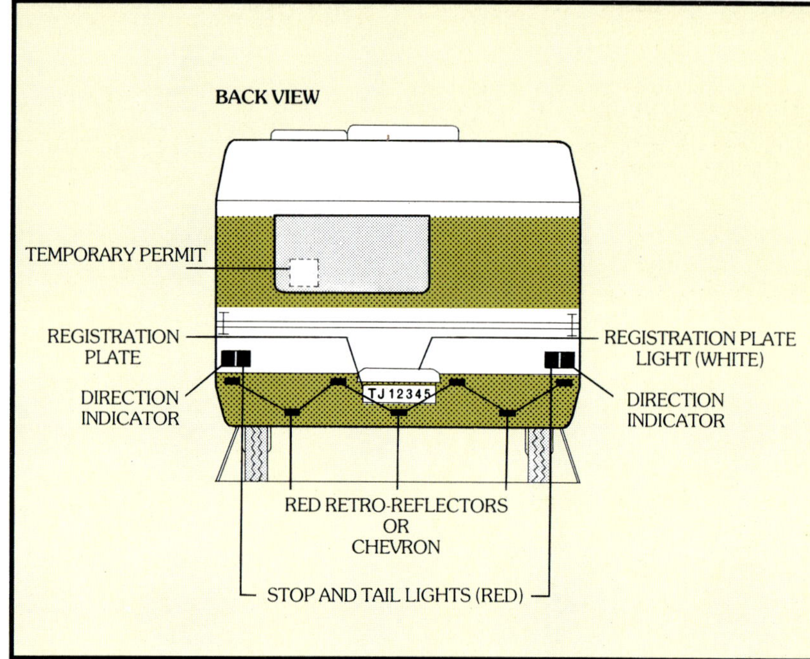

Lights

1 *Rear lights (red)*
1 lamp each side or 1 in the centre or on the right side of the caravan, not less than 300 mm or more than 1,5 m from ground level.

2 *Stop lights (red)*
Requirements the same as for rear lights but maximum height above ground level is 2,1 m.

3 *Registration plate light (white)*
At least 1 lamp must be fitted to make the registration plate "plainly distinguishable" from a distance of at least 20 m. The light must not shine directly to the rear, but must only illuminate the registration plate. Both towing vehicle and caravan must have registration plate lights.

Reflectors

1 *Front reflectors - 2 white reflectors,* one on each side, must be fitted at the same height facing forward at the front, not more than 50 mm from the outer edge of the caravan.

2 *Rear reflectors* - a chevron sign or 7 red reflectors in the prescribed pattern or an inversion of this pattern, must be fitted at the rear of the caravan, with the lower edge thereof not more than 1,1 m above ground level. The pattern of red reflectors is more easily fitted than the chevron sign and has a less "commercial" appearance. Refer to Figures 1 and 2.

3 *Side Reflectors* - 2 yellow reflectors must be fitted at all times - depending on the length, three may be required.

4 *Height* - All reflectors must be not less than 300 mm or more than 1,1 m from ground level.

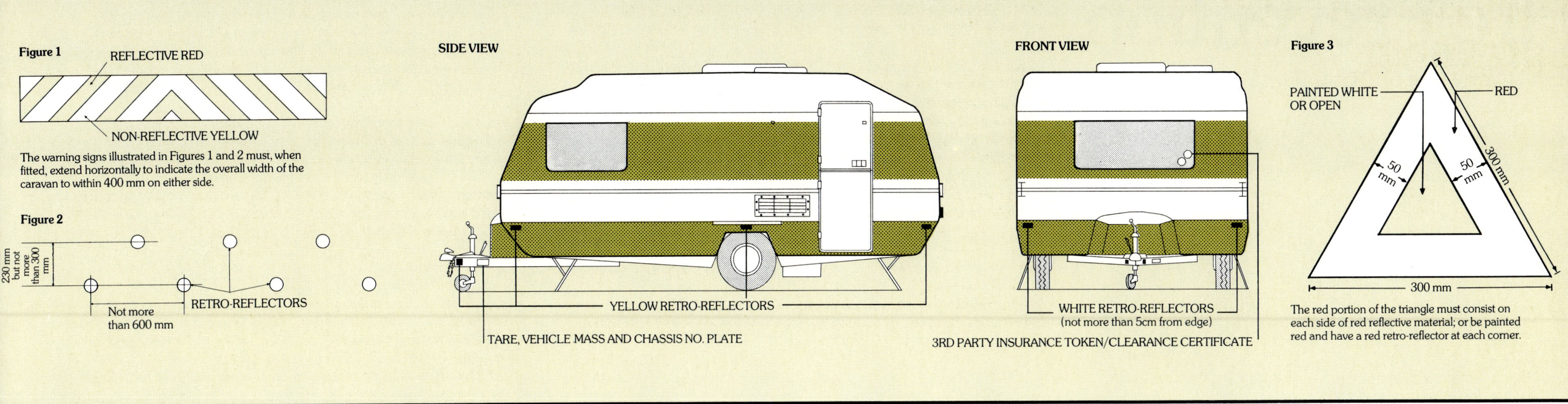

Registration Plates
These must be fitted at the rear of the caravan, not more than 1,5 m above ground level. The use of reflectorised plates having black characters on a yellow reflective background is a requirement in all provinces, but only in the case of first registration or re-registration.

Brakes
The brakes required to be fitted to a caravan are related to its gross vehicle mass (GVM) and the relationship of the GVM to the tare of the towing vehicle. These are the rules:

1 If the GVM of the caravan (namely the mass of the caravan plus its maximum load) does not exceed 570 kg and does not exceed half the tare of the towing vehicle - only a parking brake is required.

2 If the GVM is from 571 to 1 360 kg and does not exceed three-quarters of the tare of the towing vehicle - a parking brake *plus* an overrun brake or a service brake is required.

3 If the GVM exceeds 1 360 kg or the GVM does not exceed 1 360 kg but exceeds three-quarters of the tare of the towing vehicle - a parking *and* a service brake are required.

The importance of good braking cannot be over-emphasised and it is advisable to have the overrun braking system (as fitted to the majority of caravans) checked and adjusted when seasonal maintenance is carried out.

Towbar and Towing Distance
The maximum distance allowed between the towing vehicle and the caravan is 3,5 m. Manufactured caravans are built to comply with this.

Rearview Mirrors
The regulations require that a vehicle towing a caravan shall be fitted with a rearview mirror or mirrors to enable the driver to have a clear reflection of traffic to the rear.

To comply not only with the letter but the spirit of this regulation it is therefore necessary to fit two external rearview mirrors to the towing vehicle, namely one on each side, since it is virtually impossible to have a clear reflection of *all* traffic to the rear if only one external rearview mirror is fitted.

In the interests of road safety it is strongly recommended that two external rearview mirrors be fitted, as described. Before commencing a tow, the driver should specifically check their adjustment to satisfy himself that he has a satisfactory view to the rear.

Warning Triangles
Two free standing red warning triangles, as described in Figure 3 must be carried by a car/caravan combination. If for any reason the combination of vehicles, or the caravan by itself, has to be parked or is immovable in the roadway, a triangle must be placed 45 m to the front and to the rear of the vehicle/s. If only one-way traffic is involved then only one triangle need be displayed 45 m on the side of the vehicle from which the (one-way) traffic will approach.

IMPORTANT NOTE
It is forbidden to stop any vehicle (including a caravan) on a public road outside of an urban area within 1 m of the edge of the roadway - except of course in a parking place which is designated as such by an appropriate sign. Caravaners should meticulously obey this regulation which is for the safety and convenience of all road users. Severe penalties may be incurred for breaches of this law.

Carrying Persons in Caravans - PROHIBITED
Carrying persons in a caravan while it is being towed is *prohibited.* Apart from being illegal it is a dangerous practice: persons could fall and be injured, unknown to the driver; while serious consequences would certainly follow an accident involving the towing vehicle or the caravan.

Fire Prevention

for the Caravaner and Camper

As growing numbers of people are lured by the wide and beautiful countryside and the magnificent climate enjoyed in South Africa, so more and more caravans find their way on to the roads and into remote and virtually inaccessible places.

While everyone will agree that one of the most pleasant ways of getting away from the "rat race" is in a caravan, few consider the consequences of a fire involving a caravan or its towing vehicle when far from help.

The old saying "Prevention is better than cure" is an apt one and before proceeding on a trip every caravaner should stop and take stock of the situation and ask himself:

1 What causes fire to break out in a caravan?

2 Do I know what to do?

3 Am I prepared?

Let us look at the hazards involved.

Fires in Towing Vehicles
Fires occur quite commonly in motor vehicles, the most usual causes being:

1 Electrical

2 Fuel leakage

3 Careless handling of smoking material.

It is essential to be properly equipped to deal with any fire and to know how to react.

The primary requirement in dealing with fires is a cool head. Do not panic. Remember, "more haste, less speed." As with your caravan, your motor car or towing vehicle should be equipped with an approved fire extinguisher, either dry chemical or BCF (Bromochlorodifluoromethane - look for the SABS approval sign when purchasing). The extinguisher should have a capacity of at least 2,25 kg.

An important point to remember - DO NOT keep your extinguisher in the boot of your car. There are valid reasons for this - the fuel tank is usually situated below and if this is involved you may not be able to reach the extinguisher; also, you may have the boot packed with luggage and by the time you locate the extinguisher, it may be too late.

Accepting that there are three main types of fire in which motor vehicles are commonly involved, they should be dealt with as follows:

☐ ELECTRICAL FIRES (figure 1)
Disconnect a battery terminal as quickly as possible. This will, in most cases, be sufficient to bring about extinction. If, however, the fire continues to burn, it must be tackled with a fire extinguisher, with the jet of chemical being directed at the heart of the fire from as close a range as possible.

☐ FUEL FIRES (figure 2)
Fires involving fuel are easily dealt with if the correct action is taken. The fire extinguisher must be used promptly and with determination. The user should move as close to the fire as possible and work in the direction the wind is blowing, never against it. The jet of chemical should be aimed directly at that part of the fire where burning appears to be most vigorous and should be worked to and fro with a rapid sweeping motion.

☐ FIRES INVOLVING THE INTERIOR OF CARS (figure 3)
These fires are almost always caused by cigarettes or matches but occasionally by defective electrical wiring in which case they usually start off in a slow smouldering manner. If possible, whatever is involved should immediately be removed from the vehicle and the fire extinguished, either by using a fire extinguisher or by using water, which is preferable in this case.

At this stage it is appropriate to point out that with the exception of the water-filled type, modern fire extinguishers, although very swift and positive in action, have very little cooling effect and it will, in almost every case, be advisable to douse the extinguished fire with water to cool it down and prevent re-ignition. Remember though, not to use water in an attempt to extinguish a petrol fire while it is actually burning, as this could cause the fire to spread over a wider area, with disastrous results.

Fires in Caravans
☐ LIQUID PETROLEUM GAS (LPG)
The advent of LPG has made life for the caravaner and camper comfortable and civilised and if treated with due respect, the hazard occasioned by this product is negligible. However, in the case of LPG, a demon is clamouring for release and never lets up for a second.

The physical properties of this gas make it extremely dangerous in its free state (i e when unburnt gas is freely mixed with air). The flammable range is roughly between 2% and 9% of gas to air. From these figures it is apparent that a small amount of free gas could lead to disaster. To add to this, the source of ignition required is very small (a static spark or a carelessly flicked cigarette end is enough) and the amount of heat energy released is so great as to cause immediate ignition of any combustible material within the gas cloud. The gas, in its vapour state, is 1½ times heavier than air and will consequently, if allowed to escape, seek out any low-lying areas. It is not toxic, but is a simple asphyxiant (i e it could cause suffocation if breathed in in high concentrations). Fortunately a stench agent is added and very small leaks are detected by smell.

Bearing the above information in mind, the following are a few hints for the safe usage of LPG:

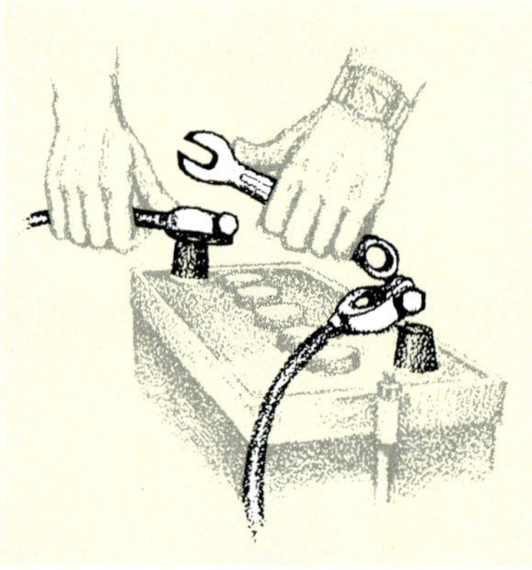

Figure 1

Figure 2

1 Never leave the main cylinder valve on when gas is not actually being consumed.

2 Unless you are properly qualified, do not attempt to install any LPG appliance.

3 Do not leave the main cylinder valve exposed to children or other persons who may tamper with it. Consideration should be given to attaching a tamper-proof lock.

4 Always carry out a check on piping and fittings before leaving on a trip and when setting up camp.

5 NEVER allow an LPG bottle to lie on its side during discharge as this will result in liquid gas being discharged, thus creating a very hazardous situation.

6 Always try to achieve maximum ventilation through your caravan, especially at low level and at night. For this a floor vent is essential.

7 If a lamp or any other appliance becomes extinguished, NEVER strike a match or lighter before turning off the main valves and ventilating the caravan thoroughly.

8 When entering a caravan that has been closed for any period, always smell for gas, especially at low level. The "nose test" is very sensitive to the gas smell. If gas is detected, ensure that the gas is turned off properly at the bottle and ventilate thoroughly. Check that all taps are closed before re-opening the gas bottle and seeking a possible leak.

9 Should a fire occur at any point on an LPG system, ALWAYS try to turn off the gas bottle valve first. This might be all that is required to extinguish the fire. Never extinguish the flame without also turning off the valve as this will lead to a further accumulation of unburnt gas and a possible explosion.

10 If you have connected to an electrical power supply , never switch on a light or any other appliance without first checking for leaking LPG.

11 If you suspect a leak, test the spot with a soap solution which will bubble if there is a leak. Do NOT light a match.

12 Do not travel with the refrigerator burning. Such action can prove very dangerous on a garage forecourt filled with petrol fumes.

Figure 3

Figure 4

Flammable Liquids

Flammable liquids present a serious fire hazard and should as far as possible be eliminated. If you *have* to use any flammable liquid, keep as small a quantity as possible. Never use indoors and always keep in an unbreakable container.

Cooking

Disastrous fires are frequently caused through cooking accidents. With a little care all danger can be avoided.

REMEMBER

- ☐ Never leave a stove unattended
- ☐ Use as little oil or fat as possible when frying
- ☐ If oil or fat ignites in a pan, *do not panic!* Simply cover the pan with a lid or a damp cloth as this will smother the flames quickly. Above all, do not attempt to carry the pan outdoors as this will almost certainly result in your burning yourself, dropping the pan and starting a serious fire. If you have NO alternative but to carry the pan outside, walk backwards very carefully. This will cause the flames to be blown away from you. Do not attempt to douse the burning oil with water - it will explode and spread the fire . . . and could blind you. (figure 4)

Siting of the Caravan

Always make sure that an area of at least 4m around the van is cleared of long grass, brush and other easily ignited material. Never build camp fires close to your vehicle or in windy conditions.

Fire Extinguishers

The most essential item of caravan equipment is an efficient fire extinguisher. There are two types, both equally efficient, which are suitable for use in caravans.

1 The dry chemical type, and

2 The vaporising liquid type (BCF)

Both, if used intelligently, will give rapid extinction of fire in its incipient stage. The fire extinguisher should preferably be mounted on a sturdy bracket outside the van and in a place that affords easy access, away from the LPG cylinders.

Experiment with your fire extinguisher, read the instructions and become used to handling it. Recharging is inexpensive and it is reassuring to know that you will be able to deal with a fire should one occur.

When camping in an urban area, make it one of your first jobs to find out if there is a fire brigade nearby. If so, memorise the telephone number and determine the position of the nearest telephone, in case of emergencies.

Veld Fires

Each year during the dry season hundreds of thousands of hectares of veld and forest in the Republic are destroyed by fire.

Apart from damage to the environment by air pollution, soil erosion and "view-pollution" caused by these fires, there is the tremendous financial loss and the untold misery suffered by wildlife.

It is known that a number of veld fires are caused by campers who treat fire in a thoughtless and haphazard manner. The senseless destruction of our beautiful countryside can be prevented if people take the following precautions:

1 Avoid making campfires when a high wind is blowing during dry seasons

2 Make campfires only in suitable places, not against logs or trees or under overhanging branches

3 Remove all combustible material, scrape away all flammable leaves, pine needles, etc., leaving a cleared area of at least 1m around your fire

4 If you dispose of paper by burning it on the campfire, screw it up tightly before putting it on to the fire. Loose sheets have a tendency to rise on the thermal current and may blow away and start a fire in nearby dry grass

5 Make sure that cigarette ends are properly extinguished by tramping on them

6 Avoid discarding burning matches by making a habit of breaking them in half before throwing them in a refuse bin

7 Fires made on the beach should be carefully extinguished, soaked and covered with sand to prevent burns to the feet of passersby

8 NEVER throw burning cigarette ends out of the window of your car; use the ashtray

9 Make absolutely sure that your campfire is properly extinguished when breaking camp. Soak the coals, turn all sticks, stir and soak again. Feel to see if the heat has gone

10 Smoke from veld fires can generally be seen from a considerable distance. Slow down when you see this and don't add to traffic congestion which can become hazardous.

With a few exceptions, all fires are caused by people. Exercise a reasonable amount of care, never leave small children on their own and you need never worry about or have any fear of fire.

First Aid

for the Caravaner and Camper

Accidents occur wherever people are found and this is no less true of the caravaner and camper who is often far from or inaccessible to skilled help when accidents happen.

A sound knowledge of first aid and of how to apply it properly may therefore save a life or limb and is of inestimable value and importance in emergencies. The following notes are of necessity brief, but will provide a good working knowledge of the action to be taken in assisting injured persons until such time as skilled assistance can be obtained.

To facilitate such emergency action, a first aid box should always be part of your equipment. It should contain the essentials for treating the injuries that are most common in accidents. Do not use the contents except in an emergency and as soon as possible after using any items you should see that they are replaced.

(First aid outfits, of various types, are available from any AA office at reasonable cost).

Essential items for inclusion in a first aid kit are:

- ☐ Ammonia
- ☐ Antiseptic lotion
- ☐ Bicarbonate of soda (for biliousness)
- ☐ Boracic crystals (for eye lotion)
- ☐ Boracic ointment
- ☐ Burn ointment
- ☐ Castor oil
- ☐ Fruit salts
- ☐ Iodine
- ☐ Sal Volatile (for fainting attacks)
- ☐ Sunburn remedies
- ☐ Petroleum jelly
- ☐ Witch hazel (paint on bruises)
- ☐ Antiseptic sticking plaster
- ☐ Boracic lint
- ☐ Crepe bandage, 75 mm
- ☐ Gauze
- ☐ Roller bandages, 25 mm to 58 mm
- ☐ Several triangular bandages
- ☐ Clinical thermometer
- ☐ Needles
- ☐ Pair of scissors
- ☐ Safety pins (various sizes)
- ☐ Torch (for use at night and for throat examinations)
- ☐ Tweezers

ACTION IN AN EMERGENCY

Do Not Panic

Your priorities of treatment are:

1 Cases of suffocation
2 Severe bleeding
3 Treatment of unconscious patient

Casualties who can help themselves can be given dressings to press on their bleeding wounds.

Unconscious patients who are breathing and not bleeding severely should be turned into the semi-prone position - see Figure 1.

Do not leave your casualties at any time to call for help. Wait for help and let others do the alerting.

Do not move casualties unless they are threatened by further injuries.

N.B. Your AA Handbook contains a list of emergency telephone numbers of the nearest hospital, police station or ambulance depot of the towns listed in the section "AA-Appointed Tow-in Service Garages."

ARTIFICIAL RESPIRATION

Steps in mouth to mouth artificial respiration:

1 Determine patient is not breathing
2 Inspect mouth and back of throat for foreign bodies or other obstruction. Clear this, especially false teeth
3 Hyper-extend neck (tilt head as far back as possible and pull chin up) - Figure 2
4 Close nose
5 Deep breath - mouth to enclose open mouth of patient - Figures 3 and 4
6 Blow firmly and watch for chest to rise
7 Remove mouth from patient's, turn face to one side and count five - Figure 5. Repeat. Continue till patient starts to breathe
8 Never leave your patient once he starts breathing, because breathing could stop again very quickly.

In drowning cases this method of respiration can - and should - be used without waiting until dry land is reached. You can blow into his nose while standing or kneeling in the water, while leaning over the side of a boat, or from the edge of a swimming pool or the bank of a river or lake. A person who has nearly drowned will have his stomach and lungs full of water. Emptying this is of lesser importance - the priority is to blow air into his lungs, and everything else must wait.

BLEEDING

Control of External Bleeding

Bleeding can be stopped by:

Pressing a clean dressing or whatever is on hand, firmly over the bleeding site for at least fifteen minutes. More dressing and firmer pressure is applied until bleeding stops. Bandage the dressing in position with pressure and tie the knot over the bleeding site if you are required for more urgent matters. Otherwise maintain pressure until help arrives. Never leave a patient who has stopped bleeding as a result of your treatment, because it can start again very quickly.

Bleeding from the armpits or deep wounds needs a dressing plug firmly pressed into it to control haemorrhage.

Direct pressure to bleeding sites is safe and effective.

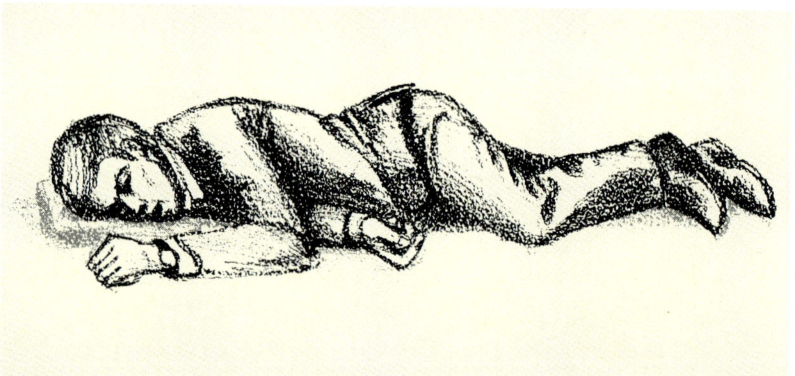

Figure 1

Bleeding Nose
Lay the patient on his back - if the bleeding continues, place something cold, such as ice, over the nose bridge or make the patient suck a block of ice.

Undo tight clothing at the neck and waist.

Tell the patient to breathe through his mouth.

Do not allow him to blow his nose.

Keep the patient quiet for a while after the bleeding has stopped.

BITES AND STINGS

Animal Bites
Allow the wound to bleed freely and then wash it with cold water and antiseptic lotion. Send for the doctor if the patient has been bitten by a dog or cat, or if it is a severe bite of any other kind.

Bees and Wasps
Carefully remove the sting. If the sting is in the mouth, hold bicarbonate of soda solution or ice in the mouth. If it is an exterior sting, apply either a blue bag, witch hazel, sal volatile, washing soda or soothe it with cold water or ice - let the patient rest.

Insect Bites
Apply a patent remedy.

Mosquito Bites
Apply a patent remedy or onion juice.

Tick Bite
To remove the tick apply paraffin or vaseline over the tick - this makes the tick withdraw. The itch can be controlled by dabbing ice, calamine or alcohol on the area. If a raised red lump with a black centre occurs, consult a doctor as soon as possible in case of tick bite fever.

SNAKE BITE

The bites of venomous snakes produce effects which are readily recognised. These symptoms determine the course of treatment. Assume that all large, unknown snakes are cobras and use serum if remote from help. *It is, however, preferable to obtain skilled medical assistance before embarking upon serum treatment.*

The Puffadder
This, the commonest of our poisonous snakes, is bold and frequents paths used by small rodents. It does not move away when it feels footsteps approaching and strikes at the walker's lower leg or foot.

Reactions: Immediate, intense and burning local pain. A rapidly occurring, gradually increasing and spreading swelling with reddening and possible bruising. There is no immediate danger to life unless the victim is bitten on the face or neck or is a small child.

Treatment: When it is anatomically possible, infiltrate the bitten area as soon as possible with as much serum as possible and inject remaining serum into a muscle or under the skin nearby. Quietly remove the victim to a hospital or doctor who can inject more serum into a vein if this is needed. Drugs for the relief of pain, such as a codeine compound, are advised. *Do not* apply a constricting bandage, make incisions or apply Condis crystal: they are useless measures and may cause increased damage.

Cobra, Ringhals and Mamba
The *cobra* and the *ringhals* are large, ground-living snakes and prefer to avoid humans. If confronted and unable to escape they rear up with expanded hood, while the ringhals may eject venom at a moving part, usually the head and eyes. In desperation they will strike.

Within South Africa, the *black mamba* is mainly confined to the Transvaal and Natal. It also occurs in South West Africa/Namibia and other neighbouring territories. It may be encountered on the ground or in trees and bush. It is aggressive, often very big, and ejects a large quantity of highly toxic venom. The *green mamba* is mainly confined to the eastern coastal belt. It is rarely seen on the ground but is common in Natal bush. It is shy, not aggressive, and its venom differs from, and is less toxic than those of all the other snakes in this group.

Reactions: There may be moderate local pain but no marked damage. Signs of general poisoning may occur within minutes but are commonly delayed from one half to two or more hours. Pallor with clammy sweaty skin, restlessness, nausea and vomiting may be followed by obvious signs of paralysis, i.e. drooping eyelids, slurred speech, drunken gait, difficult swallowing and a gradually decreasing frequency and depth of breathing which, untreated, will stop altogether and the victim will die.

Treatment: Reassure the victim and lay him down. Apply a wide (50 mm or more) constricting band on the upper part of the bitten limb and tight enough to prevent any flow of blood to or from the limb. It should not be applied longer than at most two hours and should be released for a few seconds every thirty minutes. Do not inject serum if a hospital or doctor is within reach. If this is not the case, or if the victim already shows signs of progressive systemic poisoning, inject the available serum intravenously if the attendant is experienced, otherwise under the skin and/or into the muscle at several sites on the body. Keep the air passages clear. Keep the victim's head on its side, swab away saliva and do not encourage eating or drinking if the patient has difficulty in swallowing.
Prepare for artificial respiration.

If a spitting snake has ejected venom into the eyes they will smart and burn. Washing with water or any non-irritating fluid will usually be effective; if not, a few drops of serum diluted in a little water will bring relief.

Boomslang
The boomslang, although very toxic, is nervous and lives in trees. It experiences difficulty in getting its back fangs into rounded surfaces such as limbs, but persons handling these snakes may be bitten.

Reactions: Immediate pain, with a little oozing of blood from the puncture. Within hours the victim will have a headache and will probably become aware of bruising of the skin. There may be bleeding from old cuts, from the gums and the nose in particular. The urine and stools may become bloody but such signs of serious poisoning appear late, if at all. This venom interferes with the clotting of blood and although the effect is not immediate or even rapid, it is extremely serious and may be fatal.

Treatment: Do not apply a constricting bandage but take the victim to a hospital where he can be treated with serum. Forewarn the hospital so that the serum can be ordered.

General
Incisions are not recommended, but suction should be applied to the fang marks. A mechanical suction device is included in the AA snake-bite outfit. Whether treated in the field or not, every person bitten by a snake should be taken to a hospital for observation and further treatment should this become necessary.
Serum should at all times be kept in a cool place as heat causes a loss in potency. It should be kept in a normal refrigerator except when it is being carried on a journey.
The following serums are available in South Africa and the type required is determined by the area in which it may be needed. *Snake-bite outfits are available from all AA offices.*

Type of Serum	Snake	Area
Polyvalent	Effective against the venoms of all important cobras, mambas and vipers (adders)	Throughout the Republic, South West Africa/Namibia
Boomslang*	Boomslang	Whole of Transvaal, Natal, coastal belt of the Cape Province and northern South West Africa/Namibia

* *Not supplied to the public but made available to hospitals on request by The South African Institute for Medical Research, Johannesburg. Telephone 724-1781. Telegram "BACTERIA".*

Figure 2

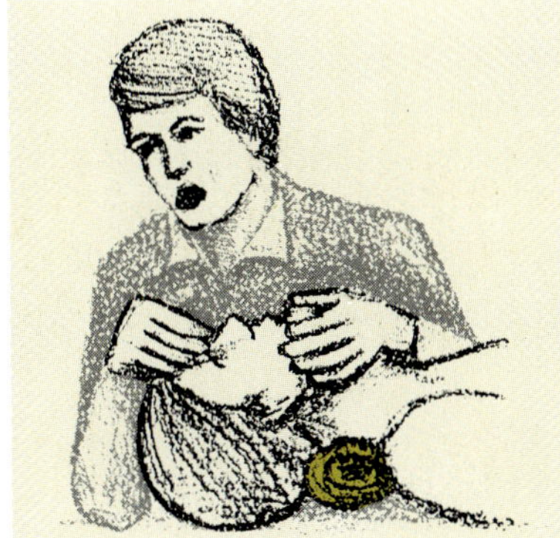
Figure 3

Figure 4

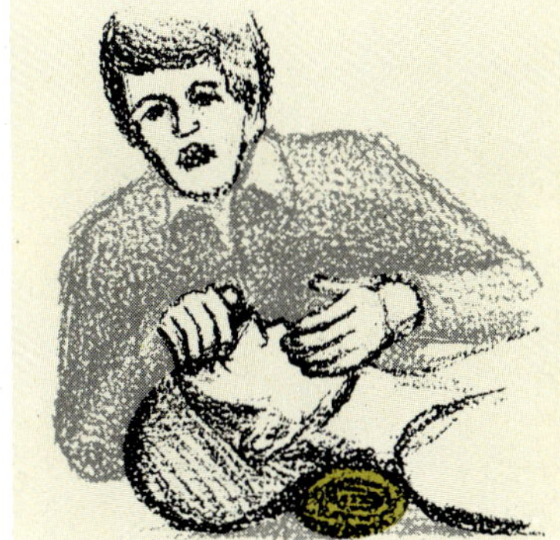
Figure 5

BURNS AND SCALDS

Burns are caused by dry heat, friction, electricity, strong acids or alkalis.
Scalds are caused by moist heat - steam, boiling water, hot fat.
DO NOT remove any clothing which is adhering to the burnt part. Carefully cut clothing away around the injured area. Do not prick or break blisters. Protect the burn from sunlight.

Treatment: Treat the patient for shock. (see "Shock", page 18). Immerse the injured part in chilled water if possible for 15 to 30 minutes, or if obtainable, apply ice. Then cover small burns with a clean dressing soaked in a solution of bicarbonate of soda. (1 dessertspoon to 2 cups of water). Cover serious burns loosely with a clean cloth and send for medical aid.

Burns by alkaline corrosive (i.e. quick lime)
Use an acid solution, e.g. lemon or lime juice, or vinegar, in equal quantities with warm water. Treat for shock and send for a doctor.

Burns by corrosive acid
Apply solution of bicarbonate of soda or washing soda.

Burns caused by clothing catching alight (see Figures 6 and 7)
Wrap rug, coat or table cloth tightly round the victim to put out the flames and keep the patient still. Treat for shock and burns. Do not use fats, oils or greasy ointments. Do not prick blisters or remove clothing which is sticking to the burnt area, as this will cause infection.

Burns caused by electricity
Switch off current or remove the patient from the contact by using a non-conductor, i.e. pole, branch, belt or rubber gloves. *Do not* touch the patient or use anything metallic or wet to pull him away while the current is still on. If the patient has stopped breathing, apply artificial respiration (see page 14).

Sunburn
AA sunburn kits are available from all AA offices at nominal cost.
Treatment:
1 Protect the burn from the sun
2 Apply calamine lotion or witch hazel
3 If blisters form, cover with a light, clean cloth, or sterile dressing

Scalded Throat
Give the patient ice to suck. If badly burnt, send for medical aid.

BROKEN BONES (see also FRACTURES)

A fracture of one of the bones of a limb may be assumed if there is pain and inability to use the limbs, or if there is any deformity; this may be apparent as a shortening of the limb or as an irregularity in the shape of the bone.

1 Handle the patient very gently where a fracture is suspected. Do not move him at all until after the fracture has been treated unless it is unsafe to treat him where he is.
2 Steady and support the whole length of the injured limb by hand, and get another person to pull *gently* on the injured limb below the seat of the fracture so as to bring it as nearly into its natural line as possible.
3 If there is a wound at the seat of the fracture or elsewhere on the injured limb, dress it as described in the paragraph on WOUNDS (page 18).
4 Fractures of the collar-bone, ribs, upper arm, forearm or hand can be secured by placing the arm in a sling and then passing a broad bandage (see Figures 10 and 11), round the middle of the upper arm on the injured side and tying it round the chest on the opposite side.
5 If the lower jaw is broken, place the centre of a narrow bandage below the chin; carry one end up one side of the face and over the top of the head to meet the other end above the opposite ear; cross the ends, carry them horizontally round the head and tie. (See figures 8 and 9).
6 Fractures of the thigh or the bones of the lower leg and foot can be secured by bandaging both legs together at four places: round the feet and ankles, below the knee and at mid-thigh.

CAR SICKNESS

Persons who suffer from car sickness should obtain a doctor's or chemist's prescribed medicine. Fresh air is a help but it is wise to take the precaution of providing suitable bags in the car.

CONCUSSION

If the patient is breathing and not bleeding, turn him into the semi-prone position and keep the airway open by having the neck in the extended position. Should the patient vomit, then this position will allow vomitus to drain out of the mouth, and it is less likely to be inhaled and so cause breathing problems.

If the patient is not breathing apply artificial respiration and establish breathing before turning the patient into the semi-prone position. If the patient is bleeding and unconscious turn him into the semi-prone position, if the control of bleeding can be performed in this position, otherwise treat bleeding and stop blood loss before treating the patient in the unconscious position.

Never leave an unconscious patient alone - stay and maintain the unconscious position, to ensure that breathing continues and bleeding is under control. Loosen tight clothing. Do not give fluids to unconscious patients. Take the patient to hospital as quickly as possible.

CUTS AND GRAZES

Carefully remove the dirt by bathing the injured part with warm water or a warm salt solution (1 teaspoonful to a tumbler of water). Apply a clean dry dressing, then cover with cotton wool and bandage. If the skin around the wound becomes inflamed and beads of pus gather in it there is probably some dirt still in the wound. Take the patient to a doctor at once. If the dressing sticks, bathe it off with warm water.

DISLOCATIONS

Make the patient comfortable on blankets; support the injured limb and await the doctor. DO NOT ATTEMPT TO PUT THE BONE BACK INTO POSITION.

DROWNING

Commence artificial respiration. (see page 14).

EXPOSURE

This can be very serious and the patient should be removed to receive proper medical attention as quickly as possible. In the meantime:
1 Cover the patient with blankets or coats to prevent his catching a chill
2 Do not apply a hot water bottle or use a heater
3 Allow the patient to take small sips of fluid from a spoon.

FAINTING

If the patient has been in the sun, move him into the shade and make sure he has plenty of fresh air. Loosen all tight clothing. If the patient is conscious give him some cold water or warm sweetened tea. If he is pale, keep his head down; if flushed, keep his head up. Let the patient inhale ammonia, smelling salts or sal volatile. If he is hot and flushed in the face, apply wet cloths to the back of his neck and bathe his face and hands in cold water.

FISH HOOK IN PATIENT'S FINGER

Where a fish hook has penetrated into a patient's finger beyond the barb, it is best removed by pushing the point gently through to the other side. Make a small cut where you can see the point pressing from the inside against the skin. Cut off the eye of the hook with pliers and then push the hook through and draw it out. Wash the wound with antiseptic lotion and dress the finger.

Figure 6

Figure 7

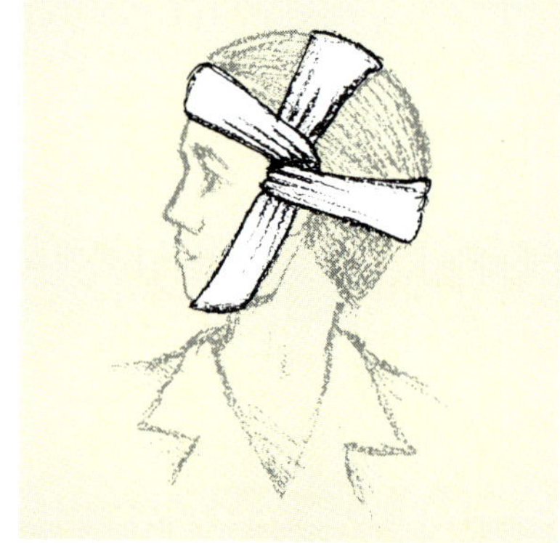
Figure 8

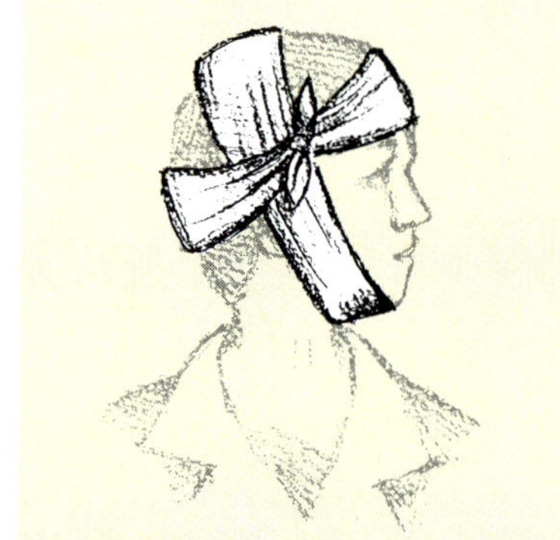
Figure 9

FOREIGN BODY IN THE EAR

1 Do not try to prod the object out of the ear
2 Turn the patient's head on one side - the object may drop out. If not -
3 Pour olive oil into the ear in order to dislodge the object
4 Take the patient to a doctor at once.

FOREIGN BODY IN THE EYE

Do not rub the eye. Blow the nose hard, which may remove the object. If this fails, seat the patient, stand behind him, steady his head and separate the eyelids, using fingers and thumb. Locate the foreign body and carefully remove it with the corner of a clean handkerchief or small piece of cotton wool. If the particle is stuck to the eyeball, do not attempt removal. If pain continues, cover the eye with a pad, bandage lightly and take the patient to a doctor.

FOREIGN BODY IN THE NOSE (peas or beads pushed up the nose)

1 Do not try to prod the object
2 Tell the patient to blow his nose violently
3 If the object has still not become dislodged, take the patient to a doctor.

FOREIGN BODY IN THE THROAT

The most effective method of dislodging a foreign body from the top of the windpipe or the back of the throat is to squeeze the stomach walls directly below the ribs suddenly and sharply towards the backbone. The abrupt rise of intrathoracic pressure should dislodge the object.

FRACTURES (see also BROKEN BONES)

Signs: Pains near the site of the fracture, loss of power of the limb, swelling, deformity of limb, irregularity along the line of the bone, unnatural mobility.

Treatment: Guard against further injury. Attend to the fracture on the spot. If bleeding, cover the wound with a clean dressing. Apply the bandage so that it does not press on to the fracture. Support the broken limb in a comfortable position. Apply slings, bandages or splints after the limb is placed in the best position. Improvise splints from wood, folded paper or cardboard; pad splints to fit limb. Fractured forearm is supported with a wide sling which includes the elbow, a fractured upper arm is supported from the wrist. A fractured thigh needs a long splint extending from the armpit to the feet. (See Figures 10 and 11).

Fractured Collar Bone

1 Support the injured arm by holding the elbow, until a sling is ready. Put a narrow fold bandage round each shoulder and tie behind.
2 Thread a belt or bandage through the shoulder loops and tie firmly to brace the shoulders back.

An arm sling can be made from a couple of large handkerchiefs. Secure the sling round the neck with a reef knot at the back on the undamaged side. Place the arm bent across the body at the elbow, in the sling. Bring the point of the scarf or cloth round the back of the arm and pin it so as to hold the elbow securely. Get a doctor as soon as possible.

Fractured Thigh and Leg

In cases of severe fracture of the thigh or lower leg, call an ambulance wherever this is practicable. If no ambulance is available the best method of moving the patient to hospital is to seat him across the rear seat of a car with his back against the locked door and with someone by his side to steady him. If you have to move him, get as many people to help as you can so that the broken limb is disturbed as little as possible. (See Figures 12 and 13).

Fracture of the Skull

Visible injuries to the head may be accompanied by fracture of the skull, of which there may or may not be obvious evidence. If there is a wound, dress it as already described. Severe head injuries frequently cause unconsciousness or semi-consciousness. This may be temporary, if the patient has been merely stunned, or it may be prolonged, indicating serious injury to the skull or brain.

If the patient's breathing is noisy it means that it is obstructed. Lack of adequate oxygen can quickly cause death and you should get the patient breathing easily as soon as possible. Turn him into the unconscious position with his head turned to one side. (See Figure 1 Page 14).

All head injuries are serious. The patient must be taken to hospital even if he appears to recover quickly. A doctor's opinion is essential as deterioration can set in later.

Fracture of the Spine

This may occur if the patient has fallen on to a raised or projecting object, or if the back or neck has been subjected to the extreme forces caused by a car's impact. By itself this injury will usually not cause loss of consciousness, but there will frequently be partial or complete loss of feeling and power of movement on both sides of the body below the seat of the fracture - for example, in both legs.

Treat with extreme care, because this injury is very serious. Unless the patient is in an unsafe place he should not be moved. If he *has* to be moved out of harm's way (and this should be avoided if at all possible) you must get two or three people to help you. He must be lifted in the position in which he is found - for instance, on his side, or his face or his back - *and the utmost care must be taken to avoid any bending of the spine.*

HEART

The brain cells are dependent upon a good supply of oxygen - after 5 minutes lack of oxygen they die or cease functioning. The heart is the pump which moves the red blood cells that transport essential oxygen supplies where they are needed. Time is the most important factor, as minutes count between life and death.

Where the heart has stopped, it can sometimes be started by squeezing the heart between the spine and the breastbone. To do this,

1 Lay the patient flat on his back on a firm surface
2 Place the palm of the hand over the breast bone and then place the other hand over the first (See Figure 14).
3 Depress both hands with a sharp jerk if the patient is an adult, but exercise care where the patient is a child (See Figure 15).
4 Repeat this rapidly or apply mouth to mouth resuscitation until skilled help arrives. (See page 14).

HICCOUGHS

Let the patient slowly sip a dessertspoonful of white vinegar.

POISONING

Berries

If someone has eaten poisonous berries:

1 Make the patient vomit to remove the poison from the system as quickly as possible by
  a) tickling the back of the throat with your fingers
  b) giving an emetic - two tablespoonsful of salt in a glass of warm water every 5 minutes until vomiting occurs
2 Take the patient to a doctor immediately.

Figure 10

Figure 11

Figure 12

Figure 13

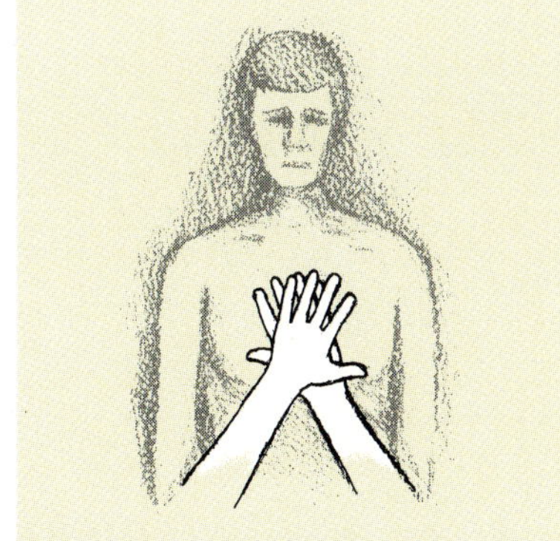

Figure 14

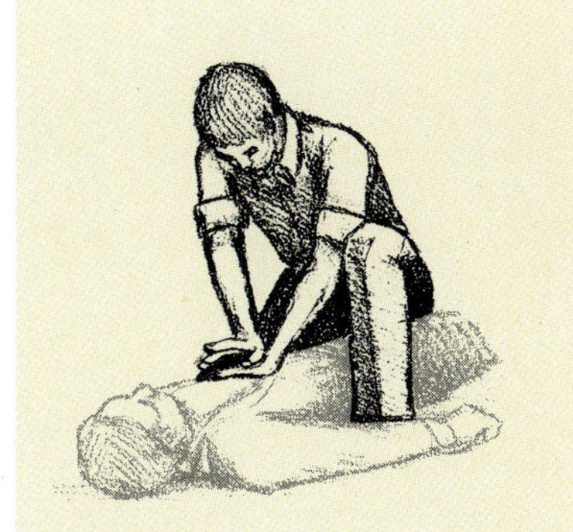

Figure 15

Figure 16

Figure 17

Figure 18

Figure 19

Carbon Monoxide
The symptoms are: headache, dizziness, difficulty in breathing, collapse and unconsciousness.

Remove the patient from the poisonous atmosphere (i.e. car engine left running in confined space).

Apply mouth to mouth resuscitation. (see page 14).

Food Poisoning
1 Induce vomiting with two tablespoons of salt or 1 teaspoon of mustard in a glass of water
2 If possible, keep the matter vomited to help the doctor diagnose the cause of the poisoning
3 Make the patient comfortable
4 Give fluid freely with a pinch of salt in each cupful of water.

SHOCK (See Figure 16)
Most people suffer from shock after having been involved in an accident. Shock is caused by a loss of blood from the general circulation system. This loss of blood in turn can be the result of external bleeding, internal bleeding, or stasis of blood in tissues of the body. Shock is aggravated by fear and anxiety. Once shock has been allowed to develop to an extreme form it cannot be treated effectively except by blood transfusions. If the injured person is treated soon enough, however, much can be done to stop the development of shock.

Symptoms are usually a pale face and lips, cold sweat on the forehead, cold and clammy skin, pulse rapid, feeble or imperceptible, weakness and giddiness.

After removing the patient from danger, you should:
1 Lay the patient flat on his back, on blankets or coats
2 Control any bleeding
3 Keep his head low and turned to one side
4 Loosen clothing round his neck, chest and waist
5 See that the patient can breathe freely - disperse onlookers
6 Reassure the patient to relieve his anxiety as far as possible - do not discuss his injuries with the patient or with others in his presence
7 Elevate the lower limbs unless they are injured
8 Use a coat or rug to keep the patient warm but not too hot
9 In severe cases, apply hot water bottles wrapped in a cover, between the legs or to the feet. DO NOT OVERHEAT TO PRODUCE SWEATING, AS THIS INCREASES SHOCK

10 Do not give anything to eat or drink - no tea, coffee, water or alcohol
11 Send for an ambulance or a doctor

SMOTHERING
This occurs when the supply of air is cut off, e.g. by gas, clothing etc. Remove the patient from the cause and apply artificial respiration.

SPLINTERS
1 Remove the splinter and apply antiseptic lotion
2 If the splinter is buried in the skin and is easily visible, it can often be removed with sterilised tweezers, a needle or a sharp penknife.
3 If the splinter is too deeply imbedded, it is advisable to leave it for the doctor to remove.

SPLINTS (See Figures 17, 18 and 19)
The patient will be made more comfortable if the fractured limb can be splinted. The best splints are flat pieces of wood long enough to extend well above and below the fracture but if these are not available any object which is of a suitable size and rigid enough to give support, may be used. Tightly rolled newspapers, a folded magazine or a rolled rubber floor-mat may be suitable for the arm, while the long handle of a jack will give support in the case of a fracture of the thigh or lower leg.

SPRAINS
Apply cold dressings to the affected joint. Keep the sprained limb comfortably supported by a pillow or coat while the patient is lying down.

SUNSTROKE
1 Place the patient in the shade
2 Apply cold wet cloths to the back of his neck and body, i.e. increase cooling.

TOOTHACHE
Temporary relief may be obtained by holding hot water in the mouth or by painting the affected part with the oil of cloves - it is preferable however, to see a dentist as soon as possible.

UNCONSCIOUSNESS
1 Stop all serious bleeding
2 Send for a doctor at once
3 Turn the patient on to his side in the semi-prone position
4 Make sure that his mouth is free of obstructions, remove froth, mucous, or blood and false teeth
5 Loosen clothing at neck, chest and waist
6 Ensure that the patient has fresh air - keep onlookers away
7 Give nothing by mouth while the patient is unconscious
8 Stay with the patient and await help.

UPSET TUMMY
1 Do not allow patient to eat any solid food for twenty-four hours
2 Make sure that he drinks only boiled or bottled water
3 If he is suffering from diarrhoea give him Kaolin mixture - one tablespoonful every four hours
4 If the symptoms persist or remain after twenty-four hours, call a doctor
5 Give fluid freely.

WOUNDS (See Figures 20 and 21, 22 and 23)
Wherever they are, wounds should be treated as follows (the utmost cleanliness is essential):
1 Try to stop local bleeding by applying local pressure, elevate the bleeding part, except in the case of fractures.
2 Expose the wound and gently swab away any dirt with clean gauze. Wherever possible it should be taken from a sealed packet.
Apply a sterile dressing, selecting a size large enough to cover the wound. If one dressing is not large enough, use more. Apply the dressings with the gauze inner surface next to the wound. Be careful not to touch the inner surface of the gauze.
3 Apply a bandage firmly over the dressing. Tie or pin it in place. (A triangular bandage can be used in various widths by folding it in two, three of four, thus making a broad, medium or narrow bandage. It can also be used unfolded as a sling for the arm, with the centre point projecting a little beyond the elbow and the ends round the neck and tied over the shoulder on the injured side).

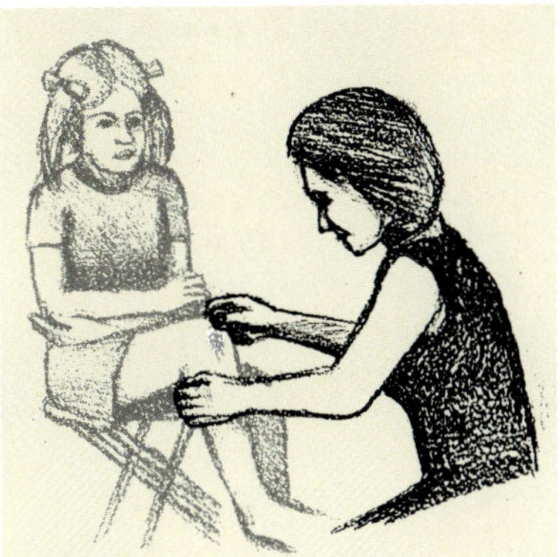
Figure 20

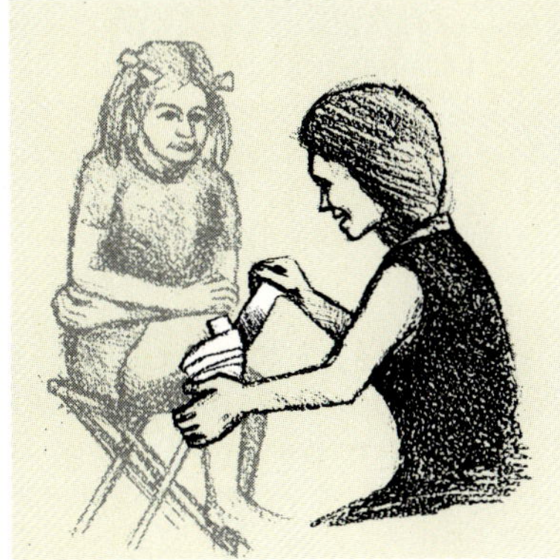
Figure 21

Figure 22

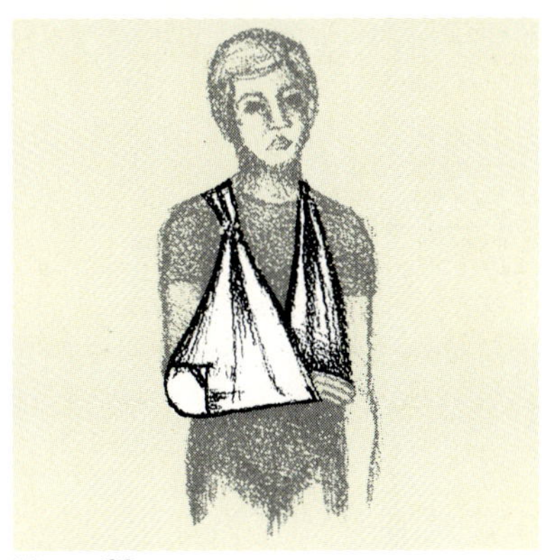
Figure 23

BLEEDING FROM WOUNDS IN THE NECK
If a large blood-vessel in the neck is cut open - for example, by a splinter of glass - fatal bleeding may occur and immediate attention is essential. In this case, of course, it will be dangerous to tie a tight bandage over the injury and you should immediately *apply direct pressure* with the fingers over a dressing in the wound. Be careful to press backwards or forwards and not sideways, otherwise the windpipe will be compressed.

HEALTH AND HYGIENE (General)

There are certain rules applying to the camping or caravaning holidaymaker, which if disregarded could have very unpleasant results or even necessitate returning home before time.

Health is a matter of commonsense and it is foolish to take unnecessary risks. Holidaymakers are always prone to sunburn. Sunbathing should not be confused with sunbaking. Over-stimulation by sunbathing in the warmest part of the day, or by working while the skin is exposed, overloads the bloodstream with toxins. The first exposure should not be for more than five minutes in direct sunlight, gradually lengthened. Protect the eyes, the back of the neck and spine from direct sunlight. Fair-skinned people should take extra care - it is wise to wear a hat.

Never dash into the water until you have cooled off a bit. Do not bathe within forty minutes of having eaten a heavy meal.

Enquire locally for safe bathing places, and make sure that there is no risk of contracting bilharzia before swimming in dams or rivers.

It is extremely important that you take the necessary prophylactic drugs if you are going to spend your holiday in an area where malaria is prevalent. These drugs are obtainable without prescription from any pharmacy and should be taken before, during and after your visit to the area.

Cramp
If you get cramp while swimming and supposing that it has as usual attacked your leg, you should turn over on your back, bend the knee of the cramped leg towards you, get hold of your big toe and pull it strongly towards you. This will make the cramped muscles relax.

It is wise to understand the principles of artificial respiration. For detailed instructions see page 14. Never allow children who cannot swim to go into the water without a competent swimmer supervising them. It is also wise to have a good knowledge of life saving procedure.

Drinking Water
Drinking water is often the cause of upsets on holiday. Whenever possible, use tap water from a mains supply. If you are in doubt as to whether the water is pure, boil it or use water-purifying tablets.

Do not scatter dirty water over vegetation but pour it into a pit. If streams are used for washing, investigate upstream to see if there is animal or human pollution.

Warmth
Protection from cold and damp is essential. If you are caught in a downpour without shelter, keep moving. At the first opportunity, strip off all wet clothing and have a brisk rub down with a dry towel. Have a warm drink as soon as you are dressed in dry clothing. Always sit on a ground sheet, never directly on the ground, which is nearly always damp.

Sore Feet
Those who are not used to doing much walking may suffer from sore feet on unaccustomed long walks in the country or climbs in the mountains. Tender feet can be hardened by soaking in a salt and water bath. This hardens the tender skin and softens the hard parts. Stronger than salt and water is a solution of a tablespoonful of alum of potassium permanganate dissolved in 4,5 litres (±4½ family sized cooldrink bottles) of water, or the soles of the feet can be rubbed with methylated spirits to harden them. After washing the feet remember to dry carefully between the toes and dust with boracic powder to absorb moisture. Never open any blisters, just protect with a light dressing which you should change every second day. In wet weather discard shoes and stockings - bare feet dry quickly in a tent or round a fire or stove.

Gas Appliances

Most of the caravans which are available today are fitted with a variety of gas appliances. In order to obtain the most benefit from the use of gas, which is dangerous if incorrectly handled, it is important that users familiarise themselves with some of its characteristics.

Liquified Petroleum Gas or LPG as it is commonly known, is a universal fuel with features that make it popular for all kinds of outdoor applications. Among its many advantages are economy, cleanliness and portability. It is also readily available from numerous sources throughout South Africa.

It is a colourless substance which is stored under pressure as a liquid in steel containers of varying sizes which are specially made to withstand the pressure, which will either increase or decrease with changes in temperature. Pure LPG is odourless, but a small amount of chemical with a distinctive odour (Mercaptan) is added for commercial use so that the gas can be smelt in case of leakage.

Should this smell be noticed at any time, locate its source immediately. To do this, check all gas connections for tightness and valves for correct operation. Then close windows and doors. Check that all taps or cookers and lighters are closed before opening the gas bottle valve. Accurate location of the leak can be made by applying a soapy water solution to the pipe joints or fittings which will bubble if gas is leaking. Do *not* look for a gas leak with a naked flame. If the leak is found at a joint, loosen the nut, apply grease to the threads and retighten, taking care not to strain the threads.

LPG is non-poisonous but when breathed in in high concentrates may induce headaches or dizziness. It is inadvisable to burn appliances in unventilated areas as the oxygen will burn up and produce carbon monoxide which is poisonous and can cause asphyxiation.

Maintain adequate ventilation in the caravan when gas lights and/or cookers are burning so that the oxygen necessary for correct combustion can be replaced as it is used up. Should any burner go out accidentally and the caravan become filled with gas, first ventilate thoroughly to get rid of accumulated gas *before* relighting.

LPG is approximately 1½ times heavier than air and will tend to collect at floor level. As adequate ventilation is essential at all times it is desirable to have permanently open floor vents, particularly in cases of spillage. When the caravan is stationary a roof vent should also be opened to allow free circulation of air. Alternatively, open the door and windows and agitate the air briskly to clear the caravan of the gas.

Gas regulators should not be tampered with but if in doubt have an authorised dealer check them.

Combustion

LPG cannot burn unless it is mixed with air. Care must be taken not to release gas into a confined space since it will mix with the air and if ignited result in a rate of combustion of explosive intensity. LPG does not pollute the atmosphere as there are no noxious products given off when complete combustion takes place.

Appliances are designed for correct combustion which requires approximately 28 parts by volume of air for one part by volume of gas. If there is insufficient air mixed with the gas when the gas is burnt i.e. overgassing, it results in a turquoise coloured flame with red tips. The correct flame colour is pale blue. In addition, insufficient air mixed with the gas results in incomplete combustion of the gas, thus producing excessive carbon monoxide instead of carbon dioxide.

Jets

Each appliance is designed for a specific quantity of gas which is controlled by the size of the hole in a jet. Use of the correct jet is therefore very important (an identification number is stamped on each jet). Since the size of the hole is very small it is easily blocked by dust or dirt. It can be cleaned with a jet cleaner - do not prick with a pin as this will enlarge the hole. An alternative method is to place some cotton wool in the back of each jet as this will prevent blockages.

If gas is found to leak around the jet sealing face, the leak can be blocked by placing an "O" ring over the jet before screwing it back into position.

Air Intake

As the density of air increases with altitude, the volume of air mixed with the gas for correct combustion is greater at high altitude than at low. Because of this, some appliances have an air intake adjustment clip which can be altered for perfect combustion.

Butane Residue

In South Africa, LPG comprises an approximately equal mixture of Propane and Butane which gives a very high heating value. A full cylinder releases a higher proportion of Propane than Butane initially, resulting in almost pure Butane being left in the bottom of the cylinder when it is nearly empty. Since this has a lower pressure than Propane it can result in less gas flowing through the jet than is required for the appliance to burn properly with the resultant low flame on the burner. The solution is merely to refill the cylinder. However, after a number of refills, the Butane residue should be burnt off or released from the cylinder by opening the valve in a safe area.

Each cylinder has an individual serial number stamped on the skirt together with its tare mass (i.e. mass when empty) and also the month and year of manufacture. To determine the amount of gas in the bottle, weigh the cylinder and subtract the tare mass - the difference gives the mass of gas still remaining. A hand or bathroom scale should be convenient for this purpose.

Overfilling

Since the liquid portion of the gas inside a cylinder expands and contracts with changes in temperature, there must always be a certain volume of gas above the liquid to act as a cushion against the expansion and so prevent the cylinder from becoming entirely filled with liquid.

Each cylinder is designed to hold a certain mass of gas. This ensures that the gas volume above the liquid is never completely taken up by expansion. Should a cylinder be filled by volume on a cold day to the level of the bleeder plug, it would contain a larger mass of gas than that for which it is designed; on a warm day this would expand with a tendency to completely fill the cylinder with liquid.

Apart from the danger of a cylinder being overfilled, it also causes the appliance to function incorrectly as liquid passes through the jet hole resulting in excessive overgassing.

To correct an overfilled cylinder, some of the gas must be released. This should be done outside in an area away from drains, basements or depressions, or any source of ignition. Open the bleeder plug gradually until liquid gas (a whitish coloured vapour) is emitted. Continue until the whitish vapour becomes colourless (indicating that gas is now being emitted) and then tighten the bleeder plug firmly. The cylinder is now ready for use.

USING YOUR GAS CYLINDER

The Gas Bottle - this needs little or no care but should be kept clean. Gas bottles should *never* be placed on top of a stove or near naked flames and must preferably be shielded from the hot sun. When changing cylinders, note that the nut on the regulator has a left-hand thread. Gas bottles should be protected from rust, particularly near the coast - a good tip is merely to insert the gas bottle in a large plastic bag sealed with a rubber band at its neck.

Mantles - before lighting gas lamps ensure that the mantle is intact and that the match is burning before turning on the gas. New mantles should be fixed in position first and then lit before opening the gas tap. When the flame has burnt out, turn on the gas and relight. If the light is not bright adjust the regulator to the best position.

When travelling it is advisable to spray the mantles lightly with a clear hair lacquer to avoid breakage through vibration.

Refrigerators - do not travel with the refrigerator burning. Before driving off, check that all gas taps are turned off and that the tank valve is closed. When the caravan is stationary and the refrigerator is switched on, ensure that there is an air vent or window open near the fridge to provide oxygen for the necessary combustion.

WASTE NOT, WANT NOT

Although bottled gas is inexpensive, observance of the tips listed below will give greater economy of use and increase the efficiency of your gas appliances. The contents of a gas bottle will last longer depending upon how well these simple rules are applied.

Cooking:

1 After filling cooking utensil, place over the burner *before* turning on and lighting the gas. Likewise turn off the gas before removing the utensil from the burner.

2 When lighting a burner, first light the match and apply near burner - then turn the gas on.

3 Where caravans are equipped with ovens, ensure that the match is alight before turning on the gas in the oven. This will prevent an accumulation of gas before igniting and so avoid a "pop".

4 Where the utensil used is smaller than the gas flame under it, reduce the flame to avoid waste of heat up past the side.

5 Turn down the burner flame as soon as food reaches steaming point.

6 Cook in as little water as possible and keep the utensil covered while cooking.

7 Use utensils with straight sides and tight-fitting covers.

8 *Mantles* - have match alight before turning on the gas.

LP GAS CYLINDERS

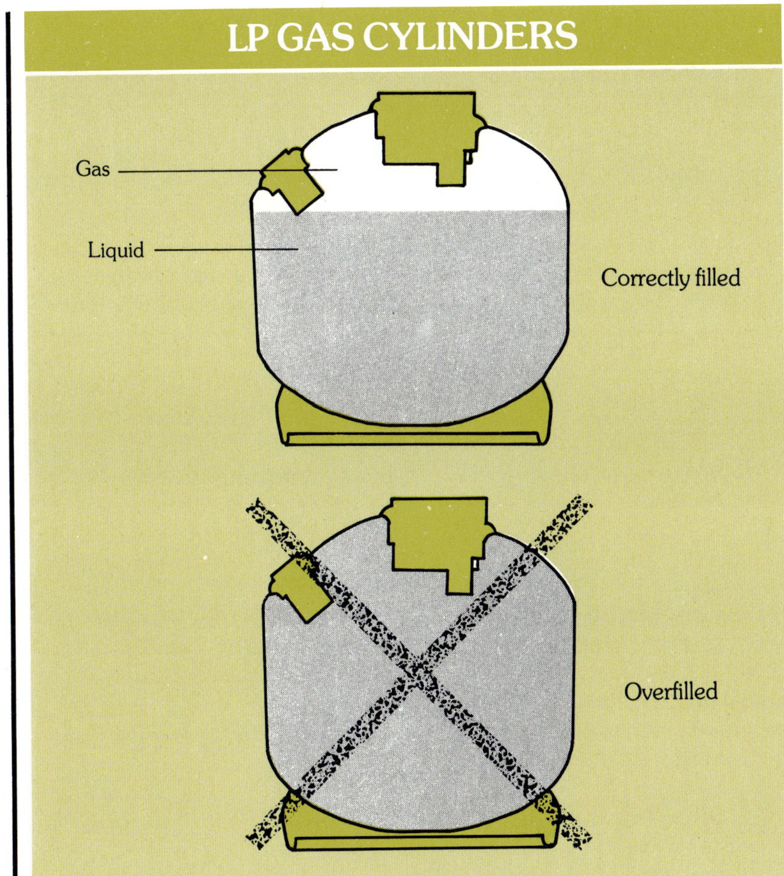

LP GAS AND AIR MIXTURE

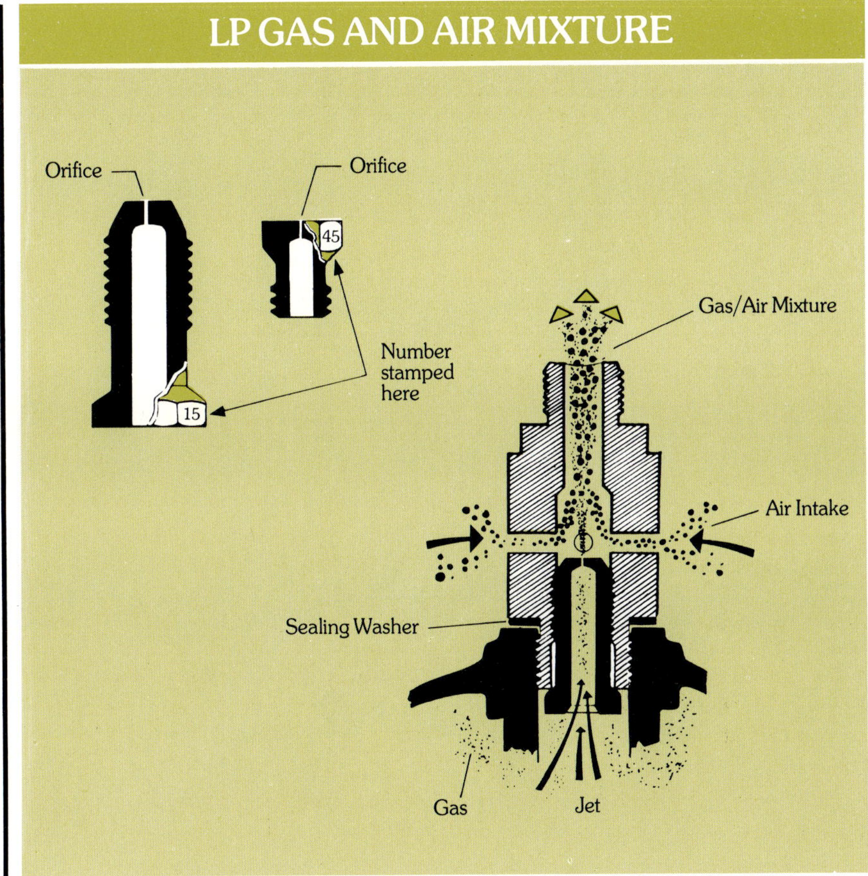

LP GAS CYLINDER

Family Camping

The tremendous advance in latter years in the design and quality of leisure-time products, the establishment of caravan parks and camping sites and the great emphasis on the protection and enjoyment of our natural heritage has contributed much to the popularity of the camping or caravaning holiday.

In the following article, no specific product brands are recommended, but the would-be purchaser is advised to consult reputable dealers, who can provide specialist advice, service and after-sales attention.

Tents

The one item which determines the success of the family's venture into leisure living in the great outdoors is the tent. This is the greatest single expense item in the camping budget.

The kind of tent needed is determined by factors of cost and the size of each family, taking into account the ages and sexes of children. Try to get the biggest tent you can afford. The type and size of car owned will also affect the buyer's decision. *NB:* It may be necessary to consider the purchase of either a roof rack or a trailer to facilitate the transport of this equipment.

Consider carefully how you are going to camp, what equipment you will require to be happy and comfortable, how much privacy each individual in the family requires and the areas where you intend camping - is mosquito-proofing necessary, for instance.

The various types of tents are -

- ☐ the single room cottage type
- ☐ the semi-frame type, with dividing sections
- ☐ the more sophisticated full-frame tent

As the cottage tent does not lend itself to congenial family living, the following notes apply to the semi-frame and full-frame designs. *NB* While the semi-frame is suitable, it is not as versatile as the full-frame design.

The following should be considered in selecting a tent to ensure that you acquire a durable, quality product.

1 *The fabric or canvas* - this should be of quality yarn and essentially pure cotton, fully water-, rot- and mildew-proofed. The colour must be of a high standard of colour fastness and the fabric closely woven to ensure good waterproof and tear-strength qualities. The roofing should preferably be of a heavier type cloth and the side-walls slightly lighter. The tent should fold up compactly and not be too heavy.

2 *Design* - the tent should be reasonably spacious, have good ventilation and a useful sidewall height, to ensure full utilisation of the floor area. Windows should give sufficient light and airiness, and be mosquito-gauzed. Transparent PVC flaps covering the gauze are useful in case of bad weather where the camper requires light but wishes to eliminate rain and wind. Outside zip-up flaps are essential as well as privacy curtains on the inside. In some tents, separate fully enclosed sleeping compartments can be made by zipping-in extra walls.

3 *Doors* - doors are important and a double zipper design which creates a stable-type door is desirable. For South African conditions, a spacious canopy forming a verandah is essential.

4 *Frames* - the frame must be sturdy, well treated against corrosion and light in mass. It is important that frame sections are versatile for easy erection and that they are of an easy packing length.

5 *Flounces* - make sure that the tent is fitted with a wide mud flounce of synthetic coated fabric. (The mud flounce is the strip of material which is constantly in contact with moisture and soil at ground level and is essential to protect the tent wall fabric from soiling and dampness).

6 *Guy Ropes* - guy ropes should be of synthetic material and tent pegs of reliable design.

7 *Cooking Areas* - a specific section for cooking is important in the living area - a PVC splash flap to avoid greasiness on the canvas is a good feature.

8 *Compartments* - inner tents which provide separate fully enclosed sleeping compartments are also popular, particularly for families.

Camp Beds, Mattresses and Sleeping Bags

Camp Beds - two types of camp bed are available, with various models of each type. The first is the sturdy folding type with tubular framework about 16 mm in diameter. This type folds flat with a bulk of about 61 cm x 91 cm x 15 cm. These beds are very comfortable and firm and are the most suitable for heavy persons.

The second kind has a frame with detachable spring steel legs and folds into a small shape - generally suitable for children.

Families with babies should obtain fold-up cots which can double as playpens if necessary.

The amount of packing space available should determine which type of bed is bought.

Camp Mattresses - these are available in various forms. Inflatable airbeds in single or double form are popular but are generally used without camp beds. (NB Don't over-inflate). Roll-up, fold-up types made in sections and filled with solid foam or foam chips are popular. The covering should be durable and suitable for cleaning. Synthetic fabrics are recommended.

Sleeping Bags - these should always be selected with quality in mind. Those with full open-ended zips are a good buy and can be zipped together with a second bag to form a double bag or, when fully opened, be used as an eiderdown.
Note: The outer fabric should be synthetic and the inner fabric cotton. Zips must be of good quality and corrosion-proof. For children, half-zip and completely washable bags are a boon.

Camp Furniture for the Kitchen and Living Areas
A great variety of furniture is available to add comfort to outdoor living. Look for sturdiness, good construction and non-corrosive qualities. Above all, ensure that the furniture you buy is lightweight and folds up completely.

Items available are:
Camp tables, kitchen shelves, fold-up wardrobes - standing type, hanging wardrobes, fold-up cabinets, wash stands with plate driers, clothes driers, folding chairs and camp stools, folding braais and grillers. Visit a specialist camping shop to select equipment to suit your needs.

Camp Cooking
Here the LP gas appliances are a boon. The double or multi-burner stove is essential for family cooking. Pay particular attention to the width, front to back, the burner spacing and overall length - this is important as narrow stoves, or burners placed too close to one another mean that only one cooking utensil at a time can be used.

Stoves with grillers are available, as are collapsible ovens with thermometers. Grids to hold pots must be firm and windshields are useful. Recessed burners provide better heat.
Note: Make sure the area under the grid can be easily cleaned.

The circular stove top, fitted on to a gas cylinder, is useful for picnics or as a standby warmer.

Lighting
Lighting by LP gas is very effective and a large variety of camp lights are available. A useful new accessary is the multi-purpose gas regulator enabling stove, lamp etc. to operate from a common cylinder.

The latest accessary is a transistorised light which operates off a car battery. Instant light at the touch of a switch makes night in the outdoors no problem. The power drain on the battery is negligible. Families with small children will find this a boon - no more scalded or blistered little fingers caused by touching hot gas lamps!

Food Preservation
One of the real problems facing the outdoor enthusiast is the preservation of perishables e.g. milk, butter, meat etc.

The products available for this purpose are the insulated type cooler box and the camping refrigerator.

For the short outing (i.e. weekend) the quality cooler box serves the purpose. It is important that you pre-freeze the perishables, pre-cool the cooler box and shortly before departure, pack the box with the goods and surround them with dry-ice or artificial ice packs. Seal well and 5 to 8 days of cooling is ensured. It is advisable to have two smaller boxes rather than one large one, as the cooling effect lasts longer if the box is not opened.

The solid metal-sided or abs. plastic type cooler boxes are more expensive but are easier to clean. They will also outlast the soft polystyrene type.

Of the camp refrigerators, the 25L or 37L box type with three-way power facility, i.e. gas, 250 volt ac or 12 volt dc power are most effective. This neat little refrigerator is plugged into the house electricity supply and frozen before departure. While you are travelling it is connected to the 12 volt car battery and on arriving at camp it is coupled to the gas cylinder! The power switch-over is instant and it is ideal for outdoor use.

For water cooling, one can select from the large variety of insulated jugs and canvas water coolers which are available.

As the outdoor enthusiast becomes more schooled in the art of outdoor living, a great variety of gadgets will be added to his collection.

The above comprises the basic equipment - the sophisticated items are for individual selection.

The following checklist for outdoor enthusiasts may be useful, particularly if adapted to individual needs.

Happy outdoor living!

CHECK LISTS
(Items are arranged alphabetically)

Clothing
Hiking shoes
Hiking slacks and shirt
Rain coats / Wellingtons
Sewing kit
Socks (extra)
Windbreaker

Personal Equipment
First aid kit
Insect repellent
Mirror
Shaving kit
Suntan lotion
Toilet paper
Toiletries
Torch and spare batteries
Towels
Wash basin

Shelter
Broom
Canvas repair kit
Floor mat
Ground sheet
Pegs and mallet
Plastic sheet for rain protection on windward side
Poles
Ropes
Tent

Bedding
Air mattress pump
Air mattress repair kit
Air or foam mattresses
Bag liners
Camp beds
Carrying cases for sleeping bags
Extra blankets
Ground sheets
Mosquito net
Pillows
Plastic cover for pillows
Sleeping bags
Zipper repair kit

Camp Tools
Axe
Clothes-line
Clothes-pegs
Fire extinguisher
Hammer
Knife
Lantern/Gas lamp/Matches
Pliers
Saw
Screwdriver
Sharpening stone
Shovel

Cleaning Equipment
Detergent
Dish mop or sponge
Scouring pads
Towels

Kitchen Equipment
Aluminium foil
Basin
Bucket
Camp stove and fuel
Can opener/Cork screw
Charcoal
Coffee pot
Cooking utensils
Cook set (nest)/saucepans
Cutlery
Food containers (plastic) with lids
Fork and spoon (long-handled)
Frying pan
Fuel can
Funnel
Icebox
Measuring cup
Mixing bowls
Mugs
Oven (folding)
Paper cups, plates, napkins
Paper towels
Plastic bags
Plates
Pressure cooker
Spatula
Table cloth
Table and chairs (folding)
Tongs
Vacuum flask
Water containers

Basic Foods
Bread
Bacon } if freezer available
Butter }
Cheese }
Eggs }
Cereal
Coffee
Cooking oil
Curry paste or powder / herbs
Drinking chocolate
Instant potato
Jam/marmalade
Packets of soup
Powdered milk
Rice
Salt, pepper, mustard
Sauces/chutney/salad cream or dressing
Stock cubes
Sugar
Tea
Tinned meats/fish
Tinned vegetables/fruit

Recreation
Binoculars
Books
Cameras and film
Cards
Fishing tackle
Games
Maps
Notebooks and pencils
Portable radio
Stamps and stationery
Sunglasses
Swim suits

Home
Advise local police
Arrange for care of plants and pets
Consider leaving house keys with neighbour
Disconnect electrical appliances
Leave fire-arms with police or at other place of safety
Lock doors and windows
Make arrangements with post office regarding mail
Remove food from refrigerator / deep freeze if away for some time
Stop milk, paper and other deliveries
Turn off water to outside taps
Turn thermostat down (geyser)

Your Caravaning Holiday

So you've made up your mind to buy a caravan - congratulations!
Before you lie the possibilities of many weekends and holidays away from home; of complete new vistas in discovering unknown parts of the country and all it has to offer.

Add to this the fun your family will experience, the feeling of "togetherness" which will flow from the various activities in which you will all participate and "hey presto", you have the magic formula for happy, healthy holidays.

To help you in your selection and in becoming familiar with caravaning, we invite you to study the following notes.

Selecting a Caravan

The overriding factors to consider are -

1 the size of your family and the amount of space needed for your comfort and enjoyment

2 how much you want to spend

3 the suitability of your towing vehicle.

The first two points will vary from family to family and are easily determined. The last point requires closer analysis. While there is no universally accepted formula for determining, within close limits, what the ideal car/caravan combination is, there are several factors to be considered which will influence the final choice - these are both technical and human.

Data such as gear and overall ratios, engine torque and mass considerations provide only half the answers. Other factors to be weighed are -

- ☐ the ability and experience of the driver
- ☐ the distance and type of terrain the vehicle is likely to be used on
- ☐ the climatic and road conditions which may be encountered, and
- ☐ the effect on engine performance of changes in altitude.

As a rule of thumb, do not allow the "all-up" mass of your caravan to exceed ¾ of the tare of the towing vehicle. Increasing caravan mass above this ratio places undue loads on the springs, tyres, clutch and brakes which can lead to their premature failure and adversely affects handling, performance and fuel consumption. Equally important, it will make the towing combination illegal unless the caravan is fitted with service brakes, as opposed to the usual overrun brakes. (NB. A service brake is one which is connected to the car's braking system and is operated by the foot brake of the towing vehicle - see Brake Table).

Caravans can be towed by vehicles with automatic or manual gear changes, but if in doubt, consult the vehicle's agents who can also advise on the towing mass capabilities of each model.

Before making a final decision regarding the purchase of a caravan, try it out on the road, preferably using the intended towing vehicle. Vary the towing speeds up to the maximum permissible. This is of particular importance when a second-hand caravan is purchased as there may be faults, caused for example by a mis-aligned axle, which are not obvious to the naked eye, but which will be detected when the caravan is being towed. Alternatively, consider hiring one to decide if you like it or not. (See gazetteer section)

NB. Check that your insurance policy covers your car when towing a unit - your insurance company can advise whether the policy or premium needs to be adjusted.

Types of Caravans

A brief description of the main categories of caravans is given below - obviously within this range there are many different types to suit varying needs and a number of visits to various manufacturers should be made to determine by comparison and elimination what is most suitable - make sure you get what you want by talking to experienced caravaners and by shopping around.

Touring Caravans - these have solid walls and are the most popular. Depending upon the size and make they offer all kinds of equipment and a variety of finishes. Generally they are equipped with sleeping berths, stoves, fridges and side tents.

Fold-down Caravans - the solid-wall fold-down model has similar facilities to the above, the main difference being that the walls and furnishings fold down to form a flat compact unit. It is easy and economical to tow even using a small vehicle.

Collapsible Caravans - these have a solid roof and base and canvas walls. They are equipped with adjoining collapsible tents and are quite versatile. Fittings such as stoves and refrigerators are generally included. Being basically trailers they can only be towed in the folded-down position.

Tent Trailer - these are generally well-designed and more spacious than most caravans, depending upon the type you buy. They comprise an easily erected tent and a trailer base to which an adjoining tent is fitted. There is ample sleeping accommodation and various items such as portable gas cookers, sink and fridges are easily accommodated. They are suitable for towing in a folded-down position by small vehicles.

Pick-up Caravans - these are not separate units but are fitted on the back of a pick-up truck or LDV for transportation "pick-a-back" style. The unit is easily moved on and off the vehicle by means of an hydraulic jack permitting the vehicle to be used independently. The great advantage of this type is that it does not require a separate licence or insurance.

Motor Caravans or Campmobiles - these are the most luxurious of models, usually fitted with a bathroom, air conditioning and water purifying unit. They are permanently fitted to the towing vehicle, usually a small truck, and are the next best thing to a permanent park home.

Features to Look For

Practical considerations are the most important, looking at it with a woman's eye (90% of caravans sold are chosen by women), and your chief concern will be the layout of the interior.

Sleeping Accommodation - this must top the list - can the bunks be left made-up or are they converted to dining setees? Are the mattresses comfortable and long enough - don't be shy to try them out (minimum mattress size for single bed ± 180 cm x 75 cm and 180 cm x 100 cm for double). A partition between sleeping and living quarters is useful, particularly if there are young children who must be put to bed early. Alternatively, provision must be made for screening sleeping areas from one another.

Kitchen - the woman's domain! Check that it is accessible from both the dining area and outside. Adequate storage space and working surfaces are also important.

Tent - examine the tent supplied with each caravan in its erected position. Bear in mind that more time will be spent in the tent than in the caravan itself. See that the tent provides all the features you feel you will require and don't be influenced purely by the advantages of a particular caravan. You may find on examination that you can do with a less luxurious caravan which has a better tent, in terms of your requirements.

Lighting and Ventilation - good lighting and ventilation are important features. Big windows make the interior light and airy but reduce storage space - find the happy medium. Roof vents give additional air. Make sure that there are reading lights over the bunks.

All permanent openings for ventilation should be covered with perforated or expanded metal or otherwise protected to keep out insects. In addition, adjustable ventilation must be available at suitable points such as over cookers and hot plates.

Toilets - where these are installed a minimum floor area of 75 cm x 50 cm is necessary. Apart from the toilet, each separate compartment that has no exterior door - such as an end bedroom or kitchen - must have an escape panel or window of suitable size at least one metre above floor level. Top-hinged windows must open through at least 70° and should stay fully open until closed manually. Exterior doors must open outwards and should have an opening of at least 50 cm width.

Wheel Boxes - these should be of such shape and size that there is a minimum clearance of 3 cm between the tyre and the wheel box at any point throughout the movement permitted by the suspension.

Gross Laden Mass - "Gross Laden Mass" is the total mass of the caravan when loaded to the maximum for which it was designed. This gross laden mass is related to the braking system in various specific points. The braking system must have a mechanism by which the brakes can be applied and set and which will prevent the uncoupled caravan from moving down a gradient of 1 in 8. For this purpose the caravan must be tested at its gross laden mass.

Fire Prevention
A fire extinguisher (2,25 kg dry powder type) should be provided in an easily accessible position.

Testing a Used Caravan
Buying a used caravan calls for great care because one must be satisfied that the caravan has not suffered deterioration in parts which are not always visible. Remember that the buyer of a used caravan has no maker's guarantee to fall back on.

Check the following -

1 The extent to which rust has affected the structure and fittings of the caravan

2 The chassis of the caravan receives the roughest treatment and should be thoroughly inspected - get underneath the caravan to see if rust has attacked or weakened the chassis anywhere

3 The presence of rust on a hitch is indicative of general neglect - check that the hitch has not been weakened through this

4 The handbrake and jockey wheel must be examined and tested and the brake drums dismantled and inspected. The ease or difficulty with which this can be done will provide useful clues. At the same time check the condition of the wheels and tyres

5 Corner stays are exposed to the elements and will tend to rust and stick if not properly cared for - as they are very important, check carefully

6 Check the interior for dampness and also the general condition of the furniture, fittings, upholstery etc.

By now you should be ready to make your purchase - remember that your caravan is an investment which will remain a valuable asset if you look after it. Bear in mind, too, that it is exposed to the elements, travels over all kinds of roads in varying conditions and is subject to wear and tear. Careful attention to the following will assist you to maintain your caravan for years of trouble-free performance.

Before you Start
Legal Requirements - these are covered under the sections on the Law and the Caravaner - see pages 10 and 11.

Servicing - the towing vehicle should be in good running order, mechanically sound and thoroughly serviced before departure. Particular attention should be paid to the cooling system, generator, front and rear spring anchorage and wheel alignment.

The vehicle should be properly tuned, radiator, oil and battery levels checked and a clean air filter installed. (Always carry a spare fan belt, radiator cap and radiator hoses).

Transmission - towing with an automatic transmission increases oil temperature and can, under severe conditions, result in costly repair work. If the towing vehicle does not have a transmission oil cooler it is a good investment to have one fitted. Avoid unnecessary up and down gear shifting as is sometimes encountered when towing up a long gradient. Should you encounter a gradient which cannot be negotiated without repeated gear changes, select the next position below "drive" and leave the gear lever there until you are on a reasonably level road again. This will allow you to vary throttle openings without repeated up and down changes and will reduce the possibility of band or clutch slippage in the gearbox.

If you are towing with a car fitted with a standard transmission, shift into the lower gear ranges early to prevent the engine labouring and to ensure that the caravan does not have to be towed from rest while against the gradient.

Lights - check the connection and adjustment of the lights. The mass of the caravan on the rear wheels of your car will probably put the headlights out of focus. Compensate for this by resetting the headlights or by driving on the dim beams if they are strong enough.

Tyres - check car and caravan tyre pressures which must conform to the maker's specifications. Make provision for the extra mass the tyres will have to cope with by increasing rear tyre pressures by up to 40 kPa each above normal - this will also minimise heat build-up at high speeds.

Check wheel nuts on the caravan for tightness, taking care not to overstrain. In addition, check -

- ☐ that all tyres are sound and have sufficient tread left
- ☐ valves
- ☐ that the front wheel alignment is correct, and
- ☐ take up steering slackness if necessary.

NB. Some caravan owners fit flaps behind the rear wheels of the towing vehicle to prevent mud and gravel being thrown against the front of the caravan.

Tow Bracket - a correctly designed tow bracket is essential and should be made and fitted by a reputable firm or person. Always check that the caravan is safely coupled up, that the hitch is locked and the safety chain connected. Apply a touch of oil or grease to the coupling ball.

The use of equaliser/stabilizer bars is recommended, but they should be correctly fitted and the bracket suitably strengthened to take the additional strain. When uncoupled, keep the ball covered (an old tennis ball is useful for this purpose although hard rubber and chrome-plated ball covers can be purchased).

Shock Absorbers - these should be in good condition. Rear car springs should not be too soft and it is advisable to have them checked if in doubt. A number of devices are available from caravan dealers for stiffening the rear suspension.

Brakes - check that -

- ☐ foot and handbrakes are in good working order and correctly adjusted
- ☐ the caravan overrun brake (cable or hydraulic type) operates correctly without excessive travel and that wheel brakes are properly adjusted. It is advisable to check for overheating of brake drums after having travelled 5 - 10 kms
- ☐ the fluid level in the master cylinder of the hydraulic brakes is adequate.

Use the table below to determine which braking system is required for your vehicle.

LEGAL REQUIREMENTS : BRAKES ON CARAVANS AND TRAILERS

Gross Mass of Trailer (kg)	Proportion Gross Mass of Trailer to Tare of Towing Vehicle (kg)		
	Up to 50%	51% - 75%	Over 75%
0 - 570 kg	Parking brake or other device for keeping trailer stationary	Parking and Overrun brake or Service brake	Parking and Service brake
571 - 1 360 kg	Parking and Overrun brake or Service brake	Parking and Overrun brake or Service brake	Parking and Service brake
1 361 kg or more	Parking and Service brake	Parking and Service brake	Parking and Service brake

Licence and Insurance - both the caravan and towing vehicle should be licensed and suitably insured. If necessary, an insurance endorsement should be obtained for the towing vehicle permitting the towing of a caravan - see Insurance and the Caravaner in gazetteer section.

Lights - test caravan tail, brake and traffic indicator rear lights for correct operation. When the caravan is fully loaded and connected to the towing vehicle, ensure that the headlights are properly adjusted, especially on "dip". Reflectors and T signs must be clean and free from dirt.

Jockey Wheel - this should be oiled, operate correctly and the clamping device work effectively. When coupling or uncoupling the caravan it is advisable to use the jockey wheel in preference to lifting the tow bar manually.

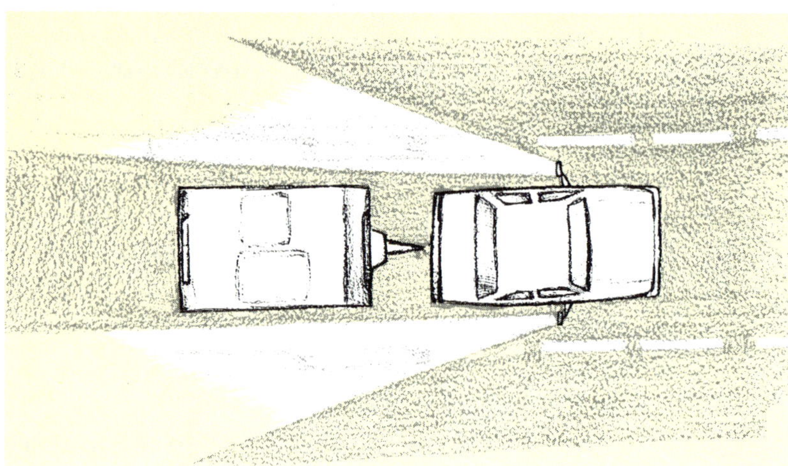

Figure 1

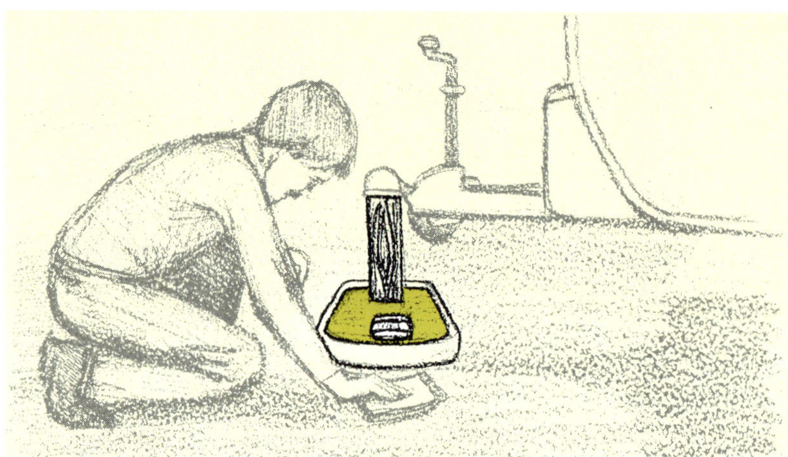

Figure 2

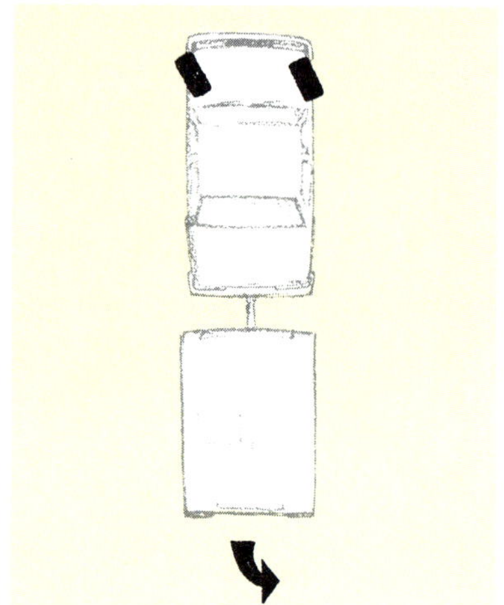

Figure 3

Figure 4

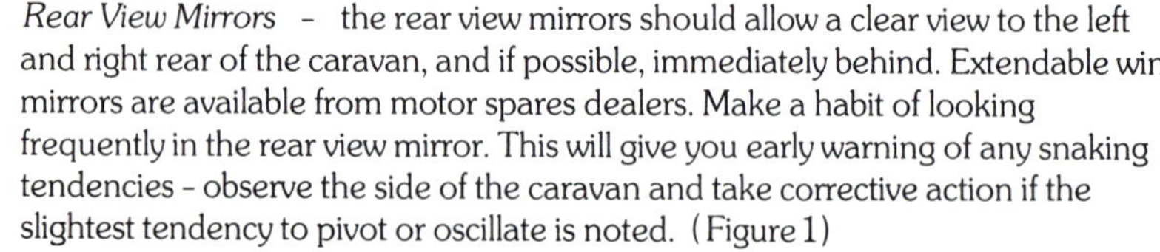

Rear View Mirrors - the rear view mirrors should allow a clear view to the left and right rear of the caravan, and if possible, immediately behind. Extendable wing mirrors are available from motor spares dealers. Make a habit of looking frequently in the rear view mirror. This will give you early warning of any snaking tendencies - observe the side of the caravan and take corrective action if the slightest tendency to pivot or oscillate is noted. (Figure 1)

Stowage - Rule number one is DON'T OVERLOAD. The structure, suspension, tyres and brakes are designed to the manufacturers' recommended gross vehicle mass. All gear must be stowed in the space provided - loose floor storage is not recommended, but should it be necessary to store items loose on the floor ensure that in the event of an emergency stop articles will not slide or displace. Heavier items should be positioned over or forward of the caravan axle.

Check all doors and drawers to ensure that they will not open while moving and secure any items carried on shelves. Plastic covered sprung curtain wire fitted onto small screw eyes is useful to hold bottles, books and so on.

NB. Groceries and provisions are best bought as you go - fresh and sufficient for a day or two.

Stability - stability can be adversely affected by incorrect caravan nose mass. Too much mass on the tow bar i.e. a caravan which has been loaded with too much mass in *front* of its axle, will result in over-sensitive steering and wander, whereas a caravan loaded with too much mass *behind* the axle will tend to sway dangerously behind the towing vehicle. Try a nose mass of between 75 and 100 kg and adjust by moving some of the equipment in the caravan until a satisfactory compromise is reached - this is why substantial movable items should be fixed securely in position.

While gauges to measure nose mass are available, a bathroom scale will do the trick. Place the caravan on a level piece of ground with the scale beneath the coupling. Then place a stout block of wood of suitable length between the scale and coupling and loosen the jockey wheel until the full mass of the caravan is transferred to the block of wood and scale in turn. Then take a reading. From this reading subtract the mass of the wooden block and the result will be the nose mass - redistribute the load inside the caravan until the correct nose mass reading is obtained. (Figure 2)

Stabilizers are available which will restrict dangerous "snaking" and if you have a rear-end sag problem, equilizer bars i.e. mass transfer bars, will not only reduce this sag on the towing unit, but will to a lesser degree, reduce tail-end sway and roll encountered on uneven road surfaces.

Roof Racks - A roof rack can be an invaluable aid to the caravaner/camper, although it should be borne in mind that bulky objects placed on the rack will increase wind resistance and fuel consumption will be affected. A heavily loaded roof rack can also under certain circumstances adversely affect the stability of the vehicle. Make sure that the roof rack itself is securely mounted to the vehicle and that any luggage on the rack is properly secured to the rack itself and does not overhang the vehicle in any way.

Fire Extinguishers - carry an effective fire extinguisher which is capable of dealing with burning liquid (i.e. petrol, paraffin) or materials. Suitable models are available from the AA - see also article on pages 12 and 13.

NB. Do not throw cigarette ends out of vehicle windows when towing - they may cause veld fires or the slipstream may carry them into the caravan.

Documents - see that you have all the necessary documents for the journey and that the caravan is included on your insurance cover.

General - at all times, before moving a caravan, see to the following -

- ☐ the supply valve on gas bottles must be fully closed
- ☐ caravan jacks must be fully raised and the brace stored - NB. do *not* use the parking jacks to lift a caravan off its wheels to rotate them or to change tyres - use an axle jack placed under a spring or as near to it as possible
- ☐ no gas or paraffin appliances must be left burning - it is dangerous to tow a caravan with any appliance burning
- ☐ the jockey wheel must be raised and clamped securely
- ☐ all vents, windows and doors must be closed and secured
- ☐ the caravan brake must be released, the coupling correctly seated and locked and safety chains engaged
- ☐ all caravan rear lights must operate correctly
- ☐ venetian blinds should be in the down position, locked in the brackets and fully tilted
- ☐ tables are best made up into bed form for travelling.

Towing a Caravan on the Road

Do not drive if you are tired - pull off the road and rest. Always ensure sufficient car interior ventilation

- ☐ Observe the legal speed limits
- ☐ Allow faster traffic to overtake as soon as possible consistent with safety
- ☐ Cause as little inconvenience to other traffic as possible : keep well to the left of the road. Travel at a reasonable speed considering the condition and width of the road, and have special regard to your ability to stop and the behaviour of your caravan at certain speeds. Avoid driving in heavy traffic which demands frequent stops and starts
- ☐ Remember the available power/mass ratio of the towing vehicle is reduced, and make allowances for this before overtaking other vehicles. Make full use of your traffic indicators
- ☐ Remember the overall length of car/towing vehicle and caravan and do not cut in front of the overtaken vehicle too soon
- ☐ Except in an emergency, do not brake hard or suddenly, especially on corners. Anticipate the movements of other road-users
- ☐ When changing direction take wider turns to allow for caravan short-cutting. However, swinging out on a corner should be avoided as much as possible
- ☐ Avoid excessive and sudden steering wheel movement at speed. Hold the car as steady as possible, don't over-correct, but correct slowly and competently. Sudden turns cause excessive caravan lurch and, if balance is incorrect, will cause caravan sway

Jack-knifing the car/caravan combination will make take-off on a steep hill easier. (Figure 5)

The bottom of the car and fully-laden caravan should be in a straight line. If the rear of the caravan dips below this line sway may result. (Figures 6 and 7)

Figure 5

Figure 6

Figure 7

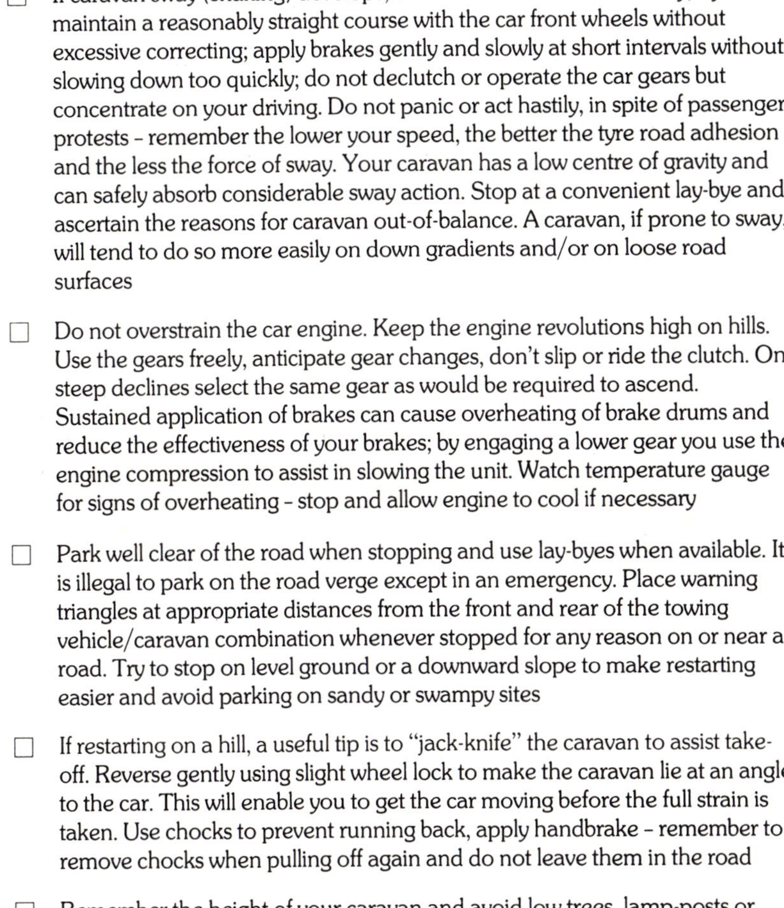

- ☐ If caravan sway (snaking) develops, do not brake hard or suddenly; try to maintain a reasonably straight course with the car front wheels without excessive correcting; apply brakes gently and slowly at short intervals without slowing down too quickly; do not declutch or operate the car gears but concentrate on your driving. Do not panic or act hastily, in spite of passenger protests - remember the lower your speed, the better the tyre road adhesion and the less the force of sway. Your caravan has a low centre of gravity and can safely absorb considerable sway action. Stop at a convenient lay-bye and ascertain the reasons for caravan out-of-balance. A caravan, if prone to sway, will tend to do so more easily on down gradients and/or on loose road surfaces

- ☐ Do not overstrain the car engine. Keep the engine revolutions high on hills. Use the gears freely, anticipate gear changes, don't slip or ride the clutch. On steep declines select the same gear as would be required to ascend. Sustained application of brakes can cause overheating of brake drums and reduce the effectiveness of your brakes; by engaging a lower gear you use the engine compression to assist in slowing the unit. Watch temperature gauge for signs of overheating - stop and allow engine to cool if necessary

- ☐ Park well clear of the road when stopping and use lay-byes when available. It is illegal to park on the road verge except in an emergency. Place warning triangles at appropriate distances from the front and rear of the towing vehicle/caravan combination whenever stopped for any reason on or near a road. Try to stop on level ground or a downward slope to make restarting easier and avoid parking on sandy or swampy sites

- ☐ If restarting on a hill, a useful tip is to "jack-knife" the caravan to assist take-off. Reverse gently using slight wheel lock to make the caravan lie at an angle to the car. This will enable you to get the car moving before the full strain is taken. Use chocks to prevent running back, apply handbrake - remember to remove chocks when pulling off again and do not leave them in the road

- ☐ Remember the height of your caravan and avoid low trees, lamp-posts or other overhanging objects

- ☐ It is illegal to carry passengers in the caravan while on the move

- ☐ If it is necessary to reverse it is often easier to unhitch the caravan and towing vehicle and turn it by hand, reconnecting after the turn. Practise reversing but ensure the overrun brake lock is in operating position and reset it when the manoeuvre has been completed. Alternatively, start off with the towing vehicle and caravan in line. Move your hands to the lower arc of the steering wheel and, using the rear end of the caravan as a reference point, *turn the wheel to the right (anti-clockwise)* if you want the tail of the caravan to move to the right and *to the left (clockwise)* if you want the tail of the caravan to move to the left (see Figure 3 and 4)

- ☐ If your caravan is not dust-proof, open the front window slightly, leaving all other windows and ventilators closed - this pressurises the interior and keeps the dust out. Remember to stop and shut this window if it starts to rain.

Camping
Consult the article "Code of Behaviour" (page 5) to ensure a happy holiday.

- ☐ If your caravan has an external sink outlet use a bucket to catch waste water. Do not foul the ground, but dispose of all waste water into a proper drain. A drop of ammonia in the bucket will prevent smells and flies. If no rubbish bins are available, bury all the rubbish before departure

- ☐ Avoid parking under trees as bird droppings, falling petals, leaves and some insects can damage the paintwork of the car and caravan. The minimum recommended distance from a neighbouring caravan is 3,5 m to reduce the hazard of fire. When camping, do not start a fire in the surrounding grass and ensure that all burning units are safe and secure. If you light a fire outside, watch it closely to avoid spreading the flame, and bury the extinguished remains when you have finished. Do not light fires on green grass

- ☐ In summer, to avoid the heat, park the caravan on the east side of trees.

Levelling
When parking it is necessary to level the caravan laterally and longitudinally; a small carpenter's level is useful for the purpose. If necessary, dig a hole for a wheel to assist levelling. Lower the jacks to stabilise the caravan and use flat stones, wood or metal under the jack foot on soft or damp ground.

The jacks should be down just firmly enough to hold the unit steady, leaving the mass on the axle where it is meant to be. Apply the handbrake to assist stabilising and to prevent movement. Do not apply the handbrake over long periods. If the caravan has been levelled by digging a hole, ensure that it is pulled out straight when moving. Pulling at an acute angle can damage axle or suspension.

Before leaving, run over the "general" check list included and after moving the caravan off the site, go back to see that nothing has been left behind and that any holes dug for levelling are filled in.

Tents and Awnings
Place the caravan and awning or tent so that it does not interfere with the convenience, privacy or enjoyment of others, and ensure that guy ropes do not present a hazard or inconvenience.

When parked on a grassy site for a considerable period do not use an awning or ground sheet as a floor covering, as it kills the grass. If a ground covering is desirable, obtain the site owner's permission. When erecting the caravan awning a periodic application of wax or soap in the caravan rope channel or on awning ropes, will facilitate erection. If ordinary manilla guy ropes are used, slacken in wet weather and at nights with heavy dew. Close awnings completely and secure all side walls and guy ropes if high winds are experienced.

Gas Appliances
Refer to the article included on pages 20 and 21.

Paraffin Appliances
Before moving the caravan ensure that all pressure valves are released to avoid fuel spillage. Carry supplies in tins with secure screw caps and not in bottles which can fall over and break. A very useful device is a plastic syphon which ensures the filling of appliances without spillage. This should not be used for petrol because of the danger of static electricity. A wide topped funnel with gauze filter is an essential item. If a metal paraffin pump is used, attach a short length of hose to the spout, using a suitable clip.

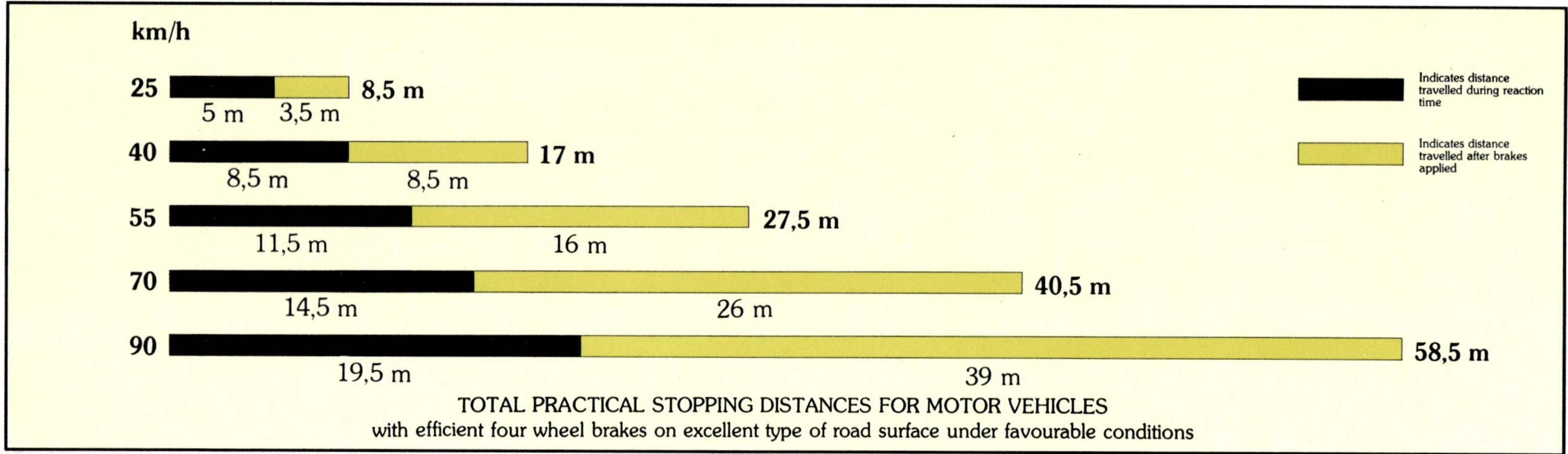

Figure 8

Methylated spirits (in unbreakable containers) or 'Meta' tablets should be carried for lighting pressure units, refrigerators or stoves.

Electricity
Before uncoupling the car from the caravan, remember to disconnect the multi-pin plug, and when wiring up car to caravan always couple caravan to car to ensure a common car battery earth.

If you want to check the polarity of the current, place the bared ends of the wire in a glass of salty water. The negative wire will bubble.

Water Tanks
Tanks should be drained and left empty if the caravan is stationary for long periods. Bicarbonate of Soda is a good cleaner and will help to keep the water untainted. The filler cap should be left loose to allow entry of air. Always drain tanks before moving.

Maintenance
Other than the various suggestions for maintenance in the previous paragraphs, the following are recommended –

- ☐ Preserve the paintwork with a good polish
- ☐ Grease coupling and spring shackles and lubricate corner jack screws frequently
- ☐ If any sign of rusting appears, paint steel parts (tow bar, chassis, step, etc) after removing the rust. Painted tow bars reveal hair line cracks which might develop
- ☐ Check over your caravan periodically including the gas installation. Attend to defects without delay. Neglect is a caravan owner's worst enemy. A well cared for caravan should last indefinitely
- ☐ Rubberising the underside of the caravan will protect the woodwork and metal against rust and rot.

Periodic Checks

- ☐ All body-holding bolts; the bolts on the coupling; the bolts holding the towing bracket on the car; the axle securing bolts and the roadwheel nuts
- ☐ Check all screws in the bodywork, especially those holding hinges, catches and locks on the doors and cupboards. Do not force these screws but tighten up where necessary
- ☐ Check wheel bearings and ensure wheels are secure and running smoothly; if in doubt check with an experienced mechanic
- ☐ Check that tyres are sound. Inspect for wall and tread cracks, uneven or excessive wear. Especially check the "invisible" side of the tyre for cracks and damage. Uneven wear of the tread should be investigated. A minimum of 2 mm depth of tread is recommended
- ☐ Check brake linings and mechanism, including the cable and its clamp. Re-line brakes when necessary
- ☐ Paint the underside of the caravan, both wood floor members and chassis frame, and inside the wheel arch, preferably with rubberised compound
- ☐ Check gas flexible couplings and hoses between bottle, regulator and metal tubing and joints, and if necessary tighten hose-clamps
- ☐ Check electrical cable for fraying and the screws at the connection.

Long Term Storage
If the caravan is to be left unused for a long period, jack the wheels off the ground and support the axle on blocks. Do not use the corner jacks to lift or keep the tyres off the ground. Cover the tyres (not with plastic) to minimise rubber deterioration through sun, light and air.

Clean the interior of the caravan regularly, but avoid harsh abrasive or scouring cleaners as much as possible.

Open all doors and windows periodically to air the caravan, especially after wet weather. Tallow or beeswax on drawer slides will ensure smooth operation.

Draw the curtains over the windows and cover all windows outside to prevent sunlight fading curtains and upholstery.

Preferably shelter the caravan from sun, wind and rain to preserve the paintwork and materials.

Caravan Check List

Air gauge
Bubble level for levelling caravan
Extension cord – 15 m
Fire extinguishers
Flashlight, standard with extra batteries and bulbs
Flashlight with red signal flasher
Fuses for car and trailer
Hose for watertank
Jack
Tent fly or awning
Tool kit
Tow rope or chain
Triangular warning signs
Tyre pump
Axe
Bedding & pillows
Braai appliances
Broom
Buckets
Detergents
Dishes
Dishpan
Emergency lantern for outside use
First aid kit
Folding chairs
Funnel for watertank
Light bulbs (spare)
Mop
Shovel (long-handled)
Snake bite kit
Sponges
Tape

Backpacking

Outdoor recreation is an essential part of the lives of many South Africans and of visitors to this country. Modern day pressures accentuate the need "to get away from it all" and our land with its magnificent climate, coastline and inland splendours, lures many to venture outdoors. Backpacking, once the preserve of the highly skilled mountaineer, is becoming increasingly popular with outdoor lovers of all types - hikers, mountaineers, motorcycle campers, motorists making frequent stops while on tour, one or two-man outings on fishing or hunting expeditions and those who just wish to get out of doors and away from the crowds.

The Department of Forestry has opened a number of sections of the National Hiking Way and these together with other wilderness areas provide plenty of scope for backpacking (see section on "Trails" following). Although being fit and properly equipped is essential, anyone with a love for the outdoors and a healthy respect for the inherent dangers involved, can enjoy backpacking.

The following information will help you to gain full enjoyment from your backpacking trip.

Equipment

The backpacker requires light, compact, multi-purpose equipment. In selecting equipment it is important to anticipate your needs and choose accordingly. The most expensive, or the cheapest, is not necessarily the most suitable. Quality is of paramount importance in purchasing equipment and these items should be regarded as an investment which will provide many years of pleasurable outdoor living. Do listen to advice from those who know, and visit a reputable stockist who will give you all the advice you need. Bear in mind that not everybody enjoys backpacking and as the equipment can be very expensive, it might be advisable, for a first trip, to borrow or hire as much as possible.

The most essential items, in order of priority, are a sturdy pair of boots, a rucksack and a sleeping bag, with a tent, stove, cooking equipment etc following a close second. As your comfort and perhaps even your survival depend on these items, they should be chosen very carefully.

Footwear

On the trail your feet are your only means of transport and therefore their comfort is of prime importance. A sturdy pair of boots will support the ankles and give protection to the soles of the feet in rough terrain. When fitting a new pair of boots be sure to wear your hiking socks. Boots should be wide enough to allow for the flattening of the feet which occurs when you walk with a heavy load. A good test for fit is to unlace the boots and push your foot as far forward as possible. You should then be able to insert your index finger snugly between your heel and the boot. A high quality boot should be water-repellent as wet feet can cause loss of body heat besides being extremely uncomfortable. Ankle support and soles should be solid but flexible. Specialised hiking boots will be relatively expensive as they are designed to be used in the roughest terrain, but if properly cared for, by rubbing with polish after each hike, they will last for a long time. Once you have bought your boots you should wear them at home for short periods before attempting a major hike. Boots, like horses, need to be broken in gradually if they are to be comfortable.

On the hike your feet must be able to perspire freely. If the moisture created is not absorbed by your socks, there will be a tendency for the sock to slip, thus causing friction and resulting in blisters. It is therefore necessary to wear thick woollen socks which contain no synthetic yarn except for nylon reinforcing in the heel and toe sections. (A thin nylon sock can be worn under the woollen sock to offset friction). Socks should be right fitting without being uncomfortable. Never choose a pair that is too large as these will tend to ruck and crease under the foot, resulting in "hot spots" and eventually blisters. Always carry a spare pair of socks.

The Rucksack

When hiking, all the gear that you need will be carried in your pack, which must therefore be well-designed and durable.

The Frame - the design of the frame should allow for effective weight distribution as a fully equipped pack can weigh in excess of 16 kg. There are two basic frame designs available - the H Frame which consists of two contoured uprights welded or screwed to cross-members which provide rigidity and strength; and the U Frame which is a one-piece outer frame bent to form a U at the base, which gives the frame added rigidity. A welded frame is considered stronger than one which is screwed together. However, the screwed adjustable frame is suitable for growing children. The recommended frame is the Butterfly version of the H Frame. To ensure that the pack fits comfortably and that the contours of the frame correspond to those of your back, you should try it on fully packed before

Pack Frame

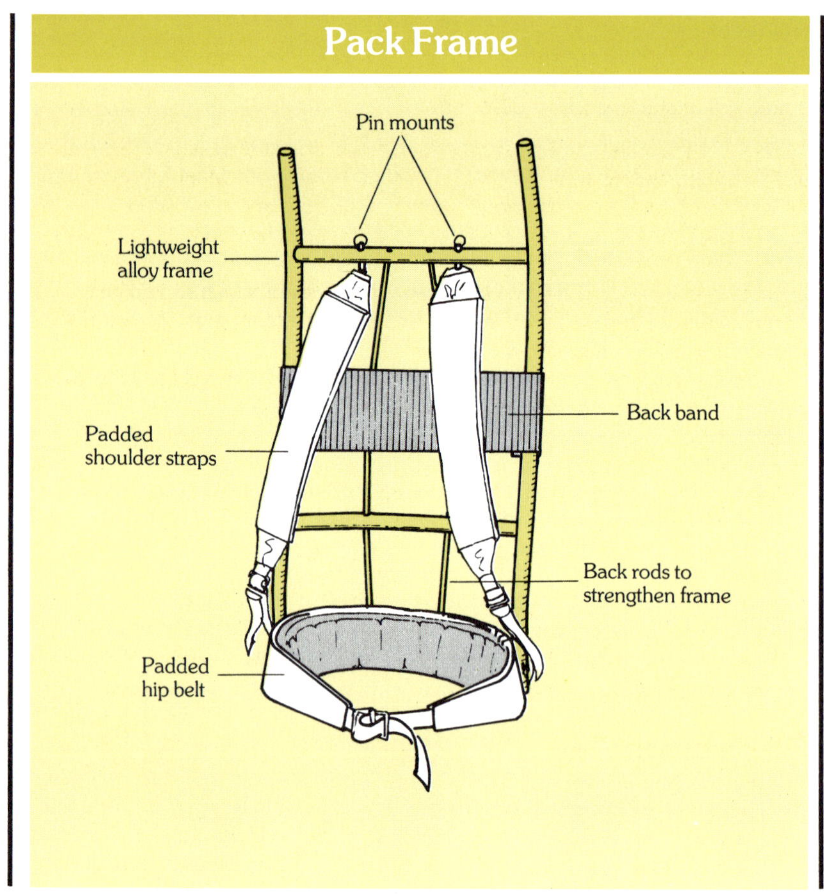

considering buying it. When shouldering the pack, the weight should bear on the hips first and the shoulder straps then be adjusted accordingly.

The Pack - most are manufactured from high count nylon, although waterproofed cotton duck is considered by some to be as good if not better. Some rucksacks have a waterproof inner coating while others are merely water repellent. The choice between the two is a matter of personal preference, bearing in mind the type of rainwear you intend carrying with you. The pack could be lined with a plastic bag for extra protection. The stitching on the bag should be small and even and the stress points well-reinforced. Nylon coil zips are preferable to metal ones which may rust or seize up in icy conditions. Zips should be covered by a protective flap. Many bags are divided into two compartments for ease of access. Outside pockets are useful for packing items which might be needed at short notice and a good rucksack should have at least two. The weather flap, which often includes a map pocket, should be large enough to cover the top opening when the bag is fully packed.

Shoulder Straps - these should be padded, well-reinforced and sufficiently long to allow for easy adjustment. They should be wide enough to prevent them cutting into your shoulders when carrying a heavy load.

Hip Belt - a padded hip belt, although not standard on all packs, allows the weight to be transferred from the shoulders to the pelvis, a useful feature when carrying a heavy load up a steep slope. This feature is a true advantage and should be considered essential.

Backbands - these keep the framework away from the back and spread the load evenly across the back. A meshed backband allows you to perspire freely.

Cross-section of a Typical Hiking or Climbing Boot

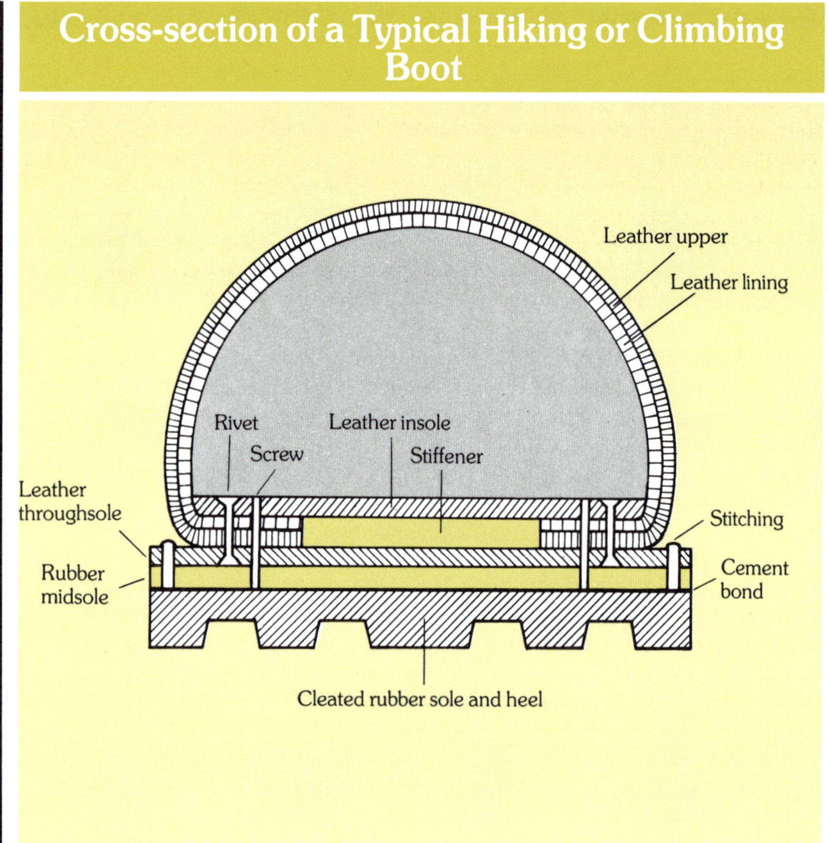

Packs not fitted with a metal frame are suitable for light loads and all the features of a good frame pack can be found in these softpacks. Packs which are fitted with an integral frame of aluminium or foam are more suitable for heavier loads.

Packing the Rucksack

Pack the rucksack systematically, with heavier items on the top and a layer of clothing against the back framework. Remember to position the articles so that they can be removed without too much upheaval. Things you will often use, such as compass, maps etc should be put in the outside pockets. (See diagram on right)

The "Outward Bound" formula for a comfortable pack: The maximum load should, where possible, be less than 16 kgs and for a long or strenuous trip you should not carry more than $^{1}/_{5}$th of your body mass, unless you are fitter than average.

Clothing

In South Africa it is seldom necessary to buy a complete set of specialised clothing for backpacking. Natural fibres are preferable to synthetic as they absorb perspiration. Always carry a woollen jersey and adequate rainwear. A change of clothing is essential as one cannot afford to remain in wet clothes in cold conditions. Remember that several layers of thin clothing are warmer than one layer of thick clothing and can be more easily adjusted for changing temperatures.

Suggested Kit Distribution

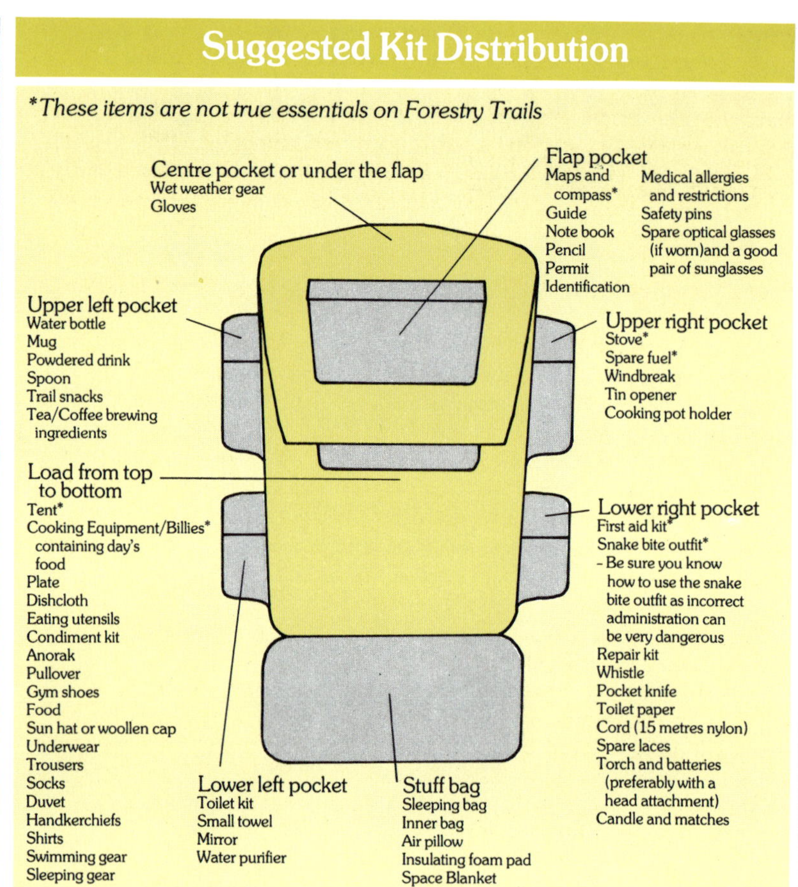

Your list should include:

2 Woollen or cotton shirts

2 Woollen slacks, jeans or shorts

2 T-shirts

2 Sets underclothing

2 Pairs woollen socks

1 Woollen sweater

1 Anorak or similar waterproof coat

A hat or balaclava

1 Pair of mittens or gloves

1 Pair of boots

Spare laces

Toilet gear, including lip ointment and small roll toilet paper - use small containers or half-used items where possible to save space

Thermal underwear, if backpacking in very high mountainous regions in mid-winter

Sleeping Bags

There is a tremendous variety of sleeping bags on the market and many factors to consider when deciding on the right one for your needs. It should be ultra lightweight, have good insulating qualities and be very compact. Down is the ideal filling, as it compresses easily into a small bundle and springs back to its original loft when the pressure is released, and also provides the best insulation to trap body heat and keep the sleeper warm. It does not however withstand water and when wet provides no insulation. There is a wide range in the quality of down fillings available, but most are better than manmade fibres. Synthetic fibres however have the advantage of being cheaper and are not as adversely affected by water.

The outer bag should be of strong water repellent nylon while the inner bag should be a breathable cotton fabric, or a cotton liner should be used. The stitching must be even and firm and the quilting pattern such that it maintains the filler in its original position. Bad quilting can lead to a shift of filler which can result in uncomfortable lumps, and also allow cold to filter in through the stitching. If there is a zip this should be corrosion-proof and covered by a protective flap.

Tapered sleeping bags which are moulded to fit the form are lighter and allow less body heat to be lost, while sleeping bags with a zip are easier to climb in or out of but the zip does allow cold to get into the bag. Some sleeping bags have cowl hoods to protect the head in very cold weather, but a balaclava could be used for this purpose. Sleeping bags will last longer if they are looked after, and this includes the use of a liner to protect the inside of the bag.

All sleeping bags need insulation to overcome loss of heat to the ground. A closed cell synthetic foam pad is the ideal article. It is also advisable, in very extreme conditions, to carry a space blanket which is made of aluminium foil and provides insulation against heat as well as cold.

The sleeping mat and space blanket can be wrapped around the sleeping bag and then put into a stuffbag and slung below the pack.

The Tent

The chief purpose of a tent is to keep you dry. Apart from rain, there is condensation to contend with. This builds up on the inner walls of the tent during the night and to overcome this problem modern tents have been designed with a waterproof nylon flysheet and a cotton inner tent. Moisture can then permeate through the cotton fabric, condense on the inside of the nylon flysheet and run down to the ground. A tent of this nature is naturally heavier than a single skin tent. Most nylon single skin tents are fitted with air vents which offset the condensation to some extent. Specialist backpacking tents now available are mostly single skin nylon with a mass as little as 2 kg.

It must be remembered that the tent has to withstand the onslaught of the elements and that in high terrain the winds can be fierce. The stitching of the tent should therefore be high quality, straight and even, the needle holes small and the stress points must be reinforced. Groundsheets should be of the sewn-in variety and poles and pegs light and strong.

Stoves and Cooking Equipment

A variety of lightweight stoves are available, some fitted with built-in pots. There are also several types of lightweight pot sets on the market, or billies can be used. The smallest stove is the solid fuel type which comprises a light metal box-type frame which supports a small billycan or kettle. A small tablet of solid fuel is inserted and lit for heating.

Small gas stoves are more effective and use disposable cartridges of LP gas. These are very popular as they are compact, light and efficient. The major disadvantage of the gas stove is the cost of the disposable cartridges.

Benzine burning stoves in compact folding containers are also popular. Fuel for these useful little stoves should be carried in an aluminium fuel bottle adequately marked for easy recognition. It is best to mark this on the bottom of the container in a bright colour.

If lighting is used, the small and efficient gas lights using disposable cartridges of LP gas are the most suitable, although it must be remembered that the backpacker usually leads a dawn to dusk existence.

Eating utensils are available in compact sets of lightweight materials, but perhaps a tablespoon and knife would suffice for most occasions.

FOOD FOR THE TRAIL

Once you have selected the most suitable equipment for your backpacking trip, the next major consideration is what food to take with you. A long trail on which you will use lots of energy requires food which is nutritious but at the same time light and compact. Bulky perishables like eggs, butter, fresh meat and vegetables will not last long on the open trail and should be replaced with dehydrated, powdered and freeze-dried foods.

As most people hike for enjoyment it would be wrong to limit the food to a spartan diet devoid of all luxuries. It is important to be aware of your capabilities and the nature of the intended trip and plan your menus accordingly. The food suggested here is intended as a basic guide which, with a little adaptation, should suit most tastes.

Before preparing your menus you should consider the availability of water in the region you intend visiting. Water is essential and if it is scarce, this heavy commodity will have to be carried. Tinned foods, while convenient, are extremely heavy. Time spent in planning and preparing the foods at home will make all the difference to your enjoyment once on the trail.

Preparation

Preparation means weighing and mixing foods for each day. If foods are to be cooked together, choose those which have roughly the same cooking time, or parboil those needing a longer cooking time before mixing - this applies to foods like rice etc. Also take into consideration the cooking time and hence the amount of fuel needed. It is wise to pack the foods you require in plastic bags and light plastic containers. Commercial packages usually contain too much for a single trip, are bulky and generate litter. Also, you can put your litter into the plastic bags when they are empty and carry it to the nearest bin. Should you decide to carry tinned food, be sure to take the containers away with you. Buried tins, although out of sight, will only slowly disintegrate and may be exposed at a later date. The same applies to tissues, sweet papers and orange peel. Peel may be biodegradable but it is nevertheless unsightly and remains around for some time.

Suggested Menus

Breakfast - Muesli, which can be bought at most supermarkets, provides a nutritious meal which is easy to prepare. It can be fortified at home with extra raisins, nuts or grated chocolate and if necessary, sugar. Dried milk can also be included. Warm or cold water is all that remains to be added on the trail. Wholewheat biscuits and jam followed by tea or coffee complete the meal. Tea bags and cube sugar which are easier to handle, together with dried milk, should be packed. If eggs are a must, it is advisable to break them and pour into an airtight plastic tub to avoid calamities en route.

Lunch - Powdered soup, wholewheat biscuits and cheese followed by a beverage will provide a sustaining lunch. Fresh fruit, while refreshing, is heavy and you should consider taking dried fruit. A tube of cheese spread is a good alternative to butter or margarine which tends to melt.

Dinner - A main course of meat substitute, mixed dehydrated vegetables and instant potato mix can taste delicious after a hard day's walk. Meat substitute can be obtained from the larger supermarkets, health shops and specialised backpacking shops. The addition of dehydrated vegetables and potato mix gives the substance to the meal. If a sweet course is desired, "instant" puddings, chocolate or tinned fruit should fill the gap. Baby desserts which should be decanted into a plastic tub are very tasty and a variety of toppings which come in tubes add a touch of luxury to the dessert.

Complete backpacker's meals which are nutritionally balanced and very tasty, can be obtained but as they are imported they are expensive.

In addition, take a supply of peanuts, dried fruit, chocolate or biltong to nibble along the trail. Emergency rations should be carried in case of unforeseen difficulties. These can consist of muesli, meat sticks, soup cubes, date blocks, glucose tablets etc.

Packing

Once you have prepared your food you may find it useful to pack each day's rations separately so that they can be selected quickly and easily. The contents of different bags should be labelled to avoid the unpleasant surprise of salt in your tea or worse still, potato mix in your coffee!

HINTS FOR THE TRAIL

On the Move

Experience will teach you the best way to tackle a long day's "slog". It is essential to save energy and walk at a speed which is as economical as possible. Small even steps rather than erratic strides will conserve energy. It is a common mistake to go too fast when first setting out. If the walker becomes out of breath, he is going too quickly; if he can whistle or sing while he is walking steadily his speed is as fast as it should be. It is much better to keep going steadily all day than to rush ahead and then stop to recover. The secret of walking is to combine this economical speed with a regular rhythmical pace. When ascending, shorten the stride, maintain the rhythm at all costs, by zig-zagging up slopes; take the outside and easiest line around curves when going up; avoid jerking and awkward movements; breathe rhythmically as you walk. Of course, the going will be far less tough if you are fit for both walking and carrying a pack.

You should be adequately equipped for any eventuality. Even if you intend sleeping in a hut overnight, you should carry emergency equipment like a space blanket in case you find yourself spending a night outside because of injury or because you have lost your way. In the wet season you should carry a full complement of equipment and adequate changes of clothing as it is essential to remain as dry as possible.

Your feet must be looked after at all costs and a first aid kit containing lint, adhesive plaster and antiseptic ointment for the treatment of blisters should be carried. Should you feel a spot on your foot becoming sore, stop and rest and take off your boot and socks. Air the spot as long as possible before putting on adhesive plaster. A change of socks will also help.

How to Keep Warm

A common danger in mountainous regions is loss of body heat or hypothermia caused by a combination of cold, wet, windy weather coupled with physical exhaustion. Once the body temperature has dropped below a certain point, loss of reason sets in. Hopefully you will not experience such extreme conditions but one must always guard against exposure by being prepared for unexpected changes in the weather. Warm protective clothing is essential and when you start to feel cold, most parts of the body should be covered. The saying, "when your feet are cold put on your hat" is no joke, as a great deal of body heat is lost through the head. You should also keep your torso warm so it can send any excess heat to your less insulated extremities. One must of course avoid overheating which causes perspiration and hence cooling.

You should find shelter from wind and rain as you must keep yourself and your equipment as dry as possible. In extremely cold conditions water should be heated before drinking to prevent further loss of body heat.

If a member of your party shows symptoms of hypothermia - violent, uncontrolled shivering and loss of reason - he should be placed in a sleeping bag and another member of the party climb in with him to restore body heat.

How to Prevent Overheating

In extreme heat body moisture and vital chemicals are lost through perspiration resulting in dehydration. In these extremes, body moisture must be conserved, i e. you should exert yourself as little as possible. Even talking leads to loss of moisture. The desire to press on or search for help must be controlled. If there is no shade a space blanket can be used to reflect heat. Salt tablets should form part of your first aid kit. If water is available it should be sipped every quarter of an hour to prevent further dehydration, even if you do not feel thirsty.

Sunstroke

If you develop a high temperature and feel ill after being in very hot sun, cool yourself with cold water sponging, drink ample fluid and take an analgesic to lower your temperature and relieve headache.

Losing your Way

Finding that you are lost is an unnerving experience. The resulting panic is minimised if you have informed the authorities of your presence in the area before commencing your hike. You should give an outline of your route, your departure time and when you propose to return. This will ensure that a search party will be organised in the event of trouble. Having notified the authorities of your route, be sure to stick to it and also to inform them when you return.

It is far better to avoid getting lost. Continually check the map and compass so that you always know where you are and if necessary retrace your steps to your last known position.

As most searches are conducted from the air, a brightly coloured object, such as a vivid anorak, placed in a conspicuous position, will help the search party to locate you. When you are lost do not try to be a hero and blunder on alone to seek help. Remain in a group and stay put.

WHERE TO GO

National Hiking Trails, Wilderness Trails and Walks.

Equipped with the aforegoing information, the intending hiker is now ready to explore. The following notes and accompanying maps serve to introduce many of the trails and walks which are open to the public and which fall respectively under the auspices of the Department of Forestry, Nature Conservation and both the National and the Natal Parks Board. A selection of private trails and walks is also included.

NATIONAL HIKING TRAILS

Bookings

The addresses for bookings and enquiries for the various trails are indicated in the tables.

Please note the following

- ☐ Bookings for forestry trails will not be accepted more than 6 months in advance. The closing date for written applications is 14 days *before* the proposed hike. Late applications may be made verbally or by telephone
- ☐ It is unnecessary to book for walks controlled by the Department of Forestry, but permits are normally required. These may be obtained from the various Forester's offices
- ☐ Any person over the age of 18 years may participate. Applications from younger persons will be permitted provided they are accompanied on the trail by at least one responsible adult
- ☐ Trails are best reserved by full parties of friends with common interests. Priority is given to full parties and it is advisable to determine the number of persons allowed at a time
- ☐ Facilities for coloured persons are provided on some forestry tails.

For information on camping/caravan sites and other accommodation in the vicinity of proposed hikes, refer to the gazetteer section of this guide.

General

All hikes are undertaken at own risk and hikers are expected to cheerfully obey the rules and regulations applicable to trails and walks. It is unnecessary to take additional sleeping and cooking equipment on trails as these are provided at the overnight huts. Intending hikers should make prior enquiries as to the times of the year when trails and walks are undertaken.

Determine starting points in relation to the route to be covered. Vehicles are left on State forest land at the owner's risk. Hikers should ensure that such vehicles are securely locked and all valuables removed. Consider the possible weather conditions (see Climate Map in Dams and Lakes section) during the proposed hike and make suitable provision for rain, cold, mist, snow and/or other emergencies. In this regard please note the following:

- ☐ Always carry a snake bite kit and ensure that you know how to use it
- ☐ Exercise meticulous care to prevent fires - smoke only where permitted and extinguish matches and cigarette butts properly. Fires should only be made where facilities are provided
- ☐ Take suitable precautions against malaria when hiking in affected areas (see map included in the Dams and Lakes section) - consult your doctor or chemist for advice
- ☐ A suitable insect repellent will be most useful
- ☐ Firearms and pets are *not* permitted and it is an offence to damage the natural surroundings in any way
- ☐ Because of the danger of bilharzia, all water must be boiled before drinking - see map included in the Dams and Lakes section
- ☐ Binoculars and a camera will add to the enjoyment and pleasant memories of your hike
- ☐ Do not litter - remember, "If it can be carried in, it can be carried out"

A list of outdoor recreation symbol signs are in use in State forests and indicate the availability of water, various amenities and also prohibitions - see figure 1.

Symbols in the form of footprints or animal silhouettes are employed on most of the trails and indicate the direction in which the trail must be traversed - see figure 2.

Many of the trees in the hiking trail areas have been marked with their respective numbers and can be identified by means of the National list of Trees - also consult the section "Roadside Identification of Trees" on pages 6 - 9.

Always remember the National Hiking Way slogan

"TAKE ONLY PHOTOGRAPHS AND LEAVE ONLY FOOTPRINTS!"

WILDERNESS TRAILS

Trails operate at Umfolozi, St Lucia and Mkuzi. Send applications to the address given in the tables.

- ☐ Advance booking is essential. Bookings open six full calendar months in advance. Lots are drawn when available space is oversubscribed at the time bookings open. At peak periods therefore, applicants should provide alternative dates in order to improve their chances of securing a booking
- ☐ Telephone bookings are accepted, but telegraphic bookings must be confirmed in writing and telegraphic replies prepaid
- ☐ A booking fee, dependent on current tariffs, is levied on each booking. This fee must be received within three weeks of the reservation being made in order to confirm the reservation, otherwise the booking may be cancelled
- ☐ Tariffs and other pertinent information is available on application, but may be altered without prior notice
- ☐ All trails are limited to six people. In the case of *bona fide* student parties, six students plus a party leader are permitted, but all participants must be over 16 years. Student parties may be granted special concession rates.

NATIONAL HIKING WAY

(Hikers must ascertain the cost of a particular trail when booking)

E = Dial code, exchange answers, ask number T = dial 0020 and book trunk call Telephone codes are included in brackets preceding each number

CAPE PROVINCE

Map	Name	Location	Bookings and Enquiries	Reservations Tel. No.	Length	No. of Huts	Persons per Hut per Night	Remarks
A page 35	Boland Hiking Trail (Hottentotsholland Section)	Between Sir Lowry's Pass and Franschhoek	The Regional Director: Western Cape, Department of Forestry, Private Bag X9005, Cape Town 8000	(021) 45-3513	84 km	2 Whites 2 Coloureds	30	Variety of fauna and flora. Proceed from south to north and from east to west. Several alternative routes
B page 36	Otter Trail	Tsitsikama Coastal National Park	The Chief Director, National Parks Board, P.O. Box 787, Pretoria 0001 **or** The Chief Nature Conservator, Tsitsikama Coastal National Park, P.O. Storms River 6308	(012) 44-1194 OR Tsitsikama 3 T	62 km	4	10	Variety of birds, marine life and animals. Forests, tidal pools, good fishing, caves, scenic views. Trail may only be followed in one direction i.e. from Storms River mouth to Groot River mouth
C page 36	Outeniqua Hiking Trail	Between Knysna and George	The Regional Director: Southern Cape, Department of Forestry, Private Bag X12, Knysna 6570	E (04452) 411	173 km	7 Whites 3 Coloureds	30 20	Traces of 19th century goldrush. Elephant and leopard may be seen as well as species of buck. Hikes must proceed from west to east
TRANSVAAL								
D page 37	Blyderivierspoort Hiking Trail	Between God's Window in the south and the Sybrand van Niekerk Public Resort in the north	The Regional Director: Eastern Transvaal, Department of Forestry, Private Bag X503, Sabie 1260	E (0131512) 196	54 km	4	30	Interesting geological formations. Six different species of protea, one of which only recently discovered. All six SA primates occur here. Breeding colony of the threatened bald ibis. The Knysna, purple-crested and grey loerie occur in the nature reserve. Hikers should proceed from south to north
E page 37	Fanie Botha Hiking Trail	Between Sabie and God's Window	See Blyderivierspoort Hiking Trail		123 km	4 (5th to be built)	30	Beautiful scenery and rich bird life, plantations. Proceed from south to north
F page 38	Soutpansberg Hiking Trail	From Hanglip near Louis Trichardt to Levubu	The Regional Director: Northern Transvaal, Department of Forestry, Private Bag X2413, Louis Trichardt 0920	(01551) 2202	98 km	4	30	Interesting remains of Venda settlements. Variety of plants and 400 species of birds. Bilharzia occurs in some streams

In addition to the above, the Department of Forestry is planning more walks and trails for the future - these are indicated by symbols on the key map (see National Hiking Way box). The following are on the high priority construction programme.

Cape Province - Franschhoek Pass to Dutoitskloof Pass; Kleinmond to Hermanus - coastal route; Nature's Valley to Storms River - inland through Tsitsikama Forest 1978/80; Pirie Walk - King William's Town 1978/79; Swellendam 1978/79

Transvaal - Morgenzon - near Pilgrim's Rest; Magaliesberg - Pretoria to Rustenburg
Natal - Drakensberg - Sani Pass to Bushmans Nek 1978/79

OUTDOOR RECREATION SYMBOL SIGNS

WILDERNESS TRAILS AND WALKS

(NB. When booking, ascertain what the costs are, if any) **Please refer to the relevant AA Touring Bulletins (available free to members) for more details of these areas*

Map	Name	Location	Bookings/Permits	Telephone	Length	Remarks
B1,B2,B3,B4 Page 36 **Cape**	Loerie, Mouth, Look-out and Dead End Trails	*Tsitsikama Coastal National Park	Not necessary	T Tsitsikama 3	B1 = 1 km, B2 = 200 m, B3 = 2 km	Beautiful scenery, cave with an exhibition of prehistoric "strandloper's" midden. Trail for underwater photographers, tidal pools
D1 Page 37 **Transvaal**	Blyde River Walk	Blyde River Canyon	Nature Conservation Headquarters at Old Mine, near Bourke's Luck	Bourke's Luck 15	9 km, 12 km, 9 km	Scenery and wildlife. There are 3 huts and a maximum of 10 persons are permitted at a time
E1 Page 37 **Transvaal**	Forest Falls Walk	Mac Mac State Forest, near Graskop	Not necessary, but hikers must register at starting point	(012) 48-2911	4 km	Waterfalls, swimming, old mines, forest
E2 Page 37 **Transvaal**	Loerie Walk	Ceylon State Forest, near Sabie	Not necessary, but hikers must register at starting point	(012) 48-2911	13,5 km	Waterfalls, forest
G Page 38 **Natal**	*Midmar Public Resort Nature Reserve	Near Howick	Natal Parks Board, Reservations Office, P.O. Box 622, Pietermaritzburg 3200	(0331) 5-3461	Various	Mgeni Cascades, bird sanctuary, fishing
H Page 38 **Natal**	*St Lucia Game Reserve *NB. Trails are conducted between April and October*	Near Hluhluwe			6 day walk (maximum of 6 persons)	Hippo reserve, crocodiles. No swimming. Primeval swamp vegetation, bird-watching. Mpophomeni pans (2½ hour walk), variety of epiphytic orchids
J Page 38 **Orange Free State**	*Golden Gate Highlands National Park	Near Bethlehem	Chief Director, National Parks Board, P.O. Box 787, Pretoria 0001	(012) 44-1194	Various	Sandstone caves, rare black eagle
K Page 38 **Transvaal**	Mount Sheba Walks	Mount Sheba Nature Reserve	Not necessary	T Pilgrim's Rest 17	Up to 4 km	Waterfalls, old mine diggings. Beautiful fauna and flora
L Page 39 **Transvaal**	Fortuna Mine Walk	Barberton	Not necessary	E (013142) 586	3 km	A torch is essential. Interesting geological formations, variety of trees and shrubs
M Page 39 **Cape**	Bushbuck Hiking Trail	Near Port Elizabeth	Permit obtainable from Forester's office, Monday to Friday 07 h 00 to 17 h 15	(014) 2-8638	16 km	Indigenous forest
C1 Page 39 **Cape**	Elephant Walk	Knysna vicinity, Deepwalls State Forest	Obtain free entry permit in advance from Regional Director, Private Bag X12, Knysna 6570 OR State Forester, Deepwalls State Forest, Private Bag X85, Knysna	E (04452) 411 or 4812	18,2 km 14,3 km 8,9 km	World-renowned Knysna elephants as well as other animals and a wide variety of birds
N Page 39 **Cape**	Goukamma Nature Reserve	Goukamma Nature Reserve, Knysna	Obtain free permit from The Responsible Officer, Goukamma Nature Reserve, P.O. Goukamma 6571 OR The Senior Nature Conservation Officer, Groenvlei, P.O. Sedgefield 6573	E (04452) 4430/1 T Sedgefield 50	1 day walk ½ day walk ½ day walk	Birds, various species of buck. Carry water and snake bite outfit
O Page 39 **Cape**	*Hogsback	At Hogsback	At the various accommodation establishments in the area		Various	Big Tree (yellow-wood) ± 2 000 years old, waterfalls
P Page 39 **Cape**	*Mountain Zebra National Park	Near Cradock	See Golden Gate Highlands National Park		Various	Bushman paintings, caves, 170 bird species, mountain zebras
Q Page 40 **Natal**	*Royal Natal National Park	Drakensberg Area	See Midmar Public Resort Nature Reserve *NB Obtain permit from Warden's office to enter Homeland*		Various	Beautiful walks and climbs to several points of interest. 2 day trip to the Mont-aux-Sources plateau. Bushman art, trout hatcheries
R Page 40 **Cape**	*Namaqualand and Cedarberg	Cedarberg Area	Obtain permit from The Government Forester, Cedarberg Forestry Station, Citrusdal 7340	E (02682) 3440	Various	Caves, mountain huts, wild flowers, beautiful viewsites
	Beaverlac	Beaverlac Nature Reserve, Porterville.	Beaverlac Nature Reserve, P.O. Box 116, Porterville 6810	E (026227) 1740	Yellow Route 12 - 14 hours. Blue Route 1 hour	Bushman paintings, variety of plant, bird and animal life
S Page 40 **Natal**	*Mkuzi Game Reserve *NB. Trails are conducted between April & December*	Near Mkuze	See Midmar Public Resort Nature Reserve OR phone	(0331) 5-1221	3 day walk	Wide variety of animals, game-viewing hides, fig forest. Black and White rhinos, profusion of bird life
T Page 40 **Natal**	*Umfolozi Game Reserve	Near Mtubatuba				Home of the square-lipped rhinoceros, lion, leopard and several antelope species
The following details are also of interest, although no covering maps are included in this section						
	Lion	Timbavati Reserve	Educational Wildlife Expeditions P.O. Box 645, Bedfordview 2008	(011) 53-1814	All are ± 15 km (Maximum 8 participants)	White lions of Timbavati
	Loskop Dam	Loskop Dam Nature Reserve				White rhino, giraffe, canoeing on river, bush camp
	Mananga Ivory	Klaserie Private Nature Reserve				Two permanent camps on river banks. 5 day duration
	Rustenburg	Rustenburg Nature Reserve	Nature Conservation Officer, Rietvlei Nature Reserve, Rustenburg	(01421) 2-5460	± 5 km	To be opened at the end of 1978
	Wolhuter	Kruger National Park (between Malelane and Pretoriuskop)	See Golden Gate Highlands National Park		2 day walk	Wildlife

REFERENCE

Title	Map No.	Bar scale (0–2 km)
Tarred road (under const.)		
Untarred road (under const.)		
Secondary road		
Minor road or Track		
Railway		
International boundary		
Provincial boundary		
Homeland boundary (approximate)		
National park, game or nature reserve		
River, with waterfall		
Dam, pan or lake		
Forest		
1426 Spot height in metres		
Towns		
Locality		
Mine		
Direction of trail		
19,2 Point to point Trail distances (km)		
Walk		
B E Beginning and end of trail/walk		
Rest camp		
Viewsite		
Place of interest		

Map symbols as shown on page 33

WHERE TO GO

National Hiking Trails, Wilderness Trails and Walks

NATIONAL HIKING WAY
- Completed Trails

PRIORITY CONSTRUCTION PROGRAMME
- High
- Medium High
- Medium Low
- Low

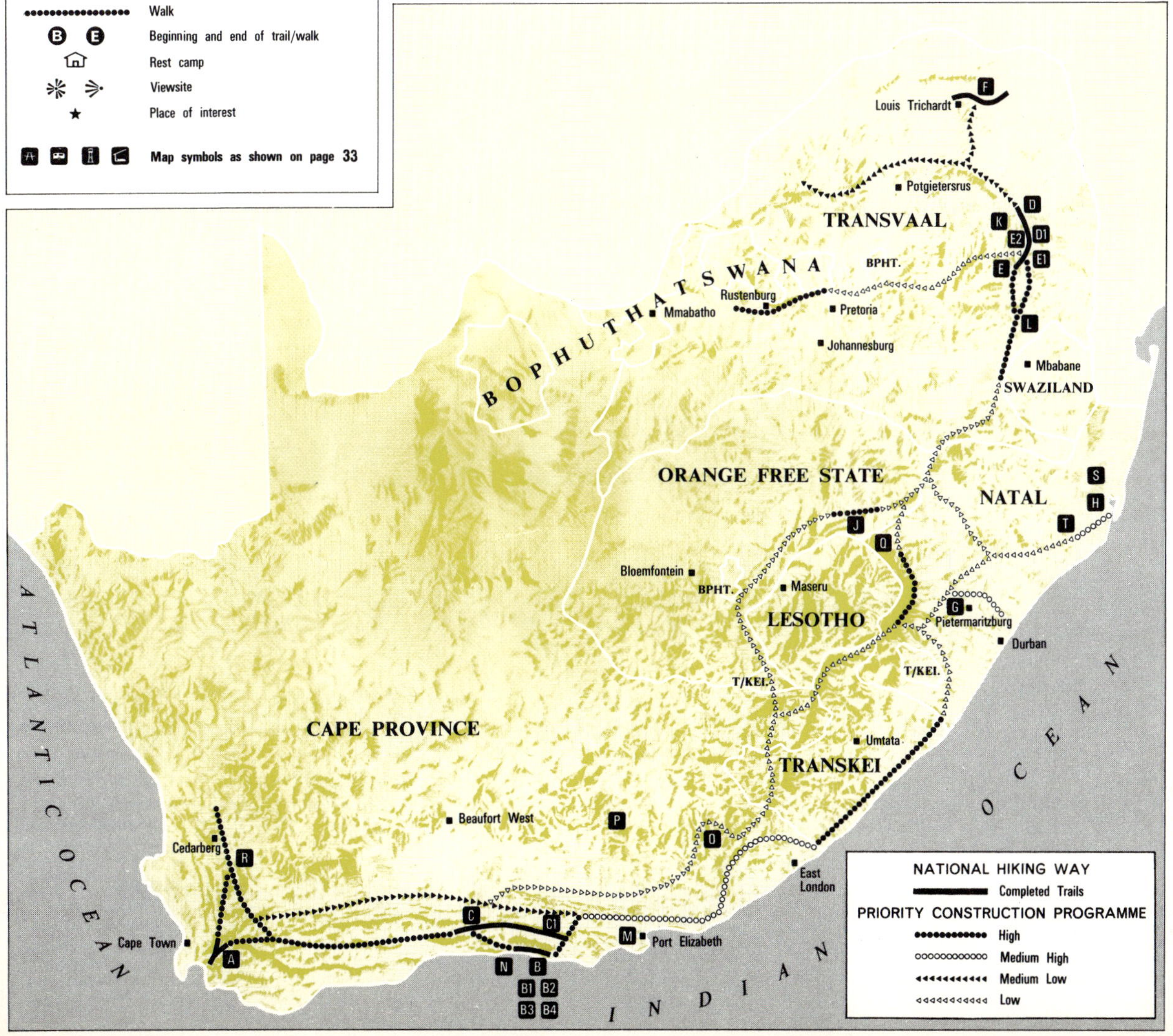

Boland Hiking Trail (Hottentotsholland Section)
Boland-voetslaanpad (Seksie Hottentotsholland)

A

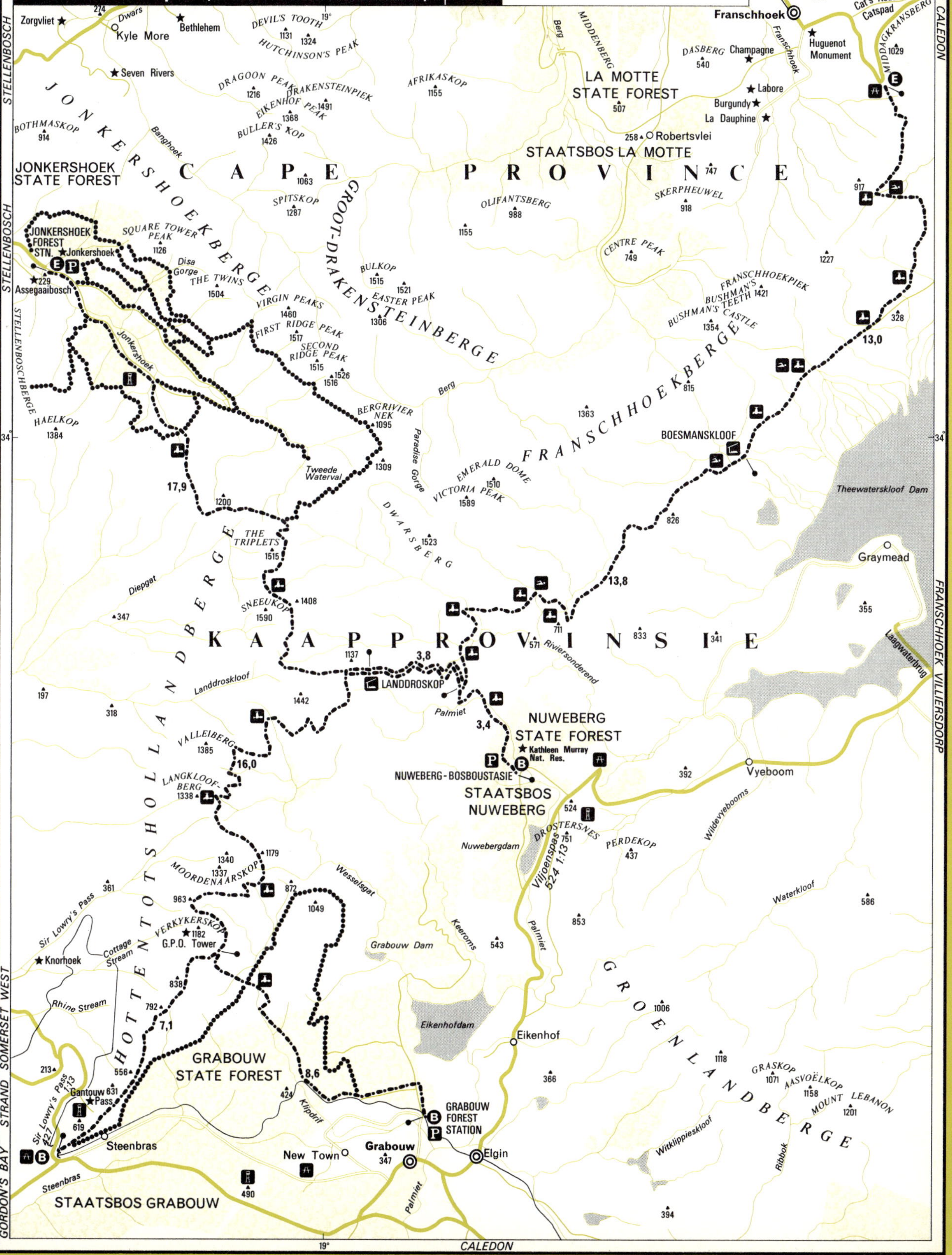

Scale: 0 1 2 3 4 5 km

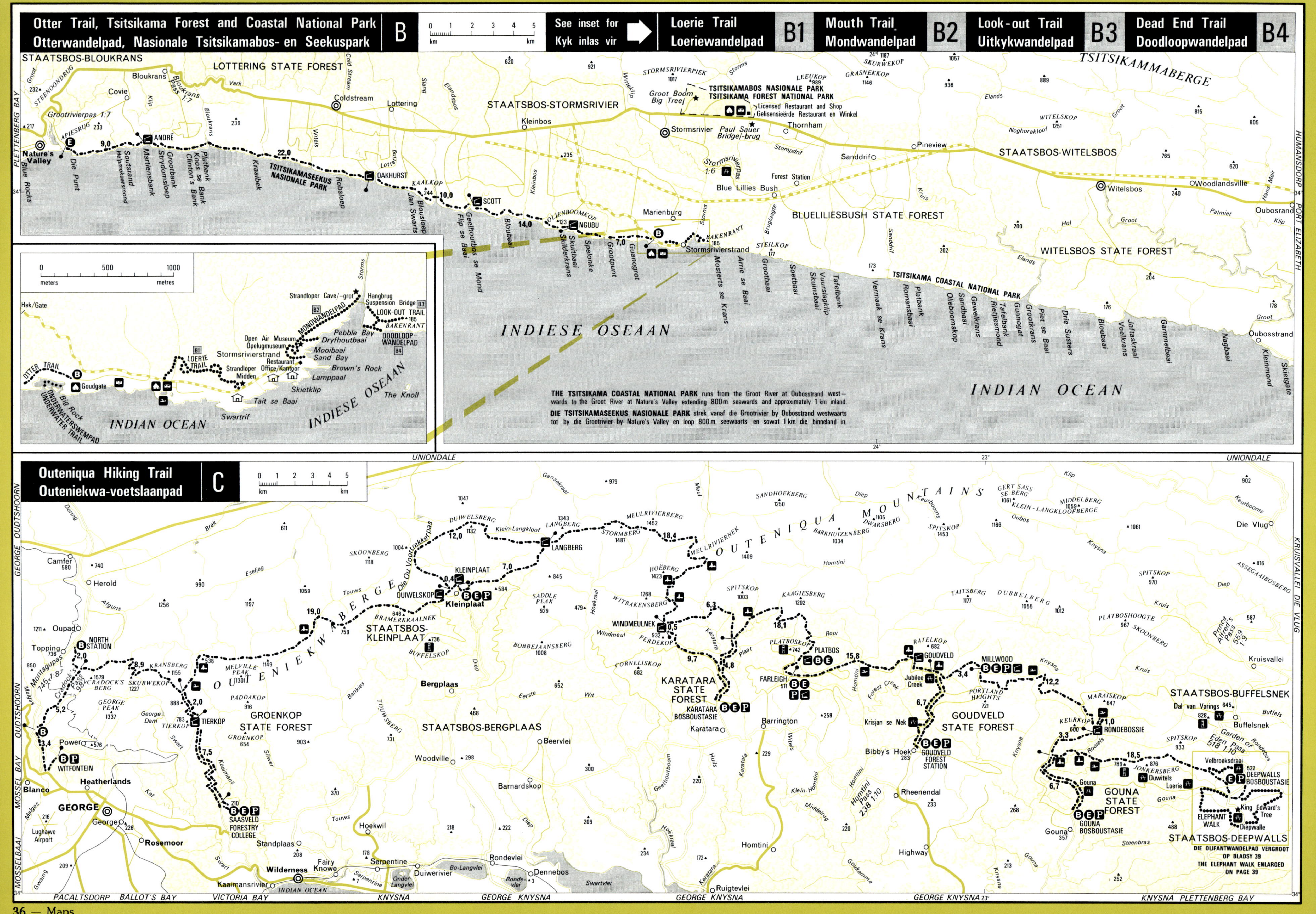

Otter Trail, Tsitsikama Forest and Coastal National Park
Otterwandelpad, Nasionale Tsitsikamabos- en Seekuspark
B
km
See inset for
Kyk inlas vir
Loerie Trail
Loeriewandelpad
B1
Mouth Trail
Mondwandelpad
B2
Look-out Trail
Uitkykwandelpad
B3
Dead End Trail
Doodloopwandelpad
B4
STAATSBOS-BLOUKRANS
LOTTERING STATE FOREST
STAATSBOS-STORMSRIVIER
TSITSIKAMABOS NASIONALE PARK
TSITSIKAMA FOREST NATIONAL PARK
Licensed Restaurant and Shop
Gelisensieërde Restaurant en Winkel
TSITSIKAMMABERGE
STAATSBOS-WITELSBOS
BLUELILIESBUSH STATE FOREST
WITELSBOS STATE FOREST
TSITSIKAMASEEKUS NASIONALE PARK
TSITSIKAMA COASTAL NATIONAL PARK
INDIESE OSEAAN
INDIAN OCEAN
Nature's Valley
Bloukrans
Coldstream
Lottering
Kleinbos
Stormsrivier
Paul Sauer Bridge/-brug
Thornham
Pineview
Sanddrif
Blue Lillies Bush
Marienburg
Stormsrivierstrand
Witelsbos
Woodlandsville
Oubosrand
Oubosstrand
ANDRÉ
OAKHURST
SCOTT
NGUBU
HUMANSDORP PORT ELIZABETH
PLETTENBERG BAY
THE TSITSIKAMA COASTAL NATIONAL PARK runs from the Groot River at Oubosstrand westwards to the Groot River at Nature's Valley extending 800 m seawards and approximately 1 km inland.
DIE TSITSIKAMASEEKUS NASIONALE PARK strek vanaf die Grootrivier by Oubosstrand westwaarts tot by die Grootrivier by Nature's Valley en loop 800 m seewaarts en sowat 1 km die binneland in.
meters
metres
Strandloper Cave/-grot
Hangbrug Suspension Bridge
LOOK-OUT TRAIL
DOODLOOP-WANDELPAD
MONDWANDELPAD
Open Air Museum Opelugmuseum
Stormsrivierstrand
Restaurant
Strandloper Midden
Office/Kantoor
LOERIE TRAIL
OTTER TRAIL
Goudgate
UNDERWATERSWEMPAD
UNDERWATER TRAIL
Outeniqua Hiking Trail
Outeniekwa-voetslaanpad
C
OUTENIQUA MOUNTAINS
OUTENIEKWABERGE
STAATSBOS-KLEINPLAAT
GROENKOP STATE FOREST
STAATSBOS-BERGPLAAS
KARATARA STATE FOREST
GOUDVELD STATE FOREST
GOUNA STATE FOREST
STAATSBOS-BUFFELSNEK
STAATSBOS-DEEPWALLS
GEORGE
Heatherlands
Blanco
Wilderness
Kaaimansrivier
WITFONTEIN
NORTH STATION
TIERKOP
SAASVELD FORESTRY COLLEGE
DUIWELSKOP
KLEINPLAAT
Kleinplaat
LANGBERG
WINDMEULNEK
KARATARA BOSBOUSTASIE
PLATBOS
FARLEIGH
GOUDVELD
GOUDVELD FOREST STATION
MILLWOOD
RONDEBOSSIE
GOUNA BOSBOUSTASIE
DEEPWALLS BOSBOUSTASIE
ELEPHANT WALK
King Edward's Tree
DIE OLIFANTWANDELPAD VERGROOT OP BLADSY 39
THE ELEPHANT WALK ENLARGED ON PAGE 39
UNIONDALE
GEORGE OUDTSHOORN
KRUISVALLEI DIE VLUG
MOSSEL BAY OUDTSHOORN
MOSSELBAAI
PACALTSDORP BALLOT'S BAY
VICTORIA BAY
KNYSNA
GEORGE KNYSNA
KNYSNA PLETTENBERG BAY

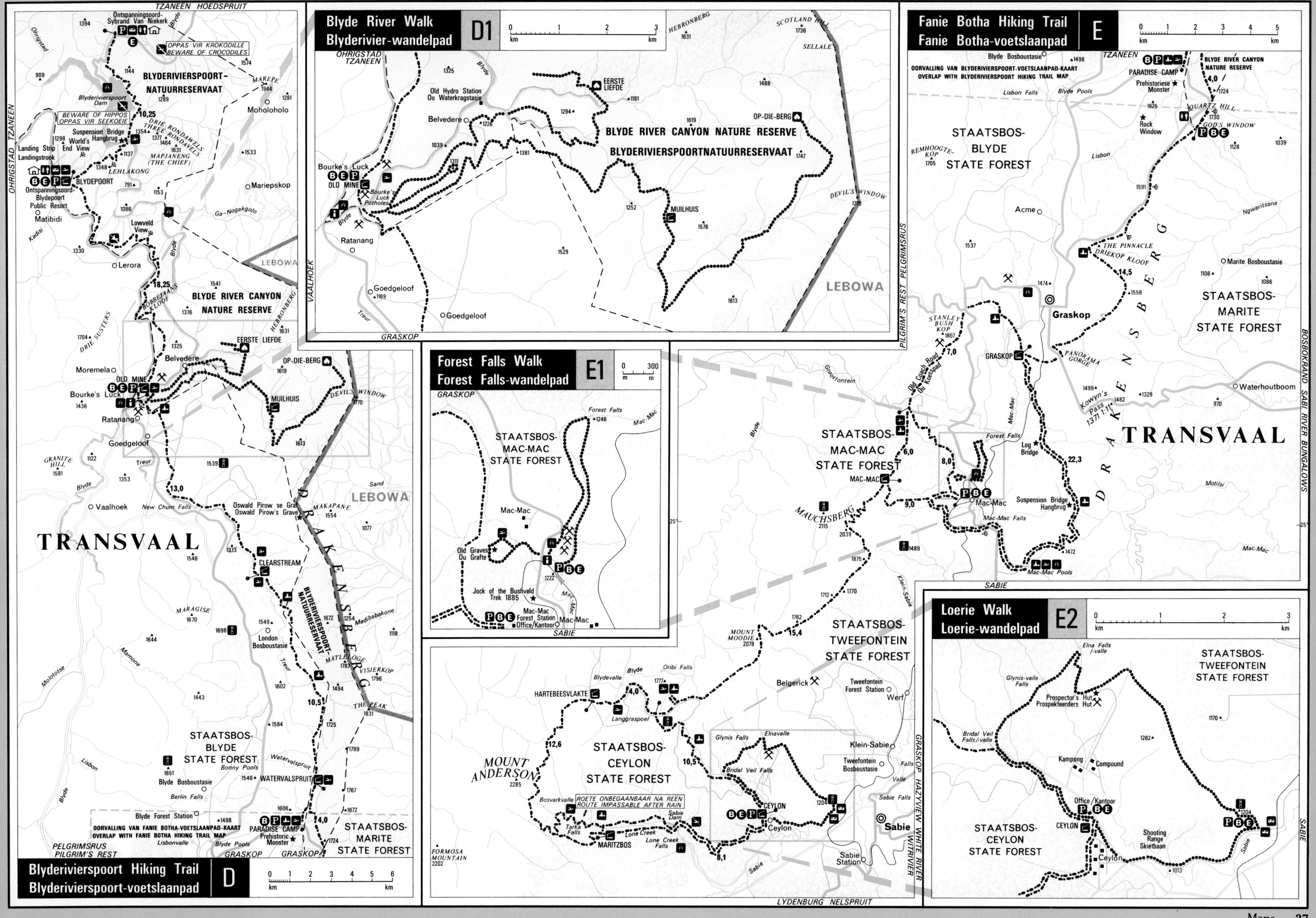
Blyderivierspoort Hiking Trail
Blyderivierspoort-voetslaanpad
D
Blyde River Walk
Blyderivier-wandelpad
D1
Fanie Botha Hiking Trail
Fanie Botha-voetslaanpad
E
Forest Falls Walk
Forest Falls-wandelpad
E1
Loerie Walk
Loerie-wandelpad
E2
TRANSVAAL
BLYDE RIVER CANYON NATURE RESERVE
BLYDERIVIERSPOORTNATUURRESERVAAT
STAATSBOS-BLYDE STATE FOREST
STAATSBOS-MARITE STATE FOREST
STAATSBOS-MAC-MAC STATE FOREST
STAATSBOS-TWEEFONTEIN STATE FOREST
STAATSBOS-CEYLON STATE FOREST
DRAKENSBERG
LEBOWA
Graskop
Sabie

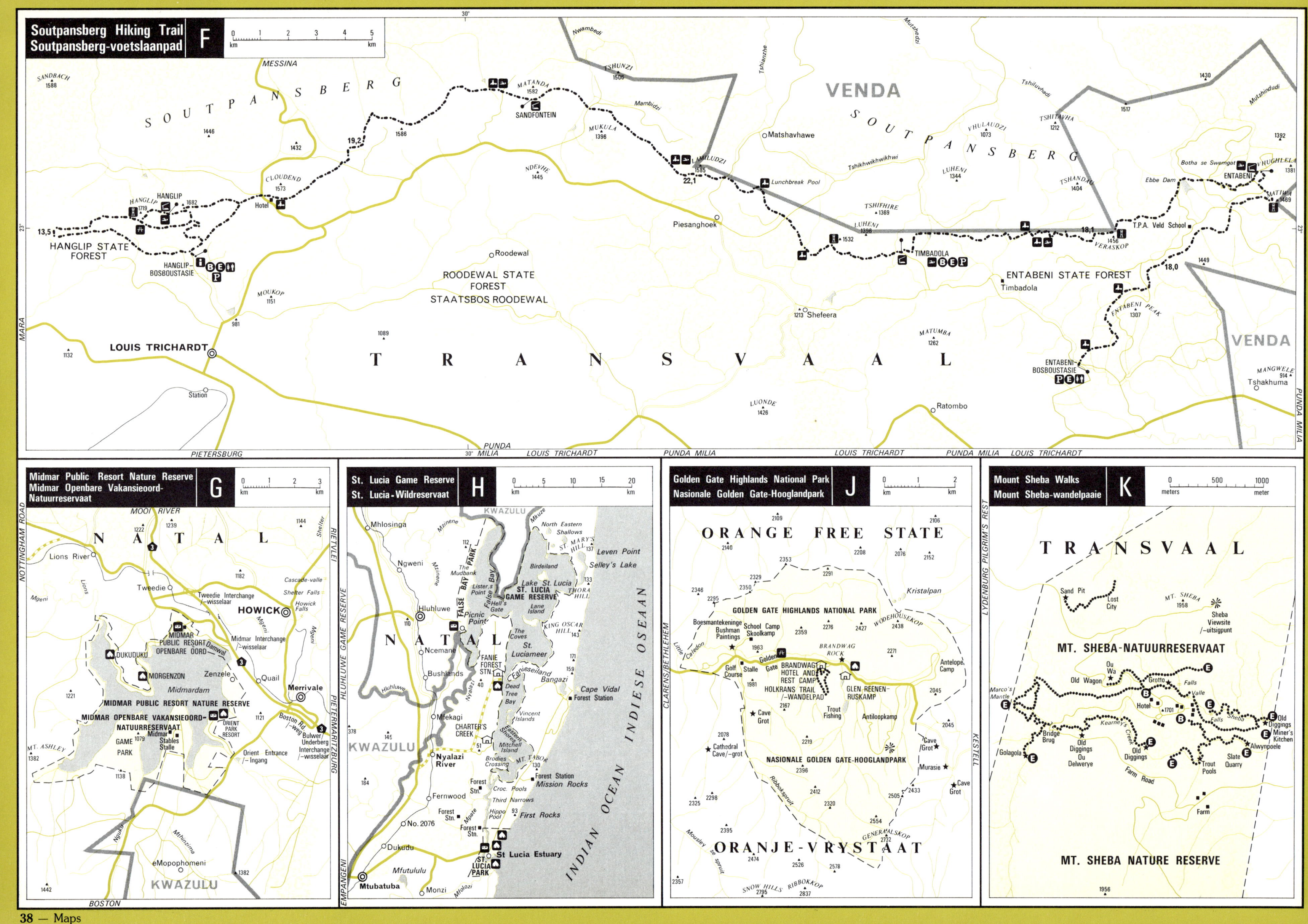

Soutpansberg Hiking Trail
Soutpansberg-voetslaanpad
F
SOUTPANSBERG
VENDA
SOUTPANSBERG
HANGLIP STATE FOREST
HANGLIP-BOSBOUSTASIE
ROODEWAL STATE FOREST
STAATSBOS ROODEWAL
ENTABENI STATE FOREST
ENTABENI-BOSBOUSTASIE
LOUIS TRICHARDT
TRANSVAAL
VENDA
MESSINA
PIETERSBURG
PUNDA MILIA
LOUIS TRICHARDT
Midmar Public Resort Nature Reserve
Midmar Openbare Vakansieoord-Natuurreservaat
G
NATAL
HOWICK
MIDMAR PUBLIC RESORT NATURE RESERVE
MIDMAR OPENBARE VAKANSIEOORD-NATUURRESERVAAT
KWAZULU
St. Lucia Game Reserve
St. Lucia-Wildreservaat
H
ST. LUCIA GAME RESERVE
NATAL
KWAZULU
INDIAN OCEAN
INDIESE OSEAAN
St Lucia Estuary
Mtubatuba
Golden Gate Highlands National Park
Nasionale Golden Gate-Hooglandpark
J
ORANGE FREE STATE
GOLDEN GATE HIGHLANDS NATIONAL PARK
NASIONALE GOLDEN GATE-HOOGLANDPARK
ORANJE-VRYSTAAT
Mount Sheba Walks
Mount Sheba-wandelpaaie
K
TRANSVAAL
MT. SHEBA-NATUURRESERVAAT
MT. SHEBA NATURE RESERVE

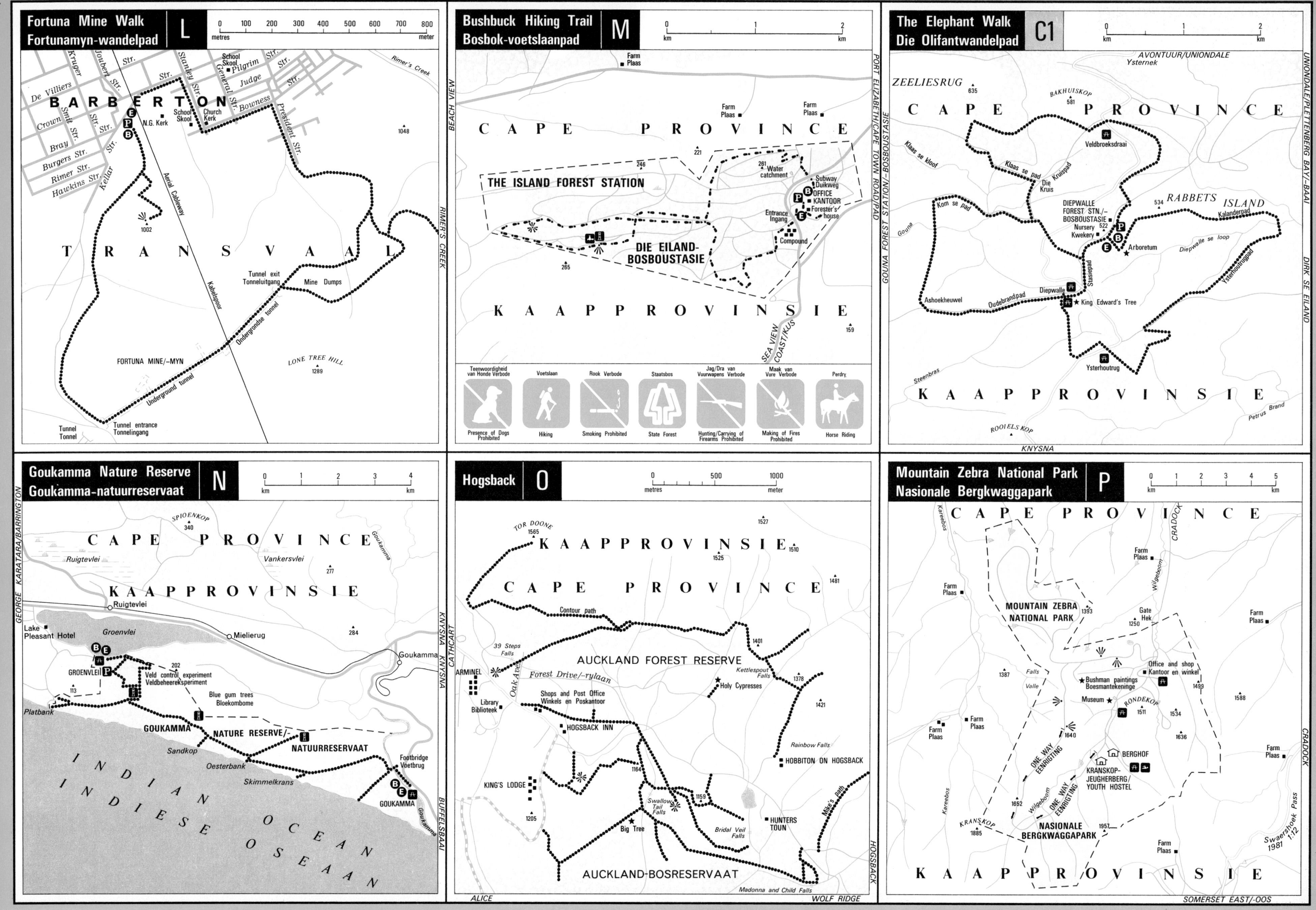

Fortuna Mine Walk
Fortunamyn-wandelpad
L
Bushbuck Hiking Trail
Bosbok-voetslaanpad
M
The Elephant Walk
Die Olifantwandelpad
C1
Goukamma Nature Reserve
Goukamma-natuurreservaat
N
Hogsback
O
Mountain Zebra National Park
Nasionale Bergkwaggapark
P
BARBERTON
TRANSVAAL
FORTUNA MINE/-MYN
LONE TREE HILL
THE ISLAND FOREST STATION
DIE EILAND-BOSBOUSTASIE
CAPE PROVINCE
KAAPPROVINSIE
Teenwoordigheid van Honde Verbode
Presence of Dogs Prohibited
Voetslaan
Hiking
Rook Verbode
Smoking Prohibited
Staatsbos
State Forest
Jag/Dra van Vuurwapens Verbode
Hunting/Carrying of Firearms Prohibited
Maak van Vure Verbode
Making of Fires Prohibited
Perdry
Horse Riding
DIEPWALLE FOREST STN./-BOSBOUSTASIE
RABBETS ISLAND
King Edward's Tree
KNYSNA
INDIAN OCEAN
INDIESE OSEAAN
GOUKAMMA NATURE RESERVE/-NATUURRESERVAAT
AUCKLAND FOREST RESERVE
AUCKLAND-BOSRESERVAAT
HOGSBACK INN
KING'S LODGE
HOBBITON ON HOGSBACK
HUNTERS TOUN
MOUNTAIN ZEBRA NATIONAL PARK
NASIONALE BERGKWAGGAPARK
KRANSKOP-JEUGHERBERG/YOUTH HOSTEL
BERGHOF
SOMERSET EAST/-OOS
CRADOCK

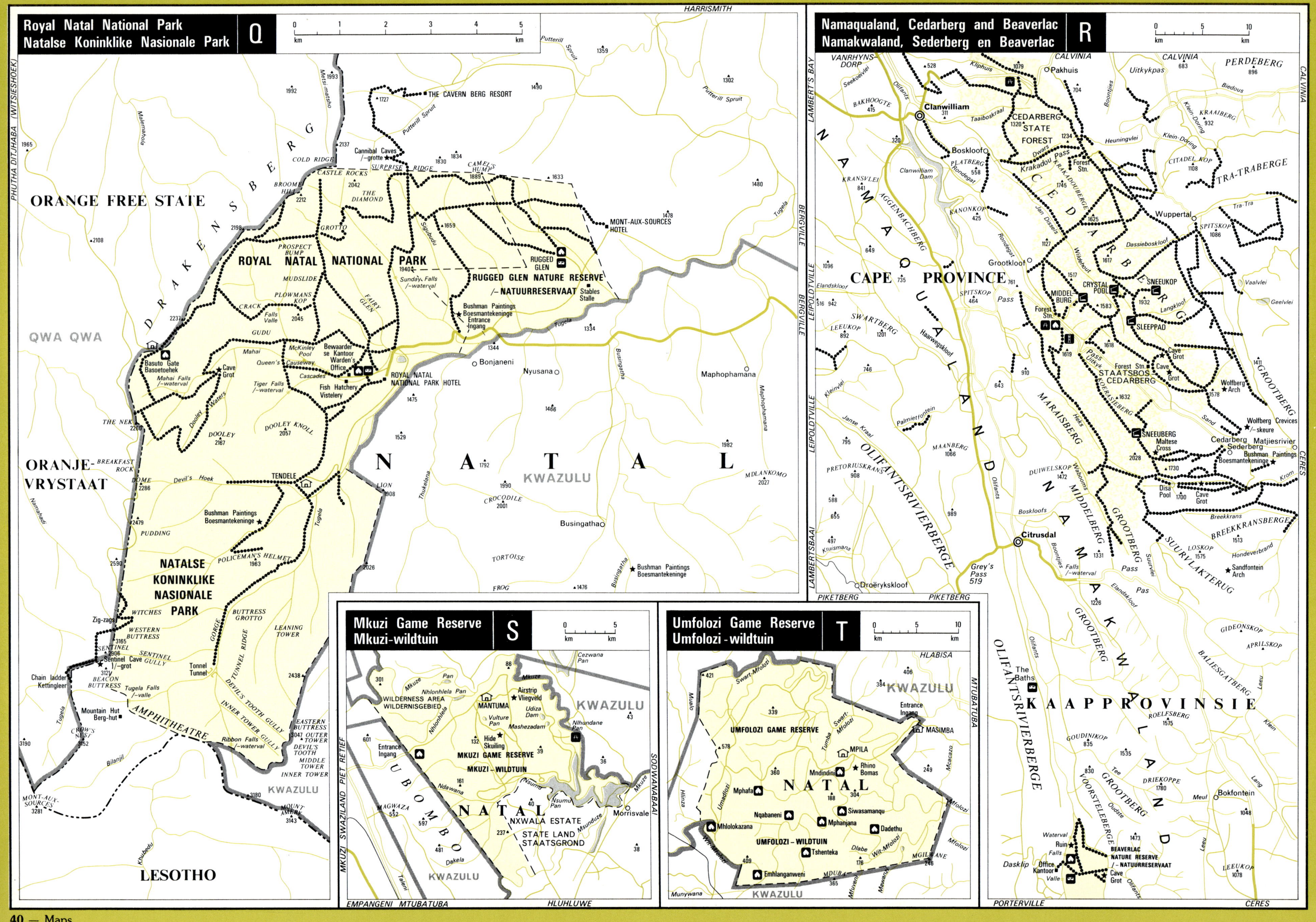

Royal Natal National Park
Natalse Koninklike Nasionale Park
Q
Namaqualand, Cedarberg and Beaverlac
Namakwaland, Sederberg en Beaverlac
R
Mkuzi Game Reserve
Mkuzi-wildtuin
S
Umfolozi Game Reserve
Umfolozi-wildtuin
T
ROYAL NATAL NATIONAL PARK
NATALSE KONINKLIKE NASIONALE PARK
RUGGED GLEN NATURE RESERVE
ORANGE FREE STATE
ORANJE-VRYSTAAT
QWA QWA
NATAL
KWAZULU
LESOTHO
DRAKENSBERG
CAPE PROVINCE
KAAPPROVINSIE
NAMAQUALAND
CEDARBERG STATE FOREST
MKUZI GAME RESERVE
MKUZI-WILDTUIN
UMFOLOZI GAME RESERVE
UMFOLOZI-WILDTUIN

The Constellations

as seen from South Africa on any night in the year

South Africa holds a favoured position in astronomy as it is one of the few parts of the Earth combining a suitable climate for viewing the rich southern skies and easy access to view-sites. Consequently, while there are a number of professional observatories engaged in research, opportunities also abound for individuals to become enthusiastic amateur astronomers.

The notes and charts which follow are valuable aids to the budding amateur astronomer spending a night out under the stars. The notes are of necessity brief, but persons desiring further information or who wish to pursue this fascinating subject, will find the programme presented by the planetaria and observatories on visiting nights helpful and instructive - See pages 46 - 47 for list of addresses. The following information will be of assistance to interested persons.

◂ **Earth as seen from space**

HOW TO USE THESE STAR CHARTS

Each chart represents the sky as it would appear to an observer at the times given if it were possible for him to take the whole sky in at one glance. The continuous circle represents the horizon at Cape Town, and the broken circle the horizon at Johannesburg. The centre of the circle is the zenith or point immediately overhead. There is no top, bottom, nor side to the charts. They are arranged so that they may be turned round to represent the portion of the sky which is under observation. For example, if the observer wishes to study the constellations in the west he will look up the chart corresponding to the night and hour, and will hold it so that the word "west" is at the bottom. The constellations in the lower half of the chart will then be those which are to be seen at that time when he is looking towards the west, and the stars in the upper half will be ignored as they are behind the observer. The names of the constellations are positioned so as to be readable when the chart is held correctly.

The charts are constructed to show all the constellations which are visible at the times given with each chart. All the stars of the first four magnitudes are shown but some fainter stars are added in order to represent constellations which contain no bright stars, such as are in the region around the South Pole. The stars are represented by discs which by their size indicate the comparative brightness of the stars.

The charts are arranged in a circular series. Chart 1 follows Chart 12, just as Chart 12 follows Chart 11. Taken in order they represent the sky at intervals of two hours on any single night, or, if the hour of observation be the same, at intervals of one month. Included below each chart is a table of the nights and hours for which the chart is correct.

The blue line which stretches from east to west on each chart indicates the celestial equator, which is the great circle in the heavens corresponding to the terrestrial equator, being in the position where the plane of the Earth's equator would intersect the celestial sphere if extended outward. To an observer on the equator the celestial equator would, in a chart of this character, be a straight line from east to west; that is, it would pass over the head of the observer. At either pole the celestial equator would be on the horizon of the observer. The departure of the equator from the zenith or centre of the chart is the measure of the observer's latitude.

The curved red line which varies with each chart marks out the ecliptic. This is the path which the Sun appears to trace in the heavens owing to the motion of the Earth in its orbit round the Sun. The ecliptic is inclined to the equator at an angle of 23½ degrees, and intersects it at two points 180 degrees apart. These points are called equinoxes, because when the Sun is at either of these positions, being then on the equator, it rises due east and sets due west, and there is equal length of day and night. The points of greatest departure from the equator are called the solstices. When the Sun reaches these points we have the longest day if the Sun is furthest south, about the 21st December. The shortest day is when the Sun is furthest north of the equator, around the 21st June.

The white line running through the centre of the chart from north to south is called the meridian. This represents the great circle which passes from horizon to horizon through the south celestial pole and the zenith of the observer. It is obvious, therefore, that when a star arrives at the meridian it is either due north or due south, according to its direction from the zenith.

Stars which rise due east will set due west. Stars rising north of east will set at a corresponding point north of west. Stars rising south of east will set at a corresponding point south of west; all reach their highest altitude when crossing the meridian. If we extend our observations further south we find that we come to stars that do not rise or set but traverse the sky in concentric circles around a certain point on the meridian. This point, where there is little apparent motion, is the South Celestial Pole. Unfortunately there is no bright star to mark the pole as in the Northern Hemisphere, but the position may be found in one of the following ways.

HOW TO FIND THE SOUTH POLE

(a) The Southern Cross, which is one of the first constellations with which the learner will become acquainted, is an indicator to the South Pole. The longer axis points very nearly in that direction. The Pole is at a point about four and a half Cross-lengths from the foot of the Cross.

(b) The South Pole lies near the centre of a line joining Achernar, the brightest star in Eridanus, with Beta Centauri, the nearer of the two pointers to the Southern Cross. ("Centauri" is the genitive case; it therefore means "of Centaurus", the Centaur. Similarly, "Alpha Crucis" indicates Alpha of Crux, the Cross, and so on.)

(c) A more accurate determination may be found by drawing a line from Alpha Crucis, the most brilliant star in the Southern Cross, to the star Beta of the constellation Hydrus. The South Pole is in this line at a point one-third of its length from the latter star. Beta Hydri may be easily identified, as it is a fairly bright star situated close to the smaller of the two white misty patches, known as the magellanic clouds, which look rather like detached portions of the Milky Way though their nature is in fact very different.

South African Astronomical Observatory at Sutherland, Cape

Pleides or the Seven Sisters

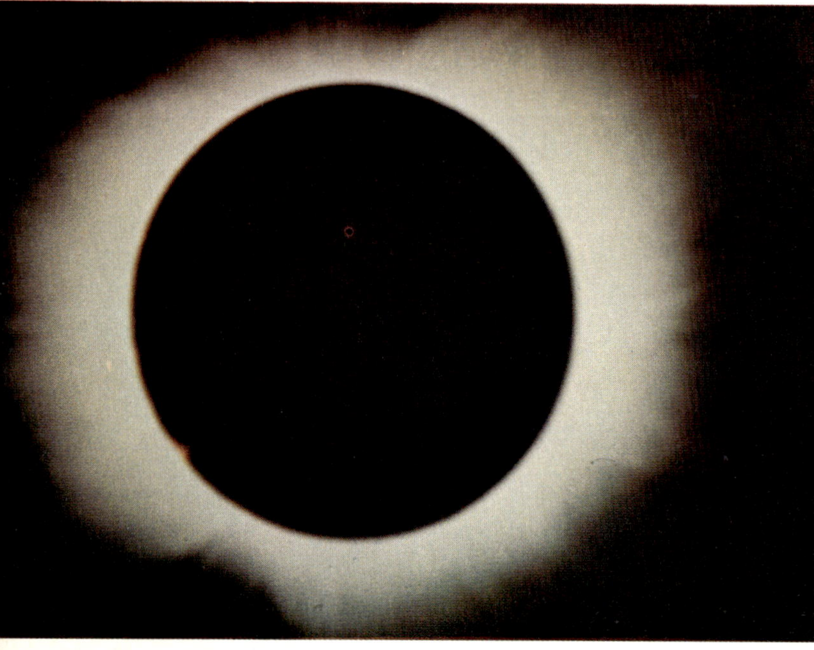

Top: The Solar System including orbit of comet

Bottom: Total Eclipse of the Sun

Right: Artist's impression of Pioneer spaceprobe to Jupiter with Earth and moon in foreground

Far Right: Orion nebula, a place where stars are born

THE CONSTELLATIONS

The constellations are arbitrary groupings of the stars. Most of them were arranged by the ancients to represent certain imaginary figures such as Leo, the lion, and Orion, the hunter, and this arrangement has since been useful in marking out the different regions of the heavens. We should not, however, try to picture the image of a lion in the stars composing the constellation Leo, nor need we wish to trace the figure of the mighty hunter in Orion, thinking that it was on account of their resemblance to animals or to mythological heroes that the groups were originally formed. In his "Primitive Constellations" Brown says: *"Writers have often told us, speaking only from the depths of their ignorance, how Chaldean shepherds were wont to gaze at the brilliant nocturne sky, and to imagine that such and such stars resemble this or that figure. But all this is merely the old effort to make capital out of nescience, and the stars are before our eyes to prove the contrary. Having already certain fixed ideas and figures in his mind, the constellation-former, when he came to his task, applied his figures to the stars and the stars to his figures as harmoniously as possible."*

Many of the constellations with which we are familiar are believed to have been named more than 4 000 years ago by the Sumerian peoples to symbolize their mythological conceptions. We in the Southern Hemisphere see a portion of the heavens which was not charted by them because they could not see it. The position of this region tells us that the heavens were first divided into constellations by a people living in a region of latitude about 40 degrees north.

Johann Bayer, in 1603 A.D., arranged the stars in this part of the sky into twelve new constellations from information furnished by southern navigators. This did not, however, complete the survey of the heavens. The Southern Cross (Crux) was added by Royer in 1679, and the less conspicuous constellations around the South Pole were grouped by La Caille, when on a visit to South Africa in 1752. La Caille's telescope was mounted in Cape Town in what is now called Strand Street, where a plaque marking the position of his observatory was erected. (On the 21st June 1977, this plaque was resited close to the site of La Caille's observatory and can be seen on a pillar inside the Old Mutual Centre, with entrance off Adderley Street and St. George's Street, corner of Strand Street.) The group of fifth magnitude stars between Chamaeleon and Hydrus was named Mons Mensa by La Caille after Table Mountain. He also subdivided the unwieldy constellation of Argo into Carina (the keel), Puppis (the poop), Vela (the sails), and Malus (the mast), though Malus is now known as Pyxis.

FIXED STARS

It will be noticed, after a preliminary study of the skies, that although the stars from time to time occupy different positions with regard to the horizon they nevertheless always preserve the same relative positions with respect to one another. For this reason the term "Fixed Stars" was used to distinguish them from those bodies which changed their positions in the constellations from time to time, and were therefore called "planets" or wanderers. The so-called fixed stars are not actually stationary, all are in motion; but they are at so great a distance from us that although their movements are very rapid their total displacement during a lifetime cannot be detected except by the aid of powerful telescopes.

Newcomb said: *"If Hipparchus or Ptolemy should rise from his sleep of two thousand years - nay, if the earliest priests of Babylon should come to life again and view the heavens, they would not perceive any change to have taken place in the relative positions of the stars. The general configurations of the constellations would be exactly that to which they were accustomed. Had they been exact observers they might notice a slight change in the position of Arcturus, but not in that of any other star".* Arcturus has a relatively large individual or "proper" motion; even so, it amounts to only 2 seconds of arc per year - a rate exceeded by Alpha Centauri (3,6 seconds).

THE PLANETS

The belt of the sky covering about 9 degrees on each side of the ecliptic is called the Zodiac, from the Greek word meaning animal, because the majority of the constellations in it have the names of animals. It is in this region of the sky that the planets appear to move.

The Inner Planets - Mercury and Venus perform their several journeys round the Sun within the Earth's orbit, and consequently cannot be seen in the opposite part of the sky to the Sun. They pass behind the Sun (superior conjunction) and are seen in the evening sky towards the west after sunset when they have attained a sufficient angular distance from the Sun. The distance increases until they reach a point beyond which they do not go. They are then said to be at greatest eastern elongation, and are seen to best advantage after sunset. Afterwards they move between us and the Sun (inferior conjunction) and appear in the morning sky before sunrise, increasing their distance from the Sun to greatest western elongation or "morning star" position, and then falling back to pass behind the Sun into the evening sky again.

The greatest elongation of Mercury never amounts to more than 28 degrees and in these latitudes this planet cannot remain above the horizon for more than about two hours after sunset, or rise more than a similar period before sunrise. Venus, being further from the Sun, attains a greater elongation, the maximum being about 47½ degrees, but must always set before midnight when in the evening sky, and rise after midnight when in the morning sky. The brightness of Mercury varies greatly according to its distance from the Earth. When at its best it rivals Sirius, the brightest star, but may at times be seen when it is only one-tenth as bright, and it is not striking, because it can never be seen against a dark background. Venus always greatly surpasses all stars and planets. Even when at minimum brightness it shines seven times more brightly than the combined lustre of all the stars in Orion, and when at maximum is three times brighter still.

Mercury revolves round the Sun in 88 days, and Venus in 225 days. As the Earth is also moving round the Sun in the same direction, a longer interval elapses between two successive conjunctions (inferior to inferior or superior to superior). This is called the synodic period and amounts in the case of Mercury to 116 days and in that of Venus to 584 days.

The Outer Planets - The other five planets, Mars, Jupiter, Saturn, Uranus and Neptune are more distant from the Sun than the Earth, the distance increasing in the order given. Although they have the same apparent daily motion as the stars, continued observations will show that they also move among the stars in an easterly direction. This is due to their movement in their orbits round the Sun, which is in the same direction as that of the Earth. When, however, the outer planets are near opposition (when Sun, Earth and planet are in a line in the order given with Earth between the Sun and the planet), the more rapid movement of the Earth causes the planets to appear to move backwards or in the opposite direction, i.e. from east to west. This is called their retrograde movement. The same effect is observed by a passenger in a train when passing another train moving in the same direction. The slower train appears to move backwards in relation to the scenery in the distant background.

Mars varies greatly in brightness owing to the great difference between its minimum and maximum distances from the Earth. When in most favourable opposition Mars may approach us to within 50 million kilometres, but when

farthest away it may be as much as 248 million kilometres from us. In the former case it outrivals the brightest stars and even excels Jupiter, whereas when most distant it is only about one-third as bright as Antares. Mars greatly resembles Antares in appearance and colour, being ruddy, and is thus easily distinguished from the other planets. Mars performs its revolution round the Sun in 687 days. Its mean synodic period (from opposition to opposition) is 780 days, or 2 years and 1 month.

Jupiter is the largest of the planets, but owing to greater distance is inferior to Venus in brightness. Jupiter always shines more brightly than Sirius. It takes nearly 12 years to complete its journey round the Sun. Its synodic period is 399 days. This planet is a very interesting object in a small telescope, which will reveal the flattening at its poles, the remarkable bands which cross its surface, and the four brightest of its moons. These four moons were the first-fruits of Galileo's observations with the newly invented telescope in 1610.

Saturn to the naked eye is the least interesting of the bright planets. When at its brightest it outshines all stars but Canopus and Sirius, and when faintest is comparable with Spica. In the telescope however, it is the most fascinating of the planets on account of the beautiful ring system which surrounds it. Saturn's sidereal period of revolution is about 29½ years. (The sidereal period of a planet is the time taken for it to complete one journey round the Sun – in the case of the Earth, 365¼ days.)

The three outermost planets were not known to the ancients. Uranus was discovered by Sir William Herschel in 1781. This planet just comes within the limit of naked eye vision, reaching 6th magnitude, somewhat fainter than Sigma Octantis, the southern polar star. Its period of revolution is 84 years.

Early in the 19th century close observations of the movement of Uranus showed discrepancies between the calculated and observed places of this planet. This led astronomers to suspect the existence of an exterior planet whose gravitational influence would account for the perturbations in the orbit of Uranus. The position of such a disturbing body was calculated independently by Adams and Le Verrier, and the planet was afterwards found in the predicted place. This planet cannot be seen with the naked eye but is visible in small telescopes as a bluish star of the eighth magnitude. Neptune occupies nearly 165 years in travelling round the Sun. Pluto, also predicted mathematically, was first observed in 1930. It is too faint to be seen with small telescopes.

As the planets are constantly changing their places in the heavens it is impossible to indicate their positions in the charts. Exact particulars as to their position from time to time, with other interesting information for the observer, are published in the Yearly Handbook of the Astronomical Society of Southern Africa, or may be obtained when visiting the Planetarium, University of Witwatersrand, Johannesburg.

WHAT TO SEE IN THE SKY

A little practice with these star charts will soon enable the enthusiastic beginner to find his (or her) way around the sky. One method is to select a few easily-identified

THE ASTRONOMICAL SOCIETY OF SOUTHERN AFRICA

The Astronomical Society of Southern Africa is a body comprising of both professional and amateur astronomers. Membership is open to all interested persons, regardless of knowledge or experience.

In addition to the issue of its handbook, the Society issues "The Monthly Notes of the Astronomical Society of Southern Africa" (MNASSA). Members also receive copies of "Sky and Telescope", an excellent and very popular monthly magazine published in the United States of America. It provides up-to-date information on both professional and amateur activities, together with news of space research and other related subjects. A small entrance fee and an annual subscription are payable.

Inquiries – Honorary Secretary, Astronomical Society of Southern Africa, c/o The South African Astronomical Observatory, P O Box 9, OBSERVATORY 7935 Cape

LOCAL CENTRES OF THE ASTRONOMICAL SOCIETY OF SOUTHERN AFRICA

Autonomous local centres of the Society hold regular meetings in Bloemfontein, Cape Town, Durban, Johannesburg, Pietermaritzburg, Pretoria and Salisbury. Visitors are welcome to attend meetings and may join a centre without becoming a full member of the society.

Bloemfontein - Free State Centre

Meetings held every third Wednesday of the month.

Inquiries: Mr F C Neser, 152 Zastron Street, BLOEMFONTEIN 9301

Cape Town - Cape Centre

Meetings are held at the South African Astronomical Observatory on the second Wednesday of the month (except January and December) at 20 h 00.

The centre possesses a small observatory housing the 30,48 cm Ron Atkins telescope and there is also an occultation section.

Inquiries: Mr J Bondietti, Electricity House, Strand Street, CAPE TOWN 8001

Durban - Natal Centre

Meetings are held on the third Wednesday of each month at the Teacher's Centre, 49 Lambert Road, Durban at 19 h 45.

Inquiries: Mr M A Gray, P O Box 2704, DURBAN 4000
Tel. 31-3021 (office) 72-3187 (home)

Johannesburg - Transvaal Centre

Alternate lecture and observing meetings are held each month. There is a very enthusiastic lunar occultation group which observes grazing occultations within a radius of about 250 km of Johannesburg.

Mirror-making classes are held at suitable intervals and the centre has its own aluminising plant.

Inquiries: Mrs A Williams, 6 Terrace Road, Eastleigh, EDENVALE 1610

Pietermaritzburg - Natal Midlands Centre

Meetings are held monthly at various venues.

Inquiries: Mrs S B Dale, 17 Yalta Road, PIETERMARITZBURG 3201
Tel. 5-4038

Pretoria - Pretoria Centre

The centre has its own observatory containing a 30 cm reflecting telescope.

Inquiries: Mr J C Bennett, 90 Malan Street, RIVIERA 0084, Pretoria
Tel. 70-4895

Salisbury

Inquiries: Mr W L Stedman, P O Box U.A.428, Union Avenue, SALISBURY

PLANETARIA

The major planetarium in Southern Africa is situated on the University of Witwatersrand campus in Yale Road across the M1 motorway from the Milner Park showgrounds (See Johannesburg Throughway Map on page 83). It is equipped with a highly complex Zeiss projector and seats over 400 persons.

Presentations:

Nightly:
Thursday to Saturday 20 h 30
(Wednesday in Afrikaans)
Tariff: Adults: R1, Children: 50c

Matinees:
Saturday 15 h 00; Sunday 16 h 00
Tariff: Adults: R1, Children: 50c

Closed Mondays, Tuesdays and public holidays.
Tel. Inquiries: 39-2926 ext. 294.

A smaller planetarium, with a Spitz projector and seating about 70 persons, is located within the South African Museum, Cape Town.

Presentations:

Saturday 15 h 00; Sunday 15 h 30
Public and school holidays 11 h 00 and 15 h 30
Inquiries: 41-2668

TEACHING DEPARTMENTS

University of Cape Town – Department of Astronomy (Optical Astronomy)
University of the Orange Free State – Department of Astronomy (Optical Astronomy)
Rhodes University – Physics Department (Radio Astronomy)
University of South Africa, Pretoria.

OBSERVATORIES OPEN TO THE PUBLIC

Visiting nights at Boyden Observatory (Maselspoort) are generally held around the time of first quarter of the moon. Numbers are restricted to twenty persons on each occasion.

constellations and use them as guides to the rest; for instance, the three stars of Orion's belt point upwards to Sirius in the Great Dog and downward to Aldebaran in the Bull.

Binoculars extend the observer's scope considerably. With a pair of, for example, 7 x 50 binoculars (that is to say a magnification of 7, with each objective 50 mm in diameter) many superb star-clusters and nebulae may be seen; look for instance at the Jewel Box in the Southern Cross, the open clusters near the tail of the Scorpion, and the two Clouds of Magellan. A telescope will extend the scope still further, but is naturally an expensive item, and on the whole a good pair of binoculars is to be preferred to a small telescope.

One point should be made. Never look directly at the sun through any telescope or binoculars, even when a dark filter is used. The sun's intense heat and brilliance will damage the observer's eye permanently. Therefore, the only safe way to observe the sunspots is to project the sun's image through the telescope on to a white screen held or fixed behind the telescope eyepiece.

Inquiries should be made direct to the observatory.

The South African Astronomical Observatory Headquarters at Observatory, Cape, is open to visitors on the second Saturday each month at 20 h 00. No tickets are necessary but parties of more than four persons should contact the observatory in advance.

OBSERVATORIES

Boyden Observatory – situated at Maselspoort, 25 km from Bloemfontein, is operated by the Department of Astronomy of the University of the Orange Free State. The site offers good observing conditions in close proximity to Bloemfontein. Inquiries should be addressed to the director.

South African Astronomical Observatory (SAAO) – This observatory is a joint venture between the South African Council for Scientific and Industrial Research and the British Science Research Council. Facilities have been merged and the larger instruments moved to a new site near Sutherland in the Karoo.

Observing continues at Cape Town, which is the headquarters of the SAAO. The SAAO outstation at Hartbeespoort, Transvaal shares the site with the Leiden Observatory Southern Station, which has a 0,9 m "light collector" reflector.

The 1,9 m Radcliffe reflector, formerly near Pretoria and the largest telescope in Southern Africa, has now been erected at Sutherland.

Radio Astronomy Observatory – A 26 metre dish erected at the newly created observatory at Hartebeeshoek, near Krugersdorp is used entirely for research work.

Rhodes University Radio Observatory – This is situated outside Grahamstown and has a number of arrays for receiving radio emission from the planet Jupiter.

In addition to the professional observatories listed above, there are numerous private ones, built and operated by amateur astronomers.

The Zeiss Planetarium Projector ▶

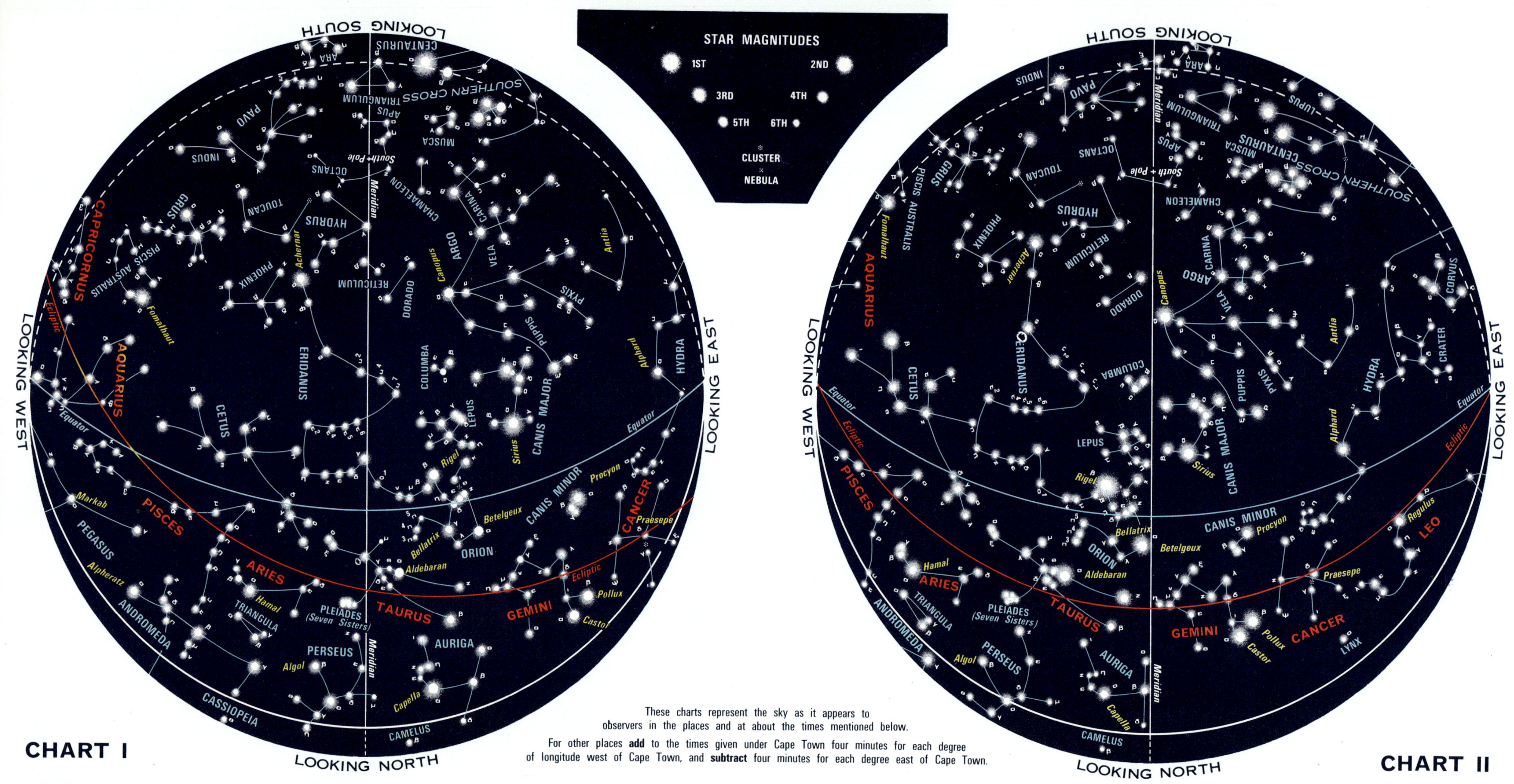

These charts represent the sky as it appears to observers in the places and at about the times mentioned below.

For other places **add** to the times given under Cape Town four minutes for each degree of longitude west of Cape Town, and **subtract** four minutes for each degree east of Cape Town.

CHART I

DATE		CAPE TOWN	BLOEMFONTEIN PORT ELIZABETH	JOHANNESBURG PRETORIA EAST LONDON	DURBAN
SEPTEMBER	1	6 a.m.	5.30 a.m.	5.22 a.m.	5.10 a.m.
	16	5 a.m.	4.30 a.m.	4.22 a.m.	4.10 a.m.
OCTOBER	1	4 a.m.	3.30 a.m.	3.22 a.m.	3.10 a.m.
	16	3 a.m.	2.30 a.m.	2.22 a.m.	2.10 a.m.
NOVEMBER	1	2 a.m.	1.30 a.m.	1.22 a.m.	1.10 a.m.
	16	1 a.m.	12.30 a.m.	12.22 a.m.	12.10 a.m.
DECEMBER	1	Midnight	11.30 p.m.	11.22 p.m.	11.10 p.m.
	16	11 p.m.	10.30 p.m.	10.22 p.m.	10.10 p.m.
JANUARY	1	10 p.m.	9.30 p.m.	9.22 p.m.	9.10 p.m.
	16	9 p.m.	8.30 p.m.	8.22 p.m.	8.10 p.m.

For intermediate days, apply the correction four minutes for each day.

THE GREEK ALPHABET

The principal stars in the constellations are denoted by the letters of the Greek alphabet, though not always in order of brightness, e.g., Alpha Crucis, Beta Crucis and Gamma Crucis.

α Alpha	η Eta	ν Nu	τ Tau
β Beta	θ Theta	ξ Xi	υ Upsilon
γ Gamma	ι Iota	ο Omicron	φ Phi
δ Delta	κ Kappa	π Pi	χ Chi
ε Epsilon	λ Lambda	ρ Rho	ψ Psi
ζ Zeta	μ Mu	σ Sigma	ω Omega

CHART II

DATE		CAPE TOWN	BLOEMFONTEIN PORT ELIZABETH	JOHANNESBURG PRETORIA EAST LONDON	DURBAN
OCTOBER	16	5 a.m.	4.30 a.m.	4.22 a.m.	4.10 a.m.
NOVEMBER	1	4 a.m.	3.30 a.m.	3.22 a.m.	3.10 a.m.
	16	3 a.m.	2.30 a.m.	2.22 a.m.	2.10 a.m.
DECEMBER	1	2 a.m.	1.30 a.m.	1.22 a.m.	1.10 a.m.
	16	1 a.m.	12.30 a.m.	12.22 a.m.	12.10 a.m.
JANUARY	1	Midnight	11.30 p.m.	11.22 p.m.	11.10 p.m.
	16	11 p.m.	10.30 p.m.	10.22 p.m.	10.10 p.m.
FEBRUARY	1	10 p.m.	9.30 p.m.	9.22 p.m.	9.10 p.m.
	16	9 p.m.	8.30 p.m.	8.22 p.m.	8.10 p.m.
MARCH	1	8 p.m.	7.30 p.m.	7.22 p.m.	7.10 p.m.

For intermediate days, apply the correction four minutes for each day.

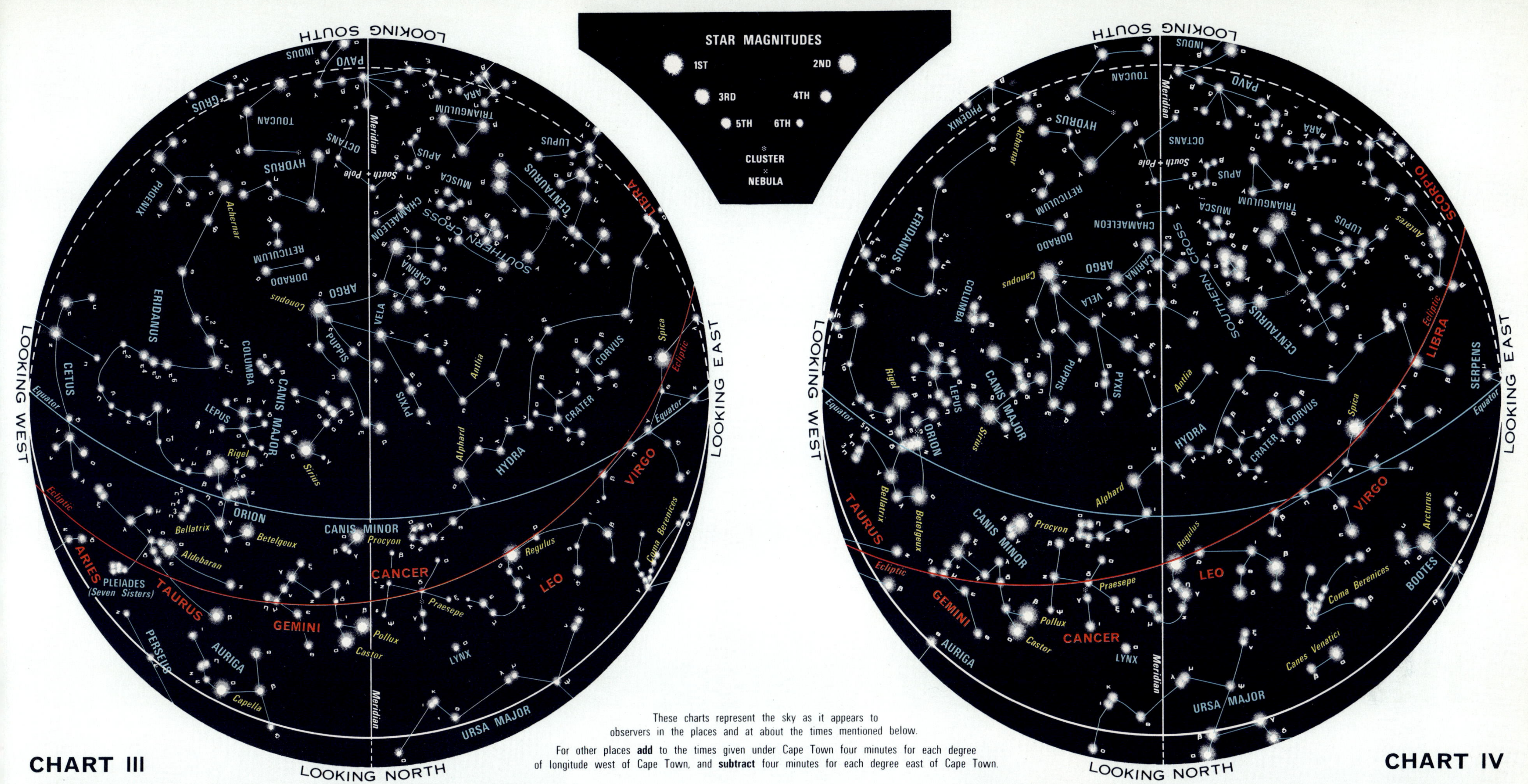

These charts represent the sky as it appears to observers in the places and at about the times mentioned below.

For other places **add** to the times given under Cape Town four minutes for each degree of longitude west of Cape Town, and **subtract** four minutes for each degree east of Cape Town.

CHART III

DATE		CAPE TOWN	BLOEMFONTEIN PORT ELIZABETH	JOHANNESBURG PRETORIA EAST LONDON	DURBAN
NOVEMBER	16	5 a.m.	4.30 a.m.	4.22 a.m.	4.10 a.m.
DECEMBER	1	4 a.m.	3.30 a.m.	3.22 a.m.	3.10 a.m.
	16	3 a.m.	2.30 a.m.	2.22 a.m.	2.10 a.m.
JANUARY	1	2 a.m.	1.30 a.m.	1.22 a.m.	1.10 a.m.
	16	1 a.m.	12.30 a.m.	12.22 a.m.	12.10 a.m.
FEBRUARY	1	Midnight	11.30 p.m.	11.22 p.m.	11.10 p.m.
	16	11 p.m.	10.30 p.m.	10.22 p.m.	10.10 p.m.
MARCH	1	10 p.m.	9.30 p.m.	9.22 p.m.	9.10 p.m.
	16	9 p.m.	8.30 p.m.	8.22 p.m.	8.10 p.m.
APRIL	1	8 p.m.	7.30 p.m.	7.22 p.m.	7.10 p.m.

For intermediate days, apply the correction four minutes for each day.

THE GREEK ALPHABET

The principal stars in the constellations are denoted by the letters of the Greek alphabet, though not always in order of brightness, e.g., Alpha Crucis, Beta Crucis and Gamma Crucis.

α Alpha	η Eta	ν Nu	τ Tau
β Beta	θ Theta	ξ Xi	υ Upsilon
γ Gamma	ι Iota	ο Omicron	φ Phi
δ Delta	κ Kappa	π Pi	χ Chi
ε Epsilon	λ Lambda	ρ Rho	ψ Psi
ζ Zeta	μ Mu	σ Sigma	ω Omega

CHART IV

DATE		CAPE TOWN	BLOEMFONTEIN PORT ELIZABETH	JOHANNESBURG PRETORIA EAST LONDON	DURBAN
JANUARY	1	4 a.m.	3.30 a.m.	3.22 a.m.	3.10 a.m.
	16	3 a.m.	2.30 a.m.	2.22 a.m.	2.10 a.m.
FEBRUARY	1	2 a.m.	1.30 a.m.	1.22 a.m.	1.10 a.m.
	16	1 a.m.	12.30 a.m.	12.22 a.m.	12.10 a.m.
MARCH	1	Midnight	11.30 p.m.	11.22 p.m.	11.10 p.m.
	16	11 p.m.	10.30 p.m.	10.22 p.m.	10.10 p.m.
APRIL	1	10 p.m.	9.30 p.m.	9.22 p.m.	9.10 p.m.
	16	9 p.m.	8.30 p.m.	8.22 p.m.	8.10 p.m.
MAY	1	8 p.m.	7.30 p.m.	7.22 p.m.	7.10 p.m.
	16	7 p.m.	6.30 p.m.	6.22 p.m.	6.10 p.m.

For intermediate days, apply the correction four minutes for each day.

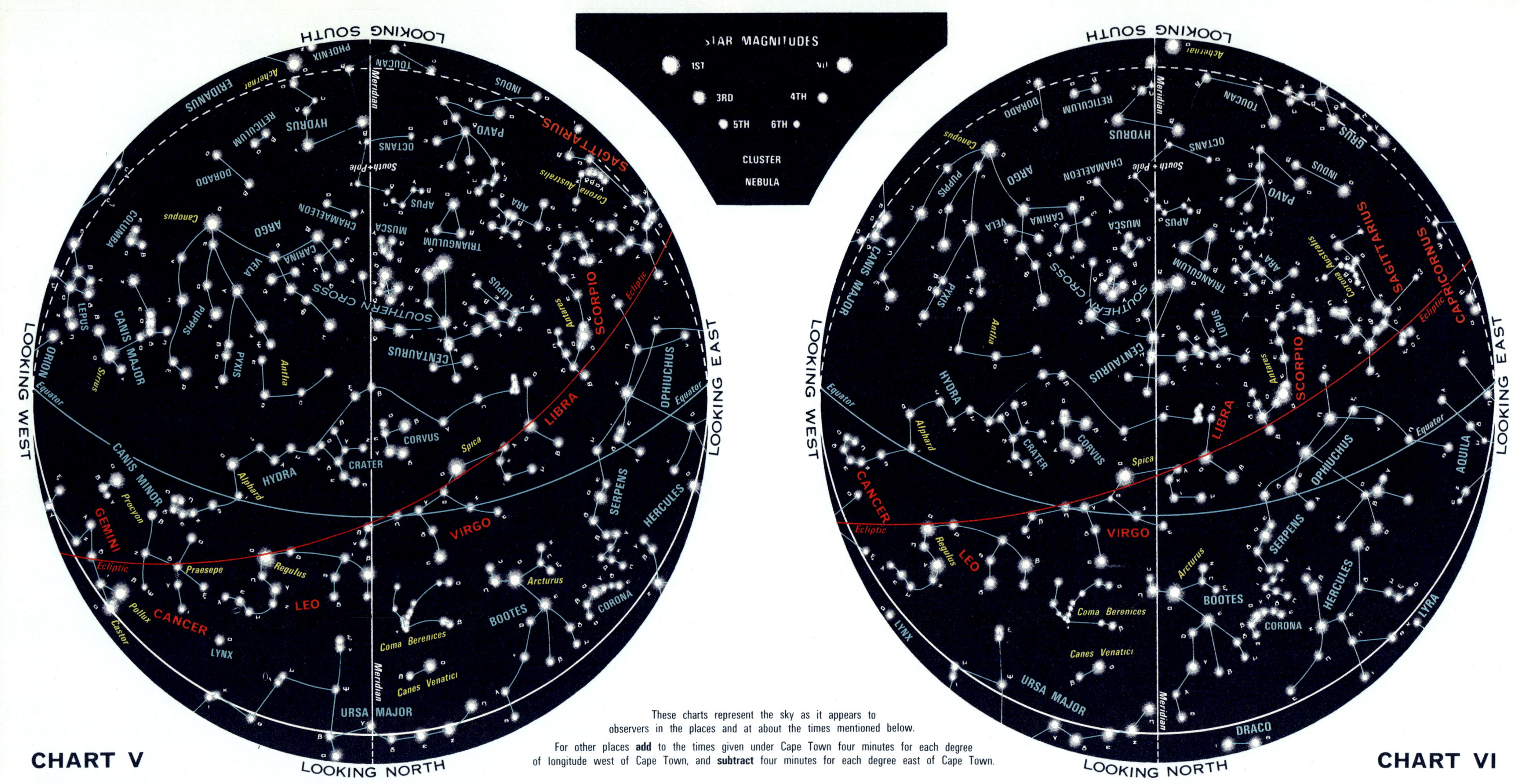

These charts represent the sky as it appears to observers in the places and at about the times mentioned below.

For other places **add** to the times given under Cape Town four minutes for each degree of longitude west of Cape Town, and **subtract** four minutes for each degree east of Cape Town.

CHART V

DATE		CAPE TOWN	BLOEMFONTEIN PORT ELIZABETH	JOHANNESBURG PRETORIA EAST LONDON	DURBAN
JANUARY	16	5 a.m.	4.30 a.m.	4.22 a.m.	4.10 a.m.
FEBRUARY	1	4 a.m.	3.30 a.m.	3.22 a.m.	3.10 a.m.
	16	3 a.m.	2.30 a.m.	2.22 a.m.	2.10 a.m.
MARCH	1	2 a.m.	1.30 a.m.	1.22 a.m.	1.10 a.m.
	16	1 a.m.	12.30 a.m.	12.22 a.m.	12.10 a.m.
APRIL	1	Midnight	11.30 p.m.	11.22 p.m.	11.10 p.m.
	16	11 p.m.	10.30 p.m.	10.22 p.m.	10.10 p.m.
MAY	1	10 p.m.	9.30 p.m.	9.22 p.m.	9.10 p.m.
	16	9 p.m.	8.30 p.m.	8.22 p.m.	8.10 p.m.
JUNE	1	8 p.m.	7.30 p.m.	7.22 p.m.	7.10 p.m.
	16	7 p.m.	6.30 p.m.	6.22 p.m.	6.10 p.m.

For intermediate days, apply the correction four minutes for each day.

THE GREEK ALPHABET

The principal stars in the constellations are denoted by the letters of the Greek alphabet, though not always in order of brightness, e.g., Alpha Crucis, Beta Crucis and Gamma Crucis.

α Alpha	η Eta	ν Nu	τ Tau
β Beta	θ Theta	ξ Xi	υ Upsilon
γ Gamma	ι Iota	ο Omicron	φ Phi
δ Delta	κ Kappa	π Pi	χ Chi
ε Epsilon	λ Lambda	ρ Rho	ψ Psi
ζ Zeta	μ Mu	σ Sigma	ω Omega

CHART VI

DATE		CAPE TOWN	BLOEMFONTEIN PORT ELIZABETH	JOHANNESBURG PRETORIA EAST LONDON	DURBAN
FEBRUARY	16	5 a.m.	4.30 a.m.	4.22 a.m.	4.10 a.m.
MARCH	1	4 a.m.	3.30 a.m.	3.22 a.m.	3.10 a.m.
	16	3 a.m.	2.30 a.m.	2.22 a.m.	2.10 a.m.
APRIL	1	2 a.m.	1.30 a.m.	1.22 a.m.	1.10 a.m.
	16	1 a.m.	12.30 a.m.	12.22 a.m.	12.10 a.m.
MAY	1	Midnight	11.30 p.m.	11.22 p.m.	11.10 p.m.
	16	11 p.m.	10.30 p.m.	10.22 p.m.	10.10 p.m.
JUNE	1	10 p.m.	9.30 p.m.	9.22 p.m.	9.10 p.m.
	16	9 p.m.	8.30 p.m.	8.22 p.m.	8.10 p.m.
JULY	1	8 p.m.	7.30 p.m.	7.22 p.m.	7.10 p.m.
	16	7 p.m.	6.30 p.m.	6.22 p.m.	6.10 p.m.

For intermediate days, apply the correction four minutes for each day.

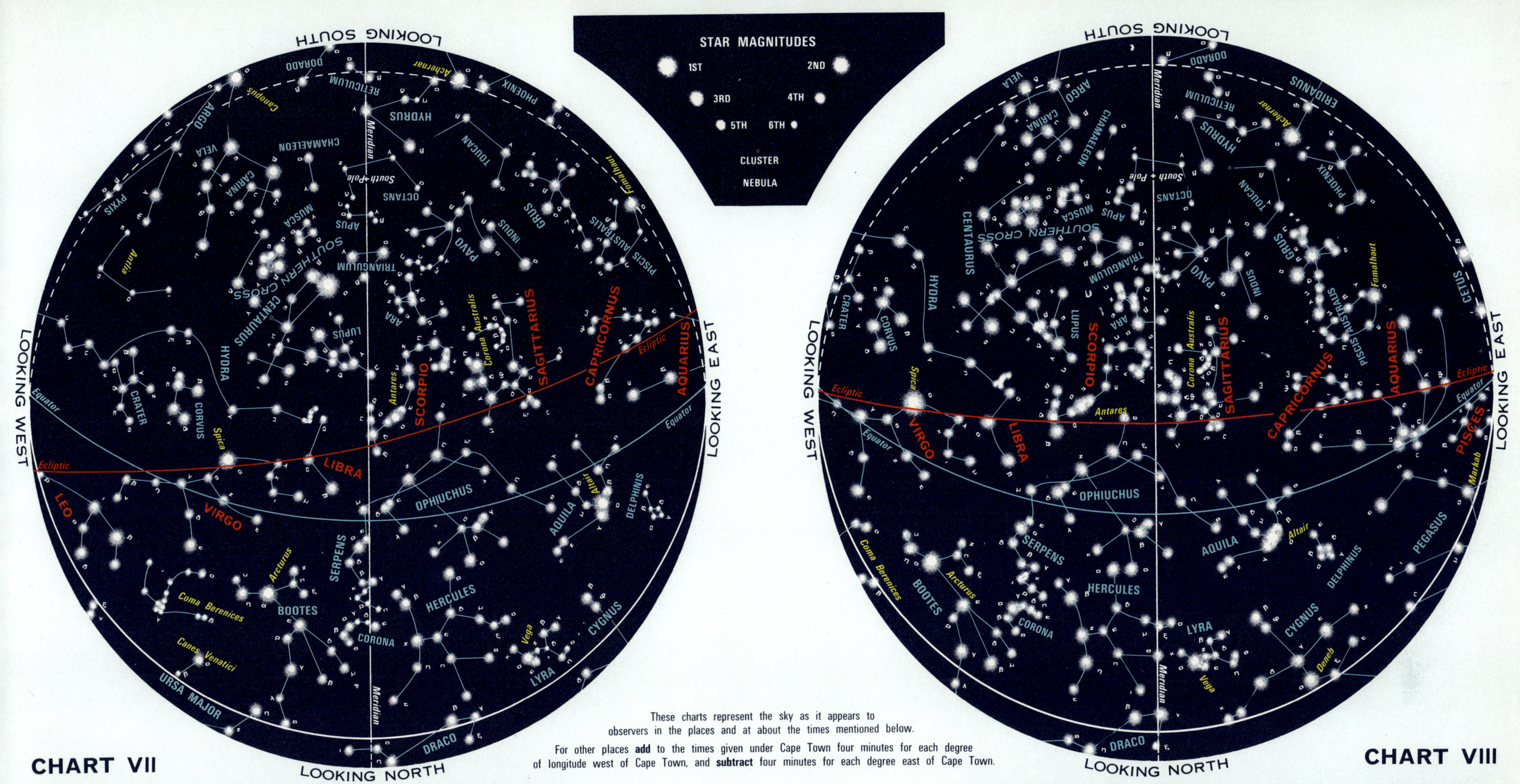

These charts represent the sky as it appears to observers in the places and at about the times mentioned below.

For other places **add** to the times given under Cape Town four minutes for each degree of longitude west of Cape Town, and **subtract** four minutes for each degree east of Cape Town.

CHART VII

DATE		CAPE TOWN	BLOEMFONTEIN PORT ELIZABETH	JOHANNESBURG PRETORIA EAST LONDON	DURBAN
MARCH	1	6 a.m.	5.30 a.m.	5.22 a.m.	5.10 a.m.
	16	5 a.m.	4.30 a.m.	4.22 a.m.	4.10 a.m.
APRIL	1	4 a.m.	3.30 a.m.	3.22 a.m.	3.10 a.m.
	16	3 a.m.	2.30 a.m.	2.22 a.m.	2.10 a.m.
MAY	1	2 a.m.	1.30 a.m.	1.22 a.m.	1.10 a.m.
	16	1 a.m.	12.30 a.m.	12.22 a.m.	12.10 a.m.
JUNE	1	Midnight	11.30 p.m.	11.22 p.m.	11.10 p.m.
	16	11 p.m.	10.30 p.m.	10.22 p.m.	10.10 p.m.
JULY	1	10 p.m.	9.30 p.m.	9.22 p.m.	9.10 p.m.
	16	9 p.m.	8.30 p.m.	8.22 p.m.	8.10 p.m.
AUGUST	1	8 p.m.	7.30 p.m.	7.22 p.m.	7.10 p.m.
	16	7 p.m.	6.30 p.m.	6.22 p.m.	6.10 p.m.

For intermediate days, apply the correction four minutes for each day.

THE GREEK ALPHABET

The principal stars in the constellations are denoted by the letters of the Greek alphabet, though not always in order of brightness, e.g., Alpha Crucis, Beta Crucis and Gamma Crucis.

α Alpha	η Eta	ν Nu	τ Tau
β Beta	θ Theta	ξ Xi	υ Upsilon
γ Gamma	ι Iota	ο Omicron	φ Phi
δ Delta	κ Kappa	π Pi	χ Chi
ε Epsilon	λ Lambda	ρ Rho	ψ Psi
ζ Zeta	μ Mu	σ Sigma	ω Omega

CHART VIII

DATE		CAPE TOWN	BLOEMFONTEIN PORT ELIZABETH	JOHANNESBURG PRETORIA EAST LONDON	DURBAN
APRIL	1	6 a.m.	5.30 a.m.	5.22 a.m.	5.10 a.m.
	16	5 a.m.	4.30 a.m.	4.22 a.m.	4.10 a.m.
MAY	1	4 a.m.	3.30 a.m.	3.22 a.m.	3.10 a.m.
	16	3 a.m.	2.30 a.m.	2.22 a.m.	2.10 a.m.
JUNE	1	2 a.m.	1.30 a.m.	1.22 a.m.	1.10 a.m.
	16	1 a.m.	12.30 a.m.	12.22 a.m.	12.10 a.m.
JULY	1	Midnight	11.30 p.m.	11.22 p.m.	11.10 p.m.
	16	11 p.m.	10.30 p.m.	10.22 p.m.	10.10 p.m.
AUGUST	1	10 p.m.	9.30 p.m.	9.22 p.m.	9.10 p.m.
	16	9 p.m.	8.30 p.m.	8.22 p.m.	8.10 p.m.
SEPTEMBER	1	8 p.m.	7.30 p.m.	7.22 p.m.	7.10 p.m.

For intermediate days, apply the correction four minutes for each day

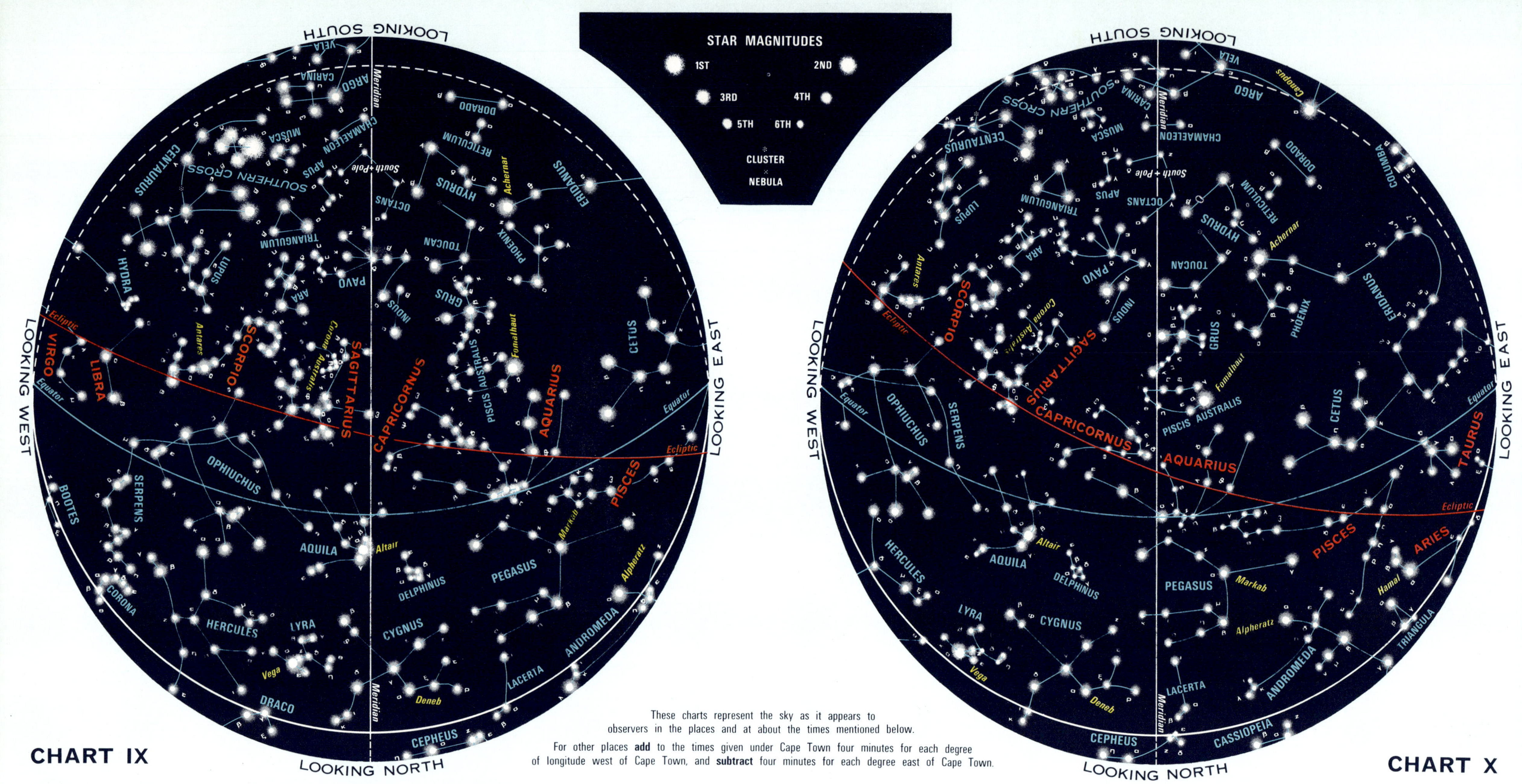

These charts represent the sky as it appears to observers in the places and at about the times mentioned below.

For other places **add** to the times given under Cape Town four minutes for each degree of longitude west of Cape Town, and **subtract** four minutes for each degree east of Cape Town.

CHART IX

DATE		CAPE TOWN	BLOEMFONTEIN PORT ELIZABETH	JOHANNESBURG PRETORIA EAST LONDON	DURBAN
MAY	1	6 a.m.	5.30 a.m.	5.22 a.m.	5.10 a.m.
	16	5 a.m.	4.30 a.m.	4.22 a.m.	4.10 a.m.
JUNE	1	4 a.m.	3.30 a.m.	3.22 a.m.	3.10 a.m.
	16	3 a.m.	2.30 a.m.	2.22 a.m.	2.10 a.m.
JULY	1	2 a.m.	1.30 a.m.	1.22 a.m.	1.10 a.m.
	16	1 a.m.	12.30 a.m.	12.22 a.m.	12.10 a.m.
AUGUST	1	Midnight	11.30 p.m.	11.22 p.m.	11.10 p.m.
	16	11 p.m.	10.30 p.m.	10.22 p.m.	10.10 p.m.
SEPTEMBER	1	10 p.m.	9.30 p.m.	9.22 p.m.	9.10 p.m.
	16	9 p.m.	8.30 p.m.	8.22 p.m.	8.10 p.m.
OCTOBER	1	8 p.m.	7.30 p.m.	7.22 p.m.	7.10 p.m.

For intermediate days, apply the correction four minutes for each day.

THE GREEK ALPHABET

The principal stars in the constellations are denoted by the letters of the Greek alphabet, though not always in order of brightness, e.g., Alpha Crucis, Beta Crucis and Gamma Crucis.

α Alpha	η Eta	ν Nu	τ Tau
β Beta	θ Theta	ξ Xi	υ Upsilon
γ Gamma	ι Iota	ο Omicron	φ Phi
δ Delta	κ Kappa	π Pi	χ Chi
ε Epsilon	λ Lambda	ρ Rho	ψ Psi
ζ Zeta	μ Mu	σ Sigma	ω Omega

CHART X

DATE		CAPE TOWN	BLOEMFONTEIN PORT ELIZABETH	JOHANNESBURG PRETORIA EAST LONDON	DURBAN
JUNE	1	6 a.m.	5.30 a.m.	5.22 a.m.	5.10 a.m.
	16	5 a.m.	4.30 a.m.	4.22 a.m.	4.10 a.m.
JULY	1	4 a.m.	3.30 a.m.	3.22 a.m.	3.10 a.m.
	16	3 a.m.	2.30 a.m.	2.22 a.m.	2.10 a.m.
AUGUST	1	2 a.m.	1.30 a.m.	1.22 a.m.	1.10 a.m.
	16	1 a.m.	12.30 a.m.	12.22 a.m.	12.10 a.m.
SEPTEMBER	1	Midnight	11.30 p.m.	11.22 p.m.	11.10 p.m.
	16	11 p.m.	10.30 p.m.	10.22 p.m.	10.10 p.m.
OCTOBER	1	10 p.m.	9.30 p.m.	9.22 p.m.	9.10 p.m.
	16	9 p.m.	8.30 p.m.	8.22 p.m.	8.10 p.m.
NOVEMBER	1	8 p.m.	7.30 p.m.	7.22 p.m.	7.10 p.m.

For intermediate days, apply the correction four minutes for each day.

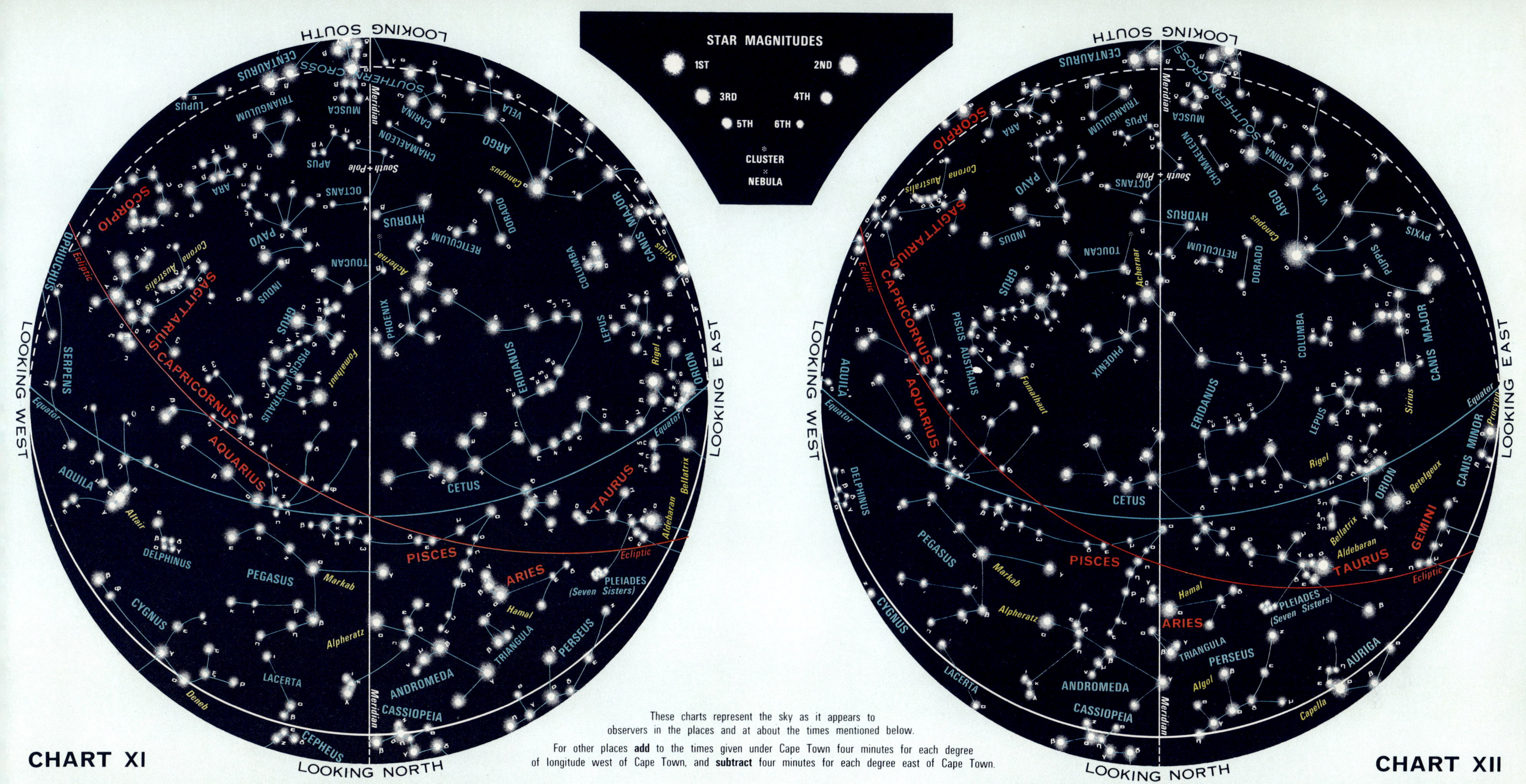

CHART XI

These charts represent the sky as it appears to observers in the places and at about the times mentioned below.

For other places **add** to the times given under Cape Town four minutes for each degree of longitude west of Cape Town, and **subtract** four minutes for each degree east of Cape Town.

CHART XII

DATE		CAPE TOWN	BLOEMFONTEIN PORT ELIZABETH	JOHANNESBURG PRETORIA EAST LONDON	DURBAN
JUNE	**16**	7 a.m.	6.30 a.m.	6.22 a.m.	6.10 a.m.
JULY	**1**	6 a.m.	5.30 a.m.	5.22 a.m.	5.10 a.m.
	16	5 a.m.	4.30 a.m.	4.22 a.m.	4.10 a.m.
AUGUST	**1**	4 a.m.	3.30 a.m.	3.22 a.m.	3.10 a.m.
	16	3 a.m.	2.30 a.m.	2.22 a.m.	2.10 a.m.
SEPTEMBER	**1**	2 a.m.	1.30 a.m.	1.22 a.m.	1.10 a.m.
	16	1 a.m.	12.30 a.m.	12.22 a.m.	12.10 a.m.
OCTOBER	**1**	Midnight	11.30 p.m.	11.22 p.m.	11.10 p.m.
	16	11 p.m.	10.30 p.m.	10.22 p.m.	10.10 p.m.
NOVEMBER	**1**	10 p.m.	9.30 p.m.	9.22 p.m.	9.10 p.m.
	16	9 p.m.	8.30 p.m.	8.22 p.m.	8.10 p.m.

For intermediate days, apply the correction four minutes for each day.

THE GREEK ALPHABET

The principal stars in the constellations are denoted by the letters of the Greek alphabet, though not always in order of brightness, e.g., Alpha Crucis, Beta Crucis and Gamma Crucis.

α Alpha	η Eta	ν Nu	τ Tau
β Beta	θ Theta	ξ Xi	υ Upsilon
γ Gamma	ι Iota	ο Omicron	φ Phi
δ Delta	κ Kappa	π Pi	χ Chi
ε Epsilon	λ Lambda	ρ Rho	ψ Psi
ζ Zeta	μ Mu	σ Sigma	ω Omega

DATE		CAPE TOWN	BLOEMFONTEIN PORT ELIZABETH	JOHANNESBURG PRETORIA EAST LONDON	DURBAN
JULY	**16**	7 a.m.	6.30 a.m.	6.22 a.m.	6.10 a.m.
AUGUST	**1**	6 a.m.	5.30 a.m.	5.22 a.m.	5.10 a.m.
	16	5 a.m.	4.30 a.m.	4.22 a.m.	4.10 a.m.
SEPTEMBER	**1**	4 a.m.	3.30 a.m.	3.22 a.m.	3.10 a.m.
	16	3 a.m.	2.30 a.m.	2.22 a.m.	2.10 a.m.
OCTOBER	**1**	2 a.m.	1.30 a.m.	1.22 a.m.	1.10 a.m.
	16	1 a.m.	12.30 a.m.	12.22 a.m.	12.10 a.m.
NOVEMBER	**1**	Midnight	11.30 p.m.	11.22 p.m.	11.10 p.m.
	16	11 p.m.	10.30 p.m.	10.22 p.m.	10.10 p.m.
DECEMBER	**1**	10 p.m.	9.30 p.m.	9.22 p.m.	9.10 p.m.
	16	9 p.m.	8.30 p.m.	8.22 p.m.	8.10 p.m.

For intermediate days, apply the correction four minutes for each day.

FREEWAYS AND OTHER ROADS
REGULATORY SIGNS

GO

STOP SIGN

NO ANIMAL-DRAWN VEHICLES

MINIMUM SPEED LIMIT

NO CYCLISTS

NO ENTRY

YIELD SIGN

NO PARKING

NO STOPPING

NO PARKING DURING CERTAIN TIMES

NO STOPPING DURING CERTAIN PERIODS

NO PARKING OR STOPPING DURING 3 PERIODS

NO OVERTAKING

ROAD CLOSED

SPEED LIMIT

SPEED LIMIT

NO LEFT TURN

NO U-TURN

NO RIGHT TURN

AXLE MASS LOAD LIMIT

PERMISSIBLE MAXIMUM MASS

KEEP LEFT

PROCEED LEFT ONLY

TURN LEFT

PROCEED STRAIGHT ON ONLY

TURN RIGHT

PROCEED RIGHT ONLY

CYCLISTS ONLY

LANE DIRECTION CONTROL SIGNALS

ILLUMINATED GREEN ARROW
Proceed in this lane only

ILLUMINATED RED CROSS
Do not enter this lane

INFORMATION SIGNS

NATIONAL ROAD ROUTE MARKER

OVERHEAD DIRECTION

DE-RESTRICTION

RAMP ENTRANCE DIRECTION

OVERHEAD DIRECTION

MAP-TYPE FREE FLOW EXIT

FREEWAY ENTRANCE AHEAD

DE-RESTRICTION

STACK-TYPE DIRECTION

DANGER WARNING SIGNS

CROSS ROADS

T-JUNCTION

SIDE-ROAD JUNCTION

STAGGERED JUNCTION

SHARP JUNCTION

SKEW JUNCTION

Y-JUNCTION

ROAD NARROWS FROM BOTH SIDES

ROAD NARROWS FROM ONE SIDE ONLY

TWO-WAY TRAFFIC

END OF DUAL ROADWAYS

BEGINNING OF DUAL ROADWAYS

MOTOR GATE ON LEFT

TRAFFIC CIRCLE

GENTLE CURVE TO RIGHT

SHARP CURVE TO RIGHT

HAIRPIN BEND

WINDING ROAD

GATE

PEDESTRIANS

PEDESTRIAN CROSSING

TEMPORARY EMERGENCY OR POLICE FLASHING LIGHT

STOP/GO CONTROL AHEAD

TRAFFIC SIGNALS AHEAD

HORSES

CATTLE

CHILDREN

SCHOLAR PATROL AHEAD

TRUCKS CROSSING

ROAD WORKMEN

GRADER WORKING

SHEEP

WILD ANIMALS

SLIPPERY ROAD

LOOSE STONES

FALLING ROCKS

CROSS-WINDS

HEIGHT RESTRICTED

DRIFT

UNEVEN ROADWAY

ONE-VEHICLE WIDTH STRUCTURE

TUNNEL

CYCLISTS

UNGUARDED LEVEL-CROSSING

STEEP DESCENT

STEEP ASCENT

JETTY EDGE OR RIVER-BANK

Level Crossing Warning Cross

ONE TRACK

2 TRACKS

3 TRACKS

INFORMATION SIGNS

STOP AHEAD

PARKING PERMITTED

ONE-WAY ROADWAY TO LEFT

ONE-WAY ROADWAY STRAIGHT ON

ONE-WAY ROADWAY TO RIGHT

DEAD-END STREET

STOPPING PLACE AHEAD

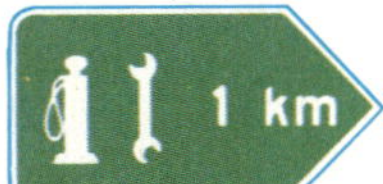

FILLING AND SERVICE STATION DIRECTION

HOSPITAL OR FIRST-AID POST DIRECTION

WATER AHEAD

CARAVAN SITE AHEAD

CARAVAN SITE DIRECTION

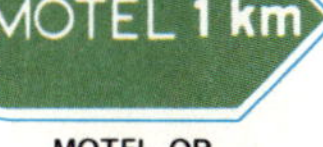

MOTEL OR HOTEL DIRECTION

MINOR AIRFIELD DIRECTION

TELEPHONE DIRECTION

CAMPING SITE DIRECTION

PARKING AREA DIRECTION

POLICE STATION DIRECTION

RESTAURANT DIRECTION

ROADWORKS AHEAD

DETOUR AHEAD

MINOR ROAD ROUTE MARKER

MAP-TYPE FOUR-LEGGED STAGGERED INTERSECTION

MAP-TYPE TRAFFIC CIRCLE JUNCTION

THANK YOU

END OF DETOUR

MAJOR PROVINCIAL OR TERRITORIAL ROUTE-MARKER

MAP-TYPE FOUR-LEGGED INTERSECTION

MINOR ROUTE DIRECTION

PROVINCIAL OR TERRITORIAL BORDER

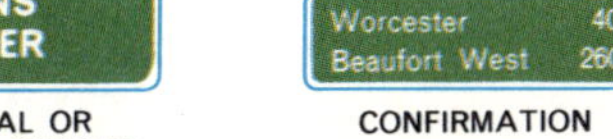

CONFIRMATION

TOWN NAME

RIVER NAME

MOUNTAIN PASS

DIRECTION

BUS STOP FOR NON-WHITES

HAZARD PLATES

BUS STOP

AIRPORT DIRECTION

SHARP CURVE CHEVRON: LEFT

RIGHT-OF-WAY

JUNCTION CHEVRON

SHARP CURVE CHEVRON: RIGHT

ROADWAY MARKINGS

Yellow Mandatory Arrow Markings

NOTE: Yellow road-markings convey a definite instruction or prohibition. For instance, the direction of a yellow arrow **must** be followed, and a taxi may not park in an ambulance bay.

PROCEED STRAIGHT ON ONLY
Left or right turn prohibited

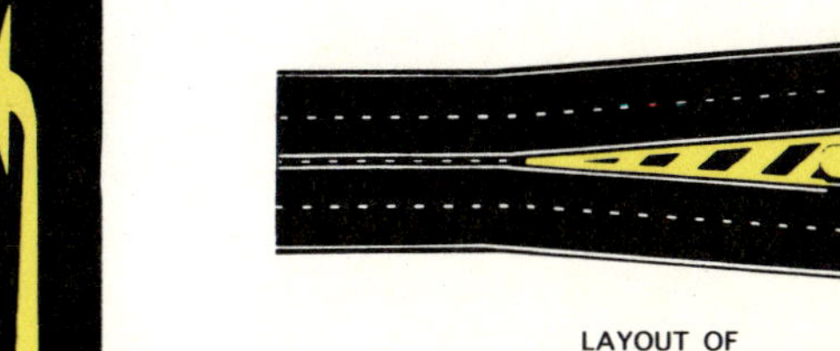

TURN LEFT ONLY
Straight on or right turn prohibited

LAYOUT OF PAINTED ISLAND

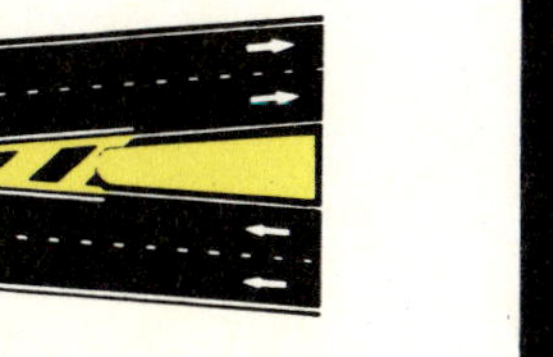

TURN RIGHT ONLY
Straight on or left turn prohibited

PROCEED STRAIGHT ON OR TURN RIGHT
Left turn prohibited

Markings for Exclusive Parking Bays

BUS | LOADING ZONE | TAXI | AMBULANCE | FIRE-FIGHTING | RICKSHA

White Roadway Lines and Markings

CENTRE-LINE

ALTERNATIVE MARKINGS FOR LEVEL CROSSING

PEDESTRIAN CROSSING LINES

CENTRE-LINE WITH BARRIER-LINES
Where the barrier-line is on the left of the centre-line, traffic must not encroach on the roadway on the right-hand side of the barrier-line.

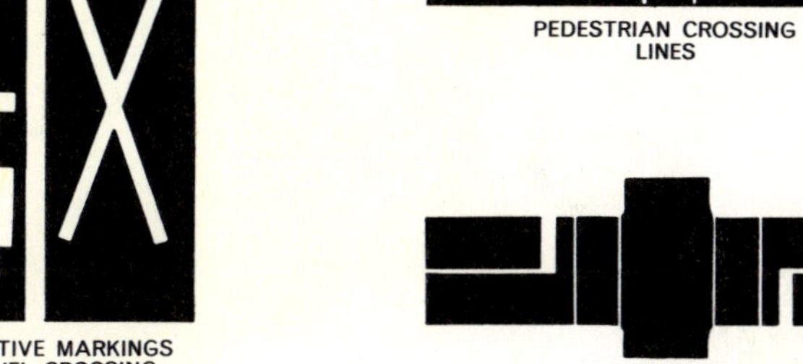

BARRIER-LINE WITH STOP-LINE AND PEDESTRIAN CROSSING LINES AT INTERSECTION

CENTRE-LINE CONVERTED TO BARRIER-LINE
Traffic must not encroach on the roadway on the right-hand side of the barrier-line.

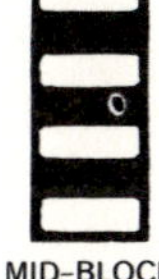

MID-BLOCK PEDESTRIAN CROSSING

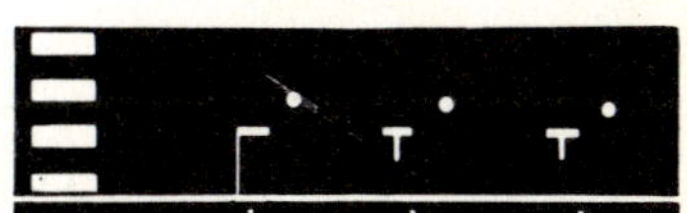

PARKING BAY LAYOUT

LANE-LINE WITH BARRIER-LINE ON ONE-WAY ROADWAY
Traffic in left lane must not cross barrier-line. Traffic in the right-hand lane may move to the left lane.

BARRIER-LINE AHEAD
Drive on left side of centre- or lane line.

INFORMATION ARROW

YIELD SIGN AHEAD
Be alert and stop for other traffic.

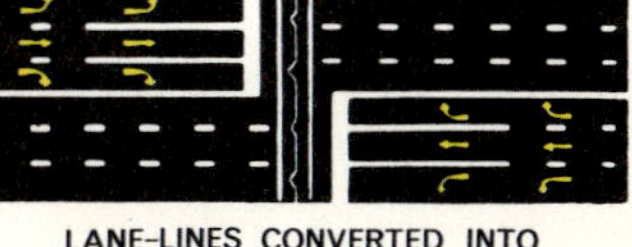

LANE-LINES CONVERTED INTO BARRIER-LINES ON APPPOACH TO INTERSECTION
Traffic must not cross from one lane to another over the barrier-line.

SOUTH AFRICA Distance Tables

ALIWAL NORTH 62 B4
503 BEAUFORT WEST 59 A2
1145 1477 BEITBRIDGE 70 B5
395 777 807 BETHLEHEM 66 C6
202 534 943 243 BLOEMFONTEIN 66 D2
366 239 1290 637 394 BRITSTOWN 61 B5
760 348 1684 1031 788 394 CALVINIA 61 C1
994 491 1968 1268 1025 730 397 CAPE TOWN 58 C3
184 319 1158 458 215 182 576 810 COLESBERG 62 B3
233 342 1351 628 408 289 683 833 193 CRADOCK 59 A5
748 1142 1059 408 651 1045 1439 1633 866 800 DURBAN 63 A4
342 607 1487 737 544 603 955 1080 422 314 656 EAST LONDON 60 B2
972 1304 543 634 780 1086 1480 1795 995 1188 958 1314 ELLISRAS 68 A5
696 1078 570 301 544 906 1300 1569 759 950 489 1011 503 ERMELO 67 A2
806 985 819 574 607 746 1140 1476 765 958 982 1151 297 587 GABORONE (B) 68 B3
654 249 1726 1003 760 488 545 445 545 480 1239 630 1553 1304 1234 GEORGE 59 B2
882 1264 824 487 730 1124 1518 1755 945 1138 382 1038 757 254 841 1490 GOLELA 67 B4
314 202 1363 663 420 249 550 693 205 140 940 405 1200 964 970 340 1150 GRAAFF-REINET 59 A4
355 510 1500 750 557 506 858 905 410 217 779 175 1327 1051 1161 460 1161 308 GRAHAMSTOWN 59 B6
486 868 827 91 334 728 1122 1359 549 719 317 828 641 268 649 1094 396 754 841 HARRISMITH 67 C2
614 946 531 276 412 728 1122 1437 627 820 600 956 358 205 366 1195 459 832 969 283 JOHANNESBURG 68 D6
382 484 1014 423 180 245 639 975 264 457 831 686 841 661 501 733 910 469 674 514 483 KIMBERLEY 66 C2
498 796 702 263 296 557 951 1287 511 704 671 840 529 382 308 1045 636 716 853 354 171 312 KLERKSDORP 66 A4
508 902 1165 514 710 849 1243 1393 658 560 240 416 1064 595 1088 999 622 700 539 423 706 890 777 KOKSTAD 63 B2
1028 1410 598 633 876 1238 1632 1901 1091 1284 638 1294 671 332 788 1636 256 1296 1383 600 479 993 650 878 KOMATIPOORT 69 C4
408 740 737 147 206 553 947 1231 421 614 555 750 564 353 424 966 590 626 763 238 206 308 116 661 685 KROONSTAD 66 B5
598 700 1041 551 396 461 700 1084 480 673 959 902 868 736 440 949 990 685 890 642 525 216 354 1106 1004 395 KURUMAN 65 B5
567 949 823 172 415 809 1203 1440 630 800 236 758 722 253 730 1175 315 835 881 81 364 595 435 342 571 319 723 LADYSMITH 67 C2
603 842 717 368 401 603 997 1333 616 809 776 945 544 485 206 1091 739 821 958 459 264 358 105 882 686 221 324 540 LICHTENBURG 68 D4
1037 1369 108 699 835 1151 1545 1860 1050 1243 951 1379 435 462 711 1618 716 1255 1392 706 423 906 594 1057 481 629 948 738 609 LOUIS TRICHARDT 70 C4
884 1285 431 489 747 1098 1492 1776 962 1117 677 1199 526 188 643 1534 391 1167 1239 456 334 849 505 783 172 541 859 441 541 323 LYDENBURG 69 C3
814 1215 501 429 687 1028 1422 1706 902 1047 607 1129 456 118 573 1464 352 1107 1169 386 264 779 435 713 215 471 789 371 471 393 70 MACHADODORP 69 C3
663 842 763 428 461 603 997 1333 622 815 836 1005 590 531 143 1091 785 827 1018 519 310 358 165 942 732 281 297 600 60 655 587 517 MAFEKING 68 C3
240 680 972 197 146 540 934 1171 361 473 605 582 799 498 659 894 684 554 595 288 441 326 351 711 830 235 542 369 456 864 686 626 516 MASERU (L) 62 A5
861 1243 664 466 709 1068 1462 1734 924 1094 544 1093 640 162 748 1492 168 1129 1216 430 430 823 544 677 208 515 898 365 649 556 223 184 692 663 MBABANE (S) 67 A4
208 308 1257 557 314 195 589 799 99 94 894 408 1094 858 864 446 1044 106 311 648 726 363 610 654 1190 520 579 729 715 1149 1046 1022 721 448 1023 MIDDELBURG (C) 62 C2
707 276 1753 1053 813 515 572 392 598 533 1292 688 1580 1354 1261 53 1540 393 513 1144 1225 760 1072 1052 1686 1016 976 1225 1118 1645 1561 1521 1118 947 1519 499 MOSSEL BAY 59 C2
921 1303 495 526 794 1131 1525 1794 1009 1154 713 1236 563 225 680 1552 327 1189 1276 493 371 886 542 820 108 578 896 478 578 387 64 107 624 723 169 1083 1607 NELSPRUIT 69 C3
980 1362 451 585 853 1180 1584 1853 1068 1213 772 1295 622 284 739 1611 386 1248 1335 552 430 945 601 879 139 637 955 537 637 343 104 166 683 782 228 1142 1666 59 NUMBI GATE 71 C5
664 189 1666 966 723 428 485 479 508 490 1299 690 1267 1267 1174 60 1453 350 520 1057 1135 673 985 1059 1599 929 899 1138 1031 1558 1474 1404 1031 869 1432 456 87 1492 1551 OUDTSHOORN 59 B2
1071 1472 346 676 934 1285 1679 1963 1149 1304 864 1386 548 375 830 1721 553 1339 1426 643 521 1036 692 970 297 728 1082 628 722 238 187 257 774 873 405 1248 1729 236 177 1661 PHALABORWA 69 A4
694 1088 979 328 571 965 1359 1579 786 746 80 602 878 409 886 1185 441 886 725 237 520 751 591 186 697 475 879 156 696 871 597 493 756 525 491 840 1238 634 693 1245 784 PIETERMARITZBURG 63 A3
938 1270 207 600 736 1052 1446 1761 951 1144 852 1309 336 363 612 1519 615 1156 1293 607 324 807 495 958 396 530 849 616 510 99 224 294 556 765 447 1050 1549 288 328 1459 212 772 PIETERSBURG 69 A2
747 1129 685 352 595 989 1383 1620 810 980 430 974 618 115 702 1378 139 1015 1102 319 320 776 496 563 322 468 850 251 600 577 303 233 646 549 114 909 1405 283 342 1318 490 377 478 PIET RETIEF 67 B3
416 571 1561 811 618 567 919 926 471 278 805 149 1388 1112 1222 481 1187 369 61 902 1030 735 914 565 1443 824 951 907 1019 1453 1300 1230 1079 656 1242 372 534 1385 1444 581 1535 751 1354 1128 PORT ALFRED 60 C1
641 1035 1230 579 822 982 1376 1526 818 693 171 549 1197 660 1153 1118 553 833 672 488 771 1023 842 133 809 726 1239 407 1015 1190 916 846 1075 844 715 787 1185 884 943 1192 1035 251 1023 601 698 PORT EDWARD 63 C3
496 462 1620 876 677 509 810 779 462 269 904 301 1457 1177 1227 334 1286 260 126 967 1089 726 973 665 1543 883 942 1007 1078 1512 1386 1310 1084 736 1342 363 387 1485 1544 394 1567 851 1413 1228 147 798 PORT ELIZABETH 59 B5
420 814 1335 684 622 752 1146 1305 570 472 410 328 1234 765 1226 911 792 612 451 593 876 802 918 170 1048 828 1018 512 1023 1227 890 883 1083 660 847 566 964 990 1049 971 1140 356 1128 733 477 207 577 PORT ST. JOHNS (X) 63 C2
670 1002 475 332 468 784 1178 1493 683 876 656 1012 302 243 344 1251 497 888 1025 339 56 539 227 762 444 262 566 420 242 367 299 229 288 497 405 782 1281 336 395 1191 486 576 268 358 1086 827 1145 932 PRETORIA 68 C6
494 352 1241 650 407 128 418 843 310 417 1173 731 1068 888 728 601 1137 377 634 741 710 227 539 968 1220 535 318 822 642 1133 1076 1006 585 553 1050 323 628 1113 1172 541 1263 978 1034 1003 695 1101 637 880 766 PRIESKA 61 A4
1171 1503 242 833 969 1285 1679 1994 1184 1377 1085 1513 569 596 845 1752 683 1389 1526 840 557 1040 728 1191 427 763 1082 849 743 134 421 491 789 1030 635 1283 1782 463 404 1692 234 1005 233 711 1644 1256 1646 1361 501 1267 PUNDA MILIA 70 B6
163 487 1308 558 365 416 810 978 243 145 655 179 1135 859 969 625 1037 285 192 649 777 507 661 415 1191 571 723 757 766 1200 1047 977 826 403 1092 221 678 1084 1143 635 1234 601 1101 978 253 548 318 309 833 544 1334 QUEENSTOWN 62 C4
935 1329 1024 505 748 1142 1536 1820 963 987 187 843 947 433 974 1426 210 1127 966 414 608 928 768 427 466 652 1056 333 873 895 621 551 933 702 378 1081 1479 658 717 1486 808 267 796 349 992 358 1092 597 676 1155 1060 842 RICHARDS BAY 67 C5
668 966 572 395 466 727 1121 1457 681 874 719 1010 399 340 247 1215 594 886 1023 402 119 482 170 825 541 286 469 483 145 464 396 326 191 521 502 780 1279 433 492 1189 583 639 365 439 1084 890 1143 995 97 709 598 831 727 RUSTENBURG 68 C5
1091 588 2065 1365 1122 827 478 177 907 930 1730 1195 1892 1666 1573 561 1852 790 1021 1456 1534 1072 1384 1490 1998 1328 1178 1537 1430 1957 1854 1803 1430 1268 1831 896 508 1910 1969 544 2060 1676 1858 1717 1082 1623 895 1402 1590 940 2091 1075 1917 1554 SALDANHA BAY 58 C2
1038 1420 508 643 911 1248 1642 1911 1126 1271 830 1313 687 342 797 1669 337 1331 1393 610 488 1003 659 937 81 695 1013 595 695 400 161 224 741 840 286 1200 1696 117 58 1609 216 751 385 457 1502 1001 1519 1107 453 1230 346 1201 775 550 2027 SKUKUZA 69 B4
1136 724 1707 1226 983 770 376 567 952 1059 1634 1331 1534 1402 1106 884 1656 926 1276 1317 1191 817 1020 1619 1670 1061 666 1398 990 1614 1525 1455 963 1129 1564 965 831 1562 1621 867 1712 1554 1515 1729 1337 1752 1218 1531 1232 590 1748 1186 1731 1135 616 1679 SPRINGBOK 60 A5
822 1216 1041 392 635 1029 1423 1707 850 874 74 730 974 455 950 1313 308 1014 853 301 584 815 655 314 564 539 943 220 760 917 643 573 820 589 470 968 1366 680 739 1373 830 162 818 356 879 245 979 484 640 1042 1067 730 113 703 1804 797 1618 STANGER 63 A4
953 466 1943 1243 1000 684 372 57 785 808 1609 1056 1770 1544 1451 421 1730 668 881 1334 1412 929 1262 1368 1876 1206 1072 1415 1287 1835 1751 1681 1308 1146 1709 774 368 1788 1847 455 1938 1554 1736 1595 902 1501 755 1280 1468 818 1969 953 1795 1432 196 1905 618 1683 STELLENBOSCH 58 C3
890 850 1423 933 778 650 764 1148 832 939 1341 1253 1250 1118 822 1099 1372 899 1156 1024 907 598 736 1398 1386 774 382 1105 706 1330 1241 1171 679 924 1280 845 1126 1278 1337 1039 1464 1261 1231 1232 1217 1531 1159 1402 948 522 1464 1066 1438 851 1242 1395 730 1325 1136 TWEE RIVIEREN 65 A2
1036 1368 232 698 834 1150 1544 1859 1049 1242 891 1378 434 402 710 1617 605 1251 1391 670 422 915 593 997 386 628 947 665 608 124 214 284 654 895 437 1148 1647 278 219 1557 114 811 98 517 1452 1062 1511 1167 366 1142 258 1199 835 463 1956 276 1613 857 1834 1329 TZANEEN 69 A3
329 723 1344 693 531 652 1046 1214 461 381 419 237 1243 774 1135 820 801 521 360 602 943 711 827 179 1057 737 927 521 935 1236 962 892 992 569 856 475 873 999 1058 880 1149 365 1137 742 386 312 486 91 999 771 1320 218 606 997 1311 1116 1422 493 1189 1309 1176 UMTATA (X) 62 C6
685 519 1308 827 584 319 433 817 501 608 1235 922 1135 1003 707 768 1257 568 825 918 792 404 621 1168 1271 662 267 999 591 1215 1126 1056 564 730 1165 514 795 1163 1222 708 1349 1155 1116 1130 886 1301 828 1071 833 191 1349 735 1332 736 911 1280 399 1219 805 331 1214 971 UPINGTON 65 C3
879 467 1803 1150 907 513 119 310 695 802 1558 1116 1599 1419 1259 627 1637 669 876 1241 1241 756 1070 1362 1751 1064 819 1322 1116 1664 1611 1541 1116 1053 1616 708 574 1648 1707 610 1798 1478 1565 1502 937 1495 961 1274 1297 537 1798 929 1655 1240 359 1765 257 1632 329 883 1663 1165 507 VANRHYNSDORP 60 C6
556 888 589 235 354 701 1104 1379 569 762 559 898 416 236 424 1137 490 774 911 242 58 456 146 665 521 148 500 323 251 481 376 306 311 432 398 668 1167 413 472 1077 563 479 382 351 972 730 1037 835 58 683 615 719 606 177 1476 530 1166 543 1354 882 480 885 767 1223 VEREENIGING 66 A5
547 924 668 152 390 737 1131 1415 605 780 476 889 482 169 507 1173 406 810 902 159 124 492 229 582 501 184 583 240 1334 547 345 287 394 349 1331 709 1203 394 453 1113 544 396 448 284 963 647 1028 752 124 719 681 710 523 260 1512 511 1249 460 1390 965 546 761 850 1248 83 VILLIERS 66 B6
1255 843 1826 1345 1102 889 495 686 1019 1178 1753 1450 1653 1521 1225 1003 1775 1045 1353 1436 1310 936 1139 1738 1789 1180 775 1517 1099 1723 1634 1564 1072 1248 1673 1084 950 1671 1717 986 1857 1673 1624 1648 1456 1871 1337 1650 1351 709 1867 1305 1850 1254 735 1798 119 1737 737 849 1732 1541 598 376 1285 1368 VIOOLSDRIF 64 E4
636 1018 674 241 484 878 1272 1509 699 869 385 907 599 104 607 1290 250 904 991 208 241 684 385 491 433 355 732 149 490 566 292 222 550 438 225 798 1343 329 388 1207 479 305 467 111 1052 556 1117 661 241 875 700 799 367 361 1606 446 1398 405 1484 1114 506 670 999 1419 239 156 1517 VOLKSRUST 67 B2
525 684 902 412 323 445 839 1175 464 657 820 867 729 597 301 933 851 669 874 503 386 200 215 926 865 253 139 584 185 794 726 650 158 466 759 563 960 757 816 873 907 740 695 712 935 1059 926 945 427 457 928 688 905 330 1272 874 805 792 1129 521 793 854 406 958 361 444 924 600 VRYBURG 66 A2
717 1099 786 322 565 959 1353 1590 780 950 329 878 719 216 757 1348 165 985 1001 231 391 745 535 462 421 469 889 150 640 678 404 334 700 519 215 879 1401 441 500 1288 591 276 579 101 1027 500 1127 632 391 972 812 877 217 510 1687 558 1555 255 1565 1271 618 671 1156 1472 389 306 1674 150 750 VRYHEID 67 B3
354 686 801 211 152 489 883 1177 367 560 619 696 628 417 452 912 671 572 709 302 270 263 157 725 749 64 354 383 263 693 605 535 322 298 579 466 965 642 701 875 792 539 594 532 770 790 829 774 326 490 827 517 716 327 1274 759 1020 603 1152 736 692 683 621 1019 212 248 1139 419 215 533 WELKOM 66 B4
644 232 1543 915 672 278 116 513 460 567 1323 839 1364 1184 1030 429 1402 434 742 1006 1006 473 785 1127 1516 781 620 1087 881 1429 1376 1252 831 818 1346 473 456 1359 1418 369 1509 1234 1330 1267 894 1260 694 1039 1062 302 1563 719 1420 955 594 1476 492 1402 488 864 1428 955 533 235 929 965 611 1156 723 1237 767 WILLISTON 61 C2
310 642 835 135 108 502 896 1133 323 516 543 652 662 451 522 868 622 528 665 226 304 288 214 649 783 98 504 307 319 727 639 569 379 137 601 422 921 676 735 831 826 463 628 487 726 714 785 730 360 515 861 473 640 384 1230 792 1170 527 1108 886 726 639 771 1015 246 282 1289 376 351 457 162 780 WINBURG 66 C5
717 1094 498 322 560 886 1280 1585 775 950 623 1059 410 135 452 1320 389 985 1072 329 143 662 314 730 336 349 668 388 350 390 191 121 396 519 297 874 1373 228 287 1283 378 544 291 250 1133 794 1198 1066 108 889 612 880 568 205 1682 345 1334 590 1560 1050 405 909 935 1384 185 170 1453 239 535 351 413 1149 447 WITBANK 69 C2
861 358 1835 1135 892 597 307 133 677 700 1500 966 1662 1436 1343 331 1622 560 971 1226 1304 842 1154 1260 1768 1098 1007 1307 1200 1727 1639 1573 1200 1038 1601 666 278 1680 1739 314 1830 1446 1628 1487 812 1393 665 1172 1360 725 1861 845 1687 1324 230 1797 553 1574 108 1071 1726 1081 740 307 1246 1282 672 1377 1042 1457 1044 423 1000 1452 WORCESTER 58 C4

REFERENCE

The page and grid reference of each place listed in this table is given to enable easy location on the relevant map.

Distance table	Kruger National Park
B Botswana	1 Rest camp
C Cape	2 Resting spot
L Lesotho	3 Picnic spot
S Swaziland	4 Gate
X Transkei	5 Tearoom

The distances given are those over the shortest practicable routes; these are not necessarily the best or the fastest.

Kruger National Park – see map on page 71

(2) BABALALA 163 324 188 260 301 130 289 349 278 230 96 343 220 159 247 64 182 333 40 154 198 33 289 193 249
(1) BALULE 173 25 105 148 33 136 199 129 77 67 190 57 7 92 227 85 186 227 9 45 136 136 40 96
(1) CROCODILE BRIDGE 174 101 79 194 35 56 65 131 228 107 125 175 169 388 246 90 364 170 126 297 67 146 75
(3) GORGE 108 151 58 139 202 132 78 92 193 58 32 95 252 110 189 228 34 48 161 139 59 99
(2) HLANGULENE 62 128 66 113 43 30 162 101 61 109 67 322 180 97 298 104 60 231 50 68 26
(4) KRUGER GATE 171 58 75 33 92 205 43 102 152 129 365 223 62 341 147 103 274 12 123 52
(1) LETABA 159 221 152 98 34 211 93 29 115 194 52 209 170 24 68 103 159 63 119
(1) LOWER SABIE 91 30 96 193 97 90 140 134 353 211 91 329 135 91 262 46 111 40
(1) MALELANE 81 142 254 73 151 203 179 416 274 63 392 198 154 325 63 174 103
(2) MKHUHLU 74 186 68 83 133 111 346 204 68 322 128 84 255 21 104 33
(2) MSANSWENI 132 132 57 79 37 292 150 128 268 74 30 201 81 38 56
(2) NSHAWU 245 127 63 149 160 86 241 136 58 102 69 193 97 153
(4) NUMBI GATE 141 192 170 405 263 10 381 187 143 314 54 163 92
(1) NWANEDZI 64 68 284 142 137 260 66 25 193 90 45 50
(1) OLIFANTS 96 223 81 188 199 5 49 132 140 44 100
(4) ORPEN 309 167 164 285 91 47 218 117 55 93
(2) PAFURI (HIPPO POOL) 246 401 56 218 262 97 353 257 313
(4) PHALABORWA GATE 259 222 76 120 155 211 115 171
(1) PRETORIUSKOP 377 183 139 310 50 159 88
(1) PUNDA MILIA 194 238 73 329 233 289
(2) RIVER VIEW 44 127 135 39 95
(1) SATARA 171 91 24 51
(1) SHINGWIDZI 262 166 222
(1) SKUKUZA 111 40
(2) TIMBAVATI 71
(5) TSHOKWANE

INTRODUCTION

OUTDOOR HOLIDAY GUIDE

ROADS

The maps show the main road system and the more important secondary and minor roads. Members requiring larger scale maps of the main touring areas can obtain a wide range of map-folders free of charge at any AA office.

The information on tarred roads was correct as at August 1978. Road construction and maintenance is constantly being done. Because of this, road conditions vary from time to time and in their own interests members should ask at the nearest AA office for the latest road information before proceeding on a tour.

Members contemplating the use of secondary or minor roads are strongly advised to make local inquiries about the condition of such roads, particularly those in mountainous or hilly country, many of which cannot be negotiated except with a high-clearance 4-wheel drive vehicle. Generally, these roads are not suited to the towing of caravans.

PLACE NAMES

Official and recognised place names from latest available sources are used throughout. In the interests of legibility, features of interest are shown in either of the official languages, with an even balance being maintained throughout.

MAP OVERLAPS

The area of map overlaps at margins lies between the solid green line and the inner black border.

Information from South African official maps reproduced under Government Printer's copyright authority no 5908 of 13/5/1977.

KEY MAP / SLEUTELKAART

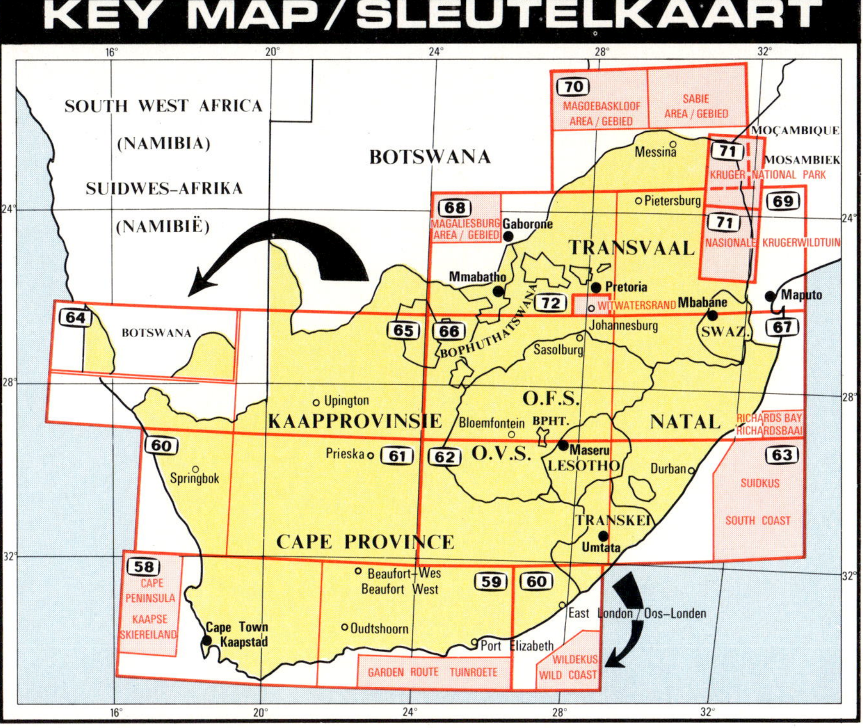

INLEIDING

BUITELUGVAKANSIEGIDS

PAAIE

Die kaarte toon die hoofpadstelsel en die belangrikste sekondêre en kleiner paaie. Lede wat kaarte van die vernaamste toergebiede op 'n groter skaal verlang, kan 'n omvattende reeks voukaarte gratis by enige AA-kantoor kry.

Die inligting aangaande teerpaaie is korrek soos in Augustus 1978. Padbouwerk en onderhoud vind gedurig plaas. Om hierdie rede wissel padtoestande van tyd tot tyd. Lede behoort dus in hulle eie belang by die naaste AA-kantoor aan te klop vir die jongste padinligting voordat hulle op reis gaan.

Lede wat dit oorweeg om sekondêre of kleiner paaie te gebruik, word ten sterkste aangeraai om plaaslik navraag te doen na die toestand van sodanige paaie, veral dié in bergagtige of heuwelagtige streke, baie van hulle onrybaar is, tensy 'n hoogloopvoertuig met vierwielaandrywing gebruik word. Hierdie paaie is oor die algemeen nie geskik vir woonwaens nie.

PLEKNAME

Amptelike en erkende plekname, verkry uit die jongste beskikbare bronne, word regdeur gebruik. Ter wille van leesbaarheid word besienswaardige plekke om die beurt in een van die amptelike tale aangedui sodat 'n goeie balans regdeur gehandhaaf word.

OORSLAG VAN KAARTE

Die strook aan die kantruimte waar die kaarte oorvleuel, lê tussen die vaste groen lyn en die binneste swart lyn.

Inligting van amptelike Suid-Afrikaanse kaarte gereproduseer ingevolge die kopieregmagtiging van die Staatsdrukker no 5908 van 13/5/77.

REFERENCE — 1:1 500 000 — VERWYSING

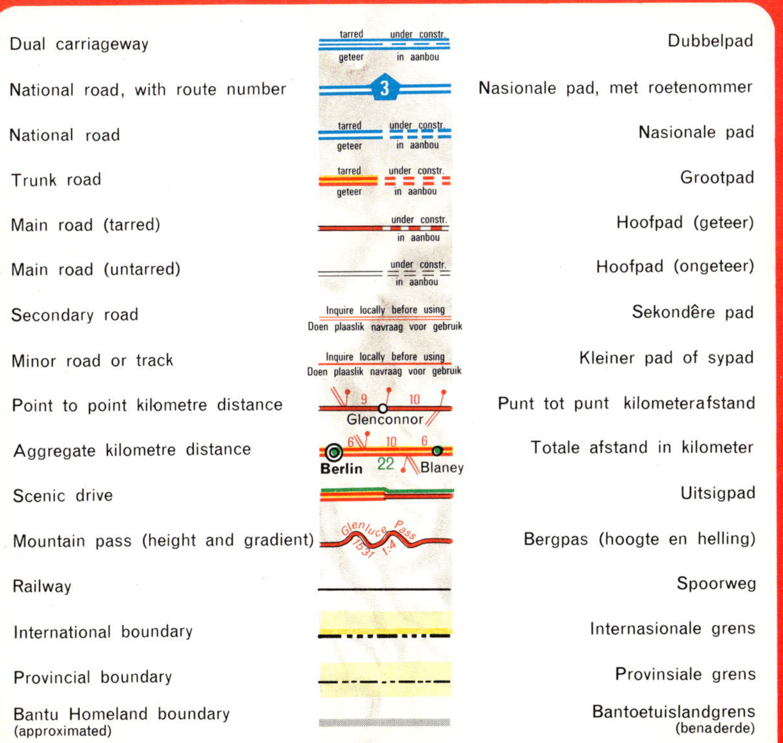

Reference	Symbol	Verwysing
Dual carriageway	tarred / under constr. — geteer / in aanbou	Dubbelpad
National road, with route number	3	Nasionale pad, met roetenommer
National road	tarred / under constr. — geteer / in aanbou	Nasionale pad
Trunk road	tarred / under constr. — geteer / in aanbou	Grootpad
Main road (tarred)	under constr. — in aanbou	Hoofpad (geteer)
Main road (untarred)	under constr. — in aanbou	Hoofpad (ongeteer)
Secondary road	Inquire locally before using — Doen plaaslik navraag voor gebruik	Sekondêre pad
Minor road or track	Inquire locally before using — Doen plaaslik navraag voor gebruik	Kleiner pad of sypad
Point to point kilometre distance	9 Glenconnor 10	Punt tot punt kilometerafstand
Aggregate kilometre distance	Berlin 6 10 6 22 Blaney	Totale afstand in kilometer
Scenic drive		Uitsigpad
Mountain pass (height and gradient)	Glenluce Pass 497 1:4	Bergpas (hoogte en helling)
Railway		Spoorweg
International boundary		Internasionale grens
Provincial boundary		Provinsiale grens
Bantu Homeland boundary (approximated)		Bantoetuislandgrens (benaderde)
National park, game or nature reserve		Nasionale park, wild- of natuurreservaat

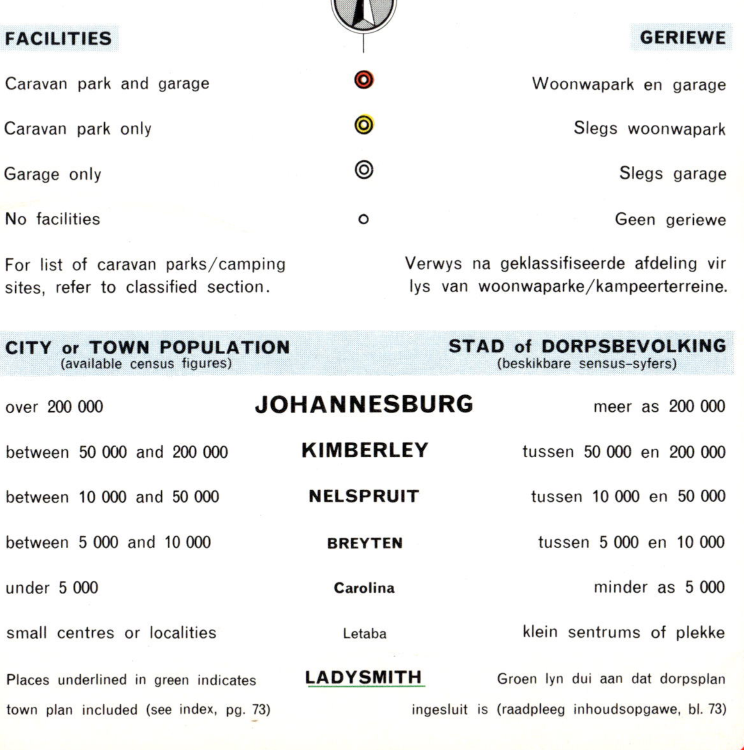

FACILITIES		GERIEWE
Caravan park and garage		Woonwapark en garage
Caravan park only		Slegs woonwapark
Garage only		Slegs garage
No facilities		Geen geriewe
For list of caravan parks/camping sites, refer to classified section.		Verwys na geklassifiseerde afdeling vir lys van woonwaparke/kampeerterreine.

CITY or TOWN POPULATION (available census figures)		STAD of DORPSBEVOLKING (beskikbare sensus-syfers)
over 200 000	JOHANNESBURG	meer as 200 000
between 50 000 and 200 000	KIMBERLEY	tussen 50 000 en 200 000
between 10 000 and 50 000	NELSPRUIT	tussen 10 000 en 50 000
between 5 000 and 10 000	BREYTEN	tussen 5 000 en 10 000
under 5 000	Carolina	minder as 5 000
small centres or localities	Letaba	klein sentrums of plekke
Places underlined in green indicates town plan included (see index, pg. 73)	LADYSMITH	Groen lyn dui aan dat dorpsplan ingesluit is (raadpleeg inhoudsopgawe, bl. 73)

Reference	Symbol	Verwysing
River, with waterfall	Mooi / Nsuze Falls	Rivier, met waterval
Marsh or swamp		Moeras of vlei
Dam, pan or lake	Soutpan / Brandvlei	Dam, pan of meer
Mineral spring		Minerale bron
Forest reserve		Bosreservaat
Rest camp		Ruskamp
National monument / Geological site (See place names gazetteer for key)		Nasionale monument / Geologiese terrein (Kyk pleknaamlys vir sleutel)
Places of interest		Besienswaardige plekke
Lighthouse / National Sea Rescue Institute		Ligtoring / Nasionale Seereddingsinstituut
Shark net		Haainet
Spot height in metres	1188	Punthoogte (in meter)
Customs post		Doeanepos
Border control post		Grensbeheerpos
Airport		Lughawe
Landing ground		Landingsveld
Map page number	70	Kaartbladsynommer
Number of adjoining map page	61	Nommer van aangrensende kaartbladsy

GAUSS CONFORM PROJECTION

km 0 10 20 30 40 50 100 km

1 cm represents 15 km — 1 cm is gelyk aan 15 km

GAUSS CONFORM-PROJEKSIE

CAPE PENINSULA / KAAPSE SKIEREILAND

CAPE PROVINCE / KAAP PROVINSIE

Abundant garage facilities
Volop garagegeriewe

THIS AREA ENLARGED OPPOSITE
HIERDIE GEBIED VERGROOT OORKANT

PEAK SNOEK SEASON MAY–JULY
Hout Bay, Kalk Bay, Hermanus, Gansbaai.

SPITS-SNOEKSEISOEN MEI–JULIE
Houtbaai, Kalkbaai, Hermanus, Gansbaai.

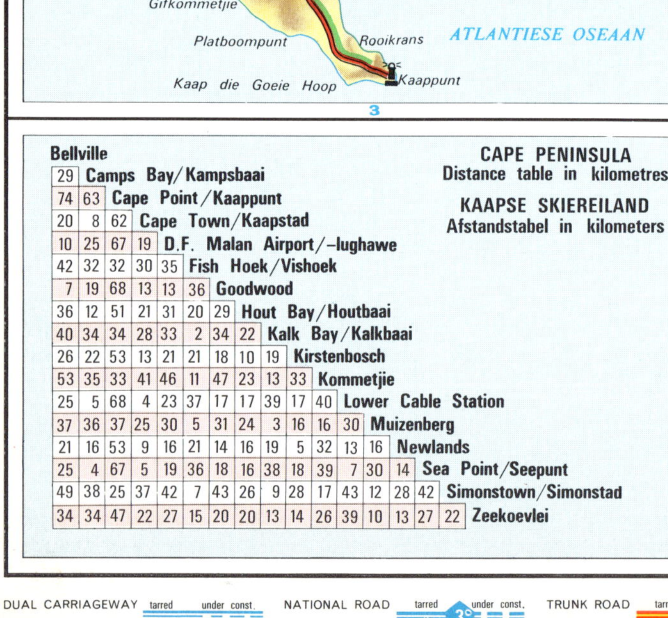

CAPE PENINSULA Distance table in kilometres
KAAPSE SKIEREILAND Afstandstabel in kilometers

	Bellville	Camps Bay/Kampsbaai	Cape Point/Kaappunt	Cape Town/Kaapstad	D.F. Malan Airport/-lughawe	Fish Hoek/Vishoek	Goodwood	Hout Bay/Houtbaai	Kalk Bay/Kalkbaai	Kirstenbosch	Kommetjie	Lower Cable Station	Muizenberg	Newlands	Sea Point/Seepunt	Simonstown/Simonstad
Camps Bay/Kampsbaai	29															
Cape Point/Kaappunt	74	63														
Cape Town/Kaapstad	20	8	62													
D.F. Malan Airport/-lughawe	10	25	67	19												
Fish Hoek/Vishoek	42	32	32	30	35											
Goodwood	7	19	68	13	13	36										
Hout Bay/Houtbaai	36	12	51	21	31	20	29									
Kalk Bay/Kalkbaai	40	34	34	28	33	2	34	22								
Kirstenbosch	26	22	53	13	21	21	18	10	19							
Kommetjie	53	35	33	41	46	11	47	23	13	33						
Lower Cable Station	25	5	68	4	23	37	17	17	39	17	40					
Muizenberg	37	36	37	25	30	5	31	24	3	16	16	30				
Newlands	21	16	53	9	16	21	14	16	19	5	32	13	16			
Sea Point/Seepunt	25	4	67	5	19	36	18	16	38	18	39	7	30	14		
Simonstown/Simonstad	49	38	25	37	42	7	43	26	9	28	17	43	12	28	42	
Zeekoevlei	34	34	47	22	27	15	20	20	13	14	26	39	10	13	27	22

DUAL CARRIAGEWAY tarred / under const. — DUBBELPAD geteer / in aanbou
NATIONAL ROAD tarred / under const. — NASIONALE PAD geteer / in aanbou
TRUNK ROAD tarred / under const. — GROOTPAD geteer / in aanbou
MAIN ROAD TARRED under const. — HOOFPAD GETEER in aanbou
MAIN ROAD UNTARRED under const. — HOOFPAD ONGETEER in aanbou
SECONDARY ROAD Inquire locally before using — SEKONDÊRE PAD Doen plaaslik navraag voor gebruik
MINOR ROAD Inquire locally before using — KLEINER PAD Doen plaaslik navraag voor gebruik
SCENIC DRIVE — UITSIGPAD
0 10 20 30 40 50 kilometres / kilometer

CAPE PROVINCE

KAAPPROVINSIE

INDIAN OCEAN

INDIESE OSEAAN

THIS AREA ENLARGED BELOW
HIERDIE GEBIED ONDERKANT VERGROOT

BEAUFORT WEST
BEAUFORT-WES

GRAAFF-REINET

CRADOCK

ABERDEEN

SOMERSET-OOS
SOMERSET EAST

ADELAIDE

BEDFORD

GRAHAMSTOWN

PRINCE ALBERT

WILLOWMORE

STEYTLERVILLE

KIRKWOOD

OUDTSHOORN

UNIONDALE

UITENHAGE

DESPATCH

PORT ELIZABETH

GEORGE

KNYSNA

MOSSEL BAY

PLETTENBERG BAY

HUMANSDORP

JEFFREYS BAY

TUINROETE
GARDEN ROUTE

DUAL CARRIAGEWAY / DUBBELPAD	NATIONAL ROAD / NASIONALE PAD	TRUNK ROAD / GROOTPAD	MAIN ROAD TARRED / HOOFPAD GETEER	MAIN ROAD UNTARRED / HOOFPAD ONGETEER	SECONDARY ROAD / SEKONDÊRE PAD	MINOR ROAD / KLEINER PAD	SCENIC DRIVE / UITSIGPAD

kilometres 0 10 20 30 40 50 kilometer

TRANSKEI

KAAPPROVINSIE

CAPE PROVINCE

NAMAQUALAND

WILD FLOWERS NAMAQUALAND
Season July/August
VELDBLOMME-NAMAKWALAND
Seisoen Julie/Augustus

DUAL CARRIAGEWAY / DUBBELPAD	NATIONAL ROAD / NASIONALE PAD	TRUNK ROAD / GROOTPAD	MAIN ROAD TARRED / HOOFPAD GETEER	MAIN ROAD UNTARRED / HOOFPAD ONGETEER	SECONDARY ROAD / SEKONDÊRE PAD	MINOR ROAD / KLEINER PAD	SCENIC DRIVE / UITSIGPAD
tarred / geteer; under const. / in aanbou	tarred / geteer; under const. / in aanbou	tarred / geteer; under const. / in aanbou	under const. / in aanbou	under const. / in aanbou	Inquire locally before using / Doen plaaslik navraag voor gebruik	Inquire locally before using / Doen plaaslik navraag voor gebruik	

0 10 20 30 40 50 kilometres / kilometer

CAPE PROVINCE

KAAPPROVINSIE

Pofadder
Namies
Houmoed
Kaimoepslaagte
Kenhardt
Putsonderwater
Koegasbrug
Westerberg
Draghoender
Springputs
Marydale
Niekerkshoop
Higg's Hope
Salt Lake
Fransenhof
PRIESKA
Kareekloof
Strydenburg
Copperton
Omdraaisvlei
Sodium
Granaatboskolk
Zwartkop
Onderstedorings
Rietkop
Vanwyksvlei
Brandvlei
Vosburg
Britstown
DE AAR
Britsville
Die Put
Mynfontein
Deelfontein
Sakrivier
Tontelbos
Loeriesfontein
CARNARVON
Pampoenpoort
Merriman
De Klerk
Klipwerf
Kootjieskolk
Williston
Sterling
Victoria West
Brakpoort
Richmond
Brandkop
Nieuwoudtville
Soetwater
CALVINIA
Downes
Loxton
Meltonwold
Hutchinson
Grootdrif
Verster
Biesiespoort
Slangfontein
Saaifontein
Nobelsfontein
Wagenaarskraal
Bonekraal
Spaarbos
Middelpos
Donkerfontein
Fraserburg
Sneeukraal
Three Sisters
Kromrivier
Murraysburg
Knolvlei
Moedverloor
Die Bos
Rosedene
Restvale
Nelspoort

DUAL CARRIAGEWAY / DUBBELPAD — tarred / geteer; under const. / in aanbou
NATIONAL ROAD / NASIONALE PAD — tarred / geteer; under const. / in aanbou
TRUNK ROAD / GROOTPAD — tarred / geteer; under const. / in aanbou
MAIN ROAD TARRED / HOOFPAD GETEER — under const. / in aanbou
MAIN ROAD UNTARRED / HOOFPAD ONGETEER — under const. / in aanbou
SECONDARY ROAD / SEKONDÊRE PAD — Inquire locally before using / Doen plaaslik navraag voor gebruik
MINOR ROAD / KLEINER PAD — Inquire locally before using / Doen plaaslik navraag voor gebruik
SCENIC DRIVE / UITSIGPAD
0 10 20 30 40 50 kilometres / kilometer

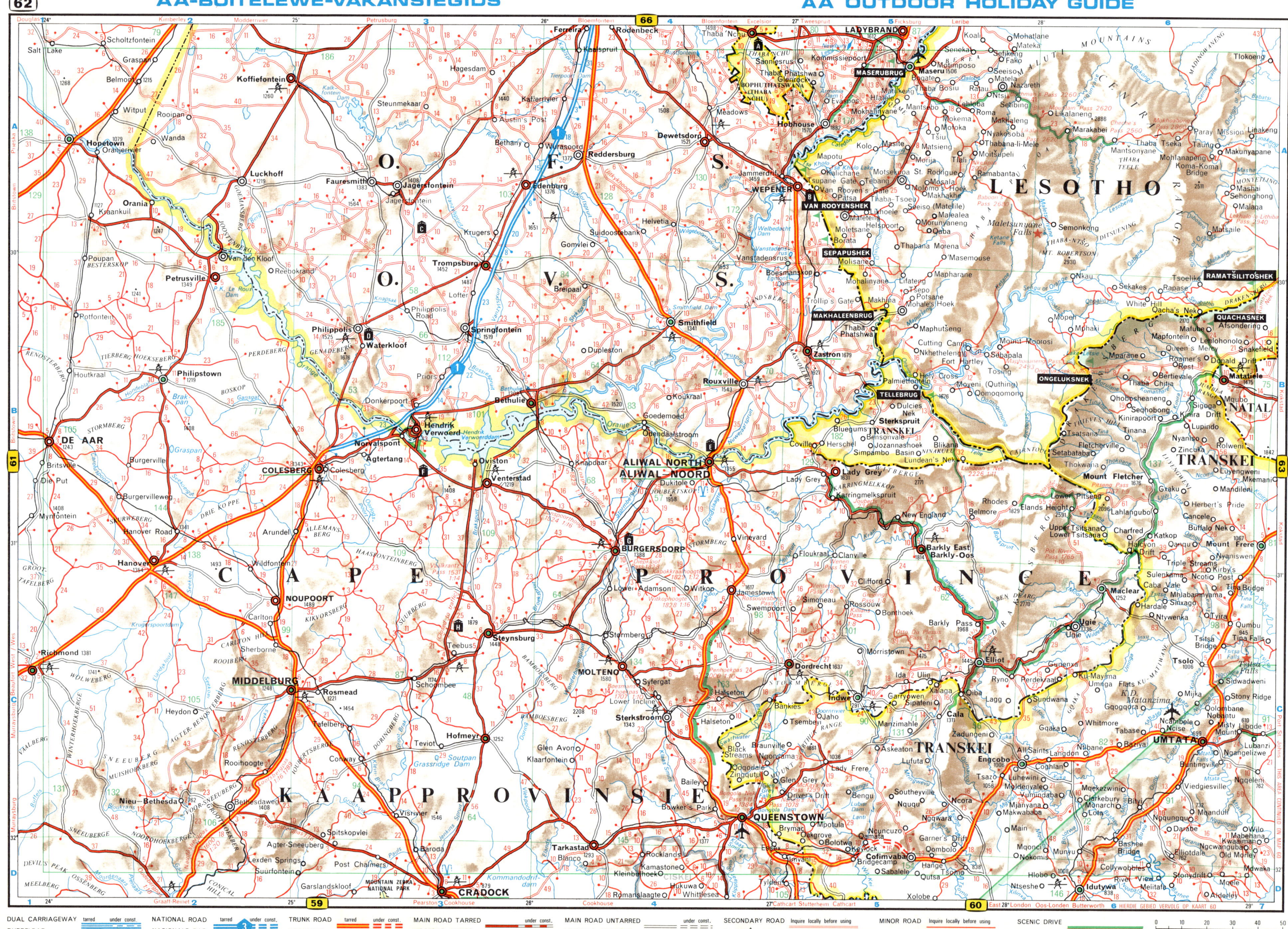

DUAL CARRIAGEWAY / DUBBELPAD — tarred / geteer; under const. / in aanbou
NATIONAL ROAD / NASIONALE PAD — tarred / geteer; under const. / in aanbou
TRUNK ROAD / GROOTPAD — tarred / geteer; under const. / in aanbou
MAIN ROAD TARRED / HOOFPAD GETEER — under const. / in aanbou
MAIN ROAD UNTARRED / HOOFPAD ONGETEER — under const. / in aanbou
SECONDARY ROAD / SEKONDÊRE PAD — Inquire locally before using / Doen plaaslik navraag voor gebruik
MINOR ROAD / KLEINER PAD — Inquire locally before using / Doen plaaslik navraag voor gebruik
SCENIC DRIVE / UITSIGPAD

0 10 20 30 40 50 kilometres / kilometer

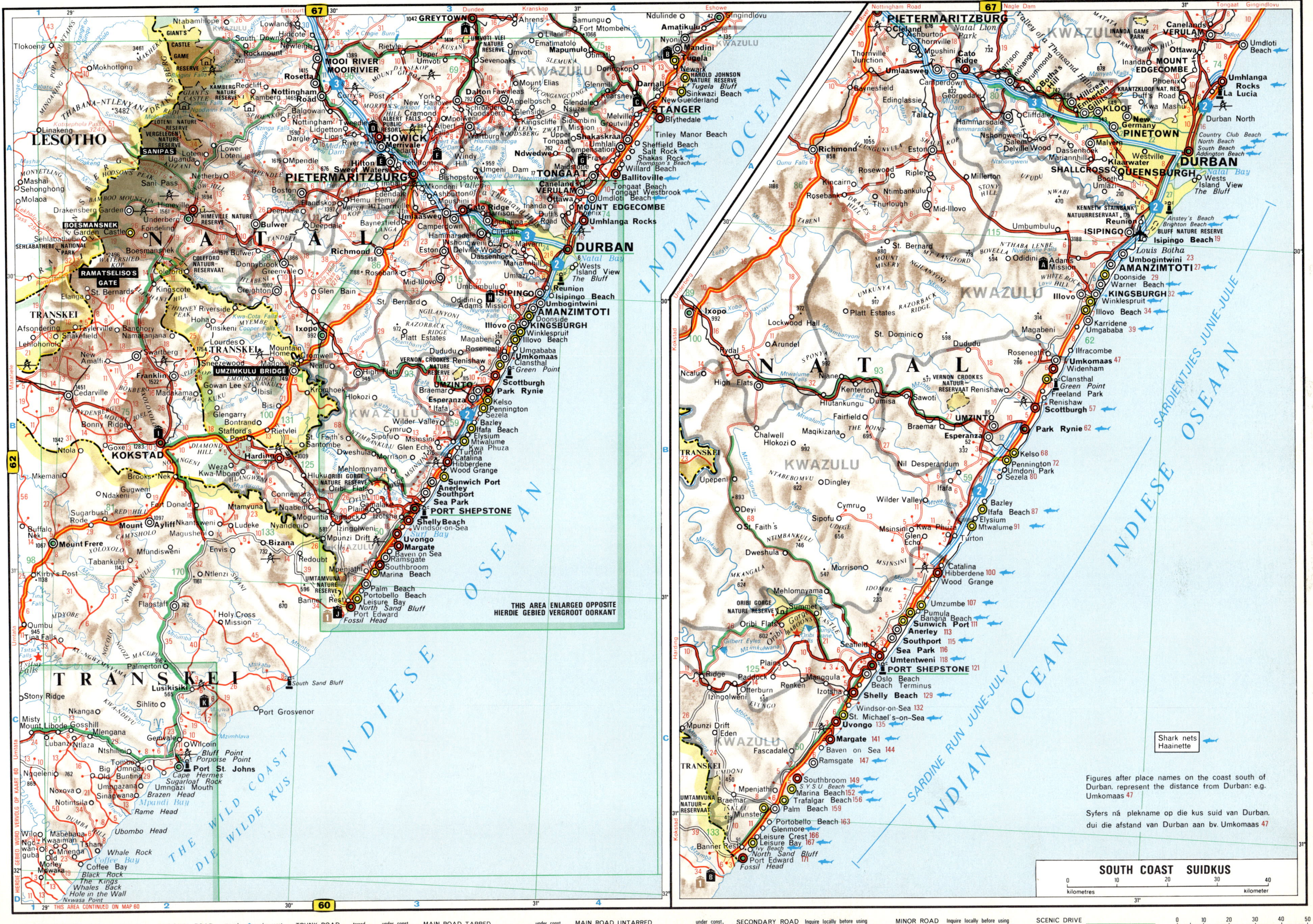
LESOTHO
NATAL
TRANSKEI
KWAZULU
INDIAN OCEAN
INDIESE OSEAAN
THE WILD COAST
DIE WILDE KUS
PIETERMARITZBURG
DURBAN
KOKSTAD
PORT SHEPSTONE
THIS AREA ENLARGED OPPOSITE
HIERDIE GEBIED VERGROOT OORKANT
SARDINE RUN JUNE-JULY
SARDIENTJIES JUNIE-JULIE
Shark nets
Haainette
Figures after place names on the coast south of Durban, represent the distance from Durban: e.g. Umkomaas 47
Syfers ná plekname op die kus suid van Durban, dui die afstand van Durban aan bv. Umkomaas 47
SOUTH COAST SUIDKUS
kilometres kilometer
DUAL CARRIAGEWAY DUBBELPAD tarred geteer under const. in aanbou
NATIONAL ROAD NASIONALE PAD tarred geteer under const. in aanbou
TRUNK ROAD GROOTPAD tarred geteer under const. in aanbou
MAIN ROAD TARRED HOOFPAD GETEER under const. in aanbou
MAIN ROAD UNTARRED HOOFPAD ONGETEER under const. in aanbou
SECONDARY ROAD SEKONDÊRE PAD Inquire locally before using Doen plaaslik navraag voor gebruik
MINOR ROAD KLEINER PAD Inquire locally before using Doen plaaslik navraag voor gebruik
SCENIC DRIVE UITSIGPAD
kilometres kilometer

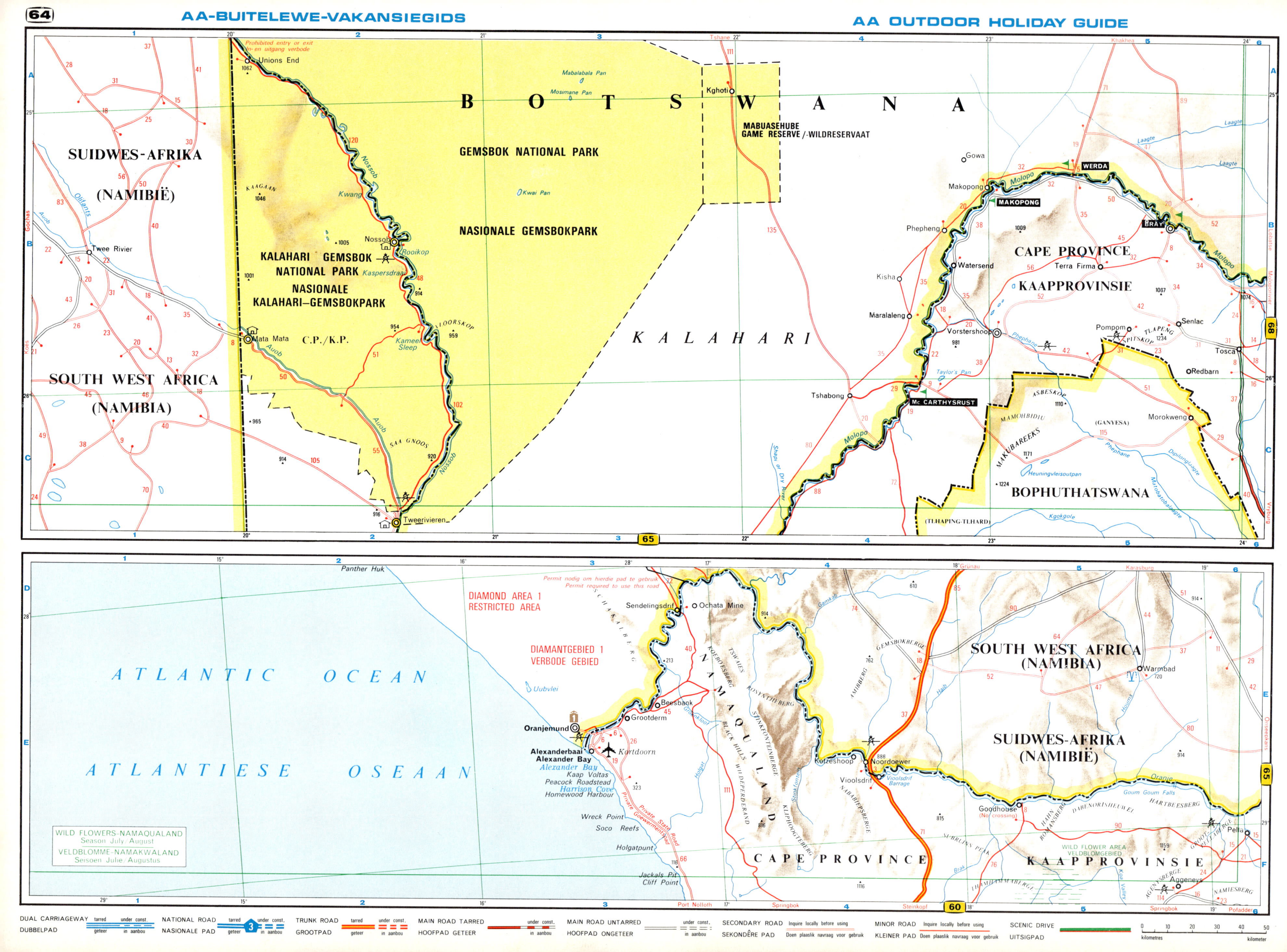
BOTSWANA
GEMSBOK NATIONAL PARK
NASIONALE GEMSBOKPARK
KALAHARI GEMSBOK NATIONAL PARK
NASIONALE KALAHARI-GEMSBOKPARK
C.P./K.P.
MABUASEHUBE GAME RESERVE /-WILDRESERVAAT
KALAHARI
SUIDWES-AFRIKA (NAMIBIË)
SOUTH WEST AFRICA (NAMIBIA)
CAPE PROVINCE
KAAPPROVINSIE
BOPHUTHATSWANA
Prohibited entry or exit
In- en uitgang verbode
Unions End
Twee Rivier
Mata Mata
Nossob
Tweerivieren
Kghoti
Gowa
Makopong
WERDA
MAKOPONG
BRAY
Phepheng
Watersend
Terra Firma
Kisha
Maralaleng
Vorstershoop
Pompom
Senlac
Tosca
Redbarn
Tshabong
Mc CARTHYSRUST
Morokweng
Molopo
Nossob
Auob
65
68
DIAMOND AREA 1 RESTRICTED AREA
DIAMANTGEBIED 1 VERBODE GEBIED
Permit nodig om hierdie pad te gebruik
Permit required to use this road
ATLANTIC OCEAN
ATLANTIESE OSEAAN
Panther Huk
Sendelingsdrif
Ochata Mine
Beesbaak
Grootderm
Oranjemund
Alexanderbaai
Alexander Bay
Kortdoorn
Kaap Voltas
Peacock Roadstead
Harrison Cove
Homewood Harbour
Wreck Point
Soco Reefs
Holgatpunt
Jackals Pit
Cliff Point
Uubvlei
NAMAQUALAND
SOUTH WEST AFRICA (NAMIBIA)
SUIDWES-AFRIKA (NAMIBIË)
Warmbad
Kotzeshoop
Noordoewer
Vioolsdrif
Vioolsdrif Barrage
Goodhouse
(No crossing)
Pella
Aggeneys
CAPE PROVINCE
KAAPPROVINSIE
WILD FLOWER AREA
VELDBLOMGEBIED
Oranje
Goum Goum Falls
WILD FLOWERS-NAMAQUALAND
Season July/August
VELDBLOMME-NAMAKWALAND
Seisoen Julie/Augustus
Port Nolloth
Springbok
Steinkopf
Pofadder
60
DUAL CARRIAGEWAY
DUBBELPAD
NATIONAL ROAD
NASIONALE PAD
TRUNK ROAD
GROOTPAD
MAIN ROAD TARRED
HOOFPAD GETEER
MAIN ROAD UNTARRED
HOOFPAD ONGETEER
SECONDARY ROAD
SEKONDÊRE PAD
MINOR ROAD
KLEINER PAD
SCENIC DRIVE
UITSIGPAD
kilometres

64

NASIONALE KALAHARI-GEMSBOKPARK
KALAHARI GEMSBOK NATIONAL PARK
GEMSBOK NATIONAL PARK
NASIONALE GEMSBOKPARK

BOTSWANA

SOUTH WEST AFRICA (NAMIBIA)

SUIDWES-AFRIKA (NAMIBIË)

CAPE PROVINCE

KAAPPROVINSIE

BOPHUTHATSWANA

(TLHAPING-TLHARO)

Twee Rivieren, Kolonkwaneng, Bogogobo, Middlepits, Khuis, MIDDELPUTS, Gakhibane, Severn, Frylinckspan, Vanzylsrus, Koopan-Noord, GEMSBOK, Bokspits, Andriesvale, Witdraai, Askham, Inkbospan, Rietfontein, Mier, Aroab, Leeubos, Hakskeenpan, Rautenbach-pan, Saulstraat-pan, Koppieskraalpan, Soutpan, Uitsakpan, Leeuvleipan, Naroegaspan, Koopan, Molopo, Kuruman, Klein-Kalpan, Kalkpan, Aasvoëlpan, Koopan-Suid, Obobogorab, Abiekwasputs, Bettastatpan, Aarpan, Rooipan, Langpan, Massaklouspan, Makalaniepan, Tellery Pan, Dead Fish Pan, Noenieput, Tsongnapan, Kongapan, Kakoerabepan, Bloupan, Witpan, Eensaamheidpan, Albion Pan, Groot-Witpan, Vrouenspan, Flanderspan, Laaistokpan, Netherlea Pan, Klein-Bloupan, Kykompan, Kuiepan, Groot-Milanipan, Vaalpan, Gamoteppan, Kakoupan, Geluksputt

Klipdam, Black, Tränental, Davignab, Fettkluft-Nord, Boesmansvlei, Nabas, Kuruman, Lower Dikgatlhong, Hotazel, Tsineng, Maipeing, Ga-Mopedi, Bothithong, Lolwane, Belcobos, Lykso, Kamden, Wesselsvlei, Tselaengwe, Riverfield, KURUMAN, Debeben, Faans Grove, Verwatersdiek, Sutton, Markramsdraai, Wincanton, Dibeng, Sishen, Dingle, Ga-Tlhose, Khosis, Gefco, Bekker, Blikfontein, Wonderwerkgrot Bushman Paintings, Grypoort, Moeswal, Olifantshoek, Cox, Lohatlha, Vroeggedeel, Manganore, Danielskuil, Swartputs, Koopmansfontein, The Great Pan, Owendale, Mancorp Mine, POSTMASBURG, Silver Streams, Lime Acres, Rooipan, Papkuil, Bermolli, Witsand, Roaring Sands and Whitesand, Matsap, Schmidtsdrif, Campbell, Glen Lyon, Griekwastad, Volop, Bucklands, Douglas, Douglas Barrage, Duikersdal, Abrahamsdam, Niekerkshoop, Higg's Hope, Kwartelspan, Dawidspan, Salt Lake

Hamrivier, Kokerboom, Kums, Ariamsvlei, Nakop, Rose Quartz Mine, Langklip, Gous, Grondneus, NOAP HILLS, Lutzputs, Upington, UPINGTON, Sultanaoord, Straussburgdam, Leerkrans, Karos, Dagbreek, Straussburg, Louisvale Road, Louisvale, Ses Brugge, Klipput, Karos Barrage, Lambrechtsdrif, Wilgenhoutsdrif, Grootdrink, Kalkwerf, Vollgraaffsig, Saalskop, Wegdraai, Opwag, Groblershoop, Skerpioenpunt, Kleinbegin, Boegoeberg, Boegoeberg Dam

DIE NASIONALE AUGRABIES-WATERVALPARK
AUGRABIES FALLS NATIONAL PARK
Augrabies Falls -waterval, Augrabies, Kalkmond, Marchand, Alheit, Kakamas, Kanoneilandweg, Keimoes, Kanoneiland, Rooikopeiland, Neilersdrif, Onseepkans, Nous, HOLLENBACHSKOP, Bladgrond, Nabies, Pella, Pofadder, Namies, Kenhardt, Putsonderwater, Koegasbrug, Westerberg, SKURWEBERGE, MOUNT INNIS, LANGEBERG, KORANNABERG, ASBESBERGE, JASPERBERG, DIKWILLEMBERG, SPELONKBERGE, NAMIESBERGE, OUSSAMOEBSBERGE, KOMSBERG, ESELBERGE, NOUKOP, STEYNKOP, Oranje, Molopo, Nossob, Hartbees, Orange, Vaal

61

DUAL CARRIAGEWAY / DUBBELPAD	tarred / geteer	under const / in aanbou
NATIONAL ROAD / NASIONALE PAD	tarred / geteer	under const. / in aanbou
TRUNK ROAD / GROOTPAD	tarred / geteer	under const. / in aanbou
MAIN ROAD TARRED / HOOFPAD GETEER		under const. / in aanbou
MAIN ROAD UNTARRED / HOOFPAD ONGETEER		under const. / in aanbou
SECONDARY ROAD / SEKONDÊRE PAD	Inquire locally before using / Doen plaaslik navraag voor gebruik	
MINOR ROAD / KLEINER PAD	Inquire locally before using / Doen plaaslik navraag voor gebruik	
SCENIC DRIVE / UITSIGPAD		

0 10 20 30 40 50 kilometres / kilometer

68

65

67

62

TRANSVAAL

CAPE PROVINCE

O.F.S.

O.V.S.

LESOTHO

BOPHUTHATSWANA

VRYBURG

SCHWEIZER-RENEKE

WOLMARANSSTAD

KLERKSDORP

POTCHEFSTROOM

CARLETONVILLE

VANDERBIJLPARK

VEREENIGING

NIGEL

HEIDELBERG

SASOLBURG

ORKNEY

PARYS

VILJOENSKROON

BOTHAVILLE

HEILBRON

FRANKFORT

BLOEMHOF

CHRISTIANA

KROONSTAD

ODENDAALSRUS

WELKOM

HENNENMAN

VIRGINIA

WARRENTON

REITZ

BETHLEHEM

SENEKAL

THEUNISSEN

WINBURG

BRANDFORT

KIMBERLEY

BLOEMFONTEIN

FICKSBURG

CLOCOLAN

LADYBRAND

DUAL CARRIAGEWAY / DUBBELPAD	tarred / geteer	under const. / in aanbou
NATIONAL ROAD / NASIONALE PAD	tarred / geteer	under const. / in aanbou
TRUNK ROAD / GROOTPAD	tarred / geteer	under const. / in aanbou
MAIN ROAD TARRED / HOOFPAD GETEER		under const. / in aanbou
MAIN ROAD UNTARRED / HOOFPAD ONGETEER		under const. / in aanbou
SECONDARY ROAD / SEKONDÊRE PAD	Inquire locally before using / Doen plaaslik navraag voor gebruik	
MINOR ROAD / KLEINER PAD	Inquire locally before using / Doen plaaslik navraag voor gebruik	
SCENIC DRIVE / UITSIGPAD		

0 10 20 30 40 50 kilometres / kilometer

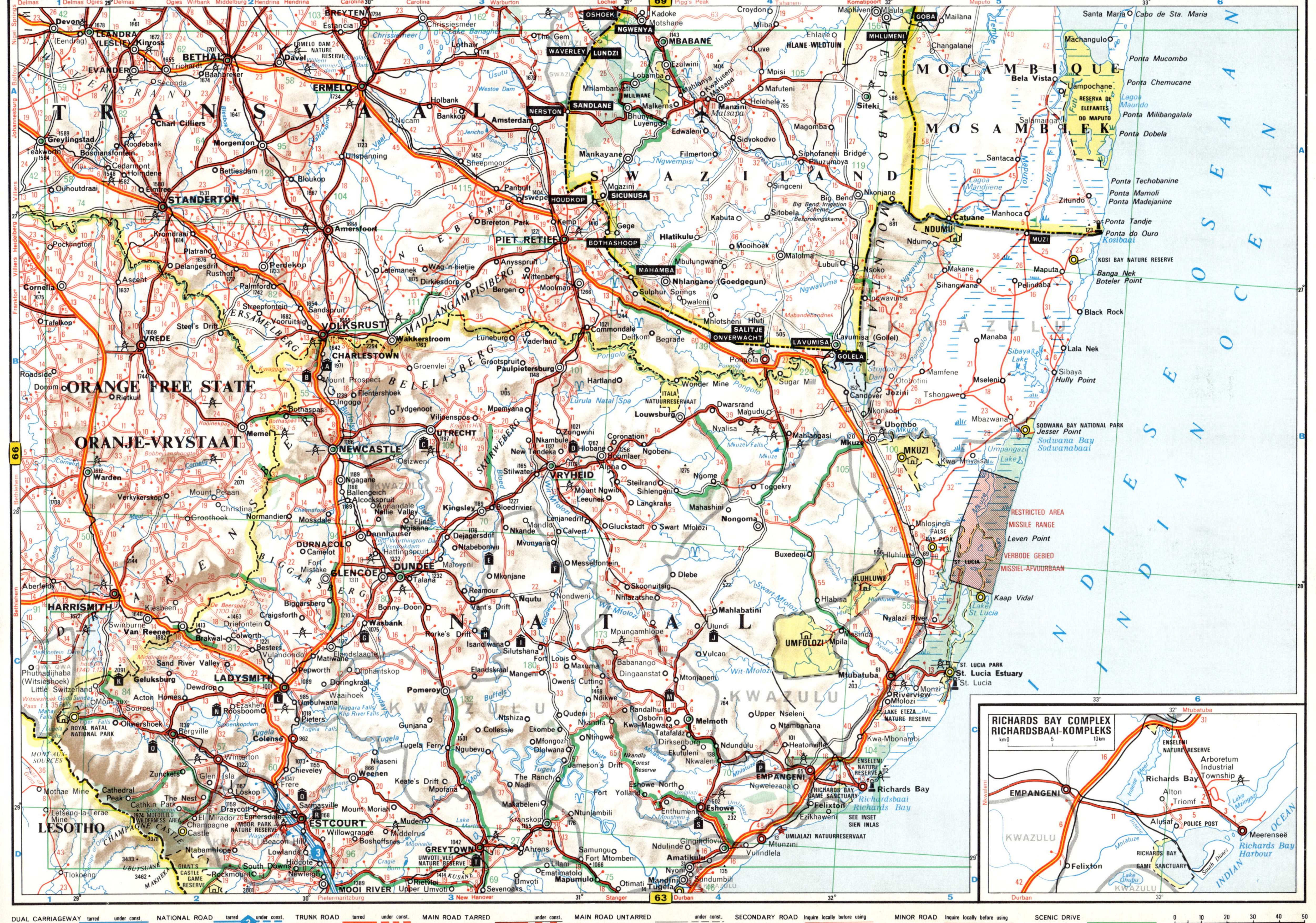

DUAL CARRIAGEWAY / DUBBELPAD	NATIONAL ROAD / NASIONALE PAD	TRUNK ROAD / GROOTPAD	MAIN ROAD TARRED / HOOFPAD GETEER	MAIN ROAD UNTARRED / HOOFPAD ONGETEER	SECONDARY ROAD / SEKONDÊRE PAD	MINOR ROAD / KLEINER PAD	SCENIC DRIVE / UITSIGPAD
tarred / geteer; under const. / in aanbou	tarred / geteer; under const. / in aanbou	tarred / geteer; under const. / in aanbou	under const. / in aanbou	under const. / in aanbou	Inquire locally before using / Doen plaaslik navraag voor gebruik	Inquire locally before using / Doen plaaslik navraag voor gebruik	

0 10 20 30 40 50 kilometres / kilometer

MAGALIESBERG AREA
MAGALIESBERG–GEBIED

kilometres 0 5 10 15 20 kilometer

Pleasure resort / Plesieroord

Rest Camp / Ruskamp

Place of interest / Besienswaardige plek

Guest Farm / Vakansieplaas

THIS AREA ENLARGED OPPOSITE

HIERDIE GEBIED VERGROOT OORKANT

BOTSWANA

TRANSVAAL

CAPE PROVINCE

BOPHUTHATSWANA

DUAL CARRIAGEWAY tarred / under const.	NATIONAL ROAD tarred / under const.	TRUNK ROAD tarred / under const.	MAIN ROAD TARRED under const.	MAIN ROAD UNTARRED under const.	SECONDARY ROAD Inquire locally before using	MINOR ROAD Inquire locally before using	SCENIC DRIVE	0 10 20 30 40 50 kilometres
DUBBELPAD geteer / in aanbou	NASIONALE PAD geteer / in aanbou	GROOTPAD geteer / in aanbou	HOOFPAD GETEER in aanbou	HOOFPAD ONGETEER in aanbou	SEKONDÊRE PAD Doen plaaslik navraag voor gebruik	KLEINER PAD Doen plaaslik navraag voor gebruik	UITSIGPAD	kilometer

70

THIS AREA ENLARGED ON PAGE 71 HIERDIE GEBIED VERGROOT OP BLADSY 71

THIS AREA ENLARGED ON PAGE 70 HIERDIE GEBIED VERGROOT OP BLADSY 70

THIS AREA ENLARGED ON PAGE 71

HIERDIE GEBIED VERGROOT OP BLADSY 71

HIERDIE GEBIED VERGROOT OP BLADSY 70

THIS AREA ENLARGED ON PAGE 70

TRANSVAAL

MOSAMBIEK

MOÇAMBIQUE

SWAZILAND

INDIAN OCEAN

INDIESE OSEAAN

KRUGER NATIONAL PARK

NASIONALE KRUGERWILDTUIN

68

67

DUAL CARRIAGEWAY / DUBBELPAD	tarred / geteer	under const. / in aanbou
NATIONAL ROAD / NASIONALE PAD	tarred / geteer	under const. / in aanbou
TRUNK ROAD / GROOTPAD	tarred / geteer	under const. / in aanbou
MAIN ROAD TARRED / HOOFPAD GETEER		under const. / in aanbou
MAIN ROAD UNTARRED / HOOFPAD ONGETEER		under const. / in aanbou
SECONDARY ROAD / SEKONDÊRE PAD	Inquire locally before using / Doen plaaslik navraag voor gebruik	
MINOR ROAD / KLEINER PAD	Inquire locally before using / Doen plaaslik navraag voor gebruik	
SCENIC DRIVE / UITSIGPAD		

0 10 20 30 40 50 kilometres kilometer

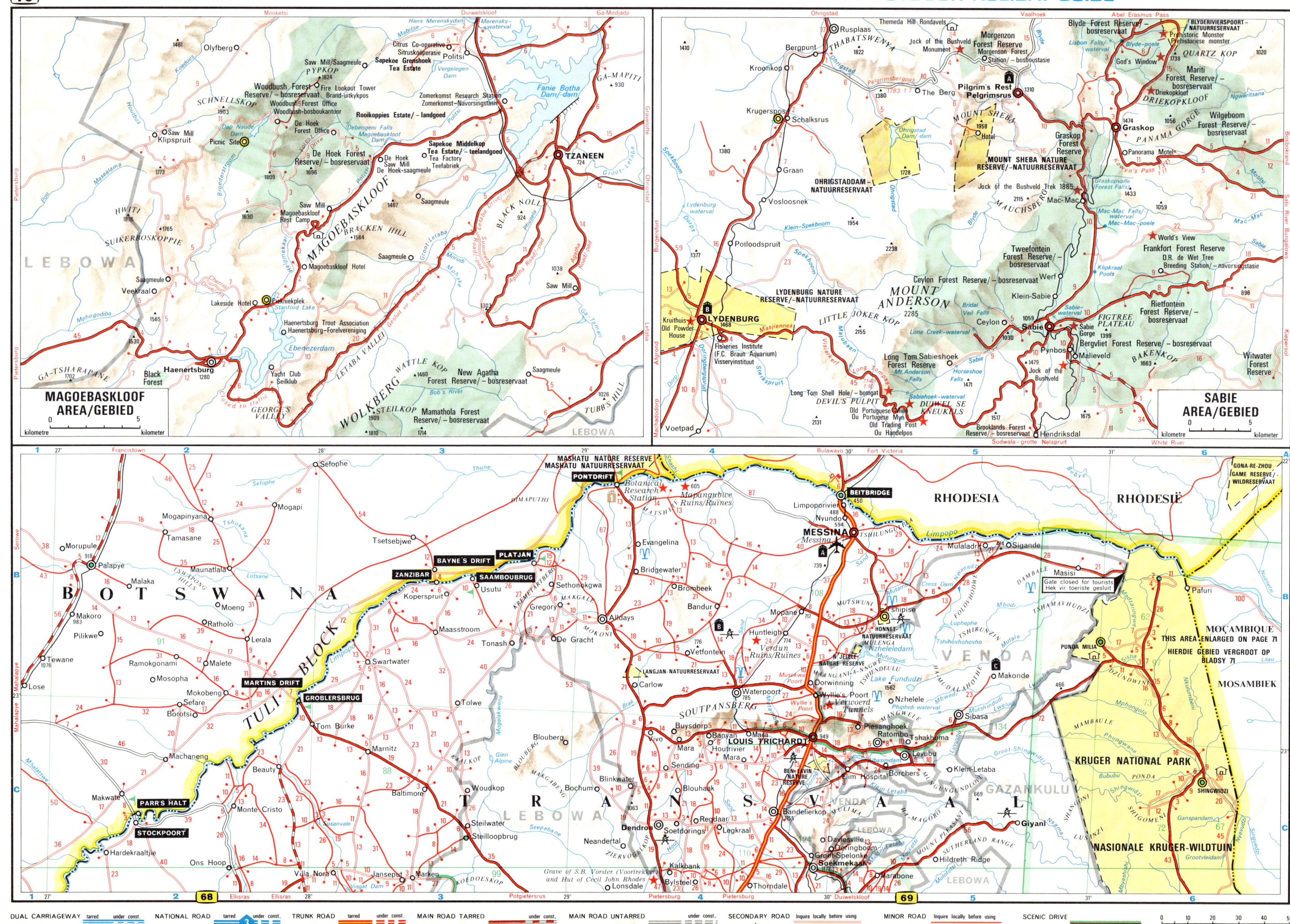
MAGOEBASKLOOF AREA/GEBIED
kilometre
kilometer
TZANEEN
Haenertsburg
MAGOEBASKLOOF
Fanie Botha Dam/-dam
Ebenezerdam
LEBOWA
Woodbush Forest Reserve/- bosreservaat
De Hoek Forest Reserve/- bosreservaat
New Agatha Forest Reserve/- bosreservaat
Mamathola Forest Reserve/- bosreservaat
Magoebaskloof Hotel
Lakeside Hotel
Piekniekplek
Picnic Site
WOLKBERG
LETABA VALLEI
SABIE AREA/GEBIED
LYDENBURG
Sabie
Graskop
Pilgrim's Rest Pelgrimsrus
MOUNT ANDERSON
MOUNT SHEBA NATURE RESERVE/-NATUURRESERVAAT
OHRIGSTADDAM-NATUURRESERVAAT
LYDENBURG NATURE RESERVE/-NATUURRESERVAAT
BLYDERIVIERSPOORT-NATUURRESERVAAT
God's Window
Mac-Mac
Bergvliet Forest Reserve/- bosreservaat
Ceylon Forest Reserve/- bosreservaat
Long Tom Sabieshoek Forest Reserve
Witwater Forest Reserve
Rietfontein Forest Reserve/- bosreservaat
Frankfort Forest Reserve
Tweefontein Forest Reserve/- bosreservaat
Mariti Forest Reserve/- bosreservaat
Wilgeboom Forest Reserve/- bosreservaat
Graskop Forest Reserve
Blyde Forest Reserve/- bosreservaat
Morgenzon Forest Reserve
BOTSWANA
TRANSVAAL
RHODESIA
RHODESIË
VENDA
GAZANKULU
LEBOWA
MOÇAMBIQUE
MOSAMBIEK
TULI BLOCK
MESSINA
BEITBRIDGE
LOUIS TRICHARDT
PONTDRIFT
PLATJAN
BAYNE'S DRIFT
ZANZIBAR
SAAMBOUBRUG
MARTINS DRIFT
GROBLERSBRUG
PARR'S HALT
STOCKPOORT
PUNDA MILIA
SHINGWIDZI
KRUGER NATIONAL PARK
NASIONALE KRUGER-WILDTUIN
THIS AREA ENLARGED ON PAGE 71
HIERDIE GEBIED VERGROOT OP BLADSY 71
MASHATU NATURE RESERVE
MASHATU NATUURRESERVAAT
GONA-RE-ZHOU GAME RESERVE/-WILDRESERVAAT
HONNET NATUURRESERVAAT
LANGJAN-NATUURRESERVAAT
BEN LAVIN NATURE RESERVE
N'JELELE NATURE RESERVE
Gate closed for tourists
Hek vir toeriste gesluit
SOUTPANSBERG
68
69
DUAL CARRIAGEWAY
DUBBELPAD
NATIONAL ROAD
NASIONALE PAD
TRUNK ROAD
GROOTPAD
MAIN ROAD TARRED
HOOFPAD GETEER
MAIN ROAD UNTARRED
HOOFPAD ONGETEER
SECONDARY ROAD
SEKONDÊRE PAD
MINOR ROAD
KLEINER PAD
SCENIC DRIVE
UITSIGPAD
tarred
geteer
under const.
in aanbou
Inquire locally before using
Doen plaaslik navraag voor gebruik
kilometres
kilometer

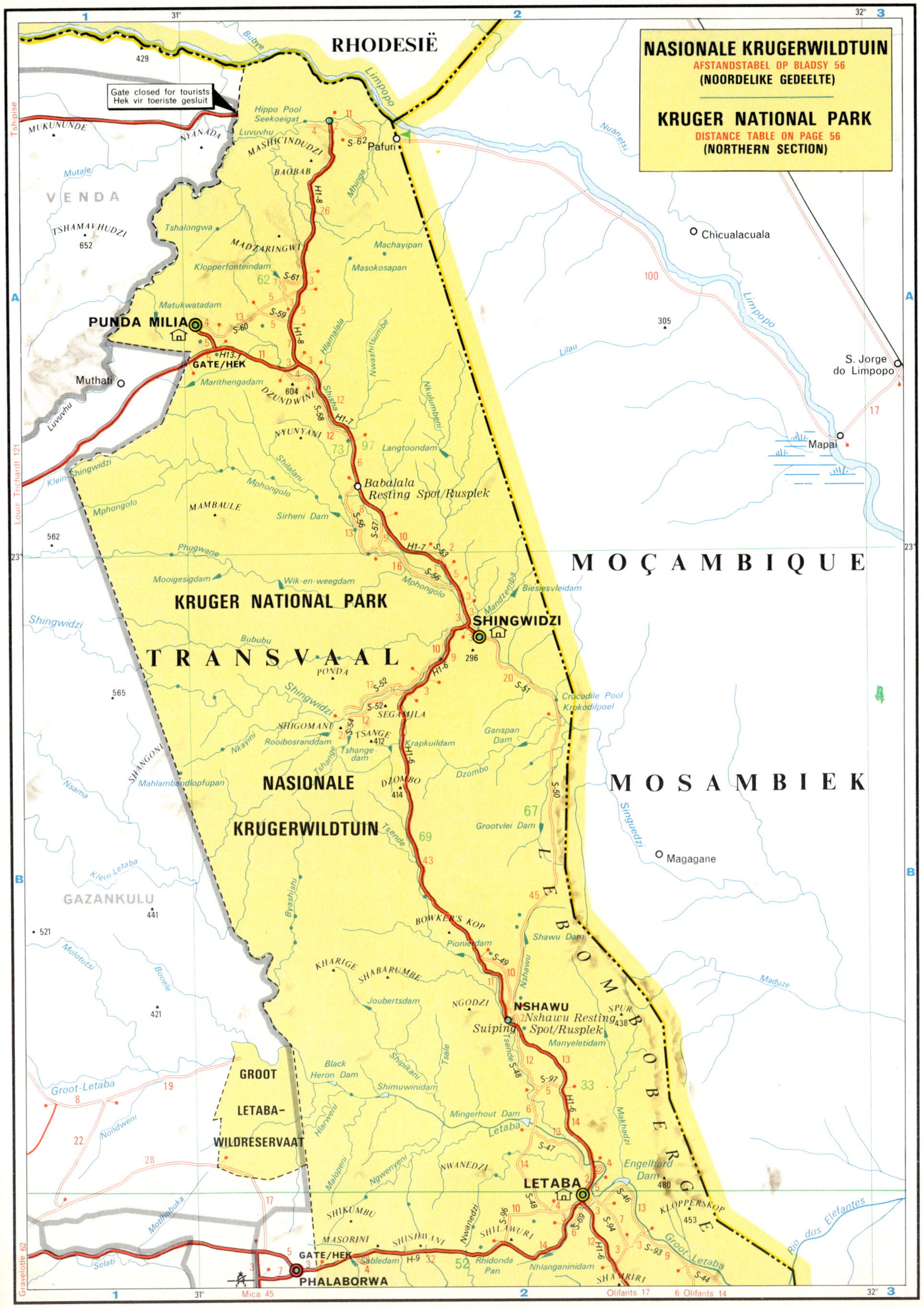

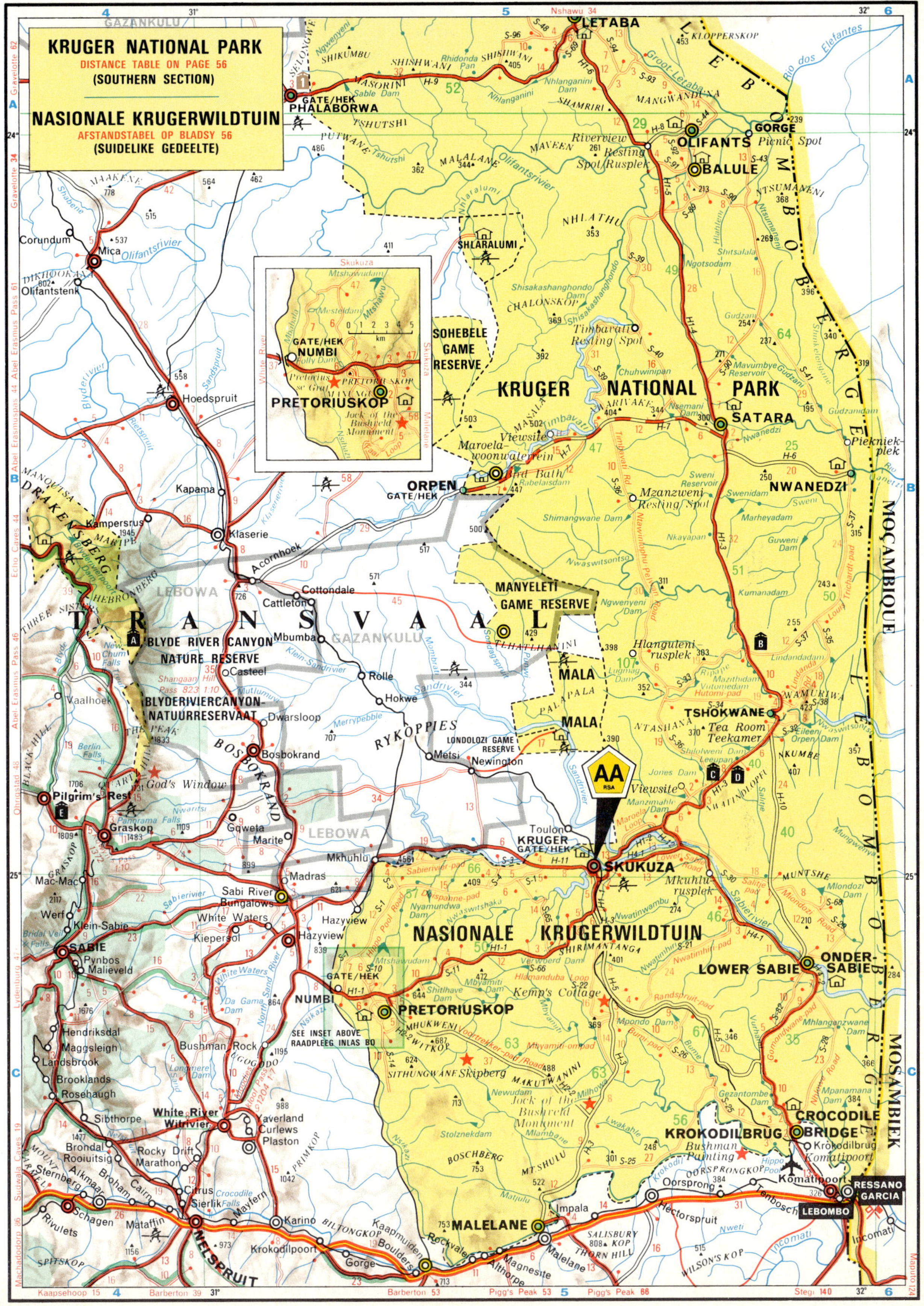

NASIONALE KRUGERWILDTUIN
AFSTANDSTABEL OP BLADSY 56
(NOORDELIKE GEDEELTE)

KRUGER NATIONAL PARK
DISTANCE TABLE ON PAGE 56
(NORTHERN SECTION)

KRUGER NATIONAL PARK
DISTANCE TABLE ON PAGE 56
(SOUTHERN SECTION)

NASIONALE KRUGERWILDTUIN
AFSTANDSTABEL OP BLADSY 56
(SUIDELIKE GEDEELTE)

WITWATERSRAND

KEEP OUR ROADS TIDY

HOU ONS PAAIE SKOON

See Town Plan section for detailed plans of places underlined in green.

Sien die Dorpsplan-deel vir gedetailleerde planne van plekke wat met groen onderstreep is.

Abundant garage facilities
Volop garagegeriewe

LUGHAWE · JAN SMUTS · AIRPORT

South Africa's Trade Centre SANSHOW
VOORGESTELDE KOMPLEKS
PROPOSED COMPLEX

DOMESTIC FLIGHTS ARRIVALS AND DEPARTURES LOWER LEVEL
BINNELANDSE VLUGTE AANKOMS EN VERTREK ONDERVLAK
INTERNASIONALE VLUGTE AANKOMS-ONDERVLAK VERTREK-BO-VLAK
INTERNATIONAL FLIGHTS ARRIVALS LOWER LEVEL DEPARTURES UPPER LEVEL

JAN SMUTS
Hotel
Heliport
International Concourse
Car Hire
Office Block
Domestic Concourse
Lugvrag
Isando

Openbare parkering P Public parking

TRANSVAAL

DUAL CARRIAGEWAY tarred under const
DUBBELPAD geteer in aanbou

NATIONAL ROAD tarred under const
NASIONALE PAD geteer in aanbou

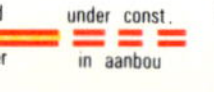

TRUNK ROAD tarred under const
GROOTPAD geteer in aanbou

MAIN ROAD TARRED under const.
HOOFPAD GETEER in aanbou

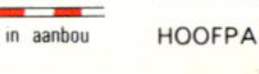

MAIN ROAD UNTARRED under const.
HOOFPAD ONGETEER in aanbou

SECONDARY ROAD Inquire locally before using
SEKONDÊRE PAD Doen plaaslik navraag voor gebruik

MINOR ROAD Inquire locally before using
KLEINER PAD Doen plaaslik navraag voor gebruik

SCENIC DRIVE
UITSIGPAD

0 2 4 6 8 10
kilometres kilometer

CITY AND TOWN PLAN REFERENCE

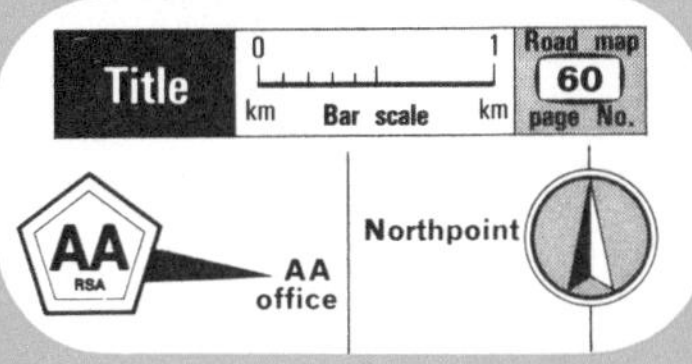

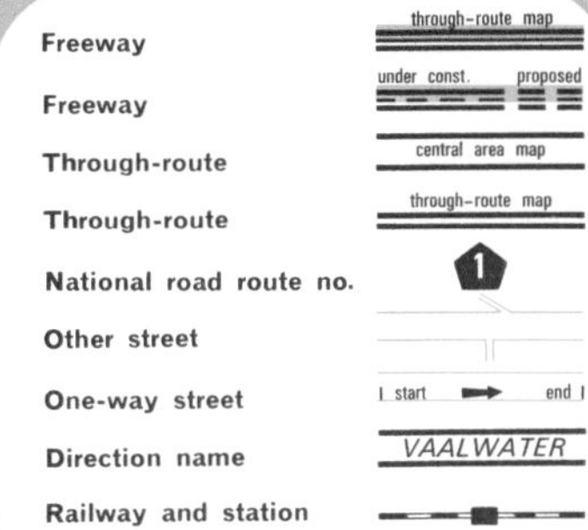

- Freeway — through-route map
- Freeway — under const. / proposed
- Through-route — central area map
- Through-route — through-route map
- National road route no.
- Other street
- One-way street — start / end
- Direction name — VAALWATER
- Railway and station

- River and bridge
- Dam, pan or lake
- Slimes dam
- Mine dump
- Cemetery
- City/Town hall
- Municipal office
- Post office
- Police station
- Fire station
- Hospital
- Car park
- Publicity/Information
- National Tourist Bureau of the Department of Tourism

- Library
- National monument *
- Airport
- Landing ground
- Dock
- Lighthouse
- Shark net
- Park
- Swimming bath
- Caravan park *
- Camping site *
- Golf course
- Racecourse
- Zoo

N.B. THESE PLANS SHOW THROUGH-ROUTES AND SOME, BUT NOT ALL, OTHER STREETS.

CITY AND TOWN PLAN INDEX

(C) CAPE PROVINCE (S) SWAZILAND (X) TRANSKEI (T) TRANSVAAL

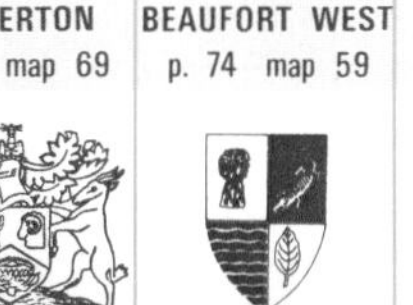

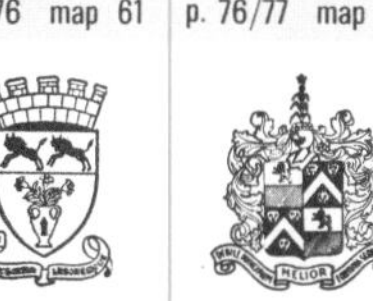
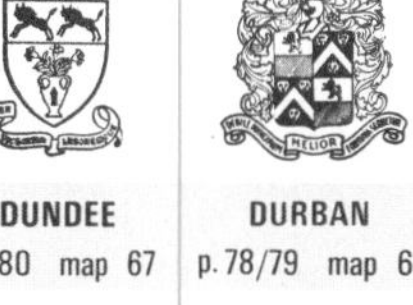

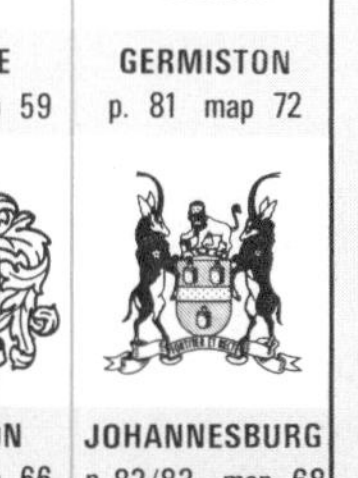

ADELAIDE	p. 74	map 59
ALBERTON	p. 74	map 72
ALICE	p. 74	map 60
ALIWAL NORTH	p. 74	map 62
BARBERTON	p. 74	map 69
BEAUFORT WEST	p. 74	map 59
BELLVILLE	p. 74	map 58
BENONI	p. 74	map 72
BETHAL	p. 75	map 67
BETHLEHEM	p. 75	map 66
BLOEMFONTEIN	p. 75	map 66
BOKSBURG	p. 75	map 72
BRAKPAN	p. 75	map 72
BREDASDORP	p. 76	map 58
BRITS	p. 76	map 68
CALEDON	p. 76	map 58
CALVINIA	p. 76	map 61
CAPE TOWN	p. 76/77	map 58
CARLETONVILLE	p. 77	map 68
CARNARVON	p. 77	map 61
CAROLINA	p. 77	map 69
CITRUSDAL	p. 78	map 58
COLESBERG	p. 78	map 62
CRADOCK	p. 78	map 59
DARLING	p. 78	map 58
DUNDEE	p. 80	map 67
DURBAN	p. 78/79	map 63
EAST LONDON	p. 79	map 60
ERMELO	p. 80	map 67
ESHOWE	p. 80	map 67
ESTCOURT	p. 80	map 67
FICKSBURG	p. 80	map 66
FLORIDA	p. 80	map 72
FORT BEAUFORT	p. 80	map 60
GEORGE	p. 81	map 59
GERMISTON	p. 81	map 72
GRAAFF-REINET	p. 81	map 59
GRAHAMSTOWN	p. 81	map 60
GREYTOWN	p. 81	map 67
GRIQUATOWN	p. 82	map 65
HARDING	p. 82	map 63
HARRISMITH	p. 82	map 67
HEIDELBERG (C)	p. 82	map 58
HEILBRON	p. 83	map 66
JOHANNESBURG	p. 82/83	map 68

* For list of National monuments/Geological sites see Place Name Gazetteer.

* Refer to classified list fo' caravan parks/camping sites.

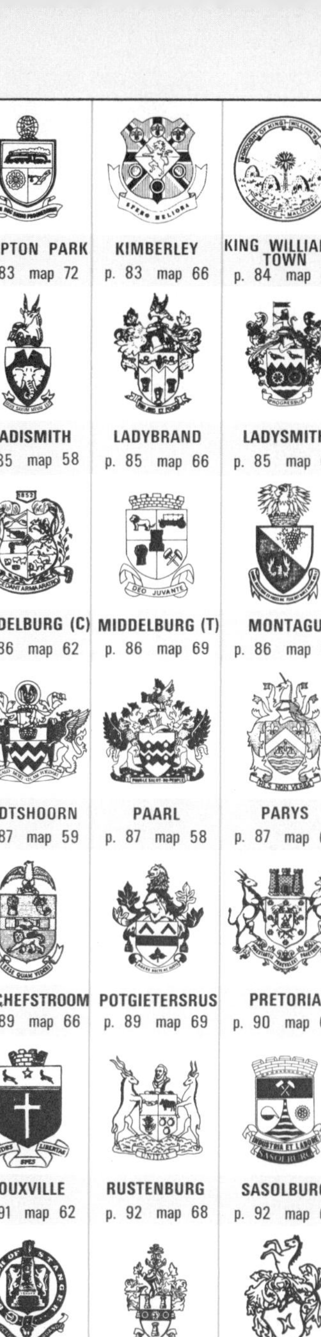
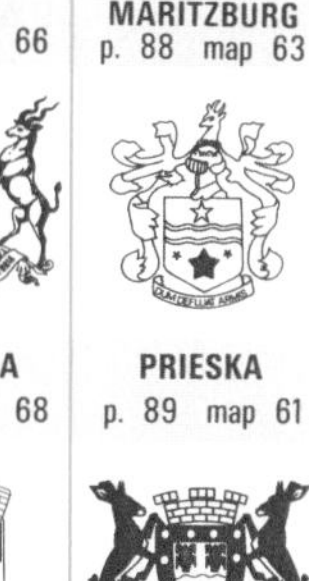
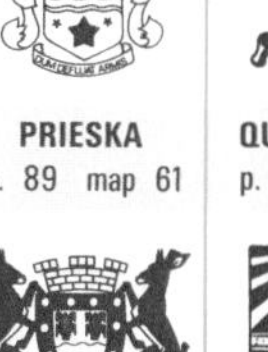

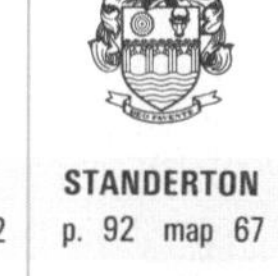

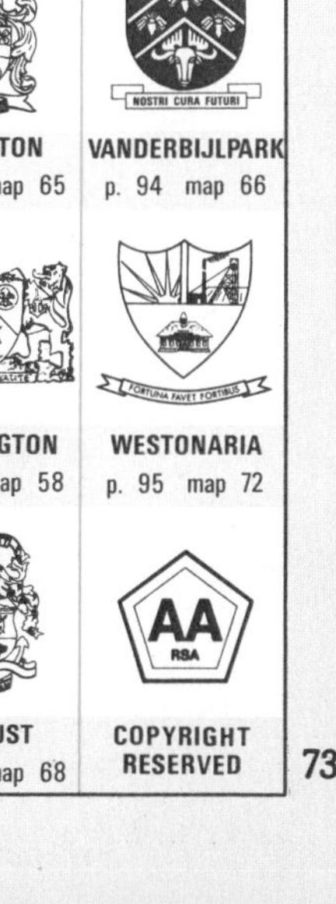

KEMPTON PARK	p. 83	map 72
KIMBERLEY	p. 83	map 66
KING WILLIAM'S TOWN	p. 84	map 60
KLERKSDORP	p. 84	map 66
KNYSNA	p. 84	map 59
KOKSTAD	p. 84	map 63
KROONSTAD	p. 84	map 66
KRUGERSDORP	p. 84	map 72
KURUMAN	p. 84	map 65
LADISMITH	p. 85	map 58
LADYBRAND	p. 85	map 66
LADYSMITH	p. 85	map 67
LICHTENBURG	p. 85	map 68
LOUIS TRICHARDT	p. 85	map 70
LYDENBURG	p. 85	map 69
MAFEKING	p. 85	map 68
MALMESBURY	p. 85	map 58
MBABANE (S)	p. 86	map 67
MIDDELBURG (C)	p. 86	map 62
MIDDELBURG (T)	p. 86	map 69
MONTAGU	p. 86	map 58
MOSSEL BAY	p. 86	map 59
NELSPRUIT	p. 86	map 69
NEWCASTLE	p. 86	map 67
NIGEL	p. 87	map 72
NYLSTROOM	p. 87	map 68
ODENDAALSRUS	p. 87	map 66
OUDTSHOORN	p. 87	map 59
PAARL	p. 87	map 58
PARYS	p. 87	map 66
PIETER–MARITZBURG	p. 88	map 63
PIETERSBURG	p. 87	map 69
PIET RETIEF	p. 88	map 67
PORT ALFRED	p. 88	map 60
PORT ELIZABETH	p. 88/89	map 59
PORT SHEPSTONE	p. 89	map 63
POTCHEFSTROOM	p. 89	map 66
POTGIETERSRUS	p. 89	map 69
PRETORIA	p. 90	map 68
PRIESKA	p. 89	map 61
QUEENSTOWN	p. 91	map 62
RANDBURG	p. 91	map 72
RANDFONTEIN	p. 91	map 72
ROBERTSON	p. 91	map 58
ROODEPOORT	p. 91	map 72
ROUXVILLE	p. 91	map 62
RUSTENBURG	p. 92	map 68
SASOLBURG	p. 92	map 66
SCHWEIZER-RENEKE	p. 92	map 66
SENEKAL	p. 92	map 66
SOMERSET EAST	p. 92	map 59
SOMERSET WEST	p. 92	map 58
SPRINGS	p. 92	map 72
STANDERTON	p. 92	map 67
STANGER	p. 93	map 63
STELLENBOSCH	p. 93	map 58
STUTTERHEIM	p. 93	map 60
SWELLENDAM	p. 93	map 58
TZANEEN	p. 93	map 69
UITENHAGE	p. 93	map 59
UMTATA (X)	p. 93	map 62
UPINGTON	p. 94	map 65
VANDERBIJLPARK	p. 94	map 66
VANRHYNSDORP	p. 94	map 60
VEREENIGING	p. 94	map 66
VOLKSRUST	p. 94	map 67
VRYBURG	p. 95	map 66
VRYHEID	p. 95	map 67
WARMBATHS	p. 95	map 68
WELKOM	p. 95	map 66
WELLINGTON	p. 95	map 58
WESTONARIA	p. 95	map 72
WHITE RIVER	p. 96	map 69
WILLISTON	p. 96	map 61
WINBURG	p. 96	map 66
WITBANK	p. 96	map 69
WOLMARANSSTAD	p. 96	map 66
WORCESTER	p. 96	map 58
ZASTRON	p. 96	map 62
ZEERUST	p. 96	map 68

Adelaide 0 500 m m 59
Alberton 0 1 km km 72
Alice 0 500 m m 60
Aliwal North 0 1 km km 62
Van Riebeeck Park
Ons Erfenismuseum
Our Heritage Museum
JOHANNESBURG
BEDFORD
PORT ELIZABETH
FORT BEAUFORT
RAND AIRPORT
RANDSE LUGHAWE
Radio Str.
ELSBURG
Grewarpark
New Market
Heidelberg Rd./-weg
VEREENIGING
HEIDELBERG
Sportterrein
Sports Ground
University of Fort Hare
Museum
KING WILLIAM'S TOWN
HOGSBACK
GRAHAMSTOWN
PEDDIE
BREAKFAST VLEI
McNab Drive
Orange
O.F.S./O.V.S.
C.P./K.P.
Sauer Park
Young Str.
LADY GREY
TRANSKEI
BURGERSDORP
QUEENSTOWN
JAMESTOWN
Kings Drive
NELSPRUIT
KAAPMUIDEN
SWAZILAND
MOSAMBIEK
President Square
De Villiers Str.
Pilgrim
THREE SISTERS
LOXTON
RICHMOND
Dam
Voortrekker Str.
ABERDEEN
WILLOWMORE
Market Square
KAAPSTAD
CAPE TOWN
LAINGSBURG
OUDTSHOORN
DURBANVILLE
PAARL
KRAAIFONTEIN
CAPE TOWN
MALMESBURY
Jack Muller Park
Karl Bremer
Voortrekker Rd./-weg
KAAPSTAD
PAROW
UNIVERSITY OF THE WESTERN CAPE
Tygerberg
D.F. MALAN AIRPORT/-LUGHAWE
KUILSRIVIER
BAPSFONTEIN
BUNNY PARK
JOHANNESBURG
PRETORIA
SPRINGS
FAR EAST RAND
WITBANK
Kleinfontein Lake/-meer
Civic Lake
Willowmoore Park
BOKSBURG
GERMISTON
DURBAN
HEIDELBERG
BRAKPAN
Barberton 0 500 m m 69
Beaufort West 0 500 m m 59
Bellville 0 1 km km 58
Benoni 0 1 km km 72

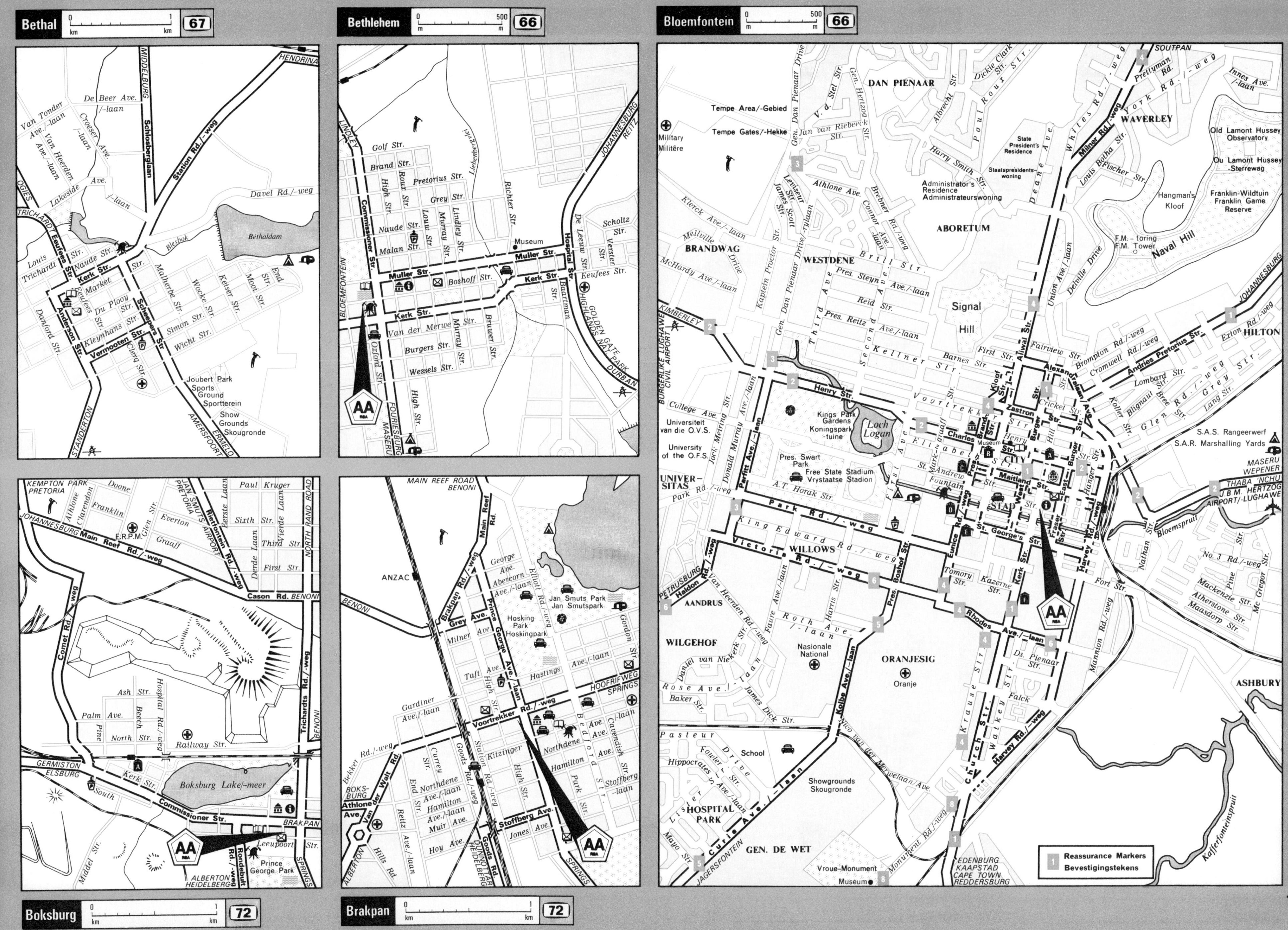
Bethal
67
Bethlehem
66
Bloemfontein
66
Boksburg
72
Brakpan
72
Reassurance Markers
Bevestigingstekens
Naval Hill
Signal Hill
Loch Logan
Bethaldam
Boksburg Lake/-meer

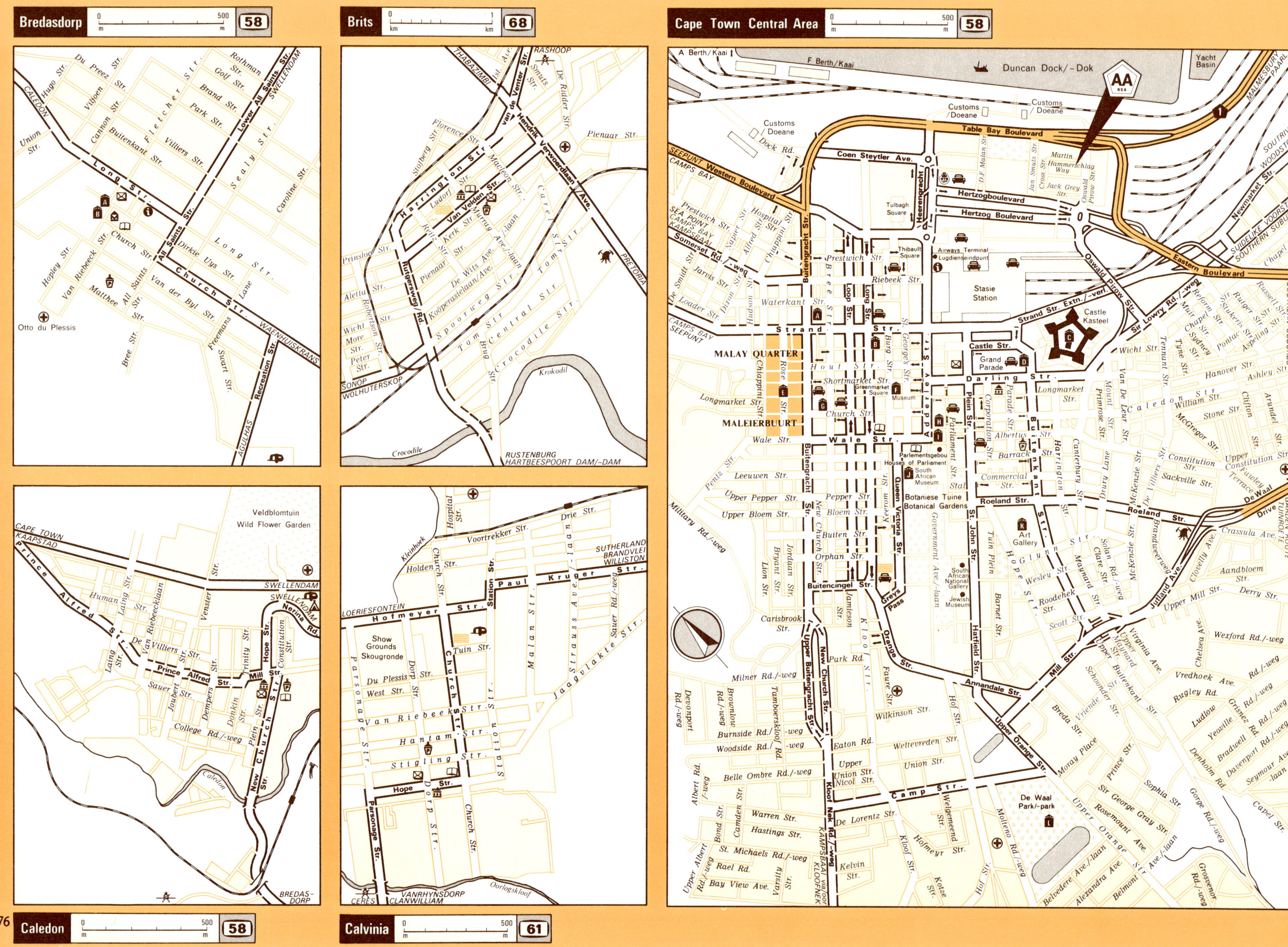
Bredasdorp
58
Brits
68
Cape Town Central Area
58
Caledon
58
Calvinia
61
Duncan Dock/-Dok
Table Bay Boulevard
Eastern Boulevard
Western Boulevard
Castle
Kasteel
Grand Parade
Stasie
Station
MALAY QUARTER
MALEIERBUURT
Houses of Parliament
Parlementsgebou
South African Museum
Botaniese Tuine
Botanical Gardens
Art Gallery
South African National Gallery
Jewish Museum
De Waal Park/-park
Veldblomtuin
Wild Flower Garden
Show Grounds
Skougronde
Otto du Plessis
RUSTENBURG
HARTBEESPOORT DAM/-DAM
PRETORIA
SWELLENDAM
CAPE TOWN
KAAPSTAD
BREDASDORP
LOERIESFONTEIN
SUTHERLAND
BRANDVLEI
WILLISTON
VANRHYNSDORP
CLANWILLIAM
CERES

Cape Town Through-routes

0 1 2 3 4 5 km **58**

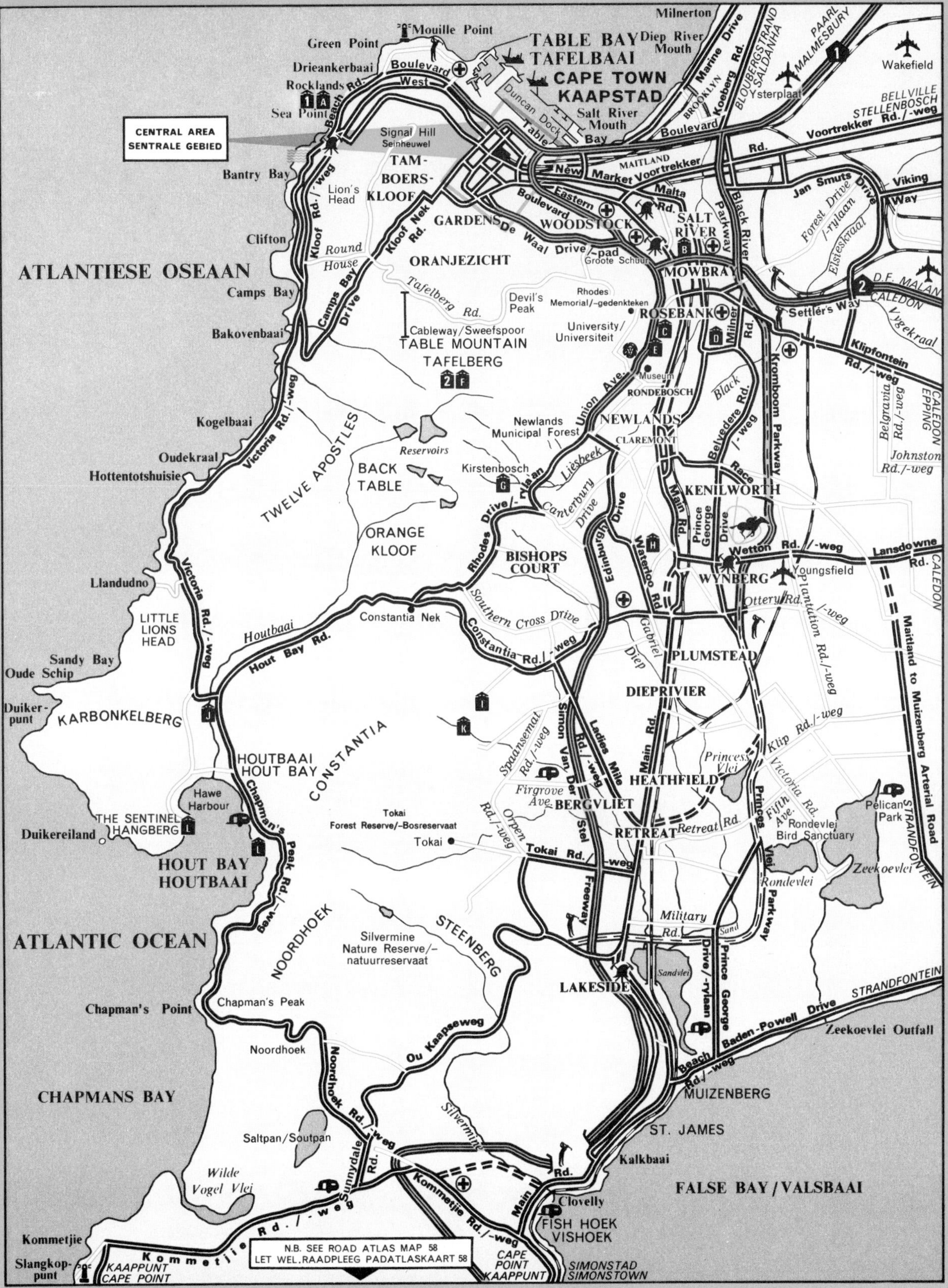

TABLE BAY
TAFELBAAI
CAPE TOWN
KAAPSTAD
Milnerton
Mouille Point
Green Point
Drieankerbaai
Rocklands
Sea Point
Diep River Mouth
Duncan Dock
Salt River Mouth
Bay
Signal Hill
Seinheuwel
CENTRAL AREA
SENTRALE GEBIED
Bantry Bay
Lion's Head
TAMBOERSKLOOF
GARDENS
WOODSTOCK
SALT RIVER
MOWBRAY
ORANJEZICHT
Clifton
ATLANTIESE OSEAAN
Camps Bay
Round House
Tafelberg Rd.
Devil's Peak
Rhodes Memorial/-gedenkteken
University/Universiteit
ROSEBANK
Bakovenbaai
Cableway/Sweefspoor
TABLE MOUNTAIN
TAFELBERG
RONDEBOSCH
Museum
Kogelbaai
Oudekraal
Hottentotshuisie
TWELVE APOSTLES
BACK TABLE
Reservoirs
Kirstenbosch
Newlands Municipal Forest
NEWLANDS
CLAREMONT
KENILWORTH
ORANGE KLOOF
BISHOPS COURT
WYNBERG
Youngsfield
Llandudno
LITTLE LIONS HEAD
Constantia Nek
Southern Cross Drive
PLUMSTEAD
DIEPRIVIER
Sandy Bay
Oude Schip
Duikerpunt
KARBONKELBERG
CONSTANTIA
HOUTBAAI
HOUT BAY
Hawe Harbour
THE SENTINEL
HANGBERG
Duikereiland
HOUT BAY
HOUTBAAI
Tokai Forest Reserve/-Bosreservaat
Tokai
BERGVLIET
HEATHFIELD
RETREAT
Princess Vlei
Rondevlei Bird Sanctuary
Pelican Park
Zeekoevlei
ATLANTIC OCEAN
NOORDHOEK
STEENBERG
Silvermine Nature Reserve/-natuurreservaat
LAKESIDE
Sandvlei
Chapman's Point
Chapman's Peak
Zeekoevlei Outfall
Noordhoek
CHAPMANS BAY
MUIZENBERG
ST. JAMES
Kalkbaai
Saltpan/Soutpan
Wilde Vogel Vlei
FALSE BAY / VALSBAAI
Clovelly
FISH HOEK
VISHOEK
Kommetjie
Slangkoppunt
KAAPPUNT
CAPE POINT
SIMONSTAD
SIMONSTOWN

N.B. SEE ROAD ATLAS MAP 58
LET WEL, RAADPLEEG PADATLASKAART 58

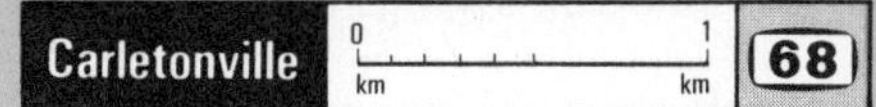

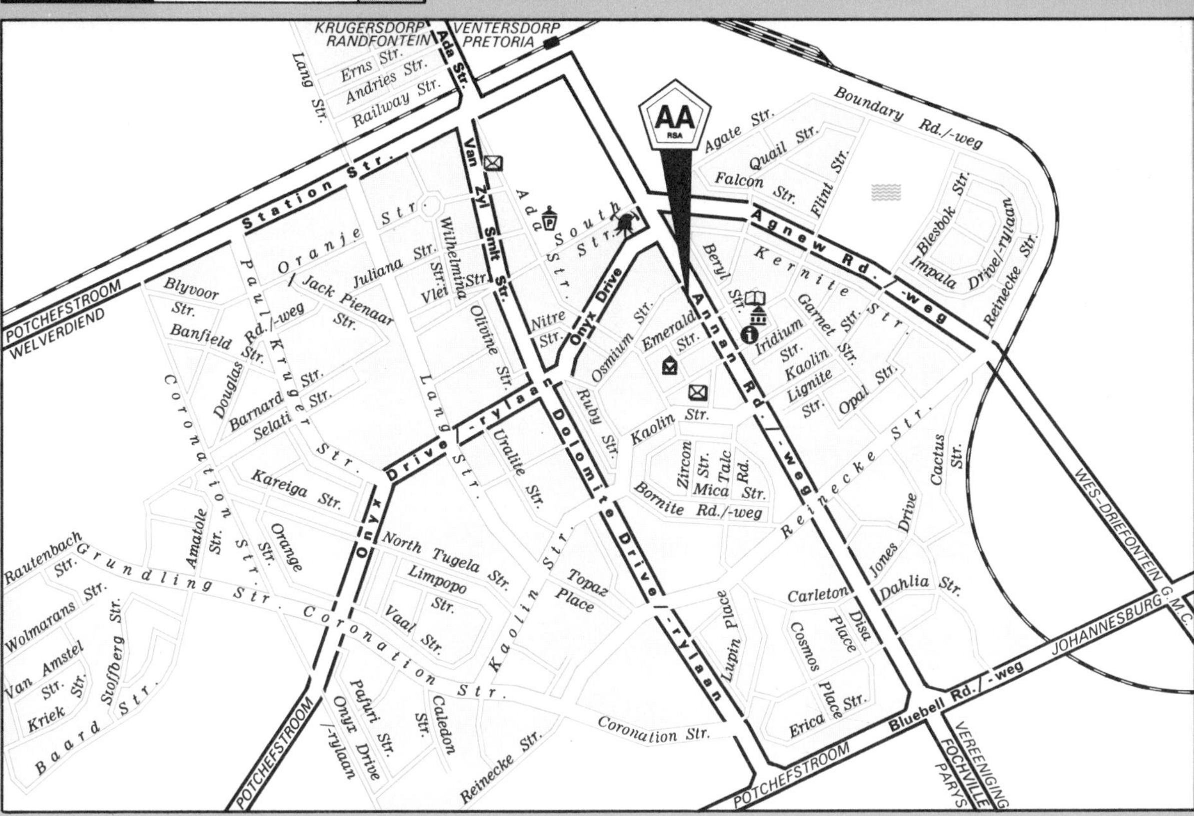

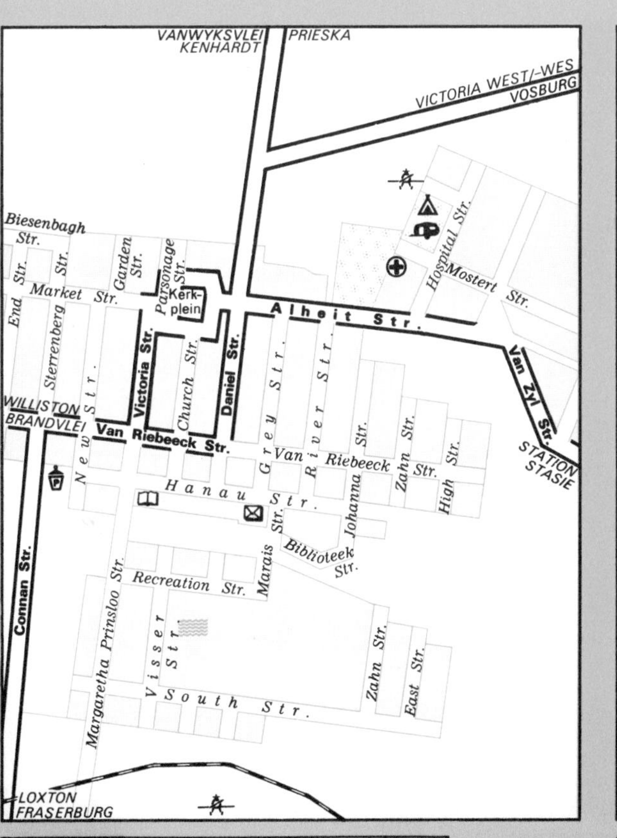

Carnarvon 0 500 m **61**

Carolina 0 500 m **69**

Citrusdal
58
Colesberg
62
Durban Central Area
63
Cradock
59
Darling
58
KRIEDOUWKRANS
Voortrekker Str.
Loop Str.
Oewer Str.
Skool Str.
Kerk Str.
Hoop Str.
Park Str.
Muller Str.
Prinsloo Str.
Orange Str.
Paul de Villiers Str.
Danckaert Str.
De Klerk Str.
Vrede Str.
CERES
BUFFELSHOEK PASS/-PAS
KEEROM
Olifants
NAMAQUALAND
CEDARBERG
CLANWILLIAM
PIKETBERG
EDENBURG
BLOEMFONTEIN
NORVALSPONT
PHILIPSTOWN
STEYNSBURG
H.F. VERWOERD DAM
Station Rd./-weg
Bypass/Verbypad
HANOVER KAAPSTAD
PORT ELIZABETH GEORGE
Church Str.
Campbell Str.
Kemper Museum
Stockenstrom Str.
Charl Cilliers Str.
Murray Str.
Kruger Str.
President Str.
Hofmeyer Str.
Grey Str.
Ventershoek Str.
Sluiters Rd.
Dam
HANOVER CAPE TOWN
PORT ELIZABETH GEORGE
Le Roux Str.
INDIAN OCEAN
INDIESE OSEAAN
NATAL BAY
North Beach
Noordstrand
South Beach
Suidstrand
West Str. Jetty/-kaai
Play Ground
Speelterrein
Cineland
Dolphinarium
Aquarium
Akwarium
Addington
Blood Transfusion Department
Marine Parade
Onder-Marineparade
Lower Marine Parade
Snake Park
Slangpark
Pretpark
Amusement Park
Amfiteater
Queens Park/-park
Shepstone Str.
Quayside Rd./-weg
T Jetty/-kaai
Spoorweggoedereloods
Railways Goods Shed
Playfair Rd./-weg
Brickhill Rd./-weg
Hoy Park
Sports Ground/
-Sportterrein
Stanger Str.
Prince Alfred Str.
Cato Str.
Point Rd./-weg
Landdroshof
Magistrate's Court
S.A.B.C.
S.A.U.K.
Kingsmead Cricket Ground/-Krieketveld
Old Fort Rd./-weg
Ordnance Rd./-weg
Walnut Str.
Victoria Embankment
Mona Rd.
S.A.R. Tourist Bureau
S.A.S-toeristeburo
Airways Terminal
Aliwal Str.
Albany Grove
Museum
Dick King's Statue
N.M.R. Avenue/-laan
City Police
Stadspolisie
City Health Dept.
Warriors Gate
Prior Rd.
Sentrale Stasie Durban
Durban Central Station
Gardiner Str.
Fort Place
Licensing Dept.
Lisensiëringsafdeling
Stadsingenieursafdeling
City Engineer's Department
Wyatt Rd./-weg
Devonshire Place
Small Craft Basin
Kleinvaartuig-bassin
Yacht Mole
Seiljaghawehoof
Railway Station (under construction)
Spoorwegstasie (in aanbou)
Soldiers Way
Field Str.
Pine Str.
Umgeni Rd.
Umgeniweg
Albert Str.
Commercial Rd.
Victoria Kaai
Broad Str.
Royal Durban
R.D.L.I. Hall/-saal
Greyville
Epsom Rd./-weg
Cathedral Rd./-weg
West Street
Weststraat
Russell Str.
AA Technical Centre
AA-Tegniese Sentrum
Albert Park
Albertpark
Alexandra Str.
Park Str.
Centenary Rd./-weg
Plakkersmark
Squatters Market
BEREA ROAD
Municipal Market
Technical College
Warwick Ave./-laan
New Natal Technical College
Sports Ground
Sportterrein
Botanic Gardens
Botaniese Tuine
Sydenham Rd./-weg
PIETERMARITZBURG
PINETOWN
SUIDKUS
SOUTH COAST
UMHLANGA ROCKS
NORTH COAST
NOORDKUS
VERULAM
ESHOWE
DURBAN NORTH/-NOORD
LA LUCIA
HOFMEYR
Sulphur Springs
Swaelbronne
Middelburg Rd.
GRAAFF-REINET MIDDELBURG
MOUNTAIN ZEBRA NAT. PARK
Voortrekker Str.
Hospital Str.
Church Str.
Mortimer Rd./-weg
Groot Vis
Barlow Canal
TARKASTAD
COOKHOUSE
PORT ELIZABETH
SOMERSET-OOS
MORTIMER
YSTERFONTEIN
HOPEFIELD
Arcadia Str.
Voortrekker Str.
Sportterrein
Sports Ground
Main Str.
Fountain Str.
Jacaranda Str.
Hibiscus Str.
Towers Rd./-weg
Langfontein Str.
KAAPSTAD
CAPE TOWN

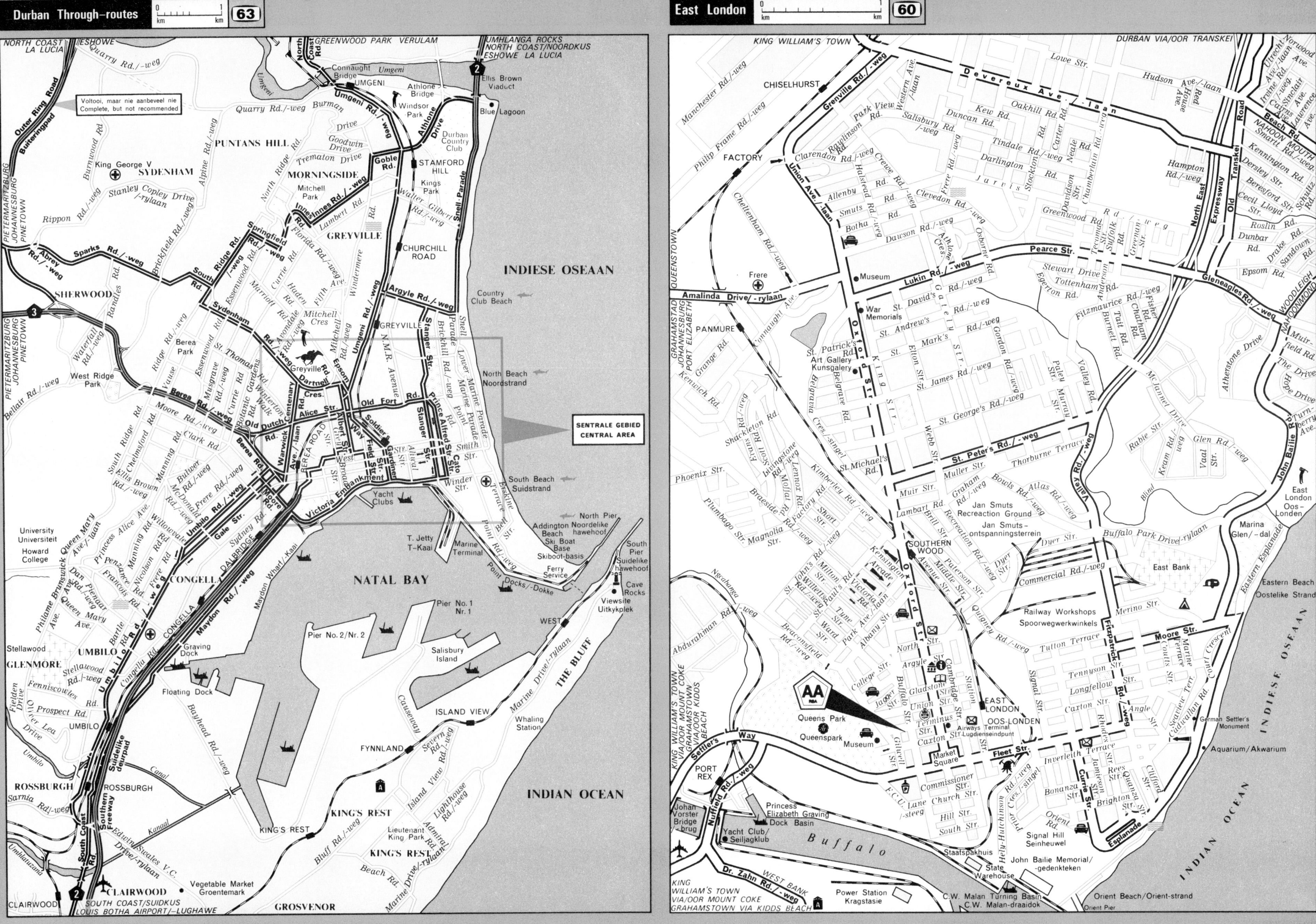
Durban Through-routes
0 1 km km
63
East London
0 1 km km
60
NORTH COAST LA LUCIA
ESHOWE
GREENWOOD PARK VERULAM
UMHLANGA ROCKS NORTH COAST/NOORDKUS ESHOWE LA LUCIA
Connaught Bridge
UMGENI
Ellis Brown Viaduct
Athlone Bridge
Windsor Park
Blue Lagoon
Voltooi, maar nie aanbeveel nie
Complete, but not recommended
Outer Ring Road
Buiteringpad
Quarry Rd./-weg
PUNTANS HILL
King George V
SYDENHAM
MORNINGSIDE
Durban Country Club
STAMFORD HILL
Kings Park
Mitchell Park
GREYVILLE
CHURCHILL ROAD
INDIESE OSEAAN
Country Club Beach
SHERWOOD
Sparks Rd./-weg
Berea Park
West Ridge Park
Greyville
North Beach
Noordstrand
SENTRALE GEBIED
CENTRAL AREA
South Beach
Suidstrand
Yacht Clubs
Victoria Embankment
North Pier
Noordelike hawehoof
Addington Beach
Ski Boat Base
Skiboot-basis
T. Jetty
T-Kaai
Marine Terminal
Ferry Service
Point Docks/-Dokke
South Pier
Suidelike hawehoof
Cave Rocks
Viewsite
Uitkykplek
University Universiteit
Howard College
CONGELLA
NATAL BAY
Pier No. 1 Nr. 1
Pier No. 2/Nr. 2
Salisbury Island
Graving Dock
Floating Dock
Stellawood
UMBILO
GLENMORE
ISLAND VIEW
THE BLUFF
Whaling Station
FYNNLAND
ROSSBURGH
KING'S REST
INDIAN OCEAN
Suidelike deurpad
Southern Freeway
South Coast Rd.
Edwin Swales V.C. Drive/-rylaan
Vegetable Market
Groentemark
CLAIRWOOD
SOUTH COAST/SUIDKUS
LOUIS BOTHA AIRPORT/-LUGHAWE
GROSVENOR
KING WILLIAM'S TOWN
DURBAN VIA/OOR TRANSKEI
CHISELHURST
Devereux Ave./-laan
FACTORY
Frere
Museum
Amalinda Drive/-rylaan
PANMURE
Queenstown
GRAHAMSTAD JOHANNESBURG PORT ELIZABETH
War Memorials
St. Patrick's Rd.
Art Gallery
Kunsgalery
Oxford Str.
Pearce Str.
Lukin Rd./-weg
St. Peter's Rd./-weg
Jan Smuts Recreaction Ground
Jan Smuts-ontspanningsterrein
SOUTHERN WOOD
Buffalo Park Drive/-rylaan
Commercial Rd./-weg
East Bank
Railway Workshops
Spoorwegwerkwinkels
Merino Str.
Moore Str.
East London Oos-Londen
Marina Glen/-dal
Eastern Esplanade
Eastern Beach
Oostelike Strand
NAHOON MOUTH
Queens Park
Queenspark
Museum
EAST LONDON
OOS-LONDEN
Airways Terminal
Lugdienseindpunt
Market Square
Fleet Str.
German Settler's Monument
Aquarium/Akwarium
PORT REX
Settler's Way
Johan Vorster Bridge
-brug
Yacht Club/ Seiljagklub
Princess Elizabeth Graving Dock Basin
Buffalo
Staatspakhuis
State Warehouse
Signal Hill
Seinheuwel
John Bailie Memorial/-gedenkteken
Esplanade
INDIAN OCEAN
INDIESE OSEAAN
Orient Beach/Orient-strand
Orient Pier
WEST BANK
Dr. Zahn Rd./-weg
KING WILLIAM'S TOWN VIA/OOR MOUNT COKE GRAHAMSTOWN VIA KIDDS BEACH
Power Station
Kragstasie
C.W. Malan Turning Basin
C.W. Malan-draaidok

Dundee
0 500
m m
67
Ermelo
0 1
km km
67
Eshowe
0 500
m m
67
Estcourt
0 1
km km
67
Roberts Str.
Pensumons Str.
Evans Str.
Chard Str.
Melville Str.
Coghill Str.
Douglas Str.
Argyll Str.
Browning Str.
Oldacre Str.
Smith Str.
Willson Str.
Union Str.
Gray Str.
Boundary
Beaconsfield Str.
Victoria Str.
VRYHEID
Steenkoolspruit
Museum
Ann Str.
NEWCASTLE
JOHANNESBURG
LADYSMITH
Karel Landman Str.
DURBAN
GLENCOE
Gladstone Str.
Commercial Rd.
Colley
GREYTOWN
McKenzie Str.
Cuthbert Str.
Bulwer Str.
Coronation Str.
WASBANK
Ryley
Tandy Str.
Handley Str.
Thorlund Str.
Comet Str.
Albert Str.
MIDDELBURG
Hospital Str.
Noord Str.
Pet Str.
Cloete Str.
Everard Str.
BREYTEN
Kerk Str.
Fourie Str.
Klein Str.
Lesar Str.
Murray Str.
Jan Van Riebeeck Str.
Burger Str.
Oosthuizen Str.
Robertson Str.
Davel
Sports Ground
Sportterrein
Naude Str.
McCabe Str.
Joubert Str.
Wedgewood Ave.
de Clerq
JOHANNESBURG
STANDERTON
Voëlpark
McDonald
Taute Str.
Joubert Park
Grobler
Smuts Str.
Kleynhans Str.
Border Str.
Buhrman
Jacobs
Jansen
Breytenbach Str.
Voortrekker Ave./-laan
VOLKSRUST
PIET RETIEF
West Str.
Stabb Str.
Curtis Str.
Wantink Rd./-weg
Maddick Str.
Ulundi Str.
Shepstone
Dickens
Hullet
Leigh Str.
Mitchell Str.
Bulwer Str.
Clarke Str.
Bale Ave./-laan
Pearson Str.
Havelock Str.
Brockwell Str.
Kangela Str.
NKANDLA
NTUMENI
Osborn Terrace
VRYHEID
Melmoth Rd.
EMPANGENI
MELMOTH
Dhlinza Forest Nature Reserve
Dhlinza-Bosnatuurreservaat
Natural Arch
Osborn Rd.
Patrick Str.
Tallantire Rd.
Parkins Rd.
Saunders Str.
Addison Str.
Main Str.
John Ross Highway
DURBAN
GINGINDLOVU
LADYSMITH
Harding Str.
Princess Park
Princesspark
Alfred
Alexandra Str.
Princess Str.
LOSKOP
Albert Str.
Connor Str.
Phillip Str.
Victoria Str.
Paterson Str.
Bushmans
Lambert Park
Lambertpark
Lorne Str.
Hellet Rd./-weg
WAGENDRIFT DAM
Martin Rd.
Breitt Rd./-weg
De Waal Drive
Wagen Rd./-weg
Macfarlane Str.
Canon Rogers Rd./-weg
Welsh Rd./-weg
Beechwood Rd.
Alexander Carr Ave.
MOOI RIVER
Roland Hellet Ave./-laan
Joycedale
Heritage Rd.
FOURIESBURG
ROSENDAL
SENEKAL
Keyter Str.
Barry Str.
Hill Str.
Veldt Str.
Taylor Str.
Kloof Str.
Ockert Str.
Brand Str.
Kort Str.
Bester Str.
LADYBRAND
BLOEMFONTEIN
McCabe Str.
Piet Retief Str.
Imperani Str.
Leipoldt Str.
CLOCOLAN
Kerk Str.
Beck Str.
Fontein Str.
Voortrekker Str.
Erwee Str.
Brand Str.
Van Soelen Str.
Toorn Str.
Kestell Str.
Bloem Str.
Villiers Str.
Lang Str.
De Jager Str.
Zon Str.
Visser Str.
Caledon Str.
Ambracht Str.
Bosch Str.
LERIBE
LESOTHO
ROODEPOORT
Daniel Malan Ave./-laan
McInerney Ave.
Lellie Str.
Petunia Str.
Barry Hertzog Drive
Louis Botha Drive/-rylaan
KRUGERSDORP
Chiltern Rd.
Cheriot Rd./-weg
Ontdekkers weg
Olympus Str.
LITTLE FALLS
NORTHCLIFF
BERARIO
Hendrik Potgieter Rd./-weg
Trezonapark
Trezona Park
Tielman Roos Ave.
The High Way
Church Str.
First Ave.
Bertha Ave.
Keith Ave.
Gavin Ave.
Gordon Rd.
Beacon Rd./-weg
Marthinus du Plessis Park
Park Lane
Alexandra Str.
Madeline Str.
Goldman Str.
Tweede Laan
Hull Str.
Die Ou Pad
Ontdekkers weg
JHB
JOHANNESBURG
Negende Laan
New Str.
Rose Str.
FLORIDA
Ruth Str.
Shamrock Str.
Florida Lake/-meer
Vierde Laan
Vyfde Laan
Sixth Ave.
Fourth Ave.
Third Ave.
Ninth Ave.
Rail Str. UNIFIED
MARAISBURG
Maud Str.
Janet Str.
Kathleen Str.
Lola Str.
Naomi Str.
Schoeman Str.
Nadine Str.
Cecil Payne Stadium
Cecil Payne-stadion
Millward Rd.
HOOFRIFWEG
MAIN REEF ROAD
Hebbard Rd.
Spencer Ave.
Charlotte Str.
Victoria Str.
HEALDTOWN
Gray Str.
Somerset Str.
Ordnance Str.
Frazer Str.
Lorenzo Str.
Kat
BALFOUR
SEYMOUR
KATBERG
QUEENSTOWN
John Str.
Durban Str.
Mitchell Str.
ALICE
Museum
Church Str.
Campbell Str.
Henriette Str.
Bell Str.
ADELAIDE
Grahamstown Str.
Victoria Bridge/-brug
Municipal Str.
Parliament Str.
Vigne Str.
Grey Str.
GRAHAMSTAD
GRAHAMSTOWN
Ficksburg
0 500
m m
66
Florida
0 1
km km
72
Fort Beaufort
0 1
km km
60

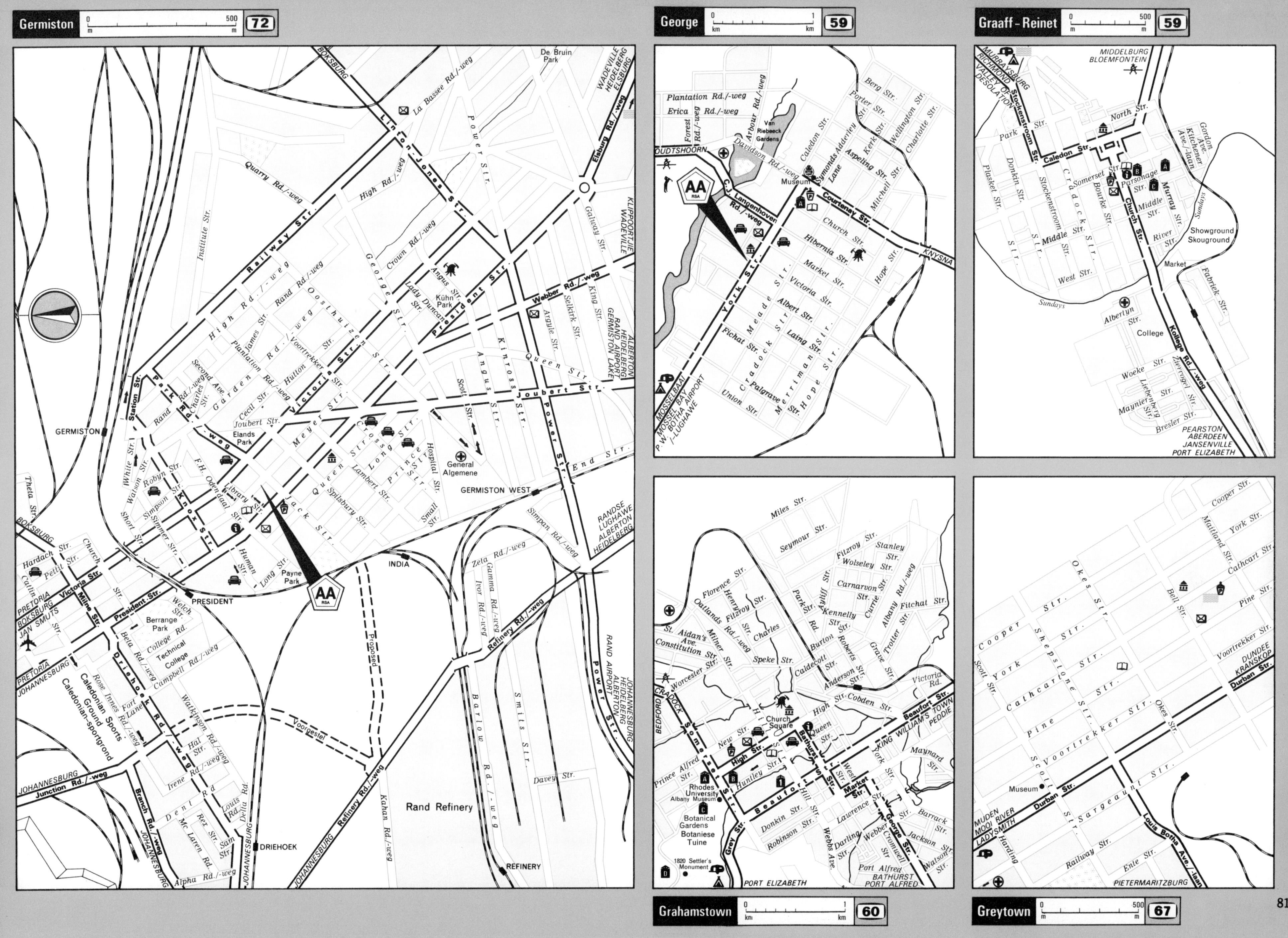

Germiston
0 500 m m
72
George
0 1 km km
59
Graaff-Reinet
0 500 m m
59
Grahamstown
0 1 km km
60
Greytown
0 500 m m
67
GERMISTON
GERMISTON WEST
PRESIDENT
INDIA
DRIEHOEK
REFINERY
Rand Refinery
General Algemene
Elands Park
Kühn Park
Berrange Park
Payne Park
Technical College
Caledonian Sports Ground
Caledonian-sportgrond
De Bruin Park
Railway Str.
Victoria Str.
President Str.
Joubert Str.
Webber Rd./-weg
Power Str.
Lnion Jones Str.
Refinery Rd./-weg
Junction Rd./-weg
Van Riebeeck Gardens
Museum
York Str.
Courtenay Str.
KNYSNA
OUDTSHOORN
MOSSELBAAI
MOSSEL BAY
P.W. BOTHA AIRPORT /-LUGHAWE
MIDDELBURG
BLOEMFONTEIN
Showground
Skougrond
Market
College
Caledon Str.
Church Str.
Kollege Rd./-weg
PEARSTON
ABERDEEN
JANSENVILLE
PORT ELIZABETH
Rhodes University
Albany Museum
Botanical Gardens
Botaniese Tuine
Church Square
1820 Settler's Monument
High Str.
Beaufort Str.
KING WILLIAM'S TOWN
PEDDIE
PORT ELIZABETH
Port Alfred
BATHURST
PORT ALFRED
Museum
Durban Str.
Voortrekker Str.
Louis Botha Ave./-laan
DUNDEE
KRANSKOP
PIETERMARITZBURG
MUDEN
MOOI RIVER
LADYSMITH

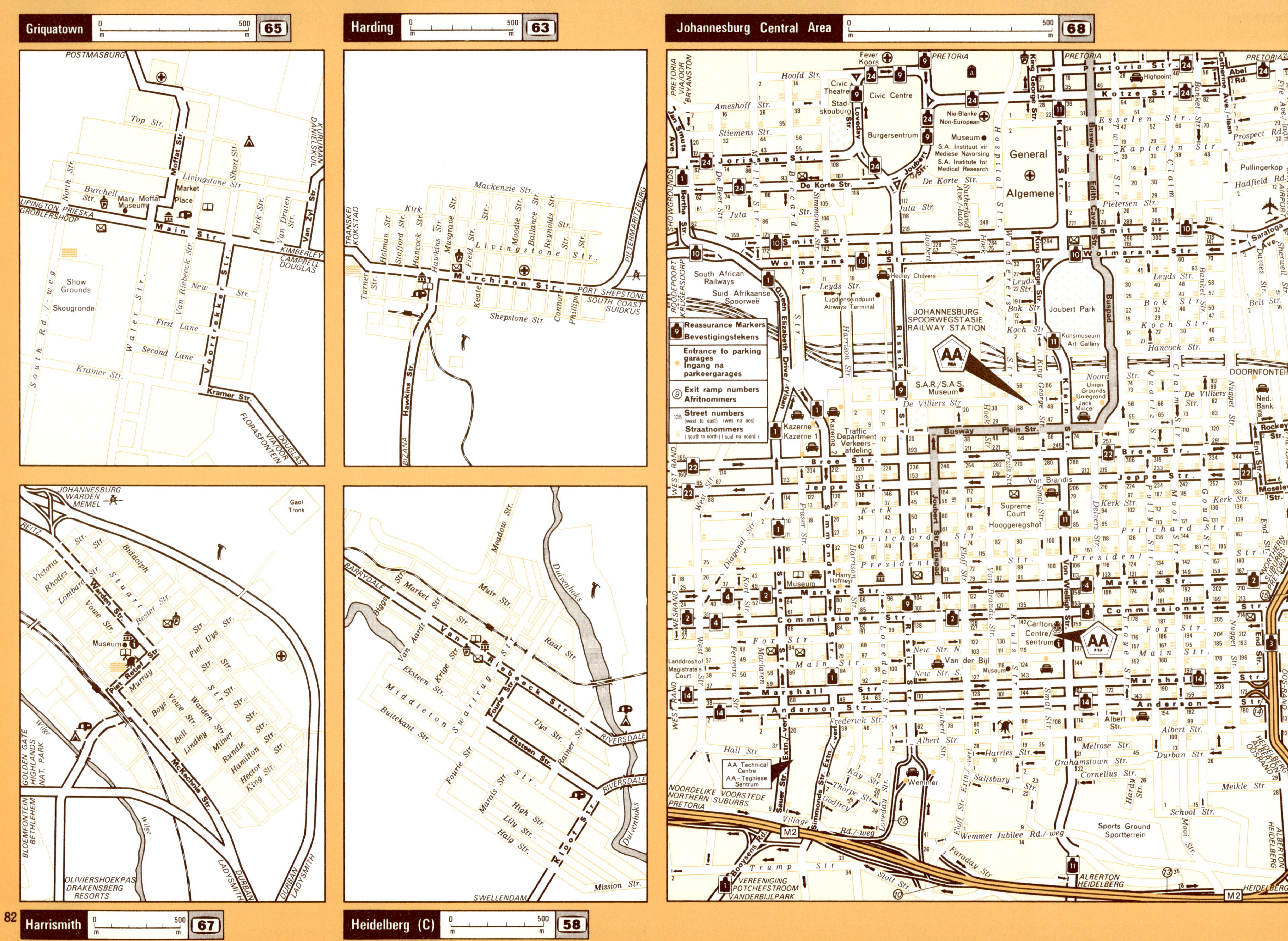
Griquatown
0
500
m
m
65
POSTMASBURG
Top Str.
Moffat Str.
Short Str.
KURUMAN
DANIELSKUIL
North Str.
Livingstone Str.
Burchell Str.
Mary Moffat Museum
Market Place
Park Str.
Van Druten Str.
Van Zyl Str.
UPINGTON PRIESKA
GROBLERSHOOP
Main Str.
KIMBERLEY
CAMPBELL
DOUGLAS
Show Grounds
Skougronde
South Rd./-weg
Water Str.
Van Riebeeck Str.
New Str.
Voortrekker Str.
First Lane
Second Lane
Kramer Str.
FLORASFONTEIN
VIA/OOR
DOUGLAS
Harding
0
500
m
m
63
Mackenzie Str.
TRANSKEI
KOKSTAD
Kirk Str.
Holman Str.
Stafford Str.
Hancock Str.
Hawkins Str.
Musgrave Str.
Field Str.
Livingstone Str.
Moodie Str.
Ballance Str.
Reynolds Str.
PIETERMARITZBURG
Turner Str.
Murchison Str.
Keate Str.
PORT SHEPSTONE
SOUTH COAST
SUIDKUS
Shepstone Str.
Connor Str.
Phillips Str.
Hawkins Str.
BIZANA
Johannesburg Central Area
0
500
m
m
68
PRETORIA
VIA/OOR
BRYANSTON
Fever Koors
Hoofd Str.
Civic Theatre
Stad-skouburg
Civic Centre
Burgersentrum
Loveday Str.
Ameshoff Str.
Stiemens Str.
Jan Smuts Ave.
Jorissen Str.
Nie-Blanke Non-European
Museum
S.A. Instituut vir Mediese Navorsing
S.A. Institute for Medical Research
General
Algemene
Hospital Str.
King George Str.
Klein Str.
Edith Cavell Str.
Busway
Pretoria Str.
Highpoint
Kotze Str.
Esselen Str.
Kapteijn Str.
Claim Str.
Banket Str.
Catherine Ave./-laan
Abel Rd.
Fife Ave./-laan
Prospect Rd.
Pullingerkop
Hadfield Rd.
JAN SMUTS AIRPORT
De Korte Str.
De Beer Str.
Juta Str.
Bertha Str.
Melle Str.
Biccard Str.
Simmonds Str.
Joubert Str.
Sutherland Ave./-laan
Pietersen Str.
Smit Str.
Wolmarans Str.
Saratoga Ave.
Davies Str.
Sherwell Str.
Beit Str.
SHOWGROUNDS
ROODEPOORT
KRUGERSDORP
South African Railways
Suid-Afrikaanse Spoorweë
Leyds Str.
Hedley Chilvers
Lugdienseindpunt
Airways Terminal
Queen Elizabeth Drive/-rylaan
Harrison Str.
Rissik Str.
JOHANNESBURG
SPOORWEGSTASIE
RAILWAY STATION
Wanderers Str.
Bok Str.
Koch Str.
Joubert Park
Kunsmuseum
Art Gallery
Buspad
Hancock Str.
Quartz Str.
DOORNFONTEIN
Reassurance Markers
Bevestigingstekens
Entrance to parking garages
Ingang na parkeergarages
Exit ramp numbers
Afritnommers
Street numbers
(west to east) (wes na oos)
Straatnommers
(south to north) (suid na noord)
S.A.R./S.A.S. Museum
Noord Str.
Union Grounds
Uniegrond
Jack Mincer
De Villiers Str.
Nugget Str.
Ned. Bank
Rockey Str.
Kazerne
Traffic Department
Verkeers-afdeling
Busway
Plein Str.
Hoek Str.
Bree Str.
Jeppe Str.
Von Brandis Str.
Kruis Str.
Small Str.
Supreme Court
Hooggeregshof
Delvers Str.
Polly Str.
Kerk Str.
Moseley Str.
WEST RAND
West Str.
Fraser Str.
Diagonal Str.
Pritchard Str.
President Str.
Harry Hofmeyr
Museum
Market Str.
Kort Str.
Sauer Str.
Commissioner Str.
Fox Str.
Main Str.
Marshall Str.
Anderson Str.
Carlton Centre/-sentrum
Von Wielligh Str.
End Str.
Goud Str.
Mooi Str.
New Str. N.
New Str. S.
Van der Bijl
Landdroshof
Magistrate's Court
Ferreira Str.
MacLaren Str.
Frederick Str.
Albert Str.
Harries Str.
Melrose Str.
Grahamstown Str.
Cornelius Str.
Hardy Str.
Durban Str.
Meikle Str.
School Str.
Hall Str.
AA Technical Centre
AA-Tegniese Sentrum
Sauer Str. Extn./-verl.
Simmonds Str. Extn./-verl.
Kay Str.
Thorpe Str.
Godfrey Str.
Wemmer
Salisbury Str.
Eloff Str. Extn./-verl.
NOORDELIKE VOORSTEDE
NORTHERN SUBURBS
PRETORIA
Village Rd./-weg
Booysens Rd.
M2
Wemmer Jubilee Rd./-weg
Sports Ground
Sportterrein
Trump Str.
Faraday Str.
Stott Str.
ALBERTON
HEIDELBERG
VEREENIGING
POTCHEFSTROOM
VANDERBIJLPARK
HEIDELBERG
ALBERTON
OOSRAND
EAST RAND
NORTHERN SUBURBS
PRETORIA
Harrismith
0
500
m
m
67
JOHANNESBURG
WARDEN
MEMEL
Gaol
Tronk
REITZ
Victoria Str.
Rhodes Str.
Lombard Str.
Warden Str.
Vowe Str.
Stuart Str.
Biddulph Str.
Bester Str.
Museum
Piet Uys Str.
Piet Retief Str.
Murray Str.
Boys Str.
Bell Str.
Lindley Str.
Milner Str.
Rundle Str.
Hamilton Str.
Hector Str.
King Str.
McKechnie Str.
Wilge
GOLDEN GATE
HIGHLANDS
NAT. PARK
BLOEMFONTEIN
BETHLEHEM
OLIVIERSHOEKPAS
DRAKENSBERG
RESORTS
LADYSMITH
DURBAN
Heidelberg (C)
0
500
m
m
58
Meadow Str.
BARRYDALE
Market Str.
Biggs Str.
Muir Str.
Duivenhoks
Van Aardt Str.
Van Riebeeck Str.
Raal Str.
Eksteen Str.
Krige Str.
Middleton Str.
Swartrug Str.
Fourie Str.
Buitekant Str.
Uys Str.
Ratmer Str.
RIVERSDALE
Marais Str.
High Str.
Lily Str.
Haig Str.
Kloof Str.
SWELLENDAM
Mission Str.

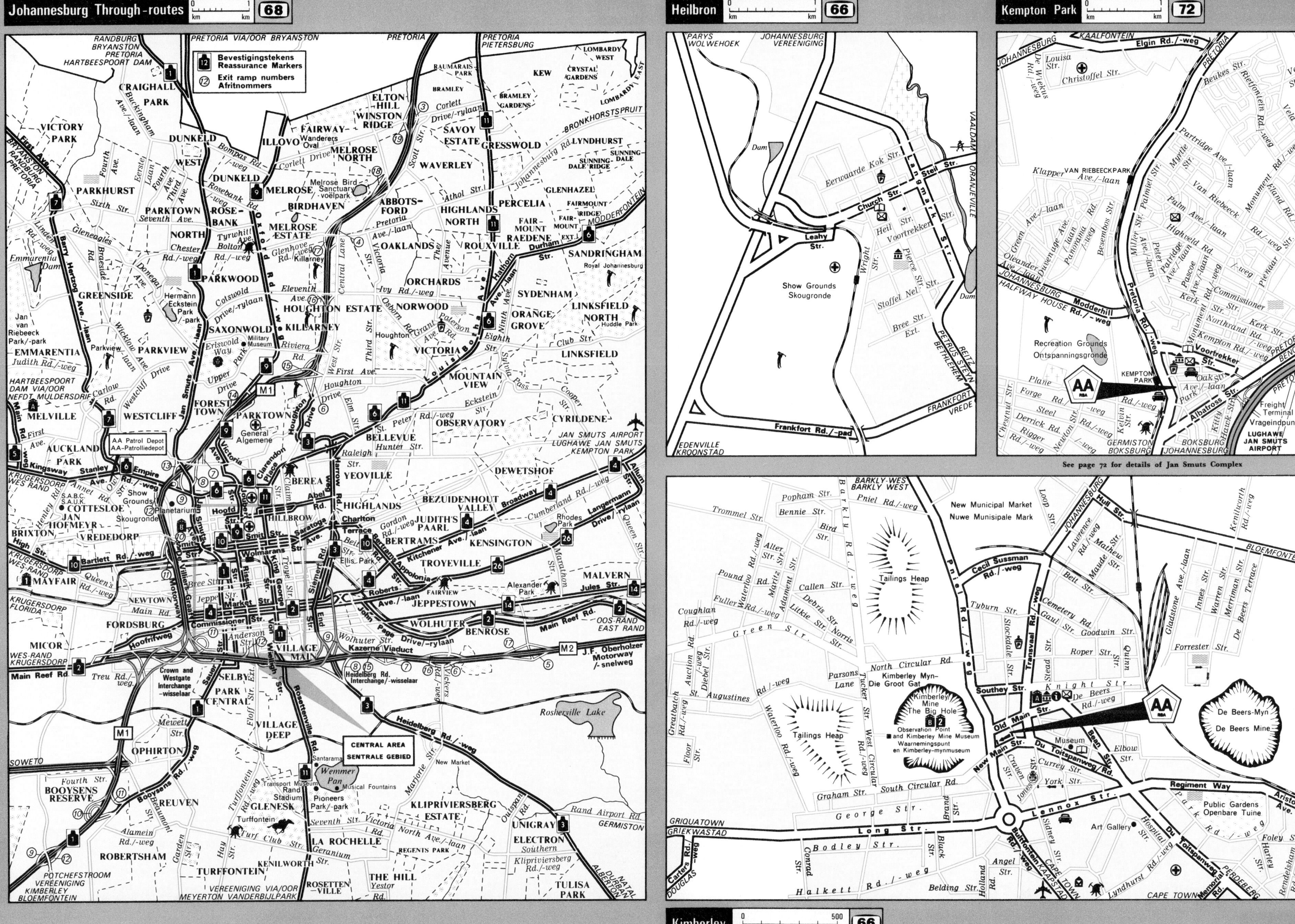
Johannesburg Through-routes
68
Bevestigingstekens Reassurance Markers
Exit ramp numbers Afritnommers
RANDBURG
BRYANSTON
PRETORIA
HARTBEESPOORT DAM
PRETORIA VIA/OOR BRYANSTON
PRETORIA PIETERSBURG
CRAIGHALL PARK
VICTORY PARK
DUNKELD WEST
DUNKELD
ILLOVO
FAIRWAY
Wanderers Oval
ELTON HILL
WINSTON RIDGE
MELROSE NORTH
SAVOY ESTATE
GRESSWOLD
WAVERLEY
KEW
LOMBARDY WEST
LOMBARDY EAST
BRAMLEY
BRAMLEY GARDENS
CRYSTAL GARDENS
RAUMARAIS PARK
LYNDHURST
SUNNINGDALE
SUNNING-DALE RIDGE
BRONKHORSTSPRUIT
PARKHURST
PARKTOWN NORTH
ROSEBANK
MELROSE
Melrose Bird Sanctuary/-voëlpark
BIRDHAVEN
MELROSE ESTATE
ABBOTSFORD
HIGHLANDS NORTH
PERCELIA
GLENHAZEL
FAIRMOUNT RIDGE
FAIRMOUNT
RAEDENE
ROUXVILLE
SANDRINGHAM
Royal Johannesburg
MODDERFONTEIN
Emmarentia Dam
GREENSIDE
PARKWOOD
Hermann Eckstein Park/-park
SAXONWOLD
Military Museum
KILLARNEY
HOUGHTON ESTATE
OAKLANDS
ORCHARDS
NORWOOD
SYDENHAM
ORANGE GROVE
LINKSFIELD NORTH
Huddle Park
LINKSFIELD
Jan van Riebeeck Park/-park
EMMARENTIA
PARKVIEW
VICTORIA
MOUNTAIN VIEW
HARTBEESPOORT DAM VIA/OOR NEFDT MULDERSDRIF
MELVILLE
WESTCLIFF
FOREST TOWN
PARKTOWN
General Algemene
OBSERVATORY
CYRILDENE
JAN SMUTS AIRPORT
LUGHAWE JAN SMUTS
KEMPTON PARK
AA Patrol Depot
AA-Patrolliedepot
AUCKLAND PARK
BELLEVUE
YEOVILLE
BEREA
DEWETSHOF
KRUGERSDORP WES RAND
S.A.B.C. S.A.U.K.
Show Grounds Skougronde
Planetarium
COTTESLOE
JAN HOFMEYR
BRIXTON
VREDEDORP
HILLBROW
HIGHLANDS
BEZUIDENHOUT VALLEY
JUDITH'S PAARL
BERTRAMS
KENSINGTON
Rhodes Park
TROYEVILLE
Ellis Park
FAIRVIEW
Alexander Park
MALVERN
MAYFAIR
NEWTOWN
JEPPESTOWN
KRUGERSDORP FLORIDA
FORDSBURG
WOLHUTER
BENROSE
OOS-RAND EAST RAND
MICOR
WES-RAND KRUGERSDORP
VILLAGE MAIN
J.F. Oberholzer Motorway/-snelweg
Crown and Westgate Interchange -wisselaar
Heidelberg Rd. Interchange/-wisselaar
SELBY
PARK CENTRAL
Rosherville Lake
VILLAGE DEEP
CENTRAL AREA
SENTRALE GEBIED
OPHIRTON
SOWETO
New Market
BOOYSENS RESERVE
Santarama
Wemmer Pan
Transport Museum
Musical Fountains
Rand Stadium
Pioneers Park/-park
REUVEN
GLENESK
Turffontein
KLIPRIVIERSBERG ESTATE
Rand Airport Rd.
GERMISTON
UNIGRAY
ELECTRON
ROBERTSHAM
Turf Club
REGENTS PARK
LA ROCHELLE
TURFFONTEIN
KENILWORTH
POTCHEFSTROOM VEREENIGING KIMBERLEY BLOEMFONTEIN
VEREENIGING VIA/OOR MEYERTON VANDERBIJLPARK
ROSETTENVILLE
THE HILL
TULISA PARK
NATAL DURBAN ALBERTON
Heilbron
66
PARYS WOLWEHOEK
JOHANNESBURG VEREENIGING
Dam
Erwaarde Kok Str.
Langmark Str.
Steil Str.
Church Str.
Leahy Str.
Heil Str.
Voortrekker Str.
Pierce Str.
Stoffel Nel Str.
Bree Str. Ext.
Show Grounds Skougronde
VAALDAM ORANJEVILLE
REITZ PETRUS STEYN BETHLEHEM
FRANKFORT VREDE
Frankfort Rd./-pad
EDENVILLE KROONSTAD
Kempton Park
72
KAALFONTEIN
Elgin Rd./-weg
JOHANNESBURG
PRETORIA
Christoffel Str.
VAN RIEBEECKPARK
Recreation Grounds Ontspanningsgronde
KEMPTON PARK
JOHANNESBURG HALFWAY HOUSE
Modderhill Rd./-weg
Voortrekker Str.
Albatross Str.
Freight Terminal Vragaindpunt
LUGHAWE JAN SMUTS AIRPORT
GERMISTON BOKSBURG
BOKSBURG JOHANNESBURG
BENONI
See page 72 for details of Jan Smuts Complex
BARKLY-WES BARKLY WEST
New Municipal Market
Nuwe Munisipale Mark
Tailings Heap
Cecil Sussman Rd./-weg
BLOEMFONTEIN
Kimberley Myn-Die Groot Gat
Kimberley Mine The Big Hole
Observation Point and Kimberley Mine Museum
Waarnemingspunt en Kimberley-mynmuseum
De Beers-Myn
De Beers Mine
North Circular Rd.
South Circular Rd.
Regiment Way
Public Gardens Openbare Tuine
Art Gallery
Long Str.
GRIQUATOWN GRIEKWASTAD
DOUGLAS
CAPE TOWN KAAPSTAD
PERDEBERG
Kimberley
66

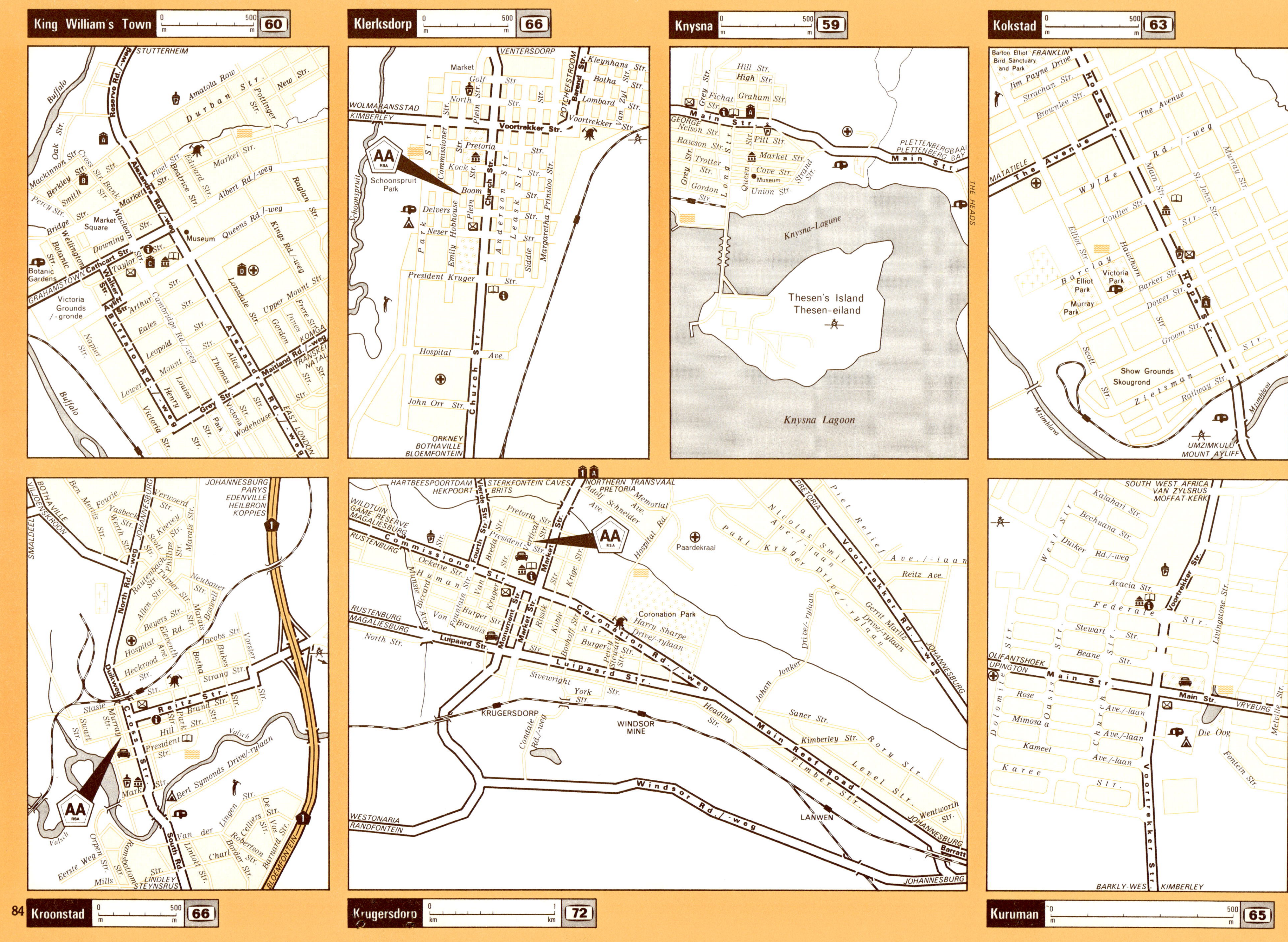

King William's Town
0 500 m m
60
STUTTERHEIM
Buffalo
Reserve Rd./-weg
Amatola Row
Durban Str.
New Str.
Pottinger Str.
Oak Str.
Mackinnon Str.
Berkley Str.
Smith Str.
Percy Str.
Cross Str.
Bank Str.
Fleet Str.
Beatrice Str.
Edward Str.
Market Str.
Alexandra Rd./-weg
Albert Rd./-weg
Raglan Str.
Bridge Str.
Market Square
Wellington Str.
Maclean Str.
Museum
Queens Rd./-weg
Kings Rd./-weg
Downing Str.
Botanic Str.
Botanic Gardens
Taylor Str.
Cathcart Str.
GRAHAMSTOWN
Victoria Grounds /-gronde
Walter Str.
Ayliff Str.
Arthur Str.
Cambridge Str.
Lonsdale Str.
Upper Mount Str.
Frere Str.
Eales Str.
Gordon Str.
Innes Str.
Napier Str.
Leopold Str.
Rd./-weg
Mount Str.
Alice Str.
Thomas Str.
Maitland Rd./-weg
KOMGA TRANSKEI NATAL
Buffalo Rd./-weg
Lower Str.
Louisa Str.
Henry Str.
Grey Str.
Victoria Str.
Park Str.
Wodehouse Str.
EAST LONDON
Klerksdorp
0 500 m m
66
VENTERSDORP
Market
Golf Str.
North Str.
Plein Str.
POTCHEFSTROOM
Barend Str.
Kleynhans Str.
Botha Str.
Lombard Str.
Van Zyl Str.
Voortrekker Str.
WOLMARANSSTAD
KIMBERLEY
Commissioner Str.
Pretoria Str.
Kock Str.
Church Str.
Anderson Str.
Leask Str.
Prinsloo Str.
Schoonspruit Park
Schoonspruit
Boom Str.
Delvers Str.
Neser Str.
Emily Hobhouse Str.
Park Str.
Siddle Str.
Margaretha Prinsloo Str.
President Kruger Str.
Hospital Ave.
John Orr Str.
ORKNEY
BOTHAVILLE
BLOEMFONTEIN
Knysna
0 500 m m
59
Hill Str.
High Str.
Graham Str.
Fichat Str.
Main Str.
GEORGE
Nelson Str.
Rawson Str.
Pitt Str.
Trotter Str.
Market Str.
Grey Str.
Long Str.
Queen Str.
Cove Str.
Museum
Strand Str.
Gordon Str.
Union Str.
PLETTENBERGBAAI
PLETTENBERG BAY
THE HEADS
Knysna-Lagune
Thesen's Island
Thesen-eiland
Knysna Lagoon
Kokstad
0 500 m m
63
Barton Elliot Bird Sanctuary and Park
FRANKLIN
Jim Payne Drive
Strachan Str.
Brownlee Str.
Hope Str.
The Avenue
MATATIELE
The Avenue
Rd./-weg
Murray Str.
Wylde
Main Str.
St. John Str.
Coulter Str.
Elliot Str.
Hawthorn
Barclay
Elliot Park
Victoria Park
Murray Park
Barker Str.
Dower Str.
Groom Str.
Scott Str.
Show Grounds
Skougrond
Zietsman
Railway Str.
Mzimhlava
UMZIMKULU
MOUNT AYLIFF
Kroonstad
0 500 m m
66
BOTHAVILLE
VILJOENSKROON
SMALDEEL
JOHANNESBURG PARYS EDENVILLE HEILBRON KOPPIES
Ben Meiring Str.
Fourie Str.
Yasbeck Str.
Werth Str.
Verwoerd Str.
Keevey Str.
Scott Str.
Phillips Str.
Marais Str.
North Rd./-weg
Rautenbach Str.
Turner Str.
Neubauer Str.
Allen Str.
Beyers Str.
Rd.
Boswell Str.
Hospital
Heckrood Str.
Eleventh Ave.
Jacobs Str.
Bukes Str.
Vorster Str.
Botha Str.
Strang Str.
Duik-weg
Reitz Str.
Staste Str.
Stuart Str.
Murray Str.
Cross Str.
Brand Str.
Park Str.
Hill Str.
President Str.
Valsch
Bert Symonds Drive/-rylaan
Mark
De Vos Str.
Van der Lingen Str.
Celliers Str.
Robertson Str.
Border Str.
Barnard Str.
Charl
South Rd.
Lintott Str.
Orpen Str.
Eerste Weg
Mills
Rumbottom Str.
LINDLEY STEYNSRUS
BLOEMFONTEIN
Krugersdorp
0 1 km km
72
HARTBEESPOORTDAM HEKPOORT
STERKFONTEIN CAVES BRITS
NORTHERN TRANSVAAL PRETORIA
Adolf Schneider Ave.
Memorial Ave.
WILDTUIN GAME RESERVE MAGALIESBURG
RUSTENBURG
Commissioner Str.
Pretoria Str.
Vierde Str.
Fourth Str.
Breda Str.
President Str.
Vertical Str.
Market Str.
Krige Str.
Hospital Rd.
Paardekraal
Paul Kruger Str.
Nicolaas Smit Ave./-laan
Piet Retief Ave./-laan
Reitz Ave.
PRETORIA
Ockerse Str.
Human Str.
Munnik Ave.
Biccard Ave.
Fountain Str.
Van Str.
Kruger Str.
Von Brandis Str.
Burger Str.
Monument Str.
Rissik Str.
Kobie Str.
Boshoff Str.
Coronation Rd./-weg
Coronation Park
Harry Sharpe Drive/-rylaan
Drive/-rylaan
Voortrekker Rd./-weg
Gerrit Maritz Drive/-rylaan
JOHANNESBURG
RUSTENBURG MAGALIESBURG
North Str.
Luipaard Str.
Percy Stewart Str.
Burger Str.
Luipaard Str.
Sivewright
York Str.
Johan Jonker
Heading Str.
KRUGERSDORP
WINDSOR MINE
Condale Rd./-weg
Saner Str.
Kimberley Str.
Rory Str.
Main Reef Road
Level Str.
Timber Str.
Windsor Rd./-weg
Wentworth Str.
WESTONARIA RANDFONTEIN
LANWEN
JOHANNESBURG
Barratt
JOHANNESBURG
Kuruman
0 500 m m
65
SOUTH WEST AFRICA VAN ZYLSRUS MOFFAT-KERK
Kalahari Str.
Bechuana Str.
West Str.
Duiker Rd./-weg
Voortrekker Str.
Acacia Str.
Federale Str.
Livingstone Str.
Stewart Str.
Beane Str.
OLIFANTSHOEK UPINGTON
Main Str.
Main Str.
VRYBURG
Melville Str.
Rose
Oasis Str.
Church Ave./-laan
Dolomite Str.
Mimosa
Ave./-laan
Die Oog
Kameel
Ave./-laan
Fontein Str.
Karee
Str.
Voortrekker Str.
BARKLY-WES
KIMBERLEY

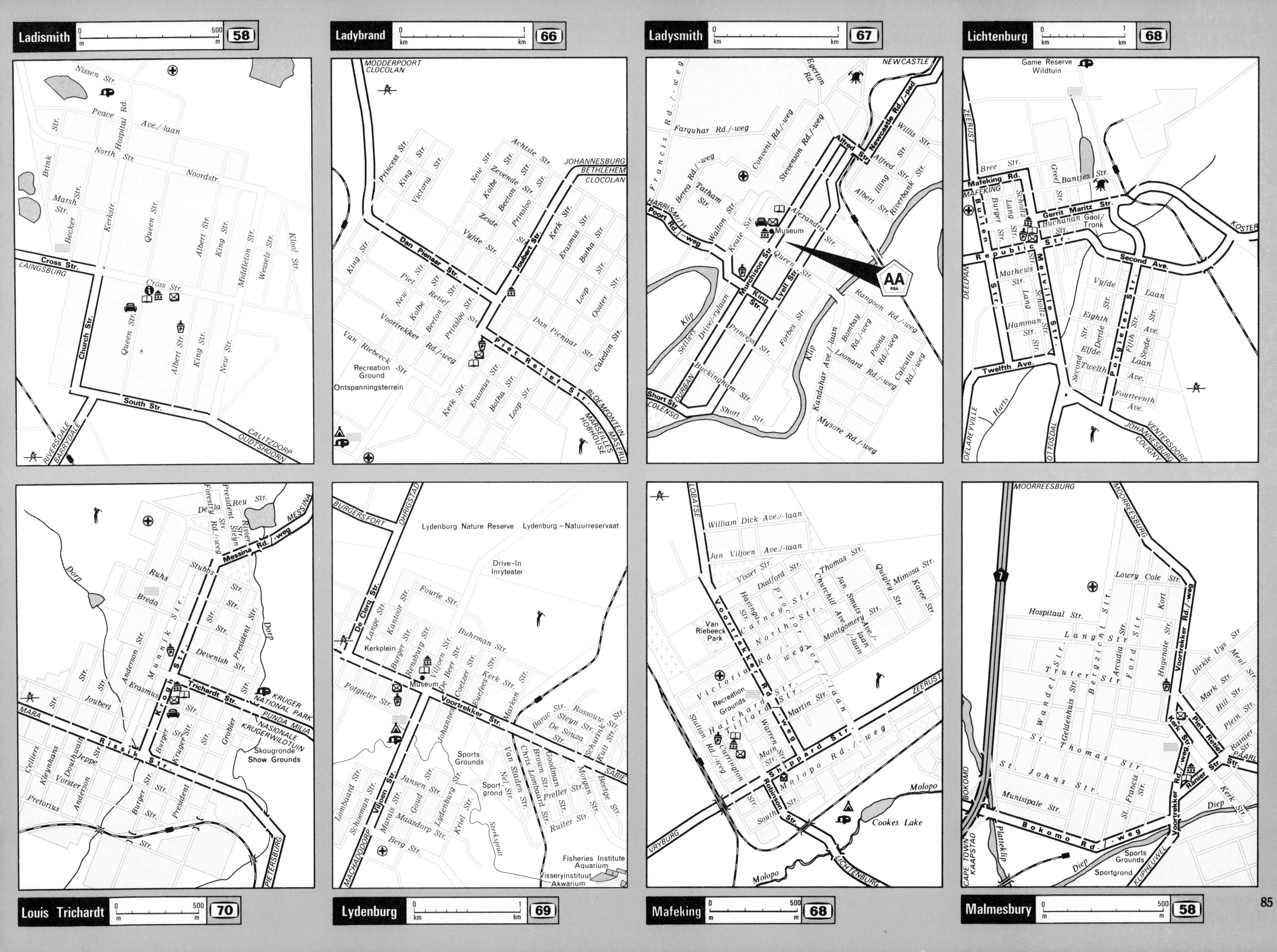
Ladismith 0 500 m m 58
Nissen Str.
Peace Ave./-laan
Hospital Rd.
North Str.
Noordstr.
Brink Str.
Marsh Str.
Becker
Kerkstr.
Queen Str.
Albert Str.
King Str.
Middleton Str.
Wessels Str.
Kloof Str.
Cross Str.
LAINGSBURG
Church Str.
Albert Str.
King Str.
New Str.
South Str.
CALITZDORP
OUDTSHOORN
RIVERSDALE
BARRYDALE
Ladybrand 0 1 km km 66
MODDERPOORT
CLOCOLAN
JOHANNESBURG
BETHLEHEM
CLOCOLAN
Princess Str.
King Str.
Victoria Str.
Achtste Str.
New Str.
Kolbe Str.
Zevende Str.
Beeton Str.
Prinsloo Str.
Zesde
Vyfde Str.
Joubert Str.
Kerk Str.
Erasmus Str.
Botha Str.
Dan Pienaar Str.
King Str.
Piet Retief Str.
New Kolbe Beeton Prinsloo Str.
Voortrekker Rd./-weg
Van Riebeeck Str.
Recreation Ground
Ontspanningsterrein
Dan Pienaar Str.
Loop Str.
Oosler Str.
Caledon Str.
Kerk Str.
Erasmus Str.
Botha Str.
Loop Str.
BLOEMFONTEIN
MASERU
MARSEILLES
HOBHOUSE
Ladysmith 0 1 km km 67
NEWCASTLE
Egerton Rd.
Francis Rd./-weg
Farquhar Rd./-weg
Convent Rd./-weg
Stevenson Rd./-weg
Alfred Str.
Newcastle Rd./-pad
Willis Str.
Alfred Str.
Illing Str.
Albert Str.
Riverbank Str.
Berea Rd./-weg
Tatham Str.
Walton Str.
HARRISMITH
Poort Rd./-weg
Alexandra Str.
Museum
Keate Str.
Murchison Str.
Queen Str.
King Str.
Lyell Str.
AA RSA
Rangoon Rd./-weg
Klip
Settlers Drive/-rylaan
Princess Str.
Forbes Str.
Bombay Rd./-weg
Poona Rd./-weg
Kandahar Ave./-laan
Leonard Rd./-weg
Calcutta Rd./-weg
Buckingham Str.
Short Str.
DURBAN
COLENSO
Short Str.
Mysore Rd./-weg
Lichtenburg 0 1 km km 68
Game Reserve
Wildtuin
ZEERUST
Bree Str.
Greef Str.
Bantjes Str.
Mafeking Rd.
MAFEKING
Burger Str.
Lang Str.
Scholtz Str.
Gerrit Maritz Str.
Buchanan Str.
Gaol/Tronk
Buiten Str.
Republic Str.
KOSTER
Second Ave.
Mathews Str.
Lang Str.
Hamman Str.
Melville Str.
Scholtz Str.
Vyfde Str.
Potgieter Str.
Laan
Eighth Str.
Fifth Ave.
Sesde Laan
Elfde Str.
Derde Str.
Second Ave.
Twelth Ave.
Fourteenth Ave.
DEELPAN
Twelfth Ave.
Harts
DELAREYVILLE
OTTOSDAL
JOHANNESBURG
COLIGNY
VENTERSDORP
Louis Trichardt 0 500 m m 70
Forestry Rd./-weg
President Str.
Rey Str.
De la Rey Str.
Steyn Str.
Rivier Str.
Messina Rd./-weg
MESSINA
Dorp
Ruhs
Stubbs
Breda
Munnik Str.
Str.
Str.
Str.
President Str.
Dorp
Anderson Str.
Devenish Str.
Krogh Str.
Erasmus
Trichardt Str.
KRUGER NATIONAL PARK
Joubert
PUNDA MILIA
NASIONALE KRUGERWILDTUIN
Skougronde
Show Grounds
MARA
Rissik Str.
Celliers
Kleynhans
Douthwaite
Jeppe Str.
Vorster
Anderson
Pretorius
Burger Str.
Kruger Str.
Grobler
Burger Str.
President
PIETERSBURG
Lydenburg 0 1 km km 69
BURGERSFORT
OHRIGSTAD
Lydenburg Nature Reserve
Lydenburg – Natuurreservaat
Drive-In
Inryteater
De Clercq Str.
Lange Str.
Kantoor Str.
Fourie Str.
Kerkplein
Burger Str.
Rensburg Str.
Viljoen Str.
De Beer Str.
Buhrman Str.
Coetzer Str.
Kerk Str.
Museum
Potgieter Str.
Voortrekker Str.
Marteen Str.
Barac Str.
Rossouw Str.
Steyn Str.
De Souza Str.
Schurink Str.
Kuit Str.
SABIE
Johannes Str.
Sports Grounds
Sportgrond
Nel Str.
Van Staden Str.
Chris Lombaard Str.
Brown Str.
Goodman Str.
Preller Str.
Morgan Str.
Beetge Str.
Ruiter Str.
Lombaard Str.
Schoeman Str.
Viljoen Str.
Jansen Str.
Marais Str.
Goud Str.
Lydenburg Str.
Maasdorp Str.
Kriel Str.
Sterkspruit
Berg Str.
MACHADODORP
Fisheries Institute
Aquarium
Visseryinstituut
Akwarium
Mafeking 0 500 m m 68
LOBATSE
William Dick Ave./-laan
Jan Viljoen Ave./-laan
Visser Str.
Dadford Str.
Thomas Str.
Quigley Str.
Mimosa Str.
Karee Str.
Havinga Str.
Carney Str.
Proctor Str.
Churchill Ave./-laan
Jan Smuts Ave./-laan
Montgomery Str.
North Str.
Van Riebeeck Park
Voortrekker Rd./-weg
Victoria Rd./-weg
Recreation Grounds
Hatchard Str.
Tillard Str.
Martin Str.
Warren Str.
Shippard Str.
Station Rd./-weg
Carrington Str.
Main Str.
Molopo Rd./-weg
ZEERUST
Robinson Str.
South Str.
Molopo
Cookes Lake
VRYBURG
Molopo
LICHTENBURG
Malmesbury 0 500 m m 58
MOORREESBURG
MOORREESBURG
Lowry Cole Str.
Hospitaal Str.
Kort
Lang Str.
Bergzicht Str.
Arcadia Str.
Ford Str.
Hugenote Str.
Voortrekker Rd./-weg
Dirkie Uys Str.
Meul Str.
Truter Str.
Wandel Str.
Geldenhuis Str.
Mark Str.
Hill Str.
Plein Str.
St. Thomas Str.
Kerk Str.
Piet Retief Str.
Rainier Str.
PAARL
St. Johns Str.
St. Francis Str.
Rainier
Munisipale Str.
Kerk Str.
Diep
BOKOMO
Voortrekker Rd./-weg
Bokomo Rd./-weg
CAPE TOWN
KAAPSTAD
Platteklip
Diep
Sports Grounds
Sportgrond
KLIPHEUWEL

Mbabane (S)
0 500 m m
67
North Str.
Matthews Str.
Mission Str.
Fitz Str.
Scott Str.
Fiddes Str.
Lanham Str.
Edwards Str.
Muir Str.
Schoch Str.
Hill Str.
PIGGS PEAK
OSHOEK
JOHANNESBURG
Murray Str.
Gilfillan Str.
Coronation Park
Allister Miller Str.
Polinjane
The Avenue
Johnson Str.
Howe Str.
Shield Str.
Smuts Str.
Bert Str.
Post Str.
Market Str.
Church Str.
Riverside Drive/-rylaan
Walker Str.
Warner Str.
Mhlonhlo Rd./-weg
Mbabane
Swazi Plaza
Swazi Market/-merk
Bypass
Verbypad
Clinic/Klinick
Coventry Cres.
Sheffield Rd./-weg
MHLAMBANYATI
Usutu Rd./-weg
MANZINI
Regeringskantore
Government Offices
Middelburg (C)
0 500 m m
62
COLESBERG
BLOEMFONTEIN
North End Str.
Meyer Str.
Camp Str.
North Str.
Van Niekerk Str.
Murray Str.
Meintjies Str.
Roode Str.
Van Niekerk Str.
New Str.
Victoria Str.
Du Plessis Str.
Van der Walt Str.
Bennie Str.
Stockenstrom Str.
Van Reenen Str.
Rosmead Str.
STEYNSBURG
Nood Str.
Du Plessis Str.
Van der Walt Str.
Smidt Str.
Smidt Str.
RICHMOND
Richmond Rd./-weg
Market Str.
Loop Str.
Church Str.
Jubilee Str.
Coetzee Str.
Naude Str.
Joubert Str.
Kruger Str.
Keerom Str.
Naude Str.
Dwars Str.
Joubert Str.
Klein-Brak
Station Rd./-weg
CRADOCK
GRAAFF REINET
Middelburg (T)
0 1 km km
69
LOSKOPDAM
Buitekant
Noordkant
Hoop Str.
Kerk Str.
Klein-Olifants
STOFFBERG
Wes Str.
Joubert Str.
Mark Str.
Coetzee Str.
Voortrekker Str.
President Kruger Str.
Hendrik Potgieter Str.
Lang Str.
Klip Str.
Rivier Str.
Joubert Str.
Lang Str.
Meyer Str.
Jan van Riebeeck Str.
Weeber Str.
MACHADODORP
BELFAST
Skougronde
Show Grounds
WITBANK
Coetzee Str.
Zuid Str.
Fontein Str.
Morkel Str.
Frame Str.
Kogel Str.
Vos Str.
Du Toitspruit
Kogel
Hoog
Francois
BETHAL
Montagu
0 500 m m
58
HOT SPRINGS
TOUWSRIVIER
MATROOSBERG
Bath
Union Str.
Cross Str.
Le Roux Str.
Smith Str.
Joubert Str.
Bloem Str.
Joubert Str.
Piet Retief Str.
Market Str.
Barry Str.
Rawson Str.
Bath Str.
Cross Str.
BARRYDALE
Berry Str.
Museum
Du Toit Str.
Long Str.
ASHTON
ROBERTSON
SWELLENDAM
Long Str.
Church Str.
Kingnas
Van Riebeeck Str.
Kohler Str.
Essen Str.
Van Huyssteen Str.
Hofmeyer Str.
Swanepoel Str.
Hospital Str.
Reitz Str.
Mossel Bay
0 500 m m
59
De Bakke Beach
GEORGE
George Rd./-weg
Long Str.
Fifth Ave.
INDIESE OSEAAN
Santos Beach/-strand
Dial Brand Str.
Long Str.
Vyfde Laan
George Rd./-weg
Seilbootklub
Yacht Club
Harbour
Hawe
Alhof Drive/-rylaan
Sesde Laan
Museum
Grave Str.
Bland Str.
Marsh Str.
Marsh Str.
Mitchell Str.
Kloof Str.
Beach Str.
Field Str.
Church Str.
CAPE TOWN
KAAPSTAD
Da Gama Str.
Seventeenth Ave.
Cape Rd.
Harry Giddey Park
Montagu Str.
Montagu Str.
Point Rd./-weg
High Str.
Eighteenth Ave.
Cape Rd./-weg
Cape St. Blaize
Eleventh Ave.
Twaalfde Laan
Sewentiende Laan
Kerk Str.
Bruns Str.
Hofmeyer Str.
Nineteenth Ave.
Hudson Str.
Hofmeyr Str.
Sportstadion
Sports Stadium
Twentyfirst Ave.
Een-en-twintigste Laan
Kerk Str.
Danie de Jager Str.
INDIAN OCEAN
Nelspruit
0 1 km km
69
WITRIVIER
WHITE RIVER
PRETORIUSKOP
Botanical Gardens
Botaniese Tuine
Noord Str.
Henshall Str.
Currie Str.
Bester Str.
KOMATIPOORT
KAAPMUIDEN
Old Pretoria Rd.
Andrew Str.
Voortrekker Str.
Paul Kruger Str.
Louis Trichardt Str.
Cameron Str.
Anderson Str.
Bester Str.
Brown Str.
Bell Str.
Brander Str.
MACHADODORP
Nell Str.
Russell Str.
Streak Str.
Rothery Str.
Marloth Str.
Van der Merwe Str.
Ferreira Str.
Piet Retief Str.
Venter Str.
Mostert Str.
BARBERTON
Sarel Cilliers Str.
Van Wyk Str.
AA
Newcastle
0 1 km km
67
MEMEL
Nagtegaal Str.
Victoria Rd./-weg
Coronation Rd./-weg
Gemsbok Str.
VOLKSRUST
Hardwick Str.
Incandu
Montague Str.
St. Dominics Str.
Lincoln Str.
Hill Str.
Kirkland Str.
Murchison Str.
Allen Str.
Voortrekker Str.
Sutherland Str.
Scott Str.
Paterson Str.
Hospital Str.
Allen Str.
Steildrift Rd./-weg
Green Str.
Church Str.
Carrington Str.
St. Bruno's Str.
Draper Str.
Boundary Str.
Midway Str.
York Rd./-weg
Oak Ave./-laan
NORMANDIEN
DURBAN

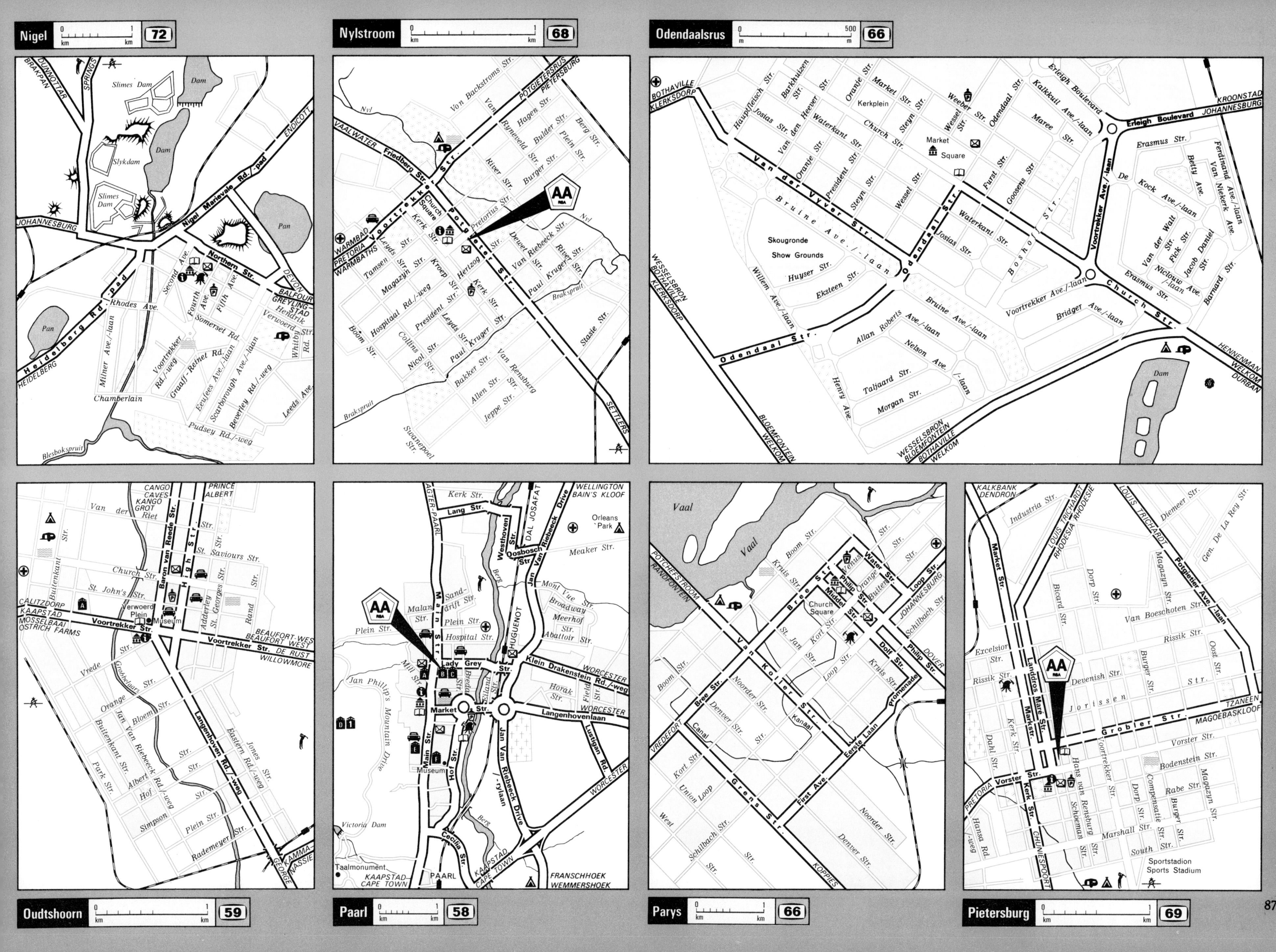
Nigel
72
Nylstroom
68
Odendaalsrus
66
Oudtshoorn
59
Paarl
58
Parys
66
Pietersburg
69
Skougronde
Show Grounds
Church Square
Market Square
Sportstadion
Sports Stadium
Taalmonument
Victoria Dam
Jan Phillip's Mountain Drive
Museum
Orleans Park

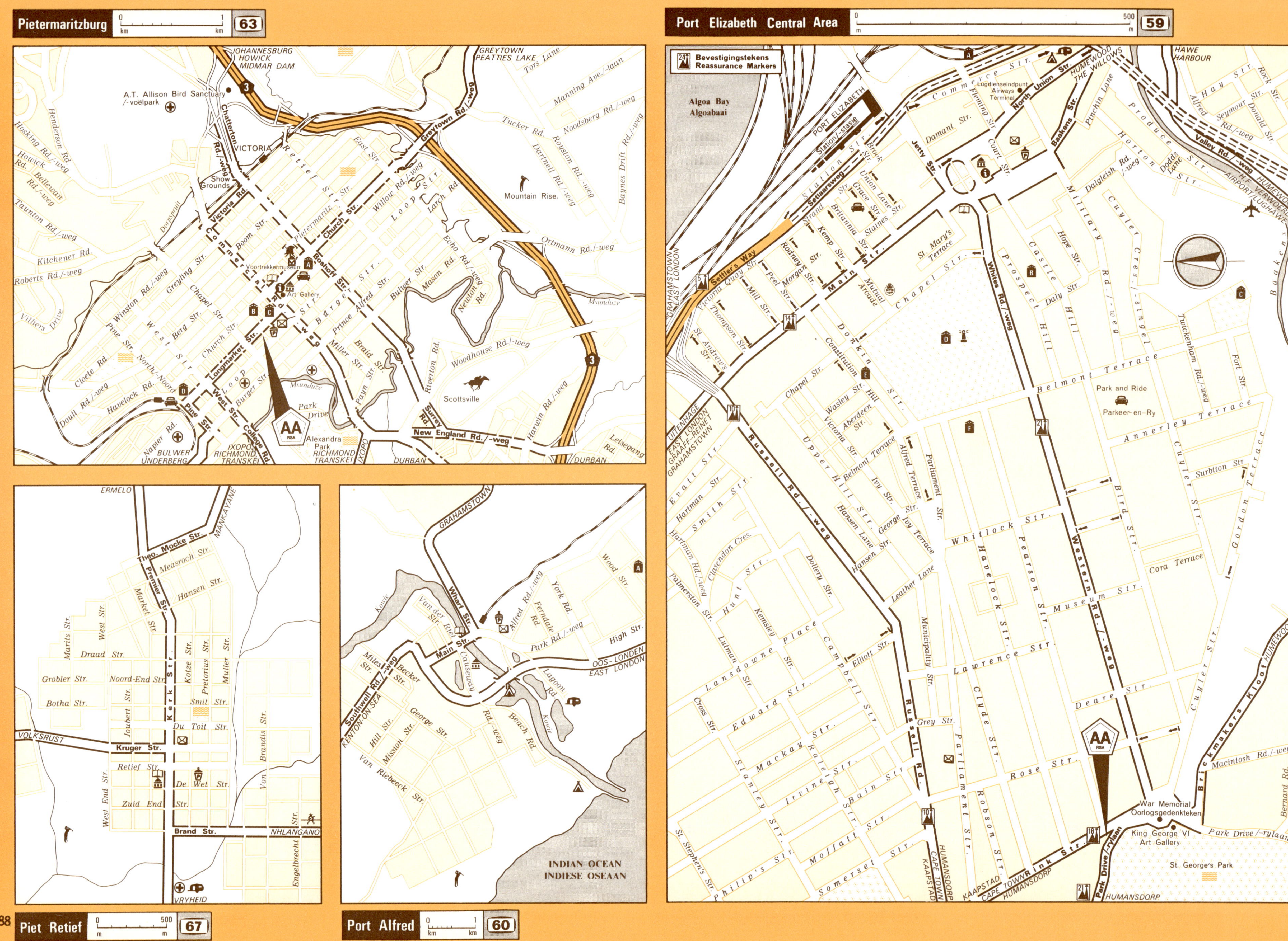
Pietermaritzburg
0 1
km km
63
JOHANNESBURG
HOWICK
MIDMAR DAM
GREYTOWN
PEATTIES LAKE
A.T. Allison Bird Sanctuary /-voëlpark
VICTORIA
Show Grounds
Voortrekkermuseum
Art Gallery
Mountain Rise.
Scottsville
Alexandra Park
BULWER
UNDERBERG
IXOPO
RICHMOND
TRANSKEI
DURBAN
Msunduze
Park Drive
Chatterton Rd./-weg
Retief Str.
Greytown Rd./-weg
Church Str.
Longmarket Str.
Loop Str.
Burger Str.
Boshoff Str.
Berg Str.
Pietermaritz Str.
Commercial Rd.
Victoria Rd.
Boom Str.
Greyling Str.
Chapel Str.
Winston Rd./-weg
Prince Alfred Str.
Bulwer Str.
Mason Rd.
Echo Rd./-weg
Newton Rd.
Woodhouse Rd./-weg
Riverton Rd.
Surrey Rd.
New England Rd./-weg
Harwin Rd./-weg
Leisegang Rd.
Ortmann Rd./-weg
Baynes Drift Rd./-weg
Noodsberg Rd./-weg
Manning Ave./-laan
Tucker Rd.
Tors Lane
Royston Rd./-weg
Dartnell Rd./-weg
Hosking Rd./-weg
Henderson Rd.
Howick Rd.
Bellevue Rd./-weg
Taunton Rd./-weg
Kitchener Rd.
Roberts Rd./-weg
Villiers Drive
Prime Str.
West Str.
North/-Noord
Havelock Rd.
Cloete Rd.
Doull Rd./-weg
Napier Rd.
Pine Str.
College Rd.
Braid Str.
Payn Str.
Miller Str.
Larch Rd.
Willow Rd./-weg
East Str.
Port Elizabeth Central Area
0 500
m m
59
Bevestigingstekens
Reassurance Markers
Algoa Bay
Algoabaai
HAWE
HARBOUR
PORT ELIZABETH
Station/-stasie
Lugdienseindpunt
Airways Terminal
H.F. VERWOERD AIRPORT/LUGHAWE
HUMEWOOD
THE WILLOWS
Commerce Str.
North Union Str.
Valley Rd./-weg
Produce Str.
Horton Str.
Main Str.
Settler's Way
Strand Str.
Russell Rd./-weg
Chapel Str.
Donkin Str.
Whites Rd./-weg
Western Rd./-weg
Belmont Terrace
Park and Ride
Parkeer-en-Ry
Annerley Terrace
Cuyler Str.
Whitlock Str.
Lawrence Str.
Deare Str.
Rose Str.
Museum Str.
Cora Terrace
Surbiton Str.
Gordon Terrace
Brickmakers Kloof
Macintosh Rd./-weg
Bernard Rd./-weg
War Memorial
Oorlogsgedenkteken
King George VI Art Gallery
St. George's Park
Park Drive/-rylaan
Rink Str.
HUMANSDORP
KAAPSTAD
CAPE TOWN
GRAHAMSTOWN
EAST LONDON
UITENHAGE
GRAAFF-REINET
Parliament Str.
Havelock Str.
Pearson Str.
Clyde Str.
Robson Str.
Military Rd./-weg
Castle Hill
Prospect Hill
Daly Str.
Hope Str.
Baakens Str.
Pinchin Lane
Dalgleish Rd./-weg
Jetty Str.
Damant Str.
Fleming Str.
Court Str.
St. Mary's Terrace
Mutual Arcade
Constitution Hill
Chapel Str.
Wasley Str.
Aberdeen Str.
Victoria Str.
Upper Hill Str.
Belmont Terrace
Alfred Terrace
Ivy Str.
George Str.
Hansen Lane
Leather Lane
Elliott Str.
Municipality Str.
Grey Str.
Bird Str.
Twickenham Rd./-weg
Fort Str.
Evatt Str.
Hartman Str.
Smith Str.
Clarendon Cres.
Hunt Str.
Dollery Str.
Kemsley Place
Campbell Str.
Lansdowne Str.
Edward Str.
Mackay Str.
Raleigh Str.
Irvine Str.
Bain Str.
Moffatt Str.
Somerset Str.
Philip's Str.
St. Stephen's Str.
Stanley Str.
Cross Str.
Lutman Str.
Palmerston Str.
Piet Retief
0 500
m m
67
ERMELO
MANKAYANE
VOLKSRUST
NHLANGANO
VRYHEID
Theo. Mocke Str.
Measroch Str.
Hansen Str.
Premier Str.
Market Str.
Marits Str.
West Str.
Draad Str.
Grobler Str.
Noord-End Str.
Botha Str.
Kerk Str.
Kotze Str.
Pretorius Str.
Muller Str.
Smit Str.
Du Toit Str.
Kruger Str.
Retief Str.
Joubert Str.
De Wet Str.
Zuid End Str.
West End Str.
Brand Str.
Brandis Str.
Von Str.
Engelbrecht Str.
Port Alfred
0 1
km km
60
GRAHAMSTOWN
OOS-LONDEN
EAST LONDON
SOUTHWELL
KENTON-ON-SEA
INDIAN OCEAN
INDIESE OSEAAN
Kowie
Wharf Str.
Van der Riet Str.
Main Str.
Causeway
Alfred Rd./-weg
York Rd.
Ferndale Rd.
Park Rd./-weg
High Str.
Wood Str.
Lagoon Rd.
Beach Rd.
Miles Str.
Becker Str.
George Str.
Hill Str.
Mission Str.
Van Riebeeck Str.

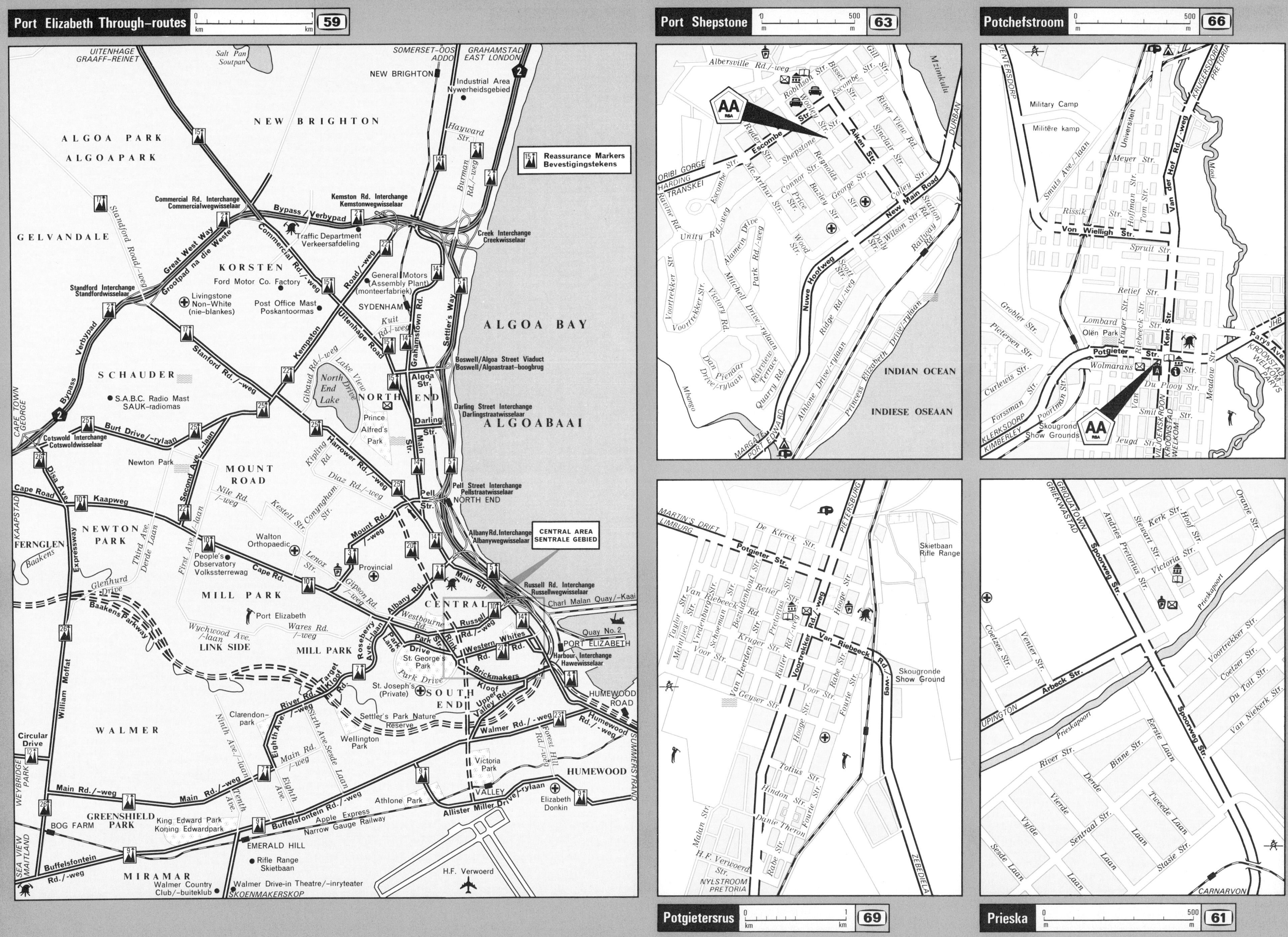

Port Elizabeth Through-routes
0
1
km
km
59
Port Shepstone
0
500
m
m
63
Potchefstroom
0
500
m
m
66
UITENHAGE
GRAAFF-REINET
Salt Pan
Soutpan
SOMERSET-OOS
ADDO
GRAHAMSTAD
EAST LONDON
NEW BRIGHTON
Industrial Area
Nywerheidsgebied
NEW BRIGHTON
ALGOA PARK
ALGOAPARK
Reassurance Markers
Bevestigingstekens
Hayward Str.
Burman Rd./-weg
Commercial Rd. Interchange
Commercialwegwisselaar
Kemston Rd. Interchange
Kemstonwegwisselaar
Bypass / Verbypad
Creek Interchange
Creekwisselaar
GELVANDALE
Standford Road/-weg
Traffic Department
Verkeersafdeling
Great West Way
Grootpad na die Weste
Commercial Rd./-weg
KORSTEN
Ford Motor Co. Factory
General Motors
(Assembly Plant)
(monteerfabriek)
Road/-weg
Standford Interchange
Standfordwisselaar
Livingstone
Non-White
(nie-blankes)
Post Office Mast
Poskantoormas
SYDENHAM
Uitenhage Road
Grahamstown Rd.
Settler's Way
Kuit Rd./-weg
ALGOA BAY
Verbypad
Stanford Rd./-weg
Kempston
Boswell/Algoa Street Viaduct
Boswell/Algoastraat-boogbrug
SCHAUDER
Gibaud Rd./-weg
Lake View Drive
North End Lake
NORTH END
Algoa Str.
S.A.B.C. Radio Mast
SAUK-radiomas
Darling Street Interchange
Darlingstraatwisselaar
ALGOABAAI
Bypass
CAPE TOWN
GEORGE
Burt Drive/-rylaan
Prince Alfred's Park
Darling Str.
Main Str.
Cotswold Interchange
Cotswoldwisselaar
Harrower Rd./-weg
Kipling Rd.
Newton Park
MOUNT ROAD
Second Ave./-laan
Diaz Rd./-weg
Pell Str.
Pell Street Interchange
Pellstraatwisselaar
NORTH END
Cape Road
Kaapweg
Disa Ave.
Nile Rd. /-weg
Kestell Str.
Conyngham Str.
KAAPSTAD
FERNGLEN
NEWTON PARK
Third Ave. Derde Laan
Walton Orthopaedic
Mount Rd. /-weg
Albany Rd. Interchange
Albanywegwisselaar
CENTRAL AREA
SENTRALE GEBIED
Expressway
Baakens
First Ave./-laan
People's Observatory
Volkssterrewag
Cape Rd.
Lenox Str.
Provincial
Main Str.
Russell Rd. Interchange
Russellwegwisselaar
Glenhurd Drive
MILL PARK
Gipson Rd. /-weg
Albany Rd.
CENTRAL
Charl Malan Quay/-Kaai
Baakens Parkway
Port Elizabeth
Westbourne Rd.
Russell Rd./-weg
Quay No. 2
Wychwood Ave. /-laan
Wares Rd. /-weg
Park Drive
Park Lane
Park Str.
Rink
Western Rd.
Whites Rd.
PORT ELIZABETH
LINK SIDE
MILL PARK
Roseberry Ave./-laan
St. George's Park
Harbour Interchange
Hawewisselaar
William Moffat
Target Kloof
Rd.
Brickmakers
St. Joseph's (Private)
Park Drive
SOUTH END
Kloof
Upper Valley Rd.
HUMEWOOD ROAD
River Rd.
Clarendon-park
Settler's Park Nature Reserve
Walmer Rd. / -weg
Humewood Rd. / -weg
WALMER
Ninth Ave./-laan
Eighth Ave.
Sixth Ave./Sesde Laan
Wellington Park
Forest Hill Rd./-weg
Circular Drive
Main Rd. /-weg
Victoria Park
HUMEWOOD
SUMMERSTRAND
WEYBRIDGE PARK
Main Rd./-weg
Main Rd./-weg
Tenth Ave.
Eighth Ave.
VALLEY
Allister Miller Drive/-rylaan
Athlone Park
Elizabeth Donkin
GREENSHIELD PARK
King Edward Park
Koning Edwardpark
BOG FARM
Buffelsfontein Rd./-weg
Apple Express
Narrow Gauge Railway
EMERALD HILL
Rifle Range
Skietbaan
SEA VIEW
MAITLAND
Buffelsfontein
Rd./-weg
MIRAMAR
Walmer Country Club/-buiteklub
Walmer Drive-in Theatre/-inryteater
SKOENMAKERSKOP
H.F. Verwoerd
Albersville Rd./-weg
Robinson Str.
Bisset Str.
Gill Str.
Mzimkulu
Escombe Str.
Woolley Str.
River View Rd.
AA
RSA
Aiken Str.
Sinclair Str.
DURBAN
Ryder Str.
Escombe
Shepstone
Reynolds
ORIBI GORGE
HARDING
TRANSKEI
Escombe Str.
McArthur Str.
Connor Str.
Price Str.
Bazley
George Str.
Colley Str.
New Main Road
Ravine Rd.
Station Rd.
Unity Rd./-weg
Alamein Drive
Park Rd./-weg
Wood Str.
Wilson Str.
Daly Str.
Railway Rd.
Voortrekker Str.
Mitchell Drive/-rylaan
Scott Str.
Nuwe Hoofweg
Voortrekker Str.
Victory Rd.
Ridge Rd./-weg
Princess Elizabeth Drive/-rylaan
Dan Pienaar Drive/-rylaan
Fairview Terrace
Quarry Rd.
Athlone Drive/-rylaan
INDIAN OCEAN
INDIESE OSEAAN
Mbango
MARGATE
PORT EDWARD
VENTERSDORP
Military Camp
Militêre kamp
Universiteit
KRUGERSDORP
PRETORIA
Van der Hof Rd./-weg
Smuts Ave./-laan
Meyer Str.
Hoffman Str.
Tom Str.
Mooi
Rissik Str.
Von Wielligh Str.
Spruit Str.
Retief Str.
Grobler Str.
Lombard Str.
Kruger Str.
Riebeeck Str.
Kerk Str.
Olën Park
JHB
Parys Ave.
KROONSTAD
WELKOM
PARYS
Pietersen Str.
Potgieter Str.
Wolmarans
Str.
Curlewis Str.
Du Plooy Str.
Meadow Str.
Forssman Str.
Poortman Str.
Van Riebeeck
Smit Str.
Skougrond
Show Grounds
KLERKSDORP
KIMBERLEY
Jeugd Str.
VILJOENSKROON
KROONSTAD
WELKOM
MARTIN'S DRIFT
LIMBURG
PIETERSBURG
De Klerck Str.
Skietbaan
Rifle Range
Potgieter Str.
Retief Str.
Van Riebeeck Str.
Vredenburg Str.
Schoeman Str.
Bezuidenhout Str.
Pretorius Str.
Rd./-weg
Hooge Str.
Taylor Str.
Mentjies Str.
Rd.
Voor Str.
Kruger Str.
Ruiter Rd./-weg
Van Riebeeck Rd.
Van Heerden Str.
Voortrekker Rd./-weg
Voor Str.
Rabe Str.
Fourie Str.
Skougronde
Show Ground
Geyser Str.
Hooge Str.
Totius Str.
Hindon Str.
Fourie Str.
Danie Theron Str.
Malan Str.
H.F. Verwoerd Str.
Rabe Str.
NYLSTROOM
PRETORIA
ZEBEDIELA
GRIQUATOWN
GRIEKWASTAD
Andries Pretorius Str.
Stewart Str.
Kerk Str.
Hoof Str.
Oranje Str.
Victoria Str.
Spoorweg Str.
Prieskapoort
Coetzee Str.
Venter Str.
Arbeck Str.
Voortrekker Str.
Coetzer Str.
Du Toit Str.
Van Niekerk Str.
UPINGTON
Prieskapoort
Spoorweg Str.
River Str.
Binne Str.
Eerste Laan
Derde
Vierde
Tweede Laan
Vyfde
Sentraal Str.
Laan
Sesde Laan
Laan
Laan
Stasie Str.
CARNARVON
Potgietersrus
0
1
km
km
69
Prieska
0
500
m
m
61

Pretoria Central Area

0 500
m m

68

2 Bevestigingstekens
Reassurance Markers

Pretoria Through-routes

0 1
km

68

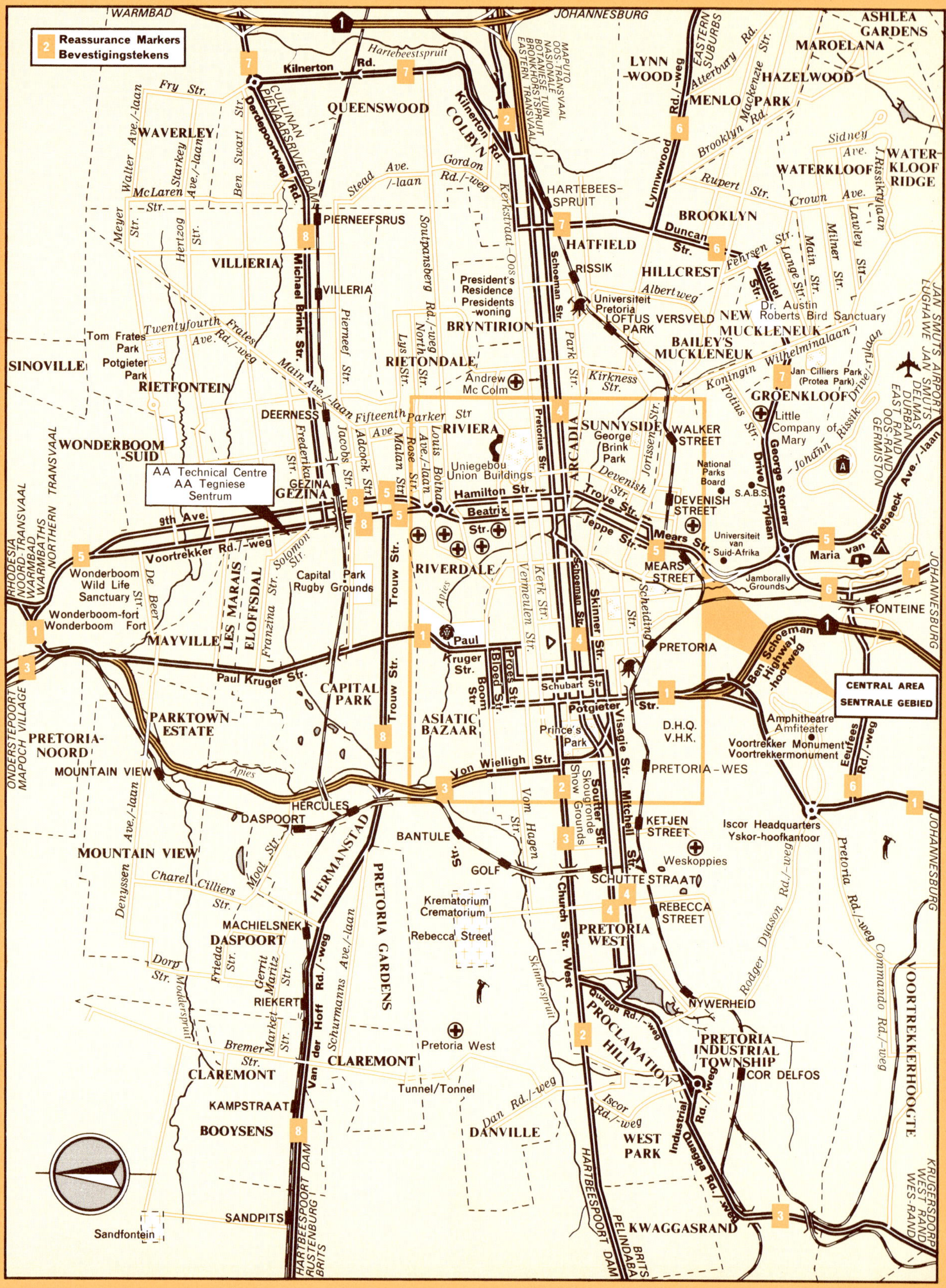

2 Reassurance Markers
Bevestigingstekens

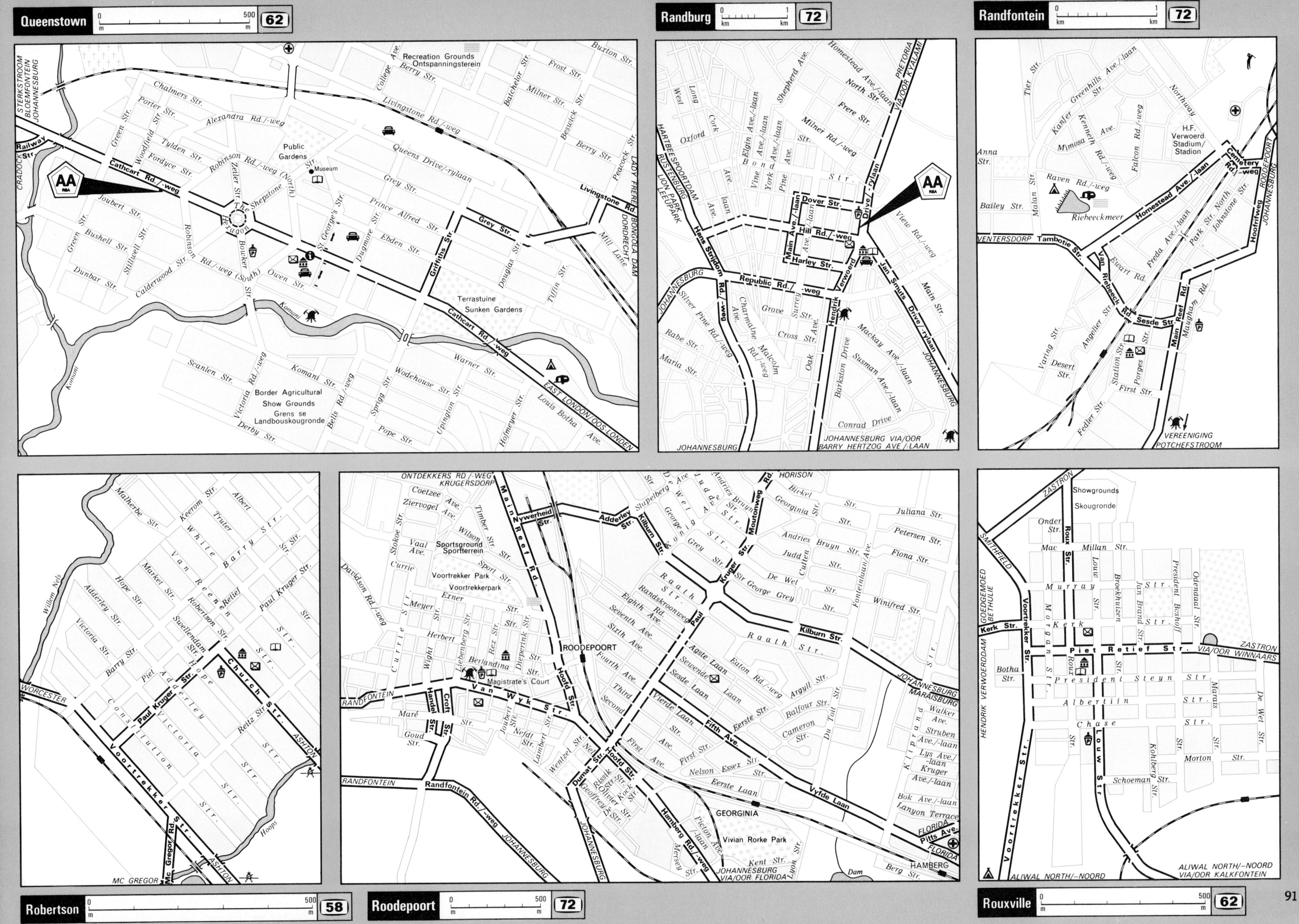

Queenstown 0 500 m m 62
Randburg 0 1 km km 72
Randfontein 0 1 km km 72
Recreation Grounds
Ontspanningsterein
Public Gardens
Museum
Terrastuine
Sunken Gardens
Border Agricultural
Show Grounds
Grens se
Landbouskougronde
Cathcart Rd./-weg
Livingstone Rd./-weg
Queens Drive/-rylaan
EAST LONDON/OOS-LONDEN
STERKSTROOM
BLOEMFONTEIN
JOHANNESBURG
LADY FRERE
BONGOLA DAM
DORDRECHT
Komani
Republic Rd./-weg
Hendrik Verwoerd Drive/-rylaan
Jan Smuts Drive/-rylaan
PRETORIA
VIA/OOR KYALAMI
HARTBEESPOORTDAM
RUSTENBURG
LION PARK
LEEUPARK
JOHANNESBURG
JOHANNESBURG VIA/OOR
BARRY HERTZOG AVE./-LAAN
H.F.
Verwoerd
Stadium/
Stadion
Riebeeckmeer
Homestead Ave./-laan
VENTERSDORP
VEREENIGING
POTCHEFSTROOM
ROODEPOORT
JOHANNESBURG
Robertson 0 500 m m 58
Roodepoort 0 500 m m 72
Rouxville 0 500 m m 62
WORCESTER
ASHTON
MC GREGOR
Voortrekker Str.
Church Str.
Paul Kruger Str.
ONTDEKKERS RD./-WEG
KRUGERSDORP
Sportsground
Sportterrein
Voortrekker Park
Voortrekkerpark
ROODEPOORT
Magistrate's Court
Main Reef Rd.
RANDFONTEIN
Randfontein Rd./-weg
GEORGINIA
Vivian Rorke Park
HORISON
MARAISBURG
FLORIDA
HAMBERG
JOHANNESBURG
VIA/OOR FLORIDA
Showgrounds
Skougronde
ZASTRON
VIA/OOR WINNAARS
SMITHFIELD
GOEDGEMOED
BETHULIE
HENDRIK VERWOERDDAM
ALIWAL NORTH/-NOORD
ALIWAL NORTH/-NOORD
VIA/OOR KALKFONTEIN
Piet Retief Str.
President Steyn Str.

Rustenburg
0 1
km km
68
Karlien Str.
Molen Str.
Lelie Str.
Rettz Str.
Burns Str.
Oxford Str.
Napoleon Str.
Foord Str.
Scheiding Str.
Smit Str.
Zendeling Str.
THABAZIMBI
Oos Str.
Buiten Str.
Malan Str.
Klopper Str.
Ridder Str.
Leyds Str.
Kruger Str.
Wolmaransplein
Van Kerk Str.
Joubert Str.
Wolmarans Str.
Beukes Str.
Kock Str.
Tuin Str.
Bosch Str.
SWARTRUGGENS
Lucas Str.
Van Zyl Str.
Berg Loop Str.
Kruis Str.
Plein Str.
Steen Str.
Burger Str.
Heysteck Str.
Van Staden Str.
Von Wielligh Str.
KLOOF
Klopper Str.
Leyds Str.
Smit Str.
Marais Str.
Kruger Str.
Kerk Str.
Joubertplein
Joubert Str.
Wolmarans Str.
Kock Str.
Skougronde
Show Grounds
Paul Bodenstein Nature Park/natuurreservaat
Bird Sanctuary/Voëlpark
PRETORIA
Wildtuin
Game Reserve
JOHANNESBURG
Kloof Rd./weg
Sasolburg
0 1
km km
66
J.G. Strijdom Rd./weg
PARYS
VANDERBIJLPARK
Provincial Rd.
Vlaardingen Str.
Felixstowe Str.
Kromellenboog Str.
Waterson Str.
D.F. Malan Rd./weg
Christiaan de Wet Rd./weg
Riemland Str.
Eric Louw Rd./weg
Van Eck Str.
Hersov Str.
Van der Bijl Str.
President Reitz Rd./weg
Pretorius Str.
Provinsiale pad
VEREENIGING
HEILBRON
Baldrif Str.
Liebenberg Str.
Fick Str.
Unie Str.
Brill Str.
Lindley Str.
Harry Smith Str.
Hertzog Rd./weg
President Brand Rd./weg
Fichardt Str.
Retief Str.
Trichardt Str.
Fraser Str.
Klasie Havenga Rd./weg
McIntyre Str.
Wedepohl Str.
Barnard Str.
President Steyn Rd.
George Grey Str.
Senekal Str.
Finlay Str.
Geduld Str.
Antrim Str.
Peeters Str.
Klasie Havenga Rd./weg
Show Grounds
Skougrond
SIGMA-MYN
VEREENIGING
HEILBRON
Schweizer-Reneke
0 500
m m
66
Wentzel Str.
Therese Str.
Barnard Str.
Groenewoud Str.
Cameron Str.
George Str.
Oertel Str.
Pauw Str.
Hospitaal Str.
DELAREYVILLE
WENTZEL DAM
Markson Str.
Buiten Str.
VRYBURG
Van Zyl Str.
Du Plessis Str.
Venter Str.
Olivier Str.
Markson Str.
Delport Str.
Buiten Str.
Homan Str.
WOLMARANSSTAD
Reneke Str.
Schweizer Str.
Buiten Str.
Jacobs Str.
Ernst Str.
Combrink Str.
Olivier Str.
Cronje Str.
Landdroshof
Magistrate's Court
AMALIA
Reneke Str.
Cronje Str.
BLOEMHOF
Senekal
0 500
m m
66
VENTERSBURG
Charl Cilliers Str.
Van Niekerk Str.
Busschau Str.
Van Rooyen Str.
Van de Wall Str.
Bester Str.
De Villiers Str.
BETHLEHEM
Sandspruit
Voortrekker Rd./weg
Bell Str.
Boje Str.
Museum
Van de Wall Str.
Boerebok Str.
WINBURG
Water Str.
Lang Str.
Malan Str.
Dreyer Str.
Landdroshof
Magistrate's Court
Van Coller Str.
Van Deventer Str.
Zuider Str.
John Duplessis Str.
Kirchner Str.
Froneman Str.
Marais Str.
Sandspruit
MARQUARD
Skougrond
Stadium
Somerset East
0 500
m m
59
Mackay Str.
Paulet Str.
Paulet Str.
Beaufort Str.
Henry Str.
Worcester Str.
Hart Str.
Bouker Str.
Bell Str.
Henry Str.
Hockley Str.
Francis Str.
Francis Str.
Bathurst Str.
War Memorial
PEARSTON
Charles Str.
Louis Trichardt Str.
Rawson Str.
Worcester Str.
Havelock Str.
Cathcart Str.
New Str.
New Str.
Scallen Str.
Hill Str.
Hill Str.
Van Riebeeck Str.
Union Str.
College Rd./weg
Railway Str.
Southey Str.
Archer Str.
Victoria Park
Victoriapark
Bird Str.
Bird Str.
Fort Str.
End Str.
Holden Ave./laan
Du Toit Ave.
Scott Str.
Dawes Ave.
Show Grounds
Skougronde
PORT ELIZABETH
COOKHOUSE
Somerset West
0 1
km km
58
Stellenbosch Rd./weg
Cyprus Rd.
Firmount Rd./weg
Bayview Rd./weg
Irene Ave./laan
STELLENBOSCH
CAPE TOWN
Main Str.
Dummer Str.
Radloff Rd.
Parel Valley Rd./weg
Upper Orange Str.
Pinewoods Rd.
Lourensford Rd./weg
Mountain Rd./weg
Firs Ave.
Erica Ave.
Willow Rd.
Keurboom Ave.
Morkel Str.
Quinan Rd./weg
Rue de Jacqueline
Andries Str.
Myburgh Str.
Reitz Str.
St. Bright Str.
St. James Str.
Pretoria Str.
Drama Str.
Pienaar Str.
Neu Str.
Oatlands Rd./weg
Pinegrove Rd./weg
Dirkie Uys Str.
CAPE TOWN
KAAPSTAD
Ave./laan
Oak Str.
Church Str.
Lourens Str.
Main Str.
Gordon Rd./weg
Lourens
De Beers
Victoria Str.
Fagan Str.
Bridgewater Rd./weg
Lourens
Van der Stel Rd./weg
STRAND
CALEDON
Springs
0 1
km km
72
PRETORIA
BENONI
Paul Kruger Rd.
Geduld Rd.
Louw Str.
Potgieter Ave.
Sixth Ave.
Geduld Rd.
Seventh Str.
Fourth Ave.
Vierde Laan
POLLAK PARK
First Ave.
Eerste Laan
WITBANK
Welgedacht Rd./pad
DELMAS
Olympia Park
Olympiapark
Boksburg Rd.
P.A.M. Brink Stadium
P.A.M. Brinkstadion
Plantation Rd./weg
Eerste Laan
BETHAL
ERMELO
Second Str.
Fourth Ave.
ZOO DIERETUIN
South Main Reef Rd./weg
BENONI
Fifth Ave.
Colliery Rd./weg
Sixth Ave.
Tenth Str.
Twelfth Str.
Middlesex Ave./laan
Main Ave.
King Ave.
Union Str.
Ernst Str.
Derde Str.
Seventh Ave.
Sixth Str.
Eighth Str.
Cornish Rd./weg
Plantation Rd.
Broad Str.
Second Str.
Third Str.
Ninth Ave.
Zigzag Rd./weg
POLLAK PARK
Springs West Road
Springs-Wespad
JOHANNESBURG
BRAKPAN
BENONI
Rorburgh Rd./weg
Nigel Rd./pad
NIGEL
HEIDELBERG
STANDERTON
Springs Country Club/-buiteklub
Standerton
0 1
km km
67
LESLIE
PRETORIA
CHARL CELLIERS
SECUNDA
BETHAL
MORGENZON
Baumann Str.
Colony Str.
Standers Str.
Kieser Str.
Caledon Str.
Lombard Str.
Leyds Str.
Charl Celliers Str.
Kerk Str.
Kruger Str.
Von Str.
Backstrom Str.
Piet Retief Str.
Joubert Str.
Berg Str.
Schwickardt Str.
GREYLINGSTAD
JOHANNESBURG
VILLIERS
Krogh Str.
Krogh Str.
Prinses Str.
Pretorius Str.
Andries Str.
Lombard Str.
Burger Str.
Minnaar Str.
Rothmann Str.
Tabard Str.
Handel Str.
Muller Str.
Van Koller Str.
Smit Str.
Van Veen Str.
Vaal
Lang Str.
Steyn Str.
Brits Str.
Botha Str.
Roberts Str.
VOLKSRUST
DURBAN
VREDE

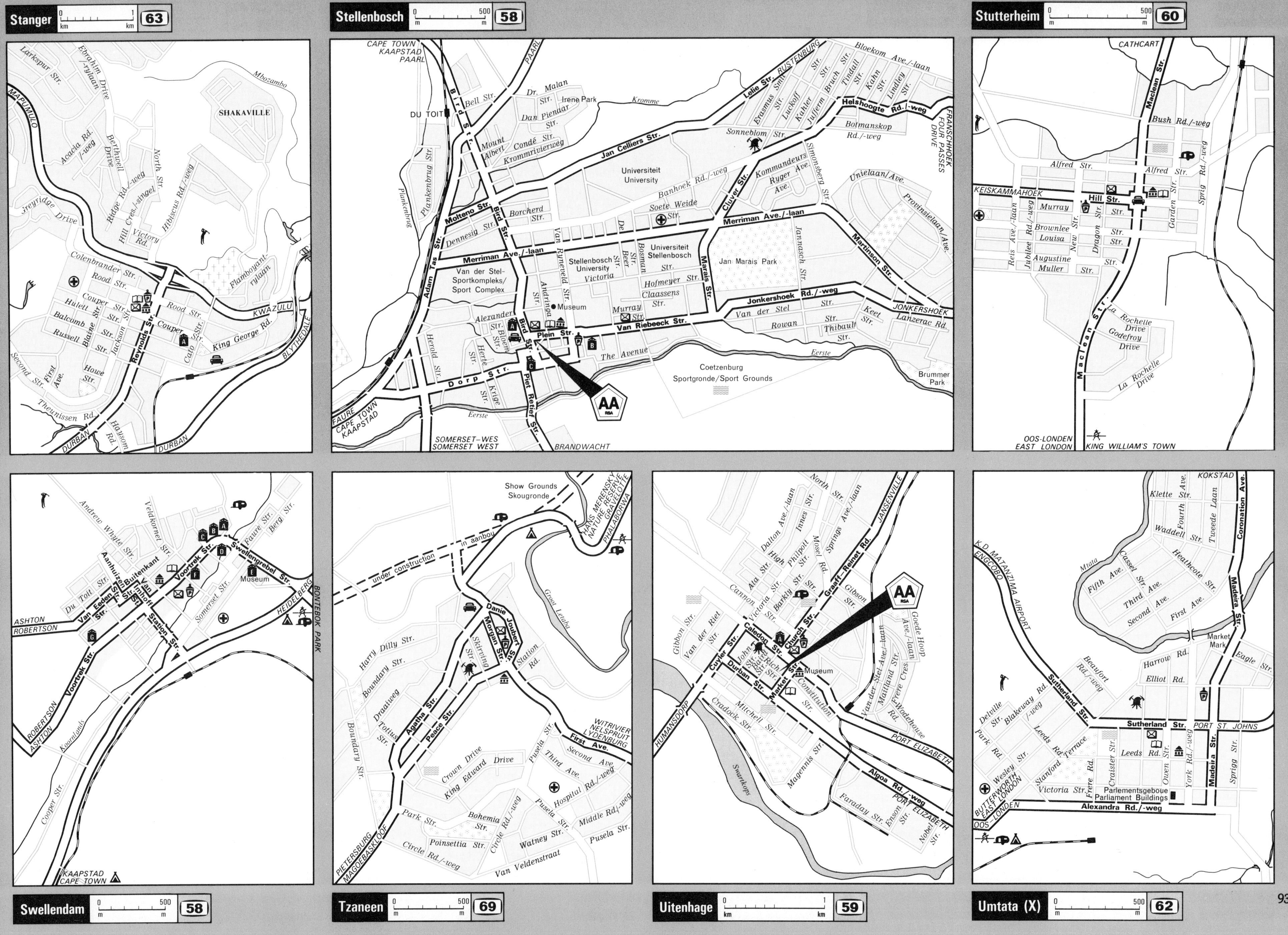
Stanger
0
1
km
km
63
Larkspur Str.
Ebrahim Drive
-rylaan
MAPUMULO
Mbozambo
SHAKAVILLE
Acacia Rd./-weg
Berthwell Drive
North Str.
Ridge Rd./-weg
Hill Cres./-singel
Hibiscus Rd./-weg
Victory Rd.
Breytidge Drive
Colenbrander Str.
Rood Str.
Flamboyant-rylaan
Couper Str.
Hulett Str.
Balcomb Str.
Russell Str.
Blaine Str.
Jackson Str.
Reynolds Str.
Rood Str.
Couper Str.
Cato Str.
King George Rd.
KWAZULU
BLYTHEDALE
Howe Str.
First Ave.
Second Str.
Theunissen Rd.
Hulsom Rd.
DURBAN
DURBAN
Stellenbosch
0
500
m
m
58
CAPE TOWN
KAAPSTAD
PAARL
PAARL
RUSTENBURG
Bloekom Ave./-laan
Lelie Str.
Erasmus Smit Str.
Luckoff Str.
Kahler Str.
Jufferm Bruch Str.
Tindall Str.
Kahn Str.
Lindley Str.
Helshoogte Rd./-weg
FRANSCHHOEK
FOUR PASSES DRIVE
Bird Str.
Bell Str.
Dr. Malan Str.
Irene Park
Kromme
DU TOIT
Dan Pienaar Str.
Mount Albert
Condé Str.
Krommrivierweg
Sonneblom Str.
Botmanskop Rd./-weg
Jan Celliers Str.
Plankenbrug Str.
Plankenbrug
Universiteit University
Cluver Str.
Kommandeurs
Ryger Ave.
Simonsberg Str.
Unielaan/Ave.
Banhoek Rd./-weg
Soete Weide Str.
Provinsielaan/Ave.
Molteno Str.
Borcherd Str.
Merriman Ave./-laan
Dennesig Str.
De Beer Str.
Martinson Str.
Merriman Ave./-laan
Van Ryneveld Str.
Bosman Str.
Universiteit Stellenbosch
Adam Tas Str.
Stellenbosch University
Victoria Str.
Hofmeyer Str.
Marais Str.
Jan Marais Park
Jannasch Str.
Van der Stel-Sportkompleks/Sport Complex
Andringa Str.
Museum
Claassens Str.
Jonkershoek Rd./-weg
Murray Str.
Van der Stel
Keet Str.
JONKERSHOEK
Alexander Str.
Bloem Str.
Plein Str.
Van Riebeeck Str.
Rowan
Lanzerac Rd.
Thibault Str.
Herold Str.
Herte Str.
The Avenue
Eerste
Dorp Str.
Krige Str.
Piet Retief Str.
Coetzenburg Sportgronde/Sport Grounds
Brummer Park
FAURE
CAPE TOWN KAAPSTAD
Eerste
AA RSA
SOMERSET-WES SOMERSET WEST
BRANDWACHT
Stutterheim
0
500
m
m
60
CATHCART
Maclean Str.
Bush Rd./-weg
Alfred Str.
Alfred Str.
Garden Str.
Sprig Rd./-weg
KEISKAMMAHOEK
Hill Str.
Murray
Str.
Str.
Reis Ave./-laan
Jubilee Rd./-weg
Brownlee
Louisa
New Str.
Dragon Str.
Str.
Augustine
Muller
Str.
Str.
La Rochelle Drive
Godefroy Drive
Maclean Str.
La Rochelle Drive
OOS-LONDEN EAST LONDON
KING WILLIAM'S TOWN
Andrew Whyte Str.
Veldkornet Str.
Faure Str.
Berg Str.
Aanhuizen Str.
Buitenkant Str.
Voortrek Str.
Swellengrebel Str.
Museum
Du Toit Str.
Van Eeden Str.
Van Oudtshoorn Str.
Station Str.
Somerset Str.
ASHTON
ROBERTSON
HEIDELBERG
BONTEBOK PARK
Voortrek Str.
ROBERTSON
ASHTON
Koornlands
Cooper Str.
KAAPSTAD CAPE TOWN
Swellendam
0
500
m
m
58
Show Grounds Skougronde
HANS MERENSKY NATURE RESERVE
GRAVELOTTE
PHALABORWA
in aanbou
under construction
Danie Joubert Str.
Morgan Str.
Stirling Str.
Station Rd.
Groot Letaba
Harry Dilly Str.
Boundary Str.
Draaiweg
Totius Str.
Agatha Str.
Peace Str.
WITRIVIER NELSPRUIT LYDENBURG
First Ave.
Second Ave.
Pusela Str.
Third Ave.
Crown Drive
King Edward Drive
Hospital Rd./-weg
Boundary Str.
Park Str.
Bohemia Str.
Circle Rd./-weg
Pusela Str.
Middle Rd./-weg
Poinsettia Str.
Watney Str.
Pusela Str.
Circle Rd./-weg
Van Veldenstraat
PIETERSBURG MAGOEBASKLOOF
Tzaneen
0
500
m
m
69
North Str.
Dalton Ave./-laan
Innes Str.
Springs Ave./-laan
JANSENVILLE
High Str.
Philpott Str.
Mosel Rd.
Graaff-Reinet Rd.
Ata Str.
Cannon Str.
Victoria Str.
Barkly Str.
Gibson Str.
AA RSA
Gibbon Str.
Van der Riet Str.
Caledon Str.
Church Str.
Goede Hoop Ave./-laan
Cuyler Str.
John Str.
Baird Str.
Museum
Van der Stel Ave./-laan
Maitland Str.
Frere Cres.
Durban Str.
Market Str.
Constitution Str.
Wodehouse Rd.
HUMANSDORP
Cradock Str.
Mitchell Str.
PORT ELIZABETH
Swartkops
Magennis Str.
Algoa Rd./-weg
PORT ELIZABETH
Faraday Str.
Enson Str.
Nobel Str.
Uitenhage
0
1
km
km
59
KOKSTAD
Klette Str.
Fourth Ave.
Tweede Laan
Coronation Ave.
Waddell Str.
K.D. MATANZIMA AIRPORT
ENGCOBO
Mtata
Cassel Str.
Heathcote Str.
Madeira Str.
Fifth Ave.
Third Ave.
Second Ave.
First Ave.
Market Mark
Harrow Rd.
Eagle Str.
Beaufort Rd./-weg
Elliot Rd.
Sutherland Str.
Delville Str.
Blakeway Rd./-weg
Sutherland Str.
PORT ST. JOHNS
Park Rd.
Leeds Rd.
Terrace
Leeds Rd.
Owen Str.
York Rd./-weg
Madeira Str.
Sprigg Str.
Wesley Str.
Stanford Rd.
Craister Str.
Frere Rd.
BUTTERWORTH
EAST LONDON
Victoria Str.
Parlementsgeboue Parliament Buildings
OOS-LONDEN
Alexandra Rd./-weg
Umtata (X)
0
500
m
m
62

Upington 0 500 m m **65**

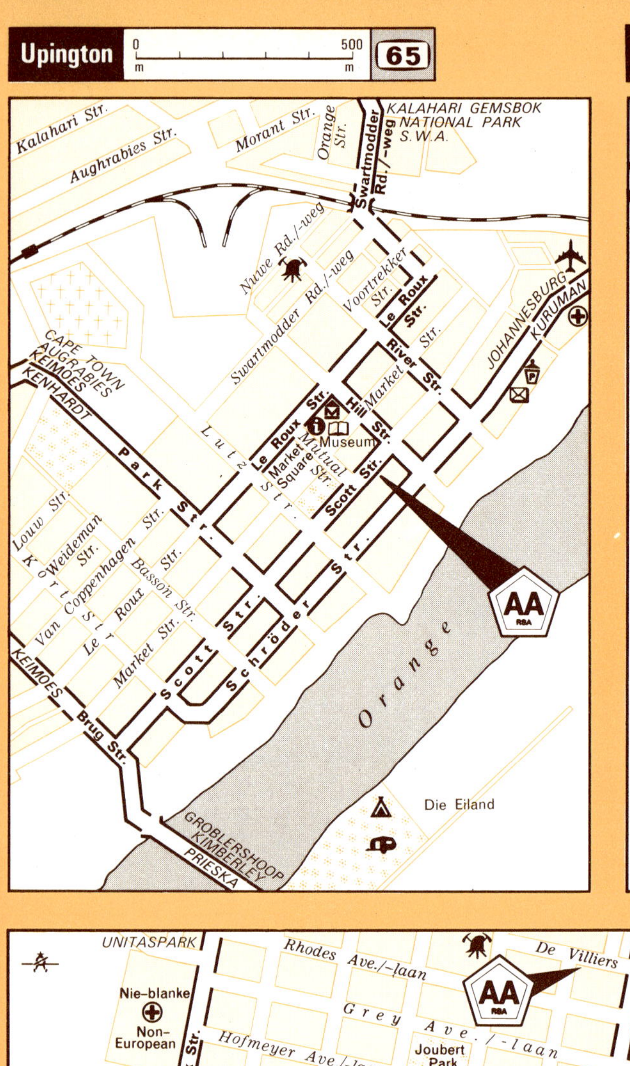

Vanderbijlpark 0 1 km km **66**

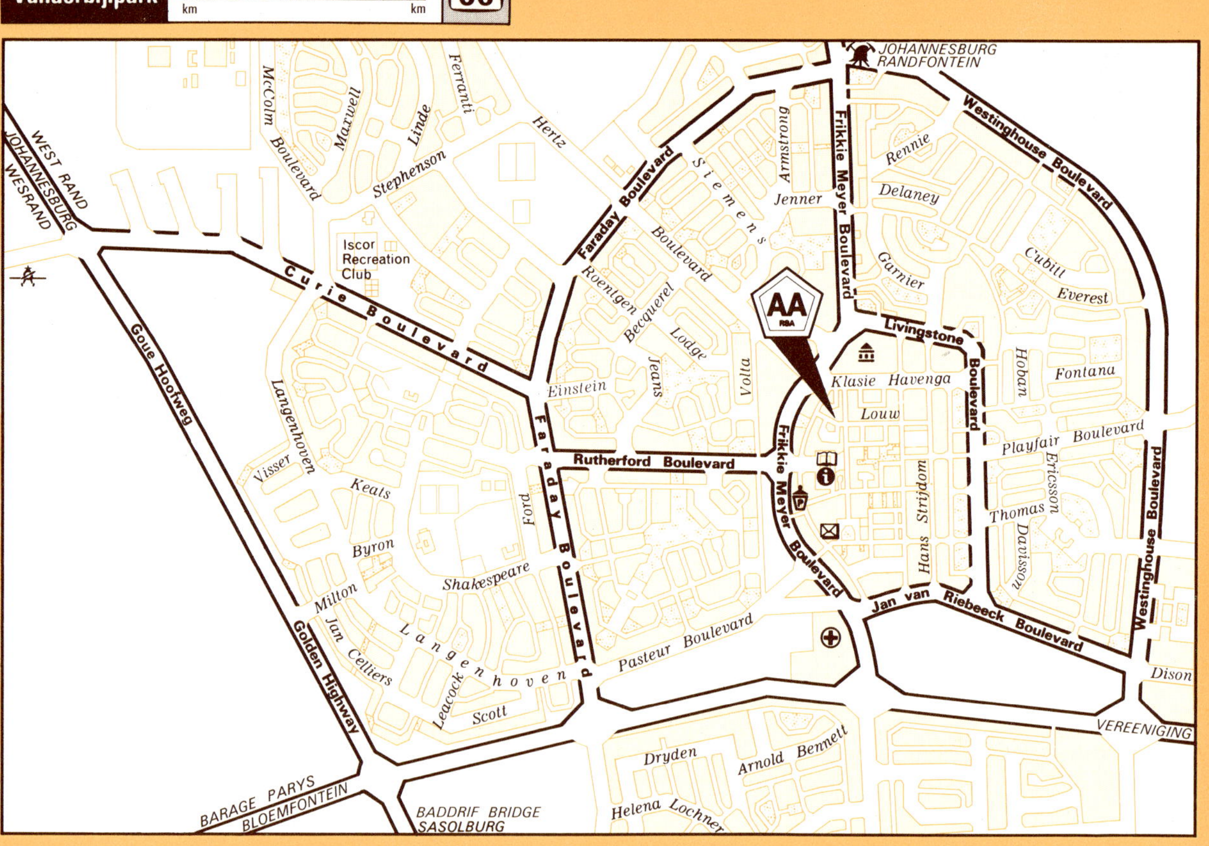

Vanrhynsdorp 0 500 m m **60**

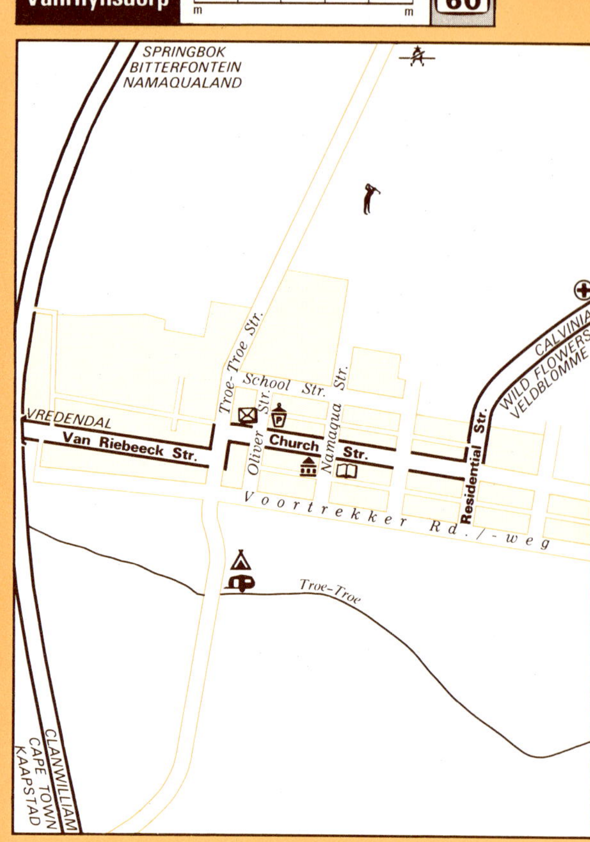

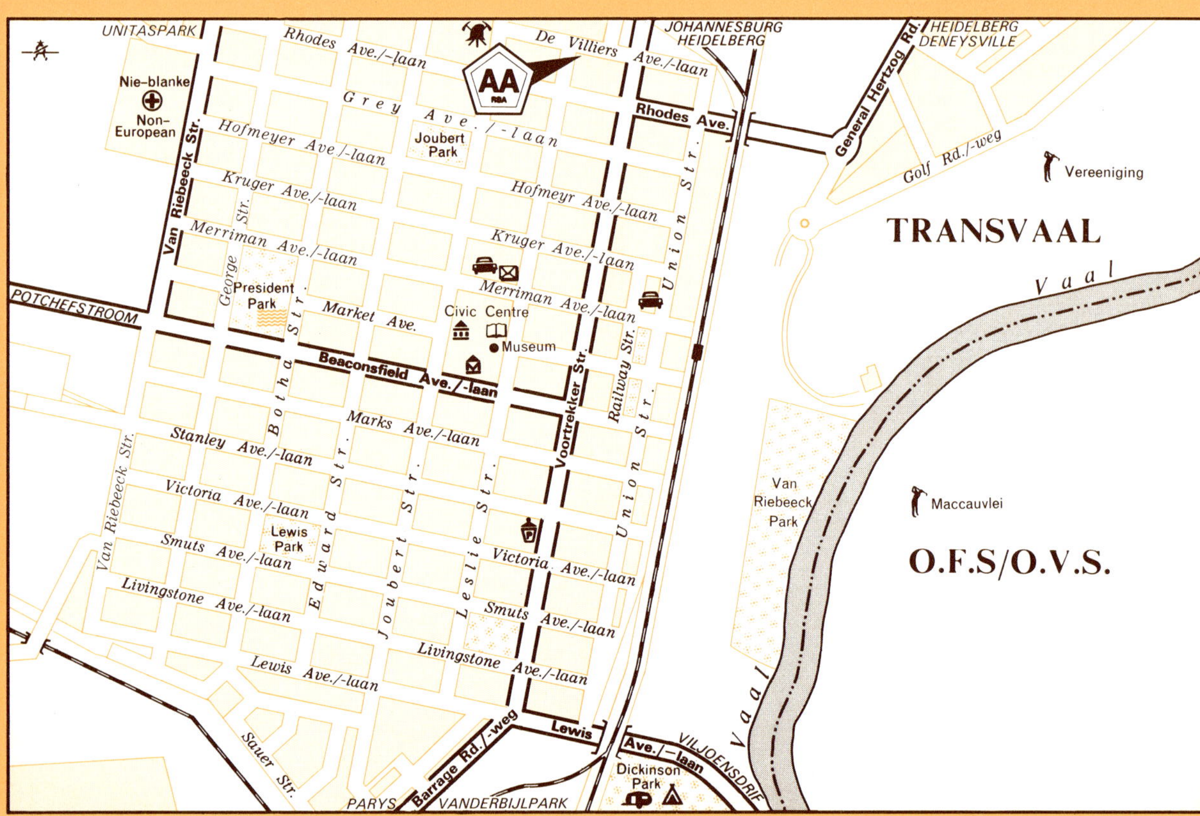

Vereeniging 0 500 m m **66**

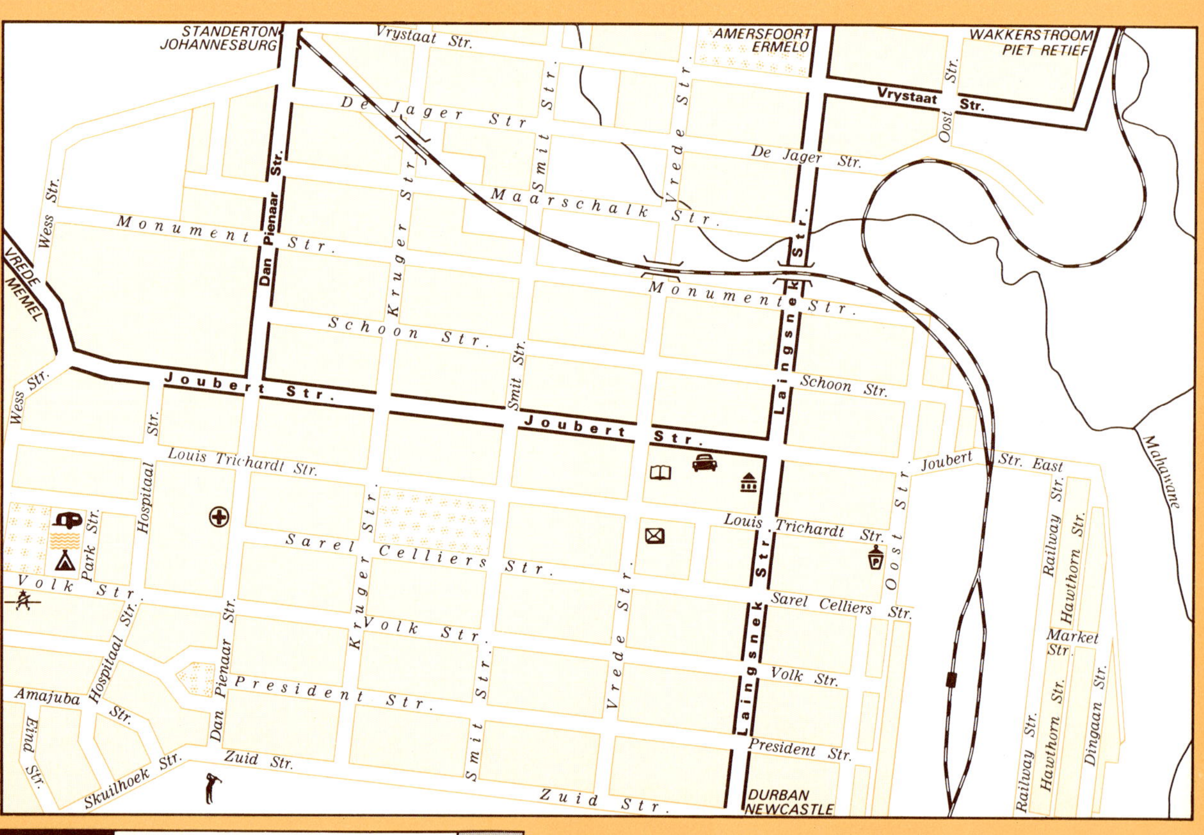

Volksrust 0 500 m m **67**

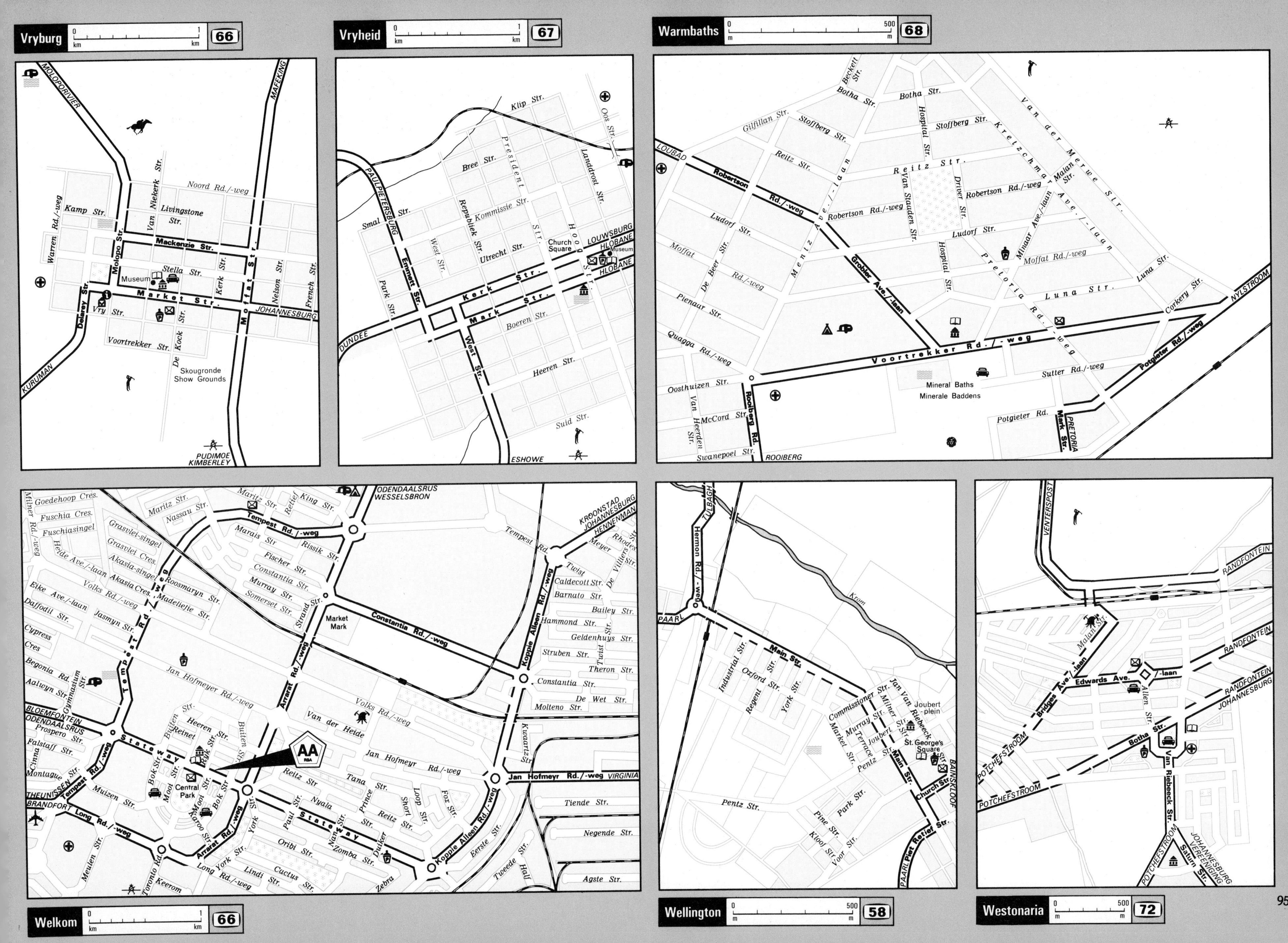
Vryburg
66
Vryheid
67
Warmbaths
68
Welkom
66
Wellington
58
Westonaria
72
Mineral Baths
Minerale Baddens
Central Park
Market Mark
Church Square
Skougronde Show Grounds
St. George's Square
Joubert -plein

White River
0 1
km km
69
LANGEMERE DAM
NASIONALE KRUGERWILDTUIN
KRUGER NATIONAL PARK
Theo Kleynhans Str.
Tom Lawrence Str.
Peter
William Lunn
PLASTON
Danie Joubert Str.
Hennie van Til Str.
Graham
Kruger Park Str.
Frank Townsend Str.
Van Riebeeck Str.
Citrus Ave./-laan
NELSPRUIT
Williston
0 500
m m
61
BRANDVLEI
Riebeeck Str.
CARNARVON
Hoog Str.
De Wet Str.
Amandelboom
New Str.
Mulder Str.
Theron Str.
Gotz Str.
Herbst Str.
Robinsky Str.
Reineke Str.
Lutz Str.
Church Str.
Kuhn Str.
Hodgson Str.
Boom Str.
Croquet Str.
Kerom
Tennis Str.
Fountain Str.
Klipheuvel Str.
South
Theron Str.
Gotz Str.
CALVINIA
SUTHERLAND
FRASERBURG
Winburg
0 500
m m
66
Northern Ave./-laan
Pres. Steyn Str.
Daantje Malherbe Str.
Central Ave. Str.
Winburgspruit
Stern Str.
Schnehage Str.
Gillespie
THEUNISSEN
De Villiers Str.
Hendrik Str.
Wilcocks Str.
Bijna Str.
La Rey Ave./-laan
DURBAN JOHANNESBURG PRETORIUS
WILLEM PRETORIUS GAME RESERVE
Pieter van der Werken Str.
Nico van der Merwe Str.
Kerk Str.
Lotz
Gen. De Str.
Leech Str.
Andries Pretoriusplein
Brand Str.
Sibella
Jac Coetzer Str.
Frikkie Cronje Str.
Achter Str.
Voortrekker Str.
Johanna
Victoria Str.
Mc Lennan Str.
Bredell Str.
Dickson Str.
Market Square Markplein
Prince Edward Str.
Ladybrand Str.
Stuart Str.
Wright
J.C.Potgieter Str.
BLOEMFONTEIN
EXCELSIOR
Witbank
0 500
m m
69
GROBLERSDAL
Retief Ave./-laan
Hertzog Str.
MIDDELBURG
Blesbok Ave./-laan
Voortrekker Rd./-weg
Van Der Stel Ave./-laan
Havenga Str.
Main Str.
Clarendon Ave./-laan
Arras Str.
Kruger
Elizabeth Ave./-laan
Rhodes Str.
Smuts Ave./-laan
Paul
Hofmeyr
President
Smuts Ave./-laan
Van Deventer Str.
Yudaken Str.
Diederichs Str.
Eadie Str.
Ave./-laan
Markplein Market Square
Botha
Ave./-laan
Arras Str.
Rhodes Str.
Haig Ave./-laan
Jellicoe Str.
Allenby Str.
Beatty Ave./-laan
AA RSA
PRETORIA SPRINGS
BETHAL
OTTOSDAL
Dundon Str.
De La Rey Str.
Van Wyk Str.
Potgieter Str.
Bodenstein
SCHWEIZER-RENEKE
Kemp Str.
Vrede Str.
Kruger Str.
Leask Str.
Van Riebeeck Rd./-weg
Piet Retief Str.
KLERKSDORP
Jansen Str.
Voortrekkerplein
Smit Str.
Kruger Str.
Bornman Str.
Kok Str.
Market Square
Makwassie
LEEUDORINGSTAD
Drive-in Theatre Inryteater
Piet Retief Str.
Bosman Str.
Broadbent Str.
Brand Str.
Rood Str.
Presidentplein
Irvin Str.
Leyds Str.
Joubert
Geyer Str.
Fels Str.
BLOEMHOF
MAKWASSIE
Wolmaransstad
0 1
km km
66
Van Riebeeck Park
Quellerie Str.
LAINGSBURG BEAUFORT-WES BEAUFORT WEST
Roux Rd./-weg
Besselaar Rd.
Willow
De La Bat Rd./-weg
KAAPSTAD CAPE TOWN
Hospital Dam
Klue Str.
AA RSA
Heyns Str.
Riebeeck Str.
Tulbagh Str.
KAAPSTAD CAPE TOWN
Rabie Ave./-laan
Afrikanermuseum
Church Str.
Porter Str.
Napier Str.
High Str.
Russell Str.
Mertring Str.
Eben Dönges
Pells Str.
ROBERTSON
Sugget Str.
Durban Str.
Fairbairn Str.
Leipoldt Str.
Trappes Str.
Porter Str.
Adderley Str.
Van Zyl Ave./-laan
Durban Str.
Le Sueur Str.
Mertring Str. Ext./-verl.
Hammer Str.
Parker Str.
Grey Str.
Gordon Str.
Buitenkant Str.
VILLIERSDORP
Worcester
0 1
km km
58
ROUXVILLE WEPENER
Boven Str.
Reichenberg
Sportgronde
De Winnaar Str.
Chase Str.
Kerk Str.
Committee Str.
Ralph Str.
Voortrekker Str.
Voortrekker Str.
MOHALE'S HOEK
Boom Str.
Vechtkop Str.
Skougronde
Boom Str.
Str.
Orange Str.
Keizers Gracht
Gustavus Str.
Kerk Str.
Mathey Str.
Mathey Str.
Hoofd Str.
Hoofd Str.
Piet Retief Gardens/-tuine
Joachim Str.
HERSCHEL LADY GREY
Reichenberg Str.
George Str.
MOYENI (QUTHING)
George Str.
Missionary Lane
Hendrik Str.
Meyer Str.
Hendrik Str.
Zastron
0 500
m m
62
GABORONE
Jeppe Str.
Joubert Str.
Jan Rossouw Ave./-laan
Jean Str.
LOBATSE
Jean Str.
Van Riebeeck Str.
Pache Str.
Park Str.
Potgieter Str.
Str.
Hendrik
Gerrit Maritz Str.
Russell Str.
Viljoen Str.
President Str.
Reid Str.
Hendrik Potgieter Str.
Sarel Cilliers Str.
Queen Str.
Voortrekker Str.
GROOT-MARICO
Kerk Str.
Coetzee Str.
Piet Retief Str.
Karreespruit
MAFEKING
Klip Str.
Rots Str.
Wolfaart Str.
Karreespruit
Du Preez Str.
Klip Str.
Loop Str.
De Lange Str.
Boom Str.
Zeerust
0 500
m m
68

Place Names

A glance at the detailed maps included in this guide reveal a multitude of names – some known, others unknown. Look a little closer and you will find towns, mountains, passes, rivers, dams, game reserves and all manner of places of interest to arouse your curiosity.

Soon you experience an increasing fascination for this inexhaustible subject – its sheer magnetism will attract and motivate you to journey into the unknown, to explore for yourself, perhaps far more so than will many a glossy travel advertisement.

Travel with the maps and it becomes a voyage of discovery as each feature is encountered – where did the name originate, when did the town come into being, what were the people like who pioneered the way and christened with such imagination the many features included?

Soon the study of place names becomes an absorbing hobby, providing endless interest, anecdote and pleasure at the uncovering of the story behind the name. A random glance at some of the names reveals stories of rich historic significance, Bloedrivier, Rorke's Drift, Isandlwana – all scenes of famous battles that gave colour and character to the country. Or there are area names such as Namaqualand, where annually daisies blossom forth in flowering carpets of magnificence after the spring rains, or the Valley of Desolation outside Graaff-Reinet, where majestic buttresses and pinnacles carved out of a dolerite plateau by the erosive forces of centuries, present an awe-inspiring and attractive scene.

The blending of so many cultures provides a variety of descriptive names; from an onomatopoeic Xhosa word like Lusikisiki, representing the sound of wind whispering through the reeds, to Hotazel, which gives one some idea of what the climate is like in that part of the world! Bourke's Luck reminds one of a miner who struck it rich in the Eastern Transvaal and who is forever immortalised thereby – lucky for some!

Names such as Avontuur, Breakfast Vlei, Discovery, Fort Mistake, Glimlag, Houmoed, Long Hope, Moedverloor, Nuwehoop, Ons Hoop, Volmoed and Oorwinning tell of the human drama behind each name; of adventure, hope, disappointment, success and humour – indeed, of the whole spectrum of living experience.

Countless other names are included in this guide and the purpose of this gazetteer, apart from capturing the romance of the subject, is to help you to locate them on the maps. Hopefully too, your appetite will be whetted and your expectation in this field awakened.

If you want to find a particular place or feature on the maps, the gazetteer will supply the answer. Here the names are arranged alphabetically (as they are in other sections of the guide) and indicate the map page number, the degree square, and the approximate direction within that degree square where the name will be located. The degree squares are formed by the green lines of latitude (East-West) and longitude (North-South) which are shown on the maps at 1° intervals.

These squares are numbered alphanumerically in blue in the borders of each map – see illustration. For example, if you wanted to locate Graskop you would look up this name in the gazetteer and find an entry reading as follows – Graskop T 71 B4 ↙. This means that Graskop is in the Transvaal and can be found on page 71 within degree square B4 more or less in the direction within that square indicated by the arrow (or in the centre if a dot is shown).

The same principle applies to all other features included in the guide, where in most instances, the names are listed exactly as shown on the map with no separate English or Afrikaans versions provided.

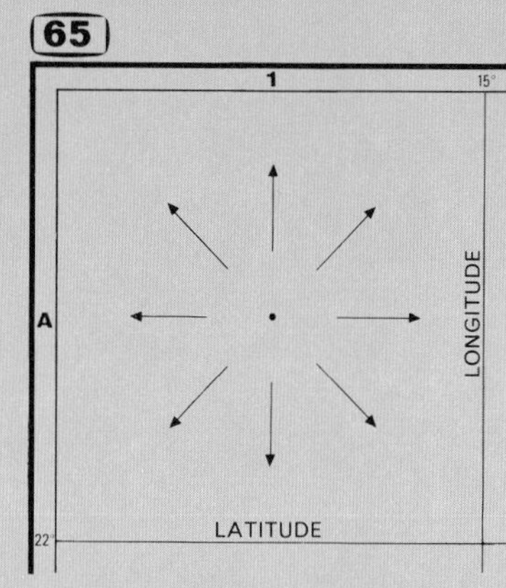

The following are abbreviations used.

Y – BophuthaTswana
B – Botswana
C – Cape
L – Lesotho
N – Natal
O – Orange Free State
T – Transvaal
X – Transkei
Z – Swaziland
NS – Inset map

So, if you want to know where a place is and how to get there, the maps will tell you – have fun!

Aalwynsfontein	C	60 B6	•
Aandster	T	66 B3	←
Aapdraai	T	68 C4	←
Abbotsdale	C	58 C3	•
Aberdeen	C	59 A4	←
Aberdeen Road	C	59 A4	↙
Aberfeldy	O	67 C1	↗
Abrahamsdam	C	65 D4	↗
Acornhoek	T	69 B4	←
Acornhoek	T	71 B5	←
Acton Homes	N	67 C2	•
Adams Mission	N	63 B3	↗
Adams Mission	N	63 NS	↗
Addo	C	59 B5	→
Adelaide	C	59 A6	↙
Adendorp	C	59 A4	↑
Adriaanshoop	T	68 B4	↘
Afgrond	T	69 C3	↖
Afguns	T	68 A5	↘
Afrikander Mine	T	66 A4	↓
Afrikaskop	O	66 C6	↗
Afsondering	X	62 B6	↗
Aggeneys	C	60 A6	↗
Agter-Sneeuberg	C	62 D3	↖
Agtertang	C	62 B3	↙
Agulhas	C	58 D5	↙
Ahrens	N	67 D3	↗
Airlie	T	69 C3	↓
Albert Falls	N	63 A3	↖
Albertinia	C	59 C1	↑
Alberton	T	68 D6	↖
Alberton	T	72 NS	↘
Albertshoek	T	66 B3	↑
Alcockspruit	N	67 B3	↙
Alderley	X	60 B3	↗
Alderley	X	63 NS	•
Alettasrus	C	66 A2	↓
Alexanderbaai	C	64 E3	↓
Alexander Bay	C	64 E3	↓
Alexandra	T	72 NS	↑
Alexandria	C	59 B6	↙
Alheit	C	65 C2	↓
Alice	C	60 B1	↘
Alicedale	C	59 B6	←
Aliwal-Noord	C	62 B4	↘
Aliwal North	C	62 B4	↘
Alkmaar	T	69 C3	→
Alkmaar	T	71 C4	→
Allandale	O	66 C5	↙
Allanridge	O	66 B4	↓
Alliance	T	72 NS	→
Alldays	T	70 B4	↙
All Saints	X	62 C6	←
Alma	T	68 B6	←
Aloe Fjord	T	66 A6	↙
Aloes	C	59 B5	↓
Alpha	N	64 B4	↙
Alrode	T	68 D6	↖
Alrode	T	72 NS	↓
Althorpe	T	71 C5	•
Alton	N	67 NS	•
Alusaf	N	67 NS	•
Amabele	C	60 B2	↓
Amaila	T	66 B3	↖
Amanzi	C	59 B5	↓
Amanzimtoti	N	63 B3	↗
Amanzimtoti	N	63 NS	↗
Amatikulu	N	67 D4	↑
Amatole Basin	C	60 B1	↘
Amersfoort	T	67 B2	↗
Amsterdam	T	67 A3	↘
Amsterdamhoek	C	59 B5	↓
Andalusia (Jan Kempdorp)	T	66 B2	↘
Andrieskraal	C	59 B4	↘
Andriesvale	C	65 A2	↓
Anerley	N	63 B3	↓
Anerley	N	63 NS	↓
Angelo	T	72 NS	→
Anglers	T	72 NS	↙
Angus	T	68 D6	←
Angus	T	72 NS	↓
Annandale	N	67 B3	↙
Ann's Villa	C	59 B5	↗
Antwerp	T	72 NS	↗
Anysberg	C	58 C5	→
Anysspruit	T	67 B3	↑
Anzac	T	72 NS	→
Apel	T	69 B2	→
Apex	T	72 NS	→
Appelbosch	N	63 A3	→
Arabta	O	66 C6	↖
Arbor	T	69 D1	↗
Arboretum Industrial Township	N	67 NS	↗
Argent	T	69 D1	↗
Arlington	O	66 C5	↗
Armmansvriend	C	59 B4	↓
Arnoldton	C	60 B2	↘
Arnot	T	69 C2	↘
Artois	C	58 C4	←
Arundel	C	62 B3	↙
Arundel	N	63 NS	↖
Ascent	O	67 B2	↖
Ashburton	N	63 A3	↓
Ashburton	N	63 NS	↑
Ashton	C	58 C5	↙
Askeaton	X	62 C5	↓
Askham	C	65 A2	↘
Askraal	C	58 D5	↗
Assegaaibos	C	59 B4	↙
Assen	T	68 C5	↗
Aston Bay	C	59 C4	↗
Atamelang	Y	66 A3	↖
Athlone	C	58 NS	↑
Atlantis	C	58 C3	↙
Atlasville	T	72 NS	→
Atoom	T	68 B6	↙
Augrabies	C	65 C2	↙
Aurora	C	58 B3	↓
Austin's Post	O	62 A3	→
Avoca	T	69 C4	↙
Avondzon	T	68 C6	↓
Avontuur	C	59 C3	↙
Baanbreker	T	67 A2	•
Baardskeerdersbos	C	58 D4	↓
Babanango	N	67 C4	↖
Babelegi	Y	68 C5	↗
Bacela	C	62 B2	↑
Badfontein	T	69 C3	↖
Badi	X	60 B3	•
Badi	X	60 NS	↙
Badplaas	T	69 C3	↓
Bailey	C	62 C4	↘
Bakenberg	T	69 A1	↘
Bakerville	T	68 C4	↙
Balderja	C	60 B1	•
Balegane	Z	69 D4	↑
Balfour	T	66 A6	↘
Balfour	C	60 B1	→
Balgowan	N	63 A3	←
Ballengeich	N	67 B2	↘
Ballitoville	N	63 A4	↙
Ballot's Bay	C	59 C2	↑
Ballot's Bay	C	59 NS	←
Balmoral	T	66 A5	→
Balmoral	T	69 C1	↘
Baltimore	T	70 C3	↑
Balule	T	69 B4	↗
Balule	T	71 B5	↗
Banana Beach	N	63 NS	↓
Banchory	N	63 B2	↖
Bandelierkop	T	70 C4	↗
Bandur	T	70 B4	↓
Bank	T	68 D5	↑
Bankies	X	62 C4	→
Bankkop	T	67 A3	•
Banner Rest	N	63 C3	↖
Banner Rest	N	63 NS	↙
Bantams	C	58 C5	↑
Bantu-Batho	T	66 A6	→
Banyan	T	70 C4	↑
Bapsfontein	T	68 C6	↓
Baragwanath	T	72 NS	↙
Barakke	C	59 A4	↗
Barandas	C	59 B3	←
Barberspan	T	66 A3	↓
Barberton	T	69 C4	↙
Barkly Bridge	C	59 B5	↘
Barkly East	C	62 B5	↓
Barkly-Oos	C	62 B5	↓
Barkly Pass	C	62 C5	↗
Barkly-Wes	C	66 C2	•
Barkly West	C	66 C2	•
Barnardskop	C	59 NS	↖
Baroda	C	62 D3	↑
Baroe	C	59 B4	↑
Barrage	T	66 A5	↘
Barretts	T	69 C3	→
Barrington	C	59 NS	↑
Barrydale	C	58 C5	↘
Bashee Bridge	X	62 C6	↓
Bashee Bridge	X	60 NS	←
Basin	X	62 B5	↓
Bassau	C	59 B2	↘
Bathurst	C	60 C1	↘
Bathusitse	Y	68 D3	↑
Battery	T	72 NS	↖
Baven on Sea	N	63 B3	↙
Baven on Sea	N	63 NS	↙
Baviaan	C	58 C5	↗
Baviaanshoek	C	58 C4	↑
Baviaansrivier	C	59 A5	→
Bayne's Drift	B	70 B3	•
Baynesfield	N	63 A3	↙
Baynesfield	N	63 NS	↖
Baziya	X	62 C6	↙
Bazley	N	63 B3	→
Bazley	N	63 NS	•
Beach Terminus	N	63 NS	↙
Beach View	C	59 C5	↑
Beacon Hill	N	67 D2	↗
Beaufort-Wes	C	59 A2	↑
Beaufort West	C	59 A2	↑
Beauty	T	70 C2	↗
Bedford	C	59 A6	↙
Bedfordview	T	72 NS	•
Bedwang	Y	68 C6	↖
Beecham Woods	X	60 B3	↗
Beecham Woods	X	60 NS	↓
Beesbank	C	64 E3	→
Beestekraal	T	68 C5	↑
Begrade	T	67 B4	↖
Behulpsaam	C	59 A4	→
Bekker	C	65 B5	↘
Bela-Bela	L	66 D6	↖
Belcobos	C	65 B5	↗
Belfast	T	69 C3	↙
Bell	C	60 C2	↖
Bellsbank	C	66 C2	↖
Bellville	C	58 C3	↓
Bellville	C	58 NS	↗
Belmont	C	62 A2	•
Belmore	C	62 B5	↘
Belvedere	C	59 NS	↓
Benadeshof	T	66 B3	↗
Bengu	X	62 C5	↙
Benoni	T	68 D6	↖
Benoni	T	72 NS	→
Bensonvale	X	62 B5	↙
Berea	C	58 D4	↑
Bergen	T	67 B3	↗
Bergnek	T	69 B2	↖
Bergplaas	C	59 B2	↘
Bergplaas	C	59 NS	↖
Bergpunt	T	70 NS	↖
Bergrivier	C	58 B3	↙
Bergville	N	67 C2	↙
Berlin	C	60 B2	↓
Bermolli	C	65 C4	→
Bertievale	X	62 B6	↑
Besters	N	67 C2	→
Bethal	T	67 A2	•
Bethanie	Y	68 C5	•
Bethanie	Y	68 NS	↖
Bethany	O	62 A3	→
Bethesdaweg	C	62 C2	↘
Bethlehem	O	66 C6	↖
Bethulie	O	62 B3	→
Bettiesdam	T	67 A2	↓
Betty's Bay	C	58 D3	→
Bewaarkloof	T	69 B2	↗
Bewley	T	68 C3	↘
Bezuidenhoutskraal	T	69 C1	↗
Bhunya	Z	67 A4	←
Bibby's Hoek	C	59 B2	↘
Bibby's Hoek	C	59 NS	↑
Biesiesfontein	C	60 C5	↗
Biesiespoort	C	61 C5	↙
Biesiesvlei	T	68 D3	→
Bietou	C	59 NS	→
Big Bend	Z	67 A4	↘
Biggarsberg	N	67 C2	↗
Big Umngazi	X	63 C2	↓
Big Umngazi	X	60 NS	↗
Bikanadale	X	60 B3	↑
Bikanadale	X	60 NS	•
Birchleigh	T	68 D6	↖
Birchleigh	T	72 NS	↗
Bishop Lavis	C	58 NS	↗
Bishopstowe	N	63 A3	↓
Bisi	X	63 B2	→
Bismark	T	69 B3	↑
Bitterfontein	C	60 C6	↖
Bityi	X	62 C6	↓
Bityi	X	60 NS	↖
Bizana	X	63 B2	↘
Blackheath	T	72 NS	↖
Blackhill	T	69 C2	↙
Black Rock	N	67 B5	↗
Black Streams	X	62 C4	↘
Bladgrond	C	65 C1	↘
Blairbeth	T	68 C4	↖
Blanco	C	59 B2	↙
Blanco	C	59 NS	←
Blanco	C	62 D4	↖
Bland's Drift	C	59 C1	↗
Bleshoender	C	59 NS	←
Blesmanspos	C	66 B2	↙
Blikana	X	62 B5	↘
Blikfontein	C	65 B5	↘
Blinkwater	T	70 C4	↖
Bloedrivier	N	67 B3	↓
Bloekomspruit	T	66 A6	↙
Bloemfontein	O	66 D4	↖
Bloemhof	T	66 B3	↓
Blouberg	T	70 C3	↗
Bloubergstrand	C	58 C3	↙
Bloudrif	O	66 C4	↗
Blouhaak	T	70 C4	↑
Bloukop	T	67 A2	↘
Bluecliff	C	59 B5	•
Bluegums	X	62 B5	←
Blue River	C	60 B2	↘
Bluewater	C	60 B2	↘
Blythedale	N	63 A4	↖
Blythswood Institute	X	60 B3	↖
Blythswood Institute	X	60 NS	↙
Blyvooruitzicht	T	66 A5	↑
Boatlaname	B	68 A3	↘
Bochum	T	70 C4	↖
Bodenstein	T	68 D4	↖
Bodiam	C	60 C2	↑
Bodibe	Y	68 D3	↗
Boegoeberg	C	65 C4	↙
Boerboonfontein	C	58 C5	↓
Boesmanskop	O	62 B5	↖
Boesmansnek	N	63 A2	↙
Boesmansriviermond	C	60 C1	↘
Boetsap	C	66 B2	↓
Bogogobo	B	65 A3	↘
Bojeni	X	60 B3	•
Bojeni	X	60 NS	↙
Bokaa	B	68 B4	←
Bokfontein	C	58 B4	↙
Bokkraal	C	60 B6	↓
Boknes	C	60 C1	↓
Boksburg	T	68 D6	↖
Boksburg	T	72 NS	→
Boksburg East	T	72 NS	→
Boksburg North	T	72 NS	→
Bokspits	B	65 A2	↘
Bo-Langverwag	C	58 C5	↙
Bolo Reserve	C	60 B2	↗
Bolotwa	X	62 C5	↙
Bon Accord	T	68 C6	←
Bon Accord	T	68 NS	↗
Bonekraal	C	61 C2	↓
Bonnievale	C	58 C5	↙
Bonny Doon	N	67 C3	↖
Bonny Ridge	N	63 B2	←
Bonthoek	C	62 C5	↑
Bontrand	X	63 B2	→
Bonza Bay	C	60 B2	↘
Boomlaer	N	67 B3	↘
Bogate	L	62 A5	↗
Boons	T	68 C5	↙
Boons	T	68 NS	↙
Booth	N	63 NS	↗
Borata	L	62 A5	↙
Borchers	T	70 C5	↖
Border Gate	T	69 C4	↘
Borotsi	B	70 C2	↑
Bosbokrand	T	69 B4	↙
Bosbokrand	T	71 B5	↙
Boshoek	T	68 C5	←
Boshof	O	66 C3	←
Boshoffsrus	N	67 D3	↖
Boskloof	C	58 B3	↗
Boskop	T	66 A5	←
Boskuil	T	66 B3	→
Bosmansfontein	T	67 A1	↘
Bospoort	T	66 A4	↙
Bosspruit	T	68 C5	←
Bosspruit	T	68 NS	↖
Boston	N	63 A2	↘
Botha	C	58 C4	←
Botha's Hill	N	63 NS	↑
Bothashoek	O	66 C3	↙
Bothashoop	T	67 A3	↘
Bothaspas	N	67 B2	↘
Bothaville	O	66 B4	↗
Bothithong	Y	65 B5	↗
Botrivier	C	58 D4	↖
Botterkloof	C	58 D6	←
Boulders	T	71 C5	←
Bourketon	O	66 B4	↗
Bo-Wadrif	C	58 B5	←
Bowker's Park	C	62 C4	↘
Boyne	T	69 A2	↘
Braamfontein	T	72 NS	•
Bracefield	C	59 B5	↗
Brackenfell	C	58 C3	↓
Bracken Hill	C	59 NS	↘
Brackenhurst	T	72 NS	↓
Braemar	N	63 B3	↑
Braemar	N	63 NS	•
Braemar	N	63 NS	↙
Brakkloof	T	68 C4	→
Brakpan	T	68 D6	↑
Brakpan	T	72 NS	→
Brakpoort	C	61 C5	↖
Brakspruit	T	66 A4	↓
Brakwal	N	67 C2	↑
Branddraai	T	69 B3	↘
Branddrif	O	66 D5	↖
Brandekraal	C	59 B4	↙
Brandfort	O	66 C4	↓
Brandkop	C	61 C1	↖
Brandrivier	C	58 C6	↙
Brandvlei	C	61 B2	•
Brandwag	C	59 C2	↖
Brandwater	O	66 C6	↙
Braunschweig	C	60 B2	↙
Braunville	X	62 C5	←
Bray	C	64 B5	→
Breakfast Vlei	C	60 C1	↗
Bredasdorp	C	58 D5	←
Breërivier	C	58 C4	←
Breidbach	C	60 B2	↓
Breipaal	O	62 B4	↖
Brenton	C	59 NS	↓
Brenton-on-Sea	C	59 NS	↓
Brentwood Park	T	72 NS	↗
Brereton Park	T	67 A3	↓
Breyten	T	69 D2	↗
Bridgecamp	C	62 D5	↑
Bridgewater	T	70 B4	←
Brits	T	68 C5	→
Brits	T	68 NS	↑
Britstown	C	61 B5	↓
Britsville	C	61 B5	↘
Britten	T	66 B3	↙
Broedersput	T	66 A3	↙
Broederstroom	T	68 NS	•
Broham	T	69 C3	→
Broham	T	71 C4	→
Brombeek	T	70 B4	←
Brondal	T	69 C3	→
Brondal	T	71 C4	→
Bronkhorstspruit	T	69 C1	↘
Broodsnyersplaas	T	69 D2	↑
Brooklands	T	69 C3	↗
Brooklands	T	71 C4	↗
Brooks Nek	X	63 B2	↓
Brownridge	T	68 B6	↙
Bruintjieshoogte	C	59 A5	↙
Bryanston	T	72 NS	↑
Brymac	X	62 C5	↙
Buccleuch	T	72 NS	↗
Bucklands	C	65 D5	↗
Buffalo Nek	X	62 B6	↘
Buffelsbaai	C	59 NS	↓
Buffelsdrif	C	59 B2	↘
Buffelsdrifthek	T	68 A4	↘
Buffelsjagsrivier	C	58 D5	↑
Buffelsklip	C	59 B2	→
Buffelsvlei	T	69 B3	↙
Buitenzorg	T	69 C2	↑
Bulembe	Z	69 C4	↙
Bulge River	T	68 B5	↗
Bulletrap	C	60 A5	→
Bull Hill	Y	66 B2	↓
Bulpan	T	69 C2	↙
Bulshoek	C	58 B3	↗
Bultfontein	O	66 C4	↖
Bulwer	N	63 A2	↘
Buntingville	X	62 C6	↘
Buntingville	X	60 NS	↑
Burgersdorp	C	62 C4	↑
Burgersfort	T	69 B3	↙
Burgerville	C	62 B2	↓
Burgervilleweg	C	62 B2	↓
Burnshill	C	60 B2	↙
Bushman Rock	T	69 C4	↖
Bushman Rock	T	71 C5	↖
Busila	X	60 B3	↖
Busila	X	60 NS	↙
Butha Buthe	L	66 C6	↙
Butterworth	X	60 B2	↖
Butterworth	X	60 NS	↙
Buxedeni	N	67 C4	↗
Buxton	C	60 B1	↘
Buysdorp	T	70 C4	↑
Bylsteel	T	69 A2	↓
Caba Vale	X	62 C6	↑
Cafutweni	X	60 B3	↖
Cafutweni	X	60 NS	↙
Cairn	T	71 C4	→
Cala	X	62 C5	→
Calderwood	C	60 B1	↘
Caledon	C	58 D4	↑
Caledonspoort	O	66 C6	↙
Calitzdorp	C	59 B1	→
Calvert	N	67 B3	↘
Calvinia	C	61 C1	→
Cambria	C	59 B4	↓
Camelot	N	67 C2	↗
Cameron's Glen	C	59 A6	←
Camfer	C	59 B2	↓
Campbell	C	65 C5	↘
Camperdown	N	63 A3	↓
Camperdown	N	63 NS	↑
Cancele	X	62 B6	↘
Candover	N	67 B4	→
Canelands	N	63 A4	↙
Canelands	N	63 NS	↗
Cape St. Francis	C	59 C4	↗
Cape Town	C	58 C3	↓
Cape Town	C	58 NS	↑
Cardoville	T	66 A5	→
Carletonville	T	66 A5	↖
Carlisle Bridge	C	59 B6	↖
Carlisonia	T	68 C4	↙
Carlow	T	70 B4	↙
Carlton	C	62 C2	↗
Carnarvon	C	61 B4	↙
Carolina	T	69 D3	↖
Carolusberg	C	60 A5	↘
Casteel	T	69 B4	↙
Casteel	T	71 B5	↙
Catalina	N	63 B3	↓
Catalina	N	63 NS	↓
Cathcart	C	60 B2	←
Cathedral Peak	N	67 C2	↙
Cathkin Park	N	67 C2	↙
Cato Ridge	N	63 A3	↓
Cato Ridge	N	63 NS	↑
Cat's Pass	X	60 B3	←
Cat's Pass	X	60 NS	↙
Cattleton	T	71 B5	←
Cebe	X	60 B3	↓
Cebe	X	60 NS	↙
Cedara	N	63 A3	←
Cedarberg	C	58 B4	↙
Cedarmont	T	67 A2	↙
Cedarville	N	63 B2	←
Cefane	C	60 B3	↙
Central	T	72 NS	↖
Centuli	X	60 B3	•
Centuli	X	60 NS	↙
Ceres	C	58 C4	↖
Ceylon	T	72 NS	↓
Chalumna	C	60 C2	↑
Chalwell	N	63 NS	→
Chamdor	T	72 NS	←
Champagne Castle	N	67 D2	↑
Charfred	X	62 B6	↓
Charl Cilliers	T	67 A2	↙
Charlestown	N	67 B2	→
Chieveley	N	67 C2	↘
Chloorkop	T	68 D6	↖
Chloorkop	T	72 NS	↗
Chrissiesmeer	T	69 D3	↖
Christiana	T	66 B3	↙
Christina	O	67 B2	↓
Christmas Rock	C	60 C2	↗
Chromite	T	68 B5	↙
Churchhaven	C	58 C3	↖
Ciko	X	60 B3	↑
Ciko	X	60 NS	↙
Cintsa	C	60 B3	↙
Cintsa Mouth East	C	60 B3	↙
Cintsa West	C	60 B3	↙
Citrus	T	71 C4	→
Citrusdal	C	58 B4	↙
Clansthal	N	63 B3	↗
Clansthal	N	63 NS	→
Clanville	C	62 B5	↗
Clanwilliam	C	58 B3	↗
Claremont	C	58 NS	↑
Clarens	O	66 C6	←
Clarkebury	X	62 C6	↙
Clarkson	C	59 C4	↑
Claudius	T	68 C6	↙
Claudius	T	68 NS	→
Clayville	T	68 C6	↙
Clayville	T	72 NS	↗
Cleland	N	63 NS	↖
Clewer	T	69 C2	↙
Cliffdale	N	63 A3	↘
Cliffdale	N	63 NS	↑
Clifford	C	62 C5	↑
Clifton	C	58 NS	↖
Clocolan	O	66 C5	↓
Clovelly	C	58 NS	•
Coalbrook	O	66 A5	↘
Coalville	T	69 D2	↖
Cobalt Mine	T	69 C2	↑
Coega	C	59 B5	↘
Coerney	C	59 B5	→

NATIONAL PARKS, GAME AND NATURE RESERVES

Name	Region	Map ref	Direction
Nasionale Kalahari-Gemsbokpark	C	64 B2	↙
Nasionale Kruger-wildtuin	T	69 A4	←
Nasionale Kruger-wildtuin	T	71 C5	↑
Ndumu	N	67 A5	↙
N'jelele Nature Reserve	T	70 B5	↙
Ohrigstaddam-natuurreservaat	T	69 B3	↓
Ohrigstaddam-natuurreservaat	T	70 NS	↑
Onderstepoort Nature Reserve	T	68 NS	↗
Oribi Gorge Nature Reserve	N	63 B3	↙
Oribi Gorge Nature Reserve	N	63 NS	↙
Percy Fyfe Nature Reserve	T	69 B2	↖
Richards Bay Game Sanctuary	N	67 C5	↙
Richards Bay Game Sanctuary	N	67 NS	↓
Royal Natal National Park	N	67 C1	↗
Rust der Winter Nature Reserve	T	68 C6	↑
St. Lucia	N	67 C5	↑
St. Lucia Park	N	67 C5	•
Salmonsdam	C	58 D4	→
Sea View Game Park	C	59 B5	↓
Sehlabathabe	L	63 A2	↙
Shlaralumi	T	69 B4	↑
Shlaralumi	T	71 B5	↑
Skihaven Game Park	C	58 D5	←
Sodwana Bay National Park	N	67 B5	→
Sohebele Game Reserve	T	69 B4	↑
Sohebele Game Reserve	T	71 B5	↑
Stormsrivier Nature Reserve	C	59 C4	↖
Suikerbosrand Nature Reserve	T	66 A6	←
Suikerbosrand Nature Reserve	T	72 NS	↓
Thomas Baines Nature Reserve	C	59 B6	•
Tsitsikama Forest and Coastal National Parks	C	59 C3	↗
Tsitsikama Forest and Coastal National Parks	C	59 NS	→
Uitenhage Nature Reserve	C	59 B5	↓
Umfolozi	N	67 C4	↗
Umlalazi-natuurreservaat	N	67 C4	↘
Umtamvuna Nature Reserve	N	63 B3	↙
Umtamvuna-natuurreservaat	N	63 NS	↙
Umvoti Vlei Nature Reserve	N	63 A3	↑
Vaaldam-natuurreservaat	T	66 B6	↑
Van Riebeeck-natuurreservaat	T	68 C6	↙
Van Riebeeck-natuurreservaat	T	68 NS	→
Vergelegen Nature Reserve	N	63 A2	•
Vernon Crookes Nature Reserve	N	63 B3	↗
Vernon Crockes-natuurreservaat	N	63 NS	•
Willem Pretorius-wildtuin	O	66 C5	↖

NATIONAL MONUMENTS

The approximate positions of the following National Monuments are shown on the relevant six-colour maps by means of white letters of the alphabet on a black rectangle, thus A. They are lettered from top to bottom and from left to right on each map or map inset.
For further information, consult the publication "The Historical Monuments of South Africa", by Prof. J. J. Oberholster.

Page		Monument	Map ref
Page 58	A	Matjiesfontein	C5 ↑
	B	Blockhouse, Laingsburg	C5 ↗
	C	Birthplace of Gen. J. C. Smuts, Riebeek West	C3 ↗
	D	Old Drostdy, Tulbagh	C4 ↖
	E	Tulbagh	C4 ↖
	F	Astronomical Relic, Touws River	C4 ↗
	G	C. J. Langenhoven's Birthplace, Hoeko	C6 ←
	H	Mamre	C3 ←
	I	Blockhouse, Wellington	C4 ←
	J	La Motte Cemetery, Franschhoek	C4 ↙
	K	Church Bell and Bridge, Genadendal	C4 ↓
	L	Old Bridge, Somerset West	D3 ↗
	M	Gantouw Pass, Sir Lowry's Pass	D4 ↖
	N	House at Zeekoeigat, Riversdale	D6 ↖
	O	"Kapstylhuise", Puntjie	D6 ↖
	P	Fishermen's Cottages, Waenhuiskrans (Arniston)	D5 ↙
	Q	Fishermen's Cottages, Struisbaai	D5 ↙
Page 58 (inset)	A	Palace Barracks, Simonstown	NS ↙
	A	Martello Tower, Simonstown	NS ↙
Page 59	A	Nooitgedacht, Graaff-Reinet	A4 ↗
	B	Glenthorn Church, Glenthorn	A6 ←
	C	Thomas Pringle's Cabin (Eildon), Thorngrove	A5 ↘
	D	Glen Lynden Church, Baviaansrivier	A5 ↘
	E	Old Mill, Prince Albert	B2 ↖
	F	Cango Caves, Oudtshoorn	B2 ←
	G	Mooimeisiesfontein, Riebeek-Oos	B6 ↖
	H	Andrew Geddes Bain Monument, Ecca Pass	B6 ↑
	I	Methodist Church, Salem	B6 •
	J	The Look-out, Sondagsrivier	B5 ↘
	K	Diaz Cross (Kwaaihoek), Boknes	B6 ↘
Page 59 (inset)	A	Old Bridge and Tollhouse, Montagu Pass	NS ↖
	B	Matjes River Cave, Keurbooms	NS ↗
	C	Belvidere Church, Belvedere	NS ↓
	D	Timber Store, Plettenberg Bay	NS ↘
	E	Redbourne Church, Plettenberg Bay	NS ↘
	F	Van Plettenberg Beacon, Plettenberg Bay	NS ↘
Page 60		Eastern Cape	
	A	Fort Armstrong, Balfour/Seymour	B1 →
	B	Sundial, Seymour	B1 →
	C	Bethal Mission Station, Stutterheim	B2 ↓
	D	Domira, Lovedale College	B1 ↘
	E	Martello Tower, Fort Beaufort	B1 ↘
	F	Fort Willshire, near Breakfast Vlei	B1 ↘
	G	Fort Murray and Mount Coke Mission Station, Mount Coke	C2 ↑
	H	Andrew Geddes Bain Monument, Ecca Pass	C1 ↖
	I	Watch Tower, Peddie	C2 ↖
	J	Governor's Kop, Grahamstown	C1 ↑
	K	Fraser's Camp Tower, Fraser's Camp	C2 ↖
	L	Churches and Wool Mill, Bathurst	C1 ↘
	M	1820-Settler Church, Port Alfred	C1 ↘
	N	Diaz Cross (Kwaaihoek) Boknes	C1 ↓
Page 60		Northern Cape	
	O	Smelting Furnace, Springbok	A5 ↘
	O	Van der Stel's Copper Mine, Springbok	A5 ↘
	P	Heerenlogement Cave, Heerenlogement	C6 ↓
Page 61	A	House of Olive Schreiner, De Aar	B5 ↘
	B	Corbelled Houses (Stuurmansfontein), near Carnarvon	B3 ↓
	C	Corbelled Houses, Williston/Carnarvon	C3 ↖
Page 62	A	Morokashoek, Voortrekker Laager Site, Thaba 'Nchu	A4 ↗
	B	Bushman Rock Paintings, Wepener	A5 ↙
	C	Battle of Boomplaats, Trompsburg/Jagersfontein	A3 ↓
	D	Dutch Reformed Church, Philippolis	B3 ↖
	E	Blockhouse, Aliwal North	B4 ↘
	F	Hebron-Farmhouse, Norvalspont	B3 ↓
	G	"Taalmonument" and Blockhouse, Burgersdorp	B4 ↓
	H	Old Trekkerhouse, Steynsburg	C3 ↗
Page 63	A	General Louis Botha's Birthplace, Greytown	A3 ↑
	B	Fort Pearson, Tugela	A4 ↖
	C	Chaka's Monument, Stanger	A4 ↖
	D	Howick Falls, Howick	A3 ←
	E	World's View, Pietermaritzburg	A3 ←
	F	Colenso's Mission, Bishopstowe	A3 •
	G	Site of first Sugarmill, Compensation	A4 ←
	H	Adams Mission, Amanzimtoti	B3 ↗
	I	Griqua National Independent Church, Kokstad	B2 ←
	J	Petrified Forest, Port Edward	C3 ↖
	K	Mkambati Palms, Lusikisiki	C2 ↗
Page 63 (inset)	A	Adams Mission, Amanzimtoti	NS ↑
	B	Petrified Forest, Port Edward	NS ↙
Page 65	A	Moffat's Church and House, Kuruman	B5 ←
	B	Battle of Kakamas, Kakamas	C2 ↓
	C	Mission Church, Campbell	C5 ↘
	D	Moffat's Pulpit, Griquatown	C5 ↙
Page 66	A	Archaeological Reserve, Vereeniging	A6 ←
	B	Prehistoric Rock Engravings (Bosworth), near Klerksdorp	A4 ↓
	C	Site of Samuel Broadbent and Thomas Hodgson's Mission Station, Witpoort	B4 ↖
	D	Battle of Vegkop, Heilbron	B5 →
	E	Aandenk Prospecting Borehole, Allanridge	B4 ↘
	F	Place where Sand River Convention was signed, Winburg/Ventersburg	C5 ↖
	G	Doornberg Beehive Huts, Willem Pretorius Game Reserve	C5 ↖
	H	Canteen Koppie, Barkly West	C2 •
	I	Voortrekker Monument, Winburg	C5 ←
	J	Bridge and Tollhouse, Barkly West	C2 ↓
	K	Prehistoric Rock Engravings (Nooitgedacht), near Barkly West	C2 ↘
	L	Doornlaagte Stone Age Settlement, Kimberley/Griquatown	C2 ↙
Page 67	A	O'Neil's Cottage, Charlestown	B2 →
	B	Amajuba Mountain, Mount Prospect	B2 →
	C	Monument of P. L. Uys, Utrecht	B3 ↙
	D	Hlobane	B3 ↘
	E	Blood River Battlefield, Bloedrivier	C3 ↑
	F	Grave of Prince Imperial Napoleon, Messelfontein	C3 ↗
	G	Battle of Elandsfontein, Wasbank	C3 ↖
	H	Rorke's Drift	C3 ↑
	I	Isandlwana Battlefield, Isandlwana	C3 ↗
	J	Ulundi Battlefield, Ulundi	C4 ↑
	K	Retief Rock Kerkenberg, Oliviershoekpas	C2 ←
	L	Platrand, Ladysmith	C2 →
	M	Dinganestat, Babanango	C4 ←
	N	Spi^enkop, Spioenkopdam	C2 ↓
	O	Emmaus Mission Station, Bergville	C2 ↙
	P	Chaka's Bulawayo Kraal, Empangeni	C4 ↘
	Q	Bloukrans, Chieveley	C2 ↘
	R	Fort Durnford and Saailaer, Estcourt	C2 ↘
	S	Fort Kwamondi and Fort Nongqai, Eshowe	C4 ↓
	T	General Louis Botha's Birthplace, Greytown	D3 ↑
Page 68	A	Blockhouse, Warmbaths	B6 ↓
	B	Boekenhoutfontein, Rustenburg	C5 ←
	C	Battlefield, Bronkhorstspruit	C6 ↘
	D	Blockhouse, Hekpoort	C5 ↓
	E	Sterkfontein Caves, Krugersdorp	D5 ↗
Page 68 (inset)	A	Blockhouse, Hekpoort	NS ↙
	B	Sterkfontein Caves, Krugersdorp	NS ↓
Page 69	A	Voortrekker Route, Pietersburg	A2 ↓
	B	Ana Trees, Potgietersrus	B1 ↗
	C	First Gold Power Plant (Eersteling), near Bergnek	B2 ↖
	D	Makapan's Caves (no access)	B2 ↖
	E	Moorddrif Monument, Potgietersrus	B1 ↗
	F	Blyde River Canyon, Blyde River	B3 →
	G	Pilgrim's Rest	B3 ↘
	H	Mapoch's Caves, Stoffberg/Steelpoort	C2 ↗
	I	Old School, Lydenburg	C3 ↑
	J	N.Z.A.S.M. Tunnel, Waterval-Boven	C3 ↙
	K	Fort Merensky, near Middelburg	C2 ↙
	L	Battlefield, Bronkhorstspruit	C1 ↘
	M	Krugerhof, Waterval-Onder	C3 ↙
	N	Stock Exchange, Barberton	C3 ↘
	O	Grobler's Bridge, Carolina/Machadodorp	C3 ↙
Page 70	A	Baobab Trees, Messina	B4 →
	B	Machema Bavenda Ruins, near Bandur	B4 ↓
	C	Dzata Bavenda Ruins, Makonde	B5 ↘
Page 70 (inset)		Sabie Area	
	A	Pilgrim's Rest	NS ↑
	B	Old School, Lydenburg	NS ↙
Page 71	A	Blyde River Canyon, Blyde River	B4 ↘
	B	Trichardt Memorial, Kruger National Park	B5 ↘
	C	Memorial Tablets, Kruger National Park	B5 ↘
	D	Eileen Orpen Memorial, Kruger National Park	B5 ↘
	E	Pilgrim's Rest	B4 ↘

TOWN PLANS

The location of the following selected National Monuments is shown on the relevant town plan by means of National Monument symbols containing a white letter of the alphabet, thus B

Where more than one monument is included on a town plan, the symbols are lettered progressively from top to bottom and from left to right.

Page 74	**ALICE**	A	Fort Hare
	ALIWAL NORTH	A	Blockhouse
	BARBERTON	A	Stock Exchange
	BEAUFORT WEST	A	Town Hall
Page 75	**BOKSBURG**	A	Old Government Building
	BLOEMFONTEIN	A	D.R. Church with Two Spires
		B	Fourth Raadsaal
		C	The Fountain
		D	The Presidency
		E	First Raadsaal
		F	Queen's or Bloemfontein Fort
Page 76	**BREDASDORP**	A	Independent Church
		B	The Rectory
	CAPE TOWN CENTRAL AREA	A	Lutheran Church, Martin Melck House and Sexton's House
		B	Koopmans de Wet House
		C	Castle
		D	Parade
		E	Malay Quarter
		F	Old Town House and Greenmarket Square
		G	St. Stephen's Church and Riebeeck Square
		H	Groote Kerk
		I	Old Supreme Court
		J	Company's Garden
		K	Rust en Vreugd
		L	De Waal Park
Page 77	**CAPE TOWN THROUGH-ROUTES (PENINSULA)**	A	Geological Exposure
		B	Corenhoop
		C	Rustenburg House and Belvedere
		D	Rondebosch Common
		E	Mostert's Mill
		F	Table Mountain
		G	Van Riebeeck's Hedge
		H	Dutch Reformed Church
		I	Groot Constantia
		J	Kronendal
		K	Hoop op Constantia
		L	West and East Battery
Page 78	**CRADOCK**	A	Dutch Reformed Church
	DURBAN CENTRAL AREA	A	Old Fort and Cemetery
		B	Post Office
		C	Old House Museum
Page 79	**DURBAN THROUGH-ROUTES**	A	Grave of J. S. King
	EAST LONDON	A	Fort Glamorgan
Page 80	**ESHOWE**	A	Fort Nongqai
		B	Fort Kwamondi
	ESTCOURT	A	Fort Durnford
	FORT BEAUFORT	A	Martello Tower
Page 81	**GEORGE**	A	Oak Tree and Van de Graaff's Beacon
	GRAAFF-REINET	A	Reinet House
		B	Hester Rupert Museum
		C	The Residency
	GRAHAMSTOWN	A	Drostdy Gateway
		B	Old Gaol
		C	Provost Building
		D	Fort Selwyn
Page 82	**JOHANNESBURG CENTRAL AREA**	A	Old Fort
Page 83	**JOHANNESBURG THROUGH-ROUTES**	A	Melville Koppies Nature Reserve
		B	Diaz Cross
	KIMBERLEY	A	Market Square
		B	Big Hole
Page 84	**KING WILLIAM'S TOWN**	A	The Residency
		B	The Baptist Manse
		C	The British Kaffrarian Savings Bank
		D	Grey Hospital
	KNYSNA	A	St. George's Church
	KOKSTAD	A	Griqua National Independent Church
	KRUGERSDORP	A	Paardekraal Monument
Page 86	**MOSSEL BAY**	A	The "Post Office Tree"
Page 87	**OUDTSHOORN**	A	Pinehurst
	PAARL	A	Gymnasium School
		B	The Oude Pastorie Museum
		C	The Printing Press of the "Genootskap van Regte Afrikaners"
		D	Paarl Mountain
		E	First Drostdy Offices
		F	The "Strooidak" Church
Page 88	**PIETERMARITZ-BURG**	A	Voortrekker Museum (Church of the Vow)
		B	St. Peter's Church
		C	Natal Legislative Council and Legislative Assembly Buildings
		D	Old Government House
	PORT ALFRED	A	1820 Settler's Church
	PORT ELIZABETH CENTRAL AREA	A	White House or Harbour Board Building
		B	Rectory, Castle Hill
		C	Fort Frederick
		D	Donkin Memorial and Reserve
		E	Donkin Street Houses
		F	Old Grey Institute
Page 89	**POTCHEFSTROOM**	A	Nederduits Hervormde Church
Page 90	**PRETORIA CENTRAL AREA**	A	"Staats Model School"
		B	Melrose House
		C	Old Government Building
		D	Kruger House
	PRETORIA THROUGH-ROUTES	A	Fort Klapperkop
Page 93	**STANGER**	A	Chaka's Memorial and Stone
	STELLENBOSCH	A	The Braak
		B	Grosvenor House
		C	Dorp Street
	SWELLENDAM	A	The Cottage
		B	Tuishuise
		C	Square
		D	Auld House
		E	Drostdy
		F	Oefeninghuis
		G	Old Boys' School
	UITENHAGE	A	Dutch Reformed Church Hall
Page 96	**WORCESTER**	A	Drostdy

GEOLOGICAL SITES

The approximate positions of the following geological sites are shown on the relevant six-colour maps by means of a white numeral on a brown rectangle, thus 1 They are numbered from top to bottom and from left to right on each map or map inset.
N.B. See also six-colour Geological Map of Southern Africa on inside back cover.

Page		Site	Map ref
Page 58 (inset)	1	Exposure of Granite Slate Contact, Sea Point, Cape Town	NS ↖
Page 59	1	Cango Caves, Oudtshoorn	B2 ←
Page 60	1	Eocene Fossil Site, Upper Need's Camp, East London	C2 ↗
	2	Cretaceous Fossil Site, Lower Need's Camp, East London	C2 ↗
	3	Andrew Geddes Bain Plaque, Ecca Pass	C1 ↑
	4	Discovery of First Diamonds in Namaqualand, 1925, Port Nolloth	A4 ↗
	5	Orbicular Granite Koppie, Nababeep	A5 →
Page 63	1	Cretaceous Fossil Site, Mzamba Beach, Port Edward	C3 ↖
Page 63 (inset)	1	Cretaceous Fossil Site, Mzamba Beach, Port Edward	NS ↙
Page 64	1	Discovery of Diamonds, 1928, Oranjemund	E3 •
Page 65	1	Discovery Site of First Diamond (Eureka), Hopetown	D5 ↗
Page 66	1	Canteen Koppie, early Alluvial Diamond Diggings, Barkly West	C2 •
	2	Glaciated Pavements (Nooitgedacht), Barkly West	C2 •
	3	Big Hole, Kimberley	C2 ↘
	4	Glaciated Pavements, Driekops Eiland	C2 ↙
Page 68	1	Old Tin Smelting Site, Rooiberg	B5 ↘
	2	Discovery Site of Cullinan Diamond, Cullinan	C6 ↓
	3	Sterkfontein Caves, Krugersdorp	D5 ↗
Page 68 (inset)	1	Kromdraai Caves, Krugersdorp	NS ↓
	2	Sterkfontein Caves, Krugersdorp	NS ↓
Page 69	1	First Gold Power and Crushing Plant (Eersteling), near Bergnek	B2 ↖
	2	First Platinum Discovery and Discovery Site of Merensky Reef (Maandagshoek), Burgersfort	B3 ←
	3	Echo Caves, Ohrigstad	B3 •
	4	Titaniferous Magnetite Exposure, Magneetshoogte	B2 ↘
	5	Outcrops of Chromitite in Anorthosite, Dwars River Bridge near Lydenburg	B3 ↙
Page 70	1	Fossil Tracks, Pontdrift	B4 ↖
Page 71	1	Large Copper/Phosphate Deposits, Phalaborwa	A5 ↙
Page 72	1	Sterkfontein Caves, Krugersdorp	NS ↖
	2	Discovery Site of Outcrop of Main Reef (Gold), Langlaagte	NS •

TOWN PLANS

The location of the following selected geological sites is shown on the relevant town plan by means of a white numeral on a black rectangle, thus 1. They are numbered from top to bottom and from left to right on each applicable town plan.
N.B. See also Geological Map of Southern Africa on inside back cover.

Page 77	**CAPE TOWN THROUGH-ROUTES (PENINSULA)**	1	Exposure of Granite Slate Contact
		2	Table Mountain
Page 81	**GRAHAMSTOWN**	1	Dr. W. G. Atherstone's House, where the first South African diamond was identified
Page 83	**JOHANNESBURG**	1	Discovery Site of outcrop of Main Reef (Gold)
	KIMBERLEY	2	Big Hole
Page 84	**KRUGERSDORP**	1	Sterkfontein Caves
Page 87	**PAARL**	1	Paarl Mountain

Inland Fishing in South Africa

'I ask a simple question
The truth I only wish
Do only fisherman lie
Or only liars fish?'

So says a humorous old fishing rhyme. But if there is one thing South Africa's anglers need not lie about, it is the wealth of inland fishing. Perhaps because of the nearness of some of our cities to a glorious coastline and a richness of sea life which is probably unparalleled in the world, there is a tendency among some to regard freshwater fishing as a "poor relation", a second best for the angler.

However, a century of fish importing and cultivation has so added to and boosted freshwater stocks that they have become an important source of food and provide sport for 160 000 registered anglers in the Transvaal alone (probably a quarter of a million people if you include minors who don't need licences), and at least as many in the other provinces.

Hundreds of dams, lakes and rivers yield eels, trout, tigerfish, carp, yellowfish, whitefish, mudfish, barbel and silver barbel, bass and kurper. There is also a horde of dwarf or minnow species regarded as more of a nuisance than of sporting interest.

Inland fishing, unlike that at the coast, is subject to licence controls, mass and bag limits, seasonal curbs and sometimes particular types of tackle and fishing methods. Wherever you go, make sure you have the provincial licence relative to the province you are fishing in.

Try to tune into local conditions through any of the many angling clubs. If you can afford it, buy club membership which gives you access to controlled waters which are litter-free and never crowded.

Good fishing areas are available to the travelling man willing to seek new waters, new horizons, new thrills. While some places have better reputations than others for fishing, the maps and information included in this guide, together with a reliable car will put you within easy reach of most without excessive travelling.

Where to Go

CAPE PROVINCE

Fishing inland is confined mainly to trout, though bass, eels and carp are sometimes of major local importance.

There are occasional reports of outstanding yellowfish and mudfish. The rival lure of coast and estuary fishing, and the enormous area of trout distribution, tend to reduce coarse fishing to local interest.

NATAL

This province is better known for its trout fishing and its coastal attractions, but it does have a great deal to offer those who seek coarse fishing. There is a species of Barbus (generally known as scalies) with a mass of up to 4,5 kg prized more than the trout as a fighter.

Natal is blessed with thousands of permanently running rivers and streams. The province also boasts an eel of 1,8 m caught on rod and line. Fine tigerfish are found in the Pongolo River near Golela and in some pans and lakes in Zululand.

Almost any town on your map is a jumping-off spot for black bass fishing (mainly dams, but also the more open waters of trout streams). Garages are sometimes particularly well-informed about where to go and how to get there. The bigger dams in the province are easily accessible, well-signposted, and nationally famous.

ORANGE FREE STATE

The rivers of the Orange Free State are all part of the Vaal-Orange system and fishing them is perhaps more seasonal because during the rains, access is often impossible. But from Parys to Christiana there are hundreds of private farms and islands with well-deserved reputations. Carp and yellowfish are the main attractions.

For the lucky few there is trout and bass fishing in the Harrismith area on the slopes of Tafelberg. Local angling societies are the key here.

TRANSVAAL

The main inland angling province is the Transvaal. It is blessed with fish species which do not occur further south because it is the limit of distribution of many tropical types. Because of the region's geographic and climatic diversity, imported breeds have done particularly well here.

The province offers year-round sport. Whatever your taste, however unusual your demands, the Transvaal can meet them.

Within 200 km of Johannesburg or Pretoria there are three main possibilities.

- ☐ The Vaal river, its dam and barrage area
- ☐ Hartbeespoort dam in the warm Magaliesberg, fed by the Magalies and Crocodile rivers and many smaller streams
- ☐ Innumerable smaller dams, from the far-flung Barberspan near Delareyville, Boskop (Potchefstroom) and Loskop (Middelburg) to the nearer Rietvlei and Bronkhorstspruit.

The Vaal is the big favourite. From the rise a little north of Standerton to the Free State border near Christiana, there is at least 450 kilometres of fishable river. More than half the Transvaal's anglers do all their fishing here.

Hartbeespoort, a giant much-loved, much-abused dam, is within an hour's drive of both Pretoria and Johannesburg.

Reaching the Transvaal's other major river system, the east-flowing Limpopo-Olifants, is more of a problem but can be just as rewarding. Access is still largely undiscovered by the masses. Any of the Eastern Transvaal towns provide jumping-off points.

Machadodorp, Waterval-Boven, Lydenburg, Belfast, Dullstroom and Pilgrim's Rest are the gateways to the trout-fishing region. The amount of good open water seems to be dwindling rapidly with the best being in club or syndicate hands. Do not venture out on "on spec" fishing expeditions. Tie up the details beforehand.

THE FISH

The following are the main fish of sporting interest inland. Also included are details of various kinds of bait. While there are no definite rules concerning bait it is always advisable to ask about local conditions.

In some areas for example, it is difficult to catch carp on anything other than a mealie pip, because generations of anglers have favoured that kind of bait in that water and the fish have become used to it.

There is a vast range of lures, spinners and flies for the predatory species and the insect world should not be neglected. Crickets and grasshoppers are good; so are flying ants. In some areas wild fruits are important bait and worth trying if you see fish feeding on ripe fruit. An unusual but effective bait on the Mgeni, for example, is the mulberry.

Barbel (Catfish)

This species includes silverbarbel and catlets and is the largest of the indigenous inland fishes with a mass of up to 25 kg. It is distinguished by its whiskers and lack of scales and/or spines. It has a brown-grey-black colour and is a good fighter although generally underrated. It can be caught on almost any kind of flesh bait e.g. fish heads or white fish, large crabs and crickets, or a bunch of worms – it will even take spinners.

Bass
A popular sporting fish of American origin. It thrives in warm, clear waters and attains a mass of up to 4 kg. Its colour is sombre, except for the eye which is red. Lures and spinners are best for bait, but the fish will also take worms and crab.

Carp
This is probably the most important inland angling fish. The mirror carp has irregular large scales while those with the full scales covering the whole body are the wild form. Mass is up to 23 kg. It is a bottom feeder and is caught mainly on mealiemeal mixtures flavoured with either aromatic oils, custard, curry or jam.

Catfish (SEE Barbel)

Eels (Madagascar mottled, African mottled and Black eel)
The skin may be either plain coloured, varying from yellow-brown to brownish black, or with a distinct mottled pattern. Eels commonly occur in all east-flowing rivers and also exceptionally in the Vaal. Mass is up to 20 kg. Flesh baits are best e.g. raw liver or fish heads.

Kurper
This is a most popular warm-water, summer fish. There are more than 450 types of this tilapia world family of which only a few are of interest to fishermen and cooks as being good for sport and eating. The fish attains a mass of up to 2,5 kg. The species includes the canary kurper, a small predator with a brightly coloured yellow belly, which is regarded as a nuisance by all anglers because it steals bait intended for other fish. Baits preferred are worms or mealiemeal mixtures flavoured with either jam, custard, curry or aromatic oils. Kurper will occasionally take an artificial fly or a small spoon.

Mudfish (including Mud Mullet)
This is an involved and differently coloured species. Its distinguishing features are the heavily lipped mouth and the sharply rising nape. Some are highly regarded and much sought-after. The mud mullet is regarded as a curse because of quick breeding and resistance to angler's baits. Mass is up to more than 3 kg. Egg-and-flour dough mixtures put on to a hook with a cake icer or pieces of earth worm threaded on to the hook are ideal bait.

Mullet (SEE Mudfish)

Scaly (SEE Yellowfish)

Springer
The freshwater grey mullet of the Eastern Cape requires skilful angling with fine nylon, corks and hooks and using white ants as bait.

Tigerfish
Can only survive in warm waters and usually only grows to about a mass of 8 kg. A fish half this size will satisfy most anglers. The ferocious appearance of the tigerfish gives a clear indication of its predatory habits - it will tackle any natural bait and anything that is shiny and moves and appears small enough to swallow.

Whitefish
Mainly found in the Berg and Breë river systems in the Cape. It is a bottom feeder and can be caught using earth worms, crickets, dough or brown bread. Mass of up to 5 kg.

Yellowfish (Scaly, Smallmouth and Largemouth)
This is a fine fighter and therefore a superb angling fish. The colour of the back varies from olive green to black and the flanks are golden or silvery. The largemouth can grow up to 20 kg, but the bigger ones are becoming rare because of slow breeding habits. Can be caught mainly on fish bait and small crabs, but mealiemeal mixtures, pastes and brown bread give good results.

GENERAL
Provincial fishing licences are essential in each province and are generally obtainable from the offices of the Receiver of Revenue and also in the larger cities from the main angling tackle dealers.

Licence fees (per person per year)

Cape Province	R1,00
Natal	R1,00
Orange Free State	R0,50
Transvaal	R3,00

The period of validity of a licence varies from province to province and it is advisable to check the position with the local division of Nature Conservation.

Closed seasons (subject to change)

Cape Province	Black bass: 1 June - 31 August
Natal	No closed season
Orange Free State	No closed season
Transvaal	No closed season, but in some cases additional local restrictions exist

Minimum size and daily bag limits
Most of the necessary information in the above regard appears on the back of the provincial licence.

Undersized fish must be returned to the water immediately. A fish is measured from the tip of the snout to the extreme tip of the tail.

Bait
It is imperative that visiting anglers ascertain locally the prevailing limitations on bait from either the divisions of Nature Conservation or the clubs.

Permits
ACCESS TO FISHING WATERS IS ALWAYS DEPENDENT ON THE PERMISSION OF THE RIPARIAN OWNER WHETHER THIS BE A PRIVATE INDIVIDUAL, A MUNICIPALITY OR A GOVERNMENT DEPARTMENT.

To fish in State Forest Reserves an additional permit from the Department of Forestry is required.

Permits to fish in areas administered by the Natal Parks, Game and Fish Preservation Board are obtainable from the Camp Superintendents.

For fishing in Trust Areas a permit is required from the Commissioner concerned.

In some instances fishing waters fall under the auspices of angling clubs from whom it is necessary to obtain membership. Temporary membership is also available to visitors who only wish to fish for one or two days. Enquiries should be made locally as almost all towns where freshwater fishing is popular, have their own clubs.

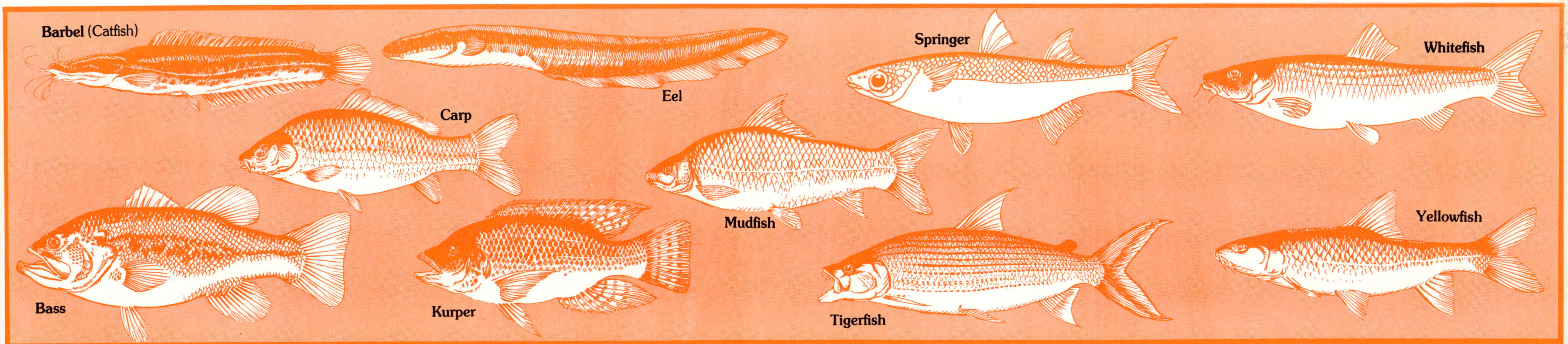

INLAND FISHING - RIVERS

For Inland Fishing - Dams - SEE Section on Dams and Lakes

CAPE

* NB Rivers listed in italics below do not appear on the maps included in this guide for reasons of scale

Area	Map Page and Grid Ref.	River(s)*	Barbel (Catfish)	Bass	Bass (black)	Bass (large-mouth)	Bass (small-mouth)	Bass (spotted)	Carp	Eel	Mudfish	Springer	White-fish	Yellow-fish (large-mouth)	Yellow-fish (small-mouth)	Yellow-fish
			1	2	3	4	5	6	7	8	9	10	11	12	13	14
Aliwal North	62 B4 ↘	Orange	1								9			12	13	
Barkly East	62 B5 ↓	Kraai	1								9					14
Barkly West	66 C2 •	Vaal	1						7		9					14
Bonnievale	58 C5 ↙	Breë		2					7	8			11			
Ceres	58 C4 ↖	Breë, *Dwars* and *Witels*					5									
Citrusdal	58 B4 ↙	Olifants					5									14
Clanwilliam	58 B3 ↗	Olifants			3		5						11			14
Douglas	65 D5 ↗	Confluence of Orange and Vaal	1						7		9					14
East London	60 B2 ↘	*Chalumna, Gxulu* and Kwelera							7			10				
		Buffalo, Nahoon				4	5				9					
Elgin	58 D4 ↖	Palmiet		2												
Grabouw	58 D4 ↖	Palmiet		2												
Groot-Drakenstein	58 C3 ↘	Berg					5						11			
Hermanus	58 D4 ←	Bot, Klein				4		6	7							
Kei Road	60 B2 ↓	Gqunube										10				
Kimberley	66 C2 ↘	Modder, Riet and Vaal	1						7							14
Komga	60 B2 →	Groot-Kei														14
Lady Grey	62 B5 ↙	Orange	1								9					14
Paarl	58 C3 ↘	Berg					5		7				11			
Rawsonville	58 C4 ↙	*Holsloot*					5									
Riversdale	58 D6 ↖	*Kafferskuil*, Vette			3											
Riverton	66 C2 →	Vaal	1						7		9					14
Robertson	58 C4 ↘	Breë					5		7	8			11			
Stanford	58 D4 •	Bot, Klein				4		6	7							
Stutterheim	60 B2 •	*Kubusi*		2					7							
Swellendam	58 D5 ↑	Breë, Riviersonderend					5		7	8			11			
Tulbagh	58 C4 ↖	*Klein-Berg*					5						11			
Uitenhage	59 B5 ↙	Swartkops		2					7	8						
Villiersdorp	58 C4 ↓	Breë, Riviersonderend				4			7	8			11			
Warrenton	66 C2 ↗	Vaal	1						7		9					14
Wellington (Bainskloof)	58 C4 ←	*Wit*					5						11			
Worcester	58 C4 ↓	Breë				4	5		7	8			11			
		Wit					5						11			

Care about your country - Don't litter

NATAL

* NB Rivers listed in italics below do not appear on the maps included in this guide for reasons of scale

Area	Map Page and Grid Ref.	River(s)*	Barbel	Bass (black)	Bass (small-mouth)	Carp	Eel	Scaly	Tigerfish
			1	2	3	4	5	6	7
Colenso	67 C2 ↘	Tugela	1					6	
Dundee	67 C3 ↖	Buffels	1				5	6	
Estcourt	67 C2 ↘	Tugela						6	
Hattingspruit	67 C3 ↖	Buffels						6	
Howick	63 A3 ←	Mgeni			3			6	
Ixopo	63 B3 ↖	Mzimkulu						6	
Ladysmith	67 C2 →	*Klip, Sand*		2					
Mooi River	63 A2 ↗	Mooi	1					6	
Newcastle	67 B2 ↘	*Ncandu, Ngogo*	1		3	4	5		
		Buffels						6	
Pongola	67 B4 ↗	Pongolo							7
Utrecht	67 B3 ↙	Bloed, Buffels	1					6	
Vryheid	67 B3 ↘	*Bivane*						6	
Weenen	67 C3 ↙	Boesmans, Mooi and Tugela	1				5	6	

ORANGE FREE STATE

* NB Rivers listed in italics below do not appear on the maps included in this guide for reasons of scale

Area	Map Page and Grid Ref.	River(s)*	Barbel (Catfish)	Bass (black)	Carp	Mudfish	Yellow-fish
			1	2	3	4	5
Bethlehem	66 C6 ↖	Jordaan, Liebenbergsvlei	1		3		5
Bethulie	62 B3 →	Orange	1		3	4	5
Bloemfontein	66 D4 ↖	Kaffer	1				5
Bothaville	66 B4 ↗	Vaal	1		3	4	5
Deneysville	66 A6 ↙	Vaal	1		3		5
Frankfort	66 B6 ↑	Wilge	1		3	4	5
Harrismith	67 C2 ↖	*Wilge*	1		3	4	5
Hobhouse	62 A5 ←	Caledon, Leeu	1		3	4	5
Koffiefontein	62 A2 →	Riet	1		3	4	5
Koppies	66 B5 ↑	Renoster	1		3	4	5
Kroonstad	66 B5 ↙	Vals	1	2	3	4	5
Lindley	66 B5 ↘	Vals	1		3	4	5
Maselspoort	66 D4 ↑	Modder	1		3	4	5
Parys	66 A5 ↓	Vaal	1		3	4	5
Philippolis	62 B3 ↖	Orange			3		5
Sasolburg	66 A5 ↘	Vaal	1		3	4	5
Smithfield	62 B4 ↑	Caledon			3		
Swinburne	67 C2 ↖	*Wilge*					5
Theunissen	66 C4 →	Vet	1		3	4	5
Villiers	66 B6 ↑	Vaal	1		3	4	5
Warden	67 B1 ↘	Cornelis, Meul and *Wilge*	1		3		5
Wepener	62 A5 ↙	Caledon	1		3	4	5

TRANSVAAL

* NB Rivers listed in italics below do not appear on the maps included in this guide for reasons of scale

Area	Map Page and Grid Ref.	River(s)*	Barbel (Catfish)	Bass (black)	Carp	Eel	Kurper	Mudfish	Scaly	Tiger-fish	Yellow-fish	Yellow-fish (large-mouth)
			1	2	3	4	5	6	7	8	9	10
Amsterdam	67 A3 ↘	Mpuluzi, Ngwempisi and Usutu				4					9	
Bloemhof	66 B3 ↓	Vaal	1		3			6			9	10
Bronkhorstspruit	69 C1 ↘	Wilge									9	
Carolina	69 D3 ↖	Komati									9	
Christiana	66 B3 ↙	Vaal	1		3							10
Ermelo	67 A2 →	Vaal	1		3						9	
Groblersdal	69 C2 ↖	Olifants					5				9	
Hazyview	69 C4 ↖	Sabie									9	
Heidelberg	66 A6 •	Blesbokspruit, *Suikerbosrand*	1		3						9	
Henley on Klip	66 A6 ←	*Klip*			3						9	
Klerksdorp	66 A4 ↘	*Skoonspruit*, Vaal	1		3							10
Komatipoort	69 C4 →	Komati, *Lumati*								8		
Louis Trichardt	70 C4 ↗	Luvuvhu	1	2	3	4	5	6			9	
Marble Hall	69 B2 ↙	Elands, Moses and Olifants	1		3		5				9	
Martins Drift	70 B2 ↘	Limpopo	1			4			7			
Nelspruit	69 C3 →	Krokodil				4		6	7		9	
Nigel	66 A6 •	Blesbokspruit	1		3						9	
Phalaborwa	69 A4 ↙	Olifants	1		3	4	5	6		8	9	
Piet Retief	67 B3 ↗	*Assegaai, Hlelo* and Pongolo							7		9	
Potchefstroom	66 A5 ↙	Mooi, Vaal			3			6				10
Sabie	69 C3 ↗	Sabie					5			8	9	
Standerton	67 A2 ↙	Vaal	1		3			6	7		9	10
Swartruggens	68 C4 ↘	Elands	1			4	5				9	
Tom Burke	70 C3 ↖	Mokolo, Palala	1			4						
Tzaneen	69 A3 ↙	Letaba, Olifants	1	2		4	5	6	7	8	9	
Vaalwater	68 B6 ↖	Mokolo, *Motlhabatsi*	1			4	5		7			
Vanderbijlpark	66 A5 ↘	Vaal	1		3						9	
Vereeniging	66 A5 ↘	*Klip Suikerbosrand* and Vaal	1		3						9	
Witbank	69 C2 ↙	Olifants					5					
Zeerust	68 C4 ←	Groot-Marico	1			4	5				9	

Don't be a litterbug - Care

Trout Fishing in Rivers

(For Trout Fishing In Dams *see* under section Dams and Lakes)

INTRODUCTION

Provincial angling licences are essential in each province and are generally obtainable from the Offices of the Receiver of Revenue and also in the larger cities from main fishing tackle dealers. In Natal and Transvaal, there is an additional charge over and above that for an ordinary angling licence, for a trout licence.

Licence fees (per person per year)

Cape Province	R1,00
Natal	R3,00
Orange Free State	R0,50
Transvaal	R6,00

Closed seasons (subject to change)

Cape Province	2 June - 31 August
Natal	16 May - 31 August
Orange Free State	No closed season
Transvaal	No closed season

Minimum size and daily bag limits

All the necessary information in the above regard appears on the back of the provincial licence.

Undersized fish must be returned to the water immediately. A fish is measured from the tip of the snout to the extreme tip of the tail.

Permits

Access to fishing waters is always dependent on the permission of the riparian owner whether this be a private individual, a municipality or a government department.

A number of popular trout areas in the Cape are in State Forest Reserves. To fish there, a permit must be obtained from the Chief Regional Officer, Private Bag 90015, Cape Town, 8000. Charges for these permits vary dependent upon whether they are per season, per day or per 3 consecutive days.

For information on trout angling conditions in the Western Cape contact the Cape Piscatorial Society, Telephone (021) 43-6723. For conditions in the Eastern Cape, contact the Eastern Province Freshwater Fish Conservancy, Telephone (041) 53-3445.

Permits to fish in areas administered by the Natal Parks, Game and Fish Preservation Board are obtainable from the Camp Superintendents.

For fishing in Non-white Areas, in any of the provinces, a permit is required from the Commissioner concerned.

In the Transvaal almost all proclaimed trout waters fall under the auspices of angling clubs from whom it is necessary to obtain membership. Temporary membership is also available to visitors who only wish to fish for one to two days. Enquiries should be made locally as almost all the towns where freshwater angling is popular, have their own clubs.

Trout
Brown and Rainbow – predators feeding mainly on waterborne fly life and small aquatic creatures. River mass is seldom above 1,5 kg and those in dams never more than 4,5 kg. If you catch anything bigger, consult the record books.

Bait
Trout may only be taken by rod and line with a non-spinning artificial fly tied to a single hook. A 'non-spinning artificial fly' is a hook with one point and one barb. To this hook, material which is not edible by fish is attached and is used without a rotating blade, spinner or spoon.

In all provinces the capture of trout is limited to the use of not more than two fly's. There is no limit to the size of the fly used when angling in the Cape. In Natal and Transvaal the size may be limited.

* Rivers listed in *italics* below do not appear on the maps included in this guide for reasons of scale.

CAPE

Area	Map Page and Grid Ref.	River(s)*	Brown Trout	Rainbow Trout
Alice	60 B1↘	Tyumie		X
Aliwal North	62 B4↘	Kraai		X
Barkly East	62 B5↓	*Bell*, Bokspruit, Kraai, Langkloofspruit and *Rifle Spruit*		X
		Telle	X	
Bontebok National Park	58 D5↑	Breë	X	X

CAPE continued

Area	Map Page and Grid Ref.	River(s)*	Brown Trout	Rainbow Trout
Cape Town	58 C3↓	*Houtbaai (Oranjekloof) and Liesbeek*		X
Cathcart	60 B2←	Klipplaat and Swart-Kei		X
Ceres	58 C4↖	*Dwars*, Olifants, Titus, *Witels* and *Wit*	X	X
Clanwilliam	58 B3↗	Breekkrans, *Krom* and *Ratel*		X
Elliot	62 C5→	Langkloofspruit, *Slang*, *Sterkspruit*, Tsomo and Xuka		X
George	59 NS↖	Gwaing	X	
Groot-Drakenstein	58 C3↘	*Dwars*	X	
Humansdorp	59 C4↗	*Klein*, *Loerie* and *Nooitgedacht*	X	
King William's Town	60 B2↓	*Buffalo*, *Keiskamma*, Swart- Kei and *Wolf*	X	X
Lady Grey	62 B5↙	*Karringmelkspruit*, Kraai		X
Maclear	62 C6↖	*Klein-Mooi*, *Klein-Pot*, Mooi and Tsitsa		X
Paarl	58 C3↘	Berg	X	X
Piketberg	58 B3↘	Ratel and *Vier-en-twintig-riviere*		X
Porterville	58 C3↗	*Vier-en-twintig-riviere*		X
Port Elizabeth	59 B5↘	*Loerie* and Van Stadens	X	
Prince Albert	59 B2↖	*Dorps*	X	
Queenstown	62 C4↘	Klipplaat		X
Rhodes	62 B5↘	*Bell*, Bokspruit, Kraai and *Rifle Spruit*		X
Somerset West	58 D3↗	*Lourens*	X	X
Stellenbosch	58 C3↘	*Eerste* and *Lourens*		X
Strand	58 D3↗	*Steenbras*	X	
Stutterheim	60 B2•	*Kubusie*		X
Thornhill (Longmore Forest Plantation)	59 B5↙	*Berg*	X	
(Otterford Forest Plantation)		*Klein*	X	
Tulbagh	58 C4↖	*Klein-Berg* and *Vier-en-twintig-riviere*		X
Ugie	62 C6↖	Mooi and Wildebees		X
Uitenhage	59 B5↙	Bulk	X	
Villiersdorp	58 C4↓	*Elands*		X
Wellington (Bainskloof Area)	58 C4←	*Wit*	X	
Worcester	58 C4↓	Hex, *Holsloot*, *Molenaars* and *Smalblaar*	X	X

NATAL

Area	Map Page and Grid Ref.	River(s)*	Brown Trout	Rainbow Trout
Bulwer	63 A2↘	*Luhane*	X	
Charlestown	67 B2→	*Cold Stream*	X	X
Coleford Nature Reserve	63 A2↓	Ngwangwane		X
Donnybrook	63 A2↘	*Nkonzo*	X	X
Estcourt	67 C2↘	Boesmans and Tugela	X	X
Giant's Castle Game Reserve	63 A2↑	Boesmans and Mooi	X	
Harding	63 B2→	Mtamvuna and *Weza*	X	X
Himeville	63 A2↓	Pholela	X	
Howick	63 A3←	Karkloof, *Lions* and Mgeni	X	X
Kamberg Nature Reserve	63 A2•	Little Mooi	X	
Loteni Nature Reserve	63 A2↑	*Loteni*	X	
Matatiele	62 B6↗	Kinira and *Mvenyane*		X
Newcastle	67 B2↘	*Ncandu*, *Ngogo* and *Slang*	X	X
Nottingham Road	63 A3↖	*Hlatikulu* and Mooi	X	
Pietermaritzburg	63 A3•	*Elands*	X	
Sevenoaks	63 A3↗	Mvoti	X	
Underberg	63 A2↓	Mzimkulu	X	X
Utrecht	67 B3↙	*Bivane*	X	X
Vergelegen Nature Reserve	63 A2•	Mkomazi	X	
Vryheid	67 B3↘	*Bivane*	X	

ORANGE FREE STATE

River trout fishing occurs only in the streams of the Golden Gate Highlands National Park

TRANSVAAL

Area	Map Page and Grid Ref.	River(s)*	Brown Trout	Rainbow Trout
Dullstroom	69 C3←	Dorps, Krokodil and *Santa*	X	X
Graskop	71 B4↙	Blyde and Sabie	X	X
Lydenburg	69 C3↑	*Kafferskraalspruit*, *Klein-Spekboom* and *Klip*	X	X
Machadodorp	69 C3↙	Elands and *Leeuspruit*		X
Magoebaskloof	70 NS•	Broederstroom and Helpmekaar	X	X
Pilgrim's Rest	69 B3↘	Blyde	X	
Sabie	69 C3↗	Sabie	X	
Waterval-Boven	69 C3↙	Elands and *Leeuspruit*		X

Coastal Fishing

No licence is necessary to catch any of the fish listed in the tables. However, strict control regulations are applicable to some protected fish eg. crayfish, mussels, crab. Details, including the bait laws and the daily bag and size limits in respect of the fish listed in the tables are given in pamphlets available from the Sea Fisheries Branch, Private Bag, Sea Point, Cape Town, 8060 and from the Natal Parks, Game and Fish Preservation Board, P.O. Box 662, Pietermaritzburg, 3200.

No closed season exists for any of the species listed. The only exception is snoek, where the season is from 1 August to 1 December. However, these dates may vary as the Department of Sea Fisheries deems fit.

For further information on Cape coastal fishing, contact the Sea Fisheries Branch, Tel. 021/44-9521 and for Natal coastal fishing contact the office of the Natal Parks Board in Durban, Tel. 031/35-4233.

It is essential that ski-boats comply with the safety requirements laid down by the respective ski-boat clubs along the whole coast.

Barracuda (Sea Pike)
Record catch: 20,4 kg
A great sporting fish and predator preferring bait such as sardines, elf, mackerel, mullet and steentjie, although live bait will produce the best results. A tasty fish but the flesh is fatty and very rich.

Blacktail (Dassie)
Record catch: 2,9 kg
Plentiful in the warmer waters of the Indian Ocean. Found mainly around rocky ledges and reefs and can be distinguished by the black spot at the root of the tail. They show a distinct preference for mussels, musselworm, crayfish tail and redbait.

Bonefish (Ladyfish)
Record catch: 8,6 kg
One of the greatest fighters on light tackle. It can be taken on crab, sand louse, prawn and sand worm.

Cape Baardman
Record catch: 10,8 kg
This is a fine fighter bearing a close resemblance to the Cob, except for its rather small mouth and the small fleshy tassel under its lower jaw from which it derives its name. Can be taken on white mussels, worms, crabs, sea fleas and lice.

Cob (Kabeljou)
Record catch: 73,5 kg
This is a much sought-after angling fish and is as much at home in the cold waters of the West coast as it is in the warm waters of the East coast. They prefer live mullet or elf but can also be caught on fresh prawns.

Elf (Shad)
Record catch: 10,2 kg
Elf are found all along the coastline. It is a very powerful fighter providing excellent fun on light tackle. As bait almost anything may be tried, but mackerel, steentjie and pilchards are favourites.

Galjoen (Damba)
Record catch: 6,5 kg
Mainly a rockfish which can be caught all along the coast. It provides great fun to the light tackle enthusiast. The most popular bait is redbait, white and black mussel, rock lobster, crab, starfish and periwinkles. Makes very tasty eating.

Garrick (Leervis)
Record catch: 32,2 kg
Normally run in small shoals and are found very close inshore. Live bait such as mullet, elf, steentjie or any other small fish found in the locality, is best.

Geelbek
Record catch: 22,6 kg
A good fighter, mainly found in deep water and therefore mostly taken from boats. They prefer sardines, mackerel, elf and steentjie as bait – the fresher the better.

Grunter
Record catch: 9,5 kg (spotted grunter)
Caught on light tackle in lagoons and river mouths. Best bait is mud-prawn, sand louse, crayfish, mud worm, sand worm and strips of mullet or sardine. Makes excellent eating.

Hottentot (Janbruin, Bronze Bream, Bluefish)
Record catch: Not available
An excellent angling fish found amongst the rocks in shallow water. Along the Cape coast they attain a mass of up to 4,5 kg and along the Natal coast they average 2 kg. For the best results use prawn, shrimp, crayfish, redbait and mussel worm as bait. The bait must be very fresh. Makes very good eating.

Katonkel (Blue Bonito)
Record catch: 3,2 kg
A summer fish found along the Cape coast as far as Plettenberg Bay. Can be caught with strips of chokka or fish such as mackerel, mullet or maasbanker.

Kingfish
Record catch: 55,3 kg
This is a warm-water fish, caught along the Natal coast where it is highly sought-after especially by ski-boat anglers, as it is easily taken on an artificial lure. Regarded as a good eating fish by some.

Mackerel (King and Spanish)
Record catches: 32,3 kg (King) and 9,4 kg (Spanish)
A great sporting fish. Being a predator it can best be taken in the early morning on artificial bait. At the time of day when the sun is at its hottest, it seeks the deeper waters and is then caught mainly from boats.

Marlin
Record catches: 491,70 kg (Black) and 79,83 kg (Striped)
A big-game fish caught from a ski-boat. Fish bait such as a small Barracuda, Bonito or Bonefish is best.

Musselcracker
Record catch: 37,6 kg
The White Musselcracker is found in warmer, relatively shallow waters, whereas the Blue Musselcracker resorts in fairly deep water as well as inshore. The White Musselcracker will take almost anything, but shows a preference to black mussel. The blue musselcracker favours octopus and fish bait.

Pompano
Record catch: 14,1 kg
A warm water fish taken mainly from river mouths and lagoons. The best bait is crab, sand worm, prawn, sea louse and shrimp.

Queenfish
Record catch: 11,68 kg
Found along the South Coast of Natal, especially during the sardine run. Sand louse, crab, shrimp, chokka, live elf, mullet and strepie give the best results.

Rock-cod
Record catch: 38,6 kg
There are three main varieties of rock -cod, namely the yellowbelly, the grey-spotted and the pink-spotted, of which the yellowbelly is probably the best-known and most often caught. In order of preference the best bait is: crab, sea-cat, crayfish tail, fish bait (mackerel and steentjie), chokka, redbait and starfish. Makes exceptionally fine eating.

Sailfish
Record catch: 63,5 kg
It derives its name from its high, round dorsal fin which resembles a sail. The sailfish is one of the fastest and most spectacular fighters in the world. The best bait is a strip of bonito, dolphin, barracuda or chokka.

Shark
Record catch: 400 kg (Blue Pointer)
There are more or less 250 types of sharks in the world, of which roughly 50 types inhabit the South African waters. It is a big gamefish and attempts to catch it can be made by trailing fish bait behind a boat. For this purpose, King mackerel is excellent.

Skate
Record catch: 98 kg
The skate spends its whole life on the sea-bed whether the water is shallow or deep. Sardine is the best bait, but chokka and prawn also give good results.

Snoek
Record catch: 8,6 kg
This is a well-known fish along the West and South-East coast as far as Mossel Bay. The conditions usually associated with snoek are clear water and dull skies. Can be caught on just about anything: strips of shark skin or pork rind, octopus leg or chokka are only a few examples. Most of the fish are cured and sold as salted or smoked snoek which makes delicious eating.

Spotted Pompano (Moonfish)
Record catch: 2,3 kg
A warm-water fish found mainly in river mouths and lagoons along the East coast. Can be caught on crab, sand worm, shrimp, prawn and sea louse.

Springer
Record Catch: 11,8 kg
As the name indicates, it is a fish that jumps high out of the water when not on a hook. The best bait is small fish such as mullet or strepie and also shrimp and prawn. They will also take strips of chokka and fish bait tied to a hook.

Steenbras (Red or Yellow)
Record catch: 44,9 kg
Found is deep water amongst rocks. It shows preference to live steentjie, strepie or mullet but can also be taken on chokka or octopus.

Steenbras (White)
Record catch: 29,9 kg
Found all along the coast from the Cape to Natal, especially in gullies. Blood worm is the best bait but they can also be taken on shrimp and sardine.

Stumpnose
Record catches: 8,2 kg (Red); 2,8 kg (White); 2,3 kg (Silver)
A migratory fish, but little is known of its migrations after the large shoals disappear from False Bay. In order of preference the best bait is chokka, fish bait such as mackerel, steentjie and maasbanker and redbait or crab. Makes delicious eating.

Torpedo Fish (Bonito)
Record catch: 9,7 kg
Found throughout the year on the Natal coast in vast shoals. Usually taken on live bait, spinner or lure.

Tunny
Record catch: 75,1 kg
Although not much is known about the general migrations of tunny, evidence proves that two main varieties, namely, the blue and yellowfin, regularly visit our shores in great shoals. They are usually taken on spinners, but will not refuse bait such as live mackerel, maasbanker, mullet or any other small fish. Makes very tasty eating.

Yellowtail
Record catch: 33,1 kg
Its most distinctive feature is its yellow tail as the name indicates. Its habitat extends roughly from the Cape to East London where it prefers water with a temperature of 16°C and higher. When it refuses to take a spinner, live mackerel, maasbanker, mullet or steentjie can be used. Makes superb eating.

Zebra (Wildeperd)
Record catch: 6,3 kg
A splendid fighter found along the coast from Saldanha to Natal throughout the year. A very popular bait is fresh redbait. Mussels, mussel worms, crabs, shrimps and crayfish tail can be used with good results.

COASTAL FISHING

NOTE: The various spots along the coast where one can fish have been arranged in the order in which they will be encountered, commencing at Saldanha on the Atlantic seaboard and proceeding south along the coast around Cape Agulhas into the Indian Ocean and then up the east coast as far as Black Rock.

A Rock and Surf Fishing in the Cape

Coast From/At *(The map page on which this section of coast appears is given in brackets)*	Coastal Fishing Spots **Places in italics are not included on the map for reasons of scale*	Some Information of Importance	Cape Baardman	Cob (Kabeljou)	Dassie (Blacktail)	Elf (Shad)	Galjoen (Damba)	Geelbek	Grunter	Hottentot, Janbruin, Bluefish, Bronze Bream	Katonkel (Blue Bonito)	Leervis (Garrick)	Musselcracker	Rock-cod	Shark	Skate	Snoek	Springer	Steenbras (Red)	Steenbras (White)	Stumpnose (Yellowfin Bream)	Tunny	Yellowtail	Zebra (Wildeperd)
			1	2	3	4	5	6	7	8	9	10	11	12	13	14	15	16	17	18	19	20	21	22
Saldanha to Milnerton (58)	*Skate Alley* (Saldanha Bay), *Donkergat, Olifantklip*			2		4	5	6		8					13	14								
	Bokbaai						5													18				
	Springfontein to *Ou Skip*	Bait in the form of white mussels and redbait is plentiful		2			5																	
	Ou Skip to Melkbosstrand						5			8											19			
	Melkbosstrand to Bloubergstrand			2		4	5								13						19			
	Bloubergstrand to Milnerton			2		4	5								13	14					19			
Milnerton to Cape Point (58)	Milnerton to Table Bay	Permits to fish in Table Bay are obtainable from the harbour authorities		2		4		6		8					13	14					19		21	
	Table Bay to Houtbaai			2			5	6		8										18	19		21	
	Houtbaai to Cape Point			2	3		5			8										18	19		21	
Cape Point to Betty's Bay (58)	*Rooikrans*			2	3	4	5	6		8	9	10	11		13	14	15		17	18	19	20	21	22
	Buffelsbaai			2	3	4	5	6		8	9	10	11		13	14	15		17	18	19	20	21	22
	Smitswinkelbaai			2	3		5	6													19		21	
	Bailey's Cottage (Muizenberg)	This is an excellent spot when the south-easter blows		2	3	4	5						11											
	Strandfontein and Macassar			2	3	4	5					10			13	14				18				
	Coastal area between Macassar and Strand is closed to public																							
	Strand to *Melkbaai*			2	3	4	5					10			13	14				18			21	
	Harmony	No jeeps allowed on the beach		2	3	4	5	6							13	14				18	19			22
	Gordon's Bay Harbour	There is a small entrance fee to the harbour		2		4		6				10											21	
	Gordon's Bay to *Hangklip*	The sea in this area is extremely treacherous and anglers must be *very careful*		2	3	4		6			9		11		13	14			17		19	20	21	
	Hangklip to Betty's Bay	— ALL SPECIES CAN BE CAUGHT FROM THE ROCKS AND IN THE BAYS —																						
Kleinmond to Agulhas (58)	Kleinmond to Hermanus	A small fee is charged to enter the harbour area at Hermanus		2	3	4		6			9									18	19		21	
	Gansbaai			2									11											
	Danger Point to Agulhas			2		4		6							13								21	
Stilbaai to Plettenberg Bay (59)	Stilbaai and surroundings (including *Blombos*)			2	3	4	5						11		13				17	18				
	Ystervarkfontein to Gouritzmond			2	3	4	5						11						17	18				
	Kanon to *Franshoek* at Mossel Bay			2	3	4	5	6		8	9	10	11	12	13				17	18		20	21	22
	Mossel Bay *Point*			2	3	4	5	6		8	9	10	11	12	13				17	18		20	21	22
	Glentana			2	3	4	5	6				10			13					18			21	22
	Heroldsbaai			2	3	4	5	6		8	9	10			13					18			21	22

Rock and Surf Fishing in the Cape (continued)

Coast From/At *(The map page on which this section of coast appears is given in brackets)*	Coastal Fishing Spots **Places in italics are not included on the map for reasons of scale*	Some Information of Importance	Cape Baardman	Cob (Kabeljou)	Dassie (Blacktail)	Elf (Shad)	Galjoen (Damba)	Geelbek	Grunter	Hottentot, Janbruin, Bluefish, Bronze Bream	Katonkel (Blue Bonito)	Leervis (Garrick)	Musselcracker	Rock-cod	Shark	Skate	Snoek	Springer	Steenbras (Red)	Steenbras (White)	Stumpnose (Yellowfin Bream)	Tunny	Yellowtail	Zebra (Wildeperd)
			1	2	3	4	5	6	7	8	9	10	11	12	13	14	15	16	17	18	19	20	21	22
Stilbaai to Plettenberg Bay (59) (continued)	Wilderness (at *Leentjiesklip* and *Die Tafel*)			2	3	4	5	6		8	9	10			13					18			21	22
	Swartvlei Beach			2		4																		
	The *Beach* at Groenvlei			2			5			8														
	Buffelsbaai			2	3	4	5								13					18				
	Knysna	Splendid rock fishing		2	3	4			7			10	11						17	18				
	Plettenberg Bay - at *Robberg*			2	3	4	5			8		10	11		13				17	18		20	21	22
Tsitsikama Coastal National Park (59)	The angling zone is strictly the 2 km stretch from *"Goudgate"* to the *"Waterfall"*, excluding the underwater trail. Anyone angling outside this zone will be liable to prosecution. Bait-collecting is strictly prohibited.			2	3		5						11		13				17	18	19			
Oyster Bay to Jeffreys Bay (59)	Oyster Bay - Angling from the beach	Angling is especially good during June and July. Rock bait is plentiful and white mussel is found on the beach				4	5						11	12						18	19			
	Cape St. Francis	Redbait, squid, periwinkle, mussels, crab and siffie are freely available	1	2	3	4	5		7	8		10	11						17	18	19		21	22
	Jeffreys Bay	Redbait and octopus freely available at low tide. Chokka can be bought from cold storage		2		4	5			8		10												
Port Elizabeth (59)	Van Stadens River Mouth - from the surf	Bait - sandmussel plentiful					5						11				15	16						
	Maitland River Mouth						5										15							
	Skoenmakerskop	Bait easily obtainable at low tide	1	2	3		5			8		10	11					16		18				22
	The Willows				3	4				8			11					16						
	Kaap Recife	Permit necessary to enter the Kaap Recife restricted area			3		5										15							
	Port Elizabeth Harbour			2		4					9	10	11	12						18				
	Sundays River Mouth				3	4			7	8			11					16		18				
Port Alfred and Surroundings (59/60)	Woody Cape, Cannon Rocks and Boesmansriviermond	Coral worm, sandmussel, pink prawn and shell-fish bait is easily obtainable		2	3	4			7			10	11		13					18				22
	Kenton-on-Sea - at *Whale's Rock, Land's End, Rocking Horse* and *Puff Adder*	Mostly low tide fishing. Coral worm, sandmussel, pink prawn and shell-fish bait is easily obtainable. Centipede may be chopped on the rocky ledges		2	3				7	8		10	11					16		18				22
	Kasuka Road - excellent spots are *Jimmies Bay, Lonely Rock, Ogilvy Rock, Dold's Rock, Ship Rock, High Bank* and *Little Bay*	Frozen bait available from bait shops; fresh bait obtainable from the rocks		2	3		5			8			11					16		18				22
	To the east of the Kowie River at *East Beach* and *Peterson's Bay*	Frozen bait obtainable from bait shops; fresh bait obtainable from the rocks	1	2	3	4	5			8		10	11	12	13			16		18				
	To the west of the Kowie River at *West Beach, Piano Rock* and *Rinkhals Beach*	Frozen bait obtainable from bait shops; fresh bait obtainable from the rocks	1	2	3	4	5			8		10	11	12	13			16		18				
East London and District (60)	Area from the Fish River to the Keiskamma River. Angling from the rocks	Beach transport is essential in this area		2	3	4	5		7	8		10	11		13		15	16		18				
	From the Keiskamma to the Chalumna River	This stretch falls in a trust area - a permit is required		2	3	4	5		7	8														
	East London Harbour	Permits are necessary to enter the harbour		2		4						10			13			16		18			21	
	Spots from the Chalumna River to Kei Mouth: *Kayser's Beach, Christmas Rock, Kidd's Beach, Hickmans River, Flat Rocks (Eastern Beach), Nahoon Reef,* Bonza Bay to *Gonubie Springs,* Sunrise-on-Sea, *Glen Eden,* Cintsa, Haga-Haga, Morgan's Bay, Kei Mouth.			2	3	4	5		7	8							15	16		18				

Rock and Surf Angling in Natal

Coast From/At *(The map page on which this section of coast appears is given in brackets)*	Coastal Fishing Spots **Places in italics are not included on the map for reasons of scale*	Some Information of Importance										Mackerel																
			Barracuda (Sea Pike)	Blacktail (Dassie)	Bonefish (Ladyfish)	Bronze Bream, Bluefish, Hottentot	Cob (Kabeljou)	Galjoen (Damba)	Garrick (Leervis)	Grunter	Kingfish	King	Spanish (Natal Snoek)	Musselcracker	Pompano	Queenfish	Rock-cod	Shad (Elf)	Shark	Skate	Spotted Pompano (Moonfish)	Springer	Steenbras (Yellow)	Stumpnose (Yellowfin Bream)	Torpedo Fish (Bonito)	Tunny	Yellowtail	Zebra (Wildeperd)
South Coast (Port Edward to Isipingo Beach) (63)	Port Edward, Munster, Trafalgar Beach, Margate, *Orange Rocks* at Uvongo, The *Sand Spit* at Port Shepstone, Umtentweni, Sunwich Port, Pumula, Umzumbe, Hibberdene, Turton, Ifafa Beach, Umdoni Park, Kelso, Park Rynie, Scottburgh, Clansthal, Umkomaas, Umgababa, Winklespruit, Warner Beach, Amanzimtoti, Isipingo Beach	For the best results, fish either at dawn or dusk or on the high tide. The famous annual sardine run occurs along this stretch of coast during June and July.	1	2	3	4	5	6	7	8	9	10	11	12	13	14	15	16	17	18	19	20	21	22	23	24	25	26
			1	2	3	4	5	6	7	8	9	10	11	12	13	14	15	16	17	18	19	20	21	22	23	24	25	26
Durban (63)	Beaches and rocks		1	2			5		7	8		10	11	12				16	17	18	19			22		24		
	Beachfront Groynes and Piers		1				5		7									16										
	In the Harbour: *Vetch's Pier* and *West Street Groyne*	A licence is required to fish in Durban harbour and is obtainable from Customs House, Esplanade, Durban								8														22				
	South Pier		1				5		7		9					14		16	17	18								
	Dick King Jetty, Fish Jetty, T-Jetty and *The Stone Wall* on the Bluff																					20						
	Off the Sandbanks																							22				
	From the Deep Water Channels						5			8														22				
	Off the piers and jetties (especially Island View and *A Shed*) and in the corners of the wharves (especially *Coaling Wharf*)									8																		
	Whale Slipway, The Stone Wall, Fish Jetty, T-Jetty, Island View, *Coaling Wharf*									8															23			
North Coast (From Umhlanga Rocks To Sinkwazi Beach) (63/7)	Umhlanga Rocks, *Peace Cottage*, Umdloti Beach, Tongaat Beach, Ballitoville, Umhlali, Salt Rock, Tinley Manor Beach, Blythedale, Sinkwazi Beach	The best fishing along this stretch of coast is between August and December	1				5		7	8	9	10	11			14	15	16	17	18	19	20		22				
	Tugela Mouth	From January to May a very rare fish, Lobotis (Flasher), is caught from the river banks or the surf	1				5		7	8	9	10	11				15	16	17	18				22				
	Richards Bay					4	5		7	8	9						15	16	17	18		20	21	22				
	St Lucia Estuary		1			4	5		7	8	9							16	17	18			21					
	Mission Rocks						5										15											
	Kaap Vidal	A four-wheel drive vehicle is essential in this area	1				5		7		9							16	17	18								
	Sodwana Bay		1						7		9																	
	Mabibi		1								9						15	16	17	18								
	Black Rock		1								9						15	16	17	18								

Keep South Africa Beautiful - Don't litter

B Deepsea, Ski-boat and Light Tackle Boat Fishing - Cape

NOTE: The various spots along the coast where one can fish have been arranged in the order in which they will be encountered, commencing at Saldanha on the Atlantic seaboard and proceeding south along the coast around Cape Agulhas into the Indian Ocean and then up the east coast as far as Black Rock.

Coast From/At *(The map page on which this section of coast appears is given in brackets)*	**Coastal Fishing Spots** **Places in italics are not included in the map for reasons of scale*	**Some Information of Importance**	**Blacktail (Dassie)**	**Cob (Kabeljou)**	**Elf (Shad)**	**Galjoen (Damba)**	**Garrick (Leervis)**	**Geelbek**	**Grunter**	**Hottentot, Janbruin, Bronze Bream, Bluefish**	**Katonkel (Blue Bonito)**	**Marlin**	**Musselcracker**	**Rock-cod**	**Shark**	**Skate**	**Snoek**	**Steenbras (Red)**	**Steenbras (White)**	**Tunny**	**Yellowtail**
			1	2	3	4	5	6	7	8	9	10	11	12	13	14	15	16	17	18	19
Saldanha to Cape Point (58)	Saldanha	Launching ramp available. Pilchard bait readily available from fish factories	1	2	3											14	15				
	Langebaan Lagoon (light tackle boat)	Launching ramp available. Visitors advised to bring own boats. (A seaworthy 4 metre dinghy with 3,73kW (5hp) outboard motor and basic safety equipment will suffice). Bait in the form of prawns, bloodworm and mullet easily obtainable	1	2	3										13	14			17		
	Melkbosstrand	Launching is through dangerous surf - four-wheel drive vehicle necessary. Bait to be purchased in Cape Town								8							15				
	Houtbaai	Launching ramp available. Pilchard bait available in harbour															15			18	19
	From Kommetjie towards Cape Point	Launching from Houtbaai										10									19
False Bay (58)	Cape Point to Buffelsbaai	Launching ramp at Buffelsbaai which is part of the Cape of Good Hope Nature Reserve. There is an entrance fee and only the first 46 boats are allowed in. The Cape Boat and Ski-boat Club offers excellent launching at *Rumbly Bay*						6			9	10					15			18	19
	Simonstown	Launching ramp available - daily launching fee payable. Entire False Bay can be reached from here. Bait in the form of squid and mackerel can often be caught in the harbour at Bull's Nose, in the early morning		2							9	10			13		15			18	19
	Roman Rock Lighthouse, Fish Hoek and Kalkbaai reef	Launching at Simonstown		2								10					15				19
	Gordon's Bay	Launching ramp available. Entrance fee to harbour payable. Bait shop in the harbour																		18	19
Kaap Hangklip to Gansbaai (58)	Kaap Hangklip	Dangerous launching ramp. Advisable to launch at Gordon's Bay or Kleinmond		2				6									15				19
	Kleinmond	Reasonably safe launching ramp - visitors to arrange permit with the town clerk. Bait is scarce, must be procured from Hermanus or Cape Town															15				19
	Hermanus	Launching ramp inside harbour - dangerous area. Bait available		2	3			6									15				19
	Hermanus Lagoon (light tackle boat)	Angler to bring own boat. Best time is in summer after the mouth has been opened. Bait in the form of bloodworm and mullet easily collected		2	3		5												17		
	Gansbaai	Launching ramp available. Bait available. Best catches are during summer		2				6									15	16			19
Kaap Agulhas (58)	Struis Bay	Primitive launching ramp but fishing is excellent. Bait readily available at local fishery		2				6				10			13			16			19
Witsand to Keurboomsriviermond (58/9)	Witsand (at Breë River Mouth)	A couple of boats with or without motors for hire at the hotel	1	2		4	5								13				17		
	Gouritzmond		1	2	3	4	5								13				17		
	Mossel Bay	Two of the Industrial fishing boats take visitors along at a charge. Launching facilities available	1	2	3							10			13				17	18	
	Knysna Lagoon (light tackle boat)	Boats of various types and sizes are for hire at the Knysna Hire Centre. Good launching from Brenton		2	3		5		7	8			11			14	15		17		
	Keurboomsriviermond (light tackle boat)	Boats, with or without motors, for hire	1	2	3	4	5			8			11		13				17		19
Oyster Bay to Jeffreys Bay (59)	Oyster Bay	Boats are launched from the surf, but a four-wheel drive vehicle is essential	SOME OF THE RICHEST FISHING GROUNDS IN THE EASTERN CAPE CAN BE REACHED FROM HERE																		
	Cape St Francis	Launching site at Sea Vista for deepsea craft		2													15	16			
	Jeffreys Bay	Launching is done over the sand, for which a four-wheel drive vehicle is essential. Bait is obtainable from cold storage		2				6					11				15	16		18	19
Port Elizabeth and Surroundings (59)	In *Sardinia Bay:* Sea View, *Kini Bay, Bushy Park,* Skoenmakerskop	Boats are launched from the beach. This area is a proclaimed nature reserve and fishing within 1 km of the shore is prohibited		2				6					11					16			19
	Thunderbolt Reef and Kaap Recife	Launching is at *Red Windmill* along Marine Drive or at Noordhoek									9									18	19
	Red Windmill: Travel to spots such as *Bell Buoy, Hugo's Diner* and *White Sands*	Safe launching area - 3 km from the city centre									9									18	19
	Port Elizabeth Harbour	Visitors to obtain special permission and clearance from the Safety Officer, P.E. Deepsea Club. Only larger boats should make the harbour their headquarters, as the fishing grounds are 50 - 60 km out to sea									9	10								18	19

B Deepsea, Ski-boat and Light Tackle Boat Fishing - Cape (continued)

Coast From/At *(The map page on which this section of coast appears is given in brackets)*	Coastal Fishing Spots **Places in italics are not included in the map for reasons of scale*	Some Information of Importance	Blacktail (Dassie)	Cob (Kabeljou)	Elf (Shad)	Galjoen (Damba)	Garrick (Leervis)	Geelbek	Grunter	Hottentot, Janbruin, Bronze Bream, Bluefish	Katonkel (Blue Bonito)	Marlin	Musselcracker	Rock-cod	Shark	Skate	Snoek	Steenbras (Red)	Steenbras (White)	Tunny	Yellowtail
			1	2	3	4	5	6	7	8	9	10	11	12	13	14	15	16	17	18	19
Port Elizabeth and Surroundings (59)	Swartkops River Mouth	Boats are launched at the slipway in front of the Rod Club. Proceed to the sea through the river mouth (this can be extremely dangerous for the inexperienced). Pencil-bait, prawns, worms and mullet easily found		2	3		5														
	Sundays River Mouth and the *Islands of St Croix, Jahleel* and *Brenton* (to the left of the mouth)	Boats are launched at the road bridge. Proceed to the sea through the river mouth		2	3		5														19
Port Alfred and Surroundings (60)	Boesmansriviermond (light tackle boat)		1	2	3		5		7	8				12							
	Kwaaihoek and Bird Island	Launching from Kenton-on-Sea. Bird Island is a very rich fishing ground		2				6						12				16			19
	Kenton-on-Sea	Launching is done from the beach. Best fishing is from behind the breakers		2				6						12				16			
	Kariega River Mouth (light tackle boat)		1	2	3		5		7	8				12							
	Kowie River Mouth	Boats are launched through the river mouth and must be registered and carry the necessary safety equipment. Limited number of boats available for charter - tackle and bait included		2				6			9	10	11					16		18	19
	Kowie River Mouth (light tackle boat)	Boats may be hired and bait in the form of prawns and mullet is easily obtainable	1	2	3		5		7										17		
East London and Surroundings (60)	Keiskamma River at Hamburg (light tackle boat)	Slipway and jetty available to public. A few boats are available for hire. Bait in the form of prawns and mullet, easily obtainable		2			5		7							14					
	Buffalo River (light tackle boat and ski-boat)	Launching facilities at local ski-boat clubs. A permit is required to fish in this river and is obtained by joining any of the clubs through a local sports shop		2	3		5		7												
	Nahoon River	Good launching area. Boats available for hire. Bait is plentiful in all forms		2	3		5		7												
	Gqunube River (light tackle boat and ski-boat)	Light tackle boats available for hire. Launching can be made from the slipway or the beach. Bait in the form of prawn and mullet, easily found		2							9									18	19
	Kei Mouth										9									18	19

Deepsea, Ski-boat and Light Tackle Boat Fishing in Natal

Coast From/At *(The map page on which this section of coast appears is given in brackets)*	Coastal Fishing Spots **Places in italics are not included in the map for reasons of scale*	Some Information of Importance	Barracuda (Sea Pike)	Bronze Bream (Bluefish)	Cob (Kabeljou)	Elf (Shad)	Garrick (Leervis)	Grunter	Marlin	Rock-cod	Sailfish	Shark	Tunny
			1	2	3	4	5	6	7	8	9	10	11
South Coast (63)	Kelso, Park Rynie, Isipingo Beach	Deepsea game fishing is at its best between May and August when the waters are calmer			3			6		8			
Durban (63)	Durban Harbour (*Fishing Jetty*)	Deepsea fishing boats which carry parties of anglers depart daily at 06 h 30 (weather permitting) for the fishing grounds. Deepsea fishing is excellent throughout the year			3				7			10	11
North Coast (63/7)	Umdloti Beach, Salt Rock, Tinley Manor Beach	Deepsea game fishing is at its best between May and August when the waters are calmer			3			6		8			
	Richards Bay Harbour (light tackle boat and ski-boat base)	Harbour very safe for launching ski-boats. Permits are necessary for both light tackle and ski-boats	1	2	3	4		6	7	8			
	Lake St Lucia (light tackle boat) at the estuary *Charter's Creek, Fanies Island* and *False Bay*	Boats without outboard motors are available for hire. Visitors wishing to use their own boats must have them registered by the Officer-in-Charge of the area, *before* they are launched. Bait is always available for purchase	1	2	3	4	5	6					
	Kaap Vidal	Safe bay for launching ski-boats	1		3		5		7		9		
	Sodwana Bay	Four-wheel drive vehicle is essential as the roads leading to Sodwana are always in a bad condition. Safe launching base for ski-boats	1		3		5		7		9		
	Kosibaai (light tackle boat)	Four-wheel drive vehicle essential to reach Kosibaai. Fishing only allowed in the second and third lakes and permits are required from the KwaZulu authorities		2				6		8			

CLIMATE — South Africa

TOWN	ZONE	AVERAGE TEMPERATURE January Max.	January Min.	July Max.	July Min.	CLIMATIC DESCRIPTION
Maputo	1	30°	21°	24°	12°	Hot summer, warm winter, mostly humid. Summer rains.
Durban	2A	27°	20°	22°	11°	Warm to hot and humid summer. Warm winter. Windy. Summer rains.
East London		25°	18°	21°	10°	
Port Elizabeth	2B	25°	16°	20°	7°	Mild, humid summer. Cool winter. All season rainfall.
Mbabane	3A	24°	15°	19°	6°	Hot summer-frequent mists. Cold winter. Summer rains.
Queenstown		30°	14°	18°	2°	
Barberton	3B	28°	18°	21°	16°	Hot summer, cool winter. Summer rains.
Bloemfontein	4A	29°	15°	16°	2°	Warm summer. Winter cool to cold, dry. Summer rains.
Pietersburg		27°	15°	19°	3°	
Pretoria	4B	28°	16°	20°	2°	Hot summer, low humidity. Cool winter.
Vryburg	5A	32°	17°	20°	-1°	Hot summer, low rainfall. Mild to warm winter.
Kimberley		32°	17°	18°	3°	
Graaff-Reinet		32°	15°	13°	6°	
Francistown	5B	31°	18°	24°	5°	Hot summer, cold winter.
Port Nolloth	6A	19°	12°	17°	7°	Cool, rainless desert. Fog in cool season. Strong sea breezes, hot "Berg" winds in winter.
Walvis Bay		29°	11°	27°	2°	
Keetmanshoop	6B	35°	18°	22°	5°	Very hot, dry summer with cold nights. Cool winter.
Windhoek	6C	30°	17°	20°	6°	Hot summer, cold winter. Little rain.
Beaufort West		32°	16°	18°	5°	
Cape Town	7	26°	16°	17°	8°	Hot, dry summer, cool winter. Windy. Winter rains.

22°S Average sea temperature in summer °C
18°W Average sea temperature in winter °C

AVERAGE YEARLY WIND DIRECTION FREQUENCIES

Calvinia
N W E S 15,3
Arcs at 5% intervals.
Number indicates % calm.

RAINFALL IN MILLIMETRES — Monthly average and average annual total at place named.

TEMPERATURES IN CELSIUS — Monthly average.

Durban 102
RAINFALL 0 5 10 15 20 25 30 35
TEMPERATURE 0° 5° 10° 15° 20° 25° 30° 35°
J F M A M J J A S O N D

Celsius × 9/5 + 32 = Fahrenheit
Fahrenheit − 32 × 5/9 = Celsius

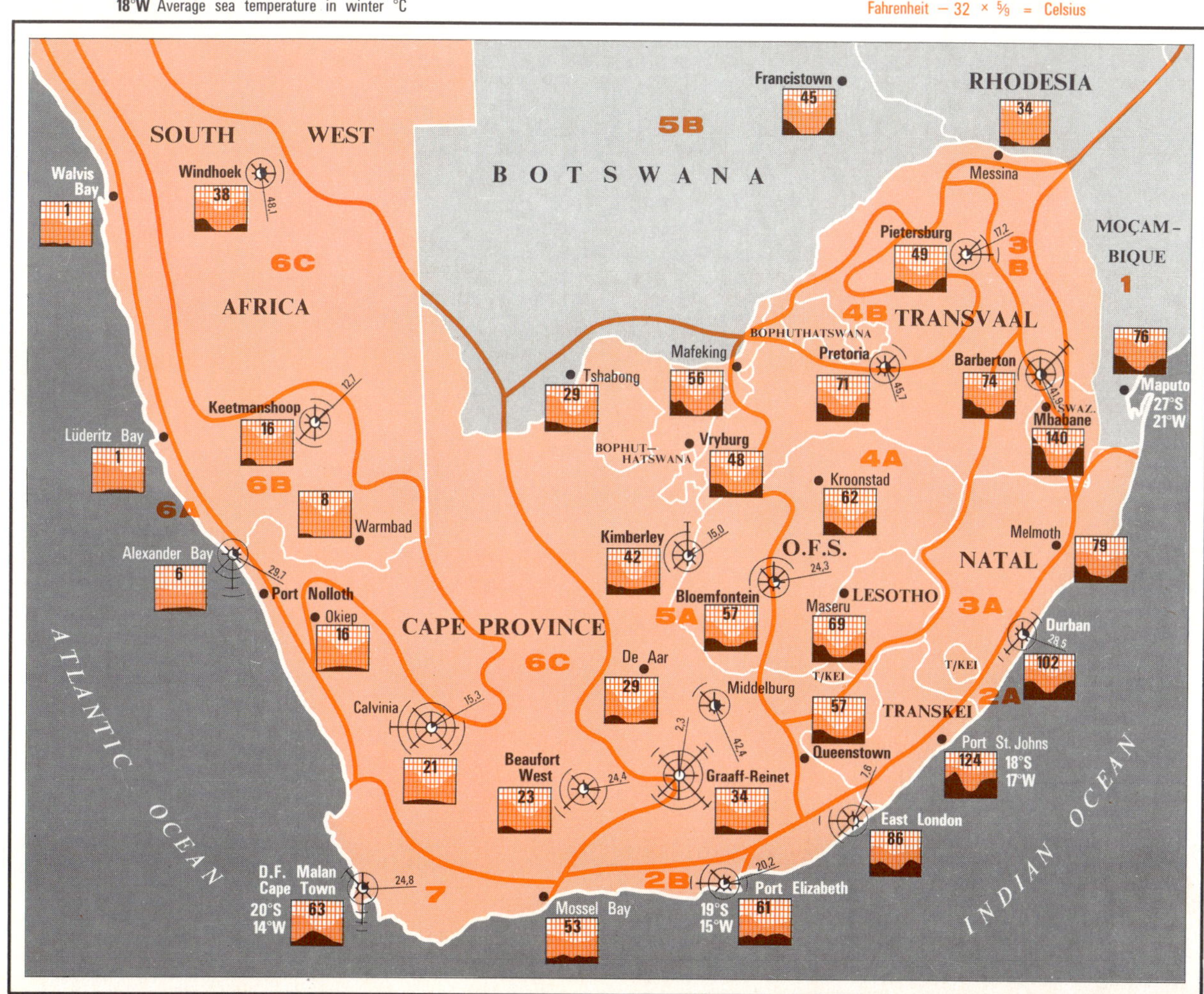

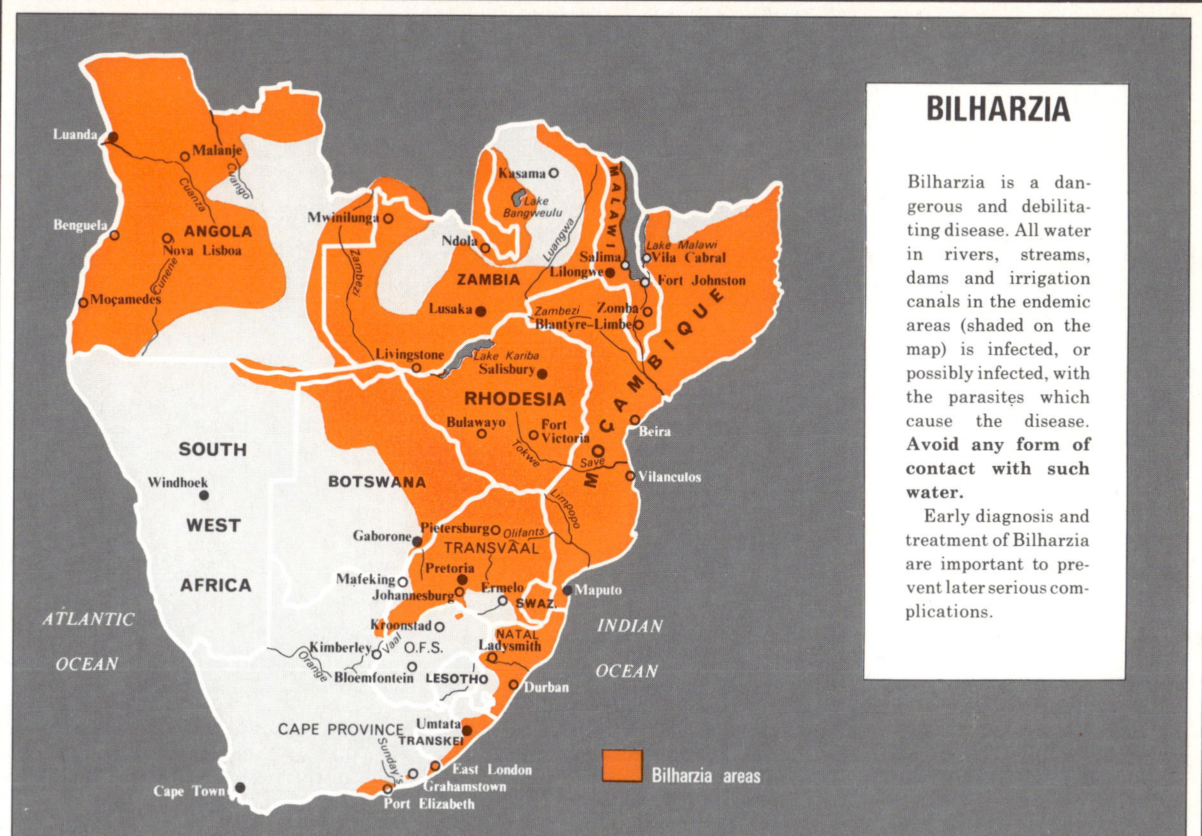

BILHARZIA

Bilharzia is a dangerous and debilitating disease. All water in rivers, streams, dams and irrigation canals in the endemic areas (shaded on the map) is infected, or possibly infected, with the parasites which cause the disease. **Avoid any form of contact with such water.**

Early diagnosis and treatment of Bilharzia are important to prevent later serious complications.

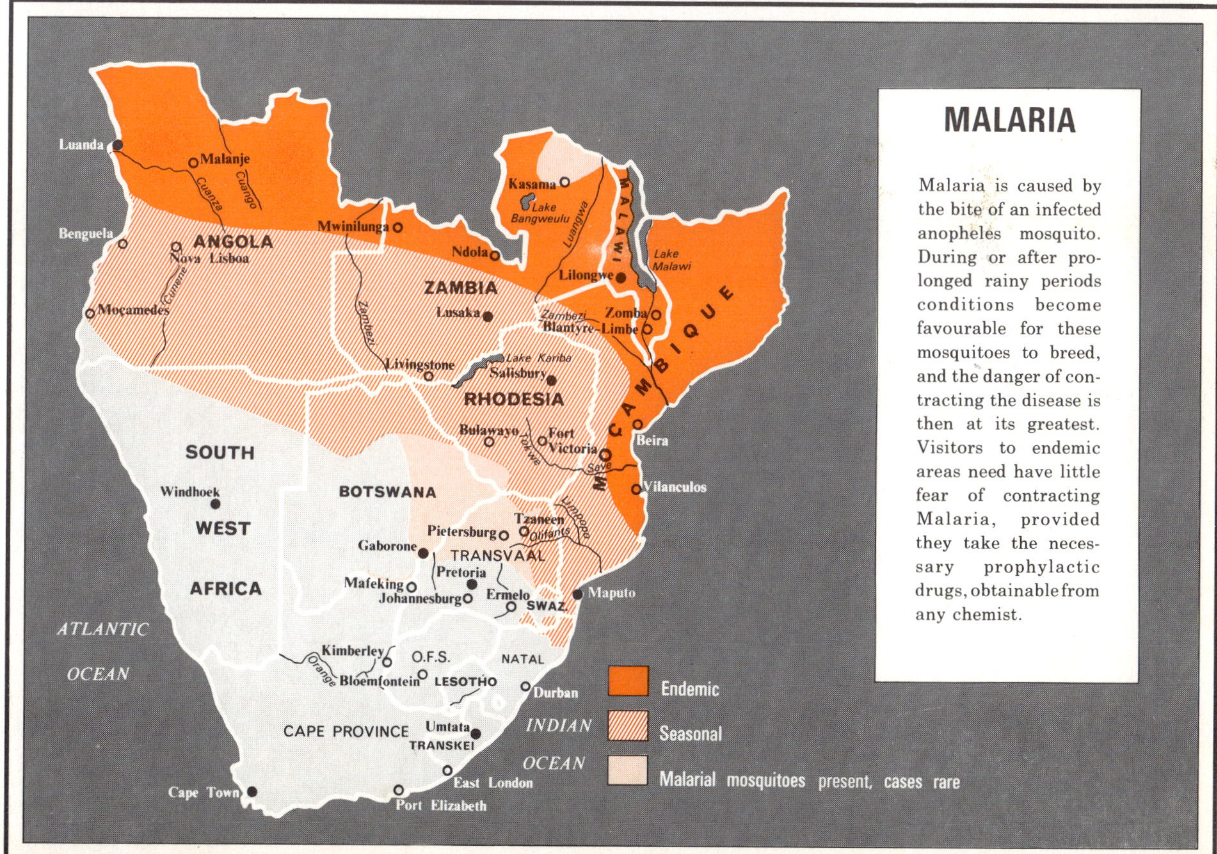

MALARIA

Malaria is caused by the bite of an infected anopheles mosquito. During or after prolonged rainy periods conditions become favourable for these mosquitoes to breed, and the danger of contracting the disease is then at its greatest. Visitors to endemic areas need have little fear of contracting Malaria, provided they take the necessary prophylactic drugs, obtainable from any chemist.

USEFUL KNOTS AND HITCHES

1. The Reef Knot
The Reef Knot is used to join two ropes of equal or nearly equal thickness, when one wants to be able to undo the knot again readily. The reef knot should *not* be used to join ropes of a different thickness or to join two wet ropes as it is liable to slip under these conditions.

To tie – first twist the running ends together.

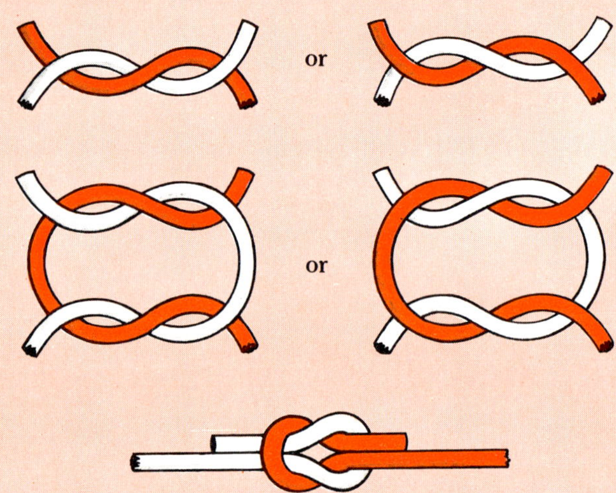

The finished knot

The Slip Reef

The slip reef will undo very quickly if required.

2. The Surgeon's Knot
It is difficult to pull a reef knot tight if the two ropes are under strain, e.g. when tying a parcel. In this case a Surgeon's Knot should be used. This is a reef knot with an extra twist in the first turn.

3. The Sheet Bend
The Sheet Bend is a good general purpose knot for joining two ropes, especially if they are of a different thickness. The initial loop or bend must be made in the thicker of the two ropes.

After having taken considerable strain the sheet bend may be difficult to untie.

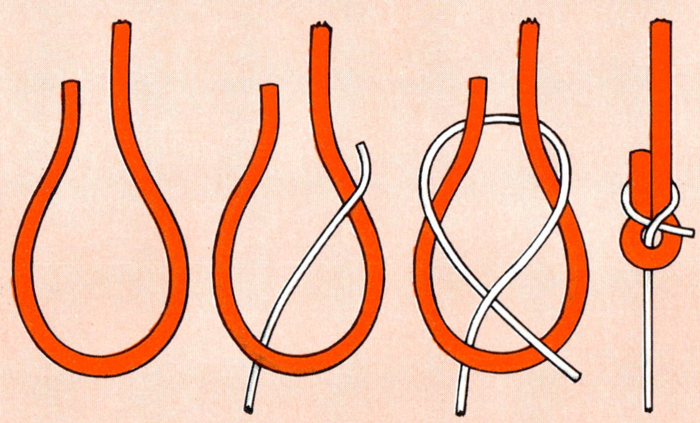

When joining wet ropes, or if the thicker of the two is appreciably greater in diameter, the single sheet bend shown above may slip. In this case use the double sheet bend as shown below.

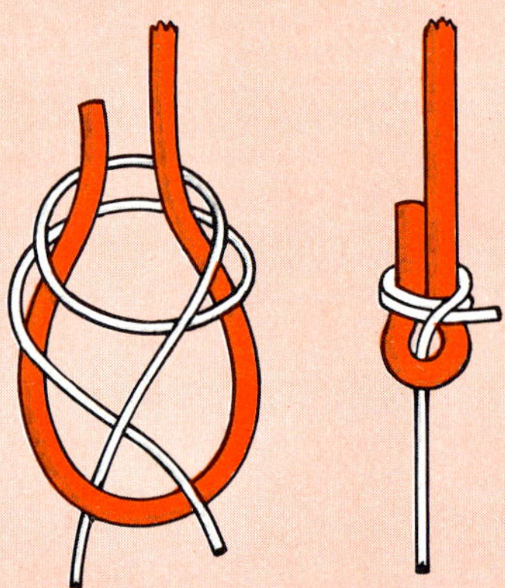

Both the single and the double sheet bend can be adapted to join a rope on to a chain or on to a hook, in which case it becomes the Blackwell Hitch; to join a length of cord on to steel wire rope and on to an existing eye splice.

4. The Clove Hitch
The Clove Hitch is one of the best knots for securing a rope to a pole or spar, provided the rope is not already under load, when it cannot be tied. There are two ways of tying the clove hitch, but whichever one you use, the hitch should end up looking exactly like this drawing.

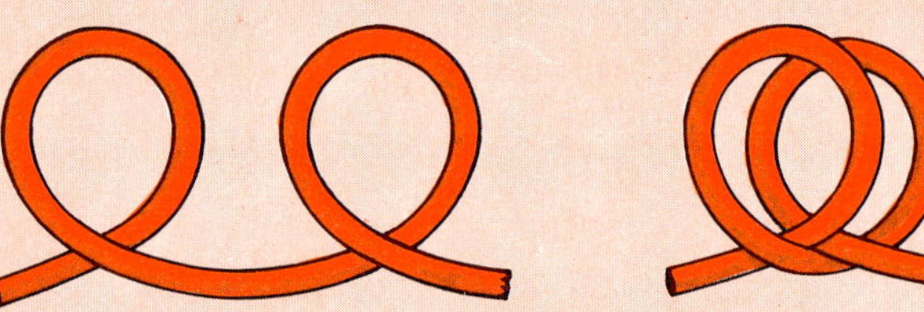

(i) If you do not have a free end of the rope, make two loops in the rope and pass one behind the other. Slip *both* loops over the pole and pull up tight.

(ii) If you have a free end of the rope, first make one turn around the pole and then a second, passing the end under itself as shown below, then pull up tight.

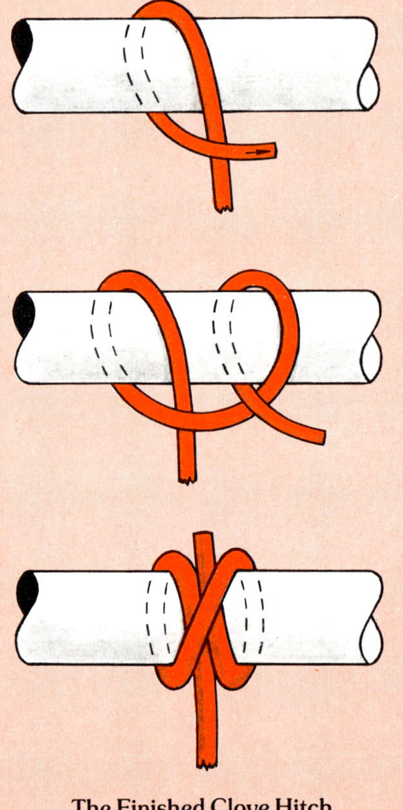

The Finished Clove Hitch

5. The Round Turn and Two Half-Hitches

The Round Turn and Two Half-Hitches is used if the rope is under strain or if you want to pull it up tight and anchor it to a post or tree trunk. The rope is pulled up tight and while still holding it tight it is worked round the post in one or even two complete turns. The strain on the free end is then minimal, and this end is secured to the starting end by two half-hitches that should then form a clove hitch.

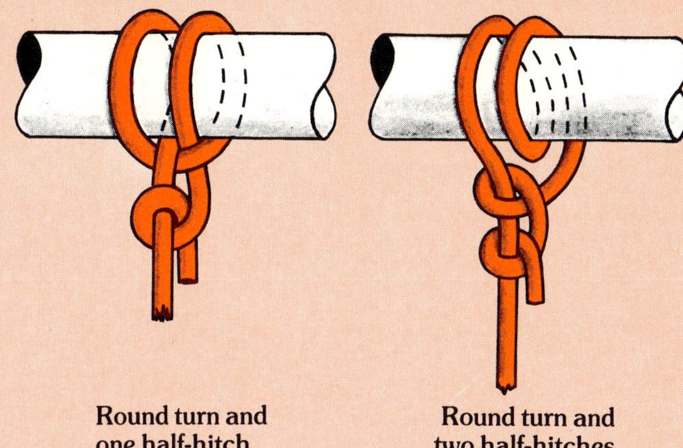

Round turn and one half-hitch **Round turn and two half-hitches**

For a neat and more or less permanent hitch, tie the free end to the standing end with string or twine.

If the running end of the rope is very long, the round turn and two half-hitches can be made with the rope doubled as shown.

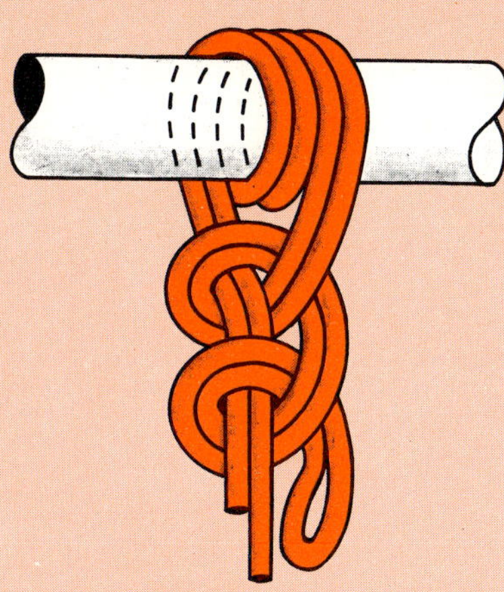

6. The Bowline

The Bowline is the knot to use to form a loop in the end of a rope that will not slip. For a really strong method of binding two ropes together, tie two bowlines, one looped through the other.

With a little bit of adjustment the bowline can be worked to fit snugly around one's waist and can thus be used for raising and lowering oneself up or down a rock face.

7. The Fisherman's Knot

The Fisherman's Knot is used for joining two wet ropes and is particularly useful for joining small lines. To make the Fisherman's Knot, tie the end of each rope with a half-hitch around the standing end of the other rope as shown.

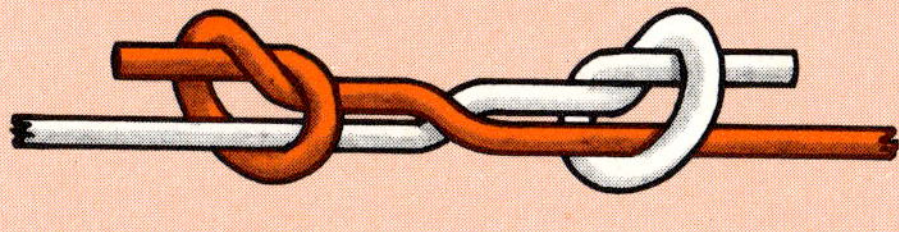

Right

Make sure that you tie it like this, when the two half-hitches will pull up snugly like this . . .

. . . which will not happen if you tie them like this.

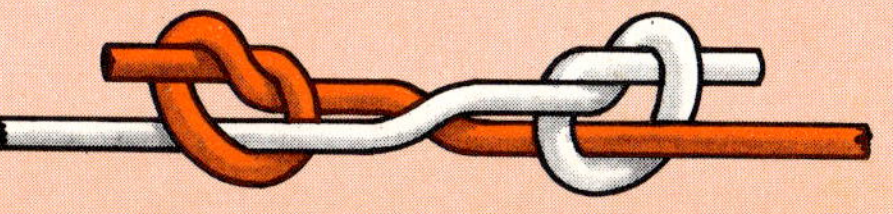

Wrong

in which case you get an ugly and untidy knot. 

Dams and Lakes

NB: See page 115 for maps on Bilharzia, Malaria and Climate.

INTRODUCTION

The casual visitor to any of the many dams and lakes listed below will, to varying degrees, find a situation which in many ways appears idyllic. The sheer magnetism which water has for the outdoor enthusiast is amply demonstrated by the number of caravans, tents, power and sailboats which are to be found at the water's edge. A mere glance at the numberplates of the many parked vehicles will also give a good idea of the various places from which people have travelled, often covering long distances to find "a place in the sun" where each person can do his "own thing," to his heart's content, whether it be sailing, swimming, paddling, boating, waterskiing or fishing.

The beauty of these natural and man-made facilities is there for all to enjoy and simple attention to the following can contribute much to the enjoyment, safe return and happy memories of such outings.

Bilharzia

Bilharzia is a dangerous and debilitating disease - the map on page 115 shows the extent of areas in which bilharzia occurs. It must be strongly emphasised that any form of contact with water in these areas must be totally avoided.

Boating

Before venturing into water with any kind of boat, make sure that you and your passengers can swim. Wherever possible wear lifejackets. This applies particularly to children. Do not overload the craft and make sure that you know what the local rules applicable to boating are. Avoid the dangerous practice of changing places in a boat, especially offshore. Pre-arrange with someone on shore, a system of hand signals which will indicate if you are in difficulties when out on the water.

In the event of the boat capsizing - DO NOT PANIC OR SHOUT - stay with the boat and either try to right it or climb on to it until help arrives - you will be more easily seen that way.

Inflatable Mattresses

These and similar inflatable toys are not designed for life-supporting use in water and anyone venturing out of their depth on one of these is asking for trouble. Beware of treacherous currents with which you may be unfamiliar.

Swimming

The greatest single safety precaution you can have near water is the ability to swim - this is of particular importance to children where constant supervision must be exercised even when paddling. DO NOT ALLOW children to go beyond waist depth. A good working knowledge of artificial respiration is a decided asset - details are included under the First Aid section of this book.

Life Saving

Do not attempt life saving unless you know what you are doing. It is foolish to risk your own life if you cannot swim well. Summon aid as quickly as you can, preferably in the form of a boat. If you are close enough, a lifebuoy, rope or even a long stick may provide the necessary assistance to keep the person afloat until more help arrives.

Sunburn

Take proper precautions - shady hats are a must and over-exposure of the body to the sun for a prolonged period will only result in pain and discomfort and spoil the fun of the outing.

The list of dams and lakes is comprehensive but is incomplete. Some dams are on private property and permission from the owners is required before venturing thereon. In some instances, membership of the local club is necessary to participate in boating and yachting and it is advisable to make prior enquiries.

Provincial fishing licences are necessary and permits are generally required but details in this regard may be found under the section on Freshwater Fishing.

Observe the rules posted at various resorts - they are there for your protection and enjoyment.

DAMS AND LAKES - CAPE

** For further information on freshwater and coastal fishing, see section on FISHING*

Dam Name	Map Page and Grid Ref.	River	Nearest Town	Distance from Town to Dam in km	Surface Area of Water in Ha (when full)	Fishing Permit Needed?	Kinds of Fish in Dam *	Caravan Park Nearby?	Camping Site Nearby?	Other Accommodation or Facilities	Facilities for Boating and Yachting?
BEAUFORT WEST	59 A2 ↗	Kuils	Beaufort West	1	14			Yes	Yes	Hotels in town	No
BEERVLEI	59 B3 ↑	Groot	Willowmore	35	2 282	Yes, but fishing potential poor	Carp	No	No	No	No
BELLAIR	58 C5 ↓	Brak	Barrydale	39	850	No	Black Bass	No	No	No	No
BLYDE RIVER	59 A5 ↙	Blyde	Pearston	12	22	No fishing		No	No	No	No
BOEGOEBERG	65 D4 ↖	Orange	Groblershoop	41	1 000	Licence only	Barbel, Carp, Mudfish, Yellowfish	No	No	Picnic sites along banks	No
BONGOLA	62 C4 ↘	Bongola	Queenstown	5		Yes	Black Bass, Carp	At Queenstown	At Queenstown	No	Yes
BOTRIVIERVLEI	58 D4 ↖	Bot	Caledon	39				Yes	Yes	Yes	Boating allowed
BRANDVLEI (LAKE MARAIS)	58 C4 ↓	Holsloot	Worcester	7	1 882 ha ultimately 4 150 ha	Yes		No	No	No	Yes
BRIDLE DRIFT (Nature Reserve)	60 B2 ↘	Buffalo	East London	25	607	Yes	Bass, Carp, Mudfish, Springer	No	No	Many pleasant picnic sites	Yes
BUFFELJAGS	58 D5 ↑	Buffeljags	Swellendam	10	130	Yes	Black Bass, Eel	In Swellendam	In Swellendam	No	No
BULK RIVER	59 B5 ↙	Bulk	Uitenhage	30	13	Permit & licence	Trout	No	No	No	Club members only
BULSHOEK	60 C6 ↘	Olifants	Clanwilliam	19	173			No	No	No	No
CHURCHILL	59 C4 ↑	Krom	Humansdorp	25	251		NO VISITORS ALLOWED				
CLANWILLIAM (A picturesque regatta held here every October	58 B3 ↗	Olifants	Clanwilliam	2	1 104	Yes	Black Bass, Yellowfish	Yes	Yes	Hotels in Clanwilliam	Yes
DE HOOPVLEI (renowned for birdlife in area)	58 D5 ←	Salt	Bredasdorp	33	1 525	No fishing		No	No	No	No
DOUGLAS BARRAGE	65 D5 ↗	Vaal	Douglas	3		Ordinary Provincial licence	Barbel, Carp, Yellowfish	No	No	Hotel in Douglas	No
DUIVENHOKS (ERWETJIESVLEI)	58 C5 ↘	Duivenhoks	Heidelberg	15	51	Yes	Black Bass	In Heidelberg	In Heidelberg	Hotel in Heidelberg	No
ELANDSKLOOF	58 C4 ↙	Elands	Villiersdorp	1	26	Yes		In Villiersdorp	No	No	No
ERWETJIESVLEI		SEE DUIVENHOKS DAM									
FLORISKRAAL	58 C6 ↖	Buffels	Laingsburg	21	806	No fishing		At dam	At dam	Hotels in town	Yes
GAMKA	59 A2 ↑	Gamka	Beaufort West	18	15	Yes	Largemouth Bass	In Beaufort West	No	Hotels in Beaufort West	No facilities, but boating and yachting allowed
GAMKAPOORT	59 B1 ↗	Gamka	Calitzdorp	74		Permit from Magistrate's office	Various kinds	No	No	Picnic and braai facilities	Rowing boats allowed
GRASSRIDGE	62 C3 ↓	Groot-Brak	Cradock	59	1 455	No	Carp, Eel, Mudfish	No	No	No	No

DAMS AND LAKES - CAPE continued

** For further information on freshwater and coastal fishing, see section on FISHING*

Dam Name	Map Page and Grid Ref.	River	Nearest Town	Distance from Town to Dam in km	Surface Area of Water in Ha (when full)	Fishing Permit Needed?	Kinds of Fish in Dam *	Caravan Park Nearby?	Camping Site Nearby?	Other Accommodation or Facilities	Facilities for Boating and Yachting?
GROENDAL	59 B5 ↙	Swartkops	Uitenhage	18		Yes, but fishing not encouraged	Bass	No	No	No	No
GROENVLEI	59 NS •		Knysna	18	250	Permit and licence	Renowned for large-mouth Bass	At the Vlei	At the Vlei	Hotel at Vlei	No powerboats
GUBU	60 B2 ↙	Gubu	Stutterheim	28	106	Yes	Trout	No	No	No	Only yachting with permission of Recreation Club
HARTENBOS	59 C2 ↖	Hartenbos	Mossel Bay	10	116	Yes		Yes	Yes	Hotels in Hartenbos and Mossel Bay	
HOWIESON'S POORT	59 B6 •	Palmiet	Grahamstown	16	15	No fishing allowed		No	No	No	No
ISLAND LAKE		SEE LOWER LANGVLEI									
JAMIESON	59 B6 ↖	New Years	Grahamstown	15	23	Yes	Black Bass, Rainbow trout	In town	In town	Hotels in town	No
KAMMANASSIE	59 B2 ↙	Kammanassie	Oudtshoorn	21	400	Yes	Yellowfish	No	No	No	No
KAROS	65 C3 →	Orange		ONLY A SMALL BARRAGE				NO FACILITIES			
KAT RIVIER	60 B1 →	Kat	Seymour	9	312	Yes	Black Bass, Carp, Kurper	No	No	Facilities for braais and picnics	At Recreation Club
KEEROM	58 C4 ↘	Nuy	Worcester	20	77			No	No	No	No
KINGNA		SEE POORTJIESKLOOF									
KLIPBERG	58 C4 ↘	Konings	McGregor	8	266	No fishing		No	No	No	No
KNYSNA LAGOON	59 NS ↓	Knysna	Knysna	Borders on Lagoon		No	Elf, Kabeljou, Leervis, Steenbras and many others	Several on banks	Several on banks	Boats, cabin cruisers and canoes for hire	Yes
KOMMANDODRIF	62 C4 ↙	Tarka	Tarkastad	28	875	No	Carp, Kurper	No	No	No	No
KOOS RAUBENHEIMER	59 B2 ←	Klein-Le Roux	Oudtshoorn	28	40	No fishing allowed		Yes	Yes	No	No
KORENTE-VETTE	58 C6 ↙	Korente-Vette	Riversdale	14	105	Yes	Barbel, Black Bass, Carp, Eel	In Riversdale	In Riversdale	Hotels in Riversdale	Yes
KRUGERSPOORT (Dam on private property)	62 C2 ↑	Elandskloof	Hanover	30		No fishing allowed		No	No	No	No
KWAGGASKLOOF	58 C4 ↓	Holsloot	Worcester	18	921	Yes		No	No	No	No
LAING	60 B2 ↓	Buffalo	King William's Town	21	206	No	Black Bass, Carp, Eel, Kurper	No	No	Many pleasant picnic sites	Yes
LAKE ARTHUR	59 A5 ↗	Tarka	Cradock	27	852	Yes	Carp, Eel, Kurper	No	No	No	Yes
LAKE MARAIS		SEE BRANDVLEI									
LAKENVALLEI	58 C4 ↑	Sanddrift	Ceres	26	112	Yes	Trout	No	No	No	No
LANGVLEI		SEE LOWER AND UPPER LANGVLEI RESPECTIVELY									
LEEUBOS (Dam mostly dry)	65 A2 ↙	Swartbos	Aroab (SWA)	50				NO FACILITIES			

DAMS AND LAKES - CAPE continued

** For further information on freshwater and coastal fishing, see section on FISHING*

Dam Name	Map Page and Grid Ref.	River	Nearest Town	Distance from Town to Dam in km	Surface Area of Water in Ha (when full)	Fishing Permit Needed?	Kinds of Fish in Dam *	Caravan Park Nearby?	Camping Site Nearby?	Other Accommodation or Facilities	Facilities for Boating and Yachting?
LEEUGAMKA (Approach roads poor)	59 A1 ↘	Leeu	Leeugamka	20	294	No fishing permitted		No	No	Hotel at Leeugamka	No
LOERIE	59 B5 ↙	Loerie	Hankey	16	107	Yes	Black Bass, Eel	No	No	No	No
LOWER LANGVLEI	59 NS ←		George	23	150	Permit needed if net is used	Various kinds	At the vlei		Rondavels	Yes
LOWER VAN STADENS	59 B5 ↙	Van Stadens	Port Elizabeth	45	6	Only members of E.P. Fresh Water Fish Conservancy	Black Bass	No	No	No	Only for members of the E.P. Fresh Water Fish Conservancy
LOXTON	61 C4 ←		Loxton	Dam situated just outside town	10	No	Carp	Yes	Yes	No	No
MADEN (Forest hiking trail along dam)	60 B2 ↙	Buffalo	King William's Town	22	30	Yes	Trout	In town	In town	Hotels in town. Picnic spots near dam wall	Yes
McGREGOR	58 D4 ↗	Hoeks	McGregor	5		No fishing		No	No	No	No
MENTZ	59 B5 ↖	Sondags	Jansenville	60	500	Yes	Carp, Eel	No	No	No	No
MIERTJIESKRAAL	58 C6 ↙	Brand	Ladismith	38		No fish yet					
MILNER	59 B6 ↖	New Years	Grahamstown	18	14	Yes	Black Bass	In town	In town	Motels and Hotels in town	No
MOORDKUIL	58 C4 ↓	Hoeks	Worcester	20	126	No fishing		No	No	No	No
NAHOON	60 B2 ↘	Nahoon	East London	18	283	No	Black Bass, Carp, Eel	No	No	No	Many pleasant picnic sites
NELSRIVIER	59 B1 →	Nels	Calitzdorp	5		Yes	Various	At Calitzdorp Spa	At Calitzdorp Spa	Braai facilities	No
PAUL SAUER	59 B4 ↓	Kouga	Patensie	27	600	No fishing allowed		No	No	No	No
PIETERSFONTEINKEISIE	58 C5 ↙	Keisies	Montagu	16	34	Yes		No	No	Picnicking allowed	No
POORTJIESKLOOF (KINGNA)	58 C5 ↙	Kingna	Montagu	35	78	Only members of Boland Fresh Water Angling Club	Black Bass, Mudfish, Yellowfish	No	No	No	No
PRINSRIVIER	58 C5 →	Prins	Ladismith	49		No fishing		No	No	No	No
RONDEVLEI (Bird sanctuary)	58 NS •		Cape Town	22		No fishing		Yes	No	No	No
RONDEVLEI	59 NS ←		George	30	170	Only required for net fishing		No	No	No	No
ROODE ELSBERG	58 C4 ↑	Sanddrift	De Doorns	15	38	Yes	Trout	No	No	Braai facilities	No
ROOIKRANS	60 B2 ↙	Buffalo	King William's Town	19	120	Yes	Trout	In town	In town	Hotels in town	Yes
SAND RIVER	59 B5 ↙	Sand	Uitenhage	44	33	An ordinary or temporary membership card of E.P. Fresh Water Fish Conservancy	Black Bass, Trout	No	No	No	No

DAMS AND LAKES - CAPE continued

** For further information on freshwater and coastal fishing, see section on FISHING*

Dam Name	Map Page and Grid Ref.	River	Nearest Town	Distance from Town to Dam in km	Surface Area of Water in Ha (when full)	Fishing Permit Needed?	Kinds of Fish in Dam *	Caravan Park Nearby?	Camping Site Nearby?	Other Accommodation or Facilities	Facilities for Boating and Yachting?
SANDVLEI	58 NS •		Cape Town	25	60	No	Mudfish, Steenbras	Yes	No	Yes	Yes
SEEKOEVLEI	58 NS •		Cape Town	22	121	Yes	Carp, Kurper	Yes	No	Yes	Yes
SETTLERS	59 B6 •	Kariega	Grahamstown	16	82,5	Yes	Black Bass, Yellowfish	In town	In town	Hotels in town	Yes
SMARTT SYNDICATE	61 B5 ↙	Ongers	Britstown	21		Yes	Barbel, Carp	In town	Yes	No	Yes, power boats freely used
SOETENDALSVLEI	58 D4 ↘	Heuningnes	Bredasdorp	29	2 250	No	Springer, Steenbras	At Struisbaai	At Struisbaai	Cottages at Struisbaai	Yes - permission from owner required
SPITSKOP	66 C2 ↑	Harts	Warrenton	34	2 141	Yes	Barbel, Carp, Mudfish, Yellowfish	No	Yes	No	No
STEENBRAS (Entry permit required. Obtain from Municipal offices Gordon's Bay, Strand or Stellenbosch)	58 D3 ↗	Steenbras	Gordon's Bay	13	379,8	Yes	Trout	At Gordon's Bay	At Gordon's Bay	A few rondavels at dam. Picnic and braai spots - these facilities are also available to Coloureds.	No
STETTYNSKLOOF	58 C4 ↙	Stettyns	Worcester	32	56	Yes	Trout	At Worcester and Goudini Spa	At Worcester and Goudini Spa	No	No
STOMPDRIFT	59 B2 •	Olifants	Oudtshoorn	37	800	Yes	Yellowfish	No	Yes	No	Yes
STRAUSSBERG	65 C3 •	Orange		ONLY A SMALL BARRAGE		- NO FACILITIES					
SWARTVLEI	59 NS ←	Karatara	George	39	1 100	Only required when net fishing	Garrick, Steenbras	At the Vlei	At the Vlei	Rondavels, Motel at Vlei	Yes
THEEWATERSKLOOF	58 D4 ↖	Rivier-sonderend	Villiersdorp	14	5 165	Yes		No	No	No	Facilities under construction
UPPER LANGVLEI	59 NS ←		George	26	200	Only required for net fishing	Black Bass	No	No	No	No
UPPER VAN STADENS	59 B5 ↙	Van Stadens	Port Elizabeth	46	4	Only members of E.P. Fresh Water Fish Conservancy	Black Bass, Trout	No	No	No	Only for members of E.P. Fresh Water Fish Conservancy
VAAL-HARTS WEIR	66 C2 ↗	Vaal	Warrenton	10	1 468	Yes	Barbel, Carp, Mudfish, Yellowfish	Yes	Yes	No	Yes
VAN RYNEVELDS PASS	59 A4 ↑	Sondags	Graaff-Reinet	Dam borders on town	1 133	Yes	Barbel, Bass, Carp, Mudfish	At dam wall	At dam wall	Chalets at caravan park	Yes
VAN STADENS DAM		SEE UPPER AND LOWER VAN STADENS RESPECTIVELY									
VANWYKSVLEI	61 B3 ↗		Vanwyksvlei	3	13	No fishing		No	No	Yes	No
VICTORIA WEST (dam situated in nature garden)	61 C5 ←	Dorpspruit	Victoria West	0,5	400	Yes		In town	No	No	No
VIOOLSDRIF	64 E4 ↘	Orange	ONLY A SMALL BARRAGE		– NO FACILITIES						
VOËLVLEI	58 C4 ↖		Tulbagh	15	1 072	Yes	Black Bass, Carp	In town	No	Hotels in town	No powerboats allowed

DAMS AND LAKES - CAPE continued

** For further information on freshwater and coastal fishing, see section on FISHING*

Dam Name	Map Page and Grid Ref.	River	Nearest Town	Distance from Town to Dam in km	Surface Area of Water in Ha (when full)	Fishing Permit Needed?	Kinds of Fish in Dam *	Caravan Park Nearby?	Camping Site Nearby?	Other Accommodation or Facilities	Facilities for Boating and Yachting?
WATERDOWN (Bushman paintings at dam site)	60 B1 →	Klipplaat	Whittlesea	16	276	Yes	Kurper, Trout, Yellowfish	No	No	No	Yes
WEMMERSHOEK (Entry permit required)	58 C4 ↙	Wemmers	Franschhoek	14	296,4	Yes	Trout	Yes	Yes	Hotel in town	No

DAMS AND LAKES - NATAL

Dam Name	Map Page and Grid Ref.	River	Nearest Town	Distance from Town to Dam in km	Surface Area of Water in Ha (when full)	Fishing Permit Needed?	Kinds of Fish in Dam *	Caravan Park Nearby?	Camping Site Nearby?	Other Accommodation or Facilities	Facilities for Boating and Yachting?
ALBERT FALLS	62 A3 ↓	Mgeni	Pietermaritzburg	28	Dam is still being filled	Yes	Bass, Mudfish	Site still being developed - at present only cold water supplied	Site still being developed - at present only cold water supplied	Rondavels and Chalets	Yes
CHELMSFORD	67 B2 ↘	Buffels	Newcastle	18	2 025	Yes	Bass, Kurper, Mudfish	No	No	Contact Natal Parks Board	Yes
CRAIGIE BURN	63 A3 ↖	Mnyamvubu	Mooi River	33	219	Yes	Bass	No	No	Beautiful picnic spots	No facilities, but boating, yachting allowed
GILBERT EYLES	63 NS ↙	Mzimkulwana	Port Shepstone	45		Yes	Bass, Eel, Mudfish	No	No	No	No
HAZELMERE	63 A3 ↘	Mdloti	Verulam	8	400						
HENLEY (Entry permits for groups of 6 or more persons needed)	63 A3 ↙	Umsinduzi	Pietermaritzburg	19	71	Yes	Bass, Mudfish, Scaly	In Pietermaritzburg	In Pietermaritzburg	Picnic and braai facilities	No
HLUHLUWE (Beware of crocodiles)	67 C5 ↖	Hluhluwe	Hluhluwe	25	357	Yes	Barbel, Eel, Kurper, Mudfish	No	No	Hutted camp in Hluhluwe Game Reserve	No
INSESE MEER	67 NS ↑	Insese	Empangeni	6	958	No fishing allowed		Yes	Yes	Hotels in town	No
J.G. STRIJDOM	67 B4 →	Pongolo	Mkuze	25	13 000	Yes	Barbel, Eel, Kurper, Tigerfish, Yellowfish	No	No	Motel at dam	No
LAKE MERTHLEY	67 D3 ↑	Keizers	Greytown	5	20	Yes	Black Bass, Carp	Yes	Yes	Cottages	Yes
LAKE MZINGAZI	67 NS →	Mzingazi	Richards Bay	2	1 064	No fishing allowed		Yes	Yes	Hotels in town	No
LAKE ST LUCIA (launch tours operate thrice daily if weather permits)	67 C5 ↑	Mkuze	Hluhluwe	13		Licence only	Mudfish	At the lake - Also for Asians, Coloureds and Blacks	At the lake - Also for Asians, Coloureds and Blacks	No	Launching of ski-boats permitted in certain areas only
MIDMAR	63 A3 ↙	Mgeni	Howick	5	1 560	Yes	Bass, Carp, Eel, Scaly	Yes - also for Asians and Coloureds	Yes - also for Asians and Coloureds	Chalets, Cottages, picnic areas with braais for Asians and Coloureds	Yes
MKUZE (Dam on private property No visitors allowed)	67 B4 ↓	Mkuze	Nongoma	31		Not allowed		No	No	No	No
NAGLE	63 A3 ↘	Mgeni	Cato Ridge	27	162	Licence only	Barbel, Black Bass, Eel	No	No		No

DAMS AND LAKES - NATAL continued

* *For further information on freshwater and coastal fishing, see section on FISHING*

Dam Name	Map Page and Grid Ref.	River	Nearest Town	Distance from Town to Dam in km	Surface Area of Water in Ha (when full)	Fishing Permit Needed?	Kinds of Fish in Dam *	Caravan Park Nearby?	Camping Site Nearby?	Other Accommodation or Facilities	Facilities for Boating and Yachting?
SPIOENKOP	67 C2 ↓	Tugela	Ladysmith	31	1 542	Yes	Bass, Mudfish	At the Dam	At the Dam	38 fully furnished chalets	Yes
TOM WORTHINGTON	67 C3 ↖	Ngobiya	Dundee	13	40	Yes	Carp, Yellowfish	In Dundee	No	No	No
UMLALAZI	67 C4 ↓	Umlalazi	Eshowe	3	8	No fishing		In Eshowe	In Eshowe	Hotels in Eshowe	No
VERDRUK	67 C3 ↖		Dundee	13	20	Yes	Carp, Yellowfish	No	No	No	No
WAGENDRIFT	67 D2 ↗	Boesman	Estcourt	8	508	Yes	Bass, Mudfish	No	No	Youth dormitories, Picnic sites	Yes

DAMS AND LAKES - ORANGE FREE STATE

Dam Name	Map Page and Grid Ref.	River	Nearest Town	Distance from Town to Dam in km	Surface Area of Water in Ha (when full)	Fishing Permit Needed?	Kinds of Fish in Dam *	Caravan Park Nearby?	Camping Site Nearby?	Other Accommodation or Facilities	Facilities for Boating and Yachting?
ALLEMANSKRAAL	66 C5 ↖	Sand	Ventersburg	28	2 771	Licence only	Barbel, Carp, Yellowfish	At Willem Pretorius Game Reserve	At Willem Pretorius Game Reserve	At Game Reserve	Yes, Permits needed
ARMENIA	62 A5 ↖	Leeu	Hobhouse	21	514	Licence only	Barbel, Carp, Yellowfish	No	No	No	No
BETHULIE	62 B3 →		Bethulie	3	153	Yes	Barbel, Black Bass, Carp, Yellowfish	Yes	Yes	Yes	Yes
BLOEMHOF	66 B3 ↘	Vaal	Bloemhof	5	23 035	Licence only	Barbel, Carp, Mudfish, Yellowfish	At the dam wall	At the dam wall	Hotel in Bloemhof	Yes
EGMONT	62 B5 ↖	Wittespruit	Zastron	27	256	Licence only	Barbel, Carp, Mudfish, Yellowfish	No	No	No	Yes
ERFENIS	66 C4 →	Groot-Vet	Theunissen	16	3 308	Yes	Barbel, Carp, Mudfish	No	Allowed, but no ablution facilities	No	Yes
HENDRIK VERWOERD	62 B3 ↘	Orange	Colesberg	40	37 400	Licence only	Barbel, Carp, Yellowfish	Yes	Yes	Yes	Yes
KALKFONTEIN	62 A3 ↙	Riet	Koffiefontein	28	4 921	Licence only	Barbel, Carp, Yellowfish	No	At dam	No	No
KOPPIES	66 B5 ↗	Renoster	Koppies	17	1 360	Licence only	Barbel, Carp, Mudfish, Yellowfish	Caravans allowed, toilets, fresh drinking water	Camping allowed, but no facilities available	Hotel at Koppies	Yes
KRUGERSDRIF	66 C4 ↙	Modder	Bloemfontein	40	1 852	Licence only	Barbel, Carp, Yellowfish	No	No	No	Not allowed
LOCH ATHLONE	66 C6 ↖	Jordaan	Bethlehem	3	1 222,2	Yes	Barbel, Carp, Yellowfish	At the dam	At the dam	Rondavels at the dam	Yes
LOCH LOMOND (Obtain permission of owners along the banks to fish or camp)	66 C6 ↖	Liebenbergsvlei	Bethlehem	18	±50	Yes	Barbel, Carp, Yellowfish	At Loch Athlone	At Loch Athlone	No	No
MASELSPOORT	66 D4 ↑	Modder	Bloemfontein	24	71	Licence only	Barbel, Carp, Yellowfish	At the dam	At the dam	Rondavels	Rowing boats only
MOCKES	66 D4 ↑	Modder	Bloemfontein	25	340	No fishing allowed		No	No	No	No
NEWBURY	66 D5 ↖	Leeu	Ladybrand	36		Licence only and permission from owners	Barbel, Carp, Mudfish, Yellowfish	In Ladybrand	No	No	Boating allowed
P.K. LE ROUX	62 B2 ↗	Orange	Petrusville	13	13 900	Licence only	Barbel, Carp, Yellowfish	Yes	Yes	Yes	In near future

DAMS AND LAKES - ORANGE FREE STATE continued

** For further information on freshwater and coastal fishing, see section on FISHING*

Dam Name	Map Page and Grid Ref.	River	Nearest Town	Distance from Town to Dam in km	Surface Area of Water in Ha (when full)	Fishing Permit Needed?	Kinds of Fish in Dam *	Caravan Park Nearby?	Camping Site Nearby?	Other Accommodation or Facilities	Facilities for Boating and Yachting?
RUSTFONTEIN	62 A4 ↑	Modder	Bloemfontein	47	1 133	Licence only	Barbel, Carp, Yellowfish	No	No	No	Yes, permit needed
SAULSPOORT	66 C6 ↖	Liebenbergsvlei	Bethlehem	8	424	Yes	Carp, Yellowfish	At Loch Athlone	At Loch Athlone	Huts at Loch Athlone	No
SMITHFIELD	62 B4 ↑	Groenspruit	Smithfield	2	117	Yes	Carp, Yellowfish	Yes	Yes	In town	Facilities for boating
STERKFONTEIN (Under construction)	67 C2 ←	Nuwejaarspruit	Harrismith	20	5 073	Fishing not allowed		No	No	No	No
TIERPOORT	62 A4 ←	Kaffer	Bloemfontein	35	938	Licence only	Barbel, Carp, Yellowfish	No	No	No	No
UNIEFEES	66 B5 ↗	Elandspruit	Heilbron	Borders on dam	52	Yes	Barbel, Carp, Yellowfish	Allowed, but no facilities	Yes	Hotels in town	Yes
VANSTADENSRUS	62 A5 ↙	Witspruit	Wepener	26	10	No	Barbel, Carp, Mudfish	Yes	Yes	Yes	Yes
WELBEDACHT	62 A4 ↘	Caledon	Wepener	40	642	Yes	Barbel, Carp, Yellowfish	No	No	No	No

DAMS AND LAKES - TRANSVAAL

Dam Name	Map Page and Grid Ref.	River	Nearest Town	Distance from Town to Dam in km	Surface Area of Water in Ha (when full)	Fishing Permit Needed?	Kinds of Fish in Dam *	Caravan Park Nearby?	Camping Site Nearby?	Other Accommodation or Facilities	Facilities for Boating and Yachting?
ALBASINI	70 C5 ↖	Luvuvhu	Louis Trichardt	22	359	Licence only	Barbel, Kurper, Yellowfish	No	Yes	Braai facilities, Toilets	Yes
BANAGHER LAKE	67 A3 ↑		Chrissiesmeer	12	600	Yes	Carp	No	No	Hotel	No
BIERSPRUIT (Obtain entry permission from Manager, Rustenburg Platinum Mine)	68 B5 ↙	Bierspruit	Thabazimbi	65	198	Yes	Barbel, Carp, Kurper, Yellowfish	No	No	Holiday Resort 8 km away	Yes
BLYDERIVIERSPOORT	69 B3 ↘	Blyde	Klaserie	33	261	Yes	To be filled with fish in near future	No	No	Yes	No inboard motors allowed
BOKSBURG LAKE	72 NS →		Boksburg	In Boksburg		No fishing allowed		No	No	Hotels in Boksburg. Pleasant picnic area.	Rowing boats for hire. Launch trips over weekends and public holidays
BON ACCORD	68 NS ↗	Apies	Pretoria	16	12	No fishing - dam choked with hyacinth		Yes	Yes	Yes	Yes
BOSKOP	66 A5 ↙	Mooi	Potchefstroom	20	335		Barbel, Bass, Carp, Kurper, Yellowfish	No	Yes	Toilets	Yes
BOSPOORT	68 NS ↖	Hex	Rustenburg	15	240	Licence only	Barbel, Bass, Carp, Eel	In Rustenburg	In Rustenburg	Picnic spots. Hotels in Rustenburg	No
BRONKHORSTSPRUIT	68 C6 ↓	Bronkhorst-spruit	Bronkhorstspruit	10	868	Yes	Barbel, Carp, Mudfish, Yellowfish	Yes	Yes	Holiday Resort	Yes
BUFFELSKLOOF	69B3 ↙	Watervals	Lydenburg	43	52	Licence only	Trout, Yellowfish	No	No	No	Yes
BUFFELSPOORT	68 NS ←	Sterkstroom	Brits	38	135	Yes	Carp, Kurper	At the dam	At the dam	Hotel, rondavels, tennis, swimming pool	Yes
CHRISSIESMEER	69 D3 ↖		Chrissiesmeer	1	1 000	Yes	Barbel, Bass, Carp	No	No	Hotel	No

DAMS AND LAKES - TRANSVAAL continued

** For further information on freshwater and coastal fishing, see section on FISHING*

Dam Name	Map Page and Grid Ref.	River	Nearest Town	Distance from Town to Dam in km	Surface Area of Water in Ha (when full)	Fishing Permit Needed?	Kinds of Fish in Dam *	Caravan Park Nearby?	Camping Site Nearby?	Other Accommodation or Facilities	Facilities for Boating and Yachting?
CIVIC LAKE	72 NS →		Benoni	In Benoni		Provincial licence required	Barbel, Carp,	No	No	Picnic area	No
CROSS	70 B5 •	Nwanedzi	Tshipise	28		No	Black Bass, Kurper, Yellowfish	No	Yes	No	No facilities but boating allowed
DA GAMA	71 NS ↙	Witwaters	White River	28	126	No	Black Bass, Carp	Plans awaiting approval	No	Picnic facilities awaiting approval	No power boats
DAP NAUDÉ	70 NS ↖	Broederstroom	Haenertsburg	28	25	Yes	Trout	Yes, permit needed	Yes	Holiday Resort	Not allowed
DONKERPOORT	68 B6 ↙	Nyl	Nylstroom	15	30	Yes	Barbel, Carp, Kurper, Largemouth Bass	In Nylstroom	No	In Nylstroom	No
DOORNDRAAI	69 B1 ↗	Sterk	Potgietersrus	38	422	Yes	Black Bass, Kurper, Yellowfish	In Potgietersrus	No	Hotels in Potgietersrus	Yes
DOORNHOEK		SEE FANIE BOTHA DAM									
DOUGLAS	67 A2 →	Kafferspruit	Ermelo	7		No		Yes	No	Holiday Resort	Yes
EBENEZER	70 NS ↙	Groot-Letaba	Haenertsburg	12	384	Yes	Black Bass, Kurper. Trout	On site	On site	Hotel 3,6 km away (Magoebaskloof)	Yes
FANIE BOTHA	70 NS ↗	Groot-Letaba	Tzaneen	2	1 000	Fishing not permitted	Barbel, Eel, Kurper, Tigerfish, Yellowfish	Yes	Planned for the future	Chalets available soon	Yes
FLORIDA LAKE	72 NS ←		Roodepoort	In Florida		Day licence from Municipal Angling Club	Barbel, Carp	On site	On site	Picnic area, swimming pool, Putt-putt course	Licence from Yacht Club needed. No power boats
GERMISTON LAKE	72 NS ↘		Germiston	In city		At a fee of R1 per day	Various kinds	No	No	Picnic area	Rowing boats and miniature motor boats for hire. Pleasure launch trips on weekends
GERT COMBRINK	69 B2 ↖	Dorps	Potgietersrus	3	50	Yes	Barbel, Carp, Kurper	In the town	No	Hotels in town	No
GLEN ALPINE	70 C3 ↗	Mogalakwena	Potgietersrus	172	469		Fishing allowed	No	Yes	No	Allowed, but no facilities
HANS MERENSKY	70 NS ↗	Mabitse	Duiwelskloof	8		Yes	Black Bass, Kurper	In Duiwelskloof	In Duiwelskloof	Hotel, Duiwelskloof	No
HARTBEESPOORT (Magnificent views from top of Magaliesberg - access by cableway)	68 NS ↑	Krokodil	Brits	12	1 883	Yes	Barbel, Bass, Carp, Kurper, Yellowfish	At the dam	At the dam	Hotel, many attractive picnic spots	Yes
HOMESTEAD LAKE	72 NS →		Benoni	In Benoni		No fishing permitted		No	No	Picnic area	No
JERICHO	67 A3 ↓	Mpama	Amsterdam	20	974	Yes	Best Black Bass fishing in the Republic; Yellowfish	Yes - only toilet facilities and purified water	Yes - only toilet facilities and purified water	No	Yes
JOHAN NESER	66 A4 ↘	Schoonspruit	Klerksdorp	10	200	Yes	Barbel, Carp, Mudfish, Yellowfish	Yes	Yes	Hotels in Klerksdorp	Yes
KAFFERSKRAAL	69 C3 ↓	Komati	Badplaas	8	662,2	Licence only	Barbel, Black Bass, Eel, Yellowfish	In Badplaas	In Badplaas	Rondavels, Hotel in Badplaas	Yes
KLASERIE	69 B4 ←	Klaserie	Klaserie	3		Yes	Kurper	In Hoedspruit	At the dam	No	No

DAMS AND LAKES - TRANSVAAL continued

* *For further information on freshwater and coastal fishing, see section on FISHING*

Dam Name	Map Page and Grid Ref.	River	Nearest Town	Distance from Town to Dam in km	Surface Area of Water in Ha (when full)	Fishing Permit Needed?	Kinds of Fish in Dam *	Caravan Park Nearby?	Camping Site Nearby?	Other Accommodation or Facilities	Facilities for Boating and Yachting?
KLEIN-MARICOPOORT	68 C4 ←	Klein-Marico	Zeerust	10	146	Yes	Barbel, Carp, Eel, Kurper	Yes	Yes	No	Yes
KLERKSKRAAL	68 D5 ↖	Mooi	Carletonville	27	557	No	Barbel, Black Bass, Mudfish, Yellowfish	No	No	No	Not allowed
KLIPDRIFT	66 A5 ↙	Loopspruit	Potchefstroom	25	329	Yes	Carp, Mudfish, Yellowfish	No	Yes	No	No, but boating allowed
KLIPVOOR (Reserved for Blacks)	68 C5 ↗	Pienaars	Brits	80		Fishing allowed					
KOSTERRIVIER	68 C4 ↘	Koster	Rustenburg	42	138	Yes	Barbel, Carp, Yellowfish	No facilities but caravans allowed	Limited facilites for all races	No	No facilities but boating allowed
KROMELLENBOOG	68 C4 ←	Klein-Marico	Zeerust	38	194,7	Yes	Barbel, Carp, Kurper	Yes	Yes	No	Yes
KRUGER (Situated in a nature reserve)	69 C2 ↓	Klein-Olifants	Middelburg	In town		Yes	Various kinds	On site	On site	Fully equipped rondavels. Swimming pool, restaurant	Yes
LAKE FUNDUDZI (Entry permit necessary. Situated in Venda Homeland - Venda's believe lake is inhabited by spirits of deceased captains)	70 B5 ↙	Mutale	Louis Trichardt			Fishing not permitted		No	No	No	No
LAKESIDE		SEE POTCHEFSTROOM DAM									
LINDLEY'S POORT (Untarred access road in poor condition)	68 C4 →	Elands	Swartruggens	20	176		Black Bass, Carp, Yellowfish	No	No	Toilet facilities for all races. Picnic spots, braais	No
LOCH VAAL		SEE VAAL RIVER BARRAGE									
LONGMERE	71 NS ↙	Witrivier	White River	10			NO FACILITIES				
LOSKOP**	69 C2 ←	Olifants	Groblersdal	32		**Yes	Barbel, Carp, Kurper, Yellowfish	**The Department of Water Affairs is raising the wall of the dam - consequently accommodation units, camping areas and existing facilities will be flooded. A complete new resort is in the planning stage.			
LOXTON		SEE VYFHOEK DAM									
LUPHEPHE	70 B5 ↙	Luphephe	Tshipise	35	137	No	Black Bass, Kurper, Yellowfish	No	Yes, at dam	No	No facilities but boating allowed
MAGOEBASKLOOF	70 NS ↗	Politsi	Tzaneen	17	45	No fishing		No	No	No	No
MARICO-BOSVELD	68 C4 ←	Groot-Marico	Zeerust	35	434,6	Yes	Black Bass, Carp, Kurper	Poor facilities but caravans allowed	Yes	No	Yes, permit needed for boating
MIDDLE LAKE	72 NS →		Benoni	In Benoni		Provincial fishing licence required	Barbel, Carp, Yellowfish	No	No	Picnic area	No
NOOITGEDACHT	69 C3 ↙	Komati	Carolina	10	770	No	Barbel, carp, Yellowfish	In Carolina	Yes, at dam	Hotel, Carolina	Yes
NYL	69 B1 ↗	Nyl	Potgietersrus	7	77	Yes	Barbel, Kurper	Potgietersrus	No	Hotels in Potgietersrus	No
NZHELELE (Beware of crocodiles)	70 B5 ↙	Nzhelele	Louis Trichardt	57	606	No	Barbel, Kurper, Yellowfish	No	Yes, at dam	No	No facilities, but boating allowed

* *For further information on freshwater and coastal fishing, see section on FISHING*

DAMS AND LAKES - TRANSVAAL continued

Dam Name	Map Page and Grid Ref.	River	Nearest Town	Distance from Town to Dam in km	Surface Area of Water in Ha (when full)	Fishing Permit Needed?	Kinds of Fish in Dam *	Caravan Park Nearby?	Camping Site Nearby?	Other Accommodation or Facilities	Facilities for Boating and Yachting?
OHRIGSTAD	70 NS ↖	Ohrigstad	Lydenburg	41	94	Licence only	Black Bass, Carp	No	Yes, at dam	No	Yes
OLIFANTSNEK	68 NS ←	Hex	Rustenburg	20	100	Licence only	Barbel, Carp, Eel, Kurper, Yellowfish	In Rustenburg	In Rustenburg	Hotel at dam	No
PHALABORWA	69 B4 ↖	Olifants	Phalaborwa	16	197	Prohibited		No	Prohibited	No	Only for members of boating club
PLATRIVIER	68 B6 ↙	Plat	Warmbaths	5	19,2	Yes	Barbel, Carp, Kurper, Yellowfish	In Warmbaths	In Warmbaths	Hotel in Warmbaths	Yes
POTCHEFSTROOM (LAKESIDE)	66 A5 ↙	Mooi	Potchefstroom	10	66	Yes	Barbel, Black Bass, Carp, Yellowfish	Yes, at dam	Yes	Rondavels	Yes
PREMIER MINE (Closed to public)	69 C1 ↘	Wilge	Bronkhorstspruit								
RIEBEECK LAKE	72 NS ←		Randfontein	2	3	Yes	Barbel, Carp	Yes	Yes	Rondavels, swimming pool	No
RIETSPRUIT	68 D4 →	Schoonspruit	Ventersdorp	13	227	Yes	Carp, Yellowfish	No	Yes	No	No
RIETVLEI	68 NS →	Sesmylspruit	Pretoria	20	12	Yes	Bass, Carp, Kurper	Yes	Yes	No	Yes
ROBINSON LAKE	72 NS ←		Randfontein	3	20	Yes	Black Bass, Carp	No	No	No	Yes
ROODEPLAAT	68 C6 ↙	Pienaars	Pretoria	20	396	Yes	Barbel, Bass, Carp, Kurper, Yellowfish	Caravans allowed, basic facilities.	Camping allowed, basic facilities. Camping site for Coloureds on Eastern bank - basic facilities	Being developed, Picnic and braai spots for Coloureds on Eastern Bank	Yes
ROOIKRAAL	69 C2 ↗	Bloed	Groblersdal	44	50	No	Barbel, Yellowfish	In Groblersdal	In Groblersdal	No	No
RUST-DE-WINTER	68 C6 ↑	Elands	Warmbaths	65	471	Licence only	Barbel, Bass, Carp, Kurper, Mudfish, Yellowfish	Basic facilities for caravans at dam (toilets, fresh drinking water)	Basic facilities at dam	Hotel 30 km away	Yes
SHIYALONGUBU	69 C4 ↙	Fed by several fountains	Barberton	33		Yes	Black Bass, Eel, Kurper	No	Yes	Hotel in Barberton	No facilities but boating allowed
STANFORD LAKE	70 NS ↓	Helpmekaar	Haenertsburg	7	5	Yes	Black Bass, Trout	Yes	Yes	Chalets nearby	No
STERKRIVIER		SEE DOORNDRAAI DAM									
TONTELDOOS	69 C2 ↗	Tonteldoos	Roossenekal	10	8		Barbel, Black Bass	No	No	No	No
VAAL	66 A6 ↙	Vaal	Vereeniging	37	29 269	Yes	Barbel, Carp, Mudfish, Yellowfish	Various parks along dam	Yes, along dam	Hotel, chalets, rondavels	Yes - permits required
VAALKOP	68 C5 ↖	Elands	Brits	52	771	No	Carp, Kurper	Yes	Yes	No	Yes
VAAL RIVER BARRAGE (LOCH VAAL)	66 A5 ↘	Vaal	Vereeniging	Borders on dam	1 683,5	Not permitted in safety area of the Barrage	Barbel, Carp, Mudfish, Yellowfish	Yes	Yes	Hotel at Loch, various resorts	Yes
VAN RYN	72 NS →		Benoni	In Benoni		Angling club may be joined	Various kinds	No	No	Picnic area	Yacht Club may be joined

DAMS AND LAKES - TRANSVAAL continued

** For further information on freshwater and coastal fishing, see section on FISHING*

Dam Name	Map Page and Grid Ref.	River	Nearest Town	Distance from Town to Dam in km	Surface Area of Water in Ha (when full)	Fishing Permit Needed?	Kinds of Fish in Dam *	Caravan Park Nearby?	Camping Site Nearby?	Other Accommodation or Facilities	Facilities for Boating and Yachting?
VERGELEGEN	70 NS ↗	Tributary of Politsi	Tzaneen	18	8,2	Fishing not allowed		In Tzaneen	No	No	No
VLUGKRAAL (Access to dam very poor)	69 C2 ↗	Vlugkraal	Roossenekal	6	11		Black Bass, Mudfish, Yellowfish	No	No	No	No
VYFHOEK (LOXTON)	66 A5 ↙	Loopspruit	Potchefstroom	8	33,5	No	Barbel, Carp, Kurper, Yellowfish	No	Yes, at dam	No	Only rowing boats allowed
WENTZEL	66 B3 ↖	Harts	Schweizer-Reneke	2	276	Licence only	Carp, Yellowfish	At dam	At dam	Hotel in town	Yes
WESTOE	67 A3 →	Usutu	Amsterdam	16	749	Yes	Black Bass, Carp, Eel, Yellowfish	Poor facilities	Poor facilities	No	Yes
WESTONARIA	72 NS ↙	Middel-vleispruit	Westonaria	2		Yes	Various kinds of fresh water fish	At dam	At dam	No	Yes
WITBANK	69 C2 ↙	Olifants	Witbank	6	970	Yes	Barbel, Black Bass, Carp, Yellowfish	Yes, at dam	Yes, at dam	Hotels in town	Yes
WOLMARANSSTAD (No swimming allowed as bilharzia prevalent)	66 B3 ↗	Makwas-siespruit	Wolmaransstad	2	8	Yes	Carp, Yellowfish	1 km from dam	Yes	Rooms at dam, hotel in town	No
ZOO LAKE (Artists in the Sun display 1st Sunday of each month)	72 NS •		Parkview, Johannesburg			Only for members of Transvaal Angling and Casting Union	Various kinds of fresh water fish	No	No	Picnic area, refreshment kiosk	Rowing boats for hire

The Climate, Bilharzia and Malaria maps will be found on page 115.

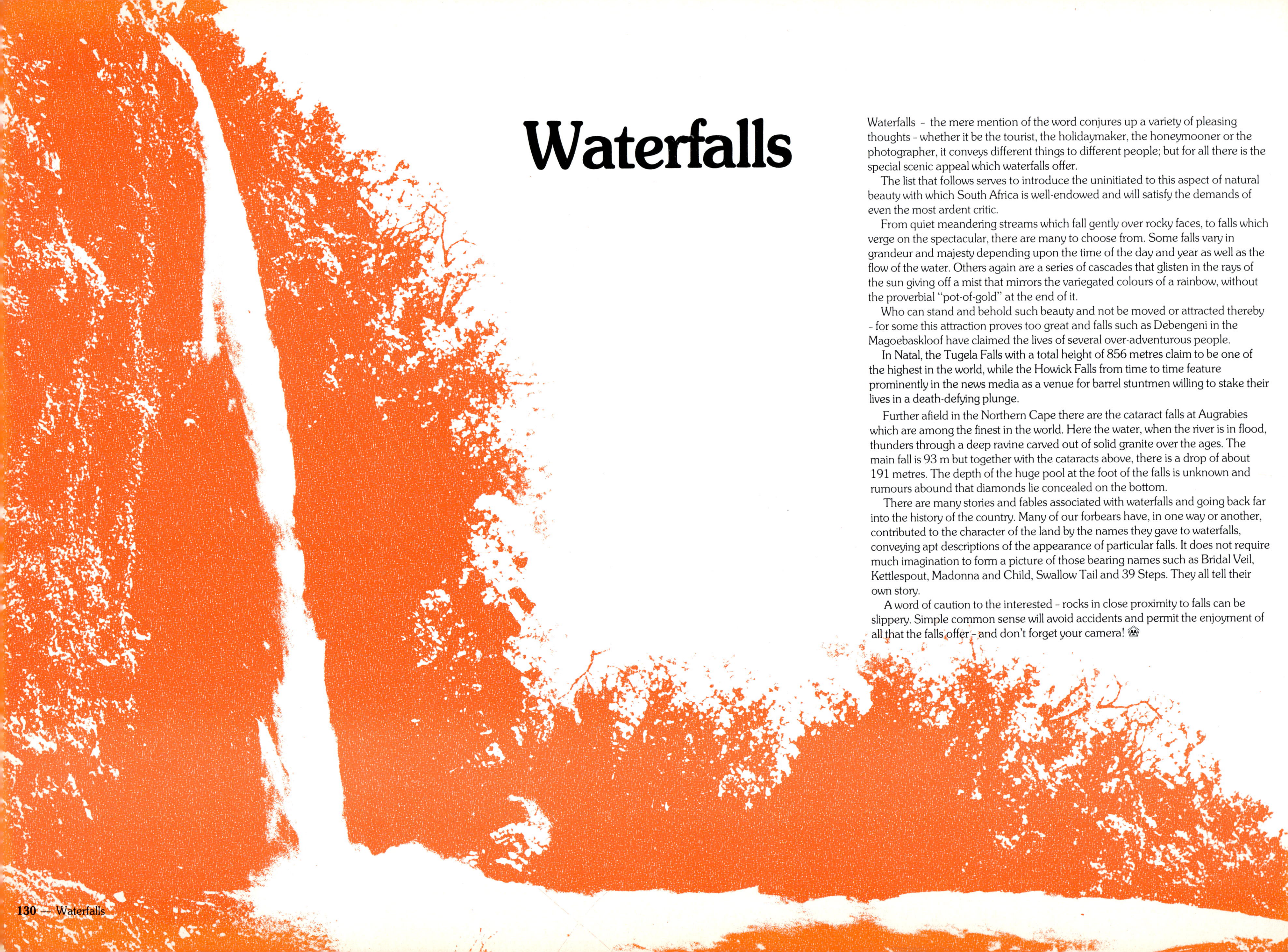

Waterfalls

Waterfalls – the mere mention of the word conjures up a variety of pleasing thoughts – whether it be the tourist, the holidaymaker, the honeymooner or the photographer, it conveys different things to different people; but for all there is the special scenic appeal which waterfalls offer.

The list that follows serves to introduce the uninitiated to this aspect of natural beauty with which South Africa is well-endowed and will satisfy the demands of even the most ardent critic.

From quiet meandering streams which fall gently over rocky faces, to falls which verge on the spectacular, there are many to choose from. Some falls vary in grandeur and majesty depending upon the time of the day and year as well as the flow of the water. Others again are a series of cascades that glisten in the rays of the sun giving off a mist that mirrors the variegated colours of a rainbow, without the proverbial "pot-of-gold" at the end of it.

Who can stand and behold such beauty and not be moved or attracted thereby – for some this attraction proves too great and falls such as Debengeni in the Magoebaskloof have claimed the lives of several over-adventurous people.

In Natal, the Tugela Falls with a total height of 856 metres claim to be one of the highest in the world, while the Howick Falls from time to time feature prominently in the news media as a venue for barrel stuntmen willing to stake their lives in a death-defying plunge.

Further afield in the Northern Cape there are the cataract falls at Augrabies which are among the finest in the world. Here the water, when the river is in flood, thunders through a deep ravine carved out of solid granite over the ages. The main fall is 93 m but together with the cataracts above, there is a drop of about 191 metres. The depth of the huge pool at the foot of the falls is unknown and rumours abound that diamonds lie concealed on the bottom.

There are many stories and fables associated with waterfalls and going back far into the history of the country. Many of our forbears have, in one way or another, contributed to the character of the land by the names they gave to waterfalls, conveying apt descriptions of the appearance of particular falls. It does not require much imagination to form a picture of those bearing names such as Bridal Veil, Kettlespout, Madonna and Child, Swallow Tail and 39 Steps. They all tell their own story.

A word of caution to the interested – rocks in close proximity to falls can be slippery. Simple common sense will avoid accidents and permit the enjoyment of all that the falls offer – and don't forget your camera!

WATERFALLS - CAPE

Name	Map Page and Grid Reference	River/Stream on which Falls are Situated	Nearest Important Town	Distance from this Town to Falls (km)	Height and Volume	Water Drinkable?	Facilities Available	Accessibility
AUGRABIES FALLS	65 C2 ↙	Orange	Kakamas	45	191 m	Yes	Picnic spot, camp site, huts	Access from tarred road
BLOUGAT WATERFALL	Not on map - obtain directions from Ladismith Municipality 58 C6 ←	Elandsvlei	Ladismith	4	15 m	Yes	None	2 km walk from where a vehicle can be parked
BRACKEN HILL FALLS	59 NS ↘	Witels	Knysna	13	Upper Falls 18 m Lower Falls 21 m	Yes	Picnic spot	1,6 km gravel road from main road
BRIDAL VEIL FALLS	See map of Hogsback in Wilderness Trail section	Tyumie	Alice	33		No	None	Situated on private land. No distinct footpath
DISA WATERFALL	58 C4 ↙	Elands	Villiersdorp	10	30 m - stronger volume in winter	Yes	Picnic spots	200 m from where a vehicle can be parked
FIRST WATERFALL	Not on map but situated in Jonkershoek Valley 58 C3 ↘	Eerste	Stellenbosch	13	50 m - Falls dry up in summer	Yes	None	15 minute walk along mountain path. Entry permits available at Jonkershoek State Forest only during winter.
GLEN AVON FALLS	59 A5 ↘	Naudés	Somerset East	8	84 m	Yes	None, on private property	Only with permission from owner of property
KETTLESPOUT FALLS	See map of Hogsback in Wilderness Trail section	Tyumie	Hogsback	Within walking distance	30 m	No	Hotels, cottages, caravan camp, picnic spots	1½ hour walk
MADONNA AND CHILD FALLS	See map of Hogsback in Wilderness Trail section	Tyumie	Hogsback	Within walking distance	30 m	No	Hotels, cottages, caravan camp, picnic spots	1½ hour walk from Alice main road
NIEUWOUDTVILLE WATERFALL	61 C1 ↖	Holdrif	Nieuwoudtville	6	Strong volume during winter	Yes	None	3 minute walk along farm road
RUST EN VREDE WATERFALL	59 B2 ↖	Groot	Oudtshoorn	40	79 m	Yes	Picnic spot, camp site - 5 km away	8 minute walk along footpath
SECOND WATERFALL	Not on map - in Jonkershoek Valley 58 C3 ↘	Eerste	Stellenbosch	15	75 m - Virtually dries up in summer	Yes	None	30 minute walk along mountain. Access only permitted in winter
SEWEWEEKSPOORT WATERFALL	59 B1 •	Seweweeks-poort	Ladismith	30	40 m	Yes	Several braai-places, camp site	100 m walk from road
SILVERMINE FALLS	58 NS ←	Silvermine	Cape Town	30	8 m - Volume just a small trickle in summer	Yes	Picnic and braai-spots	5 minute walk from car park
SWALLOW TAIL WATERFALL	See map of Hogsback area in Wilderness Trail section	Tyumie	Hogsback	Walking distance	30 m	No	Hotel, camp site, cottages, caravan camp, picnic spots	40 minute steep walk. On private property
THE WATERFALL	58 B4 ↙	Boontjies	Citrusdal	8	23 m	Yes	None	10 minute walk along footpath
THIRTY NINE STEPS	See map of Hogsback area in Wilderness Trail Section	Tyumie	Hogsback	Walking distance	30 m	No	Hotel, camp site, caravan park, cottages, picnic spots	15 minute pleasant walk
TYUMIE WATERFALL	See map of Hogsback area in Wilderness Trail section	Tyumie	Hogsback	Within walking distance	30 m	No		Access very difficult. Advice should be sought locally
VAN ZYLSKLOOF WATERFALL	Not on map - directions obtainable from Ladismith Municipality 58 C6 ←	Korlandkloof	Ladismith	3	200 m	Yes	None	800 m walk from car park

WATERFALLS - NATAL

Name	Map Page and Grid Reference	River/Stream on which Falls are Situated	Nearest Important Town	Distance from this Town to Falls (km)	Height and Volume	Water Drinkable?	Facilities Available	Accessibility
ALBERT FALLS	Not on map 63 A3 •	Mgeni	Pietermaritzburg	25		Yes	Fishing, boating, picnicking when Albert Falls public resort is completed	Next to road
BINGINI FALLS	63 A2 ↑	Ncibidwane Stream	Estcourt	65	2 x 30 m - Volume 2 M^3/S	Yes	In Giant's Castle Game Reserve. Hutted camp	1½ hour walk from camp
CASCADE FALLS	Not on map - situated on road to Rietvlei in Mgeni Valley Nature Reserve 63 A3 ←	Shelter	Howick	2,5	25 m	No	None	Next to the road
COOPER FALLS	63 B2 ↗	Mzimkulu	Creighton				None	On private land - long walk through the veld
GRYSBUCK BUSH FALLS	Not on map - situated in Giant's Castle Game Reserve 63 A2 ↑	Middle Ridge Stream	Estcourt	65	5 m - small volume	Yes	In Giant's Castle Game Reserve. Hutted camp	1 hour walk from camp
GUDU FALLS	67 C1 ↘	Gudu Stream	Bergville	45	30 m - small volume	Yes	In Royal Natal National Park. Hotel, huts, campsites. Non-White camping ground nearby	1½ hour walk from hotel
HAMMARSDALE FALLS	63 NS ↑	Sterkspruit	Hammarsdale	2	60 m	No	None	100 m walk over private land to top of falls
HLAMBAMASOGA WATERFALL	63 A3 •	Mkabela	Pietermaritzburg	28			None	Readily accessible from private farm roads
HOWICK FALLS	Not on map. Situated in the town. 63 A3 ←	Mgeni	Howick	In the town	100 m	No	Picnic spots, hotel	Situated in the town
JACOB'S LADDER	Not on map. In Loteni Nature Reserve. 63 A2 ↑	Hlatikulu	Nottingham Road	78	40 m - Volume 3 M^3/S	Yes	In Loteni Nature Reserve. Hutted camp	30 minute walk from camp
KARKLOOF FALLS	63 A3 ↖	Karkloof	Howick	16	100 m	No	Picnic spots	Visible from road
KLIP RIVER FALLS	67 C2 ↘	Klip	Ladysmith	35	Very small volume in winter	No	None	1 hour walk from road
KLOOF FALLS	Not on map. 63 NS ↗	Molweni	Durban	31	10 m - Volume 1 M^3/S	No	In Krantzkloof Nature Reserve. Commercial hotels	Road access to within metres of falls
KOCH'S WATERFALL	63 A3 →	Mkabela	Pietermaritzburg	38			None	Accessible from private farm roads
KWA-COTA FALLS	63 B2 ↗	Cota Stream	Creighton	16	21 m		None	1 km walk over veld
LITTLE NIAGARA FALLS	67 C2 ↘	Klip	Ladysmith	35		No	None	1 hour walk from nearest point where vehicle can be parked
LOTENI FALLS	63 A2 •	Loteni Stream	Nottingham Road	78	15 m - Volume 3 M^3/S	Yes	In Loteni Nature Reserve. Hutted camp	20 minute steep walk from camp
MAHAI FALLS	67 C1 ↘	Mahai Stream	Bergville	45	10 m - small volume	Yes	In Royal Natal National Park. Hutted camp, hotel	2 hour walk from hotel
MILLS FALLS	Not on map. 63 A3 ←	Mgeni	Howick	In town	7 m	No	None	2 minute walk from road

WATERFALLS - NATAL (continued)

Name	Map Page and Grid Reference	River/Stream on which Falls are Situated	Nearest Important Town	Distance from this Town to Falls (km)	Height and Volume	Water Drinkable?	Facilities Available	Accessibility
MKUZE FALLS	67 B4 ↓	Mkuze	Pongola	40 km	15 m - Very small volume in winter	No	None	Road to falls in bad condition. On private land. Permission from farmer to be obtained
MOLO FALLS	63 A2 •	Bhodla Stream	Nottingham Road	78 km	5 m - Volume 1 M³/S	Yes	In Loteni Nature Reserve. Hutted camp	30 minute walk from camp
MOOI FALLS	67 D3 ↖	Mooi	Mooi River	40 km	80 m	Yes	Picnic spot	5 minute walk from road
MPUSHENI WATERFALLS	67 C4 ↓	Mpusheni	Eshowe	2 km	13 falls over distance of 182 metres	No	Picnic spot	Easily accessible on foot
MZINYATI FALLS	63 NS ↗	Mzinyati	Mount Edgecombe	3 km	± 76 m		Picnic spot	± 3 km walk from road
NGODWINI FALLS	63 A2 •	Ngodwini	Nottingham Road	78 km	5 m	Yes	In Loteni Nature Reserve. Hutted camp	15 minute walk from camp
NUNGWANE	63 B3 ↗	Nungwane	Amanzimtoti	25	64 m	No	None	4 km drive on road in bad condition. View from top of hill. Permit required - situated in KwaZulu
NZINGA FALLS	63 A2 →	Nzinga	Nottingham Road	40 km	57 m	Yes	None	Easy 20 minute walk through veld. Permission of farmer necessary
ORIBI FALLS	63 B3 ↙	Mzimkulwana	Port Shepstone	30 km	5 m - Volume 4 M³/S	No	In Oribi Gorge Nature Reserve. Hutted camp	Access by walking from road
QUNU FALLS	63 NS ↖	Lovu	Richmond	3 km			None	Permission at farmhouse. 2 km walk from there
RED WALL FALLS	Not on map. In Giant's Castle Game Reserve 63 A2 ↑	Injasuti	Estcourt	65 km	280 m - Volume 0,5 M³/S	Yes	In Giant's Castle Game Reserve. Hutted camp	4 hour walk
SHELTER FALLS	Not on map. On Shelter Road, along road to Rietvlei. 63 A3 ↖	Shelter	Howick	2 km	20 m	No	None	10 minute walk from road. In Mgeni Valley Nature Reserve
STERKSPRUIT WATERFALL	67 D2 ↑	Sterkspruit	Estcourt	60 km	30 m	Yes	Camp site 1 km from falls	1 km walk from campsite
SUNDAY FALLS	67 C1 ↘	Sigubudu	Bergville	45 km	18 m - small volume	Yes	In Royal Natal National Park. Hotel, hutted camp	1 hour walk from hotel
TIGER FALLS	67 C1 ↘	Mahai Tributary	Bergville	45 km	7 m - small volume	Yes	In Royal Natal National Park. Hotel, hutted camp	1 hour walk from hotel
TUGELA FALLS	67 C1 ↘	Tugela	Bergville	45 km	856 m (in 3 steps)	Yes	In Royal Natal National Park. Hotel, hutted camp	3½ hour walk
TUGELA FALLS	67 C2 ↘	Tugela	Colenso	5 km		No	None	10 minute walk from where a vehicle can be parked with permission of farmer
TWO DASSIE STREAM FALLS	Not on map In Giant's Castle Game Reserve. 63 A2 ↑	Two Dassie Stream	Estcourt	65 km	18 m - small volume	Yes	In Giant's Castle Game Reserve. Hutted camp	1½ hour walk from camp

WATERFALLS - TRANSVAAL

Name	Map Page and Grid Reference	River/Stream on which Falls are Situated	Nearest Important Town	Distance from this Town to Falls (km)	Height and Volume	Water Drinkable?	Facilities Available	Accessibility
BERLIN FALLS	69 B3 ↘	Watervalspruit	Graskop	16	47,8 m	Yes	None	50 metre walk
BRIDAL VEIL FALLS	70 NS ↓	Sabie Tributary	Sabie	9	Not known	Yes	None	200 m walk from parking spot. Situated in Ceylon State Forest
CROCODILE FALLS	71 C5 ←	Crocodile	Nelspruit	5		No	None	5 minute walk through a botanical garden
DEBENGENI WATERFALL	70 NS ↑	Tributary of Politsi	Tzaneen	24	Strong volume throughout the year	Yes	Picnic spot, camp site	100 metre walk from where a vehicle can be parked
ELANDS RIVER FALLS	69 C3 ↙	Elands	Waterval-Boven	4	90 m	Yes	Camp site, picnic spots, hotel	15 minute walk
FOREST (GRASKOP) FALLS	70 NS ↗	Mac-Mac	Graskop	9	10 m	Yes	None	Path through forest. Permission to be obtained from Department of Forestry
LISBON FALLS	70 NS ↗	Lisbon	Graskop	11	82,5 m	Yes	Parking area, braais	Next to parking area
LONE CREEK FALLS	70 NS ↓	Lone Creek	Sabie	11	68 m	Yes	Picnic facilities, toilets	2 minute walk from parking spot. Situated in Ceylon State Forest
LYDENBURG WATERFALL	70 NS ←	Dorps	Lydenburg	12	182 m	No	None	5 minute walk
MAC-MAC FALLS	70 NS →	Mac-Mac	Graskop	14	68 m	Yes	None	Steps from road to a viewpoint of falls. Situated in Mac-Mac State Forest
MERENSKY WATERFALL	70 NS ↗	Ramatha	Tzaneen	15			None	Can be viewed from road. Access very difficult
MONTROSE FALLS	69 C3 →	Crocodile	Nelspruit	30	9 m	No	Hotel, camping, caravaning, chalets	3 minute walk through forest
NEW CHUM FALLS	71 B4 ↘	Treur	Graskop	28		Yes	None	At present *not* accessible to public
PANORAMA FALLS	71 B4 ↘	In the Panorama Kloof	Graskop	1	Small volume in winter	No	None	Footpath from road
PHIPHIDI WATERFALL	70 B5 ↓	Mutshindudi	Sibasa	9	15 m	Yes	Picnic spot	Can drive almost up to falls. 3 minute walk
SABIE WATERFALL	70 NS ↘	Sabie	Sabie	Just outside town		No	None	Next to road
TSHIHOVHOHOVHO WATERFALL	70 B5 ↙	Nwanedzi	Sibasa	60	25 m	Yes	None	1 km walk through dense forest

Keep South Africa Beautiful - Don't litter

Mountain Passes

INTRODUCTION

South Africa has a good network of roads with tarred and untarred surfaces and reasonable gradients. These roads climb the rugged mountains or wind their way through romantic gorges amid beautiful scenery. Many of the more spectacular mountain passes lie off the trunk and main roads.

Motorists travelling inland will find that most of the best scenery lies between the coast and the high interior plateau. There are many passes in the Cape Province and a motorist based at Cape Town can traverse several during a day-excursion.

The well-known Four Passes Drive, which includes the Helshoogte, Franschhoek, Viljoens and Sir Lowry's Passes between Stellenbosch, Villiersdorp and Somerset West, is highly recommended – see map on page 140
(NB The latter pass is being widened and construction work will last for about 3 years.)

Another suggested route takes in eight well-known passes without appreciable overlapping, over a distance of about 400 km. Two or three days should be allowed for travelling from Cape Town, via Faure to Stellenbosch, over Helshoogte to Paarl, over Bainskloof and Michell's Pass to Ceres, over the Hex River Pass to Worcester, du Toit's Kloof Pass to Paarl, then to Franschhoek and over the Franschhoek Pass, Viljoen's Pass, Sir Lowry's Pass to Faure and back to Cape Town.

Most mountain passes in the Cape Province are negotiable under normal weather conditions but there are a few which may present the caravaner with some difficulty. These include:

The Swartberg Pass (notorious for its hairpin bends) between the Cango Caves and Prince Albert; Prince Alfred's Pass between Avontuur and Knysna; Seweweekspoort between Calitzdorp and Seweweekspoort; Katberg Pass between Fort Beaufort and Queenstown (not shown on map).

Natal, with its rolling hills and high escarpment, presents a challenge to any caravaner. Roads which specifically present difficulties, include the following:

1 Caravans are not allowed on the road leading to Kosi Bay Nature Reserve – this road is only suitable for four-wheel-drive vehicles.

2 The direct road from Mkuze to Sodwana Bay is usually in poor condition, although the last 20 km, which is very sandy, can become hazardous, especially in rainy weather.

3 The road between Dundee and Greytown. This is a very steep and winding road which passes through KwaZulu. Stray dogs and cattle on the road constitute a hazard, especially at night.

4 The Sani Pass (2 000 m) climbs the wall of the Drakensberg between two notable peaks on its way to Mokhotlong. To the north looms the highest mountain peak in Southern Africa, i.e. Thabana-Ntlenyana (Thabantshonyana) (3 482 m). To the south is Hodson's Peak. From the top of the pass there are some breathtaking views.
Goods and passengers are usually transported by means of four-wheel-drive vehicles. It is very rough going in places and in winter the road is usually covered with snow. *The pass is out of bounds to caravans.* Trips up the pass can be arranged at the hotels in Sani Pass, Himeville and Underberg. Visitors must bear in mind that a passport and health certificate (smallpox inoculation) are required when visiting Lesotho.

The Orange Free State differs vastly from the other provinces in that it is small and compact and there are no great geographical differences between one area and another. The province is remarkably flat, except in the eastern districts bordering Lesotho, where the land is undulating and in some parts, mountainous.

The Oliviershoek Pass connecting the Orange Free State with Natal, should not be attempted by caravaners. This gravel pass between Harrismith and the Royal Natal National Park is usually in a poor condition and is not recommended. The alternative route via the Van Reenen's Pass is preferable although extreme care must be exercised as this pass is usually buffeted by strong cross-winds. Alternatively, the Botha's Pass between Vrede and Newcastle can be used. This is a most scenic drive.

Caravaners should not attempt the road from Kestell to the Golden Gate Highlands National Park; rather go via Clarens.

Transvaal mountain passes present no problem to the motorist towing a caravan, with the exception of Kowyns Pass in the Eastern Transvaal, which, however, is often negotiated by keen caravaners, and the Saddleback Pass between Barberton and Piggs Peak, which is an exceedingly poor gravel road which becomes very muddy in rainy weather.

The experienced driver will find that there are very few passes which cannot be negotiated with a caravan. Many caravans are not properly braked and on certain mountain passes it is recommended that motorists stop halfway on the descent to allow the brakes of their vehicles to cool off. (e.g. Swartberg Pass). Drivers are warned not to stop on bends where their vehicles are not visible to passing traffic. Warning triangles should be used.

General

In planning a trip the caravaner will find it helpful if he:

1 Considers the date and time of departure, e.g. roads are always crowded at the start and finish of school holidays.

2 Allows himself sufficient travelling time, e.g. some caravan parks close earlier than others.

3 Works out a schedule whereby he descends as many passes as possible, instead of ascending them, thereby gaining time.

4 Bears in mind that it is necessary to have permits if he wants to go off the main roads in any of the Homelands.

5 Obeys the law and does not allow anyone to remain in the caravan while it is being towed.

MOUNTAIN PASSES - CAPE

Name	Location Between	Map Page and Grid Reference	Height (in metres)	Gradient	Direction of Gradient	Road Surface	Suitable for Caravans?	Further Information of Importance
AAGEDISBERG	Stanford and Riversonderend	58 D4 •	140	1:26	South/West	Tar	Yes	
AGTER WITZENBERG	North of Ceres	58 C4 ↖	1 060	1:17	West/East	Tar	Yes	
	North of Ceres	58 C4 ↖	1 060	1:16	East/West	Tar	Yes	
ANNENOUS	Steinkopf and Port Nolloth	60 A5 ↑	950	Not much of a gradient	East/West	Tar	Yes	
BAINSKLOOF	Ceres and Wellington	58 C4 ↙	701	1:13	North/South	Tar	Yes	
BARKLY	Elliot and Barkly East	62 C5 ↗	1 979	1:9		Tar	Yes	
BERGNAARSPAD	Witsand and Bermolli	65 C4 →	1 400	1:5	East/West	Gravel - in good condition	No - too steep	
BLINKWATER	Balderja and Lower Blinkwater	60 B1 ↙	± 7 900	1:5		Gravel - in poor condition	No	
BLOMFONTEIN	Cradock and Witmos	59 A5 →	1 829	1:12	South	Gravel	No	Should not be used in rain or snow
BLOUKRANS	Calvinia and Die Bos	61 C1 ↙	± 1 083	1:7	South/North	Gravel - in good condition	Yes	
BLOUKRANS	Plettenberg Bay and Coldstream	59 B3 ↓	± 200	1:7	East/West	Tar	Yes	
BOESMANSHOEK	Sterkstroom and Molteno	62 C4 •	1 707	1:10	North/South	Gravel	Not in wet weather	
BOESMANSKLOOF	South of McGregor	58 C4 ↘	732	1:10	East/West	Gravel	No	The pass was not completed, but is kept open because of the beautiful scenery
BOMA	Middledrift and Keiskammahoek	60 B2 ↙	673	1:10		Gravel	No	
BONGOLO NEK	Queenstown and Qoqodale	62 C4 ↘	1 384	1:11		Tar	Yes	
BOSLUISKLOOF	Seweweekspoort and Gamkapoort Dam	59 B1 ↑	± 1 000		West/East	Gravel	No	
BOTHAS POST	South of Fort Beaufort	60 B1 ↓	± 500	1:5		Gravel	Under *no* circumstances	Very narrow and steep
BOTTERKLOOF	Soetwater and Moedverloor	61 C1 ↙	683		South/North	Gravel	Yes	
BRAAMBOS	North of Adelaide	59 A6 •	± 1 180	1:12			Yes, but very narrow	
BUFFELSBERG	Citrusdal and Prince Alfred Hamlet	58 B4 ↙	1 048	1:12	North/South	Gravel	Not in wet weather	
BUFFELSHOEKNEK	Pearston and Swaershoek	59 A5 ←	1 310	1:8	East	Gravel	Yes	
BURGERS	Montagu and Matroosberg	58 C4 ↘	762	1:14	East/West	Tar	Yes	
BUSHNEK	North of Adelaide	59 A6 ↓	1 022	1:10			Yes	Sharp curves
CEDARBERG (old UITKYK PASS)	Clanwilliam and Cedarberg	58 B4 ←	1 005	1:9	North/South	Gravel	No	
COGMANSKLOOF	Montagu and Ashton	58 C5 ↙	240		South/North	Tar	Yes	
DASSIESHOEK	North of Robertson	58 C4 ↘	383	1:12	South/North	Gravel	Yes	Beautiful scenery; pass leads to various farms
DE JAGERS	Beaufort West and Sneeukraal	61 D4 ↗	1 524	1:10	North/East	Gravel	Yes	
DEVIL'S BELLOWS NEK	Balfour and Whittlesea	60 B1 →	± 1 900			Gravel		
DEWAALSKLOOF	Balderja and Whittlesea	60 B1 •	± 1 450	1:10		Gravel	Yes, but very narrow	

MOUNTAIN PASSES - CAPE (continued)

Name	Location Between	Map Page and Grid Reference	Height (in metres)	Gradient	Direction of Gradient	Road Surface	Suitable for Caravans?	Further Information of Importance
DIE BERG	Niekerkshoop and Prieska	61 A4 →	1 300	1 : 12	North/South	Gravel	Yes	
DIEPKLOOF	Burgersdorp and Witkop	62 C4 ↑	1 828			Tar	Yes	
DONTSA	Keiskammahoek and Stutterheim	60 B2 ↙	1 088	1 : 12		Gravel	Yes	
DU TOITSKLOOF	Paarl and Worcester	58 C4 ↙	820	1 : 18	East/West	Tar	Yes	Stopping and parking areas along the pass road are plentiful
ECCA	Grahamstown and Fort Beaufort	60 C1 ↑	548	1 : 13	South/North	Tar	Yes	
FRANSCHHOEK	Just south of Franschhoek	58 C4 ↙	733	1 : 9	East	Tar	Yes	
GARCIA'S	Riversdale and Muiskraal	58 D6 ↖	600	1 : 14	South/North	Tar	Yes	
GARDEN OF EDEN	Knysna and Uniondale	59 NS ↗	518	1 : 10	South/North & North/South	Gravel	No	Narrow with sharp curves
GIFBERG	South of Vanrhynsdorp	60 C6 ↘	609	1 : 6	North/South	Gravel	No	
GREYLINGS	Roussouw and Clifford	62 C5 ↑	± 1 800	1 : 8		Gravel	No	
GROOTRIVIER	Keurboomsrivier and Nature's Valley	59 B3 ↓	± 200	1 : 7	East/West	Tar	Yes	
GROOTRIVIERHOOGTE	Ceres and Cedarberg	58 B4 •	975	1 : 8	North/South	Gravel	Yes	
GROOTVLEI	Kamieskroon and Wallekraal	60 B5 ↗	700		East/West	Gravel	If extreme caution is exercised	*Very* narrow in places
GYDO	North of Prince Alfred Hamlet	58 C4 ↖	1 018	1 : 15	North/South	Tar	Yes	
HELLSPOORT	Grahamstown and Carlisle Bridge	59 B6 ↖	488			Tar	Yes	
HELSHOOGTE	Stellenbosch and Pniel	58 C3 ↘	378	1 : 10	East/West	Tar	Yes	
HEXRIVIER	Touws River and De Doorns	58 C4 ↗	960	1 : 16	South/North	Tar	Yes	Stopping and parking areas are plentiful
HOEKSEBERG	Clanwilliam and Wuppertal	58 B4 ↖	722	1 : 7	South/North	Gravel	No	
HOGSBACK	Alice and Hogsback	60 B1 ↘	± 700	1 : 5	South/North	Good gravel	Yes	
HOMTINI	Rheenendal and Barrington	59 NS •	238	1 : 10	East/West & West/East	Gravel	No	Narrow, sharp curves
HOTTENTOTSKLOOF	Ceres and Hottentotskloof	58 C4 ↑	1 175	1 : 28	West/East	Tar	Yes	
HOUWHOEK	Grabouw and Botrivier	58 D4 ↖	340	1 : 15	North/West	Tar	Yes	
HOWIESONSPOORT	South of Grahamstown	59 B6 •	640	1 : 15	North/South	Tar	Yes	
HUISRIVIER	Ladismith and Calitzdorp	59 B1 •	655	1 : 14	North/South	Tar	Yes	Be on the lookout for rockfalls
JANSPOORTHOOGTE	Burgersdorp and Venterstad	62 B4 ↙	1 524	1 : 16	South/East	Tar	Yes	
JOUBERTS	Lady Grey and Barkly East	62 B5 ↙	2 349	1 : 6	East/West & South/North	Gravel	No	
KAMIESBERG	Kamieskroon and Gamoep	60 B6 ↖	1 100	Very steep	South/West & North/East	Gravel	No	
KAPOKKRAALHOOGTE	Burgersdorp and Witkop	62 C4 ↑	1 829	1 : 12	West/East	Gravel	Yes	
KATBAKKIES	North of Ceres	58 B4 ↓	1 158	1 : 8	South/North	Gravel	No	Road dangerous and very narrow

MOUNTAIN PASSES - CAPE (continued)

Name	Location Between	Map Page and Grid Reference	Height (in metres)	Gradient	Direction of Gradient	Road Surface	Suitable for Caravans?	Further Information of Importance
KILLIAN'S	Kamieskroon and Wallekraal	60 B5 ↗	500		East/West	Gravel	If extreme caution is exercised	Very narrow in places
KILLIANS	Dordrecht and Roussouw	62 C5 ↖	1 700	1 : 8		Gravel	Yes	
KINGO HILLS	Grahamstown and Douglass Heights	60 C1 ↑	564	1 : 8	West/East	Gravel	No	
KNAPDAARHOOGTE	Burgersdorp and Bethulie	62 B4 ↙	1 829	1 : 18	North/South East	Gravel	Not in wet weather	Some short and dangerous curves
KOMSBERG	South East of Sutherland	58 B5 ↘	1 721	1 : 8	South/North	Gravel	No	
KOUDEBERG	Wuppertal and Clanwilliam	58 B4 ↖	914	1 : 6	South/North	Gravel	No	
KOUEVELD	Seweweekspoort and Laingsburg	58 C6 ↖	± 1 200	1 : 12	North/South	Gravel	Yes	
KREDOUWS	Prince Albert and Klaarstroom	59 B2 ↖	1 080	1 : 14	West	Tar	Yes	
LOOTSBERG	Bethesdaweg and Rooihoogte	62 C2 ↘	1 789	1 : 16	North/South	Tar	Yes	Dangerous after a snowfall
LUNDEAN'S NEK	Sterkspruit and Belmore	62 B5 ↙	2 226	1 : 11	South/North	Gravel	Not in wet weather	Impassable after a snowfall
MCKAY'S NEK (TRANSKEI)	Queenstown and Lady Frere	62 C5 ↙	1 922		East/West	Tar	Yes	
MEIRINGSPOORT	De Rust and Klaarstroom	59 B2 •	716	Level		Tar	Yes	
MICHELL'S	South of Ceres	58 C4 ←	490	1 : 34	North/South	Concrete	Yes	
MIDDELBERG	Citrusdal and Prince Alfred Hamlet	58 B4 ↙	1 110		West/East	Gravel	Yes	Impassable after a snowfall
MOLTENO	Beaufort West and Rosedene	59 A2 ↑	1 524	1 : 10	North	Partly tarred	Yes	
MONTAGU	George and Herold	59 B2 ↓	745	1 : 8	North/South	Gravel	No	Extremely narrow in places with numerous sharp bends. Advisable to drive slowly
NAUDĒSBERG	Graaff-Reinet and Bethesdaweg	62 D2 ↑	1 600	1 : 20	West/North East	Tar	Yes	Very slippery after a snowfall
NAUDĒS NEK	Rhodes and Elands Heights	62 B6 ↙	2 623	1 : 11	West/East	Gravel	Not in wet or snowy weather	
NEW KATBERG	Balfour and Queenstown	60 B1 →	1 400	1 : 4		Gravel	Only if towed by strong vehicle	
NICO MALAN	Seymour and Whittlesea	60 B1 →	1 443	1 : 18		Tar	Yes	Frequent rockfalls
NIEKERKS	Somerset East and Bracefield	59 A5 ↓	930	1 : 14	North/South	Gravel	Yes	
NIEUWOUDTS	Clanwilliam and Cedarberg	58 B4 ↖	± 590	1 : 8	West/East	Gravel	No	
NONESI'S NEK	Queenstown and Driver's Drift	62 C5 ↙	1 078		East/West	Tar	Yes	
OTTO DU PLESSIS	Clifford and Elliot	62 C5 ↗		1 : 5		Gravel	No	
OUBERG	Montagu and Kareevlakte	58 C5 ←	990	1 : 8	South/North	Gravel	No	
OUDEBERG	Murraysburg and Graaff-Reinet	59 A4 ↖	± 1 200	1 : 18	South/North West	Tar	Yes	Very slippery after a snowfall
OU KAAPSEWEG	Cape Town and Kommetjie	58 NS •	310	1 : 16	North/South	Tar	Yes	Magnificent view from the crest of the pass
OUKLOOF	Fraserburg and Beaufort West	59 A1 ↗	1 400	1 : 10	East/West	Tar	Yes	
OUTENIQUA	George and Oudtshoorn	59 B2 ↙	800	1 : 16	North/South	Tar	Yes	In wet weather the pass is shrouded in mist

MOUNTAIN PASSES - CAPE (continued)

Name	Location Between	Map Page and Grid Reference	Height (in metres)	Gradient	Direction of Gradient	Road Surface	Suitable for Caravans?	Further Information of Importance
PADKLOOF	South of Witsand	65 C4 ↓	1 160	1 : 9	East/West	Gravel	Yes	
PAKHUIS	Clanwilliam and Pakhuis	58 B4 ↖	905	1 : 9	East/West & West/East	Gravel	Yes	
PEERBOOMSKLOOF	North East of Ceres	58 B4 ↘	792	1 : 11	West/East	Gravel	No	Road dangerous and narrow
PENHOEK	Queenstown and Jamestown	62 C4 →	2 000	1 : 10	North/South	Tar	Yes	
PHANTOM	Knysna and Rheenendal	59 NS •	185	1 : 10	South/East & North/West	Gravel	Yes	
PITSENG (TRANSKEI)	Lower Pitseng and Elands Height	62 B6 ↙	1 767	1 : 9	East	Gravel	Not in wet weather	
PLUTO'S VALE	Grahamstown and Breakfast Vlei	60 C1 ↗	533	1 : 11	West/East	Gravel	Yes	
POTJIESBERG	Speelmanskraal and Uniondale	59 B3 ↙	910		East/West	Tar	Yes	
POT RIVER	Maclear and Elands Height	62 B6 ↘	1 765	1 : 10	North	Gravel	Not in wet weather	
PRINCE ALFRED'S	Knysna and Avontuur	59 B3 ↙	853	1 : 9	South/North & North/South	Gravel	No	
RAVELSKLOOF	North of Jansenville	59 A4 ↘	797	1 : 10	North	Tar	Yes	
REMHOOGTE	Victoria West and Murraysburg	61 C5 ←	1 230		South East	Tar	Yes	
ROBINSON	Oudtshoorn and Ruitersbos	59 B2 ↙	859	1 : 14	North/South	Tar	Yes	
ROOIBERG	Vanwyksdorp and Calitzdorp	59 B1 ↓	838	1 : 8	West/East	Gravel	No	
ROOIHOOGTE	Montagu and Matroosberg	58 C4 →	1 234	1 : 12	South/North	Tar	Yes	
ROOINEK	Laingsburg and Ladismith	58 C5 ↗	914		South/North	Gravel	Yes	
ROSSOUWSBERG	Dordrecht and Clanville	62 C5 ↖	1 800	1 : 6		Gravel	No	
ROSSOUWSPOORT	Waterford and Pearston	59 A5 ↙	624	1 : 10	North/North West	Gravel	Yes	
SCHOEMANSPOORT	Schoemanshoek and the Cango Caves	59 B2 ←	610			Tar	Yes	
SEWEWEEKSPOORT	Calitzdorp and Seweweekspoort	58 C6 ↑	3 342	1 : 12	North/South	Gravel	Yes - but with some difficulty in bad weather conditions	
SHAW'S MOUNTAIN	Caledon and Hermanus	58 D4 ↖	366	1 : 17	North/East	Gravel	No	
SIR LOWRY'S	Somerset West and Grabouw	58 D3 ↗	427	1 : 13	East	Tar	Yes	The pass is being widened and construction work will last for about 3 years
SPEKTAKELBERG	Springbok and Kleinsee	60 A5 ↘	600	1 : 20	East/West	Gravel	Yes	
STRYKHOOGTE	Robertson and McGregor	58 C4 ↘	322	1 : 14	East/West	Gravel	Yes	
STUDERS	Garies and Platbakkies	60 B6 ←	400		South West/North East	Gravel	No	
SUURBERG	Suurberg and Bracefield	59 B5 ↗	960	1 : 14	South/North	Tar	Yes	
SWAARMOED	East of Ceres	58 C4 ↑	1 036	1 : 16	East/West	Tar	Yes	
SWAERSHOEK	Cradock and Swaershoek	59 A5 ↑	1 981	1 : 12	South/North	Gravel	No	
SWARTBERG	Prince Albert and the Cango Caves	59 B2 ↖	1 436	1 : 7	North/South	Gravel	No	Often closed in winter as a result of heavy snowfalls

MOUNTAIN PASSES - CAPE (continued)

Name	Location Between	Map Page and Grid Reference	Height (in metres)	Gradient	Direction of Gradient	Road Surface	Suitable for Caravans?	Further Information of Importance
THE BLES	Lower Blinkwater and Balderja	60 B1 →	± 1 180	1 : 6		Gravel	Yes	Steep with sharp curves
THEEKLOOF	Fraserburg and Leeugamka	59 A1 ↑	1 385	1 : 13	South/North	Tar	Yes	
THERONSBERG	Ceres and Hottentotskloof	58 C4 ↑	1 090	1 : 22	East/West	Tar	Yes	
TRADOUWS	Barrydale and Suurbraak	58 C5 ↘	403	1 : 10	North/South	Gravel	Yes	Under construction for tarring. Closed to traffic during the week from 10 h 00 to 17 h 00 (For 3 years)
UNIONDALE POORT	Avontuur and Uniondale	59 B3 ↙	880		North/South	Tar	Yes	
VAALKRANTZ	Steynsburg and Venterstad	62 C3 ↗	1 531	1 : 14	North/South	Tar	Yes	Watch out for rockfalls after heavy rains
VAN DER STELS	Botrivier and Vyeboom	58 D4 ↖	122		North/North West	Gravel	No	
VANRHYNS	Nieuwoudtville and Vanrhynsdorp	60 C7 ←	900			Tar	Yes	
VENTERSBERG	Dordrecht and Clanville	62 C5 ↖	± 1 900	1 : 6		Gravel	Yes	
VERLATE KLOOF	Sutherland and Matjiesfontein	58 B5 ↓	1 584	1 : 10	West/East	Tar	Yes	
VERWATERSNEK	Olifantshoek and Debeben	65 B4 ↑	1 150			Gravel	Not in wet weather	

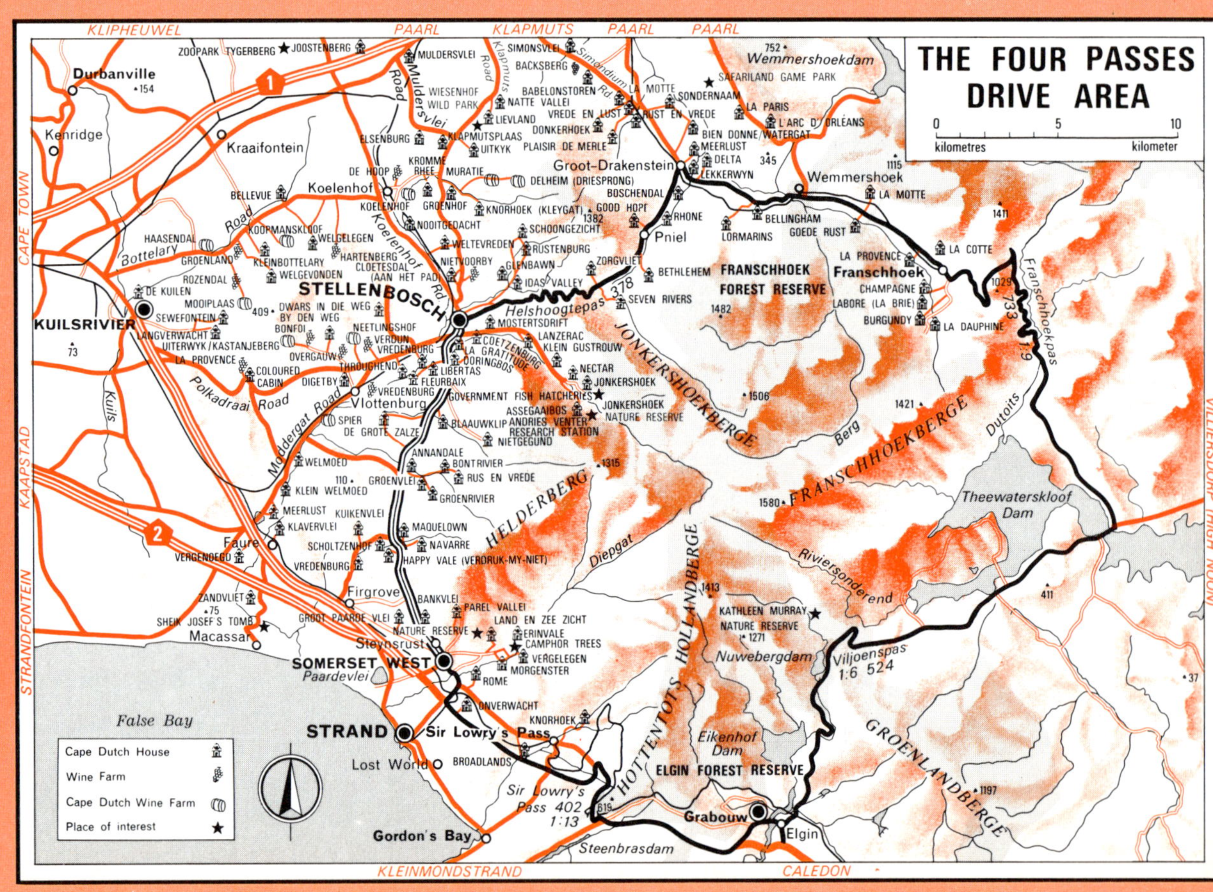

MOUNTAIN PASSES - CAPE (continued)

Name	Location Between	Map Page and Grid Reference	Height (in metres)	Gradient	Direction of Gradient	Road Surface	Suitable for Caravans?	Further Information of Importance
VILJOENS	Elgin and Vyeboom	58 D4 ↖	524	1 : 6	East/West	Tar	Yes	
WAPADSBERG	North West of Cradock	62 C2 ↘	1 700	1 : 18	West/East	Tar	Yes	
WENEN	Dordrecht and Clanville	62 C5 ↖	± 1 700	1 : 6		Gravel	Yes	
WITELSKLOOF	Clanwilliam and Paleisheuwel	58 B3 ↗	487	1 : 7	West/East	Gravel	No	
WITKOPHOOGTE	Burgersdorp and Jamestown	62 C4 ↑	1 828	1 : 16	West/South East	Gravel	Yes	

MOUNTAIN PASSES - NATAL

Name	Location Between	Map Page and Grid Reference	Height (in metres)	Gradient	Direction of Gradient	Road Surface	Suitable for Caravans?	Further Information of Importance
BOTHAS	Newcastle and Orange Free State border	67 B2 ↘	1 936	1 : 5	East/West	Tar	Yes	
COLLIN'S	Natal/Orange Free State border	67 C2 ↗	1 670	1 : 12	North/West	Gravel	Not in wet weather	
DE BEERS	Natal/Orange Free State border	67 C2 ↑	1 700	1 : 8	North/West	Gravel	No	Sharp bends
GLENLUCE	Glencoe and Wasbank	67 C3 ↖	1 247			Tar	Yes	
HELA-HELA	Richmond and Creighton	63 A3 ↙	1 218	Steep	East/West	Gravel	No	
KNIGHTS HILL	Utrecht and Viljoenspos	67 B3 ↓	1 614	1 : 6	West/East	Gravel	Not in wet weather	
MIDDLEDALE	Natal/Orange Free State border	67 C2 ←	± 1 700	1 : 12	North/West	Gravel	No	
MULLERS	Memel and Newcastle	67 B2 ↘	± 1 968	1 : 6	South/West	Gravel	No	Very slippery in wet weather
OLIVIERSHOEK	Harrismith and Royal Natal National Park	67 C2 ←	1 740	1 : 12	North/West	Gravel	Not advisable	
SANI	Himeville and Lesotho	63 A2 ↙	2 000	1 : 6	East/West	Gravel	No	
VAN REENENS	Ladysmith and Harrismith	67 C2 •	1 680	1 : 16	North/West	Tar	Yes	

MOUNTAIN PASSES - ORANGE FREE STATE

Name	Location Between	Map Page and Grid Reference	Height (in metres)	Gradient	Direction of Gradient	Road Surface	Suitable for Caravans?	Further Information of Importance
BELL'S	South West of Winburg	66 C4 ↘	± 1 387	1 : 14	North/South	Tar	Yes	
BOBBEJAANSHOOGTE	Verkykerskop and Vrede	67 B2 ↙	± 3 000	1 : 7	North/South	Gravel	No	
COLLIN'S	Orange Free State/Natal border	67 C2 ↗	1 670	1 : 12	South/West	Gravel	Not in wet weather	
DE BEERS	Orange Free State/Natal border	67 C2 ↑	1 700	1 : 8	South/West	Gravel	No	Sharp bends
GOLDEN GATE	Clarens and Kestell	66 C6 •	± 2 034	1 : 7	South/North	Gravel	No	Condition bad in wet weather
KOMMANDONEK	Fouriesburg and Ficksburg	66 C6 ↙	1 722	1 : 10	North East/South West	Tar	Yes	
KWAGGASNEK	Memel and Volksrust	67 B2 →	± 1 837		South/East	Gravel	Yes	
SAND RIVER HEIGHTS	Ventersburg and Winburg	66 C5 ↖	1 433	1 : 16	North/South	Tar	Yes	Suitable in all weather conditions
WITSIESHOEK	Witsieshoek and Mont-aux-Sources	67 C1 ↘	± 2 270	1 : 7	South/North	Gravel	No	Very steep

MOUNTAIN PASSES - TRANSVAAL

Name	Location Between	Map Page and Grid Reference	Height (in metres)	Gradient	Direction of Gradient	Road Surface	Suitable for Caravans?	Further Information of Importance
ABEL ERASMUS	Ohrigstad and Tzaneen	69 B3 •	1 242	1 : 14	North/South	Tar	Yes	
BAKKERS	Thabazimbi and Rankin's Pass	68 B5 •	1 463	1 : 30	West/East	Gravel	Yes	
BOUDERSBERG	Nelspruit and Kaapmuiden	69 C4 ←	960	1 : 8	East/West	Tar	Yes	
HILLTOP	Nelspruit and Barberton	69 C3 ↘	990	1 : 10	North/South	Gravel	Yes	
KAAPSCHE HOOP	Kaapsehoop and Nelspruit	69 C3 ↘	1 585	1 : 8	East/West	Gravel	No	
KASPERSNEK	Ohrigstad and Vaalhoek	69 B3 ↘	1 396	1 : 7	East/West	Gravel	No	
KOWYNS	Graskop and Bosbokrand	69 B3 ↘	1 371	1 : 11	East/West	Tar	Yes	
KRANSPOORT	Middelburg and Loskop Dam	69 C2 •	1 310	1 : 10	North/South	Tar	Yes	
LONG TOM	Sabie and Lydenburg	69 C3 ↗	2 149	1 : 10	East/West	Tar	Yes	
MAGOEBASKLOOF	Haenertsburg and Tzaneen	69 A2 ↘	1 370	1 : 15	West/East	Tar	Yes	Thick mist frequently occurs
MOODIESKLOOF	White River and Bushman Rock	69 C4 ↖	1 204	1 : 7	North/South	Tar	Yes	
NELSHOOGTE	Barberton and Badplaas	69 C3 ↘	1 554	1 : 12	East/West	Tar	Yes	
PELGRIMSBERG	Lydenburg and Pilgrim's Rest	70 NS ↖	1 783	1 : 7	East/West	Gravel	No	
RANKIN'S	Rankin's Pass and Maraheki	68 B5 →	1 219	1 : 10	East/West	Gravel	Yes	
SADDLEBACK	Barberton and Havelock	69 C4 ↙	1 524	1 : 7	North/South	Gravel	No	
SCHOEMANSKLOOF	Montrose and Machadodorp	69 C3 •	1 295	1 : 10	East/West	Tar	Yes	
SHANGAAN HILL	Bosbokrand and Acornhoek	71 NS ←	823		North/South	Tar	Yes	
SHIYALONGUBU	Kaapmuiden and Barberton	69 C4 ↙	1 006	1 : 7	North/South	Gravel	No	
SKURWEBERG	Machadodorp and Badplaas	69 C3 ↓	1 706	1 : 10	East/West	Gravel	No	
UITKYK	South East of Nelspruit	69 C4 ↙	1 280	1 : 10	North/South	Gravel	No	
WATERVALSRIVIER	Lydenburg and Buffelsvlei	69 B3 ↓	1 615	1 : 12	North/South	Tar	Yes	

Take nothing but pictures - leave nothing but footprints

Golf

Whether it is Alexandria or Adelaide, Pofadder or Penge, Zebediela or Zastron, you name the place they've got't. We are talking of golf courses of which you will find more than 300 listed in this book. There are the bigger clubs like Rand Park and Royal Johannesburg which boast two courses each. There is Huddle Park which has three and which probably accommodates the largest number of weekend golfers anywhere in the Republic. There are many small nine-hole courses in farflung villages.

Listening to the talk at the "nineteenth hole" of any golf club, the uninitiated may well think they have gatecrashed an executive meeting of the local branch of an ornithological society. Words like *birdies, eagles,* and sometimes even *albatrosses,* spice the usually animated "postmortems" held at this "hole". There is talk of landing in and not infrequently on the water. Of flight patterns and trajectories, of turns (not terns) and if the non-golfer stays long enough his confusion will be worse confounded when the conversation turns to *suckers* and *rough* and *nap.* But suckers are not those born every day and nap is not a card game.

The game of golf as known today is said to have first been played in Scotland in the 15th century. The precursor of the game is probably the ancient Dutch "bat" game which is recorded as having been played in the Netherlands as far back as 1390. Credence is lent to this version by the fact that Scotland imported its golf balls from the Netherlands right up to the 17th century.

The Royal and Ancient Golf Club of St. Andrews was responsible for creating unity in the game and its rules are accepted and applied throughout the world, with perhaps some small variations on the part of the American Professional Golfers' Association.

From Scotland the bug spread to other parts of the world, with serious outbreaks in various parts of the globe during the 19th century. Since the middle of the 20th century epidemics have been the order of the day and in recent years addiction has become endemic in countries as far apart as South Africa and Japan.

Like that other game bowls, to which it used to be said one migrated when becoming too crotchety and creaky for golf, there is an affinity between golfers which transcends all considerations of class, culture, intellect and whatever. The scratch player will listen to and sympathise or enthuse as the case may be, with the rabbit, because at one time or another as sure as ebb follows the flow, they can without fail be struck by maladies bearing the appellation *shank, hook, slice* and others as butcher-like.

Visitors

Like the bowling greens, golf courses throughout the country will welcome you as a visitor at most times of the day on well-nigh any day and well into the night at the nineteenth.

Where visitors are accompanied by club members, they are regarded as the responsibility of the members.

It is always wise, and polite, however to check with the secretary, club professional or manager whether the course is not being used for a tournament, reserved for men or lady members only, or for some other reason. The telephone numbers of the various clubs (correct at the time of going to press) are listed below.

Dress

Most clubs insist that players be appropriately attired when playing golf. If shorts are worn, stockings must also be worn. Proper golf shoes must be worn and casual dress like jeans and track shoes or tackies are taboo. Always take a tie or cravat and jacket along in case these have to be worn in the lounge or ladies' bar.

Etiquette of Golf

Golfers should acquaint themselves with the etiquette of golf. Rules of etiquette are usually included in the diaries which clubs issue annually to their members. These rules are more or less universal and are intended to make the game pleasant for members and visitors alike, so obey them.

Caddies and Caddy Carts

At some clubs the availability of caddies can be a problem and many golfers have acquired their own caddy carts. Most courses allow these but there are a few who frown on them, especially when competitions are played. Check before playing.

Smaller Courses

Some of the smaller courses with nine holes only use different tees to make up 18. These are also itemised below.

GOLF COURSES IN SOUTH AFRICA

GOLF CLUBS IN THE CAPE PROVINCE

City or Town	AA Road Map Ref.	Name of Club	Street Address	Tel. Code	Tel. Numbers (For Course Booking)	Length of Course (in metres)	Number of Holes	Course Par	Details for Visitors
ADELAIDE	59 A6 ↙	Adelaide Golf Club	On the Tarkastad Rd.	04662	Sec. 319	6 011	18	74	Always welcome on Wednesday and Saturday afternoons – other days by arrangement
ALEXANDRIA	59 B6 ↙	Alexandria Golf Club	Martha Oosthuizen St.	04652	Sec. 126 or 100	5 078	9	72	Special visitors' competitions arranged between Christmas and New Year
ALICE	60 B1 ↘	Alice Golf Club	Recreation Rd.	043522	Sec. 460	6 400	9	69	Welcome to play
ALIWAL NORTH	62 B4 ↘	Aliwal North Golf Club	Benson St.	05512	Club 251	5 797	9	71	Welcome to play
BARKLY EAST	62 B5 ↓	Barkly East Golf Club	Off Elliot Rd.	04542	Sec. 23	6 700	9	72	Welcome to play
BEAUFORT WEST	59 A2 ↑	Beaufort West Golf Club					18	71	Visitors to report to caretaker at course for play
BEDFORD	59 A6 ↙	Bedford Golf Club	Bourke St.	04632	Sec. 267	5 795	9	72	Contact Secretary by telephone or at his home, cnr. Bourke/Stockholm Sts.
BREDASDORP	58 D5 ←	Bredasdorp Golf Club	Recreation St.	02842	Club 599	6 024 (Men) 5 000 (Ladies)	9	72	Welcome to play and catered for by sponsored competitions from December to January. Modern clubhouse with all facilities
BRITSTOWN	61 B5 ↓	Britstown Golf Club	Market St.	05732	Sec. 56	5 979	9	70	Welcome to play on any day except Sundays
BURGERSDORP	62 C4 ↑	Burgersdorp Golf Club	Pres. Swart St.	05532	Sec. 108	6 242	9	71	Welcome to play
CALEDON	58 D4 ↑	Caledon Golf Club	Next to Railway Station	02812	Sec. 2-1861	5 900	9	73	Welcome to play. On Sundays course is reserved for non-whites
CALVINIA	61 C1 →	Calvinia Golf Club	Calvinia/Nieuwoudtville Main Rd.			5 775	18	71	Contact caretaker at the course.
CAPE TOWN	58 NS ↖	Metropolitan Golf Club	Fritz Sonnenberg Rd. (off Beach Rd.), Mouille Point	021	Professional 44-9582	5 840	9/18	72	Very welcome anytime except Tuesday afternoons and Saturdays. Bookings should be made with the professional.
	58 NS ↑	Mowbray Golf Club	Near Pinelands Railway bridge	021	Sec. 53-6491	6 095	18	74	Always welcome except Saturday afternoons
	58 NS ↑	Rondebosch Golf Club	Klipfontein Rd., Mowbray	021	Sec. 69-4176/7	5 928 (Men) 5 189 (Ladies)	18	72	Welcome at any time
	58 NS ↑	Royal Cape Golf Club	174 Ottery Rd., Wynberg	021	Sec. 71-6551	6 174	18	72	Welcome to play
CAPE PENINSULA	58 NS •	Clovelly Country Club	Clovelly Rd.	021	Sec. 8-4181	5 717	18	72	To play in competitions official handicaps are required
	58 C3 ↓	Durbanville Golf Club	Sports Rd.	021	Sec. 96-4365	6 301	18	74	Welcome at all times except during competitions which they may, however, join if they have valid handicaps
	58 NS ↗	King David Country Club	Pallotti Rd. (off Modderdam Rd.), Parow South	021	Club 93-5197	6 235	18	73	Visitors most welcome except Mondays and Saturday afternoons
	58 NS ↑	Milnerton Golf Club	Bridge Rd.	021	Sec. 52-1047	5 809	18	70	Welcome at all times except during competitions
	58 NS ↗	Parow Golf Club	Fifth Ave.	021	Sec. 92-2616	5 800	18	72	Always welcome except Saturday afternoons
	58 NS ↓	Simonstown Country Club	Froggy Pond	021	Club 86-1233	4 023	11	66	Very welcome at all times including weekends
	58 NS ↗	Welgemoed Golf Club	Kommandeur St.	021	Sec. 97-8290	5 708	9	71	Welcome at any time except public holidays
	58 NS •	Westlake Golf Club	Main Rd., Lakeside	021	Sec. 72-2234	6 155	18	71	Welcome to play at any time except Saturday afternoons
CARNARVON	61 B4 ↙	Carnarvon Golf Club	Main Rd.	03032	Sec. 7	6 000	18	72	Very welcome to play – prior arrangements to be made with secretary
CATHCART	60 B2 ←	Cathcart Golf Club		04562	Sec. 14 or 55	5 955	9	72	Welcome to play
CERES	58 C4 ↖	Ceres Golf Club		023312	Sec. 165	5 765	9	73	Visitors very welcome

GOLF CLUBS - CAPE PROVINCE (continued)

City or Town	AA Road Map Ref.	Name of Club	Street Address	Tel. Code	Tel. Numbers (For Course Booking)	Length of Course (in metres)	Number of Holes	Course Par	Details for Visitors
CLANWILLIAM	58 B3 ↗	Clanwilliam Golf Club		02682	70		9	73	Welcome to play by prior arrangement
COLESBERG	62 B3 ↙	Colesberg Golf Club		05852	Sec. 271	6 034	18	72	Very welcome to play
CRADOCK	59 A5 ↑	Cradock Golf Club		04812	Sec. 908	6 168	9	72	Very welcome at all times
DE AAR	62 B2 ↙	De Aar Country Club		0571	Office 2113 Club 3213	6 323	18	72	Full-time manager at the club will offer visitors every assistance
DE HOEK	58 B3 ↘	Cape Portland Cement Recreation Club		02612	Sec. 133	4 690	9	67	Visitors may play if introduced by members
DORDRECHT	62 C5 ←	Dordrecht Golf Club		04552	Sec. 2103	5 854	9	69	Welcome at any time, but to be signed in by a member
EAST LONDON	60 B2 ↘	Alexander Country Club	Sunningdale Ave., Sunnyridge	0431	Club 46-2141 Sec. 46-1857	5 800	18	72	Welcome at any time, phone resident professional at club
	60 B2 ↘	East London Golf Club	Gleneagles Rd.	0431	Sec. 8-8811	6 063	18	72	Very welcome to play
	60 B2 ↘	West Bank Golf Club	Adjoining the lighthouse, West Bank.	0431	Sec. 2-2768	5 726	18	73	To play in competitions certified handicaps are required
ELLIOT	62 C5 →	Elliot Country Club	On Barkly East Rd.	04522	Sec. 23 or 102	5 620	9	71	Welcome to play
FORT BEAUFORT	60 B1 ↓	Fort Beaufort Country Club Golf Course		043512	Club 391	6 157	11	72	Welcome to play at any time
FRASERBURG	61 C3 ↓	Fraserburg Golf Club		02072	Sec. 1	5 294	18	66	Welcome to play
GEORGE	59 B2 ↓	George Golf Club	Langenhoven Rd.	0441	Office 4254 Manager 2411	5 921	18	72	Visitors most welcome - they should report to the manager, or write to the secretary, P.O. Box 81, George, in advance
GONUBIE	60 B3 ↙	Gonubie Golf Club	Ocean Way	0431	Sec. 94-2018	5 292	9	69	Visitors always welcome
GRAAFF-REINET	59 A4 ↑	Graaff-Reinet Golf Club	On Middelburg Rd.	0491	Sec. 2244	6 089	18	73	Always someone at club to offer visitors assistance
GRAHAMSTOWN	59 B6 ↑	Grahamstown Golf Club	Bedford Rd.	0461	Club 2318	5 776	18	73	Club manager always in attendance to arrange games
HAGA HAGA	60 B3 ↙	Haga Haga Golf Club		04372	Sec. 2412	2 559 (Men) 2 514 (Ladies)	9	70	Welcome to play
HANKEY	59 B4 ↘	Hankey Country Club	Kleinrivier Rd.	Hankey	Sec. 17	5 371	9	72	Visitors always welcome
HANOVER	62 C2 ↑	Hanover Golf Club	17 Market St.	057212	Sec. 12 or 130	5 796	18	72	Welcome to play
HARTSWATER	66 B2 ↘	Hartswater Golf and Country Club	D.F. Malan St.	053322	Sec. 131	5 849	9	69	Welcome to play
HERMANUS	58 D4 ←	Hermanus Golf Club	Main Rd	002832	Sec. 451	5 898	18	73	Welcome to play at any time
HOPETOWN	62 A2 ↙	Hopetown Golf Club	On the Orange River Station Rd.	053242	Sec. 3030	6 328	9	72	Visitors to make prior arrangements with secretary
HUMANSDORP	59 C4 ↗	Humansdorp Country Club Golf Course		04232	Sec. 158	6 134	9	72	Visitors also encouraged to join competitions on Wednesday and Saturday afternoons
INDWE	62 C5 ←	Indwe Golf Club		Ida	Chairman 913		9	38	Welcome to play at any time
JEFFREYS BAY	59 C4 ↗	Jeffreys Bay Golf Club	Tulip Ave.			5 256	9	67	Visitors have to become temporary members of the country club
KAKAMAS	65 C2 ↓	Kakamas Golf Club	Neilersdrif Rd.	05442	Sec. 119 or 222	6 318	18	72	Welcome at all times
KEI MOUTH	60 B3 ↙	Kei Mouth Golf Club	Kei Mouth	Kei Mouth	Sec. 28	5 646	9	72	Welcome to play
KENDREW	59 A4 •	Kendrew Golf Club		Kendrew	Sec. 102	5 858	9	72	Visitors to make prior arrangements with secretary
KIMBERLEY	66 C2 ↘	Kimberley Golf Club		0531	Sec. 2-3180	6 400	18	72	Visitors very welcome

GOLF CLUBS - CAPE PROVINCE (continued)

City or Town	AA Road Map Ref.	Name of Club	Street Address	Tel. Code	Tel. Numbers (For Course Booking)	Length of Course (in metres)	Number of Holes	Course Par	Details for Visitors
KING WILLIAM'S TOWN	60 B2 ↓	King William's Town Golf Club	K.W.T./East London Rd.	0433	Sec. 2029	7 000	18	72	Always welcome
KIRKWOOD	59 B5 •	Kirkwood Golf Club		04262	Sec. 289	5 422	9	68	Visitors most welcome
KNYSNA	59 C3 ↖	Knysna Golf Club	'The Heads' Rd., Hunter's Home	04452	Club 6922	5 649	18	73	Most welcome except on Wednesday and Saturday afternoons when they may have to wait their turn
KOEGASBRUG	61 A4 ↖	Koegas Golf Club	At Recreation Club	Koegasbrug	Sec. 1 or 1512	5 804	6	72	Always welcome by prior arrangement with secretary or Mine Manager
KOMGA	60 B2 →	Komga Golf Club		04372	Sec. 69	5 170	9	70	Welcome to play
KURUMAN	65 B5 •	Kuruman Country Club		014532	Sec. 34	± 6 100	9	71	Welcome to play at any time
LADY GREY	62 B5 ↙	Lady Grey Golf Club	Church St.	05552	49 or 116	5 488	9	72	Club is open on Wednesday and Saturday afternoons. Arrangements to be made for play at other times
LIME ACRES	65 C5 ↑	Lime Acres Golf Club			Sec. 2	6 176	9	72	Always welcome
MACLEAR	62 C6 ↖	Maclear Golf Club		04742	Sec. 69	5 988	9	72	Visitors very welcome
MAFEKING	68 C3 ↓	Mafeking Golf Club	Tillard St.	014442	Club 705	6 098	9	72	Welcome to play
MALMESBURY	58 C3 →	Malmesbury Golf Club	On Moorreesburg Rd.	0224	Sec. 2-1790	5 955	9	72	Visitors most welcome
MANCORP MINE	65 C5 ↖	A.M.M.O.S.A.L. Golf Club			Sec. 56	6 029	18	70	Any time during the week
MARYDALE	61 A4 ←	Marydale Country Club	Connan St.	05482	Sec. 1202	6 900	9	70	Course is always open. Visitors may collect keys at the Standard Bank at any time
MIDDELBURG	62 C2 →	Grootfontein Golf Club	Agricultural College	04832	Sec. 531 or 455	5 847	9	72	Visitors always welcome
	62 C2 →	Middelburg Golf and Country Club		04832	Sec. 25	6 064	18	72	Welcome to play
MOLTENO	62 C4 ↖	Molteno Golf Club		04572	Sec. 55	6 158	9	72	Visitors very welcome
MONTAGU	58 C5 ↙	Montagu Golf Club	Bad St.	023412	Sec. 20	4 914	9	72	Welcome to play
MOORREESBURG	58 C3 ↗	Moorreesburg Golf Club	Rivier St.	02642	Sec. 57 or 422	5 609	9	71	Visitors very welcome - all modern facilities available at club
MOSSEL BAY	59 C2 ↘	Mossel Bay Golf Club		04441	Sec. 2730 Club 2107	5 964	18	73	Welcome to play
NABABEEP	60 A5 ↘	Klipdam Golf Club			Sec. 158	5 837	18	73	Welcome to play
NOUPOORT	62 C2 ↗	Noupoort Golf Club	Piet Retief St.	05742	Sec. 27 or 134	5 900	9	70	Visitors to contact secretary
OUDTSHOORN	59 B2 ←	Oudtshoorn Golf Club		04431	Pres. 2496		18	72	Visitors to make prior arrangements. It is the only grass course in the Karoo
PAARL	58 C3 ↘	Paarl Golf Club	Franschhoek Rd., Suider-Paarl	0251	Sec. 2-4700	6 040	18	74	Visitors welcome 7 days a week. Course closed on Christmas Day and Good Friday
PEARSTON	59 A5 ←	Pearston Golf Club		Pearston	Sec. 1522	6 120	9	68	Visitors welcome, but play is only on Saturdays
PETRUSVILLE	62 B2 ↗	Petrusville Golf Club		057232	Sec. 56	2 946	9	71	Visitors most welcome
PHILIPSTOWN	62 B2 •	Philipstown Golf Club	Slingersfontein	057222	Sec. 2321	4 000	18	72	Very welcome to play
PIKETBERG	58 B3 ↘	Piketberg Golf Club		02612	Sec. 8 or 427	5 704	9	72	Welcome to play on any day

GOLF CLUBS - CAPE PROVINCE (continued)

City or Town	AA Road Map Ref.	Name of Club	Street Address	Tel. Code	Tel. Numbers (For Course Booking)	Length of Course (in metres)	Number of Holes	Course Par	Details for Visitors
PLETTENBERG BAY	59 NS ↘	Plettenberg Bay Golf Club		04472	Club 2002	5 700	18	70	No prior arrangements necessary for play during the week. Names put on waiting list for a game during weekends and public holidays
POFADDER	65 D1 ↑	Pofadder Private Golf Club		05452	Sec. 5	5 792	9	72	Visitors very welcome
PORT ALFRED	60 C1 ↘	Royal Port Alfred Golf Club		04642	Sec. 185	5 792	18	72	Welcome to play at any time
PORT ELIZABETH	59 B5 ↘	E P Command Golf Club	Driftsands	041	Sec. 51-4185 x 143	5 528	9	70	Visitors only allowed when accompanied by a member
	59 B5 ↘	Humewood Golf Club	Summerstrand	041	Sec. 53-2137	6 276	18	73	Welcome to play
	59 B5 ↘	Northwood Golf Club	New Brighton			3 400	9	72	Non-racial club - visitors welcome
	59 B5 ↘	Port Elizabeth Golf Club	Westview Drive	041	Sec. 33-5348	6 163	18	74	Visitors are most welcome
	59 B5 ↘	Walmer Country Club	1 Victoria Drive	041	Club 51-4211 Golf Sec. 51-3401	6 291	18	73	Visitors need only make prior arrangements for play over weekends. Also welcome to enter club competitions on Saturdays and Sundays
	59 B5 ↘	Wedgewood Park Country Club	Old Cape Rd.	041	Office 2-4168 Professional 72-1075	6 372	18	74	Visitors most welcome to play
PORTERVILLE	58 C3 ↗	Porterville Golf Club		02622	Sec. 302	5 353	9	70	Very welcome
PRIESKA	61 A4 ↘	Prieska Golf Club	Park St.	05942	Sec. 9 or 299	6 150	18	73	Visitors also welcome to join competitions on Saturdays
QUEENSTOWN	62 C4 ↘	Queenstown Golf Club	Golf Rd.	0451	Sec. 3121	5 883	18	72	Welcome to play
RICHMOND	61 C5 →	Richmond Golf Club		05752		6 014	18	71	Always welcome
RIVIERSONDEREND	58 D4 ↗	Riviersonderend Golf Club		02852	Sec. 161 or 180	5 665	9	72	Welcome to play
ROBERTSON	58 C4 ↘	Robertson Golf Club	Baaiplek	02352	Sec. 601	5 999	9	72	Visitors welcome
SALDANHA	58 C2 ↗	Saldanha Golf Club	SA Navy Area	022812	Sec. 3-1263	5 857	12	72	The golf club belongs to the SA Defence Force and visitors will have to identify themselves at the gate, after which they will probably be allowed to enter
SISHEN	65 B5 ↙	Sishen Golf Club	Frikkie Meyer Rd., Kathu	05982	Sec. 120 x 263 or 549	6 440	18	72	Welcome to play
SOMERSET EAST	59 A5 ↘	Somerset East Golf Club	Bester's Hoek	04242	Sec. 750	5 846	9	72	Visitors welcome to play
SOMERSET WEST	58 D3 ↙	Somerset West Country Club	Rue de Jacqueline	024	Sec. 2-2925	6 089	18	73	Welcome to play - temporary membership also available
STELLENBOSCH	58 C3 ↖	Stellenbosch Golf Club	Strand Rd.	02231	Sec. 3279	6 270	18	73	Most welcome - visitor's membership available
STEYNSBURG	62 C3 ↙	Steynsburg Golf Club	23 van Riebeeck St.	04842	Sec. 287		10	72	Visitors very welcome
STEYTLERVILLE	59 B4 ↑	Steytlerville Golf Club		04952	Sec. 14	± 3 000	9	68	By arrangement with the secretary
STRAND	58 D3 ↗	Strand Golf Club	Gordon's Bay Rd.	024	Manager 3-1060	5 549	18	72	Welcome to play by arrangement with the manager
STUTTERHEIM	60 B2 •	Stutterheim Country Club		04362	Sec. 9902	5 882	9	72	Visitors are encouraged to play
SWELLENDAM	58 D5 ↑	Swellendam Golf Club	Andrew Whyte St.	02912	Sec. 347 Club 4303		9	72	Very welcome - course is only open on Wednesdays and Saturdays
TARKASTAD	62 D4 ↖	Tarkastad Golf Club	Off Cathcart St.	04582	Sec. 46	5 787	9	72	Visitors welcome at all times
UITENHAGE	59 B5 ↓	Uitenhage Golf Club	Winterhoek Drive	0422	Professional 2-4532	6 196	18	73	Visitors to contact the club professional for a game

GOLF CLUBS - CAPE PROVINCE (continued)

City or Town	AA Road Map Ref.	Name of Club	Street Address	Tel. Code	Tel. Numbers (For Course Booking)	Length of Course (in metres)	Number of Holes	Course Par	Details for Visitors
UPINGTON	65 C3 ←	Upington Golf Club	Toekoms Rd.	0541	Sec. 2168	5 900	18	71	Visitors most welcome
VANRHYNSDORP	60 C6 →	Vanrhynsdorp Golf Club		02712	Sec. 33	6 300	12	70	Welcome to play
VICTORIA WEST	61 C5 ↖	Victoria West Golf Club		02042	Sec. 9 or 276	6 193	18	72	Welcome to play
VRYBURG	66 A2 ↘	Vryburg Golf Club	De Kock St.	01451	Sec. 2024 or 2316		18	71	Visitors to make prior arrangements with the secretary
WELLINGTON	58 C4 ←	Wellington Golf Club	Pentz St.	0251	Club 3-1919 Sec. 3-1001		9	36	Visitors welcome to play at any time
WILLISTON	61 C2 ↗	Williston Golf Club	De Wet St.	02052	Sec. 181	2 863	9	69	Welcome to play
WILLOWMORE	59 B3 ↑	Willowmore Golf Club	Wehmeyer St.	04942	Sec. 14 or 90	5 092	18	66	Visitors to make arrangements with the secretary
WORCESTER	58 C4 ↓	Worcester Golf Club	Villiersdorp Rd.	0231	Sec. 2-1004	6 037	18	74	Visitors always welcome

GOLF CLUBS IN NATAL

City or Town	AA Road Map Ref.	Name of Club	Street Address	Tel. Code	Tel. Numbers (For Course Booking)	Length of Course (in metres)	Number of Holes	Course Par	Details for Visitors
AMANZIMTOTI	63 NS ↗	Amanzimtoti Country Club	Golf Course Rd., Athlone Park	031	Club 92-1166	5 778	18	73	Visitors welcome at any time including weekends and public holidays
AMATIKULU	67 D4 ↑	Amatikulu Golf Club		035312	Sec. 62	5 592	18	70	Welcome to play
BERGVILLE	67 C2 ↙	Bergville Golf Club	Sport Complex	03642	Sec. 26	6 100	10	70	Visitors most welcome to play
CATO RIDGE	63 NS ↑	Cato Ridge Club	Chamberlain Rd.	032512	Sec. 192	5 971	18	72	Visitors welcome – prior arrangements advisable
DUNDEE	67 C3 ↖	Dundee and District Country Club	Tandy St.	03412	Club 495 Capt. 834	6 145	18	71	Welcome to play
DURBAN	63 NS ↗	Beachwood Golf Club	Beachwood Place, off Fairway	031	Sec. 83-4206 or 83-4232	5 903	18	71	Visitors welcome to play
	63 NS ↗	Circle Country Club	Pinetown	031	Sec. 72-5198	5 880	18	71	Welcome to play
	63 NS ↗	Durban Country Club	Walter Gilbert Rd.	031	Sec. 33-5955	6 012	18	72	Welcome to play on Mondays and Tuesdays
	63 NS ↗	Kloof Country Club	Victory Rd., Kloof	031	Sec. 74-1328 or 74-1386	5 729	18	71	Welcome to play at any time except Saturday afternoon when permission from the Capt. has to be obtained.
	63 NS ↗	Royal Durban Golf Club	Mitchell Crescent	031	Sec. 33-5927	6 021	18	73	Visitors welcome except on Tuesday and Wednesday afternoons and weekends. At all times prior arrangements with the secretary must be made
	63 NS ↗	Windsor Park Golf Club	Windsor Ave.	031	Supt. 33-6880		18	72	Visitors welcome to play – a valid handicap from their home club is required
DURNACOL	67 C3 ↖	Durnacol Golf Club		03422	Sec. 611	6 255 (Men) 5 237 (Ladies)	11	72 (Men) 71 (Ladies)	Visitors welcome to play but facilities are limited during the week
EMPANGENI	67 C4 ↘	Empangeni Country Club	Pearce Crescent	0351	Sec. 2-1752	5 873	18	71	Visitors welcome
ESHOWE	67 C4 ↓	Eshowe Country Club	Hime St.	035412	Sec. 384	5 643	18	70	Welcome to play

GOLF CLUBS - NATAL (continued)

City or Town	AA Road Map Ref.	Name of Club	Street Address	Tel. Code	Tel. Numbers (For Course Booking)	Length of Course (in metres)	Number of Holes	Course Par	Details for Visitors
ESTCOURT	67 C2 ↘	Estcourt Golf Club	Louise St.	03631	Sec. 2420	5 915	9	72	Visitors welcome to play
GLENCOE	67 C3 ↖	Northfield Golf Club		0341	Sec. 7	6 264	10	71	Visitors are very welcome
GREYTOWN	67 D3 ↑	Greytown Country Club	3 Hallcar St.	03342	Sec. 302		10	70	Welcome to play
HARDING	63 B2 →	Harding Golf Club	Shepstone St.	03842	Sec. 56	6 370	9	72	Visitors most welcome
HOWICK	63 A3 ←	Howick Golf Club	Old Main Rd.	033212	Sec. 320	5 952 (Men) 5 337 (Ladies)	9	72	Visitors always welcome
IXOPO	63 NS ←	Ixopo Golf Club	Stewart Drive	03362	Sec. 65 or 100	5 504	11	69	Visitors always welcome
KOKSTAD	63 B2 ←	Kokstad Golf Club	Elliot St.	0372	Sec. 598	5 662	18	70	Very welcome to play
KWA-MBONAMBI	67 C5 ↙	Kwambonambi Club	Carissa Ave.	0352	Sec. 321	5 711 (Men) 5 020 (Ladies)	9	72	Welcome to play
LADYSMITH	67 C2 →	Ladysmith Country Club	Reservoir Rd.	0361	Sec. 3521	5 973	10	71	Visitors welcome
MANDINI	63 A4 ↖	Mandini Golf Club		032432	Sec. 7 or 516	5 540	9	71	Visitors also welcome to participate in club competitions on Saturday afternoons, if they have official handicaps
MARGATE	63 NS ↙	Margate Country Club	Gayridge Rd.	0393	Sec. 2-0571	5 573	18	36	Visitors welcome
MATATIELE	62 B6 ↗	Matatiele Golf Club	Main St. Ext.	Matatiele	Sec. 272 or 280	6 203	9	71	Visitors welcome to play
MOOI RIVER	63 A2 ↗	Mooi River Country Club	Cottage Rd.	033322	Club 9908	6 140 (Men) 5 190 (Ladies)	11	73	Welcome to play
MOUNT EDGECOMBE	63 NS ↗	Huletts Country Club	Golf Course Rd.	032132	Manager 51-2251 x 338	5 960	18	73	Visitors welcome to play
MTUBATUBA	67 C5 ←	Monzi Golf Club		03552	Sec. 1940	5 872	9	71	Visitors are very welcome
MTUNZINI	67 C4 ↘	Mtunzini Country Club	Hely Hutchinson St.	035322	Sec. 1812	5 614	9	71	Visitors are most welcome to join on Club days which are Wednesdays and Saturdays
NEWCASTLE	67 B2 ↘	Kilbarchan Golf Club	Golf Rd, Kilbarchan Village	0343	Sec. 6800 x 216	6 378	9	72	Welcome to play
	67 B2 ↘	Newcastle Golf Club	Off Hans van Rensburg Ave.	0343	Sec. 2-4885	6 365	18	73	Welcome to play at any time
PIETERMARITZBURG	63 NS ↖	Maritzburg Country Club	Duncan McKenzie Rd., Montrose	0331	Sec. 2-2442	6 054	18	71	Visitors welcome to play by prior arrangement with the secretary
	63 NS ↖	Maritzburg Golf Club	New England Rd. Ext.	0331	Club 4-2301	6 260	18	72	Visitors welcome during the week as well as weekends
PONGOLA	67 B4 ↗	Pongola Golf Club	E.G. Jansen St.	03842	Sec. 1421	6 158	9	72	Welcome to play
PORT SHEPSTONE	63 NS ↙	Port Shepstone Country Club	On the North Bank of the Mzimkulu River, Umtentweni	0391	Sec. 5-0140	5 741	18	72	Visitors welcome at all times other than closed Trophy Events
RICHMOND	63 NS ↖	Richmond (Natal) Country Club	Off Richmond/Ixopo Rd.	033222	Sec. 9908	5 828	10	72	Visitors welcome but prior arrangements are advisable
RIVERVIEW	67 C5 ←	Umfolozi Country Club	Riverview	03552	Sec. 11 x 46	5 805	9	70	Welcome to play
SCOTTBURGH	63 NS →	Scottburgh Golf Club	Williamson St.	0323	Sec. 2-0041	5 354	18	69	Visitors welcome to play - competitions arranged
SOUTHBROOM	63 NS ↙	Southbroom Golf Club	Captain Smith Rd.	0393	Sec. 6026	5 294	18	71	Welcome to play
SWARTBERG	63 B2 ↖	Swartberg Golf Club		Swartberg	Sec. 4	2 844	9	36	Visitors welcome

GOLF CLUBS - NATAL (continued)

City or Town	AA Road Map Ref.	Name of Club	Street Address	Tel. Code	Tel. Numbers (For Course Booking)	Length of Course (in metres)	Number of Holes	Course Par	Details for Visitors
ST. MICHAEL'S-ON-SEA	63 NS ↙	St. Michael's Golf Club	Marine Drive	0393	Sec. 5-0703	5 476	9	71	Visitors welcome to play and may also join the competitions on Thursdays and Saturdays
UMDONI PARK	63 NS •	Umdoni Park Golf Club		0323	Sec. 2-0051	5 443	18	72	Visitors welcome to play at any time
UMHLALI	63 A4 ←	Umhlali Country Club	500 m from Ballitoville flyover	032232	Sec. 91	5 577	9	71	Visitors most welcome - open competitions Tuesdays and Saturday afternoons
UMKOMAAS	63 NS ↗	Umkomaas Golf Club	Cnr. Moodie/Reynold Sts.	0323	Sec. 3-0121	5 436	18	70	Very welcome to play
UNDERBERG	63 A2 ↓	Underberg Golf Club	Drakensberg Garden Rd.	03372	Sec. 10 or 20	5 960	9	72	Visitors very welcome
VRYHEID	67 B3 ↘	Vryheid Golf Club	High St.	0381	Sec. 4910	6 184	9	72	Welcome to play

GOLF CLUBS IN THE ORANGE FREE STATE

City or Town	AA Road Map Ref.	Name of Club	Street Address	Tel. Code	Tel. Numbers (For Course Booking)	Length of Course (in metres)	Number of Holes	Course Par	Details for Visitors
BETHLEHEM	66 C6 ↖	Bethlehem Golf and Country Club	Golf St.	01431	Sec. 4027	6 173	18	72	Welcome to play
BLOEMFONTEIN	66 D4 ↖	Bloemfontein Golf Club	Mazelspoort Rd.	051	Sec. 8-9758	6 379	18	72	Visitors welcome
	66 D4 ↖	Defence Golf Club	Military Base, Tempe	051	Chairman 31-3611 x 106 or 22-5188	5 933	9	70	Visitors welcome to play
	66 D4 ↖	Schoemanpark Golf Club	Mazelspoort Rd.	051	Sec. 7-5996 Office 7-5973	6 419	18	72	Welcome to play
BRANDFORT	66 C4 ↓	Brandfort Golf Club	Uniefees St.	05222	Sec. 13 or 389	2 184	9	36	Visitors welcome
BULTFONTEIN	66 C4 ↖	Bultfontein Golf Club		05252	Sec. 4 or 348	6 475	18	72	Welcome to play
CLOCOLAN	66 C5 ↓	Clocolan Golf Club		05652	Sec. 378	5 777	9	72	Visitors most welcome
DEWETSDORP	62 A4 ↘	Dewetsdorp Golf Club		052112	Sec. 179 or 219	5 379	9	72	Visitors welcome
EDENBURG	62 A3 ↘	Edenburg Golf Club	Station St.	05842	Sec. 123	5 739	9	72	Visitors welcome
EXCELSIOR	66 C5 ↙	Excelsior Golf Club		Excelsior	Sec. 4	6 048	9	70	Welcome to play
FICKSBURG	66 C5 ↘	Ficksburg Golf Club	Hill St.	05632	Sec. 25	6 166	18	72	Welcome to play
FRANKFORT	66 B6 ↑	Frankfort Golf Club	Brand St.	016132	Sec. 11	6 007	9	72	All visitors welcome to play
HARRISMITH	67 C2 ↖	Harrismith Country Club Golf Course	Murray St. Ext.	014362	Sec. 200 Club 9907	6 175	18	73	Most welcome on any day and may also participate in club competitions on Wednesdays and Saturdays
HEILBRON	66 B5 ↗	Heilbron Golf Club	Sports grounds	016142	Sec. 72 or 555	6 373	9	72	Visitors welcome to play
HENNENMAN	66 B5 ↙	White's Club	Hope Ave., Whites District	017112	Sec. 3712	5 827	9	72	Welcome to play
HOOPSTAD	66 B3 ↘	Hoopstad Country Club		017122	153 or 198	5 230	9	70	Visitors most welcome
JAGERSFONTEIN	62 A3 ↓	Jagersfontein Golf Club		05832	Sec. 15 or 177	5 996	9	72	Visitors welcome to play from Monday to Saturday
KROONSTAD	66 B5 ↙	Kroonstad Country Club Golf Course	Bert Symonds Drive	01411	Club 5169	6 279	18	73	Visitors to report to the manager at the club house at any time

GOLF CLUBS - ORANGE FREE STATE (continued)

City or Town	AA Road Map Ref.	Name of Club	Street Address	Tel. Code	Tel. Numbers (For Course Booking)	Length of Course (in metres)	Number of Holes	Course Par	Details for Visitors
LADYBRAND	66 D5 ↑	Ladybrand Golf Club	Voortrekker St.	05612	Sec. 42	5 990	9	72	Very welcome
MARQUARD	66 C5 ↓	Marquard Golf Club	Kruger St. East	05272	Sec. 47 or 217	6 344	9	72	Visitors welcome to play
ODENDAALSRUS	66 B4 ↘	Freddies Golf Club	Hauptfleisch St.	017	4-1261	5 969	9	70	Welcome to play except on Monday when the course is closed
PARYS	66 A5 ↓	Parys Golf and Country Club	Golf Island	01601	Sec. 2235	6 332	9	74	Welcome to play at any time
PETRUS STEYN	66 B6 ↙	Petrus Steyn Golf Club	Steyn St.	014382	Sec. 33 or 188	6 026	9	72	Very welcome to play
PHILIPPOLIS	62 B3 ↖	Philippolis Golf Club		Philippolis	Sec. 22 or 180	5 846	18	72	Visitors welcome to play
REDDERSBURG	62 A4 ↙	Reddersburg Golf Club		052122	Sec. 64	6 639	9	72	Welcome to play
REITZ	66 B6 ↙	Reitz Golf Club		014342	Sec. 3	5 996	9	70	Visitors most welcome
ROUXVILLE	62 B4 →	Rouxville Golf Club		05572	Sec. 2712	6 362	9	72	Visitors always welcome to play
SENEKAL	66 C5 ↗	Senekal Golf Club	Voortrekker Rd.	014352	Sec. 8	6 100	9	72	Very welcome
THEUNISSEN	66 C4 →	Theunissen Golf Club		017132	Chairman 100		9	72	Visitors welcome to play at any time, but the club house is only open on Saturdays.
TROMPSBURG	62 B3 ↗	Trompsburg Golf Club		05812	Sec. 201	5 812	9	72	Visitors very welcome
TWEESPRUIT	66 D5 ↖	Tweespruit Golf Club		Tweespruit	Sec. 2	3 205	9	74	Very welcome any time during the week
VILJOENSKROON	66 B4 ↗	Viljoenskroon Golf Club	Krige St. Ext.	014132	Sec. 20	6 487	9	72	Welcome to play
VIRGINIA	66 C4 ↗	Sand River Golf Club	Valley Drive	017	Sec. 3-1676	6 238	18	71	Visitors welcome to play
VREDE	67 B2 ←	Vrede Country Club		013342	Sec. 500 or 18	6 041	9	72	Welcome to play
WELKOM	66 B4 ↘	Oppenheimer Park Golf Club		017	Club 2-3239		18	72	Visitors welcome to play at any time
WEPENER	62 A5 ↙	Wepener Golf Club	Van Rooyens Gate Rd. (3 km from Wepener)	05232	Sec. 19 or 28	5 748	9	72	Welcome to play
WESTMINSTER	66 D5 ↖	Westminster Golf Club	Westminster Estate	05642	Sec. 1240	5 942	9	70	Visitors welcome to play - course is open only from May to end October every year
WINBURG	66 C5 ←	Winburg Golf Club	Leech St.	05242	Sec. 231 or 357	5 981	9	72	Welcome to play
ZASTRON	62 B5 ↖	Zastron Golf Club		05542	Sec. 1930	6 113	9	70	Visitors always welcome

GOLF CLUBS IN TRANSVAAL

City or Town	AA Road Map Ref.	Name of Club	Street Address	Tel. Code	Tel. Numbers (For Course Booking)	Length of Course (in metres)	Number of Holes	Course Par	Details for Visitors
ALBERTON	72 NS ↘	See WITWATERSRAND							
ARNOT	69 C2 ↘	Arnot Golf Club	Near Arnot Power Station	0132272	Sec. 228	6 424 (Men) 5 549 (Ladies)	9	72 (Men) 74 (Ladies)	Welcome to play
BARBERTON	69 C4 ↙	Barberton Golf Club		013142	Sec. 280 x 115	5 393	92	72	Visitors welcome to play except on Mondays when the course is closed

GOLF CLUBS - TRANSVAAL (continued)

City or Town	AA Road Map Ref.	Name of Club	Street Address	Tel. Code	Tel. Numbers (For Course Booking)	Length of Course (in metres)	Number of Holes	Course Par	Details for Visitors
BEDFORDVIEW	72 NS •	See WITWATERSRAND							
BELFAST	69 C3 ↙	Belfast Golf Club		0132512	Sec. 1 or 93	6 031	18	72	Welcome to play
BENONI	72 NS →	See WITWATERSRAND							
BETHAL	67 A2 •	Bethal Golf Club	Myburgh St.	01361	Sec. 2011 or 4189	± 6 170	9	72	Welcome to play
BLOEMHOF	66 B3 ↓	Bloemhof Golf Club	Prins St.	018022	Sec. 9	6 039	9	72	Visitors welcome to play
BLYVOORUITZICHT	66 A5 ↑	Blyvooruitzicht Golf Club	Blyvooruitzicht Gold Mining Co. Ltd.	01491	Sec. 9151	6 376	18	72	Welcome to play
BOKSBURG	72 NS →	See WITWATERSRAND							
BOOYSENS	72 NS •	See WITWATERSRAND							
BRAKPAN	72 NS →	See WITWATERSRAND							
CARLETONVILLE	66 A5 ↖	Gold Fields West Golf Club	West Driefontein Gold Mining Co. Ltd.	01491	Sec. 2111	6 549	18	73	Welcome to play
CAROLINA	69 D3 ↖	Carolina Golf Club	Voortrekker St.	013442	Sec. 162	5 840	9	72	Very welcome - club house open on Wednesday and Saturday afternoons
CHRISTIANA	66 B3 ↙	Christiana Golf Club		05342	Sec. 1	6 030	9	72	Visitors most welcome - competitions organised Wednesday and Saturday afternoons
CULLINAN	68 C6 ↓	Premier Golf Club	Camp Rd.	012132	Sec. 23 or 157	6 186	9	72	Visitors welcome except on Saturday afternoons and Sunday mornings, unless accompanied by a member
DELAREYVILLE	66 A3 ↓	Delareyville Golf Club		014432	Sec. 82	5 935	9	72	Welcome to play
ERMELO	67 A2 →	Ermelo Golf Club	On the Hendrina Rd., opposite the Douglas Dam	01341	Sec. 4448	6 350	18	72	Visitors most welcome
EVANDER	67 A2 ←	Walker Park Golf Club	On the Kinross Main Rd.	01363	Sec. 2501	6 355	18	71 (Men) 72 (Ladies)	Visitors welcome provided they are bona fide golfers and can produce verified handicaps. Course is closed on Sundays if any competition is played on that day
GERMISTON	72 NS •	See WITWATERSRAND							
GROBLERSDAL	69 C2 ↖	Groblersdal Golf Club	On the Middelburg Rd.	012022	Sec. 248 or 38	6 322	9	72	Welcome to play
GROOTVLEI	66 A6 ↓	Springfield Collieries Golf Club	Springfield Collieries	01592	Sec. 157 Chairman 52	6 391	14	72	Visitors are encouraged to play
HAZYVIEW	71 C5 ↖	Sabi River Bungalows Golf Club	At Sabi River Bungalows	0131242	Sec. 12	2 722	9	35	Visitors welcome to play at all times
IRENE	68 NS →	Irene Country Club	Main Rd.	012	Sec. 6-5181 or 6-5556	6 414	18	72	Visitors welcome to play during the week
JAN KEMPDORP	66 B2 ↘	Jan Kempdorp Golf Club		053312	Sec. 1303	6 067	9	72	Visitors welcome and may also use the facilities of the club house.
JOHANNESBURG	72 NS •	See WITWATERSRAND							
KEMPTON PARK	72 NS ↗	See WITWATERSRAND							
KLERKSDORP	66 A4 ↘	Klerksdorp Golf Club	Swardrift St.	018	Sec. 2-5929	± 6 000	18	71	Welcome to play - no prior arrangements necessary
KRUGERSDORP	72 NS ↖	See WITWATERSRAND							
KYALAMI	72 NS ↑	See WITWATERSRAND							
LETABA	69 A3 ↙	Orangedene Golf Club	Letaba Estates	01523	Sec. 4123 or 4140	5 986	9	72	Visitors welcome to play - organised competitions on Saturday afternoons

GOLF CLUBS - TRANSVAAL (continued)

City or Town	AA Road Map Ref.	Name of Club	Street Address	Tel. Code	Tel. Numbers (For Course Booking)	Length of Course (in metres)	Number of Holes	Course Par	Details for Visitors
LICHTENBURG	68 D4 ↖	Lichtenburg Golf Club		01441	Sec. 3007	6 468	18	72	Welcome to play
LOUIS TRICHARDT	70 C4 ↗	Louis Trichardt Golf Club	Ruh St.	01551	Club 2991		19		Welcome to play - no prior arrangements necessary
LYDENBURG	70 NS ↙	Lydenburg Golf Club	Buhrman St.	013232	Sec. 874	5 920	9	70	Visitors welcome
MALELANE	69 C4 •	Malelane Golf Club		0131622	Club 52 x 240	6 070	9	71	Welcome to play
MARBLE HALL	69 B2 ↙	Marble Hall Golf Club		012082	Sec. 1712	5 305	9	72	Visitors are most welcome
MESSINA	70 B5 ↖	Messina Golf Club	Limpopo Ave.	015532	Sec. 525	6 014	9	72	Very welcome to play
MIDDELBURG	69 C2 ↓	Coronation Golf Club	On the Bethal Rd., at the Bank Colliery	01321	Sec. 1522	6 574	9	72	Visitors are very welcome
	62 C2 ↓	Middelburg Country Club	Golf St., Clubview	01321	Sec. 4961	6 469	18	72	Welcome to play
MODDERFONTEIN	72 NS ↗	See WITWATERSRAND							
NABOOMSPRUIT	69 B1 →	Naboomspruit Golf Club	Louis Trichardt Ave.	012072	Sec. 232	5 833	9	72	Course is always open to visitors and they may participate in all competitions
NELSPRUIT	69 C3 →	Nelspruit Golf Club	Miller St.	01311	Sec. 2345	6 036	18	72	Welcome to play on any day, but on Tuesdays the club house is closed
NIGEL	72 NS ↘	Nigel Golf Club	C-Shaft, Sub-Nigel	011	Sec. 739-3711	6 142 (Men) 5 276 (Ladies)	18	72	Welcome to play except when club competitions are played and on Mondays, when the course is closed
NYLSTROOM	68 B6 ↙	Nylstroom Golf Club	Kerk St. West	01532	Club 578	5 873	9	72	Most welcome to play
ORKNEY	66 A4 ↘	Orkney Golf Club	Scott Ave.	018	Sec. 3-1661	6 388	18	72	Visitors welcome to play
OTTOSDAL	66 A4 ↙	Ottosdal Golf Club	On the Klerksdorp Rd.	018032	Sec. 2104	6 100	9	72	Visitors are most welcome to play
PENGE	69 B3 ↖	Penge Golf Club	Penge Asbestos Mine	Penge	Sec. 3	5 769	9	70	Welcome to play
PHALABORWA	71 A5 ↙	Hans Merensky Club	Follow Phalaborwa Mining Co. signs	01524	Sec. 2931	6 074	18	72	Welcome to play - caddies available Tuesdays to Fridays from 13 h 00 onwards and all weekend
PIETERSBURG	69 A2 ↓	Pietersburg Golf Club	Voortrekker St.	01521	Sec. 4118	6 162	18	71	Visitors welcome to play at any time
PIET RETIEF	67 B3 ↗	Piet Retief Country Club	Follow the signs from centre of town	013432	Sec. 23	5 614	18	68	Welcome to play at any time - no prior arrangements necessary
PILGRIM'S REST	70 NS ↑	T.G.M.E. Golf Club	On the Lydenburg Rd.	Pilgrim's Rest	Sec. 33 or 10	5 514	9	70	Visitors are very welcome
POTCHEFSTROOM	66 A5 ↙	Potchefstroom Country Club	On the Johannesburg Main Rd.	01481	Sec. 4821		18	72	Welcome to play
POTGIETERSRUS	69 B2 ↖	Potgietersrus Golf Club	Pretorius St.	01542	Sec. 818 or 1618	6 322	9	72	Visitors always welcome
PRETORIA	68 NS ↗	Defence Golf Club	Voortrekkerhoogte	012	Manager 71-3916	6 495	18	72	Visitors most welcome to play by prior arrangement with the manager
	68 C6 ↙	Pretoria Country Club	Sidney Ave., Waterkloof	012	Sec. 78-6241	6 221	18	72	Visitors must be introduced by members
	68 NS ↗	Pretoria Golf Club	Rebecca St., Pretoria West	012	Club 79-4850	6 028	18	70	Members may introduce a visitor once a month or temporary membership may be taken out
	68 C6 ↙	Wingate Park Country Club	Old Military Rd., Wingate	012	Sec. 97-1001	6 573	18	72	Welcome to play
	68 C6 ↙	Zwartkop Country Club	Old Johannesburg Rd., Verwoerdburg	012	Sec. 64-1144	6 497	18	72	Visitors welcome, except on Saturday afternoons when the course is reserved for members

GOLF CLUBS - TRANSVAAL (continued)

City or Town	AA Road Map Ref.	Name of Club	Street Address	Tel. Code	Tel. Numbers (For Course Booking)	Length of Course (in metres)	Number of Holes	Course Par	Details for Visitors
RANDBURG	72 NS ↑	See WITWATERSRAND							
RANDFONTEIN	72 NS ←	See WITWATERSRAND							
ROODEPOORT	72 NS ←	See WITWATERSRAND							
ROOIBERG	68 B5 ↘	Rooiberg Golf Club		Rooiberg	Sec. 2	6 162	10	72	Welcome to play at any time
RUSTENBURG	68 NS ↖	Rustenburg Golf Club	Malan St.	01421	Sec. 2-4283	6 310	18	72	Visitors welcome 7 days a week
SANDTON	72 NS ↑	See WITWATERSRAND							
SANNIESHOF	66 A3 →	Sannieshof Golf Club		014472	Sec. 107	6 274	9	72	Visitors are very welcome to play
SCHWEIZER-RENEKE	66 B3 ↖	Schweizer-Reneke Golf Club	Vryburg Rd.	018012	Sec. 407	6 202	10	71	Welcome to play
SPRINGS	72 NS →	See WITWATERSRAND							
STANDERTON	67 A2 ↙	Standerton Country Club		01331	Sec. 2835 or 2235	± 6 300	9	72	Visitors are most welcome
STILFONTEIN	66 A4 ↘	Stilfontein Golf Club	On the Main Potchefstroom/Klerksdorp Rd.	018	Sec. 4-1852	6 443	18	72	Visitors welcome to play
THABAZIMBI	68 B5 •	Thabazimbi Golf Club	On the Rustenburg Rd.	014232	Sec. 412 x 166 or 1	6 308	9	72	Welcome to play
TZANEEN	69 A3 ↙	Letaba District Country Club	Prinsloo St.	01523	Sec. 5602	6 309	18	71	Visitors may apply to the Club Manager at the Club at any time
VANDERBIJLPARK	66 A5 ↘	Emfuleni Country Club	Opposite Vesco Caravan Park	016	Sec. 336-4361	6 482	18	72	Visitors to report to the secretary - course closed on Mondays
VANDYKSDRIF	69 D2 ↖	Douglas Golf Club		01354	Sec. 621	6 449	18	72	Visitors welcome
VENTERSDORP	68 D4 ↗	Ventersdorp Golf Club	Voortrekker St.	014832	Sec. 43	6 004	9	71	Welcome to play
VEREENIGING	66 A5 ↘	Maccauvlei Golf Club	Opposite Richmond Village	016	Sec. 22-4375 or 22-3300	6 358	18	72	Visitors welcome at all times
	66 A5 ↘	Vereeniging Country Club	Riviera Rd.	016	Sec. 22-0036/7	6 290	18	72	Welcome to play
VOLKSRUST	67 B2 ↗	Volksrust Golf Club		013332	Sec. 28	6 065	9	72	Most welcome to play
WALKERVILLE	72 NS ↙	See WITWATERSRAND							
WARMBATHS	68 B6 ↙	Warmbaths Golf Club		012062	Sec. 18	6 235	9	72	Welcome to play
WESTONARIA	72 NS ↙	See WITWATERSRAND							
WESTPLAT	68 NS ↖	Westplat Golf Club	On the Main Brits/Rustenburg Rd.	0142242	Sec. 124	6 110	9	72	Visitors are welcome to play at most times - they may also participate in competitions on Saturdays if they have official handicaps
WHITE RIVER	71 C5 ↖	White River Golf Club	The Links, Dist. Longmere	013132	Sec. 5532	6 400	9	72	Visitors welcome to play
WITBANK	69 C2 ↙	Tweefontein Golf Club	Witbank Dist.	01356	Sec. 711	6 209	10	72	Most welcome to play
	69 C2 ↙	Witbank Golf Club	Lukin St.	01351	Sec. 5031	6 209	18	72	Visitors are most welcome except on closed days approx. twice a year on Sundays
WITWATERSRAND									
ALBERTON	72 NS ↘	Reading Country Club	Fore St., Redruth	011	Sec. 869-1781	6 475	18	72	Visitors welcome to play
BEDFORDVIEW	72 NS •	Glendower Golf Club	Marais Rd.	011	Sec. 53-1331/2	6 516	18	72	Welcome to play by arrangement with the secretary

GOLF CLUBS - TRANSVAAL (continued)

City or Town	AA Road Map Ref.	Name of Club	Street Address	Tel. Code	Tel. Numbers (For Course Booking)	Length of Course (in metres)	Number of Holes	Course Par	Details for Visitors
BENONI	72 NS →	Benoni Country Club	Morris Ave., Morehill	011	Sec. 849-5211/2	6 458	18	72	Visitors who are members of another club are welcome to play except on Saturday afternoons
	72 NS →	Benoni Lake Club	Lakefield Ave.	011	Sec. 54-1341	6 314	18	71	Visitors welcome to play, preferably accompanied by a member, except Saturday afternoons and Sunday mornings
BOKSBURG	72 NS →	E.R.P.M. Golf Club	Pretoria Rd.	011	Sec. 826-2211	6 303	18	72	Visitors welcome if they are members of an affiliated club
BOOYSENS	72 NS •	Crown Mines Golf Club	Crown Mines	011	Sec. 35-3949	6 375	18	73	Visitors welcome at any time from Tuesday to Friday – prior arrangements necessary with Secretary for play on Saturday mornings and Sundays
BRAKPAN	72 NS →	John Vorster Golf Club	Main Reef Rd.	011	Sec. 55-1526		18	72	Visitors welcome to play 7 days a week
GERMISTON	72 NS •	Germiston Golf Club	Lake Grounds	011	Sec. 34-8950	6 411	18	71	Only visitors with official handicaps are allowed to play
JOHANNESBURG	72 NS •	Glenvista Country Club	Karrasberg Rd., Glenvista	011	Sec. 943-2104	6 268	18	70	Visitors must have a maximum handicap of 18 and may also join in all competitions
	72 NS •	Houghton Golf Club	2nd Ave., Lower Houghton	011	Sec. 728-1234	6 376 (White) 6 567 (Yellow)	18	71 (White) 72 (Yellow)	Visitors welcome to play on Monday and Tuesday and on Wednesday and Thursday afternoons. The course consists of a White course and a Yellow course as indicated
	72 NS •	Huddle Park Municipal Golf Club	Club St., Linksfield	011	Sec. 45-2748	6 544 (Blue) 6 011 (Yellow) 5 960 (White)	54	72 (Blue) 70 (Yellow) 71 (White)	Visitors are most welcome to play. The course consists of a Blue, a Yellow and White course
	72 NS •	Killarney Golf Club	5th St., Lower Houghton	011	Sec. 728-1316	6 070 (Men) 5 504 (Ladies)	18	70 (Men) 74 (Ladies)	Visitors welcome to play on Wednesday, Thursday, Friday, Saturday before 09 h 30 and Sunday afternoons
	72 NS •	Observatory Golf Club	Steyn St., Observatory	011	Sec. 43-7410	6 246	18	71	Welcome to play
	72 NS •	Parkview Golf Club	Wicklow Ave., Emmarentia	011	Sec. 41-5400	6 337	18	71	Visitors welcome to play by prior arrangement
	72 NS •	Royal Johannesburg Golf Club	Fairview Ave., Linksfield North	011	Sec. 45-1825 or 45-1160	6 264 (West) 6 363 (East)	18	71 (West) 72 (East)	Unintroduced persons from outside the Reef area may be permitted to play by prior arrangement with the Managing Secretary only. Parties of more than four by written application to the Committee only.
	72 NS ↓	Southdowns Country Club	Impala Rd., Kibler Park	011	Club 943-2311	6 148	18	70	Welcome to play at any time during the week
	72 NS •	The Kensington Golf Club	Langermann Drive, Kensington	011	Sec. 616-4000	6 196	18	70	Visitors have to make arrangements with the secretary and have to be members of another club. Course closed on Mondays. Tuesday ladies' day.
	72 NS •	The Wanderers Golf Club	Cnr. Corlett Drive/Rudd Rd., Illovo	011	Sec. 47-3311/3	6 372	18	71	Visitors have to introduce themselves to the secretary or manager and/or make prior arrangements
KEMPTON PARK	72 NS ↗	Kempton Park Country Club		011	Sec. 975-2092	6 268	18	72	Visitors welcome to play on weekdays, Saturday mornings and Sunday afternoons
KRUGERSDORP	72 NS ↖	Krugersdorp Golf Club	Nightingale Cres., Rant-en-Dal	011	Sec. 660-4365	6 485	18	72	Welcome to play at all times except on Saturday afternoons

GOLF CLUBS - TRANSVAAL (continued)

City or Town	AA Road Map Ref.	Name of Club	Street Address	Tel. Code	Tel. Numbers (For Course Booking)	Length of Course (in metres)	Number of Holes	Course Par	Details for Visitors
KYALAMI	72 NS ↑	Kyalami Country Club	109 Maple Rd.	011	Sec. 702-1610/1	6 431	18	72	Visitors, if recognised members of clubs affiliated to a Golf Union, are welcome to play with prior permission from the secretary
MODDERFONTEIN	72 NS ↗	Modderfontein Golf Club	Golf Club Rd., North Rand	011	Sec. 608-2033/4	6 363	18	72	Visitors welcome at all times during the week and by arrangement during the weekend
RANDBURG	72 NS ↑	Randpark Club	Setperk St., Windsor Park	011	Manager 678-5361/2	6 288 (Wind.) 6 386 (Rand.)	36	72 (Wind.) 73 (Rand.)	Both the Windsor Park and Randpark courses are used by the Randpark Club. Visitors welcome to play except on Saturday afternoons
RANDFONTEIN	72 NS ←	Randfontein Estates Golf Club	Homestead Ave. (Opp. Robinson Station)	011	Sec. 663-4391	6 638	18	72	Welcome to play
ROODEPOORT	72 NS ←	C.M.R. Golf Club	Maraisburg Rd., Maraisburg	011	Sec. 672-6169	6 097	18	70	Visitors welcome to play except Mondays when the course is closed, and when major competions take place
	72 NS ←	Durban Deep Golf Club	Durban Roodepoort Deep Ltd.	011	Sec. 763-6241 x 19	6 267	11	72	Welcome to play
SANDTON	72 NS ↑	Johannesburg Country Club	Lincoln St.,Woodmead East	011	Sec. 802-2015	6 375 (Men) 5 427 (Ladies)	18	72	Visitors must be introduced by a member
	72 NS ↑	Bryanston Country Club	Bryanston Drive	011	Manager 706-1361/2/3 or 706-6070/1	6 656	18	73	Visitors are normally only allowed to play in the company of a member, but special arrangements can be made with the manager
SPRINGS	72 NS →	Pollak Park Golf Club		011	Sec. 56-1754	6 298	18	71	Visitors are welcome to play
	72 NS →	Springs Country Club	Cnr. Nigel/Parkes Rds., Selection Park	011	Sec. 56-1977		18	72	Visitors are most welcome
WALKERVILLE	72 NS ↙	Ohenimuri Country Club	Main Vereeniging Rd. (13 km from Lido Hotel)	955	Club 7511	6 434	18	72	Visitors are welcome to play at any time
WESTONARIA	72 NS ↙	Ventersport Golf Club	Golf Drive	011	Sec. 753-1111		18	71	Visitors welcome to play
WOLMARANSSTAD	66 B3 ↗	Wolmaransstad Golf Club	Geyer St.	018112	Sec. 40 or 154	6 047	9	72	Visitors are most welcome
ZEBEDIELA	69 B2 ↖	Zebediela Country Club	Zebediela Estate	Zebediela	Sec. 11	6 144		71	Visitors are welcome to play, either in the company of a member or by prior arrangement with the Committee
ZEERUST	68 C4 ←	Zeerust Golf Club		014282	Sec. 27 or 285	5 276	9	68	Visitors very welcome to play

Pick it up - Remember, every litter bit helps

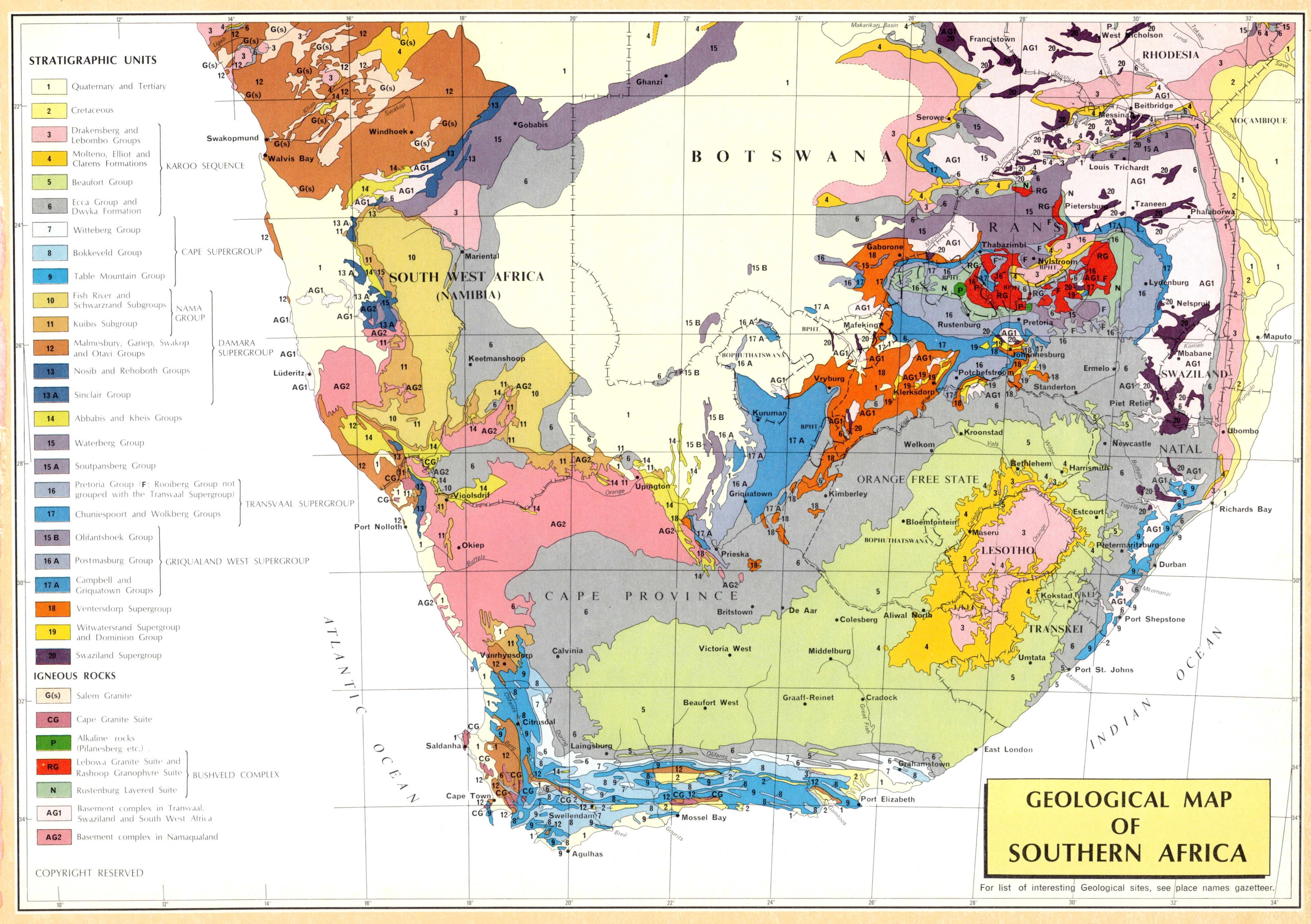

GEOLOGICAL MAP OF SOUTHERN AFRICA
For list of interesting Geological sites, see place names gazetteer.
STRATIGRAPHIC UNITS
1 Quaternary and Tertiary
2 Cretaceous
3 Drakensberg and Lebombo Groups
4 Molteno, Elliot and Clarens Formations
5 Beaufort Group
6 Ecca Group and Dwyka Formation
KAROO SEQUENCE
7 Witteberg Group
8 Bokkeveld Group
9 Table Mountain Group
CAPE SUPERGROUP
10 Fish River and Schwarzrand Subgroups
11 Kuibis Subgroup
NAMA GROUP
12 Malmesbury, Gariep, Swakop and Otavi Groups
13 Nosib and Rehoboth Groups
DAMARA SUPERGROUP
13 A Sinclair Group
14 Abbabis and Kheis Groups
15 Waterberg Group
15 A Soutpansberg Group
16 Pretoria Group (F: Rooiberg Group not grouped with the Transvaal Supergroup)
17 Chuniespoort and Wolkberg Groups
TRANSVAAL SUPERGROUP
15 B Olifantshoek Group
16 A Postmasburg Group
17 A Campbell and Griquatown Groups
GRIQUALAND WEST SUPERGROUP
18 Ventersdorp Supergroup
19 Witwatersrand Supergroup and Dominion Group
20 Swaziland Supergroup
IGNEOUS ROCKS
G(s) Salem Granite
CG Cape Granite Suite
P Alkaline rocks (Pilanesberg etc.)
RG Lebowa Granite Suite and Rashoop Granophyre Suite
N Rustenburg Layered Suite
BUSHVELD COMPLEX
AG1 Basement complex in Transvaal, Swaziland and South West Africa
AG2 Basement complex in Namaqualand
COPYRIGHT RESERVED
SOUTH WEST AFRICA (NAMIBIA)
BOTSWANA
RHODESIA
MOÇAMBIQUE
TRANSVAAL
SWAZILAND
NATAL
ORANGE FREE STATE
LESOTHO
TRANSKEI
CAPE PROVINCE
BOPHUTHATSWANA
ATLANTIC OCEAN
INDIAN OCEAN
Swakopmund
Walvis Bay
Windhoek
Gobabis
Ghanzi
Mariental
Keetmanshoop
Lüderitz
Upington
Vioolsdrif
Port Nolloth
Okiep
Prieska
Kimberley
Griquatown
Kuruman
Vryburg
Mafeking
Gaborone
Francistown
Serowe
West Nicholson
Beitbridge
Messina
Louis Trichardt
Pietersburg
Tzaneen
Phalaborwa
Thabazimbi
Nylstroom
Rustenburg
Pretoria
Johannesburg
Potchefstroom
Klerksdorp
Lydenburg
Nelspruit
Maputo
Mbabane
Ermelo
Standerton
Piet Retief
Ubombo
Kroonstad
Welkom
Bethlehem
Harrismith
Newcastle
Richards Bay
Bloemfontein
Maseru
Estcourt
Pietermaritzburg
Durban
Port Shepstone
Kokstad
Aliwal North
Umtata
Port St. Johns
Colesberg
De Aar
Britstown
Calvinia
Vanrhynsdorp
Victoria West
Middelburg
Beaufort West
Graaff-Reinet
Cradock
East London
Grahamstown
Port Elizabeth
Mossel Bay
Swellendam
Agulhas
Cape Town
Saldanha
Citrusdal
Laingsburg
Orange
Limpopo
Vaal
Olifants

ANGOLA
RHODESIA
MOÇAMBIQUE
Limpopo
BOTSWANA
SOUTH WEST
AFRICA
(NAMIBIA)
Windhoek
Walvis Bay
Mafeking
BOPHUTHATSWANA
Pretoria
Johannesburg
Maputo
SWAZ
Vaal
Tugela
Upington
Orange
Kimberley
Bloemfontein
LESOTHO
Durban
Oranjemund
ATLANTIC OCEAN
BENGUELA CURRENT
TRANSKEI
Kei
MOÇAMBIQUE CURRENT
East London
Port Elizabeth
INDIAN OCEAN
Cape Town
Agulhas
AGULHAS CURRENT
BERANN

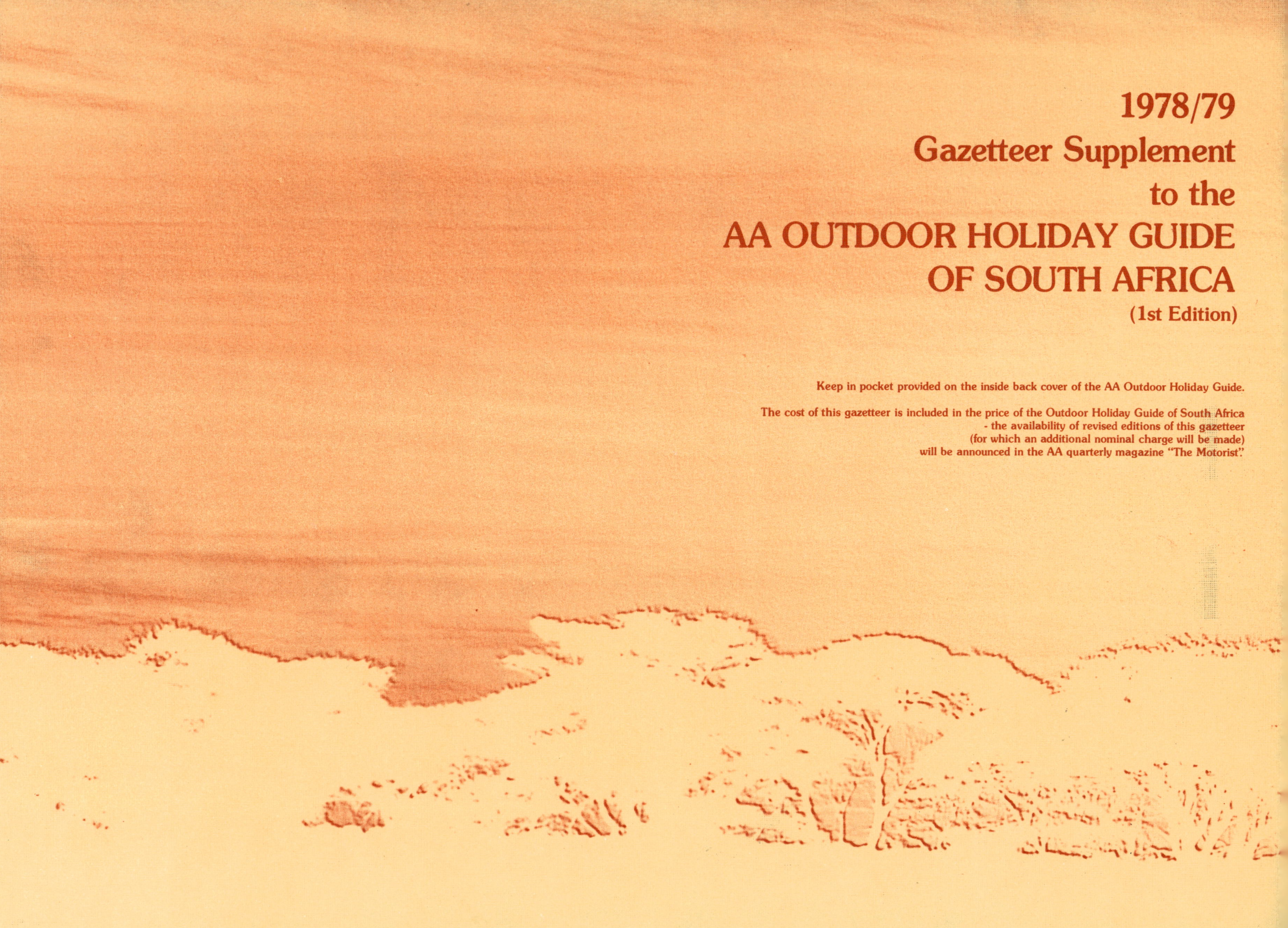

1978/79
Gazetteer Supplement
to the
AA OUTDOOR HOLIDAY GUIDE
OF SOUTH AFRICA
(1st Edition)

Keep in pocket provided on the inside back cover of the AA Outdoor Holiday Guide.

The cost of this gazetteer is included in the price of the Outdoor Holiday Guide of South Africa
- the availability of revised editions of this gazetteer
(for which an additional nominal charge will be made)
will be announced in the AA quarterly magazine "The Motorist".

1978/79 GAZETTEER SUPPLEMENT TO THE AA OUTDOOR HOLIDAY GUIDE OF SOUTH AFRICA

1st Edition © The Automobile Association of South Africa (ISBN 0 909234 13 2 - Afrikaanse uitgawe ISBN 0 909234 16 7)

INDEX

COMPILED AND PUBLISHED BY THE AUTOMOBILE ASSOCIATION OF SOUTH AFRICA
(Incorporated Association not for Gain)

Every effort has been made to ensure the accuracy of the information contained in this gazetteer, but the AA cannot accept responsibility for any errors or omissions which may occur. The AA will be indebted to members who point out any inaccuracies. Please send details to:
The Director-General
The Automobile Association of South Africa
P.O. Box 596 Johannesburg 2000

Hierdie Inligtingsgids is ook in Afrikaans beskikbaar

INTRODUCTION

This gazetteer contains the most comprehensive information of its kind available in South Africa and provides details on a wide selection of outdoor accommodation for a happy and successful holiday.

The information listed is believed to be correct at the time of publication but may be verified when booking as changes occur during the currency of the gazetteer and it is not possible to convey such changes to users before publication of the next edition. The gazetteer will be updated periodically and the availability of subsequent editions will be announced through the medium of the AA's quarterly magazine, "The Motorist".

In order to achieve maximum benefit from this guide, please familiarise yourself with the following information.

OUTDOOR HOLIDAY GUIDE

This gazetteer is designed for use in conjunction with the six colour maps included in the Outdoor Holiday Guide. The key map for these is reproduced alongside and will enable easy identification and location of the relevant map spread in which you may be interested.

Consult the map reference in the Outdoor Holiday Guide and familiarise yourself with the symbols included on the maps, particularly at towns - it will be seen that symbols for towns providing facilities for caravaners have been shown for travelling and route-planning convenience eg. the existence of caravan parks/camping sites are depicted by a black circle with a yellow centre.

Route Planning
The existence of tarred, untarred and sections of road under construction are visually depicted on the maps in the guide. Normally it is not advisable to tow a caravan for any great distance on untarred roads, but where this is unavoidable, users should make enquiries locally as to the condition of such roads before venturing forth.

Reference to the section on Mountain Passes is desirable as the information given will assist the user in avoiding passes which are unsuitable for caravans. Please also note that caravans are only permitted on tarred roads within the Kruger National Park.

The town plans included in the guide will assist travellers in finding their way through towns and will, in several instances, show the location of some of the caravan parks. Local authorities are increasingly erecting signposts to caravan parks and camping sites within towns and along the main routes. Watch out for the appropriate signs when travelling.

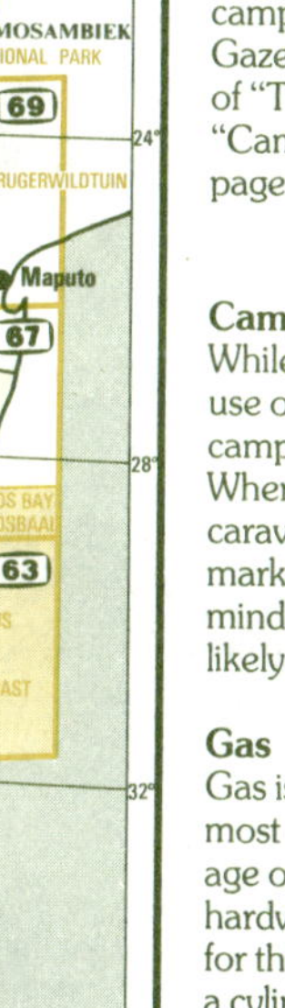

Place Names Index - see Outdoor Holiday Guide - pages 97 - 101
A detailed place names index, arranged in alphabetical sequence, is included in the Outdoor Holiday Guide and will be of assistance in identifying and locating places. In this regard, reference to the gazetteer section will indicate what caravan parks or camping sites are available at such places or in the more popular areas within close proximity.

The grid reference included will enable the user to locate these places on the six colour maps.

Early Booking
Advance bookings may be made at some of the sites listed in the Gazetteer. These have been marked for the benefit of the user and because outdoor holidays are becoming increasingly popular, it is always wise to book well in advance, in some instances as much as a year ahead, especially for coastal and mountain resorts during the main seasons. Unless you do this your holiday could get off to a bad start. Although it pays to book for the popular coastal parks during school holidays, you don't normally have to book for every step of your journey. You will then be free to move on if a particular spot doesn't appeal to you, as deposits are not usually required. Fees are paid in advance on a per night basis.

When booking, check whether the reservation is for a particular stand or not as advance booking does not necessarily guarantee the best stands. Some parks merely admit a fixed number of people who have to select from the stands available on arrival. It is wise to check with each establishment whether the caravan/camping equipment you intend using is acceptable. Give details of the size of your caravan, the number of persons in your party, your expected time of arrival and length of stay.

Always verify tariffs when booking as these are subject to change without prior notice. Check as to acceptable arrival and departure times particularly insofar as game and nature reserves are concerned, as closing times of gates are strictly enforced.

Site Rules and/or Conditions
These vary from one establishment to another and it is always wise to ascertain from the owner/manager on arrival what these are.

Additional Accommodation Facilities
Some caravan parks offer extra accommodation for hire on site in the form of bungalows, chalets, cottages, rondavels etc. Where applicable, these are listed, with tariffs, in the Gazetteer section - see columns 53, 54, 55 and 56. Several caravan parks have fully-equipped caravans for hire on site - see column 59 headed "Caravans to Rent on Site" in the Caravan Park/Camping Site list and also refer to the separate section on "Caravans for Hire on Site" in the Gazetteer.

Firms which offer caravans and/or campmobiles for hire are listed in the Gazetteer under the respective headings of "Trailer Caravans for Hire" and "Campmobiles for Hire" - see index for page numbers.

Camping Sites
While caravan parks are primarily for the use of caravaners, some will permit campers using modern equipment. Where camping sites are available at caravan parks, these have been suitably marked in the Gazetteer section. Bear in mind however, that such parks are more likely to accept campers out of season.

Gas
Gas is available at almost every town and most oil companies encourage their garage outlets to provide this service - hardware stores generally are equipped for this purpose as well. The cost of filling a cylinder varies from place to place, with coastal centres being cheaper. When a cylinder is refilled, the customer should only be charged for the actual amount of gas added to the cylinder to bring it to the required mass, but some suppliers charge a flat rate depending on the capacity of the cylinder, regardless of how much gas is actually supplied. The customer must ensure that he is not overcharged.

Telephone and Postal Codes
These have been included where applicable throughout.

Complaints
Always address complaints to the owner/manager of the establishment concerned. If no satisfaction is obtained, please write promptly and give full details for possible investigation, to: The Director-General,
The Automobile Association of South Africa,
P.O. Box 596,
Johannesburg 2000.

AA OFFICES

HEAD OFFICE: AA House,42 de Villiers Street, Johannesburg (2001)
P.O. Box 596 (2000) Telephone: 28-1400, Telegrams: "FANUMHEAD"

AREA AND REGIONAL OFFICES

Office	Area or Region	Address	Phone	Box No.	Postal Code
Bloemfontein	OFS and Northern Cape	AA House, 56 Church St. (9301)	7-6191	547	(9300)
Cape Town	Cape Western	AA House, 7 Martin Hammerschlag Way, Foreshore (8001)	21-1550	70	(8000)
Durban	Natal	AA House, 537 Smith St. (4001)	6-0341	242	(4000)
East London	Border and Midlands	AA House, 3a Terminus St. (5201)	2-1271	253	(5200)
Johannesburg	Southern Transvaal	AA House, 42 de Villiers St. (2001)	28-1400	7118	(2000)
	City Office	Shop 138, Red Route, Upper Level, Carlton Shopping Centre (2001)	21-2341	7118	(2000)
Port Elizabeth	Eastern Province	AA House, 2 Rink St. (6001)	2-8184	Centrahill 12320	(6006)
Pretoria	Northern Transvaal	AA House, 395 Schoeman St. (0002)	48-3829	477	(0001)
Windhoek	South West Africa Region	Carl List Haus, cor. Kaiser and Peter Müller Sts.	2-4201	61	(9100)

The telegraphic address of all area/regional offices is "FANUM" followed by the name of the city concerned.

BRANCH OFFICES

Office	Address	Phone	Box No.	Postal Code
Bellville	4c Anstey Centre, Teddington St.	97-2593	418	(7530)
Benoni	Lorna Court, 15 Rothsay St.	54-6381	148	(1500)
Bethlehem	30a Oxford St.	4800	152	(9700)
Boksburg	4 Pretoria St.	52-7781	278	(1460)
Brakpan	641 Voortrekker Rd.	55-8373	166	(1540)
Carletonville	87 Annan Rd.	6641	269	(2500)
Ermelo	9 Trust Bank Arcade, Joubert St.	3255	642	(2350)
Florida	Henshell House, 10 Goldman St.	672-3714	19	(1710)
George	Millwood Bldg., cor. York and Victoria Sts.	3041	130	(6530)
Germiston	186 Meyer St.(1401)	825-5170	484	(1400)
Kempton Park	West St. Arcade, 37 West St.	970-1481	178	(1620)
Kimberley	3 Stockdale St. (8301)	2-5207	397	(8300)
Klerksdorp	Clarasan Chambers, cor. Boom and Emily Hobhouse Sts.	2-4781	821	(2570)
Krugersdorp	3 President Bldg., Monument St.	660-7101	537	(1740)
Kruger National Park	Skukuza Rest Camp*	13	13	(1350)
	(* *AA Emergency Service Centre)*	13	13	(1350)
Nelspruit	56 Brown St.	4631	186	(1200)
Newcastle	10 Permanent Plaza, 58 Scott St.	2-1910	2258	(2940)
Paarl	Arcade, Backmin Centre, 39 Lady Grey St. (7646)	2-5634	382	(7620)
Pietermaritzburg	NAU Bldg., cor. Buchanan and Carbineer Sts. (3201)	2-0571	88	(3200)
Pietersburg	Talmot Bldg., 53 Schoeman St.	7-1442	7	(0700)
Pinetown	8 Nedbank Centre, 33 Hill St.	72-9701	301	(3600)
Port Shepstone	35a Wooley St.	2-2213	172	(4240)
Potchefstroom	Johan Dreyer Bldg., cor. Kerk and Potgieter Sts.	5434	397	(2520)
Queenstown	114 Cathcart Rd.	2334	109	(5320)

BRANCH OFFICES

Office	Address	Phone	Box No.	Postal Code
Randburg	79 Crossroads Shopping Centre, Hendrik Verwoerd Drive (2194)	789-1529	P/Bag X3030	(2125)
Rustenburg	146 Smit St.	2-6225	1088	(0300)
Sasolburg	102 Münchner Haus, Civic Centre	6-4572	639	(9570)
Springs	Wima Court, cor. Fourth St. and Fifth Ave.	812-2253	940	(1560)
Upington	Joe Kowen Bldg., 46 Scott St.	4701	83	(8800)
Vanderbijlpark	UBS Bldg., Eric Louw St.	33-1834	480	(1900)
Vereeniging	1a Leslie St.	22-5651	833	(1930)
Welkom	AA House, 327 Stateway	2-4231	741	(9460)
Witbank	Westra Bldg., cor. Haig and Paul Kruger Sts.	6-1231	339	(1035)

The telegraphic address of all offices is "FANUM" followed by the city or town concerned.

AA MUTUAL SUB-OFFICES

Office	Address	Phone	Box No.	Postal Code
Beaufort West	1st Floor, Trust Bank Bldg., Donkin St.	4018	131	(6970)
Kroonstad	17 Fairweather Heights, 25 Brand St.	4423	92	(9500)
Ladysmith	NBS Bldg., 174 Murchison St.	6866	17	(3370)
Nylstroom	Rentmeester Bldg. Arcade, 88 Potgieter St.	557	258	(0510)
Stellenbosch	Trust Bank Centre, Andringa St.	7-0230	369	(7600)
Uitenhage	AA Mutual Centre, Rich St.	2-6014	44	(6230)
Worcester	10 Quenets Arcade, High St.	4658	135	(6850)

The telegraphic address of all AA Mutual sub-offices is "AUTOMUTUAL" followed by the name of the city or town concerned.

AA TECHNICAL CENTRES

AA Technical Centres will be found at all area offices and most branch offices. The following are housed in separate premises at the addresses given hereunder:

Office	Address	Phone	Box No.	Postal Code
Durban	56 Alexandra St.(4001)	31-5808 2-6610	242	(4000)
Johannesburg	22 Sauer St. Ext. (2001)	834-6451	7118	(2000)
Pretoria	577 Voortrekker Rd., Gezina (0084)	76-1138	477	(0001)

OFFICE HOURS

All AA offices are open during the following hours:

Weekdays .... 08 h 30 - 17 h 00
Saturdays .... 08 h 30 - 12 h 30

Emergency breakdown service may be obtained after office hours (i.e. at night, during weekends and on public holidays) from the following offices by telephone:

Bloemfontein	**7-6191**	**Durban**	**6-0341**	**Port Elizabeth**	**2-8184**
Cape Town	**21-1550**	**Johannesburg**	**726-4230**	**Pretoria**	**48-3829**

AA SERVICES

"Is it really necessary and worthwhile?" and "I have been a member for years and have never used any of its services". A question and a statement not infrequently heard when the Automobile Association is discussed by motorists and AA members.

To this question the AA can give a resounding "Yes, certainly" and the statement is easily put in perspective after the member uttering it has been enlightened as to what he has been missing.

There are those members who support the Association largely because of what it does to further and protect the interests of motorists. And that they need protection in this age when as a sector of the community they are heavily overtaxed, cannot be gainsaid. But the member who is doubtful about the value of AA membership has not taken the trouble to read his AA Handbook, issued to him annually on renewal of membership.

Listed in that book he will find reference to the most extensive and useful range of motoring services and aids available to him to ease his cost burden. And at the modest annual subscription of only R8 a year. Put another way: the cost of a daily newspaper a day for 12 months, will cost him more than five times the annual AA subscription. Just one Sunday paper throughout the year will mean twice the AA subscription - leap years excluded!

But proof of the value of membership of the largest and most effective motoring organisation on the African continent can be seen by the fact that the AA of South Africa is supported by more than half a million members.

What are these unparalleled services?

THE CAR THAT CONKS IN

What motorist can claim that his car - used or new - has not left him in the lurch at some time or other, often at the most inconvenient moment. If it happens on the congested city street where "time is money," not only to you but to others held up by your broken down vehicle, help is only a telephone call away if you are an AA member.

In the metropolitan areas like Johannesburg, Cape Town, Durban, Pretoria, Port Elizabeth, Bloemfontein and East London the AA has a radio-controlled service which will bring a patrol to the scene of a breakdown, any time of the day or night, well within the hour - unless weather or other conditions are extremely unfavourable.

In towns or in the country car trouble during office hours need not be expensive if the cause of the breakdown is a minor electrical or mechanical failure - regularly encountered in used and new cars. The AA patrol specialises in diagnosing and fixing the "little troubles" which can spoil your day.

In country areas the AA has contracts with more than 500 garages, appointed to render tow-in services to stranded members. They are situated throughout the Republic, South West Africa/Namibia, Transkei and BophuthaTswana. This service counts among those "unknowns" which a great number of members, despite many years' membership, do not use to their benefit. They seem unaware that a refund of the tow-in service charges can be claimed from the AA as soon as the necessary supporting documents are submitted. The AA Handbook clearly sets out the way in which the tow-in vouchers, forming an integral part of the book, are to be used.

USING THE AA TECHNICAL SERVICES

Many of the AA's caravaners are among those who seem unaware of the ways in which they can consult the Association, free of charge, or use the available technical services which will assist them in planning and enjoying a trouble-free outdoor holiday. Car and caravan can be examined before the holiday - at a nominal charge - and expert advice given on a variety of technical problems. This includes roadworthiness, maintenance or the determination of values prior to sale or purchase.

BOOKING PROBLEMS

At the time of going to press with this guide, the Minister of Tourism had just returned from an overseas trip with the confident prediction that there would be a marked upward trend in the number of overseas visitors to South Africa. An interesting aspect of his forecast was that more and more people who had visited us before as individuals, would now bring their families. This could mean keener competition for South Africans who need hotel accommodation, holiday flats, caravan sites, motel and holiday bookings or guest farms.

Once again the road leads to the nearest AA office, or telephone. Provided the holiday is planned early the AA will secure the necessary accommodation for the member through one of its more than 40 offices.

EMERGENCIES

Holidays need careful budgeting and any emergency which will result in a drain on your holiday cash, could wreck your period "away from it all." While you will have peace of mind when it comes to minor breakdowns, because you are assured of AA patrol or AA-appointed garage assistance, major car trouble could be costly. The preventive here is AA emergency aid vouchers. Worth up to R150, they will take care of emergency car or caravan repairs, tow-in service charges, unforeseen medical expenses and other items. Repayments after your holiday are easily arranged with your AA office.

INSURANCE

Not only the caravan (and its contents if you so wish) may be insured by way of a special AA policy at better than generally competitive rates (see page 4 for details) but you should inquire about AA holiday insurance schemes covering medical, baggage, personal accident and loss of deposits. There is cover for the whole family or special policies covering baggage and personal accident risks.

LEGAL PROBLEMS

By prior arrangement with any AA office members can obtain legal advice from AA-appointed attorneys (the first consultation is free) on any matters arising directly out of the use/ownership of a private motor vehicle.

Free legal defence is provided in any action where a principle is involved which affects the interests of the motoring community as a whole.

MAPS

"I know my way about" are some of the famous last words chronicled. New freeways, national roads, road works which seem to go on endlessly, sudden weather changes, and a multitude of other changing "conditions" bedevil a journey. The AA can smooth the road for you from home to destination, and back, through its unrivalled range of comprehensive maps, map brochures, touring bulletins and information literature which, by and large, are available free.

GOING ABROAD

Tourist traffic is not one-way. Thousands of South Africans still go abroad every year in spite of the high inclusive cost of touring abroad. Check with the AA on the assistance it can give you in a variety of ways. The Association will help you to hire a motorised caravan or car, with or without a trailer, in Britain or on the continent. It will also arrange international camping carnets, international driving permit and introductions to affiliated motoring organisations for you.

BEATING COSTS

On the home front the AA offers the member the advantages of the AA Car, Home and Leisure Plan. This plan provides financial facilities to purchase a caravan, a combi-type vehicle, a motor-boat, a yacht, sailing dinghy, or boat trailer. The scheme offers benefits such as substantially lower hire-purchase finance charges, lower monthly repayments, the advantages of a cash buy and - on an optional basis - automatic settlement of unpaid balance of instalments in the event of the death of the buyer (age limit 18-59). Cars, tennis courts, colour television sets, home improvements and many other items can be paid for with the financial assistance provided under the scheme.

EVERYDAY MOTORING AIDS

A first aid kit, a fire extinguisher, battery cables to start a recalcitrant car, tow ropes, snake-bite outfits, travel bags, ignition drier kits and engine tyre pumps are some of the other motoring items available at all AA offices at special prices to members.

Whether you travel or holiday locally or abroad, the AA is there to help you to plan and enjoy your holiday, indoors or outdoors. And if you can think of any other motoring service which we have not thought of, call, telephone or write and we shall consider its introduction.

CAMPING CARNET

Many members have enjoyed the benefits of the International Camping Carnet in the course of camping and caravan holidays in Europe where it is issued on a huge scale by motoring and camping organisations. Recognised in the United Kingdom, virtually all countries on the Continent and many countries in North Africa, it has been a boon to lovers of the outdoors and particularly to the venturesome who have a yen to experience the outdoors in some foreign country.

In South Africa the camping carnet has been issued exclusively by the AA over a period of more than ten years to members wishing to camp and caravan in Europe and now for the first time its availability is extended to members undertaking caravan or camping holidays in South Africa.

What is the International Camping Carnet?

It is a pocket-sized identity booklet bearing the holder's photograph, name and address, AA number, signature and other identification details.

It contains a description in six different languages of what it is, the benefits it provides and how to use it.

The holder undertakes on behalf of himself and all persons travelling with him in the same private vehicle (maximum 9 persons) to obey the rules of good camping.

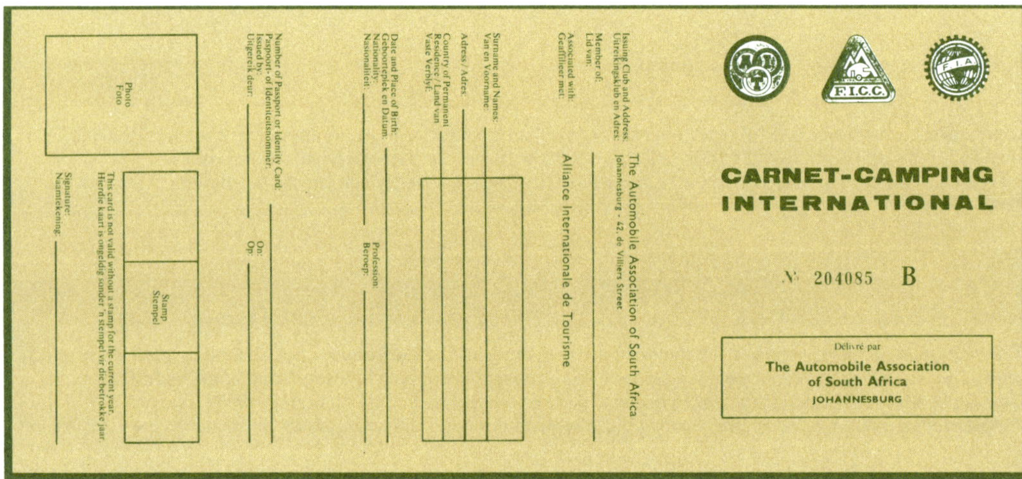

How Does it Operate?

In order to establish his *bona fides* and to encourage good relations, the holder deposits his carnet with the caravan park or camping ground proprietor or supervisor on entering the park/camping ground and collects it again on leaving.

Any complaints in regard to the conduct of the carnet holder or members of his family or other persons travelling with him in the same private vehicle are forwarded by the proprietor or supervisor to the AA.

What are the Benefits of the International Camping Carnet?

1 The holder and his family and any member of his party travelling in the same vehicle (maximum 9 persons) are insured against third party liability, i.e. claims against the holder by third parties for compensation for bodily injury and damage to property resulting from accidents occuring while the holder is camping. Members of the same family are however not regarded as third parties.

1.1 In respect of any one accident the amount of cover for personal injury is approximately R100 000 with a similar amount for loss of or damage to property. The holder may however not admit liability or offer or agree to settle any claim. Members are required to give the AA immediate notice in writing with full particulars of the happening or of any accident likely to give rise to a claim and of the receipt of any notice of any claim or of the institution of any proceedings against the holder of a camping carnet.

1.2 The insurance does not cover claims arising from

1.2.1 bodily injury or disease or damage to property:

- directly or indirectly caused by any mechanically-propelled vehicle
- directly or indirectly caused by any ship, vessel, craft or aircraft, or arising out of any work done therein or thereon by or on behalf of the insured member
- arising out of food or drink poisoning or foreign or deleterious matter in food or drink
- arising out of the pollution of air, water, or soil unless it can be demonstrably proved to have been caused by immediate discharge consequent upon an accident.
- directly or indirectly occasioned by, happening through or in consequence of war, invasion, act of foreign enemy, hostilities (whether war be declared or not), civil war, rebellion, revolution, insurrection or military or usurped power
- directly or indirectly occasioned by, happening through or in consequence of any form of large-scale entertainment where an entry fee is charged (but this shall not exclude small competitions staged for amusement)

1.2.2 bodily injury sustained by any person arising out of and in the course of his employment by the assured association or insured member under a contract of service or apprenticeship with the association or member.

1.2.3 damage to property owned or occupied by or in the care, custody or control, of the insured member or of any servant of the insured member or in the care, custody, or control of any member of his family or of any servant camping with him.

1.2.4 damage to ground or crops caused by trampling or setting up tents

1.2.5 indiscriminate disposal of garbage

1.2.6 damage to underground water-, gas- or electricity pipes or cables

1.2.7 any act committed by insured persons with malicious intent

2 **Personal Accident Insurance**

All persons travelling in the holder's vehicle and camping together are covered as follows:

Loss of index finger	R100	Death	R500
Loss of hearing of one ear	R150	Loss of hearing of both ears	R600
Loss of thumb	R200	Loss or loss of use of arm or hand	R600
Loss of sight of one eye	R300	Loss of sight of both eyes	R1 000
Loss of leg or foot	R500	Permanent total disablement	R1 000

Partial or multiple losses are paid in proportion but not exceeding R1 000 per carnet holder.
In addition, up to R50 is payable for necessary medical expenses incurred within 12 months of the accident.

Limits
Children under 5 years : 50% of benefits - maximum R250
Children 5 to 16 years : 100% of benefits - maximum R500
Maximum age : 70 years

Exclusions
War, rebellion, etc., attempted suicide, intoxication.
Winter sports, mountaineering, hunting, etc., or while boarding or alighting from a vehicle.
Transportation costs for injured or deceased persons, life saving and prosthesis.

3 Because of the protection afforded by the carnet to the holder and caravan and camping ground owners alike, it is inevitable that the latter will tend to favour those who hold camping carnets. This may in turn qualify holders for a reduction in charges at some sites.

4 **How to Obtain a Camping Carnet**

Apply to any AA office – allow a reasonable time for your application to be processed, i.e. at least two weeks before peak holiday seasons.

There is an easy-to-complete application form and one recent clear passport photograph of the applicant is required.

Note: Applicants must have a permanent home address and must not have had a previous withdrawal of a camping carnet because of any infringement of the rules of good camping or camp site regulations.

INSURANCE AND THE CARAVANER

There's a fortune to be made by someone who could design and market a crystal ball which will reveal when and where misfortune may strike. But is it ever likely to happen? Not in this century and probably not in the next one either. In the meantime fortunes will be lost by people who are not insured or inadequately insured – yes, it does cost a fortune at today's inflationary prices to replace possessions like a car and caravan and all the equipment that the ardent caravaner acquires over a period of time. One thing is therefore clear: insurance is vital and it can be obtained at reasonable premiums.

What kind of insurance should you have? Depending upon your circumstances there might be several different items which need to be insured. First of all there is the house - if it is your own. You never know what may happen while you are away on holiday - so make sure you have a house owner's policy to cover you against damage or loss arising from floods, storms, lightning, fire, etc. The premium is nominal and is usually paid to the building society with the bond repayments but it is just as well to check on this - and don't stop the insurance when the bond is fully repaid.

Householder's Policy
The householder's policy covers the contents of the house or flat, outbuildings etc. A variety of different policies are available and some of them like the AA Jumbo policy cover not only the contents of the house (including furs, jewellery, clothing, etc.) but also the contents of deep freezes, veterinary fees for injured pets, accidental damage to television and hi-fi sets, motor-cars, personal accident, and so on. Remember it is unwise and unnecessary to under-insure. To spread the financial burden the premium in respect of combination policies can be paid in monthly instalments.

Having satisfied yourself that all the items at home will be fully insured when you go away, you can now think about insuring the things you will take on holiday with you. So let's begin with the car or towing unit or the motorised caravan. Third party insurance is compulsory and failure to display a valid third party disc renders you liable to the payment of a fine, even if you have obtained the necessary disc and the insurance declaration which goes with it.

Comprehensive Insurance
Also consider comprehensive motor insurance. Here you have a choice of ordinary comprehensive motor insurance policies, combination motor insurance policies (like the AA Jumbo policy which covers the car, household goods etc.) or balance of third party policies with or without fire and theft cover. Balance of third party policies usually cost less than comprehensive policies. This is understandable as damage to the car is not covered - fire and theft risks can however be covered by paying an additional premium. Most comprehensive policies provide cover for the car while a caravan or trailer is towed but it is just as well to satisfy yourself that you are fully covered on this point.

From an insurance point of view a caravan - whether it be the trailer type or motorised type - is just another vehicle. Two different basic types of insurance are applicable - third party which is compulsory for all vehicles, and comprehensive. Fortunately the third party premium for trailer caravans is much lower than the premium for cars, LDVs, etc.

Special AA Caravan Policy
Comprehensive insurance premiums for trailer caravans are also generally lower than they are for motorised vehicles, the premium for the special AA caravan insurance policy being particularly low. It is available exclusively to AA members for their own private caravans - not hired caravans - but not for motorised caravans. Main features of the special AA caravan policy are:

- ☐ the caravan with its fittings and fixtures, tents, awnings and equipment as supplied by the manufacturer is fully covered against loss or damage - except for the first R50 of any claim. As with other comprehensive policies, mechanical and electrical breakdowns, wear and tear etc. are not covered.
- ☐ the policy-holder is covered against claims by third parties (excluding claims by employees or members of the insured's family) for bodily injury, damage to property, etc.
- ☐ the contents of the caravan - i.e. clothing, personal effects, bedding, crockery, cameras, sporting equipment, etc. but not firearms, furs and jewellery can be covered against loss or damage upon payment of an additional premium. Individual items with a value of more than R100 must be specified. Cameras, binoculars, portable radios, sporting equipment and other similar items are however only covered against loss or damage consequent upon forcible and violent entry into the locked caravan - except for this, cover is not restricted to articles inside the caravan - they are also protected as long as they are within the confines of the erected side tent section/s. All claims under this section of the policy are subject to a R50 excess.
- ☐ the caravan may be loaned or hired out to a member of the insured's family residing with him but if loaned or hired out to any other person, there is a premium loading of 50%.
- ☐ the insured may authorise repairs not exceeding R100 provided a detailed estimate is first obtained and immediately forwarded to the AA Mutual.
- ☐ the policy is operative throughout the Republic of South Africa, Botswana, Lesotho, Malawi, South West Africa/Namibia, Swaziland, Rhodesia, Transkei and BophuthaTswana.

Personal Risks
Comprehensive motor policies and combination motor policies provide a certain amount of cover in respect of medical expenses arising from accidents but not from sudden serious illness. Certain travel and holiday insurance policies such as the "AA Holiday Insurance Scheme for the Whole Family" provide cover against medical and other expenses following an accident or illness, loss of deposits through illness or accident, loss of baggage and personal effects and accidental death. The premium of R10 covers the whole family for 31 days. Specific details of the amount of cover provided in respect of each part of the policy may be obtained from any AA office.

Although the AA policies referred to above will generally meet the requirements of most members, it is inevitable that they will not meet all the requirements of all members. The AA's official insurers, the AA Mutual Insurance Association Ltd. with their very wide range of policies are however generally able to tailor any type of policy to meet a member's specific requirements.

THE SOUTH AFRICAN YOUTH HOSTELS ASSOCIATION

Over 60 years ago, a man named Richard Schirrman founded the first Youth Hostel Association in Germany. From very humble beginnings, the movement spread rapidly to other countries and in due course to America, Australia, Asia and Africa. Today the Association embraces most non-communist countries and enjoys its greatest popularity in Europe where it originated.

Internationally, the movement boasts over 6 000 hostels and exceeds four million members. The extent to which youth hostels are promoted and the very definite need which they fill in the lives of everyday people, can be gauged by the "over-night" figures of 7½ million a year recorded by the Deutsche Jugendherbergen (German Youth Hostels Association). It is thus one of the largest travel clubs in the world and helps to promote international understanding and friendship while providing facilities to enable visitors to become familiar with the host country.

Youth Hostels in South Africa
The Youth Hostels movement in South Africa was founded in 1953, following publication of a letter in a local newspaper by a South African who had used the facilities overseas. Branches were established in various large cities and the South African Youth Hostels Association was finally brought into being in 1955. This Association, like those in other countries, is run on a non-profit basis and the hostels in South Africa are managed on an independent basis.

The accommodation offered is provided at cost-price largely because of the devotion of voluntary workers and in some cases, from grants made by generous donors.

Aims
The Youth Hostels Association helps people, young and old, of limited means, to travel inexpensively by providing hostel accommodation where members can stay the night at a reasonable price. It further endeavours to help all, but especially young people, to a better understanding of one another, and to a greater knowledge, love and care of our country.

What hostels are like
Some of the attraction of youth hostels is the variety of accommodation used by the Youth Hostels Association. Places range from huts and farm-houses to mansions and even castles. All provide separate accommodation for men and women, cooking facilities (many provide meals) and a common-room where hostellers can get together to chat, read and meet socially. Beds, mattresses and pillows are provided, but each hosteller *must* provide his own sheet-sleeping bag which is made from cotton sheeting. A flap for a pillow, or for storing folded clothes is attached. These can also be hired from the hostels as sleeping bags are NOT permitted. Each hostel is supervised by a warden who ensures that a high standard of behaviour is maintained. Because of the low cost of staying at hostels, members may be requested to assist with certain chores.

How to join
Obtain and complete an application form and send it to your nearest branch of the Youth Hostels Association or to the National Secretary (see address list following). Enclose a stamped, self-addressed envelope for a reply. Allow at least seven days for the membership card to be returned to you and please mark your application URGENT if leaving South Africa within 10 days of application. Membership can also be obtained from the wardens at hostels.

Membership
NB A membership card is essential for use of the hostels and may be obtained anywhere within the Youth Hostels Movement.

i	International	R13,50
ii	S A Senior (Validity - from October 1st for 15 months)	R 3,00
iii	Life Membership (South African)	R11,00

iv Group - Groups wishing to use Youth Hostels Association facilities may make application for a Leader Card (valid for 10 members). The groups MUST comprise *bona fide* organisations and not individuals wishing to make up parties.
Applications for Leader Cards can be made to the local secretary of the Association. The names of persons utilising these cards must be given to the warden on signing into a hostel. Groups should make arrangements with the hostel warden well in advance so as to afford adequate time for catering arrangements.

Minimum age
The lowest age limit is 10 years and all children under the age of 14 must be accompanied by adults. There is no upper age limit in South Africa.

Hostel charges (usually increased by 20c a year)
At present these are R1,20 per person per night inclusive of bed, blanket and pillow. Members must provide their own sheet-sleeping bag or it can be hired at the hostel. There is no charge for the use of the kitchen, but a fee per meal is payable where these are provided at larger hostels.

Booking
Booking is not essential during the winter season in South Africa, but is advisable in summer. Telephone a few days in advance or write to the warden of the particular hostel enclosing a stamped, addressed envelope for reply.

Cancellations
Cancellation of bookings should be sent to the hostel concerned as soon as possible to avoid other hostellers being turned away unnecessarily.

Equipment
Travel as lightly as possible. If hiking, use a steel-framed rucksack. It is advisable to carry a copy of the IYHA handbook.

Cuisine
A range of typically South African dishes are provided and much of the food is similar to that of Europe.

Special interests
All sports and hobbies are catered for.

Language
The two official languages, English and Afrikaans, are used.

Travelling
Most hostellers resort to hiking, cycling or public transport to get from one place to another. Although motoring and motorcycling are not normally associated with youth hostelling, some continental countries admit motorists. However, preference is always given to non-motorists.

Regulations
Rules in force at youth hostels are very minimal and are intended for the comfort and enjoyment of all concerned. A list of these rules is contained in the I Y H A handbook and hostellers are expected to cheerfully co-operate, as indeed they normally do.

The following are of particular interest and should be noted:

1 Hostels are closed between 10 h 00 and 17 h 00. Members may only stay in hostels between these hours in exceptional cases and with the permission of the warden.

2 Members arriving after 22 h 00 are likely to be refused admission unless permission has been obtained from the warden.

3 Normally members may not stay more than three consecutive nights in one hostel unless beds are available and only at the warden's discretion.

4 No animals or pets are permitted in hostels.

ADDRESSES OF YOUTH HOSTELS IN SOUTH AFRICA

The numbers in brackets following each name indicate the map page and grid reference where the place may be located.

National Office Address
6th Floor, Boston House, Strand Street, Cape Town 8001 Tel. 43-5693 OR
P O Box 4402, CAPE TOWN 8000

CAPE

1 **Beaufort West** (59 A2)
Donkin House, 14 Donkin Street. Telephone 4287 Postal code 6970
This is not a youth hostel and no special rates are available to hostellers - apply for tariffs.
All rooms fully furnished.

2 **Cape Town** (58 C3)
Stan's Halt Youth Hostel, The Glen, Camps Bay. Telephone 48-9037 Postal code 8001
Take Bus No. 3 (Kloof Nek) and follow sign down hill. 30 beds; cooking facilities

3 **Cradock** (59 A5)
Mountain Zebra National Park, National Parks Board, P O Box 787, Pretoria 0001
Telephone 44-1194
2 x 2 bedrooms and 2 x 28 bedrooms. Accommodation available for groups of 15 people.
No cooking facilities. R1,90 per adult per night; R0,90 per child per night.

4 **East London** (60 B2)
Port Rex Youth Hostel, 128 Moore Street, Eastern Beach. Postal code 5201 Telephone 8-7515
R1,50 per person per night.

5 **Graaff-Reinet** (59 A4)
Urquhart House, Market Square, Cnr Somerset and Murray Streets, or P O Box 71,
Telephone 2121 Postal code 6280
7 - 2 bed rondavels, communal kitchen, own cooking utensils required.
R3,00 per night per rondavel.

6 **Hartenbos** (59 C2)
ATKV Camp, Cape of Good Hope Avenue, Telephone 5107 Postal code 6520
Rooms and rondavels - 50c per person per night. Meals available at restaurant at extra cost. This is not a youth hostel.

7 **Hobbiton-on-Hogsback** (60 B1)
Hobbiton-on-Hogsback. Nearest railway station is Alice and then travel by Road Motor Service to Hogsback; then 3 km walk. OR travel by rail to Cathcart with Road Motor Service to Hogsback. This is not open to the general public and caters mainly for under-privileged children. Groups permitted at management's discretion only.

8 **Muizenberg** (58 NS)
Abe Bailey Youth Hostel, Cnr Maynard and Westbury Roads. Telephone 8-4283
Postal code 7945
Take train from city station to False Bay station. The hostel is situated two blocks down from the station. 60 beds. Cooking facilities. R1,20 per person per night. Special family rates - whole family on one card at R5,00 a year. Children under 5 free. Special group rates - 10 persons or less on one card for R3,00.

9 **Port Elizabeth** (59 B5)
Lanherne Youth Hostel, "S" Bend, Humewood. Telephone 2-7739 Postal code 6001
50 beds; cooking facilities. R1,20 per person per night.

10 **Riversdale** (58 D6)
Municipal Camping Site, Meurant Tourist Camp, Meurant Street. Telephone 403. Postal code 6770
Hostellers to consult town clerk for special rate of R1,20 per person per day. 10 rondavels and 1 bungalow. No cooking facilities.

NATAL

1 **Bulwer** (63 A2)
Ashtonvale Guest Farm. Telephone 1602 Postal code 4575
R1,00 per person per night out of season. No hostellers during season.
Swimming, horse-riding, tennis, bowls, TV.

2 **Durban** (63 A4)
1 Cadogan Place, Durban North (Mrs D Griffiths). Telephone 84-2050 Postal code 4051
This is a private home. Breakfast provided, but no cooking facilities.
R1,50 per person per night. Take bus No. 740 from Field Street, Stop 1, beyond Broadway walk in direction of bus to Cadogan Drive on right.

3 **Port Edward** (63 C3)
S.A. Police Holiday Resort, P O Box 22. Telephone 823 Postal code 4295
Travel by rail from Durban to Port Shepstone. Then by Railway bus to Margate and by lift to Port Edward. Bungalows, rondavels, chalets, caravan and tent sites. Tariffs vary depending upon type of accommodation requested.

4 **Winterton** (67 C2)
Kelvin Grove Caravan Park and Camping Hostel. Telephone Winterton 2502 Postal code 3340
From Durban road, take route 35. D277 is Kelvin Grove.
R1,25 per person per day. 6 rooms with beds. Communal kitchen with cooking facilities. Swimming, walks, horse-riding, fishing.

ORANGE FREE STATE

1 **Golden Gate Highlands National Park** (66 C6)
National Parks Board, P O Box 787, Pretoria. Telephone 44-1194 Postal code 0001
2 x 2 bedrooms and 2 x 28 bedrooms. Accommodation available for groups of 15 people. No cooking facilities.
R1,90 per adult per night; R0,90 per child per night.

2 **Parys** (66 A5)
Rotary Club Camp, Sandy Beach. Telephone 2643 Postal code 9585 Furnished rondavels; no cooking facilities.
R1,20 per person per night.

TRANSVAAL

1 **Johannesburg** (68 D6)
Johannesburg Youth Hostel, 32 Main Street, Rosettenville. Telephone 26-8051 Postal code 2190
From city bus terminus, cnr Eloff and Main Streets, catch a Townsview bus (No 47) and alight at Stop 24.
Accommodation for 60 people. Cooking and camping facilities; swimming (municipal pool); film shows; bus tours over weekends; TV. R1,20 per person per night.

2 **Middelburg** (69 C2)
Midland Estate (at brickworks); ± 3 km east of Middelburg on main Eastern Transvaal road. P O Box 111, Telephone 2335
Postal code 1050
This is not a youth hostel and there are no facilities or charges. Hostellers must arrive before 17 h 00.

3 **Schoemansville** (68 NS)
Hartbeespoort Dam Hostel, Hertzog Street (just off corner Monene Street), Schoemansville. Postal code 6635.
Tel. 01211-3071
From Johannesburg take M1 North freeway and turn off into Jan Smuts Avenue until Hyde Park Corner where you turn right to Bryanston after which follows Fourways, then straight on past Riversands farm stall. Further on take the P79-1 road crossing the Hennops River, and on to a 4-way stop street. Continue straight on past Meerhof Rest Camp towards Rustenburg. Approaching the foot of the mountains ahead there are two petrol stations and approximately 200 metres beyond the Caltex station is Monene Street. Follow signs to hostel.
Accommodation for 12 persons. Cooking facilities.

CAMPMOBILES FOR HIRE

TOWN AND ESTABLISHMENT • The postal code is given in brackets following each name • The map page and grid reference follows the town entry • The telephone code is given in brackets following the telephone number • In season = I/S Out of season = O/S	Advance Booking	Makes	Sizes	RATES: Standard	RATES: Unlimited km Rates	Advance Payment/s	Insurance Details	Equipment Included: Refrigerator	Cooker	Wash Basin (Sink)	Cupboards	Lights	Crockery	Cutlery	Cooking Utensils	Side Tent/Awning	Table and/or Chairs	Gas Cylinder	Sleeping Bags	Equipment for Hire: Folding Tables	Folding Chairs	Stretchers	Tents	Gas Lamps	Chemical Toilet	Comments
CAPE TOWN (8001) 58 NS ↑ Hunts Car Hire, 77 Strand St. Tel. 22-9781 (021)		FOR DETAILS SEE HUNTS CAR HIRE, **JOHANNESBURG**																								
DURBAN (4001) 63 NS ↗ Hunts Car Hire, 89 Berea Rd. Tel. 31-8477 (031)		FOR DETAILS SEE HUNTS CAR HIRE, **JOHANNESBURG**																								
Multifleet, 22 Underwood Rd., Pinetown 3600. Tel. 72-2957/72-8836		FOR DETAILS SEE TREKLINER (PTY) LTD., **JOHANNESBURG**																								
JOHANNESBURG (2000) 72 NS • Camp and Live, 62 Blairgowrie Dve., Blairgowrie, Randburg 2194 Tel. 48-5832/3 (011)	★	VW Kombi	2 & 4 berth	R130 per week for 2 persons R160 per week for 4 persons		R75 deposit	Comprehensive Insurance with excess of R150 — can be waived at R2 per day	★	★		★	★	★	★	★	★	★		★				★			
Camp Easy, 205 Duncan Hse., de Villiers St., Tel. 725-4629/834-8529 (011)	I/S	Volkswagen Microbus & Toyota Land Cruiser	Suitable for up to 6 persons	VW: R10 per day plus 10c per km; Toyota: R16 per day plus 12c per km	VW: R22,50 per day Toyota: R36 per day	Estimated cost of hire plus 25% of cost as deposit	Comprehensive Insurance with excess of R220 (VW), R300 (Toyota)		★	★	★	★	★	★	★	★	★	★								Minimum rental period: Weekend
Free Wheel Car and Camper Hire, 50 Twist St., Joubert Park. Tel. 724-6445/724-8710 (011)	★	Volkswagen Fleetline & Hi-Line; Datsun Hi-Line	2 & 4 berth	VW Fleetline (2 berth): R155 per week (incl. 1 750 km); VW Hi-Line (4 berth): R180 per week (incl. 1 750 km); Datsun Hi-Line (4 berth): R190 per week (incl. 1 750 km)	VW Fleetline (2 berth): R465 (3 weeks), R837 (6 weeks); VW Hi-Line (4 berth): R540 (3 weeks), R972 (6 weeks); Datsun Hi-Line (4 berth): R560 (3 weeks), R995 (6 weeks)	R50 deposit plus estimated cost of hire	Comprehensive Insurance with excess of R50	★	★		★	★	★	★	★			★	★	★	★					Free delivery and return to all central hotels, stations, Jan Smuts. Elsewhere at extra charge
Hillbrow Camper Hire, 125 Twist St. P.O. Box 17385, Hillbrow 2038. Tel. 642-2412/643-1318 (011)	★	VW Jurgens Auto-Villa and Auto-Villa L	2-4 berth 2-6 berth	VW A-V: R22 per day (incl. 150 km); VW A-VL: R29 per day (incl. 150 km)	VW A-V: R700 for 3 weeks R33 per extra day; VW A-VL: R820 for 3 weeks plus R33 per extra day	R75 deposit plus estimated cost of hire	Comprehensive Insurance with R200 excess of which R150 can be waived at R12 per week	★	★	★	★	★	★	★	★	★	★	★	★					★		Drop-off charges: Cape Town: R160; Windhoek: R200; Durban: R60
Holiday Car Hire, 205 Commissioner St. Tel. 23-2288 (011)	★	Hi-Ace, Daihatsu, Mazda	2, 3, 4, 5 and 6 berth	R160-R225 per week incl. 250 km per day	Min. 3 weeks hire. Rates on application	Estimated cost of hire plus R100 deposit	Comprehensive Insurance with R250 excess — can be waived at R2 per day	★	★		★	★	★	★	★				★					★	★	Free collection and delivery within 5 km of depot. Airport: R10
Hunts Car Hire, Cnr. Von Wielligh St. & Rosettenville Rd. Tel. 21-8258/21-2531 (011)	★	VW Camper-mobile & and 'Safari' Mobile Mini Home	2, 3 and 4 berth	VW: R143 per week (incl. 200 km per day); 'Safari': R195 per week incl. 1 400 km	VW: R170 per week; 'Safari': R260 per week	Estimated cost of hire plus R75 deposit	Comprehensive Insurance with R200 excess — can be waived at R2 per day	★	★		★	★	★	★	★			★	★				★		★	
Kuoni Travel (Pty) Ltd. Delvers Sq., 91 Kerk St./P.O. Box 10733. Tel. 21-3061/6 (011)	★	Volkswagen, Toyota, Mazda, Daihatsu	2, 3, 4, 5 and 6 berth	On request	From R320-R555 for 2 weeks. High Season: Surcharge of R2 per day. Low Season: 5% discount available	Estimated cost of hire plus deposit of between R100 and R250	Comprehensive Insurance with excess of R150-R250	★	★		★	★	★	★	★				★		★		★	★		International service on five Continents. No collection or delivery on Sundays or public holidays
Lindsay Saker Interrent (Pty) Ltd. Pioneer Hse., 33 Albert St./P.O. Box 3610. Tel. 21-2511. A/Hours: 46-3944 (011)	★	VW Strato-camper, VW Jabula Cruiser, VW Campaneer	2½ and 4½ berth	R12-R18 per day plus 10c per km	From R378-R546 for 2 weeks	Estimated cost of hire plus deposit of R250	Comprehensive Insurance with an excess of R250 — can be waived at R15 per week	★	★	★	★	★	★	★	★		★	★	★	★	★	★	★			Free delivery within a 5 km radius of Lindsay Saker depot. Drop-offs made to Pretoria, Durban, Cape Town, Port Elizabeth, Windhoek at a charge
Self-Drive Motorcaravan, 228 Maritime Hse., Loveday St. Tel. 838-2830/836-0412 (011)	★	VW 'Game-viewer' and VW 'High Roof'	2¼ and 4¼ berth	'Gameviewer' (2¼ berth): R20-R22 per day incl. 170 km; 'High Roof' (4¼ berth): R22-R24 per day incl. 170 km.	'Gameviewer': R26-R28 per day 'High Roof': R28-R30 per day	Estimated cost of hire plus R100 deposit	R2 per day. Min. R25, Max. R50	★	★	★	★	★	★	★	★	★	★	★	★				★			Free delivery in central Johannesburg and city air terminal. Delivery to other cities at a charge
Trekliner (Pty) Ltd., 9 Edenvale Rd., Germiston, or Private Bag 1, Motortown 2111. Tel. 53-8815/6 (011)	★	Trekliner Standard & Deluxe	4 berth	R142-R163 per week incl. 1 000 km.	R483-R555 for 2 weeks	Estimated cost of hire plus R150 deposit	Comprehensive Insurance with excess of R150	★	★	★	★	★	★	★	★		★	★	★				★		★	Free delivery to central hotels, city air terminal and railway station. Delivery to Durban, Cape Town, Windhoek at a charge

TRAILER CARAVANS FOR HIRE

TOWN AND ESTABLISHMENT •The postal code is given in brackets following each name •The map page and grid reference follows the town entry •The telephone code is given in brackets following the telephone number •Advance booking necessary •I/S = In Season O/S = Out of Season	Makes Available	Sizes	CHARGES: In Season	CHARGES: Out of Season	Deposit	Insurance Details	Equipment Included (H = Available for Hire)											Equipment for Hire									Other Information
							Refrigerator	Cooker	Cupboards	Lights	Bedding	Crockery	Cutlery	Cooking Utensils	Side Tent	Table & Chairs	Ground Sheet	Table & Chairs	Stretchers	Bedding	Kitchenware	Side Tent	Gas Bottles	Ground Sheet	Gas Lamps	Braais	
CAPE PROVINCE **Cape Town** 58 NS ↑ Brocaar Caravan Hire, 'Shannon', Ottery Rd., Ottery (7800). Tel. 73-5803 (021)	Jurgens and Sprite	2, 3 and 4 berth	From R7 per day — negotiable for long periods	From R7 per day — negotiable for long periods	R30	Hirer **must** arrange for insurance himself	★	★	★	★		★	★	★	★												
Schus Caravans, 224 Voortrekker Rd., Goodwood (7460). Tel. 98-7821 (021)	All popular makes	2, 3, 4 and 6 berth	From R5 per day plus R5 insurance for period of hire	From R5 per day plus R5 insurance for period of hire	R30	Hirer responsible for first R50 of claim — see also under Charges	★	★	★	★					★			★	★	★	★		★			★	Also have a hire fleet for non-whites
Tyres Caravan Hire Co. (Pty) Ltd., Plantation Rd., Ottery (7800). Tel. 73-3040 (021)	Impala and other recognised makes	2 to 6 berth	From R6 per day plus R3 insurance per week	From R6 per day plus R3 insurance per week	R30	Hirer responsible for first R30 of claim — see also under Charges	★	★	★	★				★								★					Will tow caravans to Peninsula sites
Durbanville 58 D3 ↘ Boland Caravan Hire, 29 Lindenberg Ave., (7550). Tel. 96-1405 (Cape Town) (021)	Cabson, Jurgens, Travelite, Gypsey, Sprite	4 & 6 berth	From R4,50 to R8 per day	From R3,50 to R5,50 per day	R30	Hirer responsible for first R30 of claim	★	★	★	★		★	★	★	★		★	★	★								Will tow caravans to parks in vicinity at fee. (No charge to Bellville and Parow)
East London 60 B2 ↘ Caravan Hire Centre, P.O. Box 5072, Greenfields (5208). Tel. 46-1611 (0431)	Gypsey, Sprite, Jurgens	2, 4 & 6 berth	R10 per day plus 50c per day for gas	R8 per day plus 50c per day for gas	30%		★	★	★	★		★	★	★	★		★		★								Will deliver caravans anywhere in Republic at nominal fee
Verina Caravan Park, Settlers Way, P.O. Box 5102, Greenfields (5208). Tel. 46-1069 (0431)	Jurgens, Sprite	4 & 6 berth	R8 per day plus R2,50 insurance per week	R6 per day plus R2,50 insurance per week	R20	See also under Charges	★	★	★	★		★	★	★	★												
Knysna 59 NS ● Knysna Hire Centre, Main St., P.O. Box 355 (6570). Tel. 154 (04452)	Sprite, Gypsey, Jurgens	4 & 6 berth	R9 to R12 per day	R5 to R7 per day	R40	Hirer responsible for first R40 of claim	★	★	★	★		★	★	★	★		★	★	★	★		★	★	★	★	★	Will tow caravan to any spot along Garden Route at a fee
Port Elizabeth 59 B5 ↘ Conneys Caravan Hire, 241 Highfield Rd., Korsten (6016). Tel. 4-7298 (041)	Sprite, Jurgens, Wayfarer	4, 5 & 6 berth	R45 to R50 per week	R45 to R50 per week	R30		★	★	★	★					★	★							★				Free towing to Humewood Caravan Park; to other centres at a charge
East Cape Caravan Centre, 33 Lower Valley Rd. (6001). Tel. 2-1034 (041)	Sprite, Gypsey	4, 5 & 6 berth	R50 to R60 per week	R35 to R45 per week	R40		★	★	★	★		★			★		★										
EMR Caravan Hire, P.O. Box 2281 (6000) Tel. 7-4912 (041)	Sprite, Jurgens, Gypsey, Travelite, Wanderer	4 & 6 berth	R8,50 per day	R7 per day	•I/S R50; •O/S R30	Hirer responsible for first R50 of claim	★	★	★	★		★		★	★			★									Free towing to Port Elizabeth Municipal parks; at a charge to coastal resorts in Port Elizabeth area
Strand 58 D3 ↗ Karakamp (Pty) Ltd. 271 Main Rd., P.O. Box 344 (7140). Tel. 3-4525/3-6447 (024)	Sprite, Gypsey	4, 5 & 6 berth	R6 to R9 per day	By arrangement	R40	Hirer responsible for first R50 of claim	★	★	★	★		★		★	★		★	★									Will tow to local caravan parks
Strand Caravan Hire, 183 Main Rd., (7140) Tel. 3-3310 (024)	Sprite, Gypsey, Jurgens	4 & 6 berth	R6 to R10 per day	R5 to R9 per day	R30	Hirer responsible for first R50 of claim	★	★	★						★			★			★		★	★			Will tow caravans to parks in vicinity at a fee
NATAL **Pinetown** 63 NS ↗ Natal Caravans (Pty) Ltd., 6 Kirk Rd, P.O. Box 346 (3600). Tel. 72-7291/2 (Durban) (031)	Sprite, '400' Alpine, Musketeer	4 & 6 berth	R45 per week plus R2,50 insurance per week	R45 per week plus R2,50 insurance per week	R30	Hirer responsible for first R50 of claim — see also under Charges	★	★	★	★		H	H		★			★	★	★	★						Will tow caravan if park is within 50 km from Pinetown. (45c per km) Min. charge: R9
ORANGE FREE STATE **Bloemfontein** 66 D4 ↖ G. J. Reyneke Caravans, P.O. Box 2245 (9309) Tel. 22-3961 (051)	Jurgens, Gypsey, Sprite, Slipstream, Venter	4 & 6 berth	R7,50 to R12 per day	R7,50 to R12 per day	R30	Hirer responsible for first R50 of claim	★	★	★	★		★	★		★	★	★						★				Will tow caravans to parks at a charge
TRANSVAAL **Ermelo** 67 A2 → Anita's Caravan Den, 4 Clubway (2350) Tel. 100 (Nucam) (013472)	Jurgens	4, 5 & 6 berth	R6,50 to R9,50 per day	R6,50 to R9,50 per day	R50	Hirer responsible for first R50 of claim	★	★	★	★		★	★	★	★		★										Will tow caravans to parks in vicinity at 16c per km
Germiston 72 NS ↘ Caravan All Services, 25 Russell Rd., Lambton (1401). Tel. 51-1800 (011)	Jurgens, Sprite, Gypsey	4 & 6 berth	From R6,50 per day		R40	Hirer responsible for first R100 of any claim	★	★	★	★	H	H	H	H	★					★	★						
Johannesburg 72 NS ● Caravan Centre, 300 Main Reef Rd., Denver (2094). Tel. 616-2355/6 (011)	Gypsey	4, 5 & 6 berth	R45 to R80 per week	R38 to R68 per week	R30	Hirer responsible for first R50 of any claim	★	★	★	★					★		H							★			Overseas visitors can hire car and caravan fully equipped
Klerksdorp 66 A4 ↓ Mr. G. C. Erasmus, 137 Elandsheuwel St., Songloed (2570). Tel. 2-4087 (018)	Sprite, Gypsey, Jurgens	4, 5 & 6 berth	R4,50 to R9 per day	R3,50 to R8 per day	R30	Hirer responsible for first R50 of claim	★	★	★	★		★			★		★										Will tow caravans to nearby resorts ± 25c per km
Pretoria 68 C6 ↙ J & L Caravan and Trailer Hire, 653 Smook Ave., Roseville (0084). Tel. 75-2756 (012)	Sprite, Gypsey	4, 5 & 6 berth	R6 to R7 per day plus R10 insurance for the period taken	R6 to R7 per day plus R10 insurance for the period taken	R50	Hirer responsible for first R50 of claim — see also under Charges	★	★	★	★		★			★												Will tow caravans to parks in vicinity
Roodepoort 72 NS ↖ Kennis Motors (Witpoortjie) (Pty) Ltd., 6 Ontdekkers Rd. Tel. 664-7000 (011)	Jurgens	4 & 6 berth	R55 to R65 per week	R52 to R62 per week	R50		★	★	★	★					★	★											
Vanderbijlpark 66 A5 ↘ Mr. P. W. Keytel, P.O. Box 549 (1900) Tel. 33-9679 (016)	Sprite	4-6 berth	R6 per day	R6 per day	R30	Hirer responsible for R50 excess	★	★	★	★					★												
Vereeniging 66 A5 ↘ Fireman's Recreation Club, Fire Station, de Villiers Ave. (1930). Tel. 22-4431/2 (016)	Jurgens	4 berth	R6,50 per day plus R3,50 insurance for the period of hire	R6,50 per day plus R3,50 insurance for the period of hire	R20	See under Charges	★	★	★	★		★			★	★											

CARAVANS FOR HIRE ON SITE

TOWN AND ESTABLISHMENT •The postal code is given in brackets following each name •The map page and grid reference follows this entry •The telephone code is given in brackets following the telephone number *means no direct dialling — book a trunk call	Advance Bookings	Number of Caravans Available	Caravan sizes available	Tariffs		Equipment Included											Items for hire					Surroundings
				IN SEASON	OUT OF SEASON	Stove	Refrigerator	Lights	Crockery	Cutlery	Cooking Utensils	Bedding	Side Tent	Folding Tables	Folding Chairs	Groundsheet	Bedding	Stretchers	Gas Lamps	Folding Tables	Folding Chairs	
CAPE PROVINCE						P = Pillows; W/F = Wooden floor; W/A = Fixed wooden awning; S = Sleeping bag; C = Cement slab; M = Mattress																
CAPE PENINSULA **Fish Hoek (7975)** 58 NS ● Sunny Acres Caravan Park, P.O. Box 50. Tel. 82-2913 (021)	★	6	4 & 6 berth	R12-R14 per day	R7-R10 per day	★	★	★	★	★	★		★	★	★							Well-shaded, near to beach
Kraaifontein (7570) 58 D3 ↘ Impala Entertainment Park, Dan King St. Tel. 32-2511 (021)	★	7	4 & 6 berth	R5 per day	R5 per day	★	★	★	★	★	★		★	★	★	★						Plenty of trees; well-shaded
Simonstown (7995) 58 NS ↙ The Blue Lantern Caravan Park, Main Rd. Tel. 86-6184 (021)	★	4	3 & 4 berth	R26-R35 per week	R22-R30 per week	★	★	★	★		★		★			★						Near to beach
Cape St. Francis 59 C4 ↗ Cape St. Francis Caravan Park, P.O. Box 92, Humansdorp (6300). Tel. *17 Cape St. Francis	★	5		R10 per day	R6 per day	★	★	★	★	★	★		★	★	★							Situated on beach
East London and District Glen Muir 60 B3 ↙ P.O. Box 942, East London (5200). Tel. 95-1318 (0431)	★	2		R3 per day	R3 per day	★	★		★	★	★		★									Situated beside a river
Gwenshaw Caravan Park 60 B3 ↙ Eastward Ho, P.O. Box 12, Gonubie (5256). Tel. 94-1710 (0431)	★	3	4 & 6 berth	R5 per day plus park charges	R2,50 per day plus park charges	★	★	★	★	★	★		★			★		★	★	★	★	Grassy sites, well-shaded, near to beach
Pirate's Creek Holiday Resort 60 B2 ↘ P.O. Box 2065, Beacon Bay (5205) Tel. 47-1160/47-2502 (0431)	★	10		R6-R8 per day plus site fees	R5-R6 per day plus site fees	★	★	★	★	★	★		★	★	★	★	★					Situated on a lagoon which offers swimming, fishing, boating and yachting
Pixie Caravan Park 60 B2 ↘ P.O. Box 5072, Greenfields (5208). Tel. 46-1611 (0431)		20		R13 per day	R10 per day	★	★	★	★	★	★		★	★		★		★				Grassy sites; beach in immediate vicinity
Verina Caravan Park 60 B2 ↘ Settler's Way, P.O. Box 5102, Greenfields (5208). Tel. 46-1069 (0431)	★		4 & 6 berth	R10 per day	R8 per day	★	★	★	★	★	★		★									
Yellow Sands Caravan Park 60 B3 ↙ (At Kwelera Mouth) P.O. Box 920, East London (5200). Tel. 95-1336 (0431)	★	2		On application	On application	★	★	★	★	★	★		★	★	★	★						Caravans parked on beachfront beneath the trees
Keurboomsrivier (6601) 59 NS → Lagoon Holiday Resort, P.O. Box 9. Tel. *19 Keurboomsrivier	★	12		On application	On application	★	★	★					★	★	★	★		★		★	★	Situated on the banks of a lagoon; excellent for boating, yachting, skiing, fishing
San Merino Caravan Park, P.O. Box 413, Plettenberg Bay (6600). Tel.* 9 Keurboomsrivier	★	11	4 & 6 berth	R10 per day	R6,50 per day	★	★	★	★	★	★	★	★	★	★							Well-shaded, on banks of river, canoe hire, 6 km from Plettenberg Bay
Klein-Brakrivier (6503) 59 C2 ↖ Riverside Caravan Park, P.O. Box 6. Tel. 6316 (04441)	★	2		R13-R15 per day	R10-R12 per day	★	★	★	★	★	★	P	★	★	★	★						Situated on banks of river
Knysna (6570) 59 NS ● Lagoonside Holiday and Caravan Park, P.O. Box 116. Tel. 341 (04452)	Very Necessary	7	4 & 6 berth	R10-R14 per day	R8 per day	★	★	★	★	★	★		★	★	★	★						Situated on banks of lagoon; grassy sites
Waterways Caravan Park, Main St. P.O. Box 394. Tel. 557 (04452)	★	4	4 & 6 berth	R13 per day (site rental included)	R6-R10 per day (site rental included)	★	★	★	★	★	★		★	★	★	W/F	★					Well-shaded; on Knysna lagoon; braai facilities
Mossel Bay (6500) 59 C2 ↖ Mossel Bay Caravans 5 Star Park, George Rd., P.O. Box 439 Tel. 2604 (04441)	★	40	4 & 6 berth	R6,50-R8,50 per day plus site rental	R6,50-R8,50 per day plus site rental	★	★	★			★		★					★		★	★	Grassy sites; 2 km from beach
Onrus (7201) 58 D4 ← Sherwood Park, Main Rd. P.O. Box 50. Tel. *125 Onrus	★	5		R7-R10 per day	R7-R10 per day	★	★	★	★	★	★		★			★						Grassy sites; well-shaded; 1½ km from beach
Plettenberg Bay (6600) 59 NS → Piesang River Caravan Resort, Beacon Isle Drive, P.O. Box 185. Tel. 244 (04472)	★	12		On application	On application	★	★	★	★	★	★		W/A	★	★							On banks of river; within walking distance of lagoon and beach
Plettenberg Bay Caravan and Camping Park, P.O. Box 73. Tel. 199 (04472)	★	16		On application	On application	★	★	★	★	★	★		★	★	★	★		★	★			Near to lagoon and beach

CARAVANS FOR HIRE ON SITE

TOWN AND ESTABLISHMENT •The postal code is given in brackets following each name •The map page and grid reference follows this entry •The telephone code is given in brackets following the telephone number *means no direct dialling — book a trunk call	Advance Bookings	Number of Caravans Available	Caravan sizes available	Tariffs: IN SEASON	Tariffs: OUT OF SEASON	Equipment Included: Stove	Refrigerator	Lights	Crockery	Cutlery	Cooking Utensils	Bedding	Side Tent	Folding Tables	Folding Chairs	Groundsheet	Items for hire: Bedding	Stretchers	Gas Lamps	Folding Tables	Folding Chairs	Surroundings
CAPE PROVINCE continued						P = Pillows; W/F = Wooden floor; W/A = Fixed wooden awning; S = Sleeping bag; C = Cement slab; M = Mattress																
Port Alfred (6170) 60 C1 ↘ Medolino Caravan Park, 23 Stewart Rd., P.O. Box 20, Kowie West (6171). Tel. 346 (04642)	★	5	4 & 6 berth	R8,75 per night per 2 persons (site fees included)	R5 per night per 2 persons (site fees included)	★	★	★	★		★		★			★	★					Near to shops, main beach and river
Sedgefield (6573) 59 NS ← Jooris Caravan & Camping Park, On Swartvlei, P.O. Box 22. Tel. *940 Sedgefield	★	3	4 berth	R3 per night per person	R2,50 per night per person	★	★	★	★		★		★				★					Situated on Swartvlei; ideal for water sport and fishing. Short distance from many beaches
Lake Pleasant Holiday Resort, P.O. Box 16. Tel. *28 Sedgefield	★	36		R12-R15 per day	On application	★	★	★	★	★	★		★	★	★		★		★	★	★	Situated on Groenvlei; renowned for black bass fishing, boating, yachting
Landfall Caravan Park, P.O. Box 144. Tel. *44 Sedgefield	★	3	3, 5 & 6 berth	R8-R13,50 per day	R6-R10 per day	★	★	★	★	★	★		★	★	★	★						
Stellenbosch 58 C3 ↘ Bergplaas Holiday Ranch, Helshoogte Rd., P.O. Box 2172, Dennesig (7601). Tel. 7-0486 (02231)	★	2	4 & 6 berth	R8-R10 per day	R8-R10 per day	★	★	★	★	★	★		★	★	★	★						Grassy sites; park situated in heart of the wineland
Victoria Bay 59 NS ← Sea Glimpse Holiday Resort, P.O. Box 307, George (6530) Tel. 4660 (0441)	★	3		On application	On application	★	★	★	★	★	★		★	★	★	★	★					Beach in immediate vicinity; grassy sites
Vryburg (8600) 66 A2 ↘ Boereplaas Caravan Park, P.O. Box 539. Tel. 4206 (01451)	★	1		R4,50 per day	R3,50 per day	★	★	★	★	★	★	★	★	★	★							Well-shaded
Wilderness (6560) 59 NS ← Island Lake Caravan Park, P.O. Wilderness. Tel. 9194 (0441)	★	2	Up to 6 berth	R9,50 per day up to 4 persons	R5 per day for 2 persons	★	★	★	★	★	★		★	★	★		★					Situated on Island Lake, 4 km from Wilderness beach. Lake ideal for skiing, yachting and swimming
Siesta Caravan Holiday Resort, P.O. Box 35. Tel. 9197 (0441)	★	4		R8,50 per day for 2 persons	R6 per day for 2 persons	★	★	★	★	★	★		★	★								Touws River runs through park, few minutes drive from beach
The Lakes Holiday and Caravan Resort, P.O. Box 38. Tel. 9701 (0441)	★	10	4 & 6 berth	R12-R16 daily up to 4 persons	R5-R7 daily for 2 persons R9-14 for up to 4 persons	★	★	★	★	★	★		★	★	★	★	★					Situated beside the Touws River, ideal for water sport, short distance from beach
NATAL																						
Clansthal 63 NS ● Clansthal Caravan Park, P.O. Box 154, Umkomaas (4170) Tel. 3-0211 (0323)	★	4		On application	On application	★	★	★	★	★	★		★	★	★	★		★				Situated on beach
Doonside (4125) 63 NS ↗ Pot-Luck Caravan Camp, 5 Topham Rd. Tel. 93-6498 (031)	★	2		R8 per day	R6 per day	★	★	★	★	★	★		★	★	★	★						Shaded sites; beach in immediate vicinity
Ifafa Beach (4185) 63 NS ↙ Ifafa Beach Caravan Park, P.O. Box 10. Tel. 740 (03239)	★	6	Up to 6 berth	R8,50-R10,50 per day plus 75c per person daily	R4,50-R5,50 per day plus 75c per person daily	★	★	★	★	★	★		★	★	★	★						Situated right on beach, also fresh water pool
Ifafa Marina, Ifafa Marina Agencies (Pty) Ltd., Private Bag. Tel. 611 (03239)	★	50	4, 5 & 6 berth	R9-R13 per day plus 80c per person per day	R3,50-R5 per day plus 50c per per person per day	★	★	★					★	★	★	★						Situated on banks of Ifafa lagoon, free ferry service to beach
Illovo Beach (4155) 63 NS ↗ Patlyn Caravan Park, Elizabeth Ave., P.O. Box 11 Tel. 95-1339 (031)	★	5	3, 4 & 6 berth	R11-R12,50 per day	R5,50-R6 per day	★	★	★	★	★	★		★	★	★	★						Well-shaded park, ± 100 m from beach
Margate (4275) 63 NS ↙ De Wet Caravan Park, P.O. Box 71. Tel. 2-1022 (0393)	★	12	4, 5 & 6 berth	R70-R85 per week	R4,50-R5,50 per day	★	★	★	★	★	★		★	★	★	★						Situated on beach; grassy sites
Margate Caravan Park, P.O. Box 288. Tel. 2-0852 (0393)	★	3		R9 per day plus 65c per person per day	R6,50 per day plus 50c per person per day	★	★	★					★	★	★	★	M	★	★	★	★	Beach in the immediate vicinity
Marina Beach 63 NS ↙ Belle Vista Caravan Park, Write to: J. Viljoen, P.O. Box 36, Southbroom (4277). Tel. 1421 (0393)	★	42	4, 5 & 6 berth	R60-R70 per week		★	★	★	★	★	★		★	★	★	C		★				Well-shaded; 2 km from beach
Sherwood Forest Caravan Park, P.O. Box 39 (4281). Tel. 3792 (0393)	★	8		R9 per day	R5 per day	★	★	★	★	★	★		★	★	★	★						Close to beach, well-shaded sites

CARAVANS FOR HIRE ON SITE

TOWN AND ESTABLISHMENT •The postal code is given in brackets following each name •The map page and grid reference follows this entry •The telephone code is given in brackets following the telephone number *means no direct dialling — book a trunk call	Advance Bookings	Number of Caravans Available	Caravan sizes available	Tariffs: IN SEASON	Tariffs: OUT OF SEASON	Equipment Included: Stove	Refrigerator	Lights	Crockery	Cutlery	Cooking Utensils	Bedding	Side Tent	Folding Tables	Folding Chairs	Groundsheet	Items for hire: Bedding	Stretchers	Gas Lamps	Folding Tables	Folding Chairs	Surroundings
NATAL continued						P = Pillows; W/F = Wooden floor; W/A = Fixed wooden awning; S = Sleeping bag; C = Cement slab; M = Mattress																
Mtwalume (4186) 63 NS ● Longbeach Caravan Park, P.O. Box 2. Tel. 711 (03230)	★	30	Up to 6 berth	R12,50 per day for all sizes		★	★	★	★	★	★		★	★	★	★						Near to beach; transport provided
Mtwalume Caravan Park, P.O. Mtwalume. Tel. 761 (03230)	★	3		R14 per day for 4 persons	R8 per day for 4 persons	★	★	★	★	★	★		★	★	★							
Park Rynie (4182) 63·NS ● Rocky Bay Caravan Park, P.O. Box 37. Tel. 2-1701 (0323)	★	8		From R8,50 per day	From R7 per day	★	★	★	★	★	★		★	★	★	★						Grassy sites; beach in immediate vicinity
Pennington (4184) 63 NS ● Pennington Caravan Park, P.O. Box 19. Tel. 5152 (0323)	★	12		R9 per day plus 50c per person per day	R4 per day plus 50c per person per day	★	★	★	★	★	★		★	★	★	★						100 metres from beach
Shelly Beach 63 NS ↙ Blue Seas Caravan Park, P.O. Box 102, St. Michael's-on-Sea (4265). Tel. 5-1049 (0393)	★	1		R11,50 per day plus 50c per person per day	R6 per day plus 50c per person per day	★	★	★	★	★	★	S	★	★	★	★						Park terraced with lawn
Sinkwazi Beach 63 A4 ● Zinkwazi Park, P.O. Box 8, Darnall (4480). Tel. 1912 (032422)	★	4		R16 per day	R12 per day	★	★	★	★	★	★		★	★	★	★						Situated on lagoon by the beach
Southbroom (4277) 63 NS ↙ Paradise Caravan Park, Main Marine Drive, P.O. Box 55 Tel. 3725 (0393)	★	10	4 & 6 berth	R63,50-R80,50 per week	R52,65-R69,65 per week	★	★	★	★	★	★		★	★	★	★						Extensively shaded, grassy sites; beach in immediate vicinity
Umhlanga Rocks (4320) 63 NS ↗ Umhlanga Rocks Caravan Park, P.O. Box 13. Tel. 51-1533(031)	★	5	3, 4 & 6 berth	On application	On application	★	★	★	★	★	★		★	★	★	★		★		★	★	Grassy sites; minutes away from beach
Umtentweni 63 NS ↙ Umtentweni Caravan Park, P.O. Box 44, Sea Park (4241) Tel. 5-0531 (0391)	★	1		R7,60 per day for 2 persons	R7,60 per day for 2 persons	★	★	★	★	★	★		★	★								Beach in immediate vicinity
Uvongo (4270) 63 NS ↙ Oasis Caravan Park, P.O. Box 67. Tel. 5-0778 (0393)	★	2	Up to 6 berth	R9 per day (4 persons); R11 per day (6 persons)	R3 per day (4 persons); R4 per day (6 persons)	★	★	★	★	★	★		★	★	★	★	★					Beach in immediate vicinity
Winklespruit (4145) 63 NS ↗ Karavana Caravan Park, P.O. Box 5. Tel. 95-1747 (031)	★	2		R11 per day for up to 4 persons	R8 per day for up to 4 persons	★	★	★	★	★	★		★	★	★							Situated on beach
Ocean Call Caravan Park, P.O. Box 33. Tel. 95-1744 (031)	★	4		R5,80 per day plus 80c per person	R4 per day plus 80c per person	★	★	★	★	★	★		★	★	★	★		★			★	Park adjoins main beachfront
TRANSVAAL																						
Argent 69 D1 ↗ The Rocks Holiday Resort, P.O. Box 475, Delmas (2210) Tel. 1814 (01572)	★	4	3 & 4 berth	On application	On application	★	★	★	★	★	★											Situated on banks of Wilge River
Eikenhof (1872) 72 NS ↓ Blossom Valley Caravan Park, P.O. Eikenhof. Tel. 943-1508 (011)	★	9	6 berth	R4 per day	R4 per day	★	★	★					★	★	★	★		★				Well-shaded park
Protea Caravan Park, Vereeniging Main Road, P.O. Box 186. Tel. 943-1066 (011)	★	8		R70-R85 per month	R70-R85 per month	★	★	★					★	★	★	★						Swimming pool
Johannesburg 72 NS ↓ Ferreira's Caravan Park, Vereeniging Main Road, P.O. Box 82573, Southdale (2135). Tel. 942-2600 (011)	★	7		R5 per day or R86 per month	R5 per day or R86 per month	★	★	★					★	★	★	★						
Nelspruit (1200) 69 C4 ← Casarina Park, P.O. Box 398. Tel. 4012 (01311)	★	2	4 berth	R8,50 per day	R6,50 per day (up to 4 persons)	★	★	★						★	★							

PETS BOARDING EN ROUTE TO SOME GAME AND NATURE RESERVES

En Route to:	Pets Boarding in:	Name and Address of Kennels:	Tel. Code and No.	Charges	Remarks
CAPE PROVINCE ADDO ELEPHANT NATIONAL PARK	Grahamstown	SPCA, P.O. Box 21, Old Port Elizabeth Rd.	0461 3233	Dogs: 60c per day (2 in a kennel, 50c per day for the 2nd dog) Cats: 35c per day (2 in a cage, 30c per day for the 2nd cat)	Advance booking is advisable as kennels and cages are limited. Dogs to be immunised against distemper and cats against cat flu.
	Port Elizabeth	Copper Dog 'Otel Old Seaview Rd., Mount Pleasant, Walmer.	041 2-6924	70c - 90c per day depending on the size of the animal	Advance booking is advisable
		Framay Kennels, 11th Milestone, Cape Rd., Greenbushes.	041 2-7108	70c - 90c per day depending on the size of the animal	Advance booking is advisable
		SPCA, P.O. Box 7036, 8th Milestone, Cape Rd.	041 30-2281 or 30-3652	60c - R1 per day depending on the size of the animal	Advance booking is advisable
KALAHARI GEMSBOK NATIONAL PARK	Upington	SPCA	0541 2572 (Mrs Neser)	Dogs only: R1 - R1,20 per day depending on the size	Dogs may only be booked in between 17 h 30 and 18 h 30 every day
TSITSIKAMA FOREST AND COASTAL NATIONAL PARKS	Knysna	Moorlands Kennels, P.O. Highway, Dist. Knysna.	04452 5904 (Mrs Sturgess)	50c - R1 per day depending on the size of the animal	Bookings required for Christmas and mid-year holidays. Dogs to be immunised against distemper. Reception hours: Weekdays from 10 h 00 to 17 h 00; Sat. from 10 h 00 to 13 h 00.
NATAL HLUHLUWE, MKUZI, ST. LUCIA AND UMFOLOZI GAME RESERVES	Empangeni	Bulynn Pets Den, 21 Moberly Rd.	0351 2-4447	Dogs: R1 per day - large 80c per day - medium 50c per day - small Cats: 50c per day	
ROYAL NATAL NATIONAL PARK	Ladysmith	Merwood Kennels, Elandslaagte.	0361 112	Dogs: 45c - 75c per day Cats: 40c per day	
		SPCA	0361 2744	Dogs: 50c - 90c per day Cats: 50c per day	
ORANGE FREE STATE GOLDEN GATE HIGHLANDS NATIONAL PARK	Bethlehem	SPCA	01431 3553 (Miss Loubser)	Dogs: 40c - 60c per day depending on the size of the animal	
TRANSVAAL BLYDE RIVER CANYON NATURE RESERVE	Lydenburg	Spitskop Kennels, P.O. Box 142. (Take Roossenekal turn-off; 10 km further turn left at Spitskop, continue for 2 km to the kennels)	013232 1311	Dogs: 75c - R2 per day depending on size during Tvl. School Holidays. 50c - R1,50 per day out of season Cats: 75c per day during Tvl. School Holidays or 50c per day out of season	Advance booking advisable. Special rates for long periods. All pets to be healthy and inoculated.
KRUGER NATIONAL PARK	Plaston	Gundagai Kennels, P.O. Box 106, (Situated on the Andersons' citrus farm)	Plaston 72	From 65c per day for extra small dogs to R1,10 per day for extra large dogs.	It is advisable to book well in advance. Kennels are open every day, including Sun. and Public Holidays until 17 h 00
LOSKOP DAM NATURE RESERVE	Middelburg (Tvl)	SPCA, P.O. Box 400, Wicht St.	01321 4605	Dogs: R1 per day - large 90c per day - medium 60c per day - small Cats: 50c per day	It is advisable to book in advance. Hours of duty: 08 h 00 to 12 h 30 and 14 h 00 to 17 h 00. Sat. 08 h 00 to 12 h 30.

NB. PERSONS REQUIRING BOARDING FOR PETS IN CITIES OR SMALLER CENTRES, SHOULD CONSULT THE LOCAL TELEPHONE DIRECTORY OR SPCA FOR ASSISTANCE.

CARAVAN PARKS AND CAMPING SITES

INTRODUCTION

The caravan parks and camping sites listed cover the whole of South Africa and are arranged alphabetically. Where considered necessary they have been cross-referenced to enable easy location of sites listed under a different name. The information included was compiled from questionnaires completed by owners, managers or supervisors of the various establishments. Where there are gaps in the information given, it is because these facilities are missing or the questionnaire was returned incomplete to the AA. A list of parks which were contacted for information, but failed to respond, is included at the end of the list, but no guarantee can be given that these establishments so listed are still open.

A separate list gives details of facilities for Asians, Blacks and Coloureds.

Recommendation or grading of caravan parks

It is not the AA's practice to grade, appoint or recommend caravan parks or camping sites. Establishments listed are for the benefit and convenience of users. There is no official system of grading or classification of caravan parks in South Africa. However, the Caravan Club of South Africa has introduced a system of recommended parks and lays down certain basic requirements, set out below, with which establishments must comply in order to display the Caravan Club of South Africa's recommended board - see figure 1. These establishments have been marked in the gazetteer section by a dot preceding the name of the place and will serve as a guide to the more discerning traveller.

Figure 1

For the benefit of users the following are some of the more important minimum conditions laid down by the Caravan Club of South Africa (CCSA) with which a caravan park must comply to earn the CCSA's recommendation:

Stands

- ☐ there should not be more than 30 stands per ha.
- ☐ should be of adequate size (at least 10 m x 12 m) to allow for the parking of a caravan and awning and its towing vehicle without overcrowding
- ☐ should be clearly demarcated, reasonably level, well-drained and as far as possible grassed
- ☐ only one caravan or tent should be permitted on each stand with a limit to the number of people who will occupy it
- ☐ shelter in the form of hedges, windbreaks or natural bush should be provided especially at the coast
- ☐ should be so positioned as to avoid flooding during storms
- ☐ there should be one tap for every 4 stands and each tap should have a soak pit
- ☐ there should be no public access across any stand - separate, well-demarcated paths should be provided
- ☐ refuse bins, which must be emptied regularly, should be provided for every 2 stands

Toilet and Dishwashing Facilities

- ☐ Floors should be properly graded for efficient drainage
- ☐ one toilet for every 7 stands or part thereof should be provided in respect of both ladies and gentlemen
- ☐ one wash handbasin and small shelf, hot and cold water and a wall hook should be provided for every 7 stands or part thereof
- ☐ one mirror, a shower cubicle (which should have a section where clothing can be hung without getting wet) and/or baths with hot and cold water should be provided for every 10 stands or part thereof
- ☐ several open-air cold showers should be provided at the coast to ensure that sand is not carried into the ablution blocks
- ☐ the hot water system should be able to cope with the demand from the occupants of the demarcated stands
- ☐ a sufficient number of attendants should be on duty to keep the ablution blocks clean
- ☐ ablution blocks and facilities should be adequately lit during the hours of darkness
- ☐ there should be at least one disposal bin for chemical toilets
- ☐ separate facilities should be provided for the washing of utensils and garments

Roads

- ☐ adequate and durable access roads, along which speeds should be controlled, must be provided

General

- ☐ a superintendent should supervise the running of the park and see to the maintenance of all facilities, including the compliance by patrons with park regulations
- ☐ regulations and tariffs should be prominently displayed
- ☐ adequate security measures should be in force
- ☐ pets, if allowed, should be under the strict control of their owners at all times

EXPLANATION OF ENTRIES

Each entry listed commences with the name of the town in capital letters followed by the map page, alpha-numerical index and direction arrow and then the altitude of the town above sea level, thus

ILLOVO BEACH N 63 NS ˙ S.L.

Beneath the town entry are listed the various establishments at that town in alphabetical order. These entries are in bold type followed by the address to which requests for information/reservations should be sent, together with the postal code, thus

Illovo Beach P.O. Box 19 (4155)
Karridene P.O. Box 20 (4155)
Natalia Holiday Resort Manager, P.O. Box 3 (4155)
Patlyn P.O. Box 11 (4155)

The actual site address is included where applicable on the same line in italic type and is preceded by an open square, thus

☐ *17 Elizabeth Ave.*

The existence of any of the facilities listed under their respective headings is indicated by means of an X in the appropriate column. The absence of an X means that this facility is not available or that information in this regard was not provided at the time.
Please also consult the explanatory notes contained in the heading of each page to be able to fully interpret the information given.

SALES TAX

The tariffs included in the gazetteer are *exclusive* of sales tax. The following is a summary of instances for which visitors to caravan parks will, or will not be liable for tax.

Stand Charges

Sales tax (at 4% of the total charges) is payable on stand charges for any period from 1 to 45 consecutive days. Anyone intending to stay for an *unbroken* period in excess of 45 days, does not pay this tax, unless the person leaves on or before the 45th day in which case tax is payable for the actual period of stay.

Power

Charges for electricity, gas, or water supplied to patrons are not subject to sales tax where:

- ☐ the caravan is connected to plug-in electricity
- ☐ gas is provided through a meter for the heating of water for baths, basins, etc: or where
- ☐ water is supplied for baths, basins, kitchen sinks or through taps for domestic use in caravans

Sales tax is payable on gas supplied in bottles or where gas bottles are supplied for filling.

Admission of day visitors and cars

Day visitors are not required to pay tax on admission fees for themselves or their vehicles.

Boat hire

Charges for the hire of boats by the park owner to patrons is subject to tax.

Appliance hire

Hire charges of 13c or more on freezers, refrigerators, laundry machines and driers or any other domestic appliances owned by a park and rented to patrons are taxable.

Cinema shows

No sales tax is payable for cinema shows given for the entertainment of patrons for which a charge has been made which includes normal entertainment tax.

Servants' accommodation

Tax is payable up to and including 45 days of continuous stay.

CAMPMOBILES FOR HIRE - see page 7

Conditions - a valid driver's licence must be provided and the minimum driver's age ranges from 21 to 25 years depending on the company. Petrol is not included in the rates - the hirer must pay for all petrol. A deposit is necessary to secure a reservation and the estimated cost of the rental for the whole period is required at the time of delivery.

Rates and conditions of hire are subject to change without notice.

TRAILER CARAVANS FOR HIRE - see page 8

Conditions - a valid driver's licence must be produced and a deposit is usually necessary to secure a reservation. The estimated cost of hire for the whole period is payable when the caravan is taken. Normally vehicles should be fitted with a towing bracket although in some instances they may be hired. The hirer should advise his insurance company of his intention to tow a caravan otherwise his car policy could be affected.

Rates and conditions of hire are subject to change without notice.

CARAVAN PARKS AND CAMPING SITES IN SOUTH AFRICA

CARAVAN PARK / CAMP SITE TARIFF CODE – See columns 38–39 (Subject to alteration)

A = Up to R1 | C = R2–R3 | E = R4–R5 | G = R6–R7 | I = R8–R9 | K = R10–R16
B = R1–R2 | D = R3–R4 | F = R5–R6 | H = R7–R8 | J = R9–R10 | O = FREE
X = On Application

Charges are based on family of 2 adults and 2 children under 12 years

ADDITIONAL ACCOMMODATION TARIFF CODE – See columns 57–59 (Subject to alteration)

eg. Bungalows, Cabins, Cottages, Chalets, etc.
A = R1–R3 | C = R5–R7 | E = R9–R11 | G = R13–R15 | I = R17–R19 | K = R21–R30
B = R3–R5 | D = R7–R9 | F = R11–R13 | H = R15–R17 | J = R19–R21 | X = On Application

NB: Where the tariff is given in *italics* it is per person, otherwise per unit

NOTE 1 — **Columns 18, 19, 20,** — X = Stands available but not demarcated or number of stands have not been provided
NOTE 2 — **Column 35** — A = Bookings accepted for additional accommodation only i.e. cottages, bungalows, etc.
NOTE 3 — **Column 37** — Deposit refunded under certain conditions eg. less 10 % ; if site is re-let ; if cancelled well in advance (up to 2 months) or on a doctor's certificate
NOTE 4 — **Column 41** — Reductions allowed on application for youth, church, school or sport groups or caravan rallies
NOTE 5 — **Column 69** — L = Laundry facilities only
NOTE 6 — **Columns 88, 89, 90,** — I = In-Season only ; O = Out-of-Season only; X = On application
NOTE 7 — **Column 96** — I = In-Season only
NOTE 8 — **Column 102** — See section on golf in Outdoor Holiday Guide
NOTE 9 — **Column 107** — See section on freshwater angling in Outdoor Holiday Guide
NOTE 10 — **Column 108** — See section on coastal angling in Outdoor Holiday Guide

Establishments marked thus ● have the Caravan Club of South Africa recommendation — see introduction

ABBREVIATIONS
C = CAPE PROVINCE
N = NATAL
O = ORANGE FREE STATE
T = TRANSVAAL
B = BOPHUTHATSWANA
X = TRANSKEI

TELEPHONE CODE: T = DIAL 0020. BOOK TRUNK CALL. E = DIAL CODE. ASK EXCHANGE FOR NO.

	1 Telephone code	2 Telephone number	3 Owned or supervised by: Privately owned	4 Municipal	5 Divisional council	6 Provincial administration	7 Parks board	8 Site description – Locality: Beach in immediate vicinity	9 Beside river, lake or dam	10 In or near mountain area	11 Within built-up area	12 Nature of ground: Grass	13 Gravel	14 Sand	15 Shade: Unshaded	16 Partly shaded	17 Extensively shaded	18 No. of stands: Caravans only – see note 1	19 Caravans and/or tents	20 Tents only – see note 1	21 Accessibility – Approximate distance from main road to site: On main rd	22 Within 1 km	23 Within 5 km	24 Within 10 km	25 Within 15 km	26 Surface of road approach: Tar	27 Gravel	28 Sand	29 Condition of road approach: Good	30 Fair
ABERDEEN C 59 A4 ← 751m																														
Aberdeen Municipal P.O. Box 30 (6270) ☐ *Andries Pretorius St.*	T	14		X								X					X		13		X					X			X	
ACORNHOEK T See Caravan Parks for Coloureds, Asians and Blacks																														
ADDO C 59 B5 → 35m																														
Addo Elephant National Park National Parks Board, P.O. Box 787, Pretoria 0001	012	44-1194					X					X				X		20					X			X		X	X	
ADELAIDE C 59 A6 ↙ 599m																														
Dunvegan P.O. Box 87 (5760) ☐ *5 Princess St.*	04662 E	180	X						X	X	X	X				X			X		X						X		X	
AGULHAS C 58 D5 ↙ S.L.																														
Agulhas Municipal P.O. Box 178, Bredasdorp 7280 ☐ *Main Rd.*	T	Struisbaai 4212		X				X			X	X		X	X				100		X					X			X	
ALBERTON T 72 NS ↘ 1554m																														
Werda Caravan Park P.O. Box 50025, New Redruth 1452 ☐ *Vereeniging Main Rd.*	011	95-6622	X								X	X					X	30			X					X			X	
ALIWAL NORTH C 62 B4 ↘ 1355m																														
Aliwal North Hot Springs P.O. Box 206 (5530) ☐ *Levy St.*	05512 E	2951		X								X	X			X		300	250	50		X				X			X	
ALOE FJORD T 66 A6 ↙ 1494m																														
Aloe Fjord Pleasure Resort P.O. Box 84200, Greenside, Johannesburg 2034 ☐ *Vaal Dam*	016	4-0133	X						X			X	X	X		X		600	200	260		X					X		X	
AMERSFOORT T 67 B2 ↗ 1664m																														
Amersfoort Municipal P.O. Box 33 (2490) ☐ *Cnr. Plein/Bree Sts.*	013352 E	33		X							X	X				X		15			X					X			X	
ARGENT T 69 D1 ↗ 1547m																														
The Rocks Holiday Resort P.O. Box 475, Delmas 2210 ☐ *Argent/Groenfontein turn-off*	01572 E	1814	X						X			X					X	120		25			X				X		X	
ARNISTON C See Waenhuiskrans																														
ARNOT T 69 C2 ↘ 1684m																														
Uitkyk P.O. Box 50 (1051) ☐ *Middelburg/Belfast Rd.*	T	2621	X									X					X	30		30	X					X			X	
ASTON BAY C 59 C4 ↗ S.L.																														
Aston Bay P.O. Box 50, Jeffreys Bay 6330 ☐ *Barbet Cres.*	T	Jeff/Bay 8	X					X	X			X				X		48					X			X			X	
AUGRABIES C 65 C2 ← 1200m																														
Augrabies Falls National Park National Parks Board, P.O. Box 787, Pretoria 0001 ☐ *13 km from Augrabies*	012	44-1171					X		X				X				X		80			X				X			X	
BADPLAAS T 69 C3 ↓ 1189m																														
Badplaas Mineral Baths P.O. Box 15 (1190)	T	7/8				X			X	X		X				X		120		120		X				X			X	
BALLITOVILLE N 63 A4 ↙ 15m																														
● **Dolphin** P.O. Box 6 (4420) ☐ *Cnr. Dolphin/Compensation Beach Rds.*	032242 E	187	X					X				X					X		83				X			X			X	
BANANA BEACH N 63 NS ↓ 5m																														
Banana Beach Holiday Resort P.O. Box 68, Anerley 4230 ☐ *Lots 98-111, Melville*	0391	3043	X					X	X			X		X		X		45	20	20	X					X			X	
BAPSFONTEIN T 68 C6 ↓ 1612m																														
Bapsfontein P.O. Box 7092, Petit 1512 ☐ *Bapsfontein turn-off, Delmas Highway*	755 E	92	X								X		X				X		X		X					X			X	
BARBERTON T 69 C4 ↙ 877m																														
● **Fitzpatrick** P.O. Box 33 (1300) ☐ *Voortrekker St.*	013142 E	717		X						X	X	X					X		100		X					X			X	
BARKLY EAST C 62 B5 ↓ 1814m																														
Ben Macdhui Town Clerk, P/Bag 102 (5580) ☐ *Brownlee St.*	04542 E	158		X							X		X				X	20		20		X					X		X	
BARRYDALE C 58 C5 ↘ 380m																														
Anna Roux Town Clerk (6750)	02972 E	82		X					X	X	X	X					X	X	X		X						X		X	
BATHURST C 60 C1 ↘ 235m																														
Newton Walker Timm Town Clerk (6166) ☐ *Kings Rd.*	04672 E	17		X							X	X					X	24		10		X					X		X	
BEACH VIEW C 59 C5 S.L.																														
Beach View Dias Divisional Council, P.O. Box 318, Port Elizabeth 6000	041	2-8911			X			X				X	X	X		X		40	38	12		X				X			X	
Maitlands Camping Ground Bookings not accepted ☐ *Maitland River Mouth*	041	7-4884			X			X	X				X	X		X		25		25	X					X			X	
BEACON BAY C See East London																														
BEAUFORT WEST C 59 A2 ↑ 851m																														
Beaufort West Municipal Bookings not accepted ☐ *Donkin St.*	0201	2121		X						X	X	X	X				X		300		X					X			X	
Wagon Wheel Motel P.O. Box 111 (6970) ☐ *2 km from Beaufort West*	0201	2801	X								X			X		X		20		2		X					X		X	
BEDFORDVIEW T 72 NS · 1578m																														
Essexwold P.O. Box 40315, Cleveland 2022 ☐ *Chaucer Rd., St. Andrews*	011	53-4631	X						X		X	X				X			38		X						X			X
BELFAST T 69 C3 ↙ 1970m																														
Belfast Dam Town Clerk, P.O. Box 17 (1100) ☐ *Kruger St.*	0132512 E	291		X					X				X				X		84				X				X		X	
SAR Dam Town Clerk, P.O. Box 17 (1100) ☐ *Duggan St.*	0132512 E	291		X					X				X				X		15			X				X			X	
BELLA VISTA N See Marina Beach																														
BELLVILLE C 58 NS ↗ 120m																														
Gypsy P.O. Box 289 (7530) ☐ *National Rd.*	021	97-2828	X								X	X					X	40	10		X					X			X	
● **Hardekraaltjie** Bookings not accepted ☐ *Voortrekker Rd.*	021	97-1048		X							X	X					X	110		10	X					X			X	

SEASONS · TERMS FOR BOOKINGS · CARAVAN/CAMPING SITE TARIFFS (See heading) · REDUCTIONS ALLOWED FOR · RESTAURANT FACILITIES · TEAROOM/CAFE · SHOPPING FACILITIES (Provisions) · ADDITIONAL ACCOMMODATION AVAILABLE · TARIFF (See heading)

CAMP SITE FACILITIES — I = In-Season only, O = Out-of-Season only, X = On application

SPORTING AND RECREATIONAL FACILITIES — S = On Site, N = Nearby (Up to 20 km away)

33 OUT-OF-SEASON CLOSING DATE	34 RE-OPENING DATE	35 BOOKINGS ACCP./PEAK SNS. – SEE NOTE 2	36 DEPOSIT REQUIRED	37 REFUNDED IF CANCELLED – SEE NOTE 3	38 MAXIMUM IN-SEASON TARIFF	39 MAXIMUM OUT-OF-SEASON TARIFF	40 REDUCTIONS: LONG PERIODS OF STAY	41 GROUPS – SEE NOTE 4	42 AA MEMBERS	43 OTHERS (ON APPLICATION)	44 RESTAURANT: ON SITE	45 WITHIN 5 km OF SITE	46 MORE THAN 5 km FROM SITE	47 TEAROOM/CAFE: ON SITE	48 WITHIN 5 km OF SITE	49 MORE THAN 5 km FROM SITE	50 SHOPPING: ON SITE	51 WITHIN 5 km OF SITE	52 MORE THAN 5 km FROM SITE	53 BUNGALOWS	54 CABINS	55 COTTAGES (RONDAVELS)	56 CHALETS	57 MAXIMUM IN-SEASON TARIFF	58 MAXIMUM OUT-OF-SEASON TARIFF	59 CARAVANS TO RENT ON SITE – SEE SECTION	60 DRINKING WATER: PIPED	61 OTHER	62 BATHS: HOT AND COLD	63 COLD ONLY	64 SHOWERS: HOT AND COLD	65 COLD ONLY	66 WATERBORNE SANITATION	67 WASHBASINS	68 DISHWASHING FACILITIES	69 LAUNDRY AND IRONING FACILITIES – SEE NOTE 5	70 WASHING MACHINES	71 SITE LIT	72 PLUGS FOR RAZORS (VOLTAGE)	73 REFRIGERATORS	74 FIREWOOD/CHARCOAL	75 OPEN FIRE FORBIDDEN	76 CAMP FIRE PERMITTED	77 BRAAI PLACES PROVIDED	78 KITCHEN/COOKING FACILITIES	79 PETROL PUMP ON SITE	80 PETROL PUMP NEARBY	81 CAR REPAIR SHOP NEARBY	82 CAR SERVICING NEARBY	83 GAS SERVICE NEARBY	84 FIRST AID/HOSPITAL/DOCTOR NEARBY	85 POST OFFICE NEARBY	86 SITE GUARDED	87 PETS ALLOWED	88 NON-WHITE SERVANTS: SERVANTS PERMITTED – SEE NOTE 6	89 SERVANTS ACCOM. – SEE NOTE 6	90 SERVANTS FOR HIRE – SEE NOTE 6	91 TYPE OF VEHICLE PERMITTED: CAR AND TRAILER	92 TRUCK 'HORSE' AND SEMI-TRAILER	93 SELF-PROPELLED CARAVANS	94 CHILDRENS' PLAYGROUND	95 TENNIS	96 CINEMA/DRIVE-IN/TV-ROOM – SEE NOTE 7	97 HORSE-RIDING	98 GAMES ROOM	99 TRAMPOLINE	100 BOWLS	101 HOT SPRINGS	102 GOLF: GOLF COURSE – SEE NOTE 8	103 NUMBER OF HOLES	104 MINIATURE	105 MASHIE	106 PUTT-PUTT	107 FISHING: FRESHWATER – SEE NOTE 9	108 SEA – SEE NOTE 10	109 GOGGLE	110 LICENCE REQUIRED	111 SWIMMING: SWIMMING POOL	112 SEA BATHING	113 CHILDRENS' POOL	114 ADULTS ONLY	115 SHARK NETS AT BEACH	116 BOATING: BOATS FOR HIRE	117 POWER	118 SAILING	119 CANOEING	120 PLACES OF INTEREST: HISTORIC	121 SCIENTIFIC	122 NATURAL	123 NOTES
					B	B						X			X			X			X			B	B		X				X		X	X	X									X			X	X	X	X		X		X				X			N	N					N																								
		X	X	X	C	C					X			X			X					X		D	D		X		X		X		X	X	X				220		X		X	X	X	X					X		X		X	X		X	X	X																																	
		X			B	B	X	X	X	X		X			X			X									X				X		X	X	X	X		X	220		X		X	X			X	X	X	X	X	X		X	X		X	X	X	X	S	N	N		S		N		N	18				S			X	S		S				S		S	X	X	X	
					C	C				X		X	X		X	X		X	X			X		C	C		X		X		X		X	X	X			X			X		X	X	X		X	X	X	X	X	X	X	X	X			X	X	X	S	N	N			S	N								N	N			X	N	X		N	N	N	N	X		X	
		X	X	X	D	D							X		X			X									X		X		X		X	X	X	X		X			X			X									X	X				X	X	X																													←	Actually for permanent residents, but caters for en-route stopovers
					B	B						X			X			X		X	X			A	A		X		X		X		X	X	X	X		X	250		X		X	X			X	X	X	X	I	X	X					X	X	X	S	N	N			N	N	S	N	9	X		X	N			X	N		N			N			N	X		X	
		X	X		J	J	X	X			X			X			X					X		E	E		X		X		X		X	X	X	X		X			X	X	X	X		X				X	X		X	X	X	X		X	X	X	S		S	S	S	S							X	S			X			S			S	S	S	S			X	
					A	A						X			X			X									X				X		X	X				X			X		X	X			X	X	X	X	X	X	X	X	X			X		X	S	N												N			X								N	N			X	
					C	C	X				X			X			X			X				X	X	X	X		X		X		X	X	X	X		X			X		X	X		X				X	X		X		X			X	X	X	S	S	S	S	S									S				S		S						S			X	
		X	X	X	X	X	X	X	X		X			X			X					X		X	X		X		X			X	X	X				X			X	X	X	X		X		X		X	X	X	X	X			X	X	X	X	S	N	N	S	N	N	N						X	N			X	S		S									X	
May	Dec.	X	X	X	D	D		X					X			X		X		X		X		G	E		X		X		X		X	X	X	X	X	X			X		X	X			X	X	X			X						X	X	X	N	N	N	N	N	N	N		N	9				S	N			S	X	S	X				N	N		X	X	
		X	X	X	C	C		X			X			X			X			X				I	I		X	X	X		X		X	X	X	X		X	220		X		X	X		X	X	X	X	X	X	X			X		X	X	X	X	S	S																									X	X	X	
					C	C				X	X	X		X	X		X	X		X	X	X	X	B-F	B-F		X		X		X		X	X	X	X	X	X	230		X			X			X	X	X	X	X	X	X				X	X		X	S	S	S	S	S		S	S						N			X	S		S							X		X	
		X	X	X	I	F	X					X			X			X				X		B	B		X		X		X		X	X	X	X	X	X	230		X		X				X	X	X	X	X	X	X					X	X	X	N	N	N		S		N		N	18					S	S	X	S	X	S		X					X	X	X	
		X	X		H	D						X	X	X	X	X		X	X			X	X	K	F		X		X		X		X	X	X	X		X			X		X	X			X	X	X	X		X					X	X	X	X	N	N	S	N		N	N		N	18				X	X	X	X	N	X	S		X						X	X	
					A	A					X			X			X			X				C-D	B		X				X		X	X	X	X		X			X		X	X			X	X	X	X	X	X	X	X	X	X		X	X	X	S	S				N												S		S										
					E	E	X			X		X			X			X				X		X	X		X		X		X		X	X	X	X		X	220		X		X	X			X	X	X	X	X	X	X	X	X			X	X	X	S	N	N	N		N	S		N	9				N			X	N		N							X	X	X	
		X			A	A	X					X			X			X									X		X		X		X	X		X		X			X		X	X			X	X	X	X		X		X				X	X	X	N	N		N			N		N	9				N			X	N		N						N	X	X	X	
					A	A	X	X	X			X			X				X								X	X	X		X		X	X	X	X		X			X		X	X			X	X	X	X		X	X	X	X			X	X	X		N		N				N																					X	
		X			A	A							X					X	X								X		X				X	X	X	X					X		X	X			X	X	X	X	X	X		X	X		X	X	X	X	N	N	N	N	N	N	N		N	18				N	N	N	X	N	X	N	X		N	N		N	X	X	X	
		X			E	D	X				X			X			X						X	E	C		X		X		X	X	X	X	X	X		X			X		X	X							X	X						X		X	N														S				X	S									X	
					B	A						X			X				X								X			X		X	X	X							X		X	X							X							X		X	S																		X										X	
					B	B						X			X			X	X								X	X	X		X		X	X	X	X		X	220		X	X		X			X	X	X	X		X	X	X	X			X		X		N	N	N	N		N		N	18				N			X	N		N				N	N	N	X		X	
		X			B	B	X				X			X				X		X				X	X		X		X		X		X	X									X	X			X	X	X		X	X	X	X	X	X		X	X	X	S	N	N				N		N	18								S		S							X	X	X	
		X	X		D	D	X	X				X			X			X									X		X		X		X	X	X	X		X	220		X		X	X			X	X	X	X	X	X	X	X			X	X	X	X	S	N	N	N	N	N	N		N	18								N		N							X	X	X	
					A	A							X			X			X								X		X		X		X	X	X	X		X	X		X	X	X	X	X		X	X	X	X	X	X	X	X	X		X	X		X		N	N				N		N	9				S			X										X		X	
					A	A						X	X		X	X		X	X								X		X		X		X	X	X	X		X	X		X	X	X	X	X		X	X	X	X	X	X	X	X	X		X	X		X		N	N				N		N	9																	X		X	
		X	X		D	D	X					X						X									X		X		X		X	X	X	X		X	110/220		X		X	X			X	X	X	X	X	X	X					X	X	X	S	N	N	N			N		N	9								S		S							X	X	X	
					C	C						X			X			X									X		X		X		X	X	X	X		X	X					X			X	X	X			X			X			X		X	S	N	N	N			N		N	9								N		N							X	X	X	

CARAVAN PARKS AND CAMPING SITES IN SOUTH AFRICA

CARAVAN PARK / CAMP SITE TARIFF CODE – See columns 38–39 (Subject to alteration)

A = Up to R1 | B = R1–R2 | C = R2–R3 | D = R3–R4 | E = R4–R5 | F = R5–R6 | G = R6–R7 | H = R7–R8 | I = R8–R9 | J = R9–R10 | K = R10–R16 | O = FREE | X = On Application

Charges are based on family of 2 adults and 2 children under 12 years

ADDITIONAL ACCOMMODATION TARIFF CODE – See columns 57–59 (Subject to alteration)

eg. Bungalows, Cabins, Cottages, Chalets, etc.

A = R1–R3 | B = R3–R5 | C = R5–R7 | D = R7–R9 | E = R9–R11 | F = R11–R13 | G = R13–R15 | H = R15–R17 | I = R17–R19 | J = R19–R21 | K = R21–R30 | X = On Application

NB: Where the tariff is given in *italics* it is per person, otherwise per unit

NOTE 1 — **Columns 18, 19, 20**, — X = Stands available but not demarcated or number of stands have not been provided

NOTE 2 — **Column 35** — A = Bookings accepted for additional accommodation only i.e. cottages, bungalows, etc.

NOTE 3 — **Column 37** — Deposit refunded under certain conditions eg. less 10% ; if site is re-let ; if cancelled well in advance (up to 2 months) or on a doctor's certificate

NOTE 4 — **Column 41** — Reductions allowed on application for youth, church, school or sport groups or caravan rallies

NOTE 5 — **Column 69** — L = Laundry facilities only

NOTE 6 — **Columns 88, 89, 90**, — I = In-Season only ; O = Out-of-Season only; X = On application

NOTE 7 — **Column 96** — I = In-Season only

NOTE 8 — **Column 102** — See section on golf in Outdoor Holiday Guide

NOTE 9 — **Column 107** — See section on freshwater angling in Outdoor Holiday Guide

NOTE 10 — **Column 108** — See section on coastal angling in Outdoor Holiday Guide

Establishments marked thus ● have the Caravan Club of South Africa recommendation — see introduction

ABBREVIATIONS

C = CAPE PROVINCE
N = NATAL
O = ORANGE FREE STATE
T = TRANSVAAL
B = BOPHUTHATSWANA
X = TRANSKEI

	TELEPHONE CODE (T = DIAL 0020, BOOK TRUNK CALL; E = DIAL CODE, ASK EXCHANGE FOR NO.)	TELEPHONE NUMBER	OWNED OR SUPERVISED BY: PRIVATELY OWNED	MUNICIPAL	DIVISIONAL COUNCIL	PROVINCIAL COUNCIL	PARKS BOARD ADMINISTRATION	SITE DESCRIPTION – LOCALITY: BEACH IN IMMEDIATE VICINITY	BESIDE RIVER LAKE OR DAM	IN OR NEAR MOUNTAIN AREA	WITHIN BUILT-UP AREA	NATURE OF GROUND: GRASS	GRAVEL	SAND	SHADE: UNSHADED	PARTLY SHADED	EXTENSIVELY SHADED	NO. OF STANDS: CARAVANS ONLY – SEE NOTE 1	CARAVANS AND/OR TENTS – SEE NOTE 1	TENTS ONLY – SEE NOTE 1	ACCESSIBILITY – APPROXIMATE DISTANCE FROM MAIN ROAD TO SITE: ON MAIN RD	WITHIN 1 km	WITHIN 5 km	WITHIN 10 km	WITHIN 15 km	SURFACE OF ROAD APPROACH: TAR	GRAVEL	SAND	CONDITION OF ROAD APPROACH: GOOD	FAIR
	1	2	3	4	5	6	7	8	9	10	11	12	13	14	15	16	17	18	19	20	21	22	23	24	25	26	27	28	29	30
BENONI T 72 NS 1661m																														
● **Fairwinds** P.O. Box 1097 (1500) ☐ *High Rd., Norton Home Estates*	776 E	77	X								X	X					X	22	50		X						X		X	
Sonop P.O. Box 9239, Brentwood Park 1505 ☐ *6 Agate St., Rietpan*	011	973-1489	X								X		X			X	X		59			X				X			X	
BERGVILLE N 67 C2 1139m																														
Bergville Municipal P.O. Box 71 (3350)	03642 E	36		X					X	X		X	X			X			30			X					X			X
BETHAL T 67 A2 1701m																														
Bethal Municipal Park Superintendent, P.O. Box 3 (2310)	01361	2031		X					X			X				X		40	30			X					X		X	
BETHLEHEM O 66 C6 1636m																														
● **Loch Athlone Holiday Resort** P.O. Box 551 (9700) ☐ *2 km from Bethlehem*	01431	5150		X					X			X				X		78		70		X				X			X	
BETHULIE O 62 B3 1308m																														
Frank Gunn Municipal Holiday Resort Town Clerk, P.O. Box 7 (9992) ☐ *At Bethulie Dam*	05862 E	2		X					X			X	X			X		200	200			X					X		X	
BETTY'S BAY C 58 D3 S.L.																														
Hangklip P.O. Betty's Bay 7141 ☐ *Hangklip Rd.*	T	1331	X					X		X				X		X			13				X				X	X		X
BLOEMFONTEIN O 66 D4 1392m																														
Caravan and General Bookings not accepted ☐ *212 Andries Pretorius St.*	051	33-2971/2	X								X		X	X	X	X			20		X						X		X	
Maselspoort Holiday Resort Manager, P.O. Box 288 (9300) ☐ *20 km from Bloemfontein*	051	37848/75932		X					X	X			X				X	40	20					X		X	X		X	X
● **Victoria** Bookings not accepted ☐ *First Ave.*	051	8-3636 x488		X							X	X					X	80								X			X	
BLOEMHOF T 66 B3 1232m																														
Die Hoek Bookings not accepted ☐ *Rivier St.*	018022 E	17/18		X					X			X	X	X	X		X		300			X					X		X	
BLYDE RIVER CANYON NATURE RESERVE T See Graskop																														
BLYTHEDALE N 63 A4 S.L.																														
Blythedale Beach P.O. Box 483, Stanger 4450 ☐ *93 Umvoti Drive*	032412	3504	X					X				X				X			18		X					X			X	
BOESMANSRIVIERMOND C 60 C1 S.L.																														
Boesmansriviermond Town Clerk (6190) ☐ *Main St.*	T	27		X				X				X				X			45			X				X			X	
BOKNES C 60 C1 S.L.																														
Boknes Camping Ground Bookings not accepted					X			X	X		X	X				X			50			X				X			X	
Cannon Rocks P.O. Box 185, Alexandria 6185 ☐ *8 km from Boknes*	04652 E	3612	X					X			X	X				X		60		20			X				X		X	
BOKSBURG T 72 NS 1677m																														
Adventure P.O. Box 13059, Witfield 1467 ☐ *119 Madeley Rd., Boksburg West*	011	826-1074	X								X	X				X		50				X				X			X	
BONTEBOK NATIONAL PARK C See Swellendam																														
BONZA BAY C 60 B2 4m																														
● **Pirate's Creek Holiday Resort** P.O. Box 2065, Beacon Bay 5205	0431	47-1160/47-2502	X					X	X		X	X				X			60				X			X	X		X	
BOSBOKRAND T 69 B4 772m																														
Jock P.O. Box 10 (1280) ☐ *16 km from Bosbokrand*	T	Marite 9901	X							X		X				X		20			X						X			X
BOTHAVILLE O 66 B4 1311m																														
Doring Park P.O. Box 12 (9660)	014142 E	12		x					X				X			X		21				X					X		X	
BRACKENFELL C 58 C3 70m																														
Bracken Park Old Paarl Rd. (7560) ☐ *Old Paarl Rd.*	021	31-1690	X								X	X	X	X	X	X		24	24			X					X		X	
BRAKPAN T 72 NS 1615m																														
Jan Smuts Park P.O. Box 15 (1540) ☐ *Escombe Ave.*	011	55-7711		X					X		X	X				X		20					X					X		X
BRANDFORT O 66 C4 1407m																														
Brandfort Municipal P.O. Box 13 (9400)	05222 E	2		X							X	X	X			X			12		X					X			X	
BREDASDORP C 58 D5 49m																														
Suikerbossie P.O. Box 51 (7280) ☐ *Recreation St.*	02842 E	527		X								X				X			30		X						X		X	
BRENTON-ON-SEA C 59 NS S.L.																														
Lake Brenton Holiday Resort P.O. Box 235, Knysna 6570 ☐ *9 km from Knysna*	04452 E	6104	X					X	X	X		X					X	60		16				X		X			X	
BREYTEN T 69 D2 1794m																														
Lawley Park No facilities, but camping allowed ☐ *Hoy St.*	013452 E	28		X							X	X					X					X				X			X	
BRITSTOWN C 61 B5 1122m																														
Britstown Municipal Town Clerk, P.O. Box 13 (8970) ☐ *Waterkant St.*	05732 E	3		X							X		X			X			30			X					X		X	
BRONKHORSTSPRUIT T 69 C1 1426m																														
Bonamanzi Marina P.O. Box 303 (1020) ☐ *Bronkhorstspruit Dam*	012122 E	3531	X						X	X		X				X		200	50		X					X			X	
BUFFELSBAAI C 59 NS S.L.																														
● **Buffalo Bay** P.O. Box 369, Knysna 6570 ☐ *14 km from Knysna*	04452 E	6213	X					X				X			X			75	5	5				X		X			X	
BULTFONTEIN O 66 C4 1339m																														
Bultfontein Municipal P.O. Box 3 (9670) ☐ *Diamant St.*	05252 E	12		X							X	X				X		20	20			X				X			X	
BURGERSDORP C 68 B4 1388m																														
Shorten Park P.O. Box 13 (5520) ☐ *Pres. Swart Rd.*	05532 E	14 A/H 298		X						X	X	X	X				X	20	20	20		X				X	X		X	

SEASONS · TERMS FOR BOOKINGS · CARAVAN/CAMPING SITE TARIFFS (See heading) · REDUCTIONS ALLOWED FOR · RESTAURANT FACILITIES · TEAROOM/CAFE · SHOPPING FACILITIES (Provisions) · ADDITIONAL ACCOMMODATION AVAILABLE · TARIFF (See heading) · DRINKING WATER · BATHS · SHOWERS

CAMP SITE FACILITIES — I= In-Season only, O=Out-of-Season only, X=On application · NON-WHITE SERVANTS · TYPE OF VEHICLE PERMITTED

SPORTING AND RECREATIONAL FACILITIES — S=On Site, N=Nearby (Up to 20 km away) · GOLF · FISHING · SWIMMING · BOATING · PLACES OF INTEREST · NOTES

33 OUT-OF-SEASON CLOSING DATE	34 RE-OPENING DATE	35 BOOKINGS ACCP. PEAK SNS.-SEE NOTE 2	36 DEPOSIT REQUIRED	37 REFUNDED IF CANCELLED-SEE NOTE 3	38 MAXIMUM IN-SEASON TARIFF	39 MAXIMUM OUT-OF-SEASON TARIFF	40 LONG PERIODS OF STAY	41 GROUPS - SEE NOTE 4	42 AA MEMBERS	43 OTHERS (ON APPLICATION)	44 ON SITE	45 WITHIN 5 km OF SITE	46 MORE THAN 5 km FROM SITE	47 ON SITE	48 WITHIN 5 km OF SITE	49 MORE THAN 5 km FROM SITE	50 ON SITE	51 WITHIN 5 km OF SITE	52 MORE THAN 5 km FROM SITE	53 BUNGALOWS	54 CABINS	55 COTTAGES (RONDAVELS)	56 CHALETS	57 MAXIMUM IN-SEASON TARIFF	58 MAXIMUM OUT-OF-SEASON TARIFF	59 CARAVANS TO RENT ON SITE - SEE SECTION	60 PIPED	61 OTHER	62 HOT AND COLD	63 COLD ONLY	64 HOT AND COLD	65 COLD ONLY	66 WATERBORNE SANITATION	67 WASHBASINS	68 DISHWASHING FACILITIES	69 LAUNDRY AND IRONING FACILITIES - SEE NOTE 5	70 WASHING MACHINES	71 SITE LIT	72 PLUGS FOR RAZORS (VOLTAGE)	73 REFRIGERATORS	74 FIREWOOD/CHARCOAL	75 OPEN FIRE PERMITTED	76 CAMP FIRE FORBIDDEN	77 BRAAI PLACES PROVIDED	78 KITCHEN/COOKING FACILITIES	79 PETROL PUMP ON SITE	80 PETROL PUMP NEARBY	81 CAR REPAIR SHOP NEARBY	82 CAR SERVICING NEARBY	83 GAS SERVICE NEARBY	84 FIRST AID/HOSPITAL/DOCTOR NEARBY	85 POST OFFICE NEARBY	86 SITE GUARDED	87 PETS ALLOWED	88 SERVANTS PERMITTED - SEE NOTE 6	89 SERVANTS ACCOM. - SEE NOTE 6	90 SERVANTS FOR HIRE - SEE NOTE 6	91 CAR AND TRAILER	92 TRUCK, HORSE AND SEMI-TRAILER	93 SELF-PROPELLED CARAVANS	94 CHILDRENS' PLAYGROUND	95 TENNIS	96 CINEMA/DRIVE-IN/TV-ROOM - SEE NOTE 7	97 HORSE-RIDING	98 GAMES ROOM	99 TRAMPOLINE	100 BOWLS	101 HOT SPRINGS	102 GOLF COURSE - SEE NOTE 8	103 NUMBER OF HOLES	104 MINIATURE	105 MASHIE	106 PUTT-PUTT	107 FRESHWATER - SEE NOTE 9	108 SEA - SEE NOTE 10	109 GOGGLE	110 LICENCE REQUIRED	111 SWIMMING POOL	112 SEA BATHING	113 CHILDRENS' POOL	114 ADULTS ONLY	115 SHARK NETS AT BEACH	116 BOATS FOR HIRE	117 POWER	118 SAILING	119 CANOEING	120 HISTORIC	121 SCIENTIFIC	122 NATURAL	123 NOTES
		X	X		D	D	X	X				X			X			X								X		X		X		X	X	X	X	X	X	X		X			X			X	X	X	X	X	X	X		X		X	X		X	S	S	N	N	S	N	N		N	18								S		S										
		X	X	X	E	C	X		X			X			X	X		X	X							X		X		X		X	X	X	X		X					X	X	X		X	X	X	X	X	X	X	X	X	X		X		X	S	N	N	N	S	N	N		N	18								N		N							X			
		X	X		B	B									X			X		X	X	X	X	A	A		X		X		X		X	X	X	X		X	220		X	X	X	X	X		X	X	X	X	X	X			X		X	X		X	N	N					N		N	10				S			X	N						N	N	N	X	X	X	
		X	X	X	B	B						X	X		X	X		X	X							X		X		X		X	X		X		X	X				X				X	X	X			X	X					X		X	S	N		N		N	N		N	9				S		S	X	N		N										
					B	B					X			X					X	X				B-G	B-G		X		X		X		X	X	X	X		X	220	X	X			X			X	X	X	X		X	X	X	X	X	X	X	X	X	S	S	N				S		N	18	X			S			X	S		S			S	S	S	S			X	
		A	A		B	B						X						X				X		C-D	C-D		X		X		X		X	X	X	X		X			X		X	X			X	X	X	X		X		X	X		X	X	X	X	S	N		S	N	S	N							S			X	N		N				S	S	S	X		X	
		X	X	X	C	C			X			X			X				X	X				A	A		X		X		X		X	X	X						X		X	X		X				X	X	X		X	X			X	X	X	S														N	N			X											
					C	C							X		X			X								X		X		X		X	X	X	X		X			X	X		X			X	X	X			X			X			X		X																			N							X			
		X	X	X	A	A					X			X					X	X		X		B-C	A-C		X		X		X		X	X	X	X		X	220		X		X	X			X	X	X	X	X		X					X	X	X	S	S	S						N	18				S			X	S		S			S							
					B	B						X			X			X								X		X		X		X	X	X	X		X	X				X	X			X	X	X	X	X	X	X		X			X	X	X	S	N	N	N	N	N	N		N	18			X					N		N							X		X	
					B	B	X					X	X		X	X		X	X							X		X		X		X	X	X	X		X	X				X	X			X	X	X	X		X	X	X	X			X	X	X	N	S	N				N		N	9		N		S			X	S		S							X		X	
		X	X	X	F	E	X						X	X			X									X		X		X		X	X	X	X		X	X				X	X							X							X	X	X	S	N	N	N	S										N	N	X		X	N		X								
		X	X	X	J	J						X			X			X						F	F		X	X			X		X	X	X	X		X	250		X			X			X	X	X	X	X	X						X	X	X	N	N	N				N									N	N				N				N	N	N				
					A	A							X			X		X								X					X	X	X		L								X			X						X	X	X			X		X		N							N	9					N				X					N		N	X			
		X	X	X	C	C								X			X									X	X	X		X		X	X	X	L					X	X		X		X	X			X				X			X	X	X	S	N	N	N	N	N	N		N	9					N	N		N	X	N							X		X	
					D	D		X	X			X			X			X								X		X		X		X	X	X	X	X	X	X			X	X	X			X	X	X	X	X	X		X				X	X	X	S	N	N	S	S	S	N												S											
		X	X	X	E	C	X		X			X			X			X		X				I	E	X	X		X		X		X	X	X	X	X	X	X		X	X		X			X	X	X	X	X	X		X			X	X	X	X	S	N	N	N	S		N		N	18	X	X	X		N	N		N	X	S			S	S	S	S	X	X	X	
		X	X		B	B				X			X			X	X		X								X		X		X		X	X	X	X		X			X			X										X				X	X	X																															
		X			B	B							X			X			X								X		X		X		X	X	X	X		X	220		X			X			X	X	X	X		X		X	X	X		X	X	X	N	N					N							N			X	N		N										
		X	X		C	C	X					X			X			X								X		X		X		X	X	X	X							X	X			X	X	X	X		X	X	X	X			X		X	N	N							N	18								S		S	X									
					B	B						X	X		X	X		X	X							X		X		X		X	X		X		X	X								X	X	X			X								X	N	N	N	N		N	N		N	18				N			X	N		N			N		N	N			X	
					A	A						X	X			X			X							X		X		X		X	X	X	X		X					X	X			X	X	X	X		X		X				X		X	S	N	N				N		N	9								N		N							X			
					B	B	X	X					X			X			X							X		X		X		X	X	X	X			X					X			X	X	X					X	X			X		X	N	N	N				N		N	9					N				X								X		X	
		X	X	X	E	C							X			X	X		X			X	X	D-I	C-F		X		X		X		X	X	X	X		X			X	X		X			X			X				X	X	X		X		X	S	N	N		S		N		N	18				S	N	S		S	X	S			N	N	N	N	X		X	
					O	O							X			X			X								X																																																																		
					B	B						X			X				X								X				X		X	X	X	X		X	220/250				X	X			X	X	X			X		X	X			X		X		N							N	9								S		N										
		X	X	X	F	F								X			X									X				X		X	X	X						X		X	X		X		X	X			X	X	X	X			X	X	X		N												S			X	S		S				S	S	S	X			
		X	X		X	X						X			X			X								X		X		X		X	X	X	X		X			X	X	X	X			X	X	X	X		X					X	X		X	N	N	N	N			N		N	18					S	S		N	X	N							X	X	X	
		X			B	B							X			X			X								X		X		X		X	X	X	X		X						X			X	X	X			X	X					X		X	S	N	N				N		N	18	X																				
		X			B	B				X		X			X			X								X		X		X		X	X	X	X		X	220			X	X	X			X	X	X	X				X	X			X	X	X	S	S							N	9				N			X	N		N				N	N	N	X		X	

CARAVAN PARKS AND CAMPING SITES IN SOUTH AFRICA

CARAVAN PARK / CAMP SITE TARIFF CODE – See columns 38–39 (Subject to alteration)

A = Up to R1 | C = R2–R3 | E = R4–R5 | G = R6–R7 | I = R8–R9 | K = R10–R16
B = R1–R2 | D = R3–R4 | F = R5–R6 | H = R7–R8 | J = R9–R10 | O = FREE | X = On Application

Charges are based on family of 2 adults and 2 children under 12 years

ADDITIONAL ACCOMMODATION TARIFF CODE – See columns 57–59 (Subject to alteration)
eg. Bungalows, Cabins, Cottages, Chalets, etc.

A = R1–R3 | C = R5–R7 | E = R9–R11 | G = R13–R15 | I = R17–R19 | K = R21–R30
B = R3–R5 | D = R7–R9 | F = R11–R13 | H = R15–R17 | J = R19–R21 | X = On Application

NB: Where the tariff is given in *italics* it is per person, otherwise per unit

NOTE 1 — Column 18, 19, 20, — X = Stands available but not demarcated or number of stands have not been provided
NOTE 2 — Column 35 — A = Bookings accepted for additional accommodation only i.e. cottages, bungalows, etc.
NOTE 3 — Column 37 — Deposit refunded under certain conditions eg. less 10% ; if site is re-let ; if cancelled well in advance (up to 2 months) or on a doctor's certificate
NOTE 4 — Column 41 — Reductions allowed on application for youth, church, school or sport groups or caravan rallies
NOTE 5 — Column 69 — L = Laundry facilities only
NOTE 6 — Columns 88, 89, 90, — I = In-Season only ; O = Out-of Season only; X = On application
NOTE 7 — Column 96 — I = In-Season only
NOTE 8 — Column 102 — See section on golf in Outdoor Holiday Guide
NOTE 9 — Column 107 — See section on freshwater angling in Outdoor Holiday Guide
NOTE 10 — Column 108 — See section on coastal angling in Outdoor Holiday Guide

Establishments marked thus ● have the Caravan Club of South Africa recommendation — see introduction

ABBREVIATIONS
C = CAPE PROVINCE
N = NATAL
O = ORANGE FREE STATE
T = TRANSVAAL
B = BOPHUTHATSWANA
X = TRANSKEI

TELEPHONE CODE: T = DIAL 0020, BOOK TRUNK CALL; E = DIAL CODE, ASK EXCHANGE FOR NO.

Locality / Establishment	1 Telephone code	2 Telephone number	3 Owned: Privately owned	4 Municipal	5 Divisional council	6 Provincial council	7 Parks board administration	8 Locality: Beach in immediate vicinity	9 Beside river, lake or dam	10 In or near mountain area	11 Within built-up area	12 Nature of ground: Grass	13 Gravel	14 Sand	15 Shade: Unshaded	16 Partly shaded	17 Extensively shaded	18 No. of stands: Caravans only – see note 1	19 Caravans and/or tents	20 Tents only – see note 1	21 Distance from main road to site: On main rd	22 Within 1 km	23 Within 5 km	24 Within 10 km	25 Within 15 km	26 Surface of road approach: Tar	27 Gravel	28 Sand	29 Condition of road approach: Good	30 Fair
BUSHBUCKRIDGE T See Bosbokrand																														
BUSHMAN'S RIVER MOUTH C See Boesmansriviermond																														
CALITZDORP C 59 B1 → 238m																														
Calitzdorp Spa Manager, P.O. Box 169 (6660) □ *15 km from Calitzdorp*	T	Olifantsbron 1			X				X	X		X					X		150						X		X		X	
CALVINIA C 61 C1 → 988m																														
Calvinia Municipal Town Clerk, P.O. Box 28 (8190) □ *Tuin St.*	02772 E	241/11		X						X	X		X			X			23		X					X			X	
CANNON ROCKS C See Boknes																														
CAPE PENINSULA C See respectively: • Bellville • Brackenfell • Fish Hoek • Kommetjie • Kuilsrivier • Miller's Point • Milnerton • Muizenberg • Parow • Scarborough • Simonstown																														
CAPE ST. FRANCIS C 59 C4 ↗ 11m																														
Cape St. Francis P.O. Box 92, Humansdorp 6300 □ *Da Gama Rd.*	T	17	X					X				X				X		50			X						X			X
CAPE VIDAL N 67 C5 ↑ 25m																														
Cape Vidal Natal Parks Board, Cape Vidal, P.O. St. Lucia 3836	T	St. Lucia 4					X	X	X			X		X			X		36									X		
CARNARVON C 61 B4 ↙ 1253m																														
Voortrekker Park P.O. Box 10 (7060) □ *Hospital Ave.*	02032 E	116		X							X	X	X				X		X			X					X		X	
CAROLINA T 69 D3 ↖ 1718m																														
Joubert Park Town Clerk, P.O. Box 24 (1185) □ *Voortrekker St.*	013442 E	53		X							X	X				X		30	30		X					X			X	
CATHCART C 60 B2 ← 1135m																														
Cathcart Municipal P.O. Box 35 (5310) □ *Robinson St.*	04562 E	22		X							X	X				X			20		X						X		X	
CATO RIDGE N 63 NS ↗ 753m																														
● Inchanga P.O. Box 111 (3680) □ *1000 Hills Rd., Inchanga West*	032512 E	26	X							X		X				X		59			X					X			X	
CEDARBERG C 58 B4 ↖ 529m																														
Algeria Cedarberg State Forest, P.O. Citrusdal 7340 □ *27 km from Cedarberg*	02682 E	3440							X	X		X		X		X	X	10		26							X		X	
Cedarberg Recreation Area Dwarsrivier, Cedarberg, Citrusdal 7340	02682 E	1521	X						X	X			X	X	X	X	X										X			X
Cedarberg Tourist Park P/Bag Kromrivier, Citrusdal 7340	02682 E	1502	X						X	X		X	X				X		X				X				X			X
CEFANE C 60 B3 ↙ S.L.																														
Cefane Mouth P.O. Box 1474, East London 5200 □ *43 km from East London*	0431	95-1169	X					X	X			X				X		25						X		X	X		X	
CERES C 58 C4 ↖ 457m																														
● Pine Forest Public Resort Manager, P.O. Box 44 (6835) □ *Carson St.*	023312 E	543/613		X						X	X	X	X				X	240		120			X			X			X	
CHAMPAGNE CASTLE N 67 D2 ' 1300m																														
Dragon Peaks Caravan Park P.O. Loskop 3330	T	Dragon Peaks 1	X						X	X		X					X	130		30		X					X			X
CHRISTIANA T 66 B3 ↙ 1209m																														
Christiana Municipal Town Clerk, P.O. Box 13 (2680)	05342 E	13		X					X		X	X	X			X			112			X					X			X
● Rob Ferreira Mineral Baths General Manager, P.O. Box 19 (2680) □ *3 km from Christiana*	05342 E	499				X			X			X				X			400		X					X			X	
CHRISTMAS ROCK C 60 C2 ↗ S.L.																														
Christmas Rock P.O. Kidd's Beach 5264 □ *40 km west of East London*	04323	899	X					X	X			X				X		110	10				X				X			X
CINTSA MOUTH EAST C 60 B3 ↙ S.L.																														
Cintsa Mouth East P.O. Box 1711, East London 5200 □ *40 km from East London*	0431	95-1150	X					X	X			X					X		40				X				X		X	
CINTSA WEST C 60 B3 ↙ S.L.																														
Cintsa Bay Holiday Resort P.O. Box 7045 East London 5200 □ *33 km from East London*	0431	95-1178	X					X				X				X		X		X	X					X			X	
Cintsa West Holiday Resort P.O. Box 2059, Beacon Bay 5205 □ *37 km from East London*	0431	95-1177/6	X					X				X				X		X		X		X				X			X	
CITRUSDAL C 58 B4 ← 152m																														
Hennie van Zyl Tourist Camp Town Clerk, P.O. Box 57 (7340) □ *Oewer St.*	02662 E	81		X					X	X	X	X	X				X		30			X				X			X	
CITRUSDAL DISTRICT See Cedarberg																														
CLANSTHAL N 63 NS • S.L.																														
● Clansthal P.O. Box 154, Umkomaas 4170 □ *South Coast*	0323	3-0211	X					X				X				X			49		X					X			X	
CLANWILLIAM C 58 B3 ↗ 75m																														
Park Camping Site Bookings not accepted □ *Park St.*	02682 E	28		X					X	X	X			X			X	10					X			X			X	
CLARENS O 66 C6 ← 1723m																														
Clarens Municipal P.O. Box 16 (9707) □ *Van Reenen St.*	0143262 E	8		X						X	X		X				X	36		20		X					X		X	
● Glen Reenen Rest Camp National Parks Board, P.O. Box 787, Pretoria 0001 □ *Golden Gate Highlands National Park*	012	44-1194					X			X		X				X			80			X				X			X	
CLOCOLAN O 66 C5 ↓ 1617m																														
Steunmekaar Town Clerk, P.O. Box 24 (9735)	05652 E	24/63		X					X	X		X					X	40	80	150		X					X		X	
COLCHESTER C 59 B5 ↘ S.L.																														
Pearson Park 20 Alcock Rd., Walmer 6065 □ *35 km from Port Elizabeth*	T	9901	X					X	X			X			X			70	X	X		X					X			X
COLENSO N 67 C2 ↘ 962m																														
Colenso Municipal Enquiries: P.O. Box 22 (3360) □ *Botha Rd.*	0362	2111/2		X					X	X	X	X				X			25			X					X			X

OPEN THROUGHOUT THE YEAR

SEASONS: Out-of-season closing date (33)	Re-opening date (34)	TERMS FOR BOOKINGS: Bookings accp./peak sns. – see note 2 (35)	Deposit required (36)	Refunded if cancelled – see note 3 (37)	CARAVAN/CAMPING SITE TARIFFS (See heading): Maximum in-season tariff (38)	Maximum out-of-season tariff (39)	REDUCTIONS ALLOWED FOR: Long periods of stay (40)	Groups – see note 4 (41)	AA members (42)	Others (on application) (43)	RESTAURANT FACILITIES: On site (44)	Within 5 km of site (45)	More than 5 km from site (46)	TEAROOM/CAFE: On site (47)	Within 5 km of site (48)	More than 5 km from site (49)	SHOPPING FACILITIES (Provisions): On site (50)	Within 5 km of site (51)	More than 5 km from site (52)	ADDITIONAL ACCOMMODATION AVAILABLE: Bungalows (53)	Cabins (54)	Cottages (rondavels) (55)	Chalets (56)	TARIFF (See heading): Maximum in-season tariff (57)	Maximum out-of-season tariff (58)	CARAVANS TO RENT ON SITE – SEE SECTION (59)	DRINKING WATER: Piped (60)	Other (61)	BATHS: Hot and cold (62)	Cold only (63)	SHOWERS: Hot and cold (64)	Cold only (65)	CAMP SITE FACILITIES (I = In-Season only, O = Out-of-Season only, X = On application): Waterborne sanitation (66)	Washbasins (67)	Dishwashing facilities (68)	Laundry and ironing facilities – see note 5 (69)	Washing machines (70)	Site lit (71)	Plugs for razors (voltage) (72)	Refrigerators (73)	Firewood/charcoal (74)	Open fire forbidden (75)	Camp fire permitted (76)	Braai places provided (77)	Kitchen/cooking facilities (78)	Petrol pump on site (79)	Petrol pump nearby (80)	Car repair shop nearby (81)	Car servicing nearby (82)	Gas service nearby (83)	First aid/hospital/doctor nearby (84)	Post office nearby (85)	Site guarded (86)	Pets allowed (87)	NON-WHITE SERVANTS: Servants permitted – see note 6 (88)	Servants accom. – see note 6 (89)	Servants for hire – see note 6 (90)	TYPE OF VEHICLE PERMITTED: Car and trailer (91)	Truck 'horse' and semi-trailer (92)	Self-propelled caravans (93)	SPORTING AND RECREATIONAL FACILITIES (S = On Site, N = Nearby (Up to 20 km away)): Childrens playground (94)	Tennis (95)	Cinema/drive-in/TV-room – see note 7 (96)	Horse-riding (97)	Games room (98)	Trampoline (99)	Bowls (100)	Hot springs (101)	GOLF: Golf course – see note 8 (102)	Number of holes (103)	Miniature (104)	Mashie (105)	Putt-putt (106)	FISHING: Freshwater – see note 9 (107)	Sea – see note 10 (108)	Goggle (109)	Licence required (110)	SWIMMING: Swimming pool (111)	Sea bathing (112)	Childrens pool (113)	Adults only (114)	Shark nets at beach (115)	BOATING: Boats for hire (116)	Power (117)	Sailing (118)	Canoeing (119)	PLACES OF INTEREST: Historic (120)	Scientific (121)	Natural (122)	NOTES (123)
		X	X		C	C					X			X			X	X	X	X			X	D-F	B-C		X		X		X		X	X	X	X		X	225	X	X		X	X	X	X				X	X		X					X	X	X	S	N	N	N		N		S						N			X	S		S							X		X	
		X			B	B						X			X			X									X		X		X		X	X	X	X		X	220		X			X			X	X	X	X	X	X	X	X				X	X	X	S	N	N						N	18				N				S		S							X		X	
		X	X		E	E	X	X						X			X	X								X	X		X		X		X	X	X	L					X		X	X			X			X	X	X	X	X	X			X	X	X		N		N	S				N	9					N	N			X						N				X	
		X	X		X	X							X			X			X								X														X		X																X																	N	N	X		X										X	
					C	C							X						X								X		X		X		X	X	X	X		X					X	X			X	X	X	X	X	X	X	X	X			X	X	X	S	N	N	N			S		N	18								N		N									X	
		X			A	A	X					X			X			X									X		X		X		X	X	X	X		X					X	X			X	X	X	X	X	X	X	X	X			X	X	X	S	N	N				N	N	N	9				N			X										X		X	
					B	B							X			X			X								X		X			X	X	X									X	X			X	X	X	X		X	X	X	X			X		X	S	N					N		N	9				N			X	S		S					N	N	X	X	X	
		X	X	X	E	D	X						X		X	X		X	X								X		X		X		X	X	X	X	X		X		X	X					X	X	X				X	X			X	X		X	S	S		N	S		S							S																X	
		X			A	A													X								X	X	X		X		X	X	X	L					X	X	X	X															X		X	S													N			X	S						N	N	N	X		X	
June	Sept.	X			A	A		X										X	X			X		D	D		X														X		X				X			X	X	X			X			X		X																												X		X	Surroundings ideal for mountain climbing
					C	C												X				X		F	F		X	X			X		X	X	X	X				X	X		X	X		X				X		X	X					X		X														N													X		X	
		X	X	X	C	B	X					X			X			X				X		C	B		X		X		X		X	X		X					X	X		X			X			X				X			X	X		X	S	S	N		S									N	N				X										X	
		X	X		B	B						X		X	X	X		X		X	X	X		A-F	A-E		X		X		X		X	X	X	X		X	X		X		X	X			X	X	X	X	X	X	X		X		X	X	X	X	S	N	N	N		N	N	N	N	9				N			X	S		S			S			S	X		X	
		X	X		H	D	X	X				X		X			X					X	X	F	C	X	X		X		X		X	X	X	X	X	X	230		X		X			X		X	X	X	X	X	X	X	X			X		X	S	S	S	S	S	N	N		N	9				S			X	S									X		X	
		X	X		B	B							X			X			X								X				X	X	X	X									X				X	X	X	X		X		X				X	X	X	N	N	N	N		N	N	N	N	9	N			S		S	X	N		N				S	S	S			X	
		A	A	A	D	D					X	X	X	X	X	X	X	X	X			X		G	G		X		X		X		X	X	X	X		X	220		X		X	X		X	X	X	X	X	X	X	X		X	X		X		X	S	S	S	S	S		S	S	N	9				S			X	S		S				N	N	N	X			
		X	X	X	E	D	X								X		X	X	X								X		X		X		X	X	X	L					X		X				X	X	X	X		X		X			X	X		X	S	N	I	N	S		N							S	S	S			X	S				S		S			X	
		X	X		E	D	X	X	X	X			X		X			X									X		X		X		X	X	X	X		X			X	X	X	X			X			X	X		X	X	X		X	X	X	X	N	N	N	N	N										S	S			X	N				N	N	N			X	
		X	X		E	E					X	X		X	X		X	X		X		X		C	C		X		X		X		X	X	X	X		X	X	X	X		X	X	X		X	X	X	X	X	X	X		X	X	X	X	X	X	S	S	S	N	S										N				X	S									X	
		X	X		D	C	X				X			X			X					X	X	D-G	C-E		X	X		X	X		X	X		X		X						X			X	X	X	X		X			X	X	X	X	X	X	S	S	N	S	S		N								S	S			X	S				S					X	
					C	C						X	X		X	X		X	X								X		X		X		X	X	X	X		X	110/220		X	X	X	X			X	X	X	X	X	X	X	X	X			X	X	X	N	N	N					N						N			X										X		X	
		X	X	X	F	G	X						X			X	X		X							X	X		X		X			X	X	X	X	X	X	X		X		X			X	X	X	X		X		X	X			X		X	S	N	N		S		N		N	18					N	N	X	S		S										
					B	B							X			X			X								X				X		X	X	X	X		X			X		X	X			X	X	X	X	X	X			X		X	X		X	N	N		N					N	9	N			N			X										X		X	
		X	X		C	C	X	X	X			X			X			X									X	X	X		X		X	X	X	X		X	X		X		X	X			X	X	X	X	X	X	X	X	X		X	X	X	X	S	N	N	N			N							N			X	N		N							X	X	X	
		X	X	X	C	C					X			X			X			X			X	D	D		X		X		X		X	X	X	X			110/220		X	X	X	X	X	X				X	X	X	X					X	X	X		S		S			S		S	9																			X	
					A	A	X					X	X					X									X		X		X		X	X	X	X	X	X	X		X	X	X	X			X	X	X	X	X	X	X	X			X	X		X	N	N					N		N	9				N			X	N		N							N	X		X	
		X	X		C	C		X							X	X		X	X	X				B	B		X	X	X		X		X	X	X	X		X			X		X	X			X			X		X		X			X	X	X	X	S														N				X				S	S	S	S			X	
					B	B							X			X			X								X				X		X	X	X			X					X		X		X	X	X			X		X				X	X	X		N					N							S			X	N		N							X		X	

CARAVAN PARKS AND CAMPING SITES IN SOUTH AFRICA

CARAVAN PARK / CAMP SITE TARIFF CODE — See columns 38–39 (Subject to alteration)

A = Up to R1 | B = R1–R2 | C = R2–R3 | D = R3–R4 | E = R4–R5 | F = R5–R6 | G = R6–R7 | H = R7–R8 | I = R8–R9 | J = R9–R10 | K = R10–R16 | O = FREE | X = On Application

Charges are based on family of 2 adults and 2 children under 12 years

ADDITIONAL ACCOMMODATION TARIFF CODE — See columns 57–59 (Subject to alteration)

eg. Bungalows, Cabins, Cottages, Chalets, etc.

A = R1–R3 | B = R3–R5 | C = R5–R7 | D = R7–R9 | E = R9–R11 | F = R11–R13 | G = R13–R15 | H = R15–R17 | I = R17–R19 | J = R19–R21 | K = R21–R30 | X = On Application

NB: Where the tariff is given in *italics* it is per person, otherwise per unit

NOTE 1 — Columns 18, 19, 20, — X = Stands available but not demarcated or number of stands have not been provided

NOTE 2 — Column 35 — A = Bookings accepted for additional accommodation only i.e. cottages, bungalows, etc.

NOTE 3 — Column 37 — Deposit refunded under certain conditions eg less 10% ; if site is re-let ; if cancelled well in advance (up to 2 months) or on a doctor's certificate

NOTE 4 — Column 41 — Reductions allowed on application for youth, church, school or sport groups or caravan rallies

NOTE 5 — Column 69 — L = Laundry facilities only

NOTE 6 — Columns 88, 89, 90, — I = In-Season only ; O = Out-of Season only; X = On application

NOTE 7 — Column 96 — I = In-Season only

NOTE 8 — Column 102 — See section on golf in Outdoor Holiday Guide

NOTE 9 — Column 107 — See section on freshwater angling in Outdoor Holiday Guide

NOTE 10 — Column 108 — See section on coastal angling in Outdoor Holiday Guide

Establishments marked thus ● have the Caravan Club of South Africa recommendation — see introduction

ABBREVIATIONS

C = CAPE PROVINCE
N = NATAL
O = ORANGE FREE STATE
T = TRANSVAAL
B = BOPHUTHATSWANA
X = TRANSKEI

	TELEPHONE CODE (T = DIAL 0020, BOOK TRUNK CALL; E = DIAL CODE, ASK EXCHANGE FOR NO.)	TELEPHONE NUMBER	OWNED OR SUPERVISED BY: PRIVATELY OWNED	MUNICIPAL	DIVISIONAL COUNCIL	PROVINCIAL ADMINISTRATION	PARKS BOARD	SITE DESCRIPTION — LOCALITY: BEACH IN IMMEDIATE VICINITY	BESIDE RIVER, LAKE OR DAM	IN OR NEAR MOUNTAIN AREA	WITHIN BUILT-UP AREA	NATURE OF GROUND: GRASS	GRAVEL	SAND	SHADE: UNSHADED	PARTLY SHADED	EXTENSIVELY SHADED	NO. OF STANDS: CARAVANS ONLY – SEE NOTE 1	CARAVANS AND/OR TENTS	TENTS ONLY – SEE NOTE 1	ACCESSIBILITY — APPROXIMATE DISTANCE FROM MAIN ROAD TO SITE: ON MAIN RD	WITHIN 1 km	WITHIN 5 km	WITHIN 10 km	WITHIN 15 km	SURFACE OF ROAD APPROACH: TAR	GRAVEL	SAND	CONDITION OF ROAD APPROACH: GOOD	FAIR
	1	2	3	4	5	6	7	8	9	10	11	12	13	14	15	16	17	18	19	20	21	22	23	24	25	26	27	28	29	30
COLESBERG C 62 B3 ↙ 1343m																														
Colesberg Municipal P.O. Box 39 (5980)	05852 E	20		X						X	X	X	X		X			100	130			X					X		X	
Van Zyls Motel Park P.O. Box 50 (5980) ☐ *8 km from Colesberg*	05852 E	1513	X																15		X									
CRADOCK C 59 A5 ↗ 879m																														
Cradock Municipal P.O. Box 24 (5880) ☐ *Stockenstroom St.*	04812 E	719		X							X	X					X	50		50		X				X			X	
● Doornfontein P.O. Box 261 (5880) ☐ *29 km from Cradock*	04812 E	4922	X							X		X				X			X				X				X		X	
Karoo Sulphur Springs P.O. Box 24 (5880) ☐ *4 km from Cradock*	04812 E	1281		X					X			X					X		60			X					X		X	
Mountain Zebra National Park National Parks Board, P.O. Box 787, Pretoria 0001	04812 E	2113					X			X			X		X				X						X		X			X
DANIELSKUIL C 65 C5 ' 1463m																														
Danielskuil Municipal P.O. Box 43 (8405)	05381 E	13		X							X		X				X		60				X				X			X
DARNALL N See Caravan Parks for Coloureds, Asians and Blacks																														
DE AAR C 63 B2 ↙ 1243m																														
Van Der Merwe Town Clerk, P.O. Box 42 (7000) ☐ *Cilliers St.*	0571	2131		X							X			X			X		13			X				X			X	
DELPORTSHOOP C 66 C2 ↘ 1023m																														
Undeveloped area at the confluence of Vaal and Harts Rivers, but camping allowed Enquiries: Town Clerk, P.O. Box 7 (8377)	T	7		X					X			X				X		X	X	X			X			X				X
DENEYSVILLE T 66 A6 ↙ 1494m																														
Deneysville Municipal Bookings not accepted ☐ *Vaal Dam*	T	22		X					X		X	X				X						X				X			X	
Vaal Dam Nature Reserve Bookings not accepted ☐ *Dam Wall*						X			X				X				X		30				X			X			X	
DENNILTON T 69 C2 ↘ 1265m																														
Benmari Mineral Baths P.O. Box 197, Groblersdal 0470	T	Benmari 2	X						X			X				X		200		20				X			X		X	
DEWETSDORP O 62 A4 ↓ 1521m																														
Dewetsdorp Municipal P.O. Box 13 (9940)	052112 E	12		X							X	X	X				X	20		30		X					X		X	
DIE OOG T See Naboomspruit																														
DOONSIDE N 63 NS ↗ 50m																														
Pot-Luck 5 Topham Rd. (4125) ☐ *5 Topham Rd.*	031	93-6498	X					X			X	X				X		47		7		X				X			X	
DORDRECHT C 62 C5 ← 1637m																														
Dordrecht Municipal P.O. Box 20 (5435)	04552 E	17		X							X	X				X		X	X	X		X				X			X	
DRAKENSBERG N See respectively: • Champagne Castle • Garden Castle • Himeville • Mont-aux-Sources																														
DUIWELSKLOOF T 69 A3 ↙ 932m																														
Duiwelskloof Municipal P.O. Box 36 (0835) ☐ *Boltman St.*	01523	3246		X						X	X	X					X	100	100	100		X				X			X	
DURBAN N 63 NS ↗ S.L.																														
Anstey's 8 Anstey Rd., Brighton Beach 4052 ☐ *8 Anstey Rd., Brighton Beach*	031	47-7061	X					X			X	X						60			X					X			X	
Durban 55 Grays Inn Rd., Bluff 4052 ☐ *55 Grays Inn Rd., Bluff*	031	47-4791	X					X				X				X			X				X			X			X	
Q B P.O. Box 39076, Queensburgh 4070 ☐ *40 Haslam Rd., Escombe, Queensburgh*	031	44-5800	X						X		X	X				X		42				X				X		X		X
DWARSKERSBOS C 58 B3 ↙ S.L.																														
Dwarskersbos Divisional Council, P.O. Box 3, Piketberg 7320.	02612 E	60			X			X			X		X	X	X						X						X		X	
EAST LONDON C 60 B2 ↘ S.L.																														
Blue Bend Holiday Resort P.O. Box 2021, Beacon Bay 5205 ☐ *107 Hillcrest Drive, Beacon Bay*	0431	47-1537	X					X	X		X	X		X		X			32		X					X			X	
Eastern Beach Director of Parks, P.O. Box 984 (5200)	0431	2-3861		X				X				X				X			235		X					X	X		X	
● Glen Navar Holiday Resort P/Bag 502 (5200) ☐ *32 km from East London*	0431	95-1329	X					X				X				X	X		80				X			X				X
Nahoon Beach Director of Parks, P.O. Box 984 (5200) ☐ *Near Nahoon Mouth*	0431	8-7569		X				X	X			X				X	X		113			X				X				X
Pixie P.O. Box 5072, Greenfields 5208 ☐ *Chester Rd., Sunnyridge*	0431	46-1611	X					X				X				X		10				X				X				X
Rondalia Holiday Resort P.O. Box 2079, Beacon Bay 5205 ☐ *Near Sunrise-on-Sea*	0431	95-1519	X					X	X			X					X		16				X				X		X	
● Verina P.O. Box 5102, Greenfields 5208 ☐ *Settlers Way*	0431	46-1069	X								X	X				X		36		4	X					X			X	
Welcomagin Holiday Resort P.O. West Bank 5218 ☐ *Hickmans River Mouth*	0431	46-1080	X					X	X	X	X	X			X	X	X	40		7		X					X			X
EAST LONDON DISTRICT See respectively: • Bonza Bay • Cefane • Christmas Rock • Cintsa Mouth East • Cintsa West • Glengarriff • Glen Muir • Gonubie Mouth • Kidd's Beach • Rockclyffe-on-Sea																														
EDENBURG O 62 A3 ↘ 1376m																														
Edenburg Show Grounds P.O. Box 16 (9908)	05842 E	8		X							X	X				X		16	16	16	X						X		X	
EDENVALE T 72 NS ↗ 1585m																														
Willow Grove P.O. Box 23, Lyndhurst 2106 ☐ *Adrian Ave., Lombardy East*	011	608-2491	X						X			X				X			100			X				X	X			X
EIKENHOF T 72 NS ↓ 1524m																														
Blossom Valley P.O. Eikenhof 1872 ☐ *Cnr. Gordon and Alberton/Eikenhof Rds., Kibler Park*	011	943-1508	X						X		X	X					X		35	1	X					X			X	
Lion Rampant P.O. Box 141 (1872) ☐ *Plot 18, Olifantsvlei, Eikenhof/Alberton Rd.*	011	943-1802	X						X		X	X				X		36			X					X			X	
Protea P.O. Box 186 (1872) ☐ *Vereeniging Main Rd.*	011	943-1066	X						X	X	X	X				X		100	50	56	X					X			X	
EILAND MINERAL BATHS T See Letsitele																														
ELANDSFONTEIN T 72 NS → 1737m																														
Cresta North Reef Rd., P.O. Elandsfontein 1406 ☐ *North Reef Rd.*	011	36-5080	X								X	X			X	X	X	200			X					X			X	

CAMP SITE FACILITIES — I = In-Season only, O = Out-of-Season only, X = On application

SPORTING AND RECREATIONAL FACILITIES — S = On Site, N = Nearby (Up to 20 km away)

33 Seasons: Open throughout the year	34 Seasons: Out-of-season closing date / Re-opening date	35 Terms for bookings: Bookings accp./peak sns. - see note 2	36 Terms for bookings: Deposit required	37 Terms for bookings: Refunded if cancelled - see note 3	38 Caravan/camping site tariffs (see heading): Maximum in-season tariff	39 Caravan/camping site tariffs: Maximum out-of-season tariff	40 Reductions allowed for: Long periods of stay	41 Reductions allowed for: Groups - see note 4	42 Reductions allowed for: AA members	43 Reductions allowed for: Others (on application)	44 Restaurant facilities: On site	45 Restaurant facilities: Within 5 km of site	46 Restaurant facilities: More than 5 km from site	47 Tearoom/cafe: On site	48 Tearoom/cafe: Within 5 km of site	49 Tearoom/cafe: More than 5 km from site	50 Shopping facilities (provisions): On site	51 Shopping facilities: Within 5 km of site	52 Shopping facilities: More than 5 km from site	53 Additional accommodation available: Bungalows	54 Additional accommodation: Cabins	55 Additional accommodation: Cottages (rondavels)	56 Additional accommodation: Chalets	57 Tariff (see heading): Maximum in-season tariff	58 Tariff: Maximum out-of-season tariff	59 Caravans to rent on site - see section	60 Drinking water: Piped	61 Drinking water: Other	62 Baths: Hot and cold	63 Baths: Cold only	64 Showers: Hot and cold	65 Showers: Cold only	66 Waterborne sanitation	67 Washbasins	68 Dishwashing facilities	69 Laundry and ironing facilities - see note 5	70 Washing machines	71 Site lit	72 Plugs for razors (voltage)	73 Refrigerators	74 Firewood/charcoal	75 Open fire forbidden	76 Camp fire permitted	77 Braai places provided	78 Kitchen/cooking facilities	79 Petrol pump on site	80 Petrol pump nearby	81 Car repair shop nearby	82 Car servicing nearby	83 Gas service nearby	84 First aid/hospital/doctor nearby	85 Post office nearby	86 Site guarded	87 Pets allowed	88 Non-white servants: Servants permitted - see note 6	89 Non-white servants: Servants accom. - see note 6	90 Non-white servants: Servants for hire - see note 6	91 Type of vehicle permitted: Car and trailer	92 Type of vehicle permitted: Truck horse and semi-trailer	93 Type of vehicle permitted: Self-propelled caravans	94 Childrens' playground	95 Tennis	96 Cinema/drive-in/TV-room - see note 7	97 Horse-riding	98 Games room	99 Trampoline	100 Bowls	101 Hot springs	102 Golf: Golf course - see note 8	103 Golf: Number of holes	104 Golf: Miniature	105 Golf: Mashie	106 Golf: Putt-putt	107 Fishing: Freshwater - see note 9	108 Fishing: Sea - see note 10	109 Fishing: Goggle	110 Fishing: Licence required	111 Swimming: Swimming pool	112 Swimming: Sea bathing	113 Swimming: Childrens' pool	114 Swimming: Adults only	115 Swimming: Shark nets at beach	116 Boating: Boats for hire	117 Boating: Power	118 Boating: Sailing	119 Boating: Canoeing	120 Places of interest: Historic	121 Places of interest: Scientific	122 Places of interest: Natural	123 Notes
					B	B							X			X			X								X		X		X		X	X	X	X		X	X				X	X			X	X	X	X		X	X	X	X			X	X	X	S	N	N	N					N	18								N									X			
					B	B					X									X				X	X				X		X					X								X							X		X	X	X	X					S			S																							X			
																																																													S		S																											
		X			B	B	X	X				X	X			X			X								X		X		X		X	X	X	X		X	220				X	X			X	X	X		X	X		X	X		X	X	X	X	S	N	N				N	N	N	9				N			X	S		S							X		X	
		X	X		B	B		X										X									X		X		X			X	X			X			X		X	X															X	X	X		S		S				N	N	9			X					S		N									X	
		X	X	X	B	B		X					X	X		X			X			X	X	E	D		X		X		X		X	X	X	X		X	220		X		X	X			X	X	X		X	X		X	X		X	X	X	X	S	N	N				N	S	N	9				S			X	S		S							X		X	
		X			B	B		X											X				X	C	C		X				X		X	X		X		X		X	X		X	X	X	X					X	X	X		X	X		X	X	X																											X	X	X	
																				X																																																																						
			X	X	C	C							X			X			X								X		X		X		X	X	X	X							X				X	X	X	X	X	X			X		X	X	X	X														N			X							N	N	N	X		X	
					B	B							X			X			X								X		X		X		X	X	X	X		X	220					X			X	X	X	X		X		X	X			X		X	S	N	N				N		N	18								N									X		X	
					O	O						X	X		X	X		X	X																								X					X	X	X		X		X	X			X	X	X		N	N											S			X			N							X	X	X	
					O	O						X			X			X									X		X				X	X				X				X	X	X			X	X	X	X		X		X	X		X	X	X	X	N	N					N							N			X	N		N	X			N	N	N	X			
					O	O						X	X		X	X		X	X								X	X					X	X									X			X	X	X			X		X				X	X	X	N												N			X													
		X			D	C	X	X			X			X			X			X		X		C-F	B-C		X		X		X		X	X	X			X			X		X	X		X			X	X		X	X				X	X	X	X	S		S					S						S			X	S		S									X	
					A	A						X			X			X									X					X	X	X									X			X		X			X						X	X	X	N	N						N	9																				
		X	X		F	C					X	X		X	X			X								X	X		X		X		X	X	X	X	X		X		X		X				X	X	X	X		X						X	X	X			N				N								N				X			X								
					A	A						X			X			X									X						X													X	X	X	X	X	X		X	X		X	X	X	X	N	N	N	N	S	S	N		N	18																	X		X	
		X	X		B	B	X						X			X			X			X		B-D	B-D		X		X		X		X	X	X	X		X		X	X			X			X	X	X	X		X	X					X	X	X	N	S					S		N	18				N			X	S						N	N	N	X	X	X	
																																																									X	X		X		N					N		N	18				N																
		X	X		D	D	X					X			X			X									X		X		X		X	X	X	X		X	X		X	X	X	X				X	X	X	X	X	X	X	X			X	X	X	S	S	N			S	N		N	18					N		X		X	N		X								
		X	X	X	F	F	X					X		X			X										X	X	X		X		X	X	X	X	X	X	X			X		X			X	X	X	X		X	X		X			X		X	S				S		N		N	18					N			S		S		X					X		X	
		X	X		E	B	X			X		X		X			X	X									X		X		X		X	X	X	X	X				X			X			X	X	X	X	X	X	X																									S	X								X	X	X	
		X			C	C						X	X					X									X		X			X	X	X	X			X	X		X		X	X			X	X	X					X	X			X		X															N			N	X	N									X	
		X	X		E	B	X					X		X			X				X	X		A	A		X		X		X		X	X	X	X			220		X		X				X	X	X	X		X	X	O	X	X	X	X	X	X		N	N	N	S		N		N	18	X	X	X	N	N	N	X	N	X	N				N	N	N	X	X	X	
		X	X		C	C						X			X				X								X				X		X	X		X		X	220				X				X	X	X		X		X		X		X	X		X	N		N				N		N	18	X		X		N	N			X	N				N	N		X		X	
		X	X		E	D	X	X				X			X	X	X					X		H	D		X		X		X		X	X	X	X		X	220		X	X	X	X			X	X	X	X		X	X	O	X	X	X	X	X	X	S	S	S											N	N			X											
		X	X		C	C						X			X			X									X				X		X	X	X	X		X	220				X								X				X		X	X		X	N						N		N	18					N	N			X				N	N	N	N	X		X	
		X	X		C	B	X					X	X		X	X		X	X							X	X		X		X		X	X								X				X	X	X			X	X	X	X			X		X	N	N	N	N	N	N	N		N	18					N	N		S			X						X		X	
		X	X		K	G	X	X		X		X				X	X	X	X			X		C-G	C-G		X		X			X	X	X	X	X		X			X		X	X	X		X	X	X	X	X	X	X	X	X	X	X	X	X	X	S	S	N	N	S		N		N	18				N			X		X										X	
		X	X		E	C	X					X			X			X								X	X		X		X		X	X	X	X		X	32		X			X			X	X	X	X		X		X	X			X		X	S	N	N				N		N	18					N		X	S											X	
		X	X	X	J	G	X					X		X			X					X		B-E	B-E		X		X		X		X	X	X	X		X		X	X		X	X	X		X	X	X	X	X	X	X	X	X	X	X	X	X	X	S	S		N	S		N		N	18		N	N	S	S	S		S	X	S			N			N			X	
					O	O						X			X			X									X				X		X	X				X					X				X	X	X			X		X	X			X	X	X	N	N					N		N	9								N									X	X	X	
		X	X		C	C	X		X			X			X	X		X									X		X				X	X	X	X		X			X		X				X	X	X	X		X					X	X	X	X	N	N	N				N											S												
		X	X	X	C	C						X			X				X							X	X		X		X		X	X	X	X	X	X		X			X				X	X	X	X	X	X		X	X		X	X		X	S	N	N	N		S	N		N	18								N		N										
		X			C	C	X						X		X			X									X		X		X		X	X	X	X			X					X			X	X	X		X	X			X			X		X	S			N	S									N				S												
		X	X		B	B	X	X	X			X	X		X	X		X	X							X	X		X		X		X	X	X	X		X			X		X	X			X	X	X	X	X	X	X	X	X		X	X	X	X	S	N	S	N	S	N	N									N		S		S	X									
					X	X	X					X			X			X									X		X		X		X	X	X	X	X	X	220	X		X				X	X	X	X	X	X	X					X	X	X	N	N	N	N	N		N		N	18	X	X	X	N			X	N		N										

CARAVAN PARKS AND CAMPING SITES IN SOUTH AFRICA

CARAVAN PARK / CAMP SITE TARIFF CODE – See columns 38–39 (Subject to alteration)

A = Up to R1 | B = R1–R2 | C = R2–R3 | D = R3–R4 | E = R4–R5 | F = R5–R6 | G = R6–R7 | H = R7–R8 | I = R8–R9 | J = R9–R10 | K = R10–R16 | O = FREE | X = On Application

Charges are based on family of 2 adults and 2 children under 12 years

ADDITIONAL ACCOMMODATION TARIFF CODE – See columns 57–59 (Subject to alteration)

eg. Bungalows, Cabins, Cottages, Chalets, etc.

A = R1–R3 | B = R3–R5 | C = R5–R7 | D = R7–R9 | E = R9–R11 | F = R11–R13 | G = R13–R15 | H = R15–R17 | I = R17–R19 | J = R19–R21 | K = R21–R30 | X = On Application

NB: Where the tariff is given in *italics* it is per person, otherwise per unit

NOTE 1 — **Columns 18, 19, 20,** — X= Stands available but not demarcated or number of stands have not been provided

NOTE 2 — **Column 35** — A=Bookings accepted for additional accommodation only i.e. cottages, bungalows, etc.

NOTE 3 — **Column 37** — Deposit refunded under certain conditions eg. less 10% ; if site is re-let ; if cancelled well in advance (up to 2 months) or on a doctor's certificate

NOTE 4 — **Column 41** — Reductions allowed on application for youth, church, school or sport groups or caravan rallies

NOTE 5 — **Column 69** — L= Laundry facilities only

NOTE 6 — **Columns 88, 89, 90,** — I = In-Season only ; O = Out-of-Season only; X = On application

NOTE 7 — **Column 96** — I = In-Season only

NOTE 8 — **Column 102** — See section on golf in Outdoor Holiday Guide

NOTE 9 — **Column 107** — See section on freshwater angling in Outdoor Holiday Guide

NOTE 10 — **Column 108** — See section on coastal angling in Outdoor Holiday Guide

Establishments marked thus ● have the Caravan Club of South Africa recommendation — see introduction

ABBREVIATIONS

C = CAPE PROVINCE
N = NATAL
O = ORANGE FREE STATE
T = TRANSVAAL
B = BOPHUTHATSWANA
X = TRANSKEI

	TELEPHONE CODE (T = DIAL 0020, BOOK TRUNK CALL; E = DIAL CODE, ASK EXCHANGE FOR NO.)	TELEPHONE NUMBER	OWNED OR SUPERVISED BY: PRIVATELY OWNED	MUNICIPAL	DIVISIONAL COUNCIL	PROVINCIAL ADMINISTRATION	PARKS BOARD	SITE DESCRIPTION – LOCALITY: BEACH IN IMMEDIATE VICINITY	BESIDE RIVER, LAKE OR DAM	IN OR NEAR MOUNTAIN AREA	WITHIN BUILT-UP AREA	NATURE OF GROUND: GRASS	GRAVEL	SAND	SHADE: UNSHADED	PARTLY SHADED	EXTENSIVELY SHADED	NO. OF STANDS: CARAVANS ONLY – SEE NOTE 1	CARAVANS AND/OR TENTS SEE NOTE 1	TENTS ONLY – SEE NOTE 1	ACCESSIBILITY – APPROXIMATE DISTANCE FROM MAIN ROAD TO SITE: ON MAIN RD.	WITHIN 1 km	WITHIN 5 km	WITHIN 10 km	WITHIN 15 km	SURFACE OF APPROACH ROAD: TAR	GRAVEL	SAND	CONDITION OF APPROACH ROAD: GOOD	FAIR
	1	2	3	4	5	6	7	8	9	10	11	12	13	14	15	16	17	18	19	20	21	22	23	24	25	26	27	28	29	30
EMPANGENI N 67 C4 ↘ 65m																														
Empangeni P.O. Box 365 (3880) □ *10-4th St., Kuleka*	0351	2-1461	X								X	X			X			X				X				X			X	
ERMELO T 67 A2 → 1734m																														
Republiek P.O. Box 48 (2350) □ *7 km from Ermelo*	01341	4093		X					X			X				X		60		40		X				X			X	
ESHOWE N 67 C4 ↓ 502m																														
Eshowe Municipal P.O. Box 37 (3815) □ *Addison St.*	035412 E	17		X							X	X		X		X	X		22			X				X			X	
ESTCOURT N 67 D2 ↗ 1168m																														
Estcourt Municipal Bookings not accepted □ *Lorne St.*	03631	3000		X							X	X				X			25		X					X			X	
FALSE BAY PARK N See Hluhluwe																														
FANIES ISLAND N See Mtubatuba																														
FICKSBURG O 66 C5 ↘ 1630m																														
Ficksburg Municipal P.O. Box 116 (9730) □ *Bloem St.*	05632 E	12		X					X	X	X	X					X		100			X				X			X	
FISH HOEK C 58 NS • S.L.																														
Fish Hoek Municipal Bookings not accepted □ *Foreshore*	021	82-1163		X				X		X	X		X		X			24				X				X			X	
Robinvale P.O. Box 142 (7975) □ *Cnr. 20th Ave./Kommetjie Rd.*	021	82-2714/82-2162	X					X		X		X				X			40		X					X			X	
Sunnyacres P.O. Box 50 (7975)	021	82-2913	X					X				X					X		50		X						X		X	
FLORIDA T 72 NS → 1676m																														
Florida Lake Manager: Parks and Recreation, P.O. Box 217, Roodepoort 1725 □ *Westlake Rd.*	011	672-6221		X					X			X				X		65			X						X			X
FORT BEAUFORT C 60 B1 ↓ 437m																														
Fort Beaufort Municipal Town Clerk, P.O. Box 36 (5720) □ *Durban St.*	043512 E	17/162		X							X	X			X				12		X					X			X	
FOURIESBURG O 66 C2 ↙ 1829m																														
Fouriesburg Municipal P.O. Box 5 (9725) □ *Kosmos St.*	014322 E	14		X							X	X	X				X	X				X					X			X
FRANSCHHOEK C 58 C4 ↙ 100m																														
De Hollandsche Molen (Pty) Ltd. — Oude Molen P.O. Box 535, Suider-Paarl 7624 □ *Paarl-Franschhoek Rd.*	0252	2704	X						X	X		X					X				X					X			X	
FRANKFORT O 66 B6 ↘ 1574m																														
Wilgerivier P.O. Box 2 (9830)	016132 E	30		X					X			X					X		25				X			X			X	
GAMTOOS RIVER MOUTH C See Port Elizabeth																														
GANSBAAI C 58 D4 ↙ 15m																														
Uilenkraalsmond Caretaker, P.O. Box 18 (7220) □ *9 km from Gansbaai*	02834	2012			X			X	X	X		X		X			X	100	940		X	X				X				X
GARDEN CASTLE N 63 A2 ↙ 1753m																														
Drakensberg Garden Central Reservations, P.O. Box 10305, Marine Parade, Durban 4056	031	37-4222	X						X	X		X					X	4	44	25	X						X		X	
GARDEN ROUTE C See respectively: • **Brenton-on-Sea** • **Buffelsbaai** • **George** • **Glentana** • **Groot-Brakrivier** • **Gwayang River Mouth** • **Hartenbos** • **Heroldsbaai** • **Keurboomsrivier** • **Keurboomstrand** • **Klein-Brakrivier** • **Kleinkrantz** • **Knysna** • **Mossel Bay** • **Nature's Valley** • **Plettenberg Bay** • **Sedgefield** • **Stormsrivier** • **Victoria Bay** • **Wilderness**																														
GARIES C 60 B5 · 240m																														
Garies High School Sports Grounds Headmaster, Garies High School (8220)	T	3				X					X	X					X	X	X	X		X				X			X	
GEORGE C 59 NS ← 226m																														
Caravan Park International P.O. Box 617 (6530) □ *On National Rd. between George and Wilderness*	0441	4490	X					X		X		X					X		200		X						X		X	
George Municipal P.O. Box 19 (6530) □ *York St.*	0441	4115		X				X		X	X	X				X			100	65	X						X		X	
GERMISTON T 72 NS ↘ 1846m																														
Dinwoodie P.O. Box 7043, Dinwiddie 1405 □ *38 Chris St., Dinwiddie*	011	34-1861	X								X	X					X	50				X				X			X	
GLENGARRIFF C 60 B3 ↙ S.L.																														
● **Yellow Sands** P.O. Box 920, East London 5200 □ *Kwelera River Mouth*	0431	95-1336	X					X	X			X			X	X	X		100				X				X		X	
GLEN MUIR C 60 B3 ↙ 20m																														
Glen Muir P.O. Box 942, East London 5200 □ *Kwelera Dist.*	0431	95-1318	X					X	X			X			X				30			X				X	X		X	
GLENTANA C 59 C2 ↘ 2m																														
Glentana Divisional Council, P.O. Box 12, George 6530 □ *George Dist.*	0441	3001			X			X		X	X	X	X			X			53					X		X			X	
GOLDEN GATE HIGHLANDS NATIONAL PARK O See Clarens																														
GONUBIE MOUTH C 60 B3 ↙ S.L.																														
Gonubie Mouth P.O. Gonubie 5256	0431	94-1313	X					X	X		X	X		X			X		115			X				X			X	
Gwenshaw P.O. Box 12, Gonubie 5256 □ *Eastward Ho, Gonubie*	0431	94-1710	X					X	X			X				X		50		12			X				X		X	
P.S.A. Holiday Resort P.O. Box 16, Gonubie 5256 □ *Quinera River Mouth*	0431	95-1022	X					X	X			X		X			X	110		30			X				X		X	
GORDON'S BAY C 58 D3 ↗ S.L.																														
● **Gordon's Bay Municipal** P.O. Box 3 (7150) □ *Beach Rd.*	024	4-1241/4-1330		X				X				X				X			100		X					X			X	
● **Sea Breeze** P.O. Box 38 (7150) □ *Water Way*	024	4-1400	X					X		X	X	X				X			150			X				X			X	
GOURITZMOND C 59 C1 ↗ S.L.																														
Gouritzmond Caretaker, P.O. Gouritzmond 6796	02952 E	5202			X			X	X			X				X		24							X		X		X	

PEN THROUGHOUT THE YEAR

SEASONS — TERMS FOR BOOKINGS — CARAVAN/CAMPING SITE TARIFFS (See heading) — REDUCTIONS ALLOWED FOR — RESTAURANT FACILITIES — TEAROOM/CAFE — SHOPPING FACILITIES (Provisions) — ADDITIONAL ACCOMMODATION AVAILABLE — TARIFF (See heading) — CARAVANS TO RENT ON SITE – SEE SECTION — DRINKING WATER — BATHS — SHOWERS

CAMP SITE FACILITIES: I = In-Season only, O = Out-of-Season only, X = On application — NON-WHITE SERVANTS — TYPE OF VEHICLE PERMITTED

SPORTING AND RECREATIONAL FACILITIES: S = On Site, N = Nearby (Up to 20 km away) — GOLF — FISHING — SWIMMING — BOATING — PLACES OF INTEREST — NOTES

33 Out-of-season closing date	34 Re-opening date	35 Bookings accp. peak sns. – see note 2	36 Deposit required	37 Refunded if cancelled – see note 3	38 Maximum in-season tariff	39 Maximum out-of-season tariff	40 Long periods of stay	41 Groups – see note 4	42 AA members	43 Others (on application)	44 Restaurant: on site	45 Restaurant: within 5 km of site	46 Restaurant: more than 5 km from site	47 Tearoom/cafe: on site	48 Tearoom/cafe: within 5 km of site	49 Tearoom/cafe: more than 5 km from site	50 Shopping: on site	51 Shopping: within 5 km of site	52 Shopping: more than 5 km from site	53 Bungalows	54 Cabins	55 Cottages (rondavels)	56 Chalets	57 Maximum in-season tariff	58 Maximum out-of-season tariff	59 Caravans to rent on site – see section	60 Drinking water: piped	61 Drinking water: other	62 Baths: hot and cold	63 Baths: cold only	64 Showers: hot and cold	65 Showers: cold only	66 Waterborne sanitation	67 Washbasins	68 Dishwashing facilities	69 Laundry and ironing facilities – see note 5	70 Washing machines	71 Site lit	72 Plugs for razors (voltage)	73 Refrigerators	74 Firewood/charcoal	75 Open fire forbidden	76 Camp fire permitted	77 Braai places provided	78 Kitchen/cooking facilities	79 Petrol pump on site	80 Petrol pump nearby	81 Car repair shop nearby	82 Car servicing nearby	83 Gas service nearby	84 First aid/hospital/doctor nearby	85 Post office nearby	86 Site guarded	87 Pets allowed	88 Servants permitted – see note 6	89 Servants accom. – see note 6	90 Servants for hire – see note 6	91 Car and trailer	92 Truck 'horse' and semi-trailer	93 Self-propelled caravans	94 Childrens playground	95 Tennis	96 Cinema/drive-in/TV-room – see note 7	97 Horse-riding	98 Games room	99 Trampoline	100 Bowls	101 Hot springs	102 Golf course – see note 8	103 Number of holes	104 Miniature	105 Mashie	106 Putt-putt	107 Freshwater – see note 9	108 Sea – see note 10	109 Goggle	110 Licence required	111 Swimming pool	112 Sea bathing	113 Childrens pool	114 Adults only	115 Shark nets at beach	116 Boats for hire	117 Power	118 Sailing	119 Canoeing	120 Historic	121 Scientific	122 Natural	123 Notes
					E	E							X			X			X								X		X		X		X	X	X	X					X		X				X	X	X	X	X	X		X				X		X									N	18																			X	
		X	X	X	B	B							X			X						X		B	B		X		X		X		X	X	X	X		X				X																X	X	X	N								N	18				N			X							X	X	X			X	
		X	X		C	C						X	X		X	X		X	X								X		X		X		X	X	X	X		X			X	X	X	X			X	X	X	X	X	X			X			X		X	N	N	N	N			N		N	18				N	N	N	X	N	X	N	X		N	N	N	N	X		X	
					B	B						X			X				X								X		X		X		X	X	X	X		X									X	X	X					X				X		X	S	N		N			N		N	9								N		N							X		X	
					A	A						X			X			X								X	X	X		X		X	X	X	X		X	X		X		X	X			X	X	X	X	X	X		X	X		X	X	X	X	X	S	N	N	N			S		N	18	X			N			X	N		N							X	X	X	
					C	A					X	X	X	X	X	X		X	X								X				X		X	X				X				X						X	X	X	X		X								X	S																																	
		X	X	X	D	D	X						X			X			X		X	X		D	C		X		X		X		X	X	X	X			X	X	X			X					X	X	X	X	X							X	X	X	N	N	N	N			N		N	18					N	N		N	X	N			N	N	N	N	X		X	
		X	X	X	D	D	X	X				X			X		X			X	X			G	F	X	X		X		X		X	X	X	X	X		X	X	X			X			X	X	X	X	X	X	X	X	O				X	X	X	S	N	N	N	S										N	N		S	X				N	N	N		X	X	X	
					A	A						X			X			X								X		X		X		X	X	X	X		X	110/220			X					X	X	X			X						X		X	N	N	N				N							N			X	N		N					N	N	X	X	X	
		X			C	C						X			X			X								X		X		X		X	X	X	X		X	220			X	X	X			X	X	X			X		X	X			X	X	X	N	N	N				N		N	11				N			X	N									X		X	
		X			A	A							X			X			X								X		X		X		X	X	X							X	X	X			X	X	X	X	X	X	X	X	X			X		X	N	S		N			N							N			X	N									X		X	
		X	X		X	X	X	X	X		X			X			X			X	X		X	E	E		X		X		X		X	X	X	L		X			X		X	X			X	X	X	X		X	X		X			X		X	S	N	N	N	N	N	N	N						N			X	S		S							X	X	X	
		X	X		C	C							X			X			X								X		X		X		X	X	X	X		X	220		X						X	X	X	X		X	X	X	X			X	X	X	S	S	N				S		N	9		X		X				S		S										
		X	X	X	D	D							X	X		X	X		X	X				D	B		X		X		X		X	X	X			X		X	X		X	X			X	X	X	X		X	X						X	X	X	N	N	N											S	S	S			X						S	S		X		X	
		X	X	X	E	D			X			X						X				X	X	X	X		X				X		X	X	X	X		X					X	X	X		X	X	X	X	X	X	X		X	X	X	X	X	X	S	S		S	S	S	S		S	9			X	S			X	S						N	N	N			X	
					A	A	X	X				X	X		X	X		X	X								X					X		X				X					X	X			X	X	X	X	X	X	X	X	X			X	X	X	S	N	N											N						S							X	X	X	
		X	X	X	D	E	X	X			X						X					X		J	F		X		X		X		X	X	X	X		X	X	X	X			X	X		X	X	X	X	X	X	X				X	X	X	X	S	N	S	N	S	S	N		N	18					N	N		S	X	S				N	N	N	X	X	X	
		X	X	X	C	C						X	X	X	X		X	X		X		X		B-C	A-B		X		X		X		X	X	X	X		X	X		X	X	X	X			X	X	X	X	X	X	X	X	X			X		X	S	N	N	N			N		N	18					N	N		S	X	S			N	N	N	N	X		X	
		X	X	X	X	X						X	X		X	X			X																								X	X			X	X	X	X	X	X		X			X	X	X	X	S		N	N			N		N	18								S		S										
		X	X	X	F	C	X			X			X			X	X		X							X	X		X		X		X	X	X	X			220		X		X				X	X	X	X	X			O	X	X	X	X	X	X														S	S	S			X					S	S	S		X	X	
		X	X		C	C	X	X				X			X			X		X		X	X	J	F	X		X	X		X		X	X	X	X					X		X	X			X	X						X			X	X	X		S	S	N	S										N	N			X											
		X	X	X	D	B						X			X			X								X				X		X	X	X	L					X	X	X	X			X	X	X	X			X																						N	N			X										X	
		X	X	X	E	C	X	X								X						X	F	D		X		X		X		X	X	X	X		X	220		X		X				X	X	X	X		X		O	X		X	X		X	N	N	I	N	S				N	9				N	N				X	N			N	N	N	N			X	
		X	X	X	D	C	X	X				X			X		X	X	X							X	X		X		X		X	X	X	X	X	X	220		X		X	X			X	X	X	X	X	X		X	X	X	X	X	X	X	S	N	S	N	S		N		N	9					N	N		S	X	S				N	N	N	X		X	
		X	X		C	B							X			X	X									X		X		X		X	X	X	X					X	X		X			X	X	X	X	X	X	X					X	X	X	S	S	S	S					N	9					N	N	X						N	N	N			X	
		X	X	X	D	B						X			X			X		X				F-I	C-E		X		X		X		X	X	X	X		X	X				X	X			X	X	X	X	X	X	X		X			X	X	X	S		N						N	18					S				X					N	N	N	X	X	X	
		X	X	X	D	B	X	X	X			X		X	X	X	X	X	X			X		F	D		X		X		X		X	X	X	X	X	X	110/220		X	X		X			X	X	X	X	X	X	X	X	X			X	X	X	S	N	N			S	N		N	18					N	N		S	X					N	N	N	X		X	
		X			B	B						X						X								X			X		X	X	X								X	X			X						X	X	X			X	X	X															S	S	S			X	N									X	

CARAVAN PARKS AND CAMPING SITES IN SOUTH AFRICA

CARAVAN PARK / CAMP SITE TARIFF CODE – See columns 38–39 (Subject to alteration)

A = Up to R1 | B = R1–R2 | C = R2–R3 | D = R3–R4 | E = R4–R5 | F = R5–R6 | G = R6–R7 | H = R7–R8 | I = R8–R9 | J = R9–R10 | K = R10–R16 | O = FREE | X = On Application

Charges are based on family of 2 adults and 2 children under 12 years

ADDITIONAL ACCOMMODATION TARIFF CODE – See columns 57–59 (Subject to alteration)

eg. Bungalows, Cabins, Cottages, Chalets, etc.

A = R1–R3 | B = R3–R5 | C = R5–R7 | D = R7–R9 | E = R9–R11 | F = R11–R13 | G = R13–R15 | H = R15–R17 | I = R17–R19 | J = R19–R21 | K = R21–R30 | X = On Application

NB: Where the tariff is given in *italics* it is per person, otherwise per unit

NOTE 1 — Columns 18, 19, 20 – X = Stands available but not demarcated or number of stands have not been provided

NOTE 2 — Column 35 – A = Bookings accepted for additional accommodation only i.e. cottages, bungalows, etc.

NOTE 3 — Column 37 – Deposit refunded under certain conditions eg. less 10% ; if site is re-let ; if cancelled well in advance (up to 2 months) or on a doctor's certificate

NOTE 4 — Column 41 – Reductions allowed on application for youth, church, school or sport groups or caravan rallies

NOTE 5 — Column 69 – L = Laundry facilities only

NOTE 6 — Columns 88, 89, 90, – I = In-Season only ; O = Out-of Season only ; X = On application

NOTE 7 — Column 96 – I = In-Season only

NOTE 8 — Column 102 – See section on golf in Outdoor Holiday Guide

NOTE 9 — Column 107 – See section on freshwater angling in Outdoor Holiday Guide

NOTE 10 — Column 108 – See section on coastal angling in Outdoor Holiday Guide

Establishments marked thus ● have the Caravan Club of South Africa recommendation – see introduction

ABBREVIATIONS

C = CAPE PROVINCE
N = NATAL
O = ORANGE FREE STATE
T = TRANSVAAL
B = BOPHUTHATSWANA
X = TRANSKEI

TELEPHONE CODE: T = DIAL 0020. BOOK TRUNK CALL; E = DIAL CODE. ASK EXCHANGE FOR NO.

	Telephone code	Telephone number	Owned or supervised by: Privately owned	Municipal	Divisional Council	Provincial Administration	Parks Board	Site description – Locality: Beach in immediate vicinity	Beside river, lake or dam	In or near mountain area	Within built-up area	Nature of ground: Grass	Gravel	Sand	Shade: Unshaded	Partly shaded	Extensively shaded	No. of stands: Caravans only – see note 1	Caravans and/or tents	Tents only – see note 1	Accessibility – Approximate distance from main road to site: On main rd.	Within 1 km	Within 5 km	Within 10 km	Within 15 km	Surface of road approach: Tar	Gravel	Sand	Condition of road approach: Good	Fair (Poor)
	1	2	3	4	5	6	7	8	9	10	11	12	13	14	15	16	17	18	19	20	21	22	23	24	25	26	27	28	29	30
GRAAFF-REINET C 59 A4 ↑ 751m																														
● **Urquhart** P.O. Box 71 (6280) ☐ *Murraysburg Rd.*	04912 E	2121/2		X					X	X			X				X	100	150	50	X					X			X	
GRAHAMSTOWN C 59 B6 ↑ 532m																														
Grahamstown Municipal Superintendent of Parks and Forests, P.O. Box 176 (6140) ☐ *Port Elizabeth National Rd.*	0461	2043		X							X	X				X			75		X						X		X	
GRASKOP T 69 B3 → 1300m																														
Blydepoort Holiday Resort P/Bag 413 (1270) ☐ *Strijdom Tunnel Rd.*	T	Blydepoort 9				X				X		X				X		24			X					X			X	
Graskop Municipal P.O. Box 18 (1270) ☐ *Louis Trichardt Ave.*	0131522 E	126		X					X	X		X				X			36		X					X			X	
GREAT BRAK RIVER C See Groot-Brakrivier																														
GREYTOWN N 67 D3 ↑ 1324m																														
Lake Merthley Town Clerk, P.O. Box 71 (3500) ☐ *2 km from Greytown*	03342 E	21		X					X			X				X			12			X						X		X
GRIEKWASTAD C 65 C5 ↙ 1207m																														
Griekwastad Municipal P.O. Box 21 (8365)	05912 E	19		X							X	X	X				X		60			X				X			X	
GRIQUATOWN C See Griekwastad																														
GROBLERSDAL T 69 C2 ↖ 980m																														
Groblersdal Municipal Town Clerk, P.O. Box 48 (0470) ☐ *Pretoria Main Rd.*	012022 E	274/275		X							X	X					X	30	30	20	X					X			X	
GROOT-BRAKRIVIER C 59 C2 ↖ 4m																														
Pine Creek P.O. Box 80 (6525)	04442	2434	X					X	X			X					X		120			X				X			X	
GULU RIVER MOUTH C See Kidd's Beach																														
GWAYANG RIVER MOUTH C See Caravan Parks for Coloureds, Asians and Blacks																														
HAENERTSBURG T 70 NS ↙ 1380m																														
● **Lakeside Chalets** P.O. Magoebaskloof 0731 ☐ *7 km from Haenertsburg*	0152222 E	2740	X						X	X		X				X		25	25	25		X				X		X	X	
HAMBURG C 60 C2 • S.L.																														
Hamburg Municipal P.O. Hamburg 5614 ☐ *Keiskamma River Mouth Rd.*	T	16		X				X	X			X			X				35		X						X			X
HANGKLIP C See Betty's Bay																														
HANOVER C 62 C2 ↑ 1354m																														
Hanover Municipal Town Clerk, P.O. Box 15 (5960)	057212 E	53		X									X				X		35		X						X		X	
HARDING N 63 B2 ↘ 879m																														
Harding Municipal P.O. Box 23 (4680) ☐ *Murchison St.*	03942 E	13/29		X							X	X					X	4	2	8	X					X			X	
HAROLD JOHNSON NATURE RESERVE N See Darnall																														
HARRISMITH O 67 C2 ↖ 1622m																														
Harrismith Municipal P.O. Box 43 (9880)	014362 E	23		X					X			X				X			100		X					X			X	
HARTBEESPOORTDAM T See Nefdt																														
HARTENBOS C 59 C2 ↖ 6m																														
A.T.K.V. Holiday Resort P.O. Box 3 (6520) ☐ *Kaap De Goede Hoop Ave.*	04441	5107/8	X					X	X	X	X	X	X	X		X		450	400			X				X	X	X	X	
HAWSTON C See Caravan Parks for Coloureds, Asians and Blacks																														
HAZYVIEW T 69 C4 ↖ 549m																														
Hotel Numbi P.O. Box 6 (1242)	0131242 E	6	X								X	X	X			X		15				X					X		X	
HEIDELBERG C 58 D5 ↗ 84m																														
B & M Park Manager, B & M Restaurant, Eksteen St. (6760)	02962 E	475	X								X	X					X		20		X					X			X	
Heidelberg Municipal Not necessary to book ☐ *Van Riebeeck St.*	02962 E	11		X					X	X		X					X		60			X				X			X	
HEILBRON O 66 B5 ↗ 1573m																														
Langdam Pleasure Resort P.O. Box 45 (9650)	016142 E	10		X					X			X	X				X	20	20		X						X		X	
HENDRIK VERWOERD O 62 B3 ↓ 1280m																														
Hendrik Verwoerd Dam Resort Resort Manager, P/Bag X10, Hendrik Verwoerd Dam 9922	T	45				X			X	X	X	X	X		X	X			X				X			X	X		X	X
HENDRINA T 69 D2 ↗ 1768m																														
Hendrina Municipal Not necessary to book ☐ *Eeufees St.*	013282 E	1		X							X	X					X		25			X					X			X
HEROLDSBAAI C 59 NS • 2m																														
Brakfontein Divisional Council, P.O. Box 12, George 6530 ☐ *18 km from George*	0441	3001			X			X		X	X	X				X			37					X		X			X	
Duttons Cove Holiday Resort P.O. Box 722, George 6530 ☐ *18 km from George*	0441	4551	X					X				X			X	X			34			X				X	X			X
Herolds Bay Divisional Council, P.O. Box 12, George 6530 ☐ *18 km from George*	0441	3001			X			X		X	X	X	X	X	X				16					X		X			X	
HIBBERDENE N 63 NS ↙ 7m																														
Happy Days P.O. Box 1 (4220) ☐ *Marlin Drive*	0399	725	X					X	X		X	X					X	10			X					X			X	
Hibberdene P.O. Box 143 (4220)	0399	20	X					X	X		X	X					X		134		X					X			X	
Rondalia P.O. Box 14 (4220)	0399	921	X					X	X		X	X				X		85		25		X				X			X	
Umzimai P.O. Box 140 (4220) ☐ *Baracouda Boulevard*	0399	946	X					X	X			X					X		28			X						X	X	
HIMEVILLE N 63 A2 ↓ 1561m																														
Highland Nook Private Park J. D. McClean, Borreray, P.O. Himeville 4585 ☐ *5 km from Himeville/Nottingham Rd. Junction*	T	1611	X							X		X				X			20				X				X			X
Himeville Nature Reserve Officer-in-Charge, P.O. Himeville 4585	T	36					X		X	X		X				X			X			X					X			X

SEASONS (32–34) · TERMS FOR BOOKINGS (35–37) · CARAVAN/CAMPING SITE TARIFFS (See heading) (38–39) · REDUCTIONS ALLOWED FOR (40–43) · RESTAURANT FACILITIES (44–46) · TEAROOM/CAFE (47–49) · SHOPPING FACILITIES (Provisions) (50–52) · ADDITIONAL ACCOMMODATION AVAILABLE (53–56) · TARIFF (See heading) (57–58) · CARAVANS TO RENT ON SITE – SEE SECTION (59) · DRINKING WATER (60–61) · BATHS (62–63) · SHOWERS (64–65)

CAMP SITE FACILITIES — I = In-Season only, O = Out-of-Season only, X = On application

NON-WHITE SERVANTS (88–90) · TYPE OF VEHICLE PERMITTED (91–93)

SPORTING AND RECREATIONAL FACILITIES — S = On Site, N = Nearby (Up to 20 km away) · GOLF (102–106) · FISHING (107–110) · SWIMMING (111–115) · BOATING (116–119) · PLACES OF INTEREST (120–122)

32 OPEN THROUGHOUT THE YEAR	33 OUT-OF-SEASON CLOSING DATE	34 RE-OPENING DATE	35 BOOKINGS ACCP./PEAK SNS. – SEE NOTE 2	36 DEPOSIT REQUIRED	37 REFUNDED IF CANCELLED – SEE NOTE 3	38 MAXIMUM IN-SEASON TARIFF	39 MAXIMUM OUT-OF-SEASON TARIFF	40 LONG PERIODS OF STAY	41 GROUPS – SEE NOTE 4	42 AA MEMBERS	43 OTHERS (ON APPLICATION)	44 ON SITE	45 WITHIN 5 km OF SITE	46 MORE THAN 5 km FROM SITE	47 ON SITE	48 WITHIN 5 km OF SITE	49 MORE THAN 5 km FROM SITE	50 ON SITE	51 WITHIN 5 km OF SITE	52 MORE THAN 5 km FROM SITE	53 BUNGALOWS	54 CABINS	55 COTTAGES (RONDAVELS)	56 CHALETS	57 MAXIMUM IN-SEASON TARIFF	58 MAXIMUM OUT-OF-SEASON TARIFF	59 CARAVANS TO RENT ON SITE – SEE SECTION	60 PIPED	61 OTHER	62 HOT AND COLD	63 COLD ONLY	64 HOT AND COLD	65 COLD ONLY	66 WATERBORNE SANITATION	67 WASHBASINS	68 DISHWASHING FACILITIES	69 LAUNDRY AND IRONING FACILITIES – SEE NOTE 5	70 WASHING MACHINES	71 SITE LIT	72 PLUGS FOR RAZORS (VOLTAGE)	73 REFRIGERATORS	74 FIREWOOD/CHARCOAL	75 OPEN FIRE FORBIDDEN	76 CAMP FIRE PERMITTED	77 BRAAI PLACES PROVIDED	78 KITCHEN/COOKING FACILITIES	79 PETROL PUMP ON SITE	80 PETROL PUMP NEARBY	81 CAR REPAIR SHOP NEARBY	82 CAR SERVICING NEARBY	83 GAS SERVICE NEARBY	84 FIRST AID/HOSPITAL/DOCTOR NEARBY	85 POST OFFICE NEARBY	86 SITE GUARDED	87 PETS ALLOWED	88 SERVANTS PERMITTED – SEE NOTE 6	89 SERVANTS' ACCOM. – SEE NOTE 6	90 SERVANTS FOR HIRE – SEE NOTE 6	91 CAR AND TRAILER	92 TRUCK 'HORSE' AND SEMI-TRAILER	93 SELF-PROPELLED CARAVANS	94 CHILDRENS' PLAYGROUND	95 TENNIS	96 CINEMA/DRIVE-IN/TV-ROOM – SEE NOTE 7	97 HORSE-RIDING	98 GAMES ROOM	99 TRAMPOLINE	100 BOWLS	101 HOT SPRINGS	102 GOLF COURSE – SEE NOTE 8	103 NUMBER OF HOLES	104 MINIATURE	105 MASHIE	106 PUTT-PUTT	107 FRESHWATER – SEE NOTE 9	108 SEA – SEE NOTE 10	109 GOGGLE	110 LICENCE REQUIRED	111 SWIMMING POOL	112 SEA BATHING	113 CHILDRENS' POOL	114 ADULTS ONLY	115 SHARK NETS AT BEACH	116 BOATS FOR HIRE	117 POWER	118 SAILING	119 CANOEING	120 HISTORIC	121 SCIENTIFIC	122 NATURAL	123 NOTES
X			X	X	X	B	B								X			X			X			X		A	A		X		X		X		X	X	X	X		X	220		X		X	X			X	X	X	X	X	X	X	X	X	X		X	X	X	N	N	N	N			N		N	18				N			X	N		N				N	N	N	X	X	X	
X						B	B	X					X			X			X				X		B	B		X		X		X		X	X	X	X		X			X			X			X	X	X			X		X	X		X	X	X	X	S	N	N	N			N		N	18				N			X						N	N	N	X		X	
X			X	X		D	D				X			X			X						X	E-J	E-J		X		X		X		X	X	X	X	X	X	X		X		X	X		X				X	X	X	X		X	X	X	X	X	X	S	S	S	S	S												S										X	X	X	
X			X	X	X	C	C				X	X	X	X	X	X	X	X	X		X	X		D	D		X		X		X		X	X	X	X		X	250		X		X	X	X		X	X	X	X		X		X	X	X		X	X	X	S	N	N						N	9		X		N			X										X		X	
X			X	X	X	A	A	X	X	X	X		X			X			X				X		B	B		X		X		X		X	X								X		X	X			X	X	X	X	X	X		X	X			X		X	S	N	N				N		N	10				S			X	N		N				S	S	S	X		X	
X						B	B	X					X			X			X										X		X		X		X	X	X	X		X					X	X			X	X	X	X	X	X	X	X	X	X		X	X	X		N																N		N							X			
X			X			D	D					X			X			X				X		E	E		X		X		X		X	X	X	X		X	220		X		X	X			X	X	X	X	X	X	X	X	X			X	X	X	N	N	N					N	N	9								S		S										X	
X			X	X	X	D	D						X		X			X										X		X		X		X	X	X	X		X	X		X	X	X			X	X	X	X	X	X	X		X			X	X		X		N					N		N	18					N			X							N			
X			X	X	X	E	C	X	X	X	X	X			X	X		X	X	X				X	K	J		X		X		X		X	X	X	X					X		X	X			X	X	X	X	X	X		X	X	X		X	X	X	S	S	S		S		N							S			X	S		S			S	N	N	S			X	
X			X	X	X	B	B											X				X		D	C		X				X		X	X		X					X		X				X			X		X		X			X	X		X							N								N	N			X						N	N			X	
			X			B	B					X	X		X	X		X	X								X		X		X		X	X	X			X				X	X			X	X	X	X	X	X	X	X				X	X	X	N	N					N		S	18																	X			
						O	O					X			X			X										X						X	X									X				X	X	X	X	X	X	X	X				X	X	X		N	N				N		N	9				N			X	N		N										
						C	C						X			X			X								X		X		X		X	X	X	X		X	X		X		X	X			X	X	X				X					X		X	S	N	N				N		N	18				N			X	N		N							X		X	
			X	X	X	D	B		X		X	X			X			X			X	X	X	X	B-G	B-G		X		X		X		X	X	X	X		X	220	X	X	X	X				X	X	X	X	X	X	X					X	X	X	S	S	S			S	S		N	18	X		X	N	S	S		X								X		X	
			X	X		B	B					X								X		X			D	D		X		X		X		X	X		X						X		X			X	X	X	X		X	X		X			X		X	S	S	N	N			N	N	N	9		X						S									X	X	X	
			X			B	B	X	X	X		X	X		X	X				X								X		X		X		X	X		X	X	X			X	X	X	X		X	X	X	X	X				X	X		X	X	X	N	N	N	N	N	N	N											N		N									X	
						B	B	X						X			X			X								X		X		X		X	X	X	X		X	220		X		X	X			X	X	X				X	X	X			X	X	X	N	N					S		N	9		X						N		N							X		X	
														X			X			X								X															X				X	X	X	X	X	X		X	X			X		X										N	9	X			N			X	N		N				S	S	S	X			
			X	X	X	B	B		X		X	X	X	X	X	X	X	X	X	X	X			X		B	B		X	X	X		X		X	X	X	X		X			X		X	X		X	X	X	X	X		X	X	X				X	X	X	N	N	N	S					S	9		X		S			X	N		N				S	S	S	X		X	
						B	B	X						X			X		X	X								X		X		X		X	X		X					X				X	X	X	X		X		X	X			X	X	X		S	N				N						N			X												
			X	X	X	D	B					X			X			X								X				X		X	X	X	L		X			X	X	X	X			X	X	X	X	X	X	X					X	X	X			N				N		N	18					N			X	N									X	
			X	X	X	E	C					X	X	X			X			X		X		G	E		X	X	X		X		X	X	X	X		X		X	X		X	X			X	X	X	X	X	X					X	X	X	X			N				N		N	18					N	N		X								X		X	
			X	X	X	D	D					X			X			X								X				X		X	X	X	L				X	X	X	X			X	X	X	X	X		X					X	X	X			N				N		N	18					N	N		X	S								X	
			X	X	X	E	E	X	X				X			X			X		X		X		F	F		X		X		X		X	X	X	X		X	X	X	X		X	X			X	X	X	X	X	X	X	X	X			X	X		X	N	S	S			S			N	18					N	N		N		N		X							X	
			X	X		I	F				X	X	X	X	X	X	X	X	X				X	K	C		X		X		X		X	X	X	X		X		X	X	X	X				X	X	X	X	X	X	X				X	X	X	X	S	N	N		S		N		N	18					N	N		S	X	S								X	
			X	X	X	E	D	X	X		X	X	X	X	X			X	X	X			X		I	E		X		X		X		X	X	X	X		X	220		X	X	X	X			X	X	X	X	X	X	X		X	X		X		X	S	S	S			S	N		N	18					S	S		X			X	S				X	X	X	
			X	X		G	D	X	X	X			X		X				X									X		X		X			X	X	X		X	X	X		X		X			X	X	X		X	X	X		X					X	S	S	S	S	S	S	N		N	18					S			X	S								X	
			X			C	C							X			X			X								X		X		X		X	X	X					X		X	X											X				X	X					S																					X	
			X	X	X	C	C					X				X		X								X		X		X		X	X	X							X		X			X	X	X	X	X	X	X						X		X		N					N		N	9				S			X					S					X	

CARAVAN PARKS AND CAMPING SITES IN SOUTH AFRICA

CARAVAN PARK / CAMP SITE TARIFF CODE – See columns 38–39 (Subject to alteration)

A = Up to R1 | B = R1–R2 | C = R2–R3 | D = R3–R4 | E = R4–R5 | F = R5–R6 | G = R6–R7 | H = R7–R8 | I = R8–R9 | J = R9–R10 | K = R10–R16 | O = FREE | X = On Application

Charges are based on family of 2 adults and 2 children under 12 years

ADDITIONAL ACCOMMODATION TARIFF CODE – See columns 57–59 (Subject to alteration)

eg. Bungalows, Cabins, Cottages, Chalets, etc.

A = R1–R3 | B = R3–R5 | C = R5–R7 | D = R7–R9 | E = R9–R11 | F = R11–R13 | G = R13–R15 | H = R15–R17 | I = R17–R19 | J = R19–R21 | K = R21–R30 | X = On Application

NB: Where the tariff is given in *italics* it is per person, otherwise per unit

NOTE 1 — **Columns 18, 19, 20.** — X = Stands available but not demarcated or number of stands have not been provided
NOTE 2 — **Column 35** — A = Bookings accepted for additional accommodation only i.e. cottages, bungalows, etc.
NOTE 3 — **Column 37** — Deposit refunded under certain conditions eg. less 10% ; if site is re-let ; if cancelled well in advance (up to 2 months) or on a doctor's certificate
NOTE 4 — **Column 41** — Reductions allowed on application for youth, church, school or sport groups or caravan rallies
NOTE 5 — **Column 69** — L = Laundry facilities only
NOTE 6 — **Columns 88, 89, 90.** — I = In-Season only ; O = Out-of-Season only; X = On application
NOTE 7 — **Column 96** — I = In-Season only
NOTE 8 — **Column 102** — See section on golf in Outdoor Holiday Guide
NOTE 9 — **Column 107** — See section on freshwater angling in Outdoor Holiday Guide
NOTE 10 — **Column 108** — See section on coastal angling in Outdoor Holiday Guide

Establishments marked thus ● have the Caravan Club of South Africa recommendation — see introduction

ABBREVIATIONS
C = CAPE PROVINCE
N = NATAL
O = ORANGE FREE STATE
T = TRANSVAAL
B = BOPHUTHATSWANA
X = TRANSKEI

	1 TELEPHONE CODE (T = DIAL 0020, BOOK TRUNK CALL; E = DIAL CODE, ASK EXCHANGE FOR NO.)	2 TELEPHONE NUMBER	3 OWNED OR SUPERVISED BY: PRIVATELY OWNED	4 MUNICIPAL	5 DIVISIONAL COUNCIL	6 PROVINCIAL ADMINISTRATION	7 PARKS BOARD	8 SITE DESCRIPTION – LOCALITY: BEACH IN IMMEDIATE VICINITY	9 BESIDE RIVER, LAKE OR DAM	10 IN OR NEAR MOUNTAIN AREA	11 WITHIN BUILT-UP AREA	12 NATURE OF GROUND: GRASS	13 GRAVEL	14 SAND	15 SHADE: UNSHADED	16 PARTLY SHADED	17 EXTENSIVELY SHADED	18 NO. OF STANDS: CARAVANS ONLY – SEE NOTE 1	19 CARAVANS AND/OR TENTS – SEE NOTE 1	20 TENTS ONLY – SEE NOTE 1	21 ACCESSIBILITY – APPROXIMATE DISTANCE FROM MAIN ROAD TO SITE: ON MAIN RD	22 WITHIN 1km	23 WITHIN 5km	24 WITHIN 10km	25 WITHIN 15km	26 SURFACE OF ROAD APPROACH: TAR	27 GRAVEL	28 SAND	29 CONDITION OF ROAD APPROACH: GOOD	30 FAIR	POOR
HLUHLUWE N 67 B5 ↙ 5m																															
False Bay Park Officer-in-Charge, P.O. Hluhluwe 3960 ☐ *15 km from Hluhluwe*	03562 E	2911					X		X			X				X			40						X		X			X	
HOEDSPRUIT T 69 B3 → 550m																															
Manoutsa P/Bag 502 (1380)	0131732 E	623	X						X	X		X				X			40		X							X	X		
Strijdom Tunnel Motel and Rest Camp P.O. Box 53 (1380)	0131732 E	1913	X						X	X		X		X			X	30	30	30		X					X	X		X	
HOFMEYR C 62 C3 ↘ 1252m																															
Hofmeyr Municipal Town Clerk, P.O. Box 97 (5930) ☐ *Du Plessis St.*	04852 E	97/33		X								X					X	20	20			X					X		X		
HOGSBACK C 60 B1 → 1450m																															
Waterfall Park N. C. Powrie, Tanglewood (5705)	T	240	X						X	X	X	X					X		12		X						X		X		
HONEYDEW T 72 NS ↖ 1234m																															
Honeydew P.O. Box 67 (2040) ☐ *D.F. Malan Drive*	011	675-2605	X								X	X				X		51			X						X			X	
HOT SPRINGS, MINERAL BATHS AND SPA'S See respectively: • Aliwal North • Badplaas • Calitzdorp • Christiana • Cradock • Dennilton • Letsitele • Montagu • Naboomspruit • Rawsonville • Sabi River Bungalows • The Baths • Tshipise • Warmbaths																															
HOUTBOSDORP T 70 NS ↖ 1524m																															
Woodbush Forest Reserve P/Bag 4013, Tzaneen 0850	01523	5767							X				X			X	X		50						X		X			X	
HOWICK N 63 A3 ← 1048m																															
● **Midmar Dam** P/Bag (3290) ☐ *5 km from Howick*	033212 E	267					X		X	X		X				X		31					X			X			X		
HUMANSDORP C 59 C4 ↗ 144m																															
Humansdorp Tourist Park P.O. Box 26 (6300) ☐ *Main St.*	04232 E	37		X							X	X					X					X				X			X		
IFAFA BEACH N 63 NS ↙ 8m																															
● **Ifafa Beach** P.O. Box 10 (4185) ☐ *Sydney See Rd.*	03239	740	X					X				X					X	44		10		X				X			X		
● **Ifafa Marina** Ifafa Marina (Agencies) (Pty) Ltd., P/Bag (4185) ☐ *Ifafa Lagoon*	03239	611/675	X						X	X		X				X			160				X				X		X		
ILLOVO BEACH N 63 NS ↗ S.L.																															
Illovo Beach P.O. Box 19 (4155) ☐ *17 Elizabeth Ave.*	031	95-1366						X				X					X	22		6		X				X			X		
Karridene P.O. Box 20 (4155) ☐ *Main South Coast Rd.*	031	95-1020	X					X	X		X	X					X	X	X			X				X			X		
Natalia Holiday Resort Manager, P.O. Box 3 (4155) ☐ *2 Elizabeth Ave.*	031	95-1626	X					X			X	X					X		110		X					X			X		
Patlyn P.O. Box 11 (4155) ☐ *Elizabeth Ave.*	031	95-1339	X					X				X					X	77		8		X				X			X		
IRENE T 68 C6 ↙ 1524m																															
Doornkloof P.O. Box 36 (1675)	012	6-5476	X								X	X	X			X		15		5			X			X	X			X	
JAMESTOWN C 62 C4 ↗ 1617m																															
Jamestown Municipal Town Clerk, P.O. Box 30 (5510) ☐ *Main St.*	T	2/20		X					X		X	X				X	X	6	6	12	X					X			X		
JEFFREYS BAY C 59 C4 ↗ S.L.																															
Jeffreys Bay Holiday Resort 30 Goede Hoop St. (6330) ☐ *Goede Hoop St.*	T	61	X								X	X				X			50				X			X			X		
● **Jeffreys Bay Municipal** P.O. Box 21 (6330) ☐ *Da Gama Rd.*	T	21		X				X			X	X				X			140				X			X			X		
● **Kabeljous Holiday Resort** C/o Starward Estate Agency, Cnr. Friesland/Brampton Aves., Rowallan Park, Port Elizabeth 6001	041	30-1208	X					X			X	X				X			66			X				X			X		
JOHANNESBURG T 72 NS • 1800m																															
● **Bezuidenhout Park** C/o Parks and Recreation Dept., P.O. Box 282A (2000) ☐ *Observatory Ave., De Wetshof*	011	43-3399		X							X	X					X	55			X					X			X		
JONGENSFONTEIN C 58 D6 ↖ S.L.																															
Jongensfontein Caretaker, Jongensfontein 6786 (for caravans); Secretary, P.O. Box 13, Riversdale 6770 (for huts)	T (02932 E)	2212 C/van (29 Huts)			X			X				X				X		110							X					X	
KAAPMUIDEN T 69 C4 ← 409m																															
Lowveld P.O. Box 54 (1295) ☐ *1,6 km from Kaapmuiden*	T	34	X							X		X				X			40		X						X		X		
KAKAMAS C 65 C2 ↓ 657m																															
Kakamas Municipal P.O. Box 174 (8870) ☐ *Cnr. Van der Walt Rd./14th Ave.*	05442 E	102		X							X	X	X			X			8			X				X	X		X		
KALAHARI GEMSBOK NATIONAL PARK C See Parks under control of National Parks Board																															
KATBERG C 60 B1 • 1000m																															
Highlands Holiday Resort P.O. Balfour 5740	T	1002	X							X		X					X	30	40	15			X				X		X		
KEIMOES C 65 C2 ↘ 736m																															
Keimoes Municipal Town Clerk, P.O. Box 8 (8860)	05492 E	26/134		X					X	X	X	X					X	20	30	20	X						X		X		
KEI MOUTH C 60 B3 ↓ S.L.																															
Kei Mouth Municipal Municipality, P.O. Kei Mouth 5262 ☐ *Main Rd.*	T	4		X				X			X	X			X	X			87		X						X		X		
KELSO N 63 NS • 2m																															
● **Happy Wanderers** P.O. Kelso 4183	0323	5104	X					X				X	X				X		100			X					X			X	
Kelso Valley P.O. Box 20, Pennington 4184 ☐ *49 Cod-Crescent St.*	0323	5130	X					X	X			X					X		50	10		X				X			X		
KEMPTON PARK T 72 NS ↗ 1670m																															
Pomona P.O. Box 86 (1620) ☐ *Hawthorne Rd., Pomona Estates*	011	975-0013	X								X	X	X				X		24			X					X			X	
Protea P.O. Box 774 (1620) ☐ *Pomona Rd.*	011	975-6195	X								X	X					X	60	60		X					X			X		
KEURBOOMSRIVIER C 59 NS → S.L.																															
Lagoon Holiday Resort P.O. Box 9 (6601)	T	19	X					X	X			X			X	X	X		50				X			X	X		X	X	

CAMP SITE FACILITIES: I = In-Season only, O = Out-of-Season only, X = On application

SPORTING AND RECREATIONAL FACILITIES: S = On Site, N = Nearby (Up to 20 km away)

32 Open throughout the year	33 Out-of-season closing date	34 Re-opening date	35 Seasons/Terms for bookings: Bookings acc. peak sns. – see note 2	36 Deposit required	37 Refunded if cancelled – see note 3	38 Caravan/camping site tariffs (See heading): Maximum in-season tariff	39 Maximum out-of-season tariff	40 Reductions allowed for: Long periods of stay	41 Groups – see note 4	42 AA members	43 Others (on application)	44 Restaurant facilities: On site	45 Within 5 km of site	46 More than 5 km from site	47 Tearoom/cafe: On site	48 Within 5 km of site	49 More than 5 km from site	50 Shopping facilities (Provisions): On site	51 Within 5 km of site	52 More than 5 km from site	53 Additional accommodation available: Bungalows	54 Cabins	55 Cottages (rondavels)	56 Chalets	57 Tariff (See heading): Maximum in-season tariff	58 Maximum out-of-season tariff	59 Caravans to rent on site – see section	60 Drinking water: Piped	61 Other	62 Baths: Hot and cold	63 Cold only	64 Showers: Hot and cold	65 Cold only	66 Waterborne sanitation	67 Washbasins	68 Dishwashing facilities	69 Laundry and ironing facilities – see note 5	70 Washing machines	71 Site lit	72 Plugs for razors (voltage)	73 Refrigerators	74 Firewood/charcoal	75 Open fire forbidden	76 Camp fire permitted	77 Braai places provided	78 Kitchen/cooking facilities	79 Petrol pump on site	80 Petrol pump nearby	81 Car repair shop nearby	82 Car servicing nearby	83 Gas service nearby	84 First aid/hospital/doctor nearby	85 Post office nearby	86 Site guarded	87 Pets allowed	88 Non-white servants: Servants permitted – see note 6	89 Servants accom. – see note 6	90 Servants for hire – see note 6	91 Type of vehicle permitted: Car and trailer	92 Truck 'horse' and semi-trailer	93 Self-propelled caravans	94 Childrens' playground	95 Tennis	96 Cinema/drive-in/TV-room – see note 7	97 Horse-riding	98 Games room	99 Trampoline	100 Bowls	101 Hot springs	102 Golf: Golf course – see note 8	103 Number of holes	104 Miniature	105 Mashie	106 Putt-putt	107 Fishing: Freshwater – see note 9	108 Sea – see note 10	109 Goggle	110 Licence required	111 Swimming: Swimming pool	112 Sea bathing	113 Childrens pool	114 Adults only	115 Shark nets at beach	116 Boating: Boats for hire	117 Power	118 Sailing	119 Canoeing	120 Places of interest: Historic	121 Scientific	122 Natural	123 Notes
X			X	X	X	C	C							X			X			X								X		X		X		X	X	X						X		X				X	X	X	X	X		X		X			X	X	X																S									S	S					X	
X						B	B	X				X			X			X			X		X		*A*	*A*		X		X		X		X	X							X	X	X	X		X													X		X	S																													X	
X			X	X	X	C	C	X	X			X			X			X			X			X	*C*	*C*		X	X	X		X		X	X		X		X			X		X	X			X	X	X		X		X	X	X	X		X	X	X	S	S	S	N	S	N	N	N						N			X	S		N							X	X	X	
X			X			A	A	X						X			X			X								X				X		X	X		L		X			X		X	X			X	X	X			X		X	X			X	X	X	N	N									X																			
X			X			C	C						X						X									X	X	X		X		X	X	X	L					X		X	X			X			X		X		X				X	X	X				N			N		N	6				N			X	N		N							X	X	X	
X			X	X	X	D	D							X		X	X		X	X								X		X		X		X	X		X		X					X				X	X	X	X		X						X	X	X	S			N	S		N		N	18								S											
X						A	A													X									X													X	X		X											X			X		X															N			X											X	
X			X	X	X	D	D					X		X	X	X	X		X	X		X		X	C-E	C-E		X	X	X		X		X	X	X			X			X		X	X			X	X	X		X	X	X					X	X	X	S	N	N	S					N	9				S			X	S		S			S	S	S	S		X	X	
X				X		B	B						X			X			X				X		A	A		X		X		X		X	X		X		X	X				X	X			X	X	X			X	X	X	X			X		X	S	N	N				N		N	9					N				X										
X			X	X	X	G	D	X					X		X			X									X	X		X		X		X	X	X	X	X	X	220		X	X		X			X			X	X	X	X	O				X	X	X	S	N	S		S	S	N							N	N	N	X	S	X	S		X								
X			X	X		K	D	X	X	X		X		X	X		X	X	X	X				X	*K*	*D*	X	X		X		X		X	X	X	X	X	X	220	X	X		X	X	X		X	X	X	X	X	X	X	O	X	X	X	X	X	X	S	S	S		S	S	N					X			N	N	N	X	S	X	S		X	S	S		S			X	
X			X	X	X	D	C						X			X			X				X		D	B		X		X		X		X	X	X	X		X			X		X	X	X		X	X	X	X	X	X	X				X	X		X	N	N	N	N	N	N	N		N	18					N				N	X	N		X							X	
X			X	X		H	E						X	X		X	X		X	X								X		X		X		X	X	X			X	X				X				X	X	X			X					X	X		X	N	N	N		N	N	N		N	18					N	N	X	N	X	N		X								
X			X	X	X	E	C				X		X			X			X									X		X		X		X	X	X	X		X	X		X	X	X	X			X	X	X	X		X	X					X	X	X	S	N	S	N		S	N		N	18			X		N	N	X	S		S		X					X	X	X	
X			X	X		F	C	X					X		X			X									X	X		X		X		X	X	X	X		X	110/220		X		X	X			X	X	X	X	X	X	X	X	O		X	X		X	N	N	S		S		N		N	18				N	N	N		S	X			X	N			N				
X			X			B	B								X		X			X								X		X		X		X	X				X	X		X		X				X	X	X	X		X		X				X	X	X		N					N		N	18				N			X										X			
X			X	X		B	B					X				X			X									X				X	X		X									X	X			X	X	X		X	X		X			X	X	X	X	N	N												N			X			N							X	X	X	
X			X	X		B	B	X						X			X			X	X		X		X	B-C		X		X		X		X	X		X		X					X	X			X	X	X	X		X		X			X	X	X	X	N			N			N		N	9					N				N	X										X	
X			X	X	X	C	C				X			X			X			X								X		X		X		X	X	X	X		X						X			X	X	X	X		X					X	X		X		N					N		N	9					S	S		N	X	N									X	
X			X	X	X	E	B	X	X	X			X						X	X	X				E	D		X		X		X		X	X	X	X		X	220		X		X	X			X	X	X	X	X	X	X	X				X	X	X	S	S	N				N		N	9					N				N	X	S							X	X	X	
X			X			B	B						X			X			X	X								X		X		X		X	X	X	X		X	X								X	X	X	X		X	X	X				X	X	X	N		N				S		N	18				N			X	S		S							X	X	X	
X			X			C	C											X	X	X	X				E	D		X		X		X		X	X	X	X		X			X	X	X	X			X	X		X		X	X	X	X			X	X	X															S	S			X								X	X		
X						C	C	X				X			X			X					X		B-C	B-C		X		X		X		X	X	X	X							X	X			X	X	X	X		X						X	X	X	S	N					N											S		S							X		X	
X			X			B	B	X	X				X			X			X									X				X		X	X	X	X		X					X				X	X	X			X		X	X			X	X	X		S							N	18				N			X										X		X	
X			X	X		D	D	X	X	X	X		X			X		X					X	X	D	C		X		X		X		X	X	X	X		X		X	X		X	X	X		X	X	X	X	X	X		X	X	X	X	X	X	X	S	S	S	S	S		S		N	9	X	X	X	N			X	N		S							X		X	
X						B	B	X					X			X			X									X	X	X		X		X	X	X	X		X			X		X	X			X	X	X	X	X	X	X	X	X			X	X	X	N	N	N				N		N	9		X		N				N		N						N			X	
X			X	X		E	D		X		X								X		X	X	X	X	G	D		X				X		X	X	X	X					X		X				X	X	X	X	X	X	I		X		X	X	X	X	N	S	N				S		N	9					N	N			X					N	N	N			X	
X			X	X	X	G	D	X				X			X					X				X	D-G	C-F		X		X		X		X	X	X	X		X	110/220				X	X			X	X	X	X	X	X	X	X	X	X		X		X		N	N		S		N		N	18					N				S		S									X	
X			X	X	X	F	B	X	X	X	X		X		X	X		X	X									X		X		X		X	X	X	X	X	X	110/220	X	X		X	X	X		X	X	X	X	X	X	X	X			X	X		X	S		S	N	S	S	N		N	18				S	S	S		S	X	S		X	S	S		S			X	
X			X	X	X	C	C	X					X	X		X	X		X	X								X		X		X		X	X	X	X		X	220					X	X	X	X	X	X	X	X	X		X			X	X		X	S	N	N	N	S	N	N		N	18								S		S										
X			X		X	D	D	X		X			X	X		X			X									X		X		X			X	X	X	X	X	220	X	X		X	X			X	X	X	X	X	X	X	X	X			X		X	N		N	N		N	N		N	18								N		N										
X			X	X		X	X	X				X			X			X					X		X	X	X	X	X	X		X		X	X	X	X		X			X	X		X			X		X	X	X	X						X	X	X		N		N			N		N	18					N	N			X				N	N	N	N				

CARAVAN PARKS AND CAMPING SITES IN SOUTH AFRICA

CARAVAN PARK / CAMP SITE TARIFF CODE — See columns 38–39 (Subject to alteration)

A = Up to R1 | C = R2–R3 | E = R4–R5 | G = R6–R7 | I = R8–R9 | K = R10–R16
B = R1–R2 | D = R3–R4 | F = R5–R6 | H = R7–R8 | J = R9–R10 | O = FREE
X = On Application

Charges are based on family of 2 adults and 2 children under 12 years

ADDITIONAL ACCOMMODATION TARIFF CODE — See columns 57–59 (Subject to alteration)
eg. Bungalows, Cabins, Cottages, Chalets, etc.

A = R1–R3 | C = R5–R7 | E = R9–R11 | G = R13–R15 | I = R17–R19 | K = R21–R30
B = R3–R5 | D = R7–R9 | F = R11–R13 | H = R15–R17 | J = R19–R21 | X = On Application

NB: Where the tariff is given in *italics* it is per person, otherwise per unit

NOTE 1 — Columns 18, 19, 20. — X = Stands available but not demarcated or number of stands have not been provided
NOTE 2 — Column 35 — A = Bookings accepted for additional accommodation only i.e. cottages, bungalows, etc.
NOTE 3 — Column 37 — Deposit refunded under certain conditions eg. less 10% ; if site is re-let ; if cancelled well in advance (up to 2 months) or on a doctor's certificate
NOTE 4 — Column 41 — Reductions allowed on application for youth, church, school or sport groups or caravan rallies
NOTE 5 — Column 69 — L = Laundry facilities only
NOTE 6 — Columns 88, 89, 90. — I = In-Season only ; O = Out-of-Season only ; X = On application
NOTE 7 — Column 96 — I = In-Season only
NOTE 8 — Column 102 — See section on golf in Outdoor Holiday Guide
NOTE 9 — Column 107 — See section on freshwater angling in Outdoor Holiday Guide
NOTE 10 — Column 108 — See section on coastal angling in Outdoor Holiday Guide

Establishments marked thus ● have the Caravan Club of South Africa recommendation — see introduction

ABBREVIATIONS
C = CAPE PROVINCE
N = NATAL
O = ORANGE FREE STATE
T = TRANSVAAL
B = BOPHUTHATSWANA
X = TRANSKEI

TELEPHONE CODE: T = DIAL 0020. BOOK TRUNK CALL. E = DIAL CODE. ASK EXCHANGE FOR NO.

	Telephone Code	Telephone Number	Owned or supervised by: Privately owned	Municipal	Divisional Council	Provincial Council	Parks Board Administration	Site description – Locality: Beach in immediate vicinity	Beside river, lake or dam	In or near mountain area	Within built-up area	Nature of ground: Grass	Gravel	Sand	Shade: Unshaded	Partly shaded	Extensively shaded	No. of stands: Caravans only – see note 1	Caravans and/or tents	Tents only – see note 1	Accessibility – Approximate distance from main road to site: On main rd	Within 1 km	Within 5 km	Within 10 km	Within 15 km	Surface of road approach: Tar	Gravel	Sand	Condition of road approach: Good	Fair	Poor
	1	2	3	4	5	6	7	8	9	10	11	12	13	14	15	16	17	18	19	20	21	22	23	24	25	26	27	28	29	30	31
KEURBOOMSRIVIER (CONTINUED)																															
Public Resort Keurboomsrivier P.O. Keurboomsrivier (6601)	T	15				X		X	X	X		X				X	X	70		16	X					X			X		
San Merino P.O. Box 413, Plettenberg Bay 6600	T	9	X						X			X					X		X			X				X			X		
KEURBOOMSTRAND C 59 NS → S.L.																															
Arch Rock Holiday Resort P.O. Box 6, Keurboomsrivier 6601	T	1311	X					X				X					X		80	5				X		X			X		
The Dunes P.O. Box 10, Keurboomsrivier 6601	T	35	X					X		X		X					X		86			X					X	X		X	
KIDD'S BEACH C 60 C2 ↗ 5m																															
Aqualea P/Bag X817, East London 5200 □ *Gulu River Mouth, 13 km from Kidd's Beach*	04323	858	X					X	X			X			X	X	X		40		X					X			X		
Kidd's Beach C/o Kidd's Beach Hotel (5241)	04323	715	X					X			X	X				X		30		15		X					X		X		
Lincott Manor P.O. Kidd's Beach 5264 □ *1,5 km from Kidd's Beach*	04323	643	X					X				X					X	25				X					X		X		
Palm Springs Holiday Resort P.O. Box 14 (5264)	04323	879	X					X	X			X			X	X			70				X				X		X		
● **Rayner's Holiday Resort** P.O. Box 5079, Greenfields, East London 5208 □ *Gulu River Mouth, 13 km from Kidd's Beach*	0431	46-2410/9	X					X	X			X					X		30				X				X		X		
Seavale P.O. Box 23 (5264)	04323	720	X					X				X				X		70	10					X			X			X	
KIMBERLEY C 66 C2 ↘ 1223m																															
Kimberley Municipal P.O. Box 628 (8300) □ *Transvaal Rd.*	0531	2-6911		X							X	X					X	25		50		X				X			X		
KING WILLIAM'S TOWN C 60 B2 ↗ 374m																															
King William's Town Municipal P.O. Box 33 (5600) □ *Cathcart St.*	0433	2481		X					X			X				X					X					X			X		
KLAPMUTS C 58 D3 ↘ 168m																															
Pearl P.O. Box 37 (7625) □ *Protea Rd.*	0251	5338	X									X					X		60			X				X	X		X		
KLEIN-BRAKRIVIER C 59 C2 ↘ S.L.																															
Riverside P.O. Box 6 (6503)	04441	6316	X					X	X	X		X				X		X	X	X			X				X		X		
KLEINKRANTZ C See Caravan Parks for Coloureds, Asians and Blacks																															
KLEINMOND C 58 D4 ↘ S.L.																															
Palmiet Municipal P.O. Box 3 (7195)	02823	2		X				X	X	X		X	X			X			700			X				X	X		X		
KLERKSDORP T 66 A4 ↓ 1325m																															
Schoonspruit Bookings not accepted — Park only provides for overnight stops □ *Cnr. Park/Boom Sts.*	018	2-3635		X					X		X	X				X						X				X			X		
Water Paradise P.O. Box 667 (2570) □ *Ventersdorp Rd.*	018	2-7521	X						X			X					X	60		25	X					X			X		
KNYSNA C 59 NS • S.L.																															
Ashmead P.O. Box 109 (6570) □ *George Rex Drive.*	04452 E	605	X					X	X	X	X	X					X		42			X				X			X		
Lagoonside P.O. Box 116 (6570) □ *Holiday Park Cres.*	04452 E	341	X					X	X	X	X	X				X					X					X			X		
Monks P.O. Box 513 (6570) □ *Port Elizabeth Main Rd.*	04452 E	539	X						X		X	X				X			30		X					X			X		
● **Water Ways Holiday Park** P.O. Box 394 (6570) □ *Holiday Park Cres.*	04452 E	557	X						X			X							48		X					X			X		
Woodbourne Holiday Farm P.O. Box 78 (6570) □ *George Rex Drive*	04452 E	6802	X					X				X					X		50			X				X			X		
KOFFIEFONTEIN O 62 A2 → 1189m																															
Koffiefontein Bookings not necessary □ *Du Preez Drive*	05372 E	7		X							X		X			X			35			X					X		X		
KOKSTAD N 63 B2 • 1283m																															
Kokstad Municipal Town Clerk, P.O. Box 8 (4700) □ *Cnr. Hawthorn/Barker Sts.*	0372 E	1 or 7 or 298		X						X	X	X				X			60			X				X	X		X		
Mount Currie Motel P.O. Box 27 (4700)	0372 E	279 or 781	X						X	X		X	X			X			12	4	X					X			X		
KOMATIPOORT T 69 C4 → 189m																															
Komatipoort P.O. Box 146 (1340)	0131632 E	252			X				X			X					X		X		X						X			X	
KOMGA C 60 B2 ← 640m																															
Komga Municipal Bookings not accepted. Enquiries: Town Clerk, P.O. Box 21 (4950) □ *Main St.*	04372 E	36 or 28		X							X	X				X			12		X						X		X		
KOMMETJIE C 58 NS ← S.L.																															
Imhoff Park Manager, P.O. Box 18 (7976) □ *Wireless Rd.*	021	8-3634			X			X		X		X				X			120			X				X			X		
KOSI BAY N 67 A5 ↘ S.L.																															
Kosi Bay Nature Reserve Officer-in-Charge, P.O. Mkuze 3965							X		X			X		X	X	X	X		X						X			X			X
KOSTER T 68 C4 → 1588m																															
Koster River State Irrigation Board P/Bag 20 (2825) □ *Koster River Dam*	014242 E	4230							X	X		X	X			X			X			X					X		X		
Wonderbaar Rest Camp P.O. Box 396 (2825)	014242 E	7322	X						X	X		X	X			X	X						X				X			X	
KROONDAL T 68 C5 ↗ 1150m																															
Belvedere Holiday Resort P.O. Box 46 (0350) □ *Wigwam Rd., Rustenburg*	01421	9-2205	X							X		X				X		20				X					X			X	
Bergheim Holiday Resort P.O. Box 327 (0350) □ *Modderfontein, Rustenburg Dist.*	01421	9-2363	X							X		X			X	X	X	50	20	20	X					X			X		
Omaramba P.O. Box 72 (0350) □ *Adjoining Buffelspoort Dam*	0142222	2713	X						X	X		X				X			150				X				X			X	
KROONSTAD O 66 B5 ↘ 1369m																															
● **Kroon Park** Manager of Parks, P.O. Box 302 (9600) □ *Bert Symonds Drive*	01411	5670/4229		X					X			X				X	X	160		140		X				X			X		
KRUGER NATIONAL PARK T See Parks under control of National Parks Board																															
KRUGERSDORP T 72 NS ↘ 1692m																															
Pines Resort Manager, P.O. Box 18, Kenmare 1745 □ *Ivan Smuts Ave., Silverfields*	011	664-2506	X							X	X	X					X	44		20		X				X			X		

CAMP SITE FACILITIES (columns 60–93) — I = In-Season only, O = Out-of-Season only, X = On application

SPORTING AND RECREATIONAL FACILITIES (columns 94–122) — S = On Site, N = Nearby (Up to 20 km away)

SEASONS			TERMS FOR BOOKINGS			CARAVAN/CAMPING SITE TARIFFS (See heading)		REDUCTIONS ALLOWED FOR				RESTAURANT FACILITIES			TEAROOM/CAFE			SHOPPING FACILITIES (Provisions)			ADDITIONAL ACCOMMODATION AVAILABLE				TARIFF (See heading)			DRINKING WATER		BATHS		SHOWERS																								NON-WHITE SERVANTS			TYPE OF VEHICLE PERMITTED											GOLF					FISHING				SWIMMING					BOATING				PLACES OF INTEREST			
OPEN THROUGHOUT THE YEAR	OUT-OF-SEASON CLOSING DATE	RE-OPENING DATE	BOOKINGS ACCP. (PEAK SNS.–SEE NOTE 2)	DEPOSIT REQUIRED	REFUNDED IF CANCELLED – SEE NOTE 3	MAXIMUM IN-SEASON TARIFF	MAXIMUM OUT-OF-SEASON TARIFF	LONG PERIODS OF STAY	GROUPS – SEE NOTE 4	AA MEMBERS	OTHERS (ON APPLICATION)	ON SITE	WITHIN 5 km OF SITE	MORE THAN 5 km FROM SITE	ON SITE	WITHIN 5 km OF SITE	MORE THAN 5 km FROM SITE	ON SITE	WITHIN 5 km OF SITE	MORE THAN 5 km FROM SITE	BUNGALOWS	CABINS	COTTAGES (RONDAVELS)	CHALETS	MAXIMUM IN-SEASON TARIFF	MAXIMUM OUT-OF-SEASON TARIFF	CARAVANS TO RENT ON SITE – SEE SECTION	PIPED	OTHER	HOT AND COLD	COLD ONLY	HOT AND COLD	COLD ONLY	WATERBORNE SANITATION	WASHBASINS	DISHWASHING FACILITIES	LAUNDRY AND IRONING FACILITIES – SEE NOTE 5	WASHING MACHINES	SITE LIT	PLUGS FOR RAZORS (VOLTAGE)	REFRIGERATORS	FIREWOOD/CHARCOAL	OPEN FIRE FORBIDDEN	CAMP FIRE PERMITTED	BRAAI PLACES PROVIDED	KITCHEN/COOKING FACILITIES	PETROL PUMP ON SITE	PETROL PUMP NEARBY	CAR REPAIR SHOP NEARBY	CAR SERVICING NEARBY	GAS SERVICE NEARBY	FIRST AID/HOSPITAL/DOCTOR NEARBY	POST OFFICE NEARBY	SITE GUARDED	PETS ALLOWED	SERVANTS PERMITTED – SEE NOTE 6	SERVANTS ACCOM. – SEE NOTE 6	SERVANTS FOR HIRE – SEE NOTE 6	CAR AND TRAILER	TRUCK 'HORSE' AND SEMI-TRAILER	SELF-PROPELLED CARAVANS	CHILDRENS' PLAYGROUND	TENNIS	CINEMA/DRIVE-IN/TV-ROOM – SEE NOTE 7	HORSE-RIDING	GAMES ROOM	TRAMPOLINE	BOWLS	HOT SPRINGS	GOLF COURSE – SEE NOTE 8	NUMBER OF HOLES	MINIATURE	MASHIE	PUTT-PUTT	FRESHWATER – SEE NOTE 9	SEA – SEE NOTE 10	GOGGLE	LICENCE REQUIRED	SWIMMING POOL	SEA BATHING	CHILDRENS' POOL	ADULTS ONLY	SHARK NETS AT BEACH	BOATS FOR HIRE	POWER	SAILING	CANOEING	HISTORIC	SCIENTIFIC	NATURAL	NOTES
32	33	34	35	36	37	38	39	40	41	42	43	44	45	46	47	48	49	50	51	52	53	54	55	56	57	58	59	60	61	62	63	64	65	66	67	68	69	70	71	72	73	74	75	76	77	78	79	80	81	82	83	84	85	86	87	88	89	90	91	92	93	94	95	96	97	98	99	100	101	102	103	104	105	106	107	108	109	110	111	112	113	114	115	116	117	118	119	120	121	122	123
X			X	X	X	C-D	C-D						X			X			X					X	G	F		X		X		X		X	X	X	X		X	220			X		X			X	X	X			X	X					X	X	X	S	S	N	N			N		N	18					S	N			X	S				N	N	N	X		X	
X			X	X	X	F	C	X	X				X			X		X						X	X	X	X	X	X	X		X		X	X	X	X		X	X	X	X	X		X			X	X	X	X	X	X	X				X	X	X	X	S	N	N	N	S		N		N	18				S	N	N			X				S	S		S	X		X	
X			X	X	X	G	C	X	X						X			X											X	X		X		X	X	X	L		X			X	X	X	X			X		X	X	X	X		O			X	X	X	X							N		N	18					S				X								X		X	
X			X	X	X	F	C	X	X	X			X	X	X	X	X	X	X	X	X				G	D		X	X	X		X		X	X	X	X	X	X		X	X	X	X	X			X	X	X	X	X	X	X				X	X	X	X		N	N	N	S	N	N		N	18					N	N			X	N							X	X	X	
X			X	X	X	E	D	X						X			X	X		X								X	X	X	X	X	X	X	X		X		X			X	X	X	X			X	X	X	X		X	X				X	X	X	X			I		S		N							N	N	N	X		X				N	N	N	N			X	
X			X	X		F	C			X	X	X							X									X		X		X		X	X	X	X		X	X	X	X	X	X	X			X	X	X	X	X	X		X	X			X		X					N	S	N								N				X	N			N			N			X	
X			X	X		K	H						X	X		X	X	X	X				X		*B*	*B*		X				X		X	X	X	X					X	X		X			X	X	X	X		X	X				X	X		X					S		N							N	N			S	X	S										
X			X	X		E	B	X	X	X			X	X		X	X	X	X	X			X		F	C		X		X		X		X	X	X	X		X			X		X				X	X	X	X		X		X	X	X	X	X	X	X	S	N			S		N								N	N			X	N			S		S	S			X	
X			X	X	X	F	D							X			X	X	X					X	E	D		X		X		X		X	X	X	X	X	X		X	X	X	X	X			X	X	X	X		X		X			X	X		X	S		N		S		N								S				X				S			S				
X			X	X		E	C	X	X								X	X	X	X								X	X	X		X		X	X	X	X					X	X	X	X			X	X	X	X		X		O	X		X	X		X	S		S		S				N	8	X				S	S			X	N				N						
X			X			A	A							X			X			X								X		X		X		X	X	X	X						X	X	X														X		X	S		N						N	18																	X			
X			X		X	C	C	X						X			X		X									X		X		X		X	X	X	X			220		X		X	X			X	X	X	X	X	X			X		X	X	X	X	N	N	N	N	N		N		N	18				N			X	N		N				N	N	N	X	X	X	
X			X	X	X	X	X						X			X			X		X		X		B	A		X		X		X		X	X	X			X			X			X			X	X	X	X	X	X		X				X		X			N				N		N	18								S		S										
X			X	X	X	F	C	X	X	X	X		X			X		X					X	X	J	G	X	X		X		X		X	X	X	X		X	220	X	X		X	X			X	X	X	X		X	X				X	X	X	X		N	N	N	S	N	N		N	18				N	N	N			X				S			S			X	
X			X	X	X	C	B		X				X	X		X	X		X	X								X				X		X	X	X						X		X	X			X	X	X	X	X	X	X		X			X	X	X	S	N	N				N								N	N			X								X		X	
X						A	A							X		X			X									X						X	X									X	X			X	X	X	X		X		X				X	X	X	N	N	N				N		N	18				S			X	S		S							X		X	
X				X	X	D	D	X						X				X										X		X		X		X	X	X	X		X			X	X		X			X	X	X	X	X	X	X	X	X			X		X	S	N	N				N		N	18				N			X	S		S			S		S	S	X		X	
X			X	X		F	E		X				X			X		X	X		X	X		X	D-K	B-E		X		X		X		X	X	X	X		X	220		X		X	X			X	X	X		X	X		X	I	I	X	X	X	X	S	N	N	N	S		N		N	18				N	N	N			X	N			N	N		N	X	X	X	
X			X	X	X	F	B	X					X			X		X	X			X	X		J	E	X	X		X		X		X	X	X	X			X		X		X	X			X	X	X	X	X	X		O	X	X	X	X		X		N	N	N	S		N		N	18				N	N	N		S	X	S			S	S		S	X	X	X	
X			X	X		K	J						X		X			X			X		X		F	E		X		X		X		X	X	X	X		X	220		X		X	X		X	X	X	X	X	X	X	X				X	X		X	S	S	S				N		N	18					N	N			X	N			S	S	S	S	X		X	
X			X	X	X	E	E	X					X		X				X		X			X	H-J	D-H	X	X				X		X	X	X	X	X	X	220				X	X			X	X	X	X	X	X		O	X	X	X	X	X	X	N	N	N	N	S	N	N		N	18				N	N	N	X		X				S			S	X		X	
X			X	X		F	C	X	X		X		X			X		X			X				*B*	*A*		X		X		X		X	X		X		X	X		X		X	X			X	X	X	X		X	X					X	X	X	S	N	N	N			N		N	18					N	N			X								X	X	X	
X						B	B							X			X			X								X		X		X		X	X	X	X		X	X			X		X			X	X	X	X	X	X	X	X	X			X		X	N	N	N	N		N	N		N			X		N			X	N		N							X		X	
X						B	B	X						X			X			X								X		X		X		X	X	X	X		X	220				X	X			X	X	X	X		X	X	X	X			X		X	N	N					N		N	9				N			X	N		N							X	X	X	
X						B	B	X	X	X		X			X			X						X	C	C		X		X		X		X	X	X			X				X				X		X	X			X	X	X	X	X		X	X	X	N	N	S	N			N		N	9				N			X	N		N	X			N	N	N	X		X	
X						B	B							X		X			X									X		X		X		X	X	X	X		X			X		X	X			X	X	X	X	X	X	X				X	X	X	X	N	N	N											N			X	N		N						N			X	
X						C	C	X					X	X		X	X		X	X								X		X	X	X	X	X	X	X	X							X	X			X	X	X	X		X		X	X			X	X	X	N	N					N		N	9								N											X	
X			X	X	X	C	B		X		X		X	X		X	X		X	X								X		X		X		X	X	X	X	X	X	220		X		X	X			X	X	X	X	X	X	X					X	X	X	S	N	N	N	S	N	N		N	18			X		N	N			X	N							X		X	
X			X	X		C	C													X								X					X	X	X	X						X		X				X				X	X			X		X	4 — wheel																		N		X							N	N	N		X	X	Permits from KwaZulu authorities required ← to stay in Kosi Bay — details are sent at time of booking.
X						O	O							X			X		X	X								X			X			X								X	X	X	X									X	X	X			X	X	X														S		S	X							S	S	S			X	
X			X	X	X	C	C	X	X	X		X			X			X	X					X	D	B		X		X		X		X	X	X	X		X			X		X	X	X		X	X	X		X	X	X		X	X		X		X		N	N	S	S									N			X	S		S								X	X	
X			X	X		E	D	X	X	X			X	X	X	X	X	X	X	X			X	X	D	C		X		X		X		X	X		X	X	X	220	X	X			X	X		X	X	X	X	X	X	X				X	X		X	S	S		S	S		N		N	18				N			X	S		S									X	
X			X	X		E	E		X				X	X	X	X	X	X	X	X			X		D-F	D-F		X		X		X		X	X	X	X		X	220	X	X		X	X			X	X	X	X		X						X		X	S	S	N	S		S	N		N	18								S		S							X	X	X	
X			X	X		E	E				X		X		X			X										X		X		X		X	X	X	X		X	X		X		X	X			X	X	X	X	X	X	X	X	X	X		X	X	X	S	S	S	S	S		N		N	18				N			X	S		S									X	
X			X	X		C	C		X				X			X			X		X		X		A-D	A-D		X		X		X		X	X	X	X		X	X		X		X	X			X	X	X	X	X	X	X	X	X		X	X	X	X	S	S	N			S	S		S	18			X	N				S		S			S			S	X			
X			X	X		D	D		X	X				X	X				X					X				X		X			X	X	X				X	X		X		X	X			X	X	X	X	X	X	X					X		X	N	N																S		S										

CARAVAN PARKS AND CAMPING SITES IN SOUTH AFRICA

CARAVAN PARK / CAMP SITE TARIFF CODE – See columns 38–39 (Subject to alteration)

A = Up to R1	C = R2–R3	E = R4–R5	G = R6–R7	I = R8–R9	K = R10–R16
B = R1–R2	D = R3–R4	F = R5–R6	H = R7–R8	J = R9–R10	O = FREE
					X = On Application

Charges are based on family of 2 adults and 2 children under 12 years

ADDITIONAL ACCOMMODATION TARIFF CODE – See columns 57–59 (Subject to alteration)

eg. Bungalows, Cabins, Cottages, Chalets, etc.

A = R1–R3	C = R5–R7	E = R9–R11	G = R13–R15	I = R17–R19	K = R21–R30
B = R3–R5	D = R7–R9	F = R11–R13	H = R15–R17	J = R19–R21	X = On Application

NB: Where the tariff is given in *italics* it is per person, otherwise per unit

NOTE 1 — Columns 18, 19, 20. — X = Stands available but not demarcated or number of stands have not been provided

NOTE 2 — Column 35 — A = Bookings accepted for additional accommodation only i.e. cottages, bungalows, etc.

NOTE 3 — Column 37 — Deposit refunded under certain conditions eg. less 10 % ; if site is re-let ; if cancelled well in advance (up to 2 months) or on a doctor's certificate

NOTE 4 — Column 41 — Reductions allowed on application for youth, church, school or sport groups or caravan rallies

NOTE 5 — Column 69 — L = Laundry facilities only

NOTE 6 — Columns 88, 89, 90. — I = In-Season only ; O = Out-of Season only ; X = On application

NOTE 7 — Column 96 — I = In-Season only

NOTE 8 — Column 102 — See section on golf in Outdoor Holiday Guide

NOTE 9 — Column 107 — See section on freshwater angling in Outdoor Holiday Guide

NOTE 10 — Column 108 — See section on coastal angling in Outdoor Holiday Guide

Establishments marked thus ● have the Caravan Club of South Africa recommendation — see introduction

ABBREVIATIONS

C = CAPE PROVINCE
N = NATAL
O = ORANGE FREE STATE
T = TRANSVAAL
B = BOPHUTHATSWANA
X = TRANSKEI

TELEPHONE CODE: T = DIAL 0020, BOOK TRUNK CALL; E = DIAL CODE, ASK EXCHANGE FOR NO.

	1 Telephone Code	2 Telephone Number	3 Owned or supervised by: Privately owned	4 Municipal	5 Divisional council	6 Provincial council	7 Parks board administration	8 Site description – Locality: Beach in immediate vicinity	9 Beside river, lake or dam	10 In or near mountain area	11 Within built-up area	12 Nature of ground: Grass	13 Gravel	14 Sand	15 Shade: Unshaded	16 Partly shaded	17 Extensively shaded	18 No. of stands: Caravans only – see note 1	19 Caravans and/or tents	20 Tents only – see note 1	21 Accessibility – Approximate distance from main road to site: On main rd	22 Within 1 km	23 Within 5 km	24 Within 10 km	25 Within 15 km	26 Surface of road approach: Tar	27 Gravel	28 Sand	29 Condition of road approach: Good	30 Fair	31 Poor
KRUGERSPOS T 69 B3 ↓ 1326m																																
Krugerspost Krugerspost Restaurant, P.O. Krugerspos 1128	013232 E	2630	X							X		X				X		40			X							X	X		
KUILSRIVIER C 58 C3 ↘ 45m																																
● **Kuilsrivier Municipal** P.O. Box 68 (7580) ☐ *Van Riebeeck Rd.*	021	33-3113		X							X	X					X	85	30	115	X					X			X		
KURUMAN C 65 B5 • 1375m																																
● **Kuruman Municipal** P.O. Box 4 (8460) ☐ *Voortrekker St.*	014532 E	8		X							X	X	X				X		60		X						X		X		
LADISMITH C 58 C6 ← 539m																																
Ladismith Municipal P.O. Box 30 (6885) ☐ *Church St.*	02942 E	20		X					X		X						X									X		X	X		
LADYBRAND O 66 D5 ↑ 1612m																																
● **Leliehoek Recreation Resort** Town Clerk, P.O. Box 64 (9745) ☐ *Leliehoek Ave.*	05612 E	33		X						X		X					X	50	50				X			X			X		
LADY GREY C 62 B5 ↙ 1631m																																
Lady Grey P.O. Box 68 (5540) ☐ *Cnr. Burnett/Murray Sts.*	05552 E	72	X								X	X				X		15		5			X			X			X		
LADYSMITH N 67 C2 → 1001m																																
Ladysmith Municipal P.O. Box 119 (3370) ☐ *Buller Rd.*	0361	6050/4881		X					X	X	X	X				X			60		X					X			X		
LAINGSBURG C 58 C5 ↗ 660m																																
Peppertree Karroo Motors, 28 Voortrekker St. (3370) ☐ *Cape Town Main Rd.*	02372 E	94	X								X	X				X		20			X					X			X		
LAMBERT'S BAY C 58 B3 ↖ 30m																																
Lambert's Bay Municipal Town Clerk, P.O. Box 4 (8130) ☐ *Church St.*	T	9		X				X			X		X	X	X				180			X				X			X		
LANGEBAAN C 58 C3 ↖ S.L.																																
Langebaan Municipal P.O. Box 11 (7357) ☐ *Duffren St.*				X				X				X				X			70		X					X			X		
LEISURE BAY N 63 NS ↙ S.L.																																
Leisure View P.O. Box 16, Voortrekkerstrand 4279	03931	67	X					X				X					X	60	100	40		X				X			X		
LETSITELE T 69 A3 ↘ 530m																																
Eiland Mineral Baths P/Bag 527 (0885)	015238	759 or 776				X						X					X	300		120	X					X			X		
LICHTENBURG T 68 D4 ↖ 1489m																																
● **Lichtenburg Municipal** P.O. Box 7 (2740)	01441	5051		X					X			X				X			X				X			X			X		
Molopo-Dal Rest Resort P.O. Box 686 (2740)	T	Ottoshoop 902	X						X			X					X	50	50	100	X						X		X		
LINDLEY O 66 B5 ↘ 1540m																																
Lindley Municipal Bookings not necessary ☐ *Rautenbach St. Ext.*	014152 E	4		X					X			X		X			X		50			X					X		X		
LOSKOP DAM NATURE RESERVE T See Damwal																																
LOUIS TRICHARDT T 70 C4 ↗ 945m																																
● **Louis Trichardt Municipal** Town Clerk, P.O. Box 96 (0920) ☐ *Cnr. Trichardt/Grobler Sts.*	01551	2211		X							X	X					X		X		X					X			X		
Mountain P.O. Box 414 (0920) ☐ *Messina Main Rd.*	01551	9611	X							X		X				X		6			X						X	X		X	
LOXTON C 61 C4 ← 1219m																																
Loxton Municipal P.O. Box 8 (6985)	020212 E	4		X									X				X		100	100		X					X		X		
LYDENBURG T 69 C3 ↖ 1468m																																
Lydenburg Municipal P.O. Box 61 (1120) ☐ *Viljoen St.*	013232 E	495/308		X					X	X	X	X					X		40		X						X		X		
MACHADODORP T 69 C3 ↙ 1609m																																
Highway P.O. Box 194 (1170) ☐ *Nelspruit Main Rd.*	013242 E	192	X									X				X			20		X					X			X		
MAFEKING C 68 C3 ↓ 1278m																																
Cooke's Lake P.O. Box 42 (8670) ☐ *Lichtenburg Main Rd.*	0506	1091/2/3		X					X			X	X			X			110		X						X		X		
MAGALIESBURG T 68 D5 ↑ 1402m																																
Lovers Rock Pleasure Resort P.O. Box 79 (2805) ☐ *5 km from Magaliesburg*	01462 E	87	X						X			X					X		150		X						X		X		
MAGOEBASKLOOF T See Haenertsburg																																
MAITLAND RIVER MOUTH C See Beachview																																
MANYELETI GAME RESERVE T See Acornhoek																																
MARBLE HALL T 69 B2 ↙ 936m																																
Caravan's Rest P.O. Box 239 (0450) ☐ *6 km from Marble Hall*	012082 E	5102	X						X			X					X	12	12	12	X					X			X		
MARGATE N 63 NS / S.L.																																
● **De Wet** P.O. Box 71 (4275) ☐ *St. Andrews Rd.*	0393	2-1022	X					X				X	X		X	X	X	65	85	20		X				X			X		
Margate Caravan Corner P.O. Box 276 (4275)	0393	2-0321	X					X	X		X	X				X	X	73		6		X				X			X		
● **Margate Caravan Park** P.O. Box 288 (4275) ☐ *Valley Rd.*	0393	2-0852	X								X	X					X		73		X					X			X		
MARINA BEACH N 63 NS ↙ 15m																																
● **Belle Vista** P.O. Box 36, Southbroom 4277	0393	3755	X					X				X					X		100		X						X		X		
Sherwood Forest P.O. Box 39 (4281)	0393	3792	X					X			X	X				X	X	120	20	10	X					X			X		
SYSU SYSU-Vakansiebelange, P.O. Box 2347, Pretoria 0001 ☐ *Mars Rd.*	012 (0393)	79-6119 (3600)	X					X	X		X	X					X		30				X			X	X		X		
MATATIELE N 62 B6 ↗ 1475m																																
Haig Park Town Clerk, P.O. Box 35 (4730) ☐ *Cnr. West/High Sts.*				X							X	X					X		10		X					X			X		

CAMP SITE FACILITIES: I = In-Season only   O = Out-of-Season only   X = On application

SPORTING AND RECREATIONAL FACILITIES: S = On Site   N = Nearby (Up to 20 km away)

33 Out-of-season closing date (Seasons)	34 Re-opening date (Seasons)	35 Bookings accp. peak sns. – see note 2 (Terms for bookings)	36 Deposit required	37 Refunded if cancelled – see note 3	38 Maximum in-season tariff (Caravan/camping site tariffs (See heading))	39 Maximum out-of-season tariff	40 Long periods of stay (Reductions allowed for)	41 Groups – see note 4	42 AA members	43 Others (on application)	44 On site (Restaurant facilities)	45 Within 5 km of site	46 More than 5 km from site	47 On site (Tearoom/cafe)	48 Within 5 km of site	49 More than 5 km from site	50 On site (Shopping facilities (Provisions))	51 Within 5 km of site	52 More than 5 km from site	53 Bungalows (Additional accommodation available)	54 Cabins	55 Cottages (rondavels)	56 Chalets	57 Maximum in-season tariff (Tariff (See heading))	58 Maximum out-of-season tariff	59 Caravans to rent on site – see section	60 Piped (Drinking water)	61 Other	62 Hot and cold (Baths)	63 Cold only	64 Hot and cold (Showers)	65 Cold only	66 Waterborne sanitation	67 Washbasins	68 Dishwashing facilities	69 Laundry and ironing facilities – see note 5	70 Washing machines	71 Site lit	72 Plugs for razors (voltage)	73 Refrigerators	74 Firewood/charcoal	75 Open fire forbidden	76 Camp fire permitted	77 Braai places provided	78 Kitchen/cooking facilities	79 Petrol pump on site	80 Petrol pump nearby	81 Car repair shop nearby	82 Car servicing nearby	83 Gas service nearby	84 First aid/hospital/doctor nearby	85 Post office nearby	86 Site guarded	87 Pets allowed	88 Servants permitted – see note 6 (Non-white servants)	89 Servants accom. – see note 6	90 Servants for hire – see note 6	91 Car and trailer (Type of vehicle permitted)	92 Truck 'horse' and semi-trailer	93 Self-propelled caravans	94 Childrens' playground	95 Tennis	96 Cinema/drive-in/TV-room – see note 7	97 Horse-riding	98 Games room	99 Trampoline	100 Bowls	101 Hot springs	102 Golf course – see note 8 (Golf)	103 Number of holes	104 Miniature	105 Mashie	106 Putt-putt	107 Freshwater – see note 9 (Fishing)	108 Sea – see note 10	109 Goggle	110 Licence required	111 Swimming pool (Swimming)	112 Sea bathing	113 Childrens' pool	114 Adults only	115 Shark nets at beach	116 Boats for hire (Boating)	117 Power	118 Sailing	119 Canoeing	120 Historic (Places of interest)	121 Scientific	122 Natural	123 Notes
			X		C	C					X			X			X										X		X		X		X	X	X	X		X	X		X			X			X	X	X	X	X	X			X			X		X									N	9				N			X										X		X	
		X			C	C	X					X	X		X	X		X	X								X	X	X		X		X	X	X	X		X						X			X	X	X	X	X	X	X		X			X		X	S		N						N	18					N	N			N											
		X			B	B						X			X			X									X		X		X		X	X	X	X		X	230	X	X		X	X			X	X	X	X		X		X	X			X		X	N	N	N	N		N	N		N	9								N		N							X	X	X	
		X	X		B	B							X			X			X								X	X	X		X		X	X	X	X		X			X	X	X	X			X	X	X	X	X	X	X	X				X	X	X	S	N	N			N	N							N				N		N							X		X	
					B	B	X	X			X	X	X		X	X		X	X	X		X		B-D	B-C		X		X		X		X	X	X	X		X	220		X		X	X			X	X	X	X	X	X	X	X	X		X	X	X	X	S	N	N	S			N		N	9				N			X	S		S				N	N	N	X	X	X	
		X			B	B	X					X			X		X	X	X								X		X		X		X	X	X	X	X	X	220				X	X			X	X	X	X	X	X		X				X	X	X	N	N	N											N			X	N		N							X			
		X			C	C	X	X	X		X	X	X	X	X	X	X	X	X								X	X	X	X	X	X	X	X	X	X					X		X	X	X		X	X	X	X	X	X	X	X	X			X	X	X		N	N	N			N		N	10								S		S							X		X	
		X			B	B					X				X			X									X	X			X		X	X	X			X	X			X	X	X		X	X	X	X	X	X	X		X	X			X	X	X		N																											
		X			C	C						X			X			X									X		X			X	X	X	X	X			X				X	X			X	X	X	X		X	I		X			X		X	N	N	N		N				N	9					N	N			X									X		
		X			D	D						X			X			X									X		X		X		X	X	X	X		X	220				X	X			X	X	X	X	X	X	X		X			X		X															N	N			X				N	N	N	N	X		X	
		X	X	X	E	C	X	X	X			X	X		X	X		X	X								X		X		X		X	X	X	X		X		X	X		X	X			X	X	X	X	X	X	X	X			X	X	X	X	S	N	N	N			N		N	9	X	X	X	N	N	N		N	X	N		X							X	
					D	D					X			X			X					X		D-G	D-G		X		X		X		X	X	X	X	X	X	220		X		X	X		X		X	X	X	X		X		X	X		X	X	X	S	S	S	S				S					X	N		N		S		S									X	
		X			B	B							X			X			X								X		X		X		X	X				X					X				X	X	X			X	X					X	X	X									N	18				S			X	S									X		X	
		X	X		C	C								X			X					X		E	C		X		X		X		X	X	X			X		X	X		X	X	X		X						X					X	X	X	S	S																S		S									X	
					O	O							X			X			X								X		X		X		X	X								X	X															X		X														S			X	N		N									X	
		X	X	X	B	B						X			X			X									X		X		X		X	X	X	X		X			X	X		X			X	X	X			X	X	X	X			X		X		N	N				N		N	9			N	N			X	N		N					N	N	X		X	
		X			B	B	X					X			X			X									X		X		X		X	X							X	X		X			X	X	X	X		X		X	X			X	X	X		N	N				N		N	9								N											X	
					O	O							X			X			X								X															X	X	X			X			X		X		X	X		X				N	N												N																
		X			B	B						X			X			X		X	X	X		B-C	B-C		X		X		X		X	X	X	X		X	220			X	X	X			X	X	X			X	X					X		X		N	N				N		N	9				N			X	N		N							X	X	X	
					C	C	X	X	X		X							X									X		X		X		X	X	X	X		X	220		X		X	X		X		X	X			X		X	X			X	X	X	S	N	N				N							N			X	N		N							X		X	
					B	B		X					X			X			X								X	X	X	X	X	X	X	X	X			X	X		X		X	X			X	X	X	X	X	X	X	X	X			X	X	X	S	N	N				N		N	9				S			X	N		N						S	X			
		X			D	D				X				X	X			X				X		B	B		X		X		X		X	X	X	X			220		X		X	X			X	X	X	X	X	X		X				X	X	X	S	N												S				S		S										
		X			C	C	X	X	X	X				X			X										X		X		X		X	X	X	X		X			X	X	X	X			X	X	X					X				X	X	X		N	N				N		N	9				S			X											X	X	
		X	X	X	G	D	X	X				X			X			X								X	X		X		X		X	X	X	X		X	220		X		X	X			X	X	X	X		X	X	O	X	X		X		X	N	N	S	N	S	N	N		N	18	X	X	X	N	N	N		N	X	N		X	N			N			X	
		X	X		H	H			X			X	X		X	X		X	X				X	X	X		X	X	X		X	X	X	X	X	X		X	220	X		X		X			X	X	X	X	X	X	X				X	X		X	N	N	N	N		N	N		N	18	X				N	N		N	X	N		X								
		X	X	X	I	D	X			X			X			X			X							X	X		X		X		X	X	X	X		X	220	X	X		X	X			X	X	X	X		X	I		X	X	X	X		X	N	N	N	N	N	N	N		N	18	X		X		N	N		S	X	N		X							X	
		X	X	X	G	C	X	X	X			X	X		X			X								X	X		X		X		X	X	X	X		X	110/220	X	X		X	X			X	X	X	X	X	X	X	O		X	X	X		X	S	N	S	N	N		N		N	18			X		N	N			X	N		X		N	N	N	X	X	X	
		X	X		F	D	X	X	X	X	X	X	X	X	X	X	X	X	X							X	X		X		X		X	X	X	X	X	X	X	X	X		X	X		X	X	X	X	X	X	X	X	X	X	X	X	X	X	X	S	N	S	N	S	N	N		N	18					N	N	X		X	S		X		N			X	X	X	
		X	X		E	B				X			X		X				X				X	G	B		X		X		X		X	X	X	X		X				X		X			X	X	X	X	X	X	I				X	X	X	X	N	N					N		N	18					N				X			X								
					A	A						X			X			X									X						X										X				X	X	X	X	X	X		X	X			X	X	X	N	N	N	N			N		N	9				N			X	N		N							X	X	X	

CARAVAN PARKS AND CAMPING SITES IN SOUTH AFRICA

CARAVAN PARK / CAMP SITE TARIFF CODE – See columns 38–39 (Subject to alteration)

A = Up to R1 | B = R1–R2 | C = R2–R3 | D = R3–R4 | E = R4–R5 | F = R5–R6 | G = R6–R7 | H = R7–R8 | I = R8–R9 | J = R9–R10 | K = R10–R16 | O = FREE | X = On Application

Charges are based on family of 2 adults and 2 children under 12 years

ADDITIONAL ACCOMMODATION TARIFF CODE – See columns 57–59 (Subject to alteration)

eg. Bungalows, Cabins, Cottages, Chalets, etc.

A = R1–R3 | B = R3–R5 | C = R5–R7 | D = R7–R9 | E = R9–R11 | F = R11–R13 | G = R13–R15 | H = R15–R17 | I = R17–R19 | J = R19–R21 | K = R21–R30 | X = On Application

NB: Where the tariff is given in *italics* it is per person, otherwise per unit

NOTE 1 — Columns 18, 19, 20, — X= Stands available but not demarcated or number of stands have not been provided
NOTE 2 — Column 35 — A=Bookings accepted for additional accommodation only i.e. cottages, bungalows, etc.
NOTE 3 — Column 37 — Deposit refunded under certain conditions eg. less 10% ; if site is re-let ; if cancelled well in advance (up to 2 months) or on a doctor's certificate
NOTE 4 — Column 41 — Reductions allowed on application for youth, church, school or sport groups or caravan rallies
NOTE 5 — Column 69 — L= Laundry facilities only
NOTE 6 — Columns 88, 89, 90, — I = In-Season only ; O = Out-of- Season only; X = On application
NOTE 7 — Column 96 — I = In-Season only
NOTE 8 — Column 102 — See section on golf in Outdoor Holiday Guide
NOTE 9 — Column 107 — See section on freshwater angling in Outdoor Holiday Guide
NOTE 10 — Column 108 — See section on coastal angling in Outdoor Holiday Guide

Establishments marked thus ● have the Caravan Club of South Africa recommendation — see introduction

ABBREVIATIONS

C = CAPE PROVINCE
N = NATAL
O = ORANGE FREE STATE
T = TRANSVAAL
B = BOPHUTHATSWANA
X = TRANSKEI

	TELEPHONE CODE (T= DIAL 0020, BOOK TRUNK CALL; E= DIAL CODE, ASK EXCHANGE FOR NO.)	TELEPHONE NUMBER	OWNED OR SUPERVISED BY: PRIVATELY OWNED	MUNICIPAL	DIVISIONAL COUNCIL	PROVINCIAL ADMINISTRATION	PARKS BOARD	SITE DESCRIPTION – LOCALITY: BEACH IN IMMEDIATE VICINITY	BESIDE RIVER, LAKE OR DAM	IN OR NEAR MOUNTAIN AREA	WITHIN BUILT-UP AREA	NATURE OF GROUND: GRASS	SAND	GRAVEL	SHADE: UNSHADED	PARTLY SHADED	EXTENSIVELY SHADED	NO. OF STANDS: CARAVANS ONLY – SEE NOTE 1	CARAVANS AND/OR TENTS	TENTS ONLY – SEE NOTE 1	ACCESSIBILITY – DISTANCE FROM MAIN ROAD TO SITE: ON MAIN RD	WITHIN 1 km	WITHIN 5 km	WITHIN 10 km	WITHIN 15 km	SURFACE OF ROAD APPROACH: TAR	GRAVEL	SAND	CONDITION OF APPROACH: GOOD	FAIR	POOR
	1	2	3	4	5	6	7	8	9	10	11	12	13	14	15	16	17	18	19	20	21	22	23	24	25	26	27	28	29	30	31
MASELSPOORT O See Bloemfontein																															
MELKBOSSTRAND C 58 C3 S.L.																															
● **Ou Skip** Manager, P.O. Box 13 (7437) □ *Otto Du Plessis Drive*	02224	2058			X			X				X			X	X		215		21	X					X			X		
MELKRIVIER T 68 B6 1166m																															
Waterberg-Natuurpraal Holiday Resort P.O. Melkrivier 0541	T	Vaalwater 2712	X						X	X		X		X		X	X		12			X					X	X		X	
MESSINA T 70 B5 594m																															
● **Messina Municipal** P/Bag X611 (0900)	015532 E	103		X							X	X			X			200		200	X					X			X		
MICA T 69 B3 496m																															
Hippo Pools Holiday Resort P.O. Mica 1382	T	811	X						X				X		X	X		X	X	X			X				X		X		
MIDDELBURG C 62 C2 1248m																															
Middelburg Municipal P.O. Box 55 (5900) □ *Heuwel St.*	04832 E	17		X						X			X				X		30			X					X		X		
MIDDELBURG T 69 C2 1515m																															
Kruger Dam Recreation Resort Proprietor, P.O. Box 14 (1050) □ *Coetzee St.*	01321	3011/5331		X					X			X			X				100				X			X			X		
Midland Estate Midlands Brick and Engineering Works (Pty) Ltd., P.O. Box 111 (1050) □ *Witbank Main Rd.*	01321	2335	X						X			X					X		50		X					X			X		
MILLER'S POINT C 58 NS 4m																															
● **Miller's Point** P.O. Box 44, Simonstown 7995 □ *2 km from Simonstown*	021	86-1142			X			X		X		X				X		41			X					X			X		
MILNERTON C 58 NS S.L.																															
Zonnekus Holiday Resort P.O. Box 16 (7435) □ *Melkbosstrand Rd.*	02223	632	X										X	X			X	50		50		X					X		X		
MKUZE N 67 B5 137m																															
Mkuzi Game Reserve Camp Superintendent, P.O. Mkuze 3965	T	3					X					X				X			15						X		X			X	
MOLTENO C 62 C4 1580m																															
Molteno Municipal Town Clerk, P.O. Box 1 (5500) □ *Brownlee St.*	04572 E	21		X							X		X	X			X	25	25	25	X					X			X		
MONDEOR T 72 NS 1660m																															
Ferreira's P.O. Box 82573, Southdale 2135 □ *Vereeniging Main Rd.*	011	942-2600	X								X	X					X		50		X					X			X		
Meredale Pleasure Resort P.O. Box 21 (2110) □ *Vereeniging Main Rd.*	011	942-1008	X								X	X			X	X	X	50		20	X					X			X		
Safari P.O. Box 27533, Bertsham 2013 □ *Vereeniging Main Rd.*	011	942-1404	X								X	X					X	60	60		X					X			X		
MONTAGU C 58 C5 229m																															
● **Montagu Spa** Manager, P.O. Box 24 (6720) □ *Uitvlucht St. Ext.*	023412 E	109		X								X				X			X			X				X			X		
MONT-AUX-SOURCES N 67 C1 1433m																															
Royal Natal National Park — Mahai Campsite P.O. Mont-aux-Sources 3353	T	Mont-aux-Sources 3					X		X	X		X	X				X		X			X					X		X		
MONTROSE T 69 C3 808m																															
Montrose P.O. Box 20, Elandshoek 1208 □ *Boven/Schoemanskloof Junction*	T	Montrose Falls 3	X						X	X		X					X		30		X					X			X		
MOORREESBURG C 58 C3 155m																															
Amos Lambrecht Municipality, P.O. Box 3 (7310) □ *Main Rd., Hooikraal*	02642 E	56		X					X				X				X	50		30		X				X			X		
MORGAN'S BAY C 60 B3 10m																															
Morgan's Bay Morgan's Bay Hotel, P.O. Morgan's Bay 5292	T	Kei Mouth 130	X					X	X			X				X			60			X					X		X		
MOSSEL BAY C 59 C2 6m																															
De Bakke Municipality, P.O. Box 25 (6500) □ *George Rd.*	04441	2043		X				X				X			X				131		X					X			X		
Mossel Bay Caravans 5 Star Park P.O. Box 439 (6500) □ *George Rd.*	04441	2604	X					X				X				X			75		X					X			X		
Point Municipality, P.O. Box 25 (6500) □ *Point Rd.*	04441	2043		X				X				X				X			226			X				X			X		
Santos Municipality, P.O. Box 25 (6500) □ *George Rd.*	04441	2043		X				X				X			X				321		X					X			X		
MOUNTAIN ZEBRA NATIONAL PARK C See Cradock																															
MTUBATUBA N 67 C5 S.L.																															
Fanies Island Natal Parks Board, P/Bag 7205 (3935)	03552 E	1431					X		X			X		X		X			20						X	X	X		X	X	
MTUNZINI N 67 C4 S.L.																															
Casa Benri P.O. Box 64 (3867)	035322 E	197	X					X				X				X			50			X				X			X		
Forest Inn P.O. Box 44 (3867) □ *Empangeni Main Rd.*	035322 E	95/68	X							X	X	X			X		X	20			X					X			X		
Umlalazi Nature Reserve Natal Parks Board, P.O. Mtunzini 3867	035322 E	136					X	X	X					X			X		50				X				X			X	
MTWALUME N 63 NS S.L.																															
Longbeach Holiday Resort P.O. Box 2 (4186)	03230	711	X					X	X			X		X		X		100		50		X				X			X		
Mtwalume P.O. Mtwalume 4186 □ *Dek St.*	03230	761	X					X	X		X	X		X			X		100			X				X			X		
MUIZENBERG C 58 NS S.L.																															
● **Zandvlei** Manager Bathing Amenities, P.O. Box 298, Cape Town 8000 □ *The Row*	021	41-3411 x583		X				X	X	X	X	X					X	110				X				X			X		
MUNSTER N 63 NS S.L.																															
Mittenwald P.O. Munster 4278	03931	620	X					X				X					X	60		10		X				X			X		
NABOOMSPRUIT T 68 B6 1158m																															
Constantia Mineral Spa P.O. Box 20 (0560) □ *19 km from Naboomspruit*	012072 E	487	X							X		X		X			X		100			X						X	X		
Lekkerrus Mineral Baths P.O. Box 169 (0560)	012072 E	64	X							X		X	X				X	275								X			X		

SEASONS			TERMS FOR BOOKINGS			CARAVAN/CAMPING SITE TARIFFS (See heading)		REDUCTIONS ALLOWED FOR				RESTAURANT FACILITIES			TEAROOM/CAFE			SHOPPING FACILITIES (Provisions)			ADDITIONAL ACCOMMODATION AVAILABLE				TARIFF (See heading)			CAMP SITE FACILITIES (I = In-Season only; O = Out-of-Season only; X = On application) — DRINKING WATER		BATHS		SHOWERS																								NON-WHITE SERVANTS			TYPE OF VEHICLE PERMITTED			SPORTING AND RECREATIONAL FACILITIES (S = On Site; N = Nearby (Up to 20 km away))								GOLF					FISHING				SWIMMING					BOATING				PLACES OF INTEREST			NOTES
32 OPEN THROUGHOUT THE YEAR	33 OUT-OF-SEASON CLOSING DATE	34 RE-OPENING DATE	35 BOOKINGS ACCP./PEAK SNS.-SEE NOTE 2	36 DEPOSIT REQUIRED	37 REFUNDED IF CANCELLED-SEE NOTE 3	38 MAXIMUM IN-SEASON TARIFF	39 MAXIMUM OUT-OF-SEASON TARIFF	40 LONG PERIODS OF STAY	41 GROUPS-SEE NOTE 4	42 AA MEMBERS	43 OTHERS (ON APPLICATION)	44 ON SITE	45 WITHIN 5 km OF SITE	46 MORE THAN 5 km FROM SITE	47 ON SITE	48 WITHIN 5 km OF SITE	49 MORE THAN 5 km FROM SITE	50 ON SITE	51 WITHIN 5 km OF SITE	52 MORE THAN 5 km FROM SITE	53 BUNGALOWS	54 CABINS	55 COTTAGES (RONDAVELS)	56 CHALETS	57 MAXIMUM IN-SEASON TARIFF	58 MAXIMUM OUT-OF-SEASON TARIFF	59 CARAVANS TO RENT ON SITE - SEE SECTION	60 PIPED	61 OTHER	62 HOT AND COLD	63 COLD ONLY	64 HOT AND COLD	65 COLD ONLY	66 WATERBORNE SANITATION	67 WASHBASINS	68 DISHWASHING FACILITIES	69 LAUNDRY AND IRONING FACILITIES-SEE NOTE 5	70 WASHING MACHINES	71 SITE LIT	72 PLUGS FOR RAZORS (VOLTAGE)	73 REFRIGERATORS	74 FIREWOOD/CHARCOAL	75 OPEN FIRE FORBIDDEN	76 CAMP FIRE PERMITTED	77 BRAAI PLACES PROVIDED	78 KITCHEN/COOKING FACILITIES	79 PETROL PUMP ON SITE	80 PETROL PUMP NEARBY	81 CAR REPAIR SHOP NEARBY	82 CAR SERVICING NEARBY	83 GAS SERVICE NEARBY	84 FIRST AID AND HOSPITAL/DOCTOR NEARBY	85 POST OFFICE NEARBY	86 SITE GUARDED	87 PETS ALLOWED	88 SERVANTS PERMITTED-SEE NOTE 6	89 SERVANTS ACCOM.-SEE NOTE 6	90 SERVANTS FOR HIRE-SEE NOTE 6	91 CAR AND TRAILER	92 TRUCK HORSE AND SEMI-TRAILER	93 SELF-PROPELLED CARAVANS	94 CHILDRENS PLAYGROUND	95 TENNIS	96 CINEMA/DRIVE-IN/TV-ROOM-SEE NOTE 7	97 HORSE-RIDING	98 GAMES ROOM	99 TRAMPOLINE	100 BOWLS	101 HOT SPRINGS	102 GOLF COURSE-SEE NOTE 8	103 NUMBER OF HOLES	104 MINIATURE	105 MASHIE	106 PUTT-PUTT	107 FRESHWATER-SEE NOTE 9	108 SEA-SEE NOTE 10	109 GOGGLE	110 LICENCE REQUIRED	111 SWIMMING POOL	112 SEA BATHING	113 CHILDRENS POOL	114 ADULTS ONLY	115 SHARK NETS AT BEACH	116 BOATS FOR HIRE	117 POWER	118 SAILING	119 CANOEING	120 HISTORIC	121 SCIENTIFIC	122 NATURAL	123
X			X	X	X	C	C		X					X		X		X									X		X		X		X	X	X	X	X		220				X	X			X	X	X	X	X	X	X					X	X	X	S	N	N	N	S				N	18					N	N		S		S							X	X	X	
X			X	X		C	C	X	X						X	X		X	X		X		X	X	E-F	E-F		X	X			X		X	X		X		X			X		X	X		X	X	X	X	X		X		X	X	X	X	X	X	X	S	S			S									S			X	S		S			S			S			X	
X			X			C	B	X					X				X			X								X		X		X		X	X		X	X	X			X		X	X			X	X	X	X		X	X	X	X			X		X																														
X						D	D					X			X			X			X	X	X	X	H	F		X		X		X		X	X						X	X		X	X			X	X	X	X		X		X				X	X	X			S			S								N				S											X	
X			X	X		B	B							X			X			X								X	X	X		X		X	X	X	X		X					X	X			X	X	X			X		X	X			X		X	N	N	N				N		N	18								N		N							X	X	X	
X			A	A		B	B					X			X				X				X		C-D	C-D		X		X		X		X	X	X	X		X			X	X	X	X			X	X	X	X	X	X	X					X	X	X	S	S	N				N		N	18				S		S	X	S		S				N	S	S	X		X	
X			X			O	O						X			X			X									X								X	X		X		X	X		X	X			X	X	X	X	X	X	X	X	X			X		X	S		N				N		N	18				N			X	N		N						N	X	X	X	
X			X	X	X	C	C					X			X					X								X		X		X		X	X	X	X	X	X	X	X	X			X			X	X	X	X	X		X					X		X	S				S		N		N	18					N	N			X								X		X	
X			X	X		C	C								X			X			X				C-D	C-D				X			X	X	X		X			X		X		X	X			X	X	X	X								X	X	X									N	18					N			S		S				N	N	N				
X			X	X		C	C													X			X		B	B		X		X		X		X	X								X	X	X			X				X				X	X		X	X	X																											X	X	X	← Visitors are advised that, should the water supply fail, their bookings may be cancelled at short notice
X			X			B	B	X	X				X			X			X				X		X	X		X		X				X	X		X		X	220	X	X		X	X			X	X	X	X	X	X	X	X	X	X		X	X	X	N	N			N		S		N	9				N			X										X	X	X	
X			X	X		C	C	X	X				X			X			X								X	X		X		X		X	X	X	X		X	220			X	X				X	X	X		X	X			X	X	X	X		X	S	N		N	N	N			N	18								S		N	X								X	
X			X	X		X	X	X	X				X		X	X			X	X								X		X		X		X	X	X	X		X	220		X	X	X	X			X	X	X		X	X	X				X	X	X	X	S	S	N	N		S			N	18								S		S										
X			X	X		D	D						X	X		X	X		X	X								X		X		X		X	X	X	X		X	220		X	X	X				X	X	X	X	X	X	X	X			X	X	X	X	S	N	N						N	18								S												
X			X	X	X	C	C	X				X		X	X					X								X		X				X	X	X	X			220		X		X	X			X	X	X	X		X						X	X	X	N	N	N				N	S	N	9	X							S		S							X		X	
X			X	X	X	C	C													X								X		X		X		X	X	X						X		X	X			X				X	X						X	X	X	S			N										N			X			N						N			X	
X			X	X	X	X	X					X					X			X								X		X		X		X	X	X	X		X			X	X	X	X		X	X	X	X	X	X	X	X		X	X		X	X	X			S		S									S			X	S		S						S				
X			X			A	A	X		X			X	X		X	X		X	X								X		X		X		X	X		X		X			X		X	X			X	X	X			X		X	X			X	X	X	S	N							N	9								S		S	X						X		X	
X			X	X	X	C	B	X	X				X						X				X	X	E	B		X	X	X		X		X	X	X	L			220		X	X					X	X	X	X	X	X		X	X		X	X		X		N			N		S		N	9					N	N				S			S		S	S		X	X	
X			X	X	X	B	B	X					X		X				X					X	J	G		X		X		X		X	X	X	X		X	110/220				X	X			X	X	X	X		X	X		X		X	X	X	X	S	N	N	N			N		N	18			X		S	S			X					N	N	N	X		X	
X			X	X		D	C					X	X		X			X			X		X	X	G	D	X	X		X		X		X	X	X	X	X	X	220	X	X		X	X			X	X	X	X	X	X	X					X	X	X	S	N	N	N	S	S	N		N	18	X		X		N	N		S	X	S	X		N				X	X	X	
X			X	X	X	B	B	X					X		X				X			X			X	X		X		X		X		X	X	X	X		X	110/220				X	X			X	X	X	X		X	X		X		X	X	X	X	S	N	N	N			N		N	18			X		S	S			X	S				N	N	N	X		X	
X			X	X	X	B	B	X					X			X				X								X		X		X		X	X	X	X		X	110/220				X	X			X	X	X	X		X	X		X		X	X	X	X	N	N	N	N			N		N	18			X		S	S			X					N	N	N	X		X	
			X	X	X	X	X													X			X		X	X		X				X		X	X							X		X			X									X			X		X																N							N							
			X	X		E	D		X							X			X									X		X		X		X	X	X	L					X		X	X			X	X	X	X	X	X	X				X	X		X		N					N		N	9	X			N	N			N	X				N	N			X		X	
			X	X	X	D	D	X	X	X		X	X		X	X			X	X								X		X		X		X	X	X	X							X				X	X	X	X		X	X					X	X	X			S						N	9								N		N										
			X	X		F	F							X			X			X								X		X		X		X	X	X						X	X	X	X			X	X	X	X	X	X	X		X			X		X	N	N							N	9					N			N	X	N			N	N		N	X		X	
			X	X		H	H	X		X		X			X			X					X	X	X	X	X	X				X			X	X					X	X		X	X	X						X	X	X	X			X	X		X		S	S	S	S	S	N		N	18			X		S	S	X	S	X			X								
			X	X	X	F	D		X	X			X			X			X				X	X	F	D	X	X		X		X		X	X	X	X		X	220	X	X			X			X			X	X	X	X	O	O	O		X		X	S	N	N	N	S	N	N		N	18				N	N		X	N	X	N		X		N	N	N		X	X	
			X	X	X	D	B						X			X			X			X			E-H	C-D		X		X		X		X	X	X	X	X	X	220		X			X			X	X	X		X	X	X		X	X		X	X	X	N	N	N		S		N		N	18			X	N	N	N			X				N		N	N	X			
						E	E							X			X			X	X				X	X		X		X		X		X	X	X	X		X			X		X	X			X	X	X	X	X	X				X	X	X		X	S	N		N	S	N	N		N	18					N	N			X			X								
			X	X		K	J		X	X	X	X			X			X					X		X	X		X		X		X		X	X	X	X		X	X	X	X		X	X			X	X	X			X	X	X	X			X	X	X	S	S	S	N	S	S	N	S	N	9				N				S		S							X		X	
			X	X		X	X		X			X			X			X					X		X	X		X		X		X		X	X	X	X		X			X			X		X	X	X	X	X		X	X					X	X		S	N	S					S	N	9			X	S			X	S		S									X	

CARAVAN PARKS AND CAMPING SITES IN SOUTH AFRICA

CARAVAN PARK / CAMP SITE TARIFF CODE — See columns 38–39 (Subject to alteration)

A = Up to R1	**C** = R2–R3	**E** = R4–R5	**G** = R6–R7	**I** = R8–R9	**K** = R10–R16
B = R1–R2	**D** = R3–R4	**F** = R5–R6	**H** = R7–R8	**J** = R9–R10	**O** = FREE
					X = On Application

Charges are based on family of 2 adults and 2 children under 12 years

ADDITIONAL ACCOMMODATION TARIFF CODE — See columns 57–59 (Subject to alteration)

eg. Bungalows, Cabins, Cottages, Chalets, etc.

A = R1–R3	**C** = R5–R7	**E** = R9–R11	**G** = R13–R15	**I** = R17–R19	**K** = R21–R30
B = R3–R5	**D** = R7–R9	**F** = R11–R13	**H** = R15–R17	**J** = R19–R21	**X** = On Application

NB: Where the tariff is given in *italics* it is per person, otherwise per unit

NOTE 1 — **Columns 18, 19, 20,** — X = Stands available but not demarcated or number of stands have not been provided

NOTE 2 — **Column 35** — A = Bookings accepted for additional accommodation only i.e. cottages, bungalows, etc.

NOTE 3 — **Column 37** — Deposit refunded under certain conditions eg. less 10% ; if site is re-let ; if cancelled well in advance (up to 2 months) or on a doctor's certificate

NOTE 4 — **Column 41** — Reductions allowed on application for youth, church, school or sport groups or caravan rallies

NOTE 5 — **Column 69** — L = Laundry facilities only

NOTE 6 — **Columns 88, 89, 90,** — I = In-Season only ; O = Out-of-Season only; X = On application

NOTE 7 — **Column 96** — I = In-Season only

NOTE 8 — **Column 102** — See section on golf in Outdoor Holiday Guide

NOTE 9 — **Column 107** — See section on freshwater angling in Outdoor Holiday Guide

NOTE 10 — **Column 108** — See section on coastal angling in Outdoor Holiday Guide

Establishments marked thus ● have the Caravan Club of South Africa recommendation — see introduction

ABBREVIATIONS

C = CAPE PROVINCE
N = NATAL
O = ORANGE FREE STATE
T = TRANSVAAL
B = BOPHUTHATSWANA
X = TRANSKEI

	TELEPHONE CODE (T = DIAL 0020 BOOK TRUNK CALL; E = DIAL CODE, ASK EXCHANGE FOR NO.)	TELEPHONE NUMBER	OWNED OR SUPERVISED BY: PRIVATELY OWNED	MUNICIPAL	DIVISIONAL COUNCIL	PROVINCIAL COUNCIL	PARKS BOARD ADMINISTRATION	SITE DESCRIPTION — LOCALITY: BEACH IN IMMEDIATE VICINITY	BESIDE RIVER, LAKE OR DAM	IN OR NEAR MOUNTAIN AREA	WITHIN BUILT-UP AREA	NATURE OF GROUND: GRASS	GRAVEL	SAND	SHADE: UNSHADED	PARTLY SHADED	EXTENSIVELY SHADED	NO. OF STANDS: CARAVANS ONLY – SEE NOTE 1	CARAVANS AND/OR TENTS	TENTS ONLY – SEE NOTE 1	ACCESSIBILITY — APPROXIMATE DISTANCE FROM MAIN ROAD TO SITE: ON MAIN RD	WITHIN 1 km	WITHIN 5 km	WITHIN 10 km	WITHIN 15 km	SURFACE OF ROAD APPROACH: TAR	GRAVEL	SAND	CONDITION OF ROAD APPROACH: GOOD	FAIR	POOR
	1	2	3	4	5	6	7	8	9	10	11	12	13	14	15	16	17	18	19	20	21	22	23	24	25	26	27	28	29	30	3
NABOOMSPRUIT (CONTINUED)																															
Libertas Mineral Spa P.O. Box 113 (0560) ☐ *20 km from Naboomspruit*	012072 E	351	X						X	X		X	X			X		100		100		X					X		X		
Maroela Camp P.O. Box 194 (0560) ☐ *5 km from Naboomspruit*	012072 E	3111	X										X			X			15				X			X			X		
Naboomspruit Municipal Town Clerk, P.O. Box 34 (0560) ☐ *Hans van Rensburg St.*	012072 E	226/7		X						X	X	X					X	X	X	X	X					X			X		
Rondalia 'Die Oog' P.O. Box 5 (0560) ☐ *15 km from Naboomspruit*	012072 E	267	X							X		X				X						X					X		X		
NATURE'S VALLEY C 59 NS · S.L.																															
Grootrivier Dept. of Forestry, P/Bag 37, Humansdorp 6300	04472 E	656						X	X	X		X			X	X	X		45		X					X			X		
NEFDT T 68 NS ↗ 1170m																															
Lakeside Lodge P.O. Box 30, Broederstroom 0240 ☐ *Hartbeespoort Dam*	T	B/Stroom 1312	X						X	X		X	X			X			X			X					X	X		X	
NELSPRUIT T 69 C4 ← 620m																															
● **Allamanda Holiday Resort** P.O. Alkmaar 1206 ☐ *16 km from Nelspruit*	0131232 E	2831	X							X		X				X			60		X							X	X		
Casarina P.O. Box 398 (1200) ☐ *10 km from Nelspruit*	01311	4012	X							X		X				X		20	30	10		X					X		X		
Eureka P.O. Box 657 (1200) ☐ *10 km from Nelspruit*	01311	5080	X						X	X		X				X	X	15		10		X					X		X		
Kruine Rest Camp P.O. Box 244 (1200) ☐ *17 km from Nelspruit*	01311	2936	X							X		X				X	X	15	15	10		X					X		X		
Nelspruit Municipal Town Clerk, P.O. Box 45 (1200) ☐ *3 km from Nelspruit*	01311	2221		X					X			X				X			20			X				X			X		
Shonalanga P.O. Box 18 (1200) ☐ *2 km from Nelspruit*	01311	3223	X							X		X					X	40	40	20	X					X			X		
NIGEL T 72 NS ↘ 1575m																															
Nigel Municipal P.O. Box 23 (1490) ☐ *Hendrik Verwoerd St.*	011	739-2431		X							X		X			X	X	40						X		X			X		
NOUPOORT C 62 C2 ↗ 1489m																															
Drikkie du Toit P.O. Box 4 (5950) ☐ *Hospital St.*	05742 E	56		X							X	X	X			X		8	3	4		X				X	X		X		
NYLSTROOM T 68 B6 ↙ 1187m																															
● **J. G. Strijdom** P/Bag 1008 (0510) ☐ *Voortrekker Rd.*	01532 E	7605		X					X		X	X					X	35		10	X					X			X		
Stokkiesdraai Holiday Resort P.O. Box 88 (0510) ☐ *4 km from Nylstroom*	01532 E	791	X							X		X					X		100		X					X			X		
ONRUS C 58 D4 ← S.L.																															
Onrus Municipal Manager, De Villiers St. (7201)	T	23		X				X		X	X	X					X		230			X				X			X		
Paradise Park Holiday Camp P.O. Box 74, Parow 7500 ☐ *Hermanus Main Rd.*	T (021)	9901 (96-4053)	X					X		X		X				X		35		20	X					X			X		
Sea View P.O. Box 1 (7201) ☐ *Old Main Rd.*	T	33	X					X	X		X	X					X		28			X				X			X		
Sherwood Park P.O. Box 50 (7201) ☐ *Main Rd.*	T	125	X							X		X					X	58		14	X							X	X		
ORANJEVILLE O 66 A6 ↙ 1494m																															
Jim Fouché Holiday Resort Resort Manager, P.O. Fouché Resort, via Frankfort 9830 ☐ *Vaal Dam*	T	Jim Fouché 1				X			X			X				X			1 500		X					X			X		
ORKNEY T 66 A4 ↘ 1295m																															
● **Orkney-Vaal Holiday Resort** Manager, P.O. Box 34 (2620) ☐ *5 km from Orkney*	018	3-2328		X					X			X	X			X		150		50			X			X			X		
OUDTSHOORN C 59 B2 ← 306m																															
N. A. Smit Municipal Tourist Camp P.O. Box 255 (6620) ☐ *Park Rd. North, West Bank*	04431	2221 ext. 254		X						X	X	X				X		X		X		X				X			X		
Schoemanspoort Divisional Council, P.O. Box 127 (6620) ☐ *20 km from Oudtshoorn*	04431	2241			X				X			X					X	20		20	X						X		X		
OYSTER BAY C 59 C4 ↗ S.L.																															
Oyster Bay P.O. Box 114, Humansdorp 6300	T	2	X								X	X					X	16							X		X			X	
PAARL C 58 C3 ↘ 115m																															
Camper's Paradise P.O. Box 552, Suider-Paarl 7624	0251	2-4685	X						X	X		X		X		X	X	44	291	291		X					X		X	X	
Eerste Tol No Bookings accepted — Site actually meant for day visitors, but there is no objection to Caravans/Tents staying over ☐ *Bainskloof*					X				X	X		X				X					X						X			X	
PARADISE BEACH C 59 C4 ↗ S.L.																															
Paradise Beach P.O. Box 172, Humansdorp 6300 ☐ *Immergroen Ave.*	T	8/21	X					X	X	X	X	X				X		70		10				X				X	X		
PARK RYNIE N 63 NS • S.L.																															
● **Caravan Cove** P.O. Box 42 (4182)	0323	2-1161	X					X	X		X	X			X	X	X		160			X					X		X		
Rocky Bay P.O. Box 37 (4182)	0323	2-1701	X					X				X				X		80		10		X						X	X		
PARKS UNDER CONTROL OF NATAL PARKS BOARD:																															
HIMEVILLE NATURE RESERVE See Himeville																															
KOSI BAY NATURE RESERVE See Kosi Bay																															
MKUZI NATURE RESERVE See Mkuze																															
ROYAL NATAL NATIONAL PARK See Mont-aux-Sources																															
SODWANA BAY NATIONAL PARK See Sodwana Bay																															
ST. LUCIA GAME RESERVE See Hluhluwe (False Bay Park), Mtubatuba (Fanies Island), St. Lucia Estuary																															
UMLALAZI NATURE RESERVE See Mtunzini																															
PARKS UNDER CONTROL OF NATIONAL PARKS BOARD:																															
ADDO ELEPHANT NATIONAL PARK C See Addo																															
AUGRABIES FALLS NATIONAL PARK C See Augrabies																															
BONTEBOK NATIONAL PARK C See Swellendam																															
GOLDEN GATE HIGHLANDS NATIONAL PARK O See Clarens																															

OPEN THROUGHOUT THE YEAR

SEASONS		TERMS FOR BOOKINGS			CARAVAN/CAMPING SITE TARIFFS (See heading)		REDUCTIONS ALLOWED FOR				RESTAURANT FACILITIES			TEAROOM/CAFE			SHOPPING FACILITIES (Provisions)			ADDITIONAL ACCOMMODATION AVAILABLE				TARIFF (See heading)		CARAVANS TO RENT ON SITE - SEE SECTION	DRINKING WATER		BATHS		SHOWERS		CAMP SITE FACILITIES (I = In-Season only; O = Out-of-Season only; X = On application)																						NON-WHITE SERVANTS			TYPE OF VEHICLE PERMITTED			SPORTING AND RECREATIONAL FACILITIES (S = On Site; N = Nearby (Up to 20 km away))								GOLF					FISHING				SWIMMING					BOATING				PLACES OF INTEREST			NOTES
OUT-OF-SEASON CLOSING DATE	RE-OPENING DATE	BOOKINGS ACCP./PEAK SNS. - SEE NOTE 2	DEPOSIT REQUIRED	REFUNDED IF CANCELLED - SEE NOTE 3	MAXIMUM IN-SEASON TARIFF	MAXIMUM OUT-OF-SEASON TARIFF	LONG PERIODS OF STAY	GROUPS - SEE NOTE 4	AA MEMBERS	OTHERS (ON APPLICATION)	ON SITE	WITHIN 5 km OF SITE	MORE THAN 5 km FROM SITE	ON SITE	WITHIN 5 km OF SITE	MORE THAN 5 km FROM SITE	ON SITE	WITHIN 5 km OF SITE	MORE THAN 5 km FROM SITE	BUNGALOWS	CABINS	COTTAGES (RONDAVELS)	CHALETS	MAXIMUM IN-SEASON TARIFF	MAXIMUM OUT-OF-SEASON TARIFF		PIPED	OTHER	HOT AND COLD	COLD ONLY	HOT AND COLD	COLD ONLY	WATERBORNE SANITATION	WASHBASINS	DISHWASHING FACILITIES	LAUNDRY AND IRONING FACILITIES - SEE NOTE 5	WASHING MACHINES	SITE LIT	PLUGS FOR RAZORS (VOLTAGE)	REFRIGERATORS	FIREWOOD/CHARCOAL	OPEN FIRE FORBIDDEN	CAMP FIRE PERMITTED	BRAAI PLACES PROVIDED	KITCHEN/COOKING FACILITIES	PETROL PUMP ON SITE	PETROL PUMP NEARBY	CAR REPAIR SHOP NEARBY	CAR SERVICING NEARBY	GAS SERVICE NEARBY	FIRST AID/HOSPITAL/DOCTOR NEARBY	POST OFFICE NEARBY	SITE GUARDED	PETS ALLOWED	SERVANTS PERMITTED - SEE NOTE 6	SERVANTS ACCOM. - SEE NOTE 6	SERVANTS FOR HIRE - SEE NOTE 6	CAR AND TRAILER	TRUCK 'HORSE' AND SEMI-TRAILER	SELF-PROPELLED CARAVANS	CHILDRENS' PLAYGROUND	TENNIS	CINEMA/DRIVE-IN/TV-ROOM - SEE NOTE 7	HORSE-RIDING	GAMES ROOM	TRAMPOLINE	BOWLS	HOT SPRINGS	GOLF COURSE - SEE NOTE 8	NUMBER OF HOLES	MINIATURE	MASHIE	PUTT-PUTT	FRESHWATER - SEE NOTE 9	SEA - SEE NOTE 10	GOGGLE	LICENCE REQUIRED	SWIMMING POOL	SEA BATHING	CHILDRENS' POOL	ADULTS ONLY	SHARK NETS AT BEACH	BOATS FOR HIRE	POWER	SAILING	CANOEING	HISTORIC	SCIENTIFIC	NATURAL	
33	34	35	36	37	38	39	40	41	42	43	44	45	46	47	48	49	50	51	52	53	54	55	56	57	58	59	60	61	62	63	64	65	66	67	68	69	70	71	72	73	74	75	76	77	78	79	80	81	82	83	84	85	86	87	88	89	90	91	92	93	94	95	96	97	98	99	100	101	102	103	104	105	106	107	108	109	110	111	112	113	114	115	116	117	118	119	120	121	122	123
					D	B					X			X			X			X		X		F	E		X		X	X	X	X	X	X	X	X		X		X	X		X	X						X	X							X	X	X	N	N	S	N	N	S	N	S	N	9				N			X	S		S							X	X	X	
		X	X		B	B	X						X			X			X	X				X	X		X		X		X		X	X				X			X		X				X	X	X	X	X	X		X				X		X	S	N	N				N	N	N	9		X		N			X	S		S							X			
					C	C						X			X			X	X								X		X		X		X	X	X	X		X	220		X		X	X	X		X	X	X	X	X	X	X	X	X			X	X	X		N	N				N	N	N	9				N			X			N									X	
		X	X		E	D				X	X			X			X					X		H	D		X		X		X		X	X	X	X		X	X		X		X	X			X	X	X	X	X	X	X		X	X				X	S	S	S	N				S	N	9				N			X	S		S							X		X	
		X			B	B		X				X			X			X									X			X		X	X	X	X	X					X	X	X	X	X		X			X			X					X	X	X														S			X		X						N	N	X	X	X	
					X	X							X		X	X	X	X	X				X	G	E		X		X		X		X	X		X					X			X			X	X	X		X	X		X	X			X	X	X	S	N													S			X	S		S			S			S	X	X	X	
		X	X		D	C		X		X	X			X			X	X		X		X	X	D-G	D-F		X		X		X		X	X	X	X		X		X	X		X	X	X	X		X	X	X		X	X	X	X	X	X	X	X	X	S	S	N	N	S		N		N	18			X	S			X	S		S			S	S			X	X	X	
		X	X		C	C	X	X		X			X		X	X		X				X	X	F	F	X	X		X		X		X	X	X	X		X			X	X		X	X		X	X	X	X	X	X	X		X	X		X		X	S	S	N	N	S		N		N	18				N			X	S		S							X	X	X	
		X	X	X	C	C	X	X	X		X			X			X			X	X	X	X	X	X		X		X		X		X	X	X	X		X			X		X	X			X	X	X				X					X		X			N				N		N	18								S		S									X	
		X	X	X	C	C	X	X				X	X		X	X		X	X	X	X	X	X	A	A		X		X		X		X	X	X	X							X	X	X		X	X	X	X		X	X	X	X	X		X	X	X	S	N	N	N			N		N	18				N			X	N		N									X	
					C	C							X			X			X								X		X		X		X	X	X	X		X	220		X	X		X			X	X	X	X	X	X	X		X			X	X	X	S		N				N		N	18				S													X	X	X	
		X	X	X	C	C					X	X	X		X	X	X	X	X	X			X	F	F		X	X	X		X		X	X	X	X		X			X		X	X			X	X	X	X		X	X				X	X	X	X	S	N	N	N		N	N		N	18	X		X	N			X	S		S							X	X	X	
					A	A							X		X	X		X	X								X		X		X		X	X	X	X		X					X				X	X	X			X			X			X		X	N	N	N	N			N		N	18								N		N										
		X	X		A	A							X			X			X																																				X		X	X	X	X	N	N	N																N		N							X			
					C	C	X	X			X			X				X									X		X		X		X	X	X	X			220		X		X	X			X	X	X	X		X	X	X	X			X	X	X	S	N	N	N			N		N	9				S			X	S		S			S		S	S	X		X	
		X	X	X	E	E	X	X	X			X			X			X					X	F-K	F-K		X		X		X		X	X	X	X	X	X	220	X	X		X	X			X	X	X	X	X	X		X	X	X	X	X	X	X	S	N	N	N	N	N	N	N	N	9				N			X	N		N							X		X	
					B	B							X			X		X									X				X		X	X	X	X					X		X	X			X	X	X	X		X	X	X	X			X		X	S	N	N	N		N	N		N	9				S	S	S		N	X	N					N	N	X		X	
		X	X	X	B	B	X	X	X	X			X			X		X	X			X		C	B			X			X		X	X	X	X		X			X		X	X			X	X	X	X		X	X	X				X		X	S	N	N				N		N	9					N	N		S	X	S				N	N	N	X		X	
		X	X	X	E	D	X	X	X				X		X			X	X	X				D-G	C-F		X		X		X		X	X	X	X					X	X		X			X	X	X	X		X				X		X	X	X		N	N				N		N	9					N														X	
		X	X	X	D	C	X	X					X	X	X											X	X		X		X		X	X	X	X			220		X	X	X	X			X	X	X	X	X	X		O				X	X	X	S	N	N	N	S		N		N	9				N	N	N			X					N	N	N	X		X	
		X	X	X	C	C					X						X					X		C-E	C-E		X		X		X		X	X	X	X		X	X		X		X			X			X	X	X	X	X				X	X	X	X	S	S	S	S		S			S		X		X	S			X	S		S			S			S				
		A	A	A	E	E	X	X			X			X		X	X		X	X				A-E	A-E		X		X		X		X	X		X		X			X		X	X	X		X	X	X	X	X	X			X	X		X	X	X	S	S	S	N	S	S	N							S			X	S		S			S	S		S		X	X	
		X	X	X	C	C						X			X				X	X				A	A		X		X		X		X	X	X	X		X	X		X		X	X			X	X	X		X	X	X		X			X	X	X	S	N	N				N	N	N	18								S									X	X	X	
		X	X	X	B	B													X			X		C-E	B-C		X	X	X	X	X		X	X	X	X		X			X		X	X			X	X	X				X	X	X			X	X	X			N				N		N	18								S												
		X	X		E	D	X					X	X		X	X		X	X								X		X		X		X	X	X	X					X		X	X			X			X		X		X	X		X	X		X	N	N	N	N	N	S	S							N	N	N		N	X	N							X		X	
		X	X	X	B	B		X		X	X			X			X	X	X	X				B-D	B-D		X		X		X		X	X	X	X			220		X		X	X			X	X	X	X	X	X						X	X	X	S		S	S					N	18		X						S		S						S	X	X	X	
					O	O									X												X																	X	X									X	X			X	X	X																														X	
		X	X	X	E	D	X	X	X			X		X			X										X		X		X		X	X	X	X					X	X	X	X			X	X	X	X	X	X		X			X	X		X	S	N	N			S	N		N	9				N	N	N		N	X	N							X		X	
		X	X	X	H	D						X	X	X	X	X	X	X	X				X	D-E	D-E		X		X		X		X	X	X	X		X	110/220		X		X	X			X	X	X		X	X	X	X			X	X		X	S	N	N		S	N	N		N	18					N	N	X	S	X	S		X					X	X	X	
		X	X	X	G	F	X	X				X		X	X		X	X								X	X		X		X		X	X	X	X		X	220	X	X	X		X			X	X	X	X	X	X					X	X	X	X		N	S		S		N		N	18					N	N			X	N		X	N							

CARAVAN PARKS AND CAMPING SITES IN SOUTH AFRICA

CARAVAN PARK / CAMP SITE TARIFF CODE – See columns 38-39 (Subject to alteration)

A = Up to R1 | B = R1–R2 | C = R2–R3 | D = R3–R4 | E = R4–R5 | F = R5–R6 | G = R6–R7 | H = R7–R8 | I = R8–R9 | J = R9–R10 | K = R10–R16 | O = FREE | X = On Application

Charges are based on family of 2 adults and 2 children under 12 years

ADDITIONAL ACCOMMODATION TARIFF CODE – See columns 57-59 (Subject to alteration)

eg. Bungalows, Cabins, Cottages, Chalets, etc.

A = R1–R3 | B = R3–R5 | C = R5–R7 | D = R7–R9 | E = R9–R11 | F = R11–R13 | G = R13–R15 | H = R15–R17 | I = R17–R19 | J = R19–R21 | K = R21–R30 | X = On Application

NB: Where the tariff is given in *italics* it is per person, otherwise per unit

NOTE 1 — Columns 18, 19, 20, – X = Stands available but not demarcated or number of stands have not been provided

NOTE 2 — Column 35 – A = Bookings accepted for additional accommodation only i.e. cottages, bungalows, etc.

NOTE 3 — Column 37 – Deposit refunded under certain conditions eg less 10% ; if site is re-let ; if cancelled well in advance (up to 2 months) or on a doctor's certificate

NOTE 4 — Column 41 – Reductions allowed on application for youth, church, school or sport groups or caravan rallies

NOTE 5 — Column 69 – L = Laundry facilities only

NOTE 6 — Columns 88, 89, 90, – I = In-Season only ; O = Out-of Season only; X = On application

NOTE 7 — Column 96 – I = In-Season only

NOTE 8 — Column 102 – See section on golf in Outdoor Holiday Guide

NOTE 9 — Column 107 – See section on freshwater angling in Outdoor Holiday Guide

NOTE 10 — Column 108 – See section on coastal angling in Outdoor Holiday Guide

Establishments marked thus ● have the Caravan Club of South Africa recommendation – see introduction

ABBREVIATIONS

C = CAPE PROVINCE
N = NATAL
O = ORANGE FREE STATE
T = TRANSVAAL
B = BOPHUTHATSWANA
X = TRANSKEI

TELEPHONE CODE: T = DIAL 0020. BOOK TRUNK CALL. E = DIAL CODE. ASK EXCHANGE FOR NO.

Establishment	Telephone code (1)	Telephone number (2)	Owned or supervised by: Privately owned (3)	Municipal (4)	Divisional council (5)	Provincial administration (6)	Parks board (7)	Site description – Locality: Beach in immediate vicinity (8)	Beside river lake or dam (9)	In or near mountain area (10)	Within built-up area (11)	Nature of ground: Grass (12)	Gravel (13)	Sand (14)	Shade: Unshaded (15)	Partly shaded (16)	Extensively shaded (17)	No. of stands: Caravans only – see note 1 (18)	Caravans and/or tents (19)	Tents only – see note 1 (20)	Accessibility – Approximate distance from main road to site: On main rd (21)	Within 1 km (22)	Within 5 km (23)	Within 10 km (24)	Within 15 km (25)	Surface of road approach: Tar (26)	Gravel (27)	Sand (28)	Condition of road approach: Good (29)	Fair (30)
KALAHARI GEMSBOK NATIONAL PARK C 64 B2 ↙ 960m																														
Mata Mata Rest Camp National Parks Board, P.O. Box 787, Pretoria 0001	012	44-1194					X							X	X	X			10			X						X		X
Nossob Camp	012	44-1194					X							X	X				10			X						X		X
Tweerivieren	012	44-1194					X							X	X	X			10			X						X		X
KRUGER NATIONAL PARK T 71 B5 ↗ 193m																														
Balule National Parks Board, P.O. Box 787, Pretoria 0001	012	44-1194					X					X				X		10			X						X		X	
Crocodile Bridge	012	44-1194					X							X		X			15							X			X	
Letaba	012	44-1194					X					X	X			X			30							X			X	
Lower Sabie	012	44-1194					X					X				X			15							X			X	
Malelane	012	44-1194					X							X		X			X							X			X	
Maroela	012	44-1194					X									X			30								X			X
Olifants	012	44-1194					X							X		X			15							X			X	
Pretoriuskop	012	44-1194					X									X			30							X			X	
Punda Milia	012	44-1194					X												X							X			X	
Satara	012	44-1194					X							X		X			30							X			X	
Shingwidzi	012	44-1194					X							X	X				30							X			X	
Skukuza	012	44-1194					X							X		X			50							X			X	
MOUNTAIN ZEBRA NATIONAL PARK C See Cradock																														
TSITSIKAMA FOREST AND COASTAL NATIONAL PARKS C See Stormsrivier																														
PAROW C 58 NS ↗ 150m																														
● **Parow Municipal** Town Clerk, P.O. Box 11 (7500) ☐ *Off Hendrik Verwoerd Drive, Plattekloof*	021	92-1913		X								X				X		38				X				X			X	
PARYS O 66 A6 ↓ 1416m																														
Feesgrond Bookings not accepted ☐ *Sasolburg Rd.*	01601	2711		X					X			X			X				400			X					X		X	
● **Mimosa Garden** Town Clerk, P.O. Box 359 (9585) ☐ *Cnr. Van Koller/Boom Sts.*	01601	2711		X					X		X	X					X	180				X				X			X	
Smilin' Thru Chalets P.O. Box 388 (9585) ☐ *10 km from Parys*	01601	3921	X						X			X				X	X		120			X					X		X	
Wag-'n-Bietjie P.O. Box 426 (9585)	01601	2737	X						X		X	X	X				X	25	30		X	X				X			X	
PATENSIE C 59 B4 ↘ 213m																														
G. F. Rautenbach Park Municipality (6335) ☐ *Fred Ferreira Rd.*	T	83		X					X	X	X	X				X			10		X									
PEARLY BEACH C 58 D4 ↓ 30m																														
Pearly Beach Holiday Resort P/Bag Pearly Beach, via Napier 7270	02842 E	7213 or 7230	X					X				X				X	X		200			X					X		X	
PEDDIE C 60 C2 ↖ 427m																														
Mpekweni Holiday Resort P.O. Box 108, Port Alfred 6170 ☐ *Mpekweni River Mouth*	04382 E	1931	X					X	X			X			X				24			X				X			X	
PENNINGTON N 63 NS • S.L.																														
Pennington P.O. Box 19 (4184) ☐ *Impathla Rd.*	0323	5251	X					X			X	X	X			X	X		50				X			X		X	X	
Umdoni P.O. Box 15 (4184) ☐ *Main Rd.*	0323	5261	X					X			X	X					X		56		X						X			X
PETIT T 58 D6 ↑ 1646m																														
Cairngorm Tea Gardens P.O. Petit 1512	775 E	52	X									X					X		300		X					X			X	
PETRUSVILLE C 62 B2 ↑ 1349m																														
Petrusville Municipal Town Clerk, P.O. Box 43 (8770) ☐ *Visagie St.*	057232 E	31		X							X		X		X	X		10	10		X					X			X	
PHALABORWA T 69 A4 ↙ 506m																														
Kudu Rest Camp P.O. Box 884 (1390) ☐ *Phalaborwa Main Rd.*	01524	4043/4039	X										X	X		X			3		X							X	X	
Lion Inn P.O. Box 242 (1390) ☐ *Hendrik van Eck Drive.*	01524	4388	X								X			X		X			70		X						X		X	
PIETERMARITZBURG N 63 A3 ↙ 676m																														
Pietermaritzburg Director of Parks, P.O. Box 31 (3200) ☐ *Cleveland Rd., Hayfields*	0331	2-2970		X							X	X					X		120			X				X			X	
PIETERSBURG T 69 A2 ↓ 1160m																														
Rendezvous Recreation Resort P.O. Box 874 (0700) ☐ *23 km from Pietersburg*	01521	2737	X						X	X		X		X		X			X			X				X			X	
● **Union Park** P.O. Box 111 (0700)	01521	6468/2011 x145		X					X			X	X			X		40		20			X			X			X	
PIET RETIEF T 67 B3 ↗ 1271m																														
Piet Retief Municipal P.O. Box 23 (2380) ☐ *Kerk St.*	013432 E	23/218		X					X		X	X				X		50	80		X						X		X	
PILGRIM'S REST T 69 B3 ↘ 1311m																														
Ponies P.O. Box 47 (1290)	T	41	X						X	X		X				X		50		65		X				X			X	
PLETTENBERG BAY C 59 NS → 150m																														
Archerwood Estate P.O. Box 155 (6600) ☐ *Marine Way*	04472 E	184	X					X				X					X		20		X									X
● **Piesang River Resort** P.O. Box 185 (6600) ☐ *Beacon Isle Drive.*	04472 E	244/390	X					X	X		X	X					X	100	80	20			X			X			X	
Plettenberg Bay P.O. Box 73 (6600) ☐ *National Rd.*	04472 E	199	X					X	X		X	X		X			X		280			X					X		X	
Robberg Holiday Resort P.O. Box 81 (6600) ☐ *Robberg Rd.*	04472 E	766	X					X		X		X				X		90				X				X			X	
PONGOLA N 67 B4 ↑ 305m																														
Pongola Municipal P.O. Box 191 (3170) ☐ *40 Naude St.*	03842 E	23		X							X	X				X		40		40		X				X			X	

CAMP SITE FACILITIES: I = In-Season only; O = Out-of-Season only; X = On application

SPORTING AND RECREATIONAL FACILITIES: S = On Site; N = Nearby (Up to 20 km away)

33 SEASONS: OPEN THROUGHOUT THE YEAR	34 OUT-OF-SEASON CLOSING DATE / RE-OPENING DATE	35 TERMS FOR BOOKINGS: BOOKINGS ACCP. PEAK SNS.—SEE NOTE 2	36 DEPOSIT REQUIRED	37 REFUNDED IF CANCELLED—SEE NOTE 3	38 CARAVAN/CAMPING SITE TARIFFS (See heading): MAXIMUM IN-SEASON TARIFF	39 MAXIMUM OUT-OF-SEASON TARIFF	40 REDUCTIONS ALLOWED FOR: LONG PERIODS OF STAY	41 GROUPS—SEE NOTE 4	42 AA MEMBERS	43 OTHERS (ON APPLICATION)	44 RESTAURANT FACILITIES: ON SITE	45 WITHIN 5 km OF SITE	46 MORE THAN 5 km FROM SITE	47 TEAROOM/CAFE: ON SITE	48 WITHIN 5 km OF SITE	49 MORE THAN 5 km FROM SITE	50 SHOPPING FACILITIES (Provisions): ON SITE	51 WITHIN 5 km OF SITE	52 MORE THAN 5 km FROM SITE	53 ADDITIONAL ACCOMMODATION AVAILABLE: BUNGALOWS	54 CABINS	55 COTTAGES (RONDAVELS)	56 CHALETS	57 TARIFF (See heading): MAXIMUM IN-SEASON TARIFF	58 MAXIMUM OUT-OF-SEASON TARIFF	59 CARAVANS TO RENT ON SITE—SEE SECTION	60 DRINKING WATER: PIPED	61 OTHER	62 BATHS: HOT AND COLD	63 COLD ONLY	64 SHOWERS: HOT AND COLD	65 COLD ONLY	66 WATERBORNE SANITATION	67 WASHBASINS	68 DISHWASHING FACILITIES	69 LAUNDRY AND IRONING FACILITIES—SEE NOTE 5	70 WASHING MACHINES	71 SITE LIT	72 PLUGS FOR RAZORS (VOLTAGE)	73 REFRIGERATORS	74 FIREWOOD/CHARCOAL	75 OPEN FIRE FORBIDDEN	76 CAMP FIRE PERMITTED	77 BRAAI PLACES PROVIDED	78 KITCHEN/COOKING FACILITIES	79 PETROL PUMP ON SITE	80 PETROL PUMP NEARBY	81 CAR REPAIR SHOP NEARBY	82 CAR SERVICING NEARBY	83 GAS SERVICE NEARBY	84 FIRST AID/HOSPITAL/DOCTOR NEARBY	85 POST OFFICE NEARBY	86 SITE GUARDED	87 PETS ALLOWED	88 NON-WHITE SERVANTS: SERVANTS PERMITTED—SEE NOTE 6	89 SERVANTS' ACCOM.—SEE NOTE 6	90 SERVANTS FOR HIRE—SEE NOTE 6	91 TYPE OF VEHICLE PERMITTED: CAR AND TRAILER	92 TRUCK 'HORSE' AND SEMI-TRAILER	93 SELF-PROPELLED CARAVANS	94 CHILDRENS' PLAYGROUND	95 TENNIS	96 CINEMA/DRIVE-IN/TV-ROOM—SEE NOTE 7	97 HORSE-RIDING	98 GAMES ROOM	99 TRAMPOLINE	100 BOWLS	101 HOT SPRINGS	102 GOLF: GOLF COURSE—SEE NOTE 8	103 NUMBER OF HOLES	104 MINIATURE	105 MASHIE	106 PUTT-PUTT	107 FISHING: FRESHWATER—SEE NOTE 9	108 SEA—SEE NOTE 10	109 GOGGLE	110 LICENCE REQUIRED	111 SWIMMING: SWIMMING POOL	112 SEA BATHING	113 CHILDRENS' POOL	114 ADULTS ONLY	115 SHARK NETS AT BEACH	116 BOATING: BOATS FOR HIRE	117 POWER	118 SAILING	119 CANOEING	120 PLACES OF INTEREST: HISTORIC	121 SCIENTIFIC	122 NATURAL	123 NOTES
		X	X	X	D	D											X			X				C-H	C-H		X		X		X		X	X							X	X	X	X		X	X			X	X		X					X		X																													X	
		X	X	X	D	D											X	X		X				C-H	C-H		X				X		X	X		X			X		X	X	X	X		X				X	X		X					X		X																													X	
		X	X	X	D	D											X			X				C-H	C-H		X		X		X		X	X					X		X	X	X	X		X				X	X		X					X		X																													X	
		X	X	X	D	D							X			X			X	X				B-E	B-E		X		X		X		X	X	X						X		X	X	X								X					X	X	X																													X	
		X	X	X	D	D											X			X				C-E	C-E		X		X		X		X	X	X	X						X		X	X	X				X	X				X	X		X	X	X																													X	
		X	X	X	D	D					X			X			X			X				D-E	D-E		X		X		X		X	X	X	X			X			X		X	X	X	X			X	X				X	X		X	X	X																													X	
		X	X	X	D	D					X			X			X			X				D	D		X		X		X	X	X	X	X	X			X			X		X	X	X				X	X				X	X		X	X	X																													X	
		X	X	X	D	D											X			X				C	C		X		X		X		X	X	X	X			X			X		X	X	X				X	X				X	X		X	X	X																													X	
		X	X	X	D	D												X																																																																									X	
		X	X	X	D	D					X			X			X			X		X		D-J	D-J		X		X		X		X	X	X	X			X			X		X	X	X				X					X	X		X	X	X																													X	
		X	X	X	D	D					X			X			X			X		X		D-J	D-J		X		X		X		X	X	X	X			X			X	X	X	X					X	X				X	X		X	X	X																	S										X	
		X	X	X	D	D					X			X			X			X				C	C		X				X		X			X						X		X	X	X	X			X					X	X		X	X	X																													X	
		X	X	X	D	D					X			X			X			X				D-E	D-E		X		X		X		X	X	X	X			240			X		X	X	X				X					X	X		X	X	X																													X	
		X	X	X	D	D					X			X			X			X				C-D	C-D		X		X		X		X	X		X								X		X				X					X	X		X	X	X																													X	
		X	X	X	D	D					X			X			X			X		X		D-J	D-J		X		X		X		X	X	X	X			X			X		X	X	X	X	X	X	X	X	X			X	X		X	X	X																										X	X	X	
		X	X		D	C	X						X			X		X	X								X		X		X		X	X	X	X		X	220				X	X	X		X	X	X	X	X	X						X	X	X	N	N	N	N	N	N	N		N	18				N	N	N	X	N		N								X		
					C	C							X			X			X								X				X		X	X		X					X		X				X	X	X	X		X		X	X			X	X	X	N	N	N			N	N		N	18	X		X					N		N				N	N	N	X		X	
					D	C		X			X			X				X		X			X	G	E		X		X		X		X	X	X	X		X	X		X	X		X			X	X	X		X	X		X				X	X	X	S	N	N			S	N		N	18			X	S			X	S		S			S		S	S	X		X	
					E	E						X			X		X					X		D	D		X		X		X		X	X	X	X					X	X	X	X			X	X	X	X	X	X			X	X		X	X	X	S	S		S	S	N	N		N	18				S			X	S		S					S	S			X	
		X	X	X	B	B	X	X	X			X			X			X									X		X		X		X	X	X	X					X		X	X	X		X	X	X	X	X	X		X	X			X	X	X	N	N	N	N	N	N	N		N	18				N			X										X	X	X	
		X			A	A	X					X	X		X	X		X	X								X					X	X	X	X								X	X			X	X	X	X	X	X		X	X		X	X	X	X	S	N										X		N			X			N				N	N	N	X		X	
		X	X	X	B	B		X						X			X			X		X		B-G	B-G		X		X		X		X	X	X	X					X		X	X		X		X	X				X	X	X			X	X	X	S		I			S									N	N													X	
		X	X		D	D											X			X				D-E	D-E		X	X	X		X		X	X	X	X					X	X	X	X			X			X					X	X	X	X		X															N				X											
		X	X	X	G	C	X		X				X	X	X		X	X	X			X		I	F	X	X		X		X		X	X	X	X		X	220		X		X	X			X	X	X	X	X	X	X	X			X	X	X	X	S	N		N	S	S	N		N	18					N	N	X	S	X	S										
		X	X		C	X	X		X			X			X			X	X								X		X		X		X	X	X	X		X			X			X								X		X			X	X		X							N		N	18					N			S	X											
		X			C	C	X		X		X			X					X								X		X		X		X	X	X	X					X	X		X			X	X	X			X		X	X	X	X				S	S				S					X							S		S										
					A	A	X					X			X			X									X					X	X	X									X	X			X	X	X	X		X		X	X			X	X	X	S	S							N	9				N		N	X										X		X	
					B	B	X		X		X		X	X			X						X	D	D		X		X		X		X	X				X	220		X	X	X	X			X	X	X				X					X	X	X																														
					E	E		X	X			X			X			X									X		X		X		X	X	X	X			X				X				X	X	X			X	X					X		X	N	N	N	N			N											N		N								X		
		X			B	B							X		X			X									X		X		X		X	X	X	X		X	220				X	X			X	X	X			X	X	X	X			X		X	S	N	N	N			N		N	18				N				N		N						N	X	X	X	
		X	X		C	B	X	X	X		X			X			X			X		X	X	X	X		X		X		X		X	X	X	X					X		X	X		X		X	X	X	X	X			X		X	X		X	S	N	N	N		S	N		N	18																	X	X	X	
					C	C						X			X			X									X		X		X		X	X	X	X		X	X				X				X	X					X		X			X	X	X	S		N	S			N		N	18				S			X	N										X	
					B	B		X				X	X		X	X		X	X								X		X		X		X	X	X	X		X	X		X			X			X	X	X	X	X	X	X	X	X	X	X	X		X	N	N	N	N			N		N	18				N			X	N										X	X	
		X	X		C	C						X			X			X									X		X		X		X	X	X	X							X	X			X	X	X	X		X	X					X		X	N	N	N				N		N	9				N			X	N		N							X		X	
		X	X		F	F					X	X	X		X	X		X	X								X		X		X		X	X	X	X					X		X				X	X	X	X	X	X						X	X	X	N	N		N	S		N		N	18					N	N	X	S	X		X		N	N	N	N	X		X	
		X	X		X	X						X			X		X	X	X		X		X	X	X	X	X		X		X		X	X	X	X	X	X	220	X	X			X			X	X	X	X	X	X	X					X	X	X	S	N	I	N	S		N		N	18					N	N	X	S	X	S							X	X	X	
		X	X		X	X	X	X					X				X										X		X		X		X	X	X	X		X			X			X			X	X	X	X	X	X	X					X		X		N	N	N			N		N	18					N	N	X		X				N			N	X	X	X	
		X	X		F	C							X			X	X			X					D		X		X		X		X	X	X	X					X	X	X	X			X	X	X			X	X					X		X							N		N	18					N				X								X		X	
					C	C	X					X			X			X									X				X		X	X	X	X		X	220		X	X		X			X	X	X	X	X	X	X	X	X			X		X		N	N	N			N		N	9				N			X	N		N				N	N			X	X	

CARAVAN PARKS AND CAMPING SITES IN SOUTH AFRICA

CARAVAN PARK / CAMP SITE TARIFF CODE — See columns 38–39 (Subject to alteration)

A = Up to R1 | B = R1–R2 | C = R2–R3 | D = R3–R4 | E = R4–R5 | F = R5–R6 | G = R6–R7 | H = R7–R8 | I = R8–R9 | J = R9–R10 | K = R10–R16 | O = FREE | X = On Application

Charges are based on family of 2 adults and 2 children under 12 years

ADDITIONAL ACCOMMODATION TARIFF CODE — See columns 57–59 (Subject to alteration)

eg. Bungalows, Cabins, Cottages, Chalets, etc.

A = R1–R3 | B = R3–R5 | C = R5–R7 | D = R7–R9 | E = R9–R11 | F = R11–R13 | G = R13–R15 | H = R15–R17 | I = R17–R19 | J = R19–R21 | K = R21–R30 | X = On Application

NB: Where the tariff is given in *italics* it is per person, otherwise per unit

NOTE 1 — Columns 18, 19, 20, — X = Stands available but not demarcated or number of stands have not been provided

NOTE 2 — Column 35 — A = Bookings accepted for additional accommodation only i.e. cottages, bungalows, etc.

NOTE 3 — Column 37 — Deposit refunded under certain conditions eg. less 10% ; if site is re-let ; if cancelled well in advance (up to 2 months) or on a doctor's certificate

NOTE 4 — Column 41 — Reductions allowed on application for youth, church, school or sport groups or caravan rallies

NOTE 5 — Column 69 — L = Laundry facilities only

NOTE 6 — Columns 88, 89, 90, — I = In-Season only ; O = Out-of-Season only ; X = On application

NOTE 7 — Column 96 — I = In-Season only

NOTE 8 — Column 102 — See section on golf in Outdoor Holiday Guide

NOTE 9 — Column 107 — See section on freshwater angling in Outdoor Holiday Guide

NOTE 10 — Column 108 — See section on coastal angling in Outdoor Holiday Guide

Establishments marked thus ● have the Caravan Club of South Africa recommendation — see introduction

ABBREVIATIONS

C = CAPE PROVINCE
N = NATAL
O = ORANGE FREE STATE
T = TRANSVAAL
B = BOPHUTHATSWANA
X = TRANSKEI

TELEPHONE CODE: T = DIAL 0020. BOOK TRUNK CALL; E = DIAL CODE. ASK EXCHANGE FOR NO.

Name	1 Telephone code	2 Telephone number	3 Owned or supervised by: Privately owned	4 Municipal	5 Divisional council	6 Provincial council	7 Parks Board administration	8 Site description – Locality: Beach	9 Beside river, lake or dam in immediate vicinity	10 In or near mountain area	11 Within built-up area	12 Nature of ground: Grass	13 Gravel	14 Sand	15 Shade: Unshaded	16 Partly shaded	17 Extensively shaded	18 No. of stands: Caravans only – see note 1	19 Caravans and/or tents	20 Tents only – see note 1	21 Accessibility – Approximate distance from main road to site: On main rd	22 Within 1 km	23 Within 5 km	24 Within 10 km	25 Within 15 km	26 Surface of road approach: Tar	27 Gravel	28 Sand	29 Condition of road approach: Good	30 Fair	Poor
PORT ALFRED C 60 C1 S.L.																															
Lagoon P.O. Box 78 (6170) ☐ *Lagoon Rd., East Beach*	04642 E	590	X					X	X		X	X				X			90		X					X			X		
● **Medolino** P.O. Box 20, Kowie West 6171 ☐ *23 Stewart Rd.*	04642 E	346	X					X				X				X			75			X				X			X		
The Rainbow Park P.O. Box 15, Kowie West 6171 ☐ *Beach Front*	04642 E	495	X					X				X				X	X	25	10	5		X				X	X		X		
The Willows Town Clerk, P.O. Box 13 (6170)	04642 E	32		X				X			X	X				X	X		52		X					X			X		
PORT EDWARD N 63 NS S.L.																															
Pont P.O. Port Edward 4295 ☐ *Old Pont Rd.*				X				X	X	X		X	X			X	X		X				X				X		X		
S.A. Police Holiday Resort Manager, P.O. Box 22 (4295)	03930	823	X					X				X	X	X		X	X	41					X			X			X		
● **T.O. Strand** P.O. Box 86 (4295) ☐ *6 km from Port Edward*	03931	729	X					X	X			X					X		126			X				X			X		
PORT ELIZABETH C 59 B5 S.L.																															
● **Brookes Hill** Beach Manager, Humewood 6001 ☐ *Beach Rd., Humewood*	041	2-5400	X					X				X			X			130			X					X			X		
Gamtoos River Mouth Bookings not accepted ☐ *60 km from Port Elizabeth*	041	2-8911				X		X	X			X		X			X	X	X					X		X			X		
Humewood Beach Manager, Humewood 6001	041	53-3095		X				X			X	X	X	X	X	X	X	350		250	X					X			X		
St. Georges Strand Beach Manager, Humewood 6001	041	6134		X				X				X	X	X	X	X		X	X	X	X					X			X		
PORT NOLLOTH C 60 A4 S.L.																															
McDougalls Bay Municipality, P.O. Box 15 (8280)	T	11		X				X						X	X				30				X				X			X	
PORT SHEPSTONE N 63 NS S.L.																															
Port Shepstone Borough P.O. Box 5 (4240)	0391	2-1100		X				X	X			X					X		19		X					X			X		
PORT ST. JOHNS X 60 A4 3m																															
● **First Beach Municipal** P.O. Box 2 (4830)	04752 E	8		X				X	X			X					X	23			X					X			X		
Second Beach Municipal P.O. Box 2 (4830)	04752 E	8		X				X	X			X				X		50		60		X					X		X		
POTCHEFSTROOM T 66 A5 1300m																															
Lakeside Recreation Resort P.O. Box 20099, Noordbrug 2522 ☐ *Lakeside Dam*	01481	5144		X					X			X					X					X				X			X		
POTGIETERSRUS T 69 B2 1178m																															
Fiestapark Motel and Holiday Resort P.O. Box 616 (0600) ☐ *Naboomspruit Main Rd.*	01542 E	8712	X							X		X					X		8		X						X		X		
● **Potgietersrus Municipal** Parks Superintendent, P.O. Box 34 (0600) ☐ *Voortrekker Rd. Ext.*	01542 E	**624 x51**		X					X	X		X					X	19			X						X		X		
PRETORIA T 68 C6 1400m																															
● **Fountains Valley** Bookings not necessary	012	44-7131		X								X			X	X	X		74			X				X			X		
Hi-Way P.O. Box 186, Bon Accord 0009 ☐ *Warmbaths Main Rd.*	012	57-2651	X						X			X	X			X								X		X			X		
● **Joos Becker** Bookings not necessary	012	75-4029		X						X		X			X	X	X	60				X				X			X		
● **Polkadraai** P.O. Box 42, Voortrekkerhoogte 0143	012	64-2682	X						X			X				X		60	80	20	X							X		X	
PRIESKA C 61 A4 939m																															
Prieska Municipal P.O. Box 16 (8940) ☐ *Hoof St.*	05942 E	154		X							X		X			X		25					X			X			X		
PRINCE ALBERT C 59 B2 646m																															
Rap-Skrap Rest Camp 46 Kerk St. (6930) ☐ *46 Kerk St.*	044322 E	33	X							X	X		X			X			X			X					X			X	
QUEENSTOWN C 62 C4 1160m																															
Queenstown Municipal Bookings not necessary ☐ *East London Main Rd.*	**0451**	**2291 x31**		X					X			X	X			X			40		X						X		X		
QUINERA C See Gonubie Mouth																															
RANDFONTEIN T 72 NS 1600m																															
Riebeeck Lake Parks Superintendent, P.O. Box 218 (1760) ☐ *Malan St.*	011	663-4110		X					X		X	X					X	35				X				X			X		
RAWSONVILLE C 58 C4 242m																															
Goudini Spa P.O. Box 47 (6845) ☐ *±4 km from Rawsonville*	0231	9-1100	X							X	X	X		X		X		30					X			X			X		
REITZ O 66 B6 1623m																															
Reitz Municipal P.O. Box 26 (9810) ☐ *Sarel Cilliers St.*	014342 E	26/183		X							X	X					X		8		X					X			X		
RICHARDS BAY N 67 C5 S.L.																															
Richards Bay Municipal P/Bag X1004 (3900) ☐ *Beachfront*	0351	3-1971		X				X				X				X			211		X						X		X		
RICHMOND C 61 C5 1381m																															
Richmond Municipal P.O. Box 8 (7010) ☐ *Market St.*	05752 E	1		X					X				X				X		X			X					X			X	
RIVERSDALE C 58 D6 118m																															
Meurant P.O. Box 29 (6770)	02932 E	14		X					X	X			X				X		30				X			X			X		
RIVERTON C 66 C2 1097m																															
Riverton-on-Vaal P.O. Box 628, Kimberley 8300 ☐ *±27 km from Kimberley*	0531	2-2241 x221		X					X			X				X		43		50				X		X			X		
RIVIERSONDEREND C 58 D4 152m																															
Riviersonderend Municipal P.O. Box 31 (7250) ☐ *Main St.*	02852 E	30		X						X	X	X				X		30	30		X						X		X		
RIVONIA T 72 NS 1433m																															
Rivonia P.O. Box 18 (2128) ☐ *186 Rietfontein Rd.*	011	802-1108	X								X	X					X	X				X				X			X		
ROBERTSON C 58 C4 173m																															
● **Silverstrand Holiday Resort** Town Clerk, P.O. Box 52 (6705) ☐ *3 km from Robertson*	02352 E	627		X					X			X	X			X							X			X			X		

EN THROUGHOUT THE YEAR

CAMP SITE FACILITIES: I = In-Season only, O = Out-of-Season only, X = On application

SPORTING AND RECREATIONAL FACILITIES: S = On Site, N = Nearby (Up to 20 km away)

33 Seasons: Out-of-season closing date	34 Re-opening date	35 Terms for bookings: Bookings accp. peak sns. – see note 2	36 Deposit required	37 Refunded if cancelled – see note 3	38 Caravan/camping site tariffs (see heading): Maximum in-season tariff	39 Maximum out-of-season tariff	40 Reductions allowed for: Long periods of stay	41 Groups – see note 4	42 AA members	43 Others (on application)	44 Restaurant facilities: On site	45 Within 5 km of site	46 More than 5 km from site	47 Tearoom/cafe: On site	48 Within 5 km of site	49 More than 5 km from site	50 Shopping facilities (provisions): On site	51 Within 5 km of site	52 More than 5 km from site	53 Additional accommodation available: Bungalows	54 Cabins	55 Cottages (rondavels)	56 Chalets	57 Tariff (see heading): Maximum in-season tariff	58 Maximum out-of-season tariff	59 Caravans to rent on site – see section	60 Drinking water: Piped	61 Other	62 Baths: Hot and cold	63 Cold only	64 Showers: Hot and cold	65 Cold only	66 Camp site facilities: Waterborne sanitation	67 Washbasins	68 Dishwashing facilities	69 Laundry and ironing facilities – see note 5	70 Washing machines	71 Site lit	72 Plugs for razors (voltage)	73 Refrigerators	74 Firewood/charcoal	75 Open fire forbidden	76 Camp fire permitted	77 Braai places provided	78 Kitchen/cooking facilities	79 Petrol pump on site	80 Petrol pump nearby	81 Car repair shop nearby	82 Car servicing nearby	83 Gas service nearby	84 First aid/hospital/doctor nearby	85 Post office nearby	86 Site guarded	87 Pets allowed	88 Non-white servants: Servants permitted – see note 6	89 Servants accom. – see note 6	90 Servants for hire – see note 6	91 Type of vehicle permitted: Car and trailer	92 Truck 'horse' and semi-trailer	93 Self-propelled caravans	94 Childrens' playground	95 Tennis	96 Cinema/drive-in/TV-room – see note 7	97 Horse-riding	98 Games room	99 Trampoline	100 Bowls	101 Hot springs	102 Golf: Golf course – see note 8	103 Number of holes	104 Miniature	105 Mashie	106 Putt-putt	107 Fishing: Freshwater – see note 9	108 Sea – see note 10	109 Goggle	110 Licence required	111 Swimming: Swimming pool	112 Sea bathing	113 Childrens' pool	114 Adults only	115 Shark nets at beach	116 Boating: Boats for hire	117 Power	118 Sailing	119 Canoeing	120 Places of interest: Historic	121 Scientific	122 Natural	123 Notes
		X	X		C	C	X	X	X		X			X			X										X		X		X		X	X	X	X		X			X		X	X				X	X			X	X	X				X	X	X	S		S	S	S		S		N	18				N	N				X	N							X		X	
		X	X		D	C	X	X				X				X		X			X			C	B	X	X	X	X		X		X	X	X	X	X	X	110/220		X		X	X			X	X	X	X	X	X	X	X	X		X	X	X	X	S	N	N	N	S		N		N	18					N	N			X				N	N	N	N	X	X	X	
		X	X		D	D	X	X				X	X	X			X			X	X			B-C	B-C		X	X	X		X	X	X	X	X	X		X			X	X	X	X		X	X	X	X	X	X	X	X	X	X		X	X		X			N				N		N	18					N				X				N	N	N	N	X	X	X	
					B	B						X			X		X										X			X		X		X				X	X		X	X	X	X			X	X	X	X	X	X	X					X	X	X	S	N	N	N	N		N		N	18	X				N	N			X	N			N	N	N	N	X		X	
		X	X		C	C							X		X	X		X	X								X		X		X	X	X	X	X	X							X				X	X	X	X	X	X						X	X	X	S	N	N			N	N		N			X			N	N			X	S		X	N	N	N	N				
		X	X		D	C					X			X			X	X	X	X		X	X	A-E	A-D		X		X		X		X	X	X	X		X			X		X	X			X	X	X	X		X					X	X		X	S	S	S		S	S	N								N	N			X	S		X							X	
		X	X		E	C	X	X	X		X			X			X						X	G	C		X		X		X		X	X		X		X	X	X	X		X	X			X	X	X	X		X	X				X	X		X	S	S	S			S			N					N	N	N	X		X			X								
		X	X		C	C						X			X			X									X		X				X			X																			X					X	N	N	N	N		N	N		N	18			X	N	N	N		N	X	N							X	X	X	
					A	A							X			X			X								X				X	X											X	X			X	X	X	X		X						X	X	X	S														N	N			X										X	
		X	X		C	C						X			X			X		X		X		B-D	B-D		X		X	X	X	X	X	X	X	X		X	X		X			X			X	X	X	X	X	X		X	X			X		X	N	N	N	N		N	N		N	18				N	N	N		N	X	N							X	X	X	
					B	B																					X			X		X	X	X										X	X						X			X	X			X		X															N	N			X								X	X	X	
		X	X		A	A															X			A	A		X			X		X	X	X									X	X									X	X	X			X	X	X															N	N			X					N	N	N				
		X	X		B	B							X			X			X								X		X		X		X	X		X		X					X	X			X	X	X			X	X					X		X							N		N	18					N	N	X		X	N				N	N	N			X	
		X	X		C	C	X						X			X			X	X			X	C-E	C-E		X		X		X		X	X	X	X		X		X	X		X	X			X	X	X	X	X	X	X		X	X	X	X	X	X		N					N		N	9					N	N		N	X					N		N			X	
		X	X		C	C	X					X			X				X	X			X	C-E	C-E		X		X		X		X	X	X	X					X		X	X			X	X	X	X	X	X	X		X	X	X	X	X	X		N			S		N		N	9					N	N		N	X					N		N			X	
					C	C					X			X			X			X		X		B-E	B-E		X		X		X		X	X	X	X		X	X		X			X			X	X	X	X	X	X	X		X	X		X	X	X	S	S	N			S	N		N	18	X	X	X	S			X	S		S			S	S	S	S				
		X	X		C	C	X	X	X		X			X			X					X	X	F	F		X		X				X	X	X	X		X	220	X	X		X	X	X		X			X			X	X	X	X	X	X	X	X	S	S	N		S			N	N	9				N			X	S		S				N	N	N	X	X	X	
		X			B	B							X			X			X								X		X		X		X	X	X	X		X	220		X	X		X			X	X	X	X		X	X					X		X	S	N	N	N		N			N	9				N			X	N		N					N	N	X		X	
					B	B						X	X		X			X	X								X		X		X		X	X	X	X		X	250		X			X				X	X				X					X	X	X	S	N	N				N		N	18								N			X							X		X	
		X			B	B	X	X	X			X	X			X		X	X								X		X		X		X	X	X	X		X	220		X		X				X	X	X	X		X	X	X			X	X	X	X	S		N	N										N			X										X	X	X	
					B	B						X	X		X			X	X								X		X		X		X	X	X	X		X	250		X			X				X	X				X					X	X	X	S	N	N				N		N	18								S			X									
		X	X		C	C	X	X		X	X	X		X				X									X		X		X		X	X	X	X	X	X	220	X	X	X	X	X			X	X	X	X	X	X	X	X				X		X			S				N		N	18				N			X	S											X	
		X			C	C							X			X			X								X	X		X		X	X	X				X		X			X	X	X								X	X				X	X	X	N	N	N	N	N		N		N	18				N			X	N		N						N	X		X	
		X			C	C	X	X				X	X		X	X		X	X	X	X	X		B-C	B-C		X	X	X			X	X	X	X						X		X	X	X		X	X	X	X	X	X	X	X				X		X	S	N							N			X		N			X										X		X	
					B	B					X			X				X									X		X		X		X	X	X	X		X	220					X			X	X	X	X	X	X		X	X			X		X			N				N		N	18				N			X	N		N				N	N	N	X		X	
		X	X	X	B	B						X	X		X	X		X	X			X		C	C		X	X	X		X		X	X	X	X		X	110/220	X	X	X	X	X			X	X	X		X	X	X	X				X	X	X	S	N	N	N			N		N	18				S			X	S		S							X		X	
		X	X		E	E		X			X			X			X			X		X		H	I		X		X		X		X	X	X	X		X	220	X	X		X	X	X		X	X	X		X	X	X		X	X	X	X		X	S	S	S	N	S		N	S	N	18								S		S				N	N	N	X	X	X	
		X			C	C						X			X			X									X		X		X		X	X	X	X		X	220		X	X	X	X			X	X	X	X	X	X	X	X				X	X	X	S	N	N	N	N	N	N		N	9				S			X	S		S										
		X	X	X	C	C	X	X				X		X	X			X									X		X		X		X	X	X	X					X		X				X	X	X	X		X	X					X	X	X	S	N	N	N	S		N		N	9				N	N	N		N	X	S				N	N	N	X		X	
					B	B							X			X			X								X				X		X	X	X	X		X	X		X		X	X			X	X	X	X	X	X	X	X	X			X			N	N					N		N	18								N										X			
		A	A		B	B				X		X			X			X		X				B	B		X				X		X	X	X	X		X			X		X	X			X	X	X	X		X		X				X	X	X	N	N	N				N		N	18																				X	
		X	X	X	D	D					X			X			X					X	X	B-C	B-C		X		X		X		X	X	X	X		X	X	X	X	X		X			X				X		X					X		X	S	S												S			X	S		S			S				X			
					B	B	X	X				X			X			X									X				X		X	X	X	X		X	220/250		X		X	X			X	X	X	X		X	X		X			X	X	X	N	N	N						N	9								S		S	X								X	
		X			F	F	X					X	X		X	X		X	X								X		X		X		X	X	X	X	X	X	220		X		X	X			X	X	X	X	X	X	X		X	X			X	X	S	N	N	N			N		N	18				N				N			X									
		X	X	X	X	X					X			X				X		X		X	X	X	X		X		X		X		X	X	X	X		X	X	X	X		X	X			X	X	X	X	X	X						X	X	X	S	N	N				N		N	9				S			X			S				S	S	S			X	

CARAVAN PARKS AND CAMPING SITES IN SOUTH AFRICA

CARAVAN PARK / CAMP SITE TARIFF CODE – See columns 38–39 (Subject to alteration)

A = Up to R1	**C** = R2–R3	**E** = R4–R5	**G** = R6–R7	**I** = R8–R9	**K** = R10–R16
B = R1–R2	**D** = R3–R4	**F** = R5–R6	**H** = R7–R8	**J** = R9–R10	**O** = FREE
					X = On Application

Charges are based on family of 2 adults and 2 children under 12 years

ADDITIONAL ACCOMMODATION TARIFF CODE – See columns 57–59 (Subject to alteration)

eg. Bungalows, Cabins, Cottages, Chalets, etc.

A = R1–R3	**C** = R5–R7	**E** = R9–R11	**G** = R13–R15	**I** = R17–R19	**K** = R21–R30
B = R3–R5	**D** = R7–R9	**F** = R11–R13	**H** = R15–R17	**J** = R19–R21	**X** = On Application

NB: Where the tariff is given in *italics* it is per person, otherwise per unit

NOTE 1 — **Columns 18, 19, 20,** — X= Stands available but not demarcated or number of stands have not been provided
NOTE 2 — **Column 35** — A= Bookings accepted for additional accommodation only i.e. cottages, bungalows, etc.
NOTE 3 — **Column 37** — Deposit refunded under certain conditions eg. less 10% ; if site is re-let ; if cancelled well in advance (up to 2 months) or on a doctor's certificate
NOTE 4 — **Column 41** — Reductions allowed on application for youth, church, school or sport groups or caravan rallies

NOTE 5 — **Column 69** — L= Laundry facilities only
NOTE 6 — **Columns 88, 89, 90,** — I = In-Season only ; O = Out-of-Season only; X = On application
NOTE 7 — **Column 96** — I = In-Season only
NOTE 8 — **Column 102** — See section on golf in Outdoor Holiday Guide
NOTE 9 — **Column 107** — See section on freshwater angling in Outdoor Holiday Guide
NOTE 10 — **Column 108** — See section on coastal angling in Outdoor Holiday Guide

Establishments marked thus ● have the Caravan Club of South Africa recommendation — see introduction

ABBREVIATIONS
C = CAPE PROVINCE
N = NATAL
O = ORANGE FREE STATE
T = TRANSVAAL
B = BOPHUTHATSWANA
X = TRANSKEI

TELEPHONE CODE: T = DIAL 0020, BOOK TRUNK CALL; E = DIAL CODE, ASK EXCHANGE FOR NO.

Establishment	1 Telephone code	2 Telephone number	3 Owned/supervised by: Privately owned	4 Municipal	5 Divisional council	6 Provincial council	7 Parks board administration	8 Site description – Locality: Beach in immediate vicinity	9 Beside river, lake or dam	10 In or near mountain area	11 Within built-up area	12 Nature of ground: Grass	13 Gravel	14 Sand	15 Shade: Unshaded	16 Partly shaded	17 Extensively shaded	18 No. of stands: Caravans only – see note 1	19 Caravans and/or tents	20 Tents only – see note 1	21 Accessibility – Approximate distance from main road to site: On main rd	22 Within 1 km	23 Within 5 km	24 Within 10 km	25 Within 15 km	26 Surface of road approach: Tar	27 Gravel	28 Sand	29 Condition of road approach: Good	30 Fair
ROCKCLYFFE-ON-SEA C 60 C2 S.L.																														
Rockclyffe-on-Sea Holiday Resort P.O. Box 5022, Greenfields, East London 5208 □ + *17 km from East London*	0431	46-2540	X					X				X					X	25				X					X		X	
ROODEPOORT T 72 NS 1631m																														
Little Falls Pleasure Resort P.O. Box 1 (1725) □ *Little Falls Rd.*	011	679-1412	X						X	X		X				X		50		50		X				X	X		X	
Pondorosa P.O. Box 810 (1725)	011	765-0635	X						X			X				X		24			X						X		X	
ROYAL NATAL NATIONAL PARK N See Mont-aux-Sources																														
RUSTENBURG T 68 C5 1234m																														
Ananda P.O. Box 15 (0300)	01421	2-2332	X							X		X					X	45				X				X			X	
SABI RIVER BUNGALOWS T 69 C4 518m																														
Sabie River Mineral Bath P.O. Box 151, Hazyview 1242 □ *4 km from Hazyview*	0131242 E	3804	X						X	X	X	X				X	X		40			X					X		X	
Sabie Villa Rest Camp P.O. Box 148, Hazyview 1242	0131242 E	**825**	X						X	X		X					X		50			X					X		X	
SABIE T 69 C3 1059m																														
● **Castle Rock** P.O. Box 61 (1260) □ *Lydenburg Rd.*	0131512 E	203		X					X			X					X		100			X					X		X	
● **Merry Pebbles** P.O. Box 131 (1260) □ *Lydenburg Rd.*	0131512 E	323							X			X				X			X			X					X		X	
SALDANHA C 58 C2 S.L.																														
Saldanha Holiday Resort P.O. Box 22 (7395)	022802 E	204		X				X				X			X			90	90			X				X			X	
SASOLBURG O 66 A5 1449m																														
● **Abrahamsrust Recreation Resort** P.O. Box 60 (9570)	016	63-8909		X					X			X					X	45	21			X				X			X	
SCARBOROUGH C 58 NS S.L.																														
Scarborough Bookings not necessary	021	41-3266			X			X		X		X	X	X		X			X	X		X					X		X	
SCHAGEN T 69 C3 732m																														
St. Pauls Bungalows P.O. Schagen 1207 □ *Dist. Nelspruit*	0131232 E	1503	X						X	X		X					X		20		X							X		X
Sudwala Caves P.O. Box 30 (1207)	0131232 E	2613	X						X	X		X				X	X	50	100			X				X			X	
SCHWEIZER-RENEKE T 66 B3 1314m																														
Wentzel Dam Parking Area Bookings not accepted □ *3 km from Schweizer-Reneke*	018012 E	25 or 3340		X					X			X					X	X	X	X		X					X		X	
SCOTTBURGH N 63 NS S.L.																														
● **Scottburgh Municipal** Camp Officer, P.O. Box 19 (4180) □ *Beachfront*	**0323**	2-0291		X				X	X		X	X				X			330			X				X			X	
SEDGEFIELD C 59 NS S.L.																														
Cloverdale P.O. Box 21 (6573) □ *Swartvlei*	T	722	X					X	X	X		X					X		60			X				X			X	
● **Jooris Park** P.O. Box 22 (6573) □ *Swartvlei*	T	940	X					X	X	X		X					X		80			X					X		X	
Lake Pleasant Holiday Resort P.O. Box 16 (6573) □ *Groenvlei*	T	28	X					X	X	X		X					X		120			X				X			X	
Landfall P.O. Box 144 (6573) □ *Pelican Ave.*	T	44	X						X			X					X		45			X				X			X	
Pine Lake Marina P.O. Box 8 (6573) □ *Swartvlei*	T	59	X						X	X		X					X		100			X					X		X	
Swartvlei Divisional Council, P.O. Box 12, George 6530 □ *Swartvlei*	0441	3001			X			X	X			X		X		X			115				X				X			X
SENEKAL O 66 C5 1446m																														
Senekal Municipal P.O. Box 20 (9600) □ *Van Riebeeck St.*	014352 E	30		X					X		X	X				X						X					X		X	
SHELLY BEACH N 63 NS 5m																														
Blue Seas P.O. Box 102, St. Michael's-on-Sea 4265	0393	5-1049	X					X				X				X			54		X					X			X	
● **Karapark** P.O. Box 69, St. Michael's-on-Sea 4265	0393	5-1226	X								X	X				X			230		X					X			X	
SILWERSTROOMSTRAND C See Caravan Parks for Coloureds, Asians and Blacks																														
SIMONSTOWN C 58 NS S.L.																														
● **Oatlands Park** Froggy Pond (7995) □ *Main Rd.*	021	86-1410	X					X		X	X	X				X		70	10	15	X					X			X	
The Blue Lantern Winford (7995) □ *Main Rd.*	021	86 6184	X					X				X			X				6		X					X			X	
SINKWAZI N 63 A4 2m																														
● **Zinkwazi** P.O. Box 8, Darnall 4480	032422 E	1912	X					X	X			X					X	104		12	X					X			X	
SODWANA BAY N 67 B5 S.L.																														
Sodwana Bay National Park Officer in Charge, P/Bag Mkuze 3965	T	24					X	X						X	X	X	X		600								X	X		X
SOMERSET EAST C 59 A5 750m																														
Max Clarke Town Clerk, P.O. Box 21 (5850)	04242 E	8 or 272		X					X	X		X				X		20					X				X			X
Selley Town Clerk, P.O. Box 21 (5850)	04242 E	8 or 272		X					X			X				X			20		X					X			X	
SOMERSET WEST C 58 D3 10m																														
Cloetenberg P.O. Somerset West 7130 □ *National Rd.*	024	2 1019	X					X				X					X	100		30	X					X			X	
SOUTHBROOM N 63 NS 10m																														
Ooteekalia P.O. Box 27 (4277) □ *Outlook Rd.*	0393	6080	X					X	X		X	X		X			X	27	7			X				X			X	
● **Paradise** P.O. Box 55 (4277)	0393	3725	X					X				X				X	X		126		X					X			X	
SOUTH COAST N See respectively: • **Banana Beach** • **Belle Vista-See Marina Beach** • **Clansthal** • **Doonside** • **Hibberdene** • **Ifafa Beach** • **Illovo Beach** • **Kelso** • **Leisure Bay** • **Margate** • **Marina Beach** • **Munster** • **Park Rynie** • **Pennington** • **Port Shepstone** • **Scottburgh** • **Shelly Beach** • **Southbroom** • **St. Michael's-on-Sea** • **Sunwich Port** • **Trafalgar Beach** • **Umtentweni** • **Umzumbe** • **Uvongo** • **Widenham** • **Winkelstruit**																														

SEASONS (Open throughout the year)		TERMS FOR BOOKINGS			CARAVAN/CAMPING SITE TARIFFS (See heading)		REDUCTIONS ALLOWED FOR				RESTAURANT FACILITIES			TEAROOM/CAFE			SHOPPING FACILITIES (Provisions)			ADDITIONAL ACCOMMODATION AVAILABLE				TARIFF (See heading)		CARAVANS TO RENT ON SITE – SEE SECTION	DRINKING WATER		BATHS		SHOWERS		CAMP SITE FACILITIES I = In-Season only O = Out-of-Season only X = On application																						NON-WHITE SERVANTS			TYPE OF VEHICLE PERMITTED			SPORTING AND RECREATIONAL FACILITIES S = On Site N = Nearby (Up to 20 km away)								GOLF					FISHING				SWIMMING					BOATING				PLACES OF INTEREST			NOTES
OUT-OF-SEASON CLOSING DATE	RE-OPENING DATE	BOOKINGS ACCP./PEAK SNS. – SEE NOTE 2	DEPOSIT REQUIRED	REFUNDED IF CANCELLED – SEE NOTE 3	MAXIMUM IN-SEASON TARIFF	MAXIMUM OUT-OF-SEASON TARIFF	LONG PERIODS OF STAY	GROUPS – SEE NOTE 4	AA MEMBERS	OTHERS (ON APPLICATION)	ON SITE	WITHIN 5 km OF SITE	MORE THAN 5 km FROM SITE	ON SITE	WITHIN 5 km OF SITE	MORE THAN 5 km FROM SITE	ON SITE	WITHIN 5 km OF SITE	MORE THAN 5 km FROM SITE	BUNGALOWS	CABINS	COTTAGES (RONDAVELS)	CHALETS	MAXIMUM IN-SEASON TARIFF	MAXIMUM OUT-OF-SEASON TARIFF		PIPED	OTHER	HOT AND COLD	COLD ONLY	HOT AND COLD	COLD ONLY	WATERBORNE SANITATION	WASHBASINS	DISHWASHING FACILITIES	LAUNDRY AND IRONING FACILITIES – SEE NOTE 5	WASHING MACHINES	SITE LIT	PLUGS FOR RAZORS (VOLTAGE)	REFRIGERATORS	FIREWOOD/CHARCOAL	OPEN FIRE FORBIDDEN	CAMP FIRE PERMITTED	BRAAI PLACES PROVIDED	KITCHEN/COOKING FACILITIES	PETROL PUMP ON SITE	PETROL PUMP NEARBY	CAR REPAIR SHOP NEARBY	CAR SERVICING NEARBY	GAS SERVICE NEARBY	FIRST AID/HOSPITAL/DOCTOR NEARBY	POST OFFICE NEARBY	SITE GUARDED	PETS ALLOWED	SERVANTS PERMITTED – SEE NOTE 6	SERVANTS ACCOM. – SEE NOTE 6	SERVANTS FOR HIRE – SEE NOTE 6	CAR AND TRAILER	TRUCK 'HORSE' AND SEMI-TRAILER	SELF-PROPELLED CARAVANS	CHILDRENS' PLAYGROUND	TENNIS	CINEMA/DRIVE-IN/TV-ROOM – SEE NOTE 7	HORSE-RIDING	GAMES ROOM	TRAMPOLINE	BOWLS	HOT SPRINGS	GOLF COURSE – SEE NOTE 8	NUMBER OF HOLES	MINIATURE	MASHIE	PUTT-PUTT	FRESHWATER – SEE NOTE 9	SEA – SEE NOTE 10	GOGGLE	LICENCE REQUIRED	SWIMMING POOL	SEA BATHING	CHILDRENS' POOL	ADULTS ONLY	SHARK NETS AT BEACH	BOATS FOR HIRE	POWER	SAILING	CANOEING	HISTORIC	SCIENTIFIC	NATURAL	
33	34	35	36	37	38	39	40	41	42	43	44	45	46	47	48	49	50	51	52	53	54	55	56	57	58	59	60	61	62	63	64	65	66	67	68	69	70	71	72	73	74	75	76	77	78	79	80	81	82	83	84	85	86	87	88	89	90	91	92	93	94	95	96	97	98	99	100	101	102	103	104	105	106	107	108	109	110	111	112	113	114	115	116	117	118	119	120	121	122	123
					C	C							X			X			X			X		F	E		X		X		X		X	X							X		X	X			X	X	X	X		X					X	X		X																			X							X			X	
		X	X		F	F	X	X	X		X			X				X									X		X		X		X	X	X	X		X	220		X		X	X			X	X	X		X	X	X					X		X	S	S	N	S														S		S							X	X	X	
		X	X		C	C	X					X			X			X	X								X		X				X	X				X	220	X							X	X	X	X	X				X	X		X	X	X	S	N	N	S	S		N		N	9								S		S							X		X	
		X	X	X								X	X	X			X					X	X	*E*	*E*		X		X		X		X	X	X	X		X	X		X		X						X		X		X	X	X	X	X	X	X	X	S	S	S		S		S		N	18				N			X	S		S							X		X	
					D	D		X			X			X				X		X	X	X		*B*	*B*		X		X		X		X	X	X	X		X	X		X		X	X			X	X	X	X		X			X	X		X	X	X	N	N					N	S	N	9				S				S		S							X		X	
		X	X	X	D	D	X	X	X			X	X		X	X		X	X	X	X		X	*B*	*B*		X	X	X		X		X	X	X	X					X		X	X							X	X	X	X		X	X	X	X	X	N	N	N			N	N	N	N	9				S			X	S		S									X	
		X	X	X	C	C						X			X			X									X	X	X	X	X	X	X	X	X	X		X	X		X		X	X			X	X	X	X	X	X	X	X	X	X	X	X	X	X	S	N	N	N	S	N	N		N	9				S			X	S		S					N		X	X	X	
		X	X	X	C	C							X	X				X					X	C	C		X		X		X		X	X	X	X		X	X		X	X	X	X			X	X	X	X		X	X	X	X	X		X	X	X	S	N	N			S	N		N	9				S			X	S		S							X	X	X	
					B	B						X						X		X				C-E	C-E		X		X		X		X	X	X	X			X					X			X	X	X	X		X						X	X	X															X															X	
		X	X		G	G						X	X		X	X		X	X				X	J	J		X		X		X		X	X	X	X		X	220		X	X		X														X	X	X	S		N											S			X	S		S				S	S	S				
					A	A						X			X												X			X											X	X	X	X														X	X	X															N	N			X	S	X								X	
		X	X	X	A	A												X				X		B	B		X		X		X		X	X				X		X	X		X	X			X		X	X				X				X	X	X																		N		N									X	
					C	C		X			X			X			X			X			X	E	E		X		X		X		X	X	X	X		X			X		X	X			X	X	X		X	X	X	X				X	X	X	S																	S		S							X	X	X	
					C	C						X			X			X									X		X		X		X	X	X			X	X		X	X	X			X	X	X	X		X	X	X		X		X	X	X	X	S	N	N						N	10				S			X	S		S				S	S	S	X		X	
		X	X		E	D						X			X			X									X		X		X		X	X	X	X	X	X	X		X	X		X			X	X	X	X	X	X	X		X		X	X	X	X	N	N	N	N	S	S	N		N	18	X				N	N	X	N	X	N						N			X	
		X	X		X	X	X	X					X			X			X									X	X		X		X	X	X	X		X			X		X	X			X	X	X	X		X		X				X	X	X	S	N												S	N			S	X	S			S		S	S	X		X	
		X	X	X	F	D	X	X	X	X		X			X			X		X				*B*	*B*	X	X		X		X		X	X	X	X		X	220	X	X			X	X		X	X	X	X		X	X	O	O		X	X	X	X	S		N				N		N	18				S	N	N		N	X	N			S				X		X	
		X	X		G	D					X			X			X									X	X		X		X		X	X	X	X		X	220	X	X	X	X	X	X		X	X	X	X	X	X	X	O	O		X	X	X	X	S	N	S	S	S	S	N		N	18				S	N		X		X				S		S	S			X	
		X	X	X	E	C	X	X	X			X			X			X					X	J	F	X	X		X		X		X	X	X	X		X	220		X	X		X			X	X	X			X	X	X			X	X	X	X	S	N	N	N		N	N		N	18				S	N	N		S	X	S	X		N	N	N	N	X	X	X	
		X	X	X	F	E					X			X			X			X	X	X	X	*B-C*	*B*		X	X	X		X		X	X	X	X		X			X		X	X		X		X	X	X	X	X	X	O	X	X	X	X	X	X	S	N	N	N	S	N	N		N	18				S	N	N		S	X	S			S	S	S	S	X	X	X	
		X	X	X	D	B								X			X											X			X		X	X							X	X		X			X	X	X	X		X	X					X	X	X														S	N	N			X											
					B	B							X			X			X								X		X		X		X	X	X	X		X					X	X			X	X	X			X		X	X			X	X	X	N	N	N				N		N	9		X		N				N		N							X	X		
		X	X		H	D		X				X			X			X								X	X		X		X		X	X	X	X		X			X		X	X			X	X	X	X	X	X	X	X	X		X	X	X	X	S	N	N		S		N		N	18			X	N	N	N			X			X	N	N		N			X	
					G	G						X			X			X									X		X		X		X	X		X		X					X	X		X		X	X	X		X	X	X			X	X		X		S	S		S		S								X			S	X											
		X	X	X	E	D	X	X	X			X			X			X	X	X	X	X		G	F		X	X	X		X		X	X	X	X	X	X		X	X	X	X	X			X	X	X	X	X	X	X	X				X	X	X	S		S	N	S		N		N	11					N	N			X								X		X	
					C	B						X		X			X				X			B-D	B	X	X		X		X		X	X	X	X		X	X	X	X			X			X	X	X			X		O				X		X							N		N	11				N	N	N			X								X			
		X	X	X	H	E	X	X		X			X	X			X					X		J	F	X	X		X		X		X	X	X	X	X	X	110/220		X		X	X			X	X	X	X	X	X	X	X	X	X	X	X	X	X	S	S	S		S		N		N					N	N			S	X	S		X	S	S	S	S	X		X	
		X	X		D	D											X		X								X				X		X	X							X		X	X		X	X				X				X			X	X	X															N	N	X		X									X	X	
		X			B	B	X						X			X			X								X		X		X		X	X	X	X		X	220		X		X	X			X	X	X	X	X	X		X	X		X	X	X	X	S	N					N		S	9				S			X	N		N				S	S	S	X		X	
					A	A	X						X			X			X								X				X		X	X				X			X		X				X	X	X			X		X	X		X	X	X	X	N	N					N		N	9				N			X	N		N				N	N	N	X		X	
		X	X		C	C	X					X	X		X	X		X	X								X		X		X		X	X	X	X	X	X	220		X		X	X			X	X	X	X		X	X		X			X		X	N	N	N	N	N	N	N		N	18				N	N	N		S	X	S			N	N	N		X	X	X	
		X	X	X	E	E	X	X				X		X	X			X	X	X				X	X		X		X		X		X	X	X	X		X	X		X	X		X			X	X	X	X	X	X	X		X	X		X	X	X	S	N	N	N	S	N	N		N	18				N	N	N		N		N		X	N			N			X	
		X	X	X	F	F	X	X				X		X			X									X	X		X		X		X	X	X	X		X	X		X		X	X			X	X	X	X	X	X	X	O	X	X	X	X	X	X	S	N	S	N	S		N		N	18			X	N	N	N	X	S	X	S	X	X							X	

CARAVAN PARKS AND CAMPING SITES IN SOUTH AFRICA

CARAVAN PARK / CAMP SITE TARIFF CODE – See columns 38–39 (Subject to alteration)

A = Up to R1	C = R2–R3	E = R4–R5	G = R6–R7	I = R8–R9	K = R10–R16
B = R1–R2	D = R3–R4	F = R5–R6	H = R7–R8	J = R9–R10	O = FREE
					X = On Application

Charges are based on family of 2 adults and 2 children under 12 years

ADDITIONAL ACCOMMODATION TARIFF CODE – See columns 57–59 (Subject to alteration)

eg. Bungalows, Cabins, Cottages, Chalets, etc.

A = R1–R3	C = R5–R7	E = R9–R11	G = R13–R15	I = R17–R19	K = R21–R30
B = R3–R5	D = R7–R9	F = R11–R13	H = R15–R17	J = R19–R21	X = On Application

NB: Where the tariff is given in *italics* it is per person, otherwise per unit

NOTE 1 – **Columns 18, 19, 20,** – X= Stands available but not demarcated or number of stands have not been provided
NOTE 2 – **Column 35** – A=Bookings accepted for additional accommodation only i.e. cottages, bungalows, etc.
NOTE 3 – **Column 37** – Deposit refunded under certain conditions eg. less 10% ; if site is re-let ; if cancelled well in advance (up to 2 months) or on a doctor's certificate
NOTE 4 – **Column 41** – Reductions allowed on application for youth, church, school or sport groups or caravan rallies

NOTE 5 – **Column 69** – L= Laundry facilities only
NOTE 6 – **Columns 88, 89, 90,** – I= In-Season only ; O=Out-of-Season only; X= On application
NOTE 7 – **Column 96** – I= In-Season only
NOTE 8 – **Column 102** – See section on golf in Outdoor Holiday Guide
NOTE 9 – **Column 107** – See section on freshwater angling in Outdoor Holiday Guide
NOTE 10 – **Column 108** – See section on coastal angling in Outdoor Holiday Guide

Establishments marked thus ● have the Caravan Club of South Africa recommendation – see introduction

ABBREVIATIONS

C = CAPE PROVINCE
N = NATAL
O = ORANGE FREE STATE
T = TRANSVAAL
B = BOPHUTHATSWANA
X = TRANSKEI

Column groups: OWNED OR SUPERVISED BY (3–7); SITE DESCRIPTION: LOCALITY (8–11), NATURE OF GROUND (12–14), SHADE (15–17); NO. OF STANDS (18–20); ACCESSIBILITY: APPROXIMATE DISTANCE FROM MAIN ROAD TO SITE (21–25), SURFACE OF ROAD APPROACH (26–28), CONDITION OF ROAD APPROACH (29–30)

Establishment	1 TELEPHONE CODE (T= DIAL 0020, BOOK TRUNK CALL; E= DIAL CODE, ASK EXCHANGE FOR NO.)	2 TELEPHONE NUMBER	3 PRIVATELY OWNED	4 MUNICIPAL	5 DIVISIONAL COUNCIL	6 PROVINCIAL ADMINISTRATION	7 PARKS BOARD	8 BEACH IN IMMEDIATE VICINITY	9 BESIDE RIVER, LAKE OR DAM	10 IN OR NEAR MOUNTAIN AREA	11 WITHIN BUILT-UP AREA	12 GRASS	13 GRAVEL	14 SAND	15 UNSHADED	16 PARTLY SHADED	17 EXTENSIVELY SHADED	18 CARAVANS ONLY - SEE NOTE 1	19 CARAVANS AND/OR TENTS SEE NOTE 1	20 TENTS ONLY - SEE NOTE 1	21 ON MAIN RD.	22 WITHIN 1 km	23 WITHIN 5 km	24 WITHIN 10 km	25 WITHIN 15 km	26 TAR	27 GRAVEL	28 SAND	29 GOOD	30 FAIR
SPRINGBOK C 60 A5 953m																														
Kokerboom P/Bag (8240) ☐ *4 km from Springbok*	02732 E	5930	X							X			X	X		X			28			X					X			X
SPRINGS T 72 NS 1585m																														
● **Murray Park Pleasure Resort** Bookings not accepted ☐ *5 km from Springs*	011	816-2302		X					X		X	X					X	150		50			X			X			X	
STANDERTON T 67 A2 1531m																														
Standerton Municipal P.O. Box 66 (2430)	01331	3750/2332		X					X			X				X	X	50	50	50		X					X			X
STANFORD C 58 D4 1330m																														
Salmons Dam Nature Reserve Caretaker, P.O. Box 5 (7210)	02833	1330			X				X	X		X					X		150				X				X		X	
STANFORD LAKE T See Haenertsburg																														
STELLENBOSCH C 58 C3 30m																														
Bergplaas Holiday Ranch P.O. Box 2172, Dennesig 7601 ☐ *Helshoogte Rd.*	02231	7-0486	X							X		X				X			40		X					X				X
Drie Gewels P.O. Box 10, Lynedoch 7603 ☐ *Lynedoch*	02234	207	X									X				X			25		X					X				X
STEYNSBURG C 62 C3 1448m																														
Steynsburg Municipal P.O. Box 25 (5920) ☐ *8 Hendrik Potgieter St.*	04842 E	34		X							X		X			X		5	5			X					X			X
STILBAAI-OOS C 59 C1 S.L.																														
Ellensrust Town Clerk, P.O. Box 2 (6785) ☐ *1 Main Rd. East*	T	34		X				X	X			X				X			350		X					X			X	
ST. LUCIA N: See respectively: • **Hluhluwe (False Bay Park) • Mtubatuba (Fanies Island) • St.Lucia Estuary**																														
ST. LUCIA ESTUARY N 67 C5 • S.L.																														
St. Lucia Estuary The Warden, Natal Parks Board, P.O. St. Lucia Estuary 3936 ☐ *28 km from Mtubatuba*	T	St. Lucia 20					X	X						X		X			200							X			X	
ST. MICHAEL'S-ON-SEA N 63 NS S.L.																														
● **Surf Bay** P.O. Box 60 (4265)	0393	5-0233	X					X				X					X	34			X					X			X	
● **The Kingfisher** P.O. Box 7 (4265)	0393	5-0272/5-0566	X					X	X		X	X					X		X		X					X			X	
STORMSRIVIER C 59 C3 S.L.																														
Tsitsikama Coastal National Park National Parks Board, P.O. Box 787, Pretoria 0001	012	44-1194					X	X				X			X		X	50		20				X			X		X	
Tsitsikama Forest National Park — Storms River Bridge National Parks Board, P.O. Box 787, Pretoria 0001	012	44-1194					X		X			X					X	50			X					X			X	
STORMSVLEI C 58 D5 183m																														
Stormsvlei P.O. Box 218, Swellendam 6740 ☐ *38 km from Swellendam*	02852 E	1730	X						X	X				X			X		X			X					X			X
STRAND C 58 D3 S.L.																														
● **Kays** 54 Woltemade St. (7140) ☐ *Cnr. Woltemade St./Lourensrivier Rd.*	024	3-5025/3-2072	X					X	X	X		X		X			X		100			X				X			X	
● **Voortrekker Park** P.O. Box 3 (7140) ☐ *Hofmeyer St.*	024	3-2316		X				X			X	X				X			320			X				X			X	
STRANDFONTEIN C 60 C6 S.L.																														
Strandfontein Divisional Council, P.O. Box 16, Vanrhynsdorp 8170	02712 E	90			X			X					X	X	X			48	110		X					X			X	
STRUISBAAI C 58 D5 2m																														
Struisbaai Divisional Council, P.O. Box 35, Bredasdorp 7280 ☐ *Duiker St.*	02842 E	4930			X			X			X	X						300	300			X				X			X	
STRYDENBURG C 61 A5 1067m																														
Strydenburg Municipal Town Clerk, P.O. Box 60 (8765) ☐ *Park St.*	05762 E	16		X									X				X	20	10	5		X				X			X	
STUTTERHEIM C 60 B2 809m																														
Stutterheim Municipal P.O. Box 2 (4930) ☐ *Alfred St.*	04362 E	151		X							X	X				X		30				X				X			X	
SUDWALA CAVES T See Schagen																														
SUNWICH PORT N 63 NS S.L.																														
Saame Park P.O. Box 62, Pretoria 0001	0391(012)	3325(38891)	X					X				X				X		48			X						X		X	
SWELLENDAM C 58 D5 152m																														
Bontebok National Park National Parks Board, P.O. Box 787, Pretoria 0001	012	44-1194					X		X			X				X			20						X	X			X	
Die Stroom Caretaker, P.O. Box 20 (6740) ☐ *±6 km from Swellendam*	02912 E	484		X					X			X				X			X				X				X			X
● **Swellendam Municipal** Manager, P.O. Box 20 (6740) ☐ *Glenbarry Rd.*	02912 E	484		X					X		X	X					X		X			X				X			X	
TARKASTAD C 62 D4 1293m																														
Tarkastad Municipal P.O. Box 21 (5370)	04582 E	33		X							X			X		X		10			X						X		X	
THABA 'NCHU B 66 D4 1498m																														
Giel de Wet P.O. Box 22 (9780)	05262 E	1530		X						X		X					X	30		30		X					X		X	
THABAZIMBI T 68 B5 821m																														
● **Ben Alberts Nature Reserve** P.O. Box 50 (0380) ☐ *7 km from Thabazimbi*	014232 E	162	X							X		X					X		100			X					X		X	
THE BATHS C 58 B4 170m																														
The Baths McGregor & Co., Citrusdal 7340 ☐ *20 km from Citrusdal*	02662 E	1512	X						X	X		X	X				X	8							X		X			X
THE WILLOWS C 59 C5 S.L.																														
The Willows Holiday Resort P.O. Box 318, Port Elizabeth 6001	041	36-1035			X			X				X			X			46		7	X					X			X	
TOUWS RIVER C 58 C5 772m																														
Oom Loots P.O. Box 8 (6880)	02382 E	49	X							X	X	X	X	X		X		20		12	X					X			X	

SEASONS — TERMS FOR BOOKINGS — CARAVAN/CAMPING SITE TARIFFS (See heading) — REDUCTIONS ALLOWED FOR — RESTAURANT FACILITIES — TEAROOM/CAFE — SHOPPING FACILITIES (Provisions) — ADDITIONAL ACCOMMODATION AVAILABLE — TARIFF (See heading) — CARAVANS TO RENT ON SITE - SEE SECTION

CAMP SITE FACILITIES I = In-Season only O = Out-of-Season only X = On application

DRINKING WATER — BATHS — SHOWERS — NON-WHITE SERVANTS — TYPE OF VEHICLE PERMITTED

SPORTING AND RECREATIONAL FACILITIES S = On Site N = Nearby (Up to 20 km away)

GOLF — FISHING — SWIMMING — BOATING — PLACES OF INTEREST — NOTES

33 Out-of-season closing date	34 Re-opening date	35 Bookings accp./peak sns. – see note 2	36 Deposit required	37 Refunded if cancelled – see note 3	38 Maximum in-season tariff	39 Maximum out-of-season tariff	40 Long periods of stay	41 Groups – see note 4	42 AA members	43 Others (on application)	44 Restaurant: On site	45 Restaurant: Within 5 km of site	46 Restaurant: More than 5 km from site	47 Tearoom: On site	48 Tearoom: Within 5 km of site	49 Tearoom: More than 5 km from site	50 Shopping: On site	51 Shopping: Within 5 km of site	52 Shopping: More than 5 km from site	53 Bungalows	54 Cabins	55 Cottages (rondavels)	56 Chalets	57 Maximum in-season tariff	58 Maximum out-of-season tariff	59 Caravans to rent on site – see section	60 Drinking water: Piped	61 Drinking water: Other	62 Baths: Hot and cold	63 Baths: Cold only	64 Showers: Hot and cold	65 Showers: Cold only	66 Waterborne sanitation	67 Washbasins	68 Dishwashing facilities	69 Laundry and ironing facilities – see note 5	70 Washing machines	71 Site lit	72 Plugs for razors (voltage)	73 Refrigerators	74 Firewood/charcoal	75 Open fire forbidden	76 Camp fire permitted	77 Braai places provided	78 Kitchen/cooking facilities	79 Petrol pump on site	80 Petrol pump nearby	81 Car repair shop nearby	82 Car servicing nearby	83 Gas service nearby	84 First aid/hospital/doctor nearby	85 Post office nearby	86 Site guarded	87 Pets allowed	88 Servants permitted – see note 6	89 Servants accom. – see note 6	90 Servants for hire – see note 6	91 Car and trailer	92 Truck horse and semi-trailer	93 Self-propelled caravans	94 Childrens playground	95 Tennis	96 Cinema/drive-in/TV-room – see note 7	97 Horse-riding	98 Games room	99 Trampoline	100 Bowls	101 Hot springs	102 Golf course – see note 8	103 Number of holes	104 Miniature	105 Mashie	106 Putt-putt	107 Freshwater – see note 9	108 Sea – see note 10	109 Goggle	110 Licence required	111 Swimming pool	112 Sea bathing	113 Childrens pool	114 Adults only	115 Shark nets at beach	116 Boats for hire	117 Power	118 Sailing	119 Canoeing	120 Historic	121 Scientific	122 Natural	123 Notes
					C	C						X			X			X									X	X	X		X		X	X	X	X		X	X		X			X			X	X	X	X		X		X	X	X		X	X	X			N																										X	
					B	B					X	X	X	X	X	X		X	X								X		X		X		X	X	X	X		X			X		X	X			X	X	X		X	X		X	X			X	X	X	S	N	N	S		S												S		S					S	S				
		X			B	B							X			X			X								X		X		X		X	X	X	X		X				X	X	X			X	X	X	X		X	X	X	X			X		X	N	N	N	N	S		N		N		X			S			X												
		X		X	B	B							X			X			X	X				B-D	B-D		X			X		X	X	X	X					X	X		X	X			X	X	X			X	X		X			X	X	X	N																	S		N							X	X	X	
		X	X		E	D	X	X	X			X			X		X			X	X		X	G	E	X	X		X		X		X	X	X	X		X	220	X	X	X	X	X			X	X	X	X		X	X			X	X	X	X	S	N	N	N	N	N	N		N	18				N	N		X	S		S							X	X	X	
		X	X	X	C	B	X	X	X		X				X			X		X		X		D	D		X		X		X		X	X	X	X				X	X		X	X			X	X	X	X		X		X	X			X	X	X		S	N	S			N		N	18				N	N	N	X	S	X								X	X	X	
					A	A	X					X			X			X									X				X		X	X		X		X					X	X				X	X		X	X		X	X			X	X	X	N	N					N		N	18	X				N			S		S							X			
		X	X	X	C	C					X			X			X			X		X		D-E	D-E		X		X		X		X	X	X	X		X				X					X	X	X	X					X			X	X	X							N							N	N	N	X		X					N	N	N			X	
		X	X	X	C	C						X			X			X									X		X		X		X	X	X			X			X						X		X	X		X	X		X			X		X																S			S	X									X	X	
		X	X	X	G	E	X					X			X			X									X	X	X		X		X	X	X	X		X	220		X	X	X				X	X	X	X	X	X	X		X	X	X	X	X	X	S	N	S	N	S		N		N	9	X	X	X	N	N		X	N	X	N		X	N	N		N	X		X	
		X	X		G	C	X					X			X			X									X		X		X		X	X	X	X		X	X		X	X	X				X	X	X	X	X	X		X			X	X	X	X	S	N	N	N	S	N	N		N	9	X		X		N	N		S	X	S		X	N		N	N			X	
		X	X	X	C	C					X			X			X					X		G-J	G-J		X				X		X	X	X	X					X		X	X		X	X	X		X	X	X	X			X	X	X	X	X																			X	S							X	X	X	
		X	X	X	C	C					X			X			X										X		X		X		X	X	X						X		X	X		X				X	X		X					X	X	X																													X	
					B	B						X						X									X					X	X	X	X						X		X	X			X							X				X	X	X															S											S	S	S	X		X	
		X	X	X	D	C	X	X	X	X			X	X			X										X	X	X		X		X	X	X	X		X	X		X	X	X	X			X	X	X	X	X	X	X	X	X		X	X	X	X	S	N	N	N	N	N	N		N	18	X			N	N	N		S	X	S					N	N	X	X	X	
		X	X	X	X	X			X	X		X		X	X	X	X	X	X				X	X	X		X		X		X		X	X	X	X		X	220		X	X	X	X			X	X	X	X		X	X				X	X	X	S	N	N	N			N		N	18				N	N	N	X		X	N							X	X	X	
		X	X	X	E	E	X				X			X			X					X		X	X		X	X	X	X	X	X	X	X	X						X		X	X			X	X	X	X	X	X	X		X			X	X	X	S	N												S	S	S			X	S				S	S	S	X		X	
		X	X	X	D	D						X			X			X		X				D-E	D-E		X		X		X		X	X	X	X				X	X			X			X	X	X	X			X	X	X		X	X	X	X	N	N	N			N	N		N	9					N	N			X				N	N	N	N	X	X	X	
					B	B							X			X			X								X				X		X	X	X	X		X					X	X			X	X	X	X	X	X		X	X			X	X	X		N	N															S		S										
		X			A	A	X					X			X			X									X		X		X		X	X	X	X		X	220				X	X			X	X	X	X		X		X				X	X	X			N				N		N	9																	X		X	
		X	X		E-H	A-D				X			X			X		X									X		X		X		X	X		X		X	X		X						X	X	X			X						X		X		N	N			N	N		N	18				N	N	N		S				X							X	
					C	C							X			X				X							X				X		X	X							X	X	X	X		X				X	X		X					X	X	X																													X	
		X			B	B							X			X			X									X				X	X	X									X	X			X	X	X		X	X		X	X			X		X	N	N					N		N	9				N			X							N		N	X		X	
		X			C	C	X						X			X			X	X				E	E		X		X		X		X	X	X	X		X	220		X		X	X			X	X	X	X		X		X	X		X	X		X		N					N		N	9				N			X							N	N	N	X		X	
					O	O							X			X			X								X											X					X	X			X	X	X	X		X		X				X	X	X		N					N		N	9								S		S										
					B	B	X						X	X					X								X		X		X		X	X	X	X		X			X		X	X			X	X	X			X	X	X				X		X	S	N												N			X	S		S							X		X	
		X	X		C	C	X	X						X	X	X			X								X		X		X		X	X	X	X		X			X		X	X			X	X	X			X	X	X	X			X		X	S	N	N				N		S	9				N			X	S		S								X	X	
ne	Sept.	X	X	X	B	B	X						X			X	X	X	X	X				C-D	C-D		X	X	X				X	X	X					X	X		X	X	X										X	X		X		X		N						S						N			X	S											X	
		X	X	X	D	C	X				X			X			X			X		X	X	C-D	B-C		X				X	X	X	X		X			X				X	X			X	X	X	X		X	X					X	X	X	S				S				N						N	N	N		X					N						
		X			B	B	X	X			X			X			X			X	X	X		*A*	*A*		X	X	X		X		X	X	X	X		X	X					X		X		X	X	X	X	X	X	X	X			X	X	X	S	N	N		S	S	N											N		S							X	X	X	

CARAVAN PARKS AND CAMPING SITES IN SOUTH AFRICA

CARAVAN PARK / CAMP SITE TARIFF CODE — See columns 38–39 (Subject to alteration)

A = Up to R1 | C = R2–R3 | E = R4–R5 | G = R6–R7 | I = R8–R9 | K = R10–R16
B = R1–R2 | D = R3–R4 | F = R5–R6 | H = R7–R8 | J = R9–R10 | O = FREE | X = On Application

Charges are based on family of 2 adults and 2 children under 12 years

ADDITIONAL ACCOMMODATION TARIFF CODE — See columns 57–59 (Subject to alteration)

eg. Bungalows, Cabins, Cottages, Chalets, etc.
A = R1–R3 | C = R5–R7 | E = R9–R11 | G = R13–R15 | I = R17–R19 | K = R21–R30
B = R3–R5 | D = R7–R9 | F = R11–R13 | H = R15–R17 | J = R19–R21 | X = On Application

NB: Where the tariff is given in *italics* it is per person, otherwise per unit

NOTE 1 — Columns 18, 19, 20. — X= Stands available but not demarcated or number of stands have not been provided
NOTE 2 — Column 35 — A= Bookings accepted for additional accommodation only i.e. cottages, bungalows, etc.
NOTE 3 — Column 37 — Deposit refunded under certain conditions eg. less 10% ; if site is re-let ; if cancelled well in advance (up to 2 months) or on a doctor's certificate
NOTE 4 — Column 41 — Reductions allowed on application for youth, church, school or sport groups or caravan rallies

NOTE 5 — Column 69 — L= Laundry facilities only
NOTE 6 — Columns 88, 89, 90. — I = In-Season only ; O = Out-of-Season only ; X = On application
NOTE 7 — Column 96 — I = In-Season only
NOTE 8 — Column 102 — See section on golf in Outdoor Holiday Guide
NOTE 9 — Column 107 — See section on freshwater angling in Outdoor Holiday Guide
NOTE 10 — Column 108 — See section on coastal angling in Outdoor Holiday Guide

Establishments marked thus ● have the Caravan Club of South Africa recommendation — see introduction

ABBREVIATIONS
C = CAPE PROVINCE
N = NATAL
O = ORANGE FREE STATE
T = TRANSVAAL
B = BOPHUTHATSWANA
X = TRANSKEI

TELEPHONE CODE: T = DIAL 0020. BOOK TRUNK CALL; E = DIAL CODE. ASK EXCHANGE FOR NO.

	TELEPHONE CODE	TELEPHONE NUMBER	OWNED OR SUPERVISED BY: PRIVATELY OWNED	MUNICIPAL	DIVISIONAL COUNCIL	PROVINCIAL ADMINISTRATION	PARKS BOARD	SITE DESCRIPTION — LOCALITY: BEACH IN IMMEDIATE VICINITY	BESIDE RIVER, LAKE OR DAM	IN OR NEAR MOUNTAIN AREA	WITHIN BUILT-UP AREA	NATURE OF GROUND: GRASS	GRAVEL	SAND	SHADE: UNSHADED	PARTLY SHADED	EXTENSIVELY SHADED	NO. OF STANDS: CARAVANS ONLY – SEE NOTE 1	CARAVANS AND/OR TENTS	TENTS ONLY – SEE NOTE 1	ACCESSIBILITY — APPROXIMATE DISTANCE FROM MAIN ROAD TO SITE: ON MAIN RD	WITHIN 1 km	WITHIN 5 km	WITHIN 10 km	WITHIN 15 km	SURFACE OF ROAD APPROACH: TAR	GRAVEL	SAND	CONDITION OF ROAD APPROACH: GOOD	FAIR
	1	2	3	4	5	6	7	8	9	10	11	12	13	14	15	16	17	18	19	20	21	22	23	24	25	26	27	28	29	30
TRAFALGAR BEACH N 63 NS ↙ S.L.																														
Port O'Call P.O. Box 82, Ramsgate 4285	0393	3731	X					X				X					X		90			X				X			X	
TRICHARDTSDAL T 69 B3 ↖ 625m																														
Tourist Motel P.O. Box 199 (0850) ☐ *±20 km from Trichardtsdal*	0152302 E	2423	X						X	X		X					X		30		X					X			X	
TROMPSBURG O 62 B3 ↗ 1452m																														
Trompsburg Municipal Bookings not accepted ☐ *Voortrekker St.*	05812 E	23		X							X		X			X			50				X				X		X	
TSHIPISE T 70 B5 ↙ 534m																														
Tshipise Mineral Baths General Manager, P.O. Box 4 (0901)	T	4				X				X			X			X			285		X					X			X	
TUGELA N 63 A4 ↑ S.L.																														
Tugela Mouth North Bank P.O. Mandini 4490	032432 E	1703	X					X			X	X			X	X		10						X			X			X
TULBAGH C 58 C4 ↖ 122m																														
Tulbagh Municipal P.O. Box 3 (6820)	02362 E	20		X							X	X				X		40	40	40			X				X		X	
TZANEEN T 69 A3 ↙ 724m																														
Fairview P.O. Box 329 (0850)	01523	2-0085	X						X			X	X			X			20		X					X			X	
UITENHAGE C 59 B5 ↙ 52m																														
Magennis P.O. Box 45 (6230) ☐ *Cnr. High/Church Sts.*	0422	26011 x276		X							X	X				X			10		X					X			X	
Springs Pleasure Resort P.O. Box 45 (6230)	0422	2-4475		X						X		X				X			20			X				X			X	
UMHLANGA ROCKS N 63 NS ↗ S.L.																														
Bennets P.O. Box 38 (4320) ☐ *1 Park Drive*	031	51-1721	X					X			X			X			X	36				X				X			X	
● **Umhlanga Rocks** P.O. Box 13 (4320) ☐ *Weaver Crescent*	031	51-1533	X					X				X		X		X		36				X				X			X	
UMTATA X 62 C6 → 699m																														
Umtata Municipal P.O. Box 45 (5100)	0471	3204		X							X	X				X			50		X					X			X	
UMTENTWENI N 63 NS ↙ 2m																														
Umtentweni P.O. Box 44, Sea Park 4241	0391	5-0531	X					X	X			X				X		30			X					X			X	
UMZUMBE N 63 NS ↙ 94m																														
Hidaway P.O. Umzumbe 4225	0391	6603	X					X			X	X		X		X	X		33			X				X	X		X	X
UNIONDALE C 59 B3 ↙ 732m																														
Uniondale Municipal Town Clerk, P.O. Box 13 (6460)	04462 E	24		X							X	X				X			50			X					X		X	
UPINGTON C 65 C3 ← 805m																														
Die Eiland P.O. Box 17 (8800) ☐ *1 km from Upington*	0541	2101		X					X			X	X			X			50			X				X			X	
UVONGO N 63 NS ↙ S.L.																														
Oasis P.O. Box 67 (4270)	0393	5-0778	X					X				X		X			X	28		6	X					X			X	
Uvongo P.O. Box 22 (4270) ☐ *Collins St.*	0393	5-0424	X					X				X					X	42			X					X			X	
VAAL DAM: See respectively: • Aloe Fjord T • Deneysville T • Oranjeville O																														
VANRHYNSDORP C 60 C6 ↘ 84m																														
Gifberg P.O. Box 66 (8170)	02712 E	25/79	X								X	X	X			X		40				X					X		X	
VAN STADENS RIVER MOUTH C 59 B5 ↙ S.L.																														
Van Stadens River Mouth Divisional Council, P.O. Box 318, Port Elizabeth 6000 ☐ *± 42 km from Port*	T	2-8911			X			X	X	X		X				X		40		100					X	X			X	
VENTERSBURG O 66 C5 ↖ 1433m																														
● **Willem Pretorius Game Reserve** Bookings not accepted ☐ *Allemanskraal Dam*	017142 E	6				X			X			X				X		X	X	X					X	X			X	
VENTERSTAD C 62 B3 ↘ 1219m																														
Venterstad Municipal Town Clerk, P.O. Box 24 (5990) ☐ *Cnr. Bingle/Tennant Sts.*	T	24		X							X		X				X	20	20	15		X					X		X	
VEREENIGING T 66 A5 ↘ 1448m																														
● **Dickinson Park** Town Clerk, P.O. Box 35 (1930) ☐ *Lewis Ave.*	016	22-2251 x471		X					X			X				X		140		50		X				X	X		X	X
VICTORIA BAY C 59 NS ← S.L.																														
Sea Glimpse Holiday Resort P.O. Box 307, George 6530 ☐ *Victoria Bay Rd.*	0441	4660	X					X		X	X	X	X			X	X	8				X				X			X	
Victoria Bay Divisional Council, P.O. Box 12, George 6530	0441	3001			X			X		X	X	X	X			X			52			X				X			X	
VICTORIA WEST C 61 C5 ← 1261m																														
Victoria West Municipal P.O. Box 13 (7070) ☐ *Mugglestone Ave.*	02042 E	26		X							X		X			X		39	7			X					X		X	
VILLIERS O 66 B6 ↑ 1430m																														
Villiers Municipal Town Clerk, P.O. Box 23 (9840)	01382 E	202		X					X			X	X				X		200	100	X						X		X	
VILLIERSDORP C 58 C4 ↙ 244m																														
Villiersdorp Municipal P.O. Box 23 (7170) ☐ *Ham St.*	02252 E	431/2		X						X		X					X		X			X					X		X	
VOLKSRUST T 67 B2 → 1665m																														
Volksrust Municipal P.O. Box 48 (2470) ☐ *Cnr. Bad/West St.*	013332 E	28		X							X	X				X			38			X					X		X	
VREDE O 67 B2 ← 1669m																														
Vrede Municipal Town Clerk, P.O. Box 155 (2455) ☐ *1 km from Vrede*	013342 E	26		X					X	X		X				X		30	X	X		X					X		X	

SEASONS		TERMS FOR BOOKINGS			CARAVAN/CAMPING SITE TARIFFS (See heading)		REDUCTIONS ALLOWED FOR				RESTAURANT FACILITIES			TEAROOM/CAFE			SHOPPING FACILITIES (Provisions)			ADDITIONAL ACCOMMODATION AVAILABLE				TARIFF (See heading)			DRINKING WATER		BATHS		SHOWERS		CAMP SITE FACILITIES (I = In-Season only, O = Out-of-Season only, X = On application)																						NON-WHITE SERVANTS			TYPE OF VEHICLE PERMITTED			SPORTING AND RECREATIONAL FACILITIES (S = On Site, N = Nearby (Up to 20 km away))								GOLF					FISHING				SWIMMING					BOATING				PLACES OF INTEREST			NOTES
OUT-OF-SEASON CLOSING DATE	RE-OPENING DATE	BOOKINGS ACCP./PEAK SNS. - SEE NOTE 2	DEPOSIT REQUIRED	REFUNDED IF CANCELLED - SEE NOTE 3	MAXIMUM IN-SEASON TARIFF	MAXIMUM OUT-OF-SEASON TARIFF	LONG PERIODS OF STAY	GROUPS - SEE NOTE 4	AA MEMBERS	OTHERS (ON APPLICATION)	ON SITE	WITHIN 5 km OF SITE	MORE THAN 5 km FROM SITE	ON SITE	WITHIN 5 km OF SITE	MORE THAN 5 km FROM SITE	ON SITE	WITHIN 5 km OF SITE	MORE THAN 5 km FROM SITE	BUNGALOWS	CABINS	COTTAGES (RONDAVELS)	CHALETS	MAXIMUM IN-SEASON TARIFF	MAXIMUM OUT-OF-SEASON TARIFF	CARAVANS TO RENT ON SITE - SEE SECTION	PIPED	OTHER	HOT AND COLD	COLD ONLY	HOT AND COLD	COLD ONLY	WATERBORNE SANITATION	WASHBASINS	DISHWASHING FACILITIES	LAUNDRY AND IRONING FACILITIES - SEE NOTE 5	WASHING MACHINES	SITE LIT	PLUGS FOR RAZORS (VOLTAGE)	REFRIGERATORS	FIREWOOD/CHARCOAL	OPEN FIRE FORBIDDEN	CAMP FIRE PERMITTED	BRAAI PLACES PROVIDED	KITCHEN/COOKING FACILITIES	PETROL PUMP ON SITE	PETROL PUMP NEARBY	CAR REPAIR SHOP NEARBY	CAR SERVICING NEARBY	GAS SERVICE NEARBY	FIRST AID/HOSPITAL/DOCTOR NEARBY	POST OFFICE NEARBY	SITE GUARDED	PETS ALLOWED	SERVANTS PERMITTED - SEE NOTE 6	SERVANTS ACCOM. - SEE NOTE 6	SERVANTS FOR HIRE SEE NOTE 6	CAR AND TRAILER	TRUCK/HORSE AND SEMI-TRAILER	SELF-PROPELLED CARAVANS	CHILDRENS' PLAYGROUND	TENNIS	CINEMA/DRIVE-IN/TV-ROOM - SEE NOTE 7	HORSE-RIDING	GAMES ROOM	TRAMPOLINE	BOWLS	HOT SPRINGS	GOLF COURSE - SEE NOTE 8	NUMBER OF HOLES	MINIATURE	MASHIE	PUTT-PUTT	FRESHWATER - SEE NOTE 9	SEA - SEE NOTE 10	GOGGLE	LICENCE REQUIRED	SWIMMING POOL	SEA BATHING	CHILDRENS' POOL	ADULTS ONLY	SHARK NETS AT BEACH	BOATS FOR HIRE	POWER	SAILING	CANOEING	HISTORIC	SCIENTIFIC	NATURAL	
33	34	35	36	37	38	39	40	41	42	43	44	45	46	47	48	49	50	51	52	53	54	55	56	57	58	59	60	61	62	63	64	65	66	67	68	69	70	71	72	73	74	75	76	77	78	79	80	81	82	83	84	85	86	87	88	89	90	91	92	93	94	95	96	97	98	99	100	101	102	103	104	105	106	107	108	109	110	111	112	113	114	115	116	117	118	119	120	121	122	123
		X	X	X	G	E	X					X		X			X										X		X		X		X	X	X	X		X			X		X	X			X	X	X	X	X	X	X	X			X	X		X		N	N		S		N		N						N	N	N	N	X			X						X	X	
		X	X		B	B	X	X			X																X		X	X	X			X	X	X					X		X	X							X				X	X	X	X	X	X														N			X	S		S								X		
					O	O						X			X				X								X						X										X				X	X	X			X		X				X	X	X	N	N	N				N		N	9								N											
					D	D				X	X			X			X					X		G	G		X		X		X		X	X	X	X		X	220		X		X	X		X	X	X	X	X	X	X	X		X	X		X	X	X	S	S	S	S			S	S						N			X	S		S				N	N	N			X	
		X	X		C	C	X				X	X				X		X	X								X		X		X		X	X	X	X		X					X	X		X	X										X	X	X	X															N				X					N		N	X		X	
					C	C	X	X					X			X			X								X		X		X		X	X	X	X		X			X		X	X			X	X	X	X	X	X		X	X		X	X		X	N	N					N							N			X	S		S				N	N	N	X		X	
		X			B	B	X						X			X			X								X		X		X		X	X	X	X		X	X	X	X		X	X			X	X	X	X			X	X			X	X		X				S					N	18								S												
					B	B							X			X		X	X								X		X		X		X	X	X	X		X					X	X			X	X	X			X		X	X			X		X	N	S	N						N	18								N		N										
		X	X		C	C								X			X			X				A-B	A-B		X		X		X		X	X	X	X		X					X	X							X			X	X			X		X	S	S							N	18								S		S									X	
		X	X		G	D					X	X		X	X	X	X	X	X																X	X											X	X	X	X		X			X	X		X	X	X	N	N	N	N	N	N	N		N	18	X	X	X	N	N	N	X	N	X	N		X	N		N	N	X	X	X	
		X	X		E	D						X	X		X	X		X	X							X	X		X		X		X	X	X	X		X	X		X	X		X			X	X	X	X		X	X	X	X	X		X	X	X	S	N	N	N	N	N	N		N	18	X	X	X		N	N	X	N	X	N		X					X	X	X	
					B	B	X	X					X			X			X								X		X		X		X	X	X	X		X					X				X	X	X			X		X	X			X		X	N	N	N				N		N	18								N		N									X	
		X	X		E	D	X					X			X			X	X							X	X		X		X		X	X	X	X		X	110/220			X		X			X	X	X	X		X	X							X	N	N	N				N		N	18					N	N			X	N		X			N	N			X	
		X	X		G	D	X	X				X	X			X		X	X								X		X		X		X	X	X	X		X	220		X	X	X	X			X	X	X	X		X		X			X	X		X	S	N	N	N		N	N		N	18					N	N	X	S	X	N		X							X	
					A	A							X			X			X								X		X		X		X	X	X			X					X	X			X	X	X	X		X	X	X				X	X	X	N	N																									X			
					C	C							X			X		X	X	X	X			D-E	D-E		X		X		X		X	X	X	X		X					X	X			X	X	X	X	X	X	X	X	X			X	X	X	S	N	N				N		N	18				S			X	N		N				S	S	S	X	X	X	
		X	X		H	H	X	X				X			X			X			X		X	X	X	X	X		X		X		X	X	X	X	X	X	X	X		X		X			X	X	X	X	X	X		X			X	X		X	N	N	N	N	S		N		N	18	X		X		N	N			X	N		X	N			N			X	
		X	X		G	D						X			X			X									X		X		X		X	X	X	X		X	220				X	X			X	X	X	X	X	X			X	X		X	X	X	S	N	N		S	N	N		N	18			X		N			N	X	N		X	N	N	N	N			X	
		X			B	B							X			X			X	X				A	A		X		X		X		X	X	X	X		X	X		X		X	X			X	X	X	X		X		X	X		X	X	X	X														S																
		X			C	B	X							X					X			X		C	B		X		X		X	X		X		X							X	X						X	X							X	X	X			N		S									N	N	N			X				N			N			X	
					C	C					X			X			X					X	X	B-F	B-F		X	X	X		X		X	X	X	X		X			X		X	X		X				X	X	X	X					X	X	X	S	S	S			S	S		S	18			X	S			X	S		S				S	S	S	X		X	
					A	A							X			X			X								X		X		X		X	X	X								X											X				X	X	X	N	N					N		N	9	X			N			X							N	N	N				
					B	B	X					X			X			X									X		X		X		X	X	X	X		X			X	X		X			X	X	X	X	X	X	X	X	X			X		X	S			S		S								S			X							S		S	X		X	
		X	X	X	E	C	X	X	X			X	X		X	X		X	X			X		*B*	*B*	X	X		X		X		X	X	X	X		X		X	X		X	X	X		X	X	X	X		X					X	X	X	X	S	N	N	N	N	N	N		N	18					N	N			X	N			N	N	N	N	X	X	X	
		X	X	X	D	B						X			X			X									X				X		X	X	X	L					X	X		X						X			X					X	X	X															N	N			X	S										
		X	X		D	D	X	X				X	X		X	X			X			X		*A*	*A*		X		X		X		X	X	X	X		X	220		X		X	X					X	X		X	X	X	X	X		X		X	S	N	N				N		N	18				N			X	N		N								X	X	
		X	X		B	B	X	X					X			X			X	X	X	X		A-C	A-C		X		X		X		X	X	X	X		X	X	X	X		X	X				X	X	X	X	X	X	X	X			X		X	S	N	N		S				N		X		X	N			X	S		S						N			X	
					B	B							X			X			X								X		X		X		X	X	X	X		X	220				X	X			X	X	X	X	X	X	X	X	X			X		X	S	N					N											S		S									X	
		X			B	B	X						X			X			X								X	X	X		X		X	X	X	X		X	X				X				X	X	X			X	X	X	X			X		X	S		N				N		N	9		X		N			X	S		S							X			
		X			C	C						X			X			X									X		X		X		X	X	X	X					X			X			X	X	X			X	X	X	X			X	X	X	S	N	N	N			N		N	9	X			N			X	N		N						N			X	

CARAVAN PARKS AND CAMPING SITES IN SOUTH AFRICA

CARAVAN PARK / CAMP SITE TARIFF CODE – See columns 38–39 (Subject to alteration)

A = Up to R1 | B = R1–R2 | C = R2–R3 | D = R3–R4 | E = R4–R5 | F = R5–R6 | G = R6–R7 | H = R7–R8 | I = R8–R9 | J = R9–R10 | K = R10–R16 | O = FREE | X = On Application

Charges are based on family of 2 adults and 2 children under 12 years

ADDITIONAL ACCOMMODATION TARIFF CODE – See columns 57–59 (Subject to alteration)

eg. Bungalows, Cabins, Cottages, Chalets, etc.

A = R1–R3 | B = R3–R5 | C = R5–R7 | D = R7–R9 | E = R9–R11 | F = R11–R13 | G = R13–R15 | H = R15–R17 | I = R17–R19 | J = R19–R21 | K = R21–R30 | X = On Application

NB: Where the tariff is given in *italics* it is per person, otherwise per unit

NOTE 1 — **Columns 18, 19, 20.** — X= Stands available but not demarcated or number of stands have not been provided

NOTE 2 — **Column 35** — A=Bookings accepted for additional accommodation only i.e. cottages, bungalows, etc.

NOTE 3 — **Column 37** — Deposit refunded under certain conditions eg. less 10% ; if site is re-let ; if cancelled well in advance (up to 2 months) or on a doctor's certificate

NOTE 4 — **Column 41** — Reductions allowed on application for youth, church, school or sport groups or caravan rallies

NOTE 5 — **Column 69** — L= Laundry facilities only

NOTE 6 — **Columns 88, 89, 90.** — I = In-Season only ; O = Out-of-Season only; X = On application

NOTE 7 — **Column 96** — I = In-Season only

NOTE 8 — **Column 102** — See section on golf in Outdoor Holiday Guide

NOTE 9 — **Column 107** — See section on freshwater angling in Outdoor Holiday Guide

NOTE 10 — **Column 108** — See section on coastal angling in Outdoor Holiday Guide

Establishments marked thus ● have the Caravan Club of South Africa recommendation — see introduction

ABBREVIATIONS

C = CAPE PROVINCE
N = NATAL
O = ORANGE FREE STATE
T = TRANSVAAL
B = BOPHUTHATSWANA
X = TRANSKEI

Caravan park / camp site	1 Telephone code (T = Dial 0020, book trunk call; E = Dial code, ask exchange for no.)	2 Telephone number	3 Owned or supervised by: Privately owned	4 Municipal	5 Divisional council	6 Provincial administration	7 Parks board	8 Site description – Locality: Beach in immediate vicinity	9 Beside river, lake or dam	10 In or near mountain area	11 Within built-up area	12 Nature of ground: Grass	13 Gravel	14 Sand	15 Shade: Unshaded	16 Partly shaded	17 Extensively shaded	18 No. of stands: Caravans only – see note 1	19 Caravans and/or tents – see note 1	20 Tents only – see note 1	21 Accessibility – Approximate distance from main road to site: On main rd.	22 Within 1 km	23 Within 5 km	24 Within 10 km	25 Within 15 km	26 Surface of approach road: Tar	27 Gravel	28 Sand	29 Condition of approach road: Good	30 Fair
VRYBURG C 66 A2 ↘ 1187m																														
Boereplaas Holiday Resort P.O. Box 539 (8600)	01451	4206	X									X					X		X		X						X		X	
Mam's Roadhouse P.O. Box 282 (8600) □ *2 km from Vryburg*	01451	3630	X										X	X	X		X		X		X						X		X	
WAENHUISKRANS (ARNISTON) C 58 D5 ↙ 10m																														
Waenhuiskrans (Arniston) Divisional Council, P.O. Box 35, Bredasdorp 7280	02842 E	6202			X						X	X				X		100	100		X					X			X	
WARMBATHS T 68 B6 ↙ 1171m																														
Klein Kariba Manager, P.O. Box 150 (0480) □ *7 km from Warmbaths*	012062 E	571	X							X		X					X		70				X					X		X
Ronwil Holiday Resort P.O. Box 417 (0480) □ *3 km from Warmbaths*	012062 E	97	X						X			X		X			X	50	50		X							X	X	
Warmbaths Mineral Baths General Manager, P.O. Box 75 (0480)	012062 E	6				X					X	X					X	250	200			X				X			X	
WARRENTON T 66 C2 ↗ 1193m																														
Warrenton Municipal P.O. Box 10 (8530)	053332 E	1		X					X			X				X			40		X						X		X	
WATERVAL-BOVEN T 69 C3 ↙ 1471m																														
Waterval-Boven Municipal P.O. Box 53 (1195) □ *ZASM Ave.*	013262 E	58		X					X					X		X		6		10			X			X			X	
WELKOM O 66 B4 ↘ 1376m																														
● **Welkom Municipal** Bookings not accepted □ *Disa St.*	017	2-1455		X							X	X					X	36		6		X				X			X	
WELLINGTON C 58 C4 ↙ 99m																														
Katryntjiesdrif P.O. Box 517 (7655)	0251	3-1625	X						X	X		X		X					500			X						X	X	
Pinnie Joubert Bookings not accepted □ *Addy St.*	0251	3-2603		X							X	X					X	65				X				X			X	
WELVERDIEND T 68 D5 1470m																														
Safari P.O. Box 24 (2700) □ *Main Ave.*	01494	283	X								X	X					X	4			X					X			X	
WEPENER O 62 A5 ↙ 1438m																														
Geyer Park P.O. Box 31 (9944) □ *Spies St.*	05232	31		X					X		X	X	X			X		15					X			X			X	
WESTONARIA T 72 NS ← 1555m																														
Westonaria Dam Pleasure Resort Bookings not accepted □ *± 5 km from Westonaria*	011	753-1129		X					X			X					X	X	X	X		X				X			X	
WHITE RIVER T 69 C4 ↖ 962m																														
White River Municipal Bookings not necessary □ *Hennie van Til St.*	013132 E	434		X							X	X					X		40		X						X		X	
WIDENHAM N 63 NS ↗ S.L.																														
● **Widenham** P.O. Box 157, Umkomaas 4170 □ *2 Cheltenham Rd.*	0323	3-0351	X					X				X				X		40				X				X			X	
WILDERNESS C 59 NS ← S.L.																														
Ebb and Flow Nature Reserve Divisional Council, P.O. Box 12, George 6530	0441	3001			X				X	X		X				X			75				X			X	X		X	
Island Lake P.O. Wilderness 6560 □ *Island Lake*	0441	9194	X						X	X		X				X			50		X					X			X	
● **Siesta Holiday Resort** P.O. Box 35 (6560)	0441	9197	X					X	X	X		X					X	80				X					X		X	
The Lakes Holiday Resort P.O. Box 38 (6560)	0441	9101	X					X	X	X		X				X			75		X					X			X	
WILLEM PRETORIUS GAME RESERVE O See Ventersburg																														
WILLISTON C 61 C2 ↗ 1062m																														
Williston Municipal Bookings not necessary □ *Mulder St.*	02052 E	3		X							X		X			X		15				X					X		X	
WILLOWMORE C 59 B3 ↑ 844m																														
Willowmore Municipal P.O. Box 15 (6680) □ *Dam St.*	04942 E	4		X							X	X				X			20			X				X			X	
WINBURG O 66 C4 → 1440m																														
Winburg Municipal Town Clerk, P.O. Box 26 (9420) □ *Prince Edward St.*	05242 E	54 or 126		X							X	X	X			X			40			X				X			X	
WINKLESPRUIT N 63 NS ↗ S.L.																														
● **Karavana** P.O. Box 5 (4145) □ *Camp Rd.*	031	95-1747	X					X				X				X		240					X			X			X	
● **Mount Carmel** P.O. Box 14 (4145) □ *Camp Rd.*	031	95-1000	X					X				X				X		40				X					X		X	
● **Ocean-Call** P.O. Box 33 (4145) □ *3 Murray-Smith Rd.*	031	95-1744	X					X			X	X				X			70		X					X			X	
WINTERTON N 67 C2 ↓ 1022m																														
Kelvin Grove P.O. Winterton 3340	03682 E	2502	X						X	X	X	X					X	30				X						X	X	
WITBANK T 69 C2 ↙ 1622m																														
Witbank Recreation Resort P.O. Box 3 (1035) □ *Witbank Dam*	01351	71951		X					X			X				X	X	150	200	50		X				X			X	
WITSAND C 58 D5 → 5m																														
Witsand Bookings not accepted	T	27			X			X				X	X	X		X			89		X					X			X	
WITWATERSRAND T See respectively: ● Alberton ● Bapsfontein ● Bedfordview ● Benoni ● Boksburg ● Brakpan ● Edenvale ● Eikenhof ● Elandsfontein ● Florida ● Germiston ● Honeydew ● Johannesburg ● Kempton Park ● Krugersdorp ● Mondeor ● Randfontein ● Rivonia ● Roodepoort ● Springs ● Westonaria																														
WOLMARANSSTAD T 66 B3 ↗ 1376m																														
● **Wolmaransstad Municipal** Town Clerk, P.O. Box 17 (2630) □ *Broadbent St.*	018112 E	12 or 412		X					X		X	X				X		24	12		X						X		X	
WOODBUSH FOREST RESERVE T See Houtbosdorp																														
WORCESTER C 58 C4 ↙ 300m																														
Burger Park Town Clerk, Municipality (6850) □ *Riebeeck St.*	0231	2-1050		X					X	X	X	X	X			X			54		X					X			X	

CAMP SITE FACILITIES

I = In-Season only O = Out-of-Season only X = On application

SPORTING AND RECREATIONAL FACILITIES

S = On Site N = Nearby (Up to 20 km away)

33 SEASONS: …N THROUGHOUT THE YEAR	34 SEASONS: OUT-OF-SEASON CLOSING DATE / RE-OPENING DATE	35 TERMS FOR BOOKINGS: BOOKINGS ACCP. (PEAK SNS.) – SEE NOTE 2	36 DEPOSIT REQUIRED	37 REFUNDED IF CANCELLED – SEE NOTE 3	38 CARAVAN/CAMPING SITE TARIFFS (See heading): MAXIMUM IN-SEASON TARIFF	39 MAXIMUM OUT-OF-SEASON TARIFF	40 REDUCTIONS ALLOWED FOR: LONG PERIODS OF STAY	41 GROUPS – SEE NOTE 4	42 AA MEMBERS	43 OTHERS (ON APPLICATION)	44 RESTAURANT FACILITIES: ON SITE	45 WITHIN 5 km OF SITE	46 MORE THAN 5 km FROM SITE	47 TEAROOM/CAFE: ON SITE	48 WITHIN 5 km OF SITE	49 MORE THAN 5 km FROM SITE	50 SHOPPING FACILITIES (Provisions): ON SITE	51 WITHIN 5 km OF SITE	52 MORE THAN 5 km FROM SITE	53 ADDITIONAL ACCOMMODATION AVAILABLE: BUNGALOWS	54 CABINS	55 COTTAGES (RONDAVELS)	56 CHALETS	57 TARIFF (See heading): MAXIMUM IN-SEASON TARIFF	58 MAXIMUM OUT-OF-SEASON TARIFF	59 CARAVANS TO RENT ON SITE – SEE SECTION	60 DRINKING WATER: PIPED	61 OTHER	62 BATHS: HOT AND COLD
		X	X		C	B	X	X	X				X			X			X				X	C	B	X	X	X	X
		X			B	B	X	X			X							X									X		X
		X	X	X	D	D												X		X				D-E	D-E		X	X	X
		X	X	X	C	B			X	X	X			X			X					X		D-E	D-E		X		X
		X	X		B	B	X	X	X				X	X		X	X		X			X	X	C-F	C-F		X		X
		X			C	C						X			X			X					X	E-G	E-G		X		X
		X	X		B	B		X				X			X				X			X		A	A		X		X
		X			B	B						X			X			X									X		X
					B	B							X			X			X								X		X
		X	X		C	B		X	X		X				X			X		X				D	C		X	X	X
					B	B						X			X			X									X		X
					X	X					X			X			X										X		
					C	C										X		X	X								X		X
		X			C	C							X			X			X								X		X
					C	C	X					X			X			X									X		X
		X	X		G	D	X					X			X			X									X		X
		X	X	X	D	B							X			X			X	X		X		B	B		X		
		X	X	X	E	C	X	X		X		X			X			X				X		E	C	X	X		X
		X	X	X	F	C						X			X		X	X	X							X	X	X	X
		X	X	X	G	C						X					X			X			X	J	H-J	X	X		X
					B	B						X			X			X									X	X	
		X			B	B						X	X		X	X		X	X								X		X
					B	B						X	X		X	X		X	X									X	X
		X	X		F	F						X		X				X								X	X		X
		X	X		E	C						X			X			X									X		X
		X	X	X	H	G	X	X		X				X			X									X	X		X
		X	X		C	C	X	X		X			X			X			X		X	X		D	D		X		X
		X			B	B					X		X	X		X			X								X		X
					B	B									X	X		X	X									X	X
		X			B	B						X			X			X									X		X
		X	X		C	B	X				X					X			X								X		X

63 BATHS: COLD ONLY	64 SHOWERS: HOT AND COLD	65 COLD ONLY	66 WATERBORNE SANITATION	67 WASHBASINS	68 DISHWASHING FACILITIES	69 LAUNDRY AND IRONING FACILITIES – SEE NOTE 5	70 WASHING MACHINES	71 SITE LIT	72 PLUGS FOR RAZORS (VOLTAGE)	73 REFRIGERATORS	74 FIREWOOD/CHARCOAL	75 OPEN FIRE FORBIDDEN	76 CAMP FIRE PERMITTED	77 BRAAI PLACES PROVIDED	78 KITCHEN/COOKING FACILITIES	79 PETROL PUMP ON SITE	80 PETROL PUMP NEARBY	81 CAR REPAIR SHOP NEARBY	82 CAR SERVICING NEARBY	83 GAS SERVICE NEARBY	84 FIRST AID/HOSPITAL/DOCTOR NEARBY	85 POST OFFICE NEARBY	86 SITE GUARDED	87 PETS ALLOWED	88 NON-WHITE SERVANTS: SERVANTS PERMITTED – SEE NOTE 6	89 SERVANTS ACCOM. – SEE NOTE 6	90 SERVANTS FOR HIRE – SEE NOTE 6	91 TYPE OF VEHICLE PERMITTED: CAR AND TRAILER	92 TRUCK 'HORSE' AND SEMI-TRAILER
X	X	X	X	X	X	X	X	X		X	X	X	X	X			X	X	X	X		X	X	X	X	X	X	X	X
	X		X	X	X	X		X		X			X	X			X	X	X				X	X	X	X		X	X
	X		X	X	X	X				X	X		X	X			X			X	X		X	X	X		X	X	X
	X		X	X		X		X	220		X		X	X			X	X	X	X	X	X	X					X	X
	X		X	X	X	X		X	110/220		X		X	X			X	X	X		X	X		X	X		X	X	X
	X		X	X	X	X	X	X	X		X	X	X	X			X	X	X	X	X	X	X		X			X	X
	X		X	X	X	X		X	220		X		X	X			X	X	X	X		X		X	X			X	
	X		X	X	X	X		X					X				X	X	X	X	X	X	X	X	X		X	X	X
	X		X	X	X	X		X	220		X	X		X			X	X	X		Y	X	X		X	X			
	X		X	X	X	X		X		X	X		X	X	X		X	X	X	X	X	X	X		X			X	X
	X		X	X	X	X		X			X	X	X	X	X		X	X	X	X	X	X						X	X
	X		X	X									X	X		X		X	X			X	X	X				X	
	X		X	X		X		X					X	X			X	X	X			X		X				X	X
	X		X	X	X	X		X		X	X		X	X	X		X	X	X			X	X		X		X	X	X
	X		X	X	X	X		X	110/220		X		X	X			X	X	X	X	X	X	X	X	X			X	X
	X		X	X	X	X		X	220		X		X				X	X	X	X	X	X	X					X	
	X		X	X	X	X		X	X			X	X	X			X	X	X	X		X	X					X	X
	X		X	X	X	X					X		X	X			X	X	X	X	X	X		O			X	X	X
	X		X	X	X	X		X	220		X			X			X	X	X	X	X	X					I	X	
	X		X	X	X	X	X	X	110/220		X			X		X	X	X	X	X		X		O	X	X	X	X	X
	X		X	X	X	X		X	220				X	X			X	X	X	X	X	X		X	X			X	X
	X		X	X	X	X		X	220		X		X	X			X	X	X	X	X	X	X	X	X	X		X	X
	X		X	X	X			X	220		X		X	X			X	X	X	X	X	X		X	X	X		X	X
	X		X	X	X	X	X	X	220	X	X			X			X	X	X	X	X	X	X	X			X	X	
	X		X	X	X	X	X	X	220			X		X			X	X	X			X						X	X
	X		X	X	X	X	X	X	220		X	X		X			X	X	X	X	X	X	X	X	O			X	X
	X		X	X	X	X				X	X		X	X			X	X	X		X	X					X	X	X
	X		X	X	X	X		X	220		X		X	X			X	X	X	X	X	X						X	
	X		X	X	X	X		X			X		X	X	X		X			X		X	X		X			X	
	X		X	X	X	X		X	220		X			X			X	X	X			X	X				X	X	X
	X		X	X	X	X		X	X		X		X	X	X		X	X	X	X	X	X			X		X	X	X

93 SELF-PROPELLED CARAVANS	94 CHILDRENS' PLAYGROUND	95 TENNIS	96 CINEMA/DRIVE-IN/TV-ROOM – SEE NOTE 7	97 HORSE-RIDING	98 GAMES ROOM	99 TRAMPOLINE	100 BOWLS	101 HOT SPRINGS	102 GOLF: GOLF COURSE – SEE NOTE 8	103 NUMBER OF HOLES	104 MINIATURE	105 MASHIE	106 PUTT-PUTT	107 FISHING: FRESHWATER – SEE NOTE 9	108 SEA – SEE NOTE 10	109 GOGGLE	110 LICENCE REQUIRED	111 SWIMMING: SWIMMING POOL	112 SEA BATHING	113 CHILDRENS' POOL	114 ADULTS ONLY	115 SHARK NETS AT BEACH	116 BOATING: BOATS FOR HIRE	117 POWER	118 SAILING	119 CANOEING	120 PLACES OF INTEREST: HISTORIC	121 SCIENTIFIC	122 NATURAL	123	NOTES
X	S	N	N	S			N		N	18								S		S							X		X		
X			N				N		N	18																					
X	N	N	N			N	N		N	9					N	N			X				N	N		N	X	X	X		
X	S	N	N			S	N		N	9				S				S		S						S	X		X		
X	S	N	N		N	N	N	N	N	9				N			X	S		S									X		
X	S	S	N			N	N	S	N	9		X		N			X	S		S							X		X		
X	N	N	N				N							S			X	N		N						S					
X	N	N	N				N							N			X	N		N							X	X	X		
X		N	N				N		N	18			X					N		N											
X	S	N	N	N	N	N	N		N	9				N			X	S		S					N	N	X		X		
X	N	N	N				N		N	9								N		N							X		X		
X	N	N					N		N	9				N			X	N		N											
X	S	N	N	S	N	N	N		N	18				S			X	S		S				S	S	S			X		
X	N	N		N		N	N	N	N	9		X		N			X	N		N				N	N	N	X		X		
X	S	N	N		S		N		N	18				N	N	N	X	N	X	N								X	X		
X														S											S	S			X		
X	S	N	N	N			N		N	18				S	N	N			X				S	S	S	S	X	X	X		
X	S	N	N	N	S		N		N	18				S	N	N	X	N	X				S		S	S	X	X	X		
X	S	N	N	N	S		N		N	18					S	S			X				S	S	S	S	X		X		
X	N	N							N	9	X							S		S											
X	N	N					N		N	18								N		N							X		X		
X									N	9				N			X	N									X				
X		N	S		S		N		N	18				N	N			S	X	N											
X	S		S		S		N		N	18					N			S	X	S											
X	S	N			S	S	N		N	18					N	N		S	X	S		X									
X	S	N	N	S	N	N	N		N					N			X	S		N							X		X		
X	S	S	N	N			N		N	18	X			S			X	S		S				S	S	S			X		
X	S														N	N			X				N	N	N	N			X		
X	N	N	N				N		N	9				N			X	N		N							X				
X	S	N	N	N			N		N	18				N			X	S		S							X	X	X		

CARAVAN PARKS AND CAMPING SITES IN SOUTH AFRICA

CARAVAN PARK / CAMP SITE TARIFF CODE – See columns 38–39 (Subject to alteration)

A = Up to R1 | C = R2–R3 | E = R4–R5 | G = R6–R7 | I = R8–R9 | K = R10–R16
B = R1–R2 | D = R3–R4 | F = R5–R6 | H = R7–R8 | J = R9–R10 | O = FREE
X = On Application

Charges are based on family of 2 adults and 2 children under 12 years

ADDITIONAL ACCOMMODATION TARIFF CODE – See columns 57–59 (Subject to alteration)

eg. Bungalows, Cabins, Cottages, Chalets, etc.
A = R1–R3 | C = R5–R7 | E = R9–R11 | G = R13–R15 | I = R17–R19 | K = R21–R30
B = R3–R5 | D = R7–R9 | F = R11–R13 | H = R15–R17 | J = R19–R21 | X = On Application

NB: Where the tariff is given in *italics* it is per person, otherwise per unit

NOTE 1 — **Columns 18, 19, 20,** — X = Stands available but not demarcated or number of stands have not been provided
NOTE 2 — **Column 35** — A = Bookings accepted for additional accommodation only i.e. cottages, bungalows, etc.
NOTE 3 — **Column 37** — Deposit refunded under certain conditions eg. less 10% ; if site is re-let ; if cancelled well in advance (up to 2 months) or on a doctor's certificate
NOTE 4 — **Column 41** — Reductions allowed on application for youth, church, school or sport groups or caravan rallies

NOTE 5 — **Column 69** — L = Laundry facilities only
NOTE 6 — **Columns 88, 89, 90,** — I = In-Season only ; O = Out-of-Season only; X = On application
NOTE 7 — **Column 96** — I = In-Season only
NOTE 8 — **Column 102** — See section on golf in Outdoor Holiday Guide
NOTE 9 — **Column 107** — See section on freshwater angling in Outdoor Holiday Guide
NOTE 10 — **Column 108** — See section on coastal angling in Outdoor Holiday Guide

Establishments marked thus ● have the Caravan Club of South Africa recommendation — see introduction

ABBREVIATIONS

C = CAPE PROVINCE
N = NATAL
O = ORANGE FREE STATE
T = TRANSVAAL
B = BOPHUTHATSWANA
X = TRANSKEI

	TELEPHONE CODE (T = DIAL 0020, BOOK TRUNK CALL; E = DIAL CODE, ASK EXCHANGE FOR NO.)	TELEPHONE NUMBER	OWNED OR SUPERVISED BY: PRIVATELY OWNED	MUNICIPAL	DIVISIONAL COUNCIL	PROVINCIAL COUNCIL	PARKS BOARD ADMINISTRATION	SITE DESCRIPTION – LOCALITY: BEACH IN IMMEDIATE VICINITY	BESIDE RIVER LAKE OR DAM	IN OR NEAR MOUNTAIN AREA	WITHIN BUILT-UP AREA	NATURE OF GROUND: GRASS	GRAVEL	SAND	SHADE: UNSHADED	PARTLY SHADED	EXTENSIVELY SHADED	NO. OF STANDS: CARAVANS SEE NOTE 1	CARAVANS AND/OR TENTS SEE NOTE 1	TENTS ONLY SEE NOTE 1	ACCESSIBILITY – APPROXIMATE DISTANCE FROM MAIN ROAD TO SITE: ON MAIN RD	WITHIN 1 km	WITHIN 5 km	WITHIN 10 km	WITHIN 15 km	SURFACE OF APPROACH ROAD: TAR	GRAVEL	SAND	CONDITION OF APPROACH ROAD: GOOD	FAIR
	1	2	3	4	5	6	7	8	9	10	11	12	13	14	15	16	17	18	19	20	21	22	23	24	25	26	27	28	29	30
YSTERFONTEIN C 58 C3 ← S.L.																														
Ysterfontein P.O. Box 14, Malmesbury 7300 ☐ *Strand Rd.*	02245	2-2907			X			X			X		X		X			70	10			X					X		X	
ZASTRON O 62 B5 ↖ 1679m																														
● Zastron Municipal P.O. Box 20 (9950) ☐ *Mathee St. Ext.*	05542 E	18		X					X	X		X					X	30	60	30			X			X	X		X	
ZEERUST T 68 C4 · 1179m																														
Die Krans P.O. Box 193 (2865) ☐ *1,5 km from Zeerust*	014282 E	236	X						X	X						X	X	18				X				X			X	
ZINKWAZI N See Sinkwazi																														
FOR COLOUREDS, ASIANS AND BLACKS																														
ACORNHOEK T 71 B5 ↓ 387m																														
Manyeleti Game Reserve (for Blacks) Manager, P.O. Manyeleti, via Acornhoek 1362 ☐ *48 km from Acornhoek*	T	3												X		X			20								X			X
AMANZIMTOTI N 63 NS ↗ S.L.																														
Umgababa Seaside Holiday Resort (for Blacks) Manager, P.O. Box 172 (4125) ☐ *Main South Coast Rd.*	0323	31165/31120						X				X				X		50	150	130		X				X			X	
AUGRABIES C 65 C2 ← 1200m																														
Augrabies Falls National Park (camping for Coloureds, Asians and Blacks) National Parks Board, P.O. Box 787, Pretoria 0001 ☐ *13 km from Augrabies*	012	44-1171					X		X				X				X		X			X				X			X	
BUFFELSBAAI C 59 NS ↓ S.L.																														
Buffalo Bay Camping Area (for Coloureds) Superintendent, P.O. Box 9 (6582)	T	9			X			X		X		X			X				28	7	X						X			X
CALITZDORP C 59 B1 ← 238m																														
Huis River Camping and Picnic Site (for Coloureds) No bookings, no facilities but camping allowed ☐ *10 km from Calitzdorp*						X			X	X			X			X					X						X			X
CERES C 58 C4 ↖ 457m																														
Die Eiland Caravan Park and Holiday Resort (for Coloureds) P.O. Box 44 (6835)	023312 E	543/8		X															20											
DARNALL N 63 A4 • 66m																														
Harold Johnson Nature Reserve (for Blacks) Officer-in-Charge, P.O. Box 148 (4480)	032422 E	2204					X		X			X					X		6			X					X		X	
EAST LONDON C 60 B2 ↘ S.L.																														
Fullers Bay (For Asians) Bookings not accepted ☐ *10 km from city*				X				X				X				X			X			X					X	X		X
Leaches Bay (For Coloureds) Bookings not accepted ☐ *12 km from city*				X				X				X				X			X			X					X			X
Western Seafront (For Blacks) Bookings not accepted ☐ *9 km from city*				X				X				X				X			X		X						X			X
FRANSCHHOEK C 58 C4 ↙ 126m																														
Die Ou Tol Camping Area (for Coloureds, Asians and Blacks) Bookings not accepted ☐ *Franschhoek Pass*					X					X		X				X					X					X			X	
GEORGE C 59 NS ← 226m																														
Municipal Tourist Camp and Caravan Park (for Coloureds and Asians) P.O. Box 19 (6530) ☐ *Knysna Rd.*	0441	6001		X						X	X	X				X			75		X						X		X	
GRAHAMSTOWN C 59 B6 ↑ 532m																														
Grahamstown Caravan Park (for Coloureds and Indians) Superintendent, Parks and Forests Dept., P.O. Box 176 (6140) ☐ *Port Elizabeth National Rd.*	0461	2043		X								X				X			25		X					X			X	
GWAYANG RIVER MOUTH C 59 NS ← 10m																														
Caravan Park (for Coloureds) Divisional Council, P.O. Box 12, George 6530 ☐ *15 km from George*	0441	3001			X			X	X				X		X				30					X			X		X	
HAWSTON C 58 D4 ← 20m																														
Sonesta (for Coloureds) P.O. Box 25 (7202) ☐ *5 km from Hawston*	T	40						X	X	X		X					X	150					X			X			X	
HLUHLUWE N 67 B5 ↙ 5m																														
False Bay Park (for Non-Whites) Only 3 non-facility sites (i.e. pit latrines and water points). Officer-in-Charge, False Bay Park, P.O. Hluhluwe 3960 ☐ *15 km from Hluhluwe*	03562 E	2911					X		X			X				X			3						X		X			X
HOWICK N 63 A3 ← 1048m																														
Orient Park Resort (for Coloureds and Asians) P.O. Howick 3290 ☐ *Adjacent to Midmar Dam*	033212 E	367				X	X		X	X		X				X			15					X					X	
JEFFREYS BAY C 59 C4 ↖ S.L.																														
Municipal Caravan Camp (for Coloureds) Town Clerk, P.O. Box 21 (6330) ☐ *16 Duine Rd.*	T	21		X				X				X			X				60			X					X		X	
KIMBERLEY C 62 C2 ↘ 1223m																														
Langleg Pleasure Resort (for Coloureds and Asians) Resort Manager, P.O. Box 628 (8300) ☐ *28 km from Kimberley*	0531	2-2241 x221		X					X			X				X		X		X				X		X			X	
KLEINKRANTZ C 59 NS ← 4m																														
Kleinkrantz Caravan Park (for Coloureds) Divisional Council, P.O. Box 12, George 6530	0441	3001			X			X				X		X					60		X						X		X	
KOMMETJIE C 58 NS ← S.L.																														
Die Anker Camping Site (For Coloureds and Asians) Supervisor, Soetwater Recreation Area, P.O. Kommetjie 7976	021	8-3747			X			X		X		X	X	X		X				X	X					X			X	
Medusa Caravan Park (for Coloureds) Supervisor, Soetwater Recreation Area, P.O. Kommetjie 7976	021	8-3747			X			X				X				X		66					X			X			X	
KRUGER NATIONAL PARK T 75 C5 ↗ 167m																														
Lower Sabie (for Coloureds, Asians and Blacks) Bookings not accepted Enquiries: National Parks Board, P.O. Box 787, Pretoria 0001	012	44-1194					X					X				X			3							X			X	
Skukuza (for Coloureds, Asians and Blacks) Bookings not accepted Enquiries: National Parks Board, P.O. Box 787, Pretoria 0001	012	44-1194					X							X		X			10							X			X	
LANGEBAAN C 58 C3 ↑ S.L.																														
Municipal Caravan Park (for Coloureds) P.O. Box 11 (7357) ☐ *Main St.*	T	15		X				X					X		X				80			X					X			X

SEASONS		TERMS FOR BOOKINGS			CARAVAN/CAMPING SITE TARIFFS (See heading)		REDUCTIONS ALLOWED FOR				RESTAURANT FACILITIES			TEAROOM/CAFE			SHOPPING FACILITIES (Provisions)			ADDITIONAL ACCOMMODATION AVAILABLE				TARIFF (See heading)			CAMP SITE FACILITIES (I=In-Season only, O=Out-of-Season only, X=On application)																												NON-WHITE SERVANTS			TYPE OF VEHICLE PERMITTED			SPORTING AND RECREATIONAL FACILITIES (S=On Site, N=Nearby (Up to 20 km away))																													NOTES
OUT-OF-SEASON CLOSING DATE	RE-OPENING DATE	BOOKINGS ACCP./PEAK SNS.-SEE NOTE 2	DEPOSIT REQUIRED	REFUNDED IF CANCELLED - SEE NOTE 3	MAXIMUM IN-SEASON TARIFF	MAXIMUM OUT-OF-SEASON TARIFF	LONG PERIODS OF STAY	GROUPS - SEE NOTE 4	AA MEMBERS	OTHERS (ON APPLICATION)	ON SITE	WITHIN 5 km OF SITE	MORE THAN 5 km FROM SITE	ON SITE	WITHIN 5 km OF SITE	MORE THAN 5 km FROM SITE	ON SITE	WITHIN 5 km OF SITE	MORE THAN 5 km FROM SITE	BUNGALOWS	CABINS	COTTAGES (RONDAVELS)	CHALETS	MAXIMUM IN-SEASON TARIFF	MAXIMUM OUT-OF-SEASON TARIFF	CARAVANS TO RENT ON SITE - SEE SECTION	DRINKING WATER: PIPED	OTHER	BATHS: HOT AND COLD	COLD ONLY	SHOWERS: HOT AND COLD	COLD ONLY	WATERBORNE SANITATION	WASHBASINS	DISHWASHING FACILITIES	LAUNDRY AND IRONING FACILITIES - SEE NOTE 5	WASHING MACHINES	SITE LIT	PLUGS FOR RAZORS (VOLTAGE)	REFRIGERATORS	FIREWOOD/CHARCOAL	OPEN FIRE FORBIDDEN	CAMP FIRE PERMITTED	BRAAI PLACES PROVIDED	KITCHEN/COOKING FACILITIES	PETROL PUMP ON SITE	PETROL PUMP NEARBY	CAR REPAIR SHOP NEARBY	CAR SERVICING NEARBY	GAS SERVICE NEARBY	FIRST AID/HOSPITAL/DOCTOR NEARBY	POST OFFICE NEARBY	SITE GUARDED	PETS ALLOWED	SERVANTS PERMITTED - SEE NOTE 6	SERVANTS ACCOM. - SEE NOTE 6	SERVANTS FOR HIRE - SEE NOTE 6	CAR AND TRAILER	TRUCK "HORSE" AND SEMI-TRAILER	SELF-PROPELLED CARAVANS	CHILDRENS' PLAYGROUND	TENNIS	CINEMA/DRIVE-IN/TV-ROOM - SEE NOTE 7	HORSE-RIDING	GAMES ROOM	TRAMPOLINE	BOWLS	HOT SPRINGS	GOLF: GOLF COURSE - SEE NOTE 8	NUMBER OF HOLES	MINIATURE	MASHIE	PUTT-PUTT	FISHING: FRESHWATER - SEE NOTE 9	SEA - SEE NOTE 10	GOGGLE	LICENCE REQUIRED	SWIMMING: SWIMMING POOL	SEA BATHING	CHILDRENS' POOL	ADULTS ONLY	SHARK NETS AT BEACH	BOATING: BOATS FOR HIRE	POWER	SAILING	CANOEING	PLACES OF INTEREST: HISTORIC	SCIENTIFIC	NATURAL	
33	34	35	36	37	38	39	40	41	42	43	44	45	46	47	48	49	50	51	52	53	54	55	56	57	58	59	60	61	62	63	64	65	66	67	68	69	70	71	72	73	74	75	76	77	78	79	80	81	82	83	84	85	86	87	88	89	90	91	92	93	94	95	96	97	98	99	100	101	102	103	104	105	106	107	108	109	110	111	112	113	114	115	116	117	118	119	120	121	122	123
		X	X	X	B	B	X					X	X		X	X		X	X								X				X		X	X	X	X						X	X	X			X			X	X		X					X		X															N	N			X								X		X	
		X			C	C	X					X	X			X			X								X		X		X		X	X	X	X		X	220		X		X	X	X		X	X	X	X		X	X	X	X			X		X	S	N	N			N	N		N	9				S			X	N		N					S	S			X	
		X	X		C	B	X	X	X		X	X			X	X		X	X	X		X		X	X		X		X		X		X	X				X	220	X	X		X				X	X	X	X	X			X				X	X	X	N	N	S	N			N		N	18				S			X										X	X	X	
Jan	1 Mar.				A	A					X			X			X		X			X		A	A		X				X		X	X	X			X			X		X			X					X	X	X					X	X	X		S	S															S											X	
		X	X	X	E	C	X	X	X		X	X		X	X		X	X		X	X		X	E	G		X	X	X		X	X	X	X	X	X		X		X	X		X	X	X		X	X	X	X	X		X	X				X	X	X	S		S		S	S			S	18			X	N	N	N		S	X	S	X	X					X	X	X	
		X	X	X	C	C					X			X			X										X	X	X		X		X	X	X	X		X	220		X		X	X	X	X	X	X	X	X								X	X	X	S	S																									X	X	X	
hol.	& Estr.	X			B	B							X		X	X		X	X								X				X		X	X							X		X	X						X		X						X	X	X														N	N	N			X							N			X	
					Gratis	Gratis							X			X			X																								X	X										X				X	X	X																													X	
					B	B											X					X		A	A						X		X																	X																												S												
		X			B	B									X	X		X	X								X	X				X	X	X	X						X		X	X							X	X						X	X	X														N	N	N	X		X	N	X	X		N	N	N	X	X	X	
					A	A										X											X																X															X		X															S	S			X	N										X	
					A	A									X												X					X		X								X	X															X		X															N	N			X	N										X	
					A	A							X			X											X																X															X		X															N	N			X											X	
					Gratis	Gratis																					X																X	X										X				X	X	X	S																												X	
		X	X	X	C	C							X			X		X				X		C	B		X		X		X		X	X	X	X		X	X		X	X	X	X			X	X	X	X	X	X		X				X	X	X			N												N	N			X					N	N	N	X		X	
					A	A							X			X			X								X		X		X		X	X	X			X				X					X	X	X	X		X		X				X	X	X														N			X										X	X	X	
					B	B																					X					X	X	X	X							X	X	X									X					X		X														N	N	N			X											X	
					E	C		X			X	X	X	X			X			X		X		F-G	D-E		X		X		X		X	X	X	X		X	250		X		X	X							X	X	X					X	X	X	S	S	S		S				S		X	X	X		S	S		S	X	S	X				N				X	
					A	A										X			X																						X		X				X	X	X	X	X							X	X	X																							S						X	
		X	X	X	C	C							X	X									X	A	A		X		X		X		X	X	X	L		X					X	X			X				X		X					X			S	S	N	S										S			X						S	S	S			X	
		X	X	X	C	C		X				X			X			X									X		X		X		X	X	X	X		X				X		X			X	X	X	X	X	X	X					X		X	N	N													N				X										X	
		X	X	X	B	B								X								X		B	B		X				X		X	X				X		X	X	X		X									X					X	X	X	S													S			X	S		S			S			S				
					B	B					X			X			X										X					X	X	X								X		X			X	X	X				X					X		X															N				X										X	
					A	A							X		X			X									X			X		X	X	X	X						X		X									X	X					X	X	X															N	N			X											X	
		X			C	B				X		x	X		X	X	X	x	x								X		X		X		X	X	X	X		X			X	X	X	X			X	X	X	X	X	X	X					X	X	·															S	S			X	N	X							x		X	
					B	B					X						X					X		D-F	D-F		X		X		X	X	X	X	X	X						X		X		X												X	X	X																													X	
					B	B					X						X					X		E-F	E-F		X		X		X		X	X	X	X										X						X						X	X	X																											X	X	X	
		X			B	B						X			X			X									X					X	X	X	X	X			X					X	X								X					X	X	X															N				X					N	N					

CARAVAN PARKS AND CAMPING SITES IN SOUTH AFRICA

CARAVAN PARK / CAMP SITE TARIFF CODE – See columns 38–39 (Subject to alteration)

A = Up to R1 | B = R1–R2 | C = R2–R3 | D = R3–R4 | E = R4–R5 | F = R5–R6 | G = R6–R7 | H = R7–R8 | I = R8–R9 | J = R9–R10 | K = R10–R16 | O = FREE | X = On Application

Charges are based on family of 2 adults and 2 children under 12 years

ADDITIONAL ACCOMMODATION TARIFF CODE – See columns 57–59 (Subject to alteration)

eg. Bungalows, Cabins, Cottages, Chalets, etc.

A = R1–R3 | B = R3–R5 | C = R5–R7 | D = R7–R9 | E = R9–R11 | F = R11–R13 | G = R13–R15 | H = R15–R17 | I = R17–R19 | J = R19–R21 | K = R21–R30 | X = On Application

NB: Where the tariff is given in *italics* it is per person, otherwise per unit

NOTE 1 — **Columns 18, 19, 20,** — X = Stands available but not demarcated or number of stands have not been provided
NOTE 2 — **Column 35** — A = Bookings accepted for additional accommodation only i.e. cottages, bungalows, etc.
NOTE 3 — **Column 37** — Deposit refunded under certain conditions eg. less 10% ; if site is re-let ; if cancelled well in advance (up to 2 months) or on a doctor's certificate
NOTE 4 — **Column 41** — Reductions allowed on application for youth, church, school or sport groups or caravan rallies
NOTE 5 — **Column 69** — L = Laundry facilities only
NOTE 6 — **Columns 88, 89, 90,** — I = In-Season only ; O = Out-of-Season only; X = On application
NOTE 7 — **Column 96** — I = In-Season only
NOTE 8 — **Column 102** — See section on golf in Outdoor Holiday Guide
NOTE 9 — **Column 107** — See section on freshwater angling in Outdoor Holiday Guide
NOTE 10 — **Column 108** — See section on coastal angling in Outdoor Holiday Guide

Establishments marked thus ● have the Caravan Club of South Africa recommendation — see introduction

ABBREVIATIONS

C = CAPE PROVINCE
N = NATAL
O = ORANGE FREE STATE
T = TRANSVAAL
B = BOPHUTHATSWANA
X = TRANSKEI

TELEPHONE CODE T = DIAL 0020, BOOK TRUNK CALL; E = DIAL CODE, ASK EXCHANGE FOR NO.

	Telephone code	Telephone number	Owned or supervised by: Privately owned	Municipal	Divisional council	Provincial administration	Parks board	Site description – Locality: Beach in immediate vicinity	Beside river, lake or dam	In or near mountain area	Within built-up area	Nature of ground: Grass	Gravel	Sand	Shade: Unshaded	Partly shaded	Extensively shaded	No. of stands: Caravans only – see note 1	Caravans and/or tents	Tents only – see note 1	Accessibility – Approximate distance from main road to site: On main rd	Within 1 km	Within 5 km	Within 10 km	Within 15 km	Surface of road approach: Tar	Gravel	Sand	Condition of approach: Good	Fair
	1	2	3	4	5	6	7	8	9	10	11	12	13	14	15	16	17	18	19	20	21	22	23	24	25	26	27	28	29	30
FOR COLOUREDS, ASIANS AND BLACKS (CONTINUED)																														
MOSSEL BAY C 59 C2 ↖ 7m																														
Diaz Caravan Park (for Coloureds) Bookings not accepted ☐ *Diaz Strand, 2 km from Mossel Bay*	04441	2514		X				X				X					X	300		1000		X					X			X
OUDTSHOORN C 59 B2 ← 306m																														
Bridgton Camp (for Coloureds) Bookings not accepted ☐ *Blackwood St., Bridgton*	04431	2221		X							X		X			X			15			X				X			X	
De Hoek Holiday Resort (for Coloureds) P.O. Box 127 (6620) ☐ *±40 km from Oudtshoorn on the road to Prince Albert*	04431	2241			X				X	X		X					X	40		40		X					X		X	
PAARL C 58 C3 ↘ 115m																														
Orleans Park (for Coloureds) Secretary, Management Committee, P.O. Box 12 (7620) ☐ *Meaker St., Huguenot*	0251	2-4320		X					X					X		X				100			X			X			X	
PARK RYNIE N 63 NS • 15m																														
Park Rynie Caravan, Camping and Picnicking Ground (for Coloureds and Asians) Umzinto North Town Board, P.O. Box 39, Umzinto 4200 ☐ *Off First St., Park Rynie*	0323	4031		X				X				X				X		50	100	50			X			X	X			X
PORT ELIZABETH C 59 B5 ↘ S.L.																														
Joorst Park (for Coloureds and Asians) C/o Parks Dept., St. George's Park (6001) ☐ *St. George's Strand*	041	6 1463		X				X				X				X			X			X				X			X	
King Neptune Holiday Resort																														
Marine Drive Camping Site																														
PORT NOLLOTH C 60 A4 ↗ S.L.																														
Municipal Caravan Park (For Coloureds) Municipality, P.O. Box 13 (8280)	T	11		X				X						X	X				50				X				X	X		X
PORT ST. JOHNS X 60 A4 → 3m																														
● **First Beach Municipal Caravan Park (for all races)** Municipality, P.O. Box 2 (4830)	04752 E	8		X				X	X			X					X	23			X					X			X	
Second Beach Municipal Caravan Park (for all races) Municipality, P.O. Box 2 (4830)	04752 E	8		X				X	X			X				X		50		60		X					X		X	
ROYAL NATAL NATIONAL PARK N 67 C1 ↘ 1500m																														
Rugged Glen Campsite P.O. Mont-aux-Sources 3353	T	Mont-aux-Sources 3					X			X		X				X			X				X					X	X	
SILWERSTROOMSTRAND C 58 C3 ↙ S.L.																														
Silwerstroom Resort Area (for Coloureds and Asians) Divisional Council, P.O. Box 1073, Cape Town 8000	02202 E	1840			X			X				X	X	X	X	X								X		X			X	
STILBAAI-OOS C 59 C1 • S.L.																														
Preekstoel Beach Resort (for Coloureds) Caretaker, P.O. Box 13, Riversdale 6770	T	9909			X			X				X				X			325		X					X			X	
ST. LUCIA ESTUARY N 67 C5 • 50m																														
Natal Parks Board Campsite (for Coloureds, Asians and Blacks) Natal Parks Board, P.O. St. Lucia Estuary 3936	T	St. Lucia 20					X		X			X				X			12			X				X			X	
STRAND C 58 D3 ↗ S.L.																														
Harmony Park (for Coloureds) Bookings not accepted ☐ *Gordon's Bay Rd.*	024	3-6270		X				X		X	X			X		X				500	X					X			X	
STRUISBAAI C 58 D5 ↙ 2m																														
Molshoop Camping Area (for Coloureds) Bookings not accepted ☐ *1 km from Struisbaai*	02842 E	68			X			X				X			X				X			X					X			
SWELLENDAM C 58 D5 ↑ 152m																														
Bontebok National Park Non-White campers allowed, but adequate facilities will only be ready by 1979 — Bookings not accepted, arrangements made on arrival	02912 E	4403					X		X	X		X				X			X					X			X		X	
UMTATA X 62 C6 → 699m																														
Municipal Caravan Park (for all races) P.O. Box 45 (5100)	0471	3204		X							X	X				X			50		X					X			X	

Names and addresses of the following establishments are included for the benefit of interested persons. No other particulars are available.

BARKLY WEST C 66 C2 Municipal Caravan Park P.O. Box 11 (8375)
BLOEMFONTEIN O 66 D4 ↖ Rayton Caravan Park P.O. Box 451 (9300)
BROEDERSTROOM T 68 NS • Petit Chalet P.O. Broederstroom 0240
BRONKHORSTSPRUIT T 69 C1 ↘ Bronkhorstbaai Caravan Park P.O. Box 90 (1020)
CALEDON C 58 D4 ↑ Caledon Warm Baths Caravan Park P.O. Box 192 (7230)
EAST LONDON C 60 B2 ↘ Four Seasons Caravan Park P.O. Box 3177 (5200)
● **Glen Eden Caravan Park** P.O. Box 2054, Beacon Bay 5205
ELOFF T 68 D6 ↗ Hotel Mimosa Pleasure Resort P.O. Box 61 (2211)
ESTCOURT N 67 C2 ↘ Andrews Motel (Caravan overnight stops only) P.O. Box 101 (3310)
Woodleigh Farm P.O. Box 69 (3310)

GRASKOP T 71 B4 ↙ Panorama Rest Camp P.O. Box 29 (1270)
GROBLERSDAL T 69 C2 ↖ Kloof Motel Caravan Park P.O. Damwal (via Groblersdal) 0471
HARTBEESPOORT T 68 C5 ↘ Iscor Angling Resort P.O. Box 279 (0216)
HERMANUS C 58 D4 ← Die Mond Caravan and Camping Park P.O. Box 20 (7200)
HOEDSPRUIT T 69 B3 • Mariepsig Rest Camp P.O. Box 97 (1380)
JANSENVILLE C 59 A4 ↓ Municipal Caravan Park P.O. Box 12 (6265)
JOHANNESBURG T 68 D6 ↖ Johannesburg Caravan Park P.O. Box 529, Halfway House 1685
Panorama Caravan Park P.O. Box 35181, Northcliff 2115
Shangri-La Caravan Park 71-3rd Road, Linbro Park
KALKBANK T 69 A2 ← Uncle Wally's Caravan Park P.O. Kalkbank 0713

CAMP SITE FACILITIES — I = In-Season only; O = Out-of-Season only; X = On application

SPORTING AND RECREATIONAL FACILITIES — S = On Site; N = Nearby (Up to 20 km away)

Seasons: 33 Throughout the year	34 Out-of-season closing date / Re-opening date	Terms for bookings: 35 Bookings accp./peak sns. – see note 2	36 Deposit required	37 Refunded if cancelled – see note 3	Caravan/camping site tariffs (See heading): 38 Maximum in-season tariff	39 Maximum out-of-season tariff	Reductions allowed for: 40 Long periods of stay	41 Groups – see note 4	42 AA members	43 Others (on application)	Restaurant facilities: 44 On site	45 Within 5 km of site	46 More than 5 km from site	Tearoom/Cafe: 47 On site	48 Within 5 km of site	49 More than 5 km from site	Shopping facilities (Provisions): 50 On site	51 Within 5 km of site	52 More than 5 km from site	Additional accommodation available: 53 Bungalows	54 Cabins	55 Cottages (rondavels)	56 Chalets	Tariff (See heading): 57 Maximum in-season tariff	58 Maximum out-of-season tariff	59 Caravans to rent on site – see section	Drinking water: 60 Piped	61 Other	Baths: 62 Hot and cold	63 Cold only	Showers: 64 Hot and cold	65 Cold only	66 Waterborne sanitation	67 Washbasins	68 Dishwashing facilities	69 Laundry and ironing facilities – see note 5	70 Washing machines	71 Site lit	72 Plugs for razors (voltage)	73 Refrigerators	74 Firewood/charcoal	75 Open fire forbidden	76 Camp fire permitted	77 Braai places provided	78 Kitchen/cooking facilities	79 Petrol pump on site	80 Petrol pump nearby	81 Car repair shop nearby	82 Car servicing nearby	83 Gas service nearby	84 First aid/hospital/doctor nearby	85 Post office nearby	86 Site guarded	87 Pets allowed	Non-white servants: 88 Servants permitted – see note 6	89 Servants accom. – see note 6	90 Servants for hire – see note 6	Type of vehicle permitted: 91 Car and trailer	92 Truck "horse" and semi-trailer	93 Self-propelled caravans	94 Childrens' playground	95 Tennis	96 Cinema/drive-in/TV-room – see note 7	97 Horse-riding	98 Games room	99 Trampoline	100 Bowls	101 Hot springs	Golf: 102 Golf course – see note 8	103 Number of holes	104 Miniature	105 Mashie	106 Putt-putt	Fishing: 107 Freshwater – see note 9	108 Sea – see note 10	109 Goggle	110 Licence required	Swimming: 111 Swimming pool	112 Sea bathing	113 Childrens' pool	114 Adults only	115 Shark nets at beach	Boating: 116 Boats for hire	117 Power	118 Sailing	119 Canoeing	Places of interest: 120 Historic	121 Scientific	122 Natural	123 Notes
					C	B					X					X	X											X		X		X		X	X	X			X	220		X		X				X	X	X	X	X	X	X					X		X	S	S	N													N	N			X								X		X	
					A	A							X			X		X	X									X					X	X	X				X					X				X	X	X	X		X		X				X	X	X	N	N	N																N		N							X	X	X	
		X	X	X	C	B													X				X	E	D		X	X	X	X	X	X	X	X	X	X		X	220	X	X		X	X	X								X	X				X	X	X																			S		S										
					A	A							X			X			X									X					X	X	X							X		X	X			X	X	X	X	X	X	X	X				X		X	S	N	N																N		N							X		X	
					C	B						X			X			X										X			X		X	X	X	X			X				X	X				X	X	X	X	X	X	X					X		X															S	S		S	X	S										
		X	X		X	X					X	X		X	X			X	X	X			X	X	X		X					X	X	X	X	X		X	250		X		X	X			X	X	X	X	X	X	X	X				X		X	S	N	N	N	N	N									N				X								X	X	X	
		X	X		A	A						X															X			X		X	X	X									X				X		X			X		X				X	X	X															N	N			X					N	N	N				
		X	X		C	C	X						X			X			X	X		X	X	C-E	C-E		X		X		X		X	X	X	X		X		X	X		X	X			X	X	X	X	X	X	X					X	X	X		N					N		N	9					N	N		N	X					N		N			X	
		X	X		C	C	X					X			X				X	X		X	X	C-E	C-E		X		X		X		X	X	X	X					X		X	X			X	X	X	X	X	X	X					X	X	X		N					N		N	9					N	N		N	X					N		N			X	
		X	X	X	C	C									X			X									X	X			X		X	X	X						X		X				X				X	X	X					X	X	X	S			N										N			X												X	
					A	A								X			X											X			X		X	X	X	X	X					X		X	X							X		X					X	X	X																N	N			X										X	
					A	A					X			X			X											X			X		X	X	X	X						X		X	X			X	X	X	X		X	X	X				X	X	X															S	S			X										X	
		X	X	X	C	C									X	X			X								X		X		X										X		X				X	X	X	X		X						X	X	X															N				X				S						X	
					B	B								X					X									X					X									X			X			X	X	X													N													N	N			X										X	
					O	O						X							X									X					X	X	X	X						X		X				X	X	X	X		X	X	X				X	X	X															N	N			X				N	N			X		X	
					C	C							X			X			X									X														X	X	X			X	X	X	X	X								X	X	X																																
					B	B	X	X					X			X			X									X		X		X		X	X	X	X		X					X				X	X	X			X		X				X		X	N	N	N				N		N	18				N		N													X	

Names and addresses of the following establishments are included for the benefit of interested persons. No other particulars are available.

KIMBERLEY C 66 C2 ↘ De Beers Stadium Caravan Park P.O. Box 647 (8300)
KNYSNA C 59 C3 ↖ Knysna Caravan Park P.O. Box 133 (6570)
LOUIS TRICHARDT T 70 C4 ↗ Adam's Apple Motel and Caravan Park P.O. Box 338 (0920)
MARGATE N 63 NS ↙ Constantia Park P.O. Box 294 (4275)
MTUBATUBA N 67 C5 ← Mtuba Caravan Park P.O. Box 31 (3935)
Winchester Caravan Park P.O. Box 31 (3935)
MTUNZINI N 67 C4 ↘ ● Xaxaza Caravan Park, P.O. Box 101 (3867)
MTWALUME N 63 B3 → A T K B Beach Resort P.O. Box 7 (4186)
MURRAYSBURG C 61 C5 ↘ Municipal Caravan Park P.O. Box 336 (6995)
PAARL C 58 C3 ↘ ● Wateruintjiesvlei Municipal Camp Site P.O. Box 265 (7620)

PHILIPPOLIS O 62 B3 ↖ Van Rensburg's Dew Drop Caravan Park Voortrekker St. (9970)
POTGIETERSRUS T 69 B2 ↖ Tugela Mineral Springs (on the Botswana Border) Private Bag 2684 (0600)
PRETORIA T 68 C6 ↙ Kloof Pleasure Resort (20 km from Pretoria) P.O. De Wildt (0251)
Pretoria Spa Caravan Park (28 km from Pretoria), P.O. Box 301 (0001)
RUSTENBURG T 68 C5 ↘ Rustenburg Kloof Caravan Park P.O. Box 16 (0300)
SALT ROCK N 63 A4 ← Salt Rock Caravan Park P.O. Salt Rock 4391
SEDGEFIELD C 59 C2 ↗ Sedgefield Caravan Park P.O. Box 25 (6573)
ST. LUCIA N 67 C5 ↑ St. Lucia Travel Lodge and Caravan Park P.O. Box 4 (3936)
VIRGINIA O 66 C4 ↗ Virginia Park P.O. Box 4 (9430)
VRYBURG C 66 A2 ↘ Swartfontein Pleasure Resort P.O. Box 35 (8600)
WINKLESPRUIT N 63 NS ↗ ● Uitspan Caravan Park P.O. Box 71 (4145)

CARAVAN AND CAMPING CLUB ADDRESSES (as at date of publication)

CARAVAN CLUB OF SOUTH AFRICA

CENTRAL COUNCIL .... P O Box 50580, RANDBURG 2125
Tel. (011) 48-3336

REGIONS

ALFRED COUNTRY .... P O Box 349, PORT SHEPSTONE 4240

BORDER .... P O Box 388, EAST LONDON 5200

CAPE WESTERN .... "Raleigh House", 12 Raleigh Road, MOWBRAY 7700 Cape

EASTERN FREE STATE .... P O Box 100, GLEN HARMONY 9435

EASTERN PROVINCE .... 6 Willet Place, Fern Glen, PORT ELIZABETH 6001

EASTERN TRANSVAAL .... P O Box 2068, PRIMROSE 1416

FAR NORTHERN TRANSVAAL .... 38 Zebra Street, PIETERSBURG 0700

JOHANNESBURG AND DISTRICT .... 209 Rifle Range Road, ROBERTSHAM 2197

LOWVELD .... P O Box 1635, NELSPRUIT 1200

NATAL .... P O Box 315, KLOOF 3640

NATAL MIDLANDS .... P O Box 989, PIETERMARITZBURG 3200

NORTHERN CAPE .... P O Box 933, KIMBERLEY 8300

NORTHERN FREE STATE .... P O Box 427, WELKOM 9460

NORTHERN NATAL .... P O Box 1287, LADYSMITH 3370

NORTH RAND .... P O Box 50981, RANDBURG 2125

PRETORIA .... P O Box 26226, ARCADIA 0007

RUSTENBURG .... P O Box 1581, RUSTENBURG 0300

SOUTHERN CAPE .... P O Box 104, KNYSNA 6570

SOUTHERN FREE STATE .... P O Box 1983, BLOEMFONTEIN 9300

SOUTH WESTERN TRANSVAAL .... P O Box 316, ORKNEY 2620

VAAL TRIANGLE .... P O Box 1197, VEREENIGING 1930

WESTERN TRANSVAAL .... P O Box 319, CARLETONVILLE 2500

WEST RAND REGION .... 114, 7th Street, LINDEN, Johannesburg 2195

WITWATERSRAND EAST .... P O Box 177, BEDFORDVIEW 2008

CAMEO CARAVAN CLUB (for Coloured community) .... *Secretary* - George Merckel
12 Hexrivierberg Avenue, BOSMONT 2093, Tel. 27-2617

CAMP PRIDE OWNERS CLUB .... *Secretary* - 5 Fifth Avenue, Marlands, GERMISTON 1401

CAPE CARAVAN CLUB (for Coloured community) .... *Secretary* - Brian Bruyns
85 First Avenue, Fairways Estate, WYNBERG 7800

SA CAMPING CLUB .... *National Secretary* - Mr Ted Allbon,
P O Box 3731, DURBAN 4000

SUID-AFRIKAANSE WOONWA ASSOSIASIE / SOUTH AFRICAN CARAVAN ASSOCIATION .... P O Box 1346, EDENVALE 1610

TREKKERS OUTDOOR RECREATION CLUB .... *Secretary/ Treasurer* - D Estment
101 Bale Avenue, Woodlands, 4001 DURBAN
or
P O Box 4157, DURBAN 4000

Supplement to the AA OUTDOOR HOLIDAY GUIDE OF SOUTH AFRICA

(2nd Edition)

Keep in pocket provided on the inside back cover of the AA Outdoor Holiday Guide.

The availability of revised editions of this supplement (for which an additional nominal charge will be made) will be announced in the AA quarterly magazine "The Motorist".

Information listed in this supplement concerning the various categories of establishments is for the benefit and convenience of users and does not imply that the establishments or the facilities they offer are either recommended, graded or inspected by the AA. The onus is on users to satisfy themselves, when booking, that the facilities offered will meet their requirements.

CHANGES TO ROAD SURFACES

The following notes are provided for the benefit of members who possess copies of the 1st Edition of the AA Outdoor Holiday Guide of South Africa. The information given is ancilliary to and should be read in conjunction with the respective 6-colour maps included in the guide to enable users to determine what changes, of significance, have occurred to the road information as shown in the guide since it was last printed.

The information is listed as follows:

1 The page number of the map is given, followed by descriptive notes on affected roads falling within the boundaries of the map.
2 Each description is preceded by a letter and a number e.g. (B4) which indicates the respective degree square within which the road described can be found.
3 The descriptions are graded according to road classifications (see map reference on page 57).

By using the information thus provided, users will be able to amend the maps in their book to reflect the correct position as at the date of publication of this supplement.

PAGE 58

Main Roads

(C3) — There is a new tarred road connecting the KOEBERG NUCLEAR POWER STATION with the West Coast road to the east of Koeberg.

(C6) — KOUP/MERWEVILLE — this is a main gravel road and no construction work is in progress.

(D4) — PEARLY BEACH/HOTAGTERKLIP — there is no direct road between these places — use the road from PEARLY BEACH via ELIM to reach HOTAGTERKLIP.

(D5) — BREDASDORP/SWELLENDAM — tarred.

Secondary Roads

(C4) — There is no connecting road from TULBAGH to the CITRUSDAL/PRINCE ALFRED HAMLET road as is incorrectly shown on the map.

(C6) — The secondary road which extends from VOORBAAT in a south-easterly direction and connects with the junction of the LADISMITH/BARRYDALE and LADISMITH/RIVERSDALE roads is now tarred.

PAGE 59

Dual Carriageways

(C4,C5) — The new N2 national road is open from PORT ELIZABETH to KAREEDOUW.

Main Roads

(A4) — ABERDEEN/ABERDEEN ROAD — tarred for 20 km from ABERDEEN — thereafter gravel with no construction work in progress.

(B1,B2) — CALITZDORP/MATJIESRIVIER — this is an untarred main road and no construction work is in progress.

(B2) — PRINCE ALBERT/KLAARSTROOM — tarred.

(B2) — The road from BUFFELSKLIP via BARANDAS to UNIONDALE is now tarred.

(B2) — BUFFELSKLIP/ROOIRIVIER — under construction for tarring.

(B3) — WILLOWMORE/VONDELING — main gravel road and no construction work in progress.

(C1) — JOHNSON'S POST/VLEESBAAI — tarred.

GARDEN ROUTE INSET MAP

Main Roads

HOEKWIL/WOODVILLE — tarred

RUIGTEVLEI/KARATARA — tarred

PAGE 60

EAST COAST MAP

Dual Carriageways

(B2) — EAST LONDON/BERLIN — the road bypasses BERLIN on the northern side.

Trunk Roads

(B1,B2,B3) — CATHCART/STUTTERHEIM/KING WILLIAM'S TOWN — Reconstruction work is in progress and will go on for several years. The alternative recommended route from QUEENSTOWN to EAST LONDON is via WHITTLESEA/SEYMOUR/FORT BEAUFORT.

Main Roads

(B1) — FORT BEAUFORT/SEYMOUR — the tarred road is via LOWER BLINKWATER and from there to SEYMOUR — not as shown on the map.

(B1) — ALICE/HOGSBACK — 14 km of tar from ALICE with construction work being done on the remaining section.

(B2) — STUTTERHEIM/AMABELE — tarred. Thereafter construction work in progress towards KEI ROAD.

(C2) — CROSSROADS/PEDDIE — not tarred.

Secondary Roads

(B2) — The secondary road from FORT JACKSON does not join the main tarred road to the south.

INSET MAP

(A4) — PORT ST JOHNS — pont operates daily from 06 h 00 — 20 h 00. No charge.

WEST COAST MAP

Main Roads

(A5) — STEINKOPF/PORT NOLLOTH — tarred.

(A5) — SPRINGBOK/POFADDER — work has commenced for tarring of this road, which will be a long-term project.

(C6) — LUTZVILLE via LOSSAND to VREDENDAL — tarred.

PAGE 61

Main Roads

(A4,A5) — PRIESKA/DOUGLAS — tarred from PRIESKA with 35 km of untarred road before DOUGLAS.

(A4,B4) — PRIESKA/SODIUM — tarred for 30 km from PRIESKA whereafter this road joins the main PRIESKA/BRITSTOWN road.

(B1,C1) — LOERIESFONTEIN/NIEUWOUDTVILLE — tarred, but work in progress on approximately 10 km of road at halfway mark.

(B4,B5) — CARNARVON/VOSBURG/BRITSTOWN — 15 km of tarred road from CARNARVON — remainder gravel with no construction work in progress.

(B5) — DE AAR — work in progress on southern bypass.

(C1) — CALVINIA/DIE BOS — untarred gravel road.

(C2,C3) — WILLISTON/FRASERBURG — 26 km of tarred road from WILLISTON followed by gravel and then 10 km of tar into FRASERBURG.

PAGE 62

Trunk Roads

(B2) — DE AAR — construction work in progress on southern bypass.

(B3,C2) — COLESBERG/HANOVER/RICHMOND — road can be used but construction work is in progress — this is a long-term project.

(D5) — BRIDGECAMP/COFIMVABA — construction completed and road tarred.

Main Roads

(B3) — COLESBERG/NORVALSPONT — there is no link road between this road and the national road at the ORANGE RIVER as is incorrectly shown on the map.

(B6) — KINIRA DRIFT — a short section of road through the drift is tarred.

(C3,D3) — HOFMEYR/CRADOCK — tarred.

(C3,C4) — HOFMEYR/TARKASTAD — short section tarred from CRADOCK/TARKASTAD road junction — remainder gravel with no construction work in progress towards HOFMEYR.

(C4,C5) — PENHOEK PASS/DORDRECHT — first 20 km of road from PENHOEK PASS tarred — construction work in progress on the remaining section.

(C5,C6) — ELLIOT/UGIE — tarred.

(C6) — UGIE/MACLEAR — construction work in progress.

(C6) — MACLEAR/SOUTH EASTERN TRANSKEI BORDER — tarred.

Secondary Roads

(A5) — VAN ROOYEN'S GATE/MAFEKING — tarred.

PAGE 63 AND INSET MAP

Dual Carriageways

(A3,A4) — OUTER RING ROAD (DURBAN WESTERN BYPASS) — this road is not shown on the map, but is open from UMDLOTI BEACH in the north and joins the SOUTHERN FREEWAY at LOUIS BOTHA AIRPORT.

(B3) — Construction work on the SOUTHERN FREEWAY is in progress between SCOTTBURGH and PARK RYNIE.

(B3) — THE SOUTHERN FREEWAY is completed from PARK RYNIE to HIBBERDENE.

Main Roads

(A3) — LIONS RIVER/DARGLE — 11 km of tar from main road with construction work in progress on remaining 22 km.

(A3) — FAWNLEAS/MOUNT ELIAS — tarred.

(A3) — RICHMOND — work in progress on construction of western bypass.

(A3) — VERULAM/INANDA — approximately 15 km of road tarred from VERULAM — thereafter construction work.

(C2) — PORT ST JOHNS — pont operates daily from 06 h 00 to 20 h 00. No charge.

Secondary Roads

(A3) — THORNVILLE JUNCTION/ESTON — 8 km of road tarred from THORNVILLE.

Continued on inside back cover →

SUPPLEMENT TO THE AA OUTDOOR HOLIDAY GUIDE OF SOUTH AFRICA

2nd Edition

(ISBN 0 909234 25 6 – Afrikaanse uitgawe ISBN 0 909234 24 8)

INDEX

COMPILED AND PUBLISHED BY THE AUTOMOBILE ASSOCIATION OF SOUTH AFRICA
(Incorporated Association not for Gain)

Every effort has been made to ensure the accuracy of the information contained in this supplement but the AA cannot accept responsibility for any errors or omissions which may occur. The AA will be indebted to members who point out any inaccuracies.
Please send details to:
The Director-General
The Automobile Association of South Africa
P.O. Box 596 Johannesburg 2000

HIERDIE BYVOEGSEL IS OOK IN AFRIKAANS BESKIKBAAR

INTRODUCTION

This supplement contains the most comprehensive information of its kind available in South Africa and provides details on a wide selection of outdoor accommodation for a happy and successful holiday.

The information listed is believed to be correct at the time of publication but should be verified when booking as changes occur during the currency of the supplement and it is not possible to convey such changes to users before publication of the next edition. The supplement will be updated periodically and the availability of subsequent editions will be announced through the medium of the AA's quarterly magazine, "The Motorist".

In order to achieve maximum benefit from this guide, please familiarise yourself with the following information.

OUTDOOR HOLIDAY GUIDE

This supplement is designed for use in conjunction with the six colour maps included in the Outdoor Holiday Guide. The key map for these is reproduced below and will enable easy identification and location of the relevant map spread in which you may be interested.

Consult the map reference in the Outdoor Holiday Guide and familiarise yourself with the symbols included on the maps, particularly at towns — it will be seen that towns providing facilities for caravaners have been shown by circles in which the outer circle has either a red or a yellow filling.

As the information in this supplement has been prepared subsequent to the 6 colour maps, it is possible that not all towns will be indicated in this way on the maps.

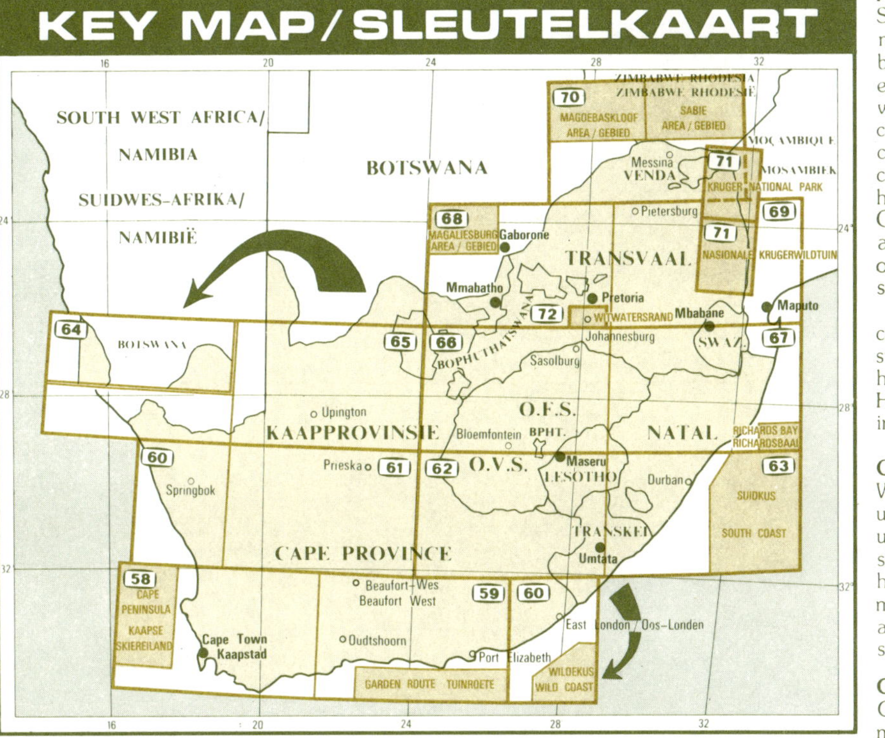

Route Planning

The existence of tarred, untarred and sections of road under construction are visually depicted on the maps in the guide. Normally it is not advisable to tow a caravan for any great distance on untarred roads, but where this is unavoidable, users should make enquiries locally as to the condition of such roads before venturing forth.

Reference to the section on Mountain Passes is advisable as the information given will assist the user in avoiding passes which are unsuitable for caravans. Please also note that caravans are only permitted on tarred roads within the Kruger National Park.

The town plans included in the guide will assist travellers in finding their way through towns and will, in several instances, show the location of some of the caravan parks. Local authorities are gradually erecting signposts to caravan parks and camping sites within towns and along the main routes. Watch for the appropriate signs when travelling.

Place Names Index — see Outdoor Holiday Guide — pages 97-101.

A detailed place names index, arranged in alphabetical sequence, is included in the Outdoor Holiday Guide and will be of assistance in identifying and locating places. In this regard, reference to the supplement will indicate what caravan parks or camping sites are available at such places or in the more popular areas within close proximity.

The grid reference included will, in turn, enable the user to locate these places on the six colour maps.

Alphabetical List of Establishments

A comprehensive list of all caravan parks/camping sites included in this supplement will be found on page 14 and 15.

Early Booking

Advance bookings may be made at some of the sites listed in the supplement. These have been marked for the benefit of the user and because outdoor holidays are becoming increasingly popular, it is always wise to book well in advance, in some instances as much as a year ahead, especially for coastal and mountain resorts, during the main seasons. Unless you do this your holiday could get off to a bad start. Although it pays to book for the popular coastal parks during school holidays, you don't normally have to book for every step of your journey. You will then be free to move on if a particular spot doesn't appeal to you, as deposits are not usually required. Fees are paid in advance on a per night basis.

When booking, check whether the reservation is for a particular stand or not as advance booking does not necessarily guarantee the best stands. Some parks merely admit a fixed number of people who have to select from the stands available on arrival. It is wise to check with each establishment whether the caravan/camping equipment you intend using is acceptable. Give details of the size of your caravan, the number of persons in your party, your expected time of arrival and length of stay.

Always verify tariffs when booking as these are subject to change without prior notice. Check as to acceptable arrival and departure times particularly insofar as game and nature reserves are concerned, as closing times of gates are strictly enforced.

Site Rules and/or Conditions

These vary from one establishment to another and it is always wise to ascertain from the owner/manager on arrival what these are.

Additional Accommodation Facilities

Some caravan parks offer extra accommodation for hire on site in the form of bungalows, chalets, cottages, rondavels etc. Where applicable, these are listed, with tariffs, in this supplement — see columns 53, 54, 55 and 56. Several caravan parks have fully-equipped caravans for hire on site — see column 59 headed "Caravans to Rent on Site" in the Caravan Park/Camping Site list and also refer to the separate section on "Caravans for Hire on Site" in the supplement.

Firms which offer caravans and/or campmobiles for hire are listed in the supplement under the respective headings of "Trailer Caravans for Hire" and "Campmobiles for Hire" — see index for page numbers.

Camping Sites

While caravan parks are primarily for the use of caravaners, most will permit campers using modern equipment. Where camping sites are available at caravan parks, these have been suitably marked in the supplement. Bear in mind however, that such parks are more likely to accept campers out of season.

Gas

Gas is available at almost every town and most oil companies encourage their garage outlets to provide this service — hardware stores generally are equipped for this purpose as well. The cost of filling a cylinder varies from place to place, with coastal centres being cheaper. When a cylinder is refilled, the customer should only be charged for the actual amount of gas added to the cylinder to bring it to the required mass, but some suppliers charge a flat rate depending on the capacity of the cylinder, regardless of how much gas is actually supplied. The customer must ensure that he is not overcharged.

Telephone and Postal Codes

These have been included where applicable throughout.

Complaints

Always address complaints to the owner/manager of the establishment concerned. If no satisfaction is obtained, please write promptly and give full details for possible investigation to:

The Director-General, The Automobile Association of South Africa, P.O. Box 596, Johannesburg 2000.

AA OFFICES

HEAD OFFICE: AA House, 66 De Korte St., Braamfontein, Johannesburg (2001).
P.O. Box 596, Johannesburg (2000) Telephone: 28-1400, Telegrams: "FANUMHEAD"

AREA AND REGIONAL OFFICES

Office	Area or Region	Address	Phone	Box No.	Postal Code
Bloemfontein	OFS and Northern Cape	AA House, 56 Church St. (9301)	7-6191	547	(9300)
Cape Town	Cape Western	AA House, 7 Martin Hammerschlag Way, Foreshore (8001)	21-1550	70	(8000)
Durban	Natal	AA House, 537 Smith St. (4001)	6-0341	242	(4000)
East London	Border and Midlands	AA House, 3a Terminus St. (5201)	2-1271	253	(5200)
Johannesburg	Southern Transvaal	AA House, 66 De Korte St., Braamfontein (2001)	28-1400	7118 (Jhb)	(2000)
	City Office	Trust Bank Centre (ground floor), cor. Main and Von Brandis Sts. (2001)	21-5852	7118 (Jhb)	(2000)
Port Elizabeth	Eastern Province	AA House, 2 Rink St. (6001)	2-8184	Centrahill 12320	(6006)
Pretoria	Northern Transvaal	AA House, 395 Schoeman St. (0002)	48-3829	477	(0001)
Windhoek	South West Africa/ Namibia Region	Carl List Haus, cor. Kaiser and Peter Müller Sts.	2-4201	61	(9100)

The telegraphic address of all area/regional offices is "FANUM" followed by the name of the city concerned.

BRANCH OFFICES

Office	Address	Phone	Box No.	Postal Code
Auckland Park, Johannesburg	AA Patrol Depot, 44 Stanley Ave.	726-7811	7118 (Jhb)	(2000)
Bedfordview	U33A Eastgate Centre, Cumberland Rd.	616-3001	7118 (Jhb)	(2000)
Bellville	4c Anstey Centre, Teddington St.	97-2593	418	(7530)
Benoni	Lorna Court, 15 Rothsay St.	54-6381	148	(1500)
Bethlehem	30a Oxford St.	4800	152	(9700)
Boksburg	4 Pretoria St.	52-7781	278	(1460)
Brakpan	641 Voortrekker Rd.	55-8373	166	(1540)
Carletonville	87 Annan Rd.	6641	269	(2500)
Ermelo	9 Trust Bank Arcade, Joubert St.	3255	642	(2350)
Florida	Henshell House, 10 Goldman St.	674-1957	19	(1710)
George	Millwood Bldg., cor. York and Victoria Sts.	3041	130	(6530)
Germiston	186 Meyer St. (1401)	825-5170	484	(1400)
Grahamstown	Publicity Assoc. Bldg., 63 High St.	2481	461	(6140)
Kempton Park	West St. Arcade, 37 West St.	970-1481	178	(1620)
Kimberley	3 Stockdale St. (8301)	2-5207	397	(8300)
Klerksdorp	Clarasan Chambers, cor. Boom and Emily Hobhouse Sts.	2-4781	821	(2570)
Krugersdorp	3 President Bldg., Monument St.	660-7101	537	(1740)
Kruger National Park	Skukuza Rest Camp*	13	13	(1350)
	(*AA Emergency Service Centre)	13	13	(1350)
Nelspruit	56 Brown St.	4631	186	(1200)
Newcastle	10 Permanent Plaza, 58 Scott St.	2-1910	2258	(2940)
Paarl	Arcade, Backmin Centre, 39 Lady Grey St. (7646)	2-5634	382	(7620)
Pietermaritzburg	NAU Bldg., cor. Buchanan and Carbineer Sts. (3201)	2-0571	88	(3200)
Pietersburg	Talmot Bldg., Schoeman St.	7-1442	7	(0700)
Pinetown	8 Nedbank Centre, 33 Hill St.	72-9701	301	(3600)
Port Shepstone	35a Wooley St.	2-2503	172	(4240)
Potchefstroom	Johan Dreyer Bldg., cor. Kerk and Potgieter Sts.	5434	397	(2520)
Queenstown	114 Cathcart Rd.	4008	109	(5320)

BRANCH OFFICES

Office	Address	Phone	Box No.	Postal Code
Randburg	79 Crossroads Shopping Centre, Hendrik Verwoerd Drive (2194)	789-1529	P/Bag X3030	(2125)
Rustenburg	146 Smit St.	2-6225	1088	(0300)
Sasolburg	102 Münchner Haus, Civic Centre	6-4572	639	(9570)
Selby, Johannesburg	AA Technical Centre, 22 Sauer St. Ext.	734-6451	7118 (Jhb)	(2000)
Springs	Wima Court, cor. Fourth St. and Fifth Ave.	812-2253	940	(1560)
Upington	Joe Kowen Bldg., 46 Scott St.	4701	83	(8800)
Vanderbijlpark	UBS Bldg., Eric Louw St.	33-1834	480	(1900)
Vereeniging	Etosha Bldg., 9b Leslie St.	22-5651	833	(1930)
Welkom	AA House, 327 Stateway	2-4231	741	(9460)
Witbank	Westra Bldg., cor. Haig and Paul Kruger Sts.	6-1231	339	(1035)

The telegraphic address of all branch offices is "FANUM" followed by the name of the city or town concerned.

AA MUTUAL SUB-OFFICES

Office	Address	Phone	Box No.	Postal Code
Beaufort West	1st Floor, Trust Bank Bldg., Donkin St.	4018	131	(6970)
Kroonstad	17 Fairweather Heights, 25 Brand St.	2-4423	92	(9500)
Ladysmith	NBS Bldg., 174 Murchison St.	6866	17	(3370)
Nylstroom	Rentmeester Bldg. Arcade, 88 Potgieter St.	2269	258	(0510)
Stellenbosch	Trust Bank Centre, Andringa St.	7-0230	369	(7600)
Uitenhage	AA Mutual Centre, Rich St.	2-6014	44	(6230)
Worcester	10 Quenets Arcade, High St.	2-2457	135	(6850)

The telegraphic address of all AA Mutual sub-offices is "AUTOMUTUAL" followed by the name of the town concerned

AA TECHNICAL CENTRES

AA Technical Centres can be found at all area offices and most branch offices. The following are housed in separate premises at the addresses given hereunder:

Office	Address	Phone	Box No.	Postal Code
Durban	56 Alexandra St. (4001)	31-5808 2-6610	242	(4000)
Johannesburg	22 Sauer St. Ext., Selby (2001)	834-6451	7118	(2000)
Pretoria	577 Voortrekker Rd., Gezina (0084)	76-1138	477	(0001)

OFFICE HOURS

All AA offices are open during the following hours:

Weekdays .... 08 h 30 - 17 h 00
Saturdays .... 08 h 30 - 12 h 30

Emergency breakdown service may be obtained after office hours (i.e. at night, during weekends and on public holidays) from the following offices by telephone:

Bloemfontein	**7-6191**	**Durban**	**6-0341**	**Port Elizabeth**	**2-8184**
Cape Town	**21-1550**	**Johannesburg**	**726-4230**	**Pretoria**	**48-3829**

AA SERVICES

"Is it really necessary and worthwhile?" and "I have been a member for years and have never used any of its services". A question and a statement not infrequently heard when the Automobile Association is discussed by motorists and AA members.

To this question the AA can give a resounding "Yes, certainly" and the statement is easily put in perspective after the member uttering it has been enlightened as to what he has been missing.

There are those members who support the Association largely because of what it does to further and protect the interests of motorists. And that they need protection in this age when as a sector of the community they are heavily overtaxed, cannot be gainsaid. But the member who is doubtful about the value of AA membership has not taken the trouble to read his AA Handbook, issued to him annually on renewal of membership.

Listed in that book he will find reference to the most extensive and useful range of motoring services and aids available to him to ease his cost burden. And at the modest annual subscription of only R8 a year. Put another way: the cost of a daily newspaper a day for 12 months, will cost him more than five times the annual AA subscription. Just one Sunday paper throughout the year will mean twice the AA subscription – leap years excluded!

But proof of the value of membership of the largest and most effective motoring organisation on the African continent can be seen by the fact that the AA of South Africa is supported by more than half a million members.

What are these unparalleled services?

THE CAR THAT CONKS IN

What motorist can claim that his car – used or new – has not left him in the lurch at some time or other, often at the most inconvenient moment. If it happens on the congested city street where "time is money", not only to you but to others held up by your broken down vehicle, help is only a telephone call away if you are an AA member.

In the metropolitan areas like Johannesburg, Cape Town, Durban, Pretoria, Port Elizabeth, Bloemfontein and East London the AA has a radio-controlled service which will bring a patrol to the scene of a breakdown, any time of the day or night, well within the hour – unless weather or other conditions are extremely unfavourable.

In towns or in the country car trouble during office hours need not be expensive if the cause of the breakdown is a minor electrical or mechanical failure – regularly encountered in used and new cars. The AA patrol specialises in diagnosing and fixing the "little troubles" which can spoil your day.

In country areas the AA has contracts with more than 500 garages, appointed to render tow-in services to stranded members. They are situated throughout the Republic, South West Africa/Namibia, Transkei and BophuthaTswana. This service counts among those "unknowns" which a great number of members, despite many years' membership, do not use to their benefit. They seem unaware that a refund of the tow-in service charges can be claimed from the AA as soon as the necessary supporting documents are submitted. The AA Handbook clearly sets out the way in which the tow-in vouchers, forming an integral part of the book, are to be used.

USING THE AA TECHNICAL SERVICES

Many of the AA's caravaners are among those who seem unaware of the ways in which they can consult the Association, free of charge, or use the available technical services which will assist them in planning and enjoying a trouble-free outdoor holiday. Car and caravan can be examined before the holiday – at a nominal charge – and expert advice given on a variety of technical problems. This includes roadworthiness, maintenance or the determination of values prior to sale or purchase.

BOOKING PROBLEMS

At the time of going to press with this supplement there was a marked upward trend in the number of overseas visitors to South Africa. An interesting aspect is that more and more people who have visited us before as individuals, will now bring their families. This could mean keener competition for South Africans who need hotel accommodation, holiday flats, caravan sites, motel and holiday bookings or guest farms.

Once again the road leads to the nearest AA office, or telephone. Provided the holiday is planned early the AA will secure the necessary accommodation for the member through one of its more than 50 offices.

EMERGENCIES

Holidays need careful budgeting and any emergency which will result in a drain on your holiday cash, could wreck your period "away from it all". While you will have peace of mind when it comes to minor breakdowns, because you are assured of AA patrol or AA-appointed garage assistance, major car trouble could be costly. The preventive here is AA emergency aid vouchers. Worth up to R150, they will take care of emergency car or caravan repairs, tow-in service charges, unforeseen medical expenses and other items. Repayments after your holiday are easily arranged with your AA office.

INSURANCE

Not only the caravan (and its contents if you so wish) may be insured by way of a special AA policy at better than generally competitive rates (see page 4 for details) but you should inquire about AA travel insurance schemes covering medical, baggage, personal accident and loss of deposits.

LEGAL PROBLEMS

By prior arrangement with any AA office members can obtain legal advice from AA-appointed attorneys (the first consultation is free) on any matters arising directly out of the use/ownership of a private motor vehicle.

Free legal defence is provided in any action where a principle is involved which affects the interests of the motoring community as a whole.

MAPS

"I know my way about" are some of the famous last words chronicled. New freeways, national roads, road works which seem to go on endlessly, sudden weather changes, and a multitude of other changing "conditions" bedevil a journey. The AA can smooth the road for you from home to destination, and back, through its unrivalled range of comprehensive maps, map brochures, touring bulletins and information literature which, by and large, are available free.

GOING ABROAD

Tourist traffic is not one-way. Thousands of South Africans still go abroad every year in spite of the high inclusive cost of touring abroad. Check with the AA on the assistance it can give you in a variety of ways. The Association will help you hire a motorised caravan or car, with or without a trailer, in Britain or on the continent. It will also arrange international camping carnets, international driving permits and introductions to affiliated motoring organisations for you.

BEATING COSTS

On the home front the AA offers its members the advantages of the AA Car, Home and Leisure Plan. This plan provides financial facilities to purchase a caravan, a combi-type vehicle, a motor-boat, a yacht, sailing dinghy or boat trailer. The scheme offers benefits such as substantially lower hire-purchase finance charges, lower monthly repayments, the advantages of a cash buy and automatic settlement of unpaid balance of instalments in the event of the death of the buyer (age limit 18-59). Cars, tennis courts, colour television sets, home improvements and many other items can be paid for with the financial assistance provided under the scheme.

EVERYDAY MOTORING AIDS

A first aid kit, fire extinguishers, battery cables to start a recalcitrant car, tow ropes, snake-bite outfits, travel bags, ignition drier kits and engine tyre pumps are some of the other motoring items available at all AA offices at special prices to members.

Whether you travel or holiday locally or abroad, the AA is there to help you to plan and enjoy your holiday, indoors or outdoors. If you can think of any other motoring service which we have not thought of, call, telephone or write and we shall consider its introduction.

INSURANCE AND THE CARAVANER

There's a fortune to be made by someone who could design and market a crystal ball which will reveal when and where misfortune will strike. But is it ever likely to happen? Not in this century and probably not in the next one either. In the meantime fortunes will be lost by people who are not insured or not adequately insured — yes, it does cost a fortune at today's inflationary prices to replace possessions like a car and caravan and all the equipment that the ardent caravaner acquires over a period of time. One thing is therefore clear: insurance is vital and it can be obtained at reasonable premiums.

What kind of insurance should you have? Depending upon your circumstances there might be several different items which need to be insured. First of all there is the house — if it is your own. You never know what might happen while you are away on holiday — so make sure you have a house owner's policy to cover you against damage or loss arising from floods, storms, lightning, fire, etc. The premium is nominal and is usually paid to the building society with the bond repayments but it is just as well to check on this — and don't stop the insurance when the bond is fully repaid.

Householder's Policy

The householder's policy covers the contents of the house or flat, outbuildings etc. A variety of different policies are available and some of them like the AA Jumbo policy cover not only the contents of the house (including furs, jewellery, clothing, etc.) but also the contents of deep freezers, veterinary fees for injured pets, accidental damage to television and hi-fi sets, motor-cars, personal accident, and so on. Remember it is unwise and unnecessary to under-insure. To spread the financial burden, the premium in respect of combination policies can be paid in monthly instalments.

Having satisfied yourself that all the items at home will be fully insured when you go away, you can now think about insuring the things you will take on holiday with you. So let's begin with the car or towing unit or the motorised caravan. Third party insurance is compulsory and failure to display a valid third party disc renders you liable to the payment of a fine, even if you have obtained the necessary disc and the insurance declaration which goes with it.

AA Breakdown Insurance Policy

This is a new type of insurance which has only recently become available in South Africa. It is the sort of insurance you need when the manufacturers' or dealers' warranty or guarantee expires. Ordinary comprehensive motor policies exclude repair costs arising from mechanical or electrical failure and it is basically these exclusions which are covered by the AA breakdown insurance policy. Repairs to the engine, transmission, steering, brakes, generator/alternator etc. up to a maximum of R1 500 but excluding the first 15% to 25% of the cost of repairs are covered. Before cover can be given, the car must be inspected and passed by the AA Technical Department. Cars not older than 5 years can be insured and policies may be taken out initially for a period of one or two years.

Comprehensive Insurance

Also consider comprehensive motor insurance. Here you have a choice of ordinary comprehensive motor insurance policies, combination motor insurance policies (like the AA Jumbo policy which covers the car, household goods etc.) or balance of third party policies with or without fire and theft cover. Balance of third party policies usually cost less than comprehensive policies. This is understandable as damage to the car is not covered — fire and theft risks can however be covered by paying an additional premium. Most comprehensive policies provide cover for the car while a caravan or trailer is being towed but it is just as well to satisfy yourself that your are fully covered on this point.

From an insurance point of view a caravan — whether it be the trailer type or motorised type — is just another vehicle. Two different basic types of insurance are applicable — third party, which is compulsory for all vehicles, and comprehensive. Fortunately the third party premium for trailer caravans is much lower than the premium for cars, LDVs, etc.

Special AA Caravan Policy

Comprehensive insurance premiums for trailer caravans are also generally lower than they are for motorised vehicles, the premium for the special AA caravan insurance policy being particularly low. It is available exclusively to AA members for their own private caravans — not hired caravans — but not for motorised caravans. Main features of the special AA caravan policy are:

- ☐ the caravan with its fittings and fixtures, tents, awnings and equipment as supplied by the manufacturer is fully covered against loss or damage – except for the first R50 of any claim. As with other comprehensive policies, mechanical and electrical breakdowns, wear and tear etc. are not covered.
- ☐ the policy-holder is covered against claims by third parties (excluding claims by employees or members of the insured's family) for bodily injury, damage to property, etc.
- ☐ the contents of the caravan – i.e. clothing, personal effects, bedding, crockery, cameras, sporting equipment, etc. but not firearms, furs and jewellery can be covered against loss or damage upon payment of an additional premium. Individual items with a value of more than R100 must be specified. Cameras, binoculars, portable radios sporting equipment and other similar items are however only covered against loss or damage consequent upon forcible and violent entry into the locked caravan. Except for this, cover is not restricted to articles inside the caravan – they are also protected as long as they are within the confines of the erected side tent section/s. All claims under this section of the policy are subject to a R50 excess.
- ☐ the caravan may be loaned or hired out to a member of the insured's family residing with him but if loaned or hired out to any other person, there is a premium loading of 50%.
- ☐ the insured may authorise repairs not exceeding R100 provided a detailed estimate is first obtained and immediately forwarded to the AA Mutual.
- ☐ the policy is operative throughout the Republic of South Africa, Botswana, Lesotho, Malawi, South West Africa/ Namibia, Swaziland, Zimbabwe Rhodesia, Transkei, BophuthaTswana and Venda.

Personal Risks

Comprehensive motor policies and combination motor policies provide a certain amount of cover in respect of medical expenses arising from accidents but not from sudden serious illness. Certain travel and holiday insurance policies such as the "AA Travelflex Policy" provide cover against medical and other expenses following an accident or illness, loss of deposits through illness or accident, loss of baggage and personal effects and accidental death.

THE SOUTH AFRICAN YOUTH HOSTELS ASSOCIATION

Over 60 years ago, a man named Richard Schirrman founded the first Youth Hostel Association in Germany. From very humble beginnings, the movement spread rapidly to other countries and in due course to America, Australia, Asia and Africa. Today the Association embraces over 50 countries and enjoys its greatest popularity in Europe where it originated.

Internationally, the movement boasts over 6 000 hostels and exceeds four million members. The extent to which youth hostels are promoted and the very definite need which they fill in the lives of everyday people, can be gauged by the "overnight" figures of 7½ million a year recorded by the Deutsche Jugendherbergen (German Youth Hostels Association). It is thus one of the largest travel clubs in the world and helps to promote international understanding and friendship while providing facilities to enable visitors to become familiar with the host country.

Youth Hostels in South Africa

The Youth Hostels movement in South Africa was founded in 1953, following publication of a letter in a local newspaper by a South African who had used the facilities overseas. Branches were established in various large cities and the South African Youth Hostels Association was finally brought into being in 1955. This Association, like those in other countries, is run on a non-profit basis and the hostels in South Africa are managed independently.

The accommodation offered is provided at cost-price largely because of the devotion of voluntary workers and in some cases, from grants made by generous donors.

Aims

The Youth Hostels Association helps people, young and old, of limited means, to travel inexpensively by providing hostel accommodation where members can stay the night at a reasonable price. It further endeavours to help all, but especially young people, to a better understanding of one another, and to a greater knowledge, love and care of our country.

What hostels are like

Some of the attraction of youth hostels is the variety of accommodation used by the Youth Hostels Association. Places range from huts and farm-houses to mansions and even castles. All provide separate accommodation for men and women, cooking facilities (many provide meals) and a common-room where hostellers can get together to chat, read and meet socially. Beds, mattresses, blankets and pillows are provided, but each hosteller *must* provide his own sheets and pillow-case, or a sheet-sleeping bag. These sheet-sleeping bags can also be hired from the hostels. Down sleeping bags are NOT permitted. Each hostel is supervised by a warden who ensures that a high standard of behaviour is maintained. Because of the low cost of staying at hostels, members may be requested to assist with certain chores.

How to join

Obtain and complete an application form and send it to your nearest branch of the Youth Hostels Association or to the National Secretary (see address list following). Enclose a stamped, self-addressed envelope for a reply. Allow at least seven days for the membership card to be sent to you and please mark your application URGENT if leaving South Africa within 10 days of application. Membership can also be obtained from the wardens at hostels.

Membership

NB A membership card is essential for use of the hostels and may be obtained anywhere within the Youth Hostels Movement.

i	International (Validity - from October 1st for 15 months)	R13,50
ii	SA Senior (Validity - from October 1st for 15 months)	R 3,00
iii	Life Membership (South African)	R11,00
iv	Group — Groups wishing to use Youth Hostels Association facilities may make application for a Leader Card (valid for 10 members). The group MUST comprise *bona fide* organisations and not individuals wishing to make up parties.	

Applications for Leader Cards can be made to the local secretary of the Association. The names of persons utilising these cards must be given to the warden on signing into a hostel. Groups should make arrangements with the hostel warden well in advance so as to afford adequate time for catering arrangements.

Minimum age

The lower age limit in South Africa is 5 years and all children under the age of 17 must be accompanied by an adult. There is no upper age limit in South Africa.

Hostel Charges (usually increased by 20c a year)

At present these are R1,20 per person per night inclusive of bed, blanket and pillow. Members must provide their own sheet-sleeping bag or it can be hired at the hostel. There is no charge for the use of the kitchen, but a fee per meal is payable where these are provided at larger hostels.

Booking

Booking is not essential during the winter season in South Africa, but is advisable in summer. Telephone a few days in advance or write to the warden of the particular hostel enclosing a stamped, self-addressed envelope for reply.

Cancellations
Cancellation of bookings should be sent to the hostel concerned as soon as possible to avoid other hostellers being turned away unnecessarily.

Equipment
Travel as lightly as possible. If hiking, use a steel-framed rucksack. It is advisable to carry a copy of the IYHA handbook.

Cuisine
A range of typically South African dishes are provided and much of the food is similar to that of Europe.

Special interests
All sports and hobbies are catered for.

Language
The two official languages, English and Afrikaans, are used.

Travelling
Most hostellers resort to hiking, cycling or public transport to get from one place to another. Although motoring and motorcycling are not normally associated with youth hostelling, some continental countries admit motorists. However, preference is always given to non-motorists.

Regulations
Rules in force at youth hostels are minimal and are intended for the comfort and enjoyment of all concerned. A list of these rules is contained in the IYHA handbook and hostellers are expected to cheerfully co-operate, as indeed they normally do.

The following are of particular interest and should be noted:

1 Hostels are closed between 10 h 00 and 17 h 00. Members may only stay in hostels between these hours in exceptional cases and with the permission of the warden.

2 Members arriving after 22 h 00 are likely to be refused admission unless permission has been obtained from the warden.

3 Normally members may not stay more than three consecutive nights in one hostel unless beds are available and then only at the warden's discretion.

4 No animals or pets are permitted in hostels.

ADDRESSES OF YOUTH HOSTELS IN SOUTH AFRICA

The numbers in brackets following each name indicate the map page and grid reference where the place may be located.

National Office Address
6th Floor, Boston House, Strand Street, Cape Town 8001. Tel. 43-5693 OR
National Secretary, PO Box 4402, CAPE TOWN 8000

CAPE

1 **Beaufort West** (59 A2 ↑)
Donkin House, 14 Donkin Street. Postal Code 6970 Telephone 4287
This is not a youth hostel and no special rates are available to hostellers — apply for tariffs.
All rooms fully furnished.

2 **Cape Town** (58 C3 ↓)
Stan's Halt Youth Hostel, The Glen, Camps Bay. Postal Code 8001 Telephone 48-9037
Take Bus No. 3 (Kloof Nek) and follow sign down hill. Thirty beds; cooking facilities

3 **Cradock** (59 A5 ↑)
Mountain Zebra National Park, National Parks Board, PO Box 787, Pretoria 0001
Telephone 44-1194
2 x 2 bedrooms and 2 x 25 bedrooms. Accommodation available for groups of 15 people.
No cooking facilities. R1,90 per adult per night; R0,90 per child per night.

4 **East London** (60 B2↘)
Port Rex Youth Hostel, 128 Moore Street, Eastern Beach. Postal Code 5201 Telephone 8-7515
R1,50 per person per night; cooking facilities available.

5 **Hartenbos** (59 C2↖)
ATKV Camp, Cape of Good Hope Avenue. Postal Code 6520 Telephone 5107
Rooms and rondavels — 50c per person per night. Meals available at restaurant at extra cost. This is not a youth hostel.

6 **Hobbiton-on-Hogsback** (60 B1 →)
Nearest railway station is Alice and then travel by Road Motor Service to Hogsback; then 3 km walk OR travel by rail to Cathcart with Road Motor Service to Hogsback. This hostel is not open to the general public and caters mainly for under-privileged children. Groups permitted at management's discretion only.

7 **Muizenberg** (58 NS •)
Abe Bailey Youth Hostel, Cnr Maynard and Westbury Roads. Postal Code 7945 Telephone 8-4283
Take train from city station to False Bay station. The hostel is situated two blocks down from the station. Sixty beds. Cooking facilities. R1,20 per person per night. Special family rates — whole family on one card at R5,00 a year. Children under 5 free. Special group rates — 10 persons or less on one card for R3,00.

8 **Port Elizabeth** (59 B5↘)
Lanherne Youth Hostel, "S" Bend, Humewood. Postal Code 6001 Telephone 2-7739
50 beds; cooking facilities. R1,20 per person per night. Special group rates — 10 persons or less on one card for R3,00

9 **Riversdale** (58 D6↖)
Municipal Camping Site, Meurant Tourist Camp, Meurant Street. Postal Code 6770 Telephone 775
Hostellers to consult Town Clerk for special rate of R1,20 per person per day. Ten rondavels and 1 bungalow. No cooking facilities.

NATAL

1 **Bulwer** (63 A2↘)
Ashtonvale Guest Farm. Postal Code 4575 Telephone 53
R1,50 per person per night out of season. No hostellers during season.
Swimming, horse-riding, tennis, bowls, TV. No cooking facilities but meals available.

2 **Durban** (63 A4↗)
15 Cadogan Place, Durban North (Mrs D Griffiths). Postal Code 4051 Telephone 84-2050
This is a private home. Breakfast provided, but no cooking facilities.
R1,25 per person per night. Take bus No. 740 from Field Street, Stop 1; beyond Broadway walk in direction of bus to Cadogan Drive on right.

3 **Port Edward** (63 C3↖)
S.A. Police Holiday Resort, PO Box 22, Postal Code 4295 Telephone 823
Travel by rail from Durban to Port Shepstone. Then by Railway bus to Margate and by lift to Port Edward. Bungalows, rondavels, chalets, caravan sites. Tariffs vary depending upon type of accommodation requested.

4 **Winterton** (67 C2 ↓)
Kelvin Grove Caravan Park and Camping Hostel. Postal Code 3340 Telephone Winterton 2502
From Durban road, take route 35. D277 is Kelvin Grove.
R1,25 per person per day. Six rooms with beds. Communal kitchen with cooking facilities. Swimming, walks, horse-riding, fishing.

ORANGE FREE STATE

1 **Golden Gate Highlands National Park** (66 C6 •)
National Parks Board, PO Box 787, Pretoria. Postal Code 0001 Telephone 44-1194
2 x 2 bedrooms and 2 x 28 bedrooms. Accommodation available for groups of 15 people. No cooking facilities.
R1,90 per adult per night; R0,90 per child per night.

2 **Parys** (66 A5 ↓)
Rotary Club Camp, Sandy Beach. Postal Code 9585 Telephone 2643. Furnished rondavels; no cooking facilities.
R1,20 per person per night.

TRANSVAAL

1 **Johannesburg** (68 D6↖)
Johannesburg Youth Hostel, 32 Main Street, Rosettenville. Postal Code 2190 Telephone 26-8051
From city bus terminus, cnr. Eloff and Main Streets, catch a Townsview bus (No. 47) and alight at Stop 24.
Accommodation for 60 people. Cooking and camping facilities; swimming (municipal pool); bus tours over weekends.
R1,20 per person per night.

2 **Middelburg** (69 C2 ↓)
Midland Estate (at brickworks); ± 3 km from Middelburg on the Witbank road. PO Box 111, Postal Code 1050
Telephone 2335
This is not a youth hostel and there are no facilities or charges. Hostellers must arrive before 17 h 00.

3 **Schoemansville** (68 NS ↑)
Hartbeespoort Dam Hostel, Hertzog Street (just off corner Monene Street), Schoemansville Postal Code 6635.
Tel. 01211-3071
From Johannesburg take M1 North freeway and turn off into Jan Smuts Avenue until Hyde Park Corner where you turn right to Bryanston after which follows Fourways. Then straight on past Riversands farm stall. Further on take the P79-1 road crossing the Hennops River, and on to a 4-way stop street. Continue straight on past Meerhof Rest Camp towards Rustenburg. Approaching the foot of the mountains ahead there are two petrol stations and approximately 200 metres beyond the Caltex station is Monene Street. Follow signs to hostel.
Accommodation for 12 persons; special group rates. Cooking facilities.

CAMPMOBILES FOR HIRE

TOWN AND ESTABLISHMENT ●The postal code is given in brackets following each name ●The map page and grid reference follows the town entry ●The telephone code is given in brackets following the telephone number	Advance Booking	Makes	Sizes	RATES Subject to alteration without prior notice Confirm charges when booking		Advance Payment/s	Insurance Details	Equipment Included												Equipment for Hire						Comments NB Towing charges may vary according to prevailing price of petrol
				Standard	Unlimited km Rates			Refrigerator	Cooker	Wash Basin (Sink)	Cupboards	Lights	Crockery	Cutlery	Cooking Utensils	Side Tent/Awning	Table and/or Chairs	Gas Cylinder	Sleeping Bags	Folding Tables	Folding Chairs	Stretchers	Tents	Gas Lamps	Chemical Toilet	
CAPE TOWN (8001) 58 NS ↑ Camperent, 20 Hudson St Tel. 43-6324 (021) 48-9975 A/hours	★	Datsun E20	4 berth	R155 per week with 1 400 km free and 10c per km thereafter	R185 per week	25% of total rental	R2 per day or R12 per week	★	★	★	★	★	★	★	★		★	★	★							Delivery and collection of vehicles at central hotels, air terminal, station
Hunts Car Hire, 77 Strand St Tel. 22-9781 (021)		FOR DETAILS SEE HUNTS CAR HIRE, **JOHANNESBURG**																								
DURBAN (4001) 63 NS ↗ Hunts Car Hire, 89 Berea Rd Tel. 31-8477 (031)		FOR DETAILS SEE HUNTS CAR HIRE, **JOHANNESBURG**																								
Multifleet, 22 Underwood Rd., Pinetown 3600 Tel. 72-2957/72-8836 (031)		Natal Agents for Trekliner FOR DETAILS SEE TREKLINER (PTY) LTD., **JOHANNESBURG**																								
JOHANNESBURG (2000) 72 NS • Auto Safari Hire, 48 Pretoria St., Hillbrow Tel. 643-1725 (011)	★	Auto-Villa	2, 4 & 6 berth	R180–R196 per week (incl. 1 400 km)	R215–R250 per week	R75 deposit	Comprehensive Insurance with excess of R75 — can be waived at R2 per day	★	★	★	★	★	★	★	★	★	★	★	★							Delivery and collection of vehicles at central hotels, air terminal, station
Camp and Live, 62 Blairgowrie Dve., Blairgowne, Randburg 2194 Tel. 48-5832/3 (011)	★	VW Kombi	2 & 5 berth	R154 per week incl. 1 750 km	R170 per week	R75 deposit	Comprehensive Insurance with excess of R150 — can be waived at R2 per day	★	★	★	★	★	★	★	★	★	★	★	★	★	★	★	★	★	★	Free delivery and return to all central hotels, stations and Jan Smuts. Elsewhere at a charge
Free Wheel Car and Camper Hire, 50 Twist St., Joubert Park Tel. 724-6445/724-8710 (011)	★	Volkswagen Fleetline & Hi-Line, Datsun Hi-Line	2 & 4 berth	VW Fleetline (2 berth): R155 per week (incl. 1 750 km); VW Hi-Line (4 berth): R180 per week (incl. 1 750 km); Datsun Hi-Line (4 berth): R190 per week (incl. 1 750 km)	VW Fleetline (2 berth): R465 (3 weeks), R837 (6 weeks); VW Hi-Line (4 berth): R540 (3 weeks), R972 (6 weeks); Datsun Hi-Line (4 berth): R560 (3 weeks), R995 (6 weeks)	R50 deposit plus estimated cost of hire	Comprehensive Insurance with excess of R50	★	★		★	★	★	★	★			★	★	★	★					Free delivery and return to all central hotels, station and Jan Smuts. Elsewhere at extra charge
Getaway Travel Car Hire, 205 Duncan Hse., 11 de Villiers St., Tel. 725-4629/834-8529 (011)	★	VW 1600 Campers	2–5 berth	R14–R16 per day plus 9c per km (150 km free per day)	R20–R24 per day	Estimated cost of hire plus R75 booking deposit	Comprehensive Insurance with excess of R220 — all but R50 can be waived at R2 per day		★	★		★	★	★	★	★	★	★		★	★	★	★	★		
Hillbrow Camper Hire, 125 Twist St P.O. Box 17385, Hillbrow 2038. Tel. 642-2412/643-1318 (011)	★	VW Jurgens Auto-Villa and Auto-Villa L	2–4 berth 2–6berth	VW A-V: R22 per day (incl. 150 km); VW A-VL: R29 per day (incl. 150 km)	VW A-V: R700 for 3 weeks R33 per extra day; VW A-VL: R820 for 3 weeks plus R33 per extra day	R75 deposit plus estimated cost of hire	Comprehensive Insurance with R200 excess of which R150 can be waived at R12 per week	★	★	★	★	★	★	★	★	★	★	★	★					★		Drop-off charges: Cape Town: R160; Windhoek: R200; Durban: R60
Holiday Car Hire, 205 Commissioner St Tel. 23-2288 (011)	★	Hi-Ace, Daihatsu, Mazda	2–6 berth	R160–R225 per week incl. 250 km per day	Min. 3 weeks hire. Rates on application	Estimated cost of hire plus R100 deposit	Comprehensive Insurance with R250 excess — can be waived at R2 per day	★	★	★	★	★	★	★	★	★	★	★	★	★	★			★	★	Free collection and delivery within 5 km of depot. Airport: R10
Hunts Car Hire, Cnr. Von Wielligh St. & Rosettenville Rd., P.O.Box 2437. Tel. 21-8258/21-2531 (011)	★	Datsun and Hunts 'Safari' Mobile Mini Home	2, 3, 4 and 6 berth	'Safari': R163 per week incl. 1 400 km per week 'Mini Home': R195 per week incl. 1 400 km per week	'Safari': R190 per week 'Mini Home': R260 per week	Estimated cost of hire plus R75 deposit	Comprehensive Insurance with R200 excess — can be waived at R2 per day or R12 per week	★	★	★	★	★	★	★	★	★	★	★	★		★		★	★	★	
interRent Rent-a-Car Ltd., Pioneer Hse., 33 Albert St./P.O. Box 3610. Tel. 21-2511. A/Hours: 46-3944 (011)	★	VW Strato-camper, VW Jabula Cruiser, VW Campaneer	2½ and 4½ berth	R21–R26 per day (incl. 150 km)	R462–R536 per day	Estimated cost of hire plus deposit of R250	Comprehensive Insurance with an excess of R250 — can be waived at R15 per week	★	★	★	★	★	★	★	★		★	★	★	★	★			★		Free delivery within a 5 km radius of interRent depot. Drop-offs made to Pretoria, Durban, Cape Town, Port Elizabeth, Windhoek at a charge
Self-Drive Motorcaravan, 60 Booysens Rd., Selby Tel. 838-2830 (011) 48-6313 A/hours	★	VW 'Game-viewer' and VW 'High Roof'	2¼ and 4¼ berth	'Gameviewer' (2¼ berth): R20–R22 per day incl. 170 km; 'High Roof' (4¼ berth): R22–R24 per day incl. 170 km.	'Gameviewer': R26–R28 per day 'High Roof': R28–R30 per day	Estimated cost of hire plus R100 deposit	R2 per day. Min. R25, Max. R50	★	★	★	★	★	★	★	★	★	★	★	★	★	★	★	★	★	★	Free delivery in central Johannesburg and city air terminal. Delivery to other cities at a charge
Trekliner (Pty) Ltd., 104 Stanhope Rd., Malvern East, Germiston (1401) or P/Bag 1, Motortown 2111 Tel. 616-3354/5 (011)	★	Trekliner Standard & Deluxe	4 berth	R174–R216 per week incl. 1 000 km.	R581–R720 for 2 weeks	Estimated cost of hire plus R150 deposit	Comprehensive Insurance with excess of R150 — can be waived at R2,50 per day	★	★	★	★	★	★	★	★		★	★	★				★		★	Free delivery to central hotels, city air terminal and railway station. Delivery to Durban, Cape Town, Windhoek at a charge

TRAILER CARAVANS FOR HIRE

TOWN AND ESTABLISHMENT ● The postal code is given in brackets following each name ● The map page and grid reference follows the town entry ● The telephone code is given in brackets following the telephone number	Makes Available	Sizes	CHARGES Subject to change without prior notice Confirm charges when booking		Deposit	Insurance Details	Equipment Included H = Available for Hire											Equipment for Hire									Other Information NB: Towing charges may vary according to prevailing price of petrol
			In Season	Out of Season			Refrigerator	Cooker	Cupboards	Lights	Bedding	Crockery	Cutlery	Cooking Utensils	Side Tent	Table and Chairs	Ground Sheet	Table and Chairs	Stretchers	Bedding	Kitchenware	Side Tent	Gas Bottles	Ground Sheet	Gas Lamps	Braais	
CAPE PROVINCE **Cape Town** 58 NS ↑ Schus Caravans, 224 Voortrekker Rd., Vasco (7460). Tel. 902-1111 (021)	All popular makes	2, 3, 4 & 6 berth	From R5 per day plus R5 insurance for period of hire	On application	R30	Hirer responsible for first R50 of claim — see also under Charges	★	★	★	★					★			★	★	★	★		★			★	Also have a hire fleet for non-whites
Tyers Caravan Hire Co. (Pty) Ltd., Plantation Rd., Ottery (7800). Tel. 73-3040 (021)	Impala and other recognised makes	2 to 6 berth	From R8 per day plus R3 insurance per week	From R8 per day plus R3 insurance per week	R30	Hirer responsible for first R50 of claim — see also under Charges	★	★	★	★				★								★					Will tow caravans to Peninsula sites at a charge
Durbanville 58 D3 ↘ Boland Caravan Hire, 29 Lindenberg Ave., (7550). Tel. 96-1405 (Cape Town) (021)	All popular makes	4 to 6 berth	From R5 to R9 per day	From R3.50 to R6 per day	R50	Hirer responsible for first R50 of claim	★	★	★	★		★	★	★	★		★	★	★								Will tow caravans to Peninsula sites at a charge
East London 60 B2 ↘ Caravan Hire Centre, P.O. Box 5072, Greenfields (5208). Tel. 46-1611 (0431)	Gypsey, Sprite, Jurgens	4 & 6 berth	R10.50 per day	R8.50 per day	R20	Hirer responsible for first R50 of claim	★	★	★	★		★	★	★	★		★		★								Will tow caravans to parks in the vicinity at a charge
Verina Caravan Park, Settlers Way, P.O. Box 5102, Greenfields (5208). Tel. 46-1069 (0431)	Jurgens, Sprite	4 & 6 berth	R8 per day plus R2.50 insurance per week	R6 per day plus R2.50 insurance per week	R20	See also under Charges	★	★	★	★		★	★	★	★												
Knysna 59 NS ● Knysna Hire Centre, 62A Main Rd. (6570). Tel. 154 (04452)	Sprite, Gypsey, Jurgens	4 & 6 berth	R9 to R12 per day	R5 to R7 per day	R40	Hirer responsible for first R40 of claim	★	★	★	★		★	★	★	★		★	★	★	★	★	★	★	★	★	★	Will tow caravan to any spot along Garden Route at a fee. (No charge to Knysna Parks)
Paarl 58 C3 ↘ Paarl-Woonwaens, 14 Louie St. P.O. Box 412 (7620). Tel. 2-4176 (0251)	Jurgens, Sprite	4, 5 & 6 berth	R7 to R9 per day – negotiable for long periods	R5 to R7 per day	R50	Hirer responsible for first R50 of claim	★	★	★	★		★			★			★			★			★	★		Will tow caravans to parks in the vicinity at a charge
Port Elizabeth 59 B5 ↘ Caravan Craft, 33 Lower Valley Rd. (6001). Tel. 2-2355 (041)	Sprite, Gypsey	4, 5 & 6 berth	R50 to R60 per week	R35 to R45 per week	R40		★	★	★	★		★			★		★										
Conneys Caravan Hire, 241 Highfield Rd. Korsten (6016). Tel. 4-7298 (041)	Sprite, Jurgens, Wayfarer	4, 5 & 6 berth	R50 to R60 per week	R50 to R60 per week	R30	Hirer responsible for first R30 of claim	★	★	★	★					★	★											Free towing to Humewood Caravan Park; to other centres at a charge
EMR Caravan Hire, P.O. Box 2281 (6000). Tel. 72-1072 (041)	All popular makes	4 & 6 berth	R7.50–R10 per day	R7.50 per day — negotiable for long periods	R50	Hirer responsible for first R50 of claim	★	★	★	★		★		★	★			★					★	★	★		Free towing to Port Elizabeth Municipal parks; at a charge to coastal resorts in Port Elizabeth area
Strand 58 D3 ↗ Karakamp (Pty) Ltd. 271 Main Rd., P.O. Box 344 (7140). Tel. 3-7357 (024)	Sprite, Gypsey	4, 5 & 6 berth	R6 to R9 per day	By arrangement	R40	Hirer responsible for first R50 of claim	★	★	★	★		★		★	★		★	★									Will tow to local caravan parks
Strand Caravan Hire, 183 Main Rd., (7140). Tel. 3-3310 (024)	Sprite, Gypsey, Jurgens	4 & 6 berth	R7 to R11 per day	R6 to R10 per day	R30	Hirer responsible for first R50 of claim	★	★	★						★			★			★		★	★			Will tow caravans to parks in vicinity at a fee
NATAL **Pinetown** 63 NS ↗ Multifleet (Pty) Ltd. 22 Underwood Rd. (3600). Tel. 72-2957/72-8836 (031)	Gypsey, Sprite, Jurgens	4 & 6 berth	R65 to R75 per week	R60 to R70 per week	R50	Hirer responsible for first R50 of claim	★	★	★	★		H	H	H	★		★										Will tow caravan to park at 60c per km, position it and erect tent
Natal Caravans (Pty) Ltd., 6 Kirk Rd., P.O. Box 346 (3600). Tel. 72-7291/2 (Durban) (031)	Sprite, '400' Alpine, Musketeer	4 & 6 berth	R62.40 per week incl. insurance	R62.40 per week incl. insurance	R50	Hirer responsible for first R100 of claim — see also under Charges	★	★	★	★	H	H	H	H	★	H		★	★	★	★						Will tow caravan if park is within 50 km from Pinetown. (50c per km) Min. charge: R12
ORANGE FREE STATE **Bloemfontein** 66 D4 ↖ G. J. Reyneke Caravans, P.O. Box 2245 (9300). Tel. 2-3603 (051)	Jurgens, Gypsey, Sprite, Slipstream, Venter	4, 5 & 6 berth	R7.50 to R12 per day	R7.50 to R12 per day	R30	Hirer responsible for first R50 of claim	★		★	★	★	★	★		★	★	★	★	★	★	★	★	★	★	★		Will tow caravans to parks at a charge
TRANSVAAL **Germiston** 72 NS ↘ Caravan All Services, 187 Elsburg Rd., Delville Ext. 4 (1401). Tel. 34-7905 (011)	Jurgens, Sprite, Gypsey	4 & 6 berth	From R8.50 per day. Weekly rates on application	R7.50 to R12.50 per day. Weekly rates on application	R40	Hirer responsible for first R100 of any claim	★	★	★	★	H	H	H	H	★	H	H	★	★	★	★	★	★	★	★	★	Will tow caravans to parks at a charge. Overseas visitors can hire car and caravan
Five Star Caravans (Pty) Ltd., Edenvale Rd., Rietfontein, P.O. Box 67, Bedfordview (2008). Tel. 53-5440 (011)	Caravette, Sprite, Jurgens, Gypsey	4, 5 & 6 berth	R65 to R75 per week — negotiable for long periods	R55 to R65 per week	R50	Hirer responsible for first R50 of any claim	★	★	★	★					★	★	★	★		★	★		★	★			Will tow caravans to parks in the vicinity at 35c per km
Johannesburg 72 NS ● Caravan Action, 302 Main Reef Rd., Denver (2094). Tel. 616-2355/6 (011)	Gypsey	4, 5 & 6 berth	R60 to R94 per week	R54 to R85 per week	R50	Hirer responsible for first R50 of any claim	★	★	★	★					★		H							★			Overseas visitors can hire car and caravan fully equipped
Klerksdorp 66 A4 ↓ Mr. G. C. Erasmus, 137 Elandsheuwel St., Songloed (2570). Tel. 2-4087 (018)	Sprite, Gypsey, Jurgens	4, 5 & 6 berth	R6 to R10 per day. R100 to R160 per month	By arrangement	R30 to R50	Hirer responsible for first R50 of claim	★	★	★	★		★			★		★										Will tow caravans to nearby resorts ± 25c per km

TRAILER CARAVANS FOR HIRE

TOWN AND ESTABLISHMENT ●The postal code is given in brackets following each name ●The map page and grid reference follows the town entry ●The telephone code is given in brackets following the telephone number	Makes Available	Sizes	CHARGES Subject to change without prior notice Confirm charges when booking		Deposit	Insurance Details	Equipment Included H = Available for Hire											Equipment for Hire									Other Information NB: Towing charges may vary according to prevailing price of petrol
			In Season	Out of Season			Refrigerator	Cooker	Cupboards	Lights	Bedding	Crockery	Cutlery	Cooking Utensils	Side Tent	Table and Chairs	Ground Sheet	Table and Chairs	Stretchers	Bedding	Kitchenware	Side Tent	Gas Bottles	Ground Sheet	Gas Lamps	Braais	
TRANSVAAL continued																											
Pretoria 68 C6 ✓ Flinke Dienste, 20 Starky Ave., Waverley (0186) Tel. 49-2316 (012)	Gypsey, Sprite	4–6 berth	R5.50–R10 per day	R5,50–R10 per day	R40	Hirer responsible for first R50 of any claim	★	★	★	★	H	★	★	★	★	H	★										Will tow caravans to parks in Pretoria vicinity at 50c per km
J & L Caravan and Trailer Hire, 653 Smook Ave., Roseville (0084). Tel. 75-2756 (012)	Gypsey, Sprite	4, 5 & 6 berth	R7 to R8 per day plus R12 insurance for the period taken	R7 to R8 per day plus R12 insurance for the period taken	R50	Hirer responsible for first R100 of claim — see also under Charges	★	★	★	★		★			★		★										Will tow caravans to parks in vicinity at a charge
Roodepoort 72 NS ↘ Kennis Motors (Witpoortjie) (Pty) Ltd., 6 Ontdekkers Rd. Tel. 664-7000 (011)	Jurgens	4 & 6 berth	R70 to R92 per week — min. period of 3 weeks	R63 to R84 per week	R50	Hirer responsible for first R50 of any claim	★	★	★	★		★			★			★									
Vanderbijlpark 66 A5 ↘ Mr. P. W. Keytel, P.O. Box 549 (1900) Tel. 33-9679 (016)	Sprite	4–6 berth	R7 per day	R7 per day	R30	Hirer responsible for R50 excess	★	★	★	★					★												
Vereeniging 66 A5 ↘ Fireman's Recreation Club, Fire Station, de Villiers Ave. (1930). Tel. 22-4431/2 (016)	Jurgens	4 berth	R6.50 per day plus R3.50 insurance for the period of hire	R6.50 per day plus R3.50 insurance for the period of hire	R20	See under Charges	★	★	★	★		★			★	★											

CARAVANS FOR HIRE ON SITE

TOWN AND ESTABLISHMENT ●The postal code is given in brackets following each name ●The map page and grid reference follows this entry ●The telephone code is given in brackets following the telephone number * means no direct dialling — book a trunk call	Advance Bookings	Number of Caravans Available	Caravan sizes available	Tariffs Subject to change without prior notice Confirm charges when booking		Equipment Included											Items for hire					Surroundings
				IN SEASON	OUT OF SEASON	Stove	Refrigerator	Lights	Crockery	Cutlery	Cooking Utensils	Bedding	Side Tent	Folding Tables	Folding Chairs	Groundsheet	Bedding	Stretchers	Gas Lamps	Folding Tables	Folding Chairs	
CAPE PROVINCE						P = Pillows; W/F = Wooden floor; W/A = Fixed wooden awning; S = Sleeping bag; C = Cement slab; M = Mattress																
CAPE PENINSULA **Fish Hoek (7975)** 58 NS • Sunny Acres Caravan Park, P.O. Box 50. Tel. 82-2913 (021)	★	6	4 & 6 berth	R12–R14 per day	R7–R10 per day	★	★	★	★	★	★		★	★	★		★	★		★	★	Well-shaded, near to beach
Simonstown (7995) 58 NS ✓ The Blue Lantern Caravan Park, Main Rd. Tel. 86-6184 (021)	★	4	3 & 4 berth	R30–R40 per week	R25–R32 per week	★	★	★	★		★		★			★	★	★			★	Near to beach
Cape St. Francis 59 C4 ✓ Cape St. Francis Caravan Park, P.O. Box 92, Humansdorp (6300) Tel. *17 Cape St. Francis	★	5		R10 per day	R6 per day	★	★	★	★	★	★		★	★	★							Situated on beach
East London and District Glen Muir 60 B3 ✓ P.O. Box 942, East London (5200). Tel. 95-1318 (0431)	★	2		On application	On application	★	★		★	★	★		★									Situated beside a stream; well-shaded; on beachfront
Gwenshaw Caravan Park 60 B3 ✓ Eastward Ho, P.O. Box 12, Gonubie (5256). Tel. 94-1710 (0431)	★	4	4 & 6 berth	R6 per day plus park charges	R3 per day plus park charges	★	★	★	★	★	★		★			★		★	★	★	★	Well-shaded, grassy sites
Pirate's Creek Holiday Resort 60 B2 ↘ P.O. Box 2065, Beacon Bay (5205) Tel. 47-1160/47-2502 (0431)	★	10		R6–R8 per day plus site fees	R5–R6 per day plus site fees	★	★	★	★	★	★		★	★	★	★	★					Situated on a lagoon which offers swimming, fishing, boating and yachting
Pixie Caravan Park 60 B2 ↘ P.O. Box 5072, Greenfields (5208). Tel. 46-1611 (0431)		20		R10 per day	R8 per day	★	★	★	★	★	★		★	★		★		★				Grassy sites; beach in immediate vicinity
Verina Caravan Park 60 B2 ↘ Settler's Way, P.O. Box 5102, Greenfields (5208) Tel. 46-1069 (0431)	★		4 & 6 berth	R10 per day	R8 per day	★	★	★	★	★	★		★			C						Large concrete sites; some shaded
Yellow Sands Caravan Park 60 B3 ✓ (At Kwelera Mouth) P.O. Box 920, East London (5200). Tel. 95-1336 (0431)	★	4		On application	On application	★	★	★	★	★	★		★	★	★	★						Caravans parked on beachfront beneath the trees
Katberg 60 B1 • Highlands Holiday Resort, P.O. Balfour (5740). Tel. *1002	★	5	3, 4 & 6 berth	From R8–R12 per day	From R5–R9 per day	★	★	★	★		★		★	★	★	★	★					Well-shaded, grassy sites

CARAVANS FOR HIRE ON SITE

TOWN AND ESTABLISHMENT ● The postal code is given in brackets following each name ● The map page and grid reference follows this entry ● The telephone code is given in brackets following the telephone number * means no direct dialling — book a trunk call	Advance Bookings	Number of Caravans Available	Caravan sizes available	Tariffs Subject to change without prior notice Confirm charges when booking IN SEASON	OUT OF SEASON	Equipment Included: Stove	Refrigerator	Lights	Crockery	Cutlery	Cooking Utensils	Bedding	Side Tent	Folding Tables	Folding Chairs	Groundsheet	Items for hire: Bedding	Stretchers	Gas Lamps	Folding Tables	Folding Chairs	Surroundings
CAPE PROVINCE continued						P = Pillows; W/F = Wooden floor; W/A = Fixed wooden awning; S = Sleeping bag; C = Cement slab; M = Mattress																
Keurboomsrivier (6601) 59 NS → Lagoon Holiday Resort, P.O. Box 9. Tel. *19 Keurboomsrivier	★	10		On application	On application	★	★	★					★	★	★	★		★		★	★	Situated on the banks of a lagoon; excellent for boating, yachting, skiing, fishing
San Merino Caravan Park, P.O. Box 413, Plettenberg Bay (6600). Tel.* 9 Keurboomsrivier	★	11	4 & 6 berth	R10 per day	R6.50 per day	★	★	★	★	★	★		★	★	★	★		★		★	★	Well-shaded, on banks of river, canoe hire, 6 km from Plettenberg Bay
Klein-Brakrivier (6503) 59 C2 ↖ Riverside Caravan Park, P.O. Box 6. Tel. 6316 (04441)	★	2		R13–R15 per day	R10–R12 per day	★	★	★	★	★	★	P	★	★	★	★			★		★	Situated on banks of river
Knysna (6570) 59 NS • Knysna Caravan and Holiday Park, Main Rd. Tel. 500 (04452)	★	8	2, 3 & 4 berth	R15 per day for 2 or 3 persons R20 per day for 4 persons	R6.50 per day for 2 persons R2 per day extra for more than 2 persons	★	★	★	★	★	★		★	★		W/F	★	★			★	Well-shaded, grassy sites; lagoon frontage
Lagoonside Holiday and Caravan Park, P.O. Box 116. Tel. 341 (04452)	★	9	4 & 6 berth	R17.50 per day	R6.50–R8.50 per day	★	★	★	★	★	★		★	★	★	W/F	★					Situated on banks of lagoon; grassy sites
Waterways Caravan Park, Main St., P.O. Box 394. Tel. 557 (04452)	★	5	4 & 6 berth	R15 per day (site rental included)	R6–R10 per day (site rental included)	★	★	★	★	★	★	P	★	★	★	W/F	★			★	★	Well-shaded; on Knysna lagoon; braai facilities
Mossel Bay (6500) 59 C2 ↖ Mossel Bay Caravans 5 Star Park, George Rd., P.O. Box 439 Tel. 2604 (04441)	★	40	4 & 6 berth	R6.50–R8.75 per day plus site rental	R6.50–R8.75 per day plus site rental	★	★	★			★		★				★	★		★	★	Grassy sites; 2 km from beach
Onrus (7201) 58 D4 ← Sherwood Park, Main Rd., P.O. Box 50. Tel. 6230 (02831)	★	6	3, 4 & 6 berth	R7.35–R8.35 per day plus site fee	R6.35–R7.35 per day plus site fee	★	★	★	★	★	★		★			★						Grassy sites; well-shaded; 1½ km from beach and lagoon
Plettenberg Bay (6600) 59 NS → Piesang River Caravan Resort, Beacon Isle Drive, P.O. Box 185. Tel. 244 (04472)	★	12	3, 4 & 6 berth	On application	On application	★	★	★	★	★	★	P	W/F	★		C						On banks of river, within walking distance of lagoon and beach
Plettenberg Bay Caravan and Camping Park, P.O. Box 73. Tel. 199 or 2604 (04472)	★	21		On application	On application	★	★	★	★	★	★		★	★	★	★		★	★			On banks of Keurbooms lagoon; foot bridge over lagoon to beach
Port Alfred (6170) 60 C1 ↖ Lagoon Caravan Park, Blue Lagoon Rd., P.O.Box 78. Tel. 590 (04642)	★	9	4 & 6 berth	R45–R53 per week	R35 per week	★	★	★	★	★	★		★									Situated on lagoon near beach
Medolino Caravan Park, 23 Stewart Rd., P.O. Box 20, Kowie West (6171). Tel. 346 (04642)	★	5	4 & 6 berth	R8.75 per night per 2 persons (site fees included)	R5 per night per 2 persons (site fees included)	★	★	★	★		★		★	★	★	★	★	★	★			Near to shops, golf course, main beach and river
Port Elizabeth 59 B5 ↖ Caracampark, P.O. Box 5054, Walmer (6065). Tel. 2-2920 (041)	★	5	4 & 6 berth	R4 per day plus R2 per person per day	R3 per day plus R1.50 per person per day	★	★	★	★		★		★			★						Sheltered sites; 5 min. from beach
Sedgefield (6573) 59 NS ← Jooris Caravan & Camping Park, On Swartvlei, P.O. Box 22. Tel. *940 Sedgefield	★	4	4 & 6 berth	R3.50 per night per person	R2.50 per night per person	★	★	★	★		★		★	★		★	★	★			★	Situated on Swartvlei; ideal for water sport and fishing Short distance from many beaches
Lake Pleasant Holiday Resort, P.O. Box 16. Tel. *28 Sedgefield	★	36		R14–R17 per day	On application	★	★	★	★	★	★		★	★	★		★		★	★	★	Situated on Groenvlei; renowned for black bass fishing, boating and yachting
Landfall Caravan Park, P.O. Box 144. Tel. *44 Sedgefield	★	2	3 & 5 berth	R8–R13.50 per day	R6–R10 per day	★	★	★	★	★	★		★	★	★	★						
Trail's End Holiday Resort, P.O. Box 31. Tel. *922 Sedgefield	★	6	4 & 5 berth	R10–R13 per day plus 50c per person	R8–R10 per day plus 50c per person	★	★	★	★	★	★		★	★	★	★		★				Situated on Swartvlei; many beaches in the vicinity
Stellenbosch 58 C3 ↖ Bergplaas Holiday Ranch, Helshoogte Rd., P.O. Box 2172, Dennesig (7601). Tel. 7-0486 (02231)	★	2	4 & 6 berth	R10–R12 per day	R8–R10 per day	★	★	★	★	★	★		★	★	★	★						Grassy sites; park situated in heart of the wineland
Stilbaai-Oos 59 C1 • Riverside Farm Caravan Park, Write to: 66 Main Rd., Fish Hoek (7975). Tel. 8-8048 (021)	★	4	4 berth	R10–R12 per day	R8–R10 per day	★	★	★	★	★	★		★									Well-shaded, grassy sites; on river bank
Victoria Bay 59 NS ← Sea Glimpse Holiday Resort, P.O. Box 307, George (6530). Tel. 4660 (0441)	★	3		On application	On application	★	★	★	★	★	★		★	★	★	★	★					Beach in immediate vicinity; grassy sites
Wilderness (6560) 59 NS ← Island Lake Caravan Park, P.O. Wilderness. Tel. 9194 (0441)	★	2	Up to 6 berth	R8.50–R12 per day	R5–R7 per day	★	★	★	★	★	★		★	★	★		★	★				Situated on Island Lake, 4 km from Wilderness beach. Lake ideal for skiing, yachting and swimming
Siesta Caravan Holiday Resort, P.O. Box 35. Tel. 9197 (0441)	★	4		R8.50 per day for 2 persons	R6 per day for 2 persons	★	★	★	★	★	★		★	★								Touws River runs through park, few minutes drive from beach

CARAVANS FOR HIRE ON SITE

TOWN AND ESTABLISHMENT ● The postal code is given in brackets following each name ● The map page and grid reference follows this entry ● The telephone code is given in brackets following the telephone number * means no direct dialling — book a trunk call	Advance Bookings	Number of Caravans Available	Caravan sizes available	Tariffs Subject to change without prior notice Confirm charges when booking IN SEASON	OUT OF SEASON	Equipment Included Stove	Refrigerator	Lights	Crockery	Cutlery	Cooking Utensils	Bedding	Side Tent	Folding Tables	Folding Chairs	Groundsheet	Items for hire Bedding	Stretchers	Gas Lamps	Folding Tables	Folding Chairs	Surroundings
CAPE PROVINCE continued						P = Pillows; W/F = Wooden floor; W/A = Fixed wooden awning; S = Sleeping bag; C = Cement slab; M = Mattress																
Wilderness (6560) 59 NS ← continued The Lakes Holiday and Caravan Resort, P.O. Box 38. Tel. 9701 (0441)	★	13	4 & 6 berth	R12–R16 daily for up to 4 persons	R5–R7 daily for 2 persons R9–R14 for up to 4 persons	★	★	★	★	★	★		★	★	★	★	★	★	★			Situated beside the Touws River, ideal for water sport, short distance from beach
NATAL																						
Clansthal 63 NS • Clansthal Caravan Park, P.O. Box 154, Umkomaas (4170) Tel. 3-0211 (0323)	★	4		On application	On application	★	★	★	★	★	★		★	★	★	★		★				Situated near beach
Doonside (4125) 63 NS / Pot-Luck Caravan Camp, 5 Topham Rd. Tel. 93-6498 (031)	★	2		R6 per day for up to 3 persons	R5 per day for up to 3 persons	★	★	★	★	★	★		★	★	★	★						Shaded sites, situated on beach
Ifafa Beach (4185) 63 NS ✓ Ifafa Beach Caravan Park, P.O. Box 10. Tel. 740 (03239)	★	6	Up to 6 berth	R8.50–R10.50 per day plus 75c per person per day	R4.50–R5.50 per day plus 75c per person per day	★	★	★	★	★	★		★	★	★	★	★	★				Situated right on beach, also fresh water pool
Ifafa Marina, Ifafa Marina Agencies (Pty) Ltd., Private Bag. Tel. 611 (03239)	★	30	4, 5 & 6 berth	R11.50–R18 per day plus 95c per person per day	R3.75–R5.50 per day plus 70c per person per day	★	★	★					★	★	★	★						Situated on banks of Ifafa Lagoon, free ferry service to beach. Lagoon ideal for water sport
Illovo Beach (4155) 63 NS / Patlyn Caravan Park, Elizabeth Ave., P.O. Box 11. Tel. 95-1339 (031)	★	5	3, 4 & 6 berth	R11–R12.50 per day	R5.50–R6 per day	★	★	★	★	★	★		★	★	★	★						Well-shaded park, ± 100 km from beach
Kingsburgh 63 NS / Uitspan Caravan Park, P.O. Box 71, Winklespruit (4145) Tel. 935-5477 (031)	★	3	4 & 6 berth	On application	On application	★	★	★	★	★	★		★	★	★	C						Well-shaded, grassy sites, near to beach
Margate (4275) 63 NS ✓ Constantia Caravan Park, P.O. Box 389. Tel. 2-0482 (0393)	★	2	4 & 6 berth	R10 per day plus 60c per person	R5 per day plus 60c per person	★	★	★	★	★	★		★	★	★	C						Well-shaded, grassy sites, beach in immediate vicinity
De Wet Caravan Park, P.O. Box 71. Tel. 2-1022 (0393)	★	12	4, 5 & 6 berth	R70–R85 per week	R5–R6.50 per day	★	★	★	★	★	★		★	★	★	★						Situated on beach, grassy sites
Margate Caravan Park, P.O. Box 288. Tel. 2-0852 (0393)	★	3		On application	On application	★	★	★					★	★	★	★	M	★	★	★	★	Beach in immediate vicinity, well-shaded grassy sites
Marina Beach 63 NS ✓ Belle Vista Caravan Park, Write to: J. Viljoen, P.O. Box 36, Southbroom (4277). Tel. 3755 (0393)	★	56	4, 5 & 6 berth	R45–R60 per week	R60–R100 per week	★	★	★	★	★	★		★	★	★	C		★				Well-shaded; 2 km from beach
Sherwood Forest Caravan Park, P.O. Box 39 (4281) Tel. 3792 (0393)	★	8		R9 per day for 4 persons	On application	★	★	★	★	★	★		★	★	★	★						Close to beach, well-shaded sites
Mtunzini (3867) 67 C4 ↘ Xaxaza Caravan Park, P.O. Box 101. Tel. 143 (035322)	★	2	4 & 6 berth	R5 – R7 per day plus park charges	R4 – R6 per day plus park charges	★	★	★	★	★	★			★	★							Shaded, grassy sites; beach and river nearby
Mtwalume (4186) 63 NS • Longbeach Caravan Park, P.O. Box 2. Tel. 711 (03230)	★	30	Up to 6 berth	R13 per day including private ablution block	R10 per day including private ablution block	★	★	★	★	★	★		★	★	★	★						Near the beach
Mtwalume Caravan Park, P.O. Box 25. Tel. 749 (03230)	★	3		R10 per day for 4 persons	R8 per day for 4 persons	★	★	★	★	★	★		★	★	★							
Park Rynie (4182) 63 NS • Rocky Bay Caravan Park, P.O. Box 37. Tel. 2-1701 (0323)	★	8		From R8.50 per day	From R7 per day	★	★	★	★	★	★		★	★	★	★						Grassy sites; beach in immediate vicinity
Pennington (4184) 63 NS • Pennington Caravan Park, P.O. Box 19. Tel. 5007 (0323)	★	12		R10 per day plus R1 per adult and 50c per child per day	R4 per day plus R1 per adult and 50c per child per day	★	★	★	★	★	★		★	★	★	★						100 metres from beach
Shelly Beach 63 NS ✓ Blue Seas Caravan Park, P.O. Box 102, St. Michael's on Sea (4265) Tel. 5-1049 (0393)	★	1		R11.50 per day plus 50c per person per day	R6 per day plus 50c per person per day	★	★	★	★	★	★	S	★	★	★	★						Grassy sites, 50 metres from beach
Karapark, P.O. Box 69, St. Michael's on Sea (4265). Tel. 5-1226 (0393)	★	10	4 & 6 berth	R10 per day	R6 per day	★	★	★	★	★	★		★	★	★	★		★				Partly shaded, grassy sites; close to beach
Sinkwazi Beach 63 A4 • Zinkwazi Park, P.O. Box 8, Darnall (4480). Tel. 1912 (032422)	★	7	4 & 6 berth	R18 per day	R12 per day	★	★	★	★	★	★		★	★	★	★						Situated on lagoon near the beach
Southbroom (4277) 63 NS ✓ Paradise Caravan Park, Main Marine Drive, P.O. Box 55. Tel. 3725 (0393)	★	10	4 & 6 berth	R75.05 – R96.25 per week	R63.50 – R80.50 per week	★	★	★	★	★	★		★	★	★	★						Extensively shaded, grassy sites; beach in immediate vicinity

CARAVANS FOR HIRE ON SITE

TOWN AND ESTABLISHMENT ● The postal code is given in brackets following each name ● The map page and grid reference follows this entry ● The telephone code is given in brackets following the telephone number * means no direct dialling — book a trunk call	Advance Bookings	Number of Caravans Available	Caravan sizes available	Tariffs Subject to change without prior notice Confirm charges when booking IN SEASON	OUT OF SEASON	Equipment Included: Stove	Refrigerator	Lights	Crockery	Cutlery	Cooking Utensils	Bedding	Side Tent	Folding Tables	Folding Chairs	Groundsheet	Items for hire: Bedding	Stretchers	Gas Lamps	Folding Tables	Folding Chairs	Surroundings
NATAL continued						P = Pillows; W/F = Wooden floor; W/A = Fixed wooden awning; S = Sleeping bag; C = Cement slab; M = Mattress																
Trafalgar Beach 63 NS ↙ Port o' Call Caravan Park, P.O. Box 82, Ramsgate (4285) Tel. 3731 (0393)	★	5	4 to 6 berth	R12,50 – R16,50 per day for 4 persons incl. site rental	R8,50 – R12,50 per day for 4 persons incl. site rental	★	★	★	★	★	★		★	★		★						Well-shaded, grassy sites adjoining beach
Umhlanga Rocks (4320) 63 NS ↗ Umhlanga Rocks Caravan Park, Weaver Cres., P.O. Box 13. Tel. 51-1533 (031)	★	5	3, 4 & 6 berth	R58 – R83 per week	R43 – R61 per week	★	★	★	★	★	★		★	★	★	W/F		★		★	★	Grassy sites; minutes away from beach
Uvongo (4270) 63 NS ↙ Oasis Caravan Park, P.O. Box 67. Tel. 5-0778 (0393)	★	2	Up to 6 berth	R11,50 per day (4 persons) R13,50 per day (6 persons)	R4 per day (4 persons) R6 per day (6 persons)	★	★	★	★	★	★		★	★	★	★	★					Beach in immediate vicinity; well-shaded park
Winklespruit (4145) 63 NS ↗ Karavana Caravan Park, P.O. Box 5. Tel. 95-1747 (031)	★	2		R13 per day for up to 4 persons	R8 per day for up to 4 persons	★	★	★	★	★	★		★	★	★							Situated on beach
Ocean Call Caravan Park, P.O. Box 33. Tel. 95-1744 (031)	★	4	6 berth	R11,80 per day plus 80c per person (Luxury Site) R10 per day plus 60c per person (Standard Site)	R8,40 per day plus 80c per person (Luxury Site) R7 per day plus 60c per person (Standard Site)	★	★	★	★	★	★		★	★	★	W/F		★			★	Park adjoins main beachfront
ORANGE FREE STATE																						
Bloemfontein 66 D4 ↖ Pitstop Caravan Park, P.O. Box 3901 (9300) Tel. 33-2129 (051)		3	4 & 6 berth	R8 per day incl. site charges	R6 per day incl. site charges	★	★	★	★	★			★			★			★	★	★	Extensively shaded sites
Parys (9585) 66 A6 ↓ Westvaal Caravan Park, P.O. Box 317. Tel. 3937 (01601)	★	2	4 to 6 berth	R5,50 – R6,50 per day	R5,50 – R6,50 per day	★	★	★						★	★							Well-shaded sites on river bank
TRANSVAAL																						
Argent 69 D1 ↗ The Rocks Holiday Resort, P.O. Box 475, Delmas (2210) Tel. 1814 or 53-8357 (01572)	★	4	3 & 4 berth	On application	On application	★	★	★	★	★	★											Situated on banks of Wilge River
Eikenhof (1872) 72 NS ↓ Blossom Valley Caravan Park, P.O. Eikenhof. Tel. 943-1508 (011)	★	9	6 berth	From R4 per day. R25 per week, R75 per month	From R4 per day. R25 per week, R75 per month	★	★	★					★	★	★	★		★				Well-shaded park
Protea Caravan Park, Vereeniging Main Road, P.O. Box 186. Tel. 943-1066 (011)	★	8		R70 – R85 per month	R70 – R85 per month	★	★	★					★	★	★	★						Swimming pool
Johannesburg 72 NS ↓ Ferreira's Caravan Park, Vereeniging Main Road, P.O. Box 82573, Southdale, (2135). Tel. 942-2600 (011)	★	7		R88 per month	R88 per month	★	★	★					★	★	★	★						Swimming pool
Kroondal 68 C5 ↙ Mountain Sanctuary Park, P.O. Box 187 (0350) Tel. 1422 (0142222)	★	2	6 berth	From R10 – R15 per day plus Sanctuary fees	From R10 – R15 per day plus Sanctuary fees	★	★	★	★	★	★		★	★	★	W/A						Situated in nature reserve — magnificent mountain scenery

PETS' BOARDING AVAILABLE WHEN EN ROUTE TO SOME GAME AND NATURE RESERVES

En Route to:	Pets Boarding in:	Name and Address of Kennels:	Tel. Code and No.	Charges (GST extra)	Remarks
CAPE PROVINCE ADDO ELEPHANT NATIONAL PARK	Grahamstown	SPCA, P.O. Box 21, Port Elizabeth Rd.	0461 3233	Dogs: 60c per day (2 in a kennel, 50c per day for the 2nd dog) Cats: 35c per day (2 in a cage, 30c per day for the 2nd cat)	Advance booking is advisable as kennels and cages are limited. Dogs to be immunised against distemper and cats against cat flu. Reception hours: 13 h 00 to 14 h 00 and 17 h 50 to 18 h 00.
	Port Elizabeth	Copper Dog 'Otel Old Seaview Rd., Mount Pleasant, Walmer.	041 32-1205	Dogs: 90c - R1,40 per day depending on their size. Cats: 85c per day	Advance booking is advisable.
		SPCA, P.O. Box 10123, 8th Milestone, Cape Rd.	041 30-7821	R1-R1,25 per day depending on the size of the animal	Advance booking is advisable. Innoculation certificate required.
KALAHARI GEMSBOK NATIONAL PARK	Upington	SPCA	0541 2572 (Mrs Neser)	Dogs only: R1,20 - R1,50 per day depending on the size	Dogs may only be booked in from 09 h 00 to 10 h 00 and 17 h 00 to 18 h 00 every day, except Sundays.
TSITSIKAMA FOREST AND COASTAL NATIONAL PARKS	Knysna	Moorlands Kennels, P.O. Highway, Dist. Knysna	04452 5904 (Mr Bell)	80c - R1,50 per day depending on the size of the animal	Bookings required for Christmas and mid-year holidays. Dogs to be immunised against distemper. Reception hours: Weekdays from 10 h 00 to 17 h 00; Sat. from 10 h 00 to 13 h 00.
NATAL HLUHLUWE, MKUZI, ST. LUCIA AND UMFOLOZI GAME RESERVES	Empangeni	Bulynn Pets Den, 21 Moberly Rd. P.O. Box 817	0351 2-4447	Dogs: R1,50 per day - large R1,20 per day - medium 85c per day - small Cats: 85c per day	Dogs to be immunised against distemper and rabies and cats against cat flu and rabies. Advance booking advisable during holiday seasons. Open 7 days a week.
ROYAL NATAL NATIONAL PARK	Ladysmith	Merwood Kennels, Elandslaagte. (26 km from Ladysmith on the main Newcastle Rd.)	0361 112	Dogs: 50c - 90c per day Cats: 45c per day	
ORANGE FREE STATE GOLDEN GATE HIGHLANDS NATIONAL PARK	Bethlehem	SPCA, 128 Cambridge St.	01431 3553 (Miss Loubser)	Dogs only: 45c - 65c depending on the size of the animal	Advance booking essential as kennels are limited. Do not cater for cats.
TRANSVAAL BLYDE RIVER CANYON NATURE RESERVE	Lydenburg	Spitskop Kennels, P.O. Box 142, (Take Roossenekal turn-off, 10 km further turn left at Spitskop, continue for 2 km to the kennels)	013232 1311	Dogs: During Tvl. School Holidays, 75c - R2 per day depending on size. Out of season, 50c - R1,50 per day. Cats: 75c per day during Tvl. School Holidays or 50c per day out of season	Advance booking advisable. Special rates for long periods. All pets to be healthy and innoculated.
KRUGER NATIONAL PARK	Plaston	Gundagai Kennels, P.O. Box 106, (Situated on the Andersons' citrus farm)	Plaston 72	From R1,05 per day for small dogs to R1,50 per day for large dogs. Cats: 85c per day	It is advisable to book well in advance. Kennels are open every day, including Sundays and Public Holidays until 17 h 00.
LOSKOP DAM NATURE RESERVE	Middelburg (Tvl)	SPCA, P.O. Box 400, Wicht St.	01321 4605	Dogs: R1 per day - large 90c per day - medium 60c per day - small Cats: 50c per day	It is advisable to book in advance. Hours of duty: 08 h 00 to 12 h 30 and 14 h 00 to 17 h 00. Sat. 08 h 00 to 12 h 30. Innoculation certificates have to be shown.

NB. PERSONS REQUIRING BOARDING FOR PETS IN CITIES OR SMALLER CENTRES, SHOULD CONSULT THE LOCAL TELEPHONE DIRECTORY OR SPCA FOR ASSISTANCE.

CARAVAN AND CAMPING CLUB ADDRESSES (as at date of publication)

CARAVAN CLUB OF SOUTH AFRICA
CENTRAL COUNCIL .... P O Box 50580, RANDBURG 2125
Tel. (011) 48-3336 and 48-3402

REGIONS

ALFRED COUNTRY .... P O Box 613, MARGATE 4275

BORDER .... P O Box 388, EAST LONDON 5200

CAPE WESTERN .... "Raleigh House", 12 Raleigh Road, MOWBRAY 7700 Cape

EASTERN FREE STATE.......... P O Box 100, GLEN HARMONY 9435

EASTERN PROVINCE .... 6 Willet Place, Fern Glen, PORT ELIZABETH 6001

EASTERN TRANSVAAL.......... P O Box 2068, PRIMROSE 1416

FAR NORTHERN TRANSVAAL.................. P O Box 710, PIETERSBURG 0700

HIGHVELD .... 11 Oak Ave., PULLENSHOPE 1096

JACARANDA .... P O Box 22028, KLOOFSIG 0034

JOHANNESBURG AND DISTRICT....................... 209 Rifle Range Road, ROBERTSHAM 2197

LOWVELD....................... P O Box 1635, NELSPRUIT 1200

NATAL.......................... 52 Vivien Road, PINETOWN 3600

NATAL MIDLANDS.............. P O Box 2001, PIETERMARITZBURG 3200

NORTH COAST................. P O Box 7179, EMPANGENI STATION 3910

NORTHERN CAPE .... P O Box 933, KIMBERLEY 8300

NORTHERN FREE STATE........ P O Box 427, WELKOM 9460

NORTHERN NATAL.............. P O Box 1287, LADYSMITH 3370

NORTH RAND .... P O Box 50981, RANDBURG 2125

ORANGE .... P O Box 295, ALIWAL NORTH 5530

PRETORIA....................... P O Box 26226, ARCADIA 0007

RUSTENBURG.................. P O Box 1581, RUSTENBURG 0300

SOUTHERN CAPE.............. P O Box 104, KNYSNA 6570

SOUTHERN FREE STATE........ P O Box 1983, BLOEMFONTEIN 9300

SOUTH WESTERN TRANSVAAL................. P O Box 316, ORKNEY 2620

VAAL TRIANGLE................ P O Box 1197, VEREENIGING 1930

WESTERN TRANSVAAL.......... P O Box 319, CARLETONVILLE 2500

WEST RAND.................... P O Box 854, ROODEPOORT 1725

WITWATERSRAND EAST........ P O Box 177, BEDFORDVIEW 2008

CAMP PRIDE OWNERS CLUB......................... *Secretary* - Machiel Eksteen, 5 Fifth Avenue, Marlands, GERMISTON 1401. Tel. (011) 58-6075

CARAVAN ORGANISATION OF SOUTHERN AFRICA (for Coloured community) ..... President - Mr Geduldt Javonne, Thornton Rd., Crawford, CAPE TOWN 8001. Tel. (021) 47-4260

SA CAMPING CLUB............ *National Secretary* - Mr Ted Allbon, P O Box 3731, DURBAN 4000

SUID-AFRIKAANSE WOONWA ASSOSIASIE/ SOUTH AFRICAN CARAVAN ASSOCIATION..... P O Box 1346, EDENVALE 1610
Tel. (011) 53-3983

TREKKERS OUTDOOR RECREATION CLUB .... *Secretary/ Treasurer* - Mrs Lunzmann
P O Box 4157, DURBAN 4000
Tel. (031) 21-3998

ALPHABETICAL LIST OF CARAVAN PARK / CAMPING SITE NAMES

NAME	LISTED UNDER
Aberdeen Municipal	Aberdeen
Abrahamsrust Recreation Resort	Sasolburg
Addo Elephant National Park	Addo
Adventure	Boksburg
Agulhas Municipal	Agulhas
Albert Falls Public Resort	Albert Falls
Algeria	Cedarberg
Aliwal North Hot Springs	Aliwal North
Allamanda Holiday Resort	Nelspruit
Aloe Fjord Pleasure Resort	Aloe Fjord
Amersfoort Municipal	Amersfoort
Amos Lambrecht	Moorreesburg
Ananda Hotel Holiday Resort	Rustenburg
Anna Roux	Barrydale
Anstey's	Durban
Aqualea	Kidd's Beach
Archerwood Estate	Plettenberg Bay
Arch Rock Holiday Resort	Keurboomstrand
Aristata	Ladismith
Ashmead	Knysna
Aston Bay	Aston Bay
A.T.K.V. Holiday Resort	Hartenbos
Augrabies Falls National Park	Augrabies
B & M Park	Heidelberg (C)
Badplaas Mineral Baths	Badplaas
Banana Beach Holiday Resort	Banana Beach
Bapsfontein	Bapsfontein
Barkly West Municipal	Barkly West
Beach View	Beach View
Beaufort West Municipal	Beaufort West
Bekkers	Vanstadensrus
Belfast Dam	Belfast
Belle Vista	Marina Beach
Ben Alberts Nature Reserve	Thabazimbi
Ben Macdhui	Barkly East
Benmari Mineral Baths	Dennilton
Bergheim Holiday Resort	Kroondal
Bergplaas Holiday Ranch	Stellenbosch
Bergville Municipal	Bergville
Bethal Municipal	Bethal
Bezuidenhout Park	Johannesburg
Blossom Valley	Eikenhof
Blue Bend Holiday Resort	East London
Blue Seas	Shelly Beach
Blydepoort Public Resort	Graskop
Bly of Gly	Beaufort West
Blythedale Beach	Blythedale
Boereplaas Holiday Resort	Vryburg
Boesmansriviermond	Boesmansrivier-mond
Boknes Camping Ground	Boknes
Bonamanzi Marina	Bronkhorstspruit
Bontebok National Park	Swellendam
Bosbokstrand	Haga-Haga
Bracken Park	Brackenfell
Braemar	Braemar
Brakfontein	Heroldsbaai
Brandfort Municipal	Brandfort
Britstown Municipal	Britstown
Bronkhorstbaai Pleasure Resort	Bronkhorstspruit
Brookes Hill	Port Elizabeth
Buffalo Bay	Buffelsbaai
Bultfontein Municipal	Bultfontein
Burger Park	Worcester

NAME	LISTED UNDER
Cairngorm Tea Gardens	Petit
Caledon Warm Baths	Caledon
Calitzdorp Spa	Calitzdorp
Calvinia Municipal	Calvinia
Camper's Paradise	Paarl
Cannon Rocks	Boknes
Cape St Francis	Cape St Francis
Cape Vidal	Cape Vidal
Caracampark	Port Elizabeth
Caravan Cove	Park Rynie
Caravan's Rest	Marble Hall
Casa Benri Camping Resort	Mtunzini
Casarina	Nelspruit
Castle Rock	Sabie
Cathcart Municipal	Cathcart
Cedarberg Recreation Area	Cedarberg
Cedarberg Tourist Park	Cedarberg
Cefane Mouth	Cefane
Chelmsford Public Resort	Newcastle
Christiana Municipal	Christiana
Christmas Rock	Christmas Rock
Cintsa Bay Holiday Resort	Cintsa West
Cintsa Mouth East	Cintsa Mouth East
Cintsa West Holiday Resort	Cintsa West
Clansthal	Clansthal
Clanwilliam Dam Resort	Clanwilliam
Clarens Municipal	Clarens
Cloetenberg	Somerset West
Cloverdale	Sedgefield
Colenso Municipal	Colenso
Colesberg Municipal	Colesberg
Con's	Keurboomsrivier
Constantia	Margate
Constantia Mineral Spa	Naboomspruit
Cooke's Lake	Mafeking
Cradock Municipal	Cradock
Cresta	Elandsfontein
Dam Recreation Resort	Potchefstroom
Danielskuil Municipal	Danielskuil
De Bakke	Mossel Bay
De Hollandsche Molen	Franschhoek
De Mond	Hermanus
Deneysville Municipal	Deneysville
De Wet	Margate
Dewetsdorp	Dewetsdorp
Dickinson Park	Vereeniging
Die Dam	Bredasdorp
Die Eiland	Upington
Die Hoek	Bloemhof
Die Krans	Zeerust
Die Stroom	Swellendam
Dinwoodie	Germiston
Dolphin	Ballitoville
Doornfontein	Cradock
Doornkloof	Irene
Dordrecht Municipal	Dordrecht
Doring Park	Bothaville
Double Mouth Camping Site	Morgan's Bay
Dragon Peaks	Champagne Castle
Drakensberg Garden	Garden Castle
Drie Gewels	Stellenbosch
Drikkie Du Toit	Noupoort
Duiwelskloof Municipal	Duiwelskloof
Dundee Municipal	Dundee
Dunvegan	Adelaide
Durban	Durban

NAME	LISTED UNDER
Duttons Cove Holiday Resort	Heroldsbaai
Dwarskersbos	Dwarskersbos
Eastern Beach	East London
Ebb and Flow Nature Reserve	Wilderness
Edenburg Show Grounds	Edenburg
Eerste Tol	Paarl
Eiland Mineral Baths	Letsitele
Elandskrans Holiday Resort	Waterval-Boven
Ellensrust	Stilbaai-Oos
Elliot Municipal	Elliot
Empangeni	Empangeni
Eshowe Municipal	Eshowe
Essexwold	Bedfordview
Estcourt Municipal	Estcourt
Eureka	Nelspruit
Fairview	Tzaneen
Fairwinds	Benoni
False Bay Park	Hluhluwe
Fanies Island	Mtubatuba
Feesgrond	Parys
Ferreira's	Mondeor
Ficksburg Municipal	Ficksburg
Fiestapark Motel and Holiday Resort	Potgietersrus
First Beach Municipal	Port St Johns
Fish Hoek Municipal	Fish Hoek
Fitzpatrick	Barberton
Florida Lake	Florida
Forest Inn	Mtunzini
Fort Beaufort Municipal	Fort Beaufort
Fountains Valley	Pretoria
Fouriesburg Municipal	Fouriesburg
Frank Gunn Municipal Holiday Resort	Bethulie
Gamtoos River Mouth	Port Elizabeth
Garies High School Sports Grounds	Garies
George Municipal	George
Geyer Park	Wepener
G F Rautenbach Park	Patensie
Giant's Castle Game Reserve – Hillside	Estcourt
Giel De Wet	Thaba Nchu
Gifberg	Vanrhynsdorp
Glen Eden	East London
Glen Muir	Glen Muir
Glen Navar Holiday Resort	East London
Glen Reenen Rest Camp (Golden Gate)	Clarens
Glentana	Glentana
Golden Sea Horse	Umhlanga Rocks
Gonubie Mouth	Gonubie Mouth
Gordon's Bay Municipal	Gordon's Bay
Goudini Spa	Rawsonville
Gouritzmond	Gouritzmond
Grahamstown Municipal	Grahamstown
Graskop Municipal	Graskop
Griekwastad Municipal	Griekwastad
Groblersdal Municipal	Groblersdal
Groen Oewers	Viljoensdrif
Grootrivier	Nature's Valley
Gwenshaw	Gonubie Mouth
Gypsy	Bellville

NAME	LISTED UNDER
Haig Park	Matatiele
Hamburg Municipal	Hamburg
Hangklip	Betty's Bay
Hanover Municipal	Hanover
Happy Days	Hibberdene
Happy Wanderers	Kelso
Hardekraaltjie	Bellville
Harding Municipal	Harding
Harrismith Municipal	Harrismith
Heidelberg Municipal	Heidelberg (C)
Hendrik Verwoerd Dam Resort	Hendrik Verwoerd
Hendrina Municipal	Hendrina
Hennie Van Zyl Tourist Camp	Citrusdal
Hennops Pride Pleasure Resort	Pretoria
Herolds Bay	Heroldsbaai
Hibberdene (Karavan Serai)	Hibberdene
Hidaway	Umzumbe
Highland Nook Private Park	Himeville
Highlands Holiday Resort	Katberg
Highway	Machadodorp
Hi-Lee	Bazley
Himeville Nature Reserve	Himeville
Hippo Pools Holiday Resort	Mica
Hofmeyr Municipal	Hofmeyr
Honeydew	Honeydew
Howick Municipal	Howick
Humansdorp Tourist Park	Humansdorp
Humewood	Port Elizabeth
Ifafa Beach	Ifafa Beach
Ifafa Marina	Ifafa Beach
Illovo Beach	Illovo Beach
Imhoff Park	Kommetjie
Impala Holiday Resort	Kraaifontein
Inchanga	Cato Ridge
International	George
Iscor Angling Resort	Kosmos
Island Lake	Wilderness
Jamestown Municipal	Jamestown
Jan Smuts Park	Brakpan
Jeffreys Bay Holiday Resort	Jeffreys Bay
Jeffreys Bay Municipal	Jeffreys Bay
J G Strijdom	Nylstroom
Jim Fouché Holiday Resort	Oranjeville
Jock	Bosbokrand
Jongensfontein	Jongensfontein
Jooris Park	Sedgefield
Joos Becker	Pretoria
Joubert Park	Carolina
Kabeljous Holiday Resort	Jeffreys Bay
Kakamas Municipal	Kakamas
Kalahari Gemsbok National Park	Parks under control of National Parks Board
Karapark	Shelly Beach
Karavana	Winklespruit
Karmosyn	Vleesbaai
Karoo Sulphur Springs	Cradock
Karridene	Illovo Beach
Katryntjiesdrif	Wellington
Kays	Strand
Keimoes Municipal	Keimoes

NAME	LISTED UNDER
Kei Mouth Municipal	Kei Mouth
Kelso Valley	Kelso
Kelvin Grove	Winterton
Keurboomsrivier Public Resort	Keurboomsrivier
Kidd's Beach	Kidd's Beach
Kimberley Municipal	Kimberley
King William's Town Municipal	King William's Town
Klein Kariba	Warmbaths
Knysna Caravan and Holiday Park	Knysna
Koffiefontein	Koffiefontein
Kokerboom	Springbok
Kokstad Municipal	Kokstad
Komatipoort	Komatipoort
Komga Municipal	Komga
Konsensus	Cullinan
Koos Taljaard	Hobhouse
Kosi Bay Nature Reserve	Kosi Bay
Koster River Dam Camping Area	Koster
Kroon Park	Kroonstad
Kruger Dam Recreation Resort	Middelburg (T)
Kruger National Park	Parks under control of National Parks Board
Krugerspos	Krugerspos
Kruine Rest Camp	Nelspruit
Kudu Rest Camp	Phalaborwa
Kuilsrivier Municipal	Kuilsrivier
Kuruman Municipal	Kuruman
Ladismith Municipal	Ladismith (C)
Lady Grey	Lady Grey
Ladysmith Municipal	Ladysmith (N)
Lagoon	Port Alfred
Lagoon Holiday Resort	Keurboomsrivier
Lagoonside	Knysna
Lake Brenton Holiday Resort	Brenton
Lake Merthley	Greytown
Lake Pleasant Holiday Resort	Sedgefield
Lakeside Chalets	Haenertsburg
Lakeside Lodge	Nefdt
Lambert's Bay Municipal	Lambert's Bay
Landfall	Sedgefield
Langdam Pleasure Resort	Heilbron
Langebaan Municipal	Langebaan
Lawley Park	Breyten
Leliehoek Recreation Resort	Ladybrand
Leisure View	Leisure Bay
Lekkerrus Mineral Baths	Naboomspruit
Libertas Mineral Spa	Naboomspruit
Lichtenburg Municipal	Lichtenburg
Lincott Manor	Kidd's Beach
Lindley Municipal Overnight Stop	Lindley
Linga Longa Christian Holiday Farm	Warmbaths
Lion Inn	Phalaborwa
Lion Rampant	Eikenhof
Little Falls Pleasure Resort	Roodepoort

NAME	LISTED UNDER
Loch Athlone Holiday Resort	Bethlehem
Longbeach Holiday Resort	Mtwalume
Loskop Dam Public Resort	Damwal
Louis Trichardt Municipal	Louis Trichardt
Lovers Rock Pleasure Resort	Magaliesburg
Lowveld	Kaapmuiden
Loxton Municipal Overnight Stop	Loxton
Lydenburg Municipal	Lydenburg
Magennis	Uitenhage
Maitlands Camping Ground	Beach View
Mam's Roadhouse	Vryburg
Manoutsa	Hoedspruit
Margate Caravan Corner	Margate
Margate Caravan Park	Margate
Mariepsig Rest Camp	Hoedspruit
Marlon Park	Sunwich Port
Maroela Camp	Naboomspruit
Marydale Camping Site	Marydale
Maselspoort Holiday Resort	Bloemfontein
Max Clarke	Somerset East
McDougalls Bay	Port Nolloth
Medolino	Port Alfred
Meredale Pleasure Resort	Mondeor
Merry Pebbles	Sabie
Messina Municipal	Messina
Meurant	Riversdale
Middelburg Municipal	Middelburg (C)
Midland Estate	Middelburg (T)
Midmar Dam	Howick
Miller's Point	Miller's Point
Mimosa Garden	Parys
Mimosa Hotel Pleasure Resort	Eloff
Mittenwald	Munster
Mkuzi Game Reserve	Mkuze
Molopo-Dal Rest Resort	Lichtenburg
Molteno Municipal	Molteno
Monks	Knysna
Montagu Spa	Montagu
Montrose	Montrose
Möreson Rest Camp	Badplaas
Morgan's Bay	Morgan's Bay
Mossel Bay Caravans Five Star Park	Mossel Bay
Mountain	Louis Trichardt
Mountain Sanctuary Park	Kroondal
Mountain Zebra National Park	Cradock
Mount Carmel	Winklespruit
Mount Currie Motel	Kokstad
Mpekweni Holiday Resort	Peddie
Mtwalume	Mtwalume
Murray Park Pleasure Resort	Springs
Murraysburg	Murraysburg
Naboomspruit Municipal	Naboomspruit
Nahoon Beach	East London
N.A. Smit Municipal Tourist Camp	Oudtshoorn
Natalia Holiday Resort	Illovo Beach
Nelspruit Municipal	Nelspruit
Newcastle Municipal	Newcastle
Newton Walker Timm	Bathurst
Numbi Hotel	Hazyview

CONTINUED →

NAME	LISTED UNDER
Oasis	Uvongo
Oatlands Park	Simonstown
Ocean-Call	Winklespruit
Olifantshoek Caravan Park and Camping Site	Olifantshoek
Omaramba	Kroondal
Onrus Municipal	Onrus
Oom Dick	Winklespruit
Oom Loots	Touws River
Ooteekalia	Southbroom
Orkney-Vaal Holiday Resort	Orkney
Ou Skip	Melkbosstrand
Oyster Bay	Oyster Bay
Palmiet Municipal	Kleinmond
Palm Springs Holiday Resort	Kidd's Beach
Panorama	Gordon's Bay
Panorama	Roodepoort
Panorama Rest Camp	Graskop
Paradise	Southbroom
Paradise Beach	Paradise Beach
Paradise Park Holiday Camp	Onrus
Parow Municipal	Parow
Patlyn	Illovo Beach
Pearl	Klapmuts
Pearly Beach Holiday Resort	Pearly Beach
Pearson Park	Colchester
Pennington	Pennington
Peppertree	Laingsburg
Petrusville Municipal	Petrusville
Philipstown Municipal	Philipstown
Piesang River Resort	Plettenberg Bay
Pietermaritzburg	Pietermaritzburg
Piet Retief Municipal	Piet Retief
Pine Creek	Groot-Brakrivier
Pine Forest Public Resort	Ceres
Pine Lake Marina	Sedgefield
Pines Resort	Krugersdorp
Pinnie Joubert	Wellington
Pirate's Creek Holiday Resort	Bonza Bay
Pitstop	Bloemfontein
Pixie	East London
Plettenberg Bay	Plettenberg Bay
Point	Mossel Bay
Polkadraai	Pretoria
Pomona	Kempton Park
Pondorosa	Roodepoort
Pongola Municipal	Pongola
Ponies	Pilgrim's Rest
Pont	Port Edward
Port O'Call	Trafalgar Beach
Potgietersrus Municipal	Potgietersrus
Pot-Luck	Doonside
Prieska Municipal	Prieska
Protea	Eikenhof
Protea	Kempton Park
P.S.A. Holiday Resort	Gonubie Mouth
QB	Durban
Queenstown Municipal	Queenstown
Quinera Lagoon Holiday Resort	Gonubie Mouth
Rap-Skrap Rest Camp	Prince Albert
Rayner's Holiday Resort	Kidd's Beach
Rayton Caravan and Picnicking Camp	Bloemfontein
Reitz Municipal	Reitz
Rendezvous Recreation Resort	Pietersburg
Republiek	Ermelo
Richards Bay Municipal	Richards Bay
Richmond Municipal	Richmond (C)
Riebeeck Lake	Randfontein
Riverside	Klein-Brakrivier
Riverside Farm	Stilbaai-Oos
Riverton-on-Vaal	Riverton
Riviersonderend Municipal	Riviersonderend
Rivonia	Rivonia
Robberg Holiday Resort	Plettenberg Bay
Rob Ferreira Mineral Baths	Christiana
Robinvale	Fish Hoek
Rockclyffe-on-Sea Holiday Resort	Rockclyffe-on-Sea
Rocky Bay	Park Rynie
Rondalia	Hibberdene
Rondalia Buffelspoort	Marikana
Rondalia Die Oog	Naboomspruit
Rondalia Holiday Resort	East London
Ronwil Holiday Resort	Warmbaths
Royal Natal National Park	Mont-aux-Sources
SA Police Holiday Resort	Port Edward
SAR Dam	Belfast
Saame Park	Sunwich Port
Sabie River Mineral Baths	Sabi River Bungalows
Sabie Villa Rest Camp	Sabi River Bungalows
Safari	Mondeor
Safari	Welverdiend
St Georges Strand	Port Elizabeth
St Lucia Public Resort	St Lucia Estuary
St Pauls Caravan Park and Bungalows	Schagen
Saldanha Holiday Resort	Saldanha
Salmons Dam Nature Reserve	Stanford
Salt Rock	Salt Rock
Sandspruit Pleasure Resort	Honeydew
San Merino	Keurboomsrivier
Santos	Mossel Bay
Scarborough	Scarborough
Schoemanspoort	Oudtshoorn
Scottburgh Municipal	Scottburgh
Sea Breeze	Gordon's Bay
Sea Glimpse Holiday Resort	Victoria Bay
Seavale	Kidd's Beach
Sea View	Onrus
Second Beach Holiday Resort	Port St Johns
Second Beach Municipal	Port St Johns
Selley	Somerset East
Senekal Municipal	Senekal
Sherwood Forest	Marina Beach
Sherwood Park	Onrus
Shonalanga	Nelspruit
Shorten Park	Burgersdorp
Siesta Holiday Resort	Wilderness
Silverstrand Holiday Resort	Robertson
Smilin' Thru Chalets	Parys
Sodwana Bay National Park	Sodwana Bay
Sonop	Benoni
Spioenkop Public Resort	Winterton
Springs Pleasure Resort	Uitenhage
Standerton Municipal	Standerton
Steenbras Holiday Resort	Gordon's Bay
Sterkstroom Municipal Rest Camp	Sterkstroom
Steunmekaar	Clocolan
Steynsburg Municipal	Steynsburg
Stokkiesdraai Holiday Resort	Nylstroom
Stormsvlei	Stormsvlei
Strandfontein	Strandfontein
Strijdom Tunnel Motel and Rest Camp	Hoedspruit
Struisbaai	Struisbaai
Strydenburg Municipal	Strydenburg
Stutterheim Municipal	Stutterheim
Stywelyne	Laaiplek
Sudwala Caves	Schagen
Suikerbossie	Bredasdorp
Sunnyacres	Fish Hoek
Surf Bay	St Michael's on Sea
Swartfontein Recreation Resort	Vryburg
Swartvlei	Sedgefield
Sweet Valley	Constantia
Swellendam Municipal	Swellendam
Swinburne	Montrose
SYSU	Marina Beach
Tarkastad Municipal	Tarkastad
The Baths	The Baths
The Blue Lantern	Simonstown
The Kingfisher	St Michael's on Sea
The Lakes Holiday Resort	Wilderness
The Rainbow Park	Port Alfred
The Rocks Holiday Resort	Argent
The Willows	Port Alfred
The Willows Holiday Resort	The Willows
T O Strand	Port Edward
Tourist Motel	Trichardtsdal
Trail's End Holiday Resort	Sedgefield
Trompsburg Municipal Overnight Stop	Trompsburg
Tshipise Mineral Baths	Tshipise
Tsitsikama Coastal National Park	Stormsrivier
Tsitsikama Forest National Park	Stormsrivier
Tugela Mouth North Bank	Tugela
Tulbagh Municipal	Tulbagh
Uilenkraalsmond	Gansbaai
Uitkyk	Arnot
Uitspan	Kingsburgh
Umdoni	Pennington
Umhlanga Rocks	Umhlanga Rocks
Umlalazi Nature Reserve	Mtunzini
Umtata Municipal	Umtata
Umtentweni	Umtentweni
Umzimai	Hibberdene
Uniondale Municipal	Uniondale
Union Park	Pietersburg
Urquhart	Graaff-Reinet
Uvongo	Uvongo
Vaal Dam Nature Reserve	Deneysville
Vaaloewer	Lindequesdrif
Van der Merwe	De Aar
Van Stadens River Mouth	Van Stadens River Mouth
Van Zyls Motel Park	Colesberg
Venterstad Municipal	Venterstad
Vergesig Beach Resort	Mtwalume
Verina	East London
Victoria	Bloemfontein
Victoria Bay	Victoria Bay
Victoria West Municipal	Victoria West
Villiersdorp Municipal	Villiersdorp
Villiers Municipal	Villiers
Volksrust Municipal	Volksrust
Voortrekker Park	Carnarvon
Voortrekker Park	Strand
Vrede Municipal	Vrede
Vryheid Municipal	Vryheid
Waenhuiskrans	Waenhuiskrans
Wagendrift Public Resort	Estcourt
Wag-'n-Bietjie	Parys
Wagon Wheel Motel	Beaufort West
Walderi	Misgund
Warmbaths Mineral Baths	Warmbaths
Warmwaterberg Guest Farm	Warmwaterberg
Warrenton Municipal	Warrenton
Waterberg-Natuurpraal Holiday Resort	Melkrivier
Waterfall Park	Hogsback
Water Paradise	Klerksdorp
Water Ways Holiday Park	Knysna
Welcomagin Holiday Resort	East London
Welkom Municipal	Welkom
Wentzel Dam Parking Area	Schweizer-Reneke
Werda Caravan Park	Alberton
Westonaria Dam Pleasure Resort	Westonaria
Westvaal	Parys
White River Municipal	White River
Widenham	Widenham
Wilgerivier	Frankfort
Willem Pretorius Game Reserve	Ventersburg
Williston Municipal	Williston
Willow Grove	Johannesburg
Willowmore Municipal	Willowmore
Winburg Municipal	Winburg
Winsome Valley Holiday Resort	Broederstroom
Witbank Recreation Resort	Witbank
Witsand	Witsand
Wolmaransstad Municipal	Wolmaransstad
Wonderbaar Rest Camp	Koster
Wonderkrater Mineral Baths	Naboomspruit
Woodbourne Holiday Farm	Knysna
Xaxaza	Mtunzini
Yellow Sands	Glengarriff
Ysterfontein	Ysterfontein
Zandvlei	Muizenberg
Zastron Municipal	Zastron
Zinkwazi	Sinkwazi
Zonnekus Holiday Resort	Milnerton

ALPHABETICAL LIST OF CARAVAN PARKS / CAMPING SITES FOR COLOUREDS, ASIANS AND BLACKS

NAME	LISTED UNDER
Arniston Park (for Coloureds)	Waenhuiskrans
Augrabies Falls National Park (for Coloureds, Asians and Blacks)	Augrabies
Bridgton Camp (for Coloureds)	Oudtshoorn
Buffalo Bay Camping Area (for Coloureds)	Buffelsbaai
Chelmsford Public Resort (for Coloureds, Asians and Blacks)	Newcastle
De Hoek Holiday Resort (for Coloureds)	Oudtshoorn
Diaz Park (for Coloureds)	Mossel Bay
Die Anker Camping Site (for Coloureds and Asians)	Kommetjie
Die Eiland Caravan Park and Holiday Resort (for Coloureds)	Ceres
Die Ou Tol Camping Area (for Coloureds, Asians and Blacks)	Franschhoek
False Bay Park (for Coloureds, Asians and Blacks)	Hluhluwe
First Beach Municipal (for all races)	Port St Johns
Fullers Bay (for Asians)	East London
George Tourist Camp and Caravan Park (for Coloureds and Asians)	George
Grahamstown Municipal (for Coloureds and Asians)	Grahamstown
Groot-Brakrivier Municipal (for Coloureds)	Groot-Brakrivier
Gwayang (for Coloureds)	Gwayang River Mouth
Harmony Park (for Coloureds)	Strand
Harold Johnson Nature Reserve (for Blacks)	Darnall
Huis River Camping and Picnic Site (for Coloureds)	Calitzdorp
Jeffreys Bay Municipal Camp (for Coloureds)	Jeffreys Bay
Joorst Park (for Coloureds and Asians)	Port Elizabeth
Kiwane Holiday Resort (for Blacks)	Chalumna
Kleinkrantz (for Coloureds)	Kleinkrantz
Kogel Bay Pleasure Resort (for Coloureds and Asians)	Gordon's Bay
Kruger National Park — Lower Sabie and Skukuza (for Coloureds, Asians and Blacks)	Kruger National Park
Laaiplek Beach Resort (for Coloureds)	Laaiplek
Langebaan Municipal (for Coloureds)	Langebaan
Langleg Pleasure Resort (for Coloureds and Asians)	Kimberley
Leach Bay (for Coloureds)	East London
Manresa Holiday Farm (for Coloureds)	Mamre
Manyeleti Game Reserve (for Blacks)	Acornhoek
McDougalls Bay (for Coloureds)	Port Nolloth
Medusa (for Coloureds)	Kommetjie
Molshoop Camping Area (for Coloureds)	Struisbaai
Orient Park Resort (for Coloureds and Asians)	Howick
Orleans Park (for Coloureds)	Paarl
Park Rynie Caravan Park and Picnicking Ground (for Coloureds and Asians)	Park Rynie
Preekstoel Beach Resort (for Coloureds)	Stilbaai-Oos
Rugged Glen Campsite (for Coloureds, Asians and Blacks)	Royal Natal National Park
Rustville (for Coloureds, Asians and Blacks)	Beaufort West
St Lucia Public Resort (for Coloureds, Asians and Blacks)	St Lucia Estuary
Second Beach Holiday Resort (for all races)	Port St Johns
Second Beach Municipal (for all races)	Port St Johns
Shalimar Pleasure Resort (for Coloureds and Asians)	Potchefstroom
Silwerstroomstrand Resort Area (for Coloureds and Asians)	Silwerstroomstrand
Sonesta (for Coloureds)	Hawston
Spioenkop Public Resort (for Coloureds, Asians and Blacks)	Winterton
The Willows Holiday Resort (for Coloureds and Asians)	The Willows
Umgababa Seaside Holiday Resort (for Blacks)	Amanzimtoti
Umtata Municipal (for all races)	Umtata
Wagendrift Public Resort (for Coloureds, Asians and Blacks)	Estcourt
Wells Estate Camping Site (for Blacks)	Port Elizabeth
Western Seafront (for Blacks)	East London

CAMPING CARNET

Many members have enjoyed the benefits of the International Camping Carnet in the course of camping and caravan holidays in Europe where it is issued on a huge scale by motoring and camping organisations. Recognised in the United Kingdom, virtually all countries on the Continent and many countries in North Africa, it has been a boon to lovers of the outdoors and particularly to the venturesome who have a yen to experience the outdoors in some foreign country.

In South Africa the camping carnet has been issued exclusively by the AA over a period of more than ten years to members wishing to camp and caravan in Europe and now its availability is extended to members undertaking caravan or camping holidays in South Africa.

What is the International Camping Carnet?
It is a pocket-sized identity booklet bearing the holder's photograph, name and address, AA number, signature and other identification details.

It contains a description in six different languages of what it is, the benefits it provides and how to use it.

The holder undertakes on behalf of himself and all persons travelling with him in the same private vehicle (maximum 9 persons) to obey the rules of good camping.

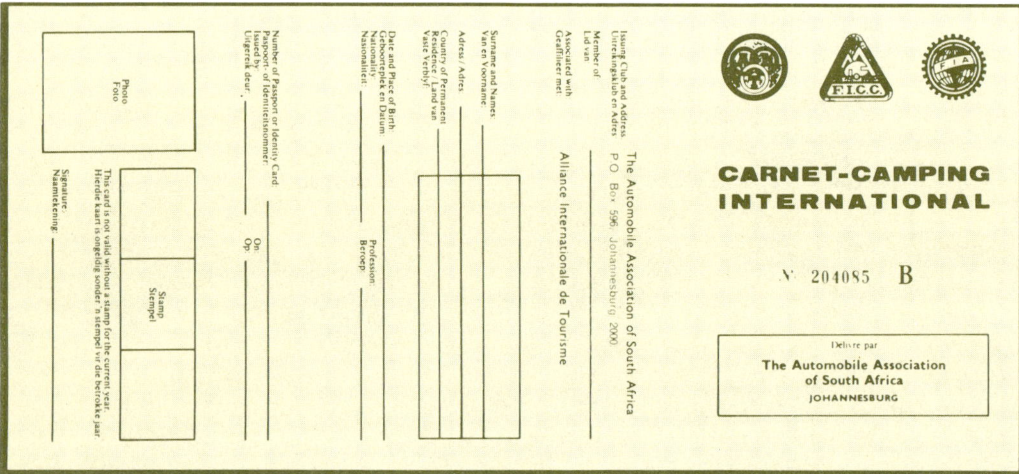

How Does it Operate?
In order to establish his *bona fides* and to encourage good relations, the holder deposits his carnet with the caravan park or camping ground proprietor or supervisor on entering the park/camping ground and collects it again on leaving.

Any complaints regarding the conduct of the carnet holder or members of his family or other persons travelling with him in the same vehicle are forwarded by the proprietor or supervisor to the AA.

What are the Benefits of the International Camping Carnet?

1. The holder and his family and any member of his party travelling in the same vehicle (maximum 9 persons) are insured against third party liability, i.e. claims against the holder by third parties for compensation for bodily injury and damage to property resulting from accidents occurring while the holder is camping. Members of the same family are however not regarded as third parties.

1.1 In respect of any one accident the amount of cover for personal injury is approximately R100 000 with a similar amount for loss of or damage to property. The holder may however not admit liability or offer or agree to settle any claim. Members are required to give the AA immediate notice in writing with full particulars of any accident likely to give rise to a claim and of the receipt of any notice of any claim or of the institution of any proceedings against the holder of a camping carnet.

1.2 The insurance does not cover claims arising from

1.2.1 bodily injury or disease or damage to property:

* directly or indirectly caused by any mechanically-propelled vehicle
* directly or indirectly caused by any ship, vessel, craft or aircraft, or arising out of any work done therein or thereon by or on behalf of the insured member
* arising out of food or drink poisoning or foreign or deleterious matter in food or drink
* arising out of the pollution of air, water, or soil unless it can be demonstrably proved to have been caused by immediate discharge consequent upon an accident
* directly or indirectly occasioned by, happening through or in consequence of war, invasion, act of foreign enemy, hostilities (whether war be declared or not), civil war, rebellion, revolution, insurrection or military or usurped power
* directly or indirectly occasioned by, happening through or in consequence of any form of large-scale entertainment where an entry fee is charged (but this shall not exclude small competitions staged for amusement)

1.2.2 bodily injury sustained by any person arising out of and in the course of his employment by the assured association or insured member under a contract of service or apprenticeship with the association or member

1.2.3 damage to property owned or occupied by or in the care, custody or control, of the insured member or of any servant of the insured member or in the care, custody, or control of any member of his family or of any servant camping with him

1.2.4 damage to ground or crops caused by trampling or setting up tents

1.2.5 indiscriminate disposal of garbage

1.2.6 damage to underground water-, gas- or electricity pipes or cables

1.2.7 any act committed by insured persons with malicious intent

2 **Personal Accident Insurance**
All persons travelling in the holder's vehicle and camping together are covered as follows:

Loss of index finger	R100	Death	R500
Loss of hearing of one ear	R150	Loss of hearing of both ears	R600
Loss of thumb	R200	Loss or loss of use of arm or hand	R600
Loss of sight of one eye	R300	Loss of sight of both eyes	R1 000
Loss of leg or foot	R500	Permanent total disablement	R1 000

Partial or multiple losses are paid in proportion but not exceeding R1 000 per carnet holder.
In addition, up to R50 is payable for necessary medical expenses incurred within 12 months of the accident.

Limits
Children under 5 years: 50% of benefits - maximum R250
Children 5 to 16 years: 100% of benefits - maximum R500
Maximum age: 70 years

Exclusions
War, rebellion, etc., attempted suicide, intoxication,
Winter sports, mountaineering, hunting, etc., or while boarding or alighting from a vehicle,
Transportation costs for injured or deceased persons, life saving and prosthesis.

3. Because of the protection afforded by the carnet to the holder and caravan and camping ground owners alike, it is inevitable that the latter will tend to favour those who hold camping carnets. This may in turn qualify holders for a reduction in charges at some sites.

4. **How to Obtain a Camping Carnet**
Apply to any AA office – allow a reasonable time for your application to be processed, i.e. at least two weeks before peak holiday seasons.

There is an easy-to-complete application form and one recent clear passport photograph of the applicant is required. The price of the Carnet is R3,00 and it is valid until the 31st December of the year of issue – apply for renewal. A camping carnet decal for cars and caravans is supplied free.

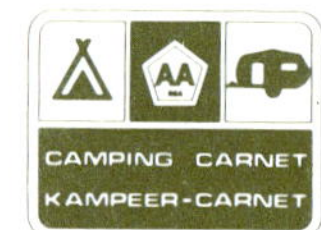

Note: Applicants must have a permanent home address and must not have had a previous withdrawal of a camping carnet because of any infringement of the rules of good camping or camp site regulations.

IMPORTANT NOTICE
All caravan parks and camping sites included in this supplement have been circularised by the AA to inform them of and to obtain their acceptance, recognition and support of the AA Camping Carnet. Establishments that have agreed to recognise the AA Camping carnet are marked in the classified list by the symbol " ⊕ " included next to the name of the establishment.
In addition, some of these establishments will *also* give a reduction in tariff of between 5-10%. These are indicated in column 42 on each page.
Establishments willing to grant tariff reductions out of season only are indicated in column 42 as well.

CARAVAN PARKS AND CAMPING SITES

INTRODUCTION

The caravan parks/camping sites listed cover the whole of South Africa and are arranged alphabetically according to the towns where, or near to which, they are situated. Where considered necessary, cross-references are included e.g. ARNISTON C see Waenhuiskrans.

In addition, an alphabetical list of caravan parks and camping site names is included, which indicates the town under which details of a particular establishment can be found e.g. Bontebok National Park will be found under Swellendam.

The information included was compiled from questionnaires completed by owners, managers or supervisors of the various establishments. Where there are gaps in the information given, it is because these facilities are missing or the questionnaire was returned incomplete to the AA.

A separate list gives details of facilities for Asians, Blacks and Coloureds.

Recommendation or grading of caravan parks

It is not the AA's practice to grade, appoint or recommend caravan parks or camping sites. Establishments listed are for the benefit and convenience of users. There is no official system of grading or classification of caravan parks in South Africa. However, the Caravan Club of South Africa has introduced a system of recommended parks and lays down certain basic requirements, set out below, with which establishments must comply in order to display the Caravan Club of South Africa's recommended board — see figure 1. These establishments have been marked in the supplement section by a ⛺ preceding the name of the place and will serve as a guide to the more discerning traveller.

Figure 1

For the benefit of users the following are some of the more important minimum conditions laid down by the Caravan Club of South Africa (CCSA) with which a caravan park must comply to earn the CCSA's recommendation:

Stands

- ☐ there should not be more than 30 stands per ha.
- ☐ should be of adequate size (at least 10 m x 12 m) to allow for the parking of a caravan and awning and its towing vehicle without overcrowding
- ☐ should be clearly demarcated, reasonably level, well-drained and as far as possible grassed
- ☐ only one caravan or tent should be permitted on each stand with a limit to the number of people who will occupy it
- ☐ shelter in the form of hedges, windbreaks or natural bush should be provided especially at the coast
- ☐ should be so positioned as to avoid flooding during storms
- ☐ there should be one tap for every 4 stands and each tap should have a soak pit
- ☐ there should be no public access across any stand – separate, well-demarcated paths should be provided
- ☐ refuse bins, which must be emptied regularly, should be provided for every 2 stands.

Toilet and Dishwashing Facilities

- ☐ Floors should be properly graded for efficient drainage
- ☐ one toilet for every 7 stands or part thereof should be provided in respect of both ladies and gentlemen
- ☐ one wash handbasin and small shelf, hot and cold water and a wall hook should be provided for every 7 stands or part thereof
- ☐ one mirror, a shower cubicle (which should have a section where clothing can be hung without getting wet) and/or baths with hot and cold water should be provided for every 10 stands or part thereof
- ☐ several open-air cold showers should be provided at the coast to ensure that sand is not carried into the ablution blocks
- ☐ the hot water system should be able to cope with the demand from the occupants of the demarcated stands
- ☐ a sufficient number of attendants should be on duty to keep the ablution blocks clean
- ☐ ablution blocks and facilities should be adequately lit during the hours of darkness
- ☐ there should be at least one disposal bin for chemical toilets
- ☐ separate facilities should be provided for the washing of utensils and garments

Roads

- ☐ adequate and durable access roads, along which speeds should be controlled, must be provided

General

- ☐ a superintendent should supervise the running of the park and see to the maintenance of all facilities, including the compliance by patrons with park regulations
- ☐ regulations and tariffs should be prominently displayed
- ☐ adequate security measures should be in force
- ☐ pets, if allowed, should be under the strict control of their owners at all times

EXPLANATION OF ENTRIES

Each entry listed commences with the name of the town in capital letters followed by a letter indicating the province in which the park falls, the map page, alpha-numerical index and direction arrow followed by the altitude of the town above sea level, thus

ILLOVO BEACH N 63 NS↗ S.L.

Beneath the town entry are listed the various establishments at that town in alphabetical order. These entries are in bold type followed by the address to which requests for information/reservations should be sent, together with the postal code, thus

Illovo Beach P.O. Box 19 (4155)
Karridene P.O. Box 20 (4155)
Natalia Holiday Resort Manager, P.O. Box 3 (4155)
Patlyn P.O. Box 11 (4155)

The actual site address is included where applicable on the same line in italic type and is preceded by an open square, thus

☐ *17 Elizabeth Ave.*

The existence of a facility as depicted under the various headings given, ■
is indicated by means of a symbol in the appropriate column. The □
symbols listed alongside are used on alternate lines to facilitate reading ●
of the information from left to right in relation to a specific establishment. ○
The symbols have no other meaning. ◆ ◇

The absence of a symbol means that this facility is not available or ▲
that information in this regard was not provided at the time. △

Please also consult the explanatory notes contained in the heading of ★
each page to be able to fully interpret the information given. ☆

SALES TAX

The tariffs included in the supplement are *exclusive* of sales tax. The following is a summary of instances for which visitors to caravan parks will, or will not be liable for tax.

Stand Charges

Sales tax (at 4% of the total charges) is payable on stand charges for any period from 1 to 45 consecutive days. Anyone intending to stay for an *unbroken* period in excess of 45 days, does not pay this tax, unless the person leaves on or before the 45th day in which case tax is payable for the actual period of stay. Advance payments are NOT exempt from tax.

Power

Charges for electricity, gas or water supplied to patrons are not subject to sales tax where:

- ☐ the caravan is connected to plug-in electricity
- ☐ gas is provided through a meter for the heating of water for baths, basins, etc. or where
- ☐ water is supplied for baths, basins, kitchen sinks or through taps for domestic use in caravans

Sales tax is payable on gas supplied in bottles or where gas bottles are supplied for filling.

Admission of day visitors and cars

Day visitors are not required to pay tax on admission fees for themselves or their vehicles.

Boat hire

Charges for the hire of boats by the park owner to patrons is subject to tax.

Appliance hire

Hire charges of 13c or more on freezers, refrigerators, laundry machines and driers or any other domestic appliances owned by a park and rented to patrons are taxable.

Cinema shows

No sales tax is payable for cinema shows given for the entertainment of patrons for which a charge has been made which includes normal entertainment tax.

Servants' accommodation

Tax is payable up to and including 45 days of continuous stay.

CAMPMOBILES FOR HIRE — see page 6

Conditions – a valid driver's licence must be provided and the minimum driver's age ranges from 21 to 25 years depending on the company. Petrol is not included in the rates – the hirer must pay for all petrol. A deposit is necessary to secure a reservation and the estimated cost of the rental for the whole period is required at the time of delivery.

Rates and conditions of hire are subject to change without notice.

TRAILER CARAVANS FOR HIRE — see page 7-8

Conditions – a valid driver's licence must be produced and a deposit is usually necessary to secure a reservation. The estimated cost of hire for the whole period is payable when the caravan is taken. Normally vehicles should be fitted with a towing bracket although in some instances they can be hired. The hirer should advise his insurance company of his intention to tow a caravan otherwise his car policy could be affected.

Rates and conditions of hire are subject to change without notice.

CARAVAN PARKS AND CAMPING SITES

Establishments marked thus [Caravan Club symbol] have the Caravan Club of South Africa recommendation – see page **17**
Establishments marked thus [AA symbol] recognise the AA Camping Carnet – see page **16** and also refer to column **42**

CARAVAN PARK / CAMP SITE TARIFF CODE – See columns 38–39 (Subject to alteration)

A = Up to R1 | C = R2–R3 | E = R4–R5 | G = R6–R7 | I = R8–R9 | K = R10–R16
B = R1–R2 | D = R3–R4 | F = R5–R6 | H = R7–R8 | J = R9–R10 | O = FREE
Charges are based on a family of 2 adults and 2 children under 12 years | X = On Application

ADDITIONAL ACCOMMODATION TARIFF CODE – See columns 57–59 (Subject to alteration)

eg. Bungalows, Cabins, Cottages, Chalets, etc.
A = R1–R3 | C = R5–R7 | E = R9–R11 | G = R13–R15 | I = R17–R19 | K = R21–R30
B = R3–R5 | D = R7–R9 | F = R11–R13 | H = R15–R17 | J = R19–R21 | X = On Application
NB: Where the tariff is given in *italics* it is per person, otherwise per unit

NOTE 1 — Columns 18, 19, 20, — Where a symbol appears instead of a number it means stands are available but not demarcated or number of stands has not been provided
NOTE 2 — Column 35 — A = Bookings accepted for additional accommodation only i.e. cottages, bungalows, etc.
NOTE 3 — Column 37 — Deposit refunded under certain conditions eg. less 10 %; if site is re-let; if cancelled well in advance (up to 2 months) or on a doctor's certificate
NOTE 4 — Column 41 — Reductions allowed on application for youth, church, school or sport groups or caravan rallies
NOTE 5 — Column 42 — R = Reduction in tariff of between 5 – 10 % to Carnet holders; O = Reduction Out-of-Season only
NOTE 6 — Column 69 — L = Laundry facilities only
NOTE 7 — Columns 88, 89, 90, — I = In-Season only; O = Out-of-Season only
NOTE 8 — Column 96 — Applicable In-Season only at some establishments
NOTE 9 — Column 102 — See section on golf in Outdoor Holiday Guide
NOTE 10 — Column 107 — See section on freshwater angling in Outdoor Holiday Guide
NOTE 11 — Column 108 — See section on coastal angling in Outdoor Holiday Guide

ABBREVIATIONS

C = CAPE PROVINCE
N = NATAL
O = ORANGE FREE STATE
T = TRANSVAAL
B = BOPHUTHATSWANA
X = TRANSKEI

			TELEPHONE CODE (T = DIAL 0020, BOOK TRUNK CALL; E = DIAL CODE, ASK EXCHANGE FOR NO.)	TELEPHONE NUMBER	OWNED OR SUPERVISED BY					SITE DESCRIPTION: LOCALITY				NATURE OF GROUND			SHADE			NO. OF STANDS			ACCESSIBILITY: APPROXIMATE DISTANCE FROM MAIN ROAD TO SITE					SURFACE OF APPROACH ROAD			CONDITION OF APPROACH ROAD	
			1	2	3 Privately owned	4 Municipality	5 Divisional council	6 Provincial administration	7 Parks board	8 Beach in immediate vicinity	9 Beside river, lake or dam	10 In or near mountain area	11 Within built-up area	12 Grass	13 Gravel	14 Sand	15 Unshaded	16 Partly shaded	17 Extensively shaded	18 Caravans only – see note 1	19 Caravans and/or tents – see note 1	20 Tents only – see note 1	21 On main rd.	22 Within 1 km	23 Within 5 km	24 Within 10 km	25 Within 15 km	26 Tar	27 Gravel	28 Sand	29 Good	30 Fair
		ABERDEEN C 59 A4 · 751m																														
□		**Aberdeen Municipal** P.O. Box 30 (6270) □ *Andries Pretorius St.*	T	14		□								□					□		13		□					□			□	
		ACORNHOEK T See Caravan Parks for Coloureds, Asians and Blacks																														
		ADDO C 59 B5 → 35m																														
◆		**Addo Elephant National Park** National Parks Board, P.O. Box 787, Pretoria 0001	012	44-1194					◆					◆				◆		20					◆			◆		◆	◆	
		ADELAIDE C 59 A6 ↙ 599m																														
▲	[AA]	**Dunvegan** P.O. Box 87 (5760) □ *5 Princess St.*	04662 E	180	▲						▲	▲	▲	▲				▲			▲		▲						▲		▲	
		AGULHAS C 58 D5 ↗ S.L.																														
★		**Agulhas Municipal** P.O. Box 178, Bredasdorp 7280 □ *Main Rd.*	T	Struisbaai 4212		★				★			★	★		★	★				100		★					★			★	
		ALBERT FALLS N 63 A3 ↖ 625m																														
■		**Albert Falls Public Resort** Officer-in-Charge, P.O. Box 31, Cramond 3420 □ *14 km from Pietermaritzburg*	0331	7-2146					■		■	■		■				■			40				■			■			■	
		ALBERTON T 72 NS ↘ 1554m																														
●		**Werda Caravan Park** P.O. Box 50025, New Redruth 1452 □ *Vereeniging Main Rd.*	T	622	●								●	●					●	30			●							●	●	
		ALIWAL NORTH C 62 B4 ↘ 1355m																														
◆		**Aliwal North Hot Springs** P.O. Box 206 (5530) □ *Levy St.*	0551 E	2951		◆								◆	◆			◆			500			◆				◆			◆	
		ALOE FJORD T 66 A6 ↙ 1494m																														
▲		**Aloe Fjord Pleasure Resort** Aloe Fjord Promotions, P.O. Box 84200, Greenside, Johannesburg 2034 □ *Vaal Dam*	016	4-0133	▲						▲			▲	▲	▲		▲		600	200	260		▲					▲		▲	
		AMERSFOORT T 67 B2 ↗ 1664m																														
★		**Amersfoort Municipal** P.O. Box 33 (2490) □ *Cnr. Plein/Bree Sts.*	013352 E	33		★							★	★				★		15			★					★			★	
		ARGENT T 69 D1 ↗ 1547m																														
■		**The Rocks Holiday Resort** P.O. Box 475, Delmas 2210 □ *Argent/Groenfontein or Arbor turn-off, 16 km from Delmas*	01572 E	1814	■						■			■					■	120		25			■				■		■	
		ARNISTON C See Waenhuiskrans																														
		ARNOT T 69 C2 ↘ 1684m																														
○		**Uitkyk** P.O. Box 50 (1051) □ *Middelburg/Belfast Rd.*	T	2621	○									○					○	30		30	○					○			○	
		ASTON BAY C 59 C4 ↗ S.L.																														
◇		**Aston Bay** P.O. Box 50, Jeffreys Bay 6330 □ *Barbet Cres.*	T	Jeff/Bay 8	◇					◇	◇			◇				◇		48					◇			◇			◇	
		AUGRABIES C 65 C2 ← 1200m																														
△		**Augrabies Falls National Park** National Parks Board, P.O. Box 787, Pretoria 0001 □ *13 km from Augrabies*	012	44-1194					△		△			△					△		80			△				△			△	
		BADPLAAS C 69 C3 ↓ 1189m																														
☆		**Badplaas Mineral Baths** P.O. Box 15 (1190)	013482 E	7/8				☆			☆	☆		☆				☆		120		120		☆				☆			☆	
■		**Mòreson Rest-camp** P.O. Box 11 (1190)	013482 E	26 or 44								■		■				■	■	■		■	■							■	■	
		BALLITOVILLE N 63 A4 ↙ 15m																														
●	[Caravan Club]	**Dolphin** P.O. Box 6 (4420) □ *Cnr, Dolphin/Compensation Beach Rds.*	032242 E	187	●					●				●					●		83				●			●			●	
		BANANA BEACH N 63 NS ↓ 5m																														
◆		**Banana Beach Holiday Resort** P.O. Box 68, Anerley 4230 □ *Lots 99–111, Melville*	0391	3043	◆					◆	◆			◆		◆		◆			30		◆					◆			◆	
		BAPSFONTEIN T 68 C6 ↓ 1612m																														
▲		**Bapsfontein** P.O. Box 7092, Petit 1512 □ *Bapsfontein turn-off, Delmas Highway*	011	844-1305	▲								▲		▲				▲		▲		▲					▲			▲	
		BARBERTON T 69 C4 ↙ 877m																														
★	[Caravan Club] [AA]	**Fitzpatrick** P.O. Box 33 (1300) □ *Voortrekker St.*	013142 E	717		★						★	★	★					★		100		★					★			★	
		BARKLY EAST C 62 B5 ↓ 1814m																														
■		**Ben Macdhui** Town Clerk, P/Bag 102 (5580) □ *Brownlee St.*	04542 E	158		■							■		■				■	20		20		■					■		■	
		BARKLY WEST C 66 C2 ● 1097m																														
●		**Barkly West Municipal** Town Clerk, P.O. Box 11 (8375) □ *Wakeford Ave.*	05352 E	17		●					●				●			●		30	50		●						●		●	
		BARRYDALE C 58 C5 ↖ 380m																														
◆		**Anna Roux** Town Clerk (6750)	02972 E	82		◆					◆	◆	◆	◆					◆	◆	◆		◆						◆		◆	
		BATHURST C 60 C1 ↘ 235m																														
▲		**Newton Walker Timm** Town Clerk (6166) □ *Kings Rd.*	04672 E	17		▲							▲	▲					▲	24		10		▲					▲		▲	
		BAZLEY N 63 NS ● S.L.																														
★		**Hi-Lee** P.O. Box 398, Scottburgh 4180	03239	763	★					★	★			★				★		40					★			★	★		★	
		BEACH VIEW C 59 C5 ↖ S.L.																														
■	[AA]	**Beach View** Dias Divisional Council, P.O. Box 318, Port Elizabeth 6000	041	2-8911			■			■				■	■	■		■		40	38	12		■				■			■	
□		**Maitlands Camping Ground** Bookings not accepted □ *Maitland River Mouth*	041	7-4884			□			□	□				□	□		□		25		25	□					□			□	
		BEACON BAY C See East London																														
		BEAUFORT WEST C 59 A2 ↑ 851m																														
◆		**Beaufort West Municipal** Bookings not accepted Enquiries: Town Clerk, P/Bag 582 (6970) □ *Donkin St.*	0201	2121		◆						◆	◆	◆	◆				◆		300		◆					◆			◆	
◇		**Bly of Gly** P.O. Box 79 (6970) □ *20 km from Beaufort West on the Cape Town Rd.*	0201	3333/1	◇									◇	◇				◇		20				◇				◇		◇	
▲		**Wagon Wheel Motel** P.O. Box 111 (6970) □ *2 km from Beaufort West*	0201	2801	▲								▲		▲			▲		20		2		▲						▲	▲	
		BEDFORDVIEW T 72 NS → 1578m																														
★		**Essexwold** P.O. Box 79160, Senderwood 2145 □ *Chaucer Rd., St. Andrews*	011	53-4631	★						★		★	★				★			38		★						★			★

SEASONS — TERMS FOR BOOKINGS — CARAVAN PARK/CAMPING SITE TARIFFS (See heading) — REDUCTIONS ALLOWED FOR — RESTAURANT FACILITIES — TEAROOM/CAFE — SHOPPING FACILITIES (Provisions) — ADDITIONAL ACCOMMODATION AVAILABLE — ADDITIONAL ACCOMMODATION TARIFF (See heading) — CARAVANS TO RENT ON SITE - SEE PAGES 8 – 11

OPEN THROUGHOUT THE YEAR / OUT-OF-SEASON CLOSING DATE / RE-OPENING DATE / BOOKINGS ACCP. PEAK SNS. - SEE NOTE 2 / DEPOSIT REQUIRED / REFUNDED IF CANCELLED - SEE NOTE 3 / MAXIMUM IN-SEASON TARIFF / MAXIMUM OUT-OF-SEASON TARIFF / LONG PERIODS OF STAY / GROUPS - SEE NOTE 4 / AA CARNET HOLDERS SEE NOTE 5 / OTHERS (ON APPLICATION) / ON SITE / WITHIN 5 km OF SITE / MORE THAN 5 km FROM SITE / ON SITE / WITHIN 5 km OF SITE / MORE THAN 5 km FROM SITE / ON SITE / WITHIN 5 km OF SITE / MORE THAN 5 km FROM SITE / BUNGALOWS / CABINS / COTTAGES (RONDAVELS) / CHALETS / MAXIMUM IN-SEASON TARIFF / MAXIMUM OUT-OF-SEASON TARIFF / CARAVANS TO RENT ON SITE - SEE PAGES 8 – 11

33	34	35	36	37	38	39	40	41	42	43	44	45	46	47	48	49	50	51	52	53	54	55	56	57	58	59
					B	B						□			□			□		□	□			D	D	
		◆	◆	◆	C	C					◆			◆			◆					◆		D	D	
		▲			B	B	▲	▲	R	▲		▲			▲			▲								
					C	C				★		★	★		★	★		★	★			★		C	C	
		■	■		D	D							■						■			■		*B*	*B*	
		●	●	●	D	D	●						●		●			●								
		◆	◆		D	D	◆	◆		◆	◆	◆		◆	◆			◆		◆	◆			B-C	B-C	
		▲	▲		D	D	▲	▲			▲			▲			▲					▲		J	G	
					A	A						★			★			★								
					C	C	■				■			■			■			■				X	X	■
		○	○	○	X	X	○	○			○			○			○					○		X	X	
May	Dec.	◇	◇	◇	E	E		◇				◇			◇			◇		◇		◇		E	E	
		△	△	△	C	C		△			△			△			△			△				I	I	
		☆	☆	☆	D	D				☆	☆	☆		☆	☆		☆	☆		☆	☆	☆	☆	B-I	B-I	
			■		D	C	■				■			■			■			■	■	■	■	F-J	D-G	
		●	●	●	I	F	●					●			●			●				●		B	B	
		◆	◆		H	D						◆	◆	◆	◆	◆		◆	◆	◆		◆	◆	K	F	
					A	A					▲			▲			▲			▲				C-D	B	
					C	C	★		R	★		★			★	★		★				★		X	X	
		■			A	A	■					■			■			■								
					A	A							●			●			●							
					A	A	◆	◆				◆			◆				◆							
		▲			B	B							▲					▲	▲							
		★	★	★	C	D				★			★	★			★									
		■			E	D	■				■			■			■						■	E	C	
					B	A						□			□				□							
					B	B						◆			◆			◆	◆							
		◇	◇	◇	D	D	◇	◇						◇					◇							
		▲	▲	▲	C	C	▲				▲							▲		▲				X	X	
		★	★		E	E	★	★				★			★			★								

CAMP SITE FACILITIES — I = In-Season only — O = Out-of-Season only

DRINKING WATER / BATHS / SHOWERS / NON-WHITE SERVANTS / TYPE OF VEHICLE PERMITTED

PIPED / OTHER / HOT AND COLD / COLD ONLY / HOT AND COLD / COLD ONLY / WATERBORNE SANITATION / WASHBASINS / DISHWASHING FACILITIES / LAUNDRY AND IRONING FACILITIES / WASHING MACHINES / SITE LIT / PLUGS FOR RAZORS (VOLTAGE) / REFRIGERATORS - SEE NOTE 6 / FIREWOOD/CHARCOAL / OPEN FIRE FORBIDDEN / CAMP FIRE PERMITTED / BRAAI PLACES PROVIDED / KITCHEN/COOKING FACILITIES / PETROL PUMP ON SITE / PETROL PUMP NEARBY / CAR REPAIR SHOP NEARBY / CAR SERVICING NEARBY / GAS SERVICE NEARBY / FIRST AID/HOSPITAL/DOCTOR NEARBY / POST OFFICE NEARBY / SITE GUARDED / PETS ALLOWED / SERVANTS PERMITTED - SEE NOTE 7 / SERVANTS ACCOM. - SEE NOTE 7 / SERVANTS FOR HIRE SEE NOTE 7 / CAR AND TRAILER / TRUCK HORSE AND SEMI-TRAILER / SELF-PROPELLED CARAVANS

60	61	62	63	64	65	66	67	68	69	70	71	72	73	74	75	76	77	78	79	80	81	82	83	84	85	86	87	88	89	90	91	92	93
□				□		□	□	□						□			□			□	□	□	□	□	□		□				□		
◆		◆		◆		◆	◆	◆				220		◆		◆	◆	◆	◆					◆		◆		◆	◆		◆	◆	◆
▲				▲		▲	▲	▲	▲		▲	220		▲		▲	▲			▲	▲	▲	▲	▲	▲		▲	▲		▲	▲	▲	▲
★		★		★		★	★	★			★			★		★	★	★		★	★	★	★	★	★	★	★	★			★	★	★
■		■		■		■	■				■					■	■			■	■	■		■	■						■	■	■
●		●		●		●	●	●	●		●				●		●									●	●			●	●	●	●
◆		◆		◆		◆	◆	◆	◆		◆	250		◆		◆	◆			◆	◆	◆	◆	◆	◆	◆					◆	◆	◆
▲		▲		▲		▲	▲	▲	▲		▲			▲	▲	▲	▲		▲				▲	▲		▲	▲	▲	▲		▲	▲	▲
★				★		★	★				★			★		★	★			★	★	★	★	★	★	★	★	★			★		★
■		■		■		■	■	■	■		■			■		■	■		■				■	■		■		■			■	■	■
○		○			○	○	○				○			○	○	○	○		○		○		○	○	○	○	○			○	○	○	○
◇		◇		◇		◇	◇	◇	◇	◇	◇			◇		◇	◇			◇	◇	◇	◇		◇						◇	◇	◇
△	△	△		△		△	△	△	△		△	220		△		△	△		△	△	△	△	△	△	△			△		△	△	△	△
☆		☆		☆		☆	☆	☆	☆	☆	☆	230		☆			☆			☆	☆	☆	☆	☆	☆	☆				☆	☆		☆
■		■	■	■	■	■	■	■	■		■		■			■	■	■		■	■	■	■		■			■	■		■		
●		●		●		●	●	●	●	●	●	230		●		●				●	●	●	●	●	●	●					●	●	●
◆		◆		◆		◆	◆	◆	◆		◆			◆		◆	◆			◆	◆	◆	◆		◆					◆	◆	◆	◆
▲				▲		▲	▲	▲	▲		▲			▲		▲	▲			▲	▲	▲	▲	▲	▲	▲	▲	▲	▲		▲	▲	▲
★		★		★		★	★	★	★		★	220		★		★	★			★	★	★	★	★	★	★	★	★			★	★	★
■		■		■		■	■		■		■					■	■			■	■	■	■		■		■				■	■	■
	●		●		●	●	●									●	●			●	●	●	●		●		●				●	●	●
◆	◆	◆		◆		◆	◆	◆	◆		◆			◆		◆	◆			◆	◆	◆	◆		◆	◆	◆	◆			◆	◆	◆
▲		▲				▲	▲	▲	▲					▲		▲	▲			▲	▲	▲	▲	▲	▲		▲	▲		▲	▲	▲	▲
★		★		★		★	★	★	★					★	★					★	★	★	★		★	★	★			★	★	★	★
■		■		■	■	■	■	■	■		■			■		■	■							■	■						■		■
□			□		□	□	□							□		□	□							□							□		□
◆	◆	◆		◆		◆	◆	◆	◆		◆	220		◆	◆		◆			◆	◆	◆	◆		◆	◆	◆	◆			◆		◆
◇		◇		◇		◇	◇	◇	◇	◇	◇		◇	◇		◇	◇	◇						◇		◇	◇			◇	◇		◇
▲		▲		▲		▲	▲									▲	▲		▲	▲	▲	▲		▲	▲	▲	▲	▲	▲		▲	▲	▲
★		★		★		★	★	★	★		★	220		★		★	★			★	★	★	★	★	★	★	★			★	★	★	★

SPORTING AND RECREATIONAL FACILITIES — S = On Site — N = Nearby (Up to 20 km away)

GOLF / FISHING / SWIMMING / BOATING / PLACES OF INTEREST / NOTES

CHILDRENS' PLAYGROUND / TENNIS / CINEMA/DRIVE-IN/TV ROOM - SEE NOTE 8 / HORSE-RIDING / GAMES ROOM / TRAMPOLINE / BOWLS / HOT SPRINGS / GOLF COURSE - SEE NOTE 9 / NUMBER OF HOLES / MINIATURE / MASHIE / PUTT-PUTT / FRESHWATER - SEE NOTE 10 / SEA - SEE NOTE 11 / GOGGLE / LICENCE REQUIRED / SWIMMING POOL / SEA BATHING / CHILDRENS' POOL / ADULTS ONLY / SHARK NETS AT BEACH / BOATS FOR HIRE / POWER / SAILING / CANOEING / HISTORIC / SCIENTIFIC / NATURAL

94	95	96	97	98	99	100	101	102	103	104	105	106	107	108	109	110	111	112	113	114	115	116	117	118	119	120	121	122	123
N	N					N																							
																												◆	
S	N	N		S		N		N	18				S			▲	S		S				S		S	▲	▲	▲	
S	N	N			S	N								N	N			★	N	★		N	N	N	N	★		★	
													S			■							S	S	S			■	
																													● Actually for permanent residents, but caters for en-route stopovers
S	S	N			S	N	S	N	9	◆		◆	N			◆	S		S							◆		◆	
S		S	S	S	S							▲	S			▲			S			S	S	S	S			▲	
S	N												N			★								N	N			★	
S	S	S	S	S									S				S		S						S			■	
S	N	N	S	N	N	N						○	N			○	S		S									○	
N	N	N	N	N	N	N		N	9				S	N			S	◇	S	◇				N	N		◇	◇	
S	S																									△	△	△	
S	S	S	S	S	S	S	S						N			☆	S		S							☆		☆	
N	N	N	N		N	N	N						■			■	S			■									
N	N	N		S		N		N	18					S	S	●	S	●	S		●					●	●	●	
N	N	S	N	S	N	N		N	18				◆	◆	◆	◆	N	◆	S		◆				N		◆	◆	
S	S				N												S		S										
S	N	N	N		N	S		N	9				N			★	N		N							★	★	★	
S	N												S			■	S								N	■	■	■	
S	N												S			●	S				●	S	S	S	S	●			
	N		N				N																					◆	
N	N	N	N	N	N	N		N	18				N	N	N	▲	N	▲	N	▲		N	N		N	▲	▲	▲	
S	N	I		S		N		N	18					N	N		S	★					S	S	S			★	
N														S				■	S									■	
S																		□										□	
	N	N	N	N		N		N	18				N			◆	N		N				N	N	N	◆		◆	
S		N	S		S	N		N	18			◇	N			◇	S		S				N	N	N	◇		◇	
S	N	N				N		N	18								S		S							▲	▲	▲	
S	N	N	N	N	N	N		N	18								N		N							★	★	★	

CARAVAN PARKS AND CAMPING SITES

Establishments marked thus [Caravan Club symbol] have the Caravan Club of South Africa recommendation – see page 17
Establishments marked thus [AA symbol] recognise the AA Camping Carnet – see page 16 and also refer to column 42

CARAVAN PARK / CAMP SITE TARIFF CODE – See columns 38–39 (Subject to alteration)

A = Up to R1 | B = R1–R2 | C = R2–R3 | D = R3–R4 | E = R4–R5 | F = R5–R6 | G = R6–R7 | H = R7–R8 | I = R8–R9 | J = R9–R10 | K = R10–R16 | O = FREE | X = On Application

Charges are based on a family of 2 adults and 2 children under 12 years

ADDITIONAL ACCOMMODATION TARIFF CODE – See columns 57–59 (Subject to alteration)

eg. Bungalows, Cabins, Cottages, Chalets, etc.

A = R1–R3 | B = R3–R5 | C = R5–R7 | D = R7–R9 | E = R9–R11 | F = R11–R13 | G = R13–R15 | H = R15–R17 | I = R17–R19 | J = R19–R21 | K = R21–R30 | X = On Application

NB: Where the tariff is given in *italics* it is per person, otherwise per unit

NOTE 1 – Columns 18, 19, 20, – Where a symbol appears instead of a number it means stands are available but not demarcated or number of stands has not been provided
NOTE 2 – Column 35 – A = Bookings accepted for additional accommodation only i.e. cottages, bungalows, etc.
NOTE 3 – Column 37 – Deposit refunded under certain conditions eg. less 10 % , if site is re-let ; if cancelled well in advance (up to 2 months) or on a doctor's certificate
NOTE 4 – Column 41 – Reductions allowed on application for youth, church, school or sport groups or caravan rallies
NOTE 5 – Column 42 – R = Reduction in tariff of between 5–10 % to Carnet holders O = Reduction Out-of-Season only
NOTE 6 – Column 69 – L = Laundry facilities only
NOTE 7 – Columns 88, 89, 90, – I = In-Season only, O = Out-of-Season only
NOTE 8 – Column 96 – Applicable In-Season only at some establishments
NOTE 9 – Column 102 – See section on golf in Outdoor Holiday Guide
NOTE 10 – Column 107 – See section on freshwater angling in Outdoor Holiday Guide
NOTE 11 – Column 108 – See section on coastal angling in Outdoor Holiday Guide

ABBREVIATIONS
C CAPE PROVINCE
N NATAL
O ORANGE FREE STATE
T TRANSVAAL
B BOPHUTHATSWANA
X TRANSKEI

TELEPHONE CODE: T – DIAL 0020, BOOK TRUNK CALL; E – DIAL CODE, ASK EXCHANGE FOR NO.

OWNED OR SUPERVISED BY: 3 Privately owned, 4 Municipality, 5 Divisional council, 6 Provincial administration, 7 Parks board
SITE DESCRIPTION – LOCALITY: 8 Beach, in immediate vicinity, 9 Beside river, lake or dam, 10 In or near mountain area, 11 Within built-up area; GROUND OF NATURE: 12 Grass, 13 Gravel, 14 Sand; SHADE: 15 Unshaded, 16 Partly shaded, 17 Extensively shaded
NO. OF STANDS: 18 Caravans only – see note 1, 19 Caravans and/or tents – see note 1, 20 Tents only – see note 1
ACCESSIBILITY – APPROXIMATE DISTANCE FROM MAIN ROAD TO SITE: 21 On main rd, 22 Within 1 km, 23 Within 5 km, 24 Within 10 km, 25 Within 15 km; SURFACE OF ROAD APPROACH: 26 Tar, 27 Gravel, 28 Sand; CONDITION OF ROAD APPROACH: 29 Good, 30 Fair, Poor

			Telephone code	Telephone number	3	4	5	6	7	8	9	10	11	12	13	14	15	16	17	18	19	20	21	22	23	24	25	26	27	28	29	30
			1	2																												
		BELFAST T 69 C3 ↙ 1970m																														
□		**Belfast Dam** Town Clerk, P.O. Box 17 (1100) □ *Kruger St.*	0132512 E	291		□					□				□				□		84				□				□		□	
●		**SAR Dam** Town Clerk, P.O. Box 17 (1100) □ *Duggan St.*	0132512 E	291		●					●				●				●		15			●				●			●	
		BELLA VISTA N See Marina Beach																														
		BELLVILLE C 58 NS ↗ 120m																														
◇		**Gypsy** P.O. Box 298 (7530) □ *National Rd.*	021	97-2828	◇								◇	◇					◇	40	10		◇					◇			◇	
▲	[Caravan Club]	**Hardekraaltjie** Bookings not accepted □ *Voortrekker Rd.*	021	97-1048		▲							▲	▲					▲	110		10	▲					▲			▲	
		BENONI T 72 NS ↗ 1661m																														
★	[Caravan Club] [AA]	**Fairwinds** P.O. Box 9297, Brentwood Park 1505 □ *High Rd., Norton Home Estates*	011	848-1819	★								★	★					★	50	50		★						★		★	
☆		**Sonop** P.O. Box 9239, Brentwood Park 1505 □ *6 Agate St., Rietpan*	011	973-1489	☆								☆		☆			☆	☆		59			☆				☆			☆	
		BERGVILLE N 67 C2 ↓ 1139m																														
□		**Bergville Municipal** P.O. Box 71 (3350) □ *3 km from Bergville*	03642 E	36		□					□	□		□	□			□			30			□					□			□
		BETHAL T 67 A2 ● 1701m																														
○		**Bethal Municipal** Park Superintendent, P.O. Box 3 (2310)	01361	2031		○					○			○				○		40	30			○					○		○	
		BETHLEHEM O 66 C6 ↑ 1636m																														
◇	[Caravan Club]	**Loch Athlone Holiday Resort** P.O. Box 551 (9700) □ *2 km from Bethlehem*	01431	5150		◇					◇			◇				◇		78	◇	100		◇				◇			◇	
		BETHULIE O 62 B3 → 1308m																														
△	[AA]	**Frank Gunn Municipal Holiday Resort** Town Clerk, P.O. Box 7 (9992) □ *At Bethulie Dam*	05862 E	2		△					△			△	△			△		200	200			△					△		△	
		BETTY'S BAY C 58 D3 → S.L.																														
☆		**Hangklip** P.O. Betty's Bay 7141 □ *Hangklip Rd.*	T	1331	☆					☆		☆				☆		☆			13				☆				☆	☆		☆
		BLOEMFONTEIN O 66 D4 ↖ 1392m																														
□		**Maselspoort Holiday Resort** Manager, P.O. Box 288 (9300) □ *20 km from Bloemfontein*	051	3-7848/3-7865		□					□	□			□				□	40	20					□		□	□		□	□
●		**Pitstop** P.O. Box 3901 (9300) □ *On the Western bypass at the Bultfontein/Eeufees Rd. Off-ramp*	051	33-2129/31-2210	●								●	●					●		120		●					●	●		●	
○		**Rayton Caravan and Picnicking Camp** P.O. Box 4182 (9300) □ *Rayton Rd.*	051	31-1348							○	○		○	○				○						○				○		○	
◆	[Caravan Club]	**Victoria** Bookings not accepted Enquiries: Director of Parks, P.O. Box 288 (9300) □ *First Ave.*	051	8-3636 x488		◆							◆	◆					◆	80								◆			◆	
		BLOEMHOF T 66 B3 ↓ 1232m																														
▲		**Die Hoek** Bookings not accepted □ *Rivier St.*	018022 E	17/18		▲					▲			▲	▲	▲	▲		▲		300			▲					▲		▲	
		BLYDE RIVER CANYON NATURE RESERVE T See Graskop																														
		BLYTHEDALE N 63 A4 ← S.L.																														
☆		**Blythedale Beach** P.O. Box 483, Stanger 4450 □ *93 Umvoti Drive*	032412	3504	☆					☆				☆				☆			18		☆					☆			☆	
		BOESMANSRIVIERMOND C 60 C1 ↘ S.L.																														
□		**Boesmansriviermond** Town Clerk (6190) □ *Main St.*	T	27		□				□				□				□			60			□				□			□	
		BOKNES C 60 C1 ↘ S.L.																														
○		**Boknes Camping Ground** Bookings not accepted	04652 E	8			○			○	○		○	○				○			50			○				○			○	
◆		**Cannon Rocks** P.O. Box 185, Alexandria 6185 □ *8 km from Boknes*	04652 E	3612	◆					◆			◆	◆				◆		60		20			◆				◆		◆	
		BOKSBURG T 72 NS → 1677m																														
▲	[AA]	**Adventure** P.O. Box 13059, Witfield 1467 □ *119 Madeley Rd., Boksburg West (Near Pick 'n Pay Hypermarket)*	011	826-1074	▲								▲	▲				▲			50			▲				▲			▲	
		BONTEBOK NATIONAL PARK C See Swellendam																														
		BONZA BAY C 60 B2 ↘ 4m																														
☆	[Caravan Club] [AA]	**Pirate's Creek Holiday Resort** P.O. Box 2065, Beacon Bay 5205	0431	47-1160/47-2502	☆					☆	☆		☆	☆				☆			60				☆			☆	☆		☆	
		BOSBOKRAND T 69 B4 ↙ 772m																														
□		**Jock** P.O. Box 10 (1280) □ *16 km from Bosbokrand*	T	Marite 9901	□							□		□				□		20			□						□			□
		BOTHAVILLE O 66 B4 ↗ 1311m																														
○		**Doring Park** P.O. Box 12 (9660)	014142 E	12		○					○				○			○		21				○					○		○	
		BRACKENFELL C 58 C3 ↓ 70m																														
◇		**Bracken Park** Old Paarl Rd. (7560) □ *Old Paarl Rd.*	021	31-1690	◇								◇	◇	◇	◇	◇	◇		24	24		◇					◇	◇		◇	
		BRAEMAR N 63 NS ● 433m																														
△	[AA]	**Braemar** Braemar Hotel, P.O. Braemar 4202	03231 E	620	△							△		△				△		18			△					△			△	
		BRAKPAN T 72 NS → 1615m																														
☆		**Jan Smuts Park** P.O. Box 15 (1540) □ *Escombe Ave.*	011	55-7711		☆					☆		☆	☆				☆		20					☆					☆		☆
		BRANDFORT O 66 C4 ↓ 1407m																														
□	[AA]	**Brandfort Municipal** P.O. Box 13 (9400)	05222 E	2		□							□	□	□			□			12		□					□			□	
		BREDASDORP C 58 D5 ← 49m																														
○		**Die Dam** Secretary, Divisional Council, P.O. Box 35 (7280)	02842 E	68			○			○				○				○			130						○		○		○	
◆		**Suikerbossie** P.O. Box 51 (7280) □ *Recreation St.*	02842 E	527		◆								◆				◆			30		◆						◆		◆	
		BRENTON C 59 NS ↓ S.L.																														
▲	[Caravan Club]	**Lake Brenton Holiday Resort** P.O. Box 235, Knysna 6570 □ *9 km from Knysna*	04452 E	6104	▲					▲	▲	▲		▲					▲	60		16				▲		▲			▲	
		BREYTEN T 69 D2 → 1794m																														
★		**Lawley Park** No facilities, but camping allowed □ *Hoy St.*	013452 E	28		★							★	★					★					★				★			★	

CAMP SITE FACILITIES — I = In-Season only; O = Out-of-Season only

SPORTING AND RECREATIONAL FACILITIES — S = On Site; N = Nearby (Up to 20 km away)

32 Seasons: Open throughout the year	33 Out-of-season closing date	34 Re-opening date	35 Terms for bookings: Bookings accp./peak sns. – see note 2	36 Deposit required	37 Refunded if cancelled – see note 3	38 Caravan park/camping site tariffs (see heading): Maximum in-season tariff	39 Maximum out-of-season tariff	40 Reductions allowed for: Long periods of stay	41 Groups – see note 4	42 AA carnet holders – see note 5	43 Others (on application)	44 Restaurant facilities: On site	45 Within 5 km of site	46 More than 5 km from site	47 Tearoom/cafe: On site	48 Within 5 km of site	49 More than 5 km from site	50 Shopping facilities (provisions): On site	51 Within 5 km of site	52 More than 5 km from site	53 Additional accommodation available: Bungalows	54 Cabins	55 Cottages (rondavels)	56 Chalets	57 Additional accommodation tariff (see heading): Maximum in-season tariff	58 Maximum out-of-season tariff	59 Caravans to rent on site – see pages 8–11	60 Drinking water: Piped	61 Other	62 Baths: Hot and cold	63 Cold only	64 Showers: Hot and cold	65 Cold only	66 Waterborne sanitation	67 Washbasins	68 Dishwashing facilities	69 Laundry and ironing facilities – see note 6	70 Washing machines	71 Site lit	72 Plugs for razors (voltage)	73 Refrigerators	74 Firewood/charcoal	75 Open fire forbidden	76 Camp fire permitted	77 Braai places provided	78 Kitchen/cooking facilities	79 Petrol pump on site	80 Petrol pump nearby	81 Car repair shop nearby	82 Car servicing nearby	83 Gas service nearby	84 First aid/hospital/doctor nearby	85 Post office nearby	86 Site guarded	87 Pets allowed	88 Non-white servants: Servants permitted – see note 7	89 Servants accom. – see note 7	90 Servants for hire – see note 7	91 Type of vehicle permitted: Car and trailer	92 Truck, horse and semi-trailer	93 Self-propelled caravans	94 Childrens' playground	95 Tennis	96 Cinema/drive-in/TV-room – see note 8	97 Horse-riding	98 Games room	99 Trampoline	100 Bowls	101 Hot springs	102 Golf: Golf course – see note 9	103 Number of holes	104 Miniature	105 Mashie	106 Putt-putt	107 Fishing: Freshwater – see note 10	108 Sea – see note 11	109 Goggle	110 Licence required	111 Swimming: Swimming pool	112 Sea bathing	113 Childrens' pool	114 Adults only	115 Shark nets at beach	116 Boating: Boats for hire	117 Power	118 Sailing	119 Canoeing	120 Places of interest: Historic	121 Scientific	122 Natural	123 Notes
□						A	A							□			□			□								□		□		□		□	□	□	□		□	□		□	□	□	□	□		□	□	□	□	□	□	□	□	□		□	□		□		N	N				N		N	9				S			□										□		□	
●						A	A						●	●		●	●		●	●								●		●		●		●	●	●	●		●	●		●	●	●	●	●		●	●	●	●	●	●	●	●	●		●	●		●		N	N				N		N	9																	●		●	
◇			◇	◇		D	D	◇					◇						◇									◇		◇		◇		◇	◇	◇	◇		◇	110/220		◇		◇	◇			◇	◇	◇	◇	◇	◇	◇					◇	◇	◇	S	N	N	N			N		N	9								S		S							◇	◇	◇	
▲						D	D						▲			▲			▲									▲		▲		▲		▲	▲	▲	▲		▲	▲					▲			▲	▲	▲			▲			▲			▲		▲	S	N	N	N			N		N	9								N		N							▲	▲	▲	
★			★	★		E	E			R			★			★			★									★		★		★		★	★	★	★	★	★	★			★		★			★	★	★	★	★	★			★			★		★	S	S	N	N			N		N	18								S		S										
☆			☆	☆	☆	E	C	☆					☆			☆	☆		☆	☆								☆		☆		☆		☆	☆	☆	☆		☆					☆	☆	☆		☆	☆	☆	☆	☆	☆	☆	☆	☆	☆		☆		☆	S	N	N	N	S	N	N		N	18								N		N							☆			
□			□	□		B	B									□			□		□	□	□	□	B	B		□		□		□		□	□	□	□		□	220		□	□	□	□	□		□	□	□	□	□	□			□		□	□		□	N	N					N		N	10				S			□	N						N	N	N	□	□	□	
○			○	○	○	C	C						○	○		○	○		○	○								○		○		○		○	○		○		○	○				○				○	○	○			○	○					○		○	S	N		N		N	N		N	9				S		S	○	N		N										
◇						C	C					◇			◇					◇	◇		◇		B-G	B-G		◇		◇		◇		◇	◇	◇	◇		◇	220	◇	◇			◇			◇	◇	◇	◇	◇	◇	◇	◇	◇	◇		◇	◇	◇	S	S	N				S		N	18	◇			S			◇	S		S			S	S	S	S			◇	
△			A	A		B	B			R			△						△				△		C-D	C-D		△		△		△		△	△	△	△		△			△		△	△			△	△	△	△		△		△	△		△	△	△	△	S	N		S	N	S	N							S			△	N		N				S	S	S	△		△	
☆			☆	☆	☆	C	C						☆			☆				☆	☆				A	A		☆		☆		☆		☆	☆	☆						☆		☆	☆		☆				☆	☆	☆		☆	☆			☆	☆	☆	S														N	N			☆											
□			□	□	□	C	C					□			□					□	□		□		D-J	D-J		□		□		□		□	□	□	□		□	220		□		□	□			□	□	□	□	□		□					□	□	□	S	S	S						N	18				S			□	S		S			S							
●			●	●		E	C	●	●		●	●		●	●		●			●							●	●	●	●		●		●	●	●	●		●	●		●		●			●	●	●	●	●			●	●	●		●	●	●	●	N	N	N	S			N		N	18				S		N														
○			○	○	○	D	D	○	○					○			○			○								○	○	○		○		○	○	○	○		○			○		○	○			○	○	○		○	○	○	○				○		○	S	S	N	N			N		N	18				S			○	S		N									○	
◆						E	E						◆			◆			◆									◆		◆		◆		◆	◆	◆	◆		◆	◆				◆	◆			◆	◆	◆	◆	◆	◆	◆		◆			◆	◆	◆	S	N	N	N	N	N	N		N	18			◆					N		N							◆		◆	
▲						B	B	▲					▲	▲		▲	▲		▲	▲								▲		▲		▲		▲	▲	▲	▲		▲	▲				▲	▲			▲	▲	▲	▲		▲	▲	▲	▲			▲	▲	▲	N	S	N				N		N	9		N		S			▲	S		S							▲		▲	
☆			☆	☆	☆	F	E	☆						☆	☆			☆										☆		☆		☆		☆	☆	☆	☆		☆	☆				☆	☆							☆							☆	☆	☆	S	N	N	N	S										N	N	☆		☆	N		☆								
□			□	□	□	E	E		□		□		□			□			□						F	F		□	□			□		□	□	□	□		□	250		□			□			□	□	□	□	□	□			□			□	□	□	N	N	N				N		N	18					N	N			N	N				N	N	N	□	□	□	
○						A	A							○			○		○									○					○	○	○		L								○			○	○	○				○	○	○			○		○		N							N	9					N				○					N		N	○		○	
◆			◆	◆	◆	C	C		◆						◆			◆										◆	◆	◆		◆		◆	◆	◆	L					◆	◆		◆		◆	◆			◆				◆			◆	◆	◆	◆	S	N	N	N	N	N	N		N	9					N	N		N	◆	N							◆		◆	
▲						D	D		▲	R			▲			▲			▲									▲		▲		▲		▲	▲	▲	▲	▲	▲	▲				▲	▲			▲	▲	▲	▲	▲	▲		▲				▲	▲	▲	S	N	N	S	S	S	N		N									S												
★			★	★	★	E	C	★		R			★			★			★		★				I	E	★	★		★		★		★	★	★	★		★	★		★	★		★			★	★	★	★	★	★		★			★	★	★	★	S	N	N	N	S		N		N	18	★	★	★		N	N		N	★	S			S			S	★	★	★	
□			□	□		B	B				□			□			□	□		□								□		□		□		□	□	□	□					□			□										□				□	□	□																														
○			○			B	B							○			○			○								○		○		○		○	○	○	○		○	220		○			○			○	○	○	○		○		○	○	○		○	○	○	N	N					N							N			○	N		N										
◇			◇	◇		C	C	◇					◇			◇			◇									◇		◇		◇		◇	◇	◇	◇							◇	◇			◇	◇	◇	◇		◇	◇	◇	◇			◇		◇	N	N							N	18								S		S	◇									
△			△	△		D	D	△			△	△			△			△										△		△		△		△	△	△	△		△																				△	△	△	S	N	N	N	S		N		N					N	N	N		S	N	S		△					△	△	△	
☆						B	B						☆	☆		☆	☆		☆	☆								☆		☆		☆		☆	☆		☆		☆	☆								☆	☆	☆			☆								☆	N	N	N	N		N	N		N	18				N			☆	N		N			N		N	N			☆	
□						B	B			R			□	□			□			□								□		□		□		□	□	□	□		□					□	□			□	□	□	□		□		□				□		□	S	N	N				N		N	9								N		N							□			
○						C	C											○		○								○		○		○		○	○	○	○					○		○	○			○			○			○	○	○			○	○	○															N	N			○					○	○	○	○			
◆						B	B	◆	◆					◆			◆			◆								◆		◆		◆		◆	◆	◆	◆			◆					◆			◆	◆	◆					◆				◆		◆	N	N	N				N		N	9					N				N								◆		◆	
▲			▲	▲	▲	G	D							▲			▲	▲		▲			▲	▲	G-K	D-H		▲		▲		▲		▲	▲	▲	▲		▲			▲	▲		▲			▲			▲				▲	▲	▲		▲		▲	S	N	N		S		N		N	18					N	S		S	▲	S			N	N	N	N	▲		▲	
★						O	O							★			★			★								★																																																																			

CARAVAN PARKS AND CAMPING SITES

Establishments marked thus [Caravan Club symbol] have the Caravan Club of South Africa recommendation – see page 17
Establishments marked thus [Camping Carnet symbol] recognise the AA Camping Carnet – see page 16 and also refer to column 42

CARAVAN PARK / CAMP SITE TARIFF CODE – See columns 38–39 (Subject to alteration)

A = Up to R1 | B = R1–R2 | C = R2–R3 | D = R3–R4 | E = R4–R5 | F = R5–R6 | G = R6–R7 | H = R7–R8 | I = R8–R9 | J = R9–R10 | K = R10–R16 | O = FREE | X = On Application

Charges are based on a family of 2 adults and 2 children under 12 years

ADDITIONAL ACCOMMODATION TARIFF CODE – See columns 57–59 (Subject to alteration)

eg. Bungalows, Cabins, Cottages, Chalets, etc.

A = R1–R3 | B = R3–R5 | C = R5–R7 | D = R7–R9 | E = R9–R11 | F = R11–R13 | G = R13–R15 | H = R15–R17 | I = R17–R19 | J = R19–R21 | K = R21–R30 | X = On Application

NB: Where the tariff is given in *italics* it is per person, otherwise per unit

NOTE 1 — Columns 18, 19, 20. — Where a symbol appears instead of a number it means stands are available but not demarcated or number of stands has not been provided
NOTE 2 — Column 35 — A = Bookings accepted for additional accommodation only i.e. cottages, bungalows, etc.
NOTE 3 — Column 37 — Deposit refunded under certain conditions eg. less 10% ; if site is re-let ; if cancelled well in advance (up to 2 months) or on a doctor's certificate
NOTE 4 — Column 41 — Reductions allowed on application for youth, church, school or sport groups or caravan rallies
NOTE 5 — Column 42 — R = Reduction in tariff of between 5–10 % to Carnet holders; O = Reduction Out-of-Season only
NOTE 6 — Column 69 — L = Laundry facilities only
NOTE 7 — Columns 88, 89, 90. — I = In-Season only ; O = Out-of-Season only
NOTE 8 — Column 96 — Applicable In-Season only at some establishments
NOTE 9 — Column 102 — See section on golf in Outdoor Holiday Guide
NOTE 10 — Column 107 — See section on freshwater angling in Outdoor Holiday Guide
NOTE 11 — Column 108 — See section on coastal angling in Outdoor Holiday Guide

ABBREVIATIONS
C = CAPE PROVINCE
N = NATAL
O = ORANGE FREE STATE
T = TRANSVAAL
B = BOPHUTHATSWANA
X = TRANSKEI

TELEPHONE CODE: T = DIAL 0020, BOOK TRUNK CALL; E = DIAL CODE, ASK EXCHANGE FOR NO.

			TELEPHONE CODE	TELEPHONE NUMBER	OWNED OR SUPERVISED BY: PRIVATELY OWNED	MUNICIPALITY	DIVISIONAL COUNCIL	PROVINCIAL ADMINISTRATION	PARKS BOARD	SITE DESCRIPTION – LOCALITY: BEACH IN IMMEDIATE VICINITY	BESIDE RIVER, LAKE OR DAM	IN OR NEAR MOUNTAIN AREA	WITHIN BUILT-UP AREA	NATURE OF GROUND: GRASS	GRAVEL	SAND	SHADE: UNSHADED	PARTLY SHADED	EXTENSIVELY SHADED	NO. OF STANDS: CARAVANS ONLY – SEE NOTE 1	CARAVANS AND/OR TENTS – SEE NOTE 1	TENTS ONLY – SEE NOTE 1	ACCESSIBILITY – APPROXIMATE DISTANCE FROM MAIN ROAD TO SITE: ON MAIN RD	WITHIN 1 km	WITHIN 5 km	WITHIN 10 km	WITHIN 15 km	SURFACE OF ROAD APPROACH: TAR	GRAVEL	SAND	CONDITION OF ROAD APPROACH: GOOD	FAIR	POOR
			1	2	3	4	5	6	7	8	9	10	11	12	13	14	15	16	17	18	19	20	21	22	23	24	25	26	27	28	29	30	31
		BRITSTOWN C 61 B5 ● 1122m																															
□		**Britstown Municipal** Town Clerk, P.O. Box 13 (8970) ☐ *Waterkant St.*	05732 E	3		□							□		□			□			30			□					□		□		
		BROEDERSTROOM T 68 NS ● 1225m																															
○		**Winsome Valley Holiday Resort** P.O. Box 46158, Orange Grove, Johannesburg 2119	011	45-3485	○						○	○		○				○		34		34			○				○		○		
		BRONKHORSTSPRUIT T 69 C1 ↘ 1426m																															
◇	[Camping Carnet]	**Bonamanzi Marina** P.O. Box 303 (1020) or P.O. Box 513, Benoni 1500 ☐ *Bronkhorstspruit Dam*	012122 E	3531	◇						◇	◇		◇				◇		200	50		◇					◇			◇		
▲		**Bronkhorstbaai Pleasure Resort** P.O. Box 26170, Arcadia, Pretoria 0007 ☐ *15 km from Bronkhorstspruit*	012122 E	520	▲						▲	▲		▲	▲	▲		▲	▲		300				▲				▲		▲		
		BUFFELSBAAI C 59 NS ↓ S.L.																															
★	[Caravan Club]	**Buffalo Bay** P.O. Box 369, Knysna 6570 ☐ *14 km from Knysna*	04452 E	6213	★					★				★			★			75	5	5				★		★			★		
		BULTFONTEIN O 66 C4 ↖ 1339m																															
■		**Bultfontein Municipal** P.O. Box 3 (9670) ☐ *Diamant St.*	05252 E	12		■							■	■				■		20	20			■				■			■		
		BURGERSDORP C 68 B4 ↙ 1388m																															
●	[Camping Carnet]	**Shorten Park** P.O. Box 13 (5520) ☐ *Pres. Swart Rd.*	05532 E	14 A/H 298		●						●	●	●	●				●	20	20	20		●				●	●		●		
		BUSHBUCKRIDGE T See Bosbokrand																															
		BUSHMAN'S RIVER MOUTH C See Boesmansriviermond																															
		CALEDON C 58 D4 ↑ 297m																															
▲		**Caledon Warm Baths** P.O. Box 192 (7230) ☐ *Off Nerena Ave.*	0281	2-2060		▲						▲		▲					▲		30		▲						▲			▲	
		CALITZDORP C 59 B1 → 238m																															
★	[Camping Carnet]	**Calitzdorp Spa** Manager, P.O. Box 169 (6660) ☐ *22 km from Calitzdorp*	T	Olifantsbron 1			★				★	★		★					★		150						★		★		★		
		CALVINIA C 61 C1 → 988m																															
■		**Calvinia Municipal** Town Clerk, P.O. Box 28 (8190) ☐ *Tuin St.*	02772 E	241/11		■					■	■			■			■			23		■					■			■		
		CANNON ROCKS C See Boknes																															
		CAPE PENINSULA C See respectively: ● **Bellville** ● **Brackenfell** ● **Constantia** ● **Fish Hoek** ● **Kommetjie** ● **Kraaifontein** ● **Kuilsrivier** ● **Miller's Point** ● **Milnerton** ● **Muizenberg** ● **Parow** ● **Scarborough** ● **Simonstown**																															
		CAPE ST. FRANCIS C 59 C4 ↗ 11m																															
◇		**Cape St. Francis** P.O. Box 92, Humansdorp 6300 ☐ *Da Gama Rd.*	T	17	◇					◇				◇				◇		50		50	◇						◇			◇	
		CAPE VIDAL N 67 C5 ↑ 25m																															
△		**Cape Vidal** Natal Parks Board, Cape Vidal, P.O. St. Lucia 3836	T	St. Lucia 1104					△	△	△			△		△			△		36									△			△
		CARNARVON C 61 B4 ↙ 1253m																															
☆		**Voortrekker Park** P.O. Box 10 (7060) ☐ *Hospital Ave.*	02032 E	397		☆							☆	☆	☆				☆		☆			☆					☆		☆		
		CAROLINA T 69 D3 ↘ 1718m																															
□		**Joubert Park** Town Clerk, P.O. Box 24 (1185) ☐ *Voortrekker St.*	013442 E	53		□							□	□				□		30	30		□					□			□		
		CATHCART C 60 B2 ← 1135m																															
○		**Cathcart Municipal** P.O. Box 35 (5310) ☐ *Robinson St.*	04562 E	22		○							○	○				○			20		○						○		○		
		CATO RIDGE N 63 NS ↗ 753m																															
◇	[Caravan Club]	**Inchanga** P.O. Box 111 (3680) ☐ *1000 Hills Rd., Inchanga West*	032512 E	26	◇							◇		◇				◇		59			◇					◇			◇		
		CEDARBERG C 58 B4 ↖ 529m																															
△		**Algeria** Cedarberg State Forest, P.O. Citrusdal 7340 ☐ *27 km from Cedarberg*	02682 E	3440							△	△		△		△		△	△		36								△		△		
★		**Cedarberg Recreation Area** Dwarsrivier, Cedarberg, P.O. Citrusdal 7340	02682 E	1521	★						★	★			★	★	★	★	★			★							★			★	
☆		**Cedarberg Tourist Park** P/Bag Kromrivier, Citrusdal 7340	02682 E	1502	☆						☆	☆		☆	☆				☆		30				☆				☆			☆	
		CEFANE C 60 B3 ↙ S.L.																															
□		**Cefane Mouth** P.O. Box 1474, East London 5200 ☐ *43 km from East London*	0431	95-1169	□					□	□			□				□		25						□		□	□		□		
		CERES C 58 C4 ↖ 457m																															
○	[Caravan Club]	**Pine Forest Public Resort** Manager, P.O. Box 44 (6835) ☐ *1 km from Ceres*	023312 E	543/613		○						○	○	○	○				○	240		120			○			○			○		
		CHAMPAGNE CASTLE N 67 D2 ↑ 1300m																															
◇		**Dragon Peaks Caravan Park** P.O. Loskop 3330	T	Dragon Peaks 1	◇						◇	◇		◇					◇	130		30		◇					◇			◇	
		CHELMSFORD PUBLIC RESORT N See Newcastle																															
		CHRISTIANA T 66 B3 ↙ 1209m																															
★		**Christiana Municipal** Town Clerk, P.O. Box 13 (2680)	05342 E	13		★					★		★	★	★			★			112 400			★					★			★	
☆	[Caravan Club]	**Rob Ferreira Mineral Baths** General Manager, P.O. Box 19 (2680) ☐ *3 km from Christiana*	05342 E	499			☆				☆			☆				☆					☆					☆			☆		
		CHRISTMAS ROCK C 60 C2 ↗ S.L.																															
□		**Christmas Rock** P.O. Kidd's Beach 5264 ☐ *40 km west of East London*	04323	899	□					□	□			□				□		110	10				□				□			□	
		CINTSA MOUTH EAST C 60 B3 ↙ S.L.																															
○	[Camping Carnet]	**Cintsa Mouth East** P.O. Box 1711, East London 5200 ☐ *40 km from East London*	0431	95-1150	○					○	○			○					○		40				○				○		○		
		CINTSA WEST C 60 B3 ↙ S.L.																															
◇		**Cintsa Bay Holiday Resort** P.O. Box 7045 East London 5200 ☐ *33 km from East London*	0431	95-1178	◇					◇				◇				◇		◇		◇	◇					◇			◇		
▲		**Cintsa West Holiday Resort** P.O. Box 2059, Beacon Bay 5205 ☐ *37 km from East London*	0431	95-1176/95-1216	▲					▲				▲				▲		▲		▲		▲				▲			▲		
		CITRUSDAL C 58 B4 ← 152m																															
★		**Hennie van Zyl Tourist Camp** Town Clerk, P.O. Box 57 (7340) ☐ *Oewer St.*	02662 E	81		★					★	★	★	★	★				★		30			★				★			★		
		CITRUSDAL DISTRICT See Cedarberg																															

CAMP SITE FACILITIES — I = In-Season only, O = Out-of-Season only

SPORTING AND RECREATIONAL FACILITIES — S = On Site, N = Nearby (Up to 20 km away)

32 Seasons: Open throughout the year	33 Out-of-season closing date	34 Re-opening date	35 Terms for bookings: Bookings accp./peak sns.—see note 2	36 Deposit required	37 Refunded if cancelled—see note 3	38 Caravan park/camping site tariffs (See heading): Maximum in-season tariff	39 Maximum out-of-season tariff	40 Reductions allowed for: Long periods of stay	41 Groups—see note 4	42 AA carnet holders—see note 5	43 Others (on application)	44 Restaurant facilities: On site	45 Within 5 km of site	46 More than 5 km from site	47 Tearoom/cafe: On site	48 Within 5 km of site	49 More than 5 km from site	50 Shopping facilities (Provisions): On site	51 Within 5 km of site	52 More than 5 km from site	53 Additional accommodation available: Bungalows	54 Cabins	55 Cottages (Rondavels)	56 Chalets	57 Additional accommodation tariff (See heading): Maximum in-season tariff	58 Maximum out-of-season tariff	59 Caravans to rent on site—see pages 8–11	60 Drinking water: Piped	61 Other	62 Baths: Hot and cold	63 Cold only	64 Showers: Hot and cold	65 Cold only	66 Waterborne sanitation	67 Washbasins	68 Dishwashing facilities	69 Laundry and ironing facilities—see note 6	70 Washing machines	71 Site lit	72 Plugs for razors (voltage)	73 Refrigerators	74 Firewood/charcoal	75 Open fire forbidden	76 Camp fire permitted	77 Braai places provided	78 Kitchen/cooking facilities	79 Petrol pump on site	80 Petrol pump nearby	81 Car repair shop nearby	82 Car servicing nearby	83 Gas service nearby	84 First aid/hospital/doctor nearby	85 Post office nearby	86 Site guarded	87 Pets allowed	88 Non-white servants: Servants permitted—see note 7	89 Servants accom.—see note 7	90 Servants for hire—see note 7	91 Type of vehicle permitted: Car and trailer	92 Truck, horse and semi-trailer	93 Self-propelled caravans	94 Childrens' playground	95 Tennis	96 Cinema/drive-in/TV-room—see note 8	97 Horse-riding	98 Games room	99 Trampoline	100 Bowls	101 Hot springs	102 Golf: Golf course—see note 9	103 Number of holes	104 Miniature	105 Mashie	106 Putt-putt	107 Fishing: Freshwater—see note 10	108 Sea—see note 11	109 Goggle	110 Licence required	111 Swimming: Swimming pool	112 Sea bathing	113 Childrens' pool	114 Adults only	115 Shark nets at beach	116 Boating: Boats for hire	117 Power	118 Sailing	119 Canoeing	120 Places of interest: Historic	121 Scientific	122 Natural	123 Notes
□			□	□	□	G	F	□		R				□			□	□		□							□	□		□		□			□	□	□	□	□	□	□		□		□			□	□	□	□		□		□	□			□		□	S	N	N		S		N		N	18					N	N	□	S		S										
○						D	c						○			○			○									○				○		○	○	○	○		○			○		○	○			○	○	○	○	○	○			○			○		○	N	N		N					N	9				N			○							S	S	S	○		○	
◇			◇	◇	◇	C	C	◇	◇				◇			◇			◇									◇	◇	◇		◇		◇	◇	◇	◇		◇	◇		◇		◇	◇			◇	◇	◇	◇	◇	◇	◇	◇				◇	◇	◇	S	N	N	N			N							N			◇	N		N							◇	◇	◇	
▲			▲	▲	▲	C	C					▲			▲			▲			▲			▲	D	D		▲		▲		▲		▲	▲	▲	▲			110/220			▲	▲	▲	▲	▲				▲	▲	▲	▲					▲	▲			S		S			S		S	9																			▲	
★						B	B						★			★			★									★		★		★		★	★	★	★	★	★	★		★	★	★	★			★	★	★	★	★	★	★	★			★	★		★	N	N					N		N	9				N			★	N		N						N	★		★	
■			■	■		D	D		■	R						■	■		■	■	■				B-F	B-F		■	■	■		■		■	■	■	■		■			■		■	■			■			■		■		■			■	■	■	■	S														N				■				S	S	S	S			■	
●						B	B							●			●			●								●				●		●	●	●			●					●		●		●	●	●			●		●				●	●	●		N					N							S			●	N		N							●		●	
◆						C	C						◆			◆			◆									◆		◆		◆		◆	◆	◆	◆		◆	◆				◆	◆			◆	◆	◆	◆	◆	◆	◆	◆	◆			◆	◆	◆	S	N	N	N			N		N	18								N									◆			
◇			◇	◇	◇	F	F	◇	◇			◇			◇			◇			◇				X	X		◇		◇		◇		◇	◇	◇	◇					◇			◇				◇	◇	◇	◇	◇	◇	◇	◇	◇		◇			S																	S									◇			
△			△	△		D	D						△			△			△									△		△		△		△	△	△	△			△			△	△	△			△	△	△			△		△	△			△	△	△			N				N	N	N	18					△			S		S							△	△	△	
☆			☆			B	B	☆	☆				☆			☆			☆									☆		☆		☆		☆	☆	☆	☆		☆	220				☆	☆			☆	☆	☆		☆	☆		☆	☆		☆	☆	☆	☆	S	N	N				N	N	N	9				N			☆	S		S							☆		☆	
■			■	■		B	B		■										■									■		■		■			■	■			■			■		■	■															■	■	■		S		S				N	N	9			■					S		N									■	
□			□	□	□	B	B		□					□	□		□			□			□	□	E	D		□		□		□		□	□	□	□		□	220		□		□	□			□	□	□		□	□		□	□		□	□	□	□	S	N	N				N	S	N	9				S			□	S		S							□		□	
●			●	●	●	B	B													●				●	C	C		●				●		●	●		●		●		●	●		●	●	●	●					●	●	●		●	●		●	●	●																											●	●	●	
◆			◆			X	X			R			◆			◆			◆					◆	X	X		◆					◆	◆	◆							◆		◆				◆	◆	◆	◆		◆	◆	◆	◆	◆		◆	◆	◆				S					N	9							S		S	◆						◆		◆	
▲			▲	▲	▲	E	E				▲	▲			▲			▲			▲	▲		▲	E+	E+		▲		▲		▲		▲	▲	▲	▲	▲	▲	220		▲	▲	▲	▲		▲				▲	▲		▲				▲	▲		▲	S	S	S		S	S								S			▲	S		S				S	S	S			▲	
★				★	★	B	B							★		★			★									★		★		★		★	★	★	★		★					★				★	★	★	★	★	★			★		★	★		★													N			★							N	N	N	★		★	
□						B	B			R				□			□				□								□		□		□		□	□	□	□		□	220					□			□	□	□	□		□		□	□			□		□	S	N	N				N		N	18								N									□		□	
○						O	O						○			○			○																									○					○	○	○		○		○	○			○	○	○		N	N											S			○			N							○	○	○	
◇						C	C	◇					◇			◇			◇		◇				X	X		◇		◇				◇	◇	◇	◇		◇			◇	◇	◇	◇			◇	◇	◇	◇	◇	◇	◇	◇	◇		◇	◇	◇	◇	N	N	N				N							N			◇	N		N	◇			N	N	N	◇			
▲						B	B						▲	▲		▲	▲		▲	▲								▲	▲					▲	▲										▲			▲	▲	▲			▲		▲				▲	▲	▲	N													N			▲													
★			★			D	C	★	★			★			★			★			★		★		C-F	B-C		★		★		★		★	★	★			★			★		★	★		★			★	★		★	★				★	★	★	★	S		S		S			S						S			★	S		S									★	
■						A	A						■			■			■									■					■	■	■										■			■		■			■						■	■	■	N	N								N	9																				
○			○	○		F	C					○	○		○	○			○								○	○		○		○		○	○	○	○	○	○	○		○		○				○	○	○	○		○						○	○	○	N	N	N				N		N						S			N	S	N		S		N	N	N			○	
◇						A	A						◇			◇			◇									◇						◇														◇	◇	◇	◇	◇	◇		◇	◇		◇	◇	◇	N	N	N	N	S	S	N		N	18																	◇		◇	
★			★	★		B	B	★						★			★		★				★		B-D	B-D		★		★		★		★	★	★	★		★		★	★			★			★	★	★	★	★	★	★					★	★	★	N	S					S		N	18				N			★	S						N	N	N	★	★	★	
■			■			c	C										■			■								■		■		■		■	■	■	■		■					■	■				■	■	■		■	■	■	■		■				N	N	N	N			N		N	18				N			■	N		N				N	N		■		■	
●			●	●		D	D						●			●			●									●		●		●		●	●	●	●		●	●		●	●	●	●				●	●	●	●	●	●	●	●			●	●	●	S	S	N			S	N		N	18					N		●		●	N		●								
○			○	○	○	F	F	○					○		○			○									○	○	○		○		○	○	○	○	○	○	○			○		○			○	○	○	○		○	○		○			○		○	S				S		N		N	18					N			S		S		○					○		○	
◆			◆	◆		E	B	◆			◆		◆		◆			◆	◆									◆		◆		◆		◆	◆	◆	◆	◆				◆			◆			◆	◆	◆	◆	◆	◆	◆				◆	◆				N					N		N	18				N				S	◆								◆	◆	◆	
▲			▲			C	C						▲	▲					▲									▲		▲			▲	▲	▲	▲			▲	▲		▲		▲	▲			▲	▲	▲					▲	▲			▲		▲															N			N	▲	N									▲	
★			★	★		E	B	★					★			★			★			★	★		X	X		★		★		★		★	★	★	★			220		★		★				★	★	★	★		★	★	0	★	★	★	★		★		N	N	N	S		N		N	18	★	★	★	N	N	N	★	N	★	N				N	N	N	★	★	★	
☆			☆	☆		D	C						☆			☆				☆								☆				☆		☆	☆		☆		☆	220				☆				☆	☆	☆		☆		☆		☆		☆	☆		☆	N	N	N				N		N	18		N	☆		N	N			☆	N				N	N		☆		☆	

CARAVAN PARKS AND CAMPING SITES

Establishments marked thus (Caravan Club symbol) have the Caravan Club of South Africa recommendation – see page **17**
Establishments marked thus (AA symbol) recognise the AA Camping Carnet – see page **16** and also refer to column **42**

CARAVAN PARK / CAMP SITE TARIFF CODE – See columns 38–39 (Subject to alteration)

A = Up to R1 | C = R2–R3 | E = R4–R5 | G = R6–R7 | I = R8–R9 | K = R10–R16
B = R1–R2 | D = R3–R4 | F = R5–R6 | H = R7–R8 | J = R9–R10 | O = FREE
Charges are based on a family of 2 adults and 2 children under 12 years | X = On Application

ADDITIONAL ACCOMMODATION TARIFF CODE – See columns 57–59 (Subject to alteration)

eg. Bungalows, Cabins, Cottages, Chalets, etc.
A = R1–R3 | C = R5–R7 | E = R9–R11 | G = R13–R15 | I = R17–R19 | K = R21–R30
B = R3–R5 | D = R7–R9 | F = R11–R13 | H = R15–R17 | J = R19–R21 | X = On Application
NB: Where the tariff is given in *italics* it is per person, otherwise per unit

NOTE 1 — Columns 18, 19, 20. — Where a symbol appears instead of a number it means stands are available but not demarcated or number of stands has not been provided
NOTE 2 — Column 35 — A = Bookings accepted for additional accommodation only i.e. cottages, bungalows, etc.
NOTE 3 — Column 37 — Deposit refunded under certain conditions eg. less 10 % ; if site is re-let ; if cancelled well in advance (up to 2 months) or on a doctor's certificate
NOTE 4 — Column 41 — Reductions allowed on application for youth, church, school or sport groups or caravan rallies
NOTE 5 — Column 42 — R = Reduction in tariff of between 5 – 10 % to Carnet holders
0 = Reduction Out-of-Season only
NOTE 6 — Column 69 — L = Laundry facilities only
NOTE 7 — Columns 88, 89, 90. — I = In-Season only ; 0 = Out-of-Season only
NOTE 8 — Column 96 — Applicable In-Season only at some establishments
NOTE 9 — Column 102 — See section on golf in Outdoor Holiday Guide
NOTE 10 — Column 107 — See section on freshwater angling in Outdoor Holiday Guide
NOTE 11 — Column 108 — See section on coastal angling in Outdoor Holiday Guide

ABBREVIATIONS
C CAPE PROVINCE
N NATAL
O ORANGE FREE STATE
T TRANSVAAL
B BOPHUTHATSWANA
X TRANSKEI

TELEPHONE CODE: T = DIAL 0020. BOOK TRUNK CALL. E = DIAL CODE. ASK EXCHANGE FOR NO.

		Telephone code (1)	Telephone number (2)	Owned or supervised by: Privately owned (3)	Municipality (4)	Divisional council (5)	Provincial administration (6)	Parks board (7)	Site description – Locality: Beach in immediate vicinity (8)	Beside river, lake or dam (9)	In or near mountain area (10)	Within built-up area (11)	Nature of ground: Grass (12)	Gravel (13)	Sand (14)	Shade: Unshaded (15)	Partly shaded (16)	Extensively shaded (17)	No. of stands: Caravans only – see note 1 (18)	Caravans and/or tents (19)	Tents only – see note 1 (20)	Accessibility – Approximate distance from main road to site: On main rd. (21)	Within 1 km (22)	Within 5 km (23)	Within 10 km (24)	Within 15 km (25)	Surface of road approach: Tar (26)	Gravel (27)	Sand (28)	Condition of approach road: Good (29)	Fair (30)	Poor (31)
	EAST LONDON (CONTINUED)																															
■	**Glen Eden** P.O. Box 2054, Beacon Bay 5205 ☐ *At Bulugha River Mouth*	0431	95-1319	■					■	■			■					■	100				■				■			■		
□	**Glen Navar Holiday Resort** P/Bag 502 (5200) ☐ *32 km from East London*	0431	95-1329	□					□				□				□	□		80				□			□				□	
●	**Nahoon Beach** Director of Parks, P.O. Box 984 (5200) ☐ *Near Nahoon Mouth*	0431	8-7569		●				●	●			●				●	●		134			●				●				●	
○	**Pixie** P.O. Box 5072, Greenfields 5208 ☐ *Chester Rd., Sunnyridge*	0431	46-1611	○					○				○				○		10				○				○				○	
◆	**Rondalia Holiday Resort** P.O. Box 2079, Beacon Bay 5205 ☐ *Near Sunrise-on-Sea*	0431	95-1519	◆					◆	◆			◆					◆		16				◆				◆		◆		
◇	**Verina** P.O. Box 5102, Greenfields 5208 ☐ *Settlers Way*	0431	46-1069	◇								◇	◇				◇		36		4	◇					◇			◇		
▲	**Welcomagin Holiday Resort** P.O. West Bank 5218 ☐ *Hickmans River Mouth*	0431	46-1080	▲					▲	▲	▲	▲	▲			▲	▲	▲	40		7		▲					▲			▲	
	EAST LONDON DISTRICT See respectively: ● **Bonza Bay** ● **Cefane** ● **Christmas Rock** ● **Cintsa Mouth East** ● **Cintsa West** ● **Glengarriff** ● **Glen Muir** ● **Gonubie Mouth** ● **Kidd's Beach** ● **Rockclyffe-on-Sea**																															
	EDENBURG O 62 A3 ↘ 1376m																															
■	**Edenburg Show Grounds** P.O. Box 16 (9908)	05842 E	8		■							■	■				■		16	16	16	■						■		■		
	EIKENHOF T 72 NS ↓ 1524m																															
●	**Blossom Valley** P.O. Eikenhof 1872 ☐ *Cnr. Gordon and Alberton/Eikenhof Rds., Kibler Park*	011	943-1508	●						●		●	●					●		35	1	●					●			●		
○	**Lion Rampant** P.O. Box 141 (1872) ☐ *Plot 18, Olifantsvlei, Eikenhof/Alberton Rd.*	011	943-1802	○						○		○	○				○		36			○					○			○		
◆	**Protea** P.O. Box 186 (1872) ☐ *Vereeniging Main Rd.*	011	943-1066	◆						◆	◆	◆	◆				◆		100	50	56	◆					◆			◆		
	EILAND MINERAL BATHS T See Letsitele																															
	ELANDSFONTEIN T 72 NS → 1737m																															
△	**Cresta** North Reef Rd., P.O. Elandsfontein 1406 ☐ *North Reef Rd.*	011	36-5081	△								△	△			△	△	△	200			△					△			△		
	ELLIOT C 62 C5 → 1448m																															
☆	**Elliot Municipal** Town Clerk, P.O. Box 21 (5460) ☐ *Maclear Ave.*	T	11		☆						☆	☆	☆				☆		25	25		☆						☆		☆		
	ELOFF T 68 C6 ↓ 1623m																															
□	**Mimosa Hotel Pleasure Resort** P.O. Box 61 (2211) ☐ *On the Witbank highway*	T	26	□								□	□					□		50		□					□			□		
	ERMELO T 67 A2 → 1734m																															
○	**Republiek** P.O. Box 48 (2350) ☐ *7 km from Ermelo*	01341	4093		○					○			○				○		60		40		○				○			○		
	ESHOWE N 67 C4 ↓ 502m																															
◇	**Eshowe Municipal** P.O. Box 37 (3815) ☐ *Addison St.*	035412 E	311/17/450		◇							◇	◇		◇		◇	◇		22			◇				◇			◇		
	ESTCOURT N 67 D2 ↗ 1168m																															
△	**Estcourt Municipal** Bookings not accepted ☐ *Lorne St.*	03631	3000		△							△	△				△			25		△					△			△		
★	**Giant's Castle Game Reserve — Hillside** Officer-in-Charge, P.O. Box 755 (3310) ☐ *69 km from Estcourt*	03631	4435					★			★		★				★			6						★		★			★	
☆	**Solitude Mountain Resort** P.O. Box 66 (3310) ☐ *3 km from Loskop*	03631	3190	☆						☆	☆		☆				☆			20						☆		☆			☆	
■	**Wagendrift Public Resort** P.O. Box 316 (3310) ☐ *8 km from Estcourt*	03631	2550					■		■			■				■			20				■			■			■		
	FALSE BAY PARK N See Hluhluwe																															
	FANIES ISLAND N See Mtubatuba																															
	FICKSBURG O 66 C5 ↘ 1630m																															
◆	**Ficksburg Municipal** P.O. Box 116 (9730) ☐ *Bloem St.*	05632 E	12		◆					◆	◆	◆	◆					◆		100			◆				◆			◆		
	FISH HOEK C 58 NS ● S.L.																															
▲	**Fish Hoek Municipal** Bookings not accepted Enquiries: Caravan/Camping Officer, 63 Main Rd. (7975) ☐ *Foreshore*	021	82-1163		▲				▲		▲	▲		▲		▲			24				▲				▲			▲		
△	**Robinvale** P.O. Box 142 (7975) ☐ *Cnr. 20th Ave./Kommetjie Rd.*	021	82-2714/82-2162	△					△		△		△				△			40		△					△			△		
★	**Sunnyacres** P.O. Box 50 (7975)	021	82-2913	★					★				★					★		50		★						★		★		
	FLORIDA T 72 NS → 1676m																															
■	**Florida Lake** Manager: Parks and Recreation, P.O. Box 217, Roodepoort 1725 ☐ *Westlake Rd.*	011	672-6221		■					■			■				■		65			■						■			■	
	FORT BEAUFORT C 60 B1 ↓ 437m																															
●	**Fort Beaufort Municipal** Town Clerk, P.O. Box 36 (5720) ☐ *Durban St.*	043512 E	17/162		●							●	●				●			12		●					●			●		
	FOURIESBURG O 66 C2 ↙ 1829m																															
◆	**Fouriesburg Municipal** P.O. Box 5 (9725) ☐ *Kosmos St.*	014322 E	14		◆							◆	◆	◆				◆	◆				◆					◆			◆	
	FRANSCHHOEK C 58 C4 ↙ 100m																															
▲	**De Hollandsche Molen (Pty) Ltd. — Oude Molen** P.O. Box 535, Suider-Paarl 7624 ☐ *Paarl-Franschhoek Rd.*	0252	2704	▲						▲	▲		▲					▲	50	20	70	▲					▲			▲		
	FRANKFORT O 66 B6 ↖ 1574m																															
★	**Wilgerivier** P.O. Box 2 (9830)	0161312 E	30		★					★			★					★		25				★			★			★		
	GAMTOOS RIVER MOUTH C See Port Elizabeth																															
	GANSBAAI C 58 D4 ↙ 15m																															
□	**Uilenkraalsmond** Caretaker, P.O. Box 18 (7220) ☐ *9 km from Gansbaai*	02834	2012			□			□	□	□		□		□			□	100	940		□	□				□				□	
	GARDEN CASTLE N 63 A2 ↙ 1753m																															
○	**Drakensberg Garden** Central Reservations, P.O. Box 2529, Marine Parade, Durban 4056	031	37-2672	○						○	○		○					○	4	44	25	○						○		○		
	GARDEN ROUTE C See respectively: ● **Brenton** ● **Buffelsbaai** ● **George** ● **Glentana** ● **Groot-Brakrivier** ● **Gwayang River Mouth** ● **Hartenbos** ● **Heroldsbaai** ● **Keurboomsrivier** ● **Keurboomstrand** ● **Klein-Brakrivier** ● **Kleinkrantz** ● **Knysna** ● **Mossel Bay** ● **Nature's Valley** ● **Plettenberg Bay** ● **Sedgefield** ● **Stormsrivier** ● **Victoria Bay** ● **Wilderness**																															
	GARIES C 60 B5 → 240m																															
★	**Garies High School Sports Grounds** Headmaster, Garies High School (8220)	T	3				★					★	★					★	★	★	★		★				★			★		

Seasons / Terms for bookings / Tariffs / Reductions / Restaurant, tearoom and shopping facilities / Additional accommodation

32 Open throughout the year	33 Out-of-season closing date	34 Re-opening date	35 Bookings acc. peak sns. – see note 2	36 Deposit required	37 Refunded if cancelled – see note 3	38 Caravan park/camping site tariffs: Maximum in-season tariff	39 Maximum out-of-season tariff	40 Reductions allowed for: Long periods of stay	41 Groups – see note 4	42 AA carnetholders – see note 5	43 Others (on application)	44 Restaurant facilities: On site	45 Within 5 km of site	46 More than 5 km from site	47 Tearoom/cafe: On site	48 Within 5 km of site	49 More than 5 km from site	50 Shopping facilities (provisions): On site	51 Within 5 km of site	52 More than 5 km from site	53 Additional accommodation available: Bungalows	54 Cabins	55 Cottages (rondavels)	56 Chalets	57 Additional accommodation tariff: Maximum in-season tariff	58 Maximum out-of-season tariff	59 Caravans to rent on site – see pages 8–11
□			□	□	□	G	F	□		R				□			□	□		□							□
○						D	c						○			○			○								
◇			◇	◇	◇	C	C	◇	◇				◇			◇			◇								
▲			▲	▲	▲	C	C					▲			▲			▲			▲			▲	D	D	
★						B	B						★			★			★								
■			■	■		D	D		■	R						■	■		■	■	■				B-F	B-F	
●						B	B							●			●			●							
◆						C	C						◆			◆			◆								
◇			◇	◇	◇	F	F	◇	◇			◇			◇			◇			◇				X	X	
△			△	△		D	D						△			△			△								
☆			☆			B	B	☆	☆				☆			☆			☆								
■			■	■		B	B		■										■								
□			□	□	□	B	B		□					□	□		□			□			□	□	E	D	
●			●	●	●	B	B													●				●	C	C	
◆			◆			X	X			R			◆			◆			◆					◆	X	X	
▲			▲	▲	▲	E	E				▲	▲			▲			▲			▲	▲		▲	E+	E+	
★				★	★	B	B							★		★			★								
□						B	B			R				□			□			□							
○						O	O						○			○			○								
◇						C	C	◇					◇			◇			◇		◇				X	X	
▲						B	B						▲	▲		▲	▲		▲	▲							
★			★			D	C	★	★			★			★			★			★		★		C-F	B-C	
■						A	A						■			■			■								
○			○	○		F	C					○	○		○	○			○								○
◇						A	A						◇			◇			◇								
★			★	★		B	B	★						★			★		★				★		B-D	B-D	
■			■			c	C										■			■							
●			●	●		D	D						●			●			●								
○			○	○	○	F	F	○					○		○			○									
◆			◆	◆		E	B	◆			◆		◆		◆			◆	◆								
▲			▲			C	C						▲	▲					▲								
★			★	★		E	B	★					★			★			★			★	★		X	X	
☆			☆	☆		D	C						☆			☆				☆							

Camp site facilities

I = In-Season only   O = Out-of-Season only

60 Drinking water: Piped	61 Other	62 Baths: Hot and cold	63 Cold only	64 Showers: Hot and cold	65 Cold only	66 Waterborne sanitation	67 Washbasins	68 Dishwashing facilities	69 Laundry and ironing facilities – see note 6	70 Washing machines	71 Site lit	72 Plugs for razors (voltage)	73 Refrigerators	74 Firewood/charcoal	75 Open fire forbidden	76 Camp fire permitted	77 Braai places provided	78 Kitchen/cooking facilities	79 Petrol pump on site	80 Petrol pump nearby	81 Car repair shop nearby	82 Car servicing nearby	83 Gas service nearby	84 First aid/hospital/doctor nearby	85 Post office nearby	86 Site guarded	87 Pets allowed	88 Non-white servants: Servants permitted – see note 7	89 Servants accom. – see note 7	90 Servants for hire – see note 7	91 Type of vehicle permitted: Car and trailer	92 Truck, horse and semi-trailer	93 Self-propelled caravans
□		□		□			□	□	□	□	□	□	□		□		□			□	□	□	□		□		□	□			□		□
○				○		○	○	○	○		○			○		○	○			○	○	○	○	○	○			○			○		○
◇	◇	◇		◇		◇	◇	◇	◇		◇	◇		◇		◇	◇			◇	◇	◇	◇	◇	◇	◇	◇				◇	◇	◇
▲		▲		▲		▲	▲	▲	▲			110/220			▲	▲	▲	▲	▲				▲	▲	▲	▲					▲	▲	
★		★		★		★	★	★	★	★	★	★		★	★	★	★			★	★	★	★	★	★	★	★			★	★		★
■	■	■		■		■	■	■	■		■			■		■	■			■			■		■		■			■	■	■	■
●				●		●	●	●			●					●		●		●	●	●			●		●				●	●	●
◆		◆		◆		◆	◆	◆	◆		◆	◆				◆	◆			◆	◆	◆	◆	◆	◆	◆	◆	◆			◆	◆	◆
◇		◇		◇		◇	◇	◇	◇					◇			◇				◇	◇	◇	◇	◇	◇	◇	◇	◇		◇		
△		△		△		△	△	△	△			△			△	△	△			△	△	△			△		△	△			△	△	△
☆		☆		☆		☆	☆	☆	☆		☆	220				☆	☆			☆	☆	☆		☆	☆		☆	☆		☆	☆	☆	☆
■		■		■			■	■			■			■		■	■														■	■	■
□		□		□		□	□	□	□		□	220		□		□	□			□	□	□		□	□		□	□		□	□	□	□
●				●		●	●		●		●		●	●		●	●	●	●					●	●	●		●	●		●	●	●
◆					◆	◆	◆							◆		◆				◆	◆	◆	◆		◆	◆	◆	◆	◆		◆	◆	◆
▲		▲		▲		▲	▲	▲	▲	▲	▲	220		▲	▲	▲	▲		▲				▲	▲		▲				▲	▲		▲
★		★		★		★	★	★	★		★					★				★	★	★	★	★	★			★		★	★	★	★
□		□		□		□	□	□	□		□	220					□			□	□	□	□		□		□	□			□		□
																○					○	○	○		○		○	○			○	○	○
◇		◇				◇	◇	◇	◇		◇			◇	◇	◇	◇			◇	◇	◇	◇	◇	◇	◇	◇	◇		◇	◇	◇	◇
▲	▲					▲	▲										▲			▲	▲	▲			▲		▲				▲	▲	▲
★		★		★		★	★	★			★			★		★	★		★			★	★		★	★				★	★	★	★
■					■	■	■										■			■		■			■						■	■	■
○		○		○		○	○	○	○	○	○	○		○		○				○	○	○	○		○						○	○	○
◇						◇														◇	◇	◇	◇	◇	◇		◇	◇		◇	◇	◇	◇
★		★		★		★	★	★	★		★		★	★			★			★	★	★	★	★	★	★					★	★	★
■		■		■		■	■	■	■		■					■	■				■	■	■		■	■	■	■		■			
●		●		●		●	●	●	●		●	●		●	●	●	●				●	●	●	●	●	●	●	●			●	●	●
○	○	○		○		○	○	○	○	○	○	○			○		○			○	○	○	○		○	○		○			○		○
◆		◆		◆		◆	◆	◆	◆	◆				◆			◆			◆	◆	◆	◆	◆	◆	◆				◆	◆		
▲		▲			▲	▲	▲	▲			▲	▲		▲		▲	▲			▲	▲	▲					▲	▲			▲		▲
★		★		★		★	★	★	★			220		★		★				★	★	★	★		★	★	0	★	★	★	★		★
☆				☆		☆	☆		☆		☆	220				☆				☆	☆	☆		☆		☆		☆		☆	☆		☆

Sporting and recreational facilities

S = On Site   N = Nearby (Up to 20 km away)

94 Childrens' playground	95 Tennis	96 Cinema/drive-in/TV-room – see note 8	97 Horse-riding	98 Games room	99 Trampoline	100 Bowls	101 Hot springs	102 Golf: Golf course – see note 9	103 Number of holes	104 Miniature	105 Mashie	106 Putt-putt	107 Fishing: Freshwater – see note 10	108 Sea – see note 11	109 Goggle	110 Licence required	111 Swimming: Swimming pool	112 Sea bathing	113 Childrens' pool	114 Adults only	115 Shark nets at beach	116 Boating: Boats for hire	117 Power	118 Sailing	119 Canoeing	120 Places of interest: Historic	121 Scientific	122 Natural	123 Notes
S	N	N		S		N		N	18					N	N	□	S		S										
N	N		N					N	9				N			○							S	S	S	○		○	
S	N	N	N			N							N			◇	N		N							◇	◇	◇	
	S		S			S		S	9																			▲	
N	N					N		N	9				N			★	N		N						N	★		★	
S														N				■				S	S	S	S			■	
	N					N							S			●	N		N							●		●	
S	N	N	N			N		N	18								N									◆			
S																	S									◇			
		N				N	N	N	18					△			S		S							△	△	△	
S	N	N				N	N	N	9				N			☆	S		S							☆		☆	
	S		S				N	N	9			■					S		N									■	
S	N	N				N	S	N	9				S			□	S		S							□		□	
																										●	●	●	
			S					N	9								S		S	◆						◆		◆	
S	S	S		S	S								S			▲	S		S				S	S	S			▲	
													N			★							N	N	N	★		★	
S	N	N				N		N	18								N									□		□	
	N	N											S			○			N							○	○	○	
N	N	N				N							N			◇	N		N	◇			N	N	N	◇			
N													N			▲													
S		S		S			S						S			★	S		S									★	
N	N							N	9																				
N	N	N				N		N						S			N	S	N		S		N	N	N			○	
N	N	N	N	S	S	N		N	18																	◇		◇	
N	S					S		N	18				N			★	S						N	N	N	★	★	★	
N	N	N	N			N		N	18				N			■	N		N				N	N		■		■	
S	S	N			S	N		N	18					N		●		●	N		●								
S				S		N		N	18					N			S		S		○					○		○	
	N					N		N	18				N				S	◆								◆	◆	◆	
														N			N	▲	N									▲	
	N	N	N	S		N		N	18	★	★	★	N	N	N	★	N	★	N				N	N	N	★	★	★	
N	N	N				N		N	18		N	☆		N	N			☆	N				N	N		☆		☆	

CARAVAN PARKS AND CAMPING SITES

Establishments marked thus [Caravan Club symbol] have the Caravan Club of South Africa recommendation – see page 17. Establishments marked thus [AA symbol] recognise the AA Camping Carnet – see page 16 and also refer to column 42.

CARAVAN PARK / CAMP SITE TARIFF CODE – See columns 38–39 (Subject to alteration)

A = Up to R1 | B = R1–R2 | C = R2–R3 | D = R3–R4 | E = R4–R5 | F = R5–R6 | G = R6–R7 | H = R7–R8 | I = R8–R9 | J = R9–R10 | K = R10–R16 | O = FREE | X = On Application

Charges are based on a family of 2 adults and 2 children under 12 years

ADDITIONAL ACCOMMODATION TARIFF CODE – See columns 57–59 (Subject to alteration)

eg. Bungalows, Cabins, Cottages, Chalets, etc.

A = R1–R3 | B = R3–R5 | C = R5–R7 | D = R7–R9 | E = R9–R11 | F = R11–R13 | G = R13–R15 | H = R15–R17 | I = R17–R19 | J = R19–R21 | K = R21–R30 | X = On Application

NB: Where the tariff is given in *italics* it is per person, otherwise per unit

NOTE 1 — Columns 18, 19, 20. — Where a symbol appears instead of a number it means stands are available but not demarcated or number of stands has not been provided
NOTE 2 — Column 35 — A = Bookings accepted for additional accommodation only i.e. cottages, bungalows, etc.
NOTE 3 — Column 37 — Deposit refunded under certain conditions eg. less 10% ; if site is re-let ; if cancelled well in advance (up to 2 months) or on a doctor's certificate
NOTE 4 — Column 41 — Reductions allowed on application for youth, church, school or sport groups or caravan rallies
NOTE 5 — Column 42 — R = Reduction in tariff of between 5–10% to Carnet holders. 0 = Reduction Out-of-Season only
NOTE 6 — Column 69 — L = Laundry facilities only
NOTE 7 — Columns 88, 89, 90. — I = In-Season only ; 0 = Out-of-Season only
NOTE 8 — Column 96 — Applicable In-Season only at some establishments
NOTE 9 — Column 102 — See section on golf in Outdoor Holiday Guide
NOTE 10 — Column 107 — See section on freshwater angling in Outdoor Holiday Guide
NOTE 11 — Column 108 — See section on coastal angling in Outdoor Holiday Guide

ABBREVIATIONS
C = CAPE PROVINCE
N = NATAL
O = ORANGE FREE STATE
T = TRANSVAAL
B = BOPHUTHATSWANA
X = TRANSKEI

TELEPHONE CODE — T = DIAL 0020, BOOK TRUNK CALL; E = DIAL CODE, ASK EXCHANGE FOR NO.

Column headings:
1 Telephone code; 2 Telephone number;
OWNED OR SUPERVISED BY: 3 Privately owned; 4 Municipality; 5 Divisional council; 6 Provincial administration; 7 Parks board;
SITE DESCRIPTION — LOCALITY: 8 Beach in immediate vicinity; 9 Beside river, lake or dam; 10 In or near mountain area; 11 Within built-up area; NATURE OF GROUND: 12 Grass; 13 Gravel; 14 Sand; SHADE: 15 Unshaded; 16 Partly shaded; 17 Extensively shaded;
NO. OF STANDS: 18 Caravans only – see note 1; 19 Caravans and/or tents – see note 1; 20 Tents only – see note 1;
ACCESSIBILITY — APPROXIMATE DISTANCE FROM MAIN ROAD TO SITE: 21 On main rd.; 22 Within 1 km; 23 Within 5 km; 24 Within 10 km; 25 Within 15 km; SURFACE OF APPROACH ROAD: 26 Tar; 27 Gravel; 28 Sand; CONDITION OF APPROACH ROAD: 29 Good; 30 Fair; 31 Poor

			1	2	3	4	5	6	7	8	9	10	11	12	13	14	15	16	17	18	19	20	21	22	23	24	25	26	27	28	29	30	31
		EAST LONDON (CONTINUED)																															
■	[Caravan Club]	**Glen Eden** P.O. Box 2054, Beacon Bay 5205 □ *At Bulugha River Mouth*	0431	95-1319	■					■	■			■					■	100				■				■			■		
□	[Caravan Club]	**Glen Navar Holiday Resort** P/Bag 502 (5200) □ *32 km from East London*	0431	95-1329	□					□				□				□	□		80				□			□				□	
●	[AA]	**Nahoon Beach** Director of Parks, P.O. Box 984 (5200) □ *Near Nahoon Mouth*	0431	8-7569		●				●	●			●				●	●		134			●				●				●	
○		**Pixie** P.O. Box 5072, Greenfields 5208 □ *Chester Rd., Sunnyridge*	0431	46-1611	○					C				○				○		10				○				○				○	
◆		**Rondalia Holiday Resort** P.O. Box 2079, Beacon Bay 5205 □ *Near Sunrise-on-Sea*	0431	95-1519	◆					◆	◆			◆					◆		16				◆				◆		◆		
◇	[Caravan Club] [AA]	**Verina** P.O. Box 5102, Greenfields 5208 □ *Settlers Way*	0431	46-1069	◇								◇	◇				◇		36		4	◇					◇			◇		
▲		**Welcomagin Holiday Resort** P.O. West Bank 5218 □ *Hickmans River Mouth*	0431	46-1080	▲					▲	▲	▲	▲	▲			▲	▲	▲	40		7		▲					▲			▲	
		EAST LONDON DISTRICT See respectively: ● **Bonza Bay** ● **Cefane** ● **Christmas Rock** ● **Cintsa Mouth East** ● **Cintsa West** ● **Glengarriff** ● **Glen Muir** ● **Gonubie Mouth** ● **Kidd's Beach** ● **Rockclyffe-on-Sea**																															
		EDENBURG O 62 A3 ↘ 1376m																															
■		**Edenburg Show Grounds** P.O. Box 16 (9908)	05842 E	8		■							■	■				■		16	16	16	■						■		■		
		EIKENHOF T 72 NS ↓ 1524m																															
●		**Blossom Valley** P.O. Eikenhof 1872 □ *Cnr. Gordon and Alberton/Eikenhof Rds., Kibler Park*	011	943-1508	●						●		●	●					●		35	1	●					●			●		
○		**Lion Rampant** P.O. Box 141 (1872) □ *Plot 18, Olifantsvlei, Eikenhof/Alberton Rd.*	011	943-1802	○						○		○	○				○		36			○					○			○		
◆		**Protea** P.O. Box 186 (1872) □ *Vereeniging Main Rd.*	011	943-1066	◆						◆	◆	◆	◆				◆		100	50	56	◆					◆			◆		
		EILAND MINERAL BATHS T See Letsitele																															
		ELANDSFONTEIN T 72 NS → 1737m																															
△		**Cresta** North Reef Rd., P.O. Elandsfontein 1406 □ *North Reef Rd.*	011	36-5081	△								△	△			△	△	△	200			△					△			△		
		ELLIOT C 62 C5 → 1448m																															
☆		**Elliot Municipal** Town Clerk, P.O. Box 21 (5460) □ *Maclear Ave.*	T	11		☆						☆	☆	☆				☆		25	25		☆						☆		☆		
		ELOFF T 68 C6 ↓ 1623m																															
□		**Mimosa Hotel Pleasure Resort** P.O. Box 61 (2211) □ *On the Witbank highway*	T	26	□								□	□					□		50		□					□			□		
		ERMELO T 67 A2 → 1734m																															
○		**Republiek** P.O. Box 48 (2350) □ *7 km from Ermelo*	01341	4093		○					○			○				○		60		40		○				○			○		
		ESHOWE N 67 C4 ↓ 502m																															
◇		**Eshowe Municipal** P.O. Box 37 (3815) □ *Addison St.*	035412 E	311/17/450		◇							◇	◇		◇		◇	◇		22			◇				◇			◇		
		ESTCOURT N 67 D2 ↗ 1168m																															
△		**Estcourt Municipal** Bookings not accepted □ *Lorne St.*	03631	3000		△							△	△				△			25		△					△			△		
★		**Giant's Castle Game Reserve — Hillside** Officer-in-Charge, P.O. Box 755 (3310) □ *69 km from Estcourt*	03631	4435					★			★		★				★			6						★		★			★	
☆		**Solitude Mountain Resort** P.O. Box 66 (3310) □ *3 km from Loskop*	03631	3190	☆						☆	☆		☆				☆			20						☆		☆			☆	
■		**Wagendrift Public Resort** P.O. Box 316 (3310) □ *8 km from Estcourt*	03631	2550					■		■			■				■			20				■			■			■		
		FALSE BAY PARK N See Hluhluwe																															
		FANIES ISLAND N See Mtubatuba																															
		FICKSBURG O 66 C5 ↘ 1630m																															
◆		**Ficksburg Municipal** P.O. Box 116 (9730) □ *Bloem St.*	05632 E	12		◆					◆	◆	◆	◆					◆		100			◆				◆			◆		
		FISH HOEK C 58 NS ● S.L.																															
▲		**Fish Hoek Municipal** Bookings not accepted Enquiries: Caravan/Camping Officer, 63 Main Rd. (7975) □ *Foreshore*	021	82-1163		▲				▲		▲	▲		▲		▲			24				▲				▲			▲		
△	[AA]	**Robinvale** P.O. Box 142 (7975) □ *Cnr. 20th Ave./Kommetjie Rd.*	021	82-2714/82-2162	△					△		△		△				△			40		△					△			△		
★		**Sunnyacres** P.O. Box 50 (7975)	021	82-2913	★					★				★					★		50		★						★		★		
		FLORIDA T 72 NS → 1676m																															
■		**Florida Lake** Manager: Parks and Recreation, P.O. Box 217, Roodepoort 1725 □ *Westlake Rd.*	011	672-6221		■					■			■				■		65			■						■			■	
		FORT BEAUFORT C 60 B1 ↓ 437m																															
●		**Fort Beaufort Municipal** Town Clerk, P.O. Box 36 (5720) □ *Durban St.*	043512 E	17/162		●							●	●				●			12		●					●			●		
		FOURIESBURG O 66 C2 ↗ 1829m																															
◆		**Fouriesburg Municipal** P.O. Box 5 (9725) □ *Kosmos St.*	014322 E	14		◆							◆	◆	◆				◆	◆				◆					◆			◆	
		FRANSCHHOEK C 58 C4 ↗ 100m																															
▲	[AA]	**De Hollandsche Molen (Pty) Ltd. — Oude Molen** P.O. Box 535, Suider-Paarl 7624 □ *Paarl-Franschhoek Rd.*	0252	2704	▲						▲	▲		▲					▲	50	20	70	▲					▲			▲		
		FRANKFORT O 66 B6 ↘ 1574m																															
★		**Wilgerivier** P.O. Box 2 (9830)	0161312 E	30		★					★			★					★		25				★			★			★		
		GAMTOOS RIVER MOUTH C See Port Elizabeth																															
		GANSBAAI C 58 D4 ↗ 15m																															
□		**Uilenkraalsmond** Caretaker, P.O. Box 18 (7220) □ *9 km from Gansbaai*	02834	2012			□			□	□	□		□		□			□	100	940		□	□				□				□	
		GARDEN CASTLE N 63 A2 ↗ 1753m																															
○		**Drakensberg Garden** Central Reservations, P.O. Box 2529, Marine Parade, Durban 4056	031	37-2672	○						○	○		○					○	4	44	25	○						○		○		
		GARDEN ROUTE C See respectively: ● **Brenton** ● **Buffelsbaai** ● **George** ● **Glentana** ● **Groot-Brakrivier** ● **Gwayang River Mouth** ● **Hartenbos** ● **Heroldsbaai** ● **Keurboomsrivier** ● **Keurboomstrand** ● **Klein-Brakrivier** ● **Kleinkrantz** ● **Knysna** ● **Mossel Bay** ● **Nature's Valley** ● **Plettenberg Bay** ● **Sedgefield** ● **Stormsrivier** ● **Victoria Bay** ● **Wilderness**																															
		GARIES C 60 B5 → 240m																															
★		**Garies High School Sports Grounds** Headmaster, Garies High School (8220)	T	3				★					★	★					★	★	★	★		★				★			★		

SEASONS: 32 Open throughout the year; 33 Out-of-season closing date; 34 Re-opening date

TERMS FOR BOOKINGS: 35 Bookings accp./peak sns. – see note 2; 36 Deposit required; 37 Refunded if cancelled – see note 3

CARAVAN PARK/CAMPING SITE TARIFFS (See heading): 38 Maximum in-season tariff; 39 Maximum out-of-season tariff

REDUCTIONS ALLOWED FOR: 40 Long periods of stay; 41 Groups – see note 4; 42 AA carnetholders – see note 5; 43 Others (on application)

RESTAURANT FACILITIES: 44 On site; 45 Within 5 km of site; 46 More than 5 km from site

TEAROOM/CAFE: 47 On site; 48 Within 5 km of site; 49 More than 5 km from site

SHOPPING FACILITIES (Provisions): 50 On site; 51 Within 5 km of site; 52 More than 5 km from site

ADDITIONAL ACCOMMODATION AVAILABLE: 53 Bungalows; 54 Cabins; 55 Cottages (rondavels); 56 Chalets

ADDITIONAL ACCOMMODATION TARIFF (See heading): 57 Maximum in-season tariff; 58 Maximum out-of-season tariff

59 CARAVANS TO RENT ON SITE – SEE PAGES 8 – 11

CAMP SITE FACILITIES (I = In-Season only; O = Out-of-Season only)

DRINKING WATER: 60 Piped; 61 Other. BATHS: 62 Hot and cold; 63 Cold only. SHOWERS: 64 Hot and cold; 65 Cold only. 66 Waterborne sanitation; 67 Washbasins; 68 Dishwashing facilities; 69 Laundry and ironing facilities – see note 6; 70 Washing machines; 71 Site lit; 72 Plugs for razors (voltage); 73 Refrigerators; 74 Firewood/charcoal; 75 Open fire permitted; 76 Camp fire forbidden; 77 Braai places provided; 78 Kitchen/cooking facilities; 79 Petrol pump on site; 80 Petrol pump nearby; 81 Car repair shop nearby; 82 Car servicing nearby; 83 Gas service nearby; 84 First aid/hospital/doctor nearby; 85 Post office nearby; 86 Site guarded; 87 Pets allowed

NON-WHITE SERVANTS: 88 Servants permitted – see note 7; 89 Servants accom. – see note 7; 90 Servants for hire – see note 7

TYPE OF VEHICLE PERMITTED: 91 Car and trailer; 92 Truck, horse and semi-trailer; 93 Self-propelled caravans

SPORTING AND RECREATIONAL FACILITIES (S = On Site; N = Nearby (Up to 20 km away))

94 Childrens' playground; 95 Tennis; 96 Cinema/drive-in/TV-room – see note 8; 97 Horse-riding; 98 Games room; 99 Trampoline; 100 Bowls; 101 Hot springs

GOLF: 102 Golf course – see note 9; 103 Number of holes; 104 Miniature; 105 Mashie; 106 Putt-putt

FISHING: 107 Freshwater – see note 10; 108 Sea – see note 11; 109 Goggle; 110 Licence required

SWIMMING: 111 Swimming pool; 112 Sea bathing; 113 Childrens' pool; 114 Adults only; 115 Shark nets at beach

BOATING: 116 Boats for hire; 117 Power; 118 Sailing; 119 Canoeing

PLACES OF INTEREST: 120 Historic; 121 Scientific; 122 Natural

NOTES

32	33	34	35	36	37	38	39	40	41	42	43	44	45	46	47	48	49	50	51	52	53	54	55	56	57	58	59	60	61	62	63	64	65	66	67	68	69	70	71	72	73	74	75	76	77	78	79	80	81	82	83	84	85	86	87	88	89	90	91	92	93	94	95	96	97	98	99	100	101	102	103	104	105	106	107	108	109	110	111	112	113	114	115	116	117	118	119	120	121	122	123	NOTES
■						F	D		■			■			■			■			■	■	■	■	A	A		■		■		■		■	■	■	■		■	■		■		■	■			■	■	■	■	■	■	■		■	■	■	■	■	■		S		N	S	S									■	■		N	■	N					N	N			■		
□			□	□		F	E	□	□				□			□	□	□					□		H	C		□		□		□		□	□	□	□		□	220		□	□	□	□			□	□	□	□		□	□	0	□	□	□	□	□	□	S	S	S												N	N			□												
●			●	●		D	C	●					●			●		●										●				●		●	●	●	●		●	220				●				●	●	●	●	●	●			●		●	●		●	N	N					N		N	18					N	N			●				N	N	N	N	●		●		
○			○	○		C	B	○					○	○		○	○		○	○							○	○		○		○		○	○									○				○	○	○			○	○	○	○			○		○	N	N	N	N	N	N	N		N	18					N	N		N	○	○	○						○		○		
◆			◆	◆		C	C	◆	◆		◆		◆				◆	◆	◆	◆			◆		C-G	C-G		◆		◆			◆	◆	◆	◆	◆		◆			◆		◆	◆	◆		◆	◆	◆	◆	◆	◆	◆	◆	◆		◆	◆	◆	◆	S	S	N	N	S		N		N	18				N			◆		◆										◆		
◇			◇	◇		E	C	◇					◇			◇			◇								◇	◇		◇		◇		◇	◇	◇	◇		◇	32		◇			◇			◇	◇	◇	◇		◇		◇	◇			◇		◇	S	N	N				N		N	18					N		◇	S											◇		
▲			▲	▲		K	G	▲					▲		▲			▲					▲		J-K	G-H		▲		▲		▲		▲	▲	▲	▲		▲		▲	▲		▲	▲	▲		▲	▲	▲	▲	▲	▲	▲	▲	▲	▲	▲	▲	▲	▲	S	S		N	S		N		N	18				S	S	S		S	▲	S			N			N			▲		
■						O	O						■			■			■									■				■		■	■				■					■				■	■	■			■		■	■			■	■	■	N	N					N		N	9								N									■	■	■		
●			●	●	●	C	C	●			●		●			●			●	●							●	●		●		●		●	●	●	●	●	●		●	●		●		●		●	●	●	●	●	●		●	●		●	●		●	S	N	N	N		S	N		N	18								N		N											
○			○			C	C	○						○		○			○									○		○		○		○	○	○	○			○					○			○	○	○		○	○			○			○		○	S			N	S									N				S													
◆			◆	◆		B	B	◆	◆				◆	◆		◆	◆		◆	◆							◆	◆		◆		◆		◆	◆	◆	◆		◆			◆		◆	◆			◆	◆	◆	◆	◆	◆	◆	◆	◆		◆	◆	◆	◆	S	N	S	N	S	N	N									N		S		S	◆										
△						E	E	△					△			△			△									△		△		△		△	△	△	△	△	△	220	△		△					△	△	△	△	△	△	△					△	△	△	N	N	N	N	N		N		N	18	△	△	△	N			△	N		N											
☆			☆			B	B						☆				☆		☆	☆								☆				☆		☆	☆	☆	L		☆					☆	☆			☆	☆	☆	☆		☆		☆				☆	☆	☆	S	N		N			N		N	9				N			☆	N		N				N	N	N	☆		☆		
□						B	B							□	□					□			□		B	B		□		□				□	□		□		□	230		□		□	□			□	□	□	□	□	□		□	□			□	□	□	S	S	N	S										N			□	S		S											
○			○	○	○	B	B							○			○						○		B	B		○		○		○		○	○	○	○		○				○																○	○	○	N								N	18				N			○							○	○	○			○		
◇			◇	◇		C	C						◇	◇		◇	◇		◇	◇								◇		◇		◇		◇	◇	◇	◇		◇			◇	◇	◇	◇			◇	◇	◇	◇	◇	◇	◇		◇			◇		◇	N	N	N	N			N		N	18				N	N	N	◇	◇	N	◇	◇		N	N	N	N	◇	◇	◇		
△						D	D						△			△			△									△		△		△		△	△	△	△		△									△	△	△					△				△		△	S	N					N		N	9								N		N							△		△		
★			★	★		D	D																					★				★		★	★									★	★							★							★	★	★				S										S			★												★		
☆			☆	☆	☆	G	F				☆						☆			☆			☆		K	K		☆	☆			☆		☆	☆	☆	L		☆			☆		☆	☆													☆							S										S			☆	S			☆						☆	☆	☆		
■			■	■	■	D	D							■			■			■								■		■		■		■	■	■						■		■	■			■	■	■		■	■	■					■	■	■	S	S					N		N	9				S			■	N		N				S	S	S	■		■		
◆						A	A						◆			◆			◆									◆	◆	◆		◆		◆	◆	◆	◆		◆	◆		◆		◆	◆			◆	◆	◆	◆	◆	◆	◆	◆	◆		◆	◆	◆	◆	S	N	N	N			S		N	18	◆			N			◆	N		N							◆	◆	◆		
▲						C	A					▲	▲	▲	▲	▲	▲		▲	▲								▲				▲		▲	▲				▲				▲					▲	▲	▲	▲		▲								▲	S																														
△			△	△	△	D	D	△						△			△			△		△	△		D	C		△		△		△		△	△	△	△			△	△	△			△				△	△	△	△	△						△	△	△	N	N	N	N			N		N	18					N	N		N	△	N			N	N	N	N	△		△		
★			★	★	★	D	D	★	★				★			★		★			★				G	F	★	★		★		★		★	★	★	★	★	★	220	★	★			★			★	★	★	★	★	★	★	★				★	★	★	S	N	N	S	S										N	N		S	N				N	N	N		★	★	★		
■						A	A						■			■			■									■		■		■		■	■	■	■		■	110/220			■					■	■	■			■						■		■	N	N	N				N							N			■	N		N					N	N	■	■	■		
●			●			C	C						●			●			●									●		●		●		●	●	●	●		●	220			●	●	●			●	●	●			●		●	●			●	●	●	N	N	N				N		N	11				N			●	N									●		●		
◆			◆			A	A							◆			◆			◆								◆		◆		◆		◆	◆	◆							◆	◆	◆			◆	◆	◆	◆	◆	◆	◆	◆	◆			◆		◆	N	S		N			N							N			◆	N									◆		◆		
▲			▲	▲		X	X	▲	▲	R		▲			▲			▲			▲	▲		▲	E	E		▲		▲		▲		▲	▲	▲	L		▲			▲		▲	▲			▲	▲	▲	▲	▲	▲	▲		▲			▲		▲	S	N	N	N	N	N	N	N						N			▲	S		S							▲	▲	▲		
★			★	★		C	C							★			★			★								★		★		★		★	★	★	★		★	220		★						★	★	★	★		★	★	★	★			★	★	★	S	S	N				S		N	9		★		★				S		S											
□			□	□	□	D	D							□	□		□	□		□	□				D	B		□				□		□	□	□					□	□		□				□	□	□	□		□	□		□			□	□	□	N	N	N											S	S	S			□					S	S		□		□		
○			○	○	○	E	D						○						○				○	○	X	X		○		○				○	○				○			○		○		○		○	○	○	○	○	○	○		○	○	○	○	○	○	S	S		S	S	S	S		S	9			○	S			○	S							N	N			○		
★						A	A	★	★				★	★		★	★		★	★								★					★		★				★					★	★			★	★	★	★	★	★	★	★	★			★	★	★	S	N	N											N						S							★	★	★		

CARAVAN PARKS AND CAMPING SITES

Establishments marked thus (Caravan Club symbol) have the Caravan Club of South Africa recommendation – see page **17**
Establishments marked thus (AA symbol) recognise the AA Camping Carnet – see page **16** and also refer to column **42**

CARAVAN PARK / CAMP SITE TARIFF CODE – See columns 38-39 (Subject to alteration)

A = Up to R1 | B = R1–R2 | C = R2–R3 | D = R3–R4 | E = R4–R5 | F = R5–R6 | G = R6–R7 | H = R7–R8 | I = R8–R9 | J = R9–R10 | K = R10–R16 | 0 = FREE | X = On Application

Charges are based on a family of 2 adults and 2 children under 12 years

ADDITIONAL ACCOMMODATION TARIFF CODE – See columns 57-59 (Subject to alteration)

eg. Bungalows, Cabins, Cottages, Chalets, etc.

A = R1–R3 | B = R3–R5 | C = R5–R7 | D = R7–R9 | E = R9–R11 | F = R11–R13 | G = R13–R15 | H = R15–R17 | I = R17–R19 | J = R19–R21 | K = R21–R30 | X = On Application

NB: Where the tariff is given in *italics* it is per person, otherwise per unit

NOTE 1 – **Columns 18, 19, 20.** – Where a symbol appears instead of a number it means stands are available but not demarcated or number of stands has not been provided
NOTE 2 – **Column 35** – A = Bookings accepted for additional accommodation only i.e. cottages, bungalows, etc.
NOTE 3 – **Column 37** – Deposit refunded under certain conditions eg. less 10%; if site is re-let; if cancelled well in advance (up to 2 months) or on a doctor's certificate
NOTE 4 – **Column 41** – Reductions allowed on application for youth, church, school or sport groups or caravan rallies
NOTE 5 – **Column 42** – R = Reduction in tariff of between 5 – 10 % to Carnet holders; 0 = Reduction Out-of-Season only
NOTE 6 – **Column 69** – L = Laundry facilities only
NOTE 7 – **Columns 88, 89, 90.** – I = In-Season only; 0 = Out-of-Season only
NOTE 8 – **Column 96** – Applicable In-Season only at some establishments
NOTE 9 – **Column 102** – See section on golf in Outdoor Holiday Guide
NOTE 10 – **Column 107** – See section on freshwater angling in Outdoor Holiday Guide
NOTE 11 – **Column 108** – See section on coastal angling in Outdoor Holiday Guide

ABBREVIATIONS
C = CAPE PROVINCE
N = NATAL
O = ORANGE FREE STATE
T = TRANSVAAL
B = BOPHUTHATSWANA
X = TRANSKEI

TELEPHONE CODE: T = DIAL 0020, BOOK TRUNK CALL; E = DIAL CODE, ASK EXCHANGE FOR NO.

Column groups: OWNED OR SUPERVISED BY (3–7); SITE DESCRIPTION: LOCALITY (8–11), NATURE OF GROUND (12–14), SHADE (15–17); NO. OF STANDS (18–20); ACCESSIBILITY: APPROXIMATE DISTANCE FROM MAIN ROAD TO SITE (21–25), SURFACE OF APPROACH ROAD (26–28), CONDITION OF APPROACH (29–31)

			Telephone code 1	Telephone number 2	3 Privately owned	4 Municipality	5 Divisional council	6 Provincial administration	7 Parks board	8 Beach in immediate vicinity	9 Beside river, lake or dam	10 In or near mountain area	11 Within built-up area	12 Grass	13 Gravel	14 Sand	15 Unshaded	16 Partly shaded	17 Extensively shaded	18 Caravans only see note 1	19 Caravans and/or tents	20 Tents only see note 1	21 On main rd	22 Within 1 km	23 Within 5 km	24 Within 10 km	25 Within 15 km	26 Tar	27 Gravel	28 Sand	29 Good	30 Fair	31 Poor
		GEORGE C 59 NS – 226m																															
□		**Caravan Park International** P.O. Box 617 (6530) □ *On National Rd. between George and Wilderness*	0441	4490	□					□		□		□					□		200		□						□		□		
●		**George Municipal** P.O. Box 19 (6530) □ *York St.*	0441	4115		●				●		●	●	●				●			400	65	●					●			●		
		GERMISTON T 72 NS 1846m																															
◆		**Dinwoodie** P.O. Box 7043, Dinwiddie 1405 □ *38 Chris St., Dinwiddie*	011	869-2865	◆								◆	◆					◆	50				◆				◆			◆		
		GIANT'S CASTLE GAME RESERVE N See Estcourt																															
		GLENGARRIFF C 60 B3 ↙ S.L.																															
△	CC	**Yellow Sands** P.O. Box 920, East London 5200 □ *Kwelera River Mouth*	0431	95-1336	△					△	△			△			△	△	△		100				△				△		△		
		GLEN MUIR C 60 B3 ↙ 20m																															
☆		**Glen Muir** P.O. Box 942, East London 5200 □ *Kwelera Dist.*	0431	95-1318	☆					☆	☆			☆					☆		30			☆				☆	☆		☆		
		GLENTANA C 59 C2 ↘ 2m																															
□		**Glentana** Divisional Council, P.O. Box 12, George 6530 □ *George Dist.*	0441	300			□			□		□	□	□	□			□			53					□		□			□		
		GOLDEN GATE HIGHLANDS NATIONAL PARK O See Clarens																															
		GONUBIE MOUTH C 60 B3 ↙ S.L.																															
◆		**Gonubie Mouth** Town Clerk, P.O. Box 20, Gonubie 5256 □ *Meier St., Gonubie*	0431	94-1313		◆				◆	◆		◆	◆		◆			◆	116				◆				◆			◆		
◇		**Gwenshaw** P.O. Box 12, Gonubie 5256 □ *Eastward Ho, Gonubie*	0431	94-1710	◇					◇	◇			◇				◇		50		12			◇				◇		◇		
▲	AA	**P.S.A. Holiday Resort** P.O. Box 284, Pretoria 0001 □ *Quinera River Mouth*	012	3-4481/2/3	▲					▲	▲			▲		▲			▲	110		30			▲				▲		▲		
△	CC	**Quinera Lagoon Holiday Resort** P.O. Box 7252, East London 5200 □ *On Quinera Lagoon*	0431	95-1462	△					△	△			△				△			100		△						△		△		
		GORDON'S BAY C 58 D3 ↗ S.L.																															
☆	CC	**Gordon's Bay Municipal** P.O. Box 3 (7150) □ *Beach Rd.*	024	41-8135		☆				☆				☆				☆			100		☆					☆			☆		
■		**Panorama** P.O. Box 346, Strand 7140 □ *Disa St.*	024	4-1730	■					■		■		■				■			120			■						■	■		
□	CC AA	**Sea Breeze** P.O. Box 38 (7150) □ *Water Way*	024	4-1400	□					□		□	□	□				□		180	200	20		□				□			□		
●		**Steenbras Holiday Resort** P.O. Box 143 (7150) □ *At Steenbras River Mouth*	024	41-8097	●						●				●	●		●			●		●					●			●		
		GOURITZMOND C 59 C1 ↗ S.L.																															
◇		**Gouritzmond** Caretaker, P.O. Gouritzmond 6796	029326	29 or 35			◇			◇	◇			◇				◇		24							◇		◇		◇		
		GRAAFF-REINET C 59 A4 ↑ 751m																															
△	CC	**Urquhart** P.O. Box 71 (6280) □ *Murraysburg Rd.*	0491	2121/2		△					△	△			△				△	100	150	50	△					△			△		
		GRAHAMSTOWN C 59 B6 ↑ 532m																															
☆	AA	**Grahamstown Municipal** Superintendent of Parks and Forests, P.O. Box 176 (6140) □ *Port Elizabeth National Rd.*	0461	2043		☆							☆	☆				☆			75		☆						☆		☆		
		GRASKOP T 69 B3 → 1300m																															
□		**Blydepoort Public Resort** P/Bag 413 (1270) □ *Strijdom Tunnel Rd.*	T	Blydepoort 9				□				□		□				□		24			□					□			□		
●		**Graskop Municipal** P.O. Box 18 (1270) □ *Louis Trichardt Ave.*	0131522 E	126		●					●	●		●				●			36		●					●			●		
○		**Panorama Rest-camp** P.O. Box 29 (1270) □ *2 km from Graskop*	0131522 E	91	○							○		○					○				○						○			○	
		GREAT BRAK RIVER C See Groot-Brakrivier																															
		GREYTOWN N 67 D3 ↑ 1324m																															
▲		**Lake Merthley** Town Clerk, P.O. Box 71 (3500) □ *2 km from Greytown*	03342 E	21		▲					▲			▲				▲			12			▲						▲		▲	
		GRIEKWASTAD C 65 C5 ↙ 1207m																															
★	AA	**Griekwastad Municipal** P.O. Box 21 (8365)	05912 E	19		★							★	★	★				★		60			★				★			★		
		GRIQUATOWN C See Griekwastad																															
		GROBLERSDAL T 69 C2 ↘ 980m																															
□		**Groblersdal Municipal** Town Clerk, P.O. Box 48 (0470) □ *Pretoria Main Rd.*	012022 E	274/275		□							□	□					□	30	30	20	□					□			□		
		GROOT-BRAKRIVIER C 59 C2 ↘ 4m																															
○		**Pine Creek** P.O. Box 80 (6525)	04442	2434	○					○	○			○					○		120			○				○			○		
		GULU RIVER MOUTH C See Kidd's Beach																															
		GWAYANG RIVER MOUTH C See Caravan Parks for Coloureds, Asians and Blacks																															
		HAENERTSBURG T 70 NS ↙ 1380m																															
△	CC AA	**Lakeside Chalets** P.O. Magoebaskloof 0731 □ *7 km from Haenertsburg*	0152222 E	2740	△						△	△		△				△		25	25	25		△				△		△	△		
		HAGA-HAGA C 60 D3 ↙ 6m																															
☆		**Bosbokstrand** P.O. Box 302, Randfontein 1760	011	696-1442	☆					☆	☆			☆					☆	50		10			☆				☆		☆		
		HAMBURG C 60 C2 ● S.L.																															
□		**Hamburg Municipal** P.O. Hamburg 5614 □ *Keiskamma River Mouth Rd.*	T	16		□				□	□			□			□				35		□						□			□	
		HANGKLIP C See Betty's Bay																															
		HANOVER C 62 C2 ↑ 1354m																															
◆		**Hanover Municipal** Town Clerk, P.O. Box 15 (5960)	057212 E	53		◆									◆				◆		35		◆						◆		◆		
		HARDING N 63 B2 ↘ 879m																															
▲		**Harding Municipal** P.O. Box 23 (4680) □ *Murchison St.*	03942 E	13/29		▲							▲	▲					▲	4	2	8	▲					▲			▲		
		HAROLD JOHNSON NATURE RESERVE N See Darnall																															
		HARRISMITH O 67 C2 ↘ 1622m																															
☆		**Harrismith Municipal** P.O. Box 43 (9880)	014362 E	23		☆					☆			☆				☆			100		☆					☆			☆		

																												CAMP SITE FACILITIES (I = In-Season only; O = Out-of-Season only)																																		SPORTING AND RECREATIONAL FACILITIES (S = On Site; N = Nearby (Up to 20 km away))																												NOTES
SEASONS			TERMS FOR BOOKINGS			CARAVAN PARK/CAMPING SITE TARIFFS (See heading)		REDUCTIONS ALLOWED FOR				RESTAURANT FACILITIES			TEAROOM/CAFE			SHOPPING FACILITIES (Provisions)			ADDITIONAL ACCOMMODATION AVAILABLE				ADDITIONAL ACCOMMODATION TARIFF (See heading)			DRINKING WATER		BATHS		SHOWERS																									NON-WHITE SERVANTS			TYPE OF VEHICLE PERMITTED											GOLF					FISHING				SWIMMING					BOATING				PLACES OF INTEREST			
32 OPEN THROUGHOUT THE YEAR	33 OUT-OF-SEASON CLOSING DATE	34 RE-OPENING DATE	35 BOOKINGS ACCP./PEAK SNS.—SEE NOTE 2	36 DEPOSIT REQUIRED	37 REFUNDED IF CANCELLED—SEE NOTE 3	38 MAXIMUM IN-SEASON TARIFF	39 MAXIMUM OUT-OF-SEASON TARIFF	40 LONG PERIODS OF STAY	41 GROUPS—SEE NOTE 4	42 AA CARNET HOLDERS—SEE NOTE 5	43 OTHERS (ON APPLICATION)	44 ON SITE	45 WITHIN 5 km OF SITE	46 MORE THAN 5 km FROM SITE	47 ON SITE	48 WITHIN 5 km OF SITE	49 MORE THAN 5 km FROM SITE	50 ON SITE	51 WITHIN 5 km OF SITE	52 MORE THAN 5 km FROM SITE	53 BUNGALOWS	54 CABINS	55 COTTAGES (RONDAVELS)	56 CHALETS	57 MAXIMUM IN-SEASON TARIFF	58 MAXIMUM OUT-OF-SEASON TARIFF	59 CARAVANS TO RENT ON SITE—SEE PAGES 8–11	60 PIPED	61 OTHER	62 HOT AND COLD	63 COLD ONLY	64 HOT AND COLD	65 COLD ONLY	66 WATERBORNE SANITATION	67 WASHBASINS	68 DISHWASHING FACILITIES	69 LAUNDRY AND IRONING FACILITIES—SEE NOTE 6	70 WASHING MACHINES	71 SITE LIT	72 PLUGS FOR RAZORS (VOLTAGE)	73 REFRIGERATORS	74 FIREWOOD CHARCOAL	75 CAMP FIRE FORBIDDEN	76 OPEN FIRE PERMITTED	77 BRAAI PLACES PROVIDED	78 KITCHEN COOKING FACILITIES	79 PETROL PUMP ON SITE	80 PETROL PUMP NEARBY	81 CAR REPAIR SHOP NEARBY	82 CAR SERVICING NEARBY	83 GAS SERVICE NEARBY	84 FIRST AID HOSPITAL DOCTOR NEARBY	85 POST OFFICE NEARBY	86 SITE GUARDED	87 PETS ALLOWED	88 SERVANTS PERMITTED—SEE NOTE 7	89 SERVANTS ACCOM.—SEE NOTE 7	90 SERVANTS FOR HIRE—SEE NOTE 7	91 CAR AND TRAILER	92 TRUCK HORSE AND SEMI-TRAILER	93 SELF-PROPELLED CARAVANS	94 CHILDRENS PLAYGROUND	95 TENNIS	96 CINEMA DRIVE-IN TV-ROOM—SEE NOTE 8	97 HORSE RIDING	98 GAMES ROOM	99 TRAMPOLINE	100 BOWLS	101 HOT SPRINGS	102 GOLF COURSE—SEE NOTE 9	103 NUMBER OF HOLES	104 MINIATURE	105 MASHIE	106 PUTT-PUTT	107 FRESHWATER—SEE NOTE 10	108 SEA—SEE NOTE 11	109 GOGGLE	110 LICENCE REQUIRED	111 SWIMMING POOL	112 SEA BATHING	113 CHILDRENS POOL	114 ADULTS ONLY	115 SHARK NETS AT BEACH	116 BOATS FOR HIRE	117 POWER	118 SAILING	119 CANOEING	120 HISTORIC	121 SCIENTIFIC	122 NATURAL	123
□			□	□	□	F	F	□	□			□			□			□					□		J	F		□		□		□		□	□	□	□		□	□	□	□			□	□		□	□	□	□	□	□	□				□	□	□	□	S	N	S	S	S	S	N		N	18					N	N		S	□	S				N	N	N	□	□	□	
●			●	●	●	C	C					●	●	●	●		●	●		●		●		B-C	A-B		●		●		●		●	●	●	●		●	●		●	●	●	●			●	●	●	●	●	●	●	●	●			●		●	S	N	N	N			N		N	18					N	N		S	●	S			N	N	N	N	●		●	
◆			◆	◆	◆	X	X					◆	◆		◆	◆			◆																									◆	◆			◆	◆	◆	◆	◆	◆		◆			◆	◆	◆	◆	S		N	N			N		N	18								S		S										
△			△	△	△	F	C	△			△			△			△	△		△							△	△		△		△		△	△	△	△					△		△			△	△	△	△	△			O	△	△	△	△	△	△													S	S	S			△						S	S	S		△	△	
☆			☆	☆		D	C	☆	☆				☆			☆		☆	☆		☆		☆	☆	J	F	☆		☆	☆		☆		☆	☆	☆	☆						☆		☆	☆			☆	☆						☆			☆	☆	☆	☆		S	S	N	S										N	N			☆											
□			□	□	□	F	D					□			□			□									□				□		□	□	□	L						□	□	□	□			□	□	□	□			□																						N	N			□											□	
◆			◆	◆	◆	E	C								◆		◆	◆									◆		◆		◆		◆	◆	◆	◆		◆	220				◆				◆	◆	◆	◆	◆	◆			◆		◆	◆		◆	N	N	N	N	S		N		N	9				N	N			N	◆	N			N	N	N	N			◆	
◇			◇	◇	◇	D	C	◇	◇				◇			◇		◇	◇								◇	◇		◇		◇		◇	◇	◇	◇	◇	◇	220		◇		◇	◇			◇	◇	◇	◇	◇	◇		◇	◇	◇	◇	◇	◇	◇	S	N	S	N	S		N		N	9						N	N		S	◇	S				N	N	N	◇		◇	
▲			▲	▲		C	B						▲			▲	▲										▲		▲		▲		▲	▲	▲	▲						▲	▲		▲			▲	▲	▲	▲	▲	▲	▲						▲	▲	▲	S	S	S	S				N	9						N	N	▲								N	N	N			▲	
△			△	△	△	C	C	△	△		△						△		△	△	△			△	F	C		△		△		△		△	△	△	△					△	△	△	△	△			△	△	△	△		△		△	△	△		△	△	△	S	N	N	N	S		N		N	9				S	S	S		S	△	S				S	S	S			△	
☆			☆	☆	☆	D	B					☆			☆			☆		☆				F-I	C-E		☆		☆		☆		☆	☆	☆	☆		☆	☆				☆	☆			☆	☆	☆	☆	☆	☆	☆		☆			☆	☆	☆	S		N						N						S			☆						N	N	N	☆	☆	☆	
■			■	■		E	D	■	■		■		■		■	■		■	■									■	■	■		■		■	■	■	■	■	■	■	■	■	■	■	■			■	■	■	■		■	■	■	■		■	■	■	■	S	N	N	N			N		N	18		N		N	N			S		S			N	N	N	N	■	■	■	
□			□	□	□	E	C	□	□	R			□			□	□	□	□	□			□		G	E		□		□		□		□	□	□	□	□	□	110/220		□	□		□			□	□	□	□	□	□	□	□	□			□	□	□	S	N	N	S	S	S	N		N	18						N	N		S	□						N	N	N	□	□	□	
●			●	●		C	C								●	●	●	●		●	●	●					G-I	D		●						●	●	●							●		●				●	●	●	●				●	●			●		●			N				N		N							N						N									●	
◇			◇			C	C							◇						◇										◇			◇		◇	◇	◇	◇									◇	◇			◇						◇	◇	◇			◇	◇	◇															S	S	S			◇	N									◇	
△			△	△	△	B	B					△			△			△				△		A	A		△		△		△		△	△	△	△		△	220		△		△	△			△	△	△	△	△	△	△	△	△	△		△	△	△	N	N	N	N			N		N	18				N			△	N		N					N	N	N	△	△	△	
☆						D	D	☆				☆			☆			☆				☆		F	F		☆		☆		☆		☆	☆	☆	☆		☆			☆			☆			☆	☆	☆			☆		☆	☆		☆	☆	☆	☆	S	N	N	N			N		N	18				N			☆								N	N	N	☆		☆	
□			□	□		D	D					□			□			□								□	E-J	E-J		□		□		□		□	□	□	□	□	□	□		□		□	□		□				□	□	□	□		□	□	□	□	□	□	S	S	S	S	S														S											□	□	□	
●						D	D					●	●	●	●	●	●	●	●	●		●	●	●	E-F	E-F		●		●		●		●	●	●	●		●			●		●	●	●		●	●	●	●		●		●	●	●		●	●	●	S	N	N						N	9		●		N			●										●		●	
○						E	E	○					○			○				○		○			X	X		○				○		○	○	○	○		○		○	○						○	○	○		○	○		○				○		○	N	N												N			○										○	○	○	
▲			▲	▲	▲	B	B					▲			▲			▲				▲		E	E		▲		▲		▲		▲	▲								▲		▲	▲			▲	▲	▲	▲	▲	▲		▲	▲			▲		▲	S	N	N				N		N	10				S			▲	N		N				S	S	S	▲		▲	
★						B	B	★				★			★			★										★		★		★		★	★	★	★		★					★	★			★	★	★	★	★	★	★	★	★	★		★	★	★		N																	N		N							★		
□			□			D	D					□			□			□				□		E	E		□		□		□		□	□	□	□		□	220		□		□	□			□	□	□	□	□	□	□	□	□			□	□	□	N	N	N					N	N	9									S		S									□	
○			○	○	○	D	D						○		○			○										○		○		○		○	○	○	○		○	○		○	○	○			○	○	○	○	○	○	○		○			○	○		○		N					N		N	18					N				○								N			
△			△	△	△	F	E	△	△	R	△	△			△	△		△	△	△				△	K	K		△		△		△		△	△	△	△					△		△	△			△	△	△	△	△	△		△	△	△		△	△	△	S	S	S		S		N							S			△	S		S			S	N	N	S			△	
☆			☆	☆		E	D										☆						☆	I	E		☆		☆		☆		☆	☆	☆	☆		☆	220		☆		☆	☆	☆		☆			☆		☆	☆		☆	☆	☆	☆	☆	☆			S	S	S				N							N	N							S	S	S	S			☆	
□			□	□	□	B	B												□				□		D	C		□				□		□	□		□						□		□				□			□		□		□			□	□		□							N								N	N			□						N	N			□	
◆			◆			B	B					◆	◆		◆	◆		◆	◆									◆		◆		◆		◆	◆	◆			◆						◆	◆			◆	◆	◆	◆	◆	◆	◆	◆				◆	◆	◆	N	N					N		S	18																		◆		
▲						O	O					▲			▲			▲									▲						▲	▲									▲				▲	▲	▲	▲	▲	▲	▲	▲				▲	▲	▲		N	N				N		N	9				N			▲	N		N											
☆						C	C					☆			☆			☆									☆		☆		☆		☆	☆	☆	☆		☆	☆		☆		☆	☆			☆	☆	☆	☆	☆	☆	☆					☆		☆	S	N	N				N		N	18				N			☆	N		N								☆		☆	

CARAVAN PARKS AND CAMPING SITES

Establishments marked thus [Caravan Club symbol] have the Caravan Club of South Africa recommendation – see page 17
Establishments marked thus [AA Carnet symbol] recognise the AA Camping Carnet – see page 16 and also refer to column 42

CARAVAN PARK / CAMP SITE TARIFF CODE – See columns 38–39 (Subject to alteration)

A = Up to R1 | B = R1–R2 | C = R2–R3 | D = R3–R4 | E = R4–R5 | F = R5–R6 | G = R6–R7 | H = R7–R8 | I = R8–R9 | J = R9–R10 | K = R10–R16 | O = FREE | X = On Application

Charges are based on a family of 2 adults and 2 children under 12 years

ADDITIONAL ACCOMMODATION TARIFF CODE – See columns 57–59 (Subject to alteration)

eg. Bungalows, Cabins, Cottages, Chalets, etc.

A = R1–R3 | B = R3–R5 | C = R5–R7 | D = R7–R9 | E = R9–R11 | F = R11–R13 | G = R13–R15 | H = R15–R17 | I = R17–R19 | J = R19–R21 | K = R21–R30 | X = On Application

NB: Where the tariff is given in *italics* it is per person, otherwise per unit

NOTE 1 – Columns 18, 19, 20, – Where a symbol appears instead of a number it means stands are available but not demarcated or number of stands has not been provided
NOTE 2 – Column 35 – A = Bookings accepted for additional accommodation only i.e. cottages, bungalows, etc.
NOTE 3 – Column 37 – Deposit refunded under certain conditions eg. less 10 % ; if site is re-let ; if cancelled well in advance (up to 2 months) or on a doctor's certificate
NOTE 4 – Column 41 – Reductions allowed on application for youth, church, school or sport groups or caravan rallies
NOTE 5 – Column 42 – R = Reduction in tariff of between 5 – 10 % to Carnet holders O = Reduction Out-of-Season only
NOTE 6 – Column 69 – L = Laundry facilities only
NOTE 7 – Columns 88, 89, 90, – I = In-Season only ; O = Out-of- Season only
NOTE 8 – Column 96 – Applicable In-Season only at some establishments
NOTE 9 – Column 102 – See section on golf in Outdoor Holiday Guide
NOTE 10 – Column 107 – See section on freshwater angling in Outdoor Holiday Guide
NOTE 11 – Column 108 – See section on coastal angling in Outdoor Holiday Guide

ABBREVIATIONS
C = CAPE PROVINCE
N = NATAL
O = ORANGE FREE STATE
T = TRANSVAAL
B = BOPHUTHATSWANA
X = TRANSKEI

			Telephone code (T = Dial 0020, book trunk call; E = Dial code, ask exchange for no.)	Telephone number	Owned or supervised by: Privately owned	Municipality	Divisional council	Provincial administration	Parks board	Site description – Locality: Beach in immediate vicinity	Beside river, lake or dam	In or near mountain area	Within built-up area	Nature of ground: Grass	Gravel	Sand	Shade: Unshaded	Partly shaded	Extensively shaded	No. of stands: Caravans only – see note 1	Caravans and/or tents – see note 1	Tents only – see note 1	Accessibility – Approximate distance from main road to site: On main rd	Within 1 km	Within 5 km	Within 10 km	Within 15 km	Surface of road approach: Tar	Gravel	Sand	Condition of road approach: Good	Fair	Poor
			1	2	3	4	5	6	7	8	9	10	11	12	13	14	15	16	17	18	19	20	21	22	23	24	25	26	27	28	29	30	31
		HARTBEESPOORTDAM T See Nefdt and Kosmos respectively																															
		HARTENBOS C 59 C2 ↖ 6m																															
●		**A.T.K.V. Holiday Resort** P.O. Box 3 (6520) ☐ *Kaap De Goede Hoop Ave.*	04441	5107/8	●					●	●	●	●	●	●	●		●		450	400			●				●			●		
		HAWSTON C See Caravan Parks for Coloureds, Asians and Blacks																															
		HAZYVIEW T 69 C4 ↖ 549m																															
◇		**Hotel Numbi** P.O. Box 6 (1242)	0131242 E	6	◇								◇	◇	◇			◇			15			◇					◇		◇		
		HEIDELBERG C 58 D5 ↗ 84m																															
△		**B & M Park** Manager, B & M Restaurant, Eksteen St. (6760)	02962 E	475	△								△	△					△		20		△					△			△		
★		**Heidelberg Municipal** Not necessary to book Enquiries: Town Clerk, P.O. Box 12 (6760) ☐ *Van Riebeeck St.*	02962 E	11		★					★	★		★					★		60			★				★			★		
		HEILBRON O 66 B5 ↗ 1573m																															
■		**Langdam Pleasure Resort** P.O. Box 45 (9650)	016142 E	10		■					■			■	■				■	20	20		■						■		■		
		HENDRIK VERWOERD O 62 B3 ↓ 1280m																															
●		**Hendrik Verwoerd Dam Resort** Resort Manager, P/Bag X10, Hendrik Verwoerd Dam 9922	T	45				●			●	●	●	●	●		●	●			●				●			●	●		●	●	●
		HENDRINA T 69 D2 ↗ 1768m																															
◆		**Hendrina Municipal** Not necessary to book ☐ *Eeufees St.*	013282 E	1		◆							◆	◆					◆		25			◆					◆			◆	
		HERMANUS C 58 D4 ← S.L.																															
▲		**De Mond** P.O. Box 20 (7200) ☐ *Cnr. 10th St/17th Ave., Voëlklip*	02831	2-1617		▲				▲	▲	▲		▲				▲		100	150		▲					▲			▲		
		HEROLDSBAAI C 59 NS ← 2m																															
★		**Brakfontein** Divisional Council, P.O. Box 12, George 6530 ☐ *18 km from George*	0441	3001			★			★		★	★	★				★			37					★		★			★		
☆	[AA Carnet]	**Duttons Cove Holiday Resort** P.O. Box 722, George 6530 ☐ *18 km from George*	0441	4557	☆					☆				☆			☆	☆			34			☆				☆	☆			☆	
■		**Herolds Bay** Divisional Council, P.O. Box 12, George 6530 ☐ *18 km from George*	0441	3001			■			■		■	■	■	■	■	■				16					■		■			■		
		HIBBERDENE N 63 NS 7m																															
●	[AA Carnet]	**Happy Days** P.O. Box 1 (4220) ☐ *Marlin Drive*	0399	2310	●					●	●		●	●					●	10			●					●			●		
○	[AA Carnet]	**Hibberdene(Karavan Serai)** P.O. Box 143 (4220)	0399	2308	○					○	○		○	○					○		134		○					○			○		
◆		**Rondalia** P.O. Box 14 (4220)	0399	2123/4	◆					◆	◆		◆	◆				◆		85				◆				◆			◆		
◇		**Umzimai** P.O. Box 140 (4220) ☐ *Baracouda Boulevard*	0399	2507	◇					◇	◇			◇					◇		28			◇						◇	◇		
		HIMEVILLE N 63 A2 ↓ 1561m																															
△		**Highland Nook Private Park** J. D. McLean, Borreray, P.O. Himeville 4585 ☐ *5 km from Himeville/Nottingham Rd. Junction*	T	1611	△							△		△				△			20				△				△			△	
★		**Himeville Nature Reserve** Officer-in-Charge, P.O. Himeville 4585	T	1521					★		★	★		★				★			★			★					★			★	
		HLUHLUWE N 67 B5 ↙ 5m																															
■		**False Bay Park** Officer-in-Charge, P.O. Hluhluwe 3960 ☐ *15 km from Hluhluwe*	03562 E	2911					■		■			■				■			40						■		■			■	
		HOBHOUSE O 62 A5 ← 1471m																															
●	[AA Carnet]	**Koos Taljaard** Town Clerk, P.O. Box 5 (9740) ☐ *Klein St.*	05662 E	13		●					●		●	●				●		10				●					●		●		
		HOEDSPRUIT T 69 B3 → 550m																															
◆		**Manoutsa** P/Bag 502 (1380)	0131732 E	623	◆						◆	◆		◆		◆		◆			40		◆							◆	◆		
◇		**Mariepsig Rest-camp** P.O. Box 97 (1380) ☐ *20 km from Hoedspruit*	0131732 E	831	◇							◇		◇		◇		◇	◇		6		◇							◇		◇	
▲		**Strijdom Tunnel Motel and Rest Camp** P.O. Box 53 (1380) ☐ *11 km from the Strijdom Tunnel*	0131732 E	1913	▲						▲	▲	▲	▲		▲			▲	30	30	30		▲					▲	▲		▲	
		HOFMEYR C 62 C3 ↘ 1252m																															
★	[AA Carnet]	**Hofmeyr Municipal** Town Clerk, P.O. Box 97 (5930) ☐ *Du Plessis St.*	04852 E	97		★								★					★	20	20			★					★		★		
		HOGSBACK C 60 B1 → 1450m																															
■	[AA Carnet]	**Waterfall Park** N. C. Powrie, Tanglewood (5705)	T	240	■						■	■	■	■					■		12		■						■		■		
		HONEYDEW T 72 NS ↖ 1234m																															
●		**Honeydew** P.O. Box 67 (2040) ☐ *D.F. Malan Drive*	011	675-2605	●								●	●				●		51			●						●			●	
○	[AA Carnet]	**Sandspruit Pleasure Resort** P.O. Box 1235 (2040) ☐ *Palora Rd.*	011	675-4023	○								○	○				○	○		40				○			○	○			○	
		HOT SPRINGS, MINERAL BATHS AND SPA'S See respectively: ● **Aliwal North** ● **Badplaas** ● **Caledon** ● **Calitzdorp** ● **Christiana** ● **Cradock** ● **Dennilton** ● **Letsitele** ● **Montagu** ● **Naboomspruit** ● **Rawsonville** ● **Sabi River Bungalows** ● **The Baths** ● **Tshipise** ● **Warmbaths** ● **Warmwaterberg**																															
		HOWICK N 63 A3 ← 1048m																															
△		**Howick Municipal** P.O. Box 5 (3290) ☐ *Falls View Drive*	033212 E	1050		△					△	△	△	△			△	△	△	20		6			△			△	△		△		
★	[Caravan Club]	**Midmar Dam** P/Bag (3290) ☐ *5 km from Howick*	033212 E	267				★			★	★		★				★		31	196				★			★			★		
		HUMANSDORP C 59 C4 ↗ 144m																															
■		**Humansdorp Tourist Park** P.O. Box 26 (6300) ☐ *Main St.*	04232 E	37		■							■	■					■	■					■			■			■		
		IFAFA BEACH N 63 NS ↙ 8m																															
●	[Caravan Club]	**Ifafa Beach** P.O. Box 10 (4185) ☐ *Sydney See Rd.*	03239	740	●					●				●					●	44		10		●				●			●		
○	[Caravan Club]	**Ifafa Marina** Ifafa Marina (Agencies) (Pty) Ltd., P/Bag (4185) ☐ *Ifafa Lagoon*	03239	611/675	○						○	○		○				○			160				○				○		○		
		ILLOVO BEACH N 63 NS ↗ S.L.																															
◇		**Illovo Beach** P.O. Box 19 (4155) ☐ *17 Elizabeth Ave.*	031	95-1366						◇				◇					◇	22		6		◇				◇			◇		
▲		**Karridene** P.O. Box 20 (4155) ☐ *Main South Coast Rd.*	031	95-1020	▲					▲	▲		▲	▲					▲	▲	▲			▲				▲			▲		
△		**Natalia Holiday Resort** Manager, P.O. Box 3 (4155) ☐ *2 Elizabeth Ave.*	031	95-1626	△					△			△	△					△		110		△					△			△		
★		**Patlyn** P.O. Box 11 (4155) ☐ *Elizabeth Ave.*	031	95-1339	★					★				★					★	77		8		★				★			★		

Column groups: SEASONS (33 Open throughout the year; 34 Out-of-season closing date / Re-opening date) · TERMS FOR BOOKINGS (35 Bookings accp. peak sns. – see note 2; 36 Deposit required; 37 Refunded if cancelled – see note 3) · CARAVAN PARK/CAMPING SITE TARIFFS (See heading) (38 Maximum in-season tariff; 39 Maximum out-of-season tariff) · REDUCTIONS ALLOWED FOR (40 Long periods of stay; 41 Groups – see note 4; 42 AA carnet holders see note 5; 43 Others (on application)) · RESTAURANT FACILITIES (44 On site; 45 Within 5 km of site; 46 More than 5 km from site) · TEAROOM/CAFE (47 On site; 48 Within 5 km of site; 49 More than 5 km from site) · SHOPPING FACILITIES (Provisions) (50 On site; 51 Within 5 km of site; 52 More than 5 km from site) · ADDITIONAL ACCOMMODATION AVAILABLE (53 Bungalows; 54 Cabins; 55 Cottages (rondavels); 56 Chalets) · ADDITIONAL ACCOMMODATION TARIFF (See heading) (57 Maximum in-season tariff; 58 Maximum out-of-season tariff) · 59 Caravans to rent on site – see pages 8–11 · CAMP SITE FACILITIES, I = In-Season only, O = Out-of-Season only (DRINKING WATER: 60 Piped; 61 Other · BATHS: 62 Hot and cold; 63 Cold only · SHOWERS: 64 Hot and cold; 65 Cold only · 66 Waterborne sanitation; 67 Washbasins; 68 Dishwashing facilities; 69 Laundry and ironing facilities – see note 6; 70 Washing machines; 71 Site lit; 72 Plugs for razors (voltage); 73 Refrigerators; 74 Firewood/charcoal; 75 Open fire permitted; 76 Camp fire forbidden; 77 Braai places provided; 78 Kitchen/cooking facilities; 79 Petrol pump on site; 80 Petrol pump nearby; 81 Car repair shop nearby; 82 Car servicing nearby; 83 Gas service nearby; 84 First aid/hospital/doctor nearby; 85 Post office nearby; 86 Site guarded; 87 Pets allowed) · NON-WHITE SERVANTS (88 Servants permitted – see note 7; 89 Servants accom. – see note 7; 90 Servants for hire – see note 7) · TYPE OF VEHICLE PERMITTED (91 Car and trailer; 92 Truck 'horse' and semi-trailer; 93 Self-propelled caravans) · SPORTING AND RECREATIONAL FACILITIES, S = On Site, N = Nearby (Up to 20 km away) (94 Childrens' playground; 95 Tennis; 96 Cinema/drive-in/TV-room – see note 8; 97 Horse-riding; 98 Games room; 99 Trampoline; 100 Bowls; 101 Hot springs · GOLF: 102 Golf course – see note 9; 103 Number of holes; 104 Miniature; 105 Mashie; 106 Putt-putt · FISHING: 107 Freshwater – see note 10; 108 Sea – see note 11; 109 Goggle; 110 Licence required · SWIMMING: 111 Swimming pool; 112 Sea bathing; 113 Childrens' pool; 114 Adults only; 115 Shark nets at beach · BOATING: 116 Boats for hire; 117 Power; 118 Sailing; 119 Canoeing · PLACES OF INTEREST: 120 Historic; 121 Scientific; 122 Natural) · 123 NOTES

33	34	35	36	37	38	39	40	41	42	43	44	45	46	47	48	49	50	51	52	53	54	55	56	57	58	59	60	61	62	63	64	65	66	67	68	69	70	71	72	73	74	75	76	77	78	79	80	81	82	83	84	85	86	87	88	89	90	91	92	93	94	95	96	97	98	99	100	101	102	103	104	105	106	107	108	109	110	111	112	113	114	115	116	117	118	119	120	121	122	123
		●	●	●	E	B		●		●	●			●			●			●	●	●	●	B-G	B-G		●		●		●		●	●	●	●		●	220	●	●		●	●			●	●	●	●	●	●	●		●	●		●	●	●	S	S	S			S	S		N	18	●		●	N	S	S			●					N			●		●	
		◇	◇		B	B					◇								◇		◇			D	D		◇		◇		◇		◇	◇		◇						◇		◇			◇	◇	◇	◇		◇	◇		◇			◇		◇	S	S	N	N			N	N	N	9		◇						S									◇	◇	◇	
		△			B	B	△	△			△	△		△	△				△								△		△		△		△	△		△	△	△			△	△	△	△		△	△	△	△	△				△	△		△	△	△	△	N	N	N	N	N	N	N											N		N									△	
					B	B	★						★			★			★								★		★		★		★	★	★	★		★	220		★		★	★			★	★	★				★	★	★			★	★	★	N	N					S		N	9		★						N		N							★		★	
					X	X							■			■			■								■																■				■	■	■	■	■	■		■	■			■		■	N								N	9	■			N			■	N		N				S	S	S	■			
		●	●	●	B	B		●		●	●	●	●	●	●	●	●	●	●			●		B	B		●	●	●		●		●	●	●	●		●			●		●	●		●	●	●	●	●		●	●	●				●	●	●	N	N	N	S					S	9		●		S			●	N		N				S	S	S	●		●	
					B	B	◆					◆			◆			◆									◆		◆		◆		◆	◆		◆							◆				◆	◆	◆	◆		◆		◆	◆			◆	◆	◆		S	N				N							N			◆												
		▲	▲	▲	D	C						▲	▲		▲	▲		▲	▲								▲		▲		▲	▲	▲	▲	▲	▲		▲	220		▲		▲	▲			▲	▲	▲	▲	▲	▲	▲		▲			▲	▲	▲	S	N	N			N	N		N	18				N	N	N			▲					N	N	N	▲	▲	▲	
		★	★	★	F	D						★			★			★									★				★		★	★	★	L		★			★	★	★	★			★	★	★	★	★	★	★					★	★	★			N				N		N	18					N				★	N									★	
		☆	☆	☆	E	C			R			☆	☆	☆			☆			☆		☆		I	E		☆	☆	☆		☆		☆	☆	☆	☆		☆		☆	☆		☆	☆			☆	☆	☆	☆	☆	☆		☆			☆	☆	☆	☆			S		S		N		N	18					N	N			☆									☆		☆	
		■	■	■	F	D						■			■			■									■				■		■	■	■	L					■	■	■	■			■	■	■	■	■		■					■	■	■			N				N		N	18					N	N			■	S									■	
		●	●	●	F	C	●	●				●			●			●		●		●		F-H	C-D		●		●		●		●	●	●	●		●	●	●	●		●	●			●	●	●	●	●	●	●	0			●	●		●	N	S	S			S			N	18					N	N		N		N		●							●	
		○	○		I	F		○	0		○	○	○	○	○	○	○	○	○				○	K	C		○		○		○		○	○	○	○		○		○	○	○	○				○	○	○	○	○	○	○				○	○	○	○	S	N	N		S		N		N	18					N	N		S	○	S									○	
		◆	◆	◆	E	D	◆	◆		◆	◆			◆			◆	◆	◆			◆		I	E		◆		◆		◆		◆	◆	◆	◆		◆	220		◆	◆	◆	◆			◆	◆	◆	◆	◆	◆	◆		◆	◆		◆		◆	S	S	S			S	N		N	18					S	S		N	◆	N		◆	S				◆	◆	◆	
		◇	◇		H	D	◇	◇				◇		◇				◇									◇		◇		◇			◇	◇	◇		◇	◇	◇		◇		◇			◇	◇	◇		◇	◇	◇		◇					◇	S	S	S	N	N	N	N		N	18					S				◇	S									◇	
		△	△	△	C	C							△			△			△								△		△		△		△	△	△						△		△	△										△				△	△	△					S																								△	
		★			C	C										★		★									★		★		★		★	★	★							★		★			★	★	★	★	★	★	★					★		★		N					N		N	9				S			★						S						★	
		■	■	■	C	C							■			■			■								■		■		■		■	■	■						■		■				■	■	■	■	■		■		■			■	■	■														S									S						■	
					C	C			R				●			●			●								●		●		●		●	●	●			●					●	●			●	●	●	●	●	●		●			●	●	●	●	N													S			●													
					C	C	◆				◆			◆			◆			◆		◆		B	B		◆		◆		◆		◆	◆				◆			◆	◆	◆	◆		◆		◆	◆		◆		◆	◆				◆		◆	S													S			◆	S		S							◆	◆	◆	
		◇	◇	◇	D	D	◇	◇					◇			◇		◇				◇		X	X		◇		◇		◇		◇	◇		◇		◇	◇	◇	◇	◇	◇				◇	◇	◇					◇	◇			◇		◇			N											N			◇												◇	
		▲	▲	▲	X	X						▲			▲		▲	▲					▲	F	F		▲		▲		▲		▲	▲		▲		▲			▲		▲	▲			▲	▲	▲	▲				▲	▲	▲		▲	▲	▲	S	S	S		S		N	N						N			▲	S									▲	▲	▲	
		★			A	A	★						★			★			★								★				★		★	★		L		★			★		★	★			★	★	★			★		★	★			★	★	★	N	N									★																			
		■			C	C						■						■									■	■	■		■		■	■	■	L					■		■	■			■			■		■		■				■	■	■							N		N	6				N			■	N		N							■	■	■	
		●	●	●	D	D							●		●	●		●	●								●		●		●		●	●		●		●					●				●	●	●	●		●						●	●	●	S			N	S		N		N	18								S												
		○	○	○	D	D			R	○	○			○				○									○		○			○	○	○	○	○					○		○	○			○	○	○	○	○	○		○				○	○	○	S	N	N	N			N		N									S		S										
		△	△	△	D	D						△			△			△									△		△		△		△	△	△	△					△		△	△			△	△	△	△	△	△						△	△	△	S	N	N	N			N		N	9				N			△	N		N			N	N	N	N	△		△	
		★	★	★	D	D					★		★	★	★	★		★	★		★		★	C-E	C-E		★	★	★		★		★	★	★			★			★		★	★			★	★	★	★	★	★	★					★	★	★	S	N	N	S			N		N	9				S			★	S		S			S	S	S	S		★	★	
			■		C	C						■			■			■				■		B	B		■		■		■		■	■	■	■		■	■				■	■			■	■	■	■	■	■	■	■	■			■		■	S	N	N				N		N	9					N				■										
		●	●	●	H	D	●					●		●			●						●	H	D	●	●		●		●		●	●	●	●	●	●	220		●	●		●			●	●	●	●	●	●	●	0			●	●	●	●	S	N	S		S	S	N							N	S	S	●	S	●	S		●							●	
		○	○		K	D	○	○			○		○	○		○	○	○	○				○	K	D		○		○		○		○	○	○	○	○	○	220	○	○		○	○	○		○	○	○	○	○	○	○	0	○	○	○	○	○	○	S	S	S		S	S	N				○			S	N	N	○	S	○	S		○	S	S		S			○	
		◇	◇	◇	F	C						◇			◇			◇				◇		D	B		◇		◇		◇		◇	◇	◇	◇		◇			◇		◇	◇	◇		◇	◇	◇	◇	◇	◇	◇				◇	◇		◇	N	N	N	N	N	N	N		N	18					N			N	◇	N		◇							◇	
		▲	▲		H	E						▲	▲		▲	▲		▲	▲								▲		▲		▲		▲	▲	▲			▲	▲				▲				▲	▲	▲			▲					▲	▲		▲	N	N	N		N	N	N		N	18					N	N	▲	N	▲	N		▲								
		△	△	△	E	C				△		△			△			△									△		△		△		△	△	△	△		△	△		△	△	△	△			△	△	△	△		△	△					△	△	△	S	N	S	N		S	N		N	18			△		N	N	△	S	△	S		△					△	△	△	
		★	★		F	C	★					★		★			★									★	★		★		★		★	★	★	★		★	110/220		★		★	★			★	★	★	★	★	★	★	★	0		★	★		★	N	N	S		S		N		N	18				N	N	N		S	★			★	N			N				

CARAVAN PARKS AND CAMPING SITES

Establishments marked thus [Caravan Club symbol] have the Caravan Club of South Africa recommendation – see page 17
Establishments marked thus [AA symbol] recognise the AA Camping Carnet – see page 16 and also refer to column 42

CARAVAN PARK / CAMP SITE TARIFF CODE – See columns 38–39 (Subject to alteration)

A = Up to R1	C = R2–R3	E = R4–R5	G = R6–R7	I = R8–R9	K = R10–R16
B = R1–R2	D = R3–R4	F = R5–R6	H = R7–R8	J = R9–R10	O = FREE
					X = On Application

Charges are based on a family of 2 adults and 2 children under 12 years

ADDITIONAL ACCOMMODATION TARIFF CODE – See columns 57–59 (Subject to alteration)

eg. Bungalows, Cabins, Cottages, Chalets, etc.

A = R1–R3	C = R5–R7	E = R9–R11	G = R13–R15	I = R17–R19	K = R21–R30
B = R3–R5	D = R7–R9	F = R11–R13	H = R15–R17	J = R19–R21	X = On Application

NB: Where the tariff is given in *italics* it is per person, otherwise per unit

NOTE 1 — Columns 18, 19, 20. — Where a symbol appears instead of a number it means stands are available but not demarcated or number of stands has not been provided
NOTE 2 — Column 35 — A = Bookings accepted for additional accommodation only i.e. cottages, bungalows, etc.
NOTE 3 — Column 37 — Deposit refunded under certain conditions eg. less 10% ; if site is re-let ; if cancelled well in advance (up to 2 months) or on a doctor's certificate
NOTE 4 — Column 41 — Reductions allowed on application for youth, church, school or sport groups or caravan rallies
NOTE 5 — Column 42 — R = Reduction in tariff of between 5–10% to Carnet holders; O = Reduction Out-of-Season only
NOTE 6 — Column 69 — L = Laundry facilities only
NOTE 7 — Columns 88, 89, 90. — I = In-Season only ; O = Out-of-Season only
NOTE 8 — Column 96 — Applicable In-Season only at some establishments
NOTE 9 — Column 102 — See section on golf in Outdoor Holiday Guide
NOTE 10 — Column 107 — See section on freshwater angling in Outdoor Holiday Guide
NOTE 11 — Column 108 — See section on coastal angling in Outdoor Holiday Guide

ABBREVIATIONS
C = CAPE PROVINCE
N = NATAL
O = ORANGE FREE STATE
T = TRANSVAAL
B = BOPHUTHATSWANA
X = TRANSKEI

Column headings: 1 TELEPHONE CODE (T = DIAL 0020, BOOK TRUNK CALL; E = DIAL CODE, ASK EXCHANGE FOR NO.); 2 TELEPHONE NUMBER; OWNED OR SUPERVISED BY: 3 PRIVATELY OWNED, 4 MUNICIPALITY, 5 DIVISIONAL COUNCIL, 6 PROVINCIAL ADMINISTRATION, 7 PARKS BOARD; SITE DESCRIPTION – LOCALITY: 8 BEACH IN IMMEDIATE VICINITY, 9 BESIDE RIVER, LAKE OR DAM, 10 IN OR NEAR MOUNTAIN AREA, 11 WITHIN BUILT-UP AREA; NATURE OF GROUND: 12 GRASS, 13 GRAVEL, 14 SAND; SHADE: 15 UNSHADED, 16 PARTLY SHADED, 17 EXTENSIVELY SHADED; NO. OF STANDS: 18 CARAVANS ONLY SEE NOTE 1, 19 CARAVANS AND/OR TENTS SEE NOTE 1, 20 TENTS ONLY SEE NOTE 1; ACCESSIBILITY – APPROXIMATE DISTANCE FROM MAIN ROAD TO SITE: 21 ON MAIN RD, 22 WITHIN 1 km, 23 WITHIN 5 km, 24 WITHIN 10 km, 25 WITHIN 15 km; SURFACE OF APPROACH ROAD: 26 TAR, 27 GRAVEL, 28 SAND; CONDITION OF APPROACH ROAD: 29 GOOD, 30 FAIR, POOR

Key	Mark	Locality / Establishment	1	2	3	4	5	6	7	8	9	10	11	12	13	14	15	16	17	18	19	20	21	22	23	24	25	26	27	28	29	30
		IRENE T 68 C6 ↙ 1524m																														
□		**Doornkloof** P.O. Box 36 (1675)	012	6-5476	□								□	□	□			□		15		5			□			□	□			□
		JAMESTOWN C 62 C4 ↗ 1617m																														
○		**Jamestown Municipal** Town Clerk, P.O. Box 30 (5510) ☐ *Main St.*	T	641 or 741		○					○		○	○				○	○	6	6	12	○								○	
		JEFFREYS BAY C 59 C4 ↗ S.L.																														
◇	AA	**Jeffreys Bay Holiday Resort** 30 Goede Hoop St. (6330) ☐ *Goede Hoop St.*	T	61	◇								◇	◇				◇			50				◇			◇			◇	
▲	CC AA	**Jeffreys Bay Municipal** P.O. Box 21 (6330) ☐ *Da Gama Rd.*	T	21		▲				▲			▲	▲				▲			140				▲			▲			▲	
△	CC	**Kabeljous Holiday Resort** P.O. Box 7190, Port Elizabeth 6000	041	30-1208	△					△			△	△				△			66			△				△			△	
		JOHANNESBURG T 72 NS ● 1800m																														
☆	CC	**Bezuidenhout Park** C/o Parks and Recreation Dept., P.O. Box 2824 (2000) ☐ *Observatory Ave., De Wetshof*	011	43-3399		☆							☆	☆					☆	55			☆					☆			☆	
■		**Willowgrove** P.O. Box 23, Lyndhurst 2106 ☐ *Adrian Ave., Lombardy East*	011	608-2491	■						■			■				■			100			■				■	■			■
		JONGENSFONTEIN C 58 D6 ↖ S.L.																														
●		**Jongensfontein** Caretaker, Jongensfontein 6786 (for caravans); Secretary, P.O. Box 13, Riversdale 6770 (for huts)	T (02932 E)	Park 2212/Huts 29			●			●				●				●		110							●					●
		KAAPMUIDEN T 69 C4 ← 409m																														
◆		**Lowveld** P.O. Box 54 (1295) ☐ *1,6 km from Kaapmuiden*	T	34	◆							◆		◆				◆			40		◆						◆		◆	
		KAKAMAS C 65 C2 ↓ 657m																														
▲		**Kakamas Municipal** P.O. Box 174 (8870) ☐ *Cnr. Van der Walt Rd./14th Ave.*	05442 E	102		▲							▲	▲	▲			▲			8			▲				▲	▲		▲	
		KALAHARI GEMSBOK NATIONAL PARK C See Parks under control of National Parks Board																														
		KATBERG C 60 B1 ● 1000m																														
☆		**Highlands Holiday Resort** P.O. Balfour 5740	T	1002	☆							☆		☆					☆	30	40	15			☆				☆		☆	
		KEIMOES C 65 C2 ↘ 736m																														
□		**Keimoes Municipal** Town Clerk, P.O. Box 8 (8860)	05492 E	26/134		□					□	□	□	□					□	20	30	20	□						□		□	
		KEI MOUTH C 60 B3 ↓ S.L.																														
○		**Kei Mouth Municipal** Municipality, P.O. Kei Mouth 5262 ☐ *Main Rd.*	T	4		○				○	○		○	○			○	○			87		○						○		○	
		KELSO N 63 NS ● 2m																														
◇	CC	**Happy Wanderers** P.O. Kelso 4183	0323	5104	◇					◇				◇	◇				◇		100			◇					◇			◇
▲		**Kelso Valley** P.O. Box 20, Pennington 4184 ☐ *49 Cod-Crescent St.*	0323	5105	▲					▲	▲			▲					▲		50	10		▲				▲			▲	
		KEMPTON PARK T 72 NS ↗ 1670m																														
★		**Pomona** P.O. Box 86 (1620) ☐ *Hawthorne Rd., Pomona Estates*	011	979-1011	★								★	★	★				★		24			★					★			★
☆		**Protea** P.O. Box 774 (1620) ☐ *Pomona Rd.*	011	979-2216	☆								☆	☆					☆	60	60		☆					☆			☆	
		KEURBOOMSRIVIER C 59 NS → S.L.																														
□	AA	**Con's** P.O. Box 11 (6601)	T	4 or 36	□					□				□			□	□			130		□					□			□	
●		**Lagoon Holiday Resort** P.O. Box 9 (6601)	T	19	●					●	●			●			●	●	●		50				●			●	●		●	●
○		**Public Resort Keurboomsrivier** P.O. Keurboomsrivier (6601)	T	15				○		○	○	○		○				○	○	70		16	○					○			○	
◆		**San Merino** P.O. Box 413, Plettenberg Bay 6600	T	9	◆					◆	◆	◆		◆					◆		◆			◆				◆			◆	
		KEURBOOMSTRAND C 59 NS → S.L.																														
▲		**Arch Rock Holiday Resort** P.O. Box 6, Keurboomsrivier 6601	T	1311	▲					▲				▲					▲		80	5				▲		▲			▲	
		KIDD'S BEACH C 60 C2 ↗ 5m																														
★		**Aqualea** P/Bag X817, East London 5200 ☐ *Gulu River Mouth, 13 km from Kidd's Beach*	04323	858	★					★	★			★			★	★	★		40		★					★			★	
☆	AA	**Kidd's Beach** C/o Kidd's Beach Hotel (5264)	04323	715	☆					☆			☆	☆				☆		30		15		☆					☆		☆	
■		**Lincott Manor** P.O. Kidd's Beach 5264 ☐ *1,5 km from Kidd's Beach*	04323	643	■					■				■					■	25		■		■					■		■	
□		**Palm Springs Holiday Resort** P.O. Box 14 (5264) ☐ *Umlele River Mouth, 4 km from Kidd's Beach*	04323	879	□					□	□			□			□	□	□		70				□				□		□	
●	CC	**Rayner's Holiday Resort** P.O. Box 5079, Greenfields, East London 5208 ☐ *Gulu River Mouth, 13 km from Kidd's Beach*	0431	46-2410/9	●					●	●			●					●		30				●				●		●	
○		**Seavale** P.O. Box 23 (5264)	04323	720	○					○				○				○		70	10					○			○			○
		KIMBERLEY C 66 C2 ↘ 1223m																														
◇	AA	**Kimberley Municipal** P.O. Box 628 (8300) ☐ *Transvaal Rd.*	0531	2-6911		◇							◇	◇					◇	25		50		◇				◇			◇	
		KINGSBURGH N 63 NS ↗ S.L.																														
△		**Uitspan** P.O. Box 71, Winklespruit 4145 ☐ *On Pietermaritzburg highway*	031	935-5477	△					△				△					△		150		△					△			△	
		KING WILLIAM'S TOWN C 60 B2 ↙ 374m																														
☆		**King William's Town Municipal** P.O. Box 33 (5600) ☐ *Cathcart St.*	0433	2-3160		☆					☆			☆				☆					☆					☆			☆	
		KLAPMUTS C 58 D3 ↘ 168m																														
□		**Pearl** P.O. Box 37 (7625) ☐ *Protea Rd.*	0251	5338	□									□					□		60			□				□	□		□	
		KLEIN-BRAKRIVIER C 59 C2 ↖ S.L.																														
○	CC AA	**Riverside** P.O. Box 6 (6503)	04441	6316	○					○	○	○		○				○		○	○	○			○				○		○	
		KLEINKRANTZ C See Caravan Parks for Coloureds, Asians and Blacks																														
		KLEINMOND C 58 D4 ↖ S.L.																														
▲		**Palmiet Municipal** P.O. Box 3 (7195)	02823	3360		▲				▲	▲	▲		▲	▲			▲			700			▲				▲	▲		▲	
		KLERKSDORP T 66 A4 ↓ 1325m																														
★		**Water Paradise** P.O. Box 667 (2570) ☐ *Ventersdorp Rd.*	018	2-7521	★						★			★					★	60		25	★					★			★	

CAMP SITE FACILITIES — I = In-Season only, O = Out-of-Season only

SPORTING AND RECREATIONAL FACILITIES — S = On Site, N = Nearby (Up to 20 km away)

SEASONS			TERMS FOR BOOKINGS			CARAVAN PARK/CAMPING SITE TARIFFS (See heading)		REDUCTIONS ALLOWED FOR				RESTAURANT FACILITIES			TEAROOM/CAFE			SHOPPING FACILITIES (Provisions)			ADDITIONAL ACCOMMODATION AVAILABLE				ADDITIONAL ACCOMMODATION TARIFF (See heading)			CAMP SITE FACILITIES: DRINKING WATER		BATHS		SHOWERS																								NON-WHITE SERVANTS			TYPE OF VEHICLE PERMITTED			SPORTING AND RECREATIONAL FACILITIES								GOLF					FISHING				SWIMMING					BOATING				PLACES OF INTEREST			
32 OPEN THROUGHOUT THE YEAR	33 OUT-OF-SEASON CLOSING DATE	34 RE-OPENING DATE	35 BOOKINGS ACCP./PEAK SNS.–SEE NOTE 2	36 DEPOSIT REQUIRED	37 REFUNDED IF CANCELLED–SEE NOTE 3	38 MAXIMUM IN-SEASON TARIFF	39 MAXIMUM OUT-OF-SEASON TARIFF	40 LONG PERIODS OF STAY	41 GROUPS–SEE NOTE 4	42 AA CARNET HOLDERS–SEE NOTE 5	43 OTHERS (ON APPLICATION)	44 ON SITE	45 WITHIN 5 km OF SITE	46 MORE THAN 5 km FROM SITE	47 ON SITE	48 WITHIN 5 km OF SITE	49 MORE THAN 5 km FROM SITE	50 ON SITE	51 WITHIN 5 km OF SITE	52 MORE THAN 5 km FROM SITE	53 BUNGALOWS	54 CABINS	55 COTTAGES (RONDAVELS)	56 CHALETS	57 MAXIMUM IN-SEASON TARIFF	58 MAXIMUM OUT-OF-SEASON TARIFF	59 CARAVANS TO RENT ON SITE–SEE PAGES 8–11	60 PIPED	61 OTHER	62 HOT AND COLD	63 COLD ONLY	64 HOT AND COLD	65 COLD ONLY	66 WATERBORNE SANITATION	67 WASHBASINS	68 DISHWASHING FACILITIES	69 LAUNDRY AND IRONING FACILITIES–SEE NOTE 6	70 WASHING MACHINES	71 SITE LIT	72 PLUGS FOR RAZORS (VOLTAGE)	73 REFRIGERATORS	74 FIREWOOD/CHARCOAL	75 OPEN FIRE FORBIDDEN	76 CAMP FIRE PERMITTED	77 BRAAI PLACES PROVIDED	78 KITCHEN/COOKING FACILITIES	79 PETROL PUMP ON SITE	80 PETROL PUMP NEARBY	81 CAR REPAIR SHOP NEARBY	82 CAR SERVICING NEARBY	83 GAS SERVICE NEARBY	84 FIRST AID/HOSPITAL/DOCTOR NEARBY	85 POST OFFICE NEARBY	86 SITE GUARDED	87 PETS ALLOWED	88 SERVANTS PERMITTED–SEE NOTE 7	89 SERVANTS' ACCOM.–SEE NOTE 7	90 SERVANTS FOR HIRE–SEE NOTE 7	91 CAR AND TRAILER	92 TRUCK, HORSE AND SEMI-TRAILER	93 SELF-PROPELLED CARAVANS	94 CHILDRENS' PLAYGROUND	95 TENNIS	96 CINEMA/DRIVE-IN/TV-ROOM–SEE NOTE 8	97 HORSE-RIDING	98 GAMES ROOM	99 TRAMPOLINE	100 BOWLS	101 HOT SPRINGS	102 GOLF COURSE–SEE NOTE 9	103 NUMBER OF HOLES	104 MINIATURE	105 MASHIE	106 PUTT-PUTT	107 FRESHWATER–SEE NOTE 10	108 SEA–SEE NOTE 11	109 GOGGLE	110 LICENCE REQUIRED	111 SWIMMING POOL	112 SEA BATHING	113 CHILDRENS' POOL	114 ADULTS ONLY	115 SHARK NETS AT BEACH	116 BOATS FOR HIRE	117 POWER	118 SAILING	119 CANOEING	120 HISTORIC	121 SCIENTIFIC	122 NATURAL	123 NOTES
□			□			B	B								□		□			□								□		□		□		□	□				□	□		□		□				□	□	□	□		□		□				□	□	□		N					N		N	18				N			□										□			
○			○	○		B	B					○				○			○									○				○	○		○									○	○			○	○	○		○	○		○			○	○	○	○	N	N												N			○			N							○	○	○	
◇			◇	◇		C	B	◇		◇				◇			◇			◇	◇		◇		B-E	B-D		◇		◇		◇		◇	◇		◇		◇					◇	◇			◇	◇	◇	◇		◇		0			◇	◇	◇	◇	N			N			N		N	9					N			N	◇										◇	
▲			▲	▲	▲	C	C				▲			▲			▲		▲									▲		▲		▲		▲	▲	▲	▲		▲						▲			▲	▲	▲	▲		▲					▲	▲		▲		N					N		N	9					S	S		N	▲	N									▲	
△			△	△	△	X	X	△	△				△						△	△	△				X	X		△		△		△		△	△	△	△		△	220		△		△	△			△	△	△	△	△	△	△	△				△	△	△	S	S	N				N		N	9					N			N	△	S							△	△	△	
☆			☆			B	B						☆			☆			☆	☆								☆		☆		☆		☆	☆	☆	☆		☆	☆								☆	☆	☆	☆		☆	☆	☆				☆	☆	☆	N		N				S		N	18				N			☆	S		S							☆	☆	☆	
■			■	■		X	X	■					■			■	■		■									■		■				■	■	■	■		■			■		■				■	■	■	■		■					■	■	■	■	N	N	N				N											S												
●			●			C	C											●	●	●	●				E-F	E-F		●		●		●		●	●	●	●		●			●	●	●	●			●	●		●		●	●	●	●			●	●	●															S	S			●								●	●		
◆						C	C	◆				◆			◆			◆					◆		B-C	B-C		◆		◆		◆		◆	◆	◆	◆							◆	◆			◆	◆	◆	◆		◆						◆	◆	◆	S	N					N											S		S							◆		◆	
▲			▲			B	B	▲	▲				▲			▲			▲									▲				▲		▲	▲	▲	▲		▲					▲				▲	▲	▲	▲	▲	▲		▲	▲			▲	▲	▲		S							N	18				N			▲										▲		▲	
☆			☆	☆		D	D	☆	☆		☆		☆			☆		☆					☆	☆	D	C	☆	☆		☆		☆		☆	☆	☆	☆		☆		☆	☆		☆	☆	☆		☆	☆	☆	☆	☆	☆		☆	☆	☆	☆	☆	☆	☆	S	S	S	S	S		S		N	9	☆	☆	☆	N			☆	N		S							☆		☆	
□						B	B	□					□			□			□									□	□	□		□		□	□	□	□		□			□		□	□			□	□	□	□	□	□	□	□	□			□	□	□	N	N	N				N		N	9		□		N				N		N						N			□	
○			○	○		E	D		○		○								○		○	○	○	○	G	D		○				○		○	○	○	○					○		○				○	○	○	○	○	○	|		○		○	○	○	○	N	S	N				S		N	9					N	N			○					N	N	N			○	
◇			◇	◇	◇	G	D	◇				◇			◇					◇				◇	E-H	D-F		◇		◇		◇		◇	◇	◇	◇		◇	110/220				◇	◇			◇	◇	◇	◇	◇	◇	◇	◇	◇	◇		◇		◇		N	N		S		N		N	18					S			S		S		N							◇	
▲			▲	▲	▲	F	B	▲	▲		▲		▲		▲	▲		▲	▲									▲		▲		▲		▲	▲	▲	▲	▲	▲	110/220	▲	▲		▲	▲	▲		▲	▲	▲	▲	▲	▲	▲	▲			▲	▲		▲	S		S	N	S	S	N		N	18				S	S	S		S	▲	S		▲	S	S		S			▲	
★			★	★	★	C	C	★					★	★		★	★		★	★								★		★		★		★	★	★	★		★	220					★	★		★	★	★	★	★	★					★	★		★	S	N	N	N	S	N	N		N	18								S		S										
☆			☆		☆	D	D	☆					☆	☆		☆			☆									☆		☆		☆			☆	☆	☆	☆	☆	220	☆	☆		☆	☆			☆	☆	☆	☆	☆	☆	☆	☆	☆			☆		☆	N		N	N		N	N		N	18								N		N										
			□	□	□	E	C	□	□	R	□		□			□			□									□		□		□		□	□	□	□	□		□	□	□	□	□	□			□	□	□	□		□	□	□			□	□	□	□	N	N	N	N	N				N	18	□				N				□				N	N	N	N	□		□	
●			●	●		H	G	●				●			●			●					●		G	G	●	●	●	●		●		●	●	●	●		●			●	●		●			●		●	●	●	●	●					●	●	●		N		N			N		N	18					N	N			●				N	N	N	N				
○			○	○	○	D-E	C-D						○			○			○					○	K	K		○		○		○		○	○	○	○		○	220			○		○			○	○	○			○	○					○	○	○	S	S	N	N			N		N	18					S	N			○	S				N	N	N	○		○	
◆			◆	◆	◆	F	C	◆	◆				◆			◆		◆						◆	X	X	◆	◆	◆	◆		◆		◆	◆	◆	◆		◆	◆	◆	◆	◆		◆			◆	◆	◆	◆	◆	◆	◆				◆	◆	◆	◆	S	N	N	N	S		N		N	18				S	N	N			◆				S	S		S	◆		◆	
▲			▲	▲	▲	G	C	▲	▲						▲			▲											▲	▲		▲		▲	▲	▲	L		▲			▲	▲	▲	▲			▲		▲	▲	▲	▲		0			▲	▲	▲	▲							N		N	18					S				▲								▲		▲	
★			★	★	★	E	D	★						★			★	★		★								★	★	★	★	★	★	★	★	★	★		★			★	★	★	★			★	★	★	★		★	★				★	★	★	★			|		S		N							N	N	N	★		★				N	N	N	N			★	
☆			☆	☆		F	C			R	☆	☆							☆									☆		☆		☆		☆	☆	☆	☆		☆	☆	☆	☆	☆	☆	☆			☆	☆	☆	☆	☆	☆		☆	☆			☆		☆					N	S	N								N				☆	N			N			N			☆	
■			■	■		H	H						■	■		■	■	■	■				■		■	■		■				■		■	■	■	■					■	■		■			■	■	■	■		■	■				■	■		■					S		N							N	N			S	■	S										
□			□	□	□	E	C	□	□		□		□			□		□	□	□				□	G	C		□		□		□		□	□	□	□		□			□		□				□	□	□	□		□		□	□	□	□	□	□	□	S	N	S		S		N								S	S			□	N			S		N	N			□	
●			●	●	●	F	D							●			●	●	●					●	E	D		●		●		●		●	●	●	●	●	●		●	●	●	●	●			●	●	●	●		●		●			●	●		●	S		N		S		N								S				●				S			S				
○			○	○		F	D	○	○								○	○	○	○								○	○	○		○		○	○	○	○					○	○	○	○			○	○	○	○		○		0	○		○	○		○	S		S		S				N	18	○				S	S			○	N				N						
◇			◇			B	B							◇			◇			◇								◇		◇		◇		◇	◇	◇	◇						◇	◇	◇														◇		◇	S		N						N	18								N									◇			
△			△	△		X	X				△	△			△			△						△	X	X	△	△		△		△		△	△	△	△	△	△	△	△	△		△			△		△	△	△	△	△	△	△	△	△	△	△		△	S	S	S	N	S		N		N	18					N	N	△	S	△	S		△	N	N					△	
☆			☆		☆	C	C							☆			☆		☆									☆		☆		☆		☆	☆	☆	☆		☆	220		☆		☆	☆			☆	☆	☆	☆	☆	☆		☆	☆		☆	☆	☆	☆	S	N	N	N	N		N		N	18				N			☆	N		N				N	N	N	☆	☆	☆	
□			□	□		D	C	□	□		□		□		□			□			□		□		G	E		□		□		□		□	□	□			□			□		□	□			□	□	□	□	□	□		□	□			□		□	N	N	N	N			N		N	18								S		S						N	□	□	□	
○			○	○	○	E	C	○	○	R	○		○			○		○			○		○	○	J	G	○	○		○		○		○	○	○	○		○	220	○	○		○	○			○	○	○	○		○	○				○	○	○	○		N		N		N	N		N	18						N			○				S						○	
▲			▲	▲	▲	D	D		▲				▲	▲		▲	▲		▲	▲								▲				▲		▲	▲	▲						▲		▲	▲			▲	▲	▲	▲		▲	▲		▲			▲	▲	▲	S	N	N				N								N	N			▲								▲		▲	
★				★	★	D	D	★						★	★			★										★		★		★		★	★	★	★		★			★	★		★			★	★	★	★	★	★	★	★	★			★		★	S	N	N				N		N	18				N			★	S		S			S		S	S	★		★	

CARAVAN PARKS AND CAMPING SITES

Establishments marked thus (CC) have the Caravan Club of South Africa recommendation – see page **17**
Establishments marked thus (AA) recognise the AA Camping Carnet – see page **16** and also refer to column **42**

CARAVAN PARK / CAMP SITE TARIFF CODE – See columns 38–39 (Subject to alteration)

A = Up to R1	C = R2–R3	E = R4–R5	G = R6–R7	I = R8–R9	K = R10–R16
B = R1–R2	D = R3–R4	F = R5–R6	H = R7–R8	J = R9–R10	O = FREE
					X = On Application

Charges are based on a family of 2 adults and 2 children under 12 years

ADDITIONAL ACCOMMODATION TARIFF CODE – See columns 57–59 (Subject to alteration)

eg. Bungalows, Cabins, Cottages, Chalets, etc.

A = R1–R3	C = R5–R7	E = R9–R11	G = R13–R15	I = R17–R19	K = R21–R30
B = R3–R5	D = R7–R9	F = R11–R13	H = R15–R17	J = R19–R21	X = On Application

NB: Where the tariff is given in *italics* it is per person, otherwise per unit

NOTE 1 – **Columns 18, 19, 20,** – Where a symbol appears instead of a number it means stands are available but not demarcated or number of stands has not been provided
NOTE 2 – **Column 35** – A = Bookings accepted for additional accommodation only i.e. cottages, bungalows, etc.
NOTE 3 – **Column 37** – Deposit refunded under certain conditions eg. less 10% ; if site is re-let ; if cancelled well in advance (up to 2 months) or on a doctor's certificate
NOTE 4 – **Column 41** – Reductions allowed on application for youth, church, school or sport groups or caravan rallies
NOTE 5 – **Column 42** – R = Reduction in tariff of between 5–10% to Carnet holders; O = Reduction Out-of-Season only
NOTE 6 – **Column 69** – L = Laundry facilities only
NOTE 7 – **Columns 88, 89, 90,** – I = In-Season only ; O = Out-of-Season only
NOTE 8 – **Column 96** – Applicable In-Season only at some establishments
NOTE 9 – **Column 102** – See section on golf in Outdoor Holiday Guide
NOTE 10 – **Column 107** – See section on freshwater angling in Outdoor Holiday Guide
NOTE 11 – **Column 108** – See section on coastal angling in Outdoor Holiday Guide

ABBREVIATIONS

C = CAPE PROVINCE
N = NATAL
O = ORANGE FREE STATE
T = TRANSVAAL
B = BOPHUTHATSWANA
X = TRANSKEI

TELEPHONE CODE: T = DIAL 0020, BOOK TRUNK CALL; E = DIAL CODE, ASK EXCHANGE FOR NO.

			Telephone code	Telephone number	Owned or supervised by: Privately owned	Municipality	Divisional council	Provincial administration	Parks board	Site description – Locality: Beach in immediate vicinity	Beside river, lake or dam	In or near mountain area	Within built-up area	Nature of ground: Grass	Gravel	Sand	Shade: Unshaded	Partly shaded	Extensively shaded	No. of stands: Caravans only – see note 1	Caravans and/or tents	Tents only – see note 1	Accessibility – Approximate distance from main road to site: On main rd.	Within 1 km	Within 5 km	Within 10 km	Within 15 km	Surface of approach road: Tar	Gravel	Sand	Condition of approach road: Good	Fair	Poor
			1	2	3	4	5	6	7	8	9	10	11	12	13	14	15	16	17	18	19	20	21	22	23	24	25	26	27	28	29	30	31
		KNYSNA C 59 NS ● S.L.																															
□		**Ashmead** P.O. Box 109 (6570) □ *George Rex Drive.*	04452 E	605	□					□	□	□	□	□					□		42			□				□			□		
●		**Knysna Caravan and Holiday Park** Main Rd. (6570) □ *Main Rd.*	04452 E	500	●						●	●		●				●		50	75		●					●			●		
○		**Lagoonside** P.O. Box 116 (6570) □ *Holiday Park Cres.*	04452 E	341	○					○	○	○	○	○				○			20		○					○			○		
◆		**Monks** P.O. Box 513 (6570) □ *Port Elizabeth Main Rd.*	04452 E	369	◆						◆		◆	◆				◆			30		◆					◆			◆		
◇	CC AA	**Water Ways Holiday Park** P.O. Box 394 (6570) □ *Holiday Park Cres.*	04452 E	557	◇						◇	◇	◇	◇					◇		48		◇					◇			◇		
▲		**Woodbourne Holiday Farm** P.O. Box 78 (6570) □ *George Rex Drive*	04452 E	6802	▲					▲				▲					▲		50			▲				▲			▲		
		KOFFIEFONTEIN O 62 A2 → 1189m																															
★		**Koffiefontein** Bookings not necessary Enquiries: Town Clerk, P.O. Box 7 (9968) □ *1 km from Koffiefontein*	05372 E	7		★							★		★			★			35			★					★		★		
		KOKSTAD N 63 B2 ● 1283m																															
■	AA	**Kokstad Municipal** Town Clerk, P.O. Box 8 (4700) □ *Cnr. Hawthorn/Barker Sts.*	0372 E	1 or 7 or 298		■						■	■	■				■			60			■				■	■		■		
□		**Mount Currie Motel** P.O. Box 27 (4700)	0372 E	279 or 781	□						□	□		□	□			□			12	4	□					□			□		
		KOMATIPOORT T 69 C4 → 189m																															
○		**Komatipoort** P.O. Box 146 (1340)	0131632 E	252			○				○			○					○		○		○						○			○	
		KOMGA C 60 B2 ← 640m																															
◇		**Komga Municipal** Bookings not accepted. Enquiries: Town Clerk, P.O. Box 21 (4950) □ *Main St.*	04372 E	113 or 28		◇							◇	◇				◇			12		◇						◇		◇		
		KOMMETJIE C 58 NS ← S.L.																															
△	CC	**Imhoff Park** Manager, P.O. Box 18 (7976) □ *Wireless Rd.*	021	8-3634			△			△		△		△				△			120			△				△			△		
		KOSI BAY N 67 A5 ↘ S.L.																															
☆		**Kosi Bay Nature Reserve** Officer-in-Charge, P.O. Box 1, Emangusi 3973							☆		☆			☆		☆	☆	☆	☆		☆									☆			☆
		KOSMOS T 68 NS ↑ 1173m																															
□		**Iscor Angling Resort** P.O. Box 279, Hartbeespoort 0216 □ *Hartbeespoort Dam*	01211	3-1035	□						□	□		□				□		75	100	25	□					□			□		
		KOSTER T 68 C4 → 1588m																															
○		**Koster River Dam Camping Area** State Irrigation Board, P/Bag 20 (2825) □ *Koster River Dam*	014242 E	4230							○	○		○	○			○			○			○					○		○		
◆		**Wonderbaar Rest Camp** P.O. Box 396 (2825)	014242 E	61 or 7322	◆						◆	◆		◆	◆			◆	◆		◆				◆				◆			◆	
		KRAAIFONTEIN C 58 C3 ↘ 107m																															
▲		**Impala Holiday Resort** Dan King Rd. (7570) □ *Dan King Rd.*	021	32-2511	▲								▲	▲				▲			50				▲					▲	▲		
		KROONDAL T 68 C5 ↙ 1150m																															
★		**Bergheim Holiday Resort** P.O. Box 327 (0350) □ *Modderfontein, Rustenburg Dist.*	01421	9-2363	★							★		★			★	★	★	50	20	20	★					★			★		
☆		**Mountain Sanctuary Park** P.O. Box 187 (0350) □ *Magaliesberg*	0142222 E	1422/1430	☆						☆	☆		☆				☆	☆		28						☆		☆			☆	
■	AA	**Omaramba** P.O. Box 72 (0350) □ *Adjoining Buffelspoort Dam*	0142222 E	2713	■						■	■		■				■			150				■				■			■	
		KROONSTAD O 66 B5 ↘ 1369m																															
●	CC	**Kroon Park** Manager of Parks, P.O. Box 302 (9500) □ *Bert Symonds Drive*	01411	2-5670/2-4229		●					●			●				●	●	160		140		●				●			●		
		KRUGER NATIONAL PARK T See Parks under control of National Parks Board																															
		KRUGERSDORP T 72 NS ↘ 1692m																															
◇		**Pines Resort** Manager, P.O. Box 3018, Kenmare 1745 □ *Ivan Smuts Ave., Silverfields*	011	664-4613	◇							◇	◇	◇					◇	44		20		◇				◇			◇		
		KRUGERSPOS T 69 B3 ↓ 1326m																															
△		**Krugerspos** Krugerspos Restaurant, P.O. Krugerspos 1128	013232 E	2630	△							△		△				△			40		△							△	△		
		KUILSRIVIER C 58 C3 ↘ 45m																															
☆	CC AA	**Kuilsrivier Municipal** P.O. Box 68 (7580) □ *Van Riebeeck Rd.*	021	903-3113		☆							☆	☆				☆			85		☆					☆			☆		
		KURUMAN C 65 B5 ● 1375m																															
□	CC	**Kuruman Municipal** P.O. Box 4 (8460) □ *Voortrekker St.*	014532 E	8		□							□	□	□				□		60		□						□		□		
		LAAIPLEK C 58 B3 ↙ 5m																															
○		**Stywelyne** Town Clerk, P.O. Box 29, Velddrif 7365 □ *Next to harbour area at Laaiplek*	022882 E	408 or 12		○				○					○				○	50	15			○					○		○		
		LADISMITH C 58 C6 ← 539m																															
◇		**Aristata** P.O. Box 14 (6885) □ *At Seweweekspoort*	02942 E	6 or 312	◇						◇	◇		◇					◇	30							◇		◇			◇	
▲	AA	**Ladismith Municipal** P.O. Box 30 (6885) □ *Church St.*	02942 E	20		▲					▲		▲		▲				▲		15			▲				▲			▲		
		LADYBRAND O 66 D5 ↑ 1612m																															
★	CC	**Leliehoek Recreation Resort** Town Clerk, P.O. Box 64 (9745) □ *Leliehoek Ave.*	05612 E	90		★						★		★					★	50	50				★			★			★		
		LADY GREY C 62 B5 ↙ 1631m																															
■		**Lady Grey** P.O. Box 68 (5540) □ *Cnr. Burnett/Murray Sts.*	05552 E	72	■								■	■				■		15		5			■			■			■		
		LADYSMITH N 67 C2 → 1001m																															
●		**Ladysmith Municipal** P.O. Box 119 (3370) □ *Buller Rd.*	0361	6050/4881		●						●	●	●				●			60		●					●			●		
		LAINGSBURG C 58 C5 ↗ 660m																															
◆		**Peppertree** Karroo Motors, 28 Voortrekker St. (3370) □ *Cape Town Main Rd.*	02372 E	94	◆								◆	◆				◆		20		◆	◆					◆			◆		
		LAMBERT'S BAY C 58 B3 ↘ 30m																															
▲		**Lambert's Bay Municipal** Town Clerk, P.O. Box 4 (8130) □ *Church St.*	T	9		▲				▲			▲		▲	▲	▲				180			▲				▲			▲		
		LANGEBAAN C 58 C3 ↘ S.L.																															
★		**Langebaan Municipal** P.O. Box 11 (7357) □ *Suffren St.*	02287	615		★				★				★				★			70		★					★			★		

Column headings (by column number):

SEASONS: OPEN THROUGHOUT THE YEAR; OUT-OF-SEASON CLOSING DATE; RE-OPENING DATE (33–34) — TERMS FOR BOOKINGS: BOOKINGS ACCP./PEAK SNS.—SEE NOTE 2 (35); DEPOSIT REQUIRED (36); REFUNDED IF CANCELLED—SEE NOTE 3 (37) — CARAVAN PARK/CAMPING SITE TARIFFS (See heading): MAXIMUM IN-SEASON TARIFF (38); MAXIMUM OUT-OF-SEASON TARIFF (39) — REDUCTIONS ALLOWED FOR: LONG PERIODS OF STAY (40); GROUPS—SEE NOTE 4 (41); AA CARNET HOLDERS—SEE NOTE 5 (42); OTHERS (ON APPLICATION) (43) — RESTAURANT FACILITIES: ON SITE (44); WITHIN 5 km OF SITE (45); MORE THAN 5 km FROM SITE (46) — TEAROOM/CAFE: ON SITE (47); WITHIN 5 km OF SITE (48); MORE THAN 5 km FROM SITE (49) — SHOPPING FACILITIES (Provisions): ON SITE (50); WITHIN 5 km OF SITE (51); MORE THAN 5 km FROM SITE (52) — ADDITIONAL ACCOMMODATION AVAILABLE: BUNGALOWS (53); CABINS (54); COTTAGES (RONDAVELS) (55); CHALETS (56) — ADDITIONAL ACCOMMODATION TARIFF (See heading): MAXIMUM IN-SEASON TARIFF (57); MAXIMUM OUT-OF-SEASON TARIFF (58) — CARAVANS TO RENT ON SITE—SEE PAGES 8–11 (59)

CAMP SITE FACILITIES (I = In-Season only; O = Out-of-Season only): DRINKING WATER: PIPED (60); OTHER (61) — BATHS: HOT AND COLD (62); COLD ONLY (63) — SHOWERS: HOT AND COLD (64); COLD ONLY (65) — WATERBORNE SANITATION (66); WASHBASINS (67); DISHWASHING FACILITIES (68); LAUNDRY AND IRONING FACILITIES—SEE NOTE 6 (69); WASHING MACHINES (70); SITE LIT (71); PLUGS FOR RAZORS (VOLTAGE) (72); REFRIGERATORS (73); FIREWOOD/CHARCOAL (74); OPEN FIRE FORBIDDEN (75); CAMP FIRE PERMITTED (76); BRAAI PLACES PROVIDED (77); KITCHEN/COOKING FACILITIES (78); PETROL PUMP ON SITE (79); PETROL PUMP NEARBY (80); CAR REPAIR SHOP NEARBY (81); CAR SERVICING NEARBY (82); GAS SERVICE NEARBY (83); FIRST AID/HOSPITAL/DOCTOR NEARBY (84); POST OFFICE NEARBY (85); SITE GUARDED (86); PETS ALLOWED (87)

NON-WHITE SERVANTS: SERVANTS PERMITTED—SEE NOTE 7 (88); SERVANTS ACCOM.—SEE NOTE 7 (89); SERVANTS FOR HIRE—SEE NOTE 7 (90) — TYPE OF VEHICLE PERMITTED: CAR AND TRAILER (91); TRUCK "HORSE" AND SEMI-TRAILER (92); SELF-PROPELLED CARAVANS (93)

SPORTING AND RECREATIONAL FACILITIES (S = On Site; N = Nearby (Up to 20 km away)): CHILDRENS' PLAYGROUND (94); TENNIS (95); CINEMA/DRIVE-IN/TV-ROOM—SEE NOTE 8 (96); HORSE-RIDING (97); GAMES ROOM (98); TRAMPOLINE (99); BOWLS (100); HOT SPRINGS (101) — GOLF: GOLF COURSE—SEE NOTE 9 (102); NUMBER OF HOLES (103); MINIATURE (104); MASHIE (105); PUTT-PUTT (106) — FISHING: FRESHWATER—SEE NOTE 10 (107); SEA—SEE NOTE 11 (108); GOGGLE (109); LICENCE REQUIRED (110) — SWIMMING: SWIMMING POOL (111); SEA BATHING (112); CHILDRENS' POOL (113); ADULTS ONLY (114); SHARK NETS AT BEACH (115) — BOATING: BOATS FOR HIRE (116); POWER (117); SAILING (118); CANOEING (119) — PLACES OF INTEREST: HISTORIC (120); SCIENTIFIC (121); NATURAL (122) — NOTES (123)

33	34	35	36	37	38	39	40	41	42	43	44	45	46	47	48	49	50	51	52	53	54	55	56	57	58	59	60	61	62	63	64	65	66	67	68	69	70	71	72	73	74	75	76	77	78	79	80	81	82	83	84	85	86	87	88	89	90	91	92	93	94	95	96	97	98	99	100	101	102	103	104	105	106	107	108	109	110	111	112	113	114	115	116	117	118	119	120	121	122	123
		□	□		H	D		□				□			□		□	□		□	□		□	D-K	B-E		□		□		□		□	□	□	□		□	220		□		□	□			□	□	□		□	□		□	I	I	□	□	□	□	S	N	N	N	S		N		N	18				N	N	N			□	N			N	N		N	□	□	□	
		●	●		G	E	●	●			●			●			●	●								●	●	●	●		●		●	●	●	●		●			●		●	●			●	●	●			●	●	O				●	●	●	S	N	N		S		N		N	18					S					N			S		S	S	●	●	●	
		○	○	○	E	C	○					○			○		○	○			○	○		X	X	○	○		○		○		○	○	○	○		○	○		○		○	○			○	○	○	○	○	○		O	○	○	○	○		○	N	N	N	N	S		N		N	18				N	N	N		S	○	S			S	S		S	○	○	○	
		◆	◆		X	X						◆		◆			◆			◆		◆		X	X		◆		◆		◆		◆	◆	◆	◆		◆	220		◆		◆	◆		◆	◆	◆	◆	◆	◆	◆	◆				◆	◆		◆	S	S	S				N		N	18					N	N			◆	N			S	S	S	S	◆		◆	
		◇	◇	◇	E	D	◇		O			◇			◇			◇		◇			◇	I-K	H-K	◇	◇				◇		◇	◇	◇	◇	◇	◇	220				◇	◇			◇	◇	◇	◇	◇	◇		O	◇	◇	◇	◇	◇	◇	N	N	N	N	S	N	N		N	18				N	N	N	◇		◇				S			S	◇		◇	
		▲	▲		F	C	▲	▲		▲		▲			▲		▲			▲				*B*	*A*		▲		▲		▲		▲	▲		▲		▲	▲		▲		▲	▲			▲	▲	▲	▲		▲	▲					▲	▲	▲	S	N	N	N			N		N	18					N	N			▲								▲	▲	▲	
					B	B						★			★			★									★		★		★		★	★	★	★		★	★			★		★			★	★	★	★	★	★	★	★	★			★		★	N	N	N	N			N		N			★		N			★	N		N							★		★	
					B	B	■						■			■			■								■		■		■		■	■	■	■		■	220				■	■			■	■	■	■		■	■	■	■			■		■	N	N					N		N	9				N			■	N		N							■	■	■	
					C	C	□	□	□		□			□			□						□	C	C		□		□		□		□	□	□	□	□	□				□				□		□	□		□	□	□	□	□	□		□	□	□	N	N	S	N			N		N	9				N			□	N		N	□			N	N	N	□		□	
					B	B							○		○			○									○		○		○		○	○	○	○		○			○		○	○			○	○	○	○	○	○	○				○	○	○	○	N	N	N											N			○	N		N						N			○	
					C	C	◇					◇			◇			◇									◇		◇	◇	◇	◇	◇	◇	◇	◇							◇	◇			◇	◇	◇	◇		◇		◇	◇			◇	◇	◇	N	N					N		N	9								N											◇	
		△	△	△	C	B		△		△		△	△		△	△		△	△								△		△		△		△	△	△	△	△	△	220		△		△	△			△	△	△	△	△	△	△					△	△	△	S	N	N	N	S	N	N		N	18			△		N	N			△	N							△	△	△	
		☆	☆		C	C													☆								☆					☆	☆	☆	☆						☆		☆				☆				☆	☆			☆			4-wheel drive																	N		☆											☆	☆	◆ Permits from KwaZulu authorities required to stay in Kosi Bay — details are sent at time of booking.
		□	□	□	C	C	□	□			□	□		□			□	□	□		□	□	□	E	C		□		□		□		□	□	□	□		□		□	□		□	□	□		□	□	□			□	□					□	□	□	S	N	N											S			□	S		S				S	S	S	□	□	□	
					O	O							○			○		○	○								○			○			○								○	○	○	○									○	○	○			○	○	○														S		S	O							S	S	S			○	
		◆	◆	◆	C	C	◆	◆			◆			◆			◆	◆					◆	D	D		◆		◆		◆		◆	◆	◆	◆		◆			◆		◆	◆	◆		◆	◆	◆		◆	◆	◆					◆		◆		N	N		S									N			◆	S		S								◆	◆	
		▲	▲		C	C	▲	▲			▲			▲				▲									▲		▲			▲	▲	▲		▲		▲			▲			▲			▲	▲	▲	▲	▲	▲		▲									S	S	S				N	18								S												
		★	★		E	E		★				★	★	★	★	★	★	★	★			★		D-H	D-F		★		★		★		★	★	★	★		★	220	★	★		★	★			★	★	★	★		★						★		★	S	S	N			S	N		N	18								S		S							★	★	★	
		☆	☆	☆	H	H															☆		☆	D-G	D-G	☆	☆					☆	☆	☆	☆	☆		☆	110/220	☆	☆		☆	☆	☆					.☆	☆		☆					☆	☆	☆							N							N			☆	S		S				N	N	N	☆	☆	☆	
		■	■		E	E			R	■		■		■			■										■		■		■		■	■	■	■		■	■		■		■	■			■	■	■	■	■	■	■	■	■	■		■	■	■	S	S	S	S	S		N		N	18				N			■	S		S				N	N	N			■	
		●	●		C	C						●			●			●		●		●		A-D	A-D		●		●		●		●	●	●	●		●	●		●		●	●			●	●	●	●	●	●	●	●	●		●	●	●	●	S	S	N				N		S	18			●	N				S		S			S	N		S	●			
		◇	◇		F	F		◇					◇	◇				◇					◇				◇		◇			◇	◇	◇				◇	◇		◇		◇	◇			◇	◇	◇	◇	◇	◇	◇					◇		◇	N	N																S		S										
		·	△		C	C					△			△			△										△		△		△		△	△	△	△		△	△		△			△			△	△	△	△	△	△			△			△		△									N	9				N			△										△		△	
		☆			D	C	☆		R			☆	☆		☆	☆		☆	☆								☆		☆		☆		☆	☆	☆	☆		☆					☆	☆			☆	☆	☆	☆	☆	☆	☆		☆			☆		☆	S	N	N				N		N	18					N	N			N											
		□			E	E						□			□			□									□		□		□		□	□	□	□		□	230	□	□		□	□			□	□	□	□		□		□	□			□		□	N	N	N	N		N	N		N	9								N		N							□	□	□	
		○			C	C							○			○			○								○		○		○		○	○	○	○		○			○		○	○			○	○	○	○	○	○	○		○			○	○	○	N	N	N	N			N							N	N	N			○				N	N	N	N			○	
		◇			B	B	◇	◇											◇								◇														◇		◇											◇	◇			◇	◇	◇																		S		S									◇	
		▲	▲		B	B	▲					▲			▲			▲									▲		▲		▲		▲	▲	▲	▲		▲			▲	▲	▲	▲			▲	▲	▲	▲	▲	▲	▲	▲				▲	▲	▲	S	N	N			N	N							N				N		N							▲		▲	
		★			C	C	★	★				★			★			★		★		★		C-E	C-D		★		★		★		★	★	★	★		★	220		★		★	★			★	★	★	★	★	★	★	★	★		★	★	★	★	S	N	N	S			N		N	9				N			★	S		S				N	N	N	★	★	★	
		■			B	B	■					■			■		■	■	■								■		■		■		■	■	■	■	■	■	220				■	■			■	■	■	■	■	■		■				■	■	■	N	N	N											N			■	N		N							■			
		●			C	C						●			●			●									●		●		●		●	●	●	●		●					●	●			●	●	●	●	●	●		●	●			●	●	●	N	N	N	N			N		N	10								S		S							●		●	
		◆			B	B					◆				◆			◆									◆	◆			◆		◆	◆	◆			◆	◆			◆	◆	◆		◆	◆	◆	◆	◆	◆	◆		◆	◆			◆	◆	◆		N																												
		▲			C	C						▲			▲			▲									▲		▲			▲	▲	▲	▲	▲			▲				▲	▲			▲	▲	▲	▲		▲	I		▲			▲		▲	N	N	N		N				N	9					N	N			▲									▲		
		★			D	C						★			★			★									★		★		★		★	★	★	★		★	220				★	★			★	★	★	★	★	★	★		★			★		★		N													N	N			★				N	N	N	N	★		★	

CARAVAN PARKS AND CAMPING SITES

Establishments marked thus (Caravan Club symbol) have the Caravan Club of South Africa recommendation – see page 17
Establishments marked thus (AA symbol) recognise the AA Camping Carnet – see page 16 and also refer to column 42

CARAVAN PARK / CAMP SITE TARIFF CODE – See columns 38–39 (Subject to alteration)

A = Up to R1 | B = R1–R2 | C = R2–R3 | D = R3–R4 | E = R4–R5 | F = R5–R6 | G = R6–R7 | H = R7–R8 | I = R8–R9 | J = R9–R10 | K = R10–R16 | O = FREE | X = On Application

Charges are based on a family of 2 adults and 2 children under 12 years

ADDITIONAL ACCOMMODATION TARIFF CODE – See columns 57–59 (Subject to alteration)

eg. Bungalows, Cabins, Cottages, Chalets, etc.
A = R1–R3 | B = R3–R5 | C = R5–R7 | D = R7–R9 | E = R9–R11 | F = R11–R13 | G = R13–R15 | H = R15–R17 | I = R17–R19 | J = R19–R21 | K = R21–R30 | X = On Application

NB: Where the tariff is given in *italics* it is per person, otherwise per unit

NOTE 1 — **Columns 18, 19, 20,** — Where a symbol appears instead of a number it means stands are available but not demarcated or number of stands has not been provided
NOTE 2 — **Column 35** — A = Bookings accepted for additional accommodation only i.e. cottages, bungalows, etc.
NOTE 3 — **Column 37** — Deposit refunded under certain conditions eg. less 10% ; if site is re-let ; if cancelled well in advance (up to 2 months) or on a doctor's certificate
NOTE 4 — **Column 41** — Reductions allowed on application for youth, church, school or sport groups or caravan rallies
NOTE 5 — **Column 42** — R = Reduction in tariff of between 5–10% to Carnet holders; O = Reduction Out-of-Season only
NOTE 6 — **Column 69** — L = Laundry facilities only
NOTE 7 — **Columns 88, 89, 90,** — I = In-Season only ; O = Out-of-Season only
NOTE 8 — **Column 96** — Applicable In-Season only at some establishments
NOTE 9 — **Column 102** — See section on golf in Outdoor Holiday Guide
NOTE 10 — **Column 107** — See section on freshwater angling in Outdoor Holiday Guide
NOTE 11 — **Column 108** — See section on coastal angling in Outdoor Holiday Guide

ABBREVIATIONS
C = CAPE PROVINCE
N = NATAL
O = ORANGE FREE STATE
T = TRANSVAAL
B = BOPHUTHATSWANA
X = TRANSKEI

			TELEPHONE CODE (T = DIAL 0020, BOOK TRUNK CALL; E = DIAL CODE, ASK EXCHANGE FOR NO.)	TELEPHONE NUMBER	OWNED OR SUPERVISED BY: PRIVATELY OWNED	MUNICIPALITY	DIVISIONAL COUNCIL	PROVINCIAL ADMINISTRATION	PARKS BOARD	SITE DESCRIPTION: LOCALITY: BEACH IN IMMEDIATE VICINITY	BESIDE RIVER LAKE OR DAM	IN OR NEAR MOUNTAIN AREA	WITHIN BUILT-UP AREA	NATURE OF GROUND: GRASS	GRAVEL	SAND	SHADE: UNSHADED	PARTLY SHADED	EXTENSIVELY SHADED	NO. OF STANDS: CARAVANS ONLY SEE NOTE 1	CARAVANS AND/OR TENTS SEE NOTE 1	TENTS ONLY SEE NOTE 1	ACCESSIBILITY: APPROXIMATE DISTANCE FROM MAIN ROAD TO SITE: ON MAIN RD	WITHIN 1 km	WITHIN 5 km	WITHIN 10 km	WITHIN 15 km	SURFACE OF APPROACH ROAD: TAR	GRAVEL	SAND	CONDITION OF APPROACH ROAD: GOOD	FAIR
			1	2	3	4	5	6	7	8	9	10	11	12	13	14	15	16	17	18	19	20	21	22	23	24	25	26	27	28	29	30
		LEISURE BAY N 63 NS ↙ S.L.																														
□		**Leisure View** P.O. Box 16, Voortrekkerstrand 4279	03931	767	□					□				□					□	60	100	40		□				□			□	
		LETSITELE T 69 A3 ↘ 530m																														
○		**Eiland Mineral Baths** P/Bag 527 (0885)	015238	759 or 667				○						○					○	300		120	○					○			○	
		LICHTENBURG T 68 D4 ↖ 1489m																														
◇	CC	**Lichtenburg Municipal** P.O. Box 7 (2740)	01441	5051		◇					◇			◇				◇			◇				◇			◇			◇	
▲		**Molopo-Dal Rest Resort** P.O. Box 107 (2740)	T	Ottoshoop 902	▲						▲			▲					▲	50	50	100	▲						▲		▲	
		LINDEQUESDRIF T 66 A5 ↓ 1417m																														
★	AA	**Vaaloewer** P.O. Box 633, Vanderbijlpark 1900 □ *10 km from the Vaal barrage*	01617 E	885	★						★			★				★			75			★					★		★	
		LINDLEY O 66 B5 ↖ 1540m																														
■		**Lindley Municipal Overnight Stop** Bookings not necessary □ *Rautenbach St. Ext.*	014152 E	4		■					■			■		■			■		50			■					■		■	
		LOSKOP DAM NATURE RESERVE T See Damwal																														
		LOUIS TRICHARDT T 70 C4 ↗ 945m																														
○	CC	**Louis Trichardt Municipal** Town Clerk, P.O. Box 96 (0920) □ *Cnr. Trichardt/Grobler Sts.*	01551	2211		○							○	○					○		○		○					○			○	
◆		**Mountain** P.O. Box 414 (0920) □ *Messina Main Rd.*	01551	9611	◆							◆		◆				◆		6		◆	◆						◆	◆		◆
		LOXTON C 61 C4 ← 1219m																														
▲		**Loxton Municipal Overnight Stop** P.O. Box 8 (6985)	020212 E	4		▲									▲				▲		100	100		▲					▲		▲	
		LYDENBURG T 69 C3 ↖ 1468m																														
★		**Lydenburg Municipal** P.O. Box 61 (1120) □ *Viljoen St.*	013232 E	495/308		★					★	★	★	★					★		40		★						★		★	
		MACHADODORP T 69 C3 ↙ 1609m																														
■	AA	**Highway** P.O. Box 194 (1170) □ *Nelspruit Main Rd.*	013242 E	192	■									■				■			20		■					■			■	
		MAFEKING C 68 C3 ↓ 1278m																														
●		**Cooke's Lake** P.O. Box 42 (8670) □ *Lichtenburg Main Rd.*	0506	1091/2/3		●					●			●	●			●			110		●						●		●	
		MAGALIESBURG T 68 D5 ↑ 1402m																														
◆		**Lovers Rock Pleasure Resort** P.O. Box 79 (2805) □ *5 km from Magaliesburg*	01462 E	87	◆						◆			◆					◆		150		◆						◆		◆	
		MAGOEBASKLOOF T See Haenertsburg																														
		MAITLAND RIVER MOUTH C See Beachview																														
		MAMRE C See Caravan Parks for Coloureds, Asians and Blacks																														
		MANYELETI GAME RESERVE T See Acornhoek																														
		MARBLE HALL T 69 B2 ↙ 936m																														
■	AA	**Caravan's Rest** P.O. Box 239 (0450) □ *6 km from Marble Hall*	012082 E	5102	■						■			■					■	12	12	12	■					■			■	
		MARGATE N 63 NS ↙ S.L.																														
●		**Constantia** P.O. Box 389 (4275) □ *Cnr. Collins/Tree Sts., Manaba Beach*	0393	2-0482	●					●				●					●	42	18			●				●			●	
○		**De Wet** P.O. Box 71 (4275) □ *St. Andrews Rd.*	0393	2-1022	○					○				○	○		○	○	○	65	85	20		○				○			○	
◆		**Margate Caravan Corner** P.O. Box 276 (4275)	0393	2-0321	◆					◆			◆	◆				◆	◆	73				◆				◆			◆	
◇	CC	**Margate Caravan Park** P.O. Box 288 (4275) □ *Valley Rd.*	0393	2-0852	◇					◇			◇	◇					◇		76		◇					◇			◇	
		MARIKANA T 68 NS ↖ 1158m																														
△		**Rondalia Buffelspoort** P.O. Box 122 (0284)	0142222 E	57	△							△		△	△		△	△		100			△					△			△	
		MARINA BEACH N 63 NS ↙ 15m																														
☆	CC	**Belle Vista** P.O. Box 36, Southbroom 4277	0393	3755	☆					☆				☆					☆		100		☆						☆		☆	
■		**Sherwood Forest** P.O. Box 39 (4281)	0393	3792	■					■			■	■				■	■	120	20	10	■					■			■	
□	AA	**SYSU** SYSU-Vakansiebelange, P.O. Box 2347, Pretoria 0001 □ *Mars Rd.*	012 (0393)	79-6119 (3600)	□					□	□		□	□					□		30				□			□	□		□	
		MARYDALE C 61 A4 ← 983m																														
○		**Marydale Camping Site** Town Clerk (8910) □ *Snyman St.*	05482 E	7		○							○		○			○			15			○				○			○	
		MATATIELE N 62 B6 ↗ 1475m																														
◇		**Haig Park** Town Clerk, P.O. Box 35 (4730) □ *Cnr. West/High Sts.*				◇							◇	◇					◇		10		◇					◇			◇	
		MASELSPOORT O See Bloemfontein																														
		MELKBOSSTRAND C 58 C3 ↙ S.L.																														
★	CC	**Ou Skip** Manager, P.O. Box 13 (7437) □ *Otto Du Plessis Drive*	02224	2058			★			★				★			★	★		215		21	★					★			★	
		MELKRIVIER T 68 B6 ↖ 1166m																														
■		**Waterberg-Natuurpraal Holiday Resort** P.O. Melkrivier 0541	015352 E	2712	■						■	■		■		■		■	■		12			■					■	■		■
		MESSINA T 70 B5 ← 594m																														
●	CC	**Messina Municipal** P/Bag X611 (0900)	015532 E	103		●							●	●			●			200		200	●					●			●	
		MICA T 69 B3 ↗ 496m																														
◆		**Hippo Pools Holiday Resort** P.O. Mica 1382	T	811	◆						◆				◆		◆	◆		◆	◆	◆			◆				◆		◆	
		MIDDELBURG C 62 C2 → 1248m																														
▲	AA	**Middelburg Municipal** P.O. Box 55 (5900) □ *Heuwel St.*	04832 E	17		▲						▲			▲				▲		30			▲					▲		▲	
		MIDDELBURG T 69 C2 ↙ 1515m																														
★		**Kruger Dam Recreation Resort** Proprietor, P.O. Box 14 (1050) □ *Coetzee St.*	01321	3011/5331		★					★			★				★			100				★			★			★	
☆	AA	**Midland Estate** Midlands Brick and Engineering Works (Pty) Ltd., P.O. Box 111 (1050) □ *Witbank Main Rd.*	01321	2335	☆						☆			☆					☆		50		☆					☆			☆	

…EN THROUGHOUT THE YEAR

SEASONS		TERMS FOR BOOKINGS			CARAVAN PARK/CAMPING SITE TARIFFS (See heading)		REDUCTIONS ALLOWED FOR				RESTAURANT FACILITIES			TEAROOM/CAFE			SHOPPING FACILITIES (Provisions)			ADDITIONAL ACCOMMODATION AVAILABLE				ADDITIONAL ACCOMMODATION TARIFF (See heading)			CAMP SITE FACILITIES (I = In-Season only; O = Out-of-Season only) — DRINKING WATER		BATHS		SHOWERS																										NON-WHITE SERVANTS			TYPE OF VEHICLE PERMITTED			SPORTING AND RECREATIONAL FACILITIES (S = On Site; N = Nearby (Up to 20 km away))								GOLF					FISHING				SWIMMING					BOATING				PLACES OF INTEREST			NOTES
OUT-OF-SEASON CLOSING DATE	RE-OPENING DATE	BOOKINGS ACCP./PEAK SNS.- SEE NOTE 2	DEPOSIT REQUIRED	REFUNDED IF CANCELLED - SEE NOTE 3	MAXIMUM IN-SEASON TARIFF	MAXIMUM OUT-OF-SEASON TARIFF	LONG PERIODS OF STAY	GROUPS - SEE NOTE 4	AA CARNET HOLDERS-SEE NOTE 5	OTHERS (ON APPLICATION)	ON SITE	WITHIN 5 km OF SITE	MORE THAN 5 km FROM SITE	ON SITE	WITHIN 5 km OF SITE	MORE THAN 5 km FROM SITE	ON SITE	WITHIN 5 km OF SITE	MORE THAN 5 km FROM SITE	BUNGALOWS	CABINS	COTTAGES (RONDAVELS)	CHALETS	MAXIMUM IN-SEASON TARIFF	MAXIMUM OUT-OF-SEASON TARIFF	CARAVANS TO RENT ON SITE - SEE PAGES 8 - 11	PIPED	OTHER	HOT AND COLD	COLD ONLY	HOT AND COLD	COLD ONLY	WATERBORNE SANITATION	WASHBASINS	DISHWASHING FACILITIES	LAUNDRY AND IRONING FACILITIES - SEE NOTE 6	WASHING MACHINES	SITE LIT	PLUGS FOR RAZORS (VOLTAGE)	REFRIGERATORS	FIREWOOD/CHARCOAL	OPEN FIRE FORBIDDEN	CAMP FIRE PERMITTED	BRAAI PLACES PROVIDED	KITCHEN/COOKING FACILITIES	PETROL PUMP ON SITE	PETROL PUMP NEARBY	CAR REPAIR SHOP NEARBY	CAR SERVICING NEARBY	GAS SERVICE NEARBY	FIRST AID/HOSPITAL/DOCTOR NEARBY	POST OFFICE NEARBY	SITE GUARDED	PETS ALLOWED	SERVANTS PERMITTED - SEE NOTE 7	SERVANTS' ACCOM. - SEE NOTE 7	SERVANTS FOR HIRE - SEE NOTE 7	CAR AND TRAILER	TRUCK 'HORSE' AND SEMI-TRAILER	SELF-PROPELLED CARAVANS	CHILDRENS' PLAYGROUND	TENNIS	CINEMA/DRIVE-IN/TV-ROOM - SEE NOTE 8	HORSE-RIDING	GAMES ROOM	TRAMPOLINE	BOWLS	HOT SPRINGS	GOLF COURSE - SEE NOTE 9	NUMBER OF HOLES	MINIATURE	MASHIE	PUTT-PUTT	FRESHWATER - SEE NOTE 10	SEA - SEE NOTE 11	GOGGLE	LICENCE REQUIRED	SWIMMING POOL	SEA BATHING	CHILDRENS' POOL	ADULTS ONLY	SHARK NETS AT BEACH	BOATS FOR HIRE	POWER	SAILING	CANOEING	HISTORIC	SCIENTIFIC	NATURAL	
33	34	35	36	37	38	39	40	41	42	43	44	45	46	47	48	49	50	51	52	53	54	55	56	57	58	59	60	61	62	63	64	65	66	67	68	69	70	71	72	73	74	75	76	77	78	79	80	81	82	83	84	85	86	87	88	89	90	91	92	93	94	95	96	97	98	99	100	101	102	103	104	105	106	107	108	109	110	111	112	113	114	115	116	117	118	119	120	121	122	123
		□	□		H	D		□				□			□		□	□		□	□		□	D-K	B-E		□		□		□		□	□	□	□		□	220		□		□	□			□	□	□		□	□		□	I	I	□	□	□	□	S	N	N	N	S		N		N	18				N	N	N			□	N			N	N		N	□	□	□	
		●	●		G	E	●	●			●			●			●	●								●	●	●	●		●		●	●	●	●		●			●		●	●			●	●	●			●	●	O				●	●	●	S	N	N		S		N		N	18					S					N			S		S	S	●	●	●	
		○	○	○	E	C	○					○			○		○	○			○	○		X	X	○	○		○		○		○	○	○	○		○	○		○		○	○			○	○	○	○	○	○		O	○	○	○	○		○	N	N	N	N	S		N		N	18				N	N	N		S	○	S			S	S		S	○	○	○	
		◆	◆		X	X						◆		◆			◆			◆		◆		X	X		◆		◆		◆		◆	◆	◆	◆		◆	220		◆		◆	◆		◆	◆	◆	◆	◆	◆	◆	◆				◆	◆		◆	S	S	S				N		N	18					N	N			◆	N			S	S	S	S	◆		◆	
		◇	◇	◇	E	D	◇		0			◇			◇			◇		◇			◇	I-K	H-K	◇	◇				◇		◇	◇	◇	◇	◇	◇	220				◇	◇			◇	◇	◇	◇	◇	◇		O	◇	◇	◇	◇	◇	◇	N	N	N	N	S	N	N		N	18				N	N	N	◇		◇				S			S	◇		◇	
		▲	▲		F	C	▲	▲		▲		▲			▲		▲			▲				*B*	*A*		▲		▲		▲		▲	▲		▲		▲	▲		▲		▲	▲			▲	▲	▲	▲		▲	▲					▲	▲	▲	S	N	N	N			N		N	18					N	N			▲								▲	▲	▲	
					B	B						★			★			★									★		★		★		★	★	★	★		★	★			★		★			★	★	★	★	★	★	★	★	★			★		★	N	N	N	N			N		N			★		N			★	N		N							★		★	
					B	B	■						■			■			■								■		■		■		■	■	■	■		■	220				■	■			■	■	■	■		■	■	■	■			■		■	N	N					N		N	9				N			■	N		N							■	■	■	
					C	C	□	□	□		□			□			□						□	C	C		□		□		□		□	□	□	□	□	□				□				□		□	□		□	□	□	□	□	□		□	□	□	N	N	S	N			N		N	9				N			□	N		N	□			N	N	N	□		□	
					B	B							○		○			○									○		○		○		○	○	○	○		○			○		○	○			○	○	○	○	○	○	○				○	○	○	○	N	N	N											N			○	N		N						N			○	
					C	C	◇					◇			◇			◇									◇		◇	◇	◇	◇	◇	◇	◇	◇							◇	◇			◇	◇	◇	◇		◇		◇	◇			◇	◇	◇	N	N					N		N	9								N											◇	
		△	△	△	C	B		△		△		△	△		△	△		△	△								△		△		△		△	△	△	△	△	△	220		△		△	△			△	△	△	△	△	△	△					△	△	△	S	N	N	N	S	N	N		N	18			△		N	N			△	N							△	△	△	
		☆	☆		C	C													☆								☆					☆	☆	☆	☆						☆		☆				☆				☆	☆			☆			4-wheel drive																	N		☆											☆	☆	Permits from KwaZulu authorities required to stay in Kosi Bay — details are sent at time of booking.
		□	□	□	C	C	□	□			□	□		□			□	□	□		□	□	□	E	C		□		□		□		□	□	□	□		□		□	□		□	□	□		□	□	□			□	□					□	□	□	S	N	N											S			□	S		S				S	S	S	□	□	□	
					O	O							○			○		○	○								○			○			○								○	○	○	○									○	○	○			○	○	○														S		S	○							S	S	S			○	
		◆	◆	◆	C	C	◆	◆			◆			◆			◆	◆					◆	D	D		◆		◆		◆		◆	◆	◆	◆		◆			◆		◆	◆	◆		◆	◆	◆		◆	◆	◆					◆		◆		N	N		S									N			◆	S		S								◆	◆	
		▲	▲		C	C	▲	▲			▲			▲				▲									▲		▲			▲	▲	▲		▲		▲			▲			▲			▲	▲	▲	▲	▲	▲		▲									S	S	S				N	18								S												
		★	★		E	E		★				★	★	★	★	★	★	★	★			★		D-H	D-F		★		★		★		★	★	★	★		★	220	★	★		★	★			★	★	★	★		★						★		★	S	S	N			S	N		N	18								S		S							★	★	★	
		☆	☆	☆	H	H															☆		☆	D-G	D-G	☆	☆					☆	☆	☆	☆	☆		☆	110/220	☆	☆		☆	☆	☆					☆	☆		☆					☆	☆	☆							N							N			☆	S		S				N	N	N	☆	☆	☆	
		■	■		E	E			R	■		■		■			■										■		■		■		■	■	■	■		■	■		■		■	■			■	■	■	■	■	■	■	■	■	■		■	■	■	S	S	S	S	S		N		N	18				N			■	S		S				N	N	N			■	
		●	●		C	C						●			●			●		●		●		A-D	A-D		●		●		●		●	●	●	●		●	●		●		●	●			●	●	●	●	●	●	●	●	●		●	●	●	●	S	S	N				N		S	18			●	N				S		S			S	N		S	●			
		◇	◇		F	F		◇					◇	◇			◇						◇				◇		◇			◇	◇	◇				◇	◇		◇		◇	◇			◇	◇	◇	◇	◇	◇	◇					◇		◇	N	N																S		S										
			△		C	C					△			△			△										△		△		△		△	△	△	△		△	△		△			△			△	△	△	△	△	△			△			△		△									N	9				N			△										△		△	
		☆			D	C	☆		R			☆	☆		☆	☆		☆	☆								☆		☆		☆		☆	☆	☆	☆		☆					☆	☆			☆	☆	☆	☆	☆	☆	☆		☆			☆		☆	S	N	N				N		N	18					N	N			N											
		□			E	E						□			□			□									□		□		□		□	□	□	□		□	230	□	□		□	□			□	□	□	□		□		□	□			□		□	N	N	N	N		N	N		N	9								N		N							□	□	□	
		○			C	C							○			○			○								○		○		○		○	○	○	○		○			○		○	○			○	○	○	○	○	○	○		○			○	○	○	N	N	N	N			N							N	N	N			○				N	N	N	N			○	
		◇			B	B	◇	◇											◇								◇														◇		◇											◇	◇			◇	◇	◇																		S		S									◇	
		▲	▲		B	B	▲					▲			▲			▲									▲		▲		▲		▲	▲	▲	▲		▲			▲	▲	▲	▲			▲	▲	▲	▲	▲	▲	▲	▲				▲	▲	▲	S	N	N			N	N							N				N		N							▲		▲	
		★			C	C	★	★				★			★			★		★		★		C-E	C-D		★		★		★		★	★	★	★		★	220		★		★	★			★	★	★	★	★	★	★	★	★		★	★	★	★	S	N	N	S			N		N	9				N			★	S		S				N	N	N	★	★	★	
		■			B	B	■					■			■		■	■	■								■		■		■		■	■	■	■	■	■	220				■	■			■	■	■	■	■	■		■				■	■	■	N	N	N											N			■	N		N							■			
		●			C	C						●			●			●									●		●		●		●	●	●	●		●					●	●			●	●	●	●	●	●		●	●			●	●	●	N	N	N	N			N		N	10								S		S							●		●	
		◆			B	B					◆				◆			◆									◆	◆			◆		◆	◆	◆			◆	◆			◆	◆	◆		◆	◆	◆	◆	◆	◆	◆		◆	◆			◆	◆	◆		N																												
		▲			C	C						▲			▲			▲									▲		▲			▲	▲	▲	▲	▲			▲				▲	▲			▲	▲	▲	▲		▲	I		▲			▲		▲	N	N	N		N				N	9					N	N			▲									▲		
		★			D	C						★			★			★									★		★		★		★	★	★	★		★	220				★	★			★	★	★	★	★	★	★		★			★		★		N													N	N			★				N	N	N	N	★		★	

CARAVAN PARKS AND CAMPING SITES

Establishments marked thus [caravan symbol] have the Caravan Club of South Africa recommendation – see page 17
Establishments marked thus [carnet symbol] recognise the AA Camping Carnet – see page 16 and also refer to column 42

CARAVAN PARK / CAMP SITE TARIFF CODE – See columns 38–39 (Subject to alteration)

A = Up to R1	C = R2–R3	E = R4–R5	G = R6–R7	I = R8–R9	K = R10–R16
B = R1–R2	D = R3–R4	F = R5–R6	H = R7–R8	J = R9–R10	O = FREE
					X = On Application

Charges are based on a family of 2 adults and 2 children under 12 years

ADDITIONAL ACCOMMODATION TARIFF CODE – See columns 57–59 (Subject to alteration)

eg. Bungalows, Cabins, Cottages, Chalets, etc.

A = R1–R3	C = R5–R7	E = R9–R11	G = R13–R15	I = R17–R19	K = R21–R30
B = R3–R5	D = R7–R9	F = R11–R13	H = R15–R17	J = R19–R21	X = On Application

NB: Where the tariff is given in *italics* it is per person, otherwise per unit

NOTE 1 – Columns 18, 19, 20, – Where a symbol appears instead of a number it means stands are available but not demarcated or number of stands has not been provided
NOTE 2 – Column 35 – A – Bookings accepted for additional accommodation only i.e. cottages, bungalows, etc.
NOTE 3 – Column 37 – Deposit refunded under certain conditions eg. less 10% ; if site is re-let ; if cancelled well in advance (up to 2 months) or on a doctor's certificate
NOTE 4 – Column 41 – Reductions allowed on application for youth, church, school or sport groups or caravan rallies
NOTE 5 – Column 42 – R – Reduction in tariff of between 5–10% to Carnet holders
O – Reduction Out-of-Season only
NOTE 6 – Column 69 – L – Laundry facilities only
NOTE 7 – Columns 88, 89, 90, – I – In-Season only ; O – Out-of-Season only
NOTE 8 – Column 96 – Applicable In-Season only at some establishments
NOTE 9 – Column 102 – See section on golf in Outdoor Holiday Guide
NOTE 10 – Column 107 – See section on freshwater angling in Outdoor Holiday Guide
NOTE 11 – Column 108 – See section on coastal angling in Outdoor Holiday Guide

ABBREVIATIONS
C CAPE PROVINCE
N NATAL
O ORANGE FREE STATE
T TRANSVAAL
B BOPHUTHATSWANA
X TRANSKEI

			1 Telephone code (T = Dial 0020. Book trunk call; E = Dial code. Ask exchange for no.)	2 Telephone number	3 Owned or supervised by: Privately owned	4 Municipality	5 Divisional council	6 Provincial administration	7 Parks board	8 Site description – Locality: Beach in immediate vicinity	9 Beside river, lake or dam	10 In or near mountain area	11 Within built-up area	12 Nature of ground: Grass	13 Gravel	14 Sand	15 Shade: Unshaded	16 Partly shaded	17 Extensively shaded	18 No. of stands: Caravans only – see note 1	19 Caravans and/or tents	20 Tents only – see note 1	21 Accessibility – Approximate distance from main road to site: On main rd	22 Within 1 km	23 Within 5 km	24 Within 10 km	25 Within 15 km	26 Surface of road approach: Tar	27 Gravel	28 Sand	29 Condition of road approach: Good	30 Fair
		LEISURE BAY N 63 NS / S.L.																														
□		**Leisure View** P.O. Box 16, Voortrekkerstrand 4279	03931	767	□					□				□					□	60	100	40		□				□			□	
		LETSITELE T 69 A3 \ 530m																														
○		**Eiland Mineral Baths** P/Bag 527 (0885)	015238	759 or 667				○						○					○	300		120	○					○			○	
		LICHTENBURG T 68 D4 \ 1489m																														
◇	[caravan symbol]	**Lichtenburg Municipal** P.O. Box 7 (2740)	01441	5051		◇					◇			◇				◇			◇				◇			◇			◇	
▲		**Molopo-Dal Rest Resort** P.O. Box 107 (2740)	T	Ottoshoop 902	▲						▲			▲					▲	50	50	100	▲						▲		▲	
		LINDEQUESDRIF T 66 A5 ↓ 1417m																														
★	[carnet symbol]	**Vaaloewer** P.O. Box 633, Vanderbijlpark 1900 □ *10 km from the Vaal barrage*	01617 E	885	★						★			★				★			75			★					★		★	
		LINDLEY O 66 B5 \ 1540m																														
■		**Lindley Municipal Overnight Stop** Bookings not necessary □ *Rautenbach St. Ext.*	014152 E	4		■					■			■		■			■		50			■					■		■	
		LOSKOP DAM NATURE RESERVE T See Damwal																														
		LOUIS TRICHARDT T 70 C4 / 945m																														
○	[caravan symbol]	**Louis Trichardt Municipal** Town Clerk, P.O. Box 96 (0920) □ *Cnr. Trichardt/Grobler Sts.*	01551	2211		○							○	○					○		○		○					○			○	
◆		**Mountain** P.O. Box 414 (0920) □ *Messina Main Rd.*	01551	9611	◆							◆		◆				◆		6		◆	◆						◆	◆		◆
		LOXTON C 61 C4 ← 1219m																														
▲		**Loxton Municipal Overnight Stop** P.O. Box 8 (6985)	020212 E	4		▲									▲				▲		100	100		▲					▲		▲	
		LYDENBURG T 69 C3 \ 1468m																														
★		**Lydenburg Municipal** P.O. Box 61 (1120) □ *Viljoen St.*	013232 E	495/308		★					★	★	★	★					★		40		★						★		★	
		MACHADODORP T 69 C3 / 1609m																														
■	[carnet symbol]	**Highway** P.O. Box 194 (1170) □ *Nelspruit Main Rd.*	013242 E	192	■									■				■			20		■					■			■	
		MAFEKING C 68 C3 ↓ 1278m																														
●		**Cooke's Lake** P.O. Box 42 (8670) □ *Lichtenburg Main Rd.*	0506	1091/2/3		●					●			●	●			●			110		●						●		●	
		MAGALIESBURG T 68 D5 ↑ 1402m																														
◆		**Lovers Rock Pleasure Resort** P.O. Box 79 (2805) □ *5 km from Magaliesburg*	01462 E	87	◆						◆			◆					◆		150		◆						◆		◆	
		MAGOEBASKLOOF T See Haenertsburg																														
		MAITLAND RIVER MOUTH C See Beachview																														
		MAMRE C See Caravan Parks for Coloureds, Asians and Blacks																														
		MANYELETI GAME RESERVE T See Acornhoek																														
		MARBLE HALL T 69 B2 / 936m																														
■	[carnet symbol]	**Caravan's Rest** P.O. Box 239 (0450) □ *6 km from Marble Hall*	012082 E	5102	■						■			■					■	12	12	12	■					■			■	
		MARGATE N 63 NS / S.L.																														
●		**Constantia** P.O. Box 389 (4275) □ *Cnr. Collins/Tree Sts., Manaba Beach*	0393	2-0482	●					●				●					●	42	18			●				●			●	
○		**De Wet** P.O. Box 71 (4275) □ *St. Andrews Rd.*	0393	2-1022	○					○				○	○		○	○	○	65	85	20		○				○			○	
◆		**Margate Caravan Corner** P.O. Box 276 (4275)	0393	2-0321	◆					◆			◆	◆				◆	◆	73				◆				◆			◆	
◇	[caravan symbol]	**Margate Caravan Park** P.O. Box 288 (4275) □ *Valley Rd.*	0393	2-0852	◇					◇			◇	◇					◇		76		◇					◇			◇	
		MARIKANA T 68 NS \ 1158m																														
△		**Rondalia Buffelspoort** P.O. Box 122 (0284)	0142222 E	57	△							△		△	△		△	△		100			△					△			△	
		MARINA BEACH N 63 NS / 15m																														
☆	[caravan symbol]	**Belle Vista** P.O. Box 36, Southbroom 4277	0393	3755	☆					☆				☆					☆		100		☆						☆		☆	
■		**Sherwood Forest** P.O. Box 39 (4281)	0393	3792	■					■			■	■				■	■	120	20	10	■					■			■	
□	[carnet symbol]	**SYSU** SYSU-Vakansiebelange, P.O. Box 2347, Pretoria 0001 □ *Mars Rd.*	012 (0393)	79-6119 (3600)	□					□	□		□	□					□		30				□			□	□		□	
		MARYDALE C 61 A4 ← 983m																														
○		**Marydale Camping Site** Town Clerk (8910) □ *Snyman St.*	05482 E	7		○							○		○			○			15			○				○			○	
		MATATIELE N 62 B6 / 1475m																														
◇		**Haig Park** Town Clerk, P.O. Box 35 (4730) □ *Cnr. West/High Sts.*				◇							◇	◇					◇		10		◇					◇			◇	
		MASELSPOORT O See Bloemfontein																														
		MELKBOSSTRAND C 58 C3 / S.L.																														
★	[caravan symbol]	**Ou Skip** Manager, P.O. Box 13 (7437) □ *Otto Du Plessis Drive*	02224	2058			★			★				★			★	★		215		21	★					★			★	
		MELKRIVIER T 68 B6 \ 1166m																														
■		**Waterberg-Natuurpraal Holiday Resort** P.O. Melkrivier 0541	015352 E	2712	■						■	■		■		■		■	■		12			■					■	■		■
		MESSINA T 70 B5 ← 594m																														
●	[caravan symbol]	**Messina Municipal** P/Bag X611 (0900)	015532 E	103		●							●	●			●			200		200	●					●			●	
		MICA T 69 B3 / 496m																														
◆		**Hippo Pools Holiday Resort** P.O. Mica 1382	T	811	◆						◆				◆		◆	◆		◆	◆	◆			◆				◆		◆	
		MIDDELBURG C 62 C2 → 1248m																														
▲	[carnet symbol]	**Middelburg Municipal** P.O. Box 55 (5900) □ *Heuwel St.*	04832 E	17		▲						▲			▲				▲		30			▲					▲		▲	
		MIDDELBURG T 69 C2 / 1515m																														
★		**Kruger Dam Recreation Resort** Proprietor, P.O. Box 14 (1050) □ *Coetzee St.*	01321	3011/5331		★					★			★				★			100				★			★			★	
☆	[carnet symbol]	**Midland Estate** Midlands Brick and Engineering Works (Pty) Ltd., P.O. Box 111 (1050) □ *Witbank Main Rd.*	01321	2335	☆						☆			☆					☆		50		☆					☆			☆	

SEASONS: OPEN THROUGHOUT THE YEAR; OUT-OF-SEASON CLOSING DATE; RE-OPENING DATE
TERMS FOR BOOKINGS: BOOKINGS ACCP. PEAK SNS. – SEE NOTE 2; DEPOSIT REQUIRED – SEE NOTE 3; REFUNDED IF CANCELLED
CARAVAN PARK/CAMPING SITE TARIFFS (See heading): MAXIMUM IN-SEASON TARIFF; MAXIMUM OUT-OF-SEASON TARIFF
REDUCTIONS ALLOWED FOR: LONG PERIODS OF STAY; GROUPS – SEE NOTE 4; AA CARNET HOLDERS SEE NOTE 5; OTHERS (ON APPLICATION)
RESTAURANT FACILITIES: ON SITE; WITHIN 5 km OF SITE; MORE THAN 5 km FROM SITE
TEAROOM/CAFE: ON SITE; WITHIN 5 km OF SITE; MORE THAN 5 km FROM SITE
SHOPPING FACILITIES (Provisions): ON SITE; WITHIN 5 km OF SITE; MORE THAN 5 km FROM SITE
ADDITIONAL ACCOMMODATION AVAILABLE: BUNGALOWS; CABINS; COTTAGES (RONDAVELS); CHALETS
ADDITIONAL ACCOMMODATION TARIFF (See heading): MAXIMUM IN-SEASON TARIFF; MAXIMUM OUT-OF-SEASON TARIFF
CARAVANS TO RENT ON SITE – SEE PAGES 8–11

CAMP SITE FACILITIES (I – In-Season only; O – Out-of-Season only): DRINKING WATER: PIPED; OTHER. BATHS: HOT AND COLD; COLD ONLY. SHOWERS: HOT AND COLD; COLD ONLY. WATERBORNE SANITATION; WASHBASINS; DISHWASHING FACILITIES; LAUNDRY AND IRONING FACILITIES – SEE NOTE 6; WASHING MACHINES; SITE LIT; PLUGS FOR RAZORS (VOLTAGE); REFRIGERATORS; FIREWOOD CHARCOAL; OPEN FIRE FORBIDDEN; CAMP FIRE PERMITTED; BRAAI PLACES PROVIDED; KITCHEN COOKING FACILITIES; PETROL PUMP ON SITE; PETROL PUMP NEARBY; CAR REPAIR SHOP NEARBY; CAR SERVICING NEARBY; GAS SERVICE NEARBY; FIRST AID HOSPITAL DOCTOR NEARBY; POST OFFICE NEARBY; SITE GUARDED; PETS ALLOWED
NON-WHITE SERVANTS: SERVANTS PERMITTED – SEE NOTE 7; SERVANTS ACCOM. – SEE NOTE 7; SERVANTS FOR HIRE – SEE NOTE 7
TYPE OF VEHICLE PERMITTED: CAR AND TRAILER; TRUCK, HORSE AND SEMI-TRAILER; SELF-PROPELLED CARAVANS

SPORTING AND RECREATIONAL FACILITIES (S – On Site; N – Nearby (Up to 20 km away)): CHILDRENS' PLAYGROUND; TENNIS; CINEMA/DRIVE-IN/TV-ROOM – SEE NOTE 8; HORSE-RIDING; GAMES ROOM; TRAMPOLINE; BOWLS; HOT SPRINGS
GOLF: GOLF COURSE – SEE NOTE 9; NUMBER OF HOLES; MINIATURE; MASHIE; PUTT-PUTT
FISHING: FRESHWATER – SEE NOTE 10; SEA – SEE NOTE 11; GOGGLE; LICENCE REQUIRED
SWIMMING: SWIMMING POOL; SEA BATHING; CHILDRENS' POOL; ADULTS ONLY; SHARK NETS AT BEACH
BOATING: BOATS FOR HIRE; POWER; SAILING; CANOEING
PLACES OF INTEREST: HISTORIC; SCIENTIFIC; NATURAL
NOTES

33	34	35	36	37	38	39	40	41	42	43	44	45	46	47	48	49	50	51	52	53	54	55	56	57	58	59	60	61	62	63	64	65	66	67	68	69	70	71	72	73	74	75	76	77	78	79	80	81	82	83	84	85	86	87	88	89	90	91	92	93	94	95	96	97	98	99	100	101	102	103	104	105	106	107	108	109	110	111	112	113	114	115	116	117	118	119	120	121	122	123 NOTES
		□	□	□	C	C					□			□					□								□		□		□		□	□	□	□	□	□	□	□	□			□			□	□	□	□	□		□					□		□	S				S		N		N	18					N	N			□								□		□	
		○	○		C	C								○			○			○				C-D	C-D				○			○	○	○	○	○			220		○		○	○			○	○	○	○			○					○	○	○					S				N	18					N			S		S				N	N	N				
		◇	◇	◇	E	E	◇	◇					◇			◇	◇		◇								◇		◇		◇		◇	◇	◇			◇			◇		◇				◇	◇	◇	◇	◇	◇	◇	◇	◇	◇	◇	◇		◇			N																									◇	
		△	△		C	C													△			△		B	B		△		△		△		△	△								△	△	△			△				△				△	△		△	△	△																											△	△	△	Visitors are advised that, should the water supply at the camping site fail, their bookings may be cancelled at short notice
		☆			B	B	☆	☆				☆			☆			☆				☆		A	A		☆		☆				☆	☆		☆		☆	220	☆	☆		☆	☆			☆	☆	☆	☆	☆	☆	☆	☆	☆	☆		☆	☆	☆	N	N			N		S		N	9				N			☆										☆	☆	☆	
		□	□		C	C	□	□				□			□			□								□	□		□		□		□	□	□	□		□	220			□	□				□	□	□		□	□			□	□	□	□		□	S	N		N	N	N			N	18								S		N	□								□	
		●	●		X	X	●	●				●		●	●			●	●								●		●		●		●	●	●	●		●	220		●	●	●	●			●	●	●	●	●	●	●				●	●	●	●	S	S	N	N		S			N	18								S		S										
		○	○		D	D						○	○		○	○		○	○								○		○		○		○	○	○	○		○	220		○	○	○				○	○	○	○	○	○	○	○			○	○	○	○	S	N	N						N	18								S												
		◇	◇	◇	C	C	◇				◇		◇	◇					◇								◇		◇				◇	◇	◇	◇			220		◇		◇	◇			◇	◇	◇	◇		◇						◇	◇	◇	N	N	N				N	S	N	9	◇							S		S							◇		◇	
		△	△	△	C	C													△								△		△		△		△	△	△						△		△	△			△				△	△						△	△	△	S			N										N			△			N						N			△	
		☆	☆	☆	X	X					☆					☆			☆								☆		☆		☆		☆	☆	☆	☆		☆			☆	☆	☆	☆		☆	☆	☆	☆	☆	☆	☆	☆		☆	☆		☆	☆	☆			S		S									S			☆	S		S						S	☆	☆	☆	
		□			B	B	□					□	□		□	□		□	□								□		□		□		□	□		□		□			□		□	□			□	□	□			□		□	□			□	□	□	S	N							N	9								S		S	□						□		□	
		○			B	B				○						○			○								○		○		○		○	○	○						○	○		○			○	○	○			○	○					○		○															N	N			○										○	
		◆	◆	◆	C	B	◆	◆	R			◆						◆				◆	◆	E	B		◆	◆	◆		◆		◆	◆	◆	L			220		◆	◆					◆	◆	◆	◆	◆	◆		◆	◆		◆	◆		◆		N			N		S		N	9					N	N				S			S		S	S		◆	◆	
		▲	▲	▲	E	C	▲					▲			▲			▲					▲	K	H		▲		▲		▲		▲	▲	▲	▲		▲	110/220				▲	▲			▲	▲	▲	▲	▲	▲	▲				▲	▲	▲	▲	S	N	N	N			N		N	18			▲		S	S			▲				N	N	N	N	▲		▲	
		△	△		D	C					△	△		△			△			△		△	△	G	D	△	△		△		△		△	△	△	△	△	△	220	△	△		△	△			△	△	△	△	△	△	△					△	△	△	S	N	N	N	S	S	N		N	18	△		△		N	N		S	△	S	△		N				△	△	△	
		★	★	★	E	C	★					★		★				★									★		★		★		★	★	★	★		★	110/220				★	★			★	★	★	★	★	★	★				★	★	★	★	S	N	N	N			N		N	18			★		S	S		S	★	S			N	N	N	N	★		★	
		☆	☆	☆	E	C	☆					☆			☆			☆									☆		☆		☆		☆	☆	☆	☆		☆	110/220				☆	☆			☆	☆	☆	☆	☆	☆	☆				☆	☆	☆	☆	N	N	N	N			N		N	18			☆		S	S			☆				N	N	N	N	☆		☆	
		●	●	●	X	X													●			●		X	X		●				●		●	●							●		●			●									●			●		●															N								N							
		◆	◆		E	D		◆	R			◆			◆			◆									◆		◆		◆		◆	◆	◆	L					◆		◆	◆			◆	◆	◆	◆	◆	◆	◆				◆	◆		◆		N					N		N	9				N	N			N	◆				N	N			◆		◆	
		◇	◇	◇	D	D	◇	◇			◇	◇		◇	◇			◇	◇								◇		◇		◇		◇	◇	◇	◇							◇				◇	◇	◇	◇		◇	◇					◇	◇	◇									N	9								N		N										
		▲	▲		F	F						▲			▲			▲			▲			C	C		▲		▲		▲		▲	▲	▲						▲	▲	▲	▲			▲	▲	▲	▲	▲	▲	▲		▲			▲		▲	N	N							N	9					N			N	▲	N			N	N	N	N	▲		▲	
		△	△	△	H	F	△	△		△			△			△	△	△				△		F	F	△	△		△		△		△	△	△	△	△	△			△	△		△			△	△	△	△	△	△	△		△	△	△	△	△	△	S	N	S		S		N		N	9					N			S	△				N	N	N	N	△		△	
		☆	☆		H	F	☆		R	☆	☆			☆			☆		☆			☆	☆	X	X	☆	☆				☆		☆	☆	☆					☆	☆		☆	☆	☆		☆	☆	☆	☆	☆	☆	☆	☆	☆		☆	☆		☆		S	S	S	S	S	N		N	18			☆		S	S	☆	S	☆			☆								
		■	■	■	D	C		■				■			■			■				■	■	E	D	■	■		■		■		■	■	■	■		■	220	■	■			■			■			■	■	■	■	■	■	■		■		■	S	N	N	N	S	N	N		N	18				N	N		■	N	■	N		■		N	N	N		■	■	
		□	□	□	F	E				□	□			□			□					□		G	F		□		□		□		□	□	□	□		□			□	□	□	□	□		□	□	□	□	□	□	□					□		□	S	S	S	N	□	S	N		N						N	N			□	N		□							□	
		○	○	○	E	C						○			○			○			○			E-H	C-E		○		○		○		○	○	○	○	○	○	220		○			○			○	○	○		○	○	○		○	○		○	○	○	N	N	N		S		N		N	18			○	N	N	N			○				N		N	N	○			
					F	F							◇			◇			◇	◇				X	X		◇		◇		◇		◇	◇	◇	◇		◇			◇		◇	◇			◇	◇	◇	◇	◇	◇				◇	◇	◇		◇	S	N		N	S	N	N		N	18					N	N			◇			◇								
		△			C	C						△			△			△									△		△		△		△	△	△	△		△					△	△			△	△	△	△	△	△	△	△			△	△	△	△	N	N					N							N			△										△	△	△	
		☆	☆		F	E		☆		☆	☆			☆			☆					☆		X	X		☆		☆		☆		☆	☆	☆	☆		☆	☆	☆	☆		☆	☆			☆	☆	☆			☆	☆	☆	☆			☆	☆	☆	S	S	S	N	S	S	N	S	N	9				N				S		S							☆		☆	
		■	■		X	X		■			■			■			■					■		X	X		■		■		■		■	■	■	■		■			■			■		■	■	■	■	■		■	■					■	■		S	N	S					S	N	9			■	N			■	S		S									■	
					D	B					□			□			□			□		□		F	E		□		□	□	□	□	□	□	□	□		□			□		□	□						□	□							□	□	□	N	N	S	N	N	S	N	S	N	9				N			□	S		S							□	□	□	
		●	●		B	B	●					●	●		●	●		●	●	●				X	X		●		●		●		●	●				●			●		●				●	●	●	●	●	●		●				●		●	S	N	N				N	N	N	9		●		N			●	S		S							●			
					C	C						○			○			○	○								○		○		○		○	○	○	○		○	220		○		○	○	○		○	○	○	○	○	○	○	○	○			○	○	○		N	N				N	N	N	9				N			○			N									○	
		◆	◆		E	D				◆	◆			◆			◆					◆		H	D		◆		◆		◆		◆	◆	◆	◆		◆	◆		◆		◆	◆			◆	◆	◆	◆	◆	◆	◆		◆	◆				◆	S	S	S	N				S	N	9				N			◆	S		S							◆		◆	
		◇	◇		B	B	◇	◇			◇	◇	◇	◇	◇	◇	◇	◇	◇			◇		E	D		◇	◇	◇	◇	◇	◇	◇	◇	◇	◇		◇	◇	◇	◇		◇	◇			◇	◇	◇	◇	◇	◇	◇	◇			◇	◇	◇	◇	S	N	S	N	◇	N	N	S	N	9				S			◇	S		S							◇	◇	◇	
		△	△		B	B		△				△			△			△									△			△		△	△	△	△	△					△	△	△	△	△		△			△			△					△	△	△														S			△		△						N	N	△	△	△	
					X	X			R				☆	☆	☆	☆	☆	☆	☆				☆	I	H		☆		☆		☆		☆	☆		☆					☆			☆			☆	☆	☆		☆	☆		☆	☆			☆	☆	☆	S													S			☆	S		S				S	S	S	☆	☆	☆	

CARAVAN PARKS AND CAMPING SITES

Establishments marked thus [Caravan Club symbol] have the Caravan Club of South Africa recommendation – see page **17**
Establishments marked thus [AA Carnet symbol] recognise the AA Camping Carnet – see page **16** and also refer to column **42**

CARAVAN PARK / CAMP SITE TARIFF CODE – See columns 38–39 (Subject to alteration)

A = Up to R1	**C** = R2–R3	**E** = R4–R5	**G** = R6–R7	**I** = R8–R9	**K** = R10–R16
B = R1–R2	**D** = R3–R4	**F** = R5–R6	**H** = R7–R8	**J** = R9–R10	**O** = FREE
					X = On Application

Charges are based on a family of 2 adults and 2 children under 12 years

ADDITIONAL ACCOMMODATION TARIFF CODE – See columns 57–59 (Subject to alteration)

eg. Bungalows, Cabins, Cottages, Chalets, etc.

A = R1–R3	**C** = R5–R7	**E** = R9–R11	**G** = R13–R15	**I** = R17–R19	**K** = R21–R30
B = R3–R5	**D** = R7–R9	**F** = R11–R13	**H** = R15–R17	**J** = R19–R21	**X** = On Application

NB: Where the tariff is given in *italics* it is per person, otherwise per unit

NOTE 1 – **Columns 18, 19, 20.** – Where a symbol appears instead of a number it means stands are available but not demarcated or number of stands has not been provided
NOTE 2 – **Column 35** – A = Bookings accepted for additional accommodation only i.e. cottages, bungalows, etc.
NOTE 3 – **Column 37** – Deposit refunded under certain conditions eg. less 10% ; if site is re-let ; if cancelled well in advance (up to 2 months) or on a doctor's certificate
NOTE 4 – **Column 41** – Reductions allowed on application for youth, church, school or sport groups or caravan rallies
NOTE 5 – **Column 42** – R = Reduction in tariff of between 5–10% to Carnet holders; O = Reduction Out-of-Season only
NOTE 6 – **Column 69** – L = Laundry facilities only
NOTE 7 – **Columns 88, 89, 90.** – I = In-Season only ; O = Out-of-Season only
NOTE 8 – **Column 96** – Applicable In-Season only at some establishments
NOTE 9 – **Column 102** – See section on golf in Outdoor Holiday Guide
NOTE 10 – **Column 107** – See section on freshwater angling in Outdoor Holiday Guide
NOTE 11 – **Column 108** – See section on coastal angling in Outdoor Holiday Guide

ABBREVIATIONS
C = CAPE PROVINCE
N = NATAL
O = ORANGE FREE STATE
T = TRANSVAAL
B = BOPHUTHATSWANA
X = TRANSKEI

TELEPHONE CODE: T = DIAL 0020, BOOK TRUNK CALL; E = DIAL CODE, ASK EXCHANGE FOR NO.

OWNED OR SUPERVISED BY: columns 3–7 · SITE DESCRIPTION – LOCALITY: 8–11; NATURE OF GROUND: 12–14; SHADE: 15–17 · NO. OF STANDS: 18–20 · ACCESSIBILITY – APPROXIMATE DISTANCE FROM MAIN ROAD TO SITE: 21–25; SURFACE OF APPROACH ROAD: 26–28; CONDITION OF APPROACH ROAD: 29–31

			1 Telephone code	2 Telephone number	3 Privately owned	4 Municipality	5 Divisional council	6 Provincial administration	7 Parks board	8 Beach in immediate vicinity	9 Beside river, lake or dam	10 In or near mountain area	11 Within built-up area	12 Grass	13 Gravel	14 Sand	15 Unshaded	16 Partly shaded	17 Extensively shaded	18 Caravans only – see note 1	19 Caravans and/or tents – see note 1	20 Tents only – see note 1	21 On main rd	22 Within 1 km	23 Within 5 km	24 Within 10 km	25 Within 15 km	26 Tar	27 Gravel	28 Sand	29 Good	30 Fair / Poor
		NELSPRUIT T 69 C4 ← 620m																														
□	[CC] [AA]	**Allamanda Holiday Resort** P.O. Alkmaar 1206 □ *16 km from Nelspruit*	0131232 E	2831	□							□		□				□			60		□							□	□	
●		**Casarina** P.O. Box 398 (1200) □ *10 km from Nelspruit*	01311	4012	●							●		●				●		20	30	10		●					●		●	
○		**Eureka** P.O. Box 657 (1200) □ *10 km from Nelspruit*	01311	5080	○						○	○		○				○	○	15		10		○					○		○	
◆		**Kruine Rest Camp** P.O. Box 244 (1200) □ *17 km from Nelspruit*	01311	2936	◆							◆		◆				◆	◆	15	15	10		◆					◆		◆	
◇		**Nelspruit Municipal** Town Clerk, P.O. Box 45 (1200) □ *3 km from Nelspruit*	01311	2221		◇					◇			◇				◇			20			◇				◇			◇	
▲	[AA]	**Shonalanga** P.O. Box 18 (1200) □ *2 km from Nelspruit*	01311	3223	▲							▲		▲					▲	40	40	20	▲					▲			▲	
		NEWCASTLE N 67 B2 ↘ 1189m																														
★		**Chelmsford Public Resort** P.O. Box 3, Ballengeich 2942 □ *40 km from Newcastle*	0343	7715					★		★	★		★				★			20						★	★			★	
☆		**Newcastle Municipal** Bookings not accepted □ *Hardwick St.*	0343	2-7211		☆							☆	☆	☆			☆			20			☆					☆			☆
		NOUPOORT C 62 C2 ↗ 1489m																														
□		**Drikkie du Toit** P.O. Box 4 (5950) □ *Hospital St.*	05742 E	56		□							□	□	□			□		8	3	4		□				□	□		□	
		NYLSTROOM T 68 B6 ↙ 1187m																														
○	[CC]	**J. G. Strijdom** P/Bag 1008 (0510) □ *Voortrekker Rd.*	01531	3481		○					○		○	○					○	35		10	○					○			○	
◆		**Stokkiesdraai Holiday Resort** P.O. Box 88 (0510) □ *4 km from Nylstroom*	01531	2091/2883	◆							◆		◆				◆	◆		100		◆					◆			◆	
		OLIFANTSHOEK C 65 B4 ↘ 1260m																														
▲	[AA]	**Olifantshoek Caravan Park and Camping Site** Town Clerk, P.O. Box 81 (8450)	05952 E	238		▲					▲	▲		▲		▲			▲		20		▲						▲		▲	
		ONRUS C 58 D4 ← S.L.																														
★		**Onrus Municipal** Manager, De Villiers St. (7201)	02831	6210		★				★		★	★	★					★		230			★				★			★	
☆	[AA]	**Paradise Park Holiday Camp** P.O. Box 74, Parow 7500 □ *Hermanus Main Rd.*	02831	6007	☆					☆		☆		☆				☆		35		20	☆					☆			☆	
■		**Sea View** P.O. Box 1 (7201) □ *Old Main Rd.*	02831	6100	■					■	■		■	■					■		28			■				■			■	
□	[AA]	**Sherwood Park** P.O. Box 50 (7201) □ *Main Rd.*	02831	6230	□					□				□					□	58		14	□							□	□	
		ORANJEVILLE O 66 A6 ↙ 1494m																														
○		**Jim Fouché Holiday Resort** Resort Manager, P.O. Fouché Resort, via Frankfort 9830 □ *Vaal Dam*	T	Jim Fouché 1				○			○			○				○			1 500		○					○			○	
		ORKNEY T 66 A4 ↘ 1295m																														
◇	[CC]	**Orkney-Vaal Holiday Resort** Manager, P.O. Box 34 (2620) □ *5 km from Orkney*	018	3-3228		◇					◇			◇	◇			◇		150		50			◇			◇			◇	
		OUDTSHOORN C 59 B2 ← 306m																														
△		**N. A. Smit Municipal Tourist Camp** P.O. Box 255 (6620) □ *Park Rd. North, West Bank*	04431	2221 ext. 254		△						△	△	△				△			150			△				△			△	
★		**Schoemanspoort** Divisional Council, P.O. Box 127 (6620) □ *16 km from Oudtshoorn*	04431	2241			★				★			★					★	20		20	★						★		★	
		OYSTER BAY C 59 C4 ↗ S.L.																														
■		**Oyster Bay** P.O. Box 114, Humansdorp 6300	T	2	■								■	■					■	16		■					■		■			■
		PAARL C 58 C3 ↘ 115m																														
●		**Camper's Paradise** P.O. Box 552, Suider-Paarl 7624 □ *3 km from Paarl on the Franschhoek/Simondium Rd.*	0251	2-4685	●						●	●		●		●		●	●	44	291	291		●					●		●	●
○		**Eerste Tol** No Bookings accepted — Site actually meant for day visitors, but there is no objection to Caravans/Tents staying over □ *Bainskloof*					○				○	○		○				○					○									○
		PARADISE BEACH C 59 C4 ↗ S.L.																														
◇		**Paradise Beach** P.O. Box 172, Humansdorp 6300 □ *Immergroen Ave.*	T	8/21	◇					◇	◇	◇	◇	◇				◇		70		10				◇				◇	◇	
		PARK RYNIE N 63 NS ● S.L.																														
△	[CC]	**Caravan Cove** P.O. Box 42 (4182)	0323	2-1215	△					△	△		△	△			△	△	△		160			△					△		△	
★	[AA]	**Rocky Bay** P.O. Box 37 (4182)	0323	2-1701	★					★				★				★		80		10		★						★	★	
		PARKS UNDER CONTROL OF NATAL PARKS BOARD:																														
		ALBERT FALLS PUBLIC RESORT See Albert Falls																														
		CHELMSFORD PUBLIC RESORT See Newcastle																														
		GIANT'S CASTLE GAME RESERVE See Estcourt																														
		HIMEVILLE NATURE RESERVE See Himeville																														
		KOSI BAY NATURE RESERVE See Kosi Bay																														
		MKUZI NATURE RESERVE See Mkuze																														
		ROYAL NATAL NATIONAL PARK See Mont-aux-Sources																														
		SODWANA BAY NATIONAL PARK See Sodwana Bay																														
		SPIOENKOP PUBLIC RESORT See Winterton																														
		ST. LUCIA GAME RESERVE See Hluhluwe (False Bay Park), Mtubatuba (Fanies Island), St. Lucia Estuary																														
		UMLALAZI NATURE RESERVE See Mtunzini																														
		WAGENDRIFT PUBLIC RESORT See Estcourt																														
		PARKS UNDER CONTROL OF NATIONAL PARKS BOARD:																														
		ADDO ELEPHANT NATIONAL PARK C See Addo																														
		AUGRABIES FALLS NATIONAL PARK C See Augrabies																														
		BONTEBOK NATIONAL PARK C See Swellendam																														
		GOLDEN GATE HIGHLANDS NATIONAL PARK O See Clarens																														
		KALAHARI GEMSBOK NATIONAL PARK C 64 B2 ↙ 960m																														
★		**Mata Mata Rest Camp** National Parks Board, P.O. Box 787, Pretoria 0001	012	44-1194					★							★	★	★			10			★						★		★
☆		**Nossob Camp**	012	44-1194					☆							☆	☆				10			☆						☆		☆

SEASONS · TERMS FOR BOOKINGS · CARAVAN PARK/CAMPING SITE TARIFFS (See heading) · REDUCTIONS ALLOWED FOR · RESTAURANT FACILITIES · TEAROOM/CAFE · SHOPPING FACILITIES (Provisions) · ADDITIONAL ACCOMMODATION AVAILABLE · ADDITIONAL ACCOMMODATION TARIFF (See heading) · DRINKING WATER · BATHS · SHOWERS

CAMP SITE FACILITIES — I = In-Season only; O = Out-of-Season only · NON-WHITE SERVANTS · TYPE OF VEHICLE PERMITTED

SPORTING AND RECREATIONAL FACILITIES — S On Site; N Nearby (Up to 20 km away) · GOLF · FISHING · SWIMMING · BOATING · PLACES OF INTEREST · NOTES

32 OPEN THROUGHOUT THE YEAR	33 OUT-OF-SEASON CLOSING DATE	34 RE-OPENING DATE	35 BOOKINGS ACCP. PEAK SNS – SEE NOTE 2	36 DEPOSIT REQUIRED	37 REFUNDED IF CANCELLED – SEE NOTE 3	38 MAXIMUM IN-SEASON TARIFF	39 MAXIMUM OUT-OF-SEASON TARIFF	40 LONG PERIODS OF STAY	41 GROUPS – SEE NOTE 4	42 AA CARNET HOLDERS SEE NOTE 5	43 OTHERS (ON APPLICATION)	44 ON SITE	45 WITHIN 5 km OF SITE	46 MORE THAN 5 km FROM SITE	47 ON SITE	48 WITHIN 5 km OF SITE	49 MORE THAN 5 km FROM SITE	50 ON SITE	51 WITHIN 5 km OF SITE	52 MORE THAN 5 km FROM SITE	53 BUNGALOWS	54 CABINS	55 COTTAGES (RONDAVELS)	56 CHALETS	57 MAXIMUM IN-SEASON TARIFF	58 MAXIMUM OUT-OF-SEASON TARIFF	59 CARAVANS TO RENT ON SITE – SEE PAGES 8 – 11	60 PIPED	61 OTHER	62 HOT AND COLD	63 COLD ONLY	64 HOT AND COLD	65 COLD ONLY	66 WATERBORNE SANITATION	67 WASHBASINS	68 DISHWASHING FACILITIES	69 LAUNDRY AND IRONING FACILITIES – SEE NOTE 6	70 WASHING MACHINES	71 SITE LIT	72 PLUGS FOR RAZORS (VOLTAGE)	73 REFRIGERATORS	74 FIREWOOD CHARCOAL	75 OPEN FIRE FORBIDDEN	76 CAMP FIRE PERMITTED	77 BRAAI PLACES PROVIDED	78 KITCHEN/COOKING FACILITIES	79 PETROL PUMP ON SITE	80 PETROL PUMP NEARBY	81 CAR REPAIR SHOP NEARBY	82 CAR SERVICING NEARBY	83 GAS SERVICE NEARBY	84 FIRST AID/HOSPITAL/DOCTOR NEARBY	85 POST OFFICE NEARBY	86 SITE GUARDED	87 PETS ALLOWED	88 SERVANTS PERMITTED – SEE NOTE 7	89 SERVANTS ACCOM. – SEE NOTE 7	90 SERVANTS FOR HIRE – SEE NOTE 7	91 CAR AND TRAILER	92 TRUCK HORSE AND SEMI-TRAILER	93 SELF-PROPELLED CARAVANS	94 CHILDRENS' PLAYGROUND	95 TENNIS	96 CINEMA/DRIVE-IN/TV-ROOM – SEE NOTE 8	97 HORSE-RIDING	98 GAMES ROOM	99 TRAMPOLINE	100 BOWLS	101 HOT SPRINGS	102 GOLF COURSE – SEE NOTE 9	103 NUMBER OF HOLES	104 MINIATURE	105 MASHIE	106 PUTT-PUTT	107 FRESHWATER – SEE NOTE 10	108 SEA – SEE NOTE 11	109 GOGGLE	110 LICENCE REQUIRED	111 SWIMMING POOL	112 SEA BATHING	113 CHILDRENS' POOL	114 ADULTS ONLY	115 SHARK NETS AT BEACH	116 BOATS FOR HIRE	117 POWER	118 SAILING	119 CANOEING	120 HISTORIC	121 SCIENTIFIC	122 NATURAL	123 NOTES
			□	□		D	C		□	R	□	□			□			□	□		□		□	□	D-G	D-F		□		□		□		□	□	□	□		□		□	□		□	□	□	□		□	□	□		□	□	□	□	□	□	□	□	□	S	S	N	N	S		N		N	18			□	S			□	S		S			S	S			□	□	□	
			●	●		C	C	●	●		●			●		●	●		●				●	●	F	F		●		●		●		●	●	●	●		●			●	●		●	●		●	●	●	●	●	●	●		●	●		●		●	S	S	N	N	S		N		N	18				N			●	S		S							●	●	●	
			○	○	○	C	C	○	○			○			○			○			○	○	○	○	X	X		○		○		○		○	○	○	○		○			○		○	○			○	○	○				○					○		○			N				N		N	18				N				S		S									○	
			◆	◆	◆	D	D	◆	◆				◆	◆		◆	◆		◆	◆	◆	◆	◆	◆	*A*	*A*		◆		◆		◆		◆	◆	◆	◆							◆	◆	◆		◆	◆	◆	◆		◆	◆	◆	◆	◆		◆	◆	◆	S	N	N	N			N		N	18				N			◆	N		N									◆	
			◇	◇		C	C						◇			◇			◇									◇		◇		◇		◇	◇	◇	◇		◇	220		◇	◇	◇	◇			◇	◇	◇	◇	◇	◇	◇		◇			◇	◇	◇	S		N				N		N	18				S													◇	◇	◇	
			▲	▲	▲	C	C			R		▲	▲	▲		▲	▲	▲	▲	▲	▲			▲	F	F		▲	▲	▲		▲		▲	▲	▲	▲		▲			▲		▲	▲			▲	▲	▲	▲		▲	▲				▲	▲	▲	▲	S	N	N	N		N	N		N	18	▲		▲	N			▲	S		S							▲	▲	▲	
			★	★		D	D																					★				★		★	★									★	★							★				★			★	★	★														S			★							S	S	S			★	
						B	B							☆		☆	☆		☆	☆								☆		☆		☆		☆	☆		☆		☆	15				☆				☆	☆	☆	☆		☆	☆				☆	☆		☆	N	N	N	N			N		N	9				N			☆	N		N				N	N	N	☆	☆	☆	
			□	□		A	A							□			□			□																																			□		□	□	□	□	N	N	N															N		N							□			
			○			C	C	○				○			○				○									○		○		○		○	○	○	○			220		○		○	○			○	○	○	○	○	○	○	○	○			○	○	○	S	N	N				N		N	9				S			○	S		S			S			S	○		○	
			◆	◆	◆	C	C	◆	◆			◆	◆		◆	◆			◆					◆	F-K	D-J		◆		◆		◆		◆	◆	◆	◆	◆	◆	220	◆	◆		◆	◆			◆	◆	◆	◆	◆	◆		◆	◆	◆	◆	◆	◆	◆	S	S	N	N	S	N	N	N	N	9				N			◆	S		S							◆		◆	
			▲			C	C					▲								▲								▲		▲		▲		▲	▲	▲	▲		▲	▲		▲	▲		▲			▲	▲	▲	▲		▲	▲	▲	▲			▲	▲	▲	S	N							N	9																				
						D	D							★			★		★									★				★		★	★	★	★					★		★	★			★	★	★	★		★	★	★	★			★		★	S	N	N	N		N	N		N	9				S	S	S		N	★	N					N	N	★		★	
			☆	☆	☆	C	C	☆	☆	R	☆			☆	☆		☆		☆	☆			☆		F	E			☆			☆		☆	☆	☆	☆		☆			☆		☆	☆			☆	☆	☆	☆		☆	☆	☆				☆		☆	S	N	N		S		N		N	9					N	N		S	☆	S				N	N	N	☆		☆	
			■	■	■	E	D	■	■					■		■			■	■	■				D-G	C-F		■		■		■		■	■	■	■					■	■		■			■	■	■	■		■				■		■	■	■		N	N				N		N	9					N														■	
			□	□	□	D	C	□	□	R				□	□	□			□				□		F	D	□	□		□		□		□	□	□	□			220		□	□	□	□			□	□	□	□	□	□		0				□	□	□	S	N	N	N	S		N		N	9				N	N	N			□					N	N	N	□		□	
			○	○	○	C	C					○						○					○		G-K	G-K		○		○		○		○	○	○	○		○	○		○		○			○			○	○	○	○	○				○	○	○	○	S	S	S	S		S			S		○		○	S			○	S		S			S			S				
			A	A	A	C	C	◇	◇			◇			◇	◇		◇		◇	◇				D-H	D-H		◇		◇		◇		◇	◇		◇	◇	◇			◇		◇	◇	◇		◇	◇	◇	◇	◇	◇			◇	◇		◇	◇	◇	S	S	S	N	S	S	N							S			◇	S		S			S	S		S		◇	◇	
			△	△	△	C	C						△			△			△		△				A	A		△		△		△		△	△	△	△	△	△	△		△		△	△			△	△	△		△	△	△		△			△	△	△	S	N	N			N	N	N	N	18								S									△	△	△	
			★	★	★	B	B													★			★		C-E	B-C		★	★	★	★	★		★	★	★	★		★			★		★	★			★	★	★				★	★	★			★	★	★			N				N		N	18								S									★	★	★	
			■	■		E	D	■					■			■			■									■		■		■		■	■	■	■					■		■	■			■			■		■		■	■		■	■		■	N	N	N	N	N	S	S							N	N	N		N	■	N							■		■	
			●	●	●	C	C		●		●	●			●			●	●	●	●				E-H	E-H		●		●		●		●	●	●	●			220		●		●	●			●	●	●	●	●	●						●	●	●	S		S	S	S				N	18		●						S		S						S	●	●	●	
						O	O									○												○																○	○											○	○			○	○	○																															○	
	Jul.	Sept.	◇	◇	◇	E	D	◇	◇				◇		◇			◇										◇		◇		◇		◇	◇	◇	◇					◇	◇	◇	◇			◇	◇	◇	◇	◇	◇		◇			◇	◇		◇	S	N	N			S	N		N	9				N	N	N		N	◇	N							◇		◇	
			△	△	△	H	D						△	△		△	△	△	△	△				△	D-E	D-E		△		△		△		△	△	△	△		△	110/220		△		△	△			△	△	△	△	△	△	△	△			△	△		△	S	N	N		S	N	N		N	18					N	N	△	S	△	S		△					△	△	△	
			★	★	★	G	F	★	★	R			★		★	★		★	★								★	★		★		★		★	★	★	★		★	220	★	★	★		★			★	★	★	★	★	★					★	★	★	★		N	S		S		N		N	18					N	N			★	N		★	N							
			★	★	★	D	D											★			★				C-H	C-H		★		★		★		★	★							★	★	★	★		★				★	★		★					★		★																														★	
			☆	☆	☆	D	D											☆			☆				C-H	C-H		☆				☆		☆	☆		☆			☆		☆	☆	☆	☆		☆				☆	☆		☆					☆		☆																														☆	

CARAVAN PARKS AND CAMPING SITES

Establishments marked thus CC have the Caravan Club of South Africa recommendation – see page 17
Establishments marked thus AA recognise the AA Camping Carnet – see page 16 and also refer to column 42

CARAVAN PARK / CAMP SITE TARIFF CODE – See columns 38–39 (Subject to alteration)

A = Up to R1 | C = R2–R3 | E = R4–R5 | G = R6–R7 | I = R8–R9 | K = R10–R16
B = R1–R2 | D = R3–R4 | F = R5–R6 | H = R7–R8 | J = R9–R10 | 0 = FREE
Charges are based on a family of 2 adults and 2 children under 12 years | X = On Application

ADDITIONAL ACCOMMODATION TARIFF CODE – See columns 57–59 (Subject to alteration)

eg. Bungalows, Cabins, Cottages, Chalets, etc.
A = R1–R3 | C = R5–R7 | E = R9–R11 | G = R13–R15 | I = R17–R19 | K = R21–R30
B = R3–R5 | D = R7–R9 | F = R11–R13 | H = R15–R17 | J = R19–R21 | X = On Application
NB: Where the tariff is given in *italics* it is per person, otherwise per unit

NOTE 1 — Columns 18, 19, 20. — Where a symbol appears instead of a number it means stands are available but not demarcated or number of stands has not been provided
NOTE 2 — Column 35 — A = Bookings accepted for additional accommodation only i.e. cottages, bungalows, etc.
NOTE 3 — Column 37 — Deposit refunded under certain conditions eg. less 10%, if site is re-let, if cancelled well in advance (up to 2 months) or on a doctor's certificate
NOTE 4 — Column 41 — Reductions allowed on application for youth, church, school or sport groups or caravan rallies
NOTE 5 — Column 42 — R = Reduction in tariff of between 5–10% to Carnet holders. 0 = Reduction Out-of-Season only
NOTE 6 — Column 69 — L = Laundry facilities only
NOTE 7 — Columns 88, 89, 90. — I = In-Season only; 0 = Out-of-Season only
NOTE 8 — Column 96 — Applicable In-Season only at some establishments
NOTE 9 — Column 102 — See section on golf in Outdoor Holiday Guide
NOTE 10 — Column 107 — See section on freshwater angling in Outdoor Holiday Guide
NOTE 11 — Column 108 — See section on coastal angling in Outdoor Holiday Guide

ABBREVIATIONS
C = CAPE PROVINCE
N = NATAL
O = ORANGE FREE STATE
T = TRANSVAAL
B = BOPHUTHATSWANA
X = TRANSKEI

TELEPHONE CODE: T – DIAL 0020, BOOK TRUNK CALL; E – DIAL CODE, ASK EXCHANGE FOR NO.

			Telephone code	Telephone number	Owned or supervised by					Site description: Locality				Nature of ground			Shade			No. of stands			Accessibility									
			1	2	3	4	5	6	7	8	9	10	11	12	13	14	15	16	17	18	19	20	21	22	23	24	25	26	27	28	29	30
		KALAHARI GEMSBOK NATIONAL PARK (Continued)																														
■		**Tweerivieren**	012	44-1194					■							■	■	■			10			■						■		■
		KRUGER NATIONAL PARK T 71 B5 ↗ 193m																														
●		**Balule** National Parks Board, P.O. Box 787, Pretoria 0001	012	44-1194					●					●				●		10			●						●		●	
○		**Crocodile Bridge**	012	44-1194					○							○		○			15		○					○			○	
◆		**Letaba**	012	44-1194					◆					◆	◆			◆			30		◆					◆			◆	
◇		**Lower Sabie**	012	44-1194					◇					◇				◇			15		◇					◇			◇	
▲		**Malelane**	012	44-1194					▲							▲		▲			15		▲					▲			▲	
△		**Maroela**	012	44-1194					△									△			30				△				△			△
★		**Olifants**	012	44-1194					★							★		★			15		★					★			★	
☆		**Pretoriuskop**	012	44-1194					☆									☆			30		☆					☆			☆	
■		**Punda Milia**	012	44-1194					■								■				15		■					■			■	
□		**Satara**	012	44-1194					□							□		□			30		□					□			□	
●		**Shingwidzi**	012	44-1194					●							●		●			30		●					●			●	
○		**Skukuza**	012	44-1194					○							○		○			50		○					○			○	
		MOUNTAIN ZEBRA NATIONAL PARK C See Cradock																														
		TSITSIKAMA FOREST AND COASTAL NATIONAL PARKS C See Stormsrivier																														
		PAROW C 58 NS ↗ 150m																														
△	CC	**Parow Municipal** Town Clerk, P.O. Box 11 (7500) □ *Off Hendrik Verwoerd Drive, Plattekloof*	021	92-1913		△								△				△		38				△				△			△	
		PARYS O 66 A6 ↓ 1416m																														
☆	AA	**Feesgrond** Bookings not accepted Enquiries: Town Clerk, P.O. Box 359 (9585) □ *Sasolburg Rd.*	01601	2711		☆					☆			☆					☆		400			☆				☆			☆	
■	CC AA	**Mimosa Garden** Town Clerk, P.O. Box 359 (9585) □ *Cnr. Van Koller/Boom Sts.*	01601	2711		■					■		■	■					■	180				■				■			■	
□		**Smilin' Thru Chalets** P.O. Box 388 (9585) □ *10 km from Parys on the Fochville Rd.*	01601	3921	□						□			□				□	□		120			□					□		□	
●		**Wag-'n-Bietjie** P.O. Box 426 (9585)	01601	2737	●						●		●	●					●	25	30		●	●				●			●	
○		**Westvaal** P.O. Box 317 (9585) □ *30 km from Parys on the Vaal River*	01601	3937	○						○			○					○	60					○				○			○
		PATENSIE C 59 B4 ↘ 213m																														
◇		**G. F. Rautenbach Park** Municipality (6335) □ *Fred Ferreira Rd.*	T	83		◇					◇	◇	◇	◇				◇			10		◇									
		PEARLY BEACH C 58 D4 ↓ 30m																														
△		**Pearly Beach Holiday Resort** P.O. Box 122, Gansbaai 7220	02842	7213 or 7230	△					△				△				△	△		300			△					△		△	
		PEDDIE C 60 C2 ↘ 427m																														
☆		**Mpekweni Holiday Resort** P.O. Box 108, Port Alfred 6170 □ *Mpekweni River Mouth*	04382 E	1931	☆					☆	☆			☆			☆				24			☆				☆			☆	
		PENNINGTON N 63 NS ● S.L.																														
□	AA	**Pennington** P.O. Box 19 (4184) □ *Impathla Rd.*	0323	5007	□					□			□	□	□			□	□		50				□			□		□	□	
●		**Umdoni** P.O. Box 15 (4184) □ *Main Rd.*	0323	5261	●					●			●	●					●		56		●						●			●
		PETIT T 68 D6 ↑ 1646m																														
◆	CC	**Cairngorm Tea Gardens** P.O. Petit 1512	775 E	52	◆									◆					◆		300		◆					◆			◆	
		PETRUSVILLE C 62 B2 ↑ 1349m																														
▲		**Petrusville Municipal** Town Clerk, P.O. Box 43 (8770) □ *Visagie St.*	057232 E	31		▲							▲		▲		▲	▲		10	10		▲					▲			▲	
		PHALABORWA T 69 A4 ↙ 506m																														
★		**Kudu Rest Camp** P.O. Box 884 (1390) □ *Phalaborwa Main Rd.*	01524	4043	★										★	★		★			3		★							★	★	
☆	AA	**Lion Inn** P.O. Box 242 (1390) □ *Hendrik van Eck Drive*	01524	3697	☆								☆	☆	☆	☆		☆			70		☆						☆		☆	
		PHILIPSTOWN C 62 B2 ● 1364m																														
□		**Philipstown Municipal** P.O. Box 36 (8795) □ *Venter St.*	057222 E	94		□							□	□					□		25		□					□			□	
		PIETERMARITZBURG N 63 A3 ↙ 676m																														
○		**Pietermaritzburg** Director of Parks, P.O. Box 31 (3200) □ *Cleland Rd., Hayfields*	0331	2-2970		○							○	○					○		120				○			○			○	
		PIETERSBURG T 69 A2 ↓ 1160m																														
◇		**Rendezvous Recreation Resort** P.O. Box 874 (0700) □ *23 km from Pietersburg*	01521	2737	◇						◇	◇		◇		◇		◇			◇			◇				◇			◇	
▲	CC	**Union Park** P.O. Box 111 (0700)	01521	6468/2011 x145		▲					▲			▲	▲			▲		40		20			▲			▲			▲	
		PIET RETIEF T 67 B3 ↗ 1271m																														
★	AA	**Piet Retief Municipal** P.O. Box 23 (2380) □ *Kerk St.*	013432 E	23/218		★					★		★	★				★		50	80		★						★		★	
		PILGRIM'S REST T 69 B3 ↘ 1311m																														
■		**Ponies** P.O. Box 47 (1290)	T	41	■						■	■		■				■		50		65		■				■			■	
		PLETTENBERG BAY C 59 NS → 150m																														
●		**Archerwood Estate** P.O. Box 155 (6600) □ *Marine Way*	04472 E	184	●					●				●					●		20		●									●
○	CC	**Piesang River Resort** P.O. Box 185 (6600) □ *Beacon Isle Drive*	04472 E	244/390	○					○	○		○	○					○	100	80	20			○			○			○	
◆		**Plettenberg Bay** P.O. Box 73 (6600) □ *National Rd.*	04472 E	199/2604	◆					◆	◆		◆	◆		◆			◆		280			◆					◆		◆	
◇		**Robberg Holiday Resort** P.O. Box 81 (6600) □ *Robberg Rd.*	04472 E	766	◇					◇		◇		◇				◇		90				◇				◇			◇	
		PONGOLA N 67 B4 ↑ 305m																														
△		**Pongola Municipal** P.O. Box 191 (3170) □ *40 Naude St.*	03842 E	23		△							△	△				△		40		40		△				△			△	
		PORT ALFRED C 60 C1 ↘ S.L.																														
☆		**Lagoon** P.O. Box 78 (6170) □ *Lagoon Rd., East Beach*	04642 E	590	☆					☆	☆		☆	☆				☆			90		☆					☆			☆	

SEASONS — OPEN THROUGHOUT THE YEAR / OUT-OF-SEASON CLOSING DATE / RE-OPENING DATE

TERMS FOR BOOKINGS — BOOKINGS ACCP./PEAK SNS. – SEE NOTE 2 / DEPOSIT REQUIRED / REFUNDED IF CANCELLED – SEE NOTE 3

CARAVAN PARK/CAMPING SITE TARIFFS (See heading) — MAXIMUM IN-SEASON TARIFF / MAXIMUM OUT-OF-SEASON TARIFF

REDUCTIONS ALLOWED FOR — LONG PERIODS OF STAY / GROUPS – SEE NOTE 4 / AA CARNET HOLDERS – SEE NOTE 5 / OTHERS (ON APPLICATION)

RESTAURANT FACILITIES — ON SITE / WITHIN 5 km OF SITE / MORE THAN 5 km FROM SITE

TEAROOM/CAFE — ON SITE / WITHIN 5 km OF SITE / MORE THAN 5 km FROM SITE

SHOPPING FACILITIES (Provisions) — ON SITE / WITHIN 5 km OF SITE / MORE THAN 5 km FROM SITE

ADDITIONAL ACCOMMODATION AVAILABLE — BUNGALOWS / CABINS / COTTAGES (RONDAVELS) / CHALETS

ADDITIONAL ACCOMMODATION TARIFF (See heading) — MAXIMUM IN-SEASON TARIFF / MAXIMUM OUT-OF-SEASON TARIFF

CARAVANS TO RENT ON SITE – SEE PAGES 8 – 11

CAMP SITE FACILITIES (I = In-Season only; O = Out-of-Season only) — DRINKING WATER: PIPED / OTHER; BATHS: HOT AND COLD / COLD ONLY; SHOWERS: HOT AND COLD / COLD ONLY; WATERBORNE SANITATION / WASHBASINS / DISHWASHING FACILITIES / LAUNDRY AND IRONING FACILITIES – SEE NOTE 6 / WASHING MACHINES / SITE LIT / PLUGS FOR RAZORS (VOLTAGE) / REFRIGERATORS / FIREWOOD/CHARCOAL / OPEN FIRE FORBIDDEN / CAMP FIRE PERMITTED / BRAAI PLACES PROVIDED / KITCHEN/COOKING FACILITIES / PETROL PUMP ON SITE / PETROL PUMP NEARBY / CAR REPAIR SHOP NEARBY / CAR SERVICING NEARBY / GAS SERVICE NEARBY / FIRST AID/HOSPITAL/DOCTOR NEARBY / POST OFFICE NEARBY / SITE GUARDED / PETS ALLOWED

NON-WHITE SERVANTS — SERVANTS PERMITTED – SEE NOTE 7 / SERVANTS ACCOM. – SEE NOTE 7 / SERVANTS FOR HIRE – SEE NOTE 7

TYPE OF VEHICLE PERMITTED — CAR AND TRAILER / TRUCK, HORSE AND SEMI-TRAILER / SELF-PROPELLED CARAVANS

SPORTING AND RECREATIONAL FACILITIES (S = On Site; N = Nearby (Up to 20 km away)) — CHILDRENS' PLAYGROUND / TENNIS / CINEMA/DRIVE-IN/TV-ROOM – SEE NOTE 8 / HORSE-RIDING / GAMES ROOM / TRAMPOLINE / BOWLS / HOT SPRINGS; GOLF: GOLF COURSE – SEE NOTE 9 / NUMBER OF HOLES / MINIATURE / MASHIE / PUTT-PUTT; FISHING: FRESHWATER – SEE NOTE 10 / SEA – SEE NOTE 11 / GOGGLE / LICENCE REQUIRED; SWIMMING: SWIMMING POOL / SEA BATHING / CHILDRENS' POOL / ADULTS ONLY / SHARK NETS AT BEACH; BOATING: BOATS FOR HIRE / POWER / SAILING / CANOEING; PLACES OF INTEREST: HISTORIC / SCIENTIFIC / NATURAL

NOTES

33	34	35	36	37	38	39	40	41	42	43	44	45	46	47	48	49	50	51	52	53	54	55	56	57	58	59	60	61	62	63	64	65	66	67	68	69	70	71	72	73	74	75	76	77	78	79	80	81	82	83	84	85	86	87	88	89	90	91	92	93	94	95	96	97	98	99	100	101	102	103	104	105	106	107	108	109	110	111	112	113	114	115	116	117	118	119	120	121	122	123
		■	■	■	D	D											■			■				C-H	C-H		■		■		■		■	■					■		■	■	■	■		■				■	■		■					■		■																												■	
		●	●	●	D	D							●			●			●	●				B-E	B-E		●		●		●		●	●	●						●		●	●	●								●					●	●	●																												●	
		○	○	○	D	D											○			○				C-E	C-E		○		○		○		○	○	○	○						○		○	○	○				○	○				○	○		○	○	○																												○	
		◆	◆	◆	D	D					◆			◆			◆			◆				D-E	D-E		◆		◆		◆		◆	◆	◆	◆			◆			◆		◆	◆	◆	◆			◆	◆				◆	◆		◆	◆	◆																												◆	
		◇	◇	◇	D	D					◇			◇			◇			◇				D	D		◇		◇		◇	◇	◇	◇	◇	◇			◇			◇		◇	◇	◇				◇	◇				◇	◇		◇	◇	◇																												◇	
		▲	▲	▲	D	D											▲			▲				C	C		▲		▲		▲		▲	▲	▲	▲			▲			▲		▲	▲	▲				▲	▲				▲	▲		▲	▲	▲																												▲	
		△	△	△	D	D												△																																																																						△	
		★	★	★	D	D					★			★			★			★		★		D-J	D-J		★		★		★		★	★	★	★			★			★		★	★	★				★					★	★		★	★	★																												★	
		☆	☆	☆	D	D					☆			☆			☆			☆		☆		D-J	D-J		☆		☆		☆		☆	☆	☆	☆			☆			☆	☆	☆	☆					☆	☆				☆	☆		☆	☆	☆																												☆	
		■	■	■	D	D					■			■			■			■				C	C		■				■		■			■						■		■	■	■	■			■					■	■		■	■	■																												■	
		□	□	□	D	D					□			□			□			□				D-E	D-E		□		□		□		□	□	□	□			240			□		□	□	□				□					□	□		□	□	□																												□	
		●	●	●	D	D					●			●			●			●				C-D	C-D		●		●		●		●	●		●								●		●				●					●	●		●	●	●																												●	
		○	○	○	D	D					○			○			○			○		○		D-J	D-J		○		○		○		○	○	○	○			○			○		○	○	○	○	○	○	○	○	○			○	○		○	○	○																										○	○	○	
		△	△		E	D	△						△			△		△	△								△		△		△		△	△	△	△		△	220				△	△	△		△	△	△	△	△	△						△	△	△	N	N	N	N	N	N	N		N	18				N	N	N	△	N		N								△		
					C	C		☆				☆			☆			☆									☆				☆		☆	☆		☆		☆			☆		☆				☆	☆	☆	☆		☆	☆	☆				☆		☆	N	N	N			N	N		N	18	N			S			☆	N		N				S		S	☆		☆	
					D	D		■			■			■				■		■			■	G	E		■		■		■		■	■	■	■		■	220		■	■		■			■	■	■		■	■	■					■		■	S	N	N			S	N		N	18	S			S			■	S		S			S			S	■		■	
					E	E						□			□		□					□		D	D		□		□		□		□	□	□	□					□	□	□	□			□	□	□	□	□	□			□	□		□	□	□	S	S		S	S	N	N		N	18				S			□	S		S					S	S	□		□	
		●	●	●	C	B	●	●				●			●			●			●	●		A	A		●		●		●		●	●	●	●					●		●	●	●		●	●	●	●	●	●		●	●			●	●	●	N	N	N	N	N	N	N		N	18				N			●										●	●	●	
					X	X							○			○			○	○				X	X	○	○		○		○		○	○					220		○	○	○	○			○						○	○	○			○	○	○	S													S			○	S		S									○	
		◇			A	A	◇					◇	◇		◇	◇		◇	◇								◇					◇	◇	◇	◇								◇	◇			◇	◇	◇	◇	◇	◇		◇	◇		◇	◇	◇	◇	S	N										◇		N			◇	N		N				N	N	N	◇		◇	
		△	△	△	B	B		△						△			△			△		△		B-G	B-G		△		△		△		△	△	△	△					△		△	△		△		△	△	△	△	△	△	△	△			△	△	△	S		I			S									N	N			△	N									△	
		☆	☆		E	E											☆			☆				E-F	E-F		☆	☆	☆		☆		☆	☆	☆	☆					☆	☆	☆	☆			☆			☆					☆	☆	☆	☆		☆																			☆												
		□	□	□	G	C	□		R				□	□	□		□	□	□			□		I	F	□	□		□		□		□	□	□	□	□	□	220		□	□	□	□			□	□	□	□	□	□	□	□			□	□	□	□	S	N		N	S	S	N		N	18					N	N	□	S	□	S										
		●	●		C	C	●					●			●			●	●								●		●		●		●	●	●	●		●			●			●								●		●			●	●		●							N		N	18					N			S	●											
		◆			C	C	◆				◆			◆				◆									◆		◆		◆		◆	◆	◆						◆	◆					◆	◆	◆	◆		◆		◆				◆	◆	◆	S	S				S					◆							S		S										
					A	A	▲					▲			▲			▲									▲					▲	▲	▲									▲	▲			▲	▲	▲	▲		▲		▲	▲			▲	▲	▲	S	S							N	9				N		N	▲										▲		▲	
					B	B	★				★		★	★			★						★	D	D		★		★		★		★	★				★	220		★	★	★	★			★	★	★				★					★	★	★																														
					D	D		☆	R			☆			☆			☆									☆		☆		☆		☆	☆	☆	☆			☆				☆				☆	☆	☆			☆	☆					☆		☆	N	N	N	N			N											N		N								☆		
		□			C	C	□					□			□			□									□		□		□		□	□	□	□		□	240				□	□			□	□	□	□	□	□	□	□	□			□		□	S	N							N	9																	□			
		○			B	B							○		○			○									○		○		○		○	○	○	○		○	220				○	○			○	○	○	○	○	○	○	○	○			○	○	○	S	N	N	N			N		N	18				N				N		N						N	○	○	○	
		◇	◇		C	B	◇	◇			◇			◇			◇	◇		◇		◇	◇	X	X		◇		◇		◇		◇	◇	◇	◇	◇	◇	◇		◇		◇	◇		◇		◇	◇	◇	◇	◇	◇	◇	◇		◇	◇		◇	S	N	N	N		S	N		N	18								S		S							◇	◇	◇	
					C	C						▲			▲			▲									▲		▲		▲		▲	▲	▲	▲		▲	▲				▲				▲	▲					▲		▲			▲	▲	▲	S		N	S			N		N	18				S			▲	N											▲	
					B	B		★				★			★			★									★		★		★		★	★	★	★		★	★		★			★			★	★	★	★	★	★	★	★	★	★	★	★		★	N	N	N	N			N		N	18				N			★	N										★	★	
		■	■		C	C						■			■			■									■		■		■		■	■	■	■							■	■			■	■	■	■		■	■					■		■	N	N	N				N		N	9				N			■	N		N							■		■	
		●	●		F	F					●	●	●		●	●		●	●		●			F	F		●		●		●		●	●	●	●					●		●				●	●	●	●	●	●						●	●	●	N	N		N	S		N		N	18					N	N	●	S	●		●		N	N	N	N	●		●	
		○	○		X	X						○		○	○		○	○	○		○		○	X	X	○	○		○		○		○	○	○	○	○	○	220	○	○			○			○	○	○	○	○	○	○					○	○	○	S	N	S	N	S		N		N	18					N	N	○	S	○	S			N	N	N	N	○	○	○	
		◆	◆		X	X	◆	◆					◆				◆									◆	◆		◆		◆		◆	◆	◆	◆		◆			◆			◆			◆	◆	◆	◆	◆	◆	◆					◆		◆		N	N	N			N		N	18					N	N	◆		◆				N			N	◆	◆	◆	
		◇	◇		F	E							◇			◇	◇			◇				E	G		◇		◇		◇		◇	◇	◇	◇					◇	◇	◇	◇			◇	◇	◇			◇	◇					◇		◇							N		N	18					N				◇								◇		◇	
					C	C	△					△			△			△									△				△		△	△	△	△		△	220		△	△		△			△	△	△	△	△	△	△	△	△			△		△		N	N	N			N		N	9				N			△	N		N				N	N			△	△	
		☆	☆		C	C	☆	☆			☆			☆			☆									☆	☆		☆		☆		☆	☆	☆	☆	☆	☆			☆		☆	☆			☆	☆	☆	☆	☆	☆	☆	☆			☆	☆	☆	☆	S	N	S	S	S		N		N	18				N	N	N		S	☆	S			N	N	N	S	☆		☆	

CARAVAN PARKS AND CAMPING SITES

Establishments marked thus [Caravan Club symbol] have the Caravan Club of South Africa recommendation – see page 17
Establishments marked thus [AA symbol] recognise the AA Camping Carnet – see page 16 and also refer to column 42

CARAVAN PARK / CAMP SITE TARIFF CODE – See columns 38–39 (Subject to alteration)

A = Up to R1 | C = R2–R3 | E = R4–R5 | G = R6–R7 | I = R8–R9 | K = R10–R16
B = R1–R2 | D = R3–R4 | F = R5–R6 | H = R7–R8 | J = R9–R10 | O = FREE
Charges are based on a family of 2 adults and 2 children under 12 years | X = On Application

ADDITIONAL ACCOMMODATION TARIFF CODE – See columns 57–59 (Subject to alteration)

eg. Bungalows, Cabins, Cottages, Chalets, etc.
A = R1–R3 | C = R5–R7 | E = R9–R11 | G = R13–R15 | I = R17–R19 | K = R21–R30
B = R3–R5 | D = R7–R9 | F = R11–R13 | H = R15–R17 | J = R19–R21 | X = On Application
NB: Where the tariff is given in *italics* it is per person, otherwise per unit

NOTE 1 — Columns 18, 19, 20. — Where a symbol appears instead of a number it means stands are available but not demarcated or number of stands has not been provided
NOTE 2 — Column 35 — A = Bookings accepted for additional accommodation only i.e. cottages, bungalows, etc.
NOTE 3 — Column 37 — Deposit refunded under certain conditions eg. less 10%, if site is re-let; if cancelled well in advance (up to 2 months) or on a doctor's certificate
NOTE 4 — Column 41 — Reductions allowed on application for youth, church, school or sport groups or caravan rallies
NOTE 5 — Column 42 — R = Reduction in tariff of between 5–10% to Carnet holders. 0 = Reduction Out-of-Season only
NOTE 6 — Column 69 — L = Laundry facilities only
NOTE 7 — Columns 88, 89, 90. — I = In-Season only; O = Out-of-Season only
NOTE 8 — Column 96 — Applicable In-Season only at some establishments
NOTE 9 — Column 102 — See section on golf in Outdoor Holiday Guide
NOTE 10 — Column 107 — See section on freshwater angling in Outdoor Holiday Guide
NOTE 11 — Column 108 — See section on coastal angling in Outdoor Holiday Guide

ABBREVIATIONS
C = CAPE PROVINCE
N = NATAL
O = ORANGE FREE STATE
T = TRANSVAAL
B = BOPHUTHATSWANA
X = TRANSKEI

Column headings: TELEPHONE CODE (T = DIAL 0020, BOOK TRUNK CALL; E = DIAL CODE, ASK EXCHANGE FOR NO.) (1); TELEPHONE NUMBER (2); OWNED OR SUPERVISED BY: Privately owned (3), Municipality (4), Divisional Council (5), Provincial Administration (6), Parks Board (7); SITE DESCRIPTION: Locality: Beach in immediate vicinity (8), Beside river, lake or dam (9), In or near mountain area (10), Within built up area (11); Nature of ground: Grass (12), Gravel (13), Sand (14); Shade: Unshaded (15), Partly shaded (16), Extensively shaded (17); NO. OF STANDS: Caravans only see note 1 (18), Caravans and/or tents see note 1 (19), Tents only see note 1 (20); ACCESSIBILITY: Approximate distance from main road to site: On main rd (21), Within 1 km (22), Within 5 km (23), Within 10 km (24), Within 15 km (25); Surface of approach road: Tar (26), Gravel (27), Sand (28); Condition of approach road: Good (29), Fair (30), Poor

		Establishment		1	2	3	4	5	6	7	8	9	10	11	12	13	14	15	16	17	18	19	20	21	22	23	24	25	26	27	28	29	30
		PORT ALFRED (Continued)																															
■	CC AA	**Medolino** P.O. Box 20, Kowie West 6171	□ *23 Stewart Rd.*	04642 E	346	■					■				■				■			75			■				■			■	
□		**The Rainbow Park** P.O. Box 15, Kowie West 6171	□ *Beach Front*	04642 E	495	□					□				□				□	□	25	10	5		□				□	□		□	
●	AA	**The Willows** Town Clerk, P.O. Box 13 (6170)		04642 E	32		●				●	●		●	●				●	●		52		●					●			●	
		PORT EDWARD N 63 NS ↙ S.L.																															
◆		**Pont** P.O. Port Edward 4295	□ *Old Pont Rd.*	03930	711		◆				◆	◆	◆		◆	◆			◆	◆		◆				◆				◆		◆	
◇		**S.A. Police Holiday Resort** Manager, P.O. Box 22 (4295)		03930	823	◇					◇				◇	◇	◇		◇	◇	41		◇			◇			◇			◇	
▲	CC	**T.O. Strand** P.O. Box 86 (4295)	□ *6 km from Port Edward*	03931	729	▲					▲	▲			▲					▲		126			▲				▲			▲	
		PORT ELIZABETH C 59 B5 ↖ S.L.																															
★	CC AA	**Brookes Hill** Beach Manager, Humewood 6001	□ *Beach Rd., Humewood*	041	2-5400		★				★				★			★			130			★					★			★	
☆		**Caracampark** P.O. Box 5054, Walmer 6065	□ *Victoria Dve., Walmer*	041	2-2920	☆					☆				☆					☆		55		☆					☆			☆	
■		**Gamtoos River Mouth** Bookings not accepted	□ *60 km from Port Elizabeth*	041	2-8911				■		■	■			■		■			■	■	■					■		■			■	
□	AA	**Humewood** Beach Manager, Humewood 6001		041	53-3095		□				□			□	□	□	□	□	□	□	350		250	□					□			□	
●	AA	**St. Georges Strand** Beach Manager, Humewood 6001		041	6134		●				●				●	●	●	●	●		●	●	●	●					●			●	
		PORT NOLLOTH C 60 A4 ↗ S.L.																															
◆	CC AA	**McDougalls Bay Municipality** P.O. Box 15 (8280)		T	11		◆				◆						◆	◆				30				◆				◆			◆
		PORT ST. JOHNS X 60 A4 → 3m																															
▲	CC	**First Beach Municipal** P.O. Box 2 (4830)		04 752 E	75 or 8		▲				▲	▲			▲					▲	23	▲		▲					▲			▲	
△		**Second Beach Holiday Resort** P.O. Box 18 (4830)		04752 E	61						△	△	△		△				△	△	30		20	△					△			△	
★		**Second Beach Municipal** P.O. Box 2 (4830)		04752 E	75 or 8		★				★	★			★				★		50		60		★					★		★	
		POTCHEFSTROOM T 66 A5 ↙ 1300m																															
■		**Dam Recreation Resort** P.O. Box 20099, Noordbrug 2522	□ *Lakeside Dam*	01481	5144		■					■			■					■		350			■				■			■	
		POTGIETERSRUS T 69 B2 ↖ 1178m																															
●		**Fiestapark Motel and Holiday Resort** P.O. Box 616 (0600)	□ *Naboomspruit Main Rd.*	01541	8712	●							●		●					●		8		●						●		●	
○	CC	**Potgietersrus Municipal** Parks Superintendent, P.O. Box 34 (0600)	□ *Voortrekker Rd. Ext.*	01541	624 x51		○					○	○		○					○	19			○						○		○	
		PRETORIA T 68 C6 ↙ 1400m																															
◇	CC	**Fountains Valley** Bookings not necessary Enquiries: P.O. Box 1454 (0001)		012	44-7131		◇								◇			◇	◇	◇		74			◇				◇			◇	
▲		**Hennops Pride Pleasure Resort** P.O. Box 1176 (0001)	□ *On Hartbeespoort Dam Rd.*	012	40-1550	▲						▲	▲		▲	▲				▲		25		▲						▲		▲	
△	CC	**Joos Becker** Bookings not necessary Enquiries: P.O. Box 1454 (0001)		012	75-4029		△						△		△			△	△	△	60		△		△				△			△	
★	CC AA	**Polkadraai** P.O. Box 42, Voortrekkerhoogte 0143		012	64-2682	★						★			★				★		60	80	20	★							★		★
		PRIESKA C 61 A4 ↘ 939m																															
■		**Prieska Municipal** P.O. Box 16 (8940)	□ *Hoof St.*	05942 E	154 or 44		■							■		■			■		25					■			■			■	
		PRINCE ALBERT C 59 B2 ↖ 646m																															
●		**Rap-Skrap Rest Camp** 46 Kerk St. (6930)	□ *46 Kerk St.*	044322 E	33	●							●	●		●			●			●			●					●			●
		QUEENSTOWN C 62 C4 ↙ 1160m																															
◆	AA	**Queenstown Municipal** Bookings not necessary	□ *East London Main Rd.*	0451	2291 x31		◆					◆			◆	◆			◆			40		◆						◆		◆	
		QUINERA C See Gonubie Mouth																															
		RANDFONTEIN T 72 NS ← 1600m																															
△	AA	**Riebeeck Lake** Parks Superintendent, P.O. Box 218 (1760)	□ *Malan St.*	011	663-5219		△					△		△	△					△	35		△		△				△			△	
		RAWSONVILLE C 58 C4 ↙ 242m																															
☆		**Goudini Spa** P.O. Box 47 (6845)	□ *±4 km from Rawsonville*	0231	9-1100	☆							☆	☆	☆		☆		☆		30					☆			☆			☆	
		REITZ O 66 B6 ↙ 1623m																															
□		**Reitz Municipal** P.O. Box 26 (9810)	□ *Sarel Cilliers St.*	01432 E	26/183		□							□	□					□		8		□					□			□	
		RICHARDS BAY N 67 C5 S.L.																															
○		**Richards Bay Municipal** P/Bag X1004 (3900)	□ *Beachfront*	0351	3-1971		○				○				○				○			211		○						○		○	
		RICHMOND C 61 C5 → 1381m																															
◇		**Richmond Municipal** P.O. Box 8 (7010)	□ *Market St.*	05752 E	1		◇					◇				◇				◇		◇			◇					◇			◇
		RIVERSDALE C 58 D6 ↖ 118m																															
△		**Meurant** P.O. Box 29 (6770)		02932 E	14		△					△	△		△	△				△		30			△				△			△	
		RIVERTON C 66 C2 → 1097m																															
☆		**Riverton-on-Vaal** P.O. Box 628, Kimberley 8300	□ *±27 km from Kimberley*	0531	2-2241 x221		☆					☆			☆				☆		43		50				☆		☆			☆	
		RIVIERSONDEREND C 58 D4 ↗ 152m																															
□		**Riviersonderend Municipal** P.O. Box 31 (7250)	□ *Main St.*	02852 E	30		□						□	□	□				□		30	30		□						□		□	
		RIVONIA T 72 NS ↑ 1433m																															
○		**Rivonia** P.O. Box 18 (2128)	□ *186 Rietfontein Rd.*	011	802-1108	○								○	○					○	○				○				○			○	
		ROBERTSON C 58 C4 ↖ 173m																															
◇	CC	**Silverstrand Holiday Resort** Town Clerk, P.O. Box 52 (6705)	□ *3 km from Robertson*	02352 E	627		◇					◇	◇		◇	◇			◇		72		35			◇			◇			◇	
		ROCKCLYFFE-ON-SEA C 60 C2 ↗ S.L.																															
△		**Rockclyffe-on-Sea Holiday Resort** P.O. Greenfields, East London 5208	□ *± 17 km from East London*	0431	46-2540	△					△				△					△	25				△					△		△	
		ROODEPOORT T 72 NS 1631m																															
☆		**Little Falls Pleasure Resort** P.O. Box 1 (1725)	□ *Little Falls (Hendrik Potgieter) Rd.*	011	679-1412	☆						☆	☆		☆				☆		50	50	50		☆				☆	☆		☆	

SEASONS · CAMP SITE FACILITIES (I = In-Season only; O = Out-of-Season only) · SPORTING AND RECREATIONAL FACILITIES (S = On Site; N = Nearby (Up to 20 km away)) · NOTES

33 OUT-OF-SEASON CLOSING DATE	34 RE-OPENING DATE	35 TERMS FOR BOOKINGS: BOOKINGS ACCP./PEAK SNS. – SEE NOTE 2	36 DEPOSIT REQUIRED	37 REFUNDED IF CANCELLED – SEE NOTE 3	38 CARAVAN PARK/CAMPING SITE TARIFFS: MAXIMUM IN-SEASON TARIFF	39 MAXIMUM OUT-OF-SEASON TARIFF	40 REDUCTIONS ALLOWED FOR: LONG PERIODS OF STAY	41 GROUPS – SEE NOTE 4	42 AA CARNET HOLDERS – SEE NOTE 5	43 OTHERS (ON APPLICATION)	44 RESTAURANT FACILITIES: ON SITE	45 WITHIN 5 km OF SITE	46 MORE THAN 5 km FROM SITE	47 TEAROOM/CAFE: ON SITE	48 WITHIN 5 km OF SITE	49 MORE THAN 5 km FROM SITE	50 SHOPPING FACILITIES (Provisions): ON SITE	51 WITHIN 5 km OF SITE	52 MORE THAN 5 km FROM SITE	53 ADDITIONAL ACCOMMODATION AVAILABLE: BUNGALOWS	54 CABINS	55 COTTAGES (RONDAVELS)	56 CHALETS	57 ADDITIONAL ACCOMMODATION TARIFF (See heading): MAXIMUM IN-SEASON TARIFF	58 MAXIMUM OUT-OF-SEASON TARIFF	59 CARAVANS TO RENT ON SITE – SEE PAGES 8–11
		■	■		D	C	■	■	R			■			■			■			■			C	B	■
		□	□		D	D	□	□				□	□	□			□			□	□			C	C	
					B	B						●			●		●									
		◆	◆		C	C							◆		◆	◆		◆	◆							
		◇	◇		D	C					◇			◇			◇	◇	◇	◇		◇	◇	A-E	A-D	
		▲	▲		E	C	▲	▲			▲			▲			▲						▲	G	C	
		★	★		C	C						★			★			★								
		☆	☆	☆	E	D	☆	☆		☆		☆			☆			☆								☆
					A	A							■			■			■							
		□	□		C	C						□			□			□		□		□		B-D	B-D	
					B	B																				
					B	B															◆			C	C	
		▲	▲		C	C	▲						▲			▲			▲	▲			▲	C-E	C-E	
		△	△	△	C	C	△	△				△					△			△		△	△	C-D	E-F	
		★	★		C	C	★					★			★				★	★			★	C-E	C-E	
					C	C					■			■			■			■		■	■	B-J	B-F	
		●	●		C	C	●	●			●			●			●					●	●	F	F	
		○			B	B						○			○			○								
					B	B						◇	◇		◇			◇	◇							
					D	B		▲			▲			▲			▲									
					B	B						△	△		△			△	△							
		★	★		C	C	★	★	R	★	★	★		★	★			★								
		■			C	C							■		■			■								
		●			C	C	●	●				●	●		●	●		●	●	●	●	●		B-C	B-C	
					B	B					◆			◆				◆								
		△	△	△	B	B						△	△		△	△		△	△			△		C	C	
		☆	☆		E	E		☆			☆			☆			☆			☆		☆		J	F	
		□			C	C						□			□			□								
		○	○	○	D	D	○	○				○		○	○			○								
					B	B							◇			◇			◇							
		A	A		B	B				△		△			△			△		△				B	B	
		☆	☆	☆	D	D					☆			☆			☆					☆	☆	B-C	B-C	
					B	B	□	□				□			□			□								
		○			F	F	○					○	○		○	○		○	○							
		◇	◇	◇	C	B					◇			◇			◇	◇		◇		◇	◇	C-E	B-D	
					F	F							△			△			△			△		F	E	
		☆	☆		F	F	☆	☆			☆			☆				☆								

60 DRINKING WATER: PIPED	61 OTHER	62 BATHS: HOT AND COLD	63 COLD ONLY	64 SHOWERS: HOT AND COLD	65 COLD ONLY	66 WATERBORNE SANITATION	67 WASHBASINS	68 DISHWASHING FACILITIES	69 LAUNDRY AND IRONING FACILITIES – SEE NOTE 6	70 WASHING MACHINES	71 SITE LIT	72 PLUGS FOR RAZORS (VOLTAGE)	73 REFRIGERATORS	74 FIREWOOD/CHARCOAL	75 OPEN FIRE FORBIDDEN	76 CAMP FIRE PERMITTED	77 BRAAI PLACES PROVIDED	78 KITCHEN/COOKING FACILITIES	79 PETROL PUMP ON SITE	80 PETROL PUMP NEARBY	81 CAR REPAIR SHOP NEARBY	82 CAR SERVICING NEARBY	83 GAS SERVICE NEARBY	84 FIRST AID HOSPITAL/DOCTOR NEARBY	85 POST OFFICE NEARBY	86 SITE GUARDED	87 PETS ALLOWED	88 NON-WHITE SERVANTS: SERVANTS PERMITTED – SEE NOTE 7	89 SERVANTS ACCOM. – SEE NOTE 7	90 SERVANTS FOR HIRE – SEE NOTE 7	91 TYPE OF VEHICLE PERMITTED: CAR AND TRAILER	92 TRUCK, HORSE AND SEMI-TRAILER	93 SELF-PROPELLED CARAVANS
■	■	■		■		■	■	■	■	■	■	110/220		■		■	■			■	■	■	■	■	■	■	■	■		■	■	■	■
□	□	□		□	□	□	□	□	□		□			□	□	□	□		□	□	□	□	□	□	□	□	□	□		□	□		□
●			●		●		●				●	●		●	●	●	●			●	●	●	●	●	●	●					●	●	●
◆		◆		◆	◆	◆	◆	◆	◆		◆					◆				◆	◆	◆	◆	◆	◆					◆	◆	◆	◆
◇		◇		◇		◇	◇	◇	◇		◇			◇		◇	◇			◇	◇	◇	◇	◇	◇					◇	◇		◇
▲		▲		▲		▲	▲		▲		▲	▲	▲	▲		▲	▲			▲	▲	▲	▲	▲	▲	▲				▲	▲		▲
★		★				★			★																			★					★
☆		☆		☆		☆	☆	☆	☆		☆			☆	☆		☆			☆	☆	☆	☆	☆	☆	☆	☆			☆	☆	☆	☆
■					■											■	■			■	■	■	■		■						■	■	■
□		□	□	□	□	□	□	□	□		□	□		□			□			□	□	□	□	□	□		□	□			□		□
●			●		●	●	●										●	●						●			●	●			●		●
◆			◆		◆	◆										◆	◆										◆	◆			◆		◆
▲		▲		▲		▲	▲	▲	▲		▲		▲	▲		▲	▲			▲	▲	▲	▲	▲	▲	▲		▲	▲	▲	▲	▲	▲
△		△		△		△	△	△	△					△		△				△	△	△	△	△	△	△	△	△	△	△	△	△	△
★		★		★		★	★	★	★					★		★	★			★	★	★	★	★	★	★		★	★	★	★	★	★
■		■		■		■	■	■	■		■	■		■			■			■	■	■	■	■	■	■		■	■	■	■	■	■
●		●				●	●	●	●		●	220	●	●		●	●	●		●			●			●	●	●	●	●	●	●	●
○		○		○		○	○	○	○		○	220		○	○		○			○	○	○	○	○	○	○					○		○
◇		◇		◇		◇	◇	◇	◇		◇	250		◇			◇				◇	◇				◇			◇		◇	◇	◇
▲					▲	▲	▲							▲		▲	▲						▲				▲	▲			▲		▲
△		△		△		△	△	△	△		△	250		△			△				△	△				△			△		△	△	△
★		★		★		★	★	★	★	★	★	220	★	★	★	★	★			★	★	★	★	★	★	★	★				★		★
■	■	■		■		■	■				■		■			■	■	■								■	■				■	■	■
●	●	●			●	●	●	●						●		●	●	●		●	●	●	●	●	●	●	●				●		●
◆		◆		◆		◆	◆	◆	◆		◆	220					◆			◆	◆	◆	◆	◆	◆		◆	◆			◆		◆
△	△	△		△		△	△	△	△		△	110/220	△	△	△	△	△			△	△	△		△	△	△	△				△	△	△
☆		☆		☆		☆	☆	☆	☆		☆	220	☆	☆		☆	☆	☆		☆	☆	☆		☆	☆	☆		☆	☆	☆	☆		☆
□		□		□		□	□	□	□		□	220		□	□	□	□			□	□	□	□	□	□	□	□	□			□	□	□
○		○		○		○	○	○	○					○		○				○	○	○	○		○	○					○	○	○
◇				◇		◇	◇	◇	◇		◇	◇		◇		◇	◇			◇	◇	◇	◇	◇	◇	◇	◇	◇			◇		
△				△		△	△	△	△		△			△		△	△			△	△	△	△	△	△		△	△			△	△	△
☆		☆		☆		☆	☆	☆	☆		☆	☆	☆	☆	☆		☆			☆				☆		☆					☆		☆
□				□		□	□	□	□		□	220/250		□		□	□			□	□	□	□		□	□		□			□	□	□
○		○		○		○	○	○	○	○	○	220		○		○	○			○	○	○	○	○	○	○		○	○		○	○	○
◇		◇		◇		◇	◇	◇			◇	◇	◇	◇		◇	◇			◇	◇	◇	◇	◇	◇	◇					◇	◇	◇
△		△		△		△	△							△		△	△			△	△	△	△		△					△	△		△
☆		☆		☆		☆	☆	☆	☆		☆	220		☆		☆	☆			☆	☆	☆		☆	☆	☆					☆		☆

94 CHILDRENS' PLAYGROUND	95 TENNIS	96 CINEMA/DRIVE-IN/TV-ROOM – SEE NOTE 8	97 HORSE-RIDING	98 GAMES ROOM	99 TRAMPOLINE	100 BOWLS	101 HOT SPRINGS	102 GOLF: GOLF COURSE – SEE NOTE 9	103 NUMBER OF HOLES	104 MINIATURE	105 MASHIE	106 PUTT-PUTT	107 FISHING: FRESHWATER – SEE NOTE 10	108 SEA – SEE NOTE 11	109 GOGGLE	110 LICENCE REQUIRED	111 SWIMMING: SWIMMING POOL	112 SEA BATHING	113 CHILDRENS' POOL	114 ADULTS ONLY	115 SHARK NETS AT BEACH	116 BOATING: BOATS FOR HIRE	117 POWER	118 SAILING	119 CANOEING	120 PLACES OF INTEREST: HISTORIC	121 SCIENTIFIC	122 NATURAL	123 NOTES
S	N	N	N	S		N		N	18					N	N			■				N	N	N	N	■	■	■	
		N				N		N	18					N				□				N	N	N	N	□	□	□	
S	N	N	N	N		N		N	18	●				N	N			●	N			N	N	N	N	●		●	
S	N	N			N	N		N	9		◆			N	N			◆	S		◆	N	N	N	N				
S	S	S		S	S	N		N	9					N	N			◇	S		◇							◇	
S	S	S			S			N	9				N	N	N	▲		▲			▲								
N	N	N	N		N	N		N	18			★	N	N	N		N	★	N							★	★	★	
S	N	S	N	N	N	N		S	18				N	N	N	☆	S	☆	S							☆	☆	☆	
S														N	N			■										■	
N	N	N	N		N	N		N	18				N	N	N		N	□	N							□	□	□	
														N	N			●								●	●	●	
														N	N			◆					N	N	N				
	N					N		N	9					N	N		N	▲					N		N			▲	
S	S	S		S	S	N		N	9				N	N	N	△		△				N			N	△	△	△	
	N			S		N		N	9					N	N		N	★					N		N			★	
S	S	N				N		N	18				S			■	S		S			S	S	S	S	■	■		
S	S	N		S			N	N	9				N			●	S		S				N	N	N	●	●	●	
S	N	N	N			N		N	9				N			○	N		N					N	N	○		○	
S	N	N				N		N	18								N			◇						◇		◇	
S													S			▲	S		S									▲	
S	N	N				N		N	18								S			△									
		S				N		N	18				N			★	S											★	
N	N		N	N		N		N	18				N			■	N		N						N	■		■	
S	N							N			●		N			●										●		●	
		N				N		N	18				N			◆	N		N				N	N	N	◆		◆	
S	N	N	N			N		N	18				S			△	S		S							△		△	
S	S	S	N	S		N	S	N	18								S		S				N	N	N	☆	☆	☆	
S	N	N	N	N	N	N		N	9				S			□	S		S										
S	N	N	N	S		N		N	9				N	N	N		N	○	S				N	N	N	○		○	
N	N					N		N	18								N									◇			
N	N	N				N		N	18																	△		△	
S	S												S			☆	S		S			S				☆			
N	N	N						N	9								S		S	□								□	
S	N	N	N			N		N	18				N				N												
S	N	N		S		N		N	9				S			◇	S		S				S	S	S			◇	
																		△							△			△	
S	S	N	S														S		S							☆	☆	☆	

CARAVAN PARKS AND CAMPING SITES

Establishments marked thus [CC] have the Caravan Club of South Africa recommendation – see page **17**
Establishments marked thus [AA] recognise the AA Camping Carnet – see page **16** and also refer to column **42**

CARAVAN PARK / CAMP SITE TARIFF CODE – See columns 38–39 (Subject to alteration)

A = Up to R1 | C = R2–R3 | E = R4–R5 | G = R6–R7 | I = R8–R9 | K = R10–R16
B = R1–R2 | D = R3–R4 | F = R5–R6 | H = R7–R8 | J = R9–R10 | O = FREE
Charges are based on a family of 2 adults and 2 children under 12 years | X = On Application

ADDITIONAL ACCOMMODATION TARIFF CODE – See columns 57–59 (Subject to alteration)
eg. Bungalows, Cabins, Cottages, Chalets, etc.
A = R1–R3 | C = R5–R7 | E = R9–R11 | G = R13–R15 | I = R17–R19 | K = R21–R30
B = R3–R5 | D = R7–R9 | F = R11–R13 | H = R15–R17 | J = R19–R21 | X = On Application
NB: Where the tariff is given in *italics* it is per person, otherwise per unit

NOTE 1 — Columns 18, 19, 20. — Where a symbol appears instead of a number it means stands are available but not demarcated or number of stands has not been provided
NOTE 2 — Column 35 — A = Bookings accepted for additional accommodation only i.e. cottages, bungalows, etc.
NOTE 3 — Column 37 — Deposit refunded under certain conditions eg. less 10 % ; if site is re-let ; if cancelled well in advance (up to 2 months) or on a doctor's certificate
NOTE 4 — Column 41 — Reductions allowed on application for youth, church, school or sport groups or caravan rallies
NOTE 5 — Column 42 — R = Reduction in tariff of between 5 – 10 % to Carnet holders; O = Reduction Out-of-Season only
NOTE 6 — Column 69 — L = Laundry facilities only
NOTE 7 — Columns 88, 89, 90. — I = In-Season only ; O = Out-of-Season only
NOTE 8 — Column 96 — Applicable In-Season only at some establishments
NOTE 9 — Column 102 — See section on golf in Outdoor Holiday Guide
NOTE 10 — Column 107 — See section on freshwater angling in Outdoor Holiday Guide
NOTE 11 — Column 108 — See section on coastal angling in Outdoor Holiday Guide

ABBREVIATIONS
C = CAPE PROVINCE
N = NATAL
O = ORANGE FREE STATE
T = TRANSVAAL
B = BOPHUTHATSWANA
X = TRANSKEI

TELEPHONE CODE: T = DIAL 0020. BOOK TRUNK CALL; E = DIAL CODE. ASK EXCHANGE FOR NO.

OWNED OR SUPERVISED BY (3–7) · SITE DESCRIPTION: LOCALITY (8–11), NATURE OF GROUND (12–14), SHADE (15–17) · NO. OF STANDS (18–20) · ACCESSIBILITY: APPROXIMATE DISTANCE FROM MAIN ROAD TO SITE (21–25), SURFACE OF APPROACH ROAD (26–28), CONDITION OF APPROACH ROAD (29–30)

			1 Telephone code	2 Telephone number	3 Privately owned	4 Municipality	5 Divisional council	6 Provincial administration	7 Parks board	8 Beach in immediate vicinity	9 Beside river, lake or dam	10 In or near mountain area	11 Within built-up area	12 Grass	13 Gravel	14 Sand	15 Unshaded	16 Partly shaded	17 Extensively shaded	18 Caravans only – see note 1	19 Caravans and/or tents – see note 1	20 Tents only – see note 1	21 On main rd.	22 Within 1 km	23 Within 5 km	24 Within 10 km	25 Within 15 km	26 Tar	27 Gravel	28 Sand	29 Good	30 Fair
		ROODEPOORT (Continued)																														
■		**Panorama** P.O. Box 35181, Northcliff 2115 □ *14 Hendrik Potgieter Rd.*	011	679-1225	■								■	■					■		60		■					■			■	
□		**Pondorosa** P.O. Box 810 (1725) □ *Impala Drive-in Rd.*	011	765-0635	□						□			□				□		24			□					□	□		□	
		ROYAL NATAL NATIONAL PARK N See Mont-aux-Sources																														
		RUSTENBURG T 68 C5 ↙ 1234m																														
◆		**Ananda Hotel Holiday Resort** P.O. Box 15 (0300)	01421	2-2332	◆							◆		◆					◆	50		◆		◆				◆			◆	
		SABIE T 69 C3 ↗ 1059m																														
▲	[CC] [AA]	**Castle Rock** P.O. Box 61 (1260) □ *Lydenburg Rd.*	0131512 E	203		▲					▲	▲		▲					▲		100			▲					▲		▲	
△	[CC] [AA]	**Merry Pebbles** P.O. Box 131 (1260) □ *Lydenburg Rd.*	0131512 E	323	△						△	△		△				△			120			△					△		△	
		SABI RIVER BUNGALOWS T 69 C4 ↖ 518m																														
☆	[AA]	**Sabie River Mineral Bath** P.O. Box 151, Hazyview 1242 □ *4 km from Hazyview*	0131242 E	3804	☆						☆	☆	☆	☆				☆	☆		40			☆					☆		☆	
■		**Sabie Villa Rest Camp** P.O. Box 148, Hazyview 1242	0131242 E	2232	■						■	■		■					■		50			■					■		■	
		SALDANHA C 58 C2 ↗ S.L.																														
●		**Saldanha Holiday Resort** P.O. Box 22 (7395)	02281	4-1525		●				●				●			●			90	90			●				●			●	
		SALT ROCK N 63 A4 ← S.L.																														
◆		**Salt Rock** Manager, Salt Rock Hotel, P.O. Salt Rock 4391	032232 E	25	◆					◆			◆	◆	◆			◆			87			◆				◆			◆	
		SASOLBURG O 66 A5 ↘ 1449m																														
▲	[CC]	**Abrahamsrust Recreation Resort** P.O. Box 60 (9570)	016	60-1909		▲					▲			▲					▲	45	21			▲				▲			▲	
		SCARBOROUGH C 58 NS ↙ S.L.																														
★		**Scarborough** Bookings not necessary Enquiries: Divisional Council, P.O. Box 1073, Cape Town 8000	021	41-3266			★			★		★		★	★	★		★			★	★		★					★		★	
		SCHAGEN T 69 C3 → 732m																														
■		**St. Pauls Caravan Park and Bungalows (at Lindale Farm)** P.O. Schagen 1207 □ *Dist. Nelspruit*	0131232 E	1503	■						■	■		■					■		20		■							■		■
□		**Sudwala Caves** P.O. Box 30 (1207)	0131232 E	2613	□						□	□		□				□	□	50	100			□				□			□	
		SCHWEIZER-RENEKE T 66 B3 ↖ 1314m																														
○		**Wentzel Dam Parking Area** Bookings not accepted □ *3 km from Schweizer-Reneke*	018012 E	25 or 3340		○					○			○					○	○	○	○		○					○		○	
		SCOTTBURGH N 63 NS ● S.L.																														
◇	[CC] [AA]	**Scottburgh Municipal** Camp Officer, P.O. Box 19 (4180) □ *Beachfront*	0323	2-0291		◇				◇	◇		◇	◇				◇			330			◇				◇			◇	
		SEDGEFIELD C 59 NS ← S.L.																														
△		**Cloverdale** P.O. Box 21 (6573) □ *Swartvlei*	T	722	△					△	△	△		△					△		60			△				△			△	
★	[CC] [AA]	**Jooris Park** P.O. Box 22 (6573) □ *Swartvlei*	T	940	★					★	★	★		★					★		80			★					★		★	
☆		**Lake Pleasant Holiday Resort** P.O. Box 16 (6573) □ *Groenvlei*	T	28	☆					☆	☆	☆		☆					☆		120			☆				☆			☆	
■	[AA]	**Landfall** P.O. Box 144 (6573) □ *Pelican Ave.*	T	44	■						■			■					■		45			■				■			■	
□	[AA]	**Pine Lake Marina** P.O. Box 8 (6573) □ *Swartvlei*	T	59	□					□	□	□		□					□		100			□					□		□	
●		**Swartvlei** Divisional Council, P.O. Box 12, George 6530 □ *Swartvlei*	0441	3001			●			●	●			●		●		●			157				●				●			●
○	[CC] [AA]	**Trail's End Holiday Resort** P.O. Box 31 (6573) □ *On banks of Swartvlei*	T	922	○					○	○	○		○		○		○	○		150				○				○		○	○
		SENEKAL O 66 C5 ↑ 1446m																														
◇		**Senekal Municipal** P.O. Box 20 (9600) □ *Van Riebeeck St.*	014352 E	30		◇					◇		◇	◇				◇						◇					◇		◇	
		SHELLY BEACH N 63 NS ↙ 5m																														
△		**Blue Seas** P.O. Box 102, St. Michael's on Sea 4265	0393	5-1049	△					△				△				△			54		△					△			△	
★	[CC]	**Karapark** P.O. Box 69, St. Michael's on Sea 4265	0393	5-1226	★								★	★				★			230		★					★			★	
		SILWERSTROOMSTRAND C See Caravan Parks for Coloureds, Asians and Blacks																														
		SIMONSTOWN C 58 NS ↙ S.L.																														
□	[CC] [AA]	**Oatlands Park** Froggy Pond (7995) □ *Main Rd.*	021	86-1410	□					□		□	□	□				□		70	10	15	□					□			□	
●		**The Blue Lantern** Winford (7995) □ *Main Rd.*	021	86-6184	●					●				●			●				6		●					●			●	
		SINKWAZI N 63 A4 ● 2m																														
◆	[CC] [AA]	**Zinkwazi Park** P.O. Box 8, Darnall 4480	032422 E	1912	◆					◆	◆			◆					◆		116		◆					◆			◆	
		SODWANA BAY N 67 B5 → S.L.																														
▲		**Sodwana Bay National Park** Officer in Charge, P/Bag X518, Mkuze 3965	T	2					▲	▲						▲	▲	▲	▲		600								▲	▲		▲
		SOMERSET EAST C 59 A5 ↓ 750m																														
★		**Max Clarke** Town Clerk, P.O. Box 21 (5850)	04242 E	8 or 272		★					★	★		★				★		20					★				★			★
☆		**Selley** Town Clerk, P.O. Box 21 (5850)	04242 E	8 or 272		☆					☆			☆				☆			20		☆					☆			☆	
		SOMERSET WEST C 58 D3 ↗ 10m																														
□		**Cloetenberg** P.O. Somerset West 7130 □ *National Rd.*	024	2-1019	□					□				□					□	100		30	□					□			□	
		SOUTHBROOM N 63 NS ↙ 10m																														
○		**Ooteekalia** P.O. Box 27 (4277) □ *Outlook Rd.*	0393	6080	○					○	○		○	○		○			○	27	7			○				○			○	
◆	[CC]	**Paradise** P.O. Box 55 (4277)	0393	3725	◆					◆				◆				◆	◆		126		◆					◆			◆	
		SOUTH COAST N See respectively: ● **Banana Beach** ● **Bazley** ● **Belle Vista-See Marina Beach** ● **Clansthal** ● **Doonside** ● **Hibberdene** ● **Ifafa Beach** ● **Illovo Beach** ● **Kelso** ● **Leisure Bay** ● **Margate** ● **Marina Beach** ● **Munster** ● **Park Rynie** ● **Pennington** ● **Port Shepstone** ● **Scottburgh** ● **Shelly Beach** ● **Southbroom** ● **St. Michael's on Sea** ● **Sunwich Port** ● **Trafalgar Beach** ● **Umtentweni** ● **Umzumbe** ● **Uvongo** ● **Widenham** ● **Winklespruit**																														
		SPIOENKOP PUBLIC RESORT N See Winterton																														

SEASONS		TERMS FOR BOOKINGS			CARAVAN PARK/CAMPING SITE TARIFFS (See heading)		REDUCTIONS ALLOWED FOR				RESTAURANT FACILITIES			TEAROOM/CAFE			SHOPPING FACILITIES (Provisions)			ADDITIONAL ACCOMMODATION AVAILABLE				ADDITIONAL ACCOMMODATION TARIFF (See heading)		CARAVANS TO RENT ON SITE – SEE PAGES 8 – 11	CAMP SITE FACILITIES (I = In-Season only, O = Out-of-Season only)																												NON-WHITE SERVANTS			TYPE OF VEHICLE PERMITTED			SPORTING AND RECREATIONAL FACILITIES (S = On Site, N = Nearby (Up to 20 km away))								GOLF					FISHING				SWIMMING					BOATING				PLACES OF INTEREST			NOTES
Out-of-season closing date	Re-opening date	Bookings accp./peak sns. – see note 2	Deposit required	Refunded if cancelled – see note 3	Maximum in-season tariff	Maximum out-of-season tariff	Long periods of stay	Groups – see note 4	AA carnet holders – see note 5	Others (on application)	On site	Within 5 km of site	More than 5 km from site	On site	Within 5 km of site	More than 5 km from site	On site	Within 5 km of site	More than 5 km from site	Bungalows	Cabins	Cottages (rondavels)	Chalets	Maximum in-season tariff	Maximum out-of-season tariff		Drinking water: Piped	Drinking water: Other	Baths: Hot and cold	Baths: Cold only	Showers: Hot and cold	Showers: Cold only	Waterborne sanitation	Washbasins	Dishwashing facilities	Laundry and ironing facilities – see note 6	Washing machines	Site lit	Plugs for razors (voltage)	Refrigerators	Firewood/charcoal	Open fire forbidden	Camp fire permitted	Braai places provided	Kitchen/cooking facilities	Petrol pump on site	Petrol pump nearby	Car repair shop nearby	Car servicing nearby	Gas service nearby	First aid/hospital/doctor nearby	Post office nearby	Site guarded	Pets allowed	Servants permitted – see note 7	Servants' accom. – see note 7	Servants for hire – see note 7	Car and trailer	Truck horse and semi-trailer	Self-propelled caravans	Childrens' playground	Tennis	Cinema/drive-in/TV-room – see note 8	Horse-riding	Games room	Trampoline	Bowls	Hot springs	Golf course – see note 9	Number of holes	Miniature	Mashie	Putt-putt	Freshwater – see note 10	Sea – see note 11	Goggle	Licence required	Swimming pool	Sea bathing	Childrens' pool	Adults only	Shark nets at beach	Boats for hire	Power	Sailing	Canoeing	Historic	Scientific	Natural	
33	34	35	36	37	38	39	40	41	42	43	44	45	46	47	48	49	50	51	52	53	54	55	56	57	58	59	60	61	62	63	64	65	66	67	68	69	70	71	72	73	74	75	76	77	78	79	80	81	82	83	84	85	86	87	88	89	90	91	92	93	94	95	96	97	98	99	100	101	102	103	104	105	106	107	108	109	110	111	112	113	114	115	116	117	118	119	120	121	122	123
		■			C	C						■			■			■									■		■		■		■	■	■	■		■	■		■		■				■	■	■	■	■	■		■	■		■	■	■	■	S		S	S		S																					■			
		□	□		D	D	□					□			□			□	□								□		□				□	□				□	220	□							□	□	□	□	□				□	□		□	□	□	S	N	N	S	S		N		N	9								S		S							□		□	
		◆	◆	◆	X	X					◆	◆		◆			◆					◆	◆	D	D		◆		◆		◆		◆	◆	◆	◆		◆	◆		◆		◆						◆		◆		◆	◆	◆	◆	◆	◆	◆	◆	S	S	S		S		S		N	18				N			◆	S		S							◆		◆	
		▲	▲	▲	E	E						▲			▲			▲									▲	▲	▲	▲	▲	▲	▲	▲	▲	▲		▲	▲		▲		▲	▲			▲	▲	▲	▲	▲	▲	▲	▲	▲	▲	▲	▲	▲	▲	S	N	N			N	N		N	9				S			▲	S		S					N		▲	▲	▲	
		△	△	△	E	E			R			△	△	△				△					△	B	B		△	△	△	△	△	△	△	△	△	△	△	△	220		△	△	△	△			△	△	△	△	△	△	△	△	△	△		△	△	△	S	N	N	N	S	S	N		N	9				S			△	S		S							△	△	△	
					D	D		☆	R		☆			☆				☆			☆	☆		B	B		☆		☆		☆		☆	☆	☆	☆		☆	220		☆		☆	☆			☆	☆	☆	☆		☆			☆	☆		☆	☆	☆	N	N					N	S	N	9				S			☆	S									☆		☆	
		■	■	■	D	D	■	■				■	■		■	■		■	■	■	■		■	B	B		■	■	■		■		■	■	■	■					■		■	■							■	■	■	■		■	■	■	■	■	N	N	N			N	N	N	N	9				S			■	S		S									■	
					B	B						●						●		●				C-E	C-E		●		●		●		●	●	●	●			●					●			●	●	●	●		●						●	●	●															●														●	
		◆	◆	◆				◆		◆		◆			◆			◆									◆		◆		◆		◆	◆	◆	◆		◆				◆					◆	◆	◆	◆		◆	◆			◆	◆	◆	◆	◆		N	N	N	N		N		N	9					N	N	◆	N	◆	S		◆							◆	
		▲	▲		G	G						▲	▲		▲	▲		▲	▲				▲	J	J		▲		▲		▲		▲	▲	▲	▲		▲	220		▲	▲		▲			▲	▲	▲	▲	▲	▲	▲					▲	▲	▲	S		N											S			▲	S		S				S	S	S				
					A	A						★			★												★			★											★	★	★	★														★	★	★															N	N			★	S	★									★	
		■	■	■	A	A												■				■		B	B		■		■		■		■	■				■		■	■		■	■			■		■	■				■				■	■	■																		N		N									■	
					C	C		□			□			□			□			□			□	E	E		□		□		□		□	□	□	□		□			□		□	□			□	□	□		□	□	□	□				□	□	□	S																	S		S							□	□	□	
					C	C						○			○			○									○		○		○		○	○	○			○	○		○	○	○			○	○	○	○		○	○	○		○		○	○	○	○	S	N	N						N	10				S			○	S		S				S	S	S	○		○	
		◇	◇		E	D					◇			◇				◇									◇		◇		◇		◇	◇	◇	◇	◇	◇	◇		◇	◇		◇			◇	◇	◇	◇	◇	◇	◇		◇		◇	◇	◇	◇	N	N	N	N	S	S	N		N	18	◇			N	N	N	◇	N	◇	N		◇				N			◇	
		△	△		X	X	△	△				△	△		△	△		△	△									△	△		△		△	△	△	△		△			△		△	△			△	△	△	△		△		△				△	△	△	S	N												S	N			S	△	S			S		S	S	△		△	
July	Sept	★	★	★	F	D	★	★	R	★		★			★			★		★				B	B	★	★		★		★		★	★	★	★		★	220		★	★	★	★			★	★	★	★		★	★	0	0		★	★	★	★	S		S				N		N	18				S	N	N		N	★	N			S	S	S	S			★	
		☆	☆		G	D					☆			☆			☆									☆	☆		☆		☆		☆	☆	☆	☆		☆	220	☆	☆	☆	☆	☆	☆		☆	☆	☆	☆	☆	☆	☆	0	0		☆	☆	☆	☆	S	N	S	S	S	S	N		N	18				S	N		☆		☆				S		S	S			☆	
		■	■	■	G	E	■	■	R			■			■			■					■	K	K	■	■		■		■		■	■	■	■		■	220		■	■		■			■	■	■			■	■	■			■	■	■	■	S	N	N	N		N	N		N	18				S	N	N		S	■	S	■		N	N	N	N	■	■	■	
		□	□	□	F	E		□	R		□			□			□			□	□	□	□	C	B-C		□	□	□		□		□	□	□	□		□	220		□	□	□	□		□		□	□	□	□	□	□	0	□	□	□	□	□	□	S	N	N	N	S	N	N		N	18				S	N	N		S	□	S			S	S	S	S	□	□	□	
		●	●	●	F	D								●			●										●				●		●	●	●						●	●		●			●	●	●	●		●	●					●	●	●														S	N	N			●											
After Easter	Oct	○	○		G	E	○			○		○	○		○	○	○	○	○		○			G	D	○		○	○		○		○	○	○	○		○	○		○	○	○	○			○	○	○	○	○	○	○				○	○	○	○	S	N	S	N	S	N	N		N	18				S	N	N		N	○	N			S	S	S	S	○		○	
					B	B						◇			◇			◇									◇		◇		◇		◇	◇	◇	◇		◇					◇	◇			◇	◇	◇			◇		◇	◇			◇	◇	◇	N	N	N				N		N	9		◇		N				N		N							◇	◇		
		△	△		H-I	D-E		△				△			△			△								△	△		△		△		△	△	△	△		△			△		△	△			△	△	△	△	△	△	△	△	△		△	△		△	S	N	N		S		N		N	18			△	N	N	N			△			△	N	N		N			△	
			★		G	G	★					★			★			★								★	★		★		★		★	★		★		★					★	★		★		★	★	★		★	★	★			★	★		★		S	S		S		S								★			S	★											
		□	□	□	G	D	□	□	R			□			□			□	□	□	□	□		J	G		□	□	□		□		□	□	□	□	□	□		□	□	□	□	□			□	□	□	□	□	□	□	□				□	□	□	S		S	N	S		N		N	11					N	N			□								□		□	
					C	B						●		●			●				●			C-D	C	●	●		●		●		●	●	●	●		●	●	●	●			●			●	●	●			●		0				●		●							N		N	11				N	N	N			●								●			
		◆	◆	◆	I	G	◆	◆	R	◆			◆	◆			◆					◆		K	I	◆	◆		◆		◆		◆	◆	◆	◆	◆	◆	110/220		◆		◆	◆			◆	◆	◆	◆	◆	◆	◆	◆	◆	◆	◆	◆	◆	◆	S	S	S		S		N		N					S	N			S	◆	S		◆	S	S	S	S	◆		◆	
		▲	▲		D	D											▲		▲								▲				▲		▲	▲							▲		▲	▲		▲	▲				▲				▲			▲	▲	▲															N	N	▲		▲									▲	▲	
		★			B	B	★						★			★			★								★		★		★		★	★	★	★		★	220		★		★	★			★	★	★	★	★	★		★	★		★	★	★	★	S	N					N		S	9				S			★	N		N				S	S	S	★		★	
					A	A	☆						☆			☆			☆								☆				☆		☆	☆				☆			☆		☆				☆	☆	☆			☆		☆	☆		☆	☆	☆	☆	N	N					N		N	9				N			☆	N		N				N	N	N	☆		☆	
		□	□		D	C	□					□			□			□									□		□		□		□	□	□	□	□	□	220				□	□			□	□	□	□		□			□			□		□	N	N	N	N	N	N	N		N	18				N	N	N		S	□	S			N	N	N		□	□	□	
		○	○	○	E	E	○	○				○		○	○			○	○	○				X	X		○		○		○		○	○	○	○		○	○		○	○		○			○	○	○	○	○	○	○		○	○		○	○	○	S	N	N	N	S	N	N		N	18				N	N	N		N		N		○	N			N			○	
		◆	◆	◆	F	F	◆	◆				◆		◆			◆									◆	◆		◆		◆		◆	◆	◆	◆		◆	◆		◆		◆	◆			◆	◆	◆	◆	◆	◆	◆	0	◆	◆	◆	◆	◆	◆	S	N	S	N	S		N		N	18			◆	N	N	N	◆	S	◆	S	◆	◆							◆	

CARAVAN PARKS AND CAMPING SITES

Establishments marked thus 🚐 have the Caravan Club of South Africa recommendation – see page **17**
Establishments marked thus ⓒ recognise the AA Camping Carnet – see page **16** and also refer to column **42**

CARAVAN PARK / CAMP SITE TARIFF CODE – See columns 38–39 (Subject to alteration)

A = Up to R1	C = R2–R3	E = R4–R5	G = R6–R7	I = R8–R9	K = R10–R16
B = R1–R2	D = R3–R4	F = R5–R6	H = R7–R8	J = R9–R10	O = FREE
Charges are based on a family of 2 adults and 2 children under 12 years					X = On Application

ADDITIONAL ACCOMMODATION TARIFF CODE – See columns 57–59 (Subject to alteration)
eg. Bungalows, Cabins, Cottages, Chalets, etc.

A = R1–R3	C = R5–R7	E = R9–R11	G = R13–R15	I = R17–R19	K = R21–R30
B = R3–R5	D = R7–R9	F = R11–R13	H = R15–R17	J = R19–R21	X = On Application

NB: Where the tariff is given in *italics* it is per person, otherwise per unit

NOTE 1 — **Columns 18, 19, 20.** — Where a symbol appears instead of a number it means stands are available but not demarcated or number of stands has not been provided
NOTE 2 — **Column 35** — A = Bookings accepted for additional accommodation only i.e. cottages, bungalows, etc.
NOTE 3 — **Column 37** — Deposit refunded under certain conditions eg. less 10%; if site is re-let; if cancelled well in advance (up to 2 months) or on a doctor's certificate
NOTE 4 — **Column 41** — Reductions allowed on application for youth, church, school or sport groups or caravan rallies
NOTE 5 — **Column 42** — R = Reduction in tariff of between 5–10% to Carnet holders; O = Reduction Out-of-Season only
NOTE 6 — **Column 69** — L = Laundry facilities only
NOTE 7 — **Columns 88, 89, 90.** — I = In-Season only; O = Out-of-Season only
NOTE 8 — **Column 96** — Applicable In-Season only at some establishments
NOTE 9 — **Column 102** — See section on golf in Outdoor Holiday Guide
NOTE 10 — **Column 107** — See section on freshwater angling in Outdoor Holiday Guide
NOTE 11 — **Column 108** — See section on coastal angling in Outdoor Holiday Guide

ABBREVIATIONS
C = CAPE PROVINCE
N = NATAL
O = ORANGE FREE STATE
T = TRANSVAAL
B = BOPHUTHATSWANA
X = TRANSKEI

			Telephone code (E = Dial code, ask exchange for no. T = Dial 0020, book trunk call)	Telephone number	Owned or supervised by					Site description: Locality				Nature of ground			Shade			No. of stands			Accessibility: Approximate distance from main road to site					Surface of road approach			Condition of road approach	
			1	2	3 Privately owned	4 Municipality	5 Divisional Council	6 Provincial Administration	7 Parks Board	8 Beach	9 Beside river, lake or dam	10 In or near mountain area	11 Within built-up area or immediate vicinity	12 Grass	13 Gravel	14 Sand	15 Unshaded	16 Partly shaded	17 Extensively shaded	18 Caravans only – see Note 1	19 Caravans and/or tents – see Note 1	20 Tents only – see Note 1	21 On main rd	22 Within 1 km	23 Within 5 km	24 Within 10 km	25 Within 15 km	26 Tar	27 Gravel	28 Sand	29 Good	30 Poor
		SPRINGBOK C 60 A5 ↘ 953m																														
□		**Kokerboom** P/Bag X35 (8240) □ *4 km from Springbok*	02732 E	5930	□							□			□	□		□			28			□					□			□
		SPRINGS T 72 NS → 1585m																														
○	🚐 ⓒ	**Murray Park Pleasure Resort** Bookings not accepted □ *5 km from Springs*	011	816-2302		○					○		○	○					○	150		50			○			○			○	
		STANDERTON T 67 A2 ↓ 1531m																														
◇		**Standerton Municipal** P.O. Box 66 (2430)	01331	3750/2332		◇					◇			◇				◇	◇	50	50	50		◇					◇			◇
		STANFORD C 58 D4 ← 1330m																														
△		**Salmons Dam Nature Reserve** Caretaker, P.O. Box 5 (7210)	02833	1330			△				△	△		△					△		150				△				△		△	
		STANFORD LAKE T See Haenertsburg																														
		STELLENBOSCH C 58 C3 ↘ 30m																														
■		**Bergplaas Holiday Ranch** P.O. Box 2172, Dennesig 7601 □ *Helshoogte Rd.*	02231	7-0486	■							■		■				■			40		■					■				■
□		**Drie Gewels** P.O. Box 10, Lynedoch 7603 □ *Lynedoch*	02234	207	□									□				□			25		□					□				□
		STERKSTROOM C 62 C4 ● 1349m																														
○		**Sterkstroom Municipal Rest Camp** Town Clerk (5425)	04592 E	8		○						○	○	○				○	○	10		10			○			○	○		○	
		STEYNSBURG C 62 C3 ↗ 1448m																														
◇		**Steynsburg Municipal** P.O. Box 35 (5920) □ *8 Hendrik Potgieter St.*	04842 E	34		◇							◇		◇			◇		5	5			◇					◇			◇
		STILBAAI-OOS C 59 C1 ● S.L.																														
△		**Ellensrust** Town Clerk, P.O. Box 2 (6785) □ *1 Main Rd. East*	T	34		△				△	△			△				△			350		△					△			△	
★	ⓒ	**Riverside Farm** C/o 66 Main Rd., Fish Hoek 7975 □ *9 km from Stilbaai-Oos*	021	88-8048	★					★	★	★		★			★	★			50			★				★			★	
		ST. LUCIA N See respectively: ● **Hluhluwe (False Bay Park)** ● **Mtubatuba (Fanies Island)** ● **St. Lucia Estuary (St. Lucia Public Resort)**																														
		ST. LUCIA ESTUARY N 67 C5 ● S.L.																														
□		**St. Lucia Public Resort** The Warden, Natal Parks Board, Private Bag, St. Lucia Estuary 3936 □ *28 km from Mtubatuba*	T	St. Lucia 20					□	□						□		□			200							□			□	
		ST MICHAEL'S ON SEA N 63 NS ✓ S.L.																														
○	🚐	**Surf Bay** P.O. Box 60 (4265)	0393	5-0233	○					○				○					○	60			○					○			○	
◆	🚐	**The Kingfisher** P.O. Box 7 (4265)	0393	5-0272/5-0566	◆					◆	◆		◆	◆					◆		◆		◆					◆			◆	
		STORMSRIVIER C 59 C3 ↗ S.L.																														
▲		**Tsitsikama Coastal National Park** National Parks Board, P.O. Box 787, Pretoria 0001	012	44-1194					▲	▲				▲			▲		▲	50		20				▲		▲			▲	
△		**Tsitsikama Forest National Park — Storms River Bridge** National Parks Board, P.O. Box 787, Pretoria 0001	012	44-1194					△		△			△					△	50			△					△			△	
		STORMSVLEI C 58 D5 ↘ 183m																														
☆		**Stormsvlei** P.O. Box 218, Swellendam 6740 □ *38 km from Swellendam*	02852 E	1730	☆						☆	☆				☆			☆		☆			☆					☆			☆
		STRAND C 58 D3 ↗ S.L.																														
□	🚐	**Kays** 54 Woltemade St. (7140) □ *Cnr. Woltemade St./Lourensrivier Rd.*	024	3-5025/3-2072	□					□	□	□		□		□			□		100			□				□			□	
●	🚐	**Voortrekker Park** P.O. Box 3 (7140) □ *Hofmeyer St.*	024	3-2316		●				●			●	●				●			320			●				●			●	
		STRANDFONTEIN C 60 C6 ✓ S.L.																														
◆		**Strandfontein** Divisional Council, P.O. Box 16, Vanrhynsdorp 8170	02712 E	90			◆			◆					◆	◆	◆			48	110		◆					◆			◆	
		STRUISBAAI C 58 D5 ← 2m																														
▲	ⓒ	**Struisbaai** Divisional Council, P.O. Box 35, Bredasdorp 7280 □ *Duiker St.*	02842 E	4930			▲			▲			▲	▲						300	300			▲				▲			▲	
		STRYDENBURG C 61 A5 ↘ 1067m																														
★		**Strydenburg Municipal** Town Clerk, P.O. Box 60 (8765) □ *Park St.*	05762 E	68 Bungalows 16		★									★				★	20	10	5		★				★			★	
		STUTTERHEIM C 60 B2 ✓ 809m																														
■		**Stutterheim Municipal** P.O. Box 2 (4930) □ *Alfred St.*	04362 E	151		■							■	■				■		30				■				■			■	
		SUDWALA CAVES T See Schagen																														
		SUNWICH PORT N 63 NS ✓ S.L.																														
○		**Marlon Park** P.O. Box 112, Anerley 4230 □ *Montgomery Rd. Ext.*	0391	3596/3477	○					○	○		○	○				○			42			○					○		○	
◆		**Saame Park** P.O. Box 62, Pretoria 0001	0391(012)	3325(38891)	◆					◆				◆				◆		48			◆						◆		◆	
		SWELLENDAM C 58 D5 ↑ 152m																														
▲		**Bontebok National Park** National Parks Board, P.O. Box 787, Pretoria 0001	012	44-1194					▲		▲			▲				▲			20						▲	▲			▲	
△		**Die Stroom** Caretaker, P.O. Box 20 (6740) □ ± *6 km from Swellendam*	02912 E	484		△					△			△				△			△				△				△			△
★	🚐	**Swellendam Municipal** Manager, P.O. Box 20 (6740) □ *Glenbarry Rd.*	02912 E	484		★					★		★	★					★		100			★				★			★	
		SWINBURNE O 67 C2 ↘ 1646m																														
■		**Montrose** P.O. Box 21 (3395) □ *On National Rd.*	T	19	■							■		■					■	25			■					■			■	
		TARKASTAD C 62 D4 ↘ 1293m																														
●		**Tarkastad Municipal** P.O. Box 21 (5370)	04582 E	33		●							●			●		●		10		●	●						●		●	
		THABA NCHU B 66 D4 ↗ 1498m																														
◆		**Giel de Wet** P.O. Box 22 (9780)	05262 E	1530		◆						◆		◆					◆	30		30		◆					◆		◆	
		THABAZIMBI T 68 B5 ● 821m																														
▲	🚐	**Ben Alberts Nature Reserve** P.O. Box 50 (0380) □ *7 km from Thabazimbi*	014232 E	162	▲							▲		▲					▲		100			▲					▲		▲	
		THE BATHS C 58 B4 ✓ 170m																														
★		**The Baths** McGregor & Co., P.O. Box 133, Citrusdal 7340 □ *20 km from Citrusdal*	02662 E	1512	★						★	★		★	★				★	8							★		★			★

CAMP SITE FACILITIES: I = In-Season only; O = Out-of-Season only

SPORTING AND RECREATIONAL FACILITIES: S = On Site; N = Nearby (Up to 20 km away)

33 SEASONS: OUT-OF-SEASON CLOSING DATE	34 RE-OPENING DATE	35 TERMS FOR BOOKINGS: BOOKINGS ACCP./PEAK SNS.–SEE NOTE 2	36 DEPOSIT REQUIRED	37 REFUNDED IF CANCELLED–SEE NOTE 3	38 CARAVAN PARK/CAMPING SITE TARIFFS (See heading): MAXIMUM IN-SEASON TARIFF	39 MAXIMUM OUT-OF-SEASON TARIFF	40 REDUCTIONS ALLOWED FOR: LONG PERIODS OF STAY	41 GROUPS–SEE NOTE 4	42 AA CARNET HOLDERS–SEE NOTE 5	43 OTHERS (ON APPLICATION)	44 RESTAURANT FACILITIES: ON SITE	45 WITHIN 5 km OF SITE	46 MORE THAN 5 km FROM SITE	47 TEAROOM/CAFE: ON SITE	48 WITHIN 5 km OF SITE	49 MORE THAN 5 km FROM SITE	50 SHOPPING FACILITIES (Provisions): ON SITE	51 WITHIN 5 km OF SITE	52 MORE THAN 5 km FROM SITE	53 ADDITIONAL ACCOMMODATION AVAILABLE: BUNGALOWS	54 CABINS	55 COTTAGES (RONDAVELS)	56 CHALETS	57 ADDITIONAL ACCOMMODATION TARIFF (See heading): MAXIMUM IN-SEASON TARIFF	58 MAXIMUM OUT-OF-SEASON TARIFF	59 CARAVANS TO RENT ON SITE–SEE PAGES 8–11	60 DRINKING WATER: PIPED	61 OTHER	62 BATHS: HOT AND COLD	63 COLD ONLY	64 SHOWERS: HOT AND COLD	65 COLD ONLY	66 WATERBORNE SANITATION	67 WASHBASINS	68 DISHWASHING FACILITIES	69 LAUNDRY AND IRONING FACILITIES–SEE NOTE 6	70 WASHING MACHINES	71 SITE LIT	72 PLUGS FOR RAZORS (VOLTAGE)	73 REFRIGERATORS	74 FIREWOOD/CHARCOAL	75 OPEN FIRE FORBIDDEN	76 CAMP FIRE PERMITTED	77 BRAAI PLACES PROVIDED	78 KITCHEN/COOKING FACILITIES	79 PETROL PUMP ON SITE	80 PETROL PUMP NEARBY	81 CAR REPAIR SHOP NEARBY	82 CAR SERVICING NEARBY	83 GAS SERVICE NEARBY	84 FIRST AID/HOSPITAL/DOCTOR NEARBY	85 POST OFFICE NEARBY	86 SITE GUARDED	87 PETS ALLOWED	88 NON-WHITE SERVANTS: SERVANTS PERMITTED–SEE NOTE 7	89 SERVANTS ACCOM.–SEE NOTE 7	90 SERVANTS FOR HIRE–SEE NOTE 7	91 TYPE OF VEHICLE PERMITTED: CAR AND TRAILER	92 TRUCK 'HORSE' AND SEMI-TRAILER	93 SELF-PROPELLED CARAVANS	94 CHILDRENS' PLAYGROUND	95 TENNIS	96 CINEMA/DRIVE-IN/TV-ROOM–SEE NOTE 8	97 HORSE-RIDING	98 GAMES ROOM	99 TRAMPOLINE	100 BOWLS	101 HOT SPRINGS	102 GOLF: GOLF COURSE–SEE NOTE 9	103 NUMBER OF HOLES	104 MINIATURE	105 MASHIE	106 PUTT-PUTT	107 FISHING: FRESHWATER–SEE NOTE 10	108 SEA–SEE NOTE 11	109 GOGGLE	110 LICENCE REQUIRED	111 SWIMMING: SWIMMING POOL	112 SEA BATHING	113 CHILDRENS' POOL	114 ADULTS ONLY	115 SHARK NETS AT BEACH	116 BOATING: BOATS FOR HIRE	117 POWER	118 SAILING	119 CANOEING	120 PLACES OF INTEREST: HISTORIC	121 SCIENTIFIC	122 NATURAL	123 NOTES
					C	C						□			□			□									□	□	□		□		□	□	□	□		□	□		□			□			□	□	□	□		□		□	□	□		□	□	□			N																										□	
					C	C					○	○	○	○	○	○		○	○								○		○		○		○	○	○	○		○			○		○	○			○	○	○		○	○		○	○			○	○	○	S	N	N	S		S												S		S					S	S				
		◇			C	C							◇			◇			◇								◇		◇		◇		◇	◇	◇	◇		◇				◇	◇	◇			◇	◇	◇	◇		◇	◇	◇	◇			◇		◇	N	N	N	N	S		N		N		◇			S			◇													
		△		△	B	B							△			△			△	△				B-D	B-D		△			△		△	△	△	△					△	△		△	△			△	△	△			△	△		△			△	△	△	N																	S		N							△	△	△	
		■	■		E	D	■	■				■			■		■			■	■		■	G	E	■	■		■		■		■	■	■	■		■	220	■	■	■	■	■			■	■	■	■		■	■				■	■	■	■	S	N	N	N	N	N	N		N	18				N	N		■	S		S							■	■	■	
		□	□	□	C	C	□	□			□				□			□		□		□		E	E		□		□		□		□	□	□	□				□	□		□	□			□	□	□	□		□		□	□			□	□	□		S	N	S			N		N	18				N	N	N	□	S	□								□	□	□	
		○			B	B						○	○			○			○								○							○								○	○	○			○	○	○	○		○			○			○	○	○		N					N																						○	
					A	A	◇					◇			◇			◇									◇				◇		◇	◇		◇		◇					◇	◇				◇	◇		◇	◇		◇	◇			◇	◇	◇	N	N					N		N	18	◇				N			S		S							◇			
		△	△	△	D	C					△			△			△			△		△		D-E	D-E		△		△		△		△	△	△	△		△				△					△	△	△	△					△			△	△	△							N							N	N	N	△		△					N	N	N			△	
		★	★		E	E	★	★	R	★		★	★		★	★	★	★	★							★	★		★		★		★	★	★	★		★			★		★	★		★	★		★	★	★	★	★	★			★	★	★	★	N		N	S	S		N		N	18				S	N	N			★				S	S	S	S			★	
		□	□	□	C	C						□			□			□									□		□		□		□	□	□			□			□						□		□	□		□	□		□			□		□															S			S	□									□	□	
		○	○	○	G	E	○					○			○			○									○	○	○		○		○	○	○	○		○	220		○	○	○				○	○	○	○	○	○	○		○	○	○	○	○	○	S	N	S	N	S		N		N	9	○	○	○	N	N		○	N	○	N		○	N	N		N	○		○	
		◆	◆		G	C	◆					◆			◆			◆									◆		◆		◆		◆	◆	◆	◆		◆	◆		◆	◆	◆				◆	◆	◆	◆	◆	◆		◆			◆	◆	◆	◆	S	N	N	N	S	N	N		N	9	◆		◆		N	N		S	◆	S		◆	N		N	N			◆	
		▲	▲	▲	C	C					▲			▲			▲					▲		G-J	G-J		▲				▲		▲	▲	▲	▲					▲		▲	▲			▲	▲		▲	▲	▲	▲					▲	▲	▲																			▲	S							▲	▲	▲	
		△	△	△	C	C					△			△			△										△		△		△		△	△	△						△		△	△		△				△	△		△					△	△	△																														△	
					B	B						☆						☆									☆					☆	☆	☆	☆						☆		☆	☆			☆							☆				☆	☆	☆														S										S	S	S	☆		☆	
		□	□	□	E	C	□	□		□		□		□	□	□	□	□	□								□	□	□		□		□	□	□	□		□	□		□	□	□	□			□	□	□	□	□	□	□	□	□		□	□	□	□	S	N	N	N	N	N	N		N	18	□			N	N	N		S	□	S					N	N	□	□	□	
		●	●	●	X	X						●		●	●	●	●	●	●				●	X	X		●		●		●		●	●	●	●		●	220		●	●	●	●			●	●	●	●	●	●	●					●	●	●	S	N	N	N			N		N	18				N	N	N	●		●	N							●	●	●	
		◆	◆	◆	E	E	◆				◆			◆			◆					◆		X	X		◆	◆	◆	◆	◆	◆	◆	◆	◆						◆		◆	◆			◆	◆	◆	◆	◆	◆	◆		◆			◆	◆	◆	S	N												S	S	S			◆	S				S	S	S	◆		◆	
		A	A	A	D	D			R			▲			▲			▲		▲				I-J	I-J		▲		▲		▲		▲	▲	▲	▲				▲	▲			▲			▲	▲	▲	▲			▲	▲	▲		▲	▲	▲	▲	N	N	N			N	N		N	9					N	N			▲				N	N	N	N	▲	▲	▲	
					B	B						★			★			★									★				★		★	★	★	★		★					★	★			★	★	★	★	★	★		★	★			★	★	★		N	N															S		S										
		■			A	A	■					■			■			■									■		■		■		■	■	■	■		■	220				■	■			■	■	■	■		■		■				■	■	■			N				N		N	9																	■		■	
		○	○	○	H	E	○			○			○		○	○		○	○								○		○		○		○	○	○	○		○			○		○	○			○	○	○	○	○	○	○					○	○	○	S	N	I		S		N		N	18					N	N	○		○			○							○	
		◆	◆		E-H	A-D				◆			◆			◆	◆						◆	J	E		◆		◆		◆		◆	◆	◆	◆		◆	◆		◆			◆			◆	◆	◆	◆		◆						◆		◆	S	N	S		S	N	N		N	18				N	N	N		S				◆							◆	
					C	C							▲			▲											▲				▲		▲	▲							▲	▲	▲	▲		▲				▲	▲		▲					▲	▲	▲																														▲	
		△			B	B							△			△			△									△				△	△	△									△	△			△	△	△		△	△		△	△			△		△	N	N					N		N	9				N			△							N		N	△		△	
		★			C	C	★					★			★			★		★				E	E		★		★		★		★	★	★	★		★	220		★		★	★			★	★	★	★	★	★		★	★		★	★		★	N	N	N				N		N	9				N			★							N	N	N	★		★	
		■			C	C					■			■				■				■		A	A		■		■		■		■	■	■	■		■	220		■		■	■		■		■	■	■	■	■	■	■	■			■	■	■	S	S	N	N	N	N	S		N	18				S			■	S		S			N			N	■	■	■	
					X	X						●			●			●									●					●	●	●				●					●	●			●	●	●	●	●	●		●	●		●	●	●	●		N					N		N	9								S		S										
					B	B	◆						◆	◆					◆								◆		◆		◆		◆	◆	◆	◆		◆			◆		◆	◆			◆	◆	◆			◆	◆	◆				◆		◆	S	N												N			◆	S		S							◆		◆	
		▲	▲		C	C	▲	▲						▲	▲	▲			▲								▲		▲		▲		▲	▲	▲	▲		▲			▲		▲	▲			▲	▲	▲			▲	▲	▲	▲			▲		▲	S	N	N				N		S	9				N			▲	S		S								▲	▲	
June	Sept.	★	★		B	B	★						★			★	★	★	★	★				C-D	C-D		★	★	★				★	★	★					★	★		★	★	★												★	★		★		★		N						S						N			★	S											★	

CARAVAN PARKS AND CAMPING SITES

Establishments marked thus 🚐 have the Caravan Club of South Africa recommendation – see page 17
Establishments marked thus Ⓒ recognise the AA Camping Carnet – see page 16 and also refer to column 42

CARAVAN PARK / CAMP SITE TARIFF CODE – See columns 38–39 (Subject to alteration)

A = Up to R1	C = R2–R3	E = R4–R5	G = R6–R7	I = R8–R9	K = R10–R16
B = R1–R2	D = R3–R4	F = R5–R6	H = R7–R8	J = R9–R10	O = FREE
					X = On Application

Charges are based on a family of 2 adults and 2 children under 12 years

ADDITIONAL ACCOMMODATION TARIFF CODE – See columns 57–59 (Subject to alteration)

eg. Bungalows, Cabins, Cottages, Chalets, etc.

A = R1–R3	C = R5–R7	E = R9–R11	G = R13–R15	I = R17–R19	K = R21–R30
B = R3–R5	D = R7–R9	F = R11–R13	H = R15–R17	J = R19–R21	X = On Application

NB: Where the tariff is given in *italics* it is per person, otherwise per unit

NOTE 1 – **Columns 18, 19, 20,** – Where a symbol appears instead of a number it means stands are available but not demarcated or number of stands has not been provided
NOTE 2 – **Column 35** – A = Bookings accepted for additional accommodation only i.e. cottages, bungalows, etc.
NOTE 3 – **Column 37** – Deposit refunded under certain conditions eg. less 10% ; if site is re-let ; if cancelled well in advance (up to 2 months) or on a doctor's certificate
NOTE 4 – **Column 41** – Reductions allowed on application for youth, church, school or sport groups or caravan rallies
NOTE 5 – **Column 42** – R = Reduction in tariff of between 5 – 10 % to Carnet holders
O = Reduction Out-of-Season only
NOTE 6 – **Column 69** – L = Laundry facilities only
NOTE 7 – **Columns 88, 89, 90,** – I = In-Season only ; O = Out-of-Season only
NOTE 8 – **Column 96** – Applicable In-Season only at some establishments
NOTE 9 – **Column 102** – See section on golf in Outdoor Holiday Guide
NOTE 10 – **Column 107** – See section on freshwater angling in Outdoor Holiday Guide
NOTE 11 – **Column 108** – See section on coastal angling in Outdoor Holiday Guide

ABBREVIATIONS

C = CAPE PROVINCE
N = NATAL
O = ORANGE FREE STATE
T = TRANSVAAL
B = BOPHUTHATSWANA
X = TRANSKEI

TELEPHONE CODE: T = DIAL 0020, BOOK TRUNK CALL; E = DIAL CODE, ASK EXCHANGE FOR NO.

Column headings: 1 Telephone code; 2 Telephone number; OWNED OR SUPERVISED BY: 3 Privately owned, 4 Municipality, 5 Divisional council, 6 Provincial administration, 7 Parks board; SITE DESCRIPTION – LOCALITY: 8 Beach in immediate vicinity, 9 Beside river, lake or dam, 10 In or near mountain area, 11 Within built-up area; NATURE OF GROUND: 12 Grass, 13 Gravel, 14 Sand; SHADE: 15 Unshaded, 16 Partly shaded, 17 Extensively shaded; NO. OF STANDS: 18 Caravans only – see note 1, 19 Caravans and/or tents, 20 Tents only – see note 1; ACCESSIBILITY – APPROXIMATE DISTANCE FROM MAIN ROAD TO SITE: 21 On main rd, 22 Within 1 km, 23 Within 5 km, 24 Within 10 km, 25 Within 15 km; SURFACE OF ROAD APPROACH: 26 Tar, 27 Gravel, 28 Sand; CONDITION OF ROAD APPROACH: 29 Good, 30 Fair, Poor

		Establishment	1	2	3	4	5	6	7	8	9	10	11	12	13	14	15	16	17	18	19	20	21	22	23	24	25	26	27	28	29	30
		THE WILLOWS C 59 C5 ↗ S.L.																														
□		**The Willows Holiday Resort** P.O. Box 318, Port Elizabeth 6000	041	36-1035			□			□				□			□			58			□					□			□	
		TOUWS RIVER C 58 C5 ↖ 772m																														
○	Ⓒ	**Oom Loots** P.O. Box 8 (6880)	02382 E	49	○							○	○	○	○	○		○		20		12	○					○			○	
		TRAFALGAR BEACH N 63 NS ↙ S.L.																														
◇	Ⓒ	**Port O'Call** P.O. Box 82, Ramsgate 4285	0393	3731	◇					◇				◇					◇		90			◇				◇			◇	
		TRICHARDTSDAL T 69 B3 ↖ 625m																														
△		**Tourist Motel** P.O. Box 199, Tzaneen 0850 □ *±20 km from Trichardtsdal*	0152302 E	2423	△						△	△		△					△		30		△					△			△	
		TROMPSBURG O 62 B3 ↗ 1452m																														
☆		**Trompsburg Municipal Camping Site** Bookings not accepted □ *Voortrekker St*	05812 E	23		☆							☆		☆			☆			50				☆				☆		☆	
		TSHIPISE T 70 B5 ↙ 534m																														
□		**Tshipise Mineral Baths** General Manager, P.O. Box 4 (0901)	T	4				□				□			□			□			285		□					□			□	
		TUGELA N 63 A4 ↑ S.L.																														
○		**Tugela Mouth North Bank** P.O. Mandini 4490	032432 E	1703	○					○			○	○			○	○		10						○			○			○
		TULBAGH C 58 C4 ↖ 122m																														
◇		**Tulbagh Municipal** P.O. Box 3 (6820)	02362 E	20		◇							◇	◇				◇		40	40	40			◇				◇		◇	
		TZANEEN T 69 A3 ↙ 724m																														
△		**Fairview** P.O. Box 329 (0850)	01523	2-0085	△						△			△	△			△			20			△				△			△	
		UITENHAGE C 59 B5 ↙ 52m																														
☆		**Magennis** P.O. Box 45 (6230) □ *Cnr. High/Church Sts.*	0422	26011 x276		☆							☆	☆				☆			10		☆					☆			☆	
■		**Springs Pleasure Resort** P.O. Box 45 (6230)	0422	2-4475		■						■		■				■			20			■				■			■	
		UMHLANGA ROCKS N 63 NS ↗ S.L.																														
●		**Golden Sea Horse** P.O. Box 38 (4320) □ *1 Park Drive*	031	51-1721	●					●			●	●		●			●	36				●				●			●	
○	🚐	**Umhlanga Rocks** P.O. Box 13 (4320) □ *Weaver Crescent*	031	51-1533	○					○			○	○		○		○		36				○				○			○	
		UMTATA X 62 C6 → 699m																														
◇		**Umtata Municipal** P.O. Box 45 (5100)	0471	3204		◇							◇	◇				◇			50		◇					◇			◇	
		UMTENTWENI N 63 NS ↙ 2m																														
△		**Umtentweni** P.O. Box 44, Sea Park 4241	0391	5-0531	△					△	△			△				△		30			△					△			△	
		UMZUMBE N 63 NS ↙ 94m																														
☆		**Hidaway** P.O. Umzumbe 4225	0391	6603	☆					☆			☆	☆		☆		☆	☆		33			☆				☆	☆		☆	☆
		UNIONDALE C 59 B3 ↙ 732m																														
□		**Uniondale Municipal** Town Clerk, P.O. Box 13 (6460)	04462 E	24		□							□	□					□		50			□					□		□	
		UPINGTON C 65 C3 ← 805m																														
○		**Die Eiland** P.O. Box 17 (8800) □ *1 km from Upington*	0541	3358		○					○			○	○				○		50			○				○			○	
		UVONGO N 63 NS ↙ S.L.																														
◇		**Oasis** P.O. Box 67 (4270)	0393	5-0778	◇					◇				◇		◇			◇	28		6	◇					◇			◇	
▲		**Uvongo** P.O. Box 22 (4270) □ *Collins St.*	0393	5-0424	▲					▲				▲					▲	42			▲					▲			▲	
		VAAL DAM: See respectively: ● **Aloe Fjord T** ● **Deneysville T** ● **Oranjeville O**																														
		VANRHYNSDORP C 60 C6 ↘ 84m																														
☆		**Gifberg** P.O. Box 66 (8170)	02712 E	25/79	☆								☆	☆	☆			☆		40		☆		☆					☆		☆	
		VAN STADENS RIVER MOUTH C 59 B5 ↙ S.L.																														
□		**Van Stadens River Mouth** Divisional Council, P.O. Box 318, Port Elizabeth 6000 □ *± 42 km from Port*	T	2-8911			□			□	□	□		□				□		40		100					□	□			□	
		VANSTADENSRUS O 62 A4 ↘ 1471m																														
○		**Bekkers** P.O. Box 16 (9945)	T	34 or 1522	○						○	○		○	○				○	12	12	12	○						○		○	
		VENTERSBURG O 66 C5 ↖ 1433m																														
◇	🚐	**Willem Pretorius Game Reserve** Bookings not accepted Enquiries: Resort Manager, P.O. Willem Pretorius Game Reserve, Via Ventersburg 9451 □ *Allemanskraal Dam*	017142 E	6				◇			◇			◇				◇		◇	◇	◇				◇		◇			◇	
		VENTERSTAD C 62 B3 ↖ 1219m																														
△	Ⓒ	**Venterstad Municipal** Town Clerk, P.O. Box 24 (5990) □ *Cnr. Bingle/Tennant Sts.*	T	24		△							△		△				△	20	20	15		△					△		△	
		VEREENIGING T 66 A5 ↖ 1448m																														
☆	🚐	**Dickinson Park** Town Clerk, P.O. Box 35 (1930) □ *Lewis Ave.*	016	22-2251 x471		☆					☆			☆				☆		140		50		☆				☆	☆		☆	☆
		VICTORIA BAY C 59 NS ← S.L.																														
□		**Sea Glimpse Holiday Resort** P.O. Box 307, George 6530 □ *Victoria Bay Rd.*	0441	4660	□					□		□	□	□	□			□	□	8		□		□				□			□	
●		**Victoria Bay** Divisional Council, P.O. Box 12, George 6530	0441	3001			●			●		●	●	●	●			●			52			●				●			●	
		VICTORIA WEST C 61 C5 ← 1261m																														
◆		**Victoria West Municipal** P.O. Box 13 (7070) □ *Mugglestone Ave.*	02042 E	26		◆							◆		◆			◆		39	7			◆					◆		◆	
		VILJOENSDRIF O 66 A5 ↖ 1490m																														
▲		**Groen Oewers** P.O. Box 17 (9580) □ *On Vaal River, 14 km from Viljoensdrif*	T	2532	▲						▲			▲				▲		150		100		▲					▲		▲	
		VILLIERS O 66 B6 ↑ 1430m																														
★		**Villiers Municipal** Town Clerk, P.O. Box 23 (9840)	01382 E	202		★					★			★	★				★		250	150		★					★		★	

…N THROUGHOUT THE YEAR

SEASONS		TERMS FOR BOOKINGS			CARAVAN PARK/CAMPING SITE TARIFFS (See heading)		REDUCTIONS ALLOWED FOR				RESTAURANT FACILITIES			TEAROOM/CAFE			SHOPPING FACILITIES (Provisions)			ADDITIONAL ACCOMMODATION AVAILABLE				ADDITIONAL ACCOMMODATION TARIFF (See heading)			CAMP SITE FACILITIES (I = In-Season only; O = Out-of-Season only)																												NON-WHITE SERVANTS			TYPE OF VEHICLE PERMITTED			SPORTING AND RECREATIONAL FACILITIES (S = On Site; N = Nearby (Up to 20 km away))								GOLF					FISHING				SWIMMING					BOATING				PLACES OF INTEREST			NOTES
OUT-OF-SEASON CLOSING DATE	RE-OPENING DATE	BOOKINGS ACCP./PEAK SNS. – SEE NOTE 2	DEPOSIT REQUIRED	REFUNDED IF CANCELLED – SEE NOTE 3	MAXIMUM IN-SEASON TARIFF	MAXIMUM OUT-OF-SEASON TARIFF	LONG PERIODS OF STAY	GROUPS – SEE NOTE 4	AA CARNET HOLDERS – SEE NOTE 5	OTHERS (ON APPLICATION)	ON SITE	WITHIN 5 km OF SITE	MORE THAN 5 km FROM SITE	ON SITE	WITHIN 5 km OF SITE	MORE THAN 5 km FROM SITE	ON SITE	WITHIN 5 km OF SITE	MORE THAN 5 km FROM SITE	BUNGALOWS	CABINS	COTTAGES (RONDAVELS)	CHALETS	MAXIMUM IN-SEASON TARIFF	MAXIMUM OUT-OF-SEASON TARIFF	CARAVANS TO RENT ON SITE – SEE PAGES 8 – 11	DRINKING WATER: PIPED	DRINKING WATER: OTHER	BATHS: HOT AND COLD	BATHS: COLD ONLY	SHOWERS: HOT AND COLD	SHOWERS: COLD ONLY	WATERBORNE SANITATION	WASHBASINS	DISHWASHING FACILITIES	LAUNDRY AND IRONING FACILITIES – SEE NOTE 6	WASHING MACHINES	SITE LIT	PLUGS FOR RAZORS (VOLTAGE)	REFRIGERATORS	FIREWOOD/CHARCOAL	OPEN FIRE FORBIDDEN	CAMP FIRE PERMITTED	BRAAI PLACES PROVIDED	KITCHEN/COOKING FACILITIES	PETROL PUMP ON SITE	PETROL PUMP NEARBY	CAR REPAIR SHOP NEARBY	CAR SERVICING NEARBY	GAS SERVICE NEARBY	FIRST AID/HOSPITAL/DOCTOR NEARBY	POST OFFICE NEARBY	SITE GUARDED	PETS ALLOWED	SERVANTS PERMITTED – SEE NOTE 7	SERVANTS ACCOM. – SEE NOTE 7	SERVANTS FOR HIRE – SEE NOTE 7	CAR AND TRAILER	TRUCK 'HORSE' AND SEMI-TRAILER	SELF-PROPELLED CARAVANS	CHILDRENS' PLAYGROUND	TENNIS	CINEMA/DRIVE-IN/TV-ROOM – SEE NOTE 8	HORSE-RIDING	GAMES ROOM	TRAMPOLINE	BOWLS	HOT SPRINGS	GOLF COURSE – SEE NOTE 9	NUMBER OF HOLES	MINIATURE	MASHIE	PUTT-PUTT	FRESHWATER – SEE NOTE 10	SEA – SEE NOTE 11	GOGGLE	LICENCE REQUIRED	SWIMMING POOL	SEA BATHING	CHILDRENS' POOL	ADULTS ONLY	SHARK NETS AT BEACH	BOATS FOR HIRE	POWER	SAILING	CANOEING	HISTORIC	SCIENTIFIC	NATURAL	
33	34	35	36	37	38	39	40	41	42	43	44	45	46	47	48	49	50	51	52	53	54	55	56	57	58	59	60	61	62	63	64	65	66	67	68	69	70	71	72	73	74	75	76	77	78	79	80	81	82	83	84	85	86	87	88	89	90	91	92	93	94	95	96	97	98	99	100	101	102	103	104	105	106	107	108	109	110	111	112	113	114	115	116	117	118	119	120	121	122	123
		□	□	□	D-G	C-E	□				□			□			□			□		□	□	C-D	B-C		□				□	□	□	□		□			□				□	□			□	□	□	□		□	□					□	□	□	S				S				N						N	N	N		□					N						
		○			C	C	○	○			○			○			○			○	○	○		*B*	*B*		○	○	○		○		○	○	○	○		○	○					○		○		○	○	○	○	○	○	○	○			○	○	○	S	N	N		S	S	N											N		S							○	○	○	
		◇	◇	◇	I	D		◇	R				◇	◇			◇									◇	◇		◇		◇		◇	◇	◇	◇					◇		◇	◇			◇	◇	◇	◇	◇	◇	◇				◇	◇		◇		N	S		S		N		N	18				N	N	N	N	N	◇			◇						◇	◇	
		△	△		B	B	△	△			△																△		△	△	△			△	△	△					△		△	△							△				△	△	△	△	△	△														N			△	S		S								△		
					O	O						☆			☆				☆								☆						☆										☆				☆	☆	☆			☆		☆				☆	☆	☆	N	N	N				N		N	9								N												
					E	E				□	□			□			□					□		B-H	B-H		□		□		□		□	□	□	□		□	220		□		□	□		□	□	□	□	□	□	□	□		□	□		□	□	□	S	S	S	S			S	S						N			□	S		S				N	N	N			□	
		○	○		C	C	○					○				○		○	○								○		○		○		○	○	○	○		○					○	○			○										○	○	○	○															N				○					N		N	○		○	
					C	C	◇	◇					◇			◇			◇								◇		◇		◇		◇	◇	◇	◇		◇			◇		◇	◇			◇	◇	◇	◇	◇	◇		◇	◇		◇	◇		◇	N	N					N							N			◇	S		S				N	N	N	◇		◇	
		△			B	B	△						△			△			△								△		△		△		△	△	△	△		△	△	△	△		△	△			△	△	△	△			△	△			△	△		△				S					N	18								S												
					B	B							☆			☆		☆	☆								☆		☆		☆		☆	☆	☆	☆		☆					☆	☆			☆	☆	☆			☆		☆	☆			☆		☆	N	S	N						N	18								N		N										
		■	■		C	C								■			■			■				B-C	A-C		■		■		■		■	■	■	■		■					■	■							■			■	■			■		■	S	S							N	18								S		S									■	
		●	●		G	D					●	●	●	●	●	●	●	●	●								●		●		●				●	●	●		220		●	●		●			●	●	●	●		●			●	●		●	●	●	N	N	N	N	N	N	N		N	18	●	●	●	N	N	N	●	N	●	N		●	N		N	N	●	●	●	
		○	○		F	E						○	○		○	○		○	○								○		○		○		○	○	○	○		○	○		○	○		○			○	○	○	○		○	○	○	○	○		○	○	○	S	N	N	N	N	N	N		N	18	○	○	○		N	N	○	N	○	N		○					○	○	○	
					C	C	◇	◇				◇			◇			◇									◇		◇		◇		◇	◇	◇	◇		◇					◇				◇	◇	◇			◇		◇	◇			◇		◇	N	N	N				N		N	18								N		N					N	N			◇	
		△	△		F	F	△					△			△			△	△								△		△		△		△	△	△	△		△	110/220			△		△			△	△	△	△		△	△							△	N	N	N				N		N	18					N	N			△	N		△			N	N			△	
		☆	☆		G	D	☆	☆				☆	☆			☆		☆	☆								☆		☆		☆		☆	☆	☆	☆		☆	220		☆	☆	☆	☆			☆	☆	☆	☆		☆		☆			☆	☆		☆	S	N	N	N		N	N		N	18					N	N	☆	S	☆	N		☆							☆	
					A	A							□			□			□								□		□		□		□	□	□			□					□	□			□	□	□	□		□	□	□				□	□	□	N	N																									□			
		○	○		E	E						○	○		○	○		○	○	○	○			K	K		○		○		○		○	○	○	○		○	○		○		○	○			○	○	○	○	○	○	○	○	○		○	○	○	○	S	S	N				S		N	18				S			○	S		N				S	S	S	○	○	○	
		◇	◇		H	C	◇	◇				◇			◇			◇			◇		◇	X	X	◇	◇		◇		◇		◇	◇	◇	◇	◇	◇	◇	◇		◇		◇			◇	◇	◇	◇	◇	◇		◇			◇	◇		◇	N	N	N	N	S		N		N	18	◇		◇		N	N			◇	N		◇	N			N			◇	
		▲	▲		G	D						▲			▲			▲									▲		▲		▲		▲	▲	▲	▲		▲	220				▲	▲			▲	▲	▲	▲	▲	▲			▲	▲		▲	▲	▲	S	N	N		S	N	N		N	18			▲		N			N	▲	N		▲	N	N	N	N			▲	
		☆			B	B						☆			☆			☆		☆				B	B		☆		☆		☆		☆	☆	☆	☆		☆	☆		☆		☆	☆			☆	☆	☆	☆		☆		☆	☆		☆	☆	☆	☆									N					S																
		□			C	B	□							□					□			□		D	C		□		□		□			□		□							□	□						□	□							□	□	□			N		S									N	N	N			□							S			□	
		○	○	○	B	B					○			○			○					○	○	E	E		○	○	○				○	○				○			○	○	○	○		○	○	○		○		○	○	○	○		○	○	○	○	S	N												N			○										○	○	○	
					C	C					◇			◇			◇					◇	◇	B-F	B-F		◇	◇	◇		◇		◇	◇	◇	◇		◇			◇		◇	◇		◇				◇	◇	◇	◇					◇	◇	◇	S	S	S			S	S		S	18			◇	S			◇	S		S				S	S	S	◇		◇	
					A	A							△			△			△								△		△		△		△	△	△								△											△				△	△	△	N	N					N		N	9	△			N			△							N	N	N				
					B	B	☆					☆			☆			☆									☆		☆		☆		☆	☆	☆	☆		☆			☆	☆		☆			☆	☆	☆	☆	☆	☆	☆	☆	☆			☆		☆	S			S		S								S			☆							S		S	☆		☆	
		□	□	□	E	C	□	□				□	□		□	□		□	□			□		*B*	*B*	□	□		□		□		□	□	□	□		□		□	□		□	□	□		□	□	□	□		□					□	□	□	□	S	N	N	N	N	N	N		N	18					N	N			□	N			N	N	N	N	□	□	□	
		●	●	●	F	D						●			●			●									●				●		●	●	●	L					●	●		●						●			●					●	●	●															N	N			●	S										
		◆	◆		D	D	◆	◆				◆	◆		◆	◆			◆			◆		*A*	*A*		◆		◆		◆		◆	◆	◆	◆		◆	220		◆		◆	◆					◆	◆		◆	◆	◆	◆	◆		◆		◆	S	N	N				N		N	18				N			◆	N		N								◆	◆	
		▲	▲		E	D	▲	▲		▲	▲			▲			▲				▲	▲		D	D		▲			▲	▲		▲	▲	▲	▲		▲			▲		▲	▲	▲		▲	▲	▲	▲	▲	▲	▲	▲	▲		▲	▲	▲	▲	S		S	S	S									S			▲	S					S	S	S	S			▲	
		★	★		C	C	★	★					★			★		★		★	★	★		C-E	C-E		★		★		★		★	★	★	★		★	★	★	★		★	★				★	★	★	★	★	★	★	★			★		★	S	N	N		S				N		★		★	N			★	S		S						N			★	

CARAVAN PARKS AND CAMPING SITES

Establishments marked thus (CC) have the Caravan Club of South Africa recommendation – see page 17
Establishments marked thus (AA) recognise the AA Camping Carnet – see page 16 and also refer to column 42

CARAVAN PARK / CAMP SITE TARIFF CODE – See columns 38–39 (Subject to alteration)

A = Up to R1 | B = R1–R2 | C = R2–R3 | D = R3–R4 | E = R4–R5 | F = R5–R6 | G = R6–R7 | H = R7–R8 | I = R8–R9 | J = R9–R10 | K = R10–R16 | O = FREE | X = On Application

Charges are based on a family of 2 adults and 2 children under 12 years

ADDITIONAL ACCOMMODATION TARIFF CODE – See columns 57–59 (Subject to alteration)

eg. Bungalows, Cabins, Cottages, Chalets, etc.

A = R1–R3 | B = R3–R5 | C = R5–R7 | D = R7–R9 | E = R9–R11 | F = R11–R13 | G = R13–R15 | H = R15–R17 | I = R17–R19 | J = R19–R21 | K = R21–R30 | X = On Application

NB: Where the tariff is given in *italics* it is per person, otherwise per unit

NOTE 1 — Columns 18, 19, 20, — Where a symbol appears instead of a number it means stands are available but not demarcated or number of stands has not been provided
NOTE 2 — Column 35 – A = Bookings accepted for additional accommodation only i.e. cottages, bungalows, etc.
NOTE 3 — Column 37 – Deposit refunded under certain conditions eg. less 10% ; if site is re-let ; if cancelled well in advance (up to 2 months) or on a doctor's certificate
NOTE 4 — Column 41 – Reductions allowed on application for youth, church, school or sport groups or caravan rallies
NOTE 5 — Column 42 – R = Reduction in tariff of between 5–10% to Carnet holders; O = Reduction Out-of-Season only
NOTE 6 — Column 69 – L = Laundry facilities only
NOTE 7 — Columns 88, 89, 90, – I = In-Season only ; O = Out-of-Season only
NOTE 8 — Column 96 — Applicable In-Season only at some establishments
NOTE 9 — Column 102 — See section on golf in Outdoor Holiday Guide
NOTE 10 — Column 107 — See section on freshwater angling in Outdoor Holiday Guide
NOTE 11 — Column 108 — See section on coastal angling in Outdoor Holiday Guide

ABBREVIATIONS
C = CAPE PROVINCE
N = NATAL
O = ORANGE FREE STATE
T = TRANSVAAL
B = BOPHUTHATSWANA
X = TRANSKEI

			TELEPHONE CODE (T = DIAL 0020, BOOK TRUNK CALL; E = DIAL CODE, ASK EXCHANGE FOR NO.)	TELEPHONE NUMBER	OWNED OR SUPERVISED BY: PRIVATELY OWNED	MUNICIPALITY	DIVISIONAL COUNCIL	PROVINCIAL ADMINISTRATION	PARKS BOARD	SITE DESCRIPTION – LOCALITY: BEACH IN IMMEDIATE VICINITY	BESIDE RIVER, LAKE OR DAM	IN OR NEAR MOUNTAIN AREA	WITHIN BUILT-UP AREA	NATURE OF GROUND: GRASS	GRAVEL	SAND	SHADE: UNSHADED	PARTLY SHADED	EXTENSIVELY SHADED	NO. OF STANDS: CARAVANS ONLY – SEE NOTE 1	CARAVANS AND/OR TENTS – SEE NOTE 1	TENTS ONLY – SEE NOTE 1	ACCESSIBILITY – APPROXIMATE DISTANCE FROM MAIN ROAD TO SITE: ON MAIN RD	WITHIN 1 km	WITHIN 5 km	WITHIN 10 km	WITHIN 15 km	SURFACE OF APPROACH ROAD: TAR	GRAVEL	SAND	CONDITION OF APPROACH: GOOD	FAIR
			1	2	3	4	5	6	7	8	9	10	11	12	13	14	15	16	17	18	19	20	21	22	23	24	25	26	27	28	29	30
		VILLIERSDORP C 58 C4 ↙ 244m																														
□		**Villiersdorp Municipal** P.O. Box 23 (7170) □ *Ham St.*	02252 E	431/2		□						□		□					□		□			□					□		□	
		VLEESBAAI C 59 C1 ↗ S.L.																														
○	(AA)	**Karmosyn** P.O. Box 333, Mossel Bay 6500 □ *35 km from Mossel Bay*	04441	3837	○					○				○				○			50						○	○			○	
		VOLKSRUST T 67 B2 → 1665m																														
◇		**Volksrust Municipal** P.O. Box 48 (2470) □ *Cnr. Bad/West St.*	013332 E	28		◇							◇	◇				◇			38			◇					◇		◇	
		VREDE O 67 B2 ← 1669m																														
△		**Vrede Municipal** Town Clerk, P.O. Box 155 (2455) □ *1 km from Vrede*	013342 E	26		△					△	△		△				△		30	△	△		△					△		△	
		VRYBURG C 66 A2 ↘ 1187m																														
☆		**Boereplaas Holiday Resort** P.O. Box 539 (8600)	01451	4206	☆									☆					☆		☆		☆						☆		☆	
■		**Mam's Roadhouse** P.O. Box 282 (8600) □ *2 km from Vryburg*	01451	3630	■										■	■	■		■		■		■						■		■	
□		**Swartfontein Recreation Resort** Manager, P.O. Box 35 (8600) □ *6 km from Vryburg*	01451	4461		□								□					□	13	10			□				□			□	
		VRYHEID N 67 B3 ↘ 1160m																														
○	(AA)	**Vryheid Municipal** P.O. Box 57 (3100) □ *Utrecht St.*	0381	2133		○							○	○					○		18			○					○		○	
		WAENHUISKRANS (ARNISTON) C 58 D5 ↙ 10m																														
◇	(AA)	**Waenhuiskrans (Arniston)** Divisional Council, P.O. Box 35, Bredasdorp 7280	02842 E	6202 (68 Bung.)			◇						◇	◇				◇		100	100		◇					◇			◇	
		WAGENDRIFT PUBLIC RESORT N See Estcourt																														
		WARMSBATHS T 68 B6 ↙ 1171m																														
★		**Klein Kariba** Manager, P.O. Box 150 (0480) □ *7 km from Warmbaths*	015332 E	571	★							★		★					★		70				★					★		★
☆		**Linga Longa Christian Holiday Farm** P.O. Box 258 (0480) □ *12 km from Warmbaths*	015332 E	6113	☆							☆		☆				☆	☆	20		10				☆		☆			☆	
■	(AA)	**Ronwil Holiday Resort** P.O. Box 417 (0480) □ *3 km from Warmbaths*	015332 E	97	■						■			■		■			■	50	50		■							■	■	
□		**Warmbaths Mineral Baths** General Manager, P.O. Box 75 (0480)	015332 E	6				□			□		□	□					□	500	80	50	□					□			□	
		WARMWATERBERG C 58 C5 ↘ 472m																														
○		**Warmwaterberg Guest Farm** P.O. Warmwaterberg (via Barrydale) 6751	02972 E	2511	○							○		○	○			○		10		10			○				○		○	
		WARRENTON T 66 C2 ↗ 1193m																														
◇	(AA)	**Warrenton Municipal** P.O. Box 10 (8530)	053332 E	1		◇					◇			◇				◇			40		◇						◇		◇	
		WATERVAL-BOVEN T 69 C3 ↙ 1471m																														
△	(AA)	**Elandskrans Holiday Resort** P.O. Box 53 (1195) □ *2 km from Waterval-Boven*	013262 E	176		△						△		△				△			115					△		△	△		△	
		WELKOM O 66 B4 ↘ 376m																														
☆	(CC)	**Welkom Municipal** Bookings not accepted □ *Disa St.*	017	2-1455		☆							☆	☆					☆	36		6		☆				☆			☆	
		WELLINGTON C 58 C4 ↙ 99m																														
□		**Katryntjiesdrif** P.O. Box 517 (7655)	0251	3-1625	□						□	□		□		□			□		500			□						□	□	
●		**Pinnie Joubert** Bookings not accepted □ *Addy St.*	0251	3-2603		●							●	●					●	65		●		●				●			●	
		WELVERDIEND T 68 D5 ← 1470m																														
◆		**Safari** P.O. Box 24 (2700) □ *Main Ave.*	01494	283	◆								◆	◆					◆	4		◆	◆					◆			◆	
		WEPENER O 62 A5 ↙ 1438m																														
▲		**Geyer Park** P.O. Box 31 (9944) □ *Spies St.*	05232	31		▲					▲		▲	▲	▲			▲		15		▲			▲			▲			▲	
		WESTONARIA T 72 NS ← 1555m																														
★		**Westonaria Dam Pleasure Resort** Bookings not accepted □ *± 5 km from Westonaria*	011	753-1129		★					★			★					★	★	★	★		★				★			★	
		WHITE RIVER T 69 C4 ↖ 962m																														
■	(AA)	**White River Municipal** Bookings not necessary Enquiries: Town Clerk, P.O. Box 2 (1240) □ *Hennie van Til St.*	013132 E	434		■							■	■					■		40		■						■		■	
		WIDENHAM N 63 NS ↗ S.L.																														
●	(CC)	**Widenham** P.O. Box 157, Umkomaas 4170 □ *2 Cheltenham Rd.*	0323	3-0351	●					●				●				●		40				●				●			●	
		WILDERNESS C 59 NS ← S.L.																														
◆		**Ebb and Flow Nature Reserve** Divisional Council, P.O. Box 12, George 6530	0441	3001			◆				◆	◆		◆				◆			75				◆			◆	◆		◆	
◇		**Island Lake** P.O. Wilderness 6560 □ *Island Lake*	0441	9194	◇					◇	◇	◇		◇				◇			55		◇					◇			◇	
▲	(CC)	**Siesta Holiday Resort** P.O. Box 35 (6560)	0441	9197	▲					▲	▲	▲		▲					▲	80				▲					▲		▲	
△		**The Lakes Holiday Resort** P.O. Box 38 (6560)	0441	9101	△					△	△	△		△				△			75		△					△			△	
		WILLEM PRETORIUS GAME RESERVE O See Ventersburg																														
☆		**WILLISTON C 61 C2 ↗ 1062m**																														
■		**Williston Municipal** Bookings not necessary □ *Mulder St.*	02052 E	3		■							■		■			■		15		■		■					■		■	
		WILLOWMORE C 59 B3 ↑ 844m																														
●		**Willowmore Municipal** P.O. Box 15 (6680) □ *Dam St.*	04942 E	4		●							●	●				●			20			●				●			●	
		WINBURG O 66 C4 → 1440m																														
◆		**Winburg Municipal** Town Clerk, P.O. Box 26 (9420) □ *Prince Edward St.*	05242 E	54 or 126		◆							◆	◆	◆			◆			40			◆				◆			◆	
		WINKLESPRUIT N 63 NS ↗ S.L.																														
▲	(CC)	**Karavana** P.O. Box 5 (4145) □ *Camp Rd.*	031	95-1747	▲					▲				▲				▲		240		▲			▲			▲			▲	
△	(CC)	**Mount Carmel** P.O. Box 14 (4145) □ *Camp Rd.*	031	95-1000	△					△				△				△		40				△					△		△	
★	(CC)	**Ocean-Call** P.O. Box 33 (4145) □ *3 Murray-Smith Rd.*	031	95-1744	★					★			★	★				★			70		★					★			★	
☆		**Oom Dick** P.O. Box 227 (4145) □ *Cnr. Camp/Eastern Glen Rd.*	031	95-1248	☆					☆	☆			☆			☆	☆			70				☆			☆			☆	

…EN THROUGHOUT THE YEAR

SEASONS · TERMS FOR BOOKINGS · CARAVAN PARK/CAMPING SITE TARIFFS (See heading) · REDUCTIONS ALLOWED FOR · RESTAURANT FACILITIES · TEAROOM/CAFE · SHOPPING FACILITIES (Provisions) · ADDITIONAL ACCOMMODATION AVAILABLE · ADDITIONAL ACCOMMODATION TARIFF (See heading) · DRINKING WATER · BATHS · SHOWERS

CAMP SITE FACILITIES — I = In-Season only; O = Out-of-Season only · NON-WHITE SERVANTS · TYPE OF VEHICLE PERMITTED

SPORTING AND RECREATIONAL FACILITIES — S = On Site; N = Nearby (Up to 20 km away) · GOLF · FISHING · SWIMMING · BOATING · PLACES OF INTEREST

33 Out-of-season closing date	34 Re-opening date	35 Bookings accp. peak sns. – see note 2	36 Deposit required	37 Refunded if cancelled – see note 3	38 Maximum in-season tariff	39 Maximum out-of-season tariff	40 Long periods of stay	41 Groups – see note 4	42 AA carnetholders – see note 5	43 Others (on application)	44 Restaurant: On site	45 Within 5 km of site	46 More than 5 km from site	47 Tearoom/cafe: On site	48 Within 5 km of site	49 More than 5 km from site	50 Shopping: On site	51 Within 5 km of site	52 More than 5 km from site	53 Bungalows	54 Cabins	55 Cottages (rondavels)	56 Chalets	57 Maximum in-season tariff	58 Maximum out-of-season tariff	59 Caravans to rent on site – see pages 8–11	60 Drinking water: Piped	61 Other	62 Baths: Hot and cold	63 Cold only	64 Showers: Hot and cold	65 Cold only	66 Waterborne sanitation	67 Washbasins	68 Dishwashing facilities	69 Laundry and ironing facilities – see note 6	70 Washing machines	71 Site lit	72 Plugs for razors (voltage)	73 Refrigerators	74 Firewood/charcoal	75 Open fire permitted	76 Camp fire forbidden	77 Braai places provided	78 Kitchen/cooking facilities	79 Petrol pump on site	80 Petrol pump nearby	81 Car repair shop nearby	82 Car servicing nearby	83 Gas service nearby	84 First aid and hospital/doctor nearby	85 Post office nearby	86 Site guarded	87 Pets allowed	88 Servants permitted – see note 7	89 Servants accom. – see note 7	90 Servants for hire – see note 7	91 Car and trailer	92 Truck, horse and semi-trailer	93 Self-propelled caravans	94 Childrens playground	95 Tennis	96 Cinema/drive-in/TV-room – see note 8	97 Horse-riding	98 Games room	99 Trampoline	100 Bowls	101 Hot springs	102 Golf course – see note 9	103 Number of holes	104 Miniature	105 Mashie	106 Putt-putt	107 Fishing: Freshwater – see note 10	108 Sea – see note 11	109 Goggle	110 Licence required	111 Swimming pool	112 Sea bathing	113 Childrens pool	114 Adults only	115 Shark nets at beach	116 Boats for hire	117 Power	118 Sailing	119 Canoeing	120 Historic	121 Scientific	122 Natural	123 Notes
					C	C						□			□			□									□		□		□		□	□	□	□		□	220				□	□			□	□	□	□	□	□	□	□	□			□		□	S	N					N											S		S									□	
		○	○	○	D	D	○	○	R								○										○		○		○		○	○	○	○		○	220		○	○	○	○			○			○		○	○	○			○	○	○	○															N	N			○						N	N			○	
		◇			B	B	◇						◇			◇			◇								◇	◇	◇		◇		◇	◇	◇	◇		◇	◇				◇				◇	◇	◇			◇	◇	◇	◇			◇		◇	S		N				N		N	9		◇		N			◇	S		S							◇			
		△			C	C						△			△			△									△		△		△		△	△	△	△					△			△			△	△	△			△	△	△	△			△	△	△	S	N	N	N			N		N	9	△			N			△	N		N						N			△	
		☆	☆		C	B	☆	☆					☆			☆			☆				☆	C	B		☆	☆	☆	☆	☆	☆	☆	☆	☆	☆	☆	☆		☆	☆	☆	☆	☆			☆	☆	☆	☆		☆	☆	☆	☆	☆	☆	☆	☆	☆	S	N	N	S			N		N	18								S		S							☆		☆	
		■			B	B	■	■			■							■									■		■		■		■	■	■	■		■		■			■	■			■	■	■				■	■	■	■		■	■	■			N				N		N	18																				
		□	□	□	C	C						□	□						□		□			*E*	*E*		□		□		□		□	□	□	□		□	220		□		□	□			□	□	□						□	□		□		□	S	N	N	N			N		N	18								S		S										
		○			B	B						○			○			○									○		○		○		○	○	○	○		○	220				○				○	○	○			○						○	○	○	S	N	N				N		N	9				N			○	N		N				N	N	N	○		○	
		◇	◇	◇	D	D			R									◇		◇				I-J	I-J		◇	◇	◇		◇		◇	◇	◇	◇				◇	◇		◇	◇			◇			◇	◇		◇	◇	◇		◇	◇	◇	◇									N	9					N	N			◇				N	N		N	◇	◇	◇	
		★	★	★	C	B				★	★			★			★					★		D-E	D-E		★		★		★		★	★		★		★	220		★		★	★			★	★	★	★	★	★	★					★	★	★	S	N	N			S	N		N	9				S				S		S						S	★		★	
		☆	☆		D	D	☆	☆		☆			☆			☆			☆								☆		☆		☆		☆	☆	☆	☆		☆	☆		☆	☆	☆	☆	☆		☆	☆	☆	☆	☆	☆	☆	☆	☆			☆		☆	S	N	N	N	S		S	N	N	9				S			☆	S			☆		N		N	N			☆	
		■	■	■	B	B	■	■	R				■	■		■	■		■			■	■	C-F	C-F		■		■		■		■	■	■	■		■	110/220		■		■	■			■	■	■	■	■	■		■	■		■	■	■	■	S	N	N		N	N	N	N	N	9				N			■	S		S									■	
		□	□	□	X	X		□			□			□			□	□				□	□	X	X		□	□	□		□		□	□	□	□	□	□	□	□	□		□	□	□		□	□	□	□	□	□	□		□	□		□			S	S	S		S		N	S	N	9		□		S			□	S		S	□						□	□	□	
		○	○	○	B	B	○	○					○			○			○			○		*A*	*A*		○		○				○	○				○				○	○	○								○		○	○			○	○	○								S										S									○	○	○	
		◇	◇		B	B		◇				◇			◇				◇			◇		A	A		◇		◇		◇		◇	◇	◇	◇		◇	220		◇		◇	◇			◇	◇	◇	◇		◇		◇	◇			◇		◇	N	N	N				N							S			◇	N		N						S				
		△			B	A					△			△			△						△	G	F		△		△		△		△	△	△	△		△	220	△			△	△			△	△	△	△	△	△	△	△	△		△	△	△	△	S	N	N				N							N			△	S		S							△	△	△	
					B	B						☆			☆			☆									☆		☆		☆		☆	☆	☆	☆		☆	220		☆	☆		☆			☆	☆	☆	☆	☆	☆	☆		☆	☆				☆		N	N				N		N	18								N		N										
		□	□		C	B		□			□				□			□		□				D	C		□	□	□		□		□	□	□	□		□		□	□		□	□	□		□	□	□	□	□	□	□		□			□	□	□	S	N	N	N	N	N	N		N	9				N			□	S		S					N	N	□		□	
					B	B		●				●			●			●									●		●		●		●	●	●	●		●			●	●	●	●	●		●	●	●	●	●	●						●	●	●	N	N	N				N		N	9								N		N							●		●	
					X	X					◆			◆			◆										◆				◆		◆	◆									◆	◆		◆		◆	◆			◆	◆	◆				◆																																
					C	C									▲			▲	▲								▲		▲		▲		▲	▲		▲		▲					▲	▲			▲	▲	▲			▲		▲				▲	▲	▲	N	N					N		N	9				N			▲	N		N										
		★			C	C							★			★			★								★		★		★		★	★	★	★		★		★	★		★	★	★		★	★	★			★	★		★		★	★	★	★	S	N	N	S	N	N	N		N	18				S			★	S		S				S	S	S			★	
					C	C	■					■			■			■									■		■		■		■	■	■	■		■	110/220		■		■	■			■	■	■	■	■	■	■	■	■			■	■	■	N	N		N		N	N	N	N	9		■		N			■	N		N				N	N	N	■		■	
		●	●		G	D	●					●			●			●									●		●		●		●	●	●	●		●	220		●		●				●	●	●	●	●	●	●					●		●	S	N	N		S		N		N	18				N	N	N	●	N	●	N								●	●	
		◆	◆	◆	E	D						◆			◆				◆	◆		◆		C	C		◆				◆		◆	◆	◆	◆		◆	◆			◆	◆	◆			◆	◆	◆	◆		◆	◆					◆	◆	◆														S											S	S			◆	
		◇	◇	◇	F	C	◇	◇		◇		◇			◇			◇				◇		E-F	C	◇	◇		◇		◇		◇	◇	◇	◇					◇		◇	◇			◇	◇	◇	◇	◇	◇		0			◇	◇	◇	◇	S	N	S	N			N		N	18				S	N	N			◇	S			S	S	S	S	◇	◇	◇	
		▲	▲	▲	F	C						▲			▲		▲	▲	▲							▲	▲	▲	▲		▲		▲	▲	▲	▲		▲	220		▲			▲			▲	▲	▲	▲	▲	▲					I	▲		▲	S	N	N	N	S		N		N	18				S	N	N	▲	N	▲				S		S	S	▲	▲	▲	
		△	△	△	G	C						△		△			△				△		△	J	H-J	△	△		△		△		△	△	△	△	△	△	110/220	△	△		△	△		△	△	△	△	△	△	△	△	0	△	△	△	△	△	△	S	N	N	N	S		N		N	18				S	S	S			△				S	S	S	S	△		△	
					B	B						■			■			■									■	■			■		■	■	■	■		■	220				■	■			■	■	■	■	■	■		■	■			■	■	■	N	N							N	9	■							S		S										
		●			C	C						●	●		●	●		●	●								●		●		●		●	●	●	●		●	220		●		●	●			●	●	●	●	●	●	●	●	●	●		●	●	●	N	N					N		N	18								N		N							●		●	
					B	B						◆	◆		◆	◆		◆	◆									◆	◆		◆		◆	◆	◆			◆	220		◆		◆	◆			◆	◆	◆	◆	◆	◆		◆	◆	◆		◆	◆	◆									N	9				N			◆	N									◆			
		▲	▲		G	C						▲		▲				▲								▲	▲		▲		▲		▲	▲	▲	▲	▲	▲	220	▲	▲			▲			▲	▲	▲	▲	▲	▲	▲	▲			▲	▲		▲		N	S		S		N		N	18				N	N			S	▲	N										
		△	△		G	E						△			△			△									△		△		△		△	△	△	△	△	△	220			△		△			△	△	△	△	△	△						△	△	△	S		S		S		N		N	18					N			S	△	S										
		★	★	★	H	G	★	★		★				★			★									★	★		★		★		★	★	★	★	★	★	220		★	★		★			★	★	★	★	★	★	★	★	0			★	★	★	S	N			S	S	N		N	18					N	N		S	★	S		★								
		☆	☆	☆	F	E	☆						☆	☆	☆	☆		☆									☆		☆		☆		☆	☆	☆	☆	☆	☆	220								☆	☆	☆			☆		☆				☆	☆	☆	S				S													S	☆											

CARAVAN PARKS AND CAMPING SITES

Establishments marked thus [Caravan Club symbol] have the Caravan Club of South Africa recommendation – see page 17. Establishments marked thus [AA symbol] recognise the AA Camping Carnet – see page 16 and also refer to column 42

CARAVAN PARK / CAMP SITE TARIFF CODE – See columns 38–39 (Subject to alteration)

A = Up to R1 | C = R2–R3 | E = R4–R5 | G = R6–R7 | I = R8–R9 | K = R10–R16
B = R1–R2 | D = R3–R4 | F = R5–R6 | H = R7–R8 | J = R9–R10 | O = FREE | X = On Application

Charges are based on a family of 2 adults and 2 children under 12 years

ADDITIONAL ACCOMMODATION TARIFF CODE – See columns 57–59 (Subject to alteration)

eg. Bungalows, Cabins, Cottages, Chalets, etc.
A = R1–R3 | C = R5–R7 | E = R9–R11 | G = R13–R15 | I = R17–R19 | K = R21–R30
B = R3–R5 | D = R7–R9 | F = R11–R13 | H = R15–R17 | J = R19–R21 | X = On Application

NB: Where the tariff is given in *italics* it is per person; otherwise per unit

NOTE 1 — Columns 18, 19, 20. – Where a symbol appears instead of a number it means stands are available but not demarcated or number of stands has not been provided
NOTE 2 — Column 35 – A = Bookings accepted for additional accommodation only, i.e. cottages, bungalows, etc.
NOTE 3 — Column 37 – Deposit refunded under certain conditions, eg. less 10%; if site is re-let; if cancelled well in advance (up to 2 months) or on a doctor's certificate
NOTE 4 — Column 41 – Reductions allowed on application for youth, church, school or sport groups or caravan rallies
NOTE 5 — Column 42 – R = Reduction in tariff of between 5–10% to Carnet holders; O = Reduction Out-of-Season only
NOTE 6 — Column 69 – L = Laundry facilities only
NOTE 7 — Columns 88, 89, 90. – I = In-Season only; O = Out-of-Season only
NOTE 8 — Column 96 – Applicable In-Season only at some establishments
NOTE 9 — Column 102 – See section on golf in Outdoor Holiday Guide
NOTE 10 — Column 107 – See section on freshwater angling in Outdoor Holiday Guide
NOTE 11 — Column 108 – See section on coastal angling in Outdoor Holiday Guide

ABBREVIATIONS
C = CAPE PROVINCE
N = NATAL
O = ORANGE FREE STATE
T = TRANSVAAL
B = BOPHUTHATSWANA
X = TRANSKEI

TELEPHONE CODE: T = DIAL 0020, BOOK TRUNK CALL; E = DIAL CODE, ASK EXCHANGE FOR NO.

Column headings: 1 Telephone code; 2 Telephone number; Owned or supervised by: 3 Privately owned, 4 Municipality, 5 Divisional council, 6 Provincial council, 7 Parks board administration; Site description – Locality: 8 Beach in immediate vicinity, 9 Beside river, lake or dam, 10 In or near mountain area, 11 Within built-up area; Nature of ground: 12 Grass, 13 Gravel, 14 Sand; Shade: 15 Unshaded, 16 Partly shaded, 17 Extensively shaded; No. of stands: 18 Caravans only – see note 1, 19 Caravans and/or tents – see note 1, 20 Tents only – see note 1; Accessibility – Distance from main road to site: 21 On main rd, 22 Within 1 km, 23 Within 5 km, 24 Within 10 km, 25 Within 15 km; Surface of approach road: 26 Tar, 27 Gravel, 28 Sand; Condition of approach road: 29 Good, 30 Fair, (Poor)

	Establishment	1	2	3	4	5	6	7	8	9	10	11	12	13	14	15	16	17	18	19	20	21	22	23	24	25	26	27	28	29	30
	WINTERTON N 67 C2 ↓ 1022m																														
□	**Kelvin Grove** P.O. Winterton 3340	03682 E	2502	□						□	□		□					□		30			□						□	□	
●	**Spioenkop Public Resort** P.O. Box 140 (3340) □ *17 km from Winterton*	03682 E	78					●		●	●		●				●			44						●		●			●
	WITBANK T 69 C2 ↗ 1622m																														
◆	[AA] **Witbank Recreation Resort** P.O. Box 3 (1035) □ *Witbank Dam*	01351	71951		◆					◆			◆				◆	◆	150	200	50		◆				◆			◆	
	WITSAND C 58 D5 → 5m																														
▲	**Witsand** Bookings not accepted	T	70147			▲			▲				▲	▲	▲		▲			89		▲					▲			▲	
	WITWATERSRAND T See respectively: ● Alberton ● Bapsfontein ● Bedfordview ● Benoni ● Boksburg ● Brakpan ● Eikenhof ● Elandsfontein ● Florida ● Germiston ● Honeydew ● Johannesburg ● Kempton Park ● Krugersdorp ● Mondeor ● Randfontein ● Rivonia ● Roodepoort ● Springs ● Westonaria																														
	WOLMARANSSTAD T 66 B3 ↗ 1376m																														
■	[Caravan Club] [AA] **Wolmaransstad Municipal** Town Clerk, P.O. Box 17 (2630) □ *Broadbent St.*	018112 E	12 or 412		■					■		■	■				■		24	12	50	■						■		■	
	WORCESTER C 58 C4 ↗ 300m																														
●	**Burger Park** Town Clerk, Municipality (6850) □ *Riebeeck St.*	0231	2-1050		●					●	●	●	●	●			●			54		●					●			●	
	YSTERFONTEIN C 58 C3 ← S.L.																														
◆	**Ysterfontein** P.O. Box 14, Malmesbury 7300 □ *Strand Rd.*	02245	2-2907			◆			◆			◆		◆		◆			70	10			◆					◆		◆	
	ZASTRON O 62 B5 ↘ 1679m																														
▲	[Caravan Club] [AA] **Zastron Municipal** P.O. Box 20 (9950) □ *Mathee St. Ext.*	05542 E	397 or 18		▲					▲	▲		▲					▲	30	60	30			▲			▲	▲		▲	
	ZEERUST T 68 C4 ← 1179m																														
★	**Die Krans** P.O. Box 193 (2865) □ *1,5 km from Zeerust*	014282 E	236	★						★	★						★	★	18				★				★			★	
	ZINKWAZI N See Sinkwazi																														

FOR COLOUREDS, ASIANS AND BLACKS

	Establishment	1	2	3	4	5	6	7	8	9	10	11	12	13	14	15	16	17	18	19	20	21	22	23	24	25	26	27	28	29	30
	ACORNHOEK T 71 B5 ↓ 387m																														
▲	[AA] **Manyeleti Game Reserve (for Blacks)** Manager, P.O. Manyeleti, via Acornhoek 1362 □ *48 km from Acornhoek*	T	3												▲		▲			20								▲			▲
	AMANZIMTOTI T 63 NS ↗ S.L.																														
★	[AA] **Umgababa Seaside Holiday Resort (for Blacks)** Manager, P.O. Box 172 (4125) □ *Main South Coast Rd.*	0323	31165/31120						★				★				★		50	150	130		★				★			★	
	ARNISTON C See Waenhuiskrans																														
	AUGRABIES C 65 C2 ← 1200m																														
□	**Augrabies Falls National Park (camping for Coloureds, Asians and Blacks)** National Parks Board, P.O. Box 787, Pretoria 0001 □ *13 km from Augrabies*	012	44-1171					□		□			□				□			□			□				□			□	
	BEAUFORT WEST C 59 A2 ↑ 851m																														
○	**Rustville (for Coloureds, Asians, Blacks)** Bookings not accepted Enquiries: Town Clerk (6970) □ *Simpson Ave.*	0201	2657		○							○		○			○			20		○					○			○	
	BUFFELSBAAI C 59 NS ↓ S.L.																														
◇	**Buffalo Bay Camping Area (for Coloureds)** Superintendent, P.O. Box 9, Knysna 6570	04452 E	9			◇			◇		◇		◇			◇				28	7	◇						◇			◇
	CALITZDORP C 59 B1 ← 238m																														
△	**Huis River Camping and Picnic Site (for Coloureds)** No bookings, no facilities but camping allowed □ *10 km from Calitzdorp*						△			△	△			△			△					△						△			△
	CERES C 58 C4 ↘ 457m																														
☆	**Die Eiland Caravan Park and Holiday Resort (for Coloureds)** P.O. Box 44 (6835)	023312 E	543/86		☆															20											
	CHALUMNA C 60 C2 ↑ S.L.																														
□	**Kiwane Holiday Resort (for Blacks)** Manager, Private Bag, Mdantsane 5219 □ *At the Chalumna River Mouth*	04342 E	64 or 65						□			□	□				□		50	200						□		□		□	
	DARNALL N 63 A4 ● 66m																														
○	**Harold Johnson Nature Reserve (for Blacks)** Officer-in-Charge, P.O. Box 148 (4480)	032422 E	2204					○		○			○					○		6			○					○		○	
	EAST LONDON C 60 B2 ↘ S.L.																														
◇	**Fullers Bay (for Asians)** Bookings not accepted □ *10 km from city* — Enquiries: Director of Parks and Amenities, P.O. Box 984 (5200)				◇				◇				◇				◇			◇			◇					◇	◇		◇
▲	**Leaches Bay (for Coloureds)** Bookings not accepted □ *12 km from city*				▲				▲				▲				▲			▲			▲					▲			▲
△	**Western Seafront (for Blacks)** Bookings not accepted □ *9 km from city*				△				△				△				△			△		△						△		△	
	ESTCOURT N 67 D2 ↗ 1168m																														
☆	**Wagendrift Public Resort (for Coloureds, Asians and Blacks)** P.O. Box 316 (3310) □ *8 km from Estcourt*	03631	2550					☆		☆	☆		☆				☆			10					☆		☆			☆	
	FRANSCHHOEK C 58 C4 ↗ 126m																														
□	**Die Ou Tol Camping Area (for Coloureds, Asians and Blacks)** Bookings not accepted □ *Franschhoek Pass*					□					□		□				□					□					□			□	
	GEORGE C 59 NS ← 226m																														
○	**Municipal Tourist Camp and Caravan Park (for Coloureds and Asians)** P.O. Box 19 (6530) □ *Knysna Rd.*	0441	6001		○						○	○	○				○			75		○						○		○	
	GORDON'S BAY C 58 D3 ↗ S.L.																														
◇	**Kogel Bay Pleasure Resort (for Coloureds and Asians)** P.O. Box 68 (7150) □ *13 km from Gordon's Bay*	024	4-1286		◇				◇		◇		◇				◇		50		300	◇					◇			◇	
	GRAHAMSTOWN C 59 B6 ↑ 532m																														
△	**Grahamstown Caravan Park (for Coloureds and Indians)** Superintendent, Parks and Forests Dept., P.O. Box 176 (6140) □ *Port Elizabeth National Rd.*	0461	2043		△								△				△			25		△					△			△	
	GROOT-BRAKRIVIER C 52 C2 ↘ 4m																														
☆	**Groot-Brakrivier Municipal (for Coloureds)** P.O. Box 15 (6525) □ *On seafront between Groot- and Kleinbrakrivier*	04442	2100		☆				☆				☆			☆				184				☆			☆			☆	

…N THROUGHOUT THE YEAR

SEASONS · TERMS FOR BOOKINGS · CARAVAN PARK/CAMPING SITE TARIFFS (See heading) · REDUCTIONS ALLOWED FOR · RESTAURANT FACILITIES · TEAROOM/CAFE · SHOPPING FACILITIES (Provisions) · ADDITIONAL ACCOMMODATION AVAILABLE · ADDITIONAL ACCOMMODATION TARIFF (See heading) · CARAVANS TO RENT ON SITE – SEE PAGES 8 – 11

CAMP SITE FACILITIES — I = In-Season only, O = Out-of-Season only — DRINKING WATER · BATHS · SHOWERS · NON-WHITE SERVANTS · TYPE OF VEHICLE PERMITTED

SPORTING AND RECREATIONAL FACILITIES — S = On Site, N = Nearby (Up to 20 km away) — GOLF · FISHING · SWIMMING · BOATING · PLACES OF INTEREST · NOTES

33 Out-of-season closing date	34 Re-opening date	35 Bookings accp./peak sns – see note 2	36 Deposit required	37 Refunded if cancelled – see note 3	38 Maximum in-season tariff	39 Maximum out-of-season tariff	40 Long periods of stay	41 Groups – see note 4	42 AA carnet holders – see note 5	43 Others (on application)	44 Restaurant: on site	45 Within 5 km of site	46 More than 5 km from site	47 Tearoom/cafe: on site	48 Within 5 km of site	49 More than 5 km from site	50 Shopping: on site	51 Within 5 km of site	52 More than 5 km from site	53 Bungalows	54 Cabins	55 Cottages (rondavels)	56 Chalets	57 Maximum in-season tariff	58 Maximum out-of-season tariff	59 Caravans to rent on site – see pages 8–11	60 Drinking water: piped	61 Other	62 Baths: hot and cold	63 Cold only	64 Showers: hot and cold	65 Cold only	66 Waterborne sanitation	67 Washbasins	68 Dishwashing facilities	69 Laundry and ironing facilities – see note 6	70 Washing machines	71 Site lit	72 Plugs for razors (voltage)	73 Refrigerators	74 Firewood/charcoal	75 Open fire permitted	76 Camp fire forbidden	77 Braai places provided	78 Kitchen/cooking facilities	79 Petrol pump on site	80 Petrol pump nearby	81 Car repair shop nearby	82 Car servicing nearby	83 Gas service nearby	84 First aid/hospital/doctor nearby	85 Post office nearby	86 Site guarded	87 Pets allowed	88 Servants permitted – see note 7	89 Servants accom. – see note 7	90 Servants for hire – see note 7	91 Car and trailer	92 Truck 'horse' and semi-trailer	93 Self-propelled caravans	94 Childrens' playground	95 Tennis	96 Cinema/drive-in/TV-room – see note 8	97 Horse-riding	98 Games room	99 Trampoline	100 Bowls	101 Hot springs	102 Golf course – see note 9	103 Number of holes	104 Miniature	105 Mashie	106 Putt-putt	107 Freshwater – see note 10	108 Sea – see note 11	109 Goggle	110 Licence required	111 Swimming pool	112 Sea bathing	113 Childrens' pool	114 Adults only	115 Shark nets at beach	116 Boats for hire	117 Power	118 Sailing	119 Canoeing	120 Historic	121 Scientific	122 Natural	123 Notes
		□	□		C	C	□	□		□			□			□			□		□	□		D	D		□		□		□		□	□	□	□				□	□		□	□			□	□	□	□	□	□					□	□	□	□	S	N	N	S	N	N	N		N					N			□	S		N							□		□	
		●	●		D	D																	●	*B*	*B*		●		●		●		●	●				●					●	●							●				●			●	●	●	S	S		S										S			●	S		S				S	S	S			●	
		◆	◆		C	C					◆		◆	◆		◆			◆				◆	H	H		◆		◆		◆		◆	◆	◆	◆		◆	220		◆		◆	◆			◆	◆	◆	◆	◆	◆	◆					◆		◆	S	S	N	N	N		N		N	18	◆			S			◆	S		S				S	S	S			◆	
					B	B									▲	▲		▲	▲									▲	▲		▲		▲	▲	▲	▲		▲			▲		▲	▲	▲		▲			▲		▲	▲		▲			▲		▲	S														N	N			▲				N	N	N	N			▲	
		■			C	C		■		■		■			■			■				■		B	B		■		■		■		■	■	■	■		■	220		■			■			■	■	■	■		■	■				■	■	■	■	N	N	N				N		N	9				N			■	N		N							■			
		●	●		C	B	●				●				●			●									●		●		●		●	●	●	●		●	●		●		●	●	●		●	●	●	●	●	●		●	●		●	●	●	●	S	N	N	N			N		N	18				N			●	S		S							●	●	●	
		◆	◆	◆	C	C	◆					◆	◆		◆	◆		◆	◆								◆		◆		◆		◆	◆	◆	◆						◆	◆	◆			◆			◆	◆		◆					◆		◆															N	N			◆								◆		◆	
		▲			C	C	▲					▲	▲			▲			▲								▲		▲		▲		▲	▲	▲	▲		▲	220		▲		▲	▲	▲		▲	▲	▲	▲	▲	▲	▲	▲	▲			▲		▲	S	N	N	S		N	N		N	9				S			▲	N		N					S	S			▲	
		★	★		C	B	★	★			★	★			★	★		★	★	★		★		X	X		★		★		★		★	★				★	220	★	★		★				★	★	★	★	★			★				★	★	★	N	N	S	N			N		N	18				S			★										★	★	★	
5 Jan.	1 Mar.				A	A					▲			▲			▲		▲			▲		*B*	*B*		▲		▲		▲		▲	▲	▲			▲			▲		▲	▲	▲	▲					▲	▲	▲					▲	▲	▲																		S											▲	
		★	★	★	E	C	★	★	R		★	★		★	★		★	★		★	★		★	E	G		★	★	★		★	★	★	★	★	★		★		★	★		★	★	★		★	★	★	★	★		★	★				★	★	★	S		S		S				S	18			★	N	N	N		S	★	S	★	★					★	★	★	
		□	□	□	C	C					□			□			□										□	□	□		□		□	□	□	□		□	220		□		□	□	□	□	□	□	□	□								□	□	□	S																										□	□	□	
					B	B							○			○			○								○		○		○		○	○		○		○			○	○		○			○	○	○	○	○	○	○	○	○			○		○		N	N											N			○										○		○	
Sch.hd.&Estr.		◇			C	C							◇		◇	◇		◇	◇								◇				◇		◇	◇							◇		◇	◇						◇		◇						◇	◇	◇														N	N	N			◇							N			◇	
					Gratis	Gratis							△			△			△									△															△	△										△				△	△	△																														△	
					B	B											☆					☆		A	A						☆		☆																	☆																												S												
		□	□	□	A	A							□			□	□	□	□	□				A	A		□			□		□						□			□		□	□			□				□		□	□				□	□	□														S			□		□											
		○			B	B									○	○		○	○								○	○				○	○	○	○						○		○	○							○	○						○	○	○														N	N	N	○		○	N	○	○		N	N	N	○	○	○	
					A	A										◇											◇															◇	◇															◇		◇															S	S			◇	N										◇	
					A	A									▲												▲					▲		▲								▲	▲															▲		▲															S	S			▲	N										▲	
					A	A										△											△															△	△															△		△															S	S			△											△	
		☆	☆	☆	D	D							☆			☆			☆								☆				☆		☆	☆										☆	☆							☆	☆			☆	☆		☆	☆	☆														S			☆							S	S	S			☆	
					Gratis	Gratis																					□																	□	□											□				□	□	□	S																													□	
		○	○	○	C	C							○			○		○				○		C	B		○		○		○		○	○	○	○		○	○		○	○	○	○			○	○	○	○	○	○		○				○	○	○			N												N	N			○					N	N	N	○		○	
					B	B								◇		◇			◇								◇					◇	◇	◇							◇	◇	◇	◇			◇	◇	◇	◇	◇	◇		◇	◇			◇		◇	S														N				◇											◇	
					A	A						△			△			△									△		△		△		△	△	△			△				△					△	△	△	△		△		△				△	△	△														N			△										△	△	△	
		☆	☆		B	B											☆	☆	☆								☆				☆		☆	☆		☆		☆				☆	☆	☆			☆	☆	☆	☆	☆	☆	☆		☆		☆	☆	☆	☆	S	N	N											N	N	N			☆								☆		☆	

CARAVAN PARKS AND CAMPING SITES

Establishments marked thus 🚐 have the Caravan Club of South Africa recommendation – see page 17
Establishments marked thus Ⓒ recognise the AA Camping Carnet – see page 16 and also refer to column 42

CARAVAN PARK / CAMP SITE TARIFF CODE – See columns 38–39 (Subject to alteration)

A = Up to R1 | C = R2–R3 | E = R4–R5 | G = R6–R7 | I = R8–R9 | K = R10–R16
B = R1–R2 | D = R3–R4 | F = R5–R6 | H = R7–R8 | J = R9–R10 | O = FREE
Charges are based on a family of 2 adults and 2 children under 12 years | X = On Application

ADDITIONAL ACCOMMODATION TARIFF CODE – See columns 57–59 (Subject to alteration)

eg. Bungalows, Cabins, Cottages, Chalets, etc.
A = R1–R3 | C = R5–R7 | E = R9–R11 | G = R13–R15 | I = R17–R19 | K = R21–R30
B = R3–R5 | D = R7–R9 | F = R11–R13 | H = R15–R17 | J = R19–R21 | X = On Application
NB: Where the tariff is given in *italics* it is per person, otherwise per unit

NOTE 1 — Columns 18, 19, 20. — Where a symbol appears instead of a number it means stands are available but not demarcated or number of stands has not been provided
NOTE 2 — Column 35 — A = Bookings accepted for additional accommodation only i.e. cottages, bungalows, etc.
NOTE 3 — Column 37 — Deposit refunded under certain conditions eg. less 10% ; if site is re-let ; if cancelled well in advance (up to 2 months) or on a doctor's certificate
NOTE 4 — Column 41 — Reductions allowed on application for youth, church, school or sport groups or caravan rallies
NOTE 5 — Column 42 — R = Reduction in tariff of between 5 – 10 % to Carnet holders
0 = Reduction Out-of-Season only
NOTE 6 — Column 69 — L = Laundry facilities only
NOTE 7 — Columns 88, 89, 90. — I = In-Season only ; 0 = Out-of-Season only
NOTE 8 — Column 96 — Applicable In-Season only at some establishments
NOTE 9 — Column 102 — See section on golf in Outdoor Holiday Guide
NOTE 10 — Column 107 — See section on freshwater angling in Outdoor Holiday Guide
NOTE 11 — Column 108 — See section on coastal angling in Outdoor Holiday Guide

ABBREVIATIONS

C = CAPE PROVINCE
N = NATAL
O = ORANGE FREE STATE
T = TRANSVAAL
B = BOPHUTHATSWANA
X = TRANSKEI

TELEPHONE CODE: T = DIAL 0020, BOOK TRUNK CALL; E = DIAL CODE, ASK EXCHANGE FOR NO.

			TELEPHONE CODE	TELEPHONE NUMBER	OWNED OR SUPERVISED BY: PRIVATELY OWNED	MUNICIPALITY	DIVISIONAL COUNCIL	PROVINCIAL COUNCIL	PARKS BOARD ADMINISTRATION	SITE DESCRIPTION – LOCALITY: BEACH IN IMMEDIATE VICINITY	BESIDE RIVER, LAKE OR DAM	IN OR NEAR MOUNTAIN AREA	WITHIN BUILT-UP AREA	NATURE OF GROUND: GRASS	GRAVEL	SAND	SHADE: UNSHADED	PARTLY SHADED	EXTENSIVELY SHADED	NO. OF STANDS: CARAVANS ONLY – SEE NOTE 1	CARAVANS AND/OR TENTS – SEE NOTE 1	TENTS ONLY – SEE NOTE 1	ACCESSIBILITY – APPROXIMATE DISTANCE FROM MAIN ROAD TO SITE: ON MAIN RD	WITHIN 1 km	WITHIN 5 km	WITHIN 10 km	WITHIN 15 km	SURFACE OF ROAD APPROACH: TAR	GRAVEL	SAND	CONDITION OF ROAD APPROACH: GOOD	FAIR
			1	2	3	4	5	6	7	8	9	10	11	12	13	14	15	16	17	18	19	20	21	22	23	24	25	26	27	28	29	30
		FOR COLOUREDS, ASIANS AND BLACKS (CONTINUED)																														
		GWAYANG RIVER MOUTH C 59 NS ← 10m																														
□		**Gwayang Caravan Park (for Coloureds)** Divisional Council, P.O. Box 12, George 6530 □ *15 km from George*	0441	3001			□			□	□				□		□				30					□			□		□	
		HAWSTON C 58 D4 ← 20m																														
○	Ⓒ	**Sonesta (for Coloureds)** P.O. Box 25 (7202) □ *5 km from Hawston*	02831	5740						○	○	○		○					○	150					○			○			○	
		HLUHLUWE N 67 B5 ↙ 5m																														
◇		**False Bay Park (for Non-Whites)** Only 3 non-facility sites (i.e. pit latrines and water points). Officer-in-Charge, False Bay Park, P.O. Hluhluwe 3960 □ *16 km from Hluhluwe*	03562 E	2911					◇		◇			◇				◇			3						◇		◇			◇
		HOWICK N 63 A3 ← 1048m																														
△		**Orient Park Resort (for Coloureds and Asians)** P.O. Howick 3290 □ *Adjacent to Midmar Dam*	033212 E	367				△	△		△	△		△				△			15					△		△			△	
		JEFFREYS BAY C 59 C4 ↖ S.L.																														
☆		**Municipal Caravan Camp (for Coloureds)** Town Clerk, P.O. Box 21 (6330) □ *16 Duine Rd.*	T	21		☆				☆				☆			☆				60			☆					☆		☆	
		KIMBERLEY C 62 C2 ↘ 1223m																														
□		**Langleg Pleasure Resort (for Coloureds and Asians)** Resort Manager, P.O. Box 628 (8300) □ *28 km from Kimberley*	0531	2-2241 x221		□					□			□				□		□		□				□		□			□	
		KLEINKRANTZ C 59 NS ← 4m																														
○		**Kleinkrantz Caravan Park (for Coloureds)** Divisional Council, P.O. Box 12, George 6530	0441	3001			○			○				○		○					60		○						○		○	
		KOMMETJIE C 58 NS ← S.L.																														
◇		**Die Anker Camping Site (for Coloureds and Asians)** Supervisor, Soetwater Recreation Area, P.O. Kommetjie 7976	021	8-3747			◇			◇		◇		◇	◇	◇		◇				◇	◇					◇			◇	
▲		**Medusa Caravan Park (for Coloureds)** Supervisor, Soetwater Recreation Area, P.O. Kommetjie 7976	021	8-3747			▲			▲				▲				▲		66					▲			▲			▲	
		KRUGER NATIONAL PARK T 75 C5 ↗ 167m																														
★		**Lower Sabie (for Coloureds, Asians and Blacks)** Bookings not accepted Enquiries: National Parks Board, P.O. Box 787, Pretoria 0001	012	44-1194					★					★				★			3							★			★	
☆		**Skukuza (for Coloureds, Asians and Blacks)** Bookings not accepted Enquiries: National Parks Board, P.O. Box 787, Pretoria 0001	012	44-1194					☆							☆		☆			10							☆			☆	
		LAAIPLEK C 58 B3 ↙ 5m																														
□		**Laaiplek Beach Resort (for Coloureds)** Town Clerk, P.O. Box 29, Velddrif 7365	022882 E	12 or 34		□				□					□		□			15	10				□				□		□	
		LANGEBAAN C 58 C3 ↑ S.L.																														
○		**Municipal Caravan Park (for Coloureds)** P.O. Box 11 (7357) □ *Main St.*	02287	615		○				○					○		○				80			○					○			○
		MAMRE C 58 C3 ← 183m																														
◇		**Manresa Holiday Farm (for Coloureds)** P.O. Box 33, Wesfleur 7349 □ *On the road between Mamre and Atlantis*	02247 E	2118/9	◇							◇		◇		◇		◇			400				◇			◇	◇			◇
		MOSSEL BAY C 59 C2 ↖ 7m																														
△		**Diaz Caravan Park (for Coloureds)** Bookings not accepted □ *Diaz Strand, 2 km from Mossel Bay*	04441	2514		△				△				△					△	300		1000		△					△			△
		NEWCASTLE N 67 B2 ↘ 1500m																														
☆		**Chelmsford Public Resort (for Coloureds, Asians and Blacks)** P.O. Box 3, Ballengeich 2942 □ *40 km from Newcastle*	0343	7715					☆		☆	☆		☆				☆			20						☆	☆			☆	
		OUDTSHOORN C 59 B2 ← 306m																														
□		**Bridgton Camp (for Coloureds)** Bookings not accepted □ *Blackwood St., Bridgton*	04431	2221		□							□		□			□			15			□				□			□	
●		**De Hoek Holiday Resort (for Coloureds)** P.O. Box 127 (6620) □ *±40 km from Oudtshoorn on the road to Prince Albert*	04431	2241			●				●	●		●					●	40		40		●				●			●	
		PAARL C 58 C3 ↘ 115m																														
◆		**Orleans Park (for Coloureds)** Secretary, Management Committee, P.O. Box 12 (7620) □ *Meaker St., Huguenot*	0251	2-4320		◆					◆					◆		◆				100			◆			◆			◆	
		PARK RYNIE N 63 NS ● 15m																														
▲		**Park Rynie Caravan, Camping and Picknicking Ground (for Coloureds and Asians)** Umzinto North Town Board, P.O. Box 39, Umzinto 4200 □ *Off First St., Park Rynie*	0323	4031		▲				▲				▲				▲		50	100	50			▲			▲	▲			▲
		PORT ELIZABETH C 59 B5 ↘ S.L.																														
★	Ⓒ	**Joorst Park (for Coloureds and Asians)** C/o Parks Dept., St. George's Park (6001) □ *St. George's Strand*	041	6-1463		★				★				★		★		★			★			★				★			★	
☆		**Wells Estate Camping Site (for Blacks)** Enquiries: Beach Manager, Humewood 6001				☆				☆				☆		☆		☆							☆				☆		☆	
		PORT NOLLOTH C 60 A4 ↗ S.L.																														
□		**McDougalls Bay Caravan Park (for Coloureds)** Municipality, P.O. Box 13 (8280)	T	11		□				□						□	□				50				□				□	□		□
		PORT ST. JOHNS X 60 A4 → 3m																														
○	🚐	**First Beach Municipal Caravan Park (for all races)** Municipality, P.O. Box 2 (4830)	04752 E	8		○				○	○			○					○	23			○					○			○	
◆		**Second Beach Holiday Resort (for all races)** P.O. Box 18 (4830)	04752 E	61						◆	◆	◆		◆				◆	◆	30		20	◆					◆			◆	
◇		**Second Beach Municipal Caravan Park (for all races)** Municipality, P.O. Box 2 (4830)	04752 E	8		◇				◇	◇			◇				◇		50		60		◇					◇		◇	
		POTCHEFSTROOM T 66 A5 ↙ 1300m																														
△		**Shalimar Pleasure Resort (for Coloureds and Asians)** 42B Krause St., Vrededorp 2141 □ *14 km from Potchefstroom*	011	35-2943	△						△			△					△	50		50	△					△			△	
		ROYAL NATAL NATIONAL PARK N 67 C1 ↘ 1500m																														
☆		**Rugged Glen Campsite (for Coloureds, Asians and Blacks)** The Officer-in-Charge, P.O. Mont-aux-Sources 3353	T	Mont-aux-Sources 3					☆			☆		☆				☆			12				☆			☆			☆	
		SILWERSTROOMSTRAND C 58 C3 ↙ S.L.																														
□		**Silwerstroom Resort Area (for Coloureds and Asians)** Divisional Council, P.O. Box 1073, Cape Town 8000	02202 E	1840			□			□				□	□	□	□	□								□		□			□	
		STILBAAI-OOS C 59 C1 ● S.L.																														
○		**Preekstoel Beach Resort (for Coloureds)** Caretaker, P.O. Box 13, Riversdale 6770	T	9909			○			○				○				○			280		○					○			○	
		ST. LUCIA ESTUARY N 67 C5 ● 50m																														
◇		**St. Lucia Public Resort (for Coloureds, Asians and Blacks)** Officer-in-Charge, P.O. St. Lucia Estuary 3936	T	St. Lucia 20					◇	◇	◇		◇	◇				◇			12			◇					◇		◇	
		STRAND C 58 D3 ↗ S.L.																														
△		**Harmony Park (for Coloureds)** Bookings not accepted □ *Gordon's Bay Rd.*	024	3-6270		△				△		△	△	△		△		△			288		△					△			△	
		STRUISBAAI C 58 D5 ↙ 2m																														
☆		**Molshoop Camping Area (for Coloureds)** Bookings not accepted □ *1 km from Struisbaai*	02842 E	68			☆			☆				☆			☆				50			☆					☆			☆

SEASONS		TERMS FOR BOOKINGS			CARAVAN PARK/CAMPING SITE TARIFFS (See heading)		REDUCTIONS ALLOWED FOR				RESTAURANT FACILITIES			TEAROOM/CAFE			SHOPPING FACILITIES (Provisions)			ADDITIONAL ACCOMMODATION AVAILABLE				ADDITIONAL ACCOMMODATION TARIFF (See heading)			CAMP SITE FACILITIES (I = In-Season only; O = Out-of-Season only) – DRINKING WATER		BATHS		SHOWERS																								NON-WHITE SERVANTS			TYPE OF VEHICLE PERMITTED			SPORTING AND RECREATIONAL FACILITIES (S = On Site; N = Nearby (Up to 20 km away))								GOLF					FISHING				SWIMMING					BOATING				PLACES OF INTEREST			NOTES
THROUGHOUT THE YEAR	OUT-OF-SEASON CLOSING DATE / RE-OPENING DATE	BOOKINGS ACCP./PEAK SNS. – SEE NOTE 2	DEPOSIT REQUIRED	REFUNDED IF CANCELLED – SEE NOTE 3	MAXIMUM IN-SEASON TARIFF	MAXIMUM OUT-OF-SEASON TARIFF	LONG PERIODS OF STAY	GROUPS – SEE NOTE 4	AA CARNET HOLDERS – SEE NOTE 5	OTHERS (ON APPLICATION)	ON SITE	WITHIN 5 km OF SITE	MORE THAN 5 km FROM SITE	ON SITE	WITHIN 5 km OF SITE	MORE THAN 5 km FROM SITE	ON SITE	WITHIN 5 km OF SITE	MORE THAN 5 km FROM SITE	BUNGALOWS	CABINS	COTTAGES (RONDAVELS)	CHALETS	MAXIMUM IN-SEASON TARIFF	MAXIMUM OUT-OF-SEASON TARIFF	CARAVANS TO RENT ON SITE – SEE PAGES 8 – 11	PIPED	OTHER	HOT AND COLD	COLD ONLY	HOT AND COLD	COLD ONLY	WATERBORNE SANITATION	WASHBASINS	DISHWASHING FACILITIES	LAUNDRY AND IRONING FACILITIES – SEE NOTE 6	WASHING MACHINES	SITE LIT	PLUGS FOR RAZORS (VOLTAGE)	REFRIGERATORS	FIREWOOD/CHARCOAL	OPEN FIRE FORBIDDEN	CAMP FIRE PERMITTED	BRAAI PLACES PROVIDED	KITCHEN/COOKING FACILITIES	PETROL PUMP ON SITE	PETROL PUMP NEARBY	CAR REPAIR SHOP NEARBY	CAR SERVICING NEARBY	GAS SERVICE NEARBY	FIRST AID/HOSPITAL/DOCTOR NEARBY	POST OFFICE NEARBY	SITE GUARDED	PETS ALLOWED	SERVANTS PERMITTED – SEE NOTE 7	SERVANTS ACCOM. – SEE NOTE 7	SERVANTS FOR HIRE – SEE NOTE 7	CAR AND TRAILER	TRUCK 'HORSE' AND SEMI-TRAILER	SELF-PROPELLED CARAVANS	CHILDRENS' PLAYGROUND	TENNIS	CINEMA/DRIVE-IN/TV-ROOM – SEE NOTE 8	HORSE-RIDING	GAMES ROOM	TRAMPOLINE	BOWLS	HOT SPRINGS	GOLF COURSE – SEE NOTE 9	NUMBER OF HOLES	MINIATURE	MASHIE	PUTT-PUTT	FRESHWATER – SEE NOTE 10	SEA – SEE NOTE 11	GOGGLE	LICENCE REQUIRED	SWIMMING POOL	SEA BATHING	CHILDRENS' POOL	ADULTS ONLY	SHARK NETS AT BEACH	BOATS FOR HIRE	POWER	SAILING	CANOEING	HISTORIC	SCIENTIFIC	NATURAL	
33	34	35	36	37	38	39	40	41	42	43	44	45	46	47	48	49	50	51	52	53	54	55	56	57	58	59	60	61	62	63	64	65	66	67	68	69	70	71	72	73	74	75	76	77	78	79	80	81	82	83	84	85	86	87	88	89	90	91	92	93	94	95	96	97	98	99	100	101	102	103	104	105	106	107	108	109	110	111	112	113	114	115	116	117	118	119	120	121	122	123
					B	B																					□					□	□	□	□							□	□	□									□					□		□														N	N	N			□										□	
			○	○	E	C		○	R	○	○	○	○	○			○			○		○		G-I	E-F		○		○		○		○	○	○	○		○	250		○		○	○						○	○	○	○					○	○	○	S	S	S		S						○	○	○		S	S		S	○	S					N				○	
		◇	◇		B	B										◇			◇								◇														◇		◇				◇	◇	◇	◇	◇							◇	◇	◇														S									S						◇	
		△	△	△	C	C							△	△									△	A	A		△		△		△		△	△	△	L		△					△	△			△				△		△					△			S	S	N	S										S			△							S	S	S			△	
		☆	☆	☆	C	C		☆				☆			☆			☆									☆		☆		☆		☆	☆	☆	☆		☆				☆		☆			☆	☆	☆	☆	☆	☆	☆					☆		☆	N	N													N				☆										☆	
		□	□	□	X	X								□								□		E	E		□		□		□		□	□				□		□	□	□		□									□					□	□	□														S			□	S					S			S				
					B	B					○			○			○										○					○	○	○								○		○			○	○	○				○					○		○															N				○										○	
					A	A							◇		◇			◇									◇			◇		◇	◇	◇	◇						◇		◇									◇	◇					◇	◇	◇															N	N			◇										◇	
		▲	▲		C	B				▲		▲	▲		▲	▲	▲	▲	▲								▲		▲		▲		▲	▲	▲	▲		▲			▲	▲	▲	▲			▲	▲	▲	▲	▲	▲	▲					▲	▲															S	S			▲	N	▲						▲		▲	
					B	B					★						★					★		D-F	D-F		★		★		★	★	★	★	★	★						★		★		★												★	★	★																														★	
					B	B					☆						☆					☆		E-F	E-F		☆		☆		☆		☆	☆	☆	☆										☆						☆							☆	☆	☆																											☆	☆	☆	
		□			B	B						□				□			□		□			D	D		□					□	□	□	□								□	□	□		□	□	□	□	□	□	□	□	□		□	□	□	□														N	N	N	□		□							N				
		○			B	B						○			○			○									○					○	○	○	○	○		○					○	○			○	○	○		○	○	○					○		○															N	N			○				N	N	N		○		○	
		◇	◇		C	C		◇			◇			◇			◇										◇		◇		◇		◇	◇	◇	◇		◇		◇	◇		◇	◇			◇	◇	◇	◇	◇	◇	◇	◇	◇			◇		◇															N			S	N	S							◇	◇	◇	
					C	C						△		△			△										△		△		△		△	△	△	△		△	220		△		△				△	△	△	△	△	△	△					△		△	S	S	N													N	N			△									△		△	
		☆	☆		C	C													☆								☆				☆		☆	☆									☆	☆								☆				☆			☆	☆	☆														S			☆							S	S	S			☆	
					A	A							□			□		□	□								□					□	□	□				□					□				□	□	□	□		□		□				□	□	□	N	N	N																N		N							□	□	□	
		●	●	●	C	B							●						●				●	E	D		●	●	●	●	●	●	●	●	●	●		●	220	●	●		●	●	●								●	●				●	●	●																		S		S									●	
					A	A							◆			◆			◆								◆					◆	◆	◆							◆		◆	◆			◆	◆	◆	◆	◆	◆	◆	◆				◆		◆	S	N	N																N		N							◆		◆	
					C	B						▲			▲			▲									▲			▲		▲	▲	▲	▲			▲				▲	▲				▲	▲	▲	▲	▲	▲	▲					▲		▲															S	S		S	▲	S									
		★	★		X	X					★	★		★	★			★	★				★	X	X		★					★	★	★	★	★		★			★		★	★			★	★	★	★	★	★	★	★				★		★	S	N	N	N	N	N									N				★									★	★	★	
					Gratis	Gratis											☆										☆			☆								☆				☆		☆										☆				☆	☆	☆															☆	☆			☆									☆	☆	☆	
		□	□		B	B						□															□			□		□	□	□									□				□		□			□		□				□	□	□															N	N			□					N	N	N				
		○	○		C	C	○						○			○			○	○		○	○	C-E	C-E		○		○		○		○	○	○	○		○		○	○		○	○			○	○	○	○	○	○	○					○	○	○		N					N		N	9					N	N		N	○					N		N			○	
		◆	◆	◆	C	C	◆	◆				◆					◆			◆		◆	◆	C-D	E-F		◆		◆		◆		◆	◆	◆	◆					◆		◆				◆	◆	◆	◆	◆	◆	◆	◆	◆	◆	◆	◆	◆	◆	S	S	S		S	S	N		N	9				N	N	N	◆		◆				N			N	◆	◆	◆	
		◇	◇		C	C	◇					◇			◇				◇	◇		◇	◇	C-E	C-E		◇		◇		◇		◇	◇	◇	◇					◇		◇	◇			◇	◇	◇	◇	◇	◇	◇					◇	◇	◇		N					N		N	9					N	N		N	◇					N		N			◇	
		△	△		X	X	△	△			△			△				△			△	△	△	H-J	H-J		△		△		△		△	△	△	△					△		△	△			△	△	△	△	△	△	△	△	△			△		△	S	S	S	S	S									N				S		S									△	
		☆	☆	☆	D	D																					☆	☆			☆												☆	☆								☆	☆			☆	☆		☆	☆	☆		N		S										S			☆												☆	
					B	B								□			□										□			□		□	□	□	□	□					□		□	□							□		□					□	□	□															N	N			□										□	
					C	B					○			○			○										○			○		○	○	○	○						○		○	○			○	○	○	○		○	○	○				○	○	○															S	S			○										○	
		◇	◇	◇	C	C									◇			◇									◇				◇		◇	◇	◇									◇	◇			◇	◇	◇	◇	◇	◇			◇			◇	◇	◇															N				◇				S						◇	
					C	B								△				△									△		△		△		△	△	△	△		△	220		△		△	△			△	△	△	△	△	△	△					△		△		N	N												N	N		S	△										△	
					B	B						☆						☆									☆					☆	☆	☆	☆						☆		☆				☆	☆	☆	☆		☆	☆	☆				☆	☆	☆															N	N			☆				N	N			☆		☆	

CARAVAN PARKS AND CAMPING SITES

Establishments marked thus [caravan symbol] have the Caravan Club of South Africa recommendation – see page **17**
Establishments marked thus [AA symbol] recognise the AA Camping Carnet – see page **16** and also refer to column **42**

CARAVAN PARK / CAMP SITE TARIFF CODE – See columns 38–39 (Subject to alteration)

A = Up to R1 | C = R2–R3 | E = R4–R5 | G = R6–R7 | I = R8–R9 | K = R10–R16
B = R1–R2 | D = R3–R4 | F = R5–R6 | H = R7–R8 | J = R9–R10 | O = FREE
Charges are based on a family of 2 adults and 2 children under 12 years | X = On Application

ADDITIONAL ACCOMMODATION TARIFF CODE – See columns 57–59 (Subject to alteration)

eg. Bungalows, Cabins, Cottages, Chalets, etc.
A = R1–R3 | C = R5–R7 | E = R9–R11 | G = R13–R15 | I = R17–R19 | K = R21–R30
B = R3–R5 | D = R7–R9 | F = R11–R13 | H = R15–R17 | J = R19–R21 | X = On Application
NB: Where the tariff is given in *italics* it is per person, otherwise per unit

NOTE 1 — Columns 18, 19, 20. — Where a symbol appears instead of a number it means stands are available but not demarcated or number of stands has not been provided
NOTE 2 — Column 35 — A = Bookings accepted for additional accommodation only i.e. cottages, bungalows, etc.
NOTE 3 — Column 37 — Deposit refunded under certain conditions eg. less 10% ; if site is re-let ; if cancelled well in advance (up to 2 months) or on a doctor's certificate
NOTE 4 — Column 41 — Reductions allowed on application for youth, church, school or sport groups or caravan rallies
NOTE 5 — Column 42 — R = Reduction in tariff of between 5 – 10 % to Carnet holders; O = Reduction Out-of-Season only
NOTE 6 — Column 69 — L = Laundry facilities only
NOTE 7 — Columns 88, 89, 90. — I = In-Season only ; O = Out-of-Season only
NOTE 8 — Column 96 — Applicable In-Season only at some establishments
NOTE 9 — Column 102 — See section on golf in Outdoor Holiday Guide
NOTE 10 — Column 107 — See section on freshwater angling in Outdoor Holiday Guide
NOTE 11 — Column 108 — See section on coastal angling in Outdoor Holiday Guide

ABBREVIATIONS
C CAPE PROVINCE
N NATAL
O ORANGE FREE STATE
T TRANSVAAL
B BOPHUTHATSWANA
X TRANSKEI

TELEPHONE CODE: T = DIAL 0020. BOOK TRUNK CALL; E = DIAL CODE. ASK EXCHANGE FOR NO.

Column groups: OWNED OR SUPERVISED BY (3–7); SITE DESCRIPTION: LOCALITY (8–11), NATURE OF GROUND (12–14), SHADE (15–17); NO. OF STANDS (18–20); ACCESSIBILITY: APPROXIMATE DISTANCE FROM MAIN ROAD TO SITE (21–25), SURFACE OF ROAD APPROACH (26–28), CONDITION OF ROAD APPROACH (29–30)

		1 TELEPHONE CODE	2 TELEPHONE NUMBER	3 PRIVATELY OWNED	4 MUNICIPALITY	5 DIVISIONAL COUNCIL	6 PROVINCIAL ADMINISTRATION	7 PARKS BOARD	8 BEACH IN IMMEDIATE VICINITY	9 BESIDE RIVER, LAKE OR DAM	10 IN OR NEAR MOUNTAIN AREA	11 WITHIN BUILT-UP AREA	12 GRASS	13 GRAVEL	14 SAND	15 UNSHADED	16 PARTLY SHADED	17 EXTENSIVELY SHADED	18 CARAVANS ONLY - SEE NOTE 1	19 CARAVANS AND/OR TENTS - SEE NOTE 1	20 TENTS ONLY - SEE NOTE 1	21 ON MAIN RD	22 WITHIN 1 km	23 WITHIN 5 km	24 WITHIN 10 km	25 WITHIN 15 km	26 TAR	27 GRAVEL	28 SAND	29 GOOD	30 FAIR
	FOR COLOUREDS, ASIANS AND BLACKS (Continued)																														
	SWELLENDAM C 58 D5 ↑ 152m																														
□	**Bontebok National Park** Non-White campers allowed, but adequate facilities will only be ready by 1979 — Bookings not accepted, arrangements made on arrival	02912 E	4403					□		□	□		□				□			□					□			□		□	
	THE WILLOWS C 59 C5 ↗ S.L.																														
○	**The Willows Holiday Resort (for Coloureds and Asians)** P.O. Box 318, Port Elizabeth 6000 □ *18 km from P.E.*	041	36-1035			○			○				○			○				○		○					○			○	
	UMTATA X 62 C6 → 699m																														
◇	**Municipal Caravan Park (for all races)** P.O. Box 45 (5100)	0471	3204		◇							◇	◇				◇			◇		◇					◇			◇	
	WAENHUISKRANS (ARNISTON) C 58 D5 ↙ 10m																														
△	**Arniston Park (for Coloureds)** Bookings not accepted □ *Arniston Coloured Township*	02842 E	6202			△			△			△	△				△			125			△					△		△	
	WINTERTON N 67 C2 ↓ 1022m																														
☆	**Spioenkop Public Resort (for Coloureds, Asians and Blacks)** P.O. Box 40 (3340) □ *17 km from Winterton*	03682 E	78					☆		☆	☆		☆				☆			5						☆		☆			☆

STOP PRESS

		1 TELEPHONE CODE	2 TELEPHONE NUMBER	3	4	5	6	7	8	9	10	11	12	13	14	15	16	17	18	19	20	21	22	23	24	25	26	27	28	29	30
	BANANA BEACH N 63 NS ↓ S.L.																														
◆	**Bendigo** P.O. Box 91, Anerley 4230	0391	3451	◆					◆	◆		◆	◆			◆	◆		100			◆					◆			◆	
◇	**Bothasrus Holiday Resort** P.O. Box 180, Anerley 4230	0391	3521	◇					◇				◇				◇			46			◇				◇			◇	
▲	**Ilanga** P.O. Box 27, Anerley 4230	0391	3280	▲					▲				▲				▲			105			▲				▲			▲	

SEASONS: 33 Throughout the year	34 Out-of-season closing date / Re-opening date	TERMS FOR BOOKINGS: 35 Bookings accp. peak sns. – see note 2	36 Deposit required	37 Refunded if cancelled – see note 3	CARAVAN PARK/CAMPING SITE TARIFFS (See heading): 38 Maximum in-season tariff	39 Maximum out-of-season tariff	REDUCTIONS ALLOWED FOR: 40 Long periods of stay	41 Groups – see note 4	42 AA carnet holders – see note 5	43 Others (on application)	RESTAURANT FACILITIES: 44 On site	45 Within 5 km of site	46 More than 5 km from site	TEAROOM/CAFE: 47 On site	48 Within 5 km of site	49 More than 5 km from site	SHOPPING FACILITIES (Provisions): 50 On site	51 Within 5 km of site	52 More than 5 km from site	ADDITIONAL ACCOMMODATION AVAILABLE: 53 Bungalows	54 Cabins	55 Cottages (rondavels)	56 Chalets	ADDITIONAL ACCOMMODATION TARIFF (See heading): 57 Maximum in-season tariff	58 Maximum out-of-season tariff	59 Caravans to rent on site – see pages 8–11
					C	C							□			□			□							
		○	○	○	A	A							○			○			○							
					C	C	◇	◇				◇			◇			◇								
					B	B													△							
		☆	☆		C	C													☆				☆	B	B	
		◆	◆	◆	H	F	◆	◆				◆			◆			◆								
		◇	◇		G	D							◇	◇				◇				◇	◇	K	E	
		▲	▲		G	F	▲	▲					▲			▲		▲								

CAMP SITE FACILITIES — I = In-Season only; O = Out-of-Season only

DRINKING WATER: 60 Piped	61 Other	BATHS: 62 Hot and cold	63 Cold only	SHOWERS: 64 Hot and cold	65 Cold only	66 Waterborne sanitation	67 Washbasins	68 Dishwashing facilities	69 Laundry and ironing facilities – see note 6	70 Washing machines	71 Site lit	72 Plugs for razors (voltage)	73 Refrigerators	74 Firewood/charcoal	75 Open fire forbidden	76 Camp fire permitted	77 Braai places provided	78 Kitchen/cooking facilities	79 Petrol pump on site	80 Petrol pump nearby	81 Car repair shop nearby	82 Car servicing nearby	83 Gas service nearby	84 First aid/hospital/doctor nearby	85 Post office nearby	86 Site guarded	87 Pets allowed	NON-WHITE SERVANTS: 88 Servants permitted – see note 7	89 Servants accom. – see note 7	90 Servants for hire – see note 7	TYPE OF VEHICLE PERMITTED: 91 Car and trailer	92 Truck "horse" and semi-trailer	93 Self-propelled caravans
□															□	□			□		□	□	□								□	□	□
	○														○		○			○	○	○	○	○	○		○	○			○	○	○
◇		◇		◇		◇	◇	◇	◇		◇					◇				◇	◇	◇			◇		◇				◇		◇
△				△		△	△	△	L					△			△			△			△	△		△	△	△		△	△	△	△
☆		☆		☆		☆	☆				☆					☆	☆							☆				☆			☆	☆	☆
◆		◆		◆		◆	◆	◆	◆		◆	◆			◆	◆	◆			◆	◆	◆	◆	◆	◆	◆	◆				◆		◆
◇	◇	◇		◇		◇	◇	◇	◇				◇	◇	◇	◇				◇	◇	◇		◇	◇	◇	◇			◇	◇	◇	◇
▲		▲		▲		▲	▲	▲	▲	▲		▲			▲	▲	▲			▲	▲	▲	▲	▲	▲	▲	▲	▲	▲		▲	▲	▲

SPORTING AND RECREATIONAL FACILITIES — S = On Site; N = Nearby (Up to 20 km away)

94 Childrens playground	95 Tennis	96 Cinema/drive-in/TV-room – see note 8	97 Horse-riding	98 Games room	99 Trampoline	100 Bowls	101 Hot springs	GOLF: 102 Golf course – see note 9	103 Number of holes	104 Miniature	105 Mashie	106 Putt-putt	FISHING: 107 Freshwater – see note 10	108 Sea – see note 11	109 Goggle	110 Licence required	SWIMMING: 111 Swimming pool	112 Sea bathing	113 Childrens pool	114 Adults only	115 Shark nets at beach	BOATING: 116 Boats for hire	117 Power	118 Sailing	119 Canoeing	PLACES OF INTEREST: 120 Historic	121 Scientific	122 Natural	123 NOTES
																												□	
														N	N			○								○	○	○	
N	N	N				N		N	18				N		N													◇	
														S	S			△				N						△	
S			S										S			☆							S	S	S			☆	
S	N	N		N									S	S	S			◆	N		◆							◆	
		S		S									N	N	N	◇		◇			◇							◇	
N	N	N											N	N				▲	S		▲	N							

COMPARATIVE ANALYSIS OF ESSENTIAL COSTS

CAR

Johannesburg – Cape Town – Johannesburg (2 874 km)
Vehicle (2,8 litre): 10,5 litres per 100 km at 55c per litre R165,97
Hotel: (Bed and Breakfast): R12,00 per person per day x 5 persons x 14 days R840,00
Meals: R4,00 per person per day x 5 persons x 14 days R280,00

TOTAL R1 285,97

TRAIN

Cost of tickets: Johannesburg – Cape Town – Johannesburg
Adults (2 x R84,30) R168,60
Children: 1 under 12 .... R42,15 .... R42,15
2 over 12 .... R84,30 x 2 .... R168,60
Taxi in Cape Town: R9,00 per day x 14 days R126,00
Hotel (Bed and Breakfast): R12,00 per person per day x 5 persons x 14 days R840,00
Meals: R4,00 per person per day x 14 days x 5 persons R280,00

TOTAL R1 625,35

BY AIR

Tickets: Johannesburg – Cape Town – Johannesburg: 5 persons at R150,00 each R750,00
Taxi in Cape Town: R9,00 per day x 14 days R126,00
Hotel (Bed and Breakfast): R12,00 per person per day x 14 days x 5 persons R840,00
Meals: R4,00 per person per day x 14 days x 5 persons R280,00

TOTAL R1 996,00

HOLIDAY FLATS

Air Tickets: Johannesburg – Cape Town – Johannesburg:5 persons at R150,00 each R750,00
Taxi in Cape Town: R9,00 per day x 14 days R126,00
Rent paid for flat: R20,00 per day x 14 days R280,00
Meals: R3,00 per person per day x 14 days x 5 persons R210,00

TOTAL R1 366,00

CARAVAN

Johannesburg – Cape Town – Johannesburg (2 874 km)
Vehicle (2,8 litre) plus caravan: 13,8 litres per 100 km at 55c per litre R218,13
Hire of caravan site: R5,00 per day x 14 days R70,00
Meals: R15,00 per day per family x 14 days R210,00

TOTAL R498,13

CARAVAN HIRE

In this case, air travel is used as a basis of comparison
Air tickets (as above) R750,00
Hire of caravan and rental of site (caravan sleeping six): R16,00 per day x 14 days R224,00
Meals: R15,00 per day per family x 14 days R210,00

TOTAL R1 184,00

NOTES